ASPEN PUBLISHERS

# KOHN ON MUSIC LICENSING

**FOURTH EDITION**

**AL KOHN**
**BOB KOHN**

*First Published as*
**The Art Of Music Licensing**

**ASPEN LAW & BUSINESS**
**A Division of Aspen Publishers, Inc.**
**New York Gaithersburg**

Wolters Kluwer
Law & Business

AUSTIN BOSTON CHICAGO NEW YORK THE NETHERLANDS

Printed in the United States of America

1 2 3 4 5 6 7 8 9 0

**Library of Congress Cataloging-in-Publication Data**

Kohn, Al.
Kohn on music licensing / Al Kohn, Bob Kohn. — 4th ed.
p. cm.
ISBN 0-7355-9090-7 (hardcover)
1. Copyright — Music — United States. 2. Copyright licenses — United States. I. Kohn, Bob. II. Title
KF3035.K64 2000
346.7304'82 — dc21

00-048510

# About Wolters Kluwer Law & Business

Wolters Kluwer Law & Business is a leading provider of research information and workflow solutions in key specialty areas. The strengths of the individual brands of Aspen Publishers, CCH, Kluwer Law International and Loislaw are aligned within Wolters Kluwer Law & Business to provide comprehensive, in-depth solutions and expert-authored content for the legal, professional and education markets.

**CCH** was founded in 1913 and has served more than four generations of business professionals and their clients. The CCH products in the Wolters Kluwer Law & Business group are highly regarded electronic and print resources for legal, securities, antitrust and trade regulation, government contracting, banking, pension, payroll, employment and labor, and healthcare reimbursement and compliance professionals.

**Aspen Publishers** is a leading information provider for attorneys, business professionals and law students. Written by preeminent authorities, Aspen products offer analytical and practical information in a range of specialty practice areas from securities law and intellectual property to mergers and acquisitions and pension/benefits. Aspen's trusted legal education resources provide professors and students with high-quality, up-to-date and effective resources for successful instruction and study in all areas of the law.

**Kluwer Law International** supplies the global business community with comprehensive English-language international legal information. Legal practitioners, corporate counsel and business executives around the world rely on the Kluwer Law International journals, loose-leafs, books and electronic products for authoritative information in many areas of international legal practice.

**Loislaw** is a premier provider of digitized legal content to small law firm practitioners of various specializations. Loislaw provides attorneys with the ability to quickly and efficiently find the necessary legal information they need, when and where they need it, by facilitating access to primary law as well as state-specific law, records, forms and treatises.

Wolters Kluwer Law & Business, a unit of Wolters Kluwer, is headquartered in New York and Riverwoods, Illinois. Wolters Kluwer is a leading multinational publisher and information services company.

## ASPEN PUBLISHERS SUBSCRIPTION NOTICE

This Aspen Publishers product is updated on a periodic basis with supplements to reflect important changes in the subject matter. If you purchased this product directly from Aspen Publishers, we have already recorded your subscription for the update service.

If, however, you purchased this product from a bookstore and wish to receive future updates and revised or related volumes billed separately with a 30-day examination review, please contact our Customer Service Department at 1-800-234-1660 or send your name, company name (if applicable), address, and the title of the product to:

**ASPEN PUBLISHERS**
**7201 McKinney Circle**
**Frederick, MD 21704**

**Important Aspen Publishers Contact Information**

- To order any Aspen Publishers title, go to *www.aspenpublishers.com* or call 1-800-638-8437.
- To reinstate your manual update service, call 1-800-638-8437.
- To contact Customer Care, e-mail *customer.care@aspenpublishers.com,* call 1-800-234-1660, fax 1-800-901-9075, or mail correspondence to Order Department, Aspen Publishers, PO Box 990, Frederick, MD 21705.
- To review your account history or pay an invoice online, visit *www.aspenpublishers.com/payinvoices.*

Wolters Kluwer
Law & Business

What neat repast shall feast us, light and choice,
Of Attic taste, with wine, whence we may rise
To hear the lute well touched, or artful voice
Warble immortal notes and Tuscan air?
He who of those delights can judge, and spare
To interpose them oft, is not unwise.

—*from a sonnet by John Milton* (*1608-1674*)

*To Edna*

# FOREWORD

Like a father talking to his son or daughter, in telling of *The Art of Music Licensing*, Al unfolds an encyclopedia of experience and information, gently and gracefully sharing the wisdom and joy of an art and expertise of which, with all humility, he reveals himself to be a master.

The fascination, affection, and almost reverential respect that Al holds for the songwriters and artists that he represents is an essential guidepost for the reader. I would venture to say that Al's whole being, as it permeates *The Art of Music Licensing*, is as much a model and resource as the technical information and good advice that he shares. Like Al, there is a gentleness to the word of caution about pitfalls and short-sightedness, and because it is Al who advises, there is the implicit instruction that the pursuit of success in the practice of licensing need never be a cutthroat game.

To Al, successful negotiation and guidance of licensing comes from an understanding and respect for the real value of the creative work, the diligent study of the extremely complex issues, precedents and processes surrounding the field of licensing, and a sympathetic view of some of the fears and confusions of those who want to do the best for their clients' work (but are unsure as to how to proceed in the volatile and ever changing world of technology and labyrinthine law); but above all, one gets the message, imbedded in each sentence of the book, that fairness and understanding of both sides of the issues is the only road to ultimate success in the practice of the art of music licensing.

Al has spent a lifetime living his art, and what he shares in this prodigious work is much more than an encyclopedic textbook. Because Al has lived the golden ages of music, has been part of its creation and has represented the titans of music history, he is able to reveal, through loving anecdotes that illustrate the themes and premises of business practice, the real fun and energy, the behind-the-scenes personality, and understandable artistic compulsivity that is the world of music we inherit.

Al, as much as he is a teacher, is a bard weaving the history of the music business into a work that might well become a model for future attempts to communicate such complexity of information of any field or art form.

This book is a remarkable gift. It's much more than facts and figures. It's even much more than sound advice and a lifetime of wisdom.

It's Al, whom we all admire and love and who has managed, with the extraordinary partnership of a loving and gifted son, to help us remember who we are and might be, as we try to meet the challenges, and share the rewards and joys, of the music business.

Peter Yarrow
September 1992

Peter Yarrow is a member of Peter, Paul & Mary and has been represented through Warner Bros. Publishing by Al Kohn for over 30 years as the writer and co-writer of such songs as *Puff The Magic Dragon, Weave Me The Sunshine, Light One Candle, Torn Between Two Lovers*, and *Day Is Done.*

# ABOUT THE AUTHORS

## Al Kohn

Al Kohn, a 50-year veteran of the music industry, was Vice President, Licensing for Warner/Chappell Music, Inc., when he retired in 1993. Prior to his 23-year association with Warner Bros., he served for over 11 years as the U.S. representative for the London-based Francis, Day & Hunter music publishing organization, developing acquisition patterns which moved them into the global pop music market.

Prior to that Al was a member of the creative team at Hummert Radio Features and was the key arranger for some of the syndicate's major network radio programs including *Waltz Time* and *Manhattan Merry-Go-Round.* During World War II, Irving Berlin tapped Al to orchestrate his all-soldier show, *This Is the Army.*

He also served as an arranger for orchestras, including those of Paul Whiteman, Abe Lyman, Ted Dale, Orrin Tucker and others, and arranged night club revues at Lou Walter's Latin Quarter, Billy Rose's Diamond Horseshoe, and the Steel Pier Music Hall. Later, he served as a television arranger for the Milton Berle, Katherine Murray, George Jessel, Martha Raye, and Jane Pickens shows. He also arranged or conducted for Bob Hope, Billy Rose, Jerry Vale, and many others.

Al lives in Tarzana, California, and serves as member of the Board of Directors of the Johnny Mercer Foundation.

*www.alkohn.com*

## Bob Kohn

Bob Kohn is an attorney, an expert in copyright and music industry matters, and a seasoned executive with experience in both the entertainment and high-tech industries. He was founder of EMusic.com, Inc. (NASDAQ:EMUS), the pioneering music download subscription service, where he served as Chairman until the company was sold to

Vivendi/Universal in June 2001. He is currently Chairman & CEO of RoyaltyShare, Inc., the premier provider of web-based royalty processing and digital revenue management solutions for the global entertainment industry. He also serves as Chairman of Laugh.com, a comedy record company, which he co-founded with the late comedian George Carlin.

He previously served as Vice Chairman of the Board of Borland Software Corporation (NASDAQ: BORL), one of the world's largest developers and marketers of computer software. He was also Vice President, Business Development of Pretty Good Privacy, Inc., a leading developer and marketer of encryption software, and Senior Vice President, Corporate Affairs, Secretary, and General Counsel of Borland International, Inc. Bob also served as Associate General Counsel for Candle Corporation, a developer of software for IBM mainframe computers, and Corporate Counsel for Ashton-Tate, a microcomputer software company.

Prior to Ashton-Tate, he was an associate attorney at the law offices of Milton A. "Mickey" Rudin in Beverly Hills, California, an entertainment law firm whose clients included Frank Sinatra, Liza Minnelli, Cher, and Warner Bros. Music. He also worked as Associate Editor of the Entertainment Law Reporter, for which he continues to serve as a member of the Advisory Board. He was also an Adjunct Professor of Law at Monterey College of Law, Monterey, California.

In 1994, Bob won the prize offered by the Encyclopedia Britannica for the best solution to a philosophical problem posed by the editors, and his winning essay, Mind and Brain: The Genius of Fortune, was published in the 1994 edition of the Britannica's The Great Ideas Today.

Bob became a member of the California Bar in 1981 after graduating from Loyola Law School, Los Angeles. He lives in Manhattan.

*www.bobkohn.com*

# THE REASONS FOR THIS BOOK

One need go no further to seek the reasons for this book than to the many friends and colleagues of mine who have urged me over the years to memorialize my thoughts on its subject in writing. Since many of these same people are lawyers, I can only assume they are more interested in the expression of my practical experience as a licensor of music, than my knowledge of the law.

It should be no surprise, therefore, that, though this book is thoroughly intertwined with, and dependent upon, the law of copyright, the primary emphasis of this book is not on the law, but on experience and practice. A book on copyright law would have been easier to write, because, in writing such a book, one can rely on the large body of statutes and legal decisions with which to adorn the pages. In the pages which follow, citations are given for few legal decisions. Presented, instead, is how music publishers and other copyright owners think, or more accurately, should think, in connection with licensing the music in their repertoire.

In contrast to the acquisition side of music publishing, which involves acquiring the publishing rights to new music and established songs, music licensing, the subject of this book, concerns the revenue side of the music publishing business — what you do after you own the song. Of course, what is revenue to the music copyright owner is cost to the music user. Consequently, this book also addresses the other side of the coin — what you need to do if you want to use the song for commercial purposes.

Music licensing can thus be viewed from two perspectives: (1) the considerations used by music publishers and songwriters in earning a living from their music copyrights, and (2) the clearance of music rights by those who desire to use copyrighted music for commercial purposes.

Because my business career in the music industry has been spent largely in the employ of music publishers, this book will more naturally reflect the perspectives of the copyright owner and songwriter. Yet, my sympathy for those whose job it is to obtain music clearances has concretely found its way into this book. The reader should find no contradiction in the expression of a music publisher's sympathies for the task of rights clearance. If the music publisher is doing its job correctly, the licensing of music rights by those who desire to use music commercially should be a simple, straightforward, and often rewarding effort. The music publisher's reward for facilitating the licensing effort is better representation of the songwriters whose livelihood may often depend on proper representation.

The reader is forewarned that some controversy may attend some of the opinions expressed in this book. Some will resent being shown that their language is confused, inconsistent, and often used unwittingly against their own best interest. At first, I hesitated to speak frankly, but, with a lifetime in this business behind me, I feel I have earned a license to finally declare, *Anything Goes.* Though some will inevitably disagree with the positions taken in this book, it is hoped that they will be viewed, if nothing more, as a call for a common understanding of the terms upon which we do business.

There's no business like show business. That issue was well settled by Ethel Merman. Yet, as Irving Berlin might have agreed, there would be no show business without music. For this reason, I could not begin without first thanking the many songwriters on behalf of whom I've had the great pleasure of working with over the years as a publisher representative and as an arranger and producer of successful radio and television productions.

AL KOHN
October 1992

# ACKNOWLEDGEMENTS TO THE FOURTH EDITION

We have several people to thank for their assistance in the preparation of this latest edition, including the following individuals who furnished some of the forms, reviewed portions of the manuscript, or provided other information that made its way into in this volume: Casey McGinty, Jonathan Kehl, Marc Ostrow, Steven Manus, James Grupenhoff, Paul John Birch, Christine Smith, Roy Kohn, Neil Gillis, Howard Singer, Bruce McKagan, Stephen Block, and Rich Bengloff. We also wish to think David Rosenberg for his legal research and providing us with copies of the recent court decisions discussed in this edition. In reviewing the proofs for this edition, we discovered an omission we correct now by providing this very special acknowledgement to Paulette Hawkins, a dedicated music licensing professional, for the helpful information and insights she has provided the authors since the publication of the first edition.

We also wish to thank the team at RoyaltyShare, especially Bob's co-founders and colleagues Steve Grady and Scott Holcombe, whose collective efforts and wealth of experience have added greatly to our understanding of what digital media will require in the coming years. The technological infrastructure that RoyaltyShare is building is destined to become the key foundation for the management of rights, revenues and royalties for the exploitation of digital music, film and ebooks.

We again gratefully acknowledge the assistance we have received over the years from our friends at Aspen Law & Business, particularly our new editor Pj, who has marshaled the many resources necessary to produce this fourth edition.

Finally, we want to especially thank our new love, Susan Kamil, for not only her expert editorial eye which helped us see the forest through the trees, but for her constant encouragement and support, without which this edition may never have happened.

Again, above all, we thank that special person to whom we continue to lovingly dedicate this book.

AL KOHN
BOB KOHN
December 2009

# ACKNOWLEDGEMENTS TO THE THIRD EDITION

The only people we really have to thank in connection with the preparation of this Third Edition are the thousands of lawyers, law students, law librarians, music industry professionals, and others who so often have expressed their desire for us to continually rekindle the flame of this work with the fuel of new material. "The only end in writing," said Dr. Samuel Johnson, "is to enable the reader better to enjoy life, or better to endure it." We had this very sentiment in mind as we wrote much of the new material on the Internet, and we hope it will be of some guidance to those who find the current challenges faced by the music industry something both to enjoy and to endure.

Of course, Dr. Johnson was also known to have said, "Sir, no man but a blockhead ever wrote except for money," which reminds us that, without those who have faithfully purchased the prior editions, and continue to purchase our annual supplements, this new edition would not have been possible.

We must also gratefully acknowledge the assistance we have received over the years from our friends at Aspen Law & Business, particularly our editor Matt Gallaway, for his tireless efforts in keeping this book up to date, and to Rick Kravitz, for his tireless support of everyone involved in its publication.

Finally, we again thank the entire Kohn family, for, without their spending, this book would not have been necessary. Above all, we thank that special person to whom we have thrice lovingly dedicated this book.

AL KOHN<br>
BOB KOHN<br>
November 2001

# ACKNOWLEDGEMENTS TO THE SECOND EDITION

We have several people to thank for their assistance in the development of the new materials we prepared for this edition. We wish to especially express our gratitude to Don Biederman, Esq. and Gary Ford for their review of selected chapters added to this work and to Lionel S. Sobel, Esq. for permission to include his materials on live musical performances. We also wish to thank the following individuals who furnished some of the forms or other information furnished in the new materials: Vincent S. Castellucci, Don Biederman, Esq., Michael Sandoval, Ronald H. Gertz, Esq., Bennett M. Lincoff, Esq., Joe DiMona, Don Williams, and Roy Kohn.

We also gratefully acknowledge the assistance of Noah J. Gordon, Esq., our editor, and the dedication, encouragement and cooperation we have received from Aspen Publishers, especially Dan Mangan and Richard Kravitz. Special thanks again to Joan Kanady for her tireless assistance in optically scanning, typing and editing the forms and other information that went into this volume and printing and copying numerous drafts of the manuscript. We also thank Joanne Butler, Esq. for her legal research.

We again thank the entire Kohn family, including Ted and Joanne Kohn, and their children Beth and Todd, for their continuous encouragement and, most especially, Lori, Katie and Joey for their patience and unwavering love and support during this intensive effort. We also thank Matthew D. Kohn, Esq. for his insight and experience in representing contemporary artists and firms in the entertainment field, and we welcome his wife Sharon, and her family, to the Kohn family. Above all, we wish to acknowledge the encouragement, support, and wisdom of the person to whom this book we lovingly dedicate.

AL KOHN
BOB KOHN
November 1995

# ACKNOWLEDGEMENTS TO THE FIRST EDITION

We have many people to thank for their assistance in the preparation of this work. We wish to especially express our gratitude to Prof. Lionel S. Sobel, Esq., Ronald H. Gertz, Esq., and Vincent S. Castellucci who made critical readings of parts of the work and provided very helpful suggestions for its improvement. We also wish to thank the following individuals who furnished some of the forms or other information included in this volume: M. William Krasilovsky, Esq., Bernard Korman, Esq., Gary Ford, Marvin L. Berenson, Esq., Ira B. Selsky, Esq., Martin Cohen, Esq., Don Biederman, Esq., Naomi Saltzman, Sid Luft, and Roy Kohn. We give special acknowledgment to Matthew D. Kohn, Esq. for his insight and experience in representing contemporary artists and firms in the entertainment field.

Our sincerest thanks and gratitude are due to those who have contributed to the cumulative experiences that have found their way into this book, including Abe Lyman, Ben Yost, Irving Caesar, Patty Andrews, Wally Weschler, Danny Gould, Arthur Hamilton, John Clark, Esq., Edward Slattery, Mrs. Frank Hummert, David Day, Bernard Sorkin, Esq., Louise Dembeck, Esq., Milton A. Rudin, Esq., Ed Perlstein, Esq., Walter Evans, Ed Silvers, Mel Blye, James Cornelius, Chuck Kaye, Les Bider, Jay Morgenstern, Michael Sandoval, Joe Guardino, and Max Berkovitz. It is painful for us to think that while we were carrying on this work, several of those to whom it would have been most interesting have passed away. We therefore wish to add to our acknowledgement the friendship and encouragement of the late Ira Gershwin, Leonore Gershwin, Harry Warren, Jerry Livingston, Herb Magidson, Milton Ager, Ben Oakland, Sammy Fain, and Howard and Lucinda Dietz.

We thank Philippe Kahn, Chairman and Chief Executive Officer of Borland International, Inc. for having the foresight to provide the company's long-term employees with the sabbatical time required to complete works such as this. We also thank Spencer Leyton, John Hansen,

Linda Wallraff, John Smart, Allen Dixon, and other members of the the law and corporate affairs department of Borland International, and its outside counsel Peter Astiz, Esq., Gary Reback, Esq., Martin Greenstein, Esq., Steven Brower, Esq., Stan Sokoloff, Esq., Peter Gelhaar, Esq., Allen Grogan, Esq., and Samuel Farb, Esq., without whom there would have been no opportunity to take advantage of that sabbatical time. Special thanks to Joan Kanady for her tireless assistance in optically scanning, typing and editing the forms that went into this volume and printing and copying numerous drafts of the manuscript. We also gratefully acknowledge the assistance of Noah J. Gordon, Esq., our editor, and the creative staff at Prentice-Hall Law and Business, and Lisa Nielsen of Borland International for a beautiful jacket design.

We also must thank the entire Kohn family, including Ted and Joanne Kohn, and their children Beth and Todd, for their continuous encouragement and, most especially, Lori, Katie and Joey for their patience and unwavering love and support during this prolonged endeavor. Above all, we wish to acknowledge the encouragement, support, and wisdom of the person to whom this book we lovingly dedicate.

Now, let's get on with the show. . . .

AL KOHN
BOB KOHN
October 1992

# SUMMARY OF CONTENTS

# Table of Contents

## CHAPTER 2
## THE ART OF MUSIC PUBLISHING

## CHAPTER 3
## SONGWRITER AGREEMENTS

## CHAPTER 4
## CO-PUBLISHING AND ADMINISTRATION AGREEMENTS

## CHAPTER 5
## INTERNATIONAL SUBPUBLISHING

## CHAPTER 6
## THE SPLIT COPYRIGHT SYNDROME



## CHAPTER 7
## THE LANGUAGE OF MUSIC LICENSING

## CHAPTER 8
## FORMALITIES OF MUSIC LICENSING

**CHAPTER 9**

**DURATION OF COPYRIGHT, ASSIGNMENTS OF COPYRIGHT, AND LICENSES**

## CHAPTER 10
## BASIC CONSIDERATIONS IN MUSIC LICENSING

## CHAPTER 11
## THE ART OF GRANTING AND CLEARING MUSIC LICENSES

## CHAPTER 12
## LICENSING MUSIC IN PRINT AND DIGITAL PRINT (PRINT LICENSES)

## CHAPTER 13
## LICENSING MUSIC IN SOUND RECORDINGS (MECHANICAL LICENSES)

**FORMS (ON CD-ROM ONLY)**



## CHAPTER 14
## LICENSING MUSIC IN BACKGROUND MUSIC SERVICES, DIGITAL JUKEBOXES, AND OTHER COMMERCIAL REPRODUCTIONS (ELECTRICAL TRANSCRIPTION LICENSES)

## CHAPTER 15
## LICENSING MUSIC IN AUDIOVISUAL WORKS (SYNCHRONIZATION LICENSES)

**FORMS (ON CD-ROM ONLY)**

## CHAPTER 16
## THE USER-GENERATED CONTENT PHENOMENON



## CHAPTER 17
## OLD LICENSES, NEW USES

## CHAPTER 18
## LICENSING MUSIC IN LIVE AND RECORDED PUBLIC PERFORMANCES
## (PUBLIC PERFORMANCE LICENSES)

## CHAPTER 19
## THE GRAND RIGHTS CONTROVERSY

## CHAPTER 20
## LICENSING MUSIC IN TELEVISION, RADIO, PRINT, AND INTERNET ADVERTISING

## CHAPTER 21
## LICENSES FOR MUSIC BOXES, CONSUMER MUSICAL PRODUCTS, AND OTHER MERCHANDISE



## CHAPTER 22
## LICENSING MUSIC IN VIDEOGAMES, OTHER NEW MEDIA, MULTIMEDIA DEVICES, AND ONLINE VERSIONS

**CHAPTER 23**

**LICENSING OF SOUND RECORDINGS**

**(MASTER USE LICENSES, DIGITAL DOWNLOADING AND DIGITAL AUDIO TRANSMISSIONS)**

## CHAPTER 24
## THE DIGITAL SAMPLING CONTROVERSY

## CHAPTER 25
## THE FAIR USE CONTROVERSY

## CHAPTER 26
## TYPICAL LICENSE FEES

CHAPTER 1

# INTRODUCTION: THE MUSIC BUSINESS — ITS PAST AND FUTURE

## SUMMARY

CHAPTER 1

# INTRODUCTION: THE MUSIC BUSINESS — ITS PAST AND FUTURE

This book is a practical guide to the art of music licensing — a guide to the process from both sides of the deal — helping copyright owners understand how to maximize the value of their songs and recordings while helping those who wish to use music for commercial purposes understand how best to obtain the licenses they need.

The life of this book, from its first edition in 1992 through the present, has not been in copyright law or court decisions as much as in practical operating knowledge of the music industry — particularly, how the music industry's long-engrained customs and practices have been affected by rapidly changing technology.

Newcomers to the industry are typically overwhelmed by the numerous "terms of art" they must embrace to gain a working knowledge of the business. Those seasoned in the business are continually overwhelmed by how changes in technology and the law affect the way they exploit their repertoire. This book attempts to satisfy the needs of both the newcomer and the seasoned music industry executive — offering the basics of music licensing, an introduction to the laws upon which the music industry relies, and a thorough exploration of the practical aspects of music licensing in a world of constant technological evolution.

As nearly everyone involved in today's music industry is aware, the digitization of recorded music and its transmission by digital means have presented daunting business and legal challenges. Notorious Internet websites and peer-to-peer (P2P) networks have facilitated the unauthorized reproduction of musical recordings to the point where it is estimated that copyright piracy in sound recordings alone accounts for over 80% of all Internet traffic.[1]

---

[1] "Digital Music Report 2009," IFPI.

Meanwhile, the sales of physical compact discs (CDs) have recently been declining at a rate of over 20% per year. Some of the bulwark retail chains of the music industry, such as Tower Records and Virgin Megastores, have closed their doors. Though revenues from digital download and subscription services are up year over year, revenues from such sources are not growing fast enough to replace the decline in CD sales. "It's a dying industry," one major record executive told us recently.

In seeking better ways to monetize the commercial use of music, online music service companies, such as digital download services and webcasters, have been trying a variety of new business models,[2] including variable-priced downloads and advertising-based services. Faced with mixed success, few service providers have achieved profitability. They wonder whether they can ever achieve a sustainable business model given the rates they are being charged for licenses to use the songs and recordings, which they complain are too high.

The angst on both sides is real, but the challenges brought about by the advent of new technologies are not new to the music industry. As we will explain below, the music industry faced similar challenges when new technologies emerging in the early twentieth century brought about a major transformation of traditional industry business models. The challenges the music industry faces today mirror the challenges of that time to a remarkable degree.

In the remainder of this chapter, we explore the music industry's present challenges, beginning with a look backward, believing that a study of the past will help us understand and address the licensing challenges we face in the twenty-first century. When William Shakespeare warned us "what's past is prologue," he had his eye on the future with his feet firmly planted in the past — because the Bard knew that only by studying the past, could we acquire the wisdom necessary to predict the future.

## I. THE WAY WE WERE

The modern music business started about the time of Al Kohn's birth in 1919. That year was perhaps the height of Tin Pan Alley — a

[2] See Chapter 23, on *Licensing of Sound Recordings.*

block of buildings on 28th Street between Fifth Avenue and Broadway in New York City where many of the nation's largest music publishers of that time were headquartered. While young boys on the fabled street below made "music" by banging on the covers of tin garbage cans,[3] songwriters like Irving Berlin and Harry Von Tilzer were writing classic songs, like *God Bless America* and *Take Me Out To The Ball Game.*

## A. The Dominance of Sheet Music

In 1919, the sale of sheet music constituted by far the most important source of a music publisher's revenue.[4] Music publishers manufactured millions of copies of sheet music and used retail stores and wholesale distribution networks to make them widely available. Many publishers operated their own retail stores where they sold sheet music, pianos, and other musical instruments.

Music publishers were quite innovative in the way they created public demand for their goods. For example, in the late nineteenth century, before the motion picture era, variety theaters would project entertaining illustrated slides onto a white screen. To promote his repertoire music publisher Edward B. Marks would have his songs performed during these presentations. M. Witmark & Sons was the first music publisher to print sheet music of songs appearing in successful Broadway shows, an excellent vehicles for the promotion of sheet music.

Musical performers on the vaudeville circuit would stop by Tin Pan Alley to discover new songs to perform in their acts. Music publishers employed *songpluggers* — one of them being a young George Gershwin[5] working for Jerome H. Remick Music and another being Jerome Kern

---

[3] Perhaps giving the street its name. Another theory as to derivation of the name "Tin Pan Alley" is provided in Chapter 2, on *The Art of Music Publishing*, together with a further history and account of the major music publishers of that era.

[4] For more on the history and licensing aspects of sheet music, see Chapter 12, on *Licensing Music in Print and Digital Print.*

[5] 1919 was also the year Mr. Gershwin co-authored with Irving Caesar, *Swanee*, a song that Al Jolson made a huge hit. The interesting tale of how the song became a hit is described in Chapter 12, on *Licensing Music in Print and Digital Print.* Tin Pan Alley also produced the likes of Milton Ager, Nacio Herb Brown, Hoagy Carmichael, George M. Cohan, Con Conrad, Buddy DeSylva, Walter Donaldson, Al Dubin, Ira Gershwin, Charles K. Harris, Scott Joplin, Gus Kahn, Jerome Kern, Johnny Mercer, Cole Porter, Harry Ruby, Fats Waller, Harry Warren, Richard A. Whiting, Jack Yellen and Vincent Youmans, among many others.

working for T.B. Harms Music — to sit at upright pianos to promote songs to performers, dance bands, and theater managers. A song added to a vaudeville act in this way would soon be winding through a nationwide network of theaters reaching an ever-widening audience. It is what we might call today, "influencing the influencers" — and it worked.

The song *After the Ball*, written and published by Charles K. Harris in 1893 was the first song to sell one million copies. By 1910, annual sales of sheet music exceeded 30 million copies. In those days, sheet music sold for 10 cents per copy. When Woolworth's decided to start selling sheet music in its five-and-ten-cents stores in 1911, it demanded from music publishers a 40% discount. The publishers acquiesced, but while their profit margins were squeezed, their volume blossomed — by 1913, Woolworth's alone was selling 150 million copies of sheet music and by 1919 over 200 million copies. By then, it was not unusual for the sheet music of a popular song to sell upwards of two to three million copies.[6]

## B. New Technologies and the Music Industry's Response

### *1. Phonograph Records and Player Piano Rolls*

Thomas Alva Edison discovered a way to store sound in 1877.[7] A columnist for the *New York Times* summarized the import of the new invention this way:

> The telephone was justly regarded as an ingenious invention when it was first brought before the public, but it is destined to be entirely eclipsed by the new invention of the phonograph. The former transmitted sound. The latter bottles it up for future use.[8]

In 1895, the player piano was invented.[9] A *player piano* is a piano equipped with a mechanical attachment, which depresses the piano's

---

[6] For the business and legal aspects of sheet music, see Chapter 12, on *Licensing Music in Print and Digital Print.*

[7] For more on the early phonographs, see Chapter 13, on *Licensing Music in Sound Recordings.*

[8] "The Phonograph," *New York Times* (November 7, 1877).

[9] For more on this player pianos, see Chapter 13, on *Licensing Music in Sound Recordings.*

keys by air pressure, reproducing notes that are represented by perforations on a paper roll. The paper rolls bearing these perforations used to play the piano keys in the proper sequence were called *piano rolls.*

Music publishers were naturally eager to license their music for use in these new "mechanical reproductions" of their music, but were stunned when, in 1908, the U.S. Supreme Court ruled that piano rolls and phonograph records were not "copies" of musical compositions and therefore were not infringements of the copyrights in their compositions.[10]

The music publishers lobbied Congress, and with the Copyright Act of 1909,[11] federal law was amended to specifically recognize the exclusive right of the copyright owner to make mechanical reproductions of their music — which included piano rolls and records. To this day, music publishers grant to record companies licenses to make *mechanical reproductions* of their songs. Even though there is virtually nothing "mechanical" about reproducing and listening to music on CDs or transmitting songs by digital download, the form of agreement used to license the reproduction and distribution of music on CDs and by digital download is still called a *mechanical license.*[12]

### *2. Radio Broadcasting*

Since the first U.S. copyright statute was enacted in 1790, music copyright owners have enjoyed an exclusive right to produce their songs in sheet music. Prior to 1897, however, it was not illegal to *perform* a song in a theater or other public place without the permission of the copyright owner. That shortcoming was remedied, in part, when Congress amended the Copyright Act to provide owners of dramatic musical compositions — such as songs written as part of musical plays — with the exclusive right to perform the work "for the purpose

---

[10] *White-Smith Music Pub. Co. v. Apollo Co.*, 209 U.S. 1 (1908).

[11] Act of March 19, 1909, ch. 320, 35 Stat. 1075, as thereafter codified in 17 U.S.C. Sec. 1 et seq., and as amended (hereinafter, the "1909 Act"). While providing copyright owners with an exclusive right to make mechanical reproductions, the 1909 Act placed severe limitations on the right which profoundly affected the way licenses for the use of songs in recordings are issued. For the history of this limitation, see Chapter 13, on *Licensing Music in Sound Recordings.*

[12] For more on mechanical licensing, see Chapter 13, on *Licensing Music in Sound Recordings.*

of public performance for profit." The Copyright Act of 1909 later extended this right to all dramatic and nondramatic musical works.[13]

The ability of music publishers to exploit their new-found right was problematic from the start. Under the terms of the Copyright Act, a license from the copyright owner is required only if the performance was rendered "publicly for profit." This provision was generally interpreted to mean that a license was required only if an admission fee was charged to hear the performance. Since most theatrical performances, such as musical plays and vaudeville shows, charge admission, there was no question the performance right could be enforced against theater owners. If, however, no admission fee was charged for entering a restaurant, performances of music at the restaurant would not be considered "for profit."

Indeed, the common wisdom among music publishers at that time was that public performances of music stimulated the sales of sheet music. Accordingly, the publishers did not want to do anything that would discourage public performances, whether authorized or not. In those days, sheet music often bore a printed notice that granted the purchaser of the sheet music the right to perform the composition in public.

But the conventional wisdom did not deter the songwriters and publishers from desiring to enforce their new right of public performance. In October 1913, at the famous theatrical club, *The Lambs* in New York City, Victor Herbert sat down to dinner with a number of his songwriter colleagues and expressed his frustration at hearing a song of his performed at a nearby swank New York restaurant without his being able to collect a royalty for the performance. Not only was it not clear whether songwriters and publishers had a right to collect for performances of their songs in restaurants, nightclubs, cabarets, and like establishments, they had no effective organization to enforce their rights.[14]

---

[13] 17 U.S.C. Sec. 1(d) (1909 Act).

[14] A year earlier, the world's first performing rights society, French Société des Auteurs, Compositeurs et Editeurs de Musique (SACEM) opened an office in New York to enforce its right of public performance in the United States. Its objective was to collect 5% of gross receipts from the producers of theatrical shows when songs authored by French writers were performed publicly for profit. Irving Berlin was among the first

It was to address these problems that the American Society of Composers, Authors and Publishers (ASCAP) was established 1914.[15] The group immediately went to work by filing lawsuits[16] and establishing a nationwide policing organization that offered licenses to amusement establishments to perform the songs of its members. ASCAP then turned to silent film theaters, which typically hired piano players to perform live music to accompany the film exhibition, successfully required the theaters to obtain a license to perform any music in ASCAP's growing repertoire. During these formative years, ASCAP set the stage and prepared the music business for the technological changes that were on the horizon.

In 1919, the Music Publisher's Protective Association (MPPA), the leading trade association of music publishers, appointed Edwin Charles Mills as its chairman. E.C. Mills had been an operator of vaudeville and silent motion picture theaters in the Southwest, and was one of the founders of the Vaudeville Managers Protective Association. Upon his joining the MPPA, he also became the chairman of administration committee of ASCAP.

At the time, wireless telegraphy had been in use for more than 20 years.[17] When E.C. Mills joined ASCAP, the U.S. government's wireless operations were being turned over to a newly formed division of General Electric called the Radio Corporation of America (RCA). In 1920, RCA received the first radio broadcasting license and commercial radio broadcasting commenced when radio station KDKA went on the air

---

songwriters to join SACEM, but the organization soon developed a poor reputation among U.S. songwriters who complained about an inequitable distribution of money and bureaucratic delays when they tried to resign.

[15] For more on the formation of ASCAP, see Chapter 18, on *Licensing Music in Live and Recorded Public Performances.*

[16] *Herbert v. Shanley*, 242 U.S. 591 (1917) (in a decision written by Justice Oliver Wendell Holmes, the U.S. Supreme Court held that the public performance of Victor Herbert's song, *Sweethearts* was infringed by its public performance in a restaurant. The business of a restaurant was to make a profit and, because the music was part of the service which the restaurant rendered to make a profit, that was enough).

[17] Guglielmo Marconi, an Italian electrical engineer, transmitted the first wireless signal in 1895 and soon formed "wireless" telegraph companies in Europe and the United States. The technology was embraced by the U.S. government when it licensed Marconi's wireless technology to replace its flock of carrier pigeons. On Good Friday, 1917, after German U-boats torpedoed and sank four American ships without warning, the U.S. declared war on Germany and President Wilson directed the Navy to take over all wireless stations during the emergency, including Marconi's ship-to-shore operations.

with the returns of the Harding-Cox presidential election. The following summer, David Sarnoff of RCA, who early on recognized the importance of offering compelling content to promote the sale of radio sets, helped arrange the radio broadcast of the heavyweight boxing match between Jack Dempsey and Georges Carpentier held on July 2, 1921. The success of the broadcast resulted in a boom in the sales of home radio sets.

### *3. E.C. Mills and the Music Industry's Response*

E.C. Mills, sensing that the radio broadcasting could threaten the very foundations of the music publishing industry, proposed something so prescient it would, as we shall see later in this chapter, only begin to resonate 90 years later: to compensate the music industry for the use of music on the radio, Mills propose a $6 annual tax on each radio listener.[18]

Under Mills's proposal, this money was to be distributed by a central organization for the benefit of composers and performers and was pitched to the broadcasting community as a way to allure the best entertainers to radio. That ambitious plan did not succeed, but it is safe to say that the modern music publishing industry owes much of its success to the extraordinary leadership of E.C. Mills.

Under Mill's direction, ASCAP quickly brought suit to require radio stations to pay for the right to use their music and in 1923 and the U.S. Supreme Court agreed.[19] On the heels of that decision, ASCAP announced that 50 radio stations had agreed to pay public performance fees for the use of music and negotiations were under way with about 350 more.[20] ASCAP was demanding $5,000 per year from each of the large broadcasters and makers of radio equipment, including RCA, Westinghouse Electric, and AT&T. The minimum fee was $200 with fees averaging $1,000 per year. With an estimated 400 commercial radio stations nationwide, ASCAP hoped to collect about $400,000 by the end of the year. As J.C. Rosenthal, the general manager of ASCAP explained the plight of his members at the time:

> Even if we should obtain $400,000 a year for our members, it would not offset the loss which they incur through radio. People are so

[18] "Edwin Mills, 77, ASCAP Aide, Dies," *New York Times* (March 15, 1959).

[19] *M. Witmark & Sons v. L. Bamberger & Co.*, 291 F. 776 (D.N.J. 1923).

[20] "Negotiations Open for Radio Music," *New York Times* (March 23, 1923).

> occupied with radio that the sales of sheet music have fallen off notably. Less than 600,000 sheets are being sold today. The reduction in the sale of phonograph records because of radio is going to be very heavy and this hits the income of the composer and writer.[21]

Broadcasters responded that the effect of broadcasting was to popularize the works owned by music publishers.[22] William H. Easton, representing the Westinghouse Electric, summarized the position of the radio broadcasters as follows:

> "A little more than a year ago there were only five broadcasting stations in the world. Today, in the United States alone, there are 576. In other words, the thing has grown too rapidly for proper development. It is a big experiment, developing an entirely new art, one of the greatest arts ever invented. To that end all of those directly concerned in the development of broadcasting have contributed all they have, their time, talent, franchises, rights and so on, gratis, to help build this up to a point where it will be profitable for all concerned."
>
> "Either broadcasting will be profitable to the composer or it won't be. If it isn't profitable, the thing will die very quickly. It will have to be profitable to all hands, not only the musicians, authors and composers, but as well to all others undertaking it before we get anywhere. But we are not at that point yet, and it seems to me that everyone concerned in this art must get together until a point is reached when it becomes established and profitable. That is the feeling of all of us here. We are far more interested than your societies. We therefore venture to suggest that you join us and the thousands of artists that have contributed their services and time in developing radio, and until the point is reached where it is showing a profit for some one, which it is not doing now."[23]

The music publishers were not the only ones concerned about the affect of radio on their businesses. Theater managers concerned that radio would reduce ticket sales on Broadway waged a short-lived

[21] *Id.*, a lament that sounds remarkably similar to what we might hear today from the Recording Industry Association of America (RIAA).

[22] *Id.*, a defense that sounds remarkably similar to what we might hear today from the Digital Media Assocication (DiMA).

[23] *Id.*

campaign, lead by Arthur Hammerstein,[24] president of the Managers Protective Association, to prevent radio stations from broadcasting music performed in current productions.[25] Nevertheless, Hammerstein remained optimistic about the prospects of live performances:

> "The present scare among the theatres," said Mr. Hammerstein, "can be likened to the introduction of the first moving pictures and will soon pass. We still have a commodity the public wants, and neither the moving picture nor radio can replace the theatre, where you can both hear and see the artist."[26]

Makers of phonograph equipment expressed not only equanimity, but some real optimism about the effect of radio broadcasting on their business. The Victor Talking Machine Company,[27] makers of phonograph players and records, issued a statement opining that artists would benefit from their radio performances despite not being paid a fee:

> "While it is considered premature to make a forecast as to the probable outcome of what has been described as an experiment to determine the practicability of broadcasting concert and opera stars, officials of Victor Company are viewing the future with optimism. It is believed radio audiences will be more eager than ever to see and hear the Victor artists as a result of the broadcasting experiment, and will attend their concert and operatic performances in even larger numbers than before."
>
> "We believe hearing such music played by the world's most famous artists will create a greater desire on the part of listeners to have in their homes for future enjoyment and education, in permanent record form, selections which they have heard and have been interested in through the radio."[28]

---

[24] Arthur Hammerstein (1872-1955), the son of Oscar Hammerstein I and uncle of Oscar Hammerstein II.

[25] "Theatre Managers Make War on Radio," *New York Times* (January 4, 1925).

[26] *Id.* It doesn't appear that he anticipated talking pictures, but history continues to prove him correct about the public's demand for the theater's unique commodity.

[27] Acquired by RCA in 1929.

[28] "Theatre Managers Make War on Radio," *New York Times* (January 4, 1925).

Interestingly, all songs performed on the radio at that time were through live performances. As we shall see, the era of the modern disc jockey, playing popular recordings over the air, did not begin until the mid-1930s.

Despite the promise of the new technologies, it was hardly a "roaring 1920s" for music publishers, whose business started experiencing a depression years before the rest of the economy would succumb to the Great Depression.

During the 1920s, revenues from sheet music experienced a precipitous decline. For example, the song *Missouri Waltz*, a hit in 1914, sold 3.5 million copies of sheet music. By 1924, it was the exception for a song to sell a million copies.[29] A year later, that figure dropped by half:

> Songs that would have exceeded a 2,000,000 circulation as in previous years are held down to slightly more than half million. This has been the experience of several of the most prominent publishing houses. A spokesman for one concern said that the radio exhausted the appeal of popular songs by over-doing them. He said he had heard one of the most promising compositions of his firm played eleven times from various stations in a single evening.
>
> "The public will not buy songs that it can hear almost at will by a brief manipulation of the radio dials," he said. "If we could control completely the broadcasting of our compositions, we would endeavor to prevent this saturating of the radio listeners with any particular song. We would try to have it broadcast for a specified period — perhaps a month — and then have it discontinued. If it had one favor, people would purchase it. Under present conditions a song is played or sung until it is a positive bore. Too much of anything becomes decidedly distasteful, and this is especially true of a piece of music."[30]

Whether this anonymous publisher was right or wrong, by 1928, a top selling song sold only about 300,000 copies of sheet music.[31]

---

[29] "Luck Eludes Songwriter," *New York Times* (September 7, 1924).

[30] "Song Pluggers By Subtle Art Purvey Wares," *New York Times* (February 15, 1925).

[31] "Mechanical Music Has Not Yet Won A Victory," *New York Times* (July 1, 1928).

At the annual convention of sheet music dealers held on June 5, 1929, one dealer addressed the audience asking, "What's the matter with the music business? Can anything be done to counteract the waning interest of the public in sheet music?"[32]

Some blamed the radio; others defended it.

> In the music-selling business the present time, there is a great hue and cry about the competition of radio. In the long run, however, the radio is likely to prove far more helpful than harmful. It is the greatest advertisement that music has ever had.[33]

Others blamed the propensity of some music publishers to sell sheet music directly to consumers by mail order or by providing equivalent discounts to mail order houses, such as Sears, which began opening large department stores:

> Are the retailers going to be eliminated by the direct-to-consumer sales policy of the music publishers? This unusual condition, as compared with other industries, has always existed in ours and is undoubtedly the reason why there are not more prosperous retailers. . . . The large mail order houses are rapidly opening an endless chain of retail stores. They undersell publisher and retailer alike, and what they advertise and offer for sale — only the "cream" of our business — that which represents a possible net profit to any music retailer. These mail order houses cannot be considered music dealers, then why should they be given any better than a school discount.[34]

In the face of declining popularity of its main source of income, and the vast deflation of the currency during the early 1930s, the music publishers decided to dramatically reduce the price of popular sheet music from 40¢ to 25¢ per copy.[35]

Meanwhile, ASCAP continued to expand its aggressive licensing campaign on behalf of music publishers and songwriters and, by 1932,

---

[32] "Sheet Music Dealers Hold Annual Convention," *Music Trade Review* (June 8, 1929).

[33] *Id.*

[34] *Id.*

[35] "Sheet Music Prices Drop," *New York Times* (May 14, 1931).

it negotiated a performance license with the radio broadcasters that, for the first time, established rates based upon a percentage of the station's advertising. That year, ASCAP collected from radio stations over $1 million in performance fees.

Nevertheless, revenues from performance licensing the use of music in recordings and for performance on radio were not making up for the decline in sheet music sales. Yet another new technology was in the wings, ready to provide another jolt of change to the music industry.

#### *4. Talking Pictures*

During the mid-1920s, two competing technologies were developed to synchronize sound with motion pictures. One was adopted by William Fox, founder of Twentieth Century Fox, who was successfully producing and distributing silent newsreels. He called the new sound-on-film system, MovieTone. When he began adding sound to his "MovieTone News," the audience not only saw famous people of their day, such as Babe Ruth and Charles Lindberg, but for the first time they heard their voices. MovieTone News recorded Lindberg's takeoff from Long Island on May 20, 1927, his arrival in France, and his subsequent ticker-tape parade in New York City.

At about the same time, Bell Laboratories and its parent company, Western Electric, were experimenting with a process of recording sound on a 16-inch phonographic disc rotated at 33⅓ revolutions per minute. Bell had already acquired the patents to a technology invented in 1907 by Dr. Lee De Forest called Audion — a photoelectric vacuum tube that made it possible to amplify sound, enabling a sound recording to be presented in a full auditorium. The combination of these recorded discs, together with an improved system of amplification, caught the interest of Jack Warner.

Warner licensed the technology and established the Vitaphone Corporation to market a complete system for talking motion pictures. With the Vitaphone system, a motion picture producer was able to synchronize a phonograph recording of various sound effects, music, and voice with the action of the picture. For replay, the disc was placed on a phonograph turntable, rotating at a uniform speed in precise relation to the motion picture.

In 1927, Warner released *The Jazz Singer* starring Al Jolson ("Wait a minute, you ain't heard nothin' yet") and the film industry changed forever.[36] The impact of "talking films" on the music publishing industry was epochal. By the end of 1929, all of the 8,000 major motion picture theaters in the United States were equipped for sound. The era of the silent film was over and the immediate popularity of talking pictures created an enormous demand for music by the Hollywood studios.

Requiring a source of popular music for his "talkies," Jack Warner had the foresight to begin acquiring some of the most important music publishers. In 1928, Warner Bros. acquired M. Witmark & Sons, which had the publishing rights to the big three of Broadway musical composers, Victor Herbert, Sigmund Romberg, and Rudolf Friml. In 1929, they purchased Remick Music Corporation, which held the rights to the works of Gus Kahn, Richard Whiting, Al Dubin, and Harry Warren.

In the same year, Warners purchased Harms, Inc. from Max Dreyfus for $11 million, but with that purchase, Warner's acquired new Broadway musical writers such as George and Ira Gershwin, Vincent Youmans, Irving Caesar, Richard Rodgers, Larry Hart, Oscar Hammerstein, and Jerome Kern. Also in 1929, MGM entered into a publishing administration agreement with Robbins Music Corp. for the publishing of music written for use in MGM pictures. Paramount Pictures established their own music publishing firm, Famous Music. Perhaps the name was adapted from Famous Players, which was Adolph Zukor's former company.

Jack Warner's acquisition of many of the major music publishers of the day couldn't have come at a better time for those publishers. The Great Depression only deepened their troubles when a slump in record sales compounded the slump in sheet music sales.

## C. Shift from Physical Sales to Licensing

During the ten-year period spanning 1922 to 1932, the music industry experienced an upheaval that would not be matched until the advent of the Internet some 70 years later. The business was being dramatically

[36] For a further history and information about licensing music in motion pictures, see Chapter 15, on *Licensing Music in Audiovisual Works.*

transformed by three new technologies — the phonograph records, radio broadcasting, and talking pictures. Sheet music sales, followed by record sales, were declining precipitously. The increase in revenues afforded by licensing public performances to the new radio broadcasting technology was not making up for the decline. The fundamental business model of the music publishing was undergoing a profound shift.

### *1. Origins of the Harry Fox Agency*

Within a few weeks after the premier of *The Jazz Singer*, E.C. Mills and the MPAA, on behalf of 63 music publishers, struck a deal with the patent licensors of both Vitaphone and Movietone, which was expected to earn the publishers more than $1 million in royalties over the following five years. Under the agreement, Vitaphone and Movietone acquired the right to use the publishers' music for which they were guaranteed royalties of $100,000 in the first year and $150,000 in the second.[37]

The following year, Mills suffered criticism for not negotiating enough on behalf of the music publishers, but it is equally plausible that by quickly providing a level of certainty to the talking picture industry that popular songs would be made available for a reasonable license fee, the music industry laid the groundwork for a healthy film industry that would later become an important source of publishing revenues. In any event, he ensured that the "synchronization" fees for the reproduction of songs on Vitaphone and Movietone recordings would get paid directly to music publishers, with songwriters sharing in the royalties through their music publishing agreements (rather than passing through ASCAP, whose activities were confined to the licensing of public performances, not reproductions).[38]

Mills left the MPPA in 1929 and was replaced by John G. Paine. Working for the MPPA during this time was a Russian immigrant in his mid-40s named Harry Fox. Fox entered the music publishing business in 1906 in Cleveland as a partner with his brother Sam Fox. Harry later moved to New York and while working for the MPPA was handed the responsibility of managing the collection and administration of the synchronization fees they were collecting from Vitaphone and Movietone.

---

[37] "Big Royalties Seen in Vitaphone Deal," *New York Times* (December 21, 1927).

[38] For more on synchronization licenses, see Chapter 15, on *Licensing Music in Audiovisual Works.*

When Paine later left to become the general manager of ASCAP, Fox was appointed as general manager of the MPPA. Fox continued to manage the administration of reproduction licenses and his responsibilities in this area became so closely associated with him that it eventually became known as the "Harry Fox Office." Today, the Harry Fox Agency is a division of the National Music Publishers Association (NMPA), the successor to the Music Publisher's Protective Association.[39]

### *2. The Maturation of Performance and Mechanical Licensing*

During the 1930s, ASCAP continued to make progress exploiting the public performance right in the new media of its day. In 1932, the radio broadcasters agreed for the first time to pay performance fees on the basis of a percentage of their revenues. By the mid 1930s, they were paying 5% of their advertising revenues for the use of music. From 1931 to 1939, ASCAP succeeded in increasing its fees from $960,000 to $4.3 million annually.

Meanwhile, phonograph record sales began to recover about the time when records were aired on the radio for the first time. Radio had been a popular media for the performance of music since 1923 and phonograph records had been around since 1912, but it was not until the mid-1930s that someone started playing recordings of popular songs on the radio. While the Lindberg kidnapping trial was being broadcast on radio, Martin Block of WNEW in New York became the first *disc jockey* when on February 2, 1935 he played records on the air as "filler" between the broadcast coverage of the closely followed Lindberg baby kidnapping trial. At the end of the trial, the program continued by popular demand and was appropriately called *Make Believe Ballroom.*

The practice of playing records on the air had been impeded by a ruling by the Federal Communications Commission (FCC), requiring stations to frequently identify the recordings they broadcast — a practice that became unpopular with radio audiences. More important, the American Federation of Musicians used their collective bargaining agreements to force record companies to include legends on their

---

[39] For more information on the Harry Fox Agency and the licensing of musical in sound recordings, see Chapter 13.

records, such as "not licensed for radio broadcast," "for home use only," or "only for noncommercial use on phonographs in home." Fred Waring, the well-known band leader and recording artist, brought suit against WDAS in Pennsylvania to enforce the restrictive language and won.[40]

However, when the jazz orchestra leader Paul Whiteman sued RCA to stop the unlicensed performance of recordings on RCA's NBC radio network, the Second Circuit Court of Appeal held that any attempts to enforce the restrictions would be preempted by federal law and federal law did not prohibit the broadcast of sound recordings.[41] Since the decision was written by the respected copyright jurist, Judge Learned Hand, whose courtroom was situated in New York, a major recording and broadcast center, performers had little hope of enforcing the restriction further in state courts or other federal courts. Seeking a second best solution, the performers proceeded to use the collective bargaining process to require record companies to pay a portion of their revenues into a trust fund for the benefit of performers and musicians.

It is estimated that in 1935 over 25 million records were sold in the United States, a number that grew fourfold by 1940. By 1941, Martin Block's *Make Believe Ballroom* show became so popular that WNEW began airing an all night disc jockey show called, *Milkman's Matinee*, making the station the first to broadcast 24 hours. Its popularity did not go unnoticed by other radio stations who followed suit and by the record companies who saw how radio began influencing record sales.

As a result, new record labels were opening up each week. Music publishers, meanwhile, were having a hard time just keeping up with the new licenses that they had to issue and the lucrative royalties they needed to collect from an increasing number of sources. To reduce the administrative costs of managing licenses issued to record labels, the Harry Fox Office expanded their work for publishers by issuing licenses and collecting royalties for the reproduction of music in phonograph records, work they continue to do for a large number of publishers to this day.

---

[40] *Waring v. WDAS Broadcasting Station, Inc.*, 327 Pa. 433, 194 Atl. 631 (1937).

[41] *RCA Manufacturing Co. v. Whiteman*, 114 F.2d 86 (2d Cir. 1940), *cert. denied*, 311 U.S. 712 (1940).

### *3. Transformation Complete*

By 1940, the transformation of the music publishing business was complete. In today's terms, we might say that evolution of technology — the development of radio, phonographs, and talking pictures during the 20-year period spanning 1920 to 1940 — transformed the music publishing business from a primarily business-to-consumer (B2C) activity, driven by the sales of physical objects (i.e., sheet music), to a primarily business-to-business (B2B) activity, driven by the licensing of rights to allow others to reproduce (e.g., in phonorecords) or perform (e.g., in theaters and by radio broadcast) their music.

Music publishers, no longer producing copies of things to distribute and sell, found themselves having to cut costs by sloughing off their expertise and infrastructure for manufacturing, distributing, and promoting of physical goods, and to make investments in acquiring expertise and relationships focused on the licensing of their musical properties to other businesses — record companies, motion picture producers, theaters, and other businesses.

This shift of business model for music publishers was, as we shall see, the shape of things to come for record companies.

## II. HISTORY REPEATS ITSELF

Since the end of World War II, the music industry grew at a relatively steady pace. By 1995, worldwide revenue of music publishers exceeded $6 billion and the record industry saw worldwide revenues grow to over $40 billion annually.

But, 1995, the year in which the second edition of this book was prepared, turned out to be the beginning of another pivotal time for the music industry.[42] It was the year the Internet arrived and began to play havoc with a record industry that was not quite prepared for the technological change the business was about to experience. The seeds of that experience were sown 20 years earlier.

---

[42] The authors wish to thank Vinton Cerf (who has become widely recognized as "the father of the Internet") for providing Bob Kohn during a cross-country flight in 1995 with his valuable insights on this subject.

## A. The Compact Disc and Digital Recording

By 1977, one hundred years after Edison's invention of the phonograph, the record industry had matured in every means but one: its technology, which was essentially the same technology invented by Edison — the analog phonograph.

In the late 1970s, Philips Electronics and Sony Corporation were each working on a new form of laser-based, permanent storage technology. In August 1980, the two companies participated in a joint press conference announcing the *compact disc* (CD). Instead of a tone arm and diamond stylus of the traditional phonograph player, the CD player used a laser beam and a photoelectric cell to read a sound pattern imprinted on the disc as a series of microscopic pits.

In addition, new recording techniques were developed that would reduce the noise and distortion unavoidable in earlier recording methods. Using a technique called *pulse code modulation* (PCM), the frequencies and amplitudes, or *analog* vibrations, of the original sound are analyzed and converted into *digital* pulses by the recording device. These digital pulses share the same basic components of the software that run modern computers: 1's and 0's, representing the *on* and *off* signals of the binary code. These "on" and "off" pulses are then processed and reconverted to ordinary sound signals when the record is cut.

Soon after the introduction of the compact disc, it was discovered that improved sound reproduction could be obtained by maintaining the digital character of the PCM recording in the process of mastering the CD. Thus, in the production of modern recordings, a digital, rather than analog, tape recorder is used during the sessions in which the sounds are (i) *recorded*, (ii) *mixed* or *edited*, and (iii) *mastered* for mass production.

Within three years after the introduction of CD technology, popular recordings in the new CD format were introduced in the United States — and none too soon. At the time, the U.S. recording industry had been experiencing its worst slump since the Great Depression. Young people, rather than buying records, were dropping quarters into videogame machines appearing in bowling alleys and game parlors all over the country. The CD format, which provided a crackle-free sound and far more convenient format for storage and handling, was such a hit that many people replaced their vinyl record collections with versions released in the CD format. By 1987, more CDs were sold in the United States than vinyl records.

## B. The Personal Computer

The digital revolution was not confined to the recording industry. By the mid-1970s, the first personal computers were being developed — with the Altair 8080 in 1975 and the Apple in 1976. With the introduction of the IBM PC in 1981, the personal computer industry was in full gear. Throughout this period, personal computer enthusiasts looked for ways to connect with each other. Necessity being the mother of invention, they found a way — through a device called a modem, which allows computers to connect with each other via telephone lines.

Here's how it worked: A *modem* (a portmanteau comprising the communications terms, *modulate* and *demodulate*) is a device that converts, or modulates, the information in your computer stored in *binary* or *digital* form (i.e., *bits* of information represented as either a one or a zero) to a form that can be transmitted over the phone line, or *analog* form. In simple terms, what happens is that the *ones* of the digital format are converted to a high pitch tone and the *zeros* are converted to a low pitch tone; the modem converts the ones and zeros generated by your computer into a series of analogous high pitched and low pitched tones and sends them over the phone lines to another modem at the receiving end of the line, which is connected to another computer. The receiving modem demodulates, or converts, the high and low pitched analog tones back into the binary ones and zeros and forwards the signals to the computer where they can be stored to disk or sent to your computer screen in the form of text or pictures.

## C. Electronic Information Services and Bulletin Board Services

The proliferation of modem-equipped personal computers gave rise to services that helped computer enthusiasts connect with each other. An *electronic information service* was like an electronic meeting place, where anyone, at any time of day or night, from virtually anywhere in the world where adequate telephone service is available, could dial in with their personal computer, leave messages for others, receive messages left by others, participate in live, *real- time* or *chat conferences*, or transfer down to their computers (i.e., *download*) virtually any kind of computer file (e.g., computer program, text, graphics, sound, etc.) that can be stored on a computer, or transfer to the online service (i.e., *upload*) any kind of computer file to enable others to download such computer file to their computers.

The larger electronic information services tended to be owned by large conglomerates, which had lots of mainframe computer time to spare during their off-peak hours. *CompuServe*, for example, was a division of H&R Block prior to its purchase by AOL. *GEnie* was a division of General Electric. *Prodigy* was originally a joint venture among IBM, CBS, and Sears. *America Online*, the most successful of the electronic information services, later merged with Time-Warner. The *Microsoft Network* (MSN) was originally an electronic information service, but was later converted to a web portal.

Even a personal computer user could operate an electronic information service at home or at the office by means of a modem, personal computer, and special electronic bulletin board software (BBS). These home BBS operators, called *sysops* (i.e., *sys*tem *op*erator*s*), ranged from professionals, such as doctors and lawyers operating a board as a forum for local colleagues, to teenagers offering electronically stored nude photographs and likenesses of favorite recording, television, and sports celebrities.[43]

Both the commercial and noncommercial online information services operated basically the same way, except the noncommercial BBSs generally did not charge a fee for their use. The fees charged by the large commercial operators, such as CompuServe and America Online, were generally about $9.95 per month for a limited number of minutes of usage (e.g., 300 minutes) and an hourly fee for use beyond the minimum (e.g., $2.95 per hour). Later, services such as AOL became Internet services providers, charging a flat $21.95 per month for unlimited Internet access and use of its electronic information service. Most personal computer bulletin board services were accessed for the price of a phone call, often free if accessed using unlimited residential phone service.

When writing the first edition of this book in 1992, the authors brought to the attention of the Harry Fox Agency the fact that numerous BBSs, including some large commercial services such as CompuServe,

---

[43] From 1985 to 1987, co-author Bob Kohn operated a BBS for lawyers (using eSoft's TBBS software), called Legacy/The Law Network, from his home in Beverly Hills, California; in 1987, he became the system operator of The Law Roundtable on GEnie, which he operated until 1992.

were offering *downloads* of MIDI files containing popular music. Within a few months, the music publishers filed a class action lawsuit against CompuServe,[44] which was later settled out of court.

The problem with electronic information services was the inefficient way one had to communicate with them: a dial-up connection using a modem through the phone line to another modem. When the session was over, you had to hang up; to reach another service, you needed to dial again. What was needed was a way to string all the services and BBS together on the same network, so that once you were on one service you could quickly switch to the next without hanging up your connection and creating a new one — a convenience we take for granted today.

## D. The Internet

The events leading up to the Internet and its effect on the music industry can be traced back to a Cold War concern about the vulnerability of the nation's telecommunications system, which could be snapped by the nuclear annihilation of just a few key metropolitan areas. The *Defense Advanced Research Projects Agency* (ARPA) project was established in 1969 to address the problem of how to keep military sites in communication across the country in the event of a nuclear war. The project, eventually to become known as ARPANET, began experimenting with various telecommunications protocols for transmitting information through various media including radio, telephone, satellites, and Ethernet.

By 1977, a packet switching protocol was designed for this purpose. That protocol formed the basis for what eventually became, the Transmission Control Protocol and Internet Protocol (TCP/IP). By 1983, each node (i.e., a computer connected to the network) on the ARPANET was required to use TCP/IP to connect to it. Essentially, the TCP/IP protocol allows any computer attached to the Internet to talk to any other computer on the Internet, as long as they both are using the TCP/IP protocol.

Being primarily a military operation, universities and the general public were not welcomed to ARPANET, but because many military contractors had ties with university research facilities, many university

[44] *Frank Music Corp. v. CompuServe, Inc.*, 93 Civ. 8153 (S.D.N.Y.), filed November 29, 1993.

researchers were given access to the network. These university researchers began a crusade to open up the network to their peers. Meanwhile, in 1984, the *National Science Foundation* opened an office to study and participate in the nation's networking efforts. By 1986, the NSF deployed a computer network called NSFNET. By contrast with ARPANET, NSFNET actively welcomed anyone who sought to connect into the network, and a number of universities and research groups were quickly given access to it. By 1988, the ARPANET evolved into the rapidly expanding NSFNET, and the resulting "Internet" was in full operation.

In 1989, Tim Berners-Lee working at CERN in Switzerland created a system to facilitate the sharing of information among researchers in high-energy particle physics. This system, called the World Wide Web, is based on a client/server model and a set of standards for information access and navigation called *hypertext.* Hypertext is a computer concept that allows one to navigate through a document or compilation of related documents by pointing and clicking on words or objects on a computer screen. For example, if you were looking at a hypertext version of this page, and you used your mouse to "point and click" on the word *synchronization*, the computer could instantly take you to the first page of Chapter 15 which covers *synchronization* licenses.

What Berners-Lee did was to extend the concept of "hypertext" not only within a document, and between documents, but also between different computer sites accessible to each other over the Internet. Thus, if you were viewing a hypertext version of this page and clicked on the word, *Kohn*, your computer, if connected to the Internet, could instantly take you to the electronic "page" published by the authors of this book,[45] and from there, you can link to any number of websites, both within the Kohns' Internet site and to other sites that are linked to our site, such as the websites of the U.S. Copyright Office, and those of ASCAP and BMI.

In 1993, a group of computer programmers at the University of Illinois developed the first computer program for the World Wide Web that had a graphical user interface, making it easy to navigate the web by clicking on links using a mouse on a personal computer.

[45] http://www.kohnmusic.com was created in July, 1995. The description of the Internet on these two pages was from our Second Edition, published in 1996.

In addition, this "browser" software allowed users to view text, such as email, and graphical images, such as photographs, and to receive just about any kind of file available over the web, including those containing sounds, video clips, and other content. The first version of this software was called *Mosaic*, and commercial versions have since been released by public companies such as Netscape (since purchased by America Online) and Microsoft (i.e., Microsoft Explorer).

Until the mid-1990s, the Internet was primarily used by academic institutions, defense contractors, and government agencies and their use was limited to remotely access other computers on the network and to send and receive *e-mail* (i.e., electronic mail). The advent of easy to use browser software for the World Wide Web fueled an explosion of growth in the number of users who access the Internet and those who set up web "servers" and web "sites" on those servers containing information and entertainment programming that users of Internet browsers may access. Each website is the equivalent of a commercial online service or BBS, with the difference being only the scale of service and content provided by the site. In fact, many BBS operators have converted their operations to websites on the World Wide Web. By the late 1990s, most electronic information services, such as BBS services, AOL, MSN, and CompuServe were converted to websites or "portals."

By this time, music copyright owners became uneasy about the potential for the easy transmission of perfect digital copies of recorded music. To the extent perfect digital copies of these transmissions could easily be made, then the transmissions posed a threat to the market for the purchase of records.

Exacerbating their fears were rumblings from the high tech community that the entire future of the music industry may be under mortal threat. Esther Dyson, the author of a highly respected technology newsletter called *Release 2.0*, suggested,

> The idea that intellectual property in a Net-based economy can lose its value horrifies most owners and creators. They'd better get over it.[46]

[46] Esther Dyson, "Intellectual Value," *Wired Magazine* (July 1995).

The advent of digital transmissions caused those who create and distribute recorded entertainment to question whether the laws designed to protect their copyrighted content. It was against this backdrop that the recording industry lobbied Congress to enact the Digital Performance Rights in Sound Recording Act of 1995, an amendment to the U.S. Copyright Act that created a limited performance right for sound recordings when they were transmitted by digital means.[47]

## E. Technological Prerequisites to Digital Commerce in Music

While files of data — such as email, word processing, spreadsheet, and MIDI files — could technically be transmitted from one computer to another, widespread adoption of digital commerce in music and recordings would have to wait until the further development of three basic market drivers: (1) bandwidth, (2) portability, and (3) ease of use.

### *1. Bandwidth*

One of the more important issues in the development of electronic commerce in digital music can be summarized by one word: *bandwidth*, which refers to the number of *bits* of information that can be transmitted *per second* through a given communications line. The bandwidth required for voice communications is 64,000 bits per second; for high fidelity music, 1.2 million bits per second; and, ideally, for video, 45 million bits per second. Copper telephone wires, sometimes called twisted-pair, can theoretically carry as much as six million bits per second — fast enough for music, but not fast enough for some transmissions of high resolution video. By comparison, the potential bandwidth of fiber optic lines exceeds 1,000 billion bits per second.

#### *a. Modem Technology*

The average modern musical recording is about 3.5 minutes long, and 3.5 minutes of musical data, in the form of 0's and 1's, is about 40 megabytes large. In the early days of personal computing, the standard

[47] The DPRSR Act of 1995 is discussed at length in Chapter 13, on *Licensing Music in Sound Recordings* and Chapter 23, on *Licensing of Sound Recordings.*

modems operated at 300 bits per second (bps). (If the words on this page were transmitted to you at the rate of 300bps, you would be able to read them twice as fast as they would appear on the page). Thus, it would take two computers each equipped with a 300bit modem over 40 hours to complete the transmission of a single recording. Moreover, computers widely in use in the early 1980s, such as the Kaypro II, were not equipped with hard drives; the maximum amount of data one could store on the 5¼-inch "floppy" drives of that time was 64k — which could be used to store only a few seconds of a single sound recording. The typical hard disk drive of that time could store only ten megabytes of data, not enough to store the data of an entire popular sound recording in digital form.

By 1984, relatively inexpensive 1,200bps modems became widely available and later 2,400bps modems became the norm. By the mid-1990s, modems operated at 28 thousand bits per second (28kbps), but even at that rate, it took nearly three hours to transmit a 40mg file. At these rates, the transmission of musical files was not very practical. Even on a network, such as the computer network of a college or university, while file transfer rates are considerably faster, there's still the problem of the limited storage space on the students' hard drives. Given the average hard disk space during the 1990s, about 2 to 4 gigabytes, it didn't take too many of these 40mg files to fill up your hard disk.

Regardless of the physical attributes of the communications line (e.g., copper wire, fiber optics, air waves), and the number of bits per second it may potentially carry, its bandwidth is further limited by the technology of the devices and software, such as modems and telecommunications protocols, used to send and receive those bits. Nevertheless, that technology began to improve rapidly.

By 2001, the standard personal computer *modem* had speeds exceeding 56,600 bits per second, over 20 times what they were just ten years before. At that time, many businesses (and many homes in communities where the service is available) began to install access to ISDN, or digital lines, offering an immediate leap to 115,000 bits per second. Many large companies access the Internet directly from their T1 lines, providing a bandwidth of over a million bits per second.

One major leap forward in bandwidth occurred upon the widespread deployment of *cable modems*, which allowed home computer users to access the Internet through their cable television lines. This greatly increased the speeds at which the Internet may be accessed from the home — as much as ten million bits per second, or about 80 times faster than an ISDN line. Another major leap was the deployment of digital signal look (DSL) technology, which provides the bandwidth of a T1 into the home at comparable speeds.

Access to the Internet using high speed bandwidth has grown to a point where virtually everyone with access to cable television in the home may subscribe to high speed Internet access. It is estimated that as of January 2005, 48% of those with Internet access at home had a high-speed or *broadband* connection,[48] and by 2008 over 90% of U.S. households enjoyed broadband access to the internet.[49]

*b. Data Compression Technology*

An important innovation that contributed to the solution to limited bandwidth, and particularly to the disk space problem, was the application of file compression technology to the problem of sound recording data. In the 1990s, a group called the Motion Pictures Experts Group (MPEG) working group developed in association with the Fraunhofer-Gesellschaft group a set of standards for compressing audio and video files.

MPEG 1, layer 3, later shortened to MP3, is simply a standard set of mathematical algorithms used for compressing sound files into an attractive format for downloading or streaming across the Internet. When the MP3 algorithms are run through a set of musical data, such as a digitally encoded recording, it eliminates virtually all of the 0's and 1's the human hear can't reasonably discern, leaving only those 0's and 1's that are recognizable. Because about 90% of the data in a typical digitally encoded musical recording are not essential to the reasonable listening experience, that 90% could be removed, leaving a greatly compressed file having only a slight reduction in sound quality. Though an audiophile or sound engineer could determine the difference between the original .wav file containing all the data of the recording and the compressed MP3 version of the recording, the latter, although degraded, still provides a quite acceptable listening experience for the average person.

As a result, a musical recording compressed with MP3 encoding software now comprised a file that was 11 times smaller than the

[48] Arbitron, *Internet and Multimedia 2005* at 2 (April 19, 2005).

[49] Nielsen Net Ratings at www.nielsen.com (2009).

original raw data file. In other words, the 40 megabyte file was now compressible to about 3.5 megabytes without a noticeable degradation in sound quality to most listeners. Now, a one gigabyte hard disk could contain over ten times as many musical recordings, and while the raw data file took nearly three hours to transfer by modem, the file encoded in MP3 could be transferred in less than 15 minutes using a 28kbps modem.

During the late 1990s, it was estimated that 60% of all college students had access to the Internet using high speed bandwidth. In other words, they were connected to the Internet at speeds offered by T1 lines. Thus, a 3.5 megabyte MP3 file could be transferred over a school's network in less than 30 seconds.

Sometime in late 1996, college students, purely on a grass roots basis, began what we now know as the MP3 phenomenon. It began with the simultaneous developments in personal computer hardware and software: the introduction of low cost CD-ROM drives for personal computers, and the development of three small utility software programs: *ripper* software, *MP3 encoder* software, and *MP3 decoder* software.

As personal computer enthusiasts discovered, CD-ROM drives not only allowed you to play interactive CD-ROM software and games, such as electronic encyclopedias and arcade games, it allowed you to use your computer to play compact discs (CDs) containing musical recordings. By downloading from the Internet and installing ripper software on your CD-ROM drive equipped personal computer, you could pop your favorite music CD into your CD-ROM drive, run the ripper software, and within minutes copy all of the tracks from your CD onto your computer's hard drive. The ripper software would actually read each digitally encoded track on your CD, recognize the 0's and 1's comprising the musical recording, and copy the track in digital form to your computer, which would appear as a .wav on your hard disk.

A sound recording ripped from a CD could be listened to, but its size made building a collection of recordings impractical. These .wav files would only be useful when they were encoded into the MP3 format. In addition, a file encoded in MP3 is only useful if you can play it, and to play an MP3 file all you needed was MP3 decoding software.

In the late 1990s, the Fraunhoffer institute posted on the Internet an example piece of MP3 encoding and decoding software, and actively encouraged their use. Software developers quickly developed various improvements in MP3 encoding and decoding software, including a 19-year old computer programmer in Sedona, Arizona, who developed what soon became the most popular MP3 software player, WinAMP. AOL later purchased this software for a reported $70 million.

In late 1997, two software executives after working at software startup Pretty Good Privacy, Inc. conceived a business plan based on the notion that a vast number of people were beginning to learn the convenience and joys of *downloadable music* and that there would soon be a demand for legally licensed MP3 files offered at an affordable price. GoodNoise Corporation was formed by Bob Kohn, your coauthor, and Gene Hoffman. In July 1998, the company began offering MP3 files for 99¢ per track. Later, the company changed its name to EMusic. com, Inc., and went public (NASDAQ: EMUS).

At about the same time eMusic was started, an entrepreneur in San Diego, California, purchased the rights to the domain name mp3.com for $5,000, and began a website devoted to news for the growing MP3 community. MP3.com later developed a free download service, offering MP3 files uploaded by unsigned bands and later went public. When MP3.com later encoded a vast number of MP3 files of recordings owned by the major record companies and offered those files to anyone who could prove they owned a CD corresponding to those files, it was sued for copyright infringement and lost.[50]

### *2. Portability*

One of the early limitations of downloading music was that you could only play the recordings on your PC. Even that experience was far from ideal, as PC speaker systems were rudimentary in 1998. More important, many people want their music on the go. There was no way to transfer an MP3 file to a CD and play it on a portable CD player.

While surfing the net in March 1998, about three months after he and Kohn started eMusic, Gene Hoffman came across an advertisement for something called MPMan. The first portable solid state digital audio player, MPMan was developed by SaeHan Information Systems of Seoul, Korea. Kohn purchased one, paying for it in advance using his American Express card, the only form of payment SaeHan would

[50] *UMG Recordings, Inc. v. mp3.com*, 92 F. Supp. 2d 349 (S.D.N.Y. 2000).

accept. When the eMusic team first saw the device a few days later, it confirmed their greatest expectations about their new endeavor: that someday, everyone would be listening to MP3 audio files on their portable solid-state music players.

The MPMan player, measuring about 91 mm tall by 70 mm wide by 16.5 mm thick and weighing just over 2 ounces, contained 32 megabytes of permanent memory — which meant that it could store and play up to about ten recordings in the MP3 format. What was nice about the solid state player was that, unlike a CD player, you could jog with it and the sound would not skip. (Joggers at the time had to use cassette players.) Kohn and Hoffman would use it to demonstrate the prospects for their digital download business when they were raising financing for eMusic and taking the company public later that year.

In September 1998, Diamond Multimedia introduced the Diamond Rio player. eMusic negotiated a deal with Diamond to bundle a coupon in the Rio package entitling the buyer to ten free downloads on the eMusic site. When the RIAA filed a lawsuit to enjoin all sales of the player, Diamond's attorney called Kohn who proceeded to outline why the Rio player was not covered by the Audio Home Recording Act of 1992. At the hearing on the RIAA's application for a temporary restraining order, Judge Andrea Collins allowed Kohn to address the court to present his arguments. Judge Collins issued the temporary order, provided that the RIAA post a $500,000 bond to compensate Diamond for the delay in shipping the device should Diamond eventually prevail in court. Diamond ultimately prevailed on appeal on the very grounds argued by Kohn on the day of the temporary restraining order.[51]

By then, Kohn and Hoffman were convinced that portability was to become one of the key market factors driving the growth of the downloadable music market. The problem was they were not happy with the functional specifications and usability of the MP3 players on the market. Hoffman had come across new miniature hard disk technology being developed by IBM and was convinced that he could build a better MP3 player. On a tip from a friend, they learned about a talented young product manager working at Philips Electronics.

---

[51] *Recording Industry Ass'n of Am. v. Diamond Multimedia Sys.*, 180 F.3d 1072 (9th Cir. 1999).

On February 1, 1999, Kohn and Hoffman met with Tony Fadell, who at that time was working in charge of the development and manufacture of Philip's Windows-based personal digital assistant (PDA). At that meeting, Fadell watched Hoffman demonstrate the MPMan music player, MPMan. Fadell was intrigued with the prospects of MP3 and digital download business and within a few weeks accepted a job with eMusic. Tony was specifically responsible for developing an eMusic-branded digital music player that would be far better than existing devices of that time.

For reasons Kohn and Hoffman never understood, Fadell left eMusic after only a few weeks with the company. For a short while, he worked at Real Networks, and then for his own startup called Fuse, but he soon went to work for Apple Computer and became one of the leading developers of the Apple iPod and later the iPhone. The first iPod was released in October 2001, six months after Kohn and Hoffman sold eMusic to Universal Music Group.

### 3. Ease of Use

A third key factor driving the growth of digital music was *ease of use.*

#### a. The Mechanics of Downloading

At the time Hoffman and Kohn founded eMusic in 1997, downloading music was easy enough — if you knew exactly what software tools were required and you knew how to use them. It was easy enough to learn, but certainly not as easy as popping a CD into a CD player. Downloading ripper and MP3 encoding software, then ripping, encoding, and naming your files, and finally installing and using MP3 player, such as the popular WinAMP, were all steps in a process. If you had purchased a portable MP3 player, such as MPMan or the Diamond Rio player, you had to use separate software to load the device with your MP3 files. It was a process that took time to learn. Many millions of people would have to change the way they acquire copies of music and play them. The process would have to be far easier for this market to grow.

For this reason, one of the key features of the eMusic store was a piece of software that eMusic developed called FreeAMP. FreeAMP was client software that operated as a music player for personal computers. It also facilitated the process of purchasing downloads in the eMusic store. When you purchased an entire album, you would normally have to click on each track and wait for several tracks to download before clicking on the rest of the tracks on the album. Then you had to be sure that the tracks were moved to the proper file folder so that you could locate the files for playback. eMusic began to receive customer service calls from purchasers who couldn't locate where on their PCs the MP3 files they had downloaded were.

With FreeAMP, you could purchase an album and FreeAMP would manage the rest of the process for you, automatically clicking on each track you purchased, managing the download process, even putting the downloaded files in the proper folders on your hard disk. Moreover, FreeAMP was developed under the "open source" license, which meant that no one, not even eMusic, could use it exclusively. FreeAMP's source code was made freely available to assure that anyone could use and customize it as an MP3 player and as client software for facilitating the download and playing of digital music from any store. Kohn and Hoffman understood the importance of open standards and compatibility to the growth of the business, so it was important to ensure the client software would not be controlled by any one company.

Recall that Hoffman charged Fadell with building a portable MP3 player for the company. The plan was to expand the functionality of FreeAMP to support not only eMusic's MP3 player but all MP3 players that would come to market. Because FreeAMP was made available under an "open source" license, any MP3 device maker could modify to work with their player and distribute it with their device at no charge.

Unfortunately, the best laid plans of mice and men often go awry. In May 2001, for the reasons described below, eMusic was sold to Universal Music Group. Shortly after the acquisition, employees of eMusic met with Apple Computer about a potential strategic partnership involving Apple's then-secret digital music player, the iPod, and the eMusic store. No strategic partnership evolved, but Apple walked out of the meeting with an insightful model for the iTunes downloadable music store.

### b. *Playlist Management*

Overall, Apple has done an admirable job of making it easier for consumers to purchase and use downloadable music. The iTunes client software not only helps you find music in the iTunes store, but facilitates the purchase and download of tracks, automatically organizes the downloads on your hard disk by creating the appropriate artist and album folders for you, and facilitates the side-loading of your tracks onto your iPod player.

However, there is still much to be done to improve the usability of downloadable music. One of the key areas of the consumer experience with downloadable music is the playlist. A *playlist* is simply the order in which a consumer wishes to hear several tracks of music. An album embodies a playlist predetermined by the record company. In the 1950s and 1960s, when 45rpm records were popular, consumers created a playlist by simply stacking the records in a certain order on their record players.

In iTunes, a user's playlist or playlists must be created in the personal computer client software before being transferred to the iPod. There currently is no way to manipulate the playlist using the iPod itself. The creation of playlists takes time and consumers are looking for more innovative ways to create, modify, and share playlists. One organization, Project Playlist which operates playlist.com, is trying to improve this important aspect of usability.

#### c. *Music Discovery*

Technological innovation has had an impact on other important areas of usability, such as music *discovery.* When you hear a recording on the radio or in a department store that you are enjoying, you often wish to know the name of the song and the recording artist so that you can later purchase the track and add it to your collection and playlist. If the title and artist are not announced, there may be little you can do — unless you have a copy of a software application called *Shazam*, released in 2009. With a mobile phone equipped with Shazam, you can point your phone in the direction of the music and Shazam will identify the recording being performed and present a list of sites, such as the iTunes store, where you can purchase the track on the spot. Similar applications, such as *Melodis*, allow you to sing the lyrics of a song into your phone and it will identify the song in a similar manner.

#### d. *Interactive Webcasting*

Internet radio stations (i.e., *webcasters*), like their terrestrial radio counterparts, play an important role in the consumer's discovery of new music. Studies show that at one time nearly 90% of all CD purchases were influenced by radio airplay. While that percentage may have declined since the advent of social networking sites and technology, which enables friends to share playlists, radio airplay is still one of the most important means of influencing the consumer's discovery of new music.

In the past few years, webcasting has grown in sophistication. Traditionally, consumers would first choose the genre of music they would like to listen to (e.g., pop, classic rock, country, classical, etc.) and select the appropriate webcast channel that restricts its broadcast to the desired genre. More recently, webcast services such as *Pandora* combine the traditional Internet radio model with technology that helps the individual listener customize the kind of music that will be transmitted to him. While listening to the station, the user may cast a vote on each recording delivered, and Pandora will begin serving up recordings more like those that the listener has approved and less like those he has disapproved. The listener may also type in the name of an artist and recordings by that artist and similar artists will begin to be included in the transmission to the user.

## F. Other Factors Affecting Digital Commerce in Music

### *1. Peer-to-Peer Software Enabling Unauthorized File Sharing*

Because ripper software was distributed on the Internet on a freeware or shareware basis, just about anyone on the Internet could download a free copy of ripper software and use it to convert recordings in their CD collections to MP3 files. Thus, millions of MP3 files were produced from virtually every popular music CD available to the public. Students could easily exchange these files over freely available computer networks, by email or by FTP file transfer, except that there was no way to search for a desired recording.

In 1998, five students at UCLA developed a website and software program called Scour.net, which greatly facilitated the exchange of MP3 files. The Scour software crawled or "scoured" all the hard disks connected on the UCLA network, and later other college networks, to determine which personal computers were storing MP3 files of recorded music. The program then permitted anyone logging on the Scour.net website to download files from those computers on the scoured networks that contained MP3 files for sharing.[52]

The facilitation of illegal *file sharing*, as it became known to defenders of this form of copyright infringement, took a giant leap forward, or backward depending upon your perspective, upon the invention and widespread deployment of *Napster.* Napster greatly facilitated the mass infringement of digital music files by operating as a client software application on your PC, cataloging the MP3 files on your hard disk, and using a peer-to-peer model that enabled any one user of the software to efficiently locate an MP3 file on the PC of any other user of the Napster software while connected to the Internet.

The notoriety and widespread deployment and use of the Napster system attracted Hummer Winblad, a Silicon Valley venture capital firm, to invest $15 million in the company. Napster was subsequently sued by the five major record companies.[53]

Investors in Napster, however, were far too optimistic about the prospects of their legal defense. A Federal District Court in California granted a preliminary injunction, ordering Napster to virtually cease operations. Napster filed an immediate appeal, and within days, the District Court's injunction was stayed pending appeal. The appeal was heard by the Ninth Circuit Court of Appeals in October 2000, and on February 12, 2001, the Ninth Circuit affirmed the lower court decision on all substantive issues.[54]

---

[52] eMusic was in discussions to acquire Scout.net, for its technology and user base, when it was approached and acquired by a company controlled by Michael Ovitz. Scour went bankrupt in 2000 under the weight of a lawsuit filed by the RIAA.

[53] Ironically, during the pendency of the lawsuit, the German media firm, Bertelsmann, which at the time owned BMG, one of the five major record companies, lent Napster over $50 million in exchange for an option to purchase a controlling interest in the firm. At a meeting that Kohn and Hoffman had with Bertelsmann's CEO Thomas Middlehoff on November 19, 1999, Middlehoff expressed interest in purchasing eMusic, but later deferred to his investment bankers who advised him to make the investment in Napster instead. That investment later cost Bertelsmann dearly when, in late 2007, after years of costly litigation, it agreed to pay $154 million in damages to the major record labels and $130 million to a group of music publishers lead by the Harry Fox Agency to settle their lawsuits against Bertelsmann for contributory copyright infringement.

[54] *A&M Records, Inc. v. Napster, Inc.*, 239 F.3d 1004 (9th Cir. 2001).

### 2. The Lack of Open Standards

By then, the damage caused by Napster to eMusic was complete. Because of the insistence of major record companies on the use of a concept known as *digital rights management*, the major record companies would not license their content in the MP3 format. That left Napster, during two years it was operating between mid-1999 to mid-2001, as the only outlet for consumers to acquire the music they wanted, the way they wanted it — that is, as downloadable music files in the MP3 format.

Digital rights management (DRM) was billed as a technical means of keeping users of music files from copying and sharing them on the Internet. To provide comfort to an industry seeking a solution to what was becoming a widespread problem a number of companies were formed in the late 1990s to develop DRM. AT&T, through a division called A2B, Liquid Audio, and Intertrust were among the first companies to develop digital rights management technologies, and later Microsoft's Windowsmedia division joined the fray.

Many of these technologies attempt to deploy one form of encryption technology or another to prevent or control the copying of copyrighted works encoded in a digitally formatted computer file. Encryption is the means by which data is scrambled into an unintelligible form in such a way that only the holder of the proper encryption key can unscramble the data back to its original state. The strength of an encryption technology depends upon the reliability of the algorithm and the length of the encryption key used in encrypting the file. Any encryption key that is over 128-bits long is considered *strong* encryption. A file of data encrypted with a 128-bit key would be virtually impossible to decrypt without the proper key. It is estimated, by the U.S. National Security Agency, that it would take 12 trillion times the age of the universe, using every computer on the planet, to break a file encrypted with a 128-bit key. Pretty strong stuff.

The problem, however, is that encryption is the wrong technology for protecting recorded music. On April 3, 1997, Bob Kohn and Gene Hoffman, working at Pretty Good Privacy, Inc., were approached by several engineers working at Philips Electronics (whose parent company at the time owned Polygram Records, the predecessor to today's Universal Music Group) to inquire whether PGP encryption technology could be used to protect downloadable music files. Hoffman replied that encryption could never be used to fully secure a digital music file, because encryption is intended to keep a communication between two parties private from a third party, not restrict one of the two parties from copying the communication.

In other words, encryption is used to solve the problem of keeping a third party, call her Cathy, from listening in to a conversation between two other parties, call them Alice and Baker. If strong encryption were used to encrypt the conversation, then Cathy could work for the CIA and she still would not be able to crack the call, using even the best of technology the intelligence agency has at its disposal. But, as Alice has to *encrypt* the sound on her end, Baker in order to listen to the sound, has to *decrypt* it on his end. Once decrypted, Baker can record it and make copies.

In other words, encryption, which is really good at keeping a third party out of the conversation, depends upon the *sender trusting the recipient.* Applying encryption to protect sound recordings is applying it to precisely the opposite situation — where the sender absolutely *does not trust* the recipient, which in this case is the consumer. The consumer must decrypt the sound in order to listen to it and if he can listen to it, he can record it. Thus, as the sound comes out of its encrypted box, it can be copied onto a hard disk in the same form it was encrypted — digital files that are easy to copy.

Because every computer contained a "digital out," the second party could always remove sounds fixed in digital form from the digital box intended to keep them secure. In addition, Hoffman explained to Philips engineers that the complications of maintaining the electronic "keys" necessary for consumers to use technically protected music files would be too complicated for the consumer to manage. Besides, there were far better means to identify and minimize the piracy of digital music files on the Internet. These included the use of encryption hashing technology to identify files shared over the Internet and business models that made it, as Hoffman coined the phrase, "easier to buy than to steal."

When Kohn and Hoffman founded eMusic in December 1997, they were committed to making music "easier to buy than to steal" and when they opened the first store to sell permanent downloads of music in July 1998, they sold the digital files in the MP3 format, the *de facto* open standard, rather than use any of various, incompatible DRM technologies that were being offered at the time. The eMusic team was convinced these DRM technologies were flawed and were committed to offering the music in the format that consumers were demanding. eMusic soon licensed hundreds of thousands of recordings from hundreds of record companies, but only from independent record companies, because the major record companies were reluctant to license their masters for sale by permanent download unless the digital files contained DRM technology.

Meanwhile, the piracy of MP3 files continued unabated. From Kohn and Hoffman's perspective, it was initially a good thing. Millions of students were becoming aware of the joys and convenience of digital downloading. An increasing number of college students began using technologies like WinAMP, an early MP3 music player for PCs, and Scour.net. Scour.net didn't always work; you had to click link after link and you were lucky to find one properly linked to the recorded music you were looking for and when you finally received the file, the quality was inconsistent, with some improperly encoded and others cut off before the end. Kohn and Hoffman were convinced that even students would pay 99¢ a track for the greater convenience of locating and downloading quality digital music files quickly and easily. The only thing eMusic needed to compete against the mass piracy was the one item they needed to level the playing field: major label content.

The fact that DRM did not work to protect music does not mean there was no effective technical means of discouraging the unauthorized file sharing by peer-to-peer networks. One promising means of enforcement was deployed by EMusic. EMusic sold downloads of MP3 files of recorded music, files that were easily copied by the consumer. For this reason, most of the EMusic catalog of MP3 files found its way onto the Napster file sharing system. But EMusic developed a system that allowed them to uniquely identify each MP3 file it offered. Using an encryption algorithm or "hash" called MD5, eMusic was able to determine if the same file was offered in the Napster system. This allowed EMusic to notify Napster in advance of its copyrighted files, and Napster could block the transfer of any MP3 files that corresponded to the list provided by EMusic. While not perfect, it significantly reduced the amount of pirating of EMusic files within the Napster system.

Through all of 1998 and 1999, Kohn and Hoffman worked furiously to try to convince the major record companies — including face-to-face meetings with Roger Ames, CEO of Warner Music, Ken Berry,

CEO of EMI, and Doug Morris and Jimmy Iovine, heads of Universal Music to abandon their hopeless allegiance to DRM. Kohn and Hoffman explained to these executives they were already selling their music in MP3 format by distributing their recordings on CDs, which are easily "ripped" and converted to MP3. You might as well offer the music in MP3 and get paid for it now than wait for some DRM solution that will never work in the first place. In the meantime, the industry could develop effective means of determining where on the Internet illegal files were being traded and stop the activity using methods such as the MD5 hash. Choosing to follow instead the advice of their "new media" strategists at the time, the major record executives remained deeply committed to only selling their music in some form of DRM format.

At a meeting on April 17, 2000, with Morris and Iovine in New York, Kohn and Hoffman offered to make available Universal Music's recordings in the eMusic download store. The eMusic executives explained they were willing to be flexible in terms of how to structure the relationship, offering an equity stake in the company and offering to sell digital downloads at a price determined by Universal, provided that eMusic got to retain some fair commission for the sale. eMusic would effectively act as an agent for the majors, giving the majors control over the pricing and even the customers.

As Kohn explained to Morris, it was imperative that the majors retain control over pricing. If they attempted to sell downloads at a wholesale price, then on the Internet, where price information could quickly and easily be compared by consumers, competition among online retailers of music would send all retail prices down to or near the wholesale price. Retailers would have to find another way to monetize their services, since they could not make a profit on selling music. In addition, Kohn offered to share the customer information with Universal. Believing that the majors would need software tools to analyze and use that information, eMusic could provide those tools for them at a cost.

In the meeting, Kohn and Hoffman also tried to explain why DRM would not work and an attempt to use anything but an open standard would impede the growth of digital music and cause more problems than it was intended to solve. As Hoffman explained, not only would DRM not work technically, "there was no customer demand for it". The most important thing the majors could do was to license their recordings in a format that consumers were demanding — the open MP3 standard. "If you don't create a legal alternative to piracy," said Kohn, "an entire generation will become more accustomed to stealing music rather than buying it."

At the end of the discussion and after seeing a live demonstration of eMusic, Doug Morris seemed perplexed, saying he saw little value — either in the technology or in the legal and royalty infrastructure that had been built to support its operation. Iovine, donning his trademark baseball cap, perked up when he discovered that eMusic, through a transaction involving Jann Wenner, owned the rights to Rollingstone.com. Other than that, it was clear they didn't quite know what to make of the presentation.

Doug Morris admitted his technological handicap years later when he sat down with *Wired Magazine* for an interview in late 2007:

> Morris insists there wasn't a thing he or anyone else could have done differently. "There's no one in the record company that's a technologist," Morris explains. "That's a misconception writers make all the time, that the record industry missed this. They didn't. They just didn't know what to do. It's like if you were suddenly asked to operate on your dog to remove his kidney. What would you do?"
>
> Personally, I would hire a vet. But to Morris, even that wasn't an option. "We didn't know who to hire," he says, becoming more agitated. "I wouldn't be able to recognize a good technology person — anyone with a good bullshit story would have gotten past me." Morris' almost willful cluelessness is telling. "He wasn't prepared for a business that was going to be so totally disrupted by technology," says a longtime industry insider who has worked with Morris. "He just doesn't have that kind of mind."[55]

Not only did these executives not understand the technical issues, they turned out to be surprisingly unschooled in the legal issues. In October 2000, Universal launched "Jimmy and Doug's Farm Club," a web-based, on-demand streaming service where it offered many of the popular recordings in its repertoire of sound recording masters. In doing so, Universal failed to obtain the necessary mechanical licenses to operate the service and within a month they were sued in federal court by several prominent music publishers. A U.S. district court later sided

[55] Seth Mnookin, "Universal's CEO Once Called iPod Users Thieves. Now He's Giving Songs Away," *Wired Magazine* Issue 15.12 (November 27, 2007).

with the music publishers, suggesting that Universal infringed music copyrights in much the same way that MP3.com had earlier infringed the sound recording copyrights of Universal.[56]

Instead of authorizing legitimate sales of their recordings under the model eMusic was proposing (i.e., 99¢ per track in the MP3 format), the majors, through the RIAA, chose instead to lead an effort beginning in 1999 called SDMI (for Secure Digital Music Initiative), to develop specifications for a technical standard that would employ DRM to protect music distributed in digital form. SDMI ceased in 2001, as a failure. The head of SDMI, Dr. Leonardo Chiariglione, later said the effort failed because, "Unfortunately it turned out that none of the technologies submitted could satisfy the requirements set out at the beginning."

eMusic was hurt greatly by Napster, not because it couldn't compete with Napster by providing better service and value to the consumer, but because it was not permitted to offer the recordings of the major record companies. While eMusic offered nearly a million tracks of independent music at a fair price, Napster offered not only independent music, but virtually all of the recordings of the major record companies. It was far from a level playing field.

Essentially, by refusing to license their recordings in the MP3 format while dithering with the patently worthless SDMI project, the major record companies essentially gave Napster a monopoly over the downloadable music business. During the two years Napster was operating outside of the law — from June 1999 through July 2001, it remained virtually the only outlet for consumers to acquire copies of music in the MP3 format other than ripping their own CDs or those of their friends.

During the course of eMusic's meetings with the five major record companies in 1998 and 1999, executives of Warner, EMI, Universal, Sony and BMG made some pretty astounding predictions, including: (1) the majors would never offer to sell music one track at a time (i.e., they would only sell digital albums), (2) that 99¢ per track was far too cheap, with one executive saying that their studies showed consumers would pay on average $1.73 per track, (3) the majors would never license their music in the MP3 format, which they expected would die out in favor of a standardized DRM format, and (4) Tower Records

[56] *Rodgers and Hammerstein Org. v. UMG Recordings, Inc.*, 2001 U.S. Dist. LEXIS 16111 (S.D.N.Y. Sept. 25, 2001).

would become the most important online retailer of downloadable music.[57]

By January 2002, three months after Apple introduced the iPod, Steve Jobs opened discussions with the major labels to try to accomplish what eMusic failed to do: to obtain the licenses he would require to operate a competitive downloadable music store. Soon thereafter, Jobs closed deals with all of the major record labels, acquiescing to the major's demands for DRM. Like eMusic, the iTunes store offered permanent downloads for 99¢ per track, but instead of using MP3 files, the tracks were encoded in the AAC compression format, and then encrypted with an additional format that renders the file exclusively compatible with the proprietary iTunes digital music player and the iPod.

Whether by design or not, the decision to use DRM was one of the best things that could have happened to Apple. In their zeal to require permanent downloads to be protected by DRM, the major record companies failed to recognize a well-known axiom of the computer business: the importance of open standards to promoting the healthy growth of an industry. In the early 1980s, the personal computer industry was stymied by the commercial availability of competing, incompatible operating systems: Unix, CP/M, Apple, and MS-DOS. Even among PCs that used MS-DOS, there were incompatibilities, so that database management or spreadsheet software that worked on one manufacturer's PC using MS-DOS could not operate on another MS-DOS based computer. It wasn't until the IBM-PC was introduced, followed by IBM-compatible personal computers, that the U.S. software industry could finally find its footing and grow.

By allowing iTunes to offer a proprietary format and a proprietary music player (i.e., the iTunes client software that operates on your PC or Apple computer), the majors allowed Apple to control the only store from which iPod-compatible digital music files licensed by the major record companies could be offered. This led to precisely the kind of problem that the executives of eMusic previously feared: the use of proprietary software like digital music players and DRM could only

[57] These were the expectations of the record industry in 1998/1999 timeframe. Needless to say, the majors eventually acquiesced to sell their recordings one track at a time and sell them at a wholesale price as low as 65¢ per a download. They also permitted the sale of their recordings in the MP3 format — but only ten years later, upon the launch of AmazonMP3 in 2008. By that time, Tower Records had long since filed for bankruptcy.

lead to incompatibilities that would lock consumers in to one brand or another and stifle the growth of the download business. It would be the equivalent of allowing Tower Records a unique version of the CD that only operated on CD players sold by Tower Records, and so on for every major chain of record stores.

iTunes succeeded in building a download business on the basis of a well-designed iPod and a sophisticated form of FreeAMP, client software that made it easy to purchase and download iTunes files and transfer them to your iPOD. Moreover, it was able to leverage its position by refusing to license its proprietary technology to what could have been iPod compatible music stores.

As a result, iTunes soon controlled over 80% of the market for downloadable music. Its only competitor was eMusic, which, although it was owned by a major record company, was still not able to offer music from any of the major record companies, because of the majors' continued insistence on DRM.[58]

It wasn't until 2008, upon the launch of the AmazonMP3 store, did the majors finally offer to consumers permanent downloads in the format they most desired. By January, 2009, Apple announced it would carry non-DRM files, though not in the MP3 format.[59]

It is no coincidence that, from 1999 to the present, the record industry has suffered a transition as painful as the one suffered by the music publishing business from 1920 through 1935 when revenues from physical sheet music sales were declining faster than new sources of licensing revenue could replace them. In 1999, U.S. revenues from sales of recordings were at a record high of $14.6 billion. The following year they declined to $14.3 billion and the decline continued unrelentingly, such that by 2005 industry revenues fell to $12.3 billion. In 2006, they fell to $11.7 billion; 2007 to 10.3 billion; and by the end of 2008, revenues dropped to less than $8.4 billion, a drop of over 40% from its high in 1999.

[58] During a short experiment in 2003, Universal permitted eMusic (which Universal owned at the time) to sell in the MP3 format a limited number of tracks from Universal's back catalog, but the terms were such that it made it uneconomical for eMusic to continue the offer. Universal hired Goldman Sachs to sell off eMusic, which it eventually did in 2003.

[59] To this day, millions of consumers are buying tracks from the iTunes music store with no assurance that these tracks will operate on personal computer and portable music players not offered by Apple Computer.

The decline in CD sales during the latter part of this period was precipitous. From 2005 to 2006, sales of recordings in physical format dropped by over 11%. From 2006 to 2007, physical sales dropped by another 19% and from 2007 to 2008 they dropped by a whopping 28%.

During the same period, digital revenues were increasing dramatically, but not nearly enough to make up for the decline in physical sales. While the record industry's transition from physical to digital was as unavoidable as the music publishing industry's transition 80 years before, a case can certainly be made that it didn't need to be quite as painful.

Executives in the music publishing industry in the 1920s took aggressive action to license their music in the new technologies, even at the risk of underpricing their repertoire. By contrast, executives in the recording industry at the turn of the millennium stood paralyzed, and by refusing to license, not only taught a whole generation to steal their recordings, they inadvertently engineered it so that there was no practical alternative to stealing.

## III. WHAT THE WORLD NEEDS NOW

The recording industry's painful transition from physical to digital is not yet complete. It is likely to continue until the last remnants of infrastructure used to support physical sales has been eliminated or outsourced. Meanwhile, a changing of the guard will give a new generation of young executives an opportunity to adopt the kinds of solutions the industry will need to embrace as the technology continues its inevitable evolution.

In previous editions of this book,[60] we made it a point to underscore the *interactive* nature of communications afforded by Internet technology. We suggested that the nature of these new digital delivery systems will transform much of our "one way" (i.e., to the listener) delivery of entertainment programming to "two way" (i.e., from the listener to the delivery system back to the listener) form of experience. The result has been the delivery of requested music, and other programming that

[60] *Kohn On Music Licensing* (2d Edition, 1996) and *Kohn On Music Licensing* (3d Edition, 2002).

contains music, to the listening public when and where they want it. That much is clear.

In addition, we pointed out that in this "two way" communication, the way back to the content provider may contain more than just the user's *requests* — or, the user's instructions as to what particular programming he or she would like to receive. What would emerge from this new interactivity is not merely communication back to the content provider, but communication *to others* on the network. This started out as electronic mail. But the low cost of personal computers, recording software, and video cameras, combined with the basic architecture of the Internet has allowed any individual to become a supplier of content delivered by digital transmission.

One consequence of this interactivity of communication has been the problem of unauthorized *file-sharing*, the best or most notorious example of which was the original *Napster.* Another has been the *user-generated content* phenomenon, as evidenced by the popularity of YouTube.[61]

Here's how we described the phenomenon in 1996:[62]

> What this all boils down to is this: Everyone will not only be a content *user* or *consumer*, everyone will become (or could easily become) a content *provider* or *supplier.* Not just traditional suppliers and distributors of entertainment programming, such as record companies and television networks, but anyone and everyone. The playing field has been leveled. Anyone on the network can become a content provider, and we believe just about everyone will become a provider of content of some sort. Just about anyone will have the ability to inexpensively become a supplier of interactive digital transmissions of content, and that content may be text, music, photographs, sounds, video, computer programs, and other data or information.
>
> What does this mean for music publishers, recording companies and other content providers? An optimist would suggest that it means the opportunity to provide music licenses to potentially millions of individuals who desire not only to receive musical works and sound recordings, but to republish them to others. A pessimist would say that

[61] For licensing issues arising from user-generated content, see Chapter 16, on *The User-Generated Content Phenomenon.*

[62] *Kohn On Music Licensing* (2d Edition, 1996).

> it means the opportunity for potentially millions of individuals to effect interactive digital transmissions of musical works and sound recordings without accounting to copyright owners. To the extent the pessimists are correct, one of the big challenges facing the music industry will be locating and prosecuting individuals and Web sites that offer unauthorized recordings of musical compositions.

In 2002, after seeing what the peer-to-peer networks had wrought, we revisited the enormity of the challenge:[63]

> Consider for a moment the challenges and difficulties inherent in locating private or semi-private electronic mail or file-sharing transmissions that contain unauthorized transmissions of musical works. Already, peer-to-peer file sharing programs, such as Gnutella, have been developed, which apparently do not require the kind of central server facilitation that Napster provides to the users of the Napster client software. Experts disagree about whether Gnutella-type programs will "scale" — that is, whether they can efficiently operate at all without someone operating a central server. This is important, because it is much easier for copyright owners to sue operators of a relatively small number of central server operators than it is to sue every individual who desires to engage in illegal file-sharing. Moreover, should anonymity technology ever be successfully applied to protect the identity and location of copyright offenders, the protection of intellectual property on the Internet may become quite problematic. Which raises the question: Should the music industry and other content providers, as one computer industry analyst suggested, just "get over it?"[64] Or will the system adjust so that both the goals of intellectual property protection and consumer freedom are equitably met?

We remain optimists and believe the system will inevitably adjust, as we suggest below, in adopting new solutions that strike a balance between the free flow of information and content among users of the network and the need to compensate authors to fulfill the objectives of copyright. Others, however, have not been so optimistic.

---

[63] *Kohn On Music Licensing* (3d Edition, 2002).

[64] Esther Dyson, "Intellectual Value," *Wired Magazine* (July 1995).

In 2002, David Bowie sat down in a rehearsal studio for an interview with the *New York Times* and mused pessimistically over the future of the record business:

> "I don't even know why I would want to be on a label in a few years, because I don't think it's going to work by labels and by distribution systems in the same way," he said. "The absolute transformation of everything that we ever thought about music will take place within 10 years, and nothing is going to be able to stop it. I see absolutely no point in pretending that it's not going to happen. I'm fully confident that copyright, for instance, will no longer exist in 10 years, and authorship and intellectual property is in for such a bashing."
>
> "Music itself is going to become like running water or electricity," he added. "So it's like, just take advantage of these last few years because none of this is ever going to happen again. You'd better be prepared for doing a lot of touring because that's really the only unique situation that's going to be left. It's terribly exciting. But on the other hand it doesn't matter if you think it's exciting or not; it's what's going to happen."[65]

Is he right? Will copyright cease to exist? Will music itself become "like running water or electricity"? Our view on these questions is: (1) Yes, copyright will exist, but music licensing will change. (2) Yes, music itself will become like running water or electricity, but we are confident that performing artists and songwriters will continue to enjoy financial remuneration from the distribution and performance of their recorded works.

The changes in music licensing required to meter the "running water or electricity" may force changes in the conventional means of providing that remuneration to creators and copyright owners. In addition, creators and copyright owners may need to cede a measure of control over the use of their copyrighted works in order to reap the rewards they seek.

---

[65] Jon Pareles, "David Bowie, 21st Century Entrepreneur," *New York Times* (June 9, 2002).

## A. Like Running Water or Electricity

That music is becoming like "running water or electricity" is a useful metaphor for what we believe is the coming, inevitable shift in the business model for digital media. This shift, in our view, will be characterized by the following: (1) a shift from a purchase model to a consumption model, (2) an increasing number and complexity of transactions, and (3) the ability and desire of consumers to become producers and distributors of original content and derivative works.

### *1. From a Purchase Model to a Consumption Model*

We are already beginning to see signs of a transition from a *purchase model*, where consumers buy CDs and individual digital downloads, to a *consumption model*, where they simply access and use the content. The first examples of the consumption model were online music subscription services, such as Rhapsody — where a consumer can pay $9.95 per month and enjoy performances of any tracks in the Rhapsody repertoire on demand. Others, of course, include peer-to-peer file sharing and the enormous success of YouTube.

This transition is closely akin to one that occured nearly a century ago — when the music publishing industry shifted from largely a purchase model (i.e., sale of sheet music) to a consumption model (i.e., the blanket licensing of public performances of live and recorded music).

#### *a. Market Drivers of the Consumption Model*

Many subscription services have been operating for some time and have not achieved nearly the same success of permanent download services such as iTunes. Nevertheless, recall the market drivers for digital media discussed above: (1) bandwidth, (2) portability, and (3) ease of use. Until very recently, none of these factors were sufficiently developed to allow high quality streaming or over-the-air (OTA) tethered downloading of recordings or videos to portable devices in a way that is easy for consumers to use and manage. As a result, subscription services had been largely confined to the personal computer and while some services offered a means to transfer tethered-downloads to portable devices, it was by no means an easy user experience.

But the prospects for on-demand, cloud-based music services are encouraging. The Pandora App for the iPhone, which provides a semi-interactive webcast experience, was already a great success when the first true, portable on-demand music service for the iPhone, the Rhapsody iPhone App, was launched in September 2009. YouTube was one of the earliest applications of the iPhone, allowing the viewing of high-quality user generated and professional videos on the go. It is only a matter of time before such services mature and truly begin to fulfill the promise of easy to use, consumption-based music services.

*b. The Download v. Streaming Debate*

There has been much debate in the Internet community about what will become prevalent: the transmission of music over the Internet by *streaming* or *downloading*? The debate is a false one. The shift from a purchase model to a consumption model should not be confused with whether a recording or video is downloaded or streamed in real-time to your player or storage device.

Suppose you want to hear the recording, *Let It Be* by the Beatles. You ask your voice recognition-equipped telephone/music player or home music system to play the song, your system notifies some celestial jukebox of your request, the recording is transmitted from the celestial jukebox to your device, which interprets the 1's and 0's for your tuner and speaker system, and you enjoy the performance. What we just described is music-on-demand, which has nothing to do with the question of streaming versus downloading.

In a world of increasing bandwidth, real-time streaming will be reserved for the delivery of live performances, such as talk radio and live concerts. Where content is pre-recorded, it will always make sense for the data comprising the content to be delivered to you by download than to be streamed in real-time.

**(1) The Importance of Cache**

Imagine during a sit-down dinner of 100 people, the waiters start serving the salad. If the salad were served one piece of lettuce at a time to each of the 100 people, how many waiters (or "servers") would it take to accomplish the task in a reasonable amount of time? Clearly, serving the salad one piece at a time would take more time using more servers than it would take if the salad were served on a plate all at once. The time that it takes to deliver the salad has little to do with the time it takes to eat it.

In other words, the time it takes to transmit a work has little to do with the time it takes to consume the work.[66] It is simply more economical to receive a pre-recorded sound recording or motion picture in a few seconds for later rendering, than to receive it in real-time — the length of time it takes to listen to the recording or view the video. It is more efficient for the equipment to send the transmission in what computer engineers call "batch" mode rather than in "interpretive" mode.

This suggests that all forms of pre-recorded works — including digitized images and text, and sound recordings and motion pictures — will be copied into RAM or, at least temporarily, onto a user's hard drive or other form of permanent storage, prior to the actual viewing or listening of the program. Even a webcast would be transmitted in this way — perhaps the next four or five recordings downloaded to your device to which you will listen one at a time at your convenience, while the next recordings are delivered to you in the same way. This would certainly improve your experience with the webcast when you enter a place where you have no Internet reception, as in a subway.

It thus appears that virtually all transmissions — other than live performances — will result in a fixation or reproduction of full copies on your device. In other words, digital life will include very little real-time broadcast.[67]

### (2) How Long Will You Save the Cache?

It is useful to consider that the download model is exactly how your Internet browser works today, with innumerable .html, .wav, .gif, and .jpg files caching on your hard disk for as long as 30 days. There is no reason to believe it will work any different with music files. This does not necessarily mean, however, that the user will maintain the copy for future private performances. The question becomes: if all pre-recorded works are downloaded to your device, how long will you keep them? Will users choose to save everything that is transmitted to them? The answer to this question is not obvious.

Virtually no one saves every piece of html, gif, jpg, java applet, and other data that is ever cached during the course of web browsing for more than the typical 30 days, the default setting on most web browsers.

[66] Negroponte, *Being Digital* (Alfred A. Knopf, New York 1995).
[67] *Id.*

Why save music any longer? Do people indefinitely save every television program ever recorded on their Tivo or DVR recording systems?

Saving everything that is downloaded to you has its costs. Recording digital transmissions does not eliminate the need for physical copies; it only transfers the cost of physical storage from the transmitter to the user who pays for the physical copies in the form of storage space (e.g., space on audiocassette tape, hard disks, optical drives, and solid-state memory). As the cost of permanent storages goes down, a consumer may tend to save more than he deletes.

One aspect of the question arises from the competition between *public* and *private* performances. When a consumer plays a DVD or a downloaded video at home, the performance of the film and the music in the film is a *private* performance. As we shall see, copyright owners only have an exclusive right in performances that are made *publicly*. The largest source of music publishing revenue is from public performances of musical works. If downloading should convert public performances into private performances, then music publishers and songwriters would need to seek ways to replace that income through another means.

It may well be that in fashioning a future solution to the problem of remunerating copyright owners, the distinction between public and private performances may become obsolete.

### 2. An Increasing Number and Complexity of Transactions

The second defining aspect of the shift from physical to digital media is a combination of (a) an increasing number of works available, (b) an increasing number of transactions, marked by a decreasing transaction size, (c) an increasing complexity of determining the share of revenues earned by each work, and (d) an increasing complexity in identifying the rightsholders of each work.

#### a. An Increasing Number of Works Available Online

In his book, *The Long Tail*,[68] Chris Anderson suggested that the low marginal cost of making available even obscure works of authorship will mean that virtually every work that could be made available

[68] Chris Anderson, *The Long Tail: Why the Future of Business is Selling Less of More* (Hyperion, 2006).

digitally will be made available digitally. We are already seeing virtually every record ever recorded, old and new, making its way on iTunes and other online music services. With companies such as Google, whose mission statement is "organizing the world's information," making huge investments in technology to drive the process, there is no reason to think this trend will not continue.

#### *b. An Increasing Number of Transactions and Decreasing Transaction Size*

The passing away of Francis Albert Sinatra in 1998 marked the end of an era, but he remained with us long enough to witness the dawn of a new age, one that was hailed as the *digital millennium.* In Sinatra's day, the singer's record company would ship copies of his classic albums to record stores and chains by the crate-load. The transaction size of such a shipment would average in the thousands or tens of thousands of dollars. By contrast, in the new millennium, iTunes delivers a monthly report to singer's record company listing tens of thousands of individual transactions, each earning the record company a royalty of about 70¢ each. iTunes is generating such reports to thousands of record labels with individual transactions numbering in the hundreds of millions.

When a subscriber to an online music subscription service, such as Rhapsody, pays a monthly fee to access performances of recordings, on-demand, as many times as they want, the number of transactions reported to the labels increase by an order of magnitude. For example, if the consumer pays $10 per month and listens to 2,000 streams of recorded music in that month, the consumer's effective cost for each transaction is ½ cent. If Rhapsody pays the labels a royalty of one-half of that amount, then the transaction size of the 2,000 transactions to the label is about ¼ cent.

In his more recent book, *Free,*[69] Anderson suggested that an increasing amount of goods and services offered online will be provided to the consumer for "free." While he admits that nothing is really truly free, we are seeing some online music services, such as iMeem, LaLa, Qtrax, and Spotify, experiment with an advertising-based model, providing music on-demand to consumers at no charge. Services that

---

[69] Chris Anderson, *Free: The Past & Future of a Radical Price* (publisher, 2009).

do not charge a subscription fee are likely to attract a greater number of potential users than those that do. The amount of transactions generated by advertising-based services is therefore likely to be much higher than those generated by subscription services. In addition, if the amount of advertising revenue generated by such services is less than subscription revenue, the transaction sizes reported by the labels, subject to some minimum, could be lower than those reported by subscription services.

### c. *An Increasing Complexity of Determining the Share of Revenue Earned by Each Work*

When a download service, such as iTunes, sells a digital download, a portion of the money collected is paid to the record label that controls the recording. For example, where iTunes sells a download for 99¢, it will pay the record label a royalty of 70¢. Each month, iTunes sends to each label a report indicating the tracks such label owns or controls that were sold, how many of each track was sold, and the applicable royalty per copy downloaded.

Likewise, when a subscription service earns a fee from a subscriber, a portion of that fee is paid to the owners of the content. But that's where the similarity ends. For example, if a subscription service charges ten subscribers a monthly fee of $10, then the service may owe one-half of the subscription revenue, or $50, to record labels. Each record label is entitled to a *pro rata* share of such $50 based upon the number of tracks controlled by such label that are actually transmitted to the subscribers during the applicable month. Thus, if 5% of the performances were of tracks owned by a particular label, the pro rata share of revenues to which that label is entitled would be $2.50.

Under most record company contracts, an artist's share of royalties will depend upon the method by which the recordings were used. The sale of a track by digital download may earn a royalty at one rate (e.g., a percentage of the retail price of the download, less various deductions defined in the contract) and the transmission of a track by an on-demand streaming service may earn the artist a royalty based on a completely different rate (e.g., 50% of gross receipts attributable to the license of the recording for such service).

Each new business model proposed by an online music service poses a challenge to the record labels and music publishers struggling to fit new ways of doing business into existing business conventions. Eventually, those conventions may need to change to accommodate the realities of technological progress.

### *d. An Increasing Complexity of Identifying the Rightsholders of Each Work*

The digital revolution not only fundamentally changed the way recordings and videos are delivered to the consumer, it also has had a profound effect on the way recordings and videos are produced. Digital recording techniques invented in the 1980s gave rise to the development of software that allows creators of recorded music to manipulate sounds in ways theretofore unimaginable.

Inexpensive personal computer software packages such as Digidesign's ProTools allows record producers to digitally sample existing recordings and include those samples in new recordings. The waveform of a sampled sound may be displayed on a computer screen and modifications may be made in the waveform to more precisely change the characteristics of the sound it produces. For example, one can change the speed at which the sound is rendered, eliminate sounds, add new ones, introduce echo or other sound effects, and, by reversing the sequence of the digital information, the sounds can even be rendered backwards.

When sounds are sampled from another's copyrighted work, legal arrangements may be made for co-ownership of the resulting new work.[70] But this is not the only way that a single copyright may be controlled by multiple owners. Collaboration between authors to create a *joint work*[71] will create multiple owners and grants of shares of copyrights, such as under a *co-publishing agreement*,[72] will further increase the number of owners of the copyright. Grants of exclusive rights to exploit a copyright overseas will split ownership or control of the copyright even further. For more on what we call *The Split Copyright Syndrome*, see Chapter 6.

When a work such as a motion picture is created, it will typically contain numerous copyrighted sound recordings, musical works, and

---

[70] For more on these arrangements, see Chapter 24, on *The Digital Sampling Controversy.*

[71] For more on joint works, see Chapter 7, on *The Language of Music Licensing.*

[72] For more on co-publishing agreements, see Chapter 4.

even other audiovisual works owned by others — each of which, of course, may be controlled by multiple owners. Where the creator of the work is in the business of producing commercial content, such as a film producer producing a theatrical motion picture, a legal and business infrastructure exists to address the complexities of identifying the rights-holders and clearing the licenses necessary for the use of the third party materials. Where, however, a noncommercial user takes or digitally samples one or more copyrighted works, incorporates the works or samples into his or her own user-generated audio or video and uploads it to YouTube, the responsibility for identifying the various right-sholders and associating with the work becomes problematic.[73]

## B. The Future of Music Licensing

In light of these challenges brought about by digital technology, will music, as David Bowie suggested, flow like water or electricity and copyright cease to exist in the digital world? These are not unreasonable questions.

Imagine we project the continuing development of technology such that the key drivers of digital media growth — bandwidth, portability, and ease of use — reach a level of advancement once the dream of science fiction writers: the realization of the "celestial jukebox" — every record ever recorded, movie ever made, book ever written, all stored on "cloud" computing servers — accessible from the web or your wireless device via easy to use browser or client software supporting voice command, drag and drop, and perhaps intelligent agent software that learns what you like and acts on your behalf to pull new music for you to discover. Or perhaps all of these works of authorship are simply loaded on to a solid-state chip you plug in to your portable device, such as your phone or "tri-corder," which could be updated over-the-air continually with new music, videos, and books.

If music did, indeed, flow like "water or electricity," or could simply be carried around in your pocket, will the exclusive rights accorded to owner of copyright cease to have any practical affect? In our view,

[73] For more on this problem, see Chapter 16, on *The User-Generated Content Phenomenon.*

copyright will survive whatever technological advances may bring; what may change, however, is nature of music licensing.

### *1. Did E.C. Mills Have the Answer?*

Recall that when the music publishing industry was first confronted with radio broadcasting, E.C. Mills called for a $6 tax on every radio listener, the spoils to be divided up by a collective administrator to assure that music publishers and songwriters get compensated for the performance of their music in radio broadcasts. As it turned out, the problem of collecting performance fees from broadcasters did not require his far reaching solution. As long as there were a limited number of broadcasters, it would be commercially feasible to reach out to each of them to negotiate on a collective basis a blanket license to authorize the performances or legally shut down broadcasters where they failed to obtain the license.

By contrast, in a world characterized by "two-way" communications, with the number of publishers of content potentially equal to the number of users — such as a peer-to-peer file-sharing network — and where users have access to technology that readily allows them to remix or readapt existing content and re-publish the adaptations — such as republication on YouTube or a peer-to-peer network — a solution that taxes all users, like the Mills Solution, may well be warranted and perhaps the only way to ensure compensation to rightsholders.

If the Mills Solution were adopted, it would involve at least the following five elements: (1) a determination of what or whom to tax and how much, (2) the identification of what works are being used, reproduced, or performed, (3) a revenue-sharing regime that divides the income collected equitably among the various works used, (4) the identification of the rightsholders of such works, and (5) the generation of royalty statements and distribution of funds among the rightsholders, with provisions for holding funds in suspense where disputes among rightsholders arise. Finally, what also may be required is a reform of the copyright law to accommodate the new compensation regime.

#### *a. Determining Who to Tax and How Much*

Determining who to tax is not as easy a question as it might seem. It is axiomatic under American law that the "power to tax involves the power to destroy,"[74] and care must be taken not to create unintended incentives or disincentives that would create an inefficient or inequitable distortion of the workings of the free market.

One economist[75] has suggested two alternatives to the taxation question: (1) add such a tax to the federal income tax, distributing the burden in accordance with existing progressive rates or (2) place a new tax on the goods and services used to gain access to the copyrighted works, such as the equipment used to hear or view the works, the media on which they are distributed, or the peer-to-peer services or Internet service providers (ISP) through which works are distributed.

The former has the advantage of low administrative costs, as the federal income tax system already exists, but has the disadvantage of being politically unpopular. Taxpayers may object to involuntarily paying for works they may never enjoy, or worse, abhor. The latter, such as a tax on ISPs, has the advantage of being somewhat voluntary in that a consumer can choose not to use an ISP for Internet access.

To compensate copyright owners for losses due to noncommercial, unauthorized use of their works on the Internet, it has been estimated that taxes would have to be raised on the nation's 90 million households by about $27 per year. To raise the same money using the second method, ISPs would have to be taxed by approximately 11.8% of their service revenue, which should increase the average monthly Internet access fee by about $5.36.[76]

### *b. Identifying the Works Used and Their Rightsholders*

The DNA of the solution would be something called, *metadata* — technically, "data about data," but really quite simple: Metadata, in the context of digital media, is a set of data that uniquely identifies a particular work or person.

For example, most professionally published books bear an ISBN number, a 13-digital number that is unique to that edition of the book.

---

[74] *McCulloch v. Maryland*, 17 U.S. 316 (1819).

[75] William W. Fisher, *Promises to Keep* (Stanford University Press, 2004).

[76] *Id.* See also, Neil Weinstock Netanel, "*Impose a Noncommercial Use Levy to Allow Free P2P File-Swapping and Remixing*," Harvard Journal of Law and Technology 17 (2003). For recent progress on ISP licensing, see Chapter 23 on *Licensing of Sound Recordings*.

ISBN, an acronym for International Standard Book Number, is an international standard for uniquely identifying books. The eBook you downloaded to your Kindle also has an ISBN number. Similarly, any form of textual work may be tagged with a code called ISTC (for International Standard Text Code); sheet music and music folios with a code called ISMN (International Sheet Music Number); sound recordings with an ISRC (International Standard Recording Code); songs with an ISWC (International Standard Musical Work Code). A new standard recently developed for tagging audiovisual works, such as films and TV programs, is called ISAN (International Standard Audiovisual Work Number).

In addition to each copyrighted work being assigned a unique identifier, each rightsholder would be assigned a unique identifier. Thus, authors and publishers, songwriters and record companies will each be assigned their own unique code. A standard in development at the International Standards Organization (ISO) is the International Standard Name Identifier (ISNI) code.

The identification of works and rightsholders would take place through a registration system, perhaps a web-based system where copyright owners can register themselves and their works, much like music publishers and songwriters become members of and register their works today with performance rights societies.

While digitization has played havoc with a copyright owner's control of distribution, the problem has ascended to another level of complexity on the production side: inexpensive digital camcorders and free video editing software has spawned the "user-generated" phenomenon — two young women dancing in their living room to the latest hit by *ColdPlay* or *Eminem*, a remix or mash-up of clips from Star Trek and Star Wars posing Captain Kirk against Darth Vader, uploaded to YouTube for millions of others to view.

This problem of derivative works that incorporate pre-existing copyrighted works would have to be accounted for in such a system. Should the maker of the remix or mash-up wish to receive a portion of the income based on the performance of their work, they would have to register the new work and by doing so would be credited with an appropriate portion of the income derived from the use of their contribution to the final work.

When every creative work, such as a book, movie, sound recording, and adaptations thereof, and every person involved in the creation or publication of a work is tagged with a unique code, then there will be no need for doors — just turnstiles.

*c. Identifying What Works Are Being Used*

In a physical world, you can count which copies and how many of them go out the door. You can easily monetize the flow, because it is *your* door — one you can open or close as you wish. In the digital realm, anyone with a website or email address — virtually everyone — has a door through which the copyrighted works of others can flow. Thus, one of the requirements and challenges of the system would be to capture information on what copyrightable works are performed or downloaded by users.

Thus, whenever a book, recording or movie is downloaded or streamed from any source, the use is tracked using the work's unique identifier. Technologies that recognize the digital fingerprint of audio and video works transmitted over the Internet could be employed to take a *census* of what works are being used and how frequently, and to counteract any potential gaming of the census, a sample, such as those taken by ASCAP or BMI or the Neilsen rating organization could be employed.

*d. Prorating the Revenue Among the Works Used*

Thus, a pool of money collected from everyone who has access to the works will be prorated among the works based on the number of times they are viewed or listened to. These individual uses — billions of them — will be associated with the unique identifiers of the appropriate rightsholders entitled to their fair share of the royalties.

Once the result of the census or sample has been collected, credits could be applied to the results that recognize the relative value of some uses over others. For example, determining the appropriate shares of revenues based on the type of work used (e.g., musical work, sound recording, audiovisual work, literary work) and the type of use made of the work (e.g., on-demand stream, derivative work, background use, advertising, etc.) could be decided by the collective much the way ASCAP or BMI today classifies types of performances to determine shares of revenue due to rightsholder members.

Such allocations of relative value are not without controversy, but appropriate results could eventually be achieved through negotiation among rightsholder representatives. Certain uses (e.g., synchronization of music in theatrical motion pictures and television programs) could be outside the scope of the collective's determination.

#### *e. Generating Royalty Statements and Distributing Royalty Shares to Rightsholders*

Using the results of the census and weighing formulas, royalty statements would be generated and payments made to rightsholders in proportion to the relative popularity of each of their works.

If the tax were to be levied directly on households through the personal income tax, the government would obviously be directly involved in the collection of the revenues. This, however, does not mean the government need be involved at all in operating the collective administration system for the registration of rightsholders and works, the taking of census and sample data, and the generation of royalty reports and payments — activities that could be done by one or more providers or non-profit enterprises representing various constituencies all linking into a central database.

### *2. Could the Mills Solution Work?*

One of the important prerequisites of the Mills Solution would be some modification of the copyright law to ensure that the exclusive rights of a copyright owner could not be exercised to prevent the uses tracked by the collective administrator. This does not mean, as Professor Lawrence Lessig has suggested, that noncommercial uses should be made exempt from the scope of the rights granted by copyright.[77] It means, rather, that such uses (e.g., peer-to-peer file sharing, amateur remixes) remain within the scope of a copyright owners exclusive rights, but that the exercise of those rights would be administered by the collective administrator (e.g., taxing ISPs and distributing royalties to rightsholders).

Lessig's suggestion that copyright law reinstitute a form of renewal registration, where owners needed to opt-in to copyright protection, rather than opt-out, would not be necessary. Under the terms of

[77] Lawrence Lessig, *Remix: Making Art and Commerce Thrive in the Hybrid Economy* (Penguin, 2008).

Google's settlement with authors and publishers (as amended), all rightsholders retain their copyright rights from inception, but if they do not show up to claim their revenues within ten years, the money that accumulated for them during such period gets redistributed to other rightsholders. Future revenues continue to accrue until the rightsholder eventually shows up to claim them.[78]

While it may seem distasteful for authors to give up a measure of creative control, particularly over the preparation of noncommercial derivative works, remixes, or mash-ups by amateurs that include their works, such control must be weighed against the practical difficulties of enforcing such exclusive rights in the first place.

The international trade association representing record labels estimated that 95% of all downloading of recording on the Internet are unauthorized and unpaid for. Meanwhile, Google estimates that 15 hours of user-generated videos are uploaded to YouTube alone every minute of every day. Traditional media organizations, working with its trade associations, have responded with a string of copyright lawsuits against both the users who "share" these infringing recordings and videos and the websites who host them — a traditional attempt to "shut the doors." Yet, the old adage, "Locks are for honest people" is as true now as before — the lawsuits do not seem to be working, at least to the degree necessary.

Simply put, we're moving from a purchase model to a consumption model and there's no turning back. It would seem that the best copyright owners can hope to get compensated for the use of their works rather than not at all. The record industry suffered unnecessarily by waiting over ten years to license their repertoire in the MP3 format. As the philosopher George Santayana admonished, "Those who cannot learn from history are doomed to repeat it."

The book publishing industry, having watched the music industry miscalculate so badly seems to have learned this lesson and forged ahead embracing the Google book scanning project rather than fighting it with protracted litigation. Under the settlement, Google will be allowed to scan and offer books online, but pay the rightsholders 63% of the revenues earned and a Book Rights Registry was established to administer the collection of revenues and distribution of payments to

---

[78] The Authors Guild, Inc., et al. v. Google Inc., Case No. 05 CV 8136 (S.D.N.Y.).

rightsholders in much the way it has been described above. Any rightsholder may remove the book from the system at any time, but books that are out of print are automatically opted-in to the system. What authors and publishers will lose by relinquishing a measure of control over the use of their works they gain by establishing a reasonable mechanism for compensating them when their works are used.

The settlement serves, in practice, as a sophisticated, privately negotiated amendment to the copyright law with respect to the use of out of print books by online service providers, demonstrating that modifying the copyright law to enable a collective administration of rights need not necessarily be accomplished through legislation.

A class action lawsuit, similar to the one filed by authors and publishers, filed on behalf of music publishers against YouTube is currently pending before the court.[79] It remains to be seen whether the music industry will follow in the footsteps of the book publishers to reach a similar rapprochement.

## C. The Future of Promotion and Marketing

In a world where music flows like water or electricity, where people listen and watch, rather than purchase copies, what becomes of promotion and marketing? What are their objectives and who will be in the best position to serve songwriters and recording artists?

### *1. Getting a Bigger Slice of the Pie*

It would seem that when commerce is dominated by a consumption model, rather than a purchase model, the objective of promotion and marketing shifts from convincing people to buy your product (e.g., CD or download) to listen to or watch it. As we have seen, in a subscription model, or a collective administration model, where a blanket license is provided in exchange for a subscription fee or a tax, shares of revenue are divided among rightsholders *pro rata* — i.e., on the basis of the popularity of the individual works. In other words, the works that are "clicked on" or listened to the most will get the greater share of the revenue pie.

The objective, therefore, of any one rightsholder would be to persuade as many people as possible to spend their time listening to or

[79] The Football Association Premier League Limited, et al. v. YouTube, Inc., et al., 07 Civ. 3582 (LLS).

watching content containing your copyrighted content rather than someone else's. The question then becomes, how is this best done?

### *a. Traditional Promotion and Marketing*

Certainly all of the promotion and marketing activity currently devoted to building artist's brands and driving consumers to their content will continue to be an important aspect of driving revenues. Live performances, traditional advertising, and public relations activities will all remain important to building the career of recording artists.

The difficulty will lie in how to get recognized by a great number of people when the width of the avenues for getting in front of them is narrowing in the new media environment. There is no equivalent today of the *Ed Sullivan Show*, where an act like the Beatles were able to appear in one evening before 74 million viewers at once, representing over 40% of the U.S. population.

### *b. Online Technology Tools*

Cable television, videogames and the Internet may have increased the challenge of promoting new acts before large audiences, but technology is beginning to provide alternative ways for artists to find or build their audiences.

Social networking websites, such as MySpace and Facebook, have become an important means for popular recording artists to keep in touch with their fans and aspiring recording artists to attract new audiences to their recordings. One relatively unknown singer and model, Tila Tequila, used the unsigned recording artist category of MySpace to rack up over 30 million pages views to become the most popular artist on the social network. She has been called "the most striking success story to come out of MySpace's unsigned artists category," a success that has spawned record sales, a clothing line, a cell-phone endorsement, and a book publishing agreement.[80]

One of the most startling uses of technology to help launch a recording artist's career occurred shortly after a little known Scottish singer named, Susan Boyle, appeared as a contestant on the popular British talent show, *Britain's Got Talent.* Her rendition that evening of the song, *I Dreamed A Dream*, from the musical *Les Misérables*, was

---

[80] Jona Weiner, *TilaTequila for President* (Slate.com, April 11, 2006).

recorded by a fan and posted on YouTube. Within 72 hours, the video was viewed by over two million people. Within a week, it was viewed over 65 million times.

The stunning publicity garnered by the performer's television appearance and the video resulted in a record deal, personal appearances and other remunerations of stardom. The singer's prospects for a long-term professional career in music can be debated, but her spectacular rise from obscurity should give hope to aspiring artists that a successful launch of a career is still possible when talent is leveraged with the right technological tools.

Online karaoke services, such as MySpace Karaoke (formerly kSolo.com), could potentially serve as an alternative form of the televised talent show. Using the karaoke website, users can listen to an instrumental recording while viewing the lyrics of the song, record their voice track, and combine it with the instrumental recording. The result is uploaded to the performer's profile page on the site where others can listen to their recordings and vote on the performances.[81]

### c. *Internet Advertising*

Of the $298.6 billion spent in 2008 on advertising in the United States, $23.4 billion, or about 8% of the total, was spent on Internet advertising. That's more than what was spent that year on terrestrial radio, network television, cable television, or magazines, and the share of advertising dollars moving from traditional media to the Internet is continuing to increase rapidly.

As we discuss in Chapter 20, on *Licensing Music in Television, Radio, Print, and Internet Advertising*, there are four basic types of Internet advertising: display, search, rich media, and sponsorships. One of the reasons for the shift from advertising on traditional media to the Internet is the way the interactive nature of the Internet affords advertisers with a way to precisely determine the rate of return on their advertising dollars.

Tracking "click-throughs" from online ads to the actual purchase decisions that result from those ads enable a fine-tuning of advertising investment not available in traditional forms of media advertising.

---

[81] The music licensing issues of operating such services are discussed in Chapter 12, on *Licensing Music in Print and Digital Print* and Chapter 22, on *Licensing Music in Videogames and Other New Media and Multimedia Devices and Online Versions.*

As we have seen, in a world of music flowing like water — the consumption model of listening and viewing as opposed to the purchase model of the past — the objective of content owners will be to increase their share of the revenue pie by getting consumers to listen to or watch their content rather than the other content available.

It is conceivable that listenings or views of content initiated directly from advertising "click-throughs" can be traceable in such a way that enables a precise calculation of the rate of return on investment made by the advertiser. When the circumstances that allow such calculations are in place, Internet advertising will play an important role in the marketing and promotion of music online.

#### *d. Audience Relationship Management*

For some time, large businesses have been employing web-based technologies to manage their sales process. Software such as Salesforce.com have improved the way large enterprises and medium sized businesses track potential customers and the process of selling additional products and services to existing customers. This same form of technology is beginning to be deployed by record labels and individual artists.

A number of technology companies have begun offering online tools to enable artists and labels a way to create awareness for their brands, to engage with their fans, such as via online newsletters and blogs, and to sell recordings and merchandise. The concept is that brands can better monetize their activities by maintaining a direct relationship, primarily through email and similar means, with as many dedicated fans as possible. Through such relationships, fans should be more likely to purchase or listen to recordings, attend live concerts, and help evangelize the artist to friends and others.

### *2. Who Will Be the Organizations That Provide These Tools and Services?*

Performers and recording artists have always outsourced their needs for many of the services necessary to advance their careers. Seeking outside help enables them to focus on what they do best: create new songs and recordings and refine their performing skills.

Artists typically engage the services of entertainment lawyers to represent them in negotiations for the various agreements touching upon their careers. Some hire accountants or business managers to manage their finances. Artists who tour will typically engage a booking agent and for all other guidance on their careers, they often rely on the help from a personal manager.

Traditionally, recording artists required the financing necessary to cut a professionally produced record album, the costs of which included not only the rental of a recording studio, but the time of studio engineers, musicians, and other performers engaged in the production. The most successful recordings often benefited by the artist's introduction to talented songwriters and record producers. Once the album is completed, they required manufacturing and distribution services to make the product readily available to the consumer. In many cases, they also required living expenses and money to support a tour of live engagements to help promote the recordings. For all these services, they typically turned to a record company — either one of the several major record companies or one of the many hundreds of independent record companies.

The shift from physical to digital distribution has greatly affected the flexibility an artist has in choosing his outsourced partners for these services. In some cases, this flexibility has become more limited, as major labels and even independents are being increasingly selective about the quantity and quality of the artist they choose to devote their time to support. By the same token, the disintermediation of distribution has allowed artists to bypass record labels and offer their content directly to the public, either from their own websites or on iTunes via a number of technology companies who will distribute the artist's recordings for relatively low fees.

There is no one best answer for each artist. Well known artists who already have established brands may no longer require the marketing, promotion and other A&R services that record companies are renowned for. These artists can make do with their booking agents, personal managers, business managers, agents, and technology companies that offer distribution and audience relationship management tools and services.

It is too soon to tell how new and established artists will eventually strike the right mix of outsourced providers to help nurture or further their careers and monetization of their talents. As the music industry continues its painful transition from physical to digital, artists and their business partners will continue to employ innovative ways to capture the public's imagination and earn enough money to keep them focused on producing new songs and recordings for the consuming public.

## IV. Future of Licensing Music on the Internet

The effects of the digital revolution on the music industry have been far reaching. Because of the ease with which potentially millions of individuals may digitally create and transmit musical works and sound recordings without accounting to copyright owners, the music industry has faced considerable challenges in enforcing the rights in their musical compositions. A series of well-publicized lawsuits have not seemed to have alleviated the problem.

Meanwhile, the Internet has provided individual songwriters and artists an alternative means of reaching the public with their artistic creations, bypassing traditional distributors and publishers, and opening up opportunities for new entrants into the publishing and recording industries.

Until the age of the Internet, the record companies added value by identifying new artists, financing the creation of recordings, providing recording expertise, promoting radio airplay and, thereby, record sales, and manufacturing and distributing records or CDs. Now, distribution requires a significantly lower investment, an activity that record companies don't necessarily have a comparative advantage over others.

Nevertheless, marketing expertise will remain as important, if not more important, than distribution. With just about everyone having access to the web and distribution, getting above the noise level will become more difficult over time, not less. Thus, artists will continue to outsource the critical function of marketing to organizations who know how to get above the noise level, and that will continue to be record labels in the foreseeable future.

It is our prediction that those music publishers, record companies, and others who are quick to adopt the new technologies and who best employ computer databases and information systems to track and analyze the musical tastes and buying habits of consumers, and to provide transparency in their reporting obligations to artists and songwriters, are likely to reap the greatest share of the digital market.

Ultimately, improvements in technology that eliminate obstacles to bandwidth, portability and ease of use, may lead us to a revised model for all content owners. E.C. Mill's suggestion in the early 1920s for an annual tax of $6 on all listeners may well finally come to pass by necessity. We may well be seeing the beginning of a new transformation in music licensing in the agreement recently reached by Google with the book publishing industry.

Indeed, the *Tin Pan Alley* of yesterday is quickly taking shape as the *Silicon Alley* of tomorrow. If Samuel Goldwyn were here today and experienced these changes, he may well have observed: "The future ain't what it used to be."

CHAPTER 2

# THE ART OF MUSIC PUBLISHING

## SUMMARY

# CHAPTER 2

# THE ART OF MUSIC PUBLISHING

*Music publishing* is the activity of (1) promoting and licensing the performance and publication of musical works or compositions, (2) administering the legal protection of the compositions and the collection of income arising from such promotion and licensing, and (3) paying the songwriters their share of the collected income.

It is important to note that the activity of music publishing concerns the copyrightable work of authorship known as a *musical work*, which should not be confused with a separate kind of copyrightable work known as a *sound recording*. A sound recording is a work that results from a fixation — in a tangible medium of expression (e.g., tape, CD, hard disk, flash memory) — of *a series of sounds*. Those sounds may embody a performance of musical work or a spoken literary work, but the copyright in the underlying musical or spoken work is entirely separate from the copyright in the series of sounds that make up the recording.

Musical works are written by *songwriters* — either composers or lyricists, or both. Sound recordings are created by performers or *recording artists*, often with the assistance of *record producers*, although many recording artists and producers are also songwriters. Unless the recording artist or producer also directly participated in the writing of the song, he would not necessarily participate in the music publishing income derived from exploiting the song he performs or helps record — to participate in music publishing income, the artist or producer, who is not also one of the songwriters, would have to enter into a separate arrangement with the songwriters to participate in a share of the music publishing income.

During the heyday of Tin Pan Alley, beginning around the turn of the last century through the 1940, the hallmark of music publishing was the creative aspects of commercial song promotion: discovering songwriting talent, teaming up one songwriter with another, and getting a song performed or recorded by popular performing artists. Today, the music publisher more closely resembles an accountancy or law firm, with emphasis primarily on the administrative aspects of publishing. The future of music publishing hangs on the course of recent technological developments and the emergence of electronic commerce in intellectual property.

This chapter sketches the historical and legal background of music publishing, describes the major sources of music publishing income, and provides an overview of the division of music publishing income among music publishers and songwriters.

## I. HISTORICAL BACKGROUND

### A. Music Publishing in Early America

When John Smith and his fellow settlers established the first permanent English settlement at Jamestown, Virginia, in 1607, they undoubtedly raised their spirits by singing verses from psalm books they brought with them from Europe. Though the first printing press in the colonies was installed at Harvard College in 1640, it was not until nearly the end of the seventeenth century that the colonies were enriched by their first printed music book. Published in 1698, the ninth edition of *The Bay Psalm Book*, derived from earlier English editions published by John Playford, was the first book printed in the United States that contained musical notation.

In 1712, the first of a series of musical instruction books appeared — written by Reverend John Tufts of Newburyport, Massachusetts, *An Introduction to the Singing of Psalm Tunes in a Plain and Easy Method with a Collection of Tunes in Three Parts*, which provided a musical notation that the author thought would be easier to read than what was available at the time. In 1764, Paul Revere and Joseph Flagg claimed that their new publication of a compilation of popular and religious music, engraved by Revere himself, was printed on the first paper made in America.

### B. The First Professional Music Publishers in America

In 1793, Benjamin Carr moved his family from England and established the first music publishing firm in the United States, printing chiefly music that had become popular in England. Other music publishers were established in many of the major cities on the eastern seaboard.

During the year 1814, following the burning of our nation's Capitol, the Library of Congress, and the White House by the British, a young lawyer named Francis Scott Key made history by writing the *Star Spangled Banner*, which became our national anthem in 1931 by an act of the 71st Congress. The years spanning 1850 through 1860 were the most productive years of one of the greatest melodists America has ever produced: Stephen Collins Foster, who wrote *Oh! Susanna, Old Folks at Home, My Old Kentucky Home, Old Black Joe, Jeannie with the Light Brown Hair*, and *Come Where My Love Lies Dreaming*.

In 1866, Gustav Schirmer, the son of a German immigrant, after working various jobs in music importing and merchandising businesses, acquired control of Kerksieg and Breusing and opened up shop as G. Schirmer, Inc. His first interest was the day's most famous and controversial composer, Wagner, which set the tone for the firm's successful importation and printing of classical music.

With the development and increasing popularity of the piano, singing became a popular form of entertainment, and sales of printed sheet music of popular songs began to flourish. Music publishers of sheet music, sometimes no more than a printer with an interest in music, would hire traveling salesmen, some of whom could actually perform the music they promoted, to sell sheet music on a commission basis to the "general stores" located within the salesman's territory. It is estimated that, during the first 25 years of the nineteenth century, over 10,000 popular songs were published in the United States. By the end of the century, *After the Ball*, written and published by Charles K. Harris in 1893, became the first song to sell a million copies.

## C. Tin Pan Alley

As we approached this section of our history, we stopped to consider a passage by Cicero — "To remain ignorant of things that happened before you were born is to remain a child." The music business, more so than others, is a business that weaves relationships with deals. We could think of no better way to convey the texture of the music publishing industry as it existed in the early part of the twentieth century than to provide the following chronicle of the place and time they called *Tin Pan Alley*.

In 1880, after winning a toy printing press from school, Isidore, Julius, and Jay Witmark — aged seventeen, thirteen, and eleven — opened a printing business in their home on West 40th Street in New York City. They earned a modest living printing Christmas cards. To augment his earnings, "Julie" became a performer of ballads in minstrel and variety shows. After achieving some success, Julie thought that if it was possible for him to establish hit songs for others, why couldn't he publish his own music? After all, Isidore could write songs, and they had a printing press on which to print the music. Because the brothers were still minors, they had their father, Marcus, become director of the company, and thus M. Witmark & Sons was established in 1886 as a publisher and printer of sheet music. After hearing a rumor that President Grover Cleveland was about to announce his engagement, Isidore quickly went to work on a wedding march for the President and, upon the announcement, the Witmarks were the first to capitalize on the event.

Within a year after their establishment, the Witmarks purchased the song catalog of the New York Variety Publishing Company; a few years later, they acquired the Dobson Banjo Music catalog, and in 1892, with the acquisition of the Prophetic Catalogue, the Witmarks became the representatives for a number of important composers, among them Gussie L. Davis. They later acquired the song catalogs of Dave Marion, the Fred J. Hamill Company, B.D. Nice, Weber & Field, the Roger Brothers, including the songs of Maurice Levi. They also acquired the Gus Edwards catalog, including *Tammany* and *In My Merry Oldsmobile*, and the Sol Bloom catalog, including Hutchinson's *Sammy* and Arthur Penn's *Carrissma.* In 1903, Witmark hired a young pianist, Ernest R. Ball who wrote, with Irish musical star Chauncy Olcott, *Mother Machree* and *When Irish Eyes Are Smiling*, and with future mayor of New York City, James J. "Jimmy" Walker, *Will You Love Me In December As You Do In May?* Perhaps one of the Witmarks' most memorable hits at that time was *Sweet Adeline*, an *echo song* (i.e., one in which the title is echoed in every line of the lyric), which caught the attention of barbershop quartets.

In the late 1880, Jerome H. Remick, a milkman, acquired a music publishing firm in Detroit known as Whitney-Warner Publishing

Company and met success with hits such as *Creole Bells* and *Hiawatha.* In 1894, Remick moved his offices to New York City. Remick's offices were located near the corner of Fourteenth Street and Fourth Avenue, but Remick was soon drawn, along with other music publishers, to where the action was — the theaters and restaurants that were opening further uptown, around Twenty Eighth Street between Fifth Avenue and Broadway.

In 1886, Joseph Stern, a necktie salesman, and Edward B. Marks, a button salesman, formed a partnership called the Joseph W. Stern Company. Both, however, had a strong desire to write songs. Their first song, *The Little Lost Child*, relates the story of a lost little girl who meets a policeman. Upon returning the child to her mother, the policeman discovers that the girl's mother was his long lost wife. One day in 1894 the songwriters came across a new device, invented by a Brooklyn electrician, which could flash a series of photographs or drawings onto a wall. Hiring professional actors to produce slides dramatizing the story of *The Little Lost Child* and engaging professional singers to perform the song while the slides were being projected on a background screen, the writers produced a sensation that resulted in the sales of over a million copies of sheet music.

Other publishers soon copied this popular new way to plug their songs, and new publishers were opening up shop nearly every month. In 1896, Maurice Shapiro and Louis Bernstein, both from retailing businesses, formed Shapiro-Bernstein Publishing, and at about the same time, Leo Feist, a corset salesman and amateur songwriter, opened his doors with his famous slogan, "You can't go wrong with a Feist song." Harry Von Tilzer, born Harry Gumm in Detroit, Michigan, ran away from home at fourteen years of age to join the circus. Working for an itinerant theatrical company, Von Tilzer began a prolific songwriting career, writing his first hit, *My Old New Hampshire Home*, which he sold to a printer named William C. Dunn. Dunn later sold out to Shapiro-Bernstein, who made Von Tilzer a staff writer and later a partner in the firm. Von Tilzer went on to write several million-copy selling songs, including *A Bird in a Gilded Cage.* In 1902, he formed his own publishing company.

The offices of nearly all the major music publishing houses of that time began to congregate on that single street: Twenty Eighth Street between Fifth Avenue and Broadway, the street that became known, beginning around 1900, as "Tin Pan Alley." The appellation is believed to have been coined by Monroe Rosenfeld, a reporter for the *New York Herald*, who after meeting with Von Tilzer wrote a column about his experience in the 28th Street "alley" that reverberated with the "tin pan" sounding cacophony of pianos blaring from the windows of the music publishing houses lined along the street.

In 1902, together with Maurice Shapiro, Remick established Shapiro-Remick & Company. In 1905, they sold several million copies of *In the Shade of the Old Apple Tree* (Harry Williams and Egbert van Alstyne), but by 1906, Shapiro split with Remick and Remick formed his own publishing company, Jerome H. Remick & Co., which went on to publish a string of hit songs, including *Pretty Baby* and *Your Eyes Have Told Me So*. In 1909, Remick published three ballads that sold more than a million copies, one being *Put On Your Old Grey Bonnet*. These were followed by other successes, including *Moonlight Bay* in 1912 and *When You Wore a Tulip* in 1914.

It was about this time that a young man by the name of George Gershwin came to Tin Pan Alley. In 1914, Remick hired Gershwin as a *song plugger* — his job was to perform the songs in the Remick catalog for theater managers, dance bands, and stores selling sheet music. He would sometimes play inside the stores for customers passing by. Sheet music was one of the prime sources of income for music publishers at the time and song plugging was an integral part of the Tin Pan Alley music publishing operation.

While working for Remick, Gershwin composed many songs hoping they would be published, but shortly after they finally published one, *Rialto Ripples*, written in 1917 with lyricist Will Donaldson, he left Remick and Tin Pan Alley. He did not have much luck until he teamed up with Irving Caesar in 1919 to write *Swanee*,[1] which sold over two million records and one million copies of sheet music within a year after it was performed by Al Jolson. Although both Gershwin and Caesar signed up with Harms, Inc., Remick met the competition by signing such young talents as Harry Warren, Al Dubin, Gus Kahn, Richard Whiting, and others.

A composer by the name of Harry Dacre came to the United States in 1891 with a bicycle for which he had to pay duty. William Jerome, a

[1] For the rest of the story, see Chapter 11, *The Art of Granting and Clearing Music Licenses*.

lyricist friend, met him at the pier and jokingly remarked that if Dacre came over with a bicycle built for two he would have to pay double duty. The phrase stuck in Dacre's mind and he used it for the first song he wrote in America. The song, *Bicycle Built for Two*, was published by Tom B. Harms in 1892 and became an instant hit.

Tom Harms became the first publisher to discover the profitability in printing the sheet music of successful Broadway shows. He published *The Bowery*, *Reuben, Reuben*, and *Push Them Clouds Away*, from the show, *A Trip to Chinatown*, in 1892. This was the first time a stage production in the United States proved an instant source of revenue for a music publisher.

Max Dreyfus joined the Tom B. Harms Company in 1901 as an arranger. He had a talent for lifting songs out of Broadway musicals and making them hits, but he also demonstrated a talent for placing many of the firm's songs in Broadway shows. This talent did not go unnoticed and he was soon promoted to an executive position with the firm. In 1904, Alex and Tom Harms left the company and Dreyfus, who by that time had acquired a 25% interest in the firm, not only became its head, but his creativity as a publisher made him one of the most influential figures in the music publishing business.

In 1905, Francis, Day & Hunter, Ltd., one of the larger British music publishing firms, opened an office in New York City. The firm soon discovered, however, that American writers and performers were too busy promoting their own material and English songs were never favored despite all of the efforts they made to promote them. As a result, Francis, Day & Hunter agreed to merge their American branch with the T.B. Harms firm, lead at the time by both Max and Louis Dreyfus. T.B. Harms and Francis Day & Hunter, Inc., was incorporated in 1908, with Fred Day, Max Dreyfus and Louis Dreyfus as equal shareholders, and the firm became the largest music publishing house in America at the time.

In 1920, William Boosey of Chappell & Co., Ltd. Approached Max and Louis Dreyfus to take over the business of Chappell & Co. Inc. in New York under a long-term contract. In return, Chappell & Co., Ltd. would become the subpublisher of the catalog of T.B. Harms for the territory of Great Britain.

Max Dreyfus was a master at signing up successful talented song pluggers, hiring, for example, a nineteen-year old Jerome Kern. Kern's job was to play the piano and sell songs at department stores such as R.H. Macy's in New York City. He also served as a rehearsal pianist for Broadway musicals. Kern's talent as a composer soon made music critics take notice. Kern became such a top contributor to the T.B. Harms catalog that Max Dreyfus gave him a partnership interest in the firm.

In 1917, Kern wrote some special material for a Victor Herbert show, *Miss 1917*. Kern was so impressed with its rehearsal pianist that he insisted that Max Dreyfus meet him. Dreyfus, therefore, arranged a time to meet this young pianist who turned out to be George Gershwin. Dreyfus hired Gershwin on the spot just to write songs and gave him a salary of $35 per week.

Like Jerome Kern and George Gershwin, Vincent Youmans became another Max Dreyfus discovery and was also employed as a staff pianist and song plugger. As M. Witmark & Sons had the big three operetta composers, Victor Herbert, Sigmund Romberg, and Rudolf Friml, so Max Dreyfus had the new popular Broadway musical writers, Jerome Kern, George Gershwin, and Vincent Youmans.

In 1925, the young members of the Theater Guild put on an intimate revue to raise money for draperies and curtains for a new Broadway theater. Richard Rodgers and Lorenz Hart contributed several songs to the successful performance. Max Dreyfus called Rodgers and Hart into his office to sign exclusive songwriter agreements with Harm, Inc. In 1924, Cole Porter contributed five songs to the Greenwich Village Follies, but it wasn't until 1928 when Irene Bordoni's rendition of *Let's Do It* in her provocative French accent caused Max Dreyfus to add another composer to his already well stocked staff of writers.

By the end of the 1920s the Harms, Inc. office at 62 West 45th Street became a "club" where composers made it a habit to meet at noon for "shoptalk" and to listen to George Gershwin play the piano. Harms, Inc. had become the top Broadway music publisher, whose songwriting staff also included Arthur Schwartz, Bert Kalmer, E.Y. Harburg, Irving Caesar, Harry Ruby, Herman Hupfeld, Howard Dietz, Vernon Duke, and Ira Gershwin.

On October 6, 1927, a startled audience at New York's Warner Theater watched and heard Al Jolson utter his famous, "Wait a minute, wait a minute, you ain't heard nothin' yet. Wait a minute, I tell ya, you ain't heard nothin'." Within months after his release of the first "talking picture," *The Jazz Singer*, film producer Jack Warner foresaw the great importance that music would play in the making of talkies. By the end of 1929, Warner Bros. had purchased the entire catalogs of M. Witmark & Sons, Remick Music Corporation, and Max Dreyfus's Harms, Inc. Tin Pan Alley would never be the same.

## II. MUSIC PUBLISHING TODAY

Today, music publishers can be classified into three main categories delineated primarily by size: (1) the major worldwide publisher, (2) the independent music publisher, and (3) the self-publishing songwriter and music publishing administrators.

### A. The Major Music Publisher

The largest publishers in the first of the above categories would include Universal Music Publishing (owned by Universal Music Group, a division of Vivendi, French conglomerate), which recently acquired one of the former majors, BMG Music (earlier owned by Bertelsmann), EMI Music (owned by EMI, a privately held firm based in the United Kingdom), and Warner/Chappell Music (owned by Warner Music Group, a publicly held firm based in New York).

### B. Independent Music Publishers and Music Publishing Administrators

The next tier of music publishers comprises the independent publishers. These include Peer Music, Abkco, Bourne Co., Cherry Lane, Chrysalis Music, Music Sales, Shapiro Bernstein, Stage Three, and Wixen. Some of the largest of these, such as Peer Music, have offices in many countries and, in addition to administering extensive catalogs of their own they provide international subpublishing services for smaller publishers around the world.

Several private equity firms have also acquired or have become the financing entities for firms looking to acquire independent publishers. Publishers closely associated with these private equity firms include Imagen, S1, and Primary Wave Music.

According to the latest research announced by Music & Copyright, a newsletter published by Informa Telecoms & Media, independent music publishers make up about 32.45% of the global market share, higher than the market share of each of the major publishers: Universal, 23.2%; EMI, 18.3%; Warner/Chappell, 14.9%; and Sony/ATV, 11.7%.

### C. Self-Publishing Songwriter and Music Publishing Administrators

Another category is the writer who maintains his own publishing rights and sets up his own publishing company. Many of these songwriters either co-publish their catalogs with one of the majors or large independent publishers, who administer their catalogs for them, or they use the services of a music publishing administrator — organizations that specialize in administering the catalogs owned by individual songwriters, their estates, and small independent publishers. Companies who specialize in providing music publishing administration services include Bug Music, Evergreen, The Royalty Network, Kobalt, and ION Music Publishing. These firms do not typically own any portion of the copyrights they administer, but provide administration services under administration agreements (discussed in Chapter 4).

Some popular songwriters not only prefer to maintain their own publishing rights, but hire their own administrators or venture with an administrator who specializes in representing the songwriter's catalog. Examples include Bob Dylan, Bruce Springsteen, Neil Diamond, and Carly Simon. Often, the objective of these composer/publishers is to maximize the control over their catalogs and seek the best subpublishing administration overseas they can at the lowest possible cost. Thus, while they may engage in some creative activities, at their core they perform the function of administering the administrators — that is, they may contract with one of the major worldwide publishers to perform their administration functions on a worldwide basis or they may engage one of the majors to administer their rights in the United States and separately contract with music publishers around the world for local overseas administration.

Many motion picture studios and production companies have their own music publishing companies, which are used to administer the compositions written for their motion pictures and television programs.

## III. SOURCES OF MUSIC PUBLISHING INCOME

The sources of a music publisher's income can be divided into two main categories: (1) major sources of income (i.e., where the largest share is derived) and (2) secondary sources of income.

The *major* sources of music publishing income include:

- Public performance income
- Mechanical reproduction income (i.e., reproduction and distribution of sound recordings and ringtones)
- Synchronization license income (i.e., reproduction, exhibition and distribution of theatrical motion pictures, television programs, and other audiovisual works)
- International subpublishing

The *secondary* sources of music publishing income include:

- Commercial advertising income
- Printed music
- Background music services
- Music boxes and other consumer musical products
- Videogames, software, and other new media products
- Reproduction and distribution of non-theatrical and corporate motion pictures and audiovisual works
- Karaoke
- Digital samples
- Dramatic performances
- Dramatic adaptations

The business and legal aspects of each of these sources of music publishing income are discussed in the chapters that follow, organized by the type of license agreement used as the basis of the underlying transaction. These sources of income and their related licenses are summarized below:

## A. Major Sources of Income

*Public Performance.* The largest source of music publishing income is from the licensing of public performances — including performances of recorded music on radio, television, places of business, and the Internet, as well as live performances. Together public performances represent about one-half of all music publishing income. Most of this income is administered and collected by organizations known as *performance rights societies*,[2] who issue public performance licenses, usually on a *blanket* basis. License for this income will be explored in Chapter 18. Performance royalties account for about 40% of all music publishing income.

*Mechanical Reproduction.* Music used in sound recordings, and distributed in compact discs, digital download, and certain forms of transmissions over the Internet are permitted by the grant of what is known, for historical reasons, as a *mechanical reproduction license*.[3] These licenses generate *mechanical royalties*, which account for about 25% of all music publishing income.

*Synchronization.* Music that is embodied in motion pictures for theatrical distribution generate *synchronization royalties*, the licensing for which is granted in a *theatrical synchronization license.* Music that is embodied in copies of television programs for television broadcast also generate *synchronization royalties*, the licensing for which is granted in a *television synchronization license.* Royalties derived from synchronization licensing[4] account for about 10% of a music publisher's income.

*International Subpublishing.* All of the licensing activities occurring in the United States, including performance licensing, mechanical licensing, and to a lesser extent, synch licensing, as well as the secondary forms of licensing discussed below, also occur outside the United States. Though the United States is the world's largest market

---

[2] For licensing music in public performances, see Chapter 18.

[3] For licensing music in sound recordings, see Chapter 13.

[4] For licensing music in audiovisual works, such as theatrical motion pictures and television shows, see Chapter 15.

for music, it only represents about 25% of worldwide music sales. A popular U.S. artist with worldwide appeal would be expected to generate for songs performed and recorded by that artist as much revenue from sources outside the United States as inside the United States, if not more. The business and licensing considerations in licensing music publishing rights overseas — known as *international subpublishing* — is discussed in Chapter 5.

## B. Secondary Sources of Income

When music is used as part of a commercial advertising campaign, a *special commercial advertising synchronization license* is required.[5] Music used in *sheet music, music folios*, and other printed copies of music — including the emerging area of *digital print* — is permitted by the grant of a *print license*.[6]

Music used in sound recordings that are intended to be used solely for closed-circuit broadcast (e.g., the music you hear in elevators and on airplanes) is permitted by the grant of what is known as an *electrical transcription license*,[7] and these generate *electrical transcription royalties.*

When music is embodied in a music box or similar musical product, such as a talking doll or singing greeting card, a *music box license* or *consumer musical product license* is required.[8] These are discussed in Chapter 13. Music used in promotional or training videos produced by corporations is licensed under a *non-theatrical synchronization license*[9] and when these videos are distributed in videocassette or laserdisc form, a *non-theatrical videogram license* is required.[10]

An emerging area of licensing concerns the use of music in videogames and other forms of software, both online and offline. These

---

[5] For licensing music in advertising, see Chapter 20.

[6] For licensing music in print, see Chapter 12.

[7] For licensing music in electrical transcriptions and background music services, see Chapter 14.

[8] For licensing music in audiovisual works distributed in videograms, or home video devices, see Chapter 15.

[9] For licensing music in non-theatrical exhibition, see Chapter 15.

[10] For licensing music in non-theatrical videograms, see Chapter 15.

licenses are discussed in Chapter 22. A new source of revenue arising from the use of digital technology in the recording process has produced the important subject of digital sampling licenses, discussed in Chapter 24.

Though rarely a significant source of publishing income, a *dramatic performance license* is required by anyone who wishes to render a dramatic performance of a song — that is, when the song is used to carry forward the plot or story of a dramatic work, such as a motion picture, television program, or theatrical play. A dramatic performance license should not be confused with a *grand performance license*, the latter of which is not a license strictly for music — it is a license to perform a grand opera or grand musical play, or portion thereof.[11]

Finally, if you desire to produce a dramatization of a musical composition — or more accurately, its lyrics (i.e., much like one would produce a motion picture adaptation of a novel or short story) — you would require a *dramatic adaptation license.* Much industry confusion over dramatic performances, grand performances, and dramatizations, is clarified in Chapter 19, regarding the *Grand Rights Controversy*.

## IV. DISTRIBUTION OF MUSIC PUBLISHING INCOME

When the promotion, publication, and performance of music results in the collection of royalty income by the music publisher, there comes a time to pay the songwriter his share. The share of the music publishing income, which the songwriter is entitled to receive, is known as the *writer's share*. The share the publisher is entitled to keep is called the *publisher's share*. Under a standard music publishing arrangement, the writer's share and the publisher's share, for the most part,[12] are equal (i.e., the publisher and writer split most of the publishing income on a 50-50 basis). The terms and conditions of this sharing of income are set forth in the agreement between the publisher and writer, discussed in Chapter 3, on *Songwriter Agreements*.

[11] The distinction is discussed at length in Chapter 19, on the *Grand Rights Controversy*.

[12] Royalties on revenues arising from print licensing comprise a notable exception.

### A. Writer's Share

If there are two or more writers, the writer's share will be shared among them, usually, but not always, in equal shares. Agreements among songwriting collaborators are discussed in Chapter 3, on *Songwriter Agreements*. With one exception, the writer's share of music publishing income is paid to the writer *by the music publisher*. The one exception is *performance royalties* (i.e., royalties generated from the public performance of the songwriter's music), which are typically paid directly to the writer *by his performance rights society* (e.g., ASCAP or BMI).[13]

### B. Publisher's Share

The publisher's share may be shared among several co-publishers, in accordance with their respective percentage interests in the publisher's share of income. Before distribution to co-publishers, the publisher's share may also be subject to the payment of an administration fee in exchange for the services of an administrator, a service one of the co-publishers often provides to the others. Arrangements among co-publishers and music publishing administrators are discussed further in Chapter 4, on *Co-Publishing and Administration Agreements*.

## V. ORGANIZATION OF THE MUSIC PUBLISHER

Though the organization of a music publisher will vary considerably depending upon its size, the typical professional music publisher will be organized along functional lines. As we have noted, music publishing can be divided between two functional aspects: *creative* and *administrative*, with the latter increasingly becoming the dominant of the two functions.

### A. Creative

The creative activities of a music publisher are generally led by the creative staff, more commonly called the *professional department*, but

[13] See Chapter 3, on *Songwriter Agreements*, and Chapter 18, on *Licensing Music in Live and Recorded Public Performances*.

sometimes referred to as the *creative department*. The domain of the *professional manager* includes: signing up songwriting talent, developing that talent, and getting songs recorded by popular performing artists. In short, the job of the professional manager involves discovering, nurturing, and plugging.

The days of a publisher hiring the likes of a young George Gershwin or Jerome Kern to perform a publisher's repertoire for theater managers, dance bands, and stores selling sheet music are long gone. Today's professional manager is more likely to be found hanging out in night clubs, listening for that new sound, in the hope of discovering a hit act just at the dawning of their career. Professional managers have played an increasing role in discovering new talent, signing them up to music publishing contracts, and then helping the act secure a recording contract.

On occasion, by bringing the right song to the right performer, the professional manager becomes the catalyst for propelling good talent to stardom. Michael Sandoval, former head of the professional management department of Warner/Chappell Music, received a movie script from Warner Bros. Pictures together with a request to have a love song written. He asked Jon Lind and John Bettis, both staff writers at the time for Warner/Chappell, to come up with something. When Joel Sill of Warner Bros. Pictures received delivery of the song, *Crazy for You*, for the motion picture, *Vision Quest*, he replied "Great, any ideas who should record it?" Sandoval suggested an unknown, but up and coming, singer named Madonna.

Opportunities such as these generally arise only after many years of building the necessary professional contacts with the people who can "make it happen." A good professional manager, therefore, works tirelessly to build long-term personal relationships with key band members, record producers, personal managers of successful performing groups and producers, executives in the A&R (i.e., artist and repertoire) departments of major record companies, and producers of motion pictures and television programs. By "doing" that lunch or dinner, keeping in touch, commissioning demo recordings and getting them to the right people, the professional manager increases his chances of leveraging his relationships into *covers* (i.e., recordings) of songs in the publisher's catalog or songs written by the publisher's exclusive staff writers.

Keeping in touch also means listening closely to trends and seeing beyond, what Sandoval calls, "the flavor of the month." The professional manager must learn to anticipate new trends and seek or nurture the talent to fill it. For this reason, it is critical for songwriters to change as the music does. To that end, the professional manager can play an invaluable role in providing guidance to songwriters, critiquing their work, and helping them develop their talent to meet the changing tastes of the listening public. Often, that development stems from a professional manager's efforts to match the talents of one songwriter with that of another. Many of today's hits are the result of collaborations suggested by professional managers.

During the first half of the twentieth century, the creative activities of the music publisher were the source of the publisher's power. Today, the center of power at a music publisher often resides in the computer software they use for computing songwriter royalties. This may all change, however, with the advent of electronic commerce. Professional managers of the future may find themselves more and more involved in discovering talent that appears on the electronic landscape and figuring out how to capitalize upon that talent through both traditional and non-traditional music publishing channels.

## B. Administrative

The administrative aspects of music publishing are traditionally distributed among the following publishing departments: Copyright Administration, Licensing, Legal Affairs, Royalty Accounting, International, and Print.

### *1. Copyright Department*

The Copyright Administration department is responsible for completing and filing of applications for copyright registration and copyright renewal (*see* Chapter 9), and the recording of copyright assignments (*see* Chapter 8), for the musical compositions in its catalog with the U.S. Copyright Office and other applicable copyright authorities.

Registering the copyright in a song, though not necessary to secure legal protection of the song, is a pre-condition to filing a copyright infringement lawsuit. In addition, recording all copyright transfers — such as when a songwriter enters into a songwriter agreement with a music publisher transferring existing copyrights to the publisher — is an important practice to avoid disputes over conflicting ownership claims.

In 2008, the U.S. Copyright Office began accepting copyright registrations over the Internet. Advantages include lower filing fees, faster processing time, and online status tracking. More information is available at www.copyright.gov.

The Copyright Department also apprises performing rights societies (e.g., ASCAP and BMI) when new songs are added to the publisher's catalog of compositions, and notifies its royalty accounting department of any changes of ownership in any of the compositions in its catalog. Such changes may occur as a result of the sale of portions of the catalog, the exercise by songwriters of termination rights (*see* Chapter 9), or by the terms of any applicable agreements with songwriters (*see* Chapter 3).

When submitting new compositions to performance rights societies, music publishers are urged to make their submissions electronically using a standard created for that purpose called the Common Works Registration (CWR) format. Certain software products, such as Musicalc and Music Maestro, have CWR capability built into them.

### *2. Licensing Department*

Often combined with the copyright administration department, the Licensing Department negotiates and issues licenses to those seeking to use any of the musical compositions in the publisher's catalog, including many of the kinds of licenses discussed in this book.

Licensing departments of many music publishers are often quite passive, generating synchronization and other license revenue simply by *taking orders* (i.e., waiting for the phone to ring), but the better licensing departments aggressively pursue new licensing opportunities by offering special services to producers of works that require music. When the music coordinator of a television or film production calls a licensing department not only to negotiate fees, but to seek a particular type of music needed, the licensing department should be able to provide a list of sample tunes from its catalog. In just this way, I was able to assist Harvey Becal, the music producer for the hit television game show, *Name That Tune*, where the contestants would bet they could name a given tune by hearing just a few bars or notes of the music. I would suggest songs from the Warner/Chappell catalog, by song genre, that were appropriate for use in the game. When a representative from Woody Allen's office expressed interest in using some of George Gershwin's music in Woody Allen's film, *Manhattan*, I was instrumental in persuading them to use strictly all Gershwin music, which they did.

Sometimes, a particular use will require the consent of the songwriter under the terms of the songwriter's agreement with the publisher. For example, Ira Gershwin had a policy of never allowing the licensing of an edited version of his brother's *Rhapsody In Blue*. When Woody Allen wanted to use an edited version of *Rhapsody In Blue* in the opening of *Manhattan*, I personally went to Ira's house, helped him understand who Woody Allen was, described the nature of the project, and ultimately persuaded him to consent to the use. When we later rendered a special screening of the movie in Ira's living room, he was delighted with the result.[14] I mention this to illustrate how far a licensing department can go to strike a deal, which benefits the publisher, the writer, and the customer.

As a result of *The Split Copyright Syndrome*, discussed in Chapter 6, producers have been finding it increasingly difficult to clear licenses for songs they desired to use. Often, the catalog of Warner/Chappell contained close substitutes for the songs requested and the advantage to the producer of using one of these substitutes is that they could quickly get a license from a single source, without having to track down and negotiate with the multiple owners of songs tainted by the split copyright problem. One day, it occurred to me that if I could compile and publish a list of standard songs in the Warner/Chappell catalog, which we could offer quickly and easily (i.e., with no need to get permission from co-publishers or consent of the songwriters), producers would more likely turn to the songs on such a list than to songs in the catalogs of other publishers. This is, in fact, just what I did: I made

[14] When I asked Ira if he had any further comments, he remarked, in jest, "They didn't give credit to the lyric writer." From that point on, I made it a point in negotiating motion picture synchronization licenses to attempt to require producers to provide screen credit to songwriters and music publishers of the licensed music.

just such a list and organized the songs by genre, such as the Roaring Twenties, Country & Western, 50's Rock & Roll, and chronologically by year of publication.

Finally, perhaps the best service a licensing manager can provide is a thorough knowledge of his catalog. Having been in music publishing for most of my professional career, and having a musician's ear and memory for good melodies, it was not difficult for me to provide a high level of service. Often, a producer need only hum a few bars and I could not only "name that tune," but "name that publisher" — that is, not only could I tell a producer if a song was in my catalog, I could often direct a caller to the publisher who owned the music — like Macy's sending a customer to Gimbel's. Today, with aging catalogs and (seemingly) younger licensing managers, it may be more difficult for a publisher to provide this level of service.

Technology is making a difference, however. Both ASCAP and BMI offer on the Internet the ability to electronically search their catalogs so that you can now easily determine the publisher of a particular composition.[15] Perhaps, someone will next develop a computer software application that will combine a song database with "song recognition" — a form of voice recognition for standard melodies.[16]

The responsibilities of the licensing department may seem to overlap with those of the professional department, but licensing managers tend to focus on issuing synchronization licenses for older, and generally *standard* songs (i.e., classics, oldies, or popular theme songs), and the professional managers tend to focus on increasing mechanical and performance license revenue by obtaining *covers* (i.e., new recordings) of the songs in the catalog, especially songs written by its *staff* songwriters (i.e., songwriters with whom the publisher has contracted on an exclusive basis for a period of years).

### *3. Legal Affairs Department*

The Legal Affairs department of a music publisher, sometimes called Business Affairs, performs many of the same functions of a

---

[15] ASCAP can be found on the Internet at www.ascap.com, BMI at www.bmi.com, and SESAC at www.sesac.com.

[16] Since the publication of the 1996 edition of this book, several song recommendation engine technologies have emerged that may well be applied to this purpose.

typical corporate in-house legal department. These include the drafting of the form agreements commonly used by the publisher, including the publisher's standard songwriter agreements, co-publishing agreements, and license agreements. The Legal Affairs department will often participate in the negotiation of particular agreements, and will at least be consulted when any changes are made to any of the legal language used in a standard form.

A very important service a Legal Affairs department can provide is something that my son emphasized in his role as general counsel to a major publisher of computer software: that is, in any transaction, *preserve your ability to change your mind.* This may be as simple as including an *out* clause (e.g., termination for convenience) or preferring non-exclusive over exclusive arrangements. If in each transaction a lawyer would ask, "What happens if you change your mind?", a solution will come to mind that will allow the publisher to negotiate, in advance, a satisfactory way out should circumstances change later on.

Finally, a responsible Legal Affairs department will assume a law enforcement role, making sure the publisher's activities are conducted within the dictates of the law. The management of a music publisher should look to its Legal Affairs department as its *corporate conscience* and should respect not only the legal, but also the ethical aspects of the advice given. Smaller publishers, as with smaller businesses, not large enough to support this function in house, will rely primarily on the services of a law firm specializing in entertainment and copyright, for its legal affairs function. Of course, songwriters who manage their own music publishing often rely on, "I have this lawyer friend . . ."

#### *4. Royalty Accounting Department*

If the check is in the mail, it was probably prepared and sent by the Royalty Accounting department. The Royalty Accounting department manages royalties that come in to the publisher, such as revenues from the issuance of mechanical, synchronization, and videogram licenses, and royalties that go out, primarily to co-publishers and songwriters with whom the publisher has entered songwriter, co-publishing, and administration agreements.

The Royalty Accounting department has, over the years, become the heart of the modern music publisher, and the heart of the Royalty

Accounting department has become the mainframe computer (and, increasingly, mini- and micro-computers). Information from royalty income statements are entered into the computer, the computer is programmed with the appropriate royalty splits, and the computer churns out royalty statements and corresponding checks for payment to the publishers and writers. An increasing share of a publisher's expenses is being devoted to improving its management information systems. The bulk of these resources are used to improve the speed and accuracy of royalty accounting, but an increasing emphasis is being placed on the storage and retrieval of copyright ownership and other information. In the future, computers will be used to enhance the licensing process itself, with storage and retrieval capabilities for sheet music, MIDI files, and other sound processing applications.

### 5. International Department

The International department[17] is responsible for managing the administration of the publisher's catalog outside the United States. Major music publishing firms have publishing subsidiaries located in each of the major markets around the world. Independent music publishers have either arrangements with a major music publisher for the administration of overseas music publishing revenue or arrangements directly with subpublishing companies located around the world. When a U.S. publisher is acting as a subpublisher for an overseas music publisher, the International department is generally responsible for managing the relationship.

### 6. Print Department

In a modern era of radio, television, motion pictures, compact disc recordings, and electronic distribution, the Print department in most music publisher's today has become little more than a file of contracts.

These contracts authorize third-party print publishing specialists to reproduce the music publisher's catalog of musical compositions in sheet music and songbook form. Since the 1930, income from licensing

[17] We prefer to use the word, "international" in place of the commonly used "foreign," because of the pejorative, and often xenophobic, connotation that the latter word tends to carry. In a global economy, it is important to avoid language that may be considered offensive in international business transactions.

the mechanical reproduction and broadcast performance of music has replaced printed music sales as the primary source of music publishing revenue to the point that, today, printed music represents only a small portion of a music publisher's income. Basic considerations in negotiating licenses for the reproduction and distribution of printed music are discussed in detail in Chapter 12, on *Licensing Music in Print and Digital Print*.

## VI. HOW TO ESTABLISH A MUSIC PUBLISHING COMPANY

Establishing a music publishing company is much the same as setting up any small business. For example, you must consider the best legal form for your business — that is, whether you will operate as a sole proprietorship, partnership, corporation, or limited liability company.[18] Before choosing the legal form for your business, however, you should first consult your legal or tax advisor.

But even before you consult the accountants and lawyers, you should first consult one of the two major performance rights societies, ASCAP or BMI. Which society you choose is often a metaphysical question, one we can't answer.[19] Nevertheless, if you are already a member of one of these societies as a songwriter, the decision is easy: you *must* join that society as a publisher as well. Ask the society for an application for publisher membership.[20]

When you apply for affiliation in the society, you must offer the society three choices for the name you wish to use for your publishing company, ranked in your order of preference. The society will tell you which of these names they will accept, if any — their objective is to avoid misdirection of performance royalty payments resulting from two publishing companies having confusingly similar names.

[18] A limited liability company (or "LLP") is often the most attractive legal form for someone just starting out — an LLP provides its owners with limited liability (i.e., the owners liability is limited to the amount he or she invests in the business), a benefit normally available only to shareholders of a corporation, but, for tax purposes, the LLP is treated as a sole proprietorship, which may be very important, particularly if you expect to operate at a loss for some period of time.

[19] For further information about the performing societies, see Chapter 18.

[20] Information on where you may contact these societies is in Chapter 18.

By first gaining the society's approval of your publishing company's name, you will avoid the expense and headache of reprinting stationery, reopening bank accounts, changing your corporate name, and the like. At the time you affiliate with your performance rights society, or shortly thereafter, you should register all of your songs with the society, which lets them know the titles of your songs and who to pay when it comes time to give royalty credit for their public performances. Note that unless you have at least one song that is either about to be recorded or used commercially in a film or television program, the society may not let you become a member.

Once you have become affiliated with a performance rights society, with a name of which they approve, you must then establish your legal form (i.e., sole proprietorship, partnership, corporation, or limited liability company). If you choose to remain a sole proprietorship, you must, in most states, publish in a newspaper, and file with the county in which your business resides, what is known in California as a *fictitious name statement* (also known as, a "DBA," or "doing business as" statement). You should first contact your local newspaper, as most newspapers will offer the service of both publishing the statement, and filing with the county, for a modest fee. You will find that, in many states, a duly filed and published fictitious business name statement will be a prerequisite to opening up a bank account under a fictitious business name.

Finally, you should register the copyrights in your songs with the U.S. Copyright Office[21] and record any assignments of copyrights[22] in the songs created by your writers from them to your publishing company.

## VII. THE FUTURE OF MUSIC PUBLISHING

During the eighteenth and early nineteenth centuries, the music publisher was someone with a printing press, an interest in music,

[21] Copies of Form PA, together with straightforward instructions on how to complete the application, may be obtained at the website of the U.S. Copyright Office, copyright.gov, where you will also find a means of registering your copyrights electronically.

[22] For a sample short form copyright assignment, see Form 8.1 on CD-ROM.

and either a storefront or a network of traveling salesmen. By 1900, music publishing became a serious, but more creative, business, with most of it concentrated in a Manhattan city block known as Tin Pan Alley. From that time on, until about the 1950, music publishing was largely a creative endeavor. It meant discovering songwriting talent, teaming up one songwriter with another, and getting a song performed or recorded.

Today, the major music publisher would seem to rely more on the talents of its Chief Information Officer than its creative staff. But, what about the future? As is suggested throughout this book, particularly in discussions regarding the application of new technologies, the digital revolution — in both the production of recordings and the means of their distribution — herald another change in the orchestration of music publishing. The emergence of electronic commerce, and the ability for virtually anyone to inexpensively become his or her own publisher and distributor of musical compositions, will have, by the end of the next decade, an impact on music publishing no less profound as the impact Tin Pan Alley had at the beginning of the last century.

CHAPTER 3

# SONGWRITER AGREEMENTS

## SUMMARY

# CHAPTER 3

# SONGWRITER AGREEMENTS

As noted in the previous chapter, income arising from the licensing of a musical composition is shared among the music publishers and songwriters who have an interest in the composition. The share of the music publishing income, which the songwriter is entitled to receive, is called the *writer's share* and the share the publisher is entitled to keep is called the *publisher's share*. The process by which this sharing of income occurs is defined and governed by an agreement between the music publisher and the songwriter called a *songwriter agreement.*

This chapter sketches the common terms and conditions contained in the typical songwriter agreement and suggests many of the common variations negotiated on behalf of songwriters.

## I. Selecting a Music Publisher

The considerations that a songwriter uses in selecting a particular music publisher vary depending upon the circumstances. Obviously, a new songwriter seeking to "break into" the business will have fewer alternatives from which to choose than a successful recording artist. Moreover, each is likely to have a different goal: the new songwriter will seek a publisher willing to commit sufficient time to effectively promote the writer's songs in the hope of obtaining a commercial recording that will launch the writer's career; by contrast, the objective of a popular recording artist, who has his own means of promoting his songs, may be to gain the largest share of music publishing income as possible while incurring the lowest possible transaction costs.

In either case, the music publisher selected may ultimately fail to achieve the writer's goal. This may not always be the fault of the music publisher, as the writer's goals may change over time. For example, the amateur songwriter may become a star, in which case his or her music publishing objectives will change accordingly; similarly, a fickle public may quickly reverse the fortunes of a successful artist, whose music publishing goals consequently shift to securing a lesser percentage of a bigger pie, with the music publisher playing a greater role in promoting the writer's published catalog.

In any case, the songwriter can reduce his risk of choosing the wrong publisher, realign his music publishing relationship to fit changing objectives — in short, preserve his ability to "change his mind" — by carefully negotiating the terms and conditions of his or her songwriter agreement in advance.

## II. Negotiating the Songwriter/Publisher Relationship

When a songwriter signs a typical songwriter agreement with a music publisher, he is granting to the publisher full ownership in the copyright in his musical compositions in exchange for the publisher's services and payment of the *writer's share*. The music publisher earns his *publisher's share* by providing creative, promotional, and administrative services intended to enhance the income upon which the writer's and publisher's shares are based. Though the songwriter who is negotiating his songwriter agreement will want to maximize the potential size of his writer's share, relative to the publisher's share, he should consider the possibility of participating in (i.e., receiving a portion of) the publisher's share itself.

Arrangements under which a songwriter receives a portion of the publisher's share of music publishing income is known as a *participation deal*. Whether the songwriter will be able to negotiate a participation deal, and take a share of the publisher's share, will depend entirely on the writer's circumstances and bargaining leverage.

### A. Negotiating for All or a Portion of the Publisher's Share

As noted, the songwriter agreement defines how the total publishing income is divided into the *writer's share* and the *publisher's share*. Negotiating the standard songwriter agreement traditionally involves reviewing and discussing solely that fundamental division. However, in the larger context of the relationship between the publisher and writer, the question of how the *publisher's share* of total publishing income is allocated often becomes the subject of additional negotiation.

A songwriter who has some bargaining power may be in a position to negotiate for all or a portion of the *publisher's share* of the total music publishing income, which, as we have said, is called a participation deal. His participation in the publisher's share would be in addition to his writer's share as defined by the songwriter agreement. For example, if the writer's share and publisher's share each amount to 50% of the total publishing income, then a writer who negotiates 50% of the publisher's share, would be entitled to receive 75% of the total publishing income (i.e., his writer's share, which equals 50% of the total publishing income, plus one-half of the publisher's share).

When the songwriter is able to retain a portion of the publisher's share, he typically enters into a *co-publishing agreement* with the music publisher, which will govern the co-ownership of the compositions and how the publisher and writer will split in the proceeds of the *publisher's share*. When the songwriter is able to retain all of the publisher's share, retaining full ownership in his compositions, he may enter into an *administration agreement*, under which the publisher agrees to perform certain administrative duties in return for an administration fee. The negotiation of co-publishing and administration agreements is discussed in detail in Chapter 4.

Most participation deals are effected by the entry of a co-publishing agreement, with administration agreements reserved for those songwriters who have a very high degree of bargaining leverage. Whether a writer retains all or a portion of the publisher's share of income under a co-publishing or administration arrangement, he will often enter into a *songwriter agreement* with a music publisher (or co-publishers), which sets forth the terms and conditions under which the writer is entitled to receive his *writer's share* of the music publishing income. Sometimes the songwriter agreement (governing the writer's share) and the co-publishing agreement (governing the writer's participation in the publisher's share) are combined into a single agreement, an example of which is set forth as Form 4.1 found on the CD-ROM. Because interests in the publisher's share are often bought and sold, even a writer who self-publishes his compositions should carefully consider the terms and conditions of the songwriter agreement he enters into with his own publishing company.

## B. Negotiating the Writer's Share (i.e., the Songwriter Agreement)

Standard songwriter publishing agreements are of two types: the *single song* agreement and the *exclusive term* agreement. Under the *single song* agreement, the songwriter grants to the publisher full ownership in the copyright in the particular musical composition or compositions involved. A misnomer in this context, the *single song* agreement may actually cover several songs, which would be listed in an exhibit or schedule attached to the agreement. Under an *exclusive term* agreement, the writer agrees to grant to the publisher any songs he writes during the term of the agreement.

Exclusive term agreements tend to be used with writers who have demonstrated a consistent ability to create successful songs or writers who are also recording artists who, by having recording contracts with record companies, have a natural opportunity to consistently effect the recording and publication of songs he or she has written. The exclusive term agreement, in this context, reduces the transaction costs of having to continually prepare and execute single song agreements for each song or group of songs written by the songwriter.

A songwriter may also enter into an exclusive term agreement to take advantage of the steady, periodic advances that are often associated with them, to gain access to a publisher's recording facilities to create high quality demonstration recordings, and to join a small circle of other talented *staff writers* through which successful collaborations may be generated. Some attorneys, however, advise songwriters against entering into exclusive term agreements unless they need the cash or unless the publisher is really in a special position to assist the writer's career through means just mentioned. They assert that any additional transaction costs associated with entering into a series of single song agreements is outweighed by the flexibility afforded by avoiding the confines of exclusivity. This flexibility, however, comes not without its costs. The songwriter should consider the additional transaction costs, such as attorneys' fees, associated with spreading his compositions among a number of different music publishers.

Many of the provisions of the *single song* and *exclusive term* agreements are the same, though the exclusive term agreement contains certain additional provisions relating to the engagement of the writer's services over a period of time. Accordingly, we will first review each material provision of a standard single song agreement and then discuss only the relevant additional provisions of the exclusive term deal.

## III. NEGOTIATING THE SINGLE SONG MUSIC PUBLISHING AGREEMENT

It seems there are as many forms of songwriter agreements as there are music publishers who use them. The CD-ROM includes several different forms that have typically been used by songwriters and music publishers over the years, and we have selected one of those forms as the starting point for the analysis which we present in the following pages.[1]

Our review here will focus only on the major business points of the transaction. Many of the legal boilerplate provisions are discussed in Chapter 10, on *Basic Considerations in Music Licensing*. Additional issues, and the way they may be resolved from the songwriter's point of view, may be found by a close review of the provisions of the AGAC and Songwriter's Guild agreements, found on the CD-ROM as Forms 3.4 to 3.7. Although few major music publishers today are willing to sign them, the AGAC and Songwriter's Guild agreements are still useful mainly for the ideas they may contribute to the negotiation of form agreements used by music publishers.

### A. Grant of Rights

The following is a typical grant of rights provision from a standard songwriter agreement:

> 1. Composer hereby sells, assigns and delivers to Publisher, its successors and assigns, the original musical composition written and composed by Composer (words of which were written by and music by and), presently entitled "______________" (the "Composition"), including the title, words and music thereof, all worldwide rights therein, all copyrights therein and thereto, all registrations with respect thereto, and the exclusive right to secure copyrights and any

[1] Form 3.2, Standard Single Song Songwriter Agreement II.

> extensions of copyrights in the same and in any arrangements and adaptations thereof, all throughout the world, and any and all other rights, claims and demands that Composer now has or to which he might be entitled or that he hereafter could or might secure throughout the world with respect thereto if these presents had not been made, and to have and to hold the same absolutely and forever unto Publisher, its successors and assigns, subject only to any existing agreements between Composer and Publisher and the Performing Rights Society (with which they are affiliated).

The grant of rights provision effects the transfer of the copyright in the composition from the songwriter to the publisher.[2] It is the entire *undivided* copyright that is being transferred or granted to the publisher, not just one or several of the exclusive rights of the author under the copyright. Note that the provision recognizes, in the last clause of its last sentence, the songwriter's prior grant to his performance rights society (e.g., ASCAP or BMI) of a license to authorize public performances of the composition, and accordingly, the songwriter's grant of copyright is specifically made subject to that license grant.[3]

The above provision also includes a grant of the *title* of the composition. (The title referred to here is not the legal title, as in ownership, but the song title, as in *Melancholy Baby*.) Though titles are not copyrightable, they may be subject to other forms of legal protection, such as the law of *unfair competition*, which, among other things, may prevent one songwriter from "palming off" or "passing off" his song as that of another. Titles can become important in certain licensing contexts.[4]

Finally, note that the above grant of rights provision does not impose any obligation upon the publisher to file appropriate applications for copyright registration. A songwriter might reasonably request that the publisher be obliged to file such registrations, and record any assignments concerning the transfer of copyright,[5] but the publisher might reasonably insist that this obligation be limited to filings with the U.S. Copyright Office.

---

[2] See Chapter 7, *The Language of Music Licensing*.

[3] See Chapter 18, *Licensing Music in Live and Recorded Public Performances.*

[4] See Chapter 20, *Licensing Music in Television, Radio, Print, and Internet Advertising*.

[5] See Chapter 8, *Formalities of Music Licensing*.

## B. Territory

The *grant of rights* provision set forth above grants to the publisher the entire copyright, including all worldwide rights. Certainly, if the writer had previously granted exclusive publishing rights for one or more territories outside the United States, the grant should specifically carve out the rights previously granted.

If international rights have not been previously granted, the writer should still consider whether a worldwide deal makes sense under the circumstances. If the writer is dealing with a large publisher that has its own publishing subsidiaries in the major international markets, the writer will benefit from having to deal with only one point of contact to manage all his worldwide publishing. If, however, the publisher is only active in the United States, and would only turn over the writer's international publishing administration to a large publisher or several overseas subpublishers, the writer may desire to restrict the publisher's territory to the United States and make his own deals for subpublishing in international markets. Worldwide music publishing administration through the use of international subpublishers is discussed at length in Chapter 5, on *International Subpublishing*.

## C. Term

Similarly, because the transfer involves the entire copyright, the term of the agreement is implicitly for the life of the copyright, subject, of course, to any statutory rights of termination under the copyright law (i.e., the right of an author or his heirs to terminate, at a later date, the grant of rights the author is making under the songwriter agreement).[6] Leaving aside any statutory termination rights, the term of the agreement will be for the life of the copyright (e.g., life of the author, plus 70 years), unless (1) the agreement specifies a fixed term (e.g., 10 years) at which point the agreement will automatically terminate and the copyrights will automatically revert to the writer, or (2) the agreement includes a *right of reversion*, in which event the agreement would terminate, and the copyrights revert, upon the writer's proper exercise of the reversion.

---

[6] See Chapter 9, *Duration of Copyright, Assignments of Copyright, and Licenses.*

## D. Reversion of Rights

Songwriters with some degree of bargaining leverage may be able to negotiate a provision under which the writer will obtain, upon certain conditions, what is known as a *reversion* of the rights granted. Typically, the writer will request that if the song is not commercially released within a specified period of time, he will have the right to terminate the agreement and demand that the copyright revert (i.e., be transferred) back to him.[7] A publisher might counter-propose that the condition could be satisfied by the composition being licensed for recording, synchronization, or public performance, within a specified period of time.

Ideally, a writer would insist that his right of reversion could be exercised if the publisher does not effect a commercial recording of the composition within six months after the agreement is signed *and* the recording is commercially released within six months thereafter.[8] The publisher may insist upon a one to two year time frame and that the termination and reversion be conditioned upon the writer returning any unrecouped advances he received for the compositions, as well as reimbursing the publisher the cost of any demo recordings made by the publisher. The precise terms will vary considerably with the bargaining leverage of the writer. The Popular Songwriter's Contract recommended by the Songwriter's Guild of America, set forth in the appendix to this chapter, contains several provisions resulting in the reversion of rights to the songwriter upon the publisher's failure to comply with specified conditions.

## E. Advances

An *advance*[9] is a lump-sum payment to the writer that is *recoupable* (i.e., deductible), by the publisher from future royalties that would otherwise be payable to writer (except performance royalties the writer

---

[7] Reversion clauses have become common in songwriter agreements entered into in the United Kingdom as a result of *Schroeder v. Macaulay* (1974) 3 All E.R. 616 (HL), discussed below.

[8] Note, the condition should be the *commercial release* of a sound or synchronized recording of the song, not merely the recording of the song, the latter of which could be effected by the recording of a demonstration record.

[9] See Chapter 10, *Basic Considerations in Music Licensing*.

receives directly from his performance rights society). The following is an example of an advance provision:

> Upon execution hereof, Publisher shall pay to Composer the amount of five hundred dollars ($500.00) as an advance, receipt of which is hereby acknowledged, which sum shall remain the property of Composer, and shall be recoupable from payments hereafter becoming due Composer under this or any other agreement with Publisher or any of its affiliated music companies.

Though the advance is recoupable, it is not *returnable* (i.e., if the advances turn out to be greater than the amount of royalties ever earned from sales, the writer will not have to pay the unearned balance of the advance back to the person who paid it, unless of course he is otherwise in breach of the agreement; in other words, an advance is not a *loan*; however, the advance may be *returnable* in certain circumstances at the option of the writer, such as when the writer exercises a reversion of rights provision). Thus, an advance is more accurately referred to as a "non-returnable, recoupable advance."

As suggested by its name, an advance is generally paid *up front*, such as upon signing of the agreement, but also may be paid on a periodic basis, regardless of whether sufficient royalties have been earned during the period in which the advance is paid. The amount of an advance in any particular deal is highly negotiable and depends entirely upon the circumstances. For example, an advance offered in a single song agreement for an unpublished composition written by an average songwriter may run anywhere from nothing to $500 or more, per song. A publisher would be willing, however, to pay higher advances if a popular recording artist has committed to recording the song or if there are other immediate prospects for licensing the work. By the same token, a publisher would tend to offer a lower advance where a reversion clause (see above) allows him only a short period of time within which to effect a commercial release of the composition. An advance for an established song could be based upon the present value of a revenue forecast; projections are usually based upon the composition's historical income and the publisher's prospects for improving upon the song's track record.

A songwriter should insist upon receiving at least some minimum advance to give the publisher some incentive, however small, to promote the song. Of course, the writer's best protection against an unpromoted song is the *reversion of rights* provision, discussed above.

## F. Cross-Collateralization

Whenever an agreement provides for an advance, a cross-collateralization[10] provision is likely to be nearby. Contracts that are *cross-collateralized* are those under which royalties earned pursuant to one contract are used to recoup advances earned under another contract. You can spot cross-collateralization by looking for the following *Three Little Words*: "or any other." For example, the last clause of the advance provision set forth above states that the advance

> "shall be deductible from payments hereafter becoming due Composer *under this or any other agreement* with Publisher or any of its affiliated music companies."

Under certain circumstances, cross-collateralization will defeat one of the primary reasons artists seek advances. If the purpose of the advance is to give the person paying the advance the proper incentive to promote a particular song, allowing the cross-collateralization of that advance against royalties payable under a contract for another song, which by reason of its popularity might sell itself, will defeat the purpose of the original advance. Accordingly, a writer might reasonably insist that the cross-collateralization provision be stricken from the agreement.

Note also that the above clause not only cross-collateralizes royalties of individual compositions with each other, but by virtue of the phrase "any other agreement with Publisher or any of its affiliated music companies," the clause may cross-collateralize the revenues generated under the songwriter contract with revenues generated under a recording agreement the songwriter may also have entered into with the music publisher's affiliated record company. Under this scenario, revenues generated under the songwriter contract could be used to recoup advances provided under the recording agreement. Even songwriters with little bargaining leverage should be able to eliminate the cross-collateralization of a songwriter agreement with a recording agreement.

---

[10] *Id.*

## G. Royalties

A typical royalty provision from a standard songwriter agreement would begin in this way:

> 3. In consideration of this agreement and of the rights and interests hereby conveyed and granted, Publisher agrees to pay to Composer the following royalties in respect of the Composition:

and then proceed to list the writer's royalty for a variety of sources of income.

### *1. Sheet Music*

The first source listed is typically the royalty for *sheet music*:

> (a) Seven cents ($.07) per copy for each copy of sheet music in standard piano-vocal notation of the Composition printed, published and sold in the United States and Canada by Publisher or its affiliates, for which payment has been received by Publisher, or been finally credited to Publisher's account in reduction of an advance after deduction of reasonable returns. (Wherever the terms "paid," "received," or the equivalent appear in this agreement, they shall be deemed to include such final credit.)

Earlier, we suggested that the *writer's share* derived from the exploitation of his musical compositions is, for the most part, 50% of the total music publishing income. Well, this is where the "for the most part" enters the picture. When a music publisher grants to a print publisher the exclusive rights to publish a composition in sheet music form,[11] the publisher typically receives a royalty of 20% of the retail price of the sheet music. If, for example, the retail price of the sheet music is $4.00, then the publisher would be entitled to receive a royalty of 80 cents.

With the writer's share of most other music publishing income being 50% (see below), then why would the writer receive only 7 cents (i.e., less than 10%) of that 80 cents received by the publisher? Very simply, the provision is considered a long-standing music

[11] See Chapter 12, *Licensing Music in Print and Digital Print.*

publishing *sacred cow* (i.e., in reference to the inviolability of the cow among the Hindus; hence, something which is considered to be exempt from criticism or questioning). Only writers with a high degree of bargaining leverage should expect to negotiate more than 10 or 12 cents per copy, but not much more.

Because sheet music sales are such a small percentage of music publishing income, and rarely does a music publisher print and publish sheet music itself (i.e., music publisher's typically license print rights to print publishers — see below — and the license revenue from such sources is split 50-50 with the writer), heated arguments about the sacrosanctity of the provision is generally not worth the writer's time or emotional resources.

### 2. Printed Folios

Closely related to sheet music royalties is income from *folios* and *songbooks* containing the compositions:

> (b) (i) If the Composition is included in any folio, songbook or similar publication ("mixed folio"), a proportionate share of a royalty of twelve and one-half percent (12½%) of the net wholesale selling price of such publication for all copies sold by Publisher or its affiliates and paid for in the United States and Canada. Said proportionate share shall be equal to the percentage computed by dividing the number "one" by the total number of all copyrighted musical compositions contained therein.

As with the foregoing sheet music royalty provision, the above provision assumes the publisher is engaging in reproducing and distributing the printed editions on its own, rather than merely sublicensing the activity to a third-party print publisher. Typically, the songwriter will receive a royalty of 10%, which, with some leverage, may be negotiated up to 12½% or even 15% in some cases. The royalty percentage should be based upon the *wholesale* selling price; if the agreement states *retail* selling price, the writer should attempt to change it.

Note that the last sentence of the above section makes it clear that the pro ration will be computed on the basis of the number of *copyrighted* compositions contained in the folio. This is to prevent the publisher from including public domain songs, like the *Star Spangled*

*Banner*, in the calculation, which would otherwise have the effect of reducing the revenue due the songwriter. A careful songwriter might add, "but not including copyrighted arrangements of musical compositions in the public domain." Alternatively, the pro ration could be computed on the basis of the number of *copyrighted, royalty-bearing* songs in the songbook.

However, this still leaves open the possibility that the publisher will promote the sale of a folio by including one or two of the writer's biggest hit songs, and adding a number of lesser known songs from the catalog of the publisher or of other publishers. Under those circumstances, pro rating the songs on an equal basis would not fairly reflect the role the writer's songs play in generating sales of the folio. To address this problem, a writer might seek to limit the proportion of compositions written by other composers that are allowed to be included in a folio that contains the writer's compositions. However, because of the popularity of mixed folios, such as "Hits of the '70s," such a limitation could severely discourage the use of the writer's songs in printed editions, which already represents a decreasing portion of total music publishing income. Of course, if the folio were comprised primarily of the writer's own songs, then the problem would not arise.

If the writer's name and likeness is used in a *personality folio* (i.e., a songbook consisting of songs written, recorded, or performed by the same artist or recording group, or written by the same songwriter),[12] the writer may insist upon an additional royalty (e.g., up to an additional 5%).

### *3. Other Printed Editions*

Royalties for other printed editions, including editions for educational use, generally carry a lower royalty:

> (ii) If the Composition is included in a "fake book," "educational edition" or an instrumental, orchestral, choral or band arrangement or other arrangement intended for pedagogical purposes, a royalty of ten percent (10%), or a proportionate share thereof (calculated in the manner prescribed above in the case of a mixed folio) of

[12] *Id.*

the net wholesale selling price for all copies of such work sold by Publisher or its affiliates and paid for in the United States and Canada.

### 4. Print Sublicensing

Where the music publisher sublicenses the printed edition activity to an unaffiliated print publisher, then the writer should receive 50% of the publisher's revenues:

> (iii) If, pursuant to a license granted by Publisher to a licensee not controlled by or affiliated with it, the Composition is included in any mixed folio in the United States and/or Canada, a pro rata share of fifty percent (50%) of the gross amount received by Publisher from the licensee as the number of uses of the Composition under the license and during the license period bears to the total number of uses of Publisher's copyrighted musical compositions (including the Composition) under the license and during the license period.

### 5. Mechanical, Synchronization, and Other Royalties

The following provision sets forth the writer's share of *mechanical, electrical transcription, synchronization,*[13] and other royalties on revenue received by the publisher in the United States and Canada:

> (c) Fifty percent (50%) of any and all net sums actually received (less any cost for collection) by Publisher or credited to Publisher's account in the United States from the exploitation in the United States and Canada by licensees of Publisher of mechanical rights, electrical transcription and reproducing rights, motion picture and television synchronization rights, and all other rights in the Composition (except print rights which are covered in paragraphs
>
> 3(a) and 3(b) above and public performance rights which are covered in (d) below), whether or not such licensees are affiliated with, owned in whole or in part by, or controlled by Publisher.

[13] See Chapters 12, 13, and 14, on *Licensing Music in Print and Digital Print, Licensing Music in Sound Recordings, Licensing Music in Background Music Services, Digital Jukeboxes, and other Commercial Reproduction (Electrical Transcription Licenses)* respectively.

A writer may seek to impose certain restrictions, discussed later in this chapter, on the publisher's ability to grant mechanical, synchronization, and other music licenses.

It is important to note that the above provision includes the all important *catchall* phrase (i.e., "and all other rights in the Composition"), which assures that the writer will receive 50% of income from uses not specifically listed. Many standard songwriter agreements limit the writer's royalties only to those derived from uses specifically listed in the agreement.

### *6. Performance Royalties*

The last clause of the above provision, together with the provision which follows, makes it clear that the writer does *not* receive any portion of the *publisher's share* of performance royalties.[14] As noted, the writer will receive *the writer's share* of performance royalties directly from his performance rights society:

> (d) (i) Composer shall receive his public performance royalties throughout the world directly from his own affiliated performing rights society and shall have no claim whatsoever against Publisher for any royalties received by Publisher from any performing rights society which makes payment directly (or indirectly other than through Publisher) to writers, authors and composers.

Because of changes in the way performance royalties are collected, it would be wise for a music publisher to include a provision, such as the following, which anticipates the possibility that the publisher may someday collect all of the writer's share of performance fees directly from licensees:

> (ii) If, however, (and to the extent that) Publisher shall collect both the Composer's and Publisher's share of performance income directly and such income shall not be collected by Composer's public performance society, Publisher shall pay to Composer fifty percent (50%) of all such net sums which are received by

[14] See Chapter 18, *Licensing Music in Live and Recorded Public Performances.*

Publisher in the United States from the exploitation of such rights in the Composition, throughout the world.

In fact, the publisher already directly collects performance royalties when granting theatrical synchronization licenses (*see* **Chapter 15**, on *Licensing Music in Audiovisual Works*) and the writer should be entitled to 50% of that income. In addition, it is not inconceivable that music publishers may in the future by-pass their performance rights organizations (e.g., ASCAP, BMI, PRS for Music) and begin licensing public performance fees directly with certain digital music services, such as background music services.

### *7. International Royalties*

The following provision sets forth the writer's share of income from publishing sources outside the United States and Canada:

> (e) Fifty percent (50%) of any and all net sums, after deduction of foreign taxes, actually received (less any reasonable costs for collection) by Publisher in the United States from sales, licenses and other uses of the Composition in countries outside of the United States and Canada (other than public performance royalties described in subparagraph 3(d)(i)) from collection agents, licensees, subpublishers or others, whether or not same are affiliated with, owned in whole or in part by, or controlled by Publisher. This provision shall not apply to copies of printed music shipped from the United States to such countries, to which the rates set forth in paragraphs 3(a) and 3(b) above shall apply.

In Chapter 5, on *International Subpublishing*, we discuss the concept of the music publisher's income from its international subpublishers being computed "at the source." Such a provision is intended to prevent the practice of using multiple layers of subpublishing companies, owned or closely affiliated with the music publisher, solely for the purpose of reducing the writer's royalties from international publishing income.[15]

---

[15] Such practices have been successful challenged in court. See *Elton John v. Dick James Music* [1982 J. No. 15026, High Court of Justice, Chancery Division].

In some circumstances, it may be difficult for a songwriter to require that the publisher have all of its subpublishing deals include an *at the source* provision, but a writer may reasonably insist upon a provision in the songwriter agreement specifying the maximum percentage that may be retained by the publisher's international subpublishers for the purpose of determining the writer's share of subpublishing income. Recognizing that the publisher may have a subsidiary in some countries and may independently contract with unaffiliated subpublishers in other countries, such percentage may vary according to territory. For example, with respect to income derived in territories in which the publisher has a subsidiary, the writer will receive 75% of publishing income, and with respect to all other territories a minimum of 50%. The percentages may also vary depending upon whether the subpublisher successfully creates language translations and *cover records* (i.e., commercially released recordings of the songwriter's composition by local artists in the territory) of the compositions.

### *8. Promotional Copies*

A publisher should not be expected to pay royalties on copies made for the purpose of promoting the compositions or on copies distributed on a consignment basis:

> (f) Publisher shall not be required to pay any royalties on reasonable numbers of professional or complimentary printed copies of the Composition or copies of mechanical derivatives of the Composition which are distributed gratuitously to performing artists, orchestra leaders and disc jockeys or for advertising, promotional or exploitation purposes for which Publisher receives no payment. Furthermore, no royalties shall be payable to Composer on consigned copies of the Composition unless paid for, and not until the accounting statement for the accounting period within which such payment is received.

The distribution of copies of the songs, in printed or recorded form, for the purpose of promoting them is an essential part of the publisher's business and should not only be permitted on a royalty-free basis, but expected and encouraged by the songwriter. Distribution of copies on a consignment basis should be royalty free unless and until the consigned copies are paid for. However, the practice is subject to abuse, as when it is used solely for the purpose of delaying the payment of royalties to writers. The writer may have a cause to claim that consignment sales, under certain circumstances, are really sales upon which royalties, subject to a reasonable reserve for returns, should be paid.

### *9. Collaborative Royalties*

In Chapter 7, on *The Language of Music Licensing*, we discuss the standard for determining whether a work is considered a *joint work*. Briefly, when the music and lyrics of a composition are originally composed and written with the knowledge and intention that they would be merged as "an inseparable or interdependent part of a unitary whole," the resulting combination is considered a *joint work*. The authors of a joint work are co-owners of copyright in the work,[16] and each author automatically acquires an *undivided* ownership interest in the entire work.

This means that, unless otherwise agreed among the co-authors, the authors will share equally in the revenues generated by *all or any portion of* the work. For example, royalties generated by the sale or performance of any instrumental version of the composition will go to both the composer and the lyricist — equally, or according to percentages otherwise agreed upon — not just to the composer of the music. Likewise, royalties from the licensing of any printed edition containing only the lyrics will go to both authors, not just the lyricist. The following provision is intended to make it clear that if lyrics are later added to an instrumental composition, the composer will only be entitled to one-half of the writer's share of publishing income and that the revenues will be split as though the work were a joint work.

> (g) If the Composition does not now have lyrics, and lyrics shall hereafter be added by Publisher, the above royalties shall be divided equally between Composer on the one hand and the writer or writers of the lyrics on the other hand.

A writer may well insist upon the right to approve any added lyrics and may, in fact, have that right, notwithstanding the terms of the

[16] 17 U.S.C. Sec. 201(a).

agreement, by virtue of the author's *moral rights* in certain countries outside the United States.[17] Moreover, the above provision leaves unanswered the question of how royalties are to be shared among the original songwriter and writers preparing changes or additions to the melodic or instrumental aspects of the composition. Some standard songwriter agreements are more specific about the division of royalties in such cases, and tend, naturally, to resolve the question in favor of the publisher. For example,

> Royalties as hereinabove specified shall be payable solely to Writer in instances where Writer is the sole author of the entire composition, including the words and music thereof. However, in the event that one or more other songwriters are authors together with Writer on any composition (including songwriters employed by Publisher to add, change or translate the words or to revise or change the music), then the foregoing royalties shall be divided equally between Writer and the other songwriters of such composition unless another division of royalties is agreed upon in writing between the parties concerned.

As discussed in more detail below in the section on *Creative Controls*, most songwriter agreements provide the publisher with a great deal of flexibility in making additions to, and modifications and translations of, the compositions covered by the agreement. That flexibility, combined with a collaborative royalties provision such as set forth above, could result in a significant and unfair reduction in the writer's royalty with the writer having little power to do anything about it. For example, if the publisher engages another writer to rewrite the lyrics, the original songwriter's royalties would be reduced to 50%. If publisher engages two other writers to write new lyrics, the original

---

[17] Moral rights include the right of an author to be named as the author of a work (the right of paternity) and the right for an author to object to uses of the work which could bring dishonor or discredit on the author's reputation (the right of integrity). The nature and scope of moral rights varies considerably from country to country, but regardless of their scope and extent, moral rights are typically not transferable and sometimes, may not be waived. In some countries, moral rights are protected by a combination of statutory provisions and common law. In the United States, for instance, this protection is found in Federal legislation, such as the Lanham Act and the Copyright Act, various state legislative provisions and the common law of privacy, defamation and the like. See *Final Report of the Ad Hoc Working Group on U.S. Adherence to the Berne Convention*, 10 Colum. VLA J.L. & Arts 513, 548-57 (1986); 2 Nimmer on Copyright § 8D.02[A] (1995).

songwriter's royalties would be reduced to 33⅓%. Further, a formula for splitting the royalties into equal shares based on the number of writers involved does not take into account the percentage each party contributed to the composition. Thus, the original songwriter's royalty share could be reduced to 33⅓%, if two other writers are used, even though it is clear the original songwriter's contribution exceeded 50% or more.

Some songwriter agreements give the publisher the sole right to determine how royalties are to be shared among collaborators. A provision that provides for equal sharing of royalties among collaborators will probably provide better protection to the original songwriter than one that leaves the matter entirely within the control of the publisher. At a minimum, the collaborators should always be given the flexibility to reach an agreement among themselves on a split acceptable to them, such as a split that is other than on an equal basis. Finally, under the collaborative royalty provision set forth above, a writer engaged to prepare a foreign language translation of lyrics could receive a share of royalties equal to that of the original songwriter, though only with respect to income derived from the exploitation of the translation (but including instrumental versions of the translation). On the one hand, it could be argued that a mere translation of lyrics does not justify a 50% share of royalties; on the other, a case can be made that the translation of lyrics, like the translation of poetry, is an art which, done well, deserves an equal share with the original writer (especially if substantial modifications or additions are required to make the translation successful). If the composition was written by a composer and lyricist in collaboration, then, under the provision set forth above, the translator would receive 33⅓% share and each of the original writers would each receive 33⅓% share of the translated composition.

It is difficult, if not impossible, to determine in advance precisely what division of royalties would be fair and appropriate under all potential circumstances. However, a songwriter may negotiate a provision that provides him with some greater control over these situations when they arise. The best solution, for the writer with a significant amount of bargaining leverage, is to obtain the complete right of approval over the engagement of other writers to make additions, changes or translations. Alternatively, a writer could negotiate a specific percentage (e.g., 50%) below which his share of royalties may not be reduced without his consent. This would give the publisher the flexibility to make changes and additions while assuring the writer of an acceptable level of royalty participation.

### *10. Demo Recordings*

The following provision allows the publisher to recoup from the writer's future royalties one-half the cost the publisher incurs in making *demo recordings* (i.e., recordings used for demonstrating or promoting the compositions):

> (h) To the extent approved by Publisher in writing in advance, Publisher shall pay the cost of making demonstration records of the Composition. One-half (½) of a pro rata share corresponding to Composer's percentage of the Composition as set forth in paragraph 1 above, of such total costs shall be deemed additional advances to Composer hereunder.

A songwriter with a high degree of bargaining power may be able to negotiate the percentage of demo costs that will be charged to him down to 25% or to 0%. Whatever the percentage charged to the writer, it should be charged against the writer's account as an *advance*; that is, the writer should not be required to pay for these costs out of his pocket, unless he records or reproduces copies of demos on his own without the approval of the publisher.

### *11. Other Publishing Expenses*

Some publishers also charge to the writers, as advances against royalties, the costs of copyright registration, advertising, the creation of lead sheets, and similar charges. A songwriter with a substantial amount of bargaining leverage might be able to negotiate these charges out of the contract on the basis that these are some of the very services the publisher is expected to provide in exchange for his publisher's share of the publishing income.

### *12. No Other Royalties*

The first sentence of the following section should be acceptable to the songwriter, because section (c) above contains a *catchall* provision, entitling the writer to 50% of all income from sources not specifically referred to in the agreement:

> (i) Except as herein expressly provided, no other royalties or moneys shall be paid to Composer.

Without a *catchall* provision, discussed above, the first sentence of the above provision would effectively limit the writer's royalties to a percentage of only those sources of publishing income specifically set forth in the royalty section of the agreement. The writer, therefore, would not be entitled to royalties based upon publishing revenues from new uses, not set forth in the agreement, because they were only conceived or devised years after the signing of the agreement.

### *13. Advances from Licenses*

Many standard songwriter agreements do not afford the writer a share in any advances received by the music publisher from its licensees. The writer would only receive these moneys when the advances are actually *earned* according to royalty statements eventually received from the licensees. But some provisions allow a writer to share in such advances under certain circumstances.

> In no event shall Composer be entitled to share in any advance payments, guarantee payments or minimum royalty payments which Publisher may receive in connection with any subpublishing agreement, collection agreement, licensing agreement or other agreement covering the Composition, unless such payment shall be solely related to the Composition; in which event Publisher shall credit Composer's royalty account with fifty percent (50%) of all such sums received by Publisher.

This refusal to share advances with the songwriter is justified in certain circumstances. For example, when a publisher receives an advance for the licensing of an entire catalog of compositions composed by several (or several hundred) writers, it would be difficult or impractical to fairly allocate the advance among the respective songs in the catalog prior to the time royalties on the catalog deal are actually earned by the respective songs. However, such proration is not necessary when the advance relates only to one song. Thus, the second clause in the above provision — affording the writer 50% of the advances received by the publisher if the advance was solely related to the composition covered by the agreement — renders the limitation on the payment of advances reasonable.

## H. Accounting

Music publishing agreements will contain a series of provisions governing the way in which royalties will be accounted and paid to the writer.

### *1. Accounting Statements*

Most music publishers will account and pay royalties to writers every six months under terms similar to the following:

> 4. (a) (i) Publisher shall compute the royalties earned by Composer pursuant to this agreement within sixty (60) days following the end of each semiannual calendar period during which moneys are received (or finally credited) with respect to the Composition, and shall thereupon submit to Composer the royalty statement for each such period together with the net amount of royalties, if any, which shall be payable after deducting any and all unrecouped advances and chargeable costs under this agreement. However, if a particular statement indicates a balance due of less than Fifty Dollars ($50.), Publisher shall not be required to make payment, and the balance due shall be carried forward until the end of the next subsequent accounting period during which the balance due exceeds Fifty Dollars ($50.), at which time such balance due shall be paid. Upon the submission of each statement, Publisher shall have the right to retain, as a reserve against subsequent charges, credits or returns, such portion of payable moneys hereunder (not exceeding 25%) with respect solely to print sales by Publisher or its affiliates as shall be necessary and appropriate in its best business judgment, but each such reserve shall be liquidated within two (2) quarter annual calendar periods following the period in respect of which such reserve is established. The payments to Composer provided for under this agreement shall be computed as of the date each such statement is due and shall be paid for in United States currency by Publisher to Composer. The rate(s) of exchange utilized by third parties in accounting to Publisher shall

also apply as between Publisher and Participant in accounting for the same moneys.

Note that, unlike similar provisions in many songwriter agreements, the above provision does *not* provide for the cross-collateralization of royalties with sums related to "any other agreement between Writer and Publisher or companies related to or affiliated with Publisher." Most publishers provide accountings to writers on a semi-annual basis. Though it would be more advantageous for a writer to receive accounting statements and royalty payments on a quarterly basis, it would be virtually impossible for many publishers to agree to change their entire royalty accounting practices to provide statements to single songwriters more frequently than their usual practices. However, a writer with high bargaining leverage may be able to negotiate that at least an advance be paid on a quarterly, monthly, or even bi-weekly basis, the amount to be determined on the basis of some percentage (e.g., in the case of quarterly advances, 25 to 50%) of the royalties earned during the most recent semi-annual accounting period.

The provision set forth above allows the publisher to dispense with sending an accounting statement when royalties earned fall under a minimum level. A publisher might be willing, albeit reluctantly, to remove this provision for writers having a moderate amount of bargaining leverage.

### *2. Reserves Against Returns*

It is customary for a publisher to maintain a *reserve against returns* by withholding a portion of the royalties due the writer. This generally only applies to royalties derived from print licensing, but some songwriter agreements do not limit the type of royalties upon which reserves may be taken. When a publisher makes sales of printed editions of a writer's compositions, the publisher may expect that some of the copies sold to distributors and retailers during one quarter will be returned to the publisher during a subsequent quarter. These returns may be the result of less than expected consumer demand or product defects or misprints. Of course, the writer is only entitled to royalties on the basis of *net revenues* (i.e., the gross revenues earned by the publisher minus the returns).

If the publisher previously paid royalties based upon the gross revenues and returns were subsequently made, then the publisher will have overpaid the writer by the amount of royalties that were based upon the returned sales. Thus, when a publisher holds a reserve against returns, he deducts a certain percentage (e.g., 25%) from the royalties he would otherwise be required to pay for sales of the work in a particular quarter, and holds on to that deduction in anticipation that there might later be a return of 25% of the copies previously sold.

The actual percentage used in calculating the reserve is intended to approximate the percentage of copies shipped that are expected, in the worst case, to be subsequently returned. Many songwriter agreements leave the determination of this percentage, and the length of time the publisher may retain the reserve, within the sole discretion of the publisher, as in the following reserve provision:

> Upon the submission of each statement, Publisher shall have the right to retain, as a reserve against subsequent charges, credits or returns, such portion of payable royalties as shall be necessary and appropriate in its best business judgment.

The *reserve* provision set forth in the section labeled 4(a)(i) above, however, reflects a compromise and limits the publisher's ability to retain a reserve in three ways: (1) by limiting the withholding of reserves solely with respect to the sales of printed editions (on the basis that returns of copies sold in the music publishing business is only applicable with respect to sales of printed editions), (2) by providing for a specific percentage limitation (i.e., 25%) on the amount that may be reserved in any one period, and (3) providing that the publisher liquidate the reserve within a specified period (i.e., two or four quarters).

### *3. Objections*

Many songwriter agreements provide that accounting statements will be deemed binding unless specific objections are submitted to the publisher within one year after the date on which the statement is rendered, as in the following example:

> (b) Each statement submitted by Publisher to Composer shall be binding upon Composer and not subject to any objection

> by Composer for any reason unless specific written objection, stating the basis thereof, is sent by Composer to Publisher within one (1) year after the date said statement is received (or deemed received as provided below).

The provision arises from the publisher's desire to achieve some level of "closure" on statements provided in the past. However, a writer is not likely to conduct an audit within one year after receiving each statement and such an audit may be necessary to provide the requisite "specific written objection, stating the basis thereof." A writer should be able to increase the one year limitation to at least two years, or perhaps as long as the typical statute of limitations period for breach of contract (e.g., four years).

#### *4. Audit Privileges*

The typical songwriter agreement will also provide the writer with the privilege to *audit* (i.e., inspect) the books and records of the publisher as follows:

> Composer or a certified public accountant in Composer's behalf may, at Composer's expense, at reasonable intervals (but not more frequently than once each year), examine Publisher's books insofar as same contain data of concern to Composer, during Publisher's usual business hours and upon thirty (30) days' notice, for the purpose of verifying the accuracy of any statement submitted to Composer hereunder. Publisher's books relating to activities during any accounting period may only be examined as aforesaid during the one (1) year period following receipt by Composer of the statement for said accounting period.

Again, a songwriter should be able to have the one year limitation in the last sentence of the previous paragraph increased to two or more years. Songwriters with some bargaining leverage should be able to negotiate the addition of a provision to the effect that, if the audit reveals that the publisher underpaid the royalties due by more than 5 or 10%, then the publisher will pay for the costs of the audit. Further, an audit provision should also contain a requirement that obligates the publisher to maintain accurate books and records in the first place. A number of accounting firms specialize in performing audits of such records, and a writer should consider having its publisher audited on a periodic basis to, as the saying goes, "keep 'em honest."

To avoid any misunderstandings regarding the calculation of the time limitations discussed above (often arising from the misdirection of accounting statements by virtue of the writer's failure to report a change of address), a publisher might include the following provision:

> (e) For the purpose of calculating the time period for audits and legal action by Composer, a statement shall be deemed to have been received thirty (30) days after the same is due unless, within such period, Publisher shall receive notice of nonreceipt of such statement from Composer. However, Composer's failure to give such notice shall not affect Composer's right to receive such statement (and any accompanying payment) thereafter.

### *5. International Payments*

The following is a typical provision setting forth the procedures under which the writer would receive royalties in the event the publisher is unable to receive payments from sources overseas due to currency control laws or other restrictions.

> (ii) If Publisher shall be unable to receive payment in United States dollars in the United States in respect of any exploitation of the Composition due to currency control laws or regulations, royalties in respect thereof shall not be credited to Composer's royalty account hereunder. Publisher shall, however, use its best efforts to accept such payments in foreign currency and deposit in a foreign bank or other depository, at Composer's expense, in such foreign currency such portion thereof, if any, as shall equal the royalties which would have actually been payable to Composer hereunder in respect of such exploitation had such payments been made to Publisher in United States dollars in the United States, and Publisher shall notify Composer thereof promptly. Deposit as aforesaid shall fulfill Publisher's royalty obligations hereunder as to such exploitation.

Because the publisher is in a better position to deal with the intricacies of foreign exchange matters, the writer should attempt to negotiate a provision to the effect that, if the Publisher is unable to receive payment in United States dollars in the United States, the Publisher shall pay to the writer an *advance* against royalties in an amount equal to the royalties that would have been payable had such payments been made to the publisher in United States dollars in the United States.

## I. Name and Likeness

A publisher will often require a license to use the name, likeness, and biography of the writer in connection with the exploitation of the composition:

> 5. Composer hereby grants to Publisher, its associates, affiliates, subsidiaries and licensees the perpetual, nonexclusive right to use and publish and to permit others to use and publish Composer's name (including any professional name heretofore or hereafter adopted by Composer), likeness and biographical material, or any reproduction or simulation thereof and the title of the Composition in connection with the exploitation of the Composition.

Writers, who are also recording artists, have been known to become film stars (e.g., Sting) or otherwise famous celebrities (e.g., Madonna), and being such, their name, likeness, and biography often become a valuable intellectual property (e.g., referred to as the artist's *right of publicity*), which may form the basis of a significant source of licensing revenue.

Some standard songwriter agreements include a very broad grant of these rights to the publisher. For example, an agreement may permit the publisher to use the writer's name, likeness, and biographical information in connection with the exploitation of the compositions and for any purpose related to the business of the publisher, or its affiliated companies, which may, of course, include, a film production company and a merchandising company (e.g., fan clubs, photographs, t-shirts, etc.). The writer should therefore carefully consider limiting the scope of the grant to uses that are directly in connection with the commercial exploitation of the compositions covered by the agreement and require the writer's consent for all other uses.

A writer with stronger bargaining leverage might insist upon the right to approve any use of his name, likeness, or biographical materials by the publisher. A publisher may insist that any use the writer permits his record company should automatically be deemed approved for use by the music publisher. Note also, as discussed above, a writer might insist upon an additional royalty, and related advance, for the use of his name and likeness in connection with the publication of a *personality folio*. Unless the agreement specifically provides for such additional royalty, by granting to the Publisher an unrestricted right to use the writer's name and likeness, the writer would be relinquishing his ability to collect additional royalties for the use of his name and likeness on personality folios and other materials.

## J. Creative Controls

A typical songwriter agreement will contain a provision that affords the publisher the privilege to make changes to the compositions covered by the agreement:

> 6. Composer hereby acknowledges that Publisher has the right hereunder, in its sole discretion, to substitute a new title or titles for the Composition, to make changes, arrangements, adaptations, translations, dramatizations and transpositions of the Composition, in whole or in part, and in connection with any other musical, literary or dramatic material, and to add new lyrics to the music of the Composition or new music to the lyrics of the Composition. Composer hereby waives any and all claims which he has or may have against Publisher, its associates, affiliates and subsidiaries and licensees by reason of the fact that the title of the Composition may be the same as or similar to that of any other musical compositions heretofore acquired by Publisher.

Many songwriters are quite sensitive to other's making changes to their compositions and will insist that some limitations, or creative controls, be imposed upon the kinds of modification privileges set forth in the above section. In general, publishers will allow some creative controls to the writer, but only to the extent the publisher believes their ability to recoup advances paid to the writer would not be impeded by the writer's unreasonable exercise of the control.

In the days when music publishers played a substantial role in the creative aspects of publishing, publishers would insist upon complete flexibility to make changes in the title, lyrics, and other aspects of the musical compositions submitted to them by songwriters. For example, Jack Robbins of Robbins Music Corp. insisted that the *title* of virtually all songs published by his company be composed of the initial few words of the lyric — e.g., *I'm in the Mood for Love, Blue Moon, Don't Blame Me, Sweet and Lovely*, and *You'll Never Know*. Today, by contrast, a publisher is not likely to resist a restriction on its right to change the title of the composition.

Nevertheless, there are circumstances under which publishers are justified in maintaining some flexibility to make changes without having to obtain the writer's consent. For example, if the title of a composition is confusingly similar to that of another song, potential errors in royalty accounting and the crediting of valuable performance fees may be avoided by a slight change in the title. Perhaps a recording artist who is in the middle of a recording session may wish to record a writer's composition, but only if the artist is permitted to make several minor changes to the lyrics; the ability of the publisher to quickly approve the change may mean the difference between the commercial release of a major cover recording, with lucrative performance royalties to follow, and no release.

The publisher's professional staff may also play a valuable role in suggesting changes that may make the composition more popular. As song lyrics become increasingly violent and indecent, and radio stations and record distributors are becoming more sensitive to the objections of their listeners and the record buying public, publishers may come under increasing pressure — particularly if they find themselves potentially liable under obscenity laws — to tone down the lyrics of songs they publish. By making changes to the lyrics for the purpose of increasing record sales and public performances of the song, the publisher may infringe upon the artistic integrity of the writer's work, but he is legitimately and justifiably intending to enhance the total music publishing income from the song.

Of course, songwriters particularly sensitive to changes to their compositions will insist on specific limitations. For example, a songwriter might insist that any changes in the music or lyrics be limited to those reasonably necessary to conform to the style of a performing or recording artist or that the writer have the opportunity to make the desired changes himself before the changes are made by anyone else. More than an issue of mere artistic integrity or vanity, such a limitation would prevent a publisher from arbitrarily or unnecessarily using third parties to alter the writer's compositions, resulting in a reduction in the writer's economic participation in the composition. Worse yet, such a limitation would prevent an unscrupulous publisher from making changes sufficient to justify a publishing executive's adding his name as co-author of the composition.

A publisher, however, may justifiably resist the requirement to obtain the songwriter's consent for the creation of foreign language translations of the lyrics, but the writer might reasonably ask to be consulted with respect to such translations.

## K. Other Restrictions

### *1. Restrictions on Mechanical Licensing*

#### *a. Statutory Rate*

A songwriter with some bargaining leverage might try to limit the publisher's right to issue mechanical licenses for a fee below the *statutory rate*,[18] but a publisher is likely to agree only to the requirement that it issue mechanical licenses at no less than the statutory rate when the licensee is a company affiliated with the publisher, such as a record or motion picture company who is a parent, subsidiary, or sister company of the publisher. As noted in Chapter 10, on *Basic Considerations in Music Licensing*, regarding the Affiliated Company Problem, a music publisher who is affiliated with a record company or motion picture studio should always be issuing licenses to their affiliates on an *arm's-length* basis (i.e., on the same rates, terms, and conditions as though they were dealing with licensees who are not affiliated with the publisher). A writer may wish to add a general provision to this effect.

#### *b. First Use Licensing*

A songwriter who is also a recording artist may request that neither the publisher, nor its subpublishers, issue a mechanical license for a *cover record* (i.e., a commercially released recording of the songwriter's composition by an artist other than the songwriter) for a specified

[18] See Chapter 12, on *Licensing Music in Print and Digital Print.*

period after the artist's own recording of the composition has been released. The publisher may wish to limit this restriction to a specified number of songs at any one time and to a specified period of time, such as nine months to one year.

As a practical matter, the publisher's ability to deny the issuance of a mechanical license may be limited in the United States by the compulsory license provision of the U.S. copyright law. After the first recording of a song is made and distributed to the public in the United States, others may acquire compulsory mechanical licenses for other recordings under Section 115 of the Copyright Act.[19]

#### *c. Controlled Compositions*

Further, a writer may require the publisher to issue licenses in accordance with any *controlled composition* clauses[20] in any recording agreement into which the writer/artist may enter. The publisher may insist in return that, if some minimum mechanical license fee cannot be collected due to the writer's controlled composition clauses, the publisher may recover the shortfall out of the writer's royalties.

### *2. Restrictions on Synchronization Licensing*

A songwriter with a high degree of bargaining power might retain the right to approve television or motion picture synchronization licenses,[21] but any approval rights over synchronization licenses the writer receives is more likely to be limited to approving the use of his compositions in (1) *X-rated films*, (2) *commercial advertisements*,[22] or at least advertisements for those specified products the writer finds distasteful (e.g., cigarettes, nuclear power plants, condoms, and the like), and (3) *political advertisements*.

---

[19] *Id.*

[20] *Id.*

[21] See Chapter 15, *Licensing Music in Audiovisual Works.*

[22] See Chapter 20, *Licensing Music in Television, Radio, Print, and Internet Advertising.*

### 3. *Restrictions on the Use of the Song's Title and on Dramatic Uses*

A writer might also obtain the right of approval over any use of the song's title as the title of a motion picture or television program or series, any dramatic adaptation of the lyrics, or any licenses for the dramatic performance of the song.[23]

### 4. *Restrictions on Print Licensing*

A songwriter may ask that he have the right to consent to, or alternatively, the right to be consulted on, the content and appearance of any printed editions of the compositions.

## IV. NEGOTIATING THE EXCLUSIVE TERM SONGWRITER AGREEMENT

The second type of songwriter agreement is known as the *exclusive term* agreement. The exclusive term agreement is sometimes referred to as a *staff writer* agreement, and the writers signed up by publishers under these agreements are called, not surprisingly, *staff writers*.

Unlike the *single song* agreement, under which the songwriter grants to the publisher the copyrights in one or more specific musical compositions, the *exclusive term* or *staff writer* agreement is used when the publisher wishes to sign up the writer on an exclusive basis for a specified period of time during which the writer is obliged to turn over to the publisher all songs he writes during that period. Note, there have evolved hybrid forms of the exclusive term songwriter agreements, such as an agreement that only covers songs written and recorded by a writer in connection with his services as a recording artist, but the discussion is essentially the same.

Because both forms of agreement define how the publisher and writer share in the income generated by the compositions covered, many of the provisions of the exclusive term agreement are the same as those in the single song agreement discussed above. Accordingly, in

---

[23] See Chapter 19, *The Grand Rights Controversy*.

the following discussion, we focus primarily on those provisions that pertain to exclusive term agreements.

## A. Exclusive Employment

Many exclusive term songwriter agreements attempt to create an employment relationship between the songwriter and publisher. Such an agreement may begin as follows:

> 1. *Employment.* Publisher hereby employs Writer to render his services as a songwriter and composer and otherwise as may be hereinafter set forth. Writer hereby accepts such employment and agrees to render such services exclusively for Publisher during the term hereof, upon the terms and conditions set forth herein.

### *1. Works Made for Hire*

Whether the relationship is deemed one of employment, rather than contractual, could affect the length of time the publisher will control the copyrights in the compositions. If the songwriter is considered an *employee* for hire of the publisher under the terms of the copyright law, then the songwriter would be unable to exercise the statutory rights he would otherwise have had to terminate the grant of rights and reacquire his copyrights after the statutory period of time.[24] The *author*, for purpose of determining an author's rights under the copyright law, is considered the employer, or the person for whom the work was made, not the actual creator of the work. In other words, given the existence of an employment relationship, the *publisher* is considered the author of the songs, not the songwriter.

However, not all work relationships are automatically deemed employment relationships. In 1989, the U.S. Supreme Court ruled that whether one is an *employee for hire* under the copyright law is determined by applying the general rules of agency law.[25] For the relationship between the publisher and the writer to be legally deemed one between an employee and employer, the publisher would have to show the publisher exercised a sufficient degree of control over the

---

[24] See Chapter 9, *Duration of Copyright, Assignments of Copyright, and Licenses.*

[25] *Community for Creative Non-Violence v. Reid*, 490 U.S. 730 (1989).

manner and means by which the work of the writer was accomplished. Factors to be considered may include the skill required, the source of the work tools, the location of the work, the duration of the relationship, the method of payment, and other factors.

Although the relationship between staff songwriter and music publisher would not typically meet this test, it may under certain circumstances. For example, arrangers employed to create lead sheets or demonstration recordings, or writers hired to create international language translations of compositions in the publisher's catalog may be deemed employees for hire. But unless circumstances show sufficient control exercised by the publisher, it is not likely that the popular musical works composed by a songwriter will be deemed a work made for hire by a mere statement in the songwriter agreement the songwriter is the employee of the publisher.

Nevertheless, a publisher may wish to include the following provision to improve the chances that the compositions created under the agreement will be considered a work made for hire of the publisher,

> 11. *Writer's Services.* Writer agrees to perform the services required hereunder conscientiously and solely and exclusively for and as requested by Publisher. Writer is deemed to be a "writer for hire" hereunder, and the works created hereunder shall be considered "works made for hire," with full rights of copyright vested in Publisher. Writer further agrees to promptly and faithfully comply with all requirements and requests made by Publisher in connection with its business as set forth herein.

There is a second way a work may be considered a work made for hire. The definition of *work for hire*, under the copyright law, is as follows:

> A "work made for hire" is
>
> (1) a work prepared by an employee within the scope of his or her employment; or
>
> (2) a work specially ordered or commissioned for use as a contribution to a collective work, as a part of a motion picture or other audiovisual work, as a translation, as a supplementary work, as a compilation, as an instructional text, as a test, as answer

> material for a test, or as an atlas, if the parties expressly agree in a written instrument signed by them that the work shall be considered a work made for hire. For the purpose of the foregoing sentence, a "supplementary work" is a work prepared for publication as a secondary adjunct to a work by another author for the purpose of introducing, concluding, illustrating, explaining, revising, commenting upon, or assisting in the use of the other work, such as forewords, afterwords, pictorial illustrations, maps, charts, tables, editorial notes, musical arrangements, answer material for tests, bibliographies, appendixes, and indexes, and an "instructional text" is a literary, pictorial, or graphic work prepared for publication and with the purpose of use in systematic instructional activities.

Thus, if a publisher engages a songwriter to write a song under a written agreement that states the work is a work made for hire, *and* it is commissioned for use in one of the works listed in subsection (2) of the above definition, then the work will be considered a work made for hire and the publisher will be considered the author of the work.

Note that general songwriting does not appear to fall within any of the categories of works set forth in section (2) of the definition. However, *audiovisual work* is listed in section (2) and, accordingly, songs written for motion pictures, television programs, music videos, and similar works will qualify as a work that may clearly be a work for hire if the publisher or other person commissioning the work enters into a written agreement with the songwriter stating that the work shall be a work made for hire. Some would assert that such an agreement must be entered into before the songwriter commences his work for hire.

### *2. Demos*

Demonstration recordings made at the music publisher's facilities could, under many circumstances, be considered the works made for hire of the publisher. In fact, many exclusive term songwriter agreements now specifically provide that demonstration recordings made by the writer during the term of the agreement are owned by the publisher. As the technology to create commercial quality demonstration has decreased, the question of who controls these demo recordings has become an increasingly important issue.

If the music publisher is to own the copyright in these demo recordings, songwriters should be certain they will be paid a fair portion of any revenues associated with their license, such as for synchronization with motion pictures, television commercials, and music videos. Though the publisher will receive a synchronization fee for the use of the underlying musical composition, half of which will be distributed as part of the writer's share of publishing income, the publisher may also receive a fee for the use of the sound recording master. At a minimum, the songwriter agreement should provide for the writer to be paid a share of these "master use" fees.

More important, however, a songwriter who is also a recording artist would want to restrict the publisher from licensing these demo recordings, by either requiring the artist's prior consent or by placing specific restrictions on the kinds of uses that may be licensed. This may be particularly important where the demo contains the performance of the songwriter and the songwriter has entered into a recording contract. Under such circumstances, the promotion of the demo may pose a conflict with the artist's recording activities.

### *3. Withholding*

By virtue of the purported employment relationship, a publisher may wish to make it clear it has the right to withhold from amounts payable to the writer any amounts required to be withheld under applicable taxation laws.

> Writer agrees and acknowledges that Publisher shall have the right to withhold from the royalties payable hereunder such amount, if any, as may be required under the applicable provisions of the California Revenue and Taxation Code, and Writer agrees to execute such forms and other documents as may be required in connection therewith.

Under California law, an employer engaging another to create a work made for hire must comply with applicable wage withholding provisions.[26]

---

[26] See California Labor Code Sec. 3351.5(c).

### *4. Consideration*

Some legal commentators have suggested that the typical exclusive term songwriter agreement is not a valid agreement because it lacks the legal requirement of sufficient *legal consideration.*

The basic legal rule is that, for a promise (i.e., agreement) to be enforceable, the promise must be supported by legal consideration. Legal consideration is the return given by one in exchange for the act or promise of another — that return may be in the form of an act, a detriment, or a return promise. It has been said that a songwriter's promise to render his services exclusively for a period of time, and to assign any compositions he writes during that time to the publisher, lacks sufficient legal consideration, because all the songwriter is getting in return is a promise to pay royalties, *if any*, to the writer, with no more than a vague and implied promise that the publisher will do something to generate income upon which such royalties could be based. Thus, the argument continues, if the publisher does not assume any express obligation under the songwriter agreement to exert any effort to generate the income upon which royalties would be based, would not his promise to pay royalties be illusory?

Under U.S. law, any detriment, such as the payment of $1.00, will constitute sufficient consideration. Most songwriter agreements don't even provide that. Instead, consideration is based upon the publisher's payment of an *advance* against future royalties or, if no advance is paid, consideration may be based upon the publisher's *implied promise* to exploit the song, together with the publisher's promise to pay royalties if and when the song generates income.[27] Though this has been the established law in the United States, a different result was reached in several cases brought by songwriters in the United Kingdom.

A U.K. court, in the seminal case of *A. Schroeder Music Publishing Company Limited v. Macaulay*,[28] ruled that an exclusive songwriter agreement was unenforceable, even though the publisher agreed to pay to the writer advances against royalties, because, under the songwriter's agreement, the publisher was not bound with a positive

[27] See *Wood v. Lucy, Lady Duff Gordon*, 222 N.Y. 88, 118 N.E. 214 (1917).

[28] (1974) 3 All E.R. 616 (HL); See also *W. Witmark & Sons v. Peters*, 149 N.Y.S. 642 (1914), *Mellencamp v. Riva Music Ltd.*, 698 F. Supp. 1154 (S.D.N.Y. 1988).

undertaking to exploit the composer's works.[29] The court in *Macaulay* suggested, however, that had the songwriter been granted the right to recover ownership of the copyrights after a reasonable time of inactivity by the publisher, the agreement probably would have been declared enforceable. As a result, reversion of rights clauses, discussed above in connection with single song agreements, have become common in songwriter agreements entered into in the United Kingdom.

### *5. Exclusivity*

The extent of *exclusivity* may be set forth in a separate provision, such as the following:

> 4. *Exclusivity*. From the date hereof and during the term of this agreement, Writer will not write or compose, or furnish or dispose of, any musical compositions, titles, lyrics or music, or any rights or interests therein whatsoever, nor participate in any manner with regard to the same for any person, firm or corporation other than Publisher, nor permit the use of his name and likeness as the writer or co-writer of any musical compositions by any person, firm or corporation other than Publisher.

A writer with some bargaining leverage might negotiate exceptions depending upon the circumstances. For example, motion picture producers typically require copyright ownership when they engage writers to compose theatrical film scores and corporations or advertising agencies typically require copyright ownership when they engage writers to compose commercial jingles. Accordingly, a writer who is likely to engage in such composing would want an exception allowing the songwriter to do so. This is typically effected by excluding compositions *written on assignment*. The publisher may wish to limit the number of

---

[29] See also *Clifford Davis Management Ltd. v. WEA Records, Ltd.*, (1975) 1 All E.R. 237 (refusing to allow the manager/publisher to enforce a publishing agreement against the rock group Fleetwood Mac, citing the Macaulay case with approval); *O'Sullivan v. Management Agency*, (1985) 3 All E.R. 351 (setting aside the songwriter agreement between Gilbert O'Sullivan and his publishing company, citing Macaulay with approval). However, in *Elton John v. Dick James Music* [1982 J. No. 15026, High Court of Justice, Chancery Division], the court refused to set aside the agreement between Elton John and his publisher, because of the long span of time that had elapsed between his first questioning the validity of the agreement and his bringing the lawsuit.

such compositions to a specified number per year, require the writer to use best efforts to retain a portion of the copyright for the music publisher, and require the writer to pay to the music publisher, to the extent of the writer's outstanding unrecouped advances, all or a portion of the composer fee earned by the writer on assignment. The exclusivity may be further circumscribed by a provision limiting the agreement to songs written and recorded by the writer in connection with his services as a recording artist. Exclusivity should certainly not apply to the artist's *recording* activities.

The exclusivity, however, will often extend not only to the writer's songwriting activity, but to the writer's name and likeness:

> Writer grants to Publisher, without any compensation other than as specified herein, the perpetual right to use and publish and to permit others to use and publish Writer's name (including any professional name heretofore or hereafter adopted by Writer), likeness and biographical material, or any reproduction or simulation thereof and titles of all compositions hereunder in connection with the printing, sale, advertising, distribution and exploitation of music, folios, recordings, performances, player rolls and otherwise concerning any of the compositions hereunder, and for any other purpose related to the business of Publisher, its affiliated and related companies, or to refrain therefrom. *This right shall be exclusive during the term hereof and nonexclusive thereafter.* Writer shall not authorize or permit the use of his name or likeness or biographical material concerning him, or other identification, or any reproduction or simulation thereof, for or in connection with any musical composition covered by this agreement, other than by or for Publisher. Writer grants Publisher the right to refer to Writer as Publisher's "Exclusive Songwriter and Composer" or other similar appropriate appellation.

As discussed in connection with single song agreements, a writer should try to limit the scope of the publisher's right to use his name, likeness, and biography to conform to the writer's career circumstances. Remember, however, unlike under single song agreements, in the context of exclusive term agreements, these rights of publicity are granted to the publisher on an *exclusive* basis, making it all the more important for the writer to carefully consider the scope of the rights granted. For example, many of the same rights of publicity granted in the above provision to the music publisher on an exclusive basis will also be required by the artist's record company. The above provision, unless modified, could be used by the music publisher as a means to affect or restrict the artist's freedom to negotiate and close his record deal.

### *6. Specific Enforcement*

The 13th Amendment to the United States Constitution outlawed slavery for good, so even a publisher may not force a writer to compose music if the latter refuses to work. Nevertheless, the exclusive term agreement will allow the publisher to enforce the exclusive nature of the relationship by legally preventing the writer from submitting compositions covered by the agreement to other publishers. The following provision clarifies the publisher's right to seek the appropriate equitable remedies necessary to enforce the publisher's exclusive rights:

> 12. *Unique Services.* Writer acknowledges that the services rendered hereunder are of a special, unique, unusual, extraordinary and intellectual character which gives them a peculiar value, the loss of which cannot be reasonably or adequately compensated in damages in an action at law, and that a breach by writer of any of the provisions of this agreement will cause Publisher great and irreparable injury and damage. Writer expressly agrees that Publisher shall be entitled to the remedies of injunction and other equitable relief to prevent a breach of this agreement or any provision thereof, which relief shall be in addition to any other remedies, for damages or otherwise, which may be available to Publisher.

## B. Term

When considering the *term*, or duration, of the exclusive term songwriter agreement, keep in mind the important distinction between the two separate contexts in which the word *term* is used. When we refer to the phrase, *exclusive term*, we are referring to the period of time, specified in the agreement, during which any songs created by the writer must be delivered and assigned to the publisher. This is sometimes referred to as the *administration period*. This should not be confused with the term, or period of time, during which the publisher will have the exclusive right to exploit any of the compositions delivered and assigned during the exclusive term — usually, the *life of copyright*, subject to any statutory termination rights or contractual rights of reversion (see above).

The exclusive term of an exclusive term songwriter agreement is typically one year with the publisher having a series of options to extend the term, usually up to an additional three years, but sometimes an additional four to six years. The exclusive term provision might be stated as follows:

> 2. *Term*. The term of this Agreement shall commence with the date hereof and shall continue in force for a period of one (1) year from said date. Writer hereby grants to Publisher four (4) separate and irrevocable options each to extend this agreement for a one (1) year term, such extension terms to run consecutively beginning at the expiration of the original term hereof, all upon the same terms and conditions as are applicable to the original term. Each option shall be automatically exercised unless written notice to the contrary is sent by Publisher to Writer at least ten (10) days prior to the expiration of the then current term. Such notice to the contrary may, at Publisher's election, be effective as to individual members of Writer or as to all members of Writer.

Publishers will seek to extend the exclusive term as long as possible. Some exclusive term agreements permit the publisher to extend the term if the advances received by the writer are unrecouped as of the date the agreement would otherwise expire. Others allow the publisher to extend the term in the event the writer does not meet certain delivery requirements. For example, the term may last for the longer of one year or until the date the writer completes the delivery to the publisher of ten acceptable songs, but these ten songs must be composed *solely* by the writer (i.e., if the writer delivers ten songs co-written with another writer, five songs remain to be delivered — to meet the delivery requirement, he must deliver either five additional songs written entirely by him or the equivalent number of songs partially written by him (e.g., two entirely written by him plus six partially written by him)). Further, the songs must be *acceptable*, or reasonably acceptable, to the publisher, which is intended to prevent the writer from, for example, composing several arrangements of songs in the public domain solely for the purpose of meeting the delivery requirement.

Songwriters might try to establish a minimum royalty level that must be achieved within any year as a condition to the publisher's exercise of the option for the following year. Alternatively, the songwriter could try to condition each option exercise with the publisher's ability to effect the commercial release of a minimum number of recordings each year. Again, the terms will vary with the bargaining leverage of the writer. A writer with a high degree of leverage may be able to require a minimum number of recordings released by artists who have been on the *charts* during the year (e.g., have had hit records listed on charts published by industry trade magazines, such as *Billboard*). Of course, if the writer possessed that degree of leverage, he would probably resist entering into an exclusive term agreement at the outset and, instead, insist upon entering a series of single song agreements having well negotiated reversion provisions (see above). Alternatively, a songwriter with a high degree of bargaining leverage would be able to command substantial advances, including advances upon the publisher's exercise of each of its options to extend the agreement. Where a music publisher has agreed to pay substantial advances, it is extremely unlikely the publisher would also agree to condition its option exercises upon either the achievement of minimum royalty levels or a minimum level of recordings released.

When a songwriter who is also a recording artist signs an exclusive term songwriter agreement with a music publishing company that is affiliated with his record company, the exclusive terms of the songwriter agreement and the recording agreement may be tied together. It should be to the writer's advantage for his exclusive term agreement to automatically terminate upon any termination of his recording contract. The following provision is an example of how the term of an exclusive term agreement may be tied with the term of a recording contract with an affiliated company:

> 8. *Other Agreements*. Simultaneously herewith Writer is entering into a recording contract with Publisher's record company affiliate. Notwithstanding any provision to the contrary herein contained, it is the intent of the parties hereto that the term of this agreement be coterminous with the term of said recording contract. Accordingly, in the event said record company affiliate fails to exercise any renewal option with respect to the recording contract, Publisher shall not have the right to exercise any extension option hereunder;

> further, any extension, renewal, suspension or termination of the recording contract by said record company affiliate shall automatically and without further notice extend, renew, suspend or terminate this agreement in like manner.

The parties to an exclusive term agreement should also be aware of any state laws that may limit the length of time a music publisher can enforce a personal services contract. For example, in California, a personal services contract cannot be enforced against the writer for more than seven years.[30] In New York, there is precedent for the enforcement of a ten-year personal services contract.[31]

## C. Advances

In the previous discussion of *single song agreements*, we mentioned that sometimes the songwriter receives, upon signing, a "nonreturnable, recoupable advance" against future royalties (except performance royalties the writer receives directly from his performance rights society). The advance tends to be higher if the songwriter has a track record, if the publisher believes the song's prospects for an early recording are good, or if the song had been previously published and has its own earnings track record.

Advances paid in the context of an exclusive term agreement are a little different in that the advance is often paid on a periodic (e.g., weekly) basis, and is paid for the purpose of providing the songwriter with a small living. These advances may range from $250 per week for a new writer to several thousands of dollars per week for established writers or writers who are also recording artists. Alternatively, advances may be paid upon the delivery of songs, but this often raises the practical difficulty of determining what really constitutes a song for purpose of meeting the delivery requirement. For example, the writer may compose an arrangement of a song in the public domain solely for the purpose of meeting the delivery requirement.

---

[30] California Labor Code Section 2855; see *Foxx v. Williams*, 244 Cal. App. 2d 223, 52 Cal. Rptr. 896 (1966).

[31] *Ketcham v. Hall Syndicate, Inc.*, 37 Misc.2d 693, 236 N.Y.S.2d 206, *aff'd*, 242 N.Y.S.2d 182.

A songwriter with some bargaining leverage may be able to negotiate an *escalation* clause, under which the amount of the minimum advance increases each year as a condition to the publisher's exercise of each of its options to extend by one year the term of the agreement. For example, each such advance may be calculated on the basis of some percentage of the songwriter's previous year's music publishing earnings, with a minimum and a maximum dollar figure set for each option year.

A songwriter who is also a recording artist may have his advances tied to the commercial release of recordings containing the compositions covered, providing him with an extra incentive to use the songs covered by the exclusive term agreement, early and often. Some attorneys suggest that songwriters should avoid entering exclusive term agreements unless they need the cash or unless the publisher is in a special position to assist the writer's career through an exclusive relationship.

## D. Cross-Collateralization

When a songwriter who is also a recording artist signs an exclusive term songwriter agreement with a music publishing company that is affiliated with his record company, the publisher may try to cross-collateralize the writer's publishing and recording agreements. In other words, the writer's songwriter agreement will permit his music publisher (1) to recoup advances the writer received from the publisher from payments due writer under the writer's recording agreement with the publisher's affiliated record company *and* (2) to recoup advances received from the affiliated record company from payments due writer under the writer's songwriter agreement. The provision might take the following form:

> 21. *Recoupments.* It is understood and acknowledged that any and all charges against royalties under this agreement which are not recouped by Publisher may be recouped by Publisher's record company affiliate from any and all royalties earned by Writer as a recording group under their recording contract of even date with said record company, and that any and all charges against royalties under said recording contract which are not recouped by said record company may be recouped by Publisher from any and all royalties earned by Writer hereunder.

Experienced writer/artists know that, because of the way their recording contracts are structured, their only true and reliable cash flow arises from their songwriter agreements. Artists who do not have the bargaining leverage to have the cross-collateral provision stricken in its entirety should at least insist that cross-collateralization be limited to payments due under other agreements with the music publisher (such as other single song publishing agreements or a co-publishing agreement), and never with his recording agreement.

## E. Compositions Covered

The compositions covered by the agreement are normally intended to include only those compositions written by the songwriter during the exclusive term of the agreement. Nevertheless, some exclusive term songwriting agreements provide that even songs composed prior to the signing of the agreement are granted to the publisher, sometimes referred to as the writer's *back catalog*. Such provisions may be found in the grant of rights clause, as illustrated by italicized language below:

> 3. *Grant of Rights.* Writer hereby irrevocably and absolutely assigns, transfers, sets over and grants to Publisher its successors and assigns each and every and all rights and interests of every kind, nature and description in and to the results and proceeds of Writer's services hereunder, including but not limited to the titles, words and music of any and all original musical compositions in any and all forms and original arrangements of musical compositions in the public domain in any and all forms, and/or all rights and interests existing under all agreements and licenses relating thereto, together with all worldwide copyrights and renewals and extensions thereof, *which musical works have been written, composed, created or conceived, in whole or in part, by Writer* alone or in collaboration with another or others, *and which hereafter, during the term hereof, be written, composed, created or conceived by Writer, in whole or in part*, alone or in collaboration with another or others, *and which are now owned or controlled and which may, during the term hereof, be owned or controlled, directly or indirectly, by Writer*, alone or with others, . . ."

A writer should independently review any of the compositions in his back catalog to determine whether the copyrights in such compositions have already been granted to another publisher. In the event the writer had previously composed some songs that are now controlled by another publisher, the back catalog provision should be limited to those compositions "owned or controlled" by the songwriter. To avoid any misunderstandings as to which songs were intended to be included, the parties would be advised to attach to the agreement a schedule listing those back catalog compositions to be covered. If the writer still controls the compositions and they are already earning publishing income, then the writer might consider either withholding the rights or offering them to the publisher for additional compensation.

Note that the foregoing grant of rights clause includes a grant of compositions composed *in whole or in part* by the writer during the term of the agreement, which means that if the writer begins the writing of a song during the exclusive term and completes it after the term expires, the composition is owned by the publisher, not the writer or the writer's new publisher. To protect themselves from writers who withhold material created until after the exclusive term expires, some publishers add a provision that grants them the publishing rights to any song written by the writer and recorded or released within six months after the exclusive term expires. This would eliminate the need to prove whether the writing of a song recorded shortly after the expiration of the exclusive term did in fact commence prior to such expiration.

The songwriter may insist, however, that only songs commercially recorded during the exclusive term should be subject to the grant and ownership in any songs previously granted that were not commercially recorded by the expiration of the exclusive term (or within six months of delivery to the publisher, whichever is later) should revert to the writer.

### F. Other Provisions

Provisions in exclusive term songwriter agreements relating to grant of rights, territory, reversion of rights, royalties, accounting, audit privileges, international payments, creative controls, and other restrictions, are generally the same as those contained in single song songwriter agreements, and the discussion regarding them in the previous section is applicable here.

## V. COLLABORATORS

It has been said that "two heads are better than one." That maxim can certainly find support in the long list of successful songwriting teams this century, including George and Ira Gershwin, Rodgers and Hart, Lennon and McCartney, and Elton John and Bernie Taupin. Several important questions arise when two or more writers work together to create musical works. Who gets the publishing rights? How are royalties shared among the collaborators? What happens when both writers sign up with the same publisher? Should the writing partners enter into a collaboration agreement? We will discuss each of these questions in turn.

### A. Who Gets the Publishing?

Where each collaborator is signed up to an exclusive term agreement with the same music publisher or each typically assigns his or her songs to the same publisher as a matter of course, the question of who gets the publishing is straightforward. But what happens when each writer is engaged to work with a different publisher? The following provision, used by some publishers to address this problem, may be found in many exclusive term agreements:

> 10. *Collaboration with Other Writers.* Whenever Writer shall collaborate with any other person in the creation of any musical composition, any such musical composition shall be subject to the terms and conditions of this agreement and Writer warrants and represents that prior to the collaboration with any other person, such other person shall be advised of this exclusive agreement and that all such compositions must be published by Publisher. In the event of such collaboration with any other person, Writer shall notify Publisher of the extent of interest that such other person may have in any such musical composition and Writer shall cause such other person to execute a separate songwriter's agreement with respect thereto, which agreement shall set forth the division of the songwriter's share of income between Writer and such other person, and Publisher shall make payment accordingly. If Publisher so desires, Publisher may request Writer to execute a separate agreement in Publisher's customary form with respect to each musical composition hereunder. Upon such request, Writer will promptly execute such agreement.

> Publisher shall have the right, pursuant to the terms and conditions hereof, to execute such agreement in behalf of Writer hereunder. Such agreement shall supplement and not supersede this agreement. In the event of any conflict between the provisions of such agreement and this agreement, the provisions of this agreement shall govern. The failure of either of the parties hereto to execute such agreement, whether requested by Publisher or not, shall not affect the rights of each of the parties hereunder, including but limited to the rights of Publisher to all of the musical compositions written and composed by Writer.

Thus, under above provision, the writer agrees to cause the copyright in the entire song, including the publishing rights of both his share and that of his collaborator, to be assigned to the writer's publisher. But how is the writer going to cause this to happen? Perhaps, before the song is written, the writer and his partner have entered into a collaboration agreement under which the partners agreed in advance that all songs they write together will be assigned to the writer's publisher. Nevertheless, unless the two writers are a standing team, that solution may not always be practical. Moreover, the writer's partner is likely to have his own ideas about who gets the right to publish his compositions. In any event, if the writer's partner had already been bound to an exclusive term agreement with another publisher at the time the composition was created, the partner may already be obligated to assign his copyright in the composition (including perhaps his partner's share) to that other publisher.

In practice, the onerous provision set forth above is rarely enforced. The typical solution is that the two publishers involved enter into a co-publishing or co-administration agreement that determines the respective rights of the parties in the composition. The several alternative forms these co-publishing and co-administration deals may take are described in the next chapter. If a songwriting team regularly collaborates on the writing of compositions, they and their publishers might agree to an arrangement under which the publishing or administration rights to the first song go to one publisher and the rights to the next song go to another publisher — in effect, alternating the allocation of rights among the parties involved. At a minimum, the songwriter should seek to limit his obligation to using *reasonable efforts* to secure the publishing of the other writer's share.

## B. How Are Royalties Shared Among Collaborators?

As discussed in the *collaborative royalties* section of our discussion of single song music publishing agreements, when the music and lyrics of a composition are originally composed and written with the knowledge and intention that they would be merged as "an inseparable or interdependent part of a unitary whole," the resulting combination is considered a *joint work.* The authors of a joint work are co-owners of copyright in the work,[32] and each author automatically acquires an *undivided* ownership interest in the entire work. This means that, unless otherwise agreed among the co-authors, the authors of the work will share equally in the revenues generated by *all or any portion of* the work.

For example, royalties generated by the sale or performance of any instrumental version of the composition will go to both the composer and the lyricist — equally, or according to percentages otherwise agreed upon — not just to the composer of the music. Likewise, royalties from the licensing of any printed edition containing only the lyrics will go to both authors, not just the lyricist.

However, this does not prevent co-authors from agreeing among themselves to another division of the copyright and the publishing royalties. For example, where one author contributed words and music and the other authored only the words, the two may agree to a 75/25% division. Composer George Gershwin always insisted upon receiving a full 50% interest in a composition, even when two lyric writers contributed to the song, each lyric writer in such an instance sharing the other 50% interest equally.

If the writers desire to agree upon a division other than in equal shares, they should notify their publisher. Many songwriter agreements specify that royalties will be paid in equal shares unless the contract specifies otherwise:

> 10. The term "Composer" shall be understood to include all the writers and composers of the Composition. If there be more than one, the covenants herein contained shall be deemed to be both joint and several on the part of the writers and composers and the royalties hereinabove specified to be paid to Composer shall, unless a different

[32] 17 U.S.C. Sec. 201(a); see also the discussion of joint works in Chapter 7, on *The Language of Music Licensing.*

division of royalties be specified herein, be due to all the writers and composers collectively, to be paid by Publisher in equal shares to each.

As noted above, some songwriter agreements give the publisher the sole right to determine how royalties are to be shared among collaborators. At a minimum, collaborators should always be given the flexibility to reach an agreement among themselves on a split acceptable to them.

## C. What Happens When Collaborators Sign Up with the Same Publisher?

When two or more co-authors grant to a publisher (or group of co-publishers) the copyright and publishing rights in their jointly created work, each writer would be advised to enter into a separate songwriter agreement with the publisher. This is to assure that if one writer breaches his songwriter agreement, the other writer's rights and obligations will not be affected.

However, if the writers are truly an inseparable team, and each has entered into an exclusive term agreement with the same publisher, each agreement should be made co-terminous with the other. In other words, if the publisher terminates, or fails to exercise an option to renew the term of one of the writer's exclusive term agreement, the other writer's exclusive term agreement is automatically terminated. Finally, a writer should try to eliminate any cross-collateralization between his songwriter agreement and that of his co-author. This will prevent any unfair distribution of royalties, and recoupment of advances, in the event that one of the writers collaborates in the writing of a song with a third writer or if the collaborators stop writing songs together.

## D. Should Co-Authors Enter into a Collaboration Agreement?

In the absence of a written agreement, the co-authors of a composition will be deemed to have equal shares in the copyright. This is because a transfer of copyright, or any exclusive rights under copyright, is not valid unless it is effected by a writing signed by the owner of the rights.[33]

---

[33] 17 U.S.C. Sec. 204(a).

Accordingly, where the co-authors agree to a division of copyright or royalties that is other than that of equal shares, they should enter into a written agreement to reflect their understanding. Alternatively, the co-authors may rely on a written communication to their music publisher evidencing their agreement, but the writer having the greater share would be advised to have his partner sign a short agreement to avoid any misunderstanding.

Members of performing groups are often advised to enter into a collaboration agreement, partnership agreement, or shareholder agreement, depending upon the circumstances, to deal with a broad range of issues concerning their respective rights to the musical works, recordings, group name, merchandising rights, and other business and legal matters arising from what is likely to be a dynamic relationship among the members over time.

## VI. SUMMARY

Whether you work for a major music publisher or are just starting your own music publishing business, you should understand the basic terms and conditions of the standard songwriter agreement. If you are a songwriter, or songwriter's representative, you should be aware of the typical variations to the terms and conditions in these agreements that may be negotiated with music publishers.

# Appendix to Chapter 3
# Songwriter Agreements

Forms (On CD-Rom Only)

| | |
|---|---|
| **Form 3.1** | **Songwriter Agreement for a Single Song I** |
| **Form 3.2** | **Songwriter Agreement for a Single Song II** |
| **Form 3.3** | **Exclusive Term Songwriter Agreement** |
| **Form 3.4** | **1939 Songwriters Protective Association Uniform Popular Songwriters Contract** |
| **Form 3.5** | **1969 American Guild of Authors & Composers Popular Songwriters Contract** |
| **Form 3.6** | **1978 American Guild of Authors & Composers Popular Songwriters Renewal Contract** |
| **Form 3.7** | **1978 Songwriters Guild of America Popular Songwriters Contract** |
| **Form 3.8** | **Standard Studio Film Music/Composer/Arranger/ Conductor Employment Agreement** |

Chapter 4

# Co-Publishing and Administration Agreements

## Summary

CHAPTER 4

# CO-PUBLISHING AND ADMINISTRATION AGREEMENTS

As noted in the previous chapter, a songwriter with some bargaining leverage can often negotiate with a publisher a variation to the standard music publishing deal, one which affords him not only the *writer's share*, but a portion of the *publisher's share* of publishing income. This is often referred to as a *participation deal*, and there are two basic ways these deals are typically done.

The first is for the writer to maintain a portion of the copyright in the compositions and enter into a *co-publishing agreement*, under which the publisher's share is split between the writer (or his own music publishing firm) and the music publisher. The second is for the writer to retain all interest in the copyrights and merely grant to the music publisher the right to administer the publishing of the compositions under what is known as an *administration agreement.* The effect of each of these deals is the same: it reduces the publisher's share by the amount of the share retained by the songwriter.

The *co-publishing* agreement, *administration* agreement, and a third form, the *collection* agreement, arise not only in the context of songwriter/publisher relationships, but as a result of a variety of music publishing circumstances. This chapter sketches the common terms and conditions contained in typical co-publishing, administration, and collection agreements.

## I. Co-Publishing Agreements

A *co-publishing agreement* is an agreement between two or more parties — generally co-owners of one or more copyrights — that defines the rights of the parties over division of ownership of copyrights, the administration of publishing activities, and the sharing of revenue relating to the musical compositions covered by the agreement.

## A. As Distinguished from Administration and Collection Agreements

An *administration agreement* is an agreement between an owner, or co-owner, of copyright and another, called the *administrator*, who is provided the right and obligation to administer the musical compositions covered by the agreement, in exchange for the payment of an administration fee. A *co-publishing* agreement is similar to an *administration* agreement, but under a co-publishing agreement each of the parties typically has some co-ownership interest in each of the copyrights covered by the agreement; under an administration agreement, the administrator acquires a license for a term of years, but does not acquire an interest in any of the copyrights.

Every co-publishing agreement will contain a provision dealing with the question of who among the parties will have the right to *administer* the exploitation of the compositions covered by the agreement. Although these *administration rights* may be allocated among the parties to a co-publishing agreement, such rights should not be confused with what is properly called an *administration agreement.*

Another difference between a *co-publishing* and an *administration* agreement is that a co-publishing agreement typically has a term that lasts the entire life of the copyrights in the compositions; by contrast, the typical administration agreement has a stated term extending for a limited period of time. However, many co-publishing agreements also carry a limited term, so the distinction between these agreements cannot generally be made on the basis of their length of term.

A *collection* agreement is virtually the same as an *administration* agreement, except that the administrator is generally not obliged or given the incentive to undertake any affirmative actions to exploit the songs.

## B. When Used

A co-publishing agreement may arise from a variety of circumstances. As stated at the outset of this chapter, a co-publishing agreement typically arises as a result of a participation deal — i.e., when a writer negotiates to maintain a portion of, or "participate in," the *publisher's share* of music publishing income. But there are other circumstances that give rise to the negotiation and entry into co-publishing agreements.

For example, where two songwriters who collaborate in the writing of a single composition have previously signed up with separate music publishing firms, the publishing firms will generally enter into a co-publishing agreement with each other to govern their respective rights in the composition. If each of these songwriters had previously negotiated for a piece of the publisher's share of income from their compositions, there would have already existed a co-publishing or administration agreement between each songwriter and his or her respective music publisher. Thus, if they should collaborate in the writing of a song, a new co-publishing agreement would be negotiated among the four publishing firms involved — the first songwriter's "self-publishing" company and the major or independent music publisher with whom he has a publishing deal, and the second songwriter's "self-publishing" company and the major or independent music publisher with whom he has a publishing deal.

Where several members of a rock band each have contributed to the writing of a single song, the complexities arising from multiple publishing companies can be daunting. Depending upon the terms of the co-publishing or partnership agreement among the members, should someone have had the presence of mind to create one for them, the resulting "split of copyright" could raise the problems that often stem from what we call the Split Copyright Syndrome, lamented in more detail in Chapter 6.

Other circumstances out of which a co-publishing agreement may arise include the situation where a writer receives control over his copyright as a result of a termination of a prior grant of rights (under statutory termination rights under the copyright law[1]) or a reversion of rights under an existing songwriter agreement, and, now, when his bargaining position is improved, wishes to gain a share in the publishing income.

An emerging area that has called for the co-publishing solution — arising from the use of digital technology in the record production process — is where a recording artist illegally takes a digital sample

[1] See Chapter 9, *Duration of Copyright, Assignments of Copyright, and Licenses.*

from a recording of another and the owner of the underlying musical composition and the sampling artist settle the matter by entering into a co-publishing agreement that calls for the sharing of income from the publication of (and, often, the sharing of the copyright in) the new work. This negotiation is covered in more detail in Chapter 24, *The Digital Sampling Controversy.*

## C. Negotiating the Co-Publishing Agreement

The primary business points on which to focus in negotiating a co-publishing agreement include: (1) copyright ownership, (2) administration rights, and (3) revenue sharing.

### *1. Copyright Ownership*

Ordinarily, when a songwriter writes a song, he assigns his entire interest in the copyright to a music publisher, which, as we have pointed out, is the arrangement set forth in the typical songwriter agreement. As a result of that transaction, the copyright is owned by a single person or entity. As discussed in the previous chapter, and later in Chapter 7, on *The Language of Music Licensing*, a copyright can also be *co-owned.* Co-ownership of a musical composition often arises from collaboration of two or more songwriters in the creation of the song — commonly, a composer and a lyricist. Traditionally, when a composer and lyricist collaborated in the writing of a song, they each assigned their respective ownership interest in the copyright to a single music publisher, resulting in the control of the composition by a single copyright owner. In recent years, however, the trend has been for songwriters to retain all or a portion of the copyright in their compositions,[2] resulting in the co-ownership of copyright among each of the songwriters and their respective publishers.

In the case of co-authorship, each co-author of a musical composition acquires an ownership interest in the song's copyright, and unless otherwise agreed between or among the several co-authors, each co-author receives an *equal share* in that copyright ownership interest. For example, where two authors collaborate in the writing of a song, each would have a 50% interest in the entire work; where there are three

---

[2] See Chapter 3, *Songwriter Agreements* and Chapter 6, *The Split Copyright Syndrome.*

authors, each would have a 33⅓% undivided interest in the entire work, etc.

Co-authors may, however, agree to another division, and that division is entirely subject to negotiation. For example, where one author contributed words and music and the other worked only on the words, the two may agree to a 75/25% division. Non-equal divisions of copyright ownership and co-publisher revenue sharing frequently arise in the context of a multiple member rock band, where the band is comprised of both songwriter and non-songwriter members. A non-songwriter member, perhaps a well known lead singer, may assert that the band as a whole should benefit from the band's recording and performance of the songs written by its members. As a result, the band itself, or each of the non-songwriter members, may receive a portion of the copyright, or a portion of the publisher's share of revenues from such songs. Such negotiations, a potential source of some heated discussions, will often pose a challenging conflict of interest problem for the attorney representing the band as a whole.

The percentage ownership of copyright usually determines the percentage that each co-author will share in the publisher's share of income, but not always — in other words, the revenue sharing percentages may not always follow the copyright ownership percentages. Copyright ownership may be split 50/50, or transferred entirely to one party (i.e., 100/0), with the revenue split under completely different terms (e.g., 75/25, 60/40). For example, if the songwriter members of a rock band are unwilling to assign a copyright ownership interest to the non-songwriter members, or to the band as a whole, they might retain the copyright, but, recognizing the band's contribution to the success of the compositions, they may be willing to share a portion of the publishing income with the other members of the band. This compromise is typically effected by the entry of a *rate participation* agreement in a form similar to Form 4.4 found on the CD-Rom.

*Term.* Because the co-publishing agreement generally involves the co-ownership of copyright, the *term* of the agreement generally lasts the life of the copyrights. Some co-publishing agreements, however, will have a term, sometimes called the *administration term*, one that is limited in much the same way as the term of an administration agreement. Of course, the term of co-ownership as between co-authors who each retain at least a portion of his undivided interest in his copyrights will always last the life of the copyrights. Where, however, co-authors with a high degree of bargaining leverage assign a co-ownership interest in their copyrights to a major music publisher, they might negotiate a limited administration term, such as three to five years, upon the expiration of which all rights will revert back to the writers. Other variations in *term* provisions are discussed below with respect to the duration of *administration agreements.*

### 2. Administration Rights

It may be recalled that *administration rights* is the term used to define who among the copyright owners, or co-publishers, has the authority to grant licenses for the use of the music. Because of the problems that arise when ownership of copyright is split among several parties,[3] how administration rights are allocated among the parties may be one of the most important factors affecting the long-term value of the copyright. Accordingly, the parties should very carefully consider how they are going to address the question of how administration rights are allocated in their co-publishing agreement.

There are three basic ways administration rights can be allocated among the parties: (a) appoint an exclusive administrator, (b) appoint an exclusive administrator, but subject his authority to certain restrictions, or (c) allow each owner to administer his own share of the copyright.

#### *a. Appoint an Exclusive Administrator*

The parties to a co-publishing agreement may appoint one of the parties as the *exclusive administrator*, who would have the exclusive right to administer all publishing matters with respect to the musical compositions covered by the agreement. This means that anyone desiring a license to use the music covered by the agreement need only locate, negotiate with, and acquire a license from a single person, the exclusive administrator, who would have the right to issue a license on behalf of all the copyright owners. The exclusive administrator collects all the income and is responsible for distributing the appropriate shares of the income, less agreed upon expenses, to the respective co-publishers. The only rights the other co-publishers have is the

[3] See Chapter 6, *The Split Copyright Syndrome.*

right to receive the share of publishing income to which they are entitled under the agreement.

Where an exclusive administrator is appointed, a copyright which is split (i.e., co-owned by several persons), — and which would otherwise be plagued by the *split copyright syndrome*[4] — can be efficiently administered, provided, of course, the exclusive administrator competently represents the co-publishing group. This leads to the question, who among the co-publishers should be appointed the exclusive administrator? This may prove to be most difficult to answer.

One commentator has suggested that the administration rights be granted to the co-publisher having the greatest percentage in the copyright. Another idea, which the present authors recommend, is what might be called, *alternating administration rights* — that is, allow each co-publisher to control the administration rights for alternating terms of two, three, or five years. The acting administrator could waive the collection of an administration fee or he could be awarded a fee for achieving a minimum level of publishing income established in advance by the parties. A potential problem with this, of course, is that potential licensees may not always know which co-owner to approach for approval to use the song. This, however, should be alleviated over time by the application of web-based technology that will make it easier for licensees to determine who controls the administration rights to individual compositions.

Co-publishers indisposed to grant exclusive administration rights to a co-publisher for financial reasons might be satisfied with a provision requiring the exclusive administrator to waive any administration fee and by requiring that shares of certain income be paid directly to each co-publisher from the source of the income, as many co-publishing agreements typically require. For example, the parties may instruct the Harry Fox Agency, and the applicable performance rights society (e.g., ASCAP or BMI), to pay any income generated by them directly to each co-publisher, according to his or her share — an arrangement which, in effect, bypasses the administrator. This should reduce any unnecessary transaction costs associated with directing these payments through to the co-publishers and reduce the amount of time it takes for these payments to reach their pockets.

[4] *Id.*

Should the parties be unable to immediately agree upon a single administrator, or alternating administration program, it may do them well to list their particular concerns, use that list to craft contractual provisions addressing their concerns, and appoint an exclusive administrator who would be subject to those restrictions.

*b. Appoint an Exclusive Administrator Subject to Restrictions*

The parties to a co-publishing agreement may appoint an *exclusive administrator*, but impose certain restrictions that affect either the administrator's authority to issue licenses or his authority to collect money on behalf of the other parties.

Just as a songwriter may wish to retain a right of consent over the licensing of certain kinds of uses by his publisher, a co-publisher granting administration rights to another may wish to retain similar rights of consent. For example, the agreement may specify that the consent of each co-publisher is required before the administrator issues a license:

(a) allowing another to make changes to the music or lyrics,

(b) allowing creation and distribution of mechanical reproductions for less than the statutory rate,

(c) allowing the use of the title of the song as the title of a play, film, or television program,

(d) allowing the use of the song in a political or commercial advertisement,

(e) allowing the synchronization of the song in a motion picture, television program, or videogram bearing a rating of "X" or its equivalent, or

(f) allowing the production of a dramatic adaptation of the song.

Any of these restrictions may vary depending upon the tastes of the particular co-publishers and nature of the relationship they have with the exclusive administrator. Restrictions such as these are becoming increasingly common.

Again, parties otherwise reluctant to appoint a single administrator, might agree to do so where the administration fee is waived, much of the income is paid directly to the co-publishers from the source, and the administrator's licensing activities are subject to adequate restrictions.

*c. Allow Each Owner to Administer His Own Share — Co-Administration*

The third alternative, and probably the least attractive of the three, is where the parties agree to *co-administer* the compositions covered by the agreement — that is, each of the parties maintains the right to administer his or her respective share.

The effect of this arrangement is to require anyone who desires a license to use a composition covered by the agreement to locate, negotiate with, and acquire a separate license from each of the co-publisher parties to the agreement. While this may not appear burdensome to the co-publishers, it generally has the effect of significantly increasing the transaction costs (which often include expensive attorneys' fees) of using the compositions covered by the agreement and will, in the long term, tend to have an adverse affect on the potential income from these compositions.

For this reason, some co-administration provisions permit any of the co-publisher parties to issue mechanical licenses provided the rate charged is at the full statutory rate. Nevertheless, this does little to ameliorate the split copyright problem, illustrated in Chapter 6, created by the co-administration of copyrights. We therefore strongly recommend that the parties attempt to work out some compromise using the suggestions set forth above.

### *3. Revenue Sharing*

As noted in Chapter 2 on *The Art of Music Publishing*, the publisher's share of music publishing income may be shared among several co-publishers in accordance with their respective percentage interests in that income. As noted above, that percentage is usually, but not always, the same as the percentage ownership interest which that co-publisher has in the copyright — which itself, as we have said, is entirely subject to negotiation.

Note that each co-owner's interest in the copyright is normally a co-ownership interest in the *entire* composition (i.e., the *undivided* copyright in the entire composition), including both the music *and* the lyrics.[5] Accordingly, any royalties generated by the sale or performance of either the music or the lyrics will normally become part of the publisher's share (and, for that matter, the writer's share) and will be divided among all the co-owners (and writers) regardless of the nature of the co-owner's (or writer's) contribution to the composition. For example, income from licensing the use of solely an instrumental version of the composition will normally be shared by all the co-publishers and writers (even the writer of only the lyrics), and income from licensing the use of a printed edition of only the lyrics will normally be shared by all the co-publishers and writers (even the composer of the music). Exceptions may exist where the parties otherwise agree or where the contributions to a composition are deemed not to be joint works.[6]

Before splitting the publisher's share among the co-publishers in accordance with their respective interests in the income, you must first determine what constitutes the publisher's share. The publisher's share is equal to the *gross receipts*, or *gross publishing income*, less (a) the amount of the *writer's share*, (b) any *direct expenses* incurred in connection with the publishing of the music, and, (c) if one of the parties has administration rights, the *administration fee*, if any. The result is referred to in most co-publishing agreements as the *net publishing income* or *net publisher's share.*

#### a. *Writer's Share*

The writer's share of music publishing income is determined in accordance with the provisions of the songwriter's agreement, discussed in Chapter 3. As we have said, with a couple of exceptions, the writer's share amounts to 50% of the income the publisher receives in connection with the publishing of the music. The first exception is that most songwriter's agreements provide for less than 50% of income generated in connection with the sale or licensing of printed editions of the music. The other exception concerns performance royalties: the writer receives his writer's share, and the publisher receives its publisher's share, of performance royalties directly from their performance rights society — because the performance rights society has already

---

[5] See generally the subject of "joint works" in Chapter 7, *The Language of Music Licensing.*

[6] *Id.*

split the performance royalties between writer and publisher, the *writer's share* of music publishing income includes no portion of the *publisher's share* of performance royalties.

*b. Direct Publishing Expenses*

In the co-publishing agreement set forth as Form 4.1 found on the CD-ROM, the following publishing expenses are listed as among those the administrator may deduct from *gross receipts:*

(a) Collection or other fees customarily charged by The Harry Fox Agency or any other collection agent which may be used by Company;

(b) Actual out-of-pocket administrative and exploitation expenses of Company with respect to the Composition for registration fees, advertising and promotion expenses directly related to the Composition, the costs of transcribing lead sheets, and the costs of producing demonstration records.

(c) Attorneys fees directly related to the defense of claims respecting the Composition, if any, actually paid by the Company;

The deduction of commissions charged by agencies like the Harry Fox Agency, and costs associated with the preparation of lead sheets, demonstration recordings, copyright office registration fees, subpublisher fees, and legal fees incurred in the collection of income or the defense of claims directly related to the compositions, is generally considered fair and acceptable. However, advertising and promotion expenses, legal fees incurred to draft license agreements, and specific overhead expenses such as word processing and secretarial expenses are typically negotiated off the list of expenses that an administrator is entitled to deduct. A party might also negotiate a specific dollar limit to the amount of such fees, which may be deducted during each payment period.

**D. Administration Fee**

The *administration fee* is the fee charged by the person responsible for administering the music publishing of the compositions covered by a co-publishing agreement. Of course, if the parties have agreed upon a co-administration arrangement, under which each party maintains the right to administer his or her own respective share, each collecting income directly from licensees, no administration fee is applied. The fee is typically calculated as a percentage of the gross publishing income, including *both* the writer's share and the publisher's share.

Administration fees vary, but usually amount anywhere from 10% to 25%. In the typical co-publishing agreement between a songwriter and a major music publisher, the publisher rarely charges an administration fee. For further details about negotiating administration fees, please refer to the discussion of administration fees in the following section regarding administration agreements.

*Revenue Sharing Example.* Assume that two parties of a co-publishing agreement, having equal shares in the publishing income, appoint one of the parties as the exclusive administrator and allow that party to deduct customary publishing expenses and a 10% administration fee. Assuming further that the gross publishing income is $100, the writer's share is $45, and direct expenses amount to $10, then the *net publishing income* is $35 (i.e., $100, less the 10% administration fee of $10, less the writer's share of $45, less the direct expenses of $10). These deductions first having been made, each publisher would then split $35 equally, or $17.50 each.

## II. ADMINISTRATION AGREEMENTS

An *administration agreement* is an agreement between two or more people that provides one of the parties, called the *administrator*, the right to administer the music publishing activities (i.e., copyright administration, use licensing, and distribution of net publishing income among the parties) relating to the musical compositions covered by the agreement, in exchange for the payment of an administration fee. Unlike an exclusive administrator under a co-publishing agreement, the administrator under an administration agreement generally does not acquire any ownership interest in the compositions covered by the agreement.

## A. When Used

As noted in the previous section, there are a variety of circumstances which may lead the owner or owners of the copyright in a musical composition to enter into a *co-publishing agreement.* Many of these circumstances may also lead to the entry of an *administration agreement*, particularly when the writer or publisher desiring to retain the entire publisher's share of income has a high degree of bargaining leverage.

A common example is where a songwriter is also a successful recording artist, circumstances that afford him the leverage to retain *all* interest in the copyrights to his compositions; but rather than devoting his personal time and resources to a self-publishing business, he finds it more attractive to grant to a music publisher the right to administer the publishing of the compositions. This is accomplished by the writer's entering into an *administration agreement* with the publisher, under which the publisher does not receive ownership of the copyrights, but only, in effect, *administration rights* and the right to receive an *administration fee* in exchange for the administration services it provides the writer.

Administration agreements are also offered by full time music publishing administrators — individuals or organizations which typically do not acquire any ownership interest in song copyrights, but provide full administration services to the copyright owner in return for an administration fee. Also, just about any situation that may call for the grant of co-publishing rights to a music publisher could instead involve the mere grant of administration rights under an administration agreement.

## B. Negotiating the Administration Agreement

Because a grant of copyrights is usually not a part of a straight administration arrangement, the primary areas on which to focus in negotiating an administration agreement only include: (1) the administration fee, (2) the term of the agreement, and (3) restrictions on the exercise of administration rights.

### *1. Administration Fee*

As noted above with respect to co-publishing agreements, the *administration fee* is the fee charged by the person responsible for administering the music publishing of the compositions. Even though the administrator under an administration agreement does not own a portion of any of the copyrights covered by the agreement, the administration fee is calculated in the same way as in the co-publishing agreement: as a percentage of the gross publishing income, including *both* the writer's share and the publisher's share.

Administration fees vary, but usually amount to 10% or 25%. If the agreement calls for the administrator to pay advances, the size of the administration fee will often be a function of the size of the advances; in other words, the higher the advance, the higher the administration fee.

Before payment is made to the publishers, the administrator is also entitled to deduct his direct expenses incurred in connection with administering the publication of the compositions. Provisions concerning what direct expenses the administrator is entitled to deduct are generally the same as that found in co-publishing agreements; please refer to the previous section for a discussion of negotiating the direct expense provision.

Because the administration fee is calculated on the basis of both the writer's share (50%) and publisher's share (50%), the administrator who receives an administration fee of 20%, will end up with an amount equal to 40% of the publisher's share. Thus, the administrator actually has some inherent incentive to promote publication and performance of the song.

*Cover Records.* Co-publishers may wish to enhance that incentive by giving the administrator additional consideration when cover records are made during the term of the agreement. A *cover record* is a commercially released recording of the songwriter's composition by an artist other than the songwriter. The structure of the incentives given to administrators to effect cover records varies widely. For example, the term of the agreement with respect to the covered song may be extended or an interest in its copyright may be transferred to the administrator. More commonly, the administration fee with respect to mechanical royalties generated by the cover recording is increased by an additional 10% or 15%. Because of the difficulty of identifying what performance royalties were associated with performances of the cover, as opposed to those generated from performances of existing recordings, the administrator might either receive no additional percentage of performance royalties or an increased percentage (i.e., the additional 10% or 15%) of that portion of performance royalties determined by the amount the mechanical royalties generated by the cover recording bears in relation to mechanical royalties generated by existing recordings.

### 2. Term

Unlike the typical co-publishing agreement, which commonly has a term lasting the life of the copyright, the term of the typical administration agreement is limited to a term of three to five years, or two or three years with several successive year options to renew. The exercise of such options may be conditioned upon the payment of advances. Other variations are entirely subject to negotiation.

For example, as noted in the previous section, should the administrator succeed in obtaining a cover record for a particular composition, the term of the administration agreement, at least with respect to that composition, may be extended for an additional period of years. However, this means of providing the administrator with the incentive to effect cover recordings is not favored, because it may result in some of the copyright owner's compositions being administered by one administrator and some being administered by another.

Thus, should the administrator insist upon extending the term of the agreement as an incentive for successful performance, that incentive should be made on the basis of achieving minimum net publishing income performance levels generated by the entire catalog. Such a provision might contain a condition that if the net publishing income for all or a selected portion of the compositions covered by the agreement fails to meet certain minimum performance levels in any year, the copyright owner may terminate the administration on 90 days' notice or any subsequent option for renewal may not be exercised.

### 3. Restrictions on the Exercise of Administration Rights

Just as a co-publisher may wish to restrict the exercise of administration rights by its co-publisher(s), a publisher may wish to impose similar controls on its appointed administrator. Recording artists with a significant amount of bargaining leverage, who maintain their own publishing, and who either have sufficient time to devote to their publishing business or sufficient publishing income to pay attorneys or others to act on their behalf, will sometimes require consent for any licensing activity proposed to be taken by the administrator, with the possible exception of issuing mechanical licenses for no less than the statutory rate.

More typically, however, the administrator will be given some greater latitude, being allowed to issue straightforward synchronization and other conventional licenses, but requiring the publisher's consent for one or more of the following kinds of uses: (a) allowing another to make changes to the music or lyrics (b) allowing creation and distribution of mechanical reproductions for less than the statutory rate, (c) allowing the use of the title of the song as the title of a play, film, or television program, (d) allowing the use of the song in a political or commercial advertisement, (e) allowing the synchronization of the song in a motion picture, television program, or videogram bearing a rating of "X" or its equivalent, or (f) allowing the production of a dramatic adaptation of the song. Any of these restrictions may vary depending upon the tastes of the particular publishers and nature of the relationship they have with the administrator.

## III. COLLECTION AGREEMENT

A *collection agreement* is virtually the same as an administration agreement, except that the fee for administering the publishing, called the *collection fee*, is generally only about 5% to 10% of the gross receipts. Because the fee is very low compared to that of administration and co-publishing deals, the music publisher has little or no incentive to promote the publication or performance of the songs covered by the agreement, and the services provided will be limited to collecting publishing income, applying for copyright registrations, and registering songs with the performance rights societies and mechanical rights agencies.

Many publishers believe that a collection fee barely covers the publisher's overhead for royalty collection and disbursement, and collection fees of less than 10% may be uneconomical for anything but catalogs that generate considerable performance royalties. However, where a catalog produces a large amount of publishing income, a publisher can earn a profit on an administration fee of less than 10%, after taking into account the *float*, or interest income, it will receive between the time it receives publishing income and the time the publisher is required to pay out the publisher's and writer's share of that income, typically on a semi-annual basis.

# Appendix to Chapter 4
# Co-Publishing and Administration Agreements

Forms (On CD-Rom Only)

| | |
|---|---|
| **Form 4.1** | **Combination Songwriter Agreement/Co-Publishing Agreement** |
| **Form 4.2** | **Co-Publishing Agreement with Exclusive Administration Rights Granted to One Co-Owner** |
| **Form 4.3** | **Co-Publishing Agreement with Exclusive Administration Rights Granted to One Co-Owner Subject to Certain Restrictions** |
| **Form 4.4** | **Administration Agreement** |
| **Form 4.5** | **Rate Participation Agreement** |

CHAPTER 5

# INTERNATIONAL SUBPUBLISHING

## SUMMARY

# CHAPTER 5

# INTERNATIONAL SUBPUBLISHING

The activity of music publishing — licensing the use of musical compositions, administering their legal protection, and collecting income arising from their use — is a worldwide effort. As the world increasingly resembles the global village projected decades ago by futurists, with cultural boundaries coming down as fast as satellites are going up, music publishers can expect an increasing portion of their income generated by the publication and performance of their compositions overseas. How a music publisher located in one country performs his responsibilities on a worldwide basis has been, traditionally, through a process called *subpublishing* — that is, by entering into an agreement with a music publishing firm located in each overseas market, called a *subpublisher*, to represent the publisher, called the *original publisher*, in promoting the use of the original publisher's compositions, and collecting the publishing income, in the subpublisher's market.

Recent developments, however, arising from the shift from the distribution of physical products (e.g., CDs) embodying musical works to the distribution and performance of music by digital means (e.g., permanent downloads, on-demand streaming, webcasting, etc.) are beginning to have a transformational effect on the way music publishers exploit their musical works outside their home countries. As a result, working with subpublishers for the exploitation of a music publisher's copyrights overseas may become less important than it has in the past. In addition, the role of performance rights and mechanical reproduction collection societies in international music publishing is undergoing an upheaval — at least with respect to the exploitation of musical works online.

This chapter sketches the business background of international subpublishing, describes certain aspects of music publishing that are unique to international subpublishing, analyzes the considerations used in selecting an international subpublishing strategy, and provides some guidelines for negotiating some of the more common terms and conditions contained in a typical *subpublishing agreement*. It will also summarize some of the recent developments in European antitrust law that are changing the way performances and mechanical reproductions of musical works are being administered in Europe.

## I. BUSINESS BACKGROUND

### A. The International Market for Music

Although the United States is the largest source of music publishing royalties in the world, it represents only about 29.3% of total worldwide music publishing revenues.[1] Clearly, given that over 70% of music publishing revenue is derived from sources outside the United States, the international aspects of music publishing international revenues cannot be ignored by today's music copyright owner.

Total worldwide music publishing royalties for the year 2001 were estimated to have been about $7.5 billion, with the United States representing about $1.9 billion of that. Germany was a close second with about $808 million, or 12.2% of worldwide revenue. Japan was next at 10.5% or $760 million, followed by the United Kingdom at 10.1% or $670 million, and France at 8.3% and $549 million. Other major countries included Italy, Spain, the Netherlands, Canada, Switzerland, Australia/New Zealand, Argentina, Belgium, Sweden, Denmark, and Brazil. The top ten markets accounted for over 85% of music publishing revenues.

### B. International Performance Rights Administration

As mentioned in Chapter 2, royalties arising from the licensing of public performances of music is one of the major sources of music publishing income. It is estimated that nearly 50% of all worldwide music publishing revenues are derived from the licensing of public performances. In 2001, this amounted to $3.69 billion, about $880

---

[1] The music publishing revenue data provided in this chapter is from a report entitled International Survey of 2001 Music Publishing Revenues, the last year such reports were issued by the National Music Publishers Association, www.nmpa.org.

million of which derived from radio performances, about $1.3 billion from various forms of television broadcast, and $1.5 billion from live and recorded performances (i.e., nightclubs, restaurants, elevators, etc.). Less than a fourth of the total worldwide performance income was generated in the United States.

In Chapter 18, on *Licensing Music in Live and Recorded Public Performances*, we provide an overview of the operation of performance rights societies operating in the United States (i.e., ASCAP, BMI, and SESAC), but these societies were modeled after performing rights societies established long before in Europe. The first European performance rights society, *Societe des Auteurs, Compositeurs et Editeurs de Musique* (SACEM), was formed in France in 1851. The first German society, *Genosenschaft Deutscher Tonsetzer* (GDT), the predecessor to today's GEMA, was founded in Berlin in 1903. The English *Performance Right Society* (PRS) was established in 1914.

Every major market for music in the world has a performance rights society collecting income on behalf of authors and publishers of music, and several of the major societies administer the collection of performance royalties in countries where no local society exists. Though each society is governed by its own unique rules, all use some form of blanket license for the collection of income, sampling surveys for the distribution of income, and all distribute income to writers and publishers. Many, like the U.S. societies, distribute income to writers and publishers on a 50/50 basis, but this varies from society to society. For example, the division of publisher and writer shares for Dutch works is approximately 2/3 to writers and 1/3 to publishers. Distributions by ASCAP and BMI arising from performance royalties collected on Dutch works performed in the United States would follow the local rule, remitting the writer's share (2/3) to the Dutch society, BUMA, and the publisher's share (1/3) to the U.S. subpublisher representing the Dutch original publisher.

## C. International Mechanical Rights Administration

Another major source of publishing income are mechanical royalties, derived from the grant by music publishers of *mechanical licenses* — the form of permission that authorizes another to make mechanical reproductions of a musical composition, such as recordings on compact discs and audiocassettes. Income derived from mechanical reproduction licensing represent about 25% of all worldwide music publishing income. Mechanical royalties are as significant a source of income in international markets as they are in the United States, but the means of collection are significantly different.

As discussed in Chapter 13, on *Licensing Music in Sound Recordings*, once a copyright owner licenses a song for mechanical reproduction for the first time, he could thereafter be compelled to license it for mechanical reproduction in the United States to anyone else for the fee set by the copyright law. The provision of the copyright statute compelling copyright owners to issue mechanical licenses is known as the *compulsory license* provision,[2] and the prescribed per unit fee set forth in the law is referred to as the *statutory rate*. Because the statutory rate is prescribed in terms of *cents per copy,* mechanical licenses in the United States are generally issued on a *cents per copy* rate for each song recorded. Moreover, the license is issued either directly by the music publisher or, at the publisher's election, by an agent, such as the Harry Fox Agency. This, however, is *not* the way mechanical licenses are generally issued overseas.

To begin with, the collection of mechanical royalties is usually conducted by a single mechanical rights collection society in each territory. Moreover, licensing from that society is typically *mandatory.* This means that all mechanical licenses in the territory are issued by the collection society, not by the individual music publishers; in other words, all record companies in the territory are required to pay mechanical royalties to the collection society, not to the individual publishers. Further, rather than being set by statute, mechanical rates overseas are generally set by some form of collective bargaining agreement between the mandatory mechanical rights organizations and the record companies, or an organization representing them. These agreements are often negotiated with the participation of a copyright tribunal, ministry of culture, or other government agency.

At one time, the record companies in a country would collectively negotiate with the single mandatory mechanical rights society in that country to set the rates and other terms of the local mechanical licenses. Consistent with the evolution of the European Community, which by

---

[2] 17 U.S.C. Sec. 115, set forth in the appendix to Chapter 13 found on the CD-ROM.

stages required the free flow of goods, services, and people among its member countries, record companies began negotiating, not with the mechanical license societies of each nation, but on a multinational basis with a coalition of mechanical licensing societies from different countries. Thus, today, IFPI, *the International Federation of Phonogram Industries*, representing the record companies, negotiates a collective bargaining agreement for mechanical licensing with a confederation of mechanical rights organizations from 30 countries called, BIEM, the *Bureau International des Societes Gerant les Droits d'Enregistrement et de Reproduction Mecanique*. The terms of the agreement negotiated by IFPI and BIEM are then administered by the member mechanical rights societies on a country-by-country basis. The mechanical fees in some territories, however, are set by the local government, which is the case in Japan and India.

Mechanical royalties overseas, whether established by a mechanical licensing society, the local government, or collective bargaining arrangement, are usually expressed as a *percentage* of either the retail selling price (RSP) or the *published price to the dealer* (PPD) of the compact disc or audiocassette recordings in which the composition is embodied. Further, the license is not issued on a per song basis, but this license is issued and the fee is collected on the entire album, regardless of the number of songs it contains. The percentage fees vary from about 6% to over 10% of PPD for the entire album. These rates are generally higher than those charged for mechanical reproduction in the United States and Canada.

The means by which the publishers get paid the mechanical royalties to which they are entitled is through a *claims* process — each local publisher registers with the collection society its claim to mechanical royalties with respect to each of its compositions, indicating its interest in the entire song or, in the case of split copyright ownership, its percentage interest in the composition. Subpublishers are often required to prove their claim by filing a copy of their subpublishing agreement with the collection society.

What happens when mechanical (or performance) royalties collected for a particular song are not claimed by any music publisher? Under the "Warsaw Rule," adopted by societies who are members of the Paris-based, *International Confederation of Societies of Authors and Composers* (CISAC), performance rights organizations will pay the entire share of performance fees to the appropriate society if they can identify at least one writer or publisher as a member of that society. Otherwise, unclaimed mechanical and performance moneys may go into what is referred to metaphorically as, a *black box*. In many countries, royalties that have not been claimed are maintained by the rights society for a specified period of time. Upon the expiration of that period, the black box moneys are paid to local publishing companies, which they may keep without any obligation to remit funds to the original publishers of the unclaimed songs. In some of these countries, the share of black box moneys paid to a local publisher is determined by dividing the amount of revenues received by the subpublisher from the society by the total revenues of the society. In other countries, the subpublisher's share is based upon seniority. Contractual terms and conditions relating to the disposition of black box moneys are discussed further below.

## D. Recent Developments in European Antitrust Law Affecting the Administration of Musical Works Distributed Digitally in Europe

Two important developments in European antitrust law threaten to change the face of international copyright administration, at least in Europe. Many of these changes have already been reflected in a variety of new alliances among some of the European rights societies and ground-breaking agreements by the large international publishers. This section will begin with an overview of just what the European Union has done, followed by an analysis of what this may mean for the administration of international rights in musical works.

### *1. 2005 Recommendation of the Competition Commission of the EU*

The European Union ("EU") was established to promote, among others things, the free flow of goods, services and people across all the member countries of the EU, reducing barrier to trade and employment opportunities, and promoting regulation and standards that facilitated trade among the member countries. For a number of years, the Competition Commission of the EU (i.e., the equivalent of the Antitrust Division of the U.S. Department of Justice) looked askance at the way mechanical rights collection societies operated. Each society has maintained strict rules on membership, generally restricting membership to those songwriters and music published domiciled in the country in which the society administers mechanical rights. In addition, these restrictions were enforced through a complex set of the bilateral agreements among the societies, facilitated by their mutual association with CISAC, a society of such societies.

On October 12, 2005, the Competition Commission adopted a recommendation on the management of online rights in musical works ("Recommendation"). (See IP/05/1261.) The Recommendation was intended to improve the European-wide licensing of musical works for online services. These improvements were deemed necessary, because new Internet-based services, such as on-demand music downloads and webcasting, need a license that covers their activities throughout the European Union. The absence of EU-wide copyright licenses, the Commission believed, was one factor that has made it difficult for new Internet-based music services to develop their full potential.

In order to improve EU-wide online licensing of music, the Commission considered three options:

**Option 1**: Do nothing (i.e., maintain the *status quo*);

**Option 2**: Improve cooperation among collecting societies allowing each society in the EU to grant a EU-wide license covering the other societies' repertoires; or

**Option 3**: Give music publishers the choice to appoint a single collection society to license and administer all the online uses of their musical works across the entire EU ("EU-wide direct licensing").

Stakeholders were consulted on the three options in July 2005 (see IP/05/872). Eighty-five stakeholders, from music publishers, mechanical reproduction collection societies, and online music services, submitted their opinions on the three options. There was broad consensus that Option 1 is not an option. Stakeholders were divided between Options 2 and 3, with online music services favoring Option 2, the majority of collection societies favoring modified versions of

Option 2, and the music publisher community, independent record labels, and certain collective rights managers favoring Option 3.

After analyzing the different options and stakeholders' comments, the Commission recommended Option 3. The Recommendation therefore proposed the elimination of territorial restrictions (in agreements among societies or between the societies and users) while leaving music publishers the right to tender their repertoire to a single society for EU-wide direct licensing.

Thus, a music publisher could appoint MCPS (now known as PRS for Music), traditionally the collection society that administers mechanical reproductions solely in the United Kingdom, to license all online uses wherever they may be initiated in Europe. (Note, the Recommendation only applied to the administration of mechanical rights with respect to online uses, not traditional or physical manufacturing and distribution. The Commission already had been involved with guidelines on *central licensing*, which protects the ability of a record company to manufacture CDs in one member country for shipment into other member countries.)

The Recommendation also included provisions on governance, transparency, dispute settlement and accountability of collective rights managers, which should introduce a culture of transparency and good governance enabling all relevant stakeholders to make an informed decision as to the licensing model best suited to their needs.

The Commission concluded that Option 3 offered the most effective long-term model for cross-border licensing of copyright-protected content in the online environment and cross-border distribution of online royalties. With respect to cross-border licensing, the music publisher's ability to choose one single collection society to license the various online uses made of its works across the EU would create an EU-wide license for his works. With respect to cross-border distribution of online royalties, the right-holders freedom to choose any collecting society in the EU (i.e., competition among societies for the rights to represent music publishers) will be a powerful incentive for collecting societies to provide optimal services to all its right-holders, irrespective of their location — thereby enhancing cross-border royalty payments.

In pursuing Option 3 as the long-term rights management model for cross-border copyright exploitation, the Commission determined that

EU action would not be based on detailed micro-regulation but would set forth a series of core principles, including the following:

- The right-holder's choice as to the online management society is based on the freedom to provide rights management services directly across borders. The freedom to provide cross-border management services by means of direct membership contracts will eliminate administrative costs inherent in channeling non-domestic right-holders' royalties through reciprocal agreements between different societies.
- The principle that a right-holders' choice of a single EU rights manager should be exercised irrespective of residence or nationality of either the rights-manager or the right-holder.
- The principle that a collecting society's online repertoire and territorial licensing power would not derive from reciprocal agreements but from right-holders concluding contractual agreements directly with a society of their choice. Right-holders should be able to withdraw online rights from their national CRMs and transfer their administration to a single rights manager of their choice. For that to work, these online rights must be withdrawn from the scope of reciprocal agreements as well.
- The principle that the individual membership contract will allow the right-holder to define precisely the categories of rights administered and the territorial scope of the society's authority. As the licensing authority would derive from the individual membership contract, the collective rights manager of choice would not be limited to managing these rights in his home territory only, but rather could manage them throughout the EU.
- Individual membership contracts create a fiduciary duty between the collecting society and its members, obliging the former to distribute royalties in an equitable manner. The principle of equitable distribution obliges CRMs to treat domestic and non-domestic members alike with respect to all elements of the management service provided. The fiduciary duty enshrined in membership contracts is thus a tool to maximize the royalties that accrue to right-holders.

- Membership cannot be refused to individual categories of right-holders who represent mainly non-domestic interests (e.g., music publishers). In addition, these right-holders should have a voice in how royalties are distributed that is commensurate with the economic value of the rights they contribute to the CRMs repertoire.
- Non-discrimination as to the service provided and the fiduciary duty of the collective rights manager vis-à-vis its members introduces a culture of transparency and good governance as to how rights are collectively managed across EU borders.

In a press release announcing the Recommendation, Charlie McCreevy, the Internal Market and Services Commissioner of the Competition Commission stated: "Today we have made workable proposals on how licensing of musical work for the Internet can be improved. I want to foster a climate where EU-wide licenses are more readily available for legitimate online music service providers. These licenses will make it easier for new European-based online services to take off. I believe that this recommendation strikes the right balance between ease of licensing and maintaining the value of copyright protected works so that content is not available on the cheap. In the interests of better regulation, for the time being and as a first step, I am making a recommendation as to how the market should develop. I will be monitoring the situation closely and, if I am not satisfied that sufficient progress is being made, I will take tougher action."

### *2. CISAC Decision of 2008*

As important as the EU's 2005 Recommendation was in bringing about change in the administration of musical works online, the practical effect was limited. The problem was that online music services required more than just a mechanical license to engage in downloading; they also required a license from the European performance rights societies — which administer on behalf of their member music publishers both performance rights and *communication rights* (i.e., the exclusive right under copyrights to communicate a musical work to the public).

Even though the mechanical collection societies could not restrict music publishers from granting pan-European licenses for mechanical reproductions, the performance rights societies could. But in a remarkable ruling dated July 16, 2008 (the "CISAC Decision"), the EU severely limited the member and territorial restrictions that the European performance rights societies have relied on for so long.

It all began in November 2000 when RTL, a large producer of television programming and broadcast facilities in Europe, filed a complaint with the EU against GEMA (i.e., the German mechanical reproduction and performance rights society). This was soon followed by a related complaint filed by Music Choice, a digital audio broadcaster, against CISAC (i.e., the meta-society to which all other European and other performance and collection societies are members).

As discussed at length in Chapter 18, on *Licensing Music in Live and Recorded Public Performances*, songwriters and music publishers grant to their local performance rights society (in the United States, ASCAP, BMI, or SESAC) the right to issue licenses to those (e.g., restaurants, nightclubs, radio and television stations, etc.) who wish to engage in the public performance of copyrighted musical works (either by live performance or the transmission of recorded performances). The society will typically issue a blanket license to each entity who wishes to make public performance of any or all of the songs in the society's repertoire. The society's repertoire includes all songs of its songwriter and music publisher members, plus those songs licensed from other performance rights societies based in other countries.

Thus, the performance rights society in each country (e.g., ASCAP in the United States, PRS in the United Kingdom, SOCAN in Canada, GEMA in Germany, SACEM in France, JASRAC in Japan, etc.) are able to collect royalties for performances of their works outside their respective countries by co-operating with their foreign counterparts. This cooperation takes the form of a network of *reciprocal representation agreements* — an agreement between two collecting societies under which the societies give each other the right to grant licenses for any public performance of musical works of their respective music publishing and songwriter members. In 1936, CISAC created a model for such reciprocal agreements, which virtually all the societies have since adopted with little substantive modification.

The focus of the EU's anti-competition inquiry focused on two provisions of these reciprocal representation agreements: (1) the membership clauses and (2) the territorial restrictions.

*Membership Clause*. Each reciprocal agreement provides:

> While this contract is in force neither of the contracting Societies may, without the consent of the other, accept as a member any member of the other society or any natural person, firm or company having the nationality of one of the countries in which the other Society operates.

In other words, a performance right society cannot accept members having the nationality of a country in which another performance right society operates. Put another way, the membership restriction obliges authors and publishers to use only their own national performance rights society.

Thus, for example, if you are a music publisher or songwriter based in the United States, you cannot join PRS (i.e., the U.K. performance right society), because PRS has agreed with ASCAP, BMI and SESAC (i.e., the U.S. performance rights societies) not to sign as members any U.S. music publisher or songwriter. To join PRS, a U.S. publisher would have to establish a legal entity under the laws of the United Kingdom and provide that entity with the rights necessary to grant PRS the means to administer the performance rights in the publisher's catalog. Individual songwriters who are citizens of the United States would not be able to become a writer member of an overseas society at all.

While this is no practical obstacle for music publishers owned by multinational conglomerates or large independent music publishers who already have offices in many countries, smaller U.S. publishers and administrators rarely have the financial means to establish independent entities around the world, which carry with them substantial legal and accounting requirements to maintain them.

*Territorial Clause*. Each reciprocal agreement lists the territory in which the performance rights society operates and provides:

> For the duration of the present contract, each of the contracting Societies shall refrain from any intervention within the territory of the other Society in the latter's exercise of the mandate conferred by the present contract.

In other words, each performance rights society agrees not to license public performance licenses to users outside their own territory.

In addition, under the reciprocal agreements, each society authorized the other to administer its repertoire in a given territory on an exclusive basis. The result of these provisions has been a practice among all performance rights societies to only license performance licenses respecting the territory they represent and to no others.

The effect on commercial users such as RTL and Music Choice, who each wished to offer a pan-European media service, was that they could not receive a license that covers more than one country in the EU, but rather had to negotiate with each individual national performance rights society for the rights to make public performances in each member country of the European Union. RTL and Music Choice wished to reduce their transaction costs, achieve some consistency in the performance royalty rates they would have to pay for their respective pan-European services, and perhaps benefit from a reduced royalty rate arising from the increased efficiencies at the society level of only one society having to issue and administer a single license (thereby reducing their costs of administration).

*CISAC Decision.* On July 16, 2008, the European Commission on Competition ruled the membership clauses and the territorial clauses are violations of the antitrust laws of the European Union (i.e., Article 81 of the EC Treaty and Article 53 of the EEA Agreement). The decision required that the performance rights societies end these violations by modifying their agreements and practices. The removal of these restrictions were specifically intended to "allow authors and publishers to choose which society manages their copyright on the basis of quality of service, efficiency of collection and the level of administration fees to be deducted." It was also intended to "make it easier for users to obtain licenses for the broadcasting of music over the Internet, by cable and by satellite in several countries from a single collection society."

The decision was addressed to 24 of the performance rights societies operating in the European Union:

AEPI (Greece)
AKKA-LAA (Latvia)
AKM (Austria)
ARTISJUS (Hungry)
BUMA (Netherlands)
EAU (Estonia)
GEMA (Germany)
IMRO (Ireland)
KODA (Denmark)
LATGA-A (Lithuania)
PRS (United Kingdom)
OSA (Czech Republic)

| | |
|---|---|
| SABAM (Belgium) | SPA (Portugal) |
| SACEM (France) | STEF (Iceland) |
| SAZAS (Slovenia) | STIM (Sweden) |
| SGAE (Spain) | TEOSTO (Finland) |
| SIAE (Italy) | TONO (Norway) |
| SOZA (Slovakia) | ZAIKAS (Poland) |

The decision would not only hold illegal the membership and territorial restrictions contained in reciprocal agreements entered into between the foregoing societies, but also in reciprocal agreements between any of the EU societies and any other non-EU society (e.g., ASCAP, JASRAC, SOCAN). The performance rights societies of Bulgaria and Romania were not addressed, as their respective countries were not part of the EU when the action was commenced. CISAC was also not directly addressed, as the organization had removed the offending clauses from its model contract during the course of the proceeding. Those clauses remained, however, in the actual reciprocal agreements in place among the societies.

### *3. Implications of the EU's 2005 Recommendation and the 2008 CISAC Decision*

The implications of the EU's 2005 Recommendation, combined with the 2008 CISAC Decision, has been far reaching — at least within Europe. They differ greatly, however, depending upon who you are: music publisher (original publisher or subpublisher), collection or performance society, or online music service.

#### *a. Music Publishers*

The implications of the EU's antitrust initiatives on music publishers, and the songwriters who they represent, is, from their perspective, very positive. As noted above, the effect of the EU's antitrust initiative is to bring about competition among collection and performance rights societies by allowing music publishers the right to choose from among the societies, or others, who shall have the right to license their repertoire to online music services and administer the collection and distribution of funds arising from such licenses. With societies having to compete for the rights to represent repertoires of large and small publishers, the result should be lower administration costs, more accurate and efficient reporting, and greater transparency — all currently the source of complaints that music publishers have about how their catalogs are administered by the societies.

Almost as soon as the EU's position on the collection societies became clear, the major music publishers not only reassessed their position with the collection societies, but also began taking actions that portend to change the face of music publishing in Europe. As of the time of this writing in 2009, all four major publishers have withdrawn (or partially withdrawn) their exclusive digital distribution rights from the European societies and reassigned them to other societies or joint venture entities.

EMI Music has granted on an exclusive basis the right to sublicense its Anglo-American works for digital purposes on a pan-European basis to CELAS, a joint venture among EMI, PRS for Music (U.K. society), and the GEMA (German society). EMI's intention was that other major publishers would join them in the venture, which would provide the "one-stop shop" for which European licensees of digital rights have been craving. But this did not happen. Each of the other major publishers has formed their pan-European licensing joint venture. Sony/ATV has, with GEMA, formed PAECOL; Universal has joined with SACEM (France) to form DEAL (for "Digital European Administration and Licensing"). Warner/Chappell has tried something a little different: joining forces with each of PRS for Music, SACEM, STIM (Sweden), and BUMA/SEMRA (Netherlands) to offer its own Anglo-American repertoire on a non-exclusive, pan-European basis through any of those partners, but under a venture called, PEDL ("Pan European Digital Licensing"). Peer Music, the largest independent music publisher, has chosen to provide its Anglo-American catalog for pan-European digital licensing to PRS for Music, and its Hispanic catalog to SGAE (Spain).

### *b. Mechanical Collection and Performance Rights Societies*

No matter how much capitalists may praise its benefits, competition is not something that any individual businessman really welcomes. Mechanical collection and performance rights societies in Europe are no exception. By virtue of the labyrinth of intramural agreements in place for decades — now declared illegal by the EU — the societies have enjoyed virtual monopolies in their respective countries. Now, the EU edicts that force these societies to compete for the affections of music publishers and songwriters are as despised by the societies as much as they are welcomed by those who the societies purpose to represent.

Though the societies will be the last to admit that their administration fees are high, their reporting is inaccurate or inefficient, and their operations opaque, only competition will truly reveal the truth on these matters. Competition will certainly force each society to devote more of their respective resources on each of these matters.

Societies who fail to satisfy their clients are destined to lose music publishers to competing societies, or joint ventures or new forms of rights administrators, who can prove they are providing better services more efficiently. The societies as a group may even find themselves confronted by new entrants into the field who are focused on better solutions to problems of efficiency, accuracy, and transparency. Advanced forms of IT services are certain to play a role in solving these problems, as much of what societies do in the online realm concerns the data processing of billions of small transactions from a relatively small number of online services. This is a rather different problem traditionally faced by the societies.

This is not to say that each society needs to build advanced IT services that meet the needs of their music publisher clients in order to survive. Like any business, a society is faced with a classic business decision: build, buy, or outsource. A small society, for example, may well find it economical to outsource its IT needs to a professional IT service company specializing in the particular requirements of music publishing revenue and royalty management. Companies like RoyaltyShare come to mind.

To the extent such outsourced IT services can be procured on a fee structure based upon percentage or revenue managed, smaller societies will be on a level playing field with the larger ones, as they will have access to the same state-of-the-art back office services as the larger societies, with no fixed cost of maintenance. By this means, the smaller societies can compete on the value-added services they've always provided: high service levels in the representation of local music publishers and songwriters in their territory.

The ability of the societies to provide monetary support for music-related cultural activities in their respective territories will be a function of the tolerance that their music publishing and songwriter members have for the reduced copyright royalties they would endure to support such activities. An argument can be made that community-supported cultural activity, to the extent that is a worthy goal, should be funded at the governmental level, so that all the citizens in the society who benefit from the activities are financing it, rather than just the individual publishers and songwriters.

The societies have asserted that it is the monopoly they have enjoyed that has resulted in higher music performance and mechanical royalties — often pointing to the higher fees they collect on behalf of their publishers and songwriters relative to the fees collected in the United States, which operates in a more competitive environment. These higher collections help finance the higher administration fees, which are, in turn, used to finance these cultural activities. Therefore, they say, the public at large (and not their members) is, at the end of the day, financing these cultural activities. But the monopolistic practices of the societies would seem to be a most opaque way of taxing the public to fund cultural activities; higher overall collections, resulting in part from higher negotiated rates, is not an excuse for inefficiency and lack of transparency in reporting.

It is too early to determine the effect of the actions taken by the four major music publishers and Peer Music, but we will begin to see clues when the terms of these deals expire and the publishers choose to renew these relationships, refine them, or look for better alternatives.

### *c. Online Music Services*

From the start, the online music services have been frustrated with the daunting task of identifying all rights and rightsholders from whom they need to acquire the licenses necessary to engage in their online music delivery activities. Because of the worldwide nature of the Internet, with no real territorial boundaries, online music services need, as a practical matter, to clear worldwide rights. But, traditionally, the music industry has been divided by territory, as reflected partly by the fact that there is a separate collection and performance society in virtually every important commercial country in the world, each claiming some monopoly over licensing activity in their individual territorial domain. Then, they must cope with the fact that they need to clear both a mechanical license and a performance (or communications) license for their activities and the entity from whom they must clear each license in each country may be different and often operate on a completely different rate structure and set of administrative procedures for monitoring and collection of royalties.

It is no surprise, therefore, that the online services have pushed for one of two kinds of models: (1) the model used in the United States for licensing permanent downloads, the *pass-through license* (discussed at length in Chapter 13, on *Licensing Music in Sound Recordings*) or (2) a *one-stop shop* where they can obtain all the mechanical and performance (or communication) licenses they need from all music publishers in a country, continent or, ideally, the world.

Although Steve Jobs of Apple Computer has purportedly told the EU that he prefers the pass-through license model, the fact is that the United States is the only country in the world which employs it. In fact, the pass-through license is far more likely to be eliminated in the United States than it is to be accepted anywhere else.

The model presented by Option 3, however, would seem to make the *one-stop shop* model less likely. With each music publisher having the freedom to choose which society gets to license its catalog on a pan-European basis, an online service like iTunes would need to obtain a license (for both mechanical reproduction and communication) from each of the societies in Europe to guarantee that it has an appropriate license for all musical works it delivers online in the EU.

In fact, the situation has become worse than that. As a result of the joint ventures established by the major publishers, an online music service must now negotiate with and obtain separate licenses from not only each society in Europe, but from each of the joint ventures as well.

However, a 24-stop, or 30-stop, shop is far better than a 100,000-stop shop (an alternative where a license would have to be cleared from each music publisher — a current requirement in the United States if you were engaging in on-demand streams and limited downloads). See Chapter 13, on *Licensing Music in Sound Recordings*. Nevertheless, the increased complexity in obtaining the licenses necessary to establish a new online music service may serve as a substantial barrier to entry in favor of the large existing services.

While the competition among societies is likely to reduce the administration fees they charge (as a percentage of revenue collected) to the music publishers and songwriters they represent, the reduction in those fees is not likely to inure to the benefit of the online services. Ironically, the entire EU inquiry of CISAC's anti-competitive practices was kicked off by a complaint by European television conglomerate, RTL, which sought changes in CISAC's practices on the basis that if those practices were changed, the societies' administration fees would be reduced and such reductions would be passed along to the music users, such as RTL, in the form of lower license fees.

Lower license fees are strictly a function of the rates negotiated between the music owners and licensees, or as established by arbitration or government edict. The administration fees associated with engaging in rate setting activities, collection, and distribution of funds is a function of the music publishers and songwriter's ability to negotiate those fees with the societies. Since the societies restricted, by contract, the ability of publishers and songwriter's to choose the society who represents them in each country in Europe, they had no leverage with which to negotiate lower administration fees. With the EU's 2005 Recommendation and the CISAC Decision, now they do.

Unless some legislative action is taken in the European Parliament to save their monopolies, the societies will begin to face competition, either among themselves or new forms of ventures organized to provide better service to the music publishers. It remains to be seen whether this will result in a one-stop shop, a 24-stop shop or something more or in between. If experience is any guide, the likely outcome is something more than a one-stop shop and something less than a 24-stop shop. Certainly, a 15-stop shop is not likely to be prohibitively burdensome to the online services, especially if data processing standards (e.g., DDEX) continue to be developed to ease the burden of reporting to multiple entities.

What the online services really require is not a one-stop shop, but a one-stop tariff, or rate setting regime for all of Europe (or the world) for the various types of deliveries they wish to make of recordings that contain copyrighted musical works — what has been called, *multi-territory licensing* for online content. In June 2009, unhappy with the fact that consumers remain in the habit of country-shopping for digital content — seeking rates that are lower than those provided by local services — the EU issued an "eYouGuide" designed to encourage the collection societies to provide a multi-territory licensing regime. The gist of the guide was the call for the removal of borders between the 27 EU countries in the offering of online services.

However European rates for the use of music by online services are set, the rate setting process should be open, fair, and easy to implement. It should also protect the services from costly copyright infringement lawsuits for delivering musical works that somehow insinuated itself onto an online music service (e.g., new songs, songs included in user-generated works, such as YouTube videos) without a proper set of licenses. Finally, it should include a mechanism that assures music rights holders of transparency — that the online services are accurately tracking uses and reporting them properly. This may require that the online services submit themselves to real-time tracking of transactions and generation of usage reports through some technical means, but it would greatly reduce auditing costs that are traditionally high — in both the management time they absorb and the legal expenses they cause when disputes become irreconcilable.

#### *d. Subpublishers*

When in 2005 the EU issued its Recommendation of Option 3 — which allowed music publishers to entrust the management of any of their online rights to their catalogs on a territorial scope of their choice, to a collection society of their choice, regardless of the nationality of either the music publisher or the collection society, the traditional structure of international rights management changed forever. The CISAC Decision, which reinforced the EU's position — felling the network of reciprocal bilateral agreements that restricted membership in the respective European performance societies to those publishers located in each society's national borders — has removed perhaps the last obstacle to systematic change in the licensing of musical works in Europe.

With music publishers now enabled to become direct members of any society in Europe, the structure of original music publishers working with local subpublishers in each European country may soon be replaced by a pan-European licensing model that bypasses the old subpublisher network. It is estimated that, in each European country, non-local catalogs represent over 40% of recorded music sales. Without the lucrative share of this revenue that European subpublishers have traditionally collected for representing foreign catalogs, subpublishers may find themselves with businesses that are no longer viable.

Accordingly, music publishers whose primary function has been to serve as subpublishers for foreign original publishers may soon either shut their doors or find themselves relegated to providing a narrow set of services, such as song-plugging, promotion, or other local marketing services. How they will be compensated for these services is up in the air.

## II. SELECTING A SUBPUBLISHER

The selection of an individual subpublisher will depend upon the nature of the overall subpublishing administration you are seeking worldwide. Determining the kind of international publishing regime that is appropriate for you is a function of five basic factors:

A. Whether you are seeking worldwide representation by the minimum number of publishers possible or by several publishers on a territory-by-territory basis,

B. Whether you are seeking to augment the publishing revenue potential of the compositions through the promotional activities of local professional staffs or you are seeking the most efficient administration of international royalty collection,

C. Whether you are seeking representation of an entire catalog of songs or the representation of your catalog on a song-by-song basis,

D. Whether you are seeking a reciprocal relationship with a subpublisher, and

E. Whether you want to engage a subpublisher at all,

F. Whether you have the ability to become your own subpublisher.

### A. Worldwide or Territory-by-Territory Representation

The first factor to consider in establishing proper representation of your compositions overseas is whether you wish to be represented by the minimum number of publishers possible or by several publishers on a territory-by-territory basis.

Spreading your publishing rights among subpublishers on a territory-by-territory basis may put you in a better position to maximize worldwide publishing income. The territory-by-territory approach allows you to select the best publisher in each region for your particular song or catalog. If one of your objectives is to receive a substantial advance against royalties, the territory-by-territory approach allows you to pit a greater number of bidders against each other, increasing your chances of obtaining the maximum advance that the circumstances and your bargaining leverage would allow. Moreover, an advance received from a subpublisher in one country will not be cross-collateralized with an advance received from another. Where you choose a single subpublisher to represent you worldwide or in many territories, the advance you receive will be recoupable from royalties earned in all covered territories unless you have the negotiating leverage to eliminate the cross-collateralization of your advance.

In addition, by entering into subpublishing deals on a territory-by-territory basis, an original publisher can avoid putting all of its "eggs in one basket," avoiding the risk of choosing one publisher who fails to meet your objectives. Similarly, if a worldwide publisher is performing poorly in one or two territories, but doing well in all others, it may be difficult to extricate the poorly performing territories from the worldwide subpublishing deal. By contrast, when deals are done on a territory-by-territory basis, if an original publisher is disappointed with the performance of a particular subpublisher, he can more easily make the necessary adjustment when the term of the agreement for that territory expires.

The territory-by-territory approach, however, carries with it significantly greater transaction costs. Obviously, this approach requires that a separate subpublishing agreement be negotiated with each and every subpublisher. The attorneys' fees alone could be a significant deterrent to this approach, especially if the original publisher has little experience in negotiating international publishing contracts. The original publisher must also consider the long distance telephone and overseas courier charges that will necessarily be incurred in conferring with the subpublishers, not only in negotiating the agreements, but also in communicating to them from time to time the information they will need to properly represent its interests. Though electronic mail and facsimile transmissions are replacing the need for many face-to-face meetings, language and cultural differences still require telephone conversations to maintain good communications. Nevertheless, telephone conversations require that each correspondent be available at the same time. In this regard, an original publisher should not underestimate the inconvenience caused by the significant differences in time zones, between both the United States and Europe, and the United States and the Far East.

By contrast with territory-by-territory representation, which has significantly high transaction costs associated with it, using a single music publisher for all territories worldwide, or all territories outside the United States, has the benefit of a single point of contact. Should any problems arise in a particular country, you can discuss it with your major publisher's international department located in the United States.

An original publisher should also consider the advantages of a single multi-national subpublisher in the area of song promotion. A multi-national subpublisher is often in a better position to conduct song promotion on a coordinated worldwide basis. For example, if a song becomes popular in one territory, the professional department of the multi-national subpublisher in that territory will often call the song to the attention of its professional departments located in other territories. It may be that the original publisher's catalog will only be a small portion of the hundreds of thousands of compositions represented by the major publisher, but an original publisher using a major worldwide publisher can improve the visibility of his catalog overseas by developing relationships, and communicate directly, with the major publisher's subsidiaries and affiliated subpublishers.

Emerging as perhaps the most important factor in whether to use a single subpublisher or multiple subpublishers is whether the entity representing your interests overseas is prepared to handle the administration of digital and mobile uses on a worldwide basis. The changes referred to earlier in this chapter — as to rapidly evolving roles of collection and performance rights societies, including competition among them, new organizations emerging to compete with them, and the ability of publishers to issue pan-European licenses — should also be considered. It is too early to tell which organizations will emerge as the best solution providers for original publishers.

An original publisher should also consider the significantly lower cost of adjudicating a dispute with a single major U.S. publisher representing its worldwide interests. If an irreconcilable dispute should arise anywhere in the world, the original publisher can file suit in the United States, even with respect to disputes relating to the U.S. publisher's overseas affiliate. As expensive as that may be, filing suit in the United States will be considerably less expensive than suing a subpublisher in his own local territory.

Often, the choice between using a single subpublisher or multiple subpublishers will depend upon the circumstances of the original publisher. If the original publisher is a busy recording artist, he may not have the time necessary to properly manage the territory-by-territory approach. He can allow his attorney to manage his subpublishing affairs, but the costs of using someone at high hourly rates may prove to be more expensive than it's worth. Alternatively, an artist who is at the height of his recording career might consider granting rights to a single subpublisher, and when the artist reaches a point at which he has more time to devote to his international publishing affairs, he can revise his worldwide subpublishing structure at that time.

Finally, anyone who chooses to manage his own international publishing by granting rights on a territory-by-territory basis should consider what has been said about market size: The top ten markets account for nearly 90% of music publishing revenues. This would suggest that a publisher considering territory-by-territory deals, should focus most of his time and resources on those ten countries. These include: the United States, Germany, France, Japan, the United Kingdom, Italy, the Netherlands, Spain, the Nordic countries (including Denmark, Sweden, Norway, and Finland), and Belgium, with Austria, Argentina, and Canada, close behind.

Accordingly, the original publisher might license these countries on a territory-by-territory basis, perhaps also considering member countries of the European Union to be a single block, and use a single major international publisher for all other countries.

## B. Promotion or Administration

The reputations of international subpublishers vary with their respective talents for promoting the use of musical compositions and administering the collection of income in their local territories. If an original publisher is seeking to augment the publishing revenue potential of its catalog, it should seek those subpublishers who have local professional staffs with good working relationships with local record companies, motion picture and television producers, and advertising agencies. If an original publisher is seeking the most efficient collection of local royalties, it should seek those subpublishers with reputations for good administrative abilities.

Ideally, a subpublisher will have a talent for both promotion and administration, but the likelihood of finding a subpublisher ideally suited to promoting and administering your catalog in each territory around the world is remote. Compromises will inevitably be made and the best an original publisher can do is to build good working relationships with both the creative and administrative personnel of his subpublishers and keep itself informed of developments.

### C. Entire Catalog or Individual Songs

In addition, the nature of your worldwide subpublishing administration, and your choice of a particular subpublisher, will be affected by whether you are seeking representation of an entire catalog of songs or merely representation on a song-by-song basis. Because of the high transaction costs of having numerous subpublishers in various territories each representing different songs in an original publisher's catalog, a strategy of splitting international subpublishing rights on a per song basis is rarely advisable.

Nevertheless, circumstances can arise that may allure the inexperienced into establishing just such a structure. For example, a song that has topped the charts in the United States may quickly attract a number of international subpublishers seeking to represent the original publisher for the subpublishing of that one song. These deals will often involve offers of substantial advances, which may be hard for an original publisher to resist. If the original publisher already has relationships with satisfactory subpublishers covering various territories, one practical solution is for the original publisher to offer the song to his existing subpublishers, giving each of them a chance to match the advances being offered by the subpublisher's competitors. If, under these circumstances, the original publisher is only just beginning to establish its worldwide subpublishing program, he should carefully consider all the factors set forth above and in the pages that follow before adopting a song-by-song disposition of his subpublishing rights.

Occasionally, however, a small publisher will be fortunate enough to come up with that one successful song that would only have the potential of being acceptable in one particular country overseas. Such a situation did arise in my career when the manager of the German branch of European music publisher, Francis, Day & Hunter, Mr. Johann Michel (presently owner/general manager of Melodie der Welt GmbH, Frankfurt/Main, Germany) sent me a cable conveying to me his interest in the theme song from John Wayne's film, *The Green Berets*. The song, *The Ballad of the Green Berets* by Sergeant Barry Sadler, had that "oom-pa-pa, oom-pa-pa" feeling that Mr. Michel believed would make it a successful hit in Germany. On his behalf, I negotiated a subpublishing agreement with the American publisher of the song through its attorney, William Krasilovsky. The song did stay in the number one position in Germany for many weeks.

### D. Reciprocal Relationships

A fourth, albeit uncommon, factor, in determining the structure of your international music publishing administration is whether you are seeking reciprocal relationships with subpublishers. In other words, an original publisher may seek to serve as the U.S. subpublishing representative for overseas catalogs that might be appropriate for the U.S. market. Under certain circumstances, the original publisher may find it advantageous to enter into subpublishing agreements with those international publishers willing to assign their U.S. subpublishing rights to the original publisher.

For London-based publishing firm Francis, Day & Hunter, Ltd., Mr. Fred Day effected very satisfactory long-term subpublishing arrangements with many American publishing firms, including Leo Feist Company and Robbins Music Corp. During the 1960, I served as U.S. representative for Francis, Day & Hunter and their affiliates throughout the world. With an office in New York provided by the Robbins-Feist-Miller music publishing companies, I not only acquired U.S. copyrights for Francis, Day & Hunter, but I was in a position to place overseas copyrights with the Robbins-Feist-Miller companies.

In this regard, in my travels abroad, I was successful in placing with The Big Three (as Robbins-Feist-Miller were called) such copyrights as *Volare, You Don't Have to Say You Love Me, The Last Waltz,* and countless others.

Though reciprocal subpublishing arrangements are not always practical, it should always remain an option for those original publishers seeking material that has hit potential in the United States.

## E. Doing Without a Subpublisher

An original publisher is not required to have a subpublisher in a territory in order to collect music publishing income generated from its catalog in that territory. If the original publisher has not appointed a subpublisher in a territory to collect its share of performance income from the local performance rights society, the performance rights society will pay the publisher's share over to the publisher's U.S. performance rights society (e.g., ASCAP or BMI), which will then pay it over to the publisher. Further, if there is no subpublisher in a territory to collect mechanical royalty income from the local mechanical rights collection society, the collection society will, if instructed, pay the publisher's mechanical royalty income from the territory over to the Harry Fox Agency in the United States, which will then remit it to the original publisher. The Harry Fox Agency has established relationships with over 23 mechanical collection societies operating in about 100 countries throughout the world for this purpose.

If this is the case, then why does one need a subpublisher? An original publisher may rely on its performance rights society to collect overseas performance income and, if it is affiliated with the Harry Fox Agency, the publisher can rely on the Agency's international relationships for the collection of its international mechanical licensing income, but the original publisher should consider that by doing so it may be foregoing many of the benefits of having a subpublisher. For some, a key benefit is simply having someone in the territory watching out for your interests. For others, having a subpublisher means having an opportunity to obtain advances against royalties and to having a local representative promote the generation of new income through local cover recordings, local performances, and local translated printed editions. If the original publisher's songwriters are also recording artists, it can be a nice touch to have a local subpublisher take out the songwriters to dinner when they are on tour overseas.

While performance rights societies claim to do a good job of collecting overseas income, some publishers claim to have experienced substantial delays in the collection of overseas income when relying solely on their performance rights society. Whether these delays are myth or reality, an original publisher will not get its fair share of international publishing income if its compositions are not being properly registered with the local performance rights and collections societies. Accordingly, to avoid any potential for delay, and to assure that it is getting its proper share of overseas income, an original publisher should appoint a subpublisher to register its compositions with the local societies and collect the performance income on behalf of the original publisher.

### F. Becoming Your Own Subpublisher

A close corollary to doing without a subpublisher is to become your own subpublisher. In the late 1990, a very innovative music publishing executive at a music publisher located in Nashville, Tennessee, tried something that no one else had seemingly tried before: Dan Ekback, a Swedish-born music publishing executive working for Bluewater Music Publishing came to the conclusion that their subpublishers in Europe were really not engaging in the added-value, creative work that would justify the subpublishing fees that were being charged to them at the time. As Ekback was quoted in Billboard magazine (January 15, 2000), "We were interested in increasing the NPS, or net publisher's share, for the original publisher. We looked at how to increase the NPS and decided to just join the societies directly. So, we have done so and are bypassing the subpublishers."

Bluewater Music, which represents writers such as Kim Richey, Jim Lauderdale, and Fred Eaglesmith, with hits recorded by the likes of George Strait and Patty Loveless, succeeded in affiliating directly with GEMA (Germany/Austria/Switzerland), BUMA/STEMRA (Netherlands), STIM/Nordisk Copyright Bureau (Sweden, Norway, Denmark, Finland and Iceland), MCPS/PRS (United Kingdom) and SOCAN/CMRRA (Canada). Speaking in early 2000, Dan said, "With today's technology, you can easily be based in Nashville and communicate directly with all the societies. Additionally, we travel to the territories and visit each society regularly. So, we're collecting directly from the societies, which means we get the money faster. In effect, we are acting as our own subpublisher in each territory. It works the same as if we had an office in each country."

As to pitching the songs locally, Ekback said that bypassing subpublishers would not hurt Bluewater's chances of getting cover songs in each territory, because (1) Bluewater pitches directly in each territory from its own database of artists, and (2) it gets most cover versions after the original version is played elsewhere.

## III. NEGOTIATING THE SUBPUBLISHING AGREEMENT

### A. Introduction

As discussed above, the choice of an international subpublisher will depend upon whether you desire worldwide representation by one publisher for all your international publishing needs, or several publishers on a territory-by-territory basis, whether you are placing a higher value on effective promotion or efficient administration, whether you have a single song or an entire catalog to offer, or you are splitting off your digital rights for pan-European subpublishing or self-subpublishing administration. To those factors you must add the specific deal points you are likely to be offered for the subpublishing rights, including the potential advances obtainable, the term or duration of the agreement, and the subpublisher fee charged for the international representation, among others.

These latter provisions are all subject to negotiation and will be discussed in this section. It may be well to remember that music publishing is a business of personal relationships, and perhaps the best way to assure that your subpublishing objectives are met is to actually arrange to meet face-to-face those with whom you expect to sign an agreement. Many of these face-to-face meetings can be achieved economically by attending the annual MIDEM music conference held in January of each year in Cannes, France. If even this is impractical for you, then it may serve you well to rely on long-standing relationships established by others, including those of a multi-national major music publisher.

On the accompanying CD-ROM are three different subpublishing agreement forms that are typical of those used by original publishers and subpublishers. Form 5.1 is a form that might commonly be used for the subpublishing of an original publisher's catalog in a single territory or group of related territories. Forms 5.2 and 5.3 each might be used by a major multi-national publisher to represent a U.S. original publisher in all territories outside the United States and Canada. The analysis in the following pages includes a review of only the business provisions of the first form, which is broad enough to illustrate nearly all the salient terms of standard subpublishing agreements.

Subpublishing agreements are very similar in nature to administration agreements. For this reason, concepts covered at length in the previous chapter, as well as those covered in Chapter 3, on *Songwriter Agreements* and Chapter 10, on *Basic Considerations in Music Licensing*, will be repeated here only where the context requires.

## B. Appointment of Subpublisher

The specific language used to engage the services of a subpublisher varies across a variety of form agreements that have been used by original publishers and subpublishers. The following provision, recommended for use by original publishers, effects the appointment of the subpublisher to serve the interests of the original publisher's catalog in a particular territory:

> Subject to the terms and conditions herein, Owner hereby appoints Subpublisher as its exclusive administrator of the Compositions throughout the Territory. Except as specifically set forth herein, all right, title and interest in and to the copyrights in the Compositions are hereby reserved by Owner.

This form of engagement avoids language that may be construed as granting to the subpublisher any of the copyrights in the compositions. Subpublishing agreements that use assignment language (e.g., "Owner hereby assigns to Subpublisher.") should be avoided. An alternative form of engagement is where the "Owner grants to Subpublisher the exclusive rights to act as administrator in the Territory of the rights in and to the Compositions." This construction would be preferred by original publishers over "Owner grants to Subpublisher the exclusive rights in and to the Compositions in the Territory . . . ," which may be construed as granting actual rights under the copyrights in the composition, rather than merely the right to administer the rights.

The difference between appointing an exclusive administrator (or granting exclusive rights to administer rights) and granting copyright rights, is important, as in certain countries, copyright owners, or those who first register copyrights in certain countries under their own name, may gain rights in the compositions that extend beyond the term of the subpublishing agreement.

## C. Compositions Covered

A subpublishing agreement may cover a specific song or existing catalog of songs, a simple provision for which may read as follows:

> The term "Compositions," as used herein, shall mean those musical works set forth in the attached Schedule "A," which is made a part of this agreement.

New compositions may be added to Schedule A by a simple amendment to the agreement. Where it is contemplated that many songs will be added to the agreement during the term, a more sophisticated definition of Compositions may be preferred:

> The term "Compositions," as used herein, shall mean each musical composition owned or controlled by Owner and presently uncommitted for the Territory and each musical composition the ownership or control of which shall be acquired by Owner during the term of this agreement in the ordinary course of business (excluding any so-called "catalog acquisitions") and which shall be uncommitted for the Territory at the time of acquisition.

The above provision would be used for a *catalog deal*, a subpublishing agreement under which the subpublisher will be representing in the territory the entire catalog of the original publisher — that is, (a) each song owned or controlled by the original publisher as of the effective date of the subpublishing agreement, and (b) each song that is later acquired by the original publisher during the term of the agreement, except "catalog acquisitions."

The exclusion of catalog acquisitions is intended to limit the songs automatically added to the subpublishing agreement to those songs acquired in the normal course of the business of the original publisher, and to exclude songs acquired by the original publisher as part of a catalog (e.g., such as when the original publisher acquires another publisher). Of course, the original publisher may always add acquired catalogs by a simple amendment to the subpublishing agreement; by withholding catalog acquisitions from the original deal, the original publisher could, in exchange for adding the acquired catalog to the existing subpublishing agreement, negotiate an additional advance, or other improved terms.

## D. Territory

Considerations of granting subpublishing rights on a territory-by-territory basis, as opposed to granting worldwide rights to a single publisher is discussed above. In the Third Edition of this book, published in 2002, we cautioned readers to consider the fact that digital transmission by streaming and download over the Internet portend to make territorial boundaries irrelevant and that careful consideration should be given to these emerging issues before granting exclusive territorial rights. The developments discussed earlier in this chapter — particularly the anti-competitive issues raised by the EU — should underscore the care that should be taken in entering into exclusive subpublishing relationships.

The territory covered by the agreement will either be set forth in the body of the contract or in a schedule attached to the agreement. This will generally be a list of countries. But, an original publisher considering the territory-by-territory approach must ask, "Which countries?" Is each country unique, requiring a separate subpublisher, or are some countries related in a way that would suggest that certain subpublishers be granted rights for more than one territory?

Though the subpublishing rights for many territories, such as Japan, are granted separately, many other countries are licensed as part of a related group. For example, if you are seeking to grant your subpublishing rights to a subpublisher in the *United Kingdom*, the subpublisher will also try to represent you in *the Republic of Ireland and South Africa.* The countries of *Germany, Austria, and Switzerland* are typically licensed together, as are *Belgium, the Netherlands, and Luxembourg* (or *Benelux*). Often *all member countries of the European Community* are licensed together. The countries of *Central America* (*including Panama*) are often licensed as a group, and the countries of *South America* (*excluding Brazil*) are also typically licensed together. The same is true for *Australia and New Zealand.* Because of the ambiguity of the terms, "English speaking territories" or "French speaking territories" (e.g., is Switzerland a French speaking country?), these terms should be avoided. However, it is not unusual for the territory to be defined as, *the country of France, its colonies, dominions and possessions, Monaco and all territories under the perception of SACEM.* Finally, it is always preferable to use the names of specific countries, rather than continents (e.g., the term, *Asia*, may or may not include the country of Russia).

It has been traditional to recognize that, from a creative perspective, Europe has been divided into two parts: The *English block*, consisting of the United Kingdom, the Nordic countries, and Holland; and the *Continental block*, consisting of Germany, Austria, France, Belgium, Switzerland, Italy, Spain, and Portugal. English-language recordings made in the United States were more likely to be successful in the English block countries, and local translations or adaptations were more likely to be necessary to extend the life of a song in the Continental countries. Nevertheless, as American entertainment has become more and more integrated with international culture, particularly as a result of satellite transmissions of U.S. television productions, the cultural and language boundaries between countries are becoming less important in the international marketing of music.

## E. Rights Covered

The subpublishing agreement will enumerate the rights covered by the agreement and any limitations on the subpublisher's rights to administer them. This section will sketch the basic considerations in negotiating the subpublishing of print rights, performance rights, mechanical and transcription rights, synchronization rights, videogram and other audiovisual rights, and those rights reserved to the original publisher.

### *1. Print Rights*

The following is typical of a grant of *print rights* in a standard subpublishing agreement:

> (i) The exclusive right to print, publish, vend, and cause to be printed, published and vended copies of Printed Music of the Compositions in the Territory.

In a world where an increasing amount of manufacturing and distribution is being conducted on a centralized basis, with many companies moving local reproduction facilities to centralized manufacturing and worldwide distribution operations in countries such as Ireland or Singapore, the exclusivity granted to the subpublisher in the above provision may cause significant problems for the original publisher. It would, in effect, allow the subpublisher, in many countries, to legally stop the importation of printed copies for sale within the territory. This may unnecessarily involve the original publisher in disputes arising from the normal activities of its distributors, and perhaps expose the original publisher to a claim of breach of contract. Accordingly, the original publisher should consider adding the following limitation on the subpublisher's exclusivity:

> provided, however, that Owner reserves to itself the right to ship or license the shipment into the Territory of printed music embodying Compositions manufactured by Owner or by its subsidiaries, affiliates or licensees outside of the Territory, and Publisher shall have no right to receive any portion of any sums received by Owner on account of such importation or licensing;

Thus, though the print rights provision is exclusive, the exclusivity is limited to copies made in the territory — that is, the original publisher is, in effect, merely agreeing not to grant to anyone other than the subpublisher the right to reproduce printed copies in the territory. Copies of printed music reproduced outside of the territory under the authority of the original publisher may be shipped into and sold within the subpublisher's territory without compensation to the subpublisher. In response, a subpublisher concerned about the bad faith circumvention of its exclusivity by the original publisher or its licensees, may insist that the limitation only be applied to copies made *in the United States* by the original publisher or its licensees.

In Chapter 12, on *Licensing Music in Print and Digital Print*, we explore the emerging market for digital print products, including downloadable sheet music, electronic guitar tablatures, and online lyrics. Because of the potential need to engage in worldwide or pan-territorial licensing of these trans-border goods, consideration should be given to excluding the digital distribution of musical notation and lyrics of any kind. One means may be to define carefully what is meant by Printed Music:

> The term "Printed Music," as that term is used herein, shall mean copies of each or any of the Compositions in printed form, whether copied, printed, lithographed, photo-offset, reproduced by xerography, by thermal processing, or by any other means of physical reproduction now known or hereafter devised, but not by digital means, such as digital sheet music, digital guitar tablatures, MIDI files, and the like.

### *2. Performance Rights*

The following is typical of a grant of *public performance rights* in a standard subpublishing agreement:

> (ii) The exclusive right of public performance of the Compositions, for profit or otherwise (including broadcasting and television), and of licensing such rights in and for the Territory;

*Writer's Share.* Recall from Chapter 3, on *Songwriter Agreements*, that the performance rights society pays the *writer's share* of performance royalties collected by the society directly to the songwriter. Where performance royalties are collected by performance rights societies overseas, such as PRS in England and SACEM in France, these societies pay the writer's share over to the writer's U.S. performance rights society, (i.e., ASCAP, BMI or SESAC), which in turn remits that share directly to the writer. Neither the subpublisher nor the original publisher is entitled to receive any portion of the writer's share.

*Publisher's Share.* Unless the original publisher appoints a subpublisher to collect the *publisher's share* from the local performance rights society in the subpublisher's territory, the performance rights society will pay the publisher's share over to the publisher's U.S. performance rights society, which will then pay it over to the publisher.

As mentioned above, however, an original publisher may consider the benefits of appointing a subpublisher to register its compositions with the local performance rights society and collect the performance income on its behalf.

In addition, be mindful that the EU's CISAC Decision, discussed above, applied to performance rights societies and opened the door to the pan-European licensing of the performance or communication right directly with the PROs or alternative organizations, bypassing the need for administration of these rights by a subpublisher. An original publisher may therefore consider excluding from this grant the making of public performances or communications of musical works in connection with digital downloads, limited downloads, on-demand streams, webcasts, and other digital uses. Since direct licensing of these rights may be some way off, the original publisher may include them on a non-exclusive basis and exclude them upon reasonable notice to the subpublisher.

The original publisher's intent with respect to reserving these rights may be clarified with the following language:

> Owner hereby reserves for itself the exclusive right to grant licenses for the entire world, or any part thereof, for the public performance or communication of any of the Compositions hereunder by means of digital delivery, including but not limited to digital permanent downloads, limited downloads, on-demand streams, webcasts, and any other digital uses, and Publisher shall not be entitled to share in any fees received by Owner in respect to such uses unless otherwise agreed in writing signed by both parties.

Alternatively, the same concept is sometimes expressed as a right to collect directly from rights societies:

> Notwithstanding anything herein to the contrary, Owner shall have the right, at any time during the term of this agreement or during any extensions thereof, to elect to collect its share of income directly from performing rights societies or mechanical rights societies, or both, either indirectly or through any other agency appointed by Owner.

To the extent the subpublisher objects to such reservations, the term of the subpublisher agreement, discussed below, might be shortened to reflect the uncertainties in the market for digital distribution of musical works.

### *3. Mechanical and Electrical Transcription Rights*

The following is typical of a grant of *mechanical and electrical transcription rights* in a standard subpublishing agreement:

> (iii) The exclusive right, for sale within the Territory only, to grant non-exclusive licenses for the manufacture of parts serving to reproduce the Compositions and the making of mechanical, electrical and similar reproductions for phonograph records, audiotapes of any configuration or type, piano rolls, transcriptions or any other method of audio reproduction as yet known or unknown, in and for the Territory.

Recall from our discussion above, regarding *International Mechanical Rights Administration*, that in most countries outside the United States, all mechanical licenses are issued by a mechanical rights collection society, not by the individual music publishers, and that mechanical rates overseas are generally set by the terms of a collective bargaining agreement between the mandatory mechanical rights organizations and the record companies, or an association representing them.

Unless the original publisher appoints a subpublisher to collect the publisher's share from the local mechanical rights collection society, the collection society will, if instructed, pay the publisher's mechanical royalty income from the territory over to the Harry Fox Agency in the United States, which will then remit it to the original publisher. An original publisher who is affiliated with the Harry Fox Agency can rely on the Agency's relationships with 23 mechanical collection societies operating in about 100 countries throughout the world for the collection of its international mechanical licensing income, but the original publisher should consider that by doing so it may be foregoing the opportunity to obtain advances against royalties and to have a local representative promote the generation of new income through local cover recordings, local performances, and local translated printed editions.

As discussed above with respect to performance rights, the CISAC Decision, combined with the EU's 2005 Recommendation, opened the door to pan-European licensing of mechanical reproduction rights to the collection societies and other entities, bypassing the need for administration of these rights by a subpublisher. An original publisher may consider excluding from this grant the right to make mechanical reproductions in connection with permanent downloads, limited downloads, on-demand streams, webcasts, or other digital uses. Since direct licensing of these rights may be some way off, the original publisher may include them on a non-exclusive basis and exclude them upon reasonable notice to the subpublisher.

The original publisher's intent with respect to reserving these rights may be clarified with the following language:

> Owner hereby reserves for itself the exclusive right to grant licenses for the entire world, or any part thereof, for the mechanical reproductions of any of the Compositions hereunder by means of digital delivery, including but not limited to digital permanent downloads, limited downloads, on-demand streams, webcasts, and any other digital uses, and Publisher shall not be entitled to share in any fees received by Owner in respect to such uses unless otherwise agreed in writing signed by both parties.

Alternatively, the same concept is sometimes expressed as a right to collect directly from rights societies:

> Notwithstanding anything herein to the contrary, Owner shall have the right, at any time during the term of this agreement or during any extensions thereof, to elect to collect its share of income directly from performing rights societies or mechanical rights societies, or both, either indirectly or through any other agency appointed by Owner.

To the extent the subpublisher objects to such reservations, the term of the subpublisher agreement, discussed below, might be shortened to reflect the uncertainties in the market for digital distribution of musical works.

### *4. Synchronization Rights*

The grant of right provision will typically go on to specify the subpublisher's authority to issue licenses for the synchronization of the compositions with motion pictures and television programs:

> (iv) Upon securing the prior written consent of Owner, the non-exclusive right to grant non-exclusive synchronization licenses

> for the recording of the Compositions in and with motion pictures and television productions produced in the Territory, and of making copies of recordings thereof, and exporting such copies to all countries of the world.

Note that the above section provides that the original publisher's consent must be obtained before the subpublisher issues any synchronization licenses. Note also, the inclusion of the language, "and of making copies of recordings thereof, and exporting such copies to all countries of the world," would allow the distribution of copies of the licensed motion pictures and television productions, not only for theatrical exhibition and broadcast, but for distribution in videocassettes, laserdiscs, and other home video devices.[3] However, this appears to be limited to the reproduction of copies of "motion pictures and television productions" produced in the territory, and there does not appear to be a separate provision for licensing the reproduction of other kinds of audiovisual works, such as multimedia programs. In any event, under this form of agreement, all forms of licensing for audiovisual reproductions would require the consent of the original publisher.

The subpublisher's authority to issue synchronization licenses is nearly always granted on a *non-exclusive* basis and limited to motion pictures and television programs *produced in the subpublisher's territory*. By the following language, the original publisher may clarify that the subpublisher's share of performance income, even when generated by the issuance of a local synchronization license, is limited to that income generated by performances occurring within the territory:

> It is specifically understood and agreed that Publisher shall not share in any fees derived from the public performance outside of the Territory of any Compositions contained in a motion picture or television production produced in the Territory, and that all such fees shall be payable to and collected by Owner or its designees. The original publisher's intent with respect to non-exclusivity may be clarified with the following language:
>
> Owner hereby reserves for itself the exclusive right to grant licenses for the entire world (including the Territory) for the synchronization and public performance of the Compositions with motion

[3] See Chapter 15, *Licensing Music in Audiovisual Works*.

> pictures or television productions produced outside the Territory, and Publisher shall not be entitled to share in any fees received by Owner in respect to such worldwide use.

Again, the emergence of the Internet has made national borders transparent. Online services like Google's YouTube — which offers millions of short videos, typically made by non-professional hobbyists, for on-demand streaming — has challenged traditional music industry business models struggling to find a means to monetize the millions of synchronization uses associated with these *user-generated* videos. An original publisher may wish to consider a familiar means of dealing with the problem:

> Owner hereby reserves for itself the exclusive right to grant licenses for the entire world, or any part thereof, for the synchronization and public performance of the Compositions with motion pictures, television productions or other audiovisual works produced anywhere in the world and made, performed or otherwise communicated by digital delivery, including but not limited to digital permanent downloads, limited downloads, on-demand streams, webcasts, and any other digital uses, anywhere in the world, and Publisher shall not be entitled to share in any fees received by Owner in respect to such uses unless otherwise agreed in writing signed by both parties.

The solution to the user-generated content problem discussed earlier in this chapter may be a form of collective licensing administered by the mechanical collection or performance rights societies, so it may be a good practice to include the following provision in all subpublishing agreements:

> Notwithstanding anything herein to the contrary, Owner shall have the right, at any time during the term of this agreement or during any extensions thereof, to elect to collect its share of income directly from performing rights societies or mechanical rights societies, or both, either indirectly or through any other agency appointed by Owner.

Again, to the extent the subpublisher objects to such reservations, the term of the subpublisher agreement, discussed below, might be shortened to reflect the uncertainties in the market for digital distribution of musical works.

### *5. Videogram and Other Audiovisual Rights*

That the subpublisher's right to issue synchronization and videogram licenses is *non-exclusive* is important. When negotiating a synchronization license for the use of music in a motion picture produced in the United States, U.S. film producers typically require that the music publisher also grant a *worldwide* license to make and distribute videocassettes and other home video devices containing the compositions licensed. For this reason, royalties for the distribution and sale of videograms overseas are paid to the original publisher in the United States. The same is true for other audiovisual works produced in the United States, such as music videos of recording artist performances, multimedia programs distributed on CD-ROM, and similar audiovisual works.

### *6. Commercial Advertising Rights*

The original publisher will typically reserve the right to license the compositions as part of any commercial advertisements. The original publisher may be required to reserve these rights to comply with any restrictions contained in its agreements with songwriters, who are increasingly demanding the right to approve the use of their songs in advertisements. At a minimum, the subpublishing agreement should contain restrictions on the grant of commercial advertising licenses that mirror any restrictions contained in the songwriter agreement with respect to the composition. Because the terms of songwriter agreements vary, and many subpublishing agreements are catalog deals (e.g., covering numerous compositions written by different songwriters), the original publisher is advised to grant the right to issue licenses for commercial advertisements, but condition the subpublisher's exercise of that right upon its obtaining the original publisher's prior written consent with respect to each proposed license.

It should be noted that performance rights societies in some countries, such as Italy, Argentina, and Mexico, do not pay performance royalties for the use of music in commercial advertising, and in Canada only commercials with musical content of 60 seconds or more are credited for payment of performance royalties. This should be considered in connection with setting synchronization license fees for the use of music in commercial advertising in these countries.

### *7. Reserved Rights*

Unless the subpublishing agreement contains a broad grant of subpublishing rights, such as the grant contained in Section 3 of the Subpublishing Agreement set forth as Form 5.2 on the CD-ROM, the scope of the subpublisher's right to issue licenses will be limited to the specific rights listed in the subpublishing agreement. Among the rights an original publisher might typically reserve, in addition to the digital uses discussed above, include:

> (a) All rights in the Compositions and the copyrights therein for the world outside the Territory, and all rights within the Territory other than as are specifically herein granted to Publisher;
>
> (b) The exclusive right to dramatize, worldwide, the Compositions, and to license the use and performance of such dramatic versions throughout the world;
>
> (c) The exclusive right to license worldwide uses of the titles of the Compositions; and
>
> (d) The exclusive right to make literary versions of the Compositions throughout the world, and to print, publish and vend such literary versions (as well as the dramatic versions aforementioned) throughout the world.

## F. Subpublisher Fees and Publishing Income

In exchange for its publishing services, the subpublisher will retain a fee similar to the administration fee charged under an administration agreement. Subpublisher fees range anywhere from 10% to 50% of publishing income, with the typical fees falling between 15% and 25%. Hybrid deals that look more like a U.S. *collection agreement* (described in the previous chapter), with the subpublisher retaining as little as 5%, but providing merely those minimum services necessary to collect and remit local publishing income, are not uncommon for catalogs owned by popular recording artists who have a great degree of bargaining leverage.

The subpublishing fee is generally reflected in the percentage of publishing income that the subpublisher pays over to the original publisher. For example, if the subpublishing fee is 25%, the agreement will provide that the subpublisher will pay to the original publisher "75% of the publisher's share . . . earned in the Territory." Provisions in a subpublishing agreement concerning the fees a subpublisher is permitted to retain from the publishing income collected may begin as follows:

> 4. All monies payable to Subpublisher with respect to the exploitation of rights granted hereunder shall be referred to herein as "Subpublishing Income." Publisher agrees that it shall have the duty to collect and to be responsible for the collection of all Subpublishing Income payable within the Territory. Subpublisher shall pay to Owner the following royalties in respect of the Compositions upon the following terms and provisions:

Under the typical subpublishing agreement, the subpublisher is not permitted to deduct its costs and expenses incurred in connection with administering the compositions. (This is unlike the typical administration agreement where the administrator is typically permitted to deduct its costs.) The foregoing provision — which defines Subpublishing Income as "all moneys payable to the Subpublisher" — implements what is referred to as a *gross receipts* deal. Under these deals, the original publisher is entitled to a percentage of gross receipts and the subpublisher does not deduct any costs or expenses prior to calculating the original publisher's share of gross receipts.

Where an original publisher's share is based on *net income*, the subpublisher is typically allowed to deduct a specified list of costs associated with exploiting the catalog, prior to calculating the original publisher's share.

### *1. Print Income*

With respect to royalties for printed editions, the subpublisher will typically pay to the original publisher,

> (a) Twelve and one-half percent (12.5%) of the marked or suggested retail selling price of each copy of each Composition in any and every printed edition sold by Publisher or its permitted subpublishers, on all gross sales (after deduction of actual returns), and that proportion of twelve and one-half percent (12.5%) of the marked or suggested retail selling price of each songbook, folio or similar compilation edition sold by Publisher or its permitted subpublishers, on all gross sales (after deduction of returns), which the number of

> Compositions included in each edition shall bear to the total number of copyrighted compositions (including the Compositions) contained therein for which a royalty is payable.

The percentage royalty may vary from 10% to 15%, with the typical being 12½%. Where the subpublisher permits local print publishers to manufacture and sell printed editions, the publishing income arising from such arrangements will be paid over to the original publisher, less the subpublisher's fee. Thus, assuming subpublisher fee rate is 25%, the subpublisher shall pay to the original publisher,

> (b) seventy-five percent (75%) of any and all gross receipts paid by printing licensees of Publisher or of its permitted subpublishers for the use of each Composition in any piano copies, songbooks, folios, books, newspapers, magazines or other printed editions.

### *2. Mechanical and Electrical Transcription Income*

The following provision is typical of one governing income from the licensing of mechanical and electrical transcription reproductions in the territory. Again, assuming the subpublisher fee is 25%, the subpublisher shall pay to the original publisher,

> (c) seventy-five percent (75%) of all monies paid by licensees of Publisher as royalties for the sale in the Territory of phonograph records or other such devices embodying mechanical, electrical or other audio reproductions of the Compositions (as described in paragraph 1(c) above), with respect to audio master recordings originally produced outside of the Territory;

*Cover Records.* Except in the case of a collection deal, where the original publisher has no expectation of the subpublisher's exerting efforts to promote the compositions covered by the agreement, the original publisher will often provide the subpublisher with an incentive to effect the recording and release of *cover records* (i.e., a recording of a composition, often translated into the local language, by an artist popular in the territory). That incentive is provided by increasing the subpublisher fee rate, with respect to income generated by cover recordings, by an amount ranging between 5% to 15%. For example, if the subpublisher fee rate is 25%, the rate may be increased to 40% with respect to cover recordings made and released in the territory.

The provision providing the incentive for the subpublisher to effect cover records might look like the following addition to paragraph (c) set forth above:

> provided, however, that if Publisher secures the release in the Territory during the term hereof of a master audio recording of a Composition originally produced within the Territory (hereinafter referred to as a "Territory-originated cover recording"), Publisher shall pay to Owner only sixty percent (60%) of all monies paid by licensees of Publisher as royalties with respect to such Territory originated cover recording.

The above language makes it clear that the subpublisher is only entitled to an increased percentage of income with respect to the *particular* cover recording originated in the territory, and does not apply to *all* recordings released in the territory (i.e., including any original hit recording released in the United States), as some subpublishing agreements provide.

However, the above language appears to leave an ambiguity as to whether the increased subpublisher fee applies merely to *mechanical* income generated by the cover recording or whether it also includes *performance* income generated from public performances of the cover recording. Clearly, if the subpublisher is to be entitled to an increased fee on performance royalties generated by cover recordings, it seems reasonable that such increase should only apply to those performance fees associated with performances of the cover recording. However, because performance rights societies do not distinguish between particular recordings when reporting public performance royalties, it is difficult to determine what portion of performance fees generated in a particular country is associated with a particular cover recording.

One solution to the problem is to limit the application of the rate increase solely to royalties generated from *mechanical* licensing of the cover recording. This is because it is fairly easy to distinguish mechanical fees generated from the cover recording from those generated by all other recordings, as collection societies receive and report mechanical collection information on the basis of particular albums and recording artists. Though the subpublisher won't benefit by the amount of the *increased rate* on performance royalties, it will benefit from the overall increase in performance royalties caused by the cover recording, as the subpublisher will be entitled to retain its normal percentage on performance royalties generated by public performances in the territory, which, of course, will include broadcasts of the cover recording. Another solution, one which is more favorable to the subpublisher, is to compute the portion of performance royalties to which the increased rate shall be applied using a ratio of the mechanical income associated with the cover recording to mechanical income associated with all recordings sold in the territory. In other words, if 30% of the total mechanical royalties generated in the territory were derived from sales of the cover recording, then the subpublisher's increased fee rate (e.g., 40%) would apply to 30% of the performance royalties and, of course, the subpublisher's normal fee rate (e.g., 25%) would apply to the balance, or 70% of the performance royalties.

*Related Restrictions*. The original publisher will typically impose the following restrictions upon the subpublisher with respect to the issuance of mechanical and transcription licenses in the territory:

> Publisher shall not license the mechanical, electrical or other reproduction of any Composition for phonorecords or other such devices at a rate less than the highest prevailing rate in the Territory. Publisher shall not refuse to grant a mechanical license for a Composition at the prevailing rate in the Territory to any authorized manufacturer in the Territory of a recording of said Composition made by Owner or its parent, affiliate or subsidiary.
>
> Notwithstanding any provision to the contrary herein contained, Publisher shall collect royalties under subparagraph (c) above only with respect to phonograph records and other devices sold in the Territory, irrespective of whether such phonorecords or devices are manufactured within the Territory or outside of the Territory. Accordingly, Publisher shall not collect royalties hereunder with respect to phonograph records and other such devices manufactured within the Territory but sold outside of the Territory.

### *3. Performance Income*

As mentioned in our discussion above regarding *International Performance Rights Administration*, unless the original publisher appoints a subpublisher to collect the *publisher's share* of performance income from the local performance rights society, the performance rights society will pay the publisher's share over to the publisher's U.S. performance rights society, which in turn will remit the amount over to the publisher. But to rely on this process is to risk substantial delays and even errors in the collection of overseas performance income. A U.S. publisher is therefore advised to appoint a subpublisher to register its compositions with the local performance rights society and collect the performance income on behalf of the original publisher. To that end, the typical subpublishing agreement contains the following provision; assuming the subpublishing fee is 25% of publishing income, the subpublisher will pay to the original publisher,

> seventy-five percent (75%) of the publisher's share of all public performance fees earned in the Territory with respect to the Compositions, it being understood and agreed that the Publisher shall authorize and direct the appropriate performance rights society in the Territory to pay to Publisher one hundred percent (100%) of said publisher's share and that Publisher shall remit to Owner its aforesaid share thereof, together with a statement signed by said performance rights society indicating in detail the titles of the Compositions and the amounts paid to Publisher on account of the public performance in the Territory of such Compositions.

Some subpublishers insist that they should receive a greater percentage for collecting performance royalties on the basis that if they apply the subpublisher fee percentage to the amount of performance income collected, the subpublisher is really only receiving one-half of the amount to which they feel entitled. Recall that the subpublisher only collects the *publisher's share* of performance income, the writer's share being paid directly to the writer through the performance rights societies. Thus, for example, if a subpublisher fee of 25% is applied to only the publisher's share, then the subpublisher is really only getting 12.5% of total performance income, yet the work the subpublisher does to maximize performance income, including the prompt and accurate registration of compositions with the local performance rights society, benefits *all* performance income, not just the publisher's share. Thus, a subpublisher may assert, that if the subpublisher fee rate is 25% for all publishing income, the rate should be 50%

for performance income. Few knowledgeable original publishers, however, concede the point.

### *4. Other Income*

The following provision confirms that all other publishing income arising from the exercise of rights granted under the agreement shall be remitted to the publisher, less the subpublisher fee:

> seventy-five percent (75%) of all gross monies paid by licensees of Publisher with respect to any other rights to the Compositions which are expressly assigned to Publisher hereunder.

The following provision makes it clear that any moneys collected by the subpublisher arising from rights not specifically granted under the agreement, including income from unauthorized licenses issued by the subpublisher, shall be paid over to the original publisher without deduction of the subpublisher's fee.

> One hundred percent (100%) of all Publishing Income received by Publisher from any exploitation of rights in and to the Compositions other than those rights expressly set forth in paragraph 1 above. Nothing herein shall in any way increase or enlarge the rights granted to Publisher hereunder, which are solely as set forth in paragraph 1.

### *5. Payment "At Source"*

Nearly all modern subpublishing agreements will contain a provision making certain that publishing income be computed "at the source." The provision may look like this:

> Notwithstanding anything to the contrary herein contained, all royalties or other monies payable to Owner hereunder are to be computed at the source from which the payments giving rise to such royalties or other monies are originally made, less only the actual commissions or collection fees (if any) retained by the performing rights society or agency and the mechanical royalty collection society or agency in the Territory.

Such a provision is intended to prevent the unscrupulous practice of using multiple layers of subpublishing companies, owned or closely affiliated with the subpublisher, solely for the purpose of reducing the original publisher's royalties from international publishing income.[4] For example, where a subpublisher, who is entitled to retain as its fee 50% of the publishing income it collects, sublicenses its subpublishing rights for the territory to an affiliated company, allowing the affiliate to retain 50% of publishing income collected by the affiliate, then the subpublisher's income will only be those receipts from its affiliate, or 50% of the true publishing income derived from the territory. Thus, if the subpublisher remits to the original publisher 50% (retaining its 50% subpublisher fee) of the 50% received from its affiliate, then the amount ultimately remitted to the original publisher will only be 25% of the true publishing income derived from the territory. If the affiliate adds another subpublishing layer under the same terms, the original publisher will only receive 12.5% of the true publishing income from the territory, and so on.

Though this practice of layering subpublishing deals to reduce royalties remitted to original publishers is no longer common, including the *at source* provision in a subpublishing agreement with a major U.S. publisher (i.e., acting as a worldwide subpublisher) will assure that intercompany agreements between the U.S. publisher and its international subsidiaries and affiliates may not be used to reduce the royalties of the original publisher. This is not to suggest that major U.S. publishers engage in this practice, but intercompany agreements among subsidiaries and affiliated companies of a multinational firm are often modified for international income tax reasons, and the at source provision will assure that such changes will not adversely affect the original publisher.

### *6. Frozen Funds*

From time to time, in certain countries, government regulations may restrict the ability of the local subpublisher to remit funds to the original publisher in the United States and in United States dollars. To

[4] Such practices have been successfully challenged in court. See *Elton John v. Dick James Music* [1982 J. No. 15026, High Court of Justice, Chancery Division].

address the problem of *frozen* or *blocked funds*, the following provision is commonly included in subpublishing agreements:

> In the event Publisher is prevented from paying any monies hereunder due to currency restrictions, Publisher shall so advise Owner by written notice accompanied by a copy of the applicable law, regulation or order (with an accurate English translation), and Owner shall have the right to elect to accept payment of such monies in foreign currency in a depository selected by Owner, and if Owner shall so elect, by written notice to Publisher, Publisher shall promptly deposit or cause to be deposited all such payable monies to the credit of Owner in such foreign currency and shall promptly give Owner written notice of said deposit. Payment so made to the depository so elected by Owner shall fulfill Publisher's obligations hereunder as to the monies so payable to Owner.

By virtue of such a provision, the original publisher gains control over the money, removing the funds from the risks of subpublisher insolvency, and enabling the original publisher to preserve the value of the funds by making interest bearing investments. The original publisher may either wait until circumstances allow the remittance of funds to the United States or use the money for defraying local expenses, as when the original publisher pays a visit to review his subpublishing affairs, or when a record or motion picture company affiliated with the original publisher produces a record, motion picture, or other work in the territory.

As noted in Chapter 3, on *Songwriter Agreements*, some songwriters are successful in negotiating a provision that requires, under circumstance where funds are frozen, that the music publisher pay to the songwriter an *advance* against royalties in an amount equal to the royalties that would have been earned had the publisher received the funds in the United States. In requesting such a provision, the songwriter would argue that the publisher is simply in a better position than the songwriter to deal with the intricacies of foreign exchange matters and therefore the publisher should bear the risks of being unable to remit frozen funds. Further, as mentioned above, even though the funds have not been paid in U.S. currency, the publisher often does have control over the funds and may actually put the funds to practical use.

For the same reasons, an original publisher signing a subpublishing agreement with a major U.S. publisher should be in the same position to request a similar provision: in circumstances where the subpublisher is prevented from paying publishing income due to currency restrictions, the subpublisher should pay to the original publisher an *advance* against publishing income in an amount equal to the publishing income that would have been earned had the major U.S. subpublisher received the funds in the United States.

### *7. Black Box Moneys*

Earlier in this chapter, under the discussion of *International Mechanical Rights Administration*, we explained the concept of the *black box* — in many countries, mechanical royalties that have not been claimed are, after a certain period of time has elapsed, paid to local publishing companies, which they may keep without any obligation to remit funds to the original publishers of the unclaimed songs. In some of these countries, the share of black box moneys entitled to be received by a local publisher is calculated by dividing the amount of mechanical revenues received by the subpublisher from the society by the total mechanical revenues of the society; in other countries, disbursement is based upon seniority and other factors.

In many cases, a major original publisher, who has placed a large catalog with a local subpublisher, may have the leverage to require the subpublisher to pay over to the original publisher a share of the black box money received by the subpublisher. This share would be calculated, roughly, by dividing the revenues the subpublisher derived from the original publisher's catalog by the total earnings of the subpublisher. The following provision, which again assumes a 25% subpublisher fee, is intended to effect such terms in favor of the original publisher:

> To the extent that authorization from Owner is necessary or desirable, Owner hereby grants to Publisher the right and authority within the Territory to collect from performing rights societies or agencies, mechanical rights licensing and/or mechanical royalty collection societies or agencies or any other persons, firms or corporations, unclaimed, unregistered or unallocated receipts, bonuses or other sums distributable to Publisher by reason of seniority or membership in or affiliation with any such society or agency, or otherwise,

not calculated on the basis of actual uses of the Compositions, to which the Publisher is or shall be entitled (hereinafter referred to as "accruals"). Publisher shall pay to Owner, with the accounting statements hereinafter provided for, seventy-five percent (75%) of that portion of such accruals which shall be calculated by multiplying the total amount of each such distribution of accruals to Publisher by a fraction, the numerator of which shall be the total public performance fee or mechanical royalty distribution, as the case may be, from such society, agency or other party, to Publisher which is allocable to identified uses of the Compositions during the relevant accounting period and the denominator of which shall be the total public performance fee or mechanical royalty distribution, as the case may be, from such society, agency or other party, to Publisher which is allocable to identified uses of any and all musical compositions controlled by Publisher, including the Compositions, during the relevant accounting period.

## G. Translations

Many subpublishing agreements drafted from the perspective of the subpublisher will include the following grant, entitling the subpublisher to make translations and adaptations:

> The exclusive right to make orchestral and other arrangements and adaptations of the Compositions, to procure any new or translated lyrics or titles thereof, and to publish, sell or use the compositions and to authorize others to do so in the Territory, either with or without any such arrangement, adaptation, new lyric or translations thereof.

Good local adaptations are not literal translations but are ones that capture the spirit and idea of the song. The creation of localized lyrics and adaptations may be necessary for a subpublisher to fully exploit a composition in its territory. In the past, this was true for a number of the continental countries of Europe, including Germany, Austria, France, Belgium, Switzerland, Italy, Spain, and Portugal. Today, however, the original English versions tend to predominate. In certain countries where English is not widely spoken, such as Japan, a localized lyric will breathe life into a song where it would not otherwise become popular. Thus, the right to create local language translations and adaptations is commonly granted to the subpublisher. Nevertheless, when the subpublisher exercises the foregoing right by engaging a writer to create new, local language lyrics, there arises the question of royalties for the local writer and who is responsible for them. Under the rules of many performance rights societies, the local lyricist will get a portion of the original *writer's share* (i.e., the total writer's share, even if there were two original writers, one being a lyricist and the other a composer) of *all* versions of the work, including the original English-language version. However, under the "Amalfi" resolution adopted by CISAC member societies, local performance rights societies are only supposed to allocate fees to local lyricists for the translated versions. In addition, a local lyric writer may receive a portion of the subpublisher's receipts arising from mechanical, synchronization and print licenses. Of course, the subpublisher would want to deduct these obligations from the original publisher's share, but it is customary for the subpublisher to bear these costs.

Recall, in Chapter 3, on *Songwriter Agreements*, that songwriters who have significant amount of bargaining leverage are generally able to obtain in their songwriter agreements the complete right of approval over the engagement of other writers to make additions, changes or translations. Under these circumstances, the original publisher would have no choice but to require its consent before the subpublisher were able to engage a lyricist to create a local language translation. It would also be advisable to make it clear that any costs incurred by the subpublisher in connection with the creation of new lyrics or local adaptations, permitted by the original publisher, will be borne by the subpublisher:

> (b) Publisher shall have the right to make and publish new adaptations and arrangements of any Composition and to translate the lyrics thereof into any language of the Territory, but only with Owner's prior written approval thereof. Publisher shall be responsible for and shall pay to local adapters, arrangers, translators and lyricists any royalties or fees for such services, solely out of Publisher's share of Publishing Income. All new matter shall be the property of Owner and shall be copyrighted solely in the name of Owner or Owner's designee.

When the original publisher provides its written consent to the creation of translations or adaptations, it should take such measures necessary to assure that publishing income is properly accounted for. For example, as noted above, the subpublisher may be entitled to retain a greater portion of publishing income with respect to cover recordings. The original publisher will want to take special care that the cover recordings of translated versions are accounted for as such, and are not confused with royalties stemming from the sale or performance of the original U.S. version. One measure is to make certain the local translation is given a different title than the original U.S. version, and that the local translation is registered separately with the local performance rights society. Another is to make sure that no more than one lyric version is released in the same language. This frequently happens with Spanish lyrics created in both Spain and Latin America, French lyrics created in both France and French Quebec, and Portuguese lyrics created in both Portugal and Brazil.

In addition, an experienced original publisher will always require that ownership in any local lyrics, modifications, or other new matter created with respect to the compositions shall remain with the original publisher. For example, Spanish lyrics created by a subpublisher in Latin America can become quite popular among the Hispanic population in the United States and the original publisher will want to collect mechanical and performance royalties in the United States without payment to the subpublisher. Further, ownership of the translation will assure the original publisher complete flexibility to exploit the song in the territory upon termination of the subpublishing agreement. Without full rights to the translation, the original publisher may find it difficult to develop new lyrics without infringing upon the translation owned by the subpublisher.

Finally, if the original songwriter has approval rights over the creation of translations, the original publisher should obtain a copy of the proposed new lyrics, together with an English translation of them, for purposes of obtaining the original writer's approval.

### H. Term

Years ago, subpublishing agreements endured for the life of the copyrights in the compositions they covered. In recent years, however, the trend has been to shorten the term of these agreements to the point that, today, the term of the typical subpublishing agreement is from *three* to *five* years. Most international performance rights societies, however, require a minimum three-year term, and some even require a five-year minimum.

As mentioned above, however, due to potential for direct licensing of digital rights on a worldwide or pan-European basis, original publishers have recently been considering a reduction in the term of their subpublishing agreements to as little as one year. Publishers who insist on such a reduced term should expect the subpublisher to reciprocate by offering little to nothing in the way of an advance.

A typical term provision might read simply as follows:

> The term of this Agreement shall be for a period of three (3) years from the date hereof.

Though it may go without saying, it would be prudent to clarify that if the original publisher loses the rights to publish any of the compositions, during the term, the term of the agreement with respect to such compositions shall expire at the time the original publisher loses such rights:

> provided, however, should Owner's rights to publish a Composition expire during the term hereof, the term of this Agreement with respect to such Composition shall terminate contemporaneously with such expiration.

The variations in structuring the durations of subpublishing agreements are as numerous as those found in co-publishing, administration, and other music publishing agreements. For example, fixed terms may be extended by exercise of options to renew, and such extensions may be conditioned upon the payment of advances or achieving minimum amounts of publishing income. These variations are entirely subject to negotiation.

For example, the term provision may provide the subpublisher with an option to renew:

> The term of this Agreement shall be for a period of three (3) years from the date hereof ("Initial Term"); provided that Subpublisher shall have the option to extend the term of this Agreement for one (1) additional three (3) year period commencing upon the expiration

> of the Initial Term upon the payment to Owner, during the last ninety (90) days of the Initial Term, of an additional advance equal to the greater of $_______ or a sum equal to fifty (50%) of Owner's receipts hereunder through the time of such payment.

When the subpublisher pays a large advance against royalties, the term is typically at the high end of the range, perhaps with the subpublisher having certain rights to extend the term beyond its originally anticipated date of expiration.

***1. Cover Records.*** For example, the subpublisher may have the right to extend the term of the agreement (e.g., typically for one to three years) with respect to compositions for which it effected cover recordings during the term. The following provision is an example of such a right:

> Notwithstanding any provision to the contrary herein contained, in the event Publisher shall secure the release during the term hereof of a Territory-originated cover recording of a Composition and said cover recording shall during the term hereof reach 20 or better on the popular single records chart of one of the two most popular record industry publications in the Territory, Publisher's rights hereunder with respect to said Composition shall continue for two (2) years after the date of release in the Territory of the first such qualifying Territory-originated cover recording.

An original publisher should be mindful, however, that such a provision may result in some of the original publisher's compositions being published in the territory by this subpublisher and some being administered by another. Splitting one's catalog in this way will, at best, be an inconvenience, and, at worst, could lead to increased transaction costs or costly errors in collection accounting.

***2. Unrecouped Advances.*** The subpublisher may also have the right to extend the term of the agreement if advances paid to the original publisher have not been fully recouped. The original publisher would seek to restrict this right by (a) limiting the exercise of such right only *to the extent* the subpublisher has not recouped a specified percentage (e.g., 75%) of the advances, and (b) providing that in no event shall such extension continue for a specified period of time (e.g., six months to one year from the stated expiration of the agreement or until such recoupment takes place, whichever is earlier).

***3. Pipeline Revenues.*** Another variation that affects the negotiated term of the agreement concerns publishing income earned during the term but not collected as of the time of its stated expiration date. A subpublisher will typically be provided the right to collect and disburse (after retaining its subpublisher's fee) these revenues, called *pipeline* revenues. The provision may look like the second sentence of the following *term* paragraph:

> 10. The term of this agreement shall commence as of the date hereof and shall continue for a period of three (3) years. At the expiration or termination of this agreement, all rights of any kind or nature granted to Publisher hereunder shall automatically revert and be the sole and exclusive property of Owner without formality or execution of any documents. Notwithstanding the foregoing, upon the expiration of this agreement (but not upon any termination of this agreement by Owner for good cause), Publisher shall have the right for six (6) months thereafter to continue to collect and disburse, in accordance with the provisions hereof, the Publishing Income which shall have been earned during the term of this agreement but which shall not have become payable until after the expiration of this agreement.

An original publisher may insist that (a) the subpublisher's right to collect pipeline revenues should cease upon the subpublisher's recoupment of most or all of the advances paid to the original publisher, (b) a time limit, such as the *six* month limit set forth in the above illustration, be placed on such rights, and (c) during the extension period, the subpublisher's rights be limited to collection and disbursement, it being understood the subpublisher shall have no right to exercise administration rights over the compositions.

***4. Reciprocal Relationships.*** A further consideration is whether the original publisher has an important reciprocal relationship with the subpublisher. In other words, if the original publisher serves as the U.S. subpublisher to the international subpublisher's overseas catalog, the international subpublisher may insist upon identical provisions with regard to the term of that agreement, and may, in fact, insist upon *co-termination* — that is, upon the termination of the overseas subpublishing agreement, the U.S. subpublishing agreement shall automatically terminate as well.

## I. Advances

Original publishers can usually expect to receive some form of advance against royalties in exchange for signing up with a subpublisher. The structure of the advance, however, varies considerably from deal to deal, and is often related to the exercise of options to renew the term of the agreement.

If the subpublisher has experience with the catalog to be represented, or access to reliable information furnished by the original publisher, the size of the advance may be determined on the basis of historical data with respect to publishing income previously generated by the compositions in the territory. Often, however, the advance is more a function of the sheer bargaining power that a popular artist with a hit album brings to the original publisher's catalog.

Typically, an original publisher receives a non-returnable *signing advance* (i.e., an advance payable upon the execution of the subpublishing agreement) recoupable from royalties earned by the original publisher during the term of the agreement.

> Within seven (7) days after the execution hereof, Publisher shall pay to Owner the sum of $_______, representing an advance recoupable by Publisher from Owner's share of Publishing Income earned hereunder.

But advance structures can often get more complicated:

> Publisher shall pay to Owner (in United States Dollars) the following amounts, at the commencement of each one (1) year period of the term hereof, as nonreturnable advances recoupable by Publisher from Owner's share of the Publishing Income earned during the applicable one (1) year period:
>
> (a) Dollars ($_______), upon the execution hereof, for the first one (1) year period.
>
> (b) Dollars ($_______), at the commencement of the second one (1) year period, for said one (1) year period.

> (c) Dollars ($________), at the commencement of the third one (1) year period, for said one (1) year period.

Note, in the above example, the advance paid at the beginning of each year is recoupable only from the publishing income generated during the one-year period immediately following the date the advance is due.

An alternative form of advance typically negotiated in subpublishing agreements is the *rolling advance* — an advance that is automatically replaced when it is recouped:

> Upon recoupment of each advance hereunder, Publisher will pay to Owner a new advance equal to the advance recouped. Such new advance shall accompany the statement in which the previous advance is first recouped; provided that such new advance shall not be due or payable after the expiration of this Agreement.

The original publisher may also negotiate an option to forego, under a rolling advance scheme, any new advance due in exchange for a reduction in the subpublisher's share of Publishing Income. A subpublisher may negotiate that if the original publisher elects to get paid the advance, the term of the Agreement would be extended by one or two years.

An original publisher should bear in mind that the subpublisher's risk/reward ratio will vary with every demand made during negotiations. The size and structure of the advance is likely to affect how the subpublisher negotiates other provisions in the agreement, particularly the subpublisher fee and the term of the agreement.

Though a higher advance may reduce certain risks of the original publisher, if the increase comes at the expense of an increase in the subpublisher's fee, it may well not be worth insisting upon. The original publisher should be considering factors other than the advance, such as the reduction of risk through a shorter agreement term. Finally, a most important consideration is to remember that music publishing is a business built upon relationships. An original publisher should not advance his short-term interests by watching an outstanding subpublisher consistently lose money on the original publisher's catalog. Because of the high costs and risks associated with adjudication of disputes overseas, good relationships are nowhere more important than in the setting of international business transactions.

## J. Currency

The original publisher should require that payments be made in its *base currency* (i.e., the currency of the publisher's domicile). For example, an original publisher based in the United States should require that it be paid in U.S. dollars, and by international wire transfer, unless it specifies otherwise, and that the costs of any currency conversion and costs associated with the wire transfer, should be borne by the subpublisher.

Because currency exchange rates can fluctuate rapidly, the rate of exchange used for converting funds received by the subpublisher in other currencies should be agreed upon and set forth in the subpublishing agreement — for example, at the rate of exchange prevailing at the close of the accounting period in which such payments were received. This would prevent the subpublisher from choosing the most advantageous rate of exchange for each payment received.

The subpublisher should agree to timely obtain any and all government approvals necessary to make all payments due the original publisher. The agreement should also make it clear that all accountings by subpublisher should be made on a *cash*, not accrual, basis. Late payments should carry an interest rate of the lesser of at least 1% per month or the lawful interest rate.

## K. Reporting

All reporting to the original publisher should be done in the English language and copies of all royalty reports from third parties (e.g., collection societies) should be made available to the original publisher upon request.

## L. Disputes

In Chapter 10, on *Basic Considerations in Music Licensing*, we discuss the important distinction between a *choice of law* provision and a *choice of forum* provision. It is important that your international subpublishing agreement contain *both* provisions, such as in the following example:

> This agreement shall be deemed to have been made in the State of California, and its validity, construction and effect shall be governed

by the laws of the State of California applicable to agreements wholly performed therein.

The venue for any action, suit or proceeding brought by either party against the other with respect to this agreement shall be in the County of Los Angeles, State of California, and both parties hereby consent to the personal jurisdiction of the courts of the State of California. Service of process may be made by registered or certified mail addressed to the defendant in accordance with the notice provisions hereof, and the time to respond to such process shall be thirty (30) days after the date of mailing thereof.

## IV. WORKING WITH YOUR SUBPUBLISHER

The working relationship between you and your subpublisher will have administrative aspects, such as providing in a timely fashion the information the subpublisher requires to effectively administer the collection of your royalties, and creative aspects, including the promotion of the musical compositions in your catalog.

A subpublisher will require a significant amount of information from the original publisher to properly represent the administration of royalty collection. For example, the subpublisher will require information about the release of any popular recordings of the compositions worldwide, copies of music cue sheets of motion pictures or television programs in which any of the compositions are featured, lead sheets or lyric sheets available for the compositions, the names of the songwriters and the amount of their percentage interests in the compositions, the performance rights affiliations of the songwriters, and if there are co-owners of any of the copyrights, their relative percentage interests in the compositions. The information in an original publisher's catalog, including updates of the catalog with information about new releases, can usually be delivered electronically — using the format of the original or subpublisher's royalty software (e.g., Musicalc, Counterpoint) or the Common Works Registration (CWR) format.

The subpublisher registers much of this information with its local mechanical license collection agency and performance rights society to improve the chances that collections by those entities with respect to the original publisher's compositions can be properly allocated and claimed as publishing income by the subpublisher. The effectiveness of the subpublisher will be as much dependent upon its diligence in using this information as upon the original publisher's diligence in supplying it.

The art of personal relationships is one of the precious keys to successful music publishing. This is why a successful working relationship with your subpublisher will often begin with a personal meeting. I will leave the reader with one example:

Murry Wilson, not to be outdone by his sons Brian, Carl, and Dennis's success as *The Beach Boys*, embarked on his own career as a songwriter and conductor of a studio size orchestra in his own album, released by Capitol Records in 1967. The album was entitled, "The Many Moods of Murry Wilson." Aiming at a global play, I set in motion on behalf of Francis, Day & Hunter, the publishing organization that handled Wilson's music interests and subpublishing for The Beach Boys' *Sea of Tunes* catalog, a campaign to help promote his music and album in Europe. Prior to a three-week visit to each of the subpublisher's offices in London and on the European continent, I arranged for a roundtable promotional meeting, at the George V Hotel in Paris, of all the subpublisher's European branch managers, together with 90-year old Mr. Fred Day, his son Eddie Day, Director, and his son, David Day. The meeting afforded Wilson the opportunity to meet the heart and soul of Francis, Day & Hunter, as well as each branch manager prior to the promotional campaign to Copenhagen, Stockholm, London, Hamburg, Berlin, Rome, and Milan. Now, eventually, Wilson's album didn't top the charts, but the meeting had the effect of satisfying Wilson that his subpublisher had the talent and enthusiasm to effectively represent his new compositions, as well as those in the *Sea of Tunes* catalog. Meanwhile, Francis, Day, knowing the importance of the Beach Boys catalog to their business, seized the opportunity to show Murry Wilson who they were and what they could do. There is simply no substitute for a face-to-face meeting to establish the *Good Vibrations* necessary for a successful subpublishing relationship.

# Appendix to Chapter 5
# International Subpublishing

## Laws and Regulations



## Forms (On CD-Rom Only)

# LAW 5.1

## EU CISAC DECISION (JULY 16, 2008)

COMMISSION OF THE EUROPEAN COMMUNITIES

Brussels, 16.07.2008
**C(2008) 3435 final**

**COMMISSION DECISION**

Of

16.07.2008

**relating to a proceeding under Article 81 of the EC Treaty and Article 53 of the EEA Agreement**

**(Case COMP/C2/38.698 – CISAC)**

(Only the Spanish, Czech, Danish, German, Estonian, Greek, English, French, Italian, Latvian, Dutch, Polish, Slovak and Slovenian texts are authentic)

(Text with EEA relevance)

**COMMISSION DECISION**

**of**

**16.07.2008**

**relating to a proceeding under Article 81 of the EC Treaty and Article 53 of the EEA Agreement**

**(Case COMP/C2/38.698 – CISAC)**

(Only the Spanish, Czech, Danish, German, Estonian, Greek, English, French, Italian, Latvian, Dutch, Polish, Slovak and Slovenian texts are authentic)

(Text with EEA relevance)

THE COMMISSION OF THE EUROPEAN COMMUNITIES,

Having regard to the Treaty establishing the European Community,

Having regard to the Agreement on the European Economic Area,

Having regard to the Council Regulation (EC) No 1/2003 of 16 December 2002 on the implementation of the rules on competition laid down in Articles 81 and 82 of the Treaty[1], and in particular Articles 7(1) thereof,

Having given the undertakings concerned the opportunity to make known their views on the objections raised by the Commission pursuant to Article 27(1) of Regulation (EC) No 1/2003 and Articles 11 and 12 of Commission Regulation (EC) No 773/2004 of 7 April 2004 relating to the conduct of proceedings by the Commission pursuant to Articles 81 and 82 of the EC Treaty[2].

After consulting the Advisory Committee on Restrictive Practices and Dominant Positions[3]

Having regard to the final report of the Hearing Officer in this case[4],

---

1 OJ L 1, 4.1.2003, p. 1. Regulation as last amended by Regulation (EC) No 1419/2006 (OJ L 269, 28.9.2006, p. 1).

2 OJ L 123, 27.4.2004, p. 18. Regulation as amended by Regulation (EC) No 1792/2006 (OJ L 362, 20.12.2006, p. 1).

3 OJ ...

4 OJ...

WHEREAS:

# 1. INTRODUCTION

1. This Decision concerns the conditions of management and licensing of authors' public performance rights of musical works by collecting societies. It is addressed to authors' collecting societies established in the EEA which are members of the International Confederation of Societies of Authors and Composers ("CISAC") and which are collectively referred to as the "EEA CISAC members".

2. CISAC advocates the use of a model contract for reciprocal representation agreements between its members for the management of public performance rights. This model contract covers all exploitation of musical works which require a public performance right licence. It is reflected to a very large extent in the bilateral reciprocal representation agreements between the EEA CISAC members. The following restrictions are at issue: clauses which restrict the right holders' ability to contract freely with the collecting societies of their choice (the "membership restrictions") and clauses and concerted practices which ensure that each collecting society will, in the territory in which it is established, enjoy absolute territorial protection from other collecting societies in granting licences to commercial users (the "territorial restrictions"). On the basis of the CISAC model contract, the EEA CISAC members conclude reciprocal representation agreements with each other.

3. The investigation concerning the CISAC model contract and the reciprocal representation agreements between the EEA CISAC members managing public performance rights has its origin in two complaints: a complaint lodged on 30 November 2000 by the RTL Group ("RTL") against GEMA which refused to grant RTL a Community-wide licence over the rights it administers for its own members as well as for the members of other collecting societies on the basis of reciprocal representation agreements for its music broadcasting activities, and a complaint lodged on 4 April 2003 by Music Choice Europe plc ("Music Choice") against CISAC concerning the CISAC model contract described in Section 4.1.

# 2. THE PARTIES

## 2.1. The complainants

Music Choice

4. Music Choice is a digital and interactive audio broadcaster that offers music channels on a multi-platform basis throughout the Community. Music Choice operates on a buyer-to-buyer-to-customer model, that is to say, it sells its programming – bundled into basic or premium subscription packages – to distributors who then retail it to end users. Music Choice provides a web-

based radio and a television service where users can watch a stream of music videos or listen to music channels. The content which Music Choice offers to distributors is already copyright-cleared by Music Choice.

RTL

5. RTL, based in Luxembourg, is a leading broadcasting group and one of the largest audiovisual content production organisations in the EEA.

**2.2. The parties against whom the complaint is made**

CISAC

6. CISAC represents 219 member societies in 115 countries[5]. CISAC is a non-governmental, non-profit making organisation registered under French law and has legal personality. Its statutes were amended at the general assembly which took place in Seoul, South Korea, in October 2004[6]. One of the major objectives of CISAC is to promote reciprocal representation among collecting societies by means of model contracts.

The EEA CISAC members

7. The EEA CISAC members manage authors' (lyricists' and composers') rights, especially their public performance rights. On behalf of their members (authors and publishers) they grant exploitation licences to commercial users.

8. The EEA CISAC members are : Ελληνική Εταιρεία Προστασίας της Πνευματικής Ιδιοκτησίας (AEPI- Greece), Autortiesibu un komunicesanas konsultaciju agentura/Latvijas Autoru apvieniba (AKKA/LAA - Latvia), Staatlich genehmigte Gesellschaft der Autoren, Komponisten und Musikverleger, reg.Gen.m.b.H (AKM - Austria), Magyar Szerzői Jogvédő Iroda Egyesület (ARTISJUS - Hungary), Vereniging Buma (BUMA - Netherlands), Eesti Autorite Ühing (EAÜ - Estonia), Gesellschaft für musikalische Aufführungs- und mechanische Vervielfältigungsrechte (GEMA - Germany), the Irish Music Rights Organisation Limited – Eagras um Chearta Cheolta Teoranta (IMRO - Ireland), Komponistrettigheder i Danmark (KODA - Denmark), Lietuvos autorių teisių gynimo asociacijos agentūra (LATGA-A - Lithuania), Performing Right Society Limited (PRS - United Kingdom), Ochranný svaz autorský pro práva k dílûm hudebním, o.s. (OSA - Czech Republic), Société Belge des Auteurs, Compositeurs et Editeurs Scrl / Belgische Vereniging van Auteurs, Componisten en Uitgevers (SABAM - Belgium), Société des Auteurs, Compositeurs et Editeurs de Musique (SACEM - France), Združenje skladateljev, avtorjev in založnikov za zaščito avtorskih pravic Slovenije (SAZAS - Slovenia), Sociedad General de Autores y Editores (SGAE - Spain), Societa Italiana degli Autori ed Editori (SIAE - Italy), Slovenský ochranný Zväz Autorský pre práva k

5 See CISAC website: www.cisac.org. The total amount of royalties collected by CISAC's member collecting societies, on their own national collection territories, amounted in 2005 to more than EUR 6,7 billion.

6 Under Article 9(4) of the current version of the statutes of CISAC, the general assembly takes place every year.

hudobným dielam (SOZA - Slovakia), Sociedade Portuguesa de Autores (SPA - Portugal), Samband Tónskalda og Eigenda Flutningsréttar (STEF - Iceland), Svenska Tonsättares Internationella Musikbyrå (STIM - Sweden), Säveltäjäin Tekijänoikeustoimisto teosto r.y. (TEOSTO - Finland), the Norwegian Performing Right Society (TONO - Norway), and Stowarzyszenie Autorów ZAiKS (ZAIKS - Poland).[7]

## 3. REGULATORY CONTEXT

9. The legal framework in which the CISAC model contract and the bilateral reciprocal representation agreements operate is composed of national laws regulating collective rights management and Community legislation. At Community level, the protection of copyright for the exploitation of music rights through the internet, cable and satellite is laid down in a number of Directives. Of particular relevance for the exploitation of copyright through the internet is Directive 2001/29/EC of the European Parliament and of the Council of 22 May 2001 on the harmonisation of certain aspects of copyright and related rights in the information society[8], the so called "EU Copyright Directive". That Directive contains a number of provisions aimed at implementing the 1996 World Intellectual Property Organisation (WIPO) Copyright Treaty within Member States[9], relating to reproduction rights, rights of communication to the public and rights of making available to the public, and distributions rights.[10]

10. Council Directive 93/83/EEC of 27 September 1993 on the co-ordination of certain rules concerning copyright and rights related to copyright applicable to satellite broadcasting and cable retransmission[11] establishes a legal framework for the legitimate trans-border exploitation of broadcast services. Article 1 of that Directive harmonises the definition of communication to the public by satellite. Article 1(2)(b) provides: "(b) The act of communication to the public by satellite occurs solely in the Member State where, under the control and responsibility of the broadcasting organization, the programme-carrying signals are introduced into an uninterrupted chain of communication leading to the satellite and down towards the earth". As a consequence of that definition, the applicable law is the law of the Member State where transmission of the signal is initiated. Authors have an exclusive right to authorise this communication of their copyrighted works by satellite (Article 2 of Directive 93/83/EEC). Concerning cable retransmission, Directive 93/83/EEC provides: "rights to grant or refuse authorization to a cable

7 The collecting societies of Bulgaria and Romania are not parties to the procedure in so far as their respective countries were not part of the EEA/Community when the procedure started.

8 OJ L 167, 22.6.2001, p. 10.

9 See Recital 15 of Directive 2001/29/EC.

10 See Articles 2, 3 and 4 of Directive 2001/29/EC.

11 OJ L 248, 6.10.1993, p. 15.

operator for a cable retransmission may be exercised only through a collecting society." (Article 9 of the Directive).

11. Lastly, Directive 2004/48/EC of the European Parliament and of the Council of 29 April 2004 on the enforcement of intellectual property rights[12] is also an important piece of Community legislation and demonstrates that the fight against piracy is of major concern to Community institutions. In that respect, it must be emphasised that this case deals only with the legal exploitation of copyrighted material, that is to say, practices which restrict the ability of collecting societies to grant licences to certain users or with a wider scope. As explained in Recitals 173 to 181 this case does not prevent collecting societies from monitoring the market in order to spot unauthorised use of copyright works, or from taking enforcement measures against such behaviour.

## 4. THE SUBJECT MATTER OF THE PRESENT DECISION

### 4.1. The CISAC model contract

12. In order to grant licences and collect royalties from commercial users abroad, the collecting societies co-operate worldwide on the basis of so-called "reciprocal representation agreements". A reciprocal representation agreement is a contract between two collecting societies whereby the societies give each other the right to grant licences for any public performance of musical works of their respective members[13].

13. The CISAC model contract is a model for reciprocal representation agreements. It was approved for the first time at the CISAC general assembly in 1936[14]. The CISAC model contract serves as a non-mandatory model[15] for reciprocal representation agreements between CISAC's members, especially for the licensing of public performance rights[16]. The CISAC model contract

12 OJ L 157, 30.4.2004, p. 45; corrected version (OJ L 195, 2.6.2004, p. 16).

13 Case 395/87 Ministère Public v. Jean-Louis Tournier [1989] ECR 2521, paragraph 17.

14 The CISAC model contract is drafted and proposed by the executive board of CISAC and is adopted by its general assembly. Over the years, the model contract has been subject to a number of revisions and amendments. The most significant modifications relate to the removal of the exclusivity clause in May 1996 and the removal of the membership clause in June 2004. When not otherwise specified, the CISAC model contract refers to the 30.8.2005 version.

15 Under Article 8 of the statutes of CISAC, the decisions taken by the different bodies of CISAC (executive board, general assembly, director-general, internal committees) are not binding on the members of CISAC but constitute recommendations.

16 "Public" performances are defined in Article 1(III) of the CISAC model contract as consisting of "all sounds and performances rendered audible to the public in any place whatever within the territories in which each of the contracting Societies operates, by any means and in any way whatever, whether the said means be already known and put to use or whether hereafter discovered and put to use during the period when this contract is in force. "Public performance" includes in particular performances provided by live means, instrumental or vocal; by mechanical means such as projection (sound film), of diffusion and transmission, etc...) as well as by any process of wireless reception (radio and television receiving apparatus, telephonic reception, etc... and similar means and devices, etc...)"

applies to all categories of exploitations of musical works requiring a public performance right licence.

## 4.2. The reciprocal representation agreements between the EEA CISAC members

14. In the EEA, each collecting society has signed a reciprocal representation agreement based on the CISAC model contract with all other EEA CISAC members. The CISAC model contract and the bilateral reciprocal representation agreements contained, or contain, clauses concerning the membership of right holders. As regards the entitlement to grant licences to users, the result of the 'web' of bilateral reciprocal representation agreements is that each collecting society is entitled to license not only the repertoire of their own members but also the repertoire of all associated collecting societies (this complete repertoire is hereinafter referred to as the "world repertoire" even though some collecting societies would occasionally not participate in the system).

15. Under that system, each collecting society collects, at the same time, royalties due as a result of exploitation of the rights in its own country, not only for its own members, but also for the authors and publishers abroad who are members of other collecting societies with which it has concluded bilateral representation agreements.

16. Each collecting society has, in principle, the right to license the repertoire of its own members for exploitation outside its domestic territory, and even on a worldwide basis. However, on the basis of the reciprocal representation agreements, each collecting society's ability to define the scope of such mono-repertoire licence may be restricted, and in fact such licences are rarely granted.

17. This also applies to exploitation using new technologies, such as for internet and cable exploitation. For satellite retransmission, collecting societies may grant a licence covering the footprint of the satellite, but only the collecting society based in the country of up link is mandated to grant the licence[17].

## 4.3. The relevant clauses of the CISAC model contract

### *4.3.1. The membership clauses*

18. Article 11(II) of the CISAC model contract provided until June 2004[18] that:

> "While this contract is in force neither of the contracting Societies may, without the consent of the other, accept as a member any member of the other society or any natural person, firm or company having the nationality of one of the countries in which the other Society operates."

---

17 See Section 7.6.1.2. of this Decision.

18 See Section 4.4.1 of this Decision.

19. In April 1990, the CISAC executive board decided to add a second sentence to Article 11(II) which reads as follows:

"Any refusal to consent to such acceptance by the other Society must be duly motivated. In the absence of reply within three months, following a request sent by recorded delivery letter, it shall be presumed that agreement has been given."

20. According to the information provided by CISAC, this new sentence was "annexed to the CISAC Model Contract"[19]. CISAC has not clarified whether this amendment was endorsed by the general assembly[20].

21. Collecting societies which implement Article 11(II) in their bilateral reciprocal representation agreements cannot, therefore, accept members of other collecting societies or right holders having the nationality of another collecting society as a member of its society, without the consent of the latter.

*4.3.2. The territorial clauses*

22. Article 1(I) of the CISAC model contract stated until May 1996[21] that:

"By virtue of the present contract, the SODIX confers on the SODAY the exclusive right, in the territories in which the latter Society operates (as they are defined and delimited in Article 6(1) hereafter), to grant the necessary authorisations for all public performances (as defined in paragraph III of this Article) of musical works, with or without lyrics, which are protected under the terms of national laws, bilateral treaties and multilateral international conventions relating to the author's right (copyright, intellectual property, etc...) now in existence or which may come into existence and enter into effect while the present contract is in force. The exclusive right referred to in the preceding paragraph is conferred insofar as the public performance right in the works concerned has been, or shall be, during the period when the present contract is in force, assigned, transferred or granted by whatever means, for the purpose of its administration, to the SODIX by its members, in accordance with its Articles of Association and Rules the said works collectively constituting "the repertoire of the SODIX".[22]

23. Article 1(II) of the CISAC model contract stated until May 1996[23] that:

---

19 See paragraph 95 of CISAC's Reply to the Statement of Objections.

20 In the CISAC Model Contract which was provided to the Commission by CISAC on 29.11. 2004, the new sentence was not integrated in the text of the agreement or referred to in a footnote in the agreement, but was only contained in the last page of the annexes to the agreement. In its notification of 3 February 1994, PRS attached a CISAC model contract, which, however, does not contain this new sentence, see annex 2 of CISAC's non-confidential Reply to the Statement of Objections.

21 See Section 4.4.1 of this Decision.

22 "SODIX" and "SODAY" refer to the parties to the reciprocal representation agreement in the CISAC model contract and are defined as *the* "society collecting public performance royalties, or public performance rights department of a unitary society".

23 See Section 4.4 1of this Decision.

"Reciprocally, by virtue of the present contract, the SODAY confers on the SODIX the exclusive right, in the territories in which this latter Society operates (as these territories are defined and delimited in Article 6(I) hereafter) to grant the necessary authorisations for all public performances (as defined in paragraph III of this Article) of musical works, with or without lyrics, which are protected under the terms of national laws, bilateral treaties and multilateral international conventions relating to the author's right (copyright, intellectual property etc...) now in existence or which may come into existence and enter into effect while the present contract is in force. The exclusive right referred to in the preceding paragraph is conferred insofar as the public performance right in the works concerned has been, or shall be, during the period when the present contract is in force, assigned, transferred or granted by whatever means, for the purpose of its administration, to the SODAY by its members, in accordance with its Articles of Association and Rules, the said works collectively constituting "the repertoire of the SODAY".

24. Article 6(I) of the CISAC model contract refers to the territories in which the respective collecting societies operate:

"The territories in which the SODIX operates are as follows: ............

The territories in which the SODAY operates are as follows: ............"

25. Article 6(II) of the CISAC model contract provides that:

"For the duration of the present contract, each of the contracting Societies shall refrain from any intervention within the territory of the other Society in the latter's exercise of the mandate conferred by the present contract."

26. The interaction between Articles 1(I), 1(II), 6(I) and 6(II) of the CISAC model contract may be described as follows: under Article 1(I), a collecting society authorises another collecting society to licence and administer its repertoire in the territory as defined in Article 6(I). The CISAC model contract leaves the definition of the territories blank. Each collecting society has to specify in its reciprocal representation agreement the scope of its territory. Under Article 6(II), the collecting society which has granted the authorisation refrains from "any intervention within the territory of the other collecting society", as defined by Article 6(I). In each reciprocal representation agreement signed by two collecting societies, this reciprocal system is implemented.

### 4.4. Application of the relevant clauses of the CISAC Model Contract

#### *4.4.1. Changes to the CISAC model contract*

Article 11(II) of the CISAC model contract (the membership clause)

27. In response to a Commission request for information of 30 September 2004, CISAC explained in a letter of 6 October 2004 that CISAC's Legal Committee proposed the deletion of Article 11(II) at its meeting of 3 June 2004. However, in response to another Commission request of 11 November

2004, CISAC sent as an annex to its answer (dated of 29 November 2004), the latest version of the CISAC model contract. That version still contains Article 11(II) but CISAC indicated that it was in the process of incorporating the latest amendments into its model contract. On 10 April 2006, CISAC replied to the Statement of Objections. CISAC attached to its Reply the 30 August 2005 version of its model contract. Footnote 42 of this model contract indicates that Article 11(II) was deleted in June 2004. Accordingly, it must be concluded that Article 11(II) remained part of the CISAC model contract until 3 June 2004.

Articles 1(I) and 1(II) of the CISAC model contract

28. Since 1996, the CISAC model contract applicable to EEA CISAC members no longer contains the exclusivity clauses in Articles 1(I) and 1(II)[24]. Indeed, CISAC demonstrated in its Reply to the Statement of Objections that its Legal Committee recommended in May 1996 not to propose the exclusivity to EEA CISAC members. This recommendation was adopted by the general assembly of CISAC on 18 and 19 September 1996[25].

Article 6 (I) and 6(II) of the CISAC model contract

29. To date, the territorial clauses laid down in Article 6(I) and 6(II) continue to be part of the CISAC model contract.

4.4.2. *Implementation of the CISAC model contract in reciprocal representation agreements between EEA CISAC members*

Implementation of Article 11(II) of the CISAC model contract (the membership clause)

30. The membership clause remains present in a significant number of bilateral reciprocal representation agreements and it has structured the relationship and the behaviour of EEA CISAC members for decades. The Commission's investigation shows that 23 of the Addressees of the Statement of Objections (all but PRS) have indicated that this model clause is present in a significant number of their bilateral reciprocal representation agreements[26]. Some of these EEA CISAC members have expressly indicated that they effectively apply this clause: BUMA, OSA, SIAE, SPA and ZAIKS. IMRO has indicated in its reply to a request for information sent in March 2005 that it "seeks the consent of an affiliate (i.e. the other society) if an applicant is already a member of that society". Some of the other EEA CISAC members claimed in their Replies to the Statement of Objections that they do not apply such a

24 See footnote 1 of the current CISAC model contract which states that any exclusivity in reciprocal representation agreements between its EEA members "is not possible".

25 See page 25 and annex 5 of CISAC's Reply to the Statement of Objections.

26 See the answers of the EEA collecting societies to the request for information sent on 11.3.2005.

clause despite the fact that it is present in the agreements, but no evidence has been put forward in order to demonstrate that assertion[27].

31. Most of the bilateral reciprocal representation agreements submitted to the Commission contain only the first sentence of Article 11(II), but not the second sentence which was "annexed" to the CISAC model contract.

32. Most of the EEA CISAC members have indicated that they have modified or wanted to modify their reciprocal representation agreements in order to remove the membership clause and have accordingly sent copies to the Commission of their correspondence with the other EEA CISAC members. This is the case for AKM[28], ARTISJUS, BUMA, GEMA, KODA, OSA, SACEM, SAZAS, SIAE, SGAE, SOZA, STIM and TONO. However, some of the documents sent by these collecting societies to the Commission were only offers to modify the agreements, which were not countersigned by the other collecting societies. KODA only sent the Commission a copy of an amended version of its reciprocal representation agreement which was, according to KODA, proposed to the other parties.[29]

33. PRS replied that only one of its reciprocal representation agreements provided for that clause and that it has been recently modified in order to eliminate the membership restriction[30]. However, it appears from the

---

27 These collecting societies are: AEPI, AKKA-LAA, ARTISJUS, EAU, GEMA, PRS, SAZAS, SGAE, SOZA, STIM and TONO.

28 In addition, AKM alleges that its bilateral reciprocal representation agreements no longer contain the membership clause because they are permanently adapted to the decisions of CISAC, see pages 8 f. and 27 of AKM's non-confidential Reply to the Statement of Objections. AKM refers to Article 12 of the CISAC model contract which is allegedly contained in all of its reciprocal representation agreements and which reads as follows: *"The present contract is subject to the provisions of the Statutes and decisions of the International Confederation of Societies of Authors and Composers."* However, the wording of this clause does not give rise to the automatic amending of the bilateral reciprocal representation agreement to conform with the CISAC model contract. The CISAC model contract contains in Article 12 a clause with the same wording. When discussing the membership clause and its use by collecting societies in the non-confidential version of its Reply to the Statement of Objections (paragraph 99 ff.), CISAC does not mention Article 12 of the CISAC model contract. On the contrary, it may be concluded from CISAC's description of the function of the CISAC model contract (paragraph 80 ff. of the non-confidential version of its Reply to the Statement of Objections) that Article 12 is not meant by CISAC to bring about the automatic amendment of bilateral reciprocal representation agreements so as to conform to the CISAC model contract. AKM itself does not seem to be of this opinion, because after 3 June 2004 – when CISAC had decided to delete the membership clause in the CISAC model contract – AKM agreed with some collecting societies to remove the membership clause from the bilateral reciprocal representation agreements without ever making the point that, in view of Article 12, the bilateral reciprocal representation agreement would no longer contain the membership clause.

29 STIM has provided evidence in their Reply to the Statement of Objections that the membership clause was deleted from its reciprocal representation agreements with most of the collecting societies in March/April 2006. In February 2008, STIM wrote to the Commission to explain that it had unilaterally 'repudiated' the restrictive membership restrictions with the remaining of the collecting societies.

30 On 18 April 2005, PRS replied to a request for information sent on 11 March 2005 concerning the implementation of the CISAC model contract by collecting societies. In its Reply, PRS indicated that it does not apply the membership restrictions: "*The bilateral agreements that PRS has entered into with other EEA collecting societies do not contain this Article. There is one exception and that is the agreement PRS has concluded with the Austrian collecting society AKM. The continued presence of the*

Commission's file that PRS has undoubtedly applied the membership restrictions: in an exchange of emails of 28 September 2004 with a Hungarian right holder, wishing to join PRS, an official of PRS wrote: "Dear Mr [...], Thank you for your recent application for membership of PRS. As you are a Hungarian national, we are required to seek permission from ARTISJUS before admitting you to membership of PRS. This is normally a formality. However, as you will see from the emails below, ARTISJUS claim that you are actually a member of ARTISJUS. This is not reflected in the internationally recognised SUISA/IPI file. If this is the case, you will have to resign from ARTISJUS before we can admit you to membership of PRS. ARTISJUS have confirmed that they do not have a problem with this, but you will need to contact them directly"[31].

34. In addition, in a letter sent to ARTISJUS on 14 September 2004, PRS wrote concerning the application of this Hungarian right holder that: "PRS have received an application for writer membership from [...]. He is a Hungarian national who was born in Budapest on... and is now a resident in the UK. Could you please confirm whether ARTISJUS have any objection to this application...?". These exchanges of correspondence are a clear application of the membership restrictions. PRS was requested to comment on these documents. It argued that it had sent the letter of 14 September 2004 to ARTISJUS because it did not know whether this right holder was a member of ARTISJUS[32]. This explanation does not appear to be consistent with either the content of the letter sent to ARTISJUS or with the exchange of e-mails between PRS and the right holder involved[33].

35. Although at least one EEA CISAC member (STIM) claims to have unilaterally brought to an end the membership clause in all its reciprocal representation agreements where it remained, taking into account that this has been done belatedly (well after the Statement of Objections) and the legal scope of such a purely unilateral removal of the membership clause is unclear, it cannot be safely concluded that any of the 24 EEA CISAC members have actually and completely removed their membership clause from its reciprocal representation agreements.

---

*above clause in that agreement is an oversight and PRS will take the steps to remove it. In any event it is not applied in practice".* See pages 1 and 2 of PRS' non-confidential Reply to the Statement of Objections dated 12 of January 2006. On 7 November 2005, PRS wrote to the Commission to inform it that the membership restrictions contained in the reciprocal representation agreement with AKM had been removed on 1 of August 2005 and provided the Commission with a copy of the amendment signed by PRS and AKM.

31 E-mail of 28 September 2004 sent by an official of PRS to a Hungarian right holder member of the Hungarian collecting society, ARTISJUS.

32 Reply dated of 2 June 2006 by PRS to the Commission's request for information dated 19 May 2006. See notably page 4 of the non-confidential version of PRS' Reply.

33 As the Court of First Instance of the European Communities stated in a recent judgment, "*...the duration of an infringement must be appraised not by reference to the period during which an agreement is in force, but by reference to the period during which the undertakings concerned adopted conduct prohibited by Article 81 EC...*" (Joined cases T-101/05 and T-111/05, BASF AG and UCB SA v Commission of the European Communities , judgment of 12 December 2007, paragraph 187).

Implementation of the exclusivity clauses of Articles 1(I) and 1(II) of the CISAC model contract.

36. The exclusivity referred to in Article 1 of the CISAC model contract is itself reflected in the bilateral reciprocal representation agreements concluded between 17 EEA CISAC members: AKKA/LAA, ARTISJUS, BUMA, EAU, IMRO, KODA LATGA-A, OSA, SAZAS, SGAE, SOZA, SPA, STIM, STEF, TONO, TEOSTO, ZAIKS[34]. Certain of these 17 collecting societies claim that all of their reciprocal representation agreements contain such exclusivity (AKKA/LAA, EAÜ, LATGA, OSA, SAZAS, SPA, TONO, and ZAIKS). The others claim that the exclusivity is not present in all their reciprocal representation agreements (ARTISJUS, BUMA, KODA, IMRO, SOZA, SGAE, STIM, STEF and TEOSTO). Finally, SGAE claims that, even though the exclusivity clause is present in some of their bilateral reciprocal representation agreements, it is not applied. However, no evidence has been brought to the Commission's attention to confirm that claim.

37. Certain EEA CISAC members have indicated that they have modified or wanted to modify their reciprocal representation agreements in order remove the exclusivity clause at issue and accordingly forwarded copies to the Commission of their correspondence with the other EEA CISAC members. This is the case for ARTISJUS, BUMA, KODA, OSA, SAZAS, SOZA, SGAE, STIM and TONO. However, some of the documents sent by these collecting societies to the Commission were only offers to modify the agreements, which were not counter signed by the other collecting societies. KODA merely provided a copy to the Commission of an amended model agreement which was, according to KODA, proposed to the other parties.[35] Although at least one collecting society (STIM) claims to have unilaterally repudiated the exclusivity clause in all its agreements where it remained, taking into account that this has been done belatedly (well after the Statement of Objections) and the legal scope of such a repudiation is unclear, it cannot be safely concluded that any of the 17 EEA CISAC members mentioned above have actually and completely removed the exclusivity clause from their reciprocal representation agreements.

Implementation of Articles 6(I) and 6(II) of the CISAC model contract

38. All the EEA CISAC members have implemented Article 6(I) of the CISAC model contract in their bilateral reciprocal representation agreements in a way which confines each collecting society's licences to its own domestic territory[36]. In practice this means that a collecting society always grants

[34] See the Replies to the request for information sent on 11 March 2005 to the EEA collecting societies.

[35] STIM has provided evidence in their Reply to the Statement of Objections that the exclusivity clause had been deleted from their reciprocal representation agreements with most of the collecting societies in March/April 2006. In February 2008, STIM wrote to the Commission to explain that it had unilaterally repudiated the exclusivity clause with the remaining of the collecting societies.

[36] The French collecting society SACEM also covers the territory of Luxembourg which has no "domestic" collecting society. The Alliance MSCP-PRS operates also in Malta where there is no "domestic" collecting society.

licences to both its own repertoire, and to the repertoires of other collecting societies, on a mono-territorial basis.

39. Reciprocal representation agreements concluded by all EEA CISAC members also contain provisions which replicate Article 6(II) of the CISAC model contract.

40. By a letter of 7 November 2005, PRS informed the Commission that it had written to the other EEA CISAC members on 12 October 2005 in order to remove Article 6(II) from the reciprocal representation agreements where this Article was present (contracts between PRS and KODA, TEOSTO, SACEM, GEMA, AEPI, STEF, SIAE, BUMA, TONO, ZAIKS, SPA, SAZAS, STIM and SGAE). PRS submitted amended reciprocal representation agreements in respect of ZAIKS, STEF, TONO and BUMA, to the Commission, wherein those parties agreed to modify their reciprocal representation agreements accordingly. Certain other EEA CISAC members have indicated that they have modified or wanted to modify their reciprocal representation agreements in order remove the exclusivity clause at issue and accordingly forwarded copies to the Commission of their correspondence with the other EEA CISAC members. This is the case, for example, for AKM, ARTISJUS, BUMA, GEMA, KODA, OSA, SAZAS, SIAE, SGAE, STIM and TONO. However, some of the documents sent by those collecting societies to the Commission were only offers to modify the agreements and were not countersigned by the other collecting societies. KODA merely sent a copy to the Commission of an amended model contract which was, according to KODA, proposed to the other parties. At present, the Commission has no evidence in its possession that any of the EEA CISAC members have actually and completely removed this clause from their reciprocal representation agreements.

## 5. THE RELEVANT MARKETS

### 5.1. Structure of the market

#### *5.1.1. The copyright held by right holders*

41. Authors hold the copyright on the musical works they have created. A copyright usually entails an exclusive right to authorise or prohibit the exploitation of the protected works. This is notably the case for public performance rights, at issue in this Decision.

42. The licensing of copyright can be ensured by individual or collective management. However, individual management is in many instances not feasible; as either the applicable national law provides for compulsory collective management, sometimes even pursuant to Community law,[37] or the market features render any individual management inefficient or impossible. Indeed, for many small or medium-sized right holders, it seems that

[37] Certain national laws provide for compulsory collective management for certain rights. At Community level, Article 9 of Directive 93/83/EEC states that: "Member States shall ensure that the right of copyright owners ...to grant or refuse authorisation to a cable operator for a cable retransmission may be exercised only through a collecting society".

individual management does not represent a viable option for the management of public performance rights. It is, therefore, often necessary to have recourse to collective management, and direct management of the rights by the author is wholly exceptional.

*5.1.2. How do collecting societies obtain the rights they licence to commercial users?*

43. Collecting societies manage copyright on behalf of their members. Collecting societies obtain rights from two sources: either by direct transfer[38] from the original right holders or via a reciprocal representation agreement with another collecting society managing the same categories of rights in another EEA country. If a right holder transfers the rights to a collecting society he or she becomes a member of that collecting society. In some cases the transfer of rights to collecting societies is made mandatory. For example, this is the situation for the cable retransmission right whereby Directive 93/83/EEC provides that such a right may be exercised only through a collecting society[39]. In certain cases, national laws provide that the collecting society may also grant licences of works of right holders who are not members of a collecting society (extended collective management system).

44. As a consequence of the transfer of rights from various right holders, a collecting society has a portfolio of works. This portfolio constitutes the national repertoire of the collecting society. However, the overall repertoire of a collecting society is much broader; it encompasses also the repertoires of other collecting societies which have signed a reciprocal representation agreement with it.

*5.1.3. The licensing of copyright*

45. A collecting society licences the rights to commercial users. In return, the collecting societies collect and distribute royalties to the right holders. Although the markets for the licensing and administration of public performance rights for satellite, cable and internet use display distinct characteristics[40], the practices of the collecting societies in terms of licensing, administration and reciprocal representation remain almost identical to the traditional ways of operating in the commercial premises licensing market (such as discos, bars) where local monitoring is necessary.

*5.1.4. Monitoring of the use of the licence, auditing of commercial users' accounts and enforcement vis-à-vis the licensee*

46. Like other entities licensing intellectual property rights, collecting societies ensure the monitoring of the use of the licensed intellectual property rights, the auditing of the commercial users' accounts and the enforcement of copyright in the case of infringement of the rights.

---

38 Under certain jurisdictions, right holders have to either transfer their rights to the collecting society or entrust them to the latter. For the purpose of this Decision, the term "transfer" covers both mechanisms.

39 Article 9 of Directive 93/83/EEC.

40 See Section 7.6.1.4 as regards the description of the distinguishing features of these markets, notably issues relating to the monitoring, auditing and enforcement of granted licences.

47. It is important to emphasise that this Decision only deals with lawful uses of works. Acts of piracy or use in the absence of an exploitation licence are therefore outside the scope of this Decision. Accordingly, the considerations and assessments in this Decision are valid only within the limits of the usual and normal relationship between collecting societies and commercial users and for specific exploitations described in Section 5.2 concerning the relevant product markets.

**5.2. Relevant product markets**

48. In its two Sony/BMG Decisions[41] as in theSeagram/Polygram Decision[42] the Commission found that exploitation on the basis of the different types of rights may lead to the defining of separate product markets for each category of rights, although the precise market definition was left open in that regard. Both demand-side (different characteristics of rights relating to different customer needs) and supply-side considerations (existence of different exploitation systems, application of dissimilar licensing rates) supported that finding.

49. Collective management of copyright covers different activities corresponding to many different relevant product markets which are all affected by the CISAC model contract:

(a) The provision of copyright administration services to right holders,

(b) The provision of copyright administration services to other collecting societies,

(c) The licensing of public performance rights for satellite, cable and internet transmissions to commercial users.

50. Due to the fact that the CISAC model contract deals with public performance rights, the product market at issue in this Decision is restricted to such rights.

*5.2.1. The copyright administration services for public performance rights*

(a) Copyright administration services to authors (the right holders' market)

51. The first relevant product market is the market for the provision of copyright administration services to right holders regarding public performance rights. On the supply side, this market is characterised by collecting societies offering the administration of public performance rights to right holders of copyright protected musical works, who on the demand side wish to engage in a collective copyright management scheme. If a right holder transfers the

---

41 Commission Decision of 19.07. 2004 (Case No COMP/M.3333 — SONY/BMG) recitals 25 and 26 (OJ L 62, 9.3.2005, p 30). and Commission Decision of 3.10.2007 (case No COMP/M.3333- SONY/BMG, recital 22 (OJ C 94, 16.4.2008, p.19). A public version in English of the two decisions can found at *http://ec.europa.eu/comm/competition/mergers/cases/index/m66.html#m_3333*.

42 Commission Decision of 21.09.1998 (Case No IV/M.1219 Seagram/Polygram) recital 17, OJ C 309, 9.10.1998. A public version in English of the decision can found at: http://ec.europa.eu/comm/competition/mergers/cases/decisions/m1219_en.pdf.

administration of his or her rights to a collecting society, he or she becomes a member of that collecting society.

(b) Copyright administration services to other collecting societies

52. The second relevant product market is the market for the provision of copyright administration services by one collecting society to another regarding public performance rights. On the supply side, this market is characterised by collecting societies that are willing and capable of administering the public performance rights of other collecting societies.

53. The demand side is characterised by collecting societies seeking to obtain the administration of their repertoire outside the EEA country where they are established. The demand side, therefore, features collecting societies which have been mandated by their members to administer the performance rights associated with their repertoires in territories other than that in which the collecting society is established. The services which the collecting societies provide to each other cover, in particular, the granting of licences for the use of the copyright work, the monitoring and auditing of such use by the licensee, the billing of users, the checking of the actual use of the music by licensees in order to allocate the royalties to different authors, and the subsequent collection of royalties and transferring of collected royalties to the recipient collecting societies. These services also include general monitoring of the market to spot those companies or individuals using music, and therefore needing a licence, and taking enforcement measures, if need be, to ensure that those companies or individuals obtain the necessary licence or otherwise cease unlawful exploitation of the work.

*5.2.2. The licensing of public performance rights for satellite, cable and internet transmissions (the licensing market)*[43]

54. The third relevant product market is the market for licensing of public performance rights to commercial users for satellite, cable and internet use. This market has specific features which are not present in the other markets covered by the CISAC model contract for public performance rights and the bilateral reciprocal representation agreements (essentially the offline environment). The main differences concern the technical possibility of remote monitoring and of copyright exploitation of public performance rights through the internet, satellite and cable environment beyond national territories. As a consequence, a distinction may be drawn between the markets covered by the preliminary rulings in Tournier and Lucazeau[44] (off-line environment) and the market at issue in this Decision. The specificities of that market and their consequences are further discussed in Section 5.3.3.

55. With respect to the licensing of public performance rights to commercial users for satellite, cable and internet use, SABAM has argued that a

43 It is understood that for the purposes of this Decision, a "cable retransmission" means a retransmission of a satellite transmission and within the satellite footprint. This Decision does not deal with the question of the liability of the different market players for acquisition of the cable retransmission right.

44 Case 395/87 - Ministère Public v. Jean-Louis Tournier [1989] ECR 2531 and Joined cases 110/88, 241/88 and 242/88 - François Lucazeau and others v Societé des Auteurs, Compositeurs et Editeurs de Musique (SACEM) and others, [1989] ECR 2811.

distinction should be drawn between multi-territorial licences of the world music repertoire, and mono-territorial (national licences) of the same world music repertoire, which would constitute a different product market. The lack of substitutability between the two products on the demand and supply side would stem from the different territorial scope of the licences that reflect different users and user needs.[45]

56. The existence of two different products is essentially the result of the practices introduced by collecting societies. In a world where territorial restrictions were removed, users would have little incentive to opt for mono-territorial licences and would accordingly request multi-territorial licences. On the demand-side, it can reasonably be argued that a certain degree of substitutability exists between the two products since users of mono-territorial and multi-territorial licences often compete on the same markets for final consumers. A content provider operating in four EEA countries could in theory sign either mono-territorial licences with the four collecting societies located in the countries where it operates, or sign one multi-territorial licence with one collecting society covering part or all of the EEA.

57. Technical and legal distinctions could militate in favour of separate product markets for each of the satellite, cable and internet transmission modes. Cable and satellite television is subject to specific regulatory frameworks and a variety of internet based transmissions display particular features. A number of users will not need a licence which covers all three modes of transmissions. However, in view of the increasing convergence between television and internet services, this might change.

### 5.3. Relevant geographic market

#### *5.3.1. The geographic scope of the market for the provision of copyright administration services to right holders*

58. The geographic scope of the market for the provision of copyright administration services to authors regarding public performance rights is national. Quite apart from factors, such as cultural or linguistic, which may influence this situation, the fact remains that membership restrictions and other measures which restrict the ability of right holders to entrust their rights on a non-exclusive basis, have contributed to this effect for decades, even in cases where such clauses have been disappearing.

59. However in the absence of the membership restrictions, the geographic market could potentially be broader, since authors could switch between collecting societies and transfer their rights to those collecting societies which would provide the best service to them.

---

45 See pages 8 to 10 of SABAM's non-confidential Reply to the Statement of Objections.

*5.3.2. The geographic scope of the market for the provision of copyright administration services to other collecting societies regarding public performance rights*

60. The geographic scope of the market for the provision of copyright administration services to other public performance rights collecting societies has both a national aspect and wider cross-border elements.

61. The collecting societies administer the repertoires of other collecting societies. Under the present bilateral reciprocal representation agreements they are confined to doing so within their own national territory. Every collecting society, therefore, holds under the current network of reciprocal representation agreements, a monopoly over services to be provided within their respective national territories for other collecting societies abroad.

62. Internet and satellite transmission activities are, however, not confined to a single EEA country. Undertakings engaged in such activities therefore demand multi-territorial licences. As a consequence, a collecting society licensing a commercial user to upload audiovisual content on the internet would, in the absence of the restrictions contained in the bilateral representation agreements, be able to grant a multi-territorial licence. Similarly, in the case of satellite transmission and cable retransmission, any collecting society located within the satellite footprint would be able to grant licences covering the footprint of the satellite.

*5.3.3. The market for the licensing of public performance rights for satellite, cable and internet broadcasting to commercial users*

63. When defining the geographic market, the Commission identifies possible obstacles and barriers isolating undertakings in a given area from the competitive pressure of undertakings located outside the area in question[46]. Historically, the Commission has defined relevant markets in the framework of traditional copyright licensing as being national[47]. The need for local monitoring and the economies of scale involved in engaging in such an activity imply that it has not been considered viable, until now, for collecting societies to operate in the territory of another collecting society. In view of the organisation of collecting societies and their current licensing practices, the relevant geographic market can be defined as being national in scope.

64. Those reasons do not, however, necessarily apply outside the traditional off-line world where remote monitoring is possible. Technical and economic barriers preventing collecting societies from entering the markets of other collecting societies have clearly diminished. The potential market is therefore much broader – the geographic market for satellite broadcasting and cable retransmission could be considered to be the entire satellite footprint; for

46 Commission Notice on the definition of the relevant market for the purposes of Community competition law (OJ C 372, 9.12.1997, p. 5) at paragraph 30.

47 Commission Decision 71/224/EEC of 2 June 1971 relating to proceedings under Article 86 of the Treaty (IV/26 760-GEMA) (OJ L 134, 20.6.1971, p. 15) at Section II.B. Decision as amended by Decision 72/268/EEC (OJ L 166, 24.7.1972, p. 22); Commission Decision 81/1030/EEC of 29 October 1981 relating to a proceeding under Article 86 of the EEC Treaty (IV/29.839 - GVL) (OJ L 370, 28.12.1981, p. 49) at Recital 45.

internet use, the geographic scope of the market is potentially worldwide, or at least regional in scope.

## 6. PROCEDURE

65. This case started in November 2000 with the lodging of a complaint by RTL against GEMA. In April 2003, another commercial user, Music Choice – a digital audio broadcaster – also complained against CISAC.

### 6.1. The Statement of Objections

66. On 31 January 2006, the Commission issued a Statement of Objections to CISAC and to the EEA CISAC members. On the same date, a CD ROM containing the Commission's file was sent to CISAC and to the EEA CISAC members as an attachment to the Statement of Objections. The addressees were granted a two month deadline to reply. LATGA-A, SPA and STEF did not lodge a Reply to the Statement of Objections.

### 6.2. The Oral Hearing

67. All addressees of the Statement of Objections, with the exception of EAÜ and those who did not reply to the Statement of Objections (namely LATGA-A, SPA and STEF), requested an oral hearing pursuant to Article 12 of Regulation (EC) No 773/2004. SOZA, ARTISJUS and OSA were represented by CISAC legal representatives.

68. The Oral Hearing took place on 14, 15 and 16 June 2006. Twenty-seven undertakings requested to be granted, and obtained, the status of interested third parties in the proceedings. Some of them did not request to be heard in a formal oral hearing.[48] All other third parties were admitted to the oral hearing.[49] They were informed about the substance of the case by means of a non-confidential version of the Statement of Objections and were requested to submit comments.

### 6.3. Further requests for information

69. Requests for information were sent after the issuing of the Statements of Objections. Access to these requests and replies thereto, as well as to comments by third parties in the Statement of Objections, were given to the addressees of the Statement of Objections on 5 July 2006. In addition, between mid-September 2006 and 20 November 2006, the Commission sent a new request for information in order to gather more financial and economic data related to the markets involved. On 18 December 2006, access was given to these requests and the replies thereto.

48 British Telecom, Deutsche Telekom, Ericsson, Infospace and the BBC.

49 They were: (i) EDIMA, (ii) IFPI, (iii) RTL Group, (iv) Music Choice, (v) Footprint, (vi) IMPALA, (vii) Universal Music International, (viii) Music users , (ix) ICMP, (x) NextRadioTv, (xi) EBU, (xii) ZDF, (xiii) ARD, (xiv) VPRT, (xv) SKAP, (xvi) EICTA, (xvii) ECCA, (xviii) ROAIM, (xix) FFACE, (xx) Vodafone, (xxi) ACT and (xxii) UTECA.

### 6.4. Notice published pursuant to Article 27(4) of Regulation (EC) No 1/2003

70. CISAC and 18 EEA CISAC members namely AEPI (Greece), AKM (Austria), ARTISJUS (Hungary), BUMA (Netherlands), GEMA (Germany), IMRO (Ireland), LATGA-A (Lithuania), PRS (United Kingdom), SABAM (Belgium), SACEM (France), SGAE (Spain), SIAE (Italy), SPA (Portugal), STEF (Iceland), STIM (Sweden), TEOSTO (Finland), TONO (Norway), SOZA (Slovakia)) offered commitments in March 2007.

71. In short, the commitments were the following: CISAC offered not to recommend the 'membership clause' for insertion into the reciprocal representation agreements between EEA CISAC members and the 18 EEA CISAC members offered to remove it from representation agreements concluded with other EEA CISAC members. In relation to the 'territoriality clauses', CISAC offered not to recommend the granting of exclusive rights between EEA CISAC members, and the 18 EEA CISAC members offered to remove such clauses from the reciprocal representation agreements concluded with other EEA CISAC members. In addition, with regard to 'territorial delineation', the signatory societies undertook to grant multi-repertoire, multi-territorial performing right licences for internet services, satellite services and cable retransmission services to each signatory society that fulfilled certain qualitative criteria.[50]

72. The commitments have been market tested by the publication of a Notice pursuant to Article 27(4) of Regulation 1/2003 on 9 June 2007[51]. More than 80 observations were submitted. Market players, that is to say, broadcasters, content providers and certain collecting societies, generally considered that the proposed commitments would not be effective and almost none of the potential licensees would be eligible under the definitions and exceptions listed in the proposed commitments, to obtain a multi-territorial multi-repertoire licence. Additionally, certain EEA CISAC members who had offered the proposed commitments took the opportunity of the market test to criticise them. It must therefore be concluded that the proposed commitments would not give an appropriate answer to the competition concerns raised in the Statement of Objections.

73. A non-confidential version of the comments made by the market players during the market test period was sent to all the addressees of the Statement of Objections.

## 7. ARTICLE 81(1) OF THE TREATY AND 53(1) OF THE EEA AGREEMENT

74. This Decision concerns:

---

[50] See paragraphs 9, 10 and 11 of the Notice published pursuant to Article 27(4) of Council Regulation No 1/2003 in Case COMP/38698- CISAC (OJ C 128, 9.6.2007, p. 12).

[51] OJ C 128, 09.06.2007, p. 12.

(a) membership restrictions contained in the reciprocal representation agreements which prevent competition between EEA CISAC members for the provision of their services to authors; and

(b) territorial restrictions which prevent competition between EEA CISAC members for the licensing of performing rights to commercial users; the territorial restrictions take the form of express exclusivities in the reciprocal representation agreements and a concerted practice on the territorial delineation of the scope of the licence.

75. As regards the membership restrictions of collecting societies, the Commission tackled certain anti-competitive practices vis-à-vis right holders in the 1971 GEMA Decision[52] and gave clear indications concerning the limitations which competition law imposes on the relationship between authors' collective societies and their members. First, the GEMA Decision precludes collecting societies from engaging in discrimination based on the nationality of right holders (notably as regards the terms of membership or the methods for distributing collected royalties). Second, the GEMA Decision gave some guidance concerning the length and the scope of the contract between collecting societies and right holders: it was made clear in that Decision that collecting societies could not impose contracts that were too long term nor oblige right holders to assign their rights on an exclusive basis and for a compulsory worldwide exploitation. In its judgement of 27 March 1974 in Belgische Radio en Televisie v SV SABAM and NV Fonior, the Court of Justice ruled that the conditions imposed by a collecting society on its members could infringe Article 82 of the Treaty if they encroached upon a member's freedom to exercise his copyright beyond that which is necessary 'for the attainment of its object'.[53]

76. In its judgment in Gesellschaft zur Verwertung von Leistungsschutzrechten mbH (GVL) v Commission of the European Communities[54], the Court of Justice upheld a Commission Decision[55] which found that GVL, a German collecting society managing certain related rights for performing artists in Germany, had breached Article 82 of the Treaty by refusing to conclude management contracts with right holders who were neither German nationals nor resident in Germany and also by refusing to protect the rights of such artists in Germany. The Court found in particular that the refusal by GVL – which had a de facto dominant position on the market in services relating to the management of secondary exploitation rights vested in performing artists – to conclude management agreements with foreign artists, having no residence in Germany, constituted discrimination on grounds of nationality and had the effect of partitioning the common market, and thereby restricting the freedom to provide services. The Court specified that the restriction on

52 Decision 71/224/EEC.

53 Case 127/73 - Belgische Radio en Televisie v SV SABAM and NV Fonior [1974] ECR 313, at paragraph 15.

54 Case 7/82 - Gesellschaft zur Verwertung von Leistungsschutzrechten mbH (GVL) v Commission of the European Communities [1983] ECR 483, paragraphs 38 and 47.

55 Decision 81/1030/EEC.

movement was appreciable "since a multitude of foreign holders of rights were prevented from exploiting their rights in Germany".[56]

77. Territorial restrictions between collecting societies were directly addressed by the Court of Justice in the cases Ministère Public v. Jean-Louis Tournier[57] and in Lucazeau v. Société des Auteurs, Compositeurs et Editeurs de Musique (Sacem) and others[58]. However, already in Greenwich Film v. Société des Auteurs, Compositeurs et Editeurs de Musique (SACEM) and Société des éditions Labrador, the Court of Justice made clear that "the activities of such associations [the collecting societies] may be conducted in such a way that their effect is to partition the Common Market and thereby restrict the freedom to provide services which constitutes one of the objectives of the Treaty"[59].

78. In the Tournier and Lucazeau preliminary rulings, the Court of Justice held that "...the reciprocal representation contracts in question are contracts for services which are not in themselves restrictive of competition...The position might be different if the contracts established exclusive rights whereby copyright-management societies undertook not to allow direct access to their repertoires by users of recorded music established abroad"[60]. In addition, the Court of Justice made clear that "any concerted practice by national copyright management societies of the Member States having as its object or effect the refusal by each society to grant direct access to its repertoire to users established in another Member States"[61] is anti-competitive.

79. The Court of Justice dealt with the reciprocal representation contracts between authors' collecting societies in the specific context of copyright licensing of performance rights for physical premises such as discos, hotels, bars and restaurants. The Court considered that "the mere parallel behaviour may amount to strong evidence of a concerted practice if it leads to conditions of competition which do not correspond to the normal conditions of competition. However, concerted action of this kind cannot be presumed where the parallel behaviour can be accounted for by reasons other than the

---

56 See paragraph 35 of the judgement.

57 Case 395/87- Ministère Public v. Jean-Louis Tournier [1989] ECR 2521, at paragraph 17.

58 Joined cases 110/88, 241/88 and 242/88 - François Lucazeau and others v Societé des Auteurs, Compositeurs et Editeurs de Musique (SACEM) and others [1989] ECR 2811.

59 Case 22/79 - Greenwich Film v Societé des Auteurs, Compositeurs et Editeurs de Musique (SACEM) and Societé des éditions Labrador [1979] ECR 3275.

60 Judgement of the Court of Justice in Case 395/87 - Ministère Public v. Jean-Louis Tournier, at paragraph 20; see also judgement of the Court of Justice in joined cases 110/88, 241/88 and 242/88 - François Lucazeau and others v Societé des Auteurs, Compositeurs et Editeurs de Musique (SACEM) and others, [1989] ECR 2811, at paragraph 14.

61 Case 395/87 - Ministère Public v. Jean-Louis Tournier, paragraph 26, Joined cases 110/88, 241/88 and 242/88 - François Lucazeau and others v Societé des Auteurs, Compositeurs et Editeurs de Musique (SACEM) and othersat paragraph 20.

existence of concerted action."[62] For copyright licensing for physical premises, the Court found that such a reason might be that collecting societies of other Member States would be obliged, in order to license their repertoire outside their own territory, to organise their own management and monitoring system in another country.

80. The present Decision assesses the systematic territorial delineation for copyright licensing of music rights for certain types of exploitation (satellite, cable broadcasting and the internet), in light of the test established in the Tournier and Lucazeau cases and the characteristics of these new forms of exploitation.

81. The Commission has adopted two Decisions concerning the relationship between collecting societies and commercial users, either in a multi-territorial and/or electronic environment; the Simulcasting Decision[63] and the Cannes Extension Agreement Decision.[64]

82. In the Cannes Extension Agreement Decision, one of the issues at stake was the price of the multi-territorial licence granted to users (record companies) for mechanical rights. Under the system put in place by authors' collecting societies (with the consent of the publishers), a record company could conclude a single licensing agreement with only one collecting society for the whole of the EEA territory or for part thereof. The record company had to pay all royalties due for the EEA exploitation of the works to the single collecting society in question. This collecting society applied the uniform rate agreed between all collecting societies and any rebate to users was practically impossible. However, the Cannes Extension Agreement Decision imposed binding commitments whereby collecting societies could introduce a mechanism to grant a certain and maximum rebate to record companies which contracted for a multi-territorial mechanical rights licence. The Cannes Extension Agreement allowed therefore for the delivery of multi-territorial licences with the guarantee that right holders revenues will not be jeopardised (due to the fixed and uniform rate), along with a certain degree of price competition (namely, the introduction of the possibility for collecting societies to offer a maximum rebate to record companies which is limited to administrative costs).

83. In the same vein, the Simulcasting Agreement enabled collecting societies managing the rights of record companies to issue multi-territorial licences for

62 Case 395/87 - Ministère Public v. Jean-Louis Tournier, paragraph 24, Joined cases 11/0/88, 241/88, 242/88 –François Lucazeau and others v Sociétés des Auteurs, Compositeurs et Editeurs de Musique (SACEM) and others, paragraph 18.

63 Commission Decision 2003/300/EC of 8 October 2002 relating to a proceeding under Article 81 of the EC Treaty and Article 53 of the EEA Agreement (Case No COMP/C2/38.014- IFPI 'Simulcasting') (OJ L107, 30.4.2003, p. 58).

64 Commission Decision 2007/735/EC of 4 October 2006 relating to a proceeding pursuant to Article 81 of the EC Treaty and Article 53 of the EEA Agreement (Case COMP/C2/38.681-The Cannes Extension Agreement) (OJ L 296, 15.11.2007, p. 27).

simulcasting[65]. The original notification provided that commercial users could be granted the licence only from the collecting society located in their national territory. The Commission granted an exemption only after collecting societies agreed that commercial users could seek a licence from any collecting society in the EEA. Collecting societies had to split the price of the licence between the administration fees and the price of the protected subject matter. Competition took place on the administration fees and not on the remuneration of the authors themselves, thus ensuring that in this respect right holders' revenues cannot be jeopardised.

### 7.1. Relationship between the Treaty and the EEA Agreement – Jurisdiction

84. As set out in Section 2.2., CISAC is an association of collecting societies which incorporates a number of members based in the Community and two based in EFTA States which are parties to the EEA Agreement, namely TONO of Norway and STEF of Iceland.

85. Insofar as the decisions adopted by CISAC, bilateral reciprocal representation agreements between collecting societies and concerted practices restrict competition in the common market and affect trade between Member States, Article 81 of the EC Treaty is applicable. Similarly insofar as the decisions adopted by CISAC, bilateral reciprocal representation agreements between collecting societies and concerted practices restrict competition within the territory covered by the EEA Agreement and have an effect on trade between the Community and EFTA States, Article 53 of the EEA Agreement is applicable.

86. In this case, the Commission is the competent authority to apply both Article 81 of the Treaty and Article 53 of the EEA Agreement on the basis of Article 56 of the EEA Agreement as both trade between Member States and between Member States and EFTA States is affected[66].

### 7.2. Agreements between undertakings and a decision of an association of undertakings

#### *7.2.1. Collecting societies are undertakings*

87. Collecting societies are undertakings within the meaning of Article 81(1) of the Treaty and Article 53(1) of the EEA Agreement. They participate in the commercial provision of services[67] and are therefore engaged in the exercise of economic activities. On various occasions, the Court of Justice has

[65] Simulcasting is the simultaneous transmission by radio and television stations via the internet of sound recordings included in their broadcast of radio and television signals. The reciprocal representation agreement is intended to facilitate the grant of internet licences to radio and television broadcasters engaged in simulcasting.

[66] See Section 7.7.

[67] See for example, Case 127/73 Belgische Radio en Televisie v. SV SABAM and NV Fonior.

considered that EC competition rules apply to the activities of collecting societies[68].

7.2.2. *CISAC is an association of undertakings*

88. CISAC is an association of collecting societies and therefore an association of undertakings within the meaning of both Article 81(1) of the Treaty and Article 53(1) of the EEA Agreement.

7.2.3. *Reciprocal representation agreements are agreements between undertakings*

89. The bilateral reciprocal representation agreements concluded between the EEA CISAC members constitute agreements between undertakings within the meaning of Article 81(1) of the Treaty and Article 53(1) of the EEA Agreement[69].

7.2.4. *The CISAC Model Contract is a decision of an association of undertakings*

90. Both Article 81(1) of the Treaty and Article 53(1) of the EEA Agreement are applicable to associations of undertakings insofar as:

(a) the activities of the association, or of the undertakings belonging to the association, are intended to produce the results which Article 81(1) of the Treaty and Article 53(1) of the EEA Agreement aim to suppress;[70] and / or

(b) the association intended, and/or did, co-ordinate the conduct of its members on the market[71].

91. CISAC argues that the model contract for reciprocal representation agreements between the collecting societies is non-binding for the EEA CISAC members[72]. CISAC indicates also that "Any CISAC member is free to make use of the model contract...The CISAC model contract has to be so adapted because it is a document which has been designed for the potential use not just in the EEA but for more than 140 societies representing musical works all over the world"[73]. In order to demonstrate its assertions, CISAC notes that "virtually none of the authors' societies has systematically used an exact reproduction of the CISAC model contract for its bilateral representation"[74].

---

68 See also the GVL and Lucazeau judgements referred to in footnotes 56 and 59.

69 TONO and STEF have concluded bilateral agreements with all collecting societies in the Community.

70 See Joined cases 209 to 215 and 218/78 - Heintz van Landewyck SARL and others v Commission of the European Communities [1980] ECR 3125, paragraph 88.

71 Case 45/85 Verband der Sachversicherer e.V. v Commission of the European Communities [1987] ECR 405, at paragraph 32; Joined cases 96-102, 104, 105, 108 and 110/82 NV IAZ International Belgium and others v Commission of the European Communities , [1983] ECR 3369, at paragraphs 20 and 21.

72 Response of 15 July 2003 to the complaint submitted by Music Choice.

73 See point 76 of CISAC's Reply to the Statement of Objections.

74 See point 80 of CISAC's reply to the Statement of Objections.

92. However, even if it takes the form of a non-binding recommendation to the members, the CISAC model contract constitutes a decision taken by an association of undertakings within the meaning of Article 81(1) of the Treaty and Article 53(1) of the EEA Agreement, on the basis of which the individual members of the association conclude bilateral reciprocal representation agreements. A recommendation made by an association has been held to amount to a decision even in circumstances where the recommendation was not binding upon its members but where members were actually complying with the recommendation[75]. As shown in Section 4.4.2, EEA CISAC members have used the relevant provisions of the CISAC model contract in their bilateral reciprocal representation agreements. The CISAC model contract therefore determined their conduct and consequently had an appreciable influence on competition. CISAC itself strongly invites its members to follow the model contract; this is indeed explained at the beginning of the model contract in a "Note of the use of the model contract", wherein it states that its purpose is the protection of right holders' interests "through harmonising the conditions in which the authors' societies represent each other..." (emphasis added). In addition,, CISAC recommends that the model contract be used "whenever that is possible" and if collecting societies cannot use the exact wording of the model contract, CISAC specifies that collecting societies are *"called upon to conclude the essential general principles contained in the model contract"* (emphasis added)[76]. The intention to coordinate, and the actual coordination of CISAC members, appears quite clearly from these statements.

## 7.3. Legal and policy context

### *7.3.1. Article 151(4) of the Treaty*

93. According to Article 151(4) of the Treaty: "The Community shall take cultural aspects into account in its action under other provisions of this Treaty, in particular in order to respect and to promote the diversity of its cultures". In this regard reference can also be made to the UNESCO Convention on the Protection and Promotion of the Diversity of Cultural Expressions which was approved by the Council on behalf of the Community[77]. The content of this Convention is therefore part of the Community acquis.

94. Some parties have argued that these proceedings would hurt cultural diversity in Europe and would not therefore be in line with the objectives of Article 151(4) of the Treaty. That assertion appears to refer only to the objection regarding the territorial delineation of the authority to licence, and not to the other elements of this case. It is based on the assumption that this Decision would prohibit territorial delineation as such and would therefore jeopardise

---

75 Joined cases 96-102, 104, 105, 108 and 110/82, at paragraphs 20 and 21 and 89.

76 See page 2 of the CISAC model contract, updated on 30 August 2005.

77 Decision 2006/515/EC of 18 May 2006 on the conclusion of the Convention on the Protection and Promotion of the Diversity of Cultural Expressions (JO L 201, 25.7.2006, p. 15).

the proper licensing of musical works. It is alleged that the intervention of the Commission would destroy the system of bilateral reciprocal representation agreements, with the effect that the world repertoire would no longer be available from one collecting society. This would lead some users to focus on the popular repertories and to leave aside repertories of smaller EEA countries[78]. In the same context, it has been argued that the prohibition of territorial delineation would lead to a concentration of the management and multi-territorial licensing of repertoires which have an international appeal to a limited number of collecting societies. Without this revenue 'stream', which according to this argument might become very significant, the management of the local repertoire would prove very costly for more traditional or other local uses thus jeopardising adequate promotion and remuneration of local talent and threatening cultural diversity.

95. Cultural diversity in the music sector is not called into question by this Decision, which neither prohibits the reciprocal representation system as such, nor the possibility for collecting societies to introduce a certain territorial delineation together with certain commercial conditions in their representation contracts. It prohibits the coordination amounting to a systematic territorial delineation by national territory[79]. As explained in Section 7.6.2.2, this Decision therefore does not constitute an incentive for collecting societies to leave the system of reciprocal representation. On the contrary, it offers collecting societies the possibility to adapt the system of reciprocal representation to the needs of the online environment and to thereby make it more attractive for both right holders and users.

96. In addition, it has also been claimed that a prohibition decision in this case would introduce competition among EEA CISAC members as to the prices of licences granted to commercial users (a so-called "race to the bottom"), to the detriment of right holders. As shown in Section 7.6.2.2, having regard to previous Commission Decisions, it cannot be expected that this Decision will lead to a race to the bottom for royalties being paid to authors.

97. It has also been argued that the cross-subsidisation for distributing royalties which is currently made by certain EEA CISAC members between 'massive-used' music and local music, or between the biggest right holders and small authors would be jeopardised[80]. However, this Decision does not interfere with the internal policy of EEA CISAC members concerning the distribution of royalties between their members, as to whether they apply some level of cross-subsidisation among members - including offering social or cultural services - or distribute royalties on the basis of the actual use of musical works only.

---

78 See, for example, paragraphs 23, 102 ff., and 155 of GEMA's non-confidential Reply to the Statement of Objections and page 26 of AKM's non-confidential Reply to the Statement of Objections.

79 See Section 7.6.

80 For example, TONO asserted in its Reply to the Statement of Objections (at page 15 of the non-confidential version) that the end of territorial delineation "would have a negative effect on the cultural diversity within the EEA. Especially for the more national repertoire such as the Norwegian, it will lead to further marginalisation of Norwegian music ... within the EEA, to the advantage of anglo-american music."

98. The tendency of certain right holders observed over the last few years to withdraw part of their rights from the reciprocal representation system of collecting societies and to appoint new rights managers for pan-European licensing is a consequence of market evolution and the emergence of new business models which developed long before these proceedings and cannot be interpreted as arising from them. It cannot be accepted that this Decision would jeopardise the viability of local repertoires as a consequence of the withdrawal of reciprocal representation agreements because this Decision does not call into question the reciprocal agreements as such, and does not constitute an incentive for collecting societies to terminate them.

99. Finally, the marketing efforts for music distribution are essentially carried out by record companies, broadcasters and radio stations, not by collecting societies. The promotion and the success of musical works are to a large extent beyond the control of authors' collecting societies.

*7.3.2. The effect of local regulations*

100. Some EEA CISAC members claim that they are assigned a monopoly position by national law. This would, allegedly, be the case in Italy, Austria, Hungary and Slovakia. In other cases (for example, SAZAS) it is claimed that local regulations require registration, or some form of authorisation, which other EEA CISAC members do not have and which would prevent those EEA CISAC members from issuing licences in a specific territory. It is not always clear whether this refers to the issuing of a licence to a user who is located in that territory or who intends to exploit the licence in that territory.

101. Without reaching a definitive conclusion, it must be observed that these alleged national monopolies or other restrictive measures do not prevent collecting societies from concluding reciprocal representation agreements with other collecting societies which would allow the counterpart to grant multi-territorial licences, or which would abolish the counterpart's protection against competition from other collecting societies. For example, Austrian law could not prevent AKM from concluding an agreement with SABAM whereby the mandate of the latter would be non-exclusive, or would also include the territory of the Netherlands. Insofar as the practices described in this Decision affect markets other than those where exclusivity is granted by law, these are the result of autonomous decisions of collecting societies, and not the result of national legislation.[81] In any event, the arguments relating to the effect of local regulations contradict the previous behaviour of certain parties, notably SIAE and AKM[82]. Both have signed the Santiago Agreement[83], which means that they do not see any difficulty with any other

81 To that extent, it is observed that in a letter sent by SIAE to BUMA dated 5 April 2006, SIAE explained to BUMA that there was no exclusivity in their reciprocal representation agreements. SIAE emphasised the fact that: "*In other words, BUMA has the right to appoint another mandatee or itself to license its repertoire in Italy*".

82 See pages 12 and 21 of AKM's non-confidential Reply to the Statement of Objections.

83 The Commission issued a Statement of Objections in 2004 concerning internet licensing made by authors' collecting societies under the so-called *Santiago Agreement.* This Agreement contained a customer allocation clause by which collecting societies undertook to issue worldwide licences only to users located in their domestic (that is to say, national) territory. The Commission considered that the

signatory of the Santiago Agreement issuing licences covering the whole EEA territory, including Italy and Austria.

102. In addition, some EEA CISAC members claim that the clauses at issue in these proceedings are in any case unenforceable, since they are contrary to certain provisions of national law[84]. However, the fact that a clause in an agreement may also be contrary to national law cannot prevent the application of Article 81 of the Treaty.

*7.3.3. The extended licensing system*

103. Certain EEA CISAC members indicated to the Commission that their national law provides for a collective licensing system. Under this system, a collecting society is entitled to issue a licence covering not only the works of the right holders it represents, but also the works of right holders who are not members of a collecting society. Notably this is a possibility for the licensing of broadcasting and cable retransmission rights[85].

104. However, such a system is aimed at ensuring that certain users can get a single licence for all rights and is not relevant for assessing the compatibility of the practices at issue in this procedure with Article 81 of the Treaty. The extended licensing system does not impede, as such, a collecting society located in another EEA country from issuing a licence covering the territory of the EEA country where such a system is in place. The usual condition for a collecting society to validly issue an extended licence is for it to be in line with local laws on the functioning of collecting societies (in terms of accountability, efficiency). Any collecting society fulfilling this condition could potentially start to issue extended licences.

105. Accordingly, it should be concluded that this Decision does not undermine the existence and the functioning of the extended licensing system.

*7.3.4. The Commission Recommendation on rights management in the online environment*

106. In 2005, Commission Recommendation 2005/737/EC of 18 May 2005 on collective cross-border management of copyright and related rights for legitimate online music serviceswas published. [86]

---

loss of territoriality brought about by the internet, as well as the digital format of music files, opened the way for multi-territorial licensing with an increasing competition between collecting societies for the delivery of this new licence. The Santiago Agreement expired at the end of 2004 and the parties did not renew it (See Commission press release IP/04/586 of 3 May 2004). BUMA and SABAM offered commitments not to sign any agreement on licensing of public performance rights for online use with other copyright management societies containing the customer allocation clause (see Notice published pursuant to Article 27(4) of Council Regulation (EC) No 1/2003 in Cases COMP/ C2/39152 — BUMA and COMP/C2/39151 SABAM (Santiago Agreement —COMP/C2/38126), OJ C 200, 17.8. 2005, p. 11).

84 See AEPI's Reply to the Statement of Objections, and points 34 and 35 of GEMA's Reply to the Statement of Objections.

85 See Articles 3(2) and 9(2) of Directive 93/83/EEC.

86 OJ L 276 of 21.10.2005, p. 54.

107. Many EEA CISAC members have argued that the Statement of Objections substantially contradicts that Recommendation. Those arguments may be summarised by quoting CISAC observations: "This study strongly criticises and clearly rejects "option" 2 which enhances cross-border management of copyright by introducing multi territorial licences with a free choice for access point. It introduces competition at the level of the commercial user and thus enhances the user's bargaining power further". CISAC considered therefore that: "The position taken by the Statement of Objections regarding competition in relation to music services over the internet is unjustified and clearly at odds with the 2005 study in which the Commission concludes that the competition promoted in the Statement of Objections would be detrimental to authors and commercial users in the cultural sector"[87].

108. From the outset, the Commission observes that the EEA CISAC members confused Recommendation 2005/737/EC (which does not propose any "option") with the impact assessment contained in a Staff working paper drafted prior to that Recommendation. The Staff working paper was merely a preparatory work and was not adopted by the Commission. [88]

109. In substance, Recommendation 2005/737/EC strongly advocates that right holders should be free to choose their rights managers and to choose the scope of the rights managed, irrespective of the residence or the nationality of the right holder[89]. In addition, that Recommendation clearly states that collective rights managers should grant licences to commercial users on the basis of objective criteria and "without any discrimination among users"[90] and advocates the emergence of multi-territorial licences. Recommendation 2005/737/EC and this Decision are therefore consistent in that they both encourage the removal of anti-competitive barriers impeding right holders from freely choosing their collecting societies and rights managers from delivering multi-territorial licences.

110. Finally, a Recommendation, which is a non-binding act, must be read and interpreted in light of the provisions of the Treaty, notably Articles 81 and 82 thereof.

---

87 See pages 11 and 12 of CISAC's Reply to the Statement of Objections.

88 See Commission Staff Working Document –Impact Assessment reforming cross border collective management of copyright and related rights for legitimate online music services SEC(2005) 1254 dated 11.10.2005, available at http://ec.europa.eu/internal_market/copyright/docs/management/sec_2005_1254_en.pdf. In this respect, it is noted that CISAC has made references to language that is not part of the study as regards the assessment made by the staff of option 2 (see in particular citations made in paragraph 175 of CISAC's Reply to the Statement of Objections).

89 See points 3 and 5 of Recommendation 2005/737/EC.

90 See point 9 of Recommendation 2005/737/EC.

*7.3.5. The affected forms of competition*

111. Paragraph 18 of the Guidelines on the application of Article 81(3) of the Treaty [91] provides a framework for analysing which sources of competition may be affected by agreements that have as their object or effect the restriction of competition within the meaning of Article 81(1). In the context of this case, two forms of competition are affected. First, competition between collecting societies relating to their own services or repertoires. Such (actual or potential) competition could take place on the three markets described in Section 5.2, namely, the market for the provision of copyright administration services to right holders, the market for the provision of administration services to other collecting societies and the market for the licensing of public performance rights for satellite, cable and internet to commercial users.

112. Some EEA CISAC members have argued that competition between collecting societies for the licensing of their own repertoire to commercial users via direct licensing could not occur, since the collecting societies' repertoires are complementary. It is true that some users, such as radio and television channels, have only a limited opportunity to select individual national repertoires. Other users, such as ringtone providers might be more flexible in the repertoires they need for their own offers to the market. In addition, the high degree of complementarity of the repertoires of the collecting societies is significantly increased by restrictions which are imposed, or have been imposed, on a member's ability to join a different collecting society or to split his/her own repertoire amongst several collecting societies. These restrictions have divided the worldwide repertoire into strictly national ones.

113. The second form of competition is competition between collecting societies offering similar repertoires. It would occur, in the absence of the territorial restrictions contained in the reciprocal representation agreements, between collecting societies on the basis of rights that they have obtained from other collecting societies as a result of reciprocal representation agreements. This form of (actual or potential) competition which affects the offer of music repertoires to commercial users comes into play only on the market for the licensing of public performance rights.

114. Agreements that restrict a licence to a particular territory and which prevent other collecting societies from licensing into that territory affect competition on the repertoire concerned. In short, if an agreement restricts actual or potential competition, that would have existed but for the contractual restraints, then such an agreement may be 'caught' by Article 81(1) of the Treaty.

115. Before it may be concluded whether such a restriction of competition is caught by Article 81(1) of the Treaty due to its restrictive object or effect, it is necessary, according to paragraph 18(2) of the Commission Guidelines on the application of Article 81(3) of the Treaty, to consider whether licensing between collecting societies would be likely to occur in the absence of the

91 Communication from the Commission – Notice - Guidelines on the application of Article 81(3) of the Treaty of 24.4.2004 (2004/OJ C 101, p. 97).

34

contractual restraints in question. If the restraint is objectively necessary for the existence of such licensing, the restraint is not 'caught' by Article 81(1) of the Treaty[92]. Article 81(1) therefore does not apply if, in the absence of the restraint, the type of agreement in question would not have been concluded. In that case, there is no competition to restrict. As indicated by the reference to "objective necessity" this assessment is not based on the subjective views of the parties. As stated in paragraph 18(2) of those Guidelines, the question is not whether the parties in their particular situation would not have accepted the conclusion of a less restrictive agreement, but rather, given the nature of the agreement and the characteristics of the market, whether a less restrictive agreement would have been concluded by undertakings in a similar setting. In this regard, it is necessary to assess the actual economic context in which the CISAC model contract and the EEA CISAC members function, as well as the characteristics of the relevant markets.

116. That framework is applied in the Sections dealing both with the various restrictions contained in the bilateral reciprocal representation agreements (Sections 7.4 and 7.5) and with the concerted practices between EEA CISAC members, and the compatibility of such restrictions with Article 81(1) of the Treaty and Article 53(1) of the EEA Agreement (Section 7.6).

*7.3.6. The comfort letter sent to PRS in 1999*

117. Prior to the Statement of Objections, and within the framework of another procedure (Case IV/34.991), the Commission sent a comfort letter to PRS concerning its internal membership rules and its reciprocal representation contract with SACEM[93].

118. PRS notified its membership rules to the Commission on 3 February 1994. According to the Annex to Form A/B, the members' assignment of rights to PRS was exclusive for the whole body of performance rights (Point 5.2.2. of Annex to Form A/B). In an update made to the notification on 12 January 1999 PRS notified its amended membership terms to allow for the withdrawal of live performance rights. PRS likewise notified its reciprocal representation agreements with other EEA CISAC members, which, according to the text of the Annex to Form A/B, "...are not exclusive..." According to the text of the Annex to Form A/B, PRS provided its agreement with SACEM in Appendix 8 to the notification. However, the document which is in Annex 8 is actually the CISAC model contract. A comfort letter was issued to PRS on 16 February 1999.

119. PRS and other Addressees of the Statement of Objections argued that in light of this comfort letter it was not readily comprehensible why the Commission had changed its assessment and how the Commission could fine PRS and the other Addressees of the Statement of Objections for having proposed or

---

92 Case 258/78 L.C. Nungesser KG and Kurt Eisele v Commission of the European Communities [1978] ECR 2015.

93 In the context of these proceedings, PRS requested access to the Commission file relating to Case IV/34.991. PRS was granted access to this file on 28 March 2006. It was also afforded the opportunity to take photocopies of whichever accessible documents they deemed appropriate.

implemented the membership and territorial restrictions of the CISAC model contract.

120. However, a comfort letter does not preclude the Commission from reassessing the agreement or the practice at stake, as indicated in the comfort letter itself.

121. In substance, considerable new market developments have occurred since 1999 and the present case also brought new information to the Commission's attention. In short, the emergence of the internet radically modifies the way copyright is exploited. In addition, market players have developed new business models, as explained in Recital 98. In its complaint, RTL submitted information concerning satellite and cable exploitation which was not known at the date of the PRS notification. That additional information included evidence that the reciprocal representation agreements have precluded the development of the international business activities of broadcasters. The PRS notification only contained information relating to procedural aspects of the membership rules and agreements with other EEA CISAC members.

122. To conclude, the comfort letter sent to PRS in 1999 does not prevent the Commission from finding an infringement on the basis of the facts which are relevant for this Decision.

### 7.4. Membership restrictions

123. This Section concerns the membership restrictions in the bilateral reciprocal representation agreements between EEA CISAC members, which constitute agreements between undertakings within the meaning of Article 81(1) of the Treaty and Article 53(1) of the EEA Agreement.

124. Article 11(II) of the CISAC model contract provides[94] that neither of the contracting collecting societies may, without the consent of the other, accept as member any member of the other society or any natural person, firm or company having the nationality of one of the countries in which the other society operates. When implemented in bilateral reciprocal representation agreements, Article 11(II) implied that a collecting society needed to ask for permission from another collecting society – a potential competitor in the market for administration of rights to authors – before it could accept an author who was either already a member of another collecting society, or who was a national of the territory where the other collecting society operated, which is normally the country where the other collecting society was located.

125. That provision restricts the ability of an author from becoming a member of the collecting society of their choice or to be simultaneously a member of different EEA collecting societies for the management of his or her rights in different EEA territories.

94 Although the clause was formally removed from the CISAC model contract in June 2004 it continues to be implemented by a number of collecting societies in their bilateral reciprocal agreements as explained in Recitals 30 to 34.

126. The membership restrictions affect two forms of competition. First and foremost, they restrict competition between collecting societies on the market for the provision of services to right holders. Second, and more indirectly, the resulting impact on the repertoires held by each collecting society may also affect competition between collecting societies on the market for the licensing of rights to commercial users. The clauses are liable to limit the repertoires of each collecting society to the rights of right holders of the same EEA country, thereby rendering the repertoires more complementary than would otherwise be the case. Therefore, the restrictions are liable to reduce potential competition between collecting societies on the licensing of their own repertoires. The membership restrictions must also be taken into account in the assessment of the territorial restrictions confining the licensing activities of the collecting societies to a single EEA country. The more the repertoires of individual collecting societies maybe considered substitutable, the more the territorial restrictions restrict the competition that would otherwise occur in the absence of the bilateral reciprocal representation agreements. The membership restrictions contribute to bringing about clearly separated national repertoires since they make it more difficult for authors to become members of other collecting societies. Without the membership restriction this distinction by nationality is less likely to exist, and this would potentially render the repertoires more homogeneous in the long term.

127. The membership restrictions are therefore caught by the prohibition in Article 81(1) of the Treaty and Article 53(1) of the EEA Agreement and constitute an infringement by object.

128. The Commission's investigation and the Oral Hearing have shown that some EEA CISAC members themselves consider this model clause to be anti-competitive [95].

129. IMRO contends that some practical reasons justify the need to obtain the consent of the other collecting society and that this provision was applied only where an author was already a member of another collecting society and sought to transfer membership[96]. It seems indeed necessary that collecting

---

95 For example, in an exchange of letters of April 2005 with STIM, SACEM wrote concerning Article 11(II) of the CISAC model contract that: "Une telle clause n'est pas conforme à l'article 81(1) du Traité de Rome. Par conséquent, il apparaît nécessaire de (la) supprimer du contrat de représentation réciproque conclu entre la SACEM et la STIM... »" Such a clause does not comply with Article 81(1) of the Treaty of Rome. For this reason, it appears necessary to remove it from the reciprocal representation agreement between SACEM and STIM" (See the letter of M. Thierry Desurmont, SACEM, of 4 April 2005 sent to M. Kenth Muldin, STIM, page 1). In a letter to SACEM dated 18 May 2005, ZAIKS wrote that: " l' article 11(II) ...n'est pas conforme aux dispositions de l'article 81(1) du traité de Rome". "Article 11(II)... does not comply with Article 81(1) of the Treaty of Rome". AKKA-LAA wrote on substance similar observations to SACEM in a letter dated 7 June 2005: "Referring to your letter dated 13 May 2005 concerning reciprocal representation agreement in compliance with Article 81(1) of Rome Treaty, I would like to confirm that AKKA-LAA agrees to consider as excluded Article 11(II) from the signed reciprocal representation agreement between SACEM and AKKA-LAA". Other collecting societies started, during the procedure, to remove the clause from their reciprocal representation agreements which indicates that either this clause is not necessary for the smooth operation of these contracts or that the clause is implicitly perceived as anti-competitive by these parties (for example, ARTISJUS, BUMA, KODA, OSA).

96 IMRO limits these reasons to the scenario whereby a member of another collecting society decides to join IMRO and to consequently leave their own collecting society. IMRO considers that it is obliged to

societies should communicate between each other in order to smoothly transfer a right holder's membership from one collecting society to another. However, this is not what is suggested by the clause and requiring consent on whether or not the right holder is entitled to choose another collecting society should not be necessary irrespective of whether refusal of consent must be motivated or not.

130. The argument raised by some EEA CISAC members that the membership clause has not been applied does not change the restrictive nature of the clause. As the clause has the object of allocating authors according to their nationality, by putting the decision into the hands of the "domestic" collecting society as to whether or not authors may join a different collecting society, it is not necessary to show that the clause was applied or enforced. The mere existence of the clause creates a "visual and psychological" background which deters collecting societies from attracting authors who are currently either members of other collecting societies or who are not nationals of their domestic territory[97]. Similarly, the argument raised by some EEA CISAC members that there were simply no requests by authors to become members of a collecting society, other than the one in the country of which they are a national, does not negate the restrictive nature of the clause. On the contrary, there would be no need for such a clause if this statement was correct.

131. In addition, the investigation has shown that there is a low proportion of members who are not nationals of the domestic territory of the collecting society. In March 2005, the Commission asked EEA CISAC members, via a request for information, if they had any non-national members. AKKA/LAA replied that it had no non-national members. Certain EEA CISAC members presented very low figures: AEPI replied that it had 11 non-national members. Non-nationals represented 0,8% for TEOSTO, 1% for ARTISJUS and OSA, 1,43% for SGAE. Other EEA CISAC members did not provide figures (ZAIKS, TONO, SPA, SOZA, STIM, SIAE, SABAM, LATGA-A, KODA, EAÜ, STIM, AKM). GEMA indicated that 6,83% of its members were not German. According to PRS (which does not have an explicit membership clause in its reciprocal contracts) 11,3% of its members were not British. Non-nationals comprised 19% of SACEM's membership, though that figure can be explained by the fact that SACEM operates directly in several countries, either in the Community (Luxemburg) or outside the Community (mainly in Africa).

132. There are clear indications that competition between collecting societies on the provision of copyright administration services to right holders of musical works could benefit the latter. This is because, in most instances, the international royalties are subject to multiple or different deductions for the

---

obtain the consent of the other collecting society in relation to the start and end dates of the membership of the right holder in question. See paragraphs 38 and 39 of IMRO's Reply to the Statement of Objections of 31.1.2008, and its letter of 28.9. 2005.

97 To this effect see Case 19/77 *Miller International Schallplatten GmbH* v Commission of the European Communities [1978] ECR 131, at paragraph 7; Joined cases 32/78, 36/78 and 82/78 BMW Belgium SA v Commission of the European Communities [1979] ECR 2435, at paragraphs 27 to36; Case 246/86 *SC Belasco and others v* Commission of the European [1989] ECR 2117, at paragraph 15.

administrative costs of other collecting societies situated in various jurisdictions. Therefore, the revenue finally accruing to the right holder may vary depending on the collecting society which is managing his or her right. The Commission asked EEA CISAC members for their typical fee and royalty structure and whether they apply different administration fees for the rights flowing from their reciprocal representation agreements[98]. The answers were threefold: (i) certain collecting societies do not charge further administration fees on revenues coming from other societies[99]; (ii) other societies charge a specific rate which varies from one society to another;[100] and finally (iii) certain societies do not apply a different rate for rights collected directly by them or flowing from the reciprocal representation agreements[101]. As a whole, the rates applied by EEA CISAC members for the rights flowing from the reciprocal representation contracts vary from 0% to around 27,7%[102].

133. Another indication related to the efficiency of services provided by EEA CISAC members to right holders is the level of administration fees or the so-called "administrative overhead ratio". STIM has indicated in its Reply to the Statement of Objections that: "collecting societies use an international benchmark called "administrative overhead ratio" for the purpose of measuring efficiency"[103]. In that respect, it appears that the administration fees charged by the EEA CISAC members to their members vary significantly[104].

134. Thus, right holders would have an incentive to choose copyright administration services on the basis of many criteria, notably: (i) the cost elements (commission related deductions, membership fees and associated costs such as pension or cultural deductions); (ii) the quality of service (transparency, accountability, royalty payment terms, information, legal protection and enforcement); (iii) the benefits derived from the membership (such as pension or illness schemes); and (iv) the ability to collect the highest proportion of rights due to the authors.

---

98 Request for Information of September 2006 sent to all EEA collecting societies.

99 For example, IMRO (see the Section entitled "International administration costs" or its non-confidential Reply to the request for information of September 2006) or KODA (see Section I.B.1.2 in its non-confidential Reply to the Request for Information of September 2006).

100 For example, OSA (see Section I.B of its non-confidential Reply to the Request for Information of September 2006).

101 For example, GEMA (see page 3 of its non-confidential Reply to the Request for Information of September 2006).

102 See page 2 of the non-confidential version of STEF Reply. It should be emphasised that these examples are provided on the basis of the available data. Indeed, certain collecting societies did not reply to this question.

103 See point 14 of STIM Reply to the Statement of Objections.

104 The result of the request for information sent to the EEA collecting societies in September 2006 shows that the administration fees charged by collecting societies vary from 10 % to 27% of the collected rights.

135. The interest that right holders have in increased competition between collecting societies is not a merely theoretical hypothesis. For example, in 1998, a French right holder (the "Daft Punk" group) wanted to transfer only certain categories of its copyright to SACEM and only for its domestic territory (France). SACEM considered that request to be incompatible with its statutes and therefore rejected it. Following a complaint lodged by the band, the Commission considered that SACEM's refusal could constitute an abuse of its dominant position. Accordingly, SACEM modified its statutes and established the option for its right holders to individually manage certain categories of their rights or to transfer them to another collecting society[105].

136. Collecting societies may also have an interest in competing for the signing up of authors, as this could have a positive impact on their total turnover which is the basis for the administration fees they charge. In the absence of the membership clause, collecting societies would be less restricted in competing for the 'signing up' of right holders.

137. To conclude, in the absence of the membership clause, competition would intensify between collecting societies in the market for copyright administration services to right holders. In addition, in the absence of the membership restrictions, collecting societies could negotiate directly with members of other collecting societies and could therefore try to build their own "global" repertoire, or at least repertoires which have more variety than purely national repertories because they include works of authors from different countries. The restrictions therefore create artificial dependence between collecting societies because purely national repertoires, although an important part of the repertoire of any society, are rarely a commercially attractive product for commercial users.

### 7.5. The exclusive representation

#### *7.5.1. General observations*

138. Some EEA CISAC members have raised the argument that the reciprocal representation agreements between the collecting societies constitute agency contracts and would consequently not fall under Article 81(1) of the Treaty. This argument cannot be accepted. First, only obligations which are inherent in an agency agreement fall outside Article 81(1).[106] Agreeing that the authority to licence be granted on an exclusive basis, or implementing a concerted practice as regards the definition of limitations on the territory in which a collecting society may licence, are certainly not covered by such obligations. Second, a collecting society has normally no authority over "prices" (the royalties) charged by the collecting society exercising the mandate; the latter will apply the same royalty rates as it does to its own repertoire.

105 Commission Decision in Case COMP/C2/37.219 Banghalter and Homem Christo (Daft Punk) v SACEM of 12.8.2002.

106 See Commission Notice - "Guidelines on Vertical Restraints", OJ C 291, 13.10.2000, pgs. 1–44, paragraph 18.

139. Third, agency agreements cover the situation in which an agent is vested with the power to negotiate on behalf of another person who alone carries the risks connected to the contracts concluded and to market-specific investments.[107] Collecting societies make investments, for example, in the electronic processing of large amounts of data relating to the administration of or the monitoring of the use of such rights in new applications (for example, online music services). The risks connected with these investments are borne by the collecting societies who undertake such investments and not by their partners in the reciprocal system who assign their rights to them. Fourth, EEA CISAC members have submitted, in the context of the discussion on the scope of Article 6(II) of the CISAC model contract that the collecting society giving the mandate cannot interfere at all with the work of the collecting society exercising the mandate, so that, for example, it cannot give it any instructions[108]. This appears to contradict the argument that the collecting society exercising the mandate is simply an agent of the other collecting society. Fifth, the Court of Justice has clearly confirmed, in its Lucazeau judgement, the applicability of Article 81(1) to reciprocal representation agreements when they provide for exclusivity, or to concerted practices which would have a similar object or effect.

### 7.5.2. *Article 1 of the CISAC model contract: the exclusivity clause*

140. Article 1 of the CISAC model contract stated, until May 1996[109], that the reciprocal representation of repertoires was to be done on an exclusive basis. This exclusivity is restrictive of competition and has a foreclosure effect in the domestic market of collecting societies which are granted exclusivity insofar as no other collecting society may licence the relevant repertoire for exploitation within the territory of that collecting society. For example, if KODA grants the Danish repertoire to SGAE for licensing in Spain on an exclusive basis it thereby guarantees to SGAE not only that no other collecting society will be granted the Danish repertoire for exploitation in Spain, but also that KODA itself will not grant a licence over its own repertoire in Spain and therefore will not allow direct access to its repertoire. The exclusivity clause therefore restricts competition on two levels: (i) competition on the market for administration services provided by collecting societies to each other; and (ii) competition on the licensing market.

141. On the market for administration services granted to other collecting societies, each collecting society is assured that no other collecting society will be appointed in its territory. Accordingly, no other collecting society will be able to grant multi-repertoire licences (or indeed, any licence at all) for exploitation in that territory, whether or not the users are located in that territory. This restriction equally applies to the market for licensing, since users face a monopolistic collecting society in each country and, regardless of their own location, must obtain a mono-territorial licence from each

107 See Commission Notice - "Guidelines on Vertical Restraints", at paragraph 12 et seq.

108 See Section 7.5.3.

109 As of that date, CISAC no longer proposed the use of exclusive reciprocal representation agreements to its EEA members, under Article 1 of its model contract.

collecting society if the use of the copyright work is considered to take place in several countries. The exclusivity clause restricts competition since collecting societies do not compete against each other on the basis of the same foreign repertoire, for the administration of which they could be appointed in parallel.

142. Therefore, the bilateral reciprocal representation agreements, insofar as they contain clauses similar to Article 1 of the CISAC model contract as worded until May 1996, restrict competition contrary to Article 81(1) of the Treaty and Article 53(1) of the EEA Agreement.

143. The EEA CISAC members did not challenge this element of the Statement of Objections and recognised, both in their written replies and during the Oral Hearing, that the exclusivity clause was contrary to EC competition rules, as interpreted in the Tournier and Lucazeau judgements by the Court of Justice. The position of the addressees of the Statement of Objections may be summarised by the CISAC Reply: "The (Legal and Legislation) Committee stated that, in accordance with EC competition law, these authors' societies could not obtain exclusive mandates from foreign authors' societies"[110].

144. It is noted that 12 years after the CISAC recommendation of May 1996 to its EEA members to avoid usage of any exclusivity clause in their reciprocal representation agreements, and 19 years after the Tournier and Lucazeau rulings, the majority of the EEA CISAC members have not yet modified their reciprocal representation agreements in compliance with these judgments, even though they all recognised that the exclusivity clause is contrary to EC competition rules.

### 7.5.3. *Article 6(II) of the CISAC model contract*

145. The Commission considered in its Statement of Objections that pursuant to Article 6(II) of the CISAC model contract, the EEA CISAC members agreed to abstain from operating in the territory of the other collecting society. The Commission considered that Articles 1 and 6(II) fully protected the exclusive and reciprocal representation[111]. As explained in Recital 78, the Court of Justice made clear in its Tournier and Lucazeau preliminary rulings that there are competition concerns if collecting societies undertake not to allow access to their own repertoire for users outside of their domestic territory.

146. CISAC and most EEA CISAC members replied that the Commission had completely misinterpreted Article 6(II). These replies may be summarised by quoting the position of SACEM: "Article 6(II) only aims at ensuring a rational management of our reciprocal agreement. Indeed when a society has been given a mandate to manage the repertoire of the other society in its territory this mandate itself can be exercised only by the society which holds the mandate. In other words it is up to the society which holds the mandate to negotiate with users...But it must be underlined that such a rule does not prevent the society which has given a mandate to the other to deliver directly,

[110] See paragraph 111 of the non-confidential version of CISAC's Reply to the Statement of Objections.

[111] See paragraphs 29, 91 and 92 of the Statement of Objections.

at its own conditions and regardless of this mandate, licenses to users established in the territory of the other"[112].

147. It appears that that reply is largely shared by CISAC and the EEA CISAC members. For example, PRS explained in its Reply to the Statement of Objections that: "PRS believes that the Commission has entirely misconstrued Article 6(II) of the CISAC model contract...PRS understands this clause simply to mean that it will not interfere with the other society's ability to grant licences"[113].

148. However, this position is at odds with other elements in the Commission's file. In a letter sent by PRS to SACEM on 3 January 2006, PRS seems to have a completely different interpretation of Article 6(II): PRS indicates to SACEM that the interpretation made by SACEM in its letter dated 4 November 2005 has "perplexed us" and that "we do not understand the point you have made". PRS also emphasises that Article 6(II) "contains the very broad obligation to refrain from any intervention within the territory of the other society in relation to the mandate....it is open to misinterpretation that it negates or conflicts with the non-exclusive nature of the contract"[114]. That letter, which is not in line with the explanation made by PRS in its Reply to the Statement of Objections, indicates that Article 6(II) can indeed be understood as a clause which grants some degree of protection to the collecting societies in their domestic territories for the management of the respective foreign repertoires and that collecting societies do indeed interpret it in such a manner.

149. In the same vein, the position of CISAC or SACEM is also contradicted by SOZA, which, in its Reply to the Statement of Objections, considers that Article 6(II) is a "purely coordinative and logical" provision, because "any representation in the execution of delegated rights, which allow parallel action by the represented and representing, as well as other represented parties, would be confusing and lead to legal uncertainty"[115].

150. CISAC stated that the reciprocal representation agreements signed between IMRO and BUMA, STIM and BUMA and between SABAM and BUMA contained a provision in their respective Article 1 clauses by which the licensing society remained entitled to directly license its repertoire in the territory of the licensee society[116]. The Commission takes note of this information, but observes that CISAC (or the other parties) presented a very limited number of reciprocal representation agreements containing such a

112 See notably the letter sent by SACEM to PRS on 4 November 2005. This letter is attached to the non-confidential version of SACEM's Reply to the Statement of Objections.

113 See paragraph 33 of PRS' non-confidential Reply to the Statement of Objections dated 14.4. 2006.

114 See letter from PRS to SACEM dated 3.1. 2006. This letter is attached to the non-confidential version of SACEM's Reply to the Statement of Objections.

115 See Section 2.3.1. e) of SOZA's Reply to the Statement of Objections.

116 The sentence reads as follows: "BUMA reserves the right to issue the authorisations referred to above directly in (IMRO) territory...". See footnote 86 of CISAC Reply to the Statement of Objections.

provision. It cannot therefore be considered that this provision is the result of a general practice of collecting societies. Furthermore, the addition of such a provision is an indication that these collecting societies perceived a need to clarify the issue possibly in view of the interpretation of Article 6(II) as a clause which grants or reinforces exclusivity.

151. In addition, some EEA CISAC members started suggesting at the end of 2005 and in 2006 (before and after the sending of the Statement of Objections) that other EEA CISAC members should delete Article 6(II) in order to comply with Community competition rules. For example, BUMA sent a letter to all the other EEA CISAC members on 20 March 2006 requesting the removal of Article 6(II) from its own reciprocal representation agreements[117]. SGAE, SIAE[118], STIM[119] and EAÜ[120] also sent similar letters to other EEA CISAC members. The removal of the clause has been accepted by some EEA CISAC members, notably AEPI, AKKA/LAA, AKM, ARTISJUS, EAÜ, GEMA, LATGA-A, OSA, PRS, SAZAS, SOZA, SPA, STEF, STIM, TONO and ZAIKS.

152. The Commission takes account of the understanding according to which, and in spite of its unclear wording, Article 6(II) should not be interpreted as imposing any form of exclusivity. The Commission also takes into account the fact that some parties started to remove Article 6(II) from their reciprocal representation agreements. The Commission therefore refrains from intervening in relation to this provision insofar as CISAC and its EEA members understand it simply to mean that a collecting society will not interfere with the other society's ability to grant licences and that the clause is not interpreted as in any way limiting the possibility for the former to grant direct licences covering its own repertoire.

**7.6. The territorial delineation of the authority to licence**

153. This Section covers the management and the licensing of public performance rights for internet, satellite and cable exploitation of musical works.

154. The territorial limitation is reflected in the bilateral reciprocal representation agreements concluded by all the Addressees of the Statement of Objections[121]. Under Article 1 of the CISAC model contract, the licensor

117 A copy of the letters is attached to BUMA's Reply to the Statement of Objections. In this letter, BUMA wrote: "We have decided not to oppose the Commission findings...We will consider Article 6(II) as null and void and deleted from the agreement".

118 See page 10 of SIAE's Reply to the Statement of Objections.

119 In a letter dated 8 March 2006 STIM wrote to SIAE that "As for Article 6(II), we cannot see any reason to keep this clause. Given the non exclusive nature of our reciprocal agreement, this clause is in any case not significant". In a standard letter sent to the other parties, STIM wrote " We consider that Article 6(II) and 11(II) as null and void. Accordingly, *these clauses have not been applied*" (see, for example, the letter sent to BUMA on 8 March 2006).

120 See point 3.2 of EAÜ's Reply to the Statement of Objections.

121 See the Replies to the Commission's Request for Information of 11.3. 2005. All the Addressees apply Article 1 of the CISAC model contract and reciprocally transfer their repertoire for the respective territory of the other collecting societies. PRS applies its specific model contract which also contains a

limits the transfer of its repertoire to the territory of the licensee, as defined in Article 6(I). When implementing the CISAC model contract, all EEA CISAC members have defined the territory within the EEA as corresponding to the domestic territory of the licensee of the respective bilateral reciprocal representation agreement. The defined territory of a collecting society does not extend to the domestic territory of another collecting society. Each collecting society thereby limits its authority to licence to its own domestic territory[122].

155. This Section firstly examines why this parallel practice of collecting societies should be considered to be a concerted practice (Section 7.6.1). Second, it is explained why this practice is restrictive of competition. CISAC and the EEA CISAC members have presented a number of arguments intended to contest the preliminary finding that this behaviour would constitute an infringement of Article 81(1) of the Treaty(Section 7.6.2). In most cases, it is not clear whether the Addressees are contesting the existence of a concerted practice or a restriction of competition. For explanatory purposes, certain arguments are dealt with in Section 7.6.1 on the existence of a concerted practice, although some may also be relevant to Section 7.6.2. As shown in these Sections, none of the contrary arguments presented by the EEA CISAC members appear convincing.

*7.6.1. The parallel territorial delineation constitutes a concerted practice*

156. In essence, it must be noted that the fact that all the reciprocal representation agreements contain a clause limiting the mandate of a collecting society to the territory where it is established, is not the result of normal competitive conditions. These clauses are based on the CISAC model contract and limit themselves to uniformly defining the relevant territory as the domestic territory of the respective collecting society. Therefore, these clauses cannot simply be explained by autonomous behaviour prompted by market forces. By coordinating their behaviour on the basis of the CISAC model contract the risks of competition are substituted for practical cooperation between the EEA CISAC members.

157. Due to this uniform approach in the context of CISAC, each participating collecting society is granted a certain degree of certainty that national territorial delineation will not only be reciprocally accepted by the other collecting society, but will also be implemented in all the bilateral reciprocal representation agreements signed by the EEA CISAC members[123]. This certainty also results from the mutual dependency of all EEA CISAC members which exists, in particular, in the field of offline applications. The rights management in this sector requires local monitoring networks. For the licensing of rights and the collection of royalties abroad, each collecting society is therefore dependent on the other collecting societies with respect to

similar territorial allocation (see the sections entitled "Administration" and "Allocation" in its "ABCD2" contract).

122 See point 102 of the Statement of Objections.

123 See paragraph 104 of the Statement of Objections.

most traditional offline applications. Any collecting society which would be unwilling to perpetuate the historical market segmentation in the field of online rights might face the risk of losing support in offline rights management. This allows for discipline of collecting societies which consider deviating from the coordinated approach.

158. The existence of a concerted practice is supported by a number of elements, which will be examined in more detail in response to the arguments by the Addressees of the Statement of Objections. Collecting societies discuss the standardisation of their model contracts in the context of CISAC. The issue of territorial limitation of the reciprocal mandates, in particular for the new forms of exploitation, has been the subject-matter of multilateral discussions among the collecting societies, as illustrated by the Santiago agreement. This parallel behaviour has to be assessed in light of the previous situation where reciprocal agreements were granted on an explicitly exclusive basis. The deletion of express exclusivity has not led to any material change in the behaviour of the collecting societies. Further, parallel behaviour is strong evidence for a concerted practice, unless there are other reasons which may show that market segmentation results from autonomous behaviour. As will be shown below, this is not the case here.

*7.6.1.1. Territorial restrictions are not explained by the territorial nature of copyright*

159. Some EEA CISAC members argue that territorial delineation is part of the specific subject matter of this kind of intellectual property right. An elimination of territoriality would therefore affect the substance of such a right[124].

160. However, the territoriality of copyright does not require a national assignment of rights for the purpose of administration abroad on a strictly national basis. The fact that national legislations define copyright, as well as the scope of its protection and the consequences for infringements, does not mean that licences in a specific country have to be granted by the incumbent national collecting society. Authors assign their rights to collecting societies mostly for worldwide exploitation. Without exclusivity clauses in the reciprocal representation agreements, every collecting society would therefore be entitled to grant licences over their own members' repertoires on a worldwide basis. The former Santiago Agreement concerning multi-territorial multi-repertoire licensing, or the alleged claim that collecting societies can licence their own repertoire on a multi-territorial basis, show that there is no legal or practical requirement that only the collecting society located where the exploitation takes place can grant a copyright licence.

124 See, for example, paragraph 48 of the non-confidential version of PRS' Reply to the Statement of Objections.

7.6.1.2. *In the context of satellite transmission, the behaviour of the 24 EEA CISAC members cannot be justified by legislative provisions and the Sydney Agreement is not an appropriate answer to the objections.*

(a) The practice of the 24 EEA CISAC members cannot be justified by legislative provisions

161. It has been argued by a number of Addressees that the Commission has misunderstood Directive 93/83/EEC. It is claimed that this Directive "provides that it is the uplink Member State whose copyright rules apply"[125]. It seems that EEA CISAC members consider therefore that that Directive implies that only the collecting society located in the Member State where the uplink takes place can deliver the licence for satellite transmission. According to certain EEA CISAC members the system put in place by CISAC would be necessary to comply with Community legislation[126] and would also be an appropriate answer to the objections raised by the Commission concerning territorial restrictions[127].

162. The interpretation of Directive 93/83/EEC made by the Addressees of the Statement of Objections cannot be accepted. That Directive does not provide that the applicable law is the law of the Member State where the uplink takes place. Directive 93/83/EEC specifies that the act of communication to the public is the act of introducing the programme-carrying signal into an uninterrupted chain of communication leading to the satellite and down towards the earth[128]. Consequently, the applicable law will be the law of the Member State where this act of communication takes place[129]. However, this act does not automatically start with the uplink. As an example, the act of communication can be the signal sent by the television studio to the uplink radio station. The television studio and the radio station may not be located in the same Member State. In that example, the applicable law will be the law of the Member State where the television studio is located.

163. In addition, even in the situation where the uplink is indeed the place where the first act of communication takes place, this still does not imply that the collecting society established in the country of the uplink should be the only one competent to grant the licence. In fact, Directive 93/83/EC established the applicable law for satellite exploitation of copyright works. The fact that the law of a specific Member State is applicable is not relevant to making a determination on which collecting society can grant the licence. It merely means that in cases of conflict, the conflict should be resolved according to the applicable law. The law may well not be the law of the territory where the collecting society is located, as happens whenever a collecting society, which

125 See, for example, paragraph 8 of the non-confidential version of the PRS' Reply to the Statement of Objections.

126 See paragraph 9 of the non-confidential version of the PRS' Reply to the Statement of Objections.

127 See paragraph 47 of CISAC's Reply to the Statement of Objections.

128 See Article 1(2)(a) of Directive 93/83/EEC.

129 See Article 1(2)(b) of Directive 93/83/EEC.

is not located where the first act of communication of the public takes place, grants a licence. It is noted that neither CISAC, nor the EEA CISAC members, explained why it is necessary for the collecting society located within the satellite footprint to be the only one which can issue the licence for satellite exploitation of musical works. It must be recalled that Directive 93/83/EEC does not, and cannot, imply that only one collecting society would be entitled to deliver the licence for satellite exploitation; such a provision could be contrary to the Treaty, notably Article 49 thereof which establishes the principle of the freedom to provide services, and which is one of the legal bases of Directive 93/83/EEC.

(b) The "Sydney Agreement" is not an appropriate answer to the objections

164. In relation to satellite exploitation, CISAC and certain EEA CISAC members[130] stated in their Replies to the Statement of Objections that the so-called "Sydney Agreement" signed between CISAC members in 1987 is an integral part of the CISAC model contract and extends the rights conferred under Article 1 of the CISAC model contract to all countries within the footprint of the satellite. Under Article 2(III) of the CISAC model contract, when the satellite's footprint covers several countries, the collecting society located in the country where the satellite uplink takes place can issue a licence covering the entire footprint of that satellite. The "Sydney Agreement" offers three possible formulae:

(a) Under the first formula, collecting societies agree to allow the licensor collecting society located in the country of uplink to offer a licence for satellite transmission which covers the entire footprint of the satellite;

(b) Under the second formula, collecting societies agree to allow the licensor collecting society located in the country of uplink to offer a licence for satellite transmission which covers the entire footprint of the satellite, but with the prior agreement of collecting societies operating within the footprint;

(c) Under the third formula, collecting societies agree to allow the licensor collecting society located in the country of uplink to offer a licence for satellite transmission which covers the entire footprint of the satellite, but with prior consultation with collecting societies operating within the footprint.

165. The Commission takes note of Article 2(III) of the CISAC model contract which was agreed between the CISAC members in the Sydney Agreement[131], but does not consider that it gives any relevant answer to the objections related to the concerted practice on territorial delineation. As explained in Recitals 161-162, under Directive 93/83/EC, only one single licence has to be obtained by the broadcaster for rights exploitation within the entire satellite footprint. The applicable law governing the licence will be the law of the country where the first signal is introduced (usually the uplink). As the act of communication takes place in that EEA country, a licence is needed only for

130 GEMA, PRS, SACEM, SGAE, SIAE, STIM and ZAIKS.

131 The "Sydney Agreement" is not an element assessed by this Decision. The Commission reserves the right to examine that Agreement in the context of competition rules.

that EEA country. Consequently, the Sydney Agreement is obsolete in this respect and is not required for ensuring that the granted licence covers the entire satellite footprint[132].

*7.6.1.3. The practice cannot be said to be the outcome of individual market reaction*

166. It cannot be assumed that the parallel behaviour is the outcome of individual market action. Every collecting society needs to have a reciprocal representation agreement with every other collecting society if it wants to gather all available repertoires and offer a multi-repertoire licence. However, this equal exchange of repertoires should not prevent collecting societies from granting their rights to more than one collecting society for the same territory. GEMA could, for example, have a reciprocal representation agreement with SACEM and with SABAM in order to get in exchange the French, as well as the Belgian rights, for exploitation in Germany. This would not prevent GEMA from granting the German rights for the combined territories of Belgium and France to both collecting societies thereby allowing for competition between them.

167. The collecting societies are very different. They differ in terms of efficiency and administration costs as well as in terms of size and number of works[133]. PRS (in the United Kingdom) has a very large international repertoire whereas many smaller collecting societies have smaller repertoires which are mostly used nationally.

168. Despite these differences, all collecting societies mutually grant each other access to their own repertoires on an equal footing. Given that collecting societies show differing degrees of efficiency, they could have an interest in mandating one collecting society, with a particularly good record, to grant a licence for exploitation in a territory wider than the one in which it is located, or to mandate more than one collecting society in some regions, in order to increase the coverage of their licensing and thereby the remuneration for their authors.

169. Negotiations leading to bilateral reciprocal representation agreements had been preceded by previous coordination. When the issue of satellite or internet use arose, EEA CISAC members did not simply try to find a solution

---

132 This is especially clearly explained by KODA in its Reply to the Statement of Objections: "The reciprocal representation agreements do not distinguish between the different usage forms and thus, they also cover broadcasting via satellite, cable retransmission and the internet. With regard to broadcasting via satellite, the satellite and cable directive (93/83/EC) states that the restricted act takes place in the uplink country, which means that the sister societies are able to license KODA's repertoire in the entire footprint of the satellite. Article 1 of the satellite and cable Directive entails that the restricted act only takes place in the uplink country, and therefore it is not necessary to have specific provisions in the reciprocal agreements regarding satellite (emphasis added)", see page 8 of KODA's Reply to the Statement of Objections.

133 It appears from various requests for information and public sources that the level of administration fees varies considerably between the EEA CISAC members (from 11% to more than 25% in 2005). This huge difference is also reflected in the amount of collected rights (from EUR 3,4 million to EUR 823 million in 2005). Other factors also suggest substantial differences between collecting societies. Examples are the timing of payments between collecting societies or the method for calculating and allocating royalties (either a calculation per second or via regular samples).

in the context of their bilateral relations. As a reaction, for example, to the increasing importance of the internet in the EEA, EEA CISAC members coordinated their positions and agreed on the so-called Santiago Agreement, which was jointly notified for a possible exemption pursuant to Article 81(3) of the Treaty. That it was decided not to renew the Santiago Agreement, which resulted again in a strict domestic territorial delineation, is yet another indication of the fact that EEA CISAC members do coordinate their behaviour as regards the scope of licences for internet use. This can hardly be said to be independent undertakings acting autonomously in the market.

170. Finally, it must be recalled that even in cases where no exclusivity clauses were inserted into the bilateral representation agreements, where such clauses have allegedly not been applied, or where they have been removed, the practice has continued whereby collecting societies limit the licences they grant to the exploitation of domestic territories only. This practice results from the continued existence of the territorial delineation in clauses replicating Article 6(I) of the CISAC model contract. In the Lucazeau judgment, the Court of Justice stated that, if even without explicit exclusivity clauses no change in behaviour occurs, this might be taken as indication of a concerted practice. The Court further ruled that the observed parallel behaviour may be considered as "strong evidence" for a concerted practice and therefore for coordination, unless there are other reasons which may show that the market segmentation is the result of individual market behaviour.[134]

*7.6.1.4. The need for local presence does not explain the systematic delineation of the territory as the territory of the country where the collecting society is established*

171. The Addressees of the Statement of Objections [135] alleged in their Replies to the Statement of Objections and during the Oral Hearing that local presence is necessary for the monitoring of right uses. As one Addressee puts it: "As the use of copyrighted work via cable, satellite or the internet virtually always requires local verification outside the territory in which the authors' society operates, it is impossible for an author's society to issue authorisations for use of its repertoire outside its own territory (emphasis added) " [136]. "It would be not realistic for authors' societies to monitor from their domestic territory the very large number of cable or internet operators active abroad"[137]. "Remote monitoring is ineffective. For example the Finnish authors' society would

134 Joined cases 110/88, 241/88 and 242/88 François Lucazeau and others v Societé des Auteurs, Compositeurs et Editeurs de Musique (SACEM) and others, [1989] ECR 2811, paragraph 18.

135 See, for example, paragraph 54 of GEMA's non-confidential Reply to the Statement of Objections.

136 This assertion contradicts the statements of certain collecting societies concerning the meaning of Article 6(II) of the CISAC model contract. It has been claimed that Article 6(II) does not prevent collecting societies from issuing a licence covering their own repertoire outside their domestic territory. Certain collecting societies claim that they can issue such a licence, but apparently only to certain of their domestic commercial users. However, it is at least an indication that collecting societies can technically issue multi-territorial licenses. See, for example, points 17 and 183 of SGAE's non-confidential Reply to the Statement of Objections.

137 See paragraph 198 of CISAC's non-confidential Reply to the Statement of Objections.

have no other effective means of controlling physical acts of exploitation of the works of its members in Ireland"[138].

172. Those assertions are based on this assumption, that it would be necessary to have geographic proximity between the licensor (namely, the collecting society) and the licensee (namely, the commercial user). Some EEA CISAC members stressed, in addition, that litigation addressing infringements of their authors' copyrights abroad would be difficult and costly for any collecting society. It has also been argued that knowledge of local laws is important.

173. As regards proximity with the licensee, the current system is not based on such proximity. Under the current system, the territorial limitation of the mandate means that each collecting society grants licences or exploitation within its territory, irrespective of the residence of the licensee. As an example, if a website is directed to the German territory, GEMA would be competent to grant the licence, even if the company which offers the services on this website is based in France.

174. As regards internet, satellite and cable retransmission there are technical solutions which allow monitoring of the licensee even if the use is made outside the domestic territory of the collecting society or if the licensee is located outside the domestic territory of the collecting society. Collecting societies have already put in place licensing practices which demonstrate their capability to monitor uses and users outside their domestic territory and which show that different local laws are not an obstacle to multi-territory licensing. In addition, most EEA CISAC members argued (in the context of the discussion of objections relating to Article 6(II) of the CISAC model contract and its implementation) that they can grant multi-territorial licences.

175. As to the confusion which has been said to occur when one user may obtain licences from other collecting societies, and the effect this may have in carrying out monitoring activities in the market and searching for unauthorised use of music, it should be stressed that a commercial user would need to prove, if so requested, that it had obtained a licence for exploitation, and would thereby need to identify the scope of the licence and the licensor collecting society. According to some EEA CISAC members, already today it is possible to get a licence from another collecting society in certain circumstances (for example, direct licensing from the collecting society for its own repertoire).

176. As regards the link between litigation and enforcement, first, a distinction should be drawn between monitoring the market in general, as regards the unauthorised use of copyright work, and monitoring the activities of a licensee, in order to ensure that it acts in accordance with the licence and pays the royalties due to the licensor. Every time a collecting society grants a multi-territorial licence of its own repertoire it already relies on effective monitoring outside its domestic territory. Since acts of exploitation may be carried out abroad (indeed, potentially anywhere in the world), unauthorised

138 See paragraph 198 of CISAC's non-confidential Reply to the Statement of Objections.

use in another country, contrary to the licence, may require that action be taken in that other country.

177. Second, it is perfectly conceivable to dissociate litigation from enforcement. In cases of litigation, geographic proximity and good local knowledge of the country where the user is located is necessary. However, whenever collecting societies grant a licence to an undertaking located in another country, such litigation can at present be initiated by another person, such as the local collecting society. Therefore, the granting of the licence is not inextricably linked to the ability of the licensor to itself litigate in another country.

178. Third, during the Oral Hearing, it was argued that the monitoring, auditing and controlling activities in the on-line environment need not be exercised by the licensor himself in each of the territories covered by the licence. SABAM explained that it is possible to adapt the CISAC model contract and the existing network of reciprocal representation agreements. Under the model suggested by SABAM, the collecting society which issues a multi-territorial multi-repertoire licence could, if necessary, ask other collecting societies to locally monitor and enforce the granted licence.

179. Fourth, in the same line of arguments raised by SABAM, Nordic collecting societies presented the "Nordic and Baltic" cooperation model (NCB). They explained that they operate a multi-territorial online licensing scheme which provides for one single licence covering both the requisite mechanical reproduction and the performing rights. In addition, this system allows a commercial user to obtain such a licence in respect of both sets of rights which covers Sweden, Norway, Finland, Denmark, Iceland, Estonia, Latvia, and Lithuania. The NCB is based on explicit contractual cooperation between the societies as mandated by the right holders. Nordic Baltic collecting societies argued that the NCB experience has shown that: (i) in any multi-territorial licensing model, the existence of a network of national societies cooperating in preserving the rights and interest of the right holders is essential (local presence is necessary in order to detect and monitor usage); and (ii) multi-territorial blanket licensing would require the provision of the requisite mandate by right holders and their representatives.

180. OSA seems to support the views and practices expressed by SABAM and the Nordic societies. OSA indicated in its Reply to the Statement of Objections that: "We believe that there is no substance to the claim that these days collecting societies issue licences for the use of a musical repertoire over the Internet and in satellite broadcasting covering solely the territory of a single country (in the case of the OSA the Czech Republic). Such a licence, at least in the case of users licensed by the OSA, would not be accepted by users, and it is doubtful whether the OSA could even grant such a licence under the Copyright Act, according to which the extent of a licence, including its territorial scope, stems from the purpose of the licence. We are convinced that the granting of a licence, for example, for Internet broadcasting solely within the territory of the Czech Republic would require excessive technical measures on the part of the user or the de facto impossibility of complying with the conditions of such a licence"[139].

[139] See section 4.A of the OSA's Reply to the Statement of Objections.

181. OSA also indicated that it grants multi-territorial licences for webcasting: "At present, the OSA licences several original webcastings, especially radio broadcasting; all the licences are granted without territorial limitation. All the licences have been granted to Czech entities; as yet we have received no licensing requests from foreign broadcasters."[140] It is obvious that OSA does not believe that technical issues impede the delivery of multi-territorial licences and considers that users need such a type of licence.

182. Finally, it needs to be stressed that the findings set out in the previous Recitals are without prejudice to the fact that, in specific circumstances, the decision not to grant authority to licence outside the territory where the collecting society is established may be due to the fact that the other collecting society may not be seen as having the technical capability to ensure proper monitoring and enforcement. Equally, the legal system of an EEA country may present features which will normally lead to the domestic society being the preferred choice, due, for example, to the particular status which it may enjoy in litigation before domestic courts. A territorial delineation which is the result of the assessment of the individual capabilities of the parties to the bilateral reciprocal representation agreement is not normally a concerted practice restrictive of competition.

183. However, the concerted practice, which is systematic, cannot be explained by the particular situation in a given legal system or by the limited technical capability of one or the other collecting society. Therefore, this Decision cannot be interpreted as precluding collecting societies as independent market actors, from taking account of each other's capabilities to monitor the market and ensure proper enforcement of authors' rights in their bilateral negotiations.

184. Admittedly, the Court of Justice[141] has considered, in light of the need for local and physical monitoring of many premises in the case of off-line applications (bars, restaurants, discos, etc.), that the territorial delineation of licences along national borders might be justified on the basis that duplication of copyright usage monitoring structures in all territories would lack economic rationale. The cost of establishing a network of contracts with commercial users in another country and the implementation of own local monitoring arrangements would be simply excessive and would prevent collecting societies from becoming active outside their home territories. The necessity of having a local network of agents could, therefore, explain in the off-line world the strictly national definition of licensing areas and the absolutely symmetric mutual exchange between the collecting societies as the "natural" market outcome not based on a concerted practice.

---

140 See the Section on "Original webcasting" in the OSA's Reply to the Statement of Objections.

141 Joined cases 110/88, 241/88 and 242/88 François Lucazeau and others v Societé des Auteurs, Compositeurs et Editeurs de Musique (SACEM) and others , paragraph 18. Collecting societies could, nevertheless, be actual competitors in the off-line environment if they establish a network of monitoring operations outside their domestic territory.

185. As explained in the following Recitals, this is not the case as regards, satellite, internet and cable transmission.

186. Satellite transmission: The Statement of Objections found that "...any satellite transmission can be monitored within the entire footprint. A collecting society may control content from any location within the footprint of the satellite. For example, this can be illustrated by a reciprocal representation agreement concluded by PRS which authorises each signatory of the contract to grant a licence not only for its own domestic territory but for the entire footprint of the satellite in case of a direct broadcasting use"[142].

187. Some EEA CISAC members allege that geographical presence in the country of the broadcaster is necessary to collect information about the rights used and to enforce claims against the broadcasters. For instance, encrypted channels could only be monitored from the country to which they are directed. [143]

188. However, the encrypted channels argument is flawed: collecting societies which intend to grant a licence to a broadcaster can perfectly tackle this issue during the negotiations for the granting of the licence and the broadcaster can always give to the licensor collecting society the required device for decrypting the broadcast. Concerning the need for a local presence, EEA CISAC members merely presented the arguments already discussed and rebutted above[144].

189. Internet use: The internet presents new features which are radically different from those of the traditional exploitation of music at issue in the Tournier and Lucazeau cases. During the Oral Hearing, it was demonstrated, especially by EDIMA[145], that remote monitoring for the online delivery of music (both streaming and downloading) can be accomplished in practice. Each musical work has an electronic identity and each personal computer has an internet protocol address. As a consequence of this information, the collecting society can ensure, when it delivers the licence, that the commercial user is in a position to know precisely which musical work is used, by which computer, and for which kind of use. The commercial user can then send this data to collecting societies which will exploit this information in order to accurately distribute royalties to right holders. In other words, collecting societies can agree on the modalities of the monitoring.

190. As already explained in the Statement of Objections, recent market developments in the field of collective management of intellectual property rights for online use do not support the claim that territorial limitations are

142 See paragraph 111 of the Statement of Objections.

143 See paragraphs 62 et seq. of GEMA's non-confidential Reply to the Statement of Objections; page 10 of AKM's non-confidential Reply to the Statement of Objections.

144 See paragraphs 173 et seq. of this Decision.

145 EDIMA is an association representing firms involved in the provision of audio and audio-visual content on-line. EDIMA's members represent 70% of the online digital media market.

indispensable, notably for ensuring proper monitoring, auditing and enforcement activities by collecting societies.

191. First, in the *Simulcasting* case[146], subsequent to discussions with the Commission, IFPI (the "International Federation of the Phonographic Industry") notified an amended version of the reciprocal representation agreement to the Commission which allowed broadcasters whose signals originated in the EEA to approach any collecting society established in the EEA which was party to the reciprocal representation agreement, in order to obtain a multi-territorial and multi-repertoire internet simulcasting licence. In addition, on 11 November 2003, IFPI announced the conclusion of a standard agreement between phonogram producers' collecting societies for the purposes of delivering multi-repertoire multi-territory webcasting licences[147]. The *Webcasting* agreement mirrors the structure of the *Simulcasting* agreement in that it allows participating societies to grant worldwide licences to commercial users located anywhere in the EEA. Thus the outcome in the *Simulcasting* case and the terms of the subsequent Webcasting agreement illustrate that it is not technically necessary for intellectual property rights collecting societies to have a territorial (that is to say, a local) presence in order to offer multi-territory multi-repertoire licences for internet use and to properly monitor such use.

192. In addition, the *Santiago* Agreement already provided for the granting of multi-territorial licences, even if this possibility was limited to users having their economic residence in the same domestic territory. This demonstrates that local presence in the countries of use was not deemed to be necessary.

193. Second, in January 2006, PRS and GEMA established a joint venture which will act as a pan-European one-stop-shop for the licensing of online and mobile rights of EMI's Anglo-American repertoire. It is understood that this joint venture will deliver pan-European licences to commercial users located in any EEA country. Adam Singer, Group CEO of the MCPS-PRS Alliance recognised that "In online, no-one can hear your borders" and Jürgen Becker, then Head of the Executive Board of GEMA said: "This will provide licensees and consumers with a one-stop-shop and also guarantee that right holders and sister societies are efficiently protected in the global digital networks"[148]. Accordingly, this new model is an example which demonstrates the technical possibility for collecting societies to offer a multi-territory licence and that the arguments related to the auditing, monitoring and enforcement tasks of collecting societies and the required geographic proximity between the licensor and the licensee do not validate the current parallel behaviour as regards territorial limitations. Some of the same

[146] Commission Decision 2003/300/EC of October 2002 relating to a proceeding under Article 81 of the EC Treaty and Article 53 of the EEA Agreement (Case No COMP/C2/38.014 *IFPI* 'Simulcasting') (OJ L107, 30.4.2003, p. 58), at paragraphs 3 and 27.

[147] See press release "Recording industry announces new one-stop-shop for webcast licensing" of 11.11.2003 at www.ifpi.org

[148] See GEMA press release of 23.1. 2006 at www.gema.de

collecting societies which raised these arguments do not consider them as obstacles to concluding agreements such as the PRS/GEMA joint venture.

194. Third, certain EEA CISAC members put forward other solutions or mechanisms in order to offer multi-territorial licences in a competitive environment. It is notably relevant to quote a proposal made by some small and medium size EEA collecting societies which are EEA CISAC members. They suggest that a new and adequate model could emerge: under this model, "Every European collective right management society is entitled to grant European-wide online cross-border licences to every user having an economic residence within the EU/EEA...the licensing collective right management society applies the tariff and conditions of the country of destination"[149]. This proposal made by some licensors demonstrates that no technical or economic reasons preclude the emergence of a multi-repertoire multi-territory licence granted to any commercial user located within the EEA rather than simply within the domestic territory of the licensor.

195. Cable retransmission of musical works: the Addressees of the Statement of Objections generally consider that the cable retransmission market presents features similar to the off-line market where a local presence and a local knowledge of the market remain necessary.

196. It is not challenged that cable exploitation of musical works remains for the time being national or local in scope. Channels retransmitted by cable are indeed usually proposed to consumers on a local scale (for example, cable operators offer a package of channels to consumers located in a specific area or in a city). This does not imply, however, that this market has no EEA interest. On the contrary certain programmes are retransmitted through cable in many EEA countries, such as major national television channels or programmes with a potential international appeal (for example, BBC World, TV5 and Euronews).

197. It is also not contested that cable operators need a specific licence for cable exploitation which is different from that of the satellite broadcaster.

198. As was made clear in the Statement of Objections[150], the retransmitted programmes at issue are only those which are first transmitted by satellite and then retransmitted by cable, insofar as the retransmission does not go beyond the footprint of the satellite. As a consequence, the content of the cable retransmission at issue would be strictly identical to the satellite transmission. Considering the fact that all collecting societies located within the satellite footprint can potentially issue a licence covering the entire satellite footprint and can properly monitor the use of that licence, it can be assumed in normal circumstances and unless there is a problem specific to the monitoring of a

149 See the position paper of 29.8.2005 "Cross border collective management of online rights in Europe" signed by ARTISJUS, AKM, KODA, SPA, STIM, TEOSTO and TONO, page 2. These collecting societies which include some of the Addressees of the Statement of Objections took this position in the framework of the working document released on 7.7. 2005 by the Commission on "The cross-border collective management of copyright".

150 See paragraphs 109, 110 and 111 of the Statement of Objections.

given cable operator, that those collecting societies can also properly licence and monitor the cable exploitation of a work previously transmitted by the satellite transmission. Should a specific problem be encountered, due to the business model of the cable operator, it may be legitimate to refuse to deliver such a licence or otherwise agree on specific measures for monitoring, but the current reciprocal representation agreements do not even provide for the possibility of the delivery of such a licence in the first place.

199. To conclude, there is no objective reason which may explain why all collecting societies have implemented the same parallel behaviour in the market or why they have maintained their exclusive position in their domestic market for the delivery of cable retransmission licences, in so far as the retransmitted content takes place within the satellite footprint where the first transmission took place.

*7.6.2. The concerted practice is restrictive of competition*

200. The following Recitals explain why the concerted practice is restrictive of competition. It is explained, first, that it produces a segmentation of the market and, second, that it is not objectively necessary, from an economic and commercial point of view, to have a set of bilateral reciprocal representation agreements among collecting societies which impose national territorial delineation.

201. In examining each of the different issues relating to this topic, it is important to bear in mind the scope of the Commission's objections. This Decision does not take issue with the mere fact of delineating the scope of the mandate, but rather with the coordinated approach by all EEA CISAC members as regards such delineation. From the outset, it has to be noted that, in isolation, the granting of a licence limited to a certain territory, even to the domestic territory, is not automatically restrictive of competition. A licensor is normally entitled to limit a licence to a particular territory without falling foul of Article 81(1) of the Treaty and Article 53(1) of the EEA Agreement.

202. In the assessment of the effects of the bilateral reciprocal representation agreements concluded by collecting societies, it is necessary to take into account the actual conditions in which they function, the economic context in which the undertakings operate, the products and services covered by those agreements and the actual structure of the market concerned[151].

*7.6.2.1. Territorial delineation and exclusivity*

203. Even in the absence of explicit exclusivity described in Section 7.5.2, limiting the territorial delineation of the authority to licence to the domestic territory (that is to say, the national territory) of the collecting society amounts to the granting of exclusivity to the domestic collecting society and the segmentation of the market into national monopolies. [152]

---

151 Case 23/67 SA Brasserie de Haecht v Consorts Wilkin-Janssen[1967] ECR 407.

152 See paragraph 99 of the Statement of Objections.

204. The uniform territorial delineation has the effect of indirectly granting exclusivity insofar as it standardises the reciprocal representation between the EEA CISAC members: each collecting society's authority to licence is limited in the sense that it can only grant access to its portfolio of works for exploitation in its "domestic" territory (regardless of where the user is located). By including this territorial delineation in all such agreements, the end result is that only one collecting society per country is able to grant multi-repertoire licences for the use of the covered music in that country.

205. That delineation reflects, to some extent, the explicit exclusivity which had been set out in the CISAC model contract and the bilateral reciprocal representation agreements implementing it. If exclusivity is explicitly granted to the other collecting society concluding the bilateral agreement, collecting societies will delineate the authority to licence in the other bilateral agreements on the basis of the domestic territory of each collecting society. Any territorial delineation which would go beyond the borders of the domestic territory could encroach upon the exclusivity granted to another collecting society.

206. However, this also shows that since the two clauses concerning explicit exclusivity and territorial delineation go hand in hand, dropping the clauses on explicit exclusivity will not remove exclusivity altogether. Even in the absence of explicit exclusivity, collecting societies can achieve the same result by simply coordinating their behaviour so that the authority to licence is limited to the domestic territory of the collecting society. Even where collecting societies have, in individual cases, dropped the explicit exclusivity, no change in the allocation of territories among the collecting societies could be observed[153]. Although a number of collecting societies claimed that they did not apply the existing exclusivity clauses, the collecting societies neither granted their own repertoires for exploitation in another country by a collecting society, other than the respective incumbent one, nor did they grant their repertoire to more than one collecting society in parallel for the same territory (covering several countries).

207. This effectively leads to national monopolies for the multi-repertoire licensing of public performance rights and has the effect of segmenting the EEA into national markets. Competition is restricted on two levels: (i) on the market for administration services which collecting societies provide to each other; and (ii) on the licensing market.

208. On the market for administration services which collecting societies provide to each other, the uniform territorial delineation ensures that each collecting society provides these administration services exclusively for its own home territory and also that it will not face competition from other collecting societies there. As an example, GEMA could in principle select the French SACEM to provide administrative services to GEMA in Belgium in parallel with the Belgian SABAM. However, on the basis of the coordinated rules applied by the collecting societies, GEMA selects SACEM only for France and SABAM for Belgium. In turn, SACEM and SABAM do not appoint

153 See Section 7.6.2.1. of this Decision and paragraph 102 of the Statement of Objections.

anyone else other than GEMA, for the administration of French and Belgian rights in Germany.

209. The corresponding effect is reached on the market for the licensing of rights. Due to the allocation of the authority to license on a strictly national basis, the right users have no alternative for the acquisition of multi-repertoire licences other than the national collecting society for the respective country. A right user, regardless of its location, wishing to use music in Germany, for example, may only revert to GEMA for the necessary licence – no other collecting society may, on the basis of the concerted practice, grant licences to a user located in Germany. In principle, any collecting society could grant its rights to more than one collecting society per country. For example, SACEM could grant the rights over its repertoire (the French repertoire) for exploitation in Austria and Germany to both Austria's AKM and Germany's GEMA. Both collecting societies would then be able to grant licences over the French repertoire in Germany and Austria and the right-users would have a clear alternative with respect to that repertoire between two competing collecting societies.

210. The mutually guaranteed territorial monopolies for the licensing of public performance rights ensure that each collecting society will be able to charge administration costs for the management of rights and the delivery of the licence without facing competitive pressure on these fees from other collecting societies. Competition is thereby restricted. This lack of competition, as explained above, might also have negative repercussions at right holders' level.

211. The uniform territorial delineation creates effects which cement the structure of the market, exclude other forms of multi-repertoire licensing and confine each collecting society to operate only in its domestic territory. This network of reciprocal representation agreements has led to a situation where there is no scope for other means of organising and competing in the administration of copyright. It also creates barriers preventing access to the market by new competitors capable of administering the copyright in question, or new ways in administering copyright by existing players, and has the effect of constraining copyright distribution to the advantage of certain existing players.

212. In the absence of concerted practices on territorial delineations, collecting societies would be more likely to compete against each other by finding the most efficient means of rights administration. This would create differences between them in the territorial delineation of their licensing areas as well as in the number of collecting societies asked to administer their rights in another territory. The authors would consequently have an incentive to become members of those collecting societies which have found more efficient means of rights administration.

*7.6.2.2. Is the concerted practice objectively necessary for ensuring that EEA CISAC members grant each other reciprocal mandates?*

213. Some EEA CISAC members have submitted that in the absence of territorial delimitation, collecting societies would have no incentive to grant each other

reciprocal mandates to licence since it would force them to compete against each other in their respective territory and grant licence to the collecting societies in territories for which the latter may not have the prerequisite expertise or competence [154].

214. On the contrary, SABAM argued in its Reply to the Statement of Objections that: "there is no advantage for authors from obstructing the activities of legitimate multi national users of the world music repertoire who embark on modes of exploitation that are technologically new and inherently borderless"[155]. SABAM also considers in its Reply that: "far from imperilling the quality of collective management of authors' rights, a multi territorial licence produces advantages to authors and users alike... The territorial restrictions of the CISAC model contract generate the opposite from an improvement in collective management and preclude the emergence, growth and future maturity of this new market"[156]. Competition will: "heighten the quality of services rendered to authors and users and no argument related to the existence of national exclusive rights can justify a non application of Article 81 of the EC Treaty. ... The national nature of copyright law can in no way sustain the claim of some collecting societies to be a natural and contractual national monopoly." [157]

215. First, it must again be observed that the ability of collecting societies to include territorial limitations in their reciprocal mandates is not contested. It is only the parallel territorial limitation applied to domestic territories which constitutes the objection raised by the Commission. There is no indication that such parallel conduct is objectively justified for having a network of reciprocal representation agreements, and the arguments of the Addressees of the Statement of Objections are mainly aimed at contesting the idea that territorial limitation would be, as such, restrictive of competition.

216. Second, the arguments developed by the EEA CISAC members are not convincing in general. The Addressees of the Statement of Objections have reiterated that monitoring abroad is difficult, and therefore that concluding reciprocal representation agreements with other collecting societies is vital in order to protect the interest of their members abroad. Without prejudice to the fact that some of the difficulties vis-à-vis monitoring exploitation beyond the domestic territory are exaggerated, the fact remains that it would hardly appear to be credible that collecting societies would simply give up the protection of their members abroad just because some degree of competition would arise as a result of the prohibition of such a concerted practice. In addition, since collecting societies have a fiduciary duty towards their members and are not entitled to discriminate as regard the royalties applied, a "race to the bottom" would imply that the collecting society would also

154 See, for example, paragraph 53 of PRS's non-confidential Reply to the Statement of Objections.

155 See p. 19, first paragraph of SABAM's Reply to the Statement of Objections

156 See p. 19, second paragraph of SABAM's Reply to the Statement of Objections.

157 See p. 20, last paragraph of SABAM's Reply to the Statement of Objections.

decide to charge lower royalties as regards its own members, which does not appear to be a realistic situation.

217. Third, collecting societies are not prevented from protecting the interests that their members may have in ensuring that revenues do not suffer as a result of the existence of some degree of competition in the granting of licences. Certain EEA CISAC members argued during the Oral Hearing that the main problem for issuing a multi-territorial licence is not related to the remote monitoring, auditing and enforcement activities of collecting societies, but to the price-setting of such a licence[158]. According to this opinion, a collecting society would not have an interest in having other collecting societies compete against each other to licence its own repertoire abroad. This would mean – if the example mentioned in Recital 208 is used – that GEMA would, according to this opinion, not have an interest in SACEM and SABAM competing against each other to grant licences for the German repertoire since this would result in a race to the bottom for the prices for this repertoire and therefore in losses for GEMA (as opposed to the model with separate national territories per collecting society).

218. The Commission's position concerning this specific element has already been clarified in a similar case, in which all territorial delineations were dropped, and accepted a price mechanism in order to retain some control over revenues arising from such a mandate and to avoid any race to the bottom concerning the income of right holders. Indeed, in the *Simulcasting* Decision, it was stated that "the need for a collecting society to guarantee an appropriate level of remuneration for its own repertoire certainly results from the essential function of copyright and neighbouring rights, and consequently it is only natural that agreements between collecting societies will contain provisions on this issue"[159]. As a consequence, the Commission accepted, as being exempted under Article 81(3) of the Treaty, the setting of a tariff mechanism: the price of a simulcasting licence is based on a global tariff to be charged by the licensor society and will reflect the different national tariffs determined by each of the participating collecting societies[160]. The price of the licence issued by collecting societies is a combination of the administration fees and the price of the protected subject matter. Competition takes place on the administration fees and not on the rights themselves. It appears therefore that collecting societies have the option of securing the income of their members in a competitive environment for the delivery of multi-territorial multi-repertoire licences[161].

---

158 With regard to the price setting mechanism, see paragraphs 16 f. of GEMA's non-confidential Reply to the Statement of Objections.

159 See paragraph 70 of Decision 2003/300/EC.

160 A certain degree of competition concerning the price has been introduced, but only for the administration fees for licensors. Under this system, the "copyright" part of the price is not subject to competition, but only the level of administrative fees.

161 A similar system is currently applied by collecting societies in the EEA in the framework of the Cannes Extension Agreement, see Recital 82.

219. In addition, even without any such mechanism as used in the *Simulcasting* Decision, the mere deviation from the concerted approach and any resulting parallel assignment of identical licensing areas to more than one collecting society, does not necessarily lead to a race to the bottom. Currently a collecting society granting licences abroad for another collecting society which has given it a mandate, uses its own national tariffs and passes on a certain percentage of this income to the original collecting society. In order to avoid a race to the bottom on the repertoire of its own members which is licensed abroad by another collecting society, the collecting society giving a mandate could merely define a level of revenue (a sort of price) for its repertoire vis-à-vis the other collecting societies which grant licences abroad. It would thereby receive a guaranteed "wholesale" price for its repertoire and the distributor collecting societies would consequently compete on the margin they add to this wholesale price.

220. It cannot be assumed that even with certain adaptations of the pricing system, collecting societies would not have an incentive to create competition between their distributor collecting societies. A recent market trend clearly confirms that it may be an efficient strategy for right holders and therefore also for their trustees – the collecting societies – to grant their rights to several competing collecting societies. In the field of Anglo-American mechanical rights for online use, several initiatives have been initiated by the large publishers to withdraw these rights (which are in the hands of the publishers) from the current collecting societies system and to select one or several collecting societies for the EEA-wide administration of these rights. Warner Chappell has announced that it intends to designate several collecting societies who will have the power to grant, to commercial users, pan-European licences to exploit the Anglo-American mechanical rights of the Warner Chappell repertoire for online use[162]. This means that several collecting societies will compete for the granting of the corresponding licences in an identical territory. Warner Chappell considers that this will give it scope to withdraw its repertoire from any collecting society if the latter does not operate efficiently, without affecting the licensing market, because the other collecting societies will continue to be able to issue pan-European licenses.

221. It can therefore be concluded that the practice at issue is not objectively necessary, in that there are less restrictive methods for ensuring that collecting societies have incentives to grant reciprocal mandates to licence.

### *7.6.3. Conclusion*

222. Accordingly, a concerted practice between the EEA CISAC members is the only possible explanation for the current market outcome.

223. This concerted practice restricts competition within the meaning of Article 81(1) of the Treaty and Article 53(1) of the EEA Agreement since it prevents

[162] See press release of Warner Chappell dated 2.6. 2006, "*Warner Chappell music launches its pan-European digital licensing (P.E.D.L.) initiative.*"

EEA CISAC members from choosing collecting societies, other than the domestic one, for the licensing of their repertoires abroad.

### 7.7. Effect on trade between Member States and between Contracting Parties to the EEA Agreement

224. In order to ascertain if the reciprocal representation agreements affect trade between Member States it must be determined whether they "may have an influence, direct or indirect, actual or potential, on the pattern of trade between Member States"[163].

225. For the purposes of that analysis the Commission should consider "all the consequences of the conduct complained of for the competitive structure in the common market"[164].

226. The Court of Justice has consistently adopted the view that the activities of collecting societies are capable of affecting trade between Member States[165]. In this case, the effects on trade are two-fold:

(a) Membership restrictions restrict the ability of authors to obtain copyright administration services for their works from a collecting society outside their national jurisdiction; and

(b) Territorial restrictions and concerted practices on the uniform application of territorial delineations limit the ability of a prospective satellite, cable or internet broadcasters to obtain licences from several alternate collecting societies. In addition, a collecting society is prevented under the current system from offering licensing and administration services beyond its own national territory.

227. TONO from Norway and STEF from Iceland are both members of CISAC and have concluded reciprocal representation agreements with each collecting society in the Community.[166]

---

163 Case 42/84 Remia BV and others v Commission of the European Communities [1985] ECR 2545.

164 Joined cases 6/73 and 7/73 Istituto Chemioterapico Italiano Spa and Commercial Solvents Corporation v Commission of the European Communities [1973] ECR 223, paragraph 33.

165 Case 22/79 Greenwich Film Production v Société des Auteurs, compositeurs et éditeurs de musique (SACEM) and Société des Éditions Labrador; Case 7/82 Gesellschaft zur Verwertung von Leistungsschutzrechten mbH (GVL) v Commission of the European Communities, at paragraph 38.

166 All reciprocal representation agreements of TONO and STEF contain Article 6(II) of the CISAC model contract. TONO and STEF take part in the concerted practice. Some of the reciprocal representation agreements concluded with collecting societies in the Community contain the membership clause and the exclusivity clause. Nevertheless, regarding those two restrictions, there is an effect on trade between Member States and EFTA States within the meaning of Article 53(1) of the EEA Agreement for the reciprocal representation agreements of all collecting societies in the Community. A membership clause between two collecting societies in the Community can have an impact on an author from Norway or Iceland if he or she is currently a member of one of those Community collecting societies. An exclusivity clause between two collecting societies in the Community has an impact on TONO and STEF because it prevents TONO and STEF from offering the repertoires covered by the exclusivity in the territories of those Community collecting societies.

228. Accordingly, the reciprocal representation agreements affect trade between Member States within the meaning of Article 81(1) of the Treaty and between Member States and EFTA States within the meaning of Article 53(1) of the EEA Agreement.

## 8. ARTICLE 81(3) OF THE TREATY AND ARTICLE 53(3) OF THE EEA AGREEMENT

### 8.1. Overview

229. In order to fulfil the conditions of Article 81(3) of the Treaty and of Article 53(3) of the EEA Agreement, the reciprocal representation agreements at bilateral level between collecting societies and the concerted practice of territorial delineation must satisfy four conditions, namely:

(a) contribute to improving the production or distribution of goods or to promoting technical or economic progress;

(b) allow consumers a fair share of the resulting benefits;

(c) not impose on the undertakings concerned restrictions which are not indispensable to the attainment of these objectives; and

(d) not afford such undertakings the possibility of eliminating competition in respect of a substantial part of the products in question.

Those conditions are cumulative and must be satisfied in full. It is for the Addressees of the Statement of Objections to prove that the practice satisfies the cumulative conditions laid down by Article 81(3) of the Treaty[167].

230. The Addressees of the Statement of Objections did not put forward arguments which specifically address the application of Article 81(3) of the Treaty to the membership and exclusivity clauses. The following Section therefore assesses the application of Article 81(3) of the Treaty only to the coordinated approach which amounts to systematic territorial delineation by domestic territory.

231. Several EEA CISAC members have stated that the territorial restrictions in their bilateral reciprocal representation agreements constitute a pre-requisite for the mutual exchange of repertoires and, therefore, for collecting societies to offer multi-repertoire licences. It was stated that, without territorial limitations, no reciprocal representation agreements would be concluded, since collecting societies would not allow other collecting societies compete against them with their own repertoire. This would, as a consequence, destroy the one-stop shop which currently exists on national level on the basis of the reciprocal representation agreements.

232. However, the comments referred in the previous Recital address a scenario in which EEA CISAC members could not use any kind of territorial delineation

167 Order of the Court of 28.9.2006, C-552/03-P Unilever Bestfoods (Ireland) Ltd v Commission of the European Communities, [2006] ECR I-09091, at paragraph 103.

in their reciprocal representation agreements. Since this Decision prohibits a concerted practice among the EEA CISAC members with respect to the definition and application of territorial delineation, the arguments raised by the EEA CISAC members do not apply. EEA CISAC members are not prevented from defining, on an individual basis, the licensing areas for their own repertoire abroad. As explained in Section 7.6.2.2., it cannot be accepted that, in the absence of the concerted practice, EEA CISAC members would refrain from entering into reciprocal representation agreements. There is therefore no need for EEA CISAC members to leave the reciprocal system following this Decision.

### 8.2. Contribution to improving the production or distribution of goods or the promotion of technical or economic progress

233. Under the first condition of Article 81(3) of the Treaty and of Article 53(3) of the EEA Agreement the decision, an agreement or practice must contribute to improving the production or distribution of products or to promoting technical or economic progress. This condition entails an examination of all the economic benefits flowing from the economic activity covered by the agreement. Efficiency claims must be substantiated[168] and only objective benefits, as opposed to the subjective views of the parties, may be taken into account[169]. The improvement "must in particular show appreciable objective advantages of such a character as to compensate for the disadvantages which they cause in the field of competition".[170]

234. It is not disputed that the network of bilateral reciprocal representation agreements between collecting societies provides a national one-stop shop for a worldwide management of rights. Within a particular territory, the CISAC model contract and the bilateral reciprocal representation agreements implementing it, allow a collecting society to provide a one-stop shop for the licensing of public performance rights within that particular territory. As a result, a potential commercial user which intends to perform acts in Germany which require a licence from the right holder needs only approach GEMA for the relevant multi-repertoire licence within the German territory. The network of bilateral reciprocal representation agreements generally facilitates the licensing of public performance rights through increased simplicity.[171]

168 Communication from the Commission - Notice - Guidelines the on the application of Article 81(3) of the Treaty.

169 Joined cases 56/64 and 58/66 Établissements Consten S.à.R.L. and Grundig-Verkaufs-GmbH v Commission of the European Economic Community [1966] ECR 299.

170 Order of the Court of 28.9.2006 in Case C-552/03-P Unilever Bestfoods (Ireland) Ltd v Commission of the European Communities, at paragraph 103: "as regards the first of those conditions, HB was required in particular to establish that the exclusivity clause contributed to improving the production or distribution of the goods in question, so that, were restrictions to be imposed on the possibility of implementing that clause, such an improvement could no longer be realised".

171 See, for example, paragraphs 13 and 154 f. of GEMA's non-confidential Reply to the Statement of Objections.

235. However, the arguments of the EEA CISAC members address a scenario in which EEA CISAC members could not use any kind of territorial delineation in their reciprocal representation agreements. As explained in Recital 232, there is therefore no need for EEA CISAC members to leave the reciprocal system following this Decision.

236. None of the parties raised the argument that a concerted practice on uniform national territorial delineation between CISAC members contributes to preserving these potential benefits. The prohibition of a concerted practice on territorial delineation does not call into question the system of reciprocal representation agreements. It may only change the degree of participation of each collecting society within this system. Individually concluded, reciprocal representation agreements would lead to the result that some EEA CISAC members would be granted the opportunity to issue licences for the administration and licensing of foreign repertoires beyond their home territory. This would be the case where particular collecting societies offer a better service in terms of, for example, better monitoring and recording of royalty collection, lower administrative fees. Due to the incentive to have reciprocal representation agreements with all collecting societies so as to have access to all repertoires, there is no risk for the national one-stop shop even if there were to be an increase in the number of alternative licensors with respect to certain territories.

237. To conclude, the Addressees of the Statement of Objections did not demonstrate that the concerted practice, amounting to the systematic territorial delineation of the authority to license by domestic territory, improves the delivery of public performance rights licences for internet, satellite and cable exploitation.

### 8.3. The indispensability of restrictions

238. The issue of indispensability raises the question as to "whether or not the restrictive agreement and individual restrictions make it possible to perform the activity in question more efficiently than would likely have been the case in the absence of the agreement or the restriction concerned"[172]. To assess the indispensability of individual restrictions, as is required in this Decision, it is particularly relevant to examine whether the Addressees of the Statement of Objections could have achieved the efficiencies by means of a less restrictive agreement.

239. In order to justify the territorial restriction, EEA CISAC members have referred to the need to ensure proper reporting, auditing and enforcement of rights.

240. As explained in Section 8.2, the current network of bilateral reciprocal representation agreements between collecting societies offers certain efficiencies: from a commercial user's perspective, the system offers a one-stopshop for the granting of a national multi-repertoire licence. Each collecting society fulfils this one-stop shop function within respective

172 See Communication from the Commission - Notice - Guidelines on the application of Article 81(3) of the Treaty, at paragraph 74.

domestic territories. The collecting societies' arguments seem to indicate that only in the current system proper monitoring, reporting, auditing and enforcement of rights may take place.

241. As indicated in Recital 236, the national one-stop shop is not put at risk by the prohibition of the concerted practice relating to the territorial delimitation based on domestic territories. The one-stop shop does not require a concerted definition of territorial restrictions. In the absence of the coordination on territorial restrictions, each collecting society will likely remain a one-stop shop within its territory for the granting of a multi-repertoire licence, since every collecting society has a strong incentive to conclude a reciprocal representation agreement with every other collecting society in order to receive all repertoires. However, any collecting society will have the opportunity to be selected for the administration of foreign repertoires for a broader geographic scope (that is to say, to grant licences beyond its home territory in competition with the incumbent collecting society).

242. The Commission's market investigation has shown that collecting societies are able to guarantee the proper administration of rights on a larger geographic basis. The recent market developments (the joint venture between PRS and GEMA for the management of the online rights of the Anglo-American repertoire of EMI[173], the tender launched by Warner Chappell for the management of its online rights[174] and the agreement between SACEM and Universal Publishing for online and mobile licensing[175]) demonstrate that authors' collecting societies have solutions for licensing on a multi-territorial basis and for ensuring proper remote monitoring, auditing and local enforcement if necessary. In addition, the licensor of a multi-territorial licence may not automatically be the entity which will perform the tasks of monitoring, auditing and enforcement[176].

243. To conclude, the concerted practice on territorial delineation, which limits the licence to the domestic territory of each collecting society, cannot be considered as indispensable within the meaning of Article 81(3) of the Treaty or of Article 53(3) of the EEA Agreement.

### 8.4. Allowing consumers a fair share of the resulting benefit

244. Under the second condition of Article 81(3) of the Treaty and of Article 53(3) of the EEA Agreement, economic benefits must be shown to favour not only the parties to the agreement, or to the concerted practice, but also consumers,

173 See Section 7.6.1.4, Recital 193.

174 See Section 7.6.2.2., Recital 220.

175 SACEM and Universal Publishing announced on 28 January 2008 that they have signed an agreement to allow SACEM to licence Universal Publishing's rights for online and mobile exploitation in Europe. Notably, Universal emphasises the technical capacities of SACEM – The Executive Vice President of Universal Publishing said "I have great confidence that SACEM's remarkable IDOLS system will facilitate the pan European administration of our repertoire". See joint press release of SACEM and Universal published on 28.1.2008.

176 See Recital 178 et seq.

and these benefits must outweigh the negative effects caused to them by the restrictions on competition.

245. As indicated above, this Decision does not affect the potential benefits connected to a national one-stop shop on the basis of the reciprocal representation agreements. It does not put into question cultural diversity, whether at the level of creation (authors) or access (consumers), as explained above[177].

246. Whilst the issue of a "fair share" can therefore in principle be left open in the framework of this Decision, there are in any case doubts that consumers receive a fair share of the potential benefits provided by the system of uniform national territorial delineations.

247. It is recalled that the concept of "consumer" within the meaning of Article 81(3) of the Treaty and of Article 53(3) of the EEA Agreement is not synonymous with the final consumer. The term covers the customers of the parties to the agreement, in this case the right holders (that is to say, authors of musical works) and commercial users of public performance rights for satellite, cable and internet exploitation[178].

248. From a right holder's perspective, the existing network of reciprocal representation by domestic territory ensures that in each EEA country one collecting society (the incumbent collecting society) is in charge of the exploitation of their works. However, this only translates into an economic advantage if all the local collecting societies efficiently manage the repertoires they have been granted. As has been demonstrated[179], based on certain criteria such as the administration fee rates, the level of efficiency of the various collecting societies significantly varies.. The advantage of the restriction of competition resulting from the existing network of bilateral reciprocal representation agreements is therefore not evident from a right holders' perspective[180].

249. From a commercial user's perspective, the coordination on a uniform national territorial delineation enables the incumbent collecting society to offer a comprehensive repertoire to their domestic commercial users. This solution generates efficiency insofar as each collecting society is a one-stop shop for the delivery of a multi-repertoire licence. However, the disadvantages of this

177 See Section 7.3.1.

178 See Communication from the Commission - Notice Guidelines on the application of Article 81(3) of the Treaty, at paragraph 84.

179 See Recital 133.

180 In addition, as mentioned by SABAM in its Reply to the Statement of Objections, "The exercise of authors' rights by the collecting societies appointed by these authors requires to be carried out to these authors' advantage. No such advantage is gained from materially obstructing the activities of legitimate multi national users of the world music repertoire who embark on modes of reproductions and, specifically, of performance that are technologically new in that they are inherently borderless and allow the dissemination of protected works towards a number of national populations" (emphasis added) (see page 19 of SABAM's Reply to the Statement of Objections).

one-stop shop include the fact that any licence granted is strictly limited to single national territories and that the emergence of alternative providers of licences for the same territory are excluded. It can, therefore, be left open whether this would represent a fair share, since the application of Article 81(3) of the Treaty already fails on the basis of the other conditions.

### 8.5. No elimination of competition

250. According to the fourth condition of Article 81(3) of the Treaty and of Article 53(3) of the EEA Agreement, an agreement must not afford the undertakings concerned the possibility of eliminating competition in respect of a substantial part of the products (or services) concerned[181]. For the assessment of the market situation in the light of the above criteria, both actual and potential competition must be considered.

251. Due to the territorial restrictions resulting from the concerted practice, a collecting society cannot offer administration services beyond its own territory and may not, as a consequence, offer licences which include more repertoires than its own one, for use by commercial users outside of its own territory. Commercial users have no choice but to obtain a multi-repertoire licence from the local collecting society for only that local territory. The coordination on territorial restrictions means, therefore, that collecting societies totally eliminate competition between each other in relation to licensing of the other collecting societies' repertoires for satellite, cable and internet broadcasting use and create a market partitioning between EEA CISAC members.

252. Due to the complementary nature of individual repertoires, which is exacerbated by the membership restrictions, the main source of competition in this market is at present competition on the repertoire which collecting societies would receive via the reciprocal representation agreements but for the territorial restrictions. The elimination of competition is particularly serious because the collecting societies themselves are the only ones who could realistically enter the other national markets. Their long-entrenched monopolistic positions, caused by exclusivity granted directly (through explicit provisions) and indirectly (through the concerted practice on territorial delineation), creates a barrier to entry which is impossible for a newcomer to overcome. The prospects for market entry by newcomers are consequently poor. In light of the above, the territorial restrictions eliminate competition in the relevant markets for the administration of rights and the licensing of repertoires.

### 8.6. Conclusion on Article 81(3) of the Treaty and on Article 53(3) of the EEA Agreement

253. The Addresses of the Statement of Objections have failed to demonstrate that the CISAC model contract and its application at bilateral level between EEA CISAC members, including the concerted practice on territorial delineation,

---

181 See Communication from the Commission - Notice - Guidelines on the application of Article 81(3) of the Treaty, at paragraph 105.

fulfil all the requirements of Article 81(3) of the Treaty and of Article 53(3) of the EEA Agreement.

254. Even without the restrictions, the alleged benefits, in particular national one-stop shops and proper monitoring and reporting can still be provided. The restrictions are consequently not indispensable. In addition, they eliminate competition on the markets for the administration of repertoires for other EEA CISAC members and the licensing of rights.

255. Accordingly, it must be concluded that neither the membership clause, the territorial restrictions in the bilateral reciprocal representation agreements, nor the concerted practice on the uniform national territorial delineation fulfil Article 81(3) of the Treaty or Article 53(3) of the EEA Agreement.

## 9. ARTICLE 86(2) OF THE TREATY

256. Some EEA CISAC members submit that they are undertakings entrusted with 'the operation of services of general economic interest' within the meaning of Article 86(2) of the Treaty and that therefore they are subject to the rules on competition only insofar as the application of such rules 'does not obstruct' the performance of the particular tasks assigned to them[182].

257. The Court of Justice held in Case 7/82, the *GVL* judgment regarding the German performing artists' collecting society, that the fact that a company must be officially authorised, be subject to monitoring by a public authority and be under a duty to conclude certain management agreements, is not sufficient for it to be included in the category of undertakings referred to in Article 86(2) of the Treaty[183]. The Court underlined that the German legislation does not confer the management of copyright or related rights on specific undertakings but defines in a general manner the rules applying to collecting societies[184]. It can be left open whether the relevant laws of certain EEA countries describe the function and the status of the collecting society in a way which allows the assumption that the collecting society is entrusted with the operation of services of general economic interest[185].

258. In any case, as has been shown in Section 7.6.2.2, it has not been demonstrated by the EEA CISAC members who have raised this issue that the concerted practice on the territorial delineation, which limits a licence to the domestic territory of each collecting society, is necessary for the proper functioning of collective rights management. AKM puts forward that only a

---

182 See in particular pages 34 et seq. of AKM's non-confidential Reply to the Statement of Objections. GEMA is of the opinion that Article 86(2) of the Treaty should at least be applied by analogy – see paragraph 122 of GEMA's non-confidential Reply to the Statement of Objections.

183 Case 7/82 Gesellschaft zur Verwertung von Leistungsschutzrechten mbH (GVL) v Commission of the European Communities , at paragraph 31 et seq.

184 Ibid at paragraph 32.

185 In particular AKM argues that the legal situation in Austria differs appreciably from the one existing in Germany – see pages 35 et seq. of AKM's non-confidential Reply to the Statement of Objections.

territorial delineation of the licence could best guarantee its members' rights abroad because in the case of licences unlimited in their territorial scope, foreign collecting societies could compete on AKM's repertoire, which would put pressure on the right holders' royalties[186].

259. First, this Decision does not prohibit any territorial delineation, but the concerted practice among all EEA CISAC members relating to strict domestic territorial delineation. Second, as demonstrated in Section 7.6.2.2., there are mechanisms which allow collecting societies to retain some control over revenues in case they grant licences to several collecting societies for the same territory, in particular by limiting price competition to the administrative fees. On the contrary, granting a mandate to a very efficient collecting society in addition to, or instead of the domestic collecting society, could increase the number of licences granted to commercial users, which would have a positive impact on the royalties paid to the members of AKM. In addition, insofar as national laws have created exclusive or special rights, this Decision, which limits itself to assess the restrictions of competition which result from the collecting societies' autonomous behaviour (see Section 7.3.2.), does not affect the national laws. The prohibition of the concerted practice does not therefore obstruct the public performance of the tasks which might be assigned to certain collecting societies.

## 10. REMEDIES

### 10.1. Practices infringing Article 81(1) of the Treaty and Article 53(1) of the EEA Agreement

260. Certain of the infringements covered by this Decision have been terminated. The exclusivity clause (in Article 1(I) and (II)) and the membership clause (in Article 11(II)) are no longer part of the CISAC model contract.[187] However, on the basis of the information in the Commission' possession, a series of clauses are still included in a number of reciprocal representation agreements and certain practices contrary to both Article 81(1) of the Treaty and Article 53 (1) EEA continue to be in place. This is true in particular for:

(a) the membership restriction clauses contained in reciprocal representation agreements concluded by certain collecting societies;

(b) the exclusive rights conferred in the reciprocal representation agreements concluded by certain collecting societies;

(c) the concerted practices relating to the territorial delineation by the collecting societies.

186 See page 38 of AKM's non-confidential Reply to the Statement of Objections.

187 These clauses were respectively removed from the CISAC model contract in 1996 and 2004. See Section 4.4.1. of this Decision, Recital 27 et seq.

### 10.2. Article 7(1) of Regulation (EC) No 1/2003

261. Where the Commission finds that there is an infringement of Article 81 of the Treaty it may, in accordance with Article 7(1) of Regulation (EC) No 1/2003 require, by decision, the undertakings and/or associations of undertakings concerned to bring such an infringement to an end. Pursuant to Article 5 of Council Regulation (EC) No 2894/94 of 28 November 1994, concerning arrangements for implementing the Agreement of the European Economic Area[188], "the Community rules giving effect to the principles set out in Articles 85 and 86 [now Articles 81 and 82] of the EC Treaty [...] shall apply mutatis mutandis" in respect of the EEA.

262. For that purpose, the Commission may impose on the undertakings any behavioural or structural remedies which are proportionate to the infringement committed and necessary to effectively bring the infringement to an end.

263. First, a series of clauses are still included in certain agreements and some practices are still in place. Second, although some EEA CISAC members claim to have removed restrictive clauses from all the bilateral reciprocal representation agreements, it cannot be safely assumed that such belated removal completely removes the need to order the undertakings in question to bring the infringement to an end. Third, bearing in mind that Article 81 of the Treaty may apply with regard to agreements which are no longer in force, if they continue to produce their effects after they have formally ceased to be in force,[189] it is not certain that the infringement has come to a complete end as regards certain anti-competitive practices carried out by certain collecting societies. Accordingly, the addressees of this Decision must first:

(a) immediately bring to an end, if they have not already done so, the infringements concerning the membership restriction clauses and exclusive rights clauses contained in reciprocal representation agreements; and

(b) within 120 days of the date of notification of this Decision, bring to an end the infringement concerning the concerted practice relating to the territorial delineation.

264. The addressees of the Decision should also communicate to the Commission all the measures they have taken to implement these remedies. As regards the concerted practice on territorial delineation, it is first necessary to stop any concertation in the future of the type addressed in this decision. Second, although the fact of limiting the mandate to the territory of the other collecting society is not in itself restrictive of competition, it is also

188 OJ L 305, 30.11.1994, p. 6.

189 See, to this effect, Case 51/75 *EMI Records Limited v CBS United Kingdom Limited* [1976] ECR 811, paragraph 15; Case 243/83 SA Binon & Cie v SA Agence et messageries de la presse [1985] ECR 2015, paragraph 17; Case T-2/89 *Petrofina* SA v *Commission of the European Communities* [1991] ECR II-1087, paragraph 212; Case T-14/89 Montecatini SpA (formerly Montedipe SpA) v Commission of the European Communities [1992] ECR II-2409, paragraph 231; Case T-327/94 *SCA Holding Ltd* v *Commission of the European Communities* [1998] ECR II-1373, paragraph 95; joined cases T-109/02, T-118/02, T-122/02, T-125/02, T-126/02, T-128/02, T-129/02, T-132/02 and T-136/02, *Bolloré SA and Others* v *Commission of the European Communities* [2007] ECR II-00947, at paragraph 186.

necessary, insofar as past concertation is still reflected in existing agreements, to make sure that the bilateral agreements in the future are, as regards the territorial delineation of the reciprocal mandates, the result of bilateral negotiations and are not anymore influenced by the existence of a concerted practice which limits the territory of the mandate.

265. Further, the addressees of the decision should refrain from any agreement or concerted practice which might have the same or similar object or effect as the conduct described in Recital 260,

HAS ADOPTED THIS DECISION:

Article 1

The following undertakings have infringed Article 81 of the Treaty and Article 53 of the EEA Agreement by using, in their reciprocal representation agreements, the membership restrictions which were contained in Article 11(II) of the model contract of the International Confederation of Societies of Authors and Composers (' the CISAC model contract'), or by de facto applying those membership restrictions:

AEPI
AKKA/LAA
AKM
ARTISJUS
BUMA
EAÜ
GEMA
IMRO
KODA
LATGA-A
PRS
OSA
SABAM
SACEM
SAZAS
SGAE
SIAE
SOZA
SPA
STEF
STIM
TEOSTO
TONO
ZAIKS

Article 2

The following 17 undertakings have infringed Article 81 of the Treaty and Article 53 of the EEA Agreement by conferring, in their reciprocal representation agreements, exclusive rights as provided for in Article 1(I) and (II) of the CISAC model contract:

AKKA/LAA
ARTISJUS
BUMA
EAÜ
IMRO
KODA
LATGA-A
OSA
SAZAS
SGAE
SOZA
SPA
STEF
STIM
TEOSTO
TONO
ZAIKS

Article 3

The following undertakings have infringed Article 81 of the Treaty and Article 53 of the EEA Agreement by coordinating the territorial delineations in a way which limits a licence to the domestic territory of each collecting society:

AEPI
AKKA/LAA
AKM
ARTISJUS
BUMA
EAÜ
GEMA
IMRO
KODA
LATGA-A
PRS
OSA
SABAM
SACEM
SAZAS
SGAE
SIAE
SOZA
SPA

STEF
STIM
TEOSTO
TONO
ZAIKS

Article 4

1. The undertakings listed in Articles 1 and 2 shall immediately bring to an end the infringements referred to in those Articles, insofar as they have not already done so, and shall communicate to the Commission all the measures they have taken for that purpose.

2. The undertakings listed in Article 3 shall, within 120 days of the date of notification of this Decision, bring to an end the infringement referred to in that Article and shall, within that period of time, communicate to the Commission all the measures they have taken for that purpose.

   In particular, the undertakings listed in Article 3 shall review bilaterally with each other undertaking listed in Article 3 the territorial delineation of their mandates for satellite, cable retransmission and internet use in each of their reciprocal representation agreements and shall provide the Commission with copies of the reviewed agreements.

3. The addressees of this Decision shall refrain from repeating any act or conduct described in Articles 1, 2 and 3, and from any act or conduct having the same, or similar, object or effect.

Article 5

The Commission may at its sole discretion and upon reasoned and timely request by one or several undertakings listed in Article 3 grant an extension of the time provided for in Article 4 second paragraph.

Article 6

This Decision is addressed to:

(1) Ελληνική Εταιρεία Προστασίας της Πνευματικής Ιδιοκτησίας (AEPI), Fragoklissias and Samou street n° 51, 151 25 Amaroussio, Athens, Greece

(2) Autortiesibu un komunicesanas konsultaciju agentura – Latvijas Autoru apvieniba (AKKA/LAA), A.Čaka street 97, 1011 Riga, Latvia

(3) Staatlich genehmigte Gesellschaft der Autorem, Komponisten und Musikverleger, reg.Gen.m.b.H (AKM), Baumannstrasse 10, Postfach 259, 1031 Vienna, Austria

(4) Magyar Szerzői Jogvédő Iroda Egyesület (ARTISJUS, Meszaros u. 15-17, 1016 Budapest, Hungary

(5) Vereniging Buma (BUMA), Siriusdreef 22-28, 2130 KB Hoofddorp, Netherlands

(6) Eesti Autorite Ühing (EAÜ), Lille 13, 10614 Tallinn, Estonia

(7) Gesellschaft für musikalische Aufführungs- und mechanische Vervielfältigungsrechte (GEMA), Rosenheimer Strasse 11, 81667 Munich, Germany

(8) the Irish Music Rights Organisation Limited – Eagras um Chearta Cheolta Teoranta (IMRO), Copyright House, Pembroke Row, Lower Baggot Street, Dublin 2, Ireland

(9) Komponistrettigheder i Danmark (KODA), Landemaerket 23-25, Postboks 2154, 1016 Copenhagen, Denmark

(10) Lietuvos autorių teisių gynimo asociacijos agentūra (LATGA-A), J. Basanaviciaus G. 4h, 2600 Vilnius, Lithuania

(11) Ochranný svaz autorský pro práva k dílům hudebním, o.s. (OSA), Cs. Armady 786/20,16056 Prague 6, Czech Republic

(12) Performing Right Society Limited (PRS), Berners Street 29-33, London WIT 3AB, United Kingdom

(13) Société Belge des Auteurs, Compositeurs et Editeurs Scrl / Belgische Vereniging van Auteurs, Componisten en Uitgevers (SABAM), Rue d'Arlon 75-77, 1040 Brussels, Belgium

(14) Société des Auteurs, Compositeurs et Editeurs de Musique (SACEM), 225 av Charles de Gaulle, 92528 Neuilly sur Seine Cedex, France

(15) Združenje skladateljev, avtorjev in založnikov za zaščito avtorskih pravic Slovenije (SAZAS), Trzaska cesta 34, 1000 Ljubljana, Slovenia

(16) Sociedad General de Autores y Editores (SGAE), Fernando VI-4, 28004 Madrid, Spain

(17) Societa Italiana degli Autori ed Editori (SIAE), VIALE della Letteratura 30, 00144 Rome, Italy

(18) Slovenský ochranný Zväz Autorský pre práva k hudobným dielam (SOZA), Rastislavova 3, 2108 Bratislava 2, Slovakia

(19) Sociedade Portuguesa de Autores (SPA), Avenue Duque de Loulé 31, 1069-153 Lisbon, Portugal

(20) Samband Tónskalda og Eigenda Flutningsréttar (STEF), Laufasvegi 40, 101 Reykjavik, Iceland

76

(21) Svenska Tonsättares Internationella Musikbyrå (STIM), BOX 27327, 10254 Stockholm, Sweden

(22) Säveltäjäin Tekijänoikeustoimisto teosto r.y.(TEOSTO), Lauttasaarentie 1, 00200 Helsinki, Finland

(23) The Norwegian Performing Right Society (TONO), Postboks 9171, Gronland, 0134 Oslo, Norway

(24) Stowarzyszenie Autorów ZAiKS (ZAIKS), 2, Hipoteczna Street, PO Box P-16, 00092 Warsaw, Poland

This Decision shall be enforceable pursuant to Article 256 of the Treaty and Article 110 of the EEA Agreement.

Done at Brussels, 16.07.2008

*For the Commission*
*Neelie KROES*
*Member of the Commission*

# LAW 5.2

# EU RECOMMENDATION (ADOPTED OCTOBER 12, 2005)

II

*(Acts whose publication is not obligatory)*

## COMMISSION

### COMMISSION RECOMMENDATION

### of 18 May 2005

### on collective cross-border management of copyright and related rights for legitimate online music services

**(Text with EEA relevance)**

(2005/737/EC)

THE COMMISSION OF THE EUROPEAN COMMUNITIES,

Having regard to the Treaty establishing the European Community, and in particular Article 211 thereof,

Whereas:

(1) In April 2004 the Commission adopted a Communication on the Management of Copyright and Related Rights in the Internal Market.

(2) The European Parliament, in its report of 15 January 2004 (1), stated that right-holders should be able to enjoy copyright and related rights protection wherever such rights are established, independent of national borders or modes of use during the whole term of their validity.

(3) The European Parliament further emphasised that any action by the Community in respect of the collective cross-border management of copyright and related rights should strengthen the confidence of artists, including writers and musicians, that the pan-European use of their creative works will be financially rewarded (2).

(4) New technologies have led to the emergence of a new generation of commercial users that make use of musical works and other subject matter online. The provision of legitimate online music services requires management of a series of copyright and related rights.

(5) One category of those rights is the exclusive right of reproduction which covers all reproductions made in the process of online distribution of a musical work. Other categories of rights are the right of communication to the public of musical works, the right to equitable remuneration for the communication to the public of other subject matter and the exclusive right of making available a musical work or other subject matter.

(6) Pursuant to Directive 2001/29/EC of the European Parliament and of the Council of 22 May 2001 on the harmonisation of certain aspects of copyright and related rights in the information society (3) and Council Directive 92/100/EEC of 19 November 1992 on rental right and lending right and on certain rights related to copyright in the field of intellectual property (4), a licence is required for each of the rights in the online exploitation of musical works. These rights may be managed by collective rights managers that provide certain management services to right-holders as agents or by individual right-holders themselves.

(7) Licensing of online rights is often restricted by territory, and commercial users negotiate in each Member State with each of the respective collective rights managers for each right that is included in the online exploitation.

(8) In the era of online exploitation of musical works, however, commercial users need a licensing policy that corresponds to the ubiquity of the online environment and which is multi-territorial. It is therefore appropriate to provide for multi-territorial licensing in order to enhance greater legal certainty to commercial users in relation to their activity and to foster the development of legitimate online services, increasing, in turn, the revenue stream for right-holders.

(1) A5-0478/2003.
(2) See recital 29.
(3) OJ L 167, 22.6.2001, p. 10.
(4) OJ L 346, 27.11.1992, p. 61. Directive as amended by Directive 2001/29/EC.

(9) Freedom to provide collective management services across national borders entails that right-holders are able to freely choose the collective rights manager for the management of the rights necessary to operate legitimate online music services across the Community. That right implies the possibility to entrust or transfer all or a part of the online rights to another collective rights manager irrespective of the Member State of residence or the nationality of either the collective rights manager or the rights-holder.

(10) Fostering effective structures for cross-border management of rights should also ensure that collective rights managers achieve a higher level of rationalisation and transparency, with regard to compliance with competition rules, especially in the light of the requirements arising out of the digital environment.

(11) The relationship between right-holders and collective rights managers, whether based on contract or statutory membership rules, should include a minimum protection for right-holders with respect to all categories of rights that are necessary for the provision of legitimate online music services. There should be no difference in treatment of right-holders by rights managers on the basis of the Member State of residence or nationality.

(12) Royalties collected on behalf of right-holders should be distributed equitably and without discrimination on the grounds of residence, nationality, or category of right-holder. In particular, royalties collected on behalf of right-holders in Member States other than those in which the right-holders are resident or of which they are nationals should be distributed as effectively and efficiently as possible.

(13) Additional recommendations on accountability, right-holder representation in the decision-making bodies of collective rights managers and dispute resolution should ensure that collective rights managers achieve a higher level of rationalisation and transparency and that right-holders and commercial users can make informed choices. There should be no difference in treatment on the basis of category of membership in the collective rights management society: all right-holders, be they authors, composers, publishers, record producers, performers or others, should be treated equally.

(14) It is appropriate to continuously assess the development of the online music market,

HEREBY RECOMMENDS:

*Definitions*

1. For the purposes of this Recommendation the following definitions are applied:

(a) 'management of copyright and related rights for the provision of legitimate online music services at Community level' means the provision of the following services: the grant of licences to commercial users, the auditing and monitoring of rights, the enforcement of copyright and related rights, the collection of royalties and the distribution of royalties to right-holders;

(b) 'musical works' means any musical work or other protected subject matter;

(c) 'repertoire' means the catalogue of musical works which is administered by a collective rights manager;

(d) 'multi-territorial licence' means a licence which covers the territory of more than one Member state;

(e) 'collective rights manager' means any person providing the services set out in point (a) to several right-holders;

(f) 'online rights' means any of the following rights:

(i) the exclusive right of reproduction that covers all reproductions provided for under Directive 2001/29/EC in the form of intangible copies, made in the process of online distribution of musical works;

(ii) the right of communication to the public of a musical work, either in the form of a right to authorise or prohibit pursuant to Directive 2001/29/EC or a right to equitable remuneration in accordance with Directive 92/100/EEC, which includes webcasting, internet radio and simulcasting or near-on-demand services received either on a personal computer or on a mobile telephone;

(iii) the exclusive right of making available a musical work pursuant to Directive 2001/29/EC, which includes on-demand or other interactive services;

(g) 'right-holder' means any natural or legal person that holds online rights;

(h) 'commercial user' means any person involved in the provision of online music services who needs a licence from right-holders in order to provide legitimate online music services;

(i) 'reciprocal representation agreement' means any bilateral agreement between collective rights managers whereby one collective rights manager grants to the other the right to represent its repertoire in the territory of the other.

*General*

2. Member States are invited to take the steps necessary to facilitate the growth of legitimate online services in the Community by promoting a regulatory environment which is best suited to the management, at Community level, of copyright and related rights for the provision of legitimate online music services.

*The relationship between right-holders, collective rights managers and commercial users*

3. Right-holders should have the right to entrust the management of any of the online rights necessary to operate legitimate online music services, on a territorial scope of their choice, to a collective rights manager of their choice, irrespective of the Member State of residence or the nationality of either the collective rights manager or the right-holder.

4. Collective rights managers should apply the utmost diligence in representing the interests of right-holders.

5. With respect to the licensing of online rights the relationship between right-holders and collective rights managers, whether based on contract or statutory membership rules, should, at least be governed by the following:

   (a) right-holders should be able to determine the online rights to be entrusted for collective management;

   (b) right-holders should be able to determine the territorial scope of the mandate of the collective rights managers;

   (c) right-holders should, upon reasonable notice of their intention to do so, have the right to withdraw any of the online rights and transfer the multi territorial management of those rights to another collective rights manager, irrespective of the Member State of residence or the nationality of either the collective rights manager or the right-holder;

   (d) where a right-holder has transferred the management of an online right to another collective rights manager, without prejudice to other forms of cooperation among rights managers, all collective rights managers concerned should ensure that those online rights are withdrawn from any existing reciprocal representation agreement concluded amongst them.

6. Collective rights managers should inform right-holders and commercial users of the repertoire they represent, any existing reciprocal representation agreements, the territorial scope of their mandates for that repertoire and the applicable tariffs.

7. Collective rights managers should give reasonable notice to each other and commercial users of changes in the repertoire they represent.

8. Commercial users should inform collective right managers of the different features of the services for which they want to acquire online rights.

9. Collective rights managers should grant commercial users licences on the basis of objective criteria and without any discrimination among users.

*Equitable distribution and deductions*

10. Collective rights managers should distribute royalties to all right-holders or category of right-holders they represent in an equitable manner.

11. Contracts and statutory membership rules governing the relationship between collective rights managers and right-holders for the management, at Community level, of musical works for online use should specify whether and to what extent, there will be deductions from the royalties to be distributed for purposes other than for the management services provided.

12. Upon payment of the royalties collective rights managers should specify vis-à-vis all the right-holders they represent, the deductions made for purposes other than for the management services provided.

*Non-discrimination and representation*

13. The relationship between collective rights managers and right-holders, whether based on contract or statutory membership rules should be based on the following principles:

    (a) any category of right-holder is treated equally in relation to all elements of the management service provided;

    (b) the representation of right-holders in the internal decision making process is fair and balanced.

*Accountability*

14. Collective rights managers should report regularly to all right-holders they represent, whether directly or under reciprocal representation agreements, on any licences granted, applicable tariffs and royalties collected and distributed.

*Dispute settlement*

15. Member States are invited to provide for effective dispute resolution mechanisms, in particular in relation to tariffs, licensing conditions, entrustment of online rights for management and withdrawal of online rights.

*Follow-up*

16. Member States and collective rights managers are invited to report, on a yearly basis, to the Commission on the measures they have taken in relation to this Recommendation and on the management, at Community level, of copyright and related rights for the provision of legitimate online music services.

17. The Commission intends to assess, on a continuous basis, the development of the online music sector and in the light of this Recommendation.

18. The Commission will to consider, on the basis of the assessment referred to in point 17, the need for further action at Community level.

*Addressees*

19. This Recommendation is addressed to the Member States and to all economic operators which are involved in the management of copyright and related rights within the Community.

Done at Brussels, 18 May 2005.

*For the Commission*

Charlie McCREEVY

*Member of the Commission*

CHAPTER 6

# THE SPLIT COPYRIGHT SYNDROME

## SUMMARY

CHAPTER 6

# THE SPLIT COPYRIGHT SYNDROME

A *split copyright* is a copyright owned by two or more people (i.e., one in which two or more persons own an undivided interest). Anyone who regularly seeks to clear licenses for the use of music in motion pictures, television programs, or advertisements should be quite familiar with the challenges posed when a musical copyright is controlled by more than one person or entity. Situations in which there is agreement among the co-owners assigning the song's administration rights to one of the co-owners often poses one of the most frustrating barriers to clearing licenses: locating and obtaining permission from each of the several owners of the copyright.

This chapter sketches the chaos that can result from co-ownership of copyright and suggests to copyright co-owners a solution that should enhance the value of their copyrights and simplify the task of persons seeking to clear permission for the use of copyrighted compositions.

## I. Legal Background

### A. Undivided Co-Ownership of Copyright

As discussed at length in Chapter 7, on *The Language of Music Licensing*, when a composer and lyricist collaborate in the writing of a song, a copyright is said to *subsist* in the composer and lyricist the moment that they fix the song on paper or recording tape. From that moment, the composer and lyricist co-own the *undivided* interest in the entire copyright of the song. The co-owners of a copyright are much like tenants in common of real property. Each author automatically acquires an undivided ownership interest in the *entire* work.

Unless they agree otherwise, the composer and lyricist each acquire a 50% undivided interest in the entire work, and they will share equally in the revenues generated by the song. When there are three writers, each will have a 33⅓% undivided interest in the entire work; when there are four, each will own a 25% interest, and so forth. The writers may, however, agree to another division. For example, when one writer's contribution involved words and music and the other's involved only the words, the two may agree to a 75/25% division.

A concept discussed in Chapter 8, on the *Formalities of Music Licensing*, is the *assignment* (i.e., transfer or sale) of copyrights. In other words, copyrights, and exclusive rights under copyright, may be transferred from one person to another, much like other forms of property. The composer, in the above example, may sell to another his 50% undivided interest in the copyright. If he does so, he will then own no part of the copyright, and the person to whom the assignment is made, the "assignee," will become the owner of that 50% undivided interest in the copyright. This is typically the effect of the standard songwriter agreement between a composer and a music publisher, discussed in Chapter 3, on *Songwriter Agreements*. In exchange for granting his 50% undivided interest in the copyright to the music publisher, the composer is given contractual rights under which he receives the benefits of the publisher's administration services, including the administration of the copyright, the promotion of the song, the collection of revenues from licensing use of the song, and payment of royalties to the composer, representing the composer's share of such revenues.

In short, when a writer signs a standard songwriter agreement, he is generally agreeing to assign to the music publisher all his undivided interest in his song. In some cases, however, the composer assigns only one-half of his undivided interest in the song to the music publisher, with the composer retaining the other half personally or in a separate sole proprietorship music publishing company established for the purpose of holding that interest. This is typically the effect of the standard co-publishing agreement between a composer's publishing company and a major music publisher, discussed in Chapter 4, on *Co-Publishing and Administration.*

In the example of our composer, who started out owning only 50% of the song (his lyricist collaborator owning the other 50%), if the composer should assign half of his 50% undivided interest to a music publisher, then the composer and his music publisher would each own a 25% undivided interest in the copyright, leaving the lyricist, of course, with his 50% undivided interest, which he may retain or assign to the same or another music publisher. Thus, in the above example, concerning one song written by two collaborators, as many as four music publishing companies may claim to have an undivided interest in the whole copyright in the song — i.e., the two respective major music publishers normally used by the composer and lyricist and the two respective sole proprietorship music publishing companies operated by the composer and lyricist or their respective attorneys, agents, or business managers.

Co-ownership of copyright can also result from a variety of other circumstances. Copyright ownership may be split by a statutory termination of a prior grant of copyright. When a grant of copyright is terminated under the 35-year termination rule[1] or the 39-year termination rule[2] (discussed in Chapter 9, on *Duration of Copyright, Assignments of Copyright, and Licenses*), the copyright reverts to the author or authors of the work, or to other persons owning the termination interests, such as a deceased author's surviving spouse or children. Each author or other person to whom an undivided interest in the copyright reverts under a statutory termination is in a position to make a further grant of his or her interest to another, such as a music publisher of that person's choosing. Each may choose to grant the reverted rights to a different music publisher or choose to administer those rights himself. A similar split may occur where the *renewal* rights of a co-writer, discussed in Chapter 9, are assigned to a different publisher from the publisher of the rights of another co-writer.

The provisions of U.S. copyright law concerning termination of grants and renewal rights in no way impact rights arising under any foreign laws. Laws of certain countries provide similar statutory mechanisms that may cause a split copyright. For example, under the old British copyright law, all rights under copyright reverted to an author's heirs upon the 25th anniversary of the author's death. Thus, a split copyright results when the British reversionary rights of a co-writer are assigned to a different publisher from the publisher of the rights of another co-writer.

---

[1] 17 U.S.C. Sec. 203.

[2] 17 U.S.C. Sec. 115(b)(1).

Finally, a division by percentage of ownership between writers is not the only way that a copyright may be split. As we have seen in Chapter 5, on *International Subpublishing*, a copyright also may be split by territory. For example, one publisher may own exclusive rights to a composition for exploitation in the United States and several others may own rights for the rest of the world.

## B. Licensing Rights of Co-Owners

The general rule in the United States governing the right of a co-owner to grant non-exclusive licenses for use of the work is this: unless co-owners have a contract among them that states otherwise, a co-owner can grant a license for the use of the song without the consent of the co-owners, as long as the licensing co-owner accounts and pays to the others their share of the license fee collected.[3]

However, this rule is not entirely settled law. Courts have held that one co-owner may not unilaterally grant a license that will effectively destroy the value of the copyright. Just what kinds of licenses would be construed as having destroyed the value of the copyright is not clear. Further, and perhaps more important, this rule is not followed in many countries around the world. In the United Kingdom, France, and many other countries, the rule is: a license is not valid unless all co-owners consent to it.

Relying solely on the U.S. rule, persons seeking to clear permission should feel comfortable in accepting a license offered by only one of several co-owners, provided that the territory of the license is limited to the United States and that the licensee has no reason to believe that there exists an agreement among the co-owners restricting the granting of licenses by the other co-owners. The licensee might also rely on a written warranty from the licensing co-owner that the latter has the right to grant the license without the consent of any of the co-owners.

The practical problem faced by producers of works that include music licensed from one co-owner is the risk that another co-owner will later make an objection. The consequences of having an ineffectual license are great: the producer risks having the distribution of his entire work enjoined by a court. A more important practical problem stems

[3] See generally 1 Nimmer On Copyright, Sec. 6.10.

from the fact that advances in worldwide telecommunications are making the economies of countries increasingly interdependent. As a result, licensees are increasingly demanding that the territories of music licenses be made worldwide. If the territory of the license is worldwide, the producer must insist upon receiving the written permission from *all* of the co-owners of the song.

## II. THE PROBLEM — AN ILLUSTRATIVE EXAMPLE

Let us consider an example in which the five members of a rock band collaborated in the writing of a song. Suppose that, upon formation of the band, they had agreed that each contributor would own an equal share of the copyright in any songs composed in collaboration. Thus, in this example, each writer owns a 20% interest in the undivided copyright in the composition.

The first member had previously established his own publishing company, to which he promptly assigned his entire 20% undivided interest.

The second member had previously signed an exclusive songwriter's contract with a major music publisher and, under that contract, was obligated to assign his entire 20% undivided interest to the publisher. Since this member had no contractual control over his colleagues' music publishing rights, he was unable to assist his major publisher in obtaining the remaining undivided interest in the copyright.

The third member had also signed an exclusive songwriter's agreement, but with a publisher affiliated with the record company with which the band had signed, and his deal was a "co-publishing" deal, under which he agreed to assign only half of any undivided interest in any songs that he wrote during the term of the contract. This resulted in his assigning a 10% undivided interest in the copyright to his music publisher, but still retaining the other 10%, which he assigned to his own publishing company.

The fourth member also had previously signed an exclusive songwriter's agreement, but his deal was an administration agreement, under which he maintained his entire 20% undivided interest in the copyright, but granted to a major music publisher exclusive administration rights for the United States and Canada. The publisher will be issuing licenses in and for that territory and collecting income in exchange for retaining a 15% administration fee. This member's own music publishing company is run by his attorney. In exchange for a large advance against royalties, this fourth member also promptly assigned his subpublishing rights, with respect to his 20% undivided interest, to a major European music publishing company for exploitation in member countries of the European Community. He received additional advances for parceling out his remaining subpublishing rights for all other territories on a territory-by-territory, song-by-song basis.

The fifth member didn't know anything about copyright, but was satisfied that the other members placed his name on the copyright registration form and took no further action, except to send a letter to ASCAP requesting a membership application form.

After several years, the song was becoming recognized as a standard hit, and motion picture producers began to seek worldwide synchronization licenses and advertisers began offering large sums for permission to use the song in national television commercials. The band, of course, has long since broken up. One member died of a drug overdose, leaving a widow and two children, and another committed suicide over the frustration of determining his music rights, leaving no heirs except the Chase Manhattan Bank as the executor of his estate.

## III. THE MUSIC CLEARANCE INDUSTRY — A PARTIAL SOLUTION

The foregoing is an example of what might be called the "Split Copyright Syndrome," and it is not as far-fetched as it might initially appear. The Split Copyright Syndrome has spawned a new industry: music clearance companies. As noted and discussed in Chapter 6, *music clearance* is the process of (a) ascertaining whether a musical composition is protected by copyright, (b) if it is protected, determining who owns the copyright or, more important, who has the right to administer its licensing, and (c) obtaining permission for the proposed use. Responding to the complexities posed by an increasing number of split copyrights, several entrepreneurs have established companies that specialize in performing the task of music clearance on behalf of motion picture producers, television producers, advertising agencies, and virtually anyone seeking to clear a license for the use of music.

For any clearance projects involving multiple music compositions or new technologies, such as multimedia works, the services of a professional clearance firm are highly recommended.

The Clearing House, Ltd. is one such firm that specializes in representing producers of television programs and motion pictures and others in clearing the use of copyrighted music by its clients. Ronald H. Gertz, Esq., a lawyer and the chief executive officer of Clearing House, Ltd., makes his living on the chaos resulting from the split copyright problem. In his commentary entitled *Hung Up on Splintered Rights*, which appeared in a January 1984 issue of *Billboard* magazine, Mr. Gertz artfully describes the problem of split copyrights. The article is so instructive that we have obtained his permission to reprint it here in its entirety:

> Everyone has heard variations of the oft recycled joke about the three biggest lies in Hollywood. The first two usually are, "The Mercedes is paid for," and "The check is in the mail." The third always seems to be rooted in social comment, like "It's only a cold sore."
>
> My vote for lie number three is, "Don't worry, I control the rights." Accordingly, I am treating all publishers who say that as though they have some bizarre social disease, until proven otherwise.
>
> Behind lie number three are the issues of terminated rights, reversionary rights, split copyrights and separate administration. These concepts and practices have a tendency to fragment the bundle of rights we call a song into a number of separately controlled pieces, creating havoc for anyone wishing to license its use.
>
> The problems engendered apply in any licensing situation, whether the song is to be performed on a television show or the lyrics are to be reprinted on T-shirts.
>
> Terminations and reversions aren't the only way that compositions get split up into little pieces. It happens as a result of legitimate collaboration. It happens when six members of a musical group cowrite a song with each member keeping his own publishing and administration. It also happens when an artist, as an inducement to record a song, takes a percentage of the copyright and administers his

or her own share. I've seen situations like the latter with shares as small as 6¼%. At that rate, the income generated doesn't even pay the fees of the attorney handling the administration.

When a song is divided into several parts, whether by percentages, territories or both, the result is invariably chaos. How does one locate all the owners? Which owner has the right to give a license to a potential user? What happens when all the owners can't agree on a price for their respective shares?

At what point will an owner, relying on joint ownership rules, tire of the game and license the whole song without regard to the feelings of his co-owners? Will that owner ever account to the other parties? Will he first deduct the cost of traveling to Hollywood to complete the negotiation?

Can the potential music user trust the publisher who says, "Don't worry, I control the rights"?

I have always believed that the basic rule in the music publishing business is to get songs performed. Performances mean royalties and royalties make people happy. But a split copyright, for whatever reason, frequently means fewer performances and less royalties.

While most publishers approach the administration of their catalogs in a professional manner, a growing number fail to grasp the practical and business issues presented. The inability to contact these publishers by phone or letter, and their own lack of knowledge about what causes royalties to be generated, will frequently result in a composition being deleted from a program.

Perhaps a recent experience in attempting to license a song in a two-hour television variety special will serve to illustrate the problem. I squared off against a composition which was to be used as a vocal bridge for about 30 seconds during the course of a 10-song production number. The rights to the song were divided into four separate interests. One publisher controlled the rights in all territories of the world, excluding the United States. The other three publishers each owned 33⅓% of the U.S. rights.

Publisher number one demanded a laughably high license fee. Number two referred us to his agent, who wouldn't do anything until all the others agreed. Number three, an obvious disciple of Newton Minnow, didn't want his part of the song to contribute to television's vast wasteland, and wouldn't grant permission. Number four was on vacation and could not be reached.

When I told the producer that we could not obtain the rights he needed within his time frame, his musical director came up with a substitute song that, as fate would have it, was divided into only three parts. The owners were willing to grant a license, but each wanted a full license fee for his fractional interest.

When I told the producer that his second choice was going to be the most expensive song in the show, he decided to find a new clearance company. I'm sure that in his mind, with production costs mounting and the minutes ticking by, the most logical thing to do in the face of the message was to kill the messenger.

Since Old Testament prophets frequently suffered the same fate, I didn't feel so bad. But I lost a client, and the publishers lost their respective share of about $5,000 income over the network and syndicated runs. Although the mutuality of loss also softened the blow, I have the hollow feeling that the publishers I dealt with didn't care, and that is what I find so disturbing.

It is clear to me that fragmentation of rights will make it harder and harder for television and film producers to use certain songs. When that occurs, the royalties generated by those songs will begin to decrease. The widows and the publishers will wake up one morning to the startling revelation that "the checks are no longer in the mail."

The solution might be as simple as letting the party with the greatest percentage have the administration rights. That way each party would take his share of the total fee rather than require a user to negotiate a separate dollar amount for each share.

In conclusion, all is again well in Hollywood, the Mercedes is on a lease, and my producer friend is back in the fold. He read the first draft of this commentary and now realizes what the problem really was. His next project is going to be a star-studded musical salute to Stephen "Public Domain" Foster.

## IV. TIP ON CLEARING LICENSES FROM MULTIPLE CO-OWNERS

When you are seeking to clear a license requiring permission from more than one owner, you should condition any obligation to pay license fees to any one co-owner upon your obtaining the necessary license from all the other co-owners. Thus, if you cannot obtain the consent of all other co-owners of the composition, it would then be clear that you have no obligation to pay the negotiated fee to the co-owners from whom you were able to obtain a license, provided, of course, that you make no use of the song.

Alternatively, you may negotiate all the necessary licenses from the various co-owners and then sign them all at once. The problem is that you may find, as co-owners have an opportunity to confer with each other, that one or more may have a change of mind and you may find yourself in an endless circle of negotiation. It would be better to get each co-owner to sign an agreement when the fire is hot and condition your obligations to pay upon your obtaining the consent of the other co-owners.

## V. COMMENT ON PRUDENT COPYRIGHT ADMINISTRATION

It is ironic that the most common cause of lost licensing opportunities is the inexperienced co-owner, or the co-owner's attorney, manager, or publisher representative, who, in insisting upon a fee that is far higher than any reasonable fee that should be charged for the license, loses the licensing opportunity entirely, not just for him or his client, but for all co-owners — indeed, for the song itself.

It has been the experience of both music clearance firms and professional publishers that too many songwriters who own their own publishing companies turn over absolute control of their publishing activities to an inexperienced or inappropriate representative, often an attorney. Many of these writers do not keep track of what their own attorney is doing. In some cases, the writer fails to realize that, as much as an attorney can be valued for providing legal advice and drafting contracts, the basic business skills of managing the copyright of a song are an entirely different matter. How many times have we seen, when a copyright is split, that a poor co-writer is losing thousands of dollars of revenue due to one co-writer's stubborn lawyer?

And when years after a song was a hit, when the songwriter is old and gray and wonders why the licensing revenue for that song has been reduced to a trickle in his retirement years, it may never have occurred to him that the reason for his circumstances is that his attorneys and managers have over the years either asked for exorbitant fees for synchronization licenses or withheld licenses under the assumption that his client didn't want the song used.

It is therefore strongly recommended that the administration of copyright should be (a) exercised directly by the writer, (b) given to one of several co-owners, or (c) turned over to a professional music publisher that can make the delicate judgments required to keep their copyrights returning revenues well into the writer's retirement. The risks of turning over administration of rights to a single co-owner or the wrong publisher may be reduced by many of the means suggested in the next section.

## VI. CURING THE SPLIT COPYRIGHT SYNDROME

An economist would view the problem of split copyright as one that unnecessarily increases the transaction costs of deriving income from the copyright. Clearly, transaction costs would be reduced if only one person owned or controlled the administration of the copyright.[4] When only one person controls the administration of a copyright, the person seeking to clear a license for use of the copyrighted material would need to locate and negotiate with only that one person; the sole copyright owner or administrator could make the appropriate decisions without requiring the consent of the co-owners. The risk that one of the co-owners, or their representatives or heirs, will impede the income potential of the copyright will be significantly reduced.

[4] Landes and Posner, *An Economic Analysis of Copyright Law*, 18 Journal of Legal Studies 325 (1989).

The most obvious way to effect the administration of publishing rights by one party is one that provides the exclusive right to administer the copyright to just one of the co-owners of the copyright or to an independent third party that has an incentive and the appropriate resources to maximize the value of the copyright for all concerned.

### A. Co-Publishing Agreement

Control over the administration of the copyright by one co-owner or an independent third party does not require the other co-owners to transfer their ownership interest in the copyright. As noted above, co-owners of copyright can always enter into an agreement that specifically governs their respective rights to grant licenses. This may be accomplished by the signing of a Co-Publishing Agreement, discussed at length in Chapter 4, which would define and govern the respective administration rights of co-owners of copyright. An example of a co-publishing agreement that vests in one of the parties the exclusive right to issue non-exclusive licenses for the use of the music they co-own is set forth as Form 4.1 on the CD-ROM.

### B. Restrictions

If a co-owner has certain sensitivities about the licensing of his or her music, then appropriate safeguards can be built into the co-publishing agreement. To that end, the agreement could provide that the writer's consent be obtained when the permission being requested broaches that area of sensitivity.

For example, a co-owner may grant exclusive administration rights to another co-owner, but still require that his consent be obtained to permit any change in the lyrics or harmonic structure of the music, to issue any mechanical license at less than the prevailing statutory rate, to authorize the use of the title of the song as the title of a play, film, or TV program, to authorize the production of a dramatic adaptation of the song, to authorize the synchronization of the song in a motion picture, television program, or videogram bearing a rating of "X" or its equivalent, or authorize the use of the song in any political advertisement. Any of these restrictions may vary depending upon the tastes of the particular co-owners and nature of the relationship that they have with the administrative co-owner.

## C. Who Controls?

After a decision is made among the co-owners to grant exclusive administration rights to one of the parties, what still remains is the question of who among the co-owners should be given administrative control. As noted in Chapter 4, on *Co-Publishing and Administration*, there are several alternatives.

Of course, prudent co-owners should each grant their respective administration rights to the one co-owner who has shown the greatest amount of business acumen and interest in spending the time required to properly manage the copyright. Needless to say, this is easier said than done. If it is not readily apparent who among the co-owners would be best for this job, perhaps, as Ron Gertz has suggested, the solution is as simple as letting the party with the greatest percentage have the administration rights.

Another idea, which the present authors recommend, is what might be called *alternating administration rights* — that is, allow each co-publisher to control the administration rights for alternating terms of two, three, or five years. The acting administrator could waive the collection of an administration fee or he could be awarded a fee for achieving a minimum level of publishing income established in advance by the parties. The co-owners may also impose restrictions that affect the administrator's authority to issue licenses, including many of the restrictions set forth in the preceding section.

To improve the efficiency of distributing publishing income among the co-owners, or if a co-owner doesn't completely trust the efficiency of the administrative co-owner, the co-owners may require that shares of certain income be paid directly to each co-publisher from the source of the income. For example, the parties may instruct the Harry Fox Agency, and the applicable performance rights society (e.g., ASCAP or BMI), to pay any income generated by it directly to each co-publisher, according to his or her share, in effect bypassing the administrator. This will reduce any unnecessary transaction costs associated with flowing these payments through to the co-publishers and reduce the amount of time that it takes for these payments to reach their pockets.

Should the parties be unable to immediately agree upon a single administrator or alternating administration program, it may do them well to list their particular concerns, use that list to craft contractual provisions addressing their concerns, and appoint an exclusive administrator who would be subject to those restrictions.

### D. Major Music Publisher

Should the co-owners fail to reach an agreement on an effective co-publishing arrangement, they could still accomplish exclusive control of administration rights in one party by turning to one independent, professional music publisher to administer the copyright on their behalf. Under this arrangement, each writer can maintain his own publishing company and his share of the publishing revenues, but each would agree to grant to a professional music publisher the exclusive right to administer those rights, without restriction or subject only to restrictions on licensing uses over which one or more of the co-owners may be particularly sensitive.

As noted in Chapter 4, many music publishers will agree to administer the copyrights owned by others for an administration fee — usually 10%–15% of net revenues — without taking an ownership interest in the copyright of the song. An example of a music publishing *administration agreement* is set forth as Form 4.4 on the CD-ROM.

Granting administration rights to an independent music publisher may be the only solution that assures each of the co-owners that the copyright will be administered with each of their interests in mind. The only key decision that would remain is choosing the right music publisher. The risks of that decision can be alleviated in part by limiting the term of the administration agreement to three to five years. Granting administration rights to a professional music publisher may, in fact, be the best solution for the co-owners under many circumstances. Because of its access to vast amounts of information regarding the standard terms and conditions and going rates and practices in licensing music, the professional music publisher is in a better position than most others to maximize the value of the musical composition.

What has been said about administering copyrights in the United States applies equally to international subpublishing administration. As noted in Chapter 5, because of the high transaction costs of having numerous subpublishers in various territories each representing different songs in an original publisher's catalog, a strategy of splitting international subpublishing rights on a per-song basis is rarely advisable. When a U.S. publisher is being offered substantial advances overseas under deals that would split up the international exclusive rights under the copyright, the U.S. publisher should first consider offering the song to its existing subpublishers, preferably a single major publisher handling all rights outside of the United States and Canada. If, under these circumstances, a U.S. publisher is only just beginning to establish its worldwide subpublishing program, it should carefully consider all the factors set forth in Chapter 5 before adopting a song-by-song or territory-by-territory disposition of its subpublishing rights. Such a splitting of rights would only compound the split copyright problems that have such a detrimental effect on the long-term value of copyrights.

## VII. THE FINAL SOLUTION — COMPULSORY LICENSE?

As discussed in Chapter 13, owners of copyright in music may be compelled to issue licenses for the use of their works in audio recordings, provided that they pay the copyright owners the rate set forth in the law. One of the benefits of this compulsory license provision is that it appears to be an effective solution to the split copyright syndrome insofar as it facilitates the clearing of licenses to use music in sound recordings (that are not accompanied by audiovisual works).

Split copyright does not become an issue when all the co-owners are required to accept no more than the statutory rate. Further, when the person seeking to clear a mechanical license cannot identify or locate the owner of the copyright, the compulsory license provision provides a safe harbor: if the public records of the Copyright Office do not identify the copyright owner and include an address at which notice under the provision can be served, it is sufficient to file the required notice with the Copyright Office.[5] By properly following the procedure and paying the statutory rate set forth in the compulsory license provision, a person seeking to clear permission will be assured a license without taking any risk of liability for copyright infringement.

It has been suggested that a compulsory license provision may be an effective solution to the split copyright problem with respect to the use

[5] 17 U.S.C. Sec. 115(b)(1).

of music in audiovisual works, multimedia works, and certain transmissions of musical works occurring over the Internet. A compulsory license may well be what's needed to resolve the challenges arising from the *user-generated content* phenomenon discussed in Chapter 16. It remains to be seen whether this solution will result in the fair compensation to owners of copyrighted works or will ever receive legislative attention.

## VIII. CONCLUSION

Each of the foregoing alternatives will almost always be superior to a copyright that is excessively split up. The reduced transaction costs of having only one person control the administration rights will surely increase the net income to the copyright owners. More important, however, is the direct effect on the long-term value of the copyright. The more co-owners of a song there are, the more difficult it is to obtain the consent of all of the owners, and the result will be fewer licenses granted. Fewer licenses will lead to fewer performances; with fewer performances, the song will begin to lose its share of mind of the listening public, resulting in even fewer performances and fewer requests for licenses. The ultimate result will be a lower income stream for the copyright owners, equating to a reduced copyright value. In cases of three or more co-owners, the solution of a single administrator of all rights should always be superior to each co-owner's maintaining full control over his or her share of a split copyright. In the absence of a single administrator solution, it is hoped that co-owners of copyright who insist upon full control of the administration of his or her co-ownership interest will at least recognize the benefits of maintaining a long-term outlook when considering what fees to charge for permission to use his or her music.

CHAPTER 7

# THE LANGUAGE OF MUSIC LICENSING

## SUMMARY

E. Videogram Licenses

F. Commercial Synchronization Licenses

G. Musical Product Licenses

H. Multimedia or "New Media" License

I. Digital Transmission Licenses and Digital Reproduction Licenses

J. Performance Licenses

K. Dramatic Performance Licenses and Grand Performance Licenses

L. Dramatic Adaptation Licenses

## X. DIFFERENCES IN THE RIGHTS AND PRIVILEGES OF HOLDERS OF EXCLUSIVE RIGHTS AND NON-EXCLUSIVE LICENSES

## XI. AVOIDING CONFUSION — EXCLUSIVE RIGHT VERSUS NON-EXCLUSIVE LICENSE

## XII. AVOIDING CONFUSION — UNDERSTANDING OWNERSHIP OF THE "UNDIVIDED" COPYRIGHT

## XIII. AVOIDING CONFUSION — SELLING, ASSIGNING, GRANTING, AND LICENSING

## XIV. THE LANGUAGE OF THE ART

# CHAPTER 7

# THE LANGUAGE OF MUSIC LICENSING

The rules and symbols of musical notation is the language with which composers and arrangers communicate with musicians and singers. The language is precise and the better the writer and the reader understand the common rules of the language the better the performance is likely to be. The same is true with music licensing. The better the owners of music and users of music each understand the basic language of music licensing, the better the chances that they will each get what they expected out of a licensing arrangement. Though this chapter is technical, a better understanding of the language of music licensing will form the basis of successful music licensing.

## I. Music as Property

The term *property* should not be confused with the term *property right*. A *property right* represents a relationship among people, recognized and defined by law, with respect to a certain thing or *object*. *Property* is the object over which the *right of property* is exercised. An acre of land, a diamond ring, or a song about a diamond ring lost on an acre of land are all objects that might be the subject of property rights. The property right with respect to a particular diamond ring is a relationship among people, enforceable by law, that dictates that a particular person, for example, has the privilege of possessing, using, and disposing of the diamond ring as that person sees fit and, more important, the right to exclude all others from possessing, using, or even looking at it.

Though there are some obvious differences between them, it should be clear that a song is just as much an object as a diamond ring. Like a diamond ring, a song is an object of perception, the former perceivable by the sense of sight and touch and the latter perceivable by the sense of hearing. As one music industry professional observed, a piece of sheet music is not a song; it becomes a song only when the music is sung.[1]

Unlike a diamond ring, however, music is more than an object of perception. It is also an object of conceptual, or intellectual, thought — a song's organized patterns of sounds and silences, whether written in musical notation or performed live, can be understood only by man. While many animals have the sensory perceptions necessary to hear the sounds of music, only man has the intellect necessary to understand and appreciate its beauty. It is, perhaps, for this reason, that music is often referred to as a subject of *intellectual* property.

The property right — or relationship among people — established by law to which an acre of land is the object is called the law of *real property*. The property right to which a diamond ring is the object is called the law of *personal property*. Although a right in music is a form of personal property right, the specific form of personal property right to which music is the object is called *copyright*. The set of laws defining property rights in music is known as the *copyright law*, or *law of copyright*. When used in this book, the term, "Copyright Act" shall refer to the law of copyright in the United States as enacted by the Congress of the United States and which took effect on January 1, 1978, with all subsequent amendments.[2] The term *copyright law* or *law of copyright* shall refer to general principles of copyright as agreed upon by international treaty. The Copyright Act is set forth in Title 17 of the United States Code, and citations in this book to the Act will take the form of "17 U.S.C. Sec. 101 et seq."

## II. COPYRIGHT

Copyright has been defined as, quite simply, *the exclusive right to copy*. More specifically, the law of copyright provides the owner of

---

[1] Leonard Feist, *An Introduction to Popular Music Publishing in America* (National Music Publishers Association, Inc., N.Y., New York 1980).

[2] 17 U.S.C. Sec. 101, et seq. Act of Oct. 19, 1976, Pub. L. 94-553, 90 Stat. 2541 (the "1976 Act"). An extensive treatment of the law of copyright is beyond the scope of this book. For comprehensive coverage, the reader is referred to the following legal treatises: Nimmer on Copyright (Matthew Bender 2009); Goldstein, Copyright, 2d Edition (Aspen 2000).

copyright in a musical work with the exclusive right to make and publish copies of the musical work, to make other versions of the work, to make recordings of the work, and to perform the work in public.[3] The concept of *exclusivity* signifies that it is illegal for anyone other than the copyright owner of the work to perform any of the foregoing activities. It is this power to *exclude* others from using the music that forms the basis of one's *claim* to ownership in the music.

When someone makes a copy of or performs a song without the copyright owner's permission, he is said to *infringe upon* the copyright in the song.[4] The copyright owner may file a lawsuit against an infringer to collect damages arising from the infringement and to stop the further infringement of the copyright owner's exclusive rights.

This ability to take legal action to exclude others from doing the things that the copyright owner has the exclusive right to do empowers the copyright owner with the ability to allow (i.e., authorize) others the privilege to make copies or render performances of a copyrighted musical composition and to require the payment of compensation in exchange for that privilege. The income that the copyright owner can collect in exchange for granting permission to do such acts is precisely the reward the law of copyright seeks to provide to creators of copyrightable works. Without such a reward, anyone would be free to use an author's works without payment.

If authors were not compensated for the use by others of the works they create, few authors could afford to devote sufficient efforts to fully exercise their talents. By providing a means by which talented authors can earn a living by creating works of authorship, more works of authorship by a greater number of people, regardless of their economic background, will be created. The assumption is that society benefits when more original works of authorship are created by a greater number of talented individuals from a wide variety of backgrounds. Few would argue with that assumption.

---

[3] 17 U.S.C. Sec. 106.

[4] 17 U.S.C. Sec. 501.

## III. RIGHT VERSUS LICENSE

The terms *right* and *license* are often used interchangeably, but they refer to two entirely different concepts and much confusion can be avoided by using these terms with all the precision the law demands.

As we have said, although music is property, the property right in music properly refers to the *legal relation* that the law recognizes between one person and all other persons. The legal relation of one who has a property right in an object is an ownership *claim* to the object. It is a claim to a certain object in relation to all other persons. That claim allows him to exclude all others from making copies of the work. A *right*, properly defined, is a claim in the sense just used. When one is said to have a *right*, one has the ability, enforceable by law, to exclude others from exercising the *privilege* of possessing, using, or disposing of the object. And therein lies a most important point: The term *right* should never be used to describe what really is a *privilege*.

A *right*, as we have said, is a claim to property that enables the owner of the right to exclude others from doing some act. A *license* is a permission to exercise a privilege. A *privilege* is a freedom from the claim of another, allowing you to do an act regardless of someone else's claim. A license, therefore, is not a right (i.e., claim of ownership) but merely a *permission* to do something you would not otherwise have the *privilege* to do.

For example, if you have a right, or claim of ownership, in a song, it means that you have the right to exclude, or prevent, all others from publicly performing the song. While your *right* affords you the *privilege* to perform the song yourself, others have a duty not to perform the song, unless you give them permission to do so. When you grant to me a license, or permission, to perform a song publicly, I do not acquire any *right* in, or claim to, the song; I acquire only a limited *privilege* to perform it. My privilege, or license, is limited by the scope of the permission, or license, which you gave to me.

It should thus be apparent that the term *right* and *license* refer to two completely different concepts — the former a *claim to ownership* and the latter *a permission or privilege to act*. Unfortunately, the term *right* is too often confounded with the term *license*.[5] Some examples of these errors, as well as their consequences, will be called to the reader's attention at later points in this book. Although we have no expectation that these errors will be rectified by practitioners overnight, we do hope that recognition of the issue will aid the reader in understanding and finding solutions to practical problems in the licensing and administration of copyrights.

## IV. OWNERSHIP OF MUSIC

When a composer writes a song, a copyright is said to *subsist* in the author or composer the moment he fixes the song in tangible form (for example, on paper or recording tape). Because the copyright automatically "subsists" at that moment, the composer does not need to do anything else to "secure" protection;[6] copyright protection is automatically secured at the moment the work is fixed in some tangible medium of expression.[7] From that moment, the author is the copyright owner and is considered to *own* a 100% "undivided" interest in the copyright of the song.

## V. WORKS MADE FOR HIRE

The one exception to this principal — that the copyright in the work subsists initially in the person who created it — is when the work was *made for hire*. In the case of a "work made for hire," the employer or other person for whom the work was prepared, not the actual creator of the work, is considered to be the *author* of the work and becomes the owner of the 100% undivided interest in the copyright the moment the work is fixed in tangible form.

---

[5] This imprecision in language even extends to many of the major treatises on copyright law. In the social sphere, it leads to some pretty astounding errors in thinking about such fundamental concepts as "property rights," "civil rights," "human rights," and "individual liberty."

[6] Prior to 1978, copyright under the U.S. Copyright Act was *secured* by publication of the work with a proper copyright notice. 17 U.S.C. Sec. 10 (1909 Act).

[7] 17 U.S.C. Sec. 102(a).

A *work made for hire* is (i) a work prepared by an employee within the scope of his employment or (ii) a work that is specially ordered or commissioned in a writing that says the work is made for hire and that falls within one of several categories enumerated in the copyright law, such as a language translation, a musical arrangement, a contribution to a collective work, a compilation, or a work created for use as part of a motion picture or other audiovisual work.[8]

In 1989, the U.S. Supreme Court ruled that whether a creator of a work is an "employee" under the "scope of employment" clause (i.e., clause (i) above) is to be determined by applying the general rules of agency.[9] Among the criteria to be considered in making such a determination are the hiring party's right to control the manner and means by which the work is accomplished, the skill required, the source of the work tools, the location of the work, the duration of the relationship between the parties, the method of payment, and similar factors.

If the creator of the work is not found to be "an employee acting within the scope of employment," then the work product can be considered a work for hire only if the specific criteria set forth in the "specially ordered or commissioned" works clause of the work for hire definition are met — namely, that the work falls within one of the categories specified in clause (ii) and that the parties expressly agree in a written instrument signed by them that the work shall be considered a work made for hire.

## VI. JOINT OWNERSHIP OF MUSIC

Like any other piece of property, a copyright can be *co-owned.* In other words, a copyright may be owned by more than one person, each of whom is called a *co-owner* of the copyright. In the music business, co-ownership most likely arises from the fact that two or more authors collaborated in the creation of the musical composition — commonly, a composer and a lyricist. Such a work is known as a *joint work.* In the case of a joint work, the co-authors of the work are likewise co-owners of the copyright.

---

[8] 17 U.S.C. Sec. 101.

[9] *Community for Creative Non-Violence v. Reid,* 490 U.S. 730 (1989).

A work is considered a *joint work* if the authors collaborated with each other in the creation of the work, or if each of the authors prepared his or her contribution with the "knowledge and intention" that it would be merged with the contributions of other authors as "inseparable or interdependent parts of a unitary whole."[10] The key fact is the intention of the collaborators. The parts themselves may be either "inseparable" (as in the case of a novel or painting) or "interdependent" (as in the case of a motion picture, opera, or the words and music of a song). If it was the authors' intention at the time the writing was done that the parts be absorbed or combined into an integrated unit, then the work is considered a "joint work."

The contributions of words and music are usually intended by their authors to be merged to form a joint work. The authors of a joint work are co-owners of copyright in the work,[11] and each author automatically acquires an *undivided* ownership interest in the entire work. Unless otherwise agreed among the co-authors, the authors of a joint work usually share equally in the revenues generated by the work. Thus, when two authors collaborate in the creation of a work, each will have a 50% undivided interest in the entire work; when there are three authors, each will have a 33⅓% undivided interest in the entire work, and so on.

The authors may, however, agree to another division. For example, when one author contributed words and music and the other worked only on the words, the two may agree to a 75/25% division. Composer George Gershwin always insisted upon receiving a full 50% interest in a composition, even when two lyrics writers contributed to the song, each lyrics writer in such an instance sharing the other 50% interest equally.

Because each has an interest in the "entire work," each author will benefit to the extent of his or her percentage share in the licensing or exploitation of all or any portion of the joint work. For example, where two authors collaborate in the writing of a song, one writing the words and the other the music, royalties generated by the sale or performance of any instrumental version of the composition will go to both the authors — equally, or according to percentages otherwise agreed upon — not just the composer of the music. Likewise, royalties from

---

[10] 17 U.S.C. Sec. 101.

[11] 17 U.S.C. Sec. 201(a).

the licensing of any printed edition containing only the lyrics will go to both authors, not just the writer of the words.

Co-owners of copyright are generally treated as *tenants-in-common*, with each co-owner having, unless otherwise agreed, an independent right to use, or issue non-exclusive licenses for use of the work, subject to the duty of accounting to the other co-owners for any profits. Co-owners may not issue exclusive licenses without the consent of the other co-owners, and a co-owner may transfer or assign only that portion of the copyright that he or she owns.

## VII. NON-OWNERSHIP OF MUSIC — THE PUBLIC DOMAIN

If a musical composition is in the *public domain*, then no one owns it. Obviously, if no one has a legal claim to the work, providing them with exclusive copyright rights in the work, then no one else has a legal duty to refrain from using it. Accordingly, no permission is required to use a work that is in the public domain.

A work in the *public domain* (also referred to as "PD") is a work (1) for which copyright protection was never available, (2) for which copyright protection was never properly secured, or (3) for which copyright protection, though it may have once existed, has expired or otherwise has been lost. For this last reason, public domain has been called the place where copyrights go to die.

In the remainder of this section, we will review some of the considerations used in determining whether a work is in the public domain. The reader should be aware, however, such a determination can be extremely complex. Moreover, recent changes in the copyright law[12] have actually brought within U.S. copyright protection certain works that had previously fallen into the public domain in the United States — an action that has no precedent.

### A. Where No Copyright Protection Was Ever Available

Determining whether copyright protection is, or was ever, available for a particular musical composition depends upon the characteristics of

[12] 17 U.S.C. Sec. 104A.

the work and whether they, taken together, amount to an *original work of authorship*. Thus, to be a subject of copyright protection under U.S. law, a composition must meet two tests: It must be (1) original and (2) a work of authorship.

The requirement of *originality* does not mean the work must be novel, unique, or meet any particular standard of esthetic merit. A work is *original* if it is merely original with the author — that is, it was created by the author and not copied from another source. The merest level of creativity is enough. A copyrighted work may be based upon or derived from another work that is not copyrightable, but the test is applied to the *new matter* the author created. For example, a view of the Eiffel Tower from a street in Paris is not copyrightable subject matter, but a photograph of that view is copyrightable by virtue of the photographer's selecting the position from which the photograph was taken, the time of day and year at which it was taken, the type of film used, and other elements that contribute to the resulting work. If what the author added comprises the requisite minimal level of creativity and was not merely copied from another source, then it is *original* for purposes of determining whether it is subject to copyright protection.

Nevertheless, that a work is original with its creator is not enough; to be the subject of a copyright, the work must also be a *work of authorship*. It would seem we would have no trouble considering most musical compositions, no matter how bizarre, as works of authorship, but there is more than some doubt about whether simple drum beats, rhythms, or lyrics comprised merely of common short phrases, such as "I love you, I love you," would be considered a musical work.

Justice Oliver Wendell Holmes once defined a musical composition as "a rational collocation of sounds apart from concepts, reduced to a tangible expression from which the collocation can be reproduced either with or without continuous human intervention."[13] Yet that definition may provide little help in drawing the line in particular cases, which are generally decided by the "I know it when I see it" standard. For example, a single taped track of a long repetitive drum beat is not likely to constitute a musical work (though it clearly would be a copyrightable sound recording), but that track, creatively combined with others similar to it, could very well constitute a copyrightable *techno* song.

[13] *White-Smith Music Pub. Co. v. Apollo Co.*, 209 U.S. 1, 18 (1908).

Whether a work constitutes a copyrightable *work of authorship* may be easier defined in negative terms. Section 102(b) of the Copyright Act states,

> In no case does copyright protection for an original work of authorship extend to any idea, procedure, process, system, method of operation, concept, principle, or discovery, regardless of the form in which it is described, explained, illustrated, or embodied in such work.[14]

A well-known axiom of copyright law is that copyright will not protect an *idea*, only an *expression of an idea*. Distinguishing between ideas and expressions of ideas, however, is not always easy. A clear example is the protectability of a particular composition, but not the idea, concept, or genre of the composition (e.g., *disco* or *rap*), or the protectability of the lyrics of *I Want to Hold Your Hand*, but not lyrics about hand holding. A more difficult case might be posed when the story line of one lyric is substantially similar to the story line of another.

In a recent decision concerning Section 102(b), one federal court ruled that the words "idea," "system," "method of operation," "discovery," etc. were synonymous (e.g., suggesting that, just as there are "ideas" contrasted with "expressions of ideas," there are "discoveries" contrasted with "expressions of discoveries"). Subsequently, a court of appeals reversed that decision, recognizing that "systems," "procedures," "methods of operation," "processes," "discoveries," etc. may be more than mere abstractions.[15] Thus, a new system of musical notation used to record, publish, perform, or display a composition (such as the command structure of MIDI, the Musical Instrument Digital Interface) is not copyrightable, though a musical composition written using those commands would be protectable by copyright.[16] Similarly, a new lyric form would be no more copyrightable than an

---

[14] 17 U.S.C. 102(b).

[15] *Lotus v. Borland*, 49 F.3d 807 (1st Cir. 1995) (holding that the commands constituting the method by which a user operated a computer program constituted an uncopyrightable "method of operation"). The co-author of the present work was General Counsel to defendant and filed a brief with the U.S. Supreme Court, which upheld the First Circuit's decision.

[16] Inventors of command languages with which people use to instruct computers, or to write computer programs that instruct computers, should look to the patent law for protection of their languages.

original variation of the form of sonnet created by Shakespeare or Milton.

## B. Where Proper Copyright Protection Was Never Secured

Under the Copyright Act in effect in the United States prior to 1978,[17] a copyright in a work was *secured* by publication of the work with a proper copyright notice. If you published the work without affixing to copies of the work a proper copyright notice, the work failed to acquire federal copyright protection, and, because publication of the work meant the automatic loss of common law copyright protection (under state law), the work fell into the public domain. Such works, being in the public domain, may be freely used.

Under the Copyright Act of 1978, and under most copyright laws around the world, copyright is not *secured*; rather, it automatically *subsists* in original works of authorship the moment the work is fixed in a tangible medium of expression, such as on paper or audiotape. Thus, as of January 1, 1978, the concept of common law copyright, governed by the laws of the individual states, ended, and a work immediately acquired copyright protection upon its creation.

## C. Copyright Protection Has Expired or Has Been Lost

When the duration of protection for copyright expires, the work falls into the public domain. The duration of copyright protection must be determined with respect to each country in which you expect to reproduce, distribute, or perform the work. As discussed in Chapter 9, on the *Duration of Copyright, Assignments of Copyright, and Licenses*, the duration of copyright protection in the United States depends upon when the work was created. The reader is referred to that chapter for further details.

Generally, beginning January 1, 2001, works first published in the United States before January 1, 1923 will have fallen into the public domain. Great songs such as, *Rock-A-Bye-Your Baby With a Dixie Melody*, *Oh! How I Hate to Get Up in the Morning*, and *K-K-K-Katy*, all originally published in 1918, have already passed into the public domain in the United States.

---

[17] 17 U.S.C. Sec. 10 (1909 Act).

In addition, works created before January 1, 1964, the copyrights in which expired after its initial 28-year term because of a failure to properly effect the copyright's renewal term, are in the public domain.[18] And as mentioned above, a work that had been protected by common law copyright under state law lost that protection upon publication, and, if such publication occurred without copies of the work bearing a valid copyright notice, copyright protection under the federal copyright act was never secured.

Before March 1, 1989, the effective date of the Berne Convention Implementation Act, which amended the Copyright Act of 1978, a work for which copyright had been secured by proper publication with notice could lose its copyright protection in the United States if copies of the work were subsequently published in the United States without bearing a valid copyright notice.[19] However, the law provided some exceptions, including the right of the copyright owner to cure the defect within a certain period of time. Subsequent to March 1, 1989, failure to affix a copyright notice on a copy of a work no longer jeopardized the U.S. copyright status of the work.

Note, because a work falls in the public domain in the United States does not mean that it loses copyright protection overseas. Determining the copyright status of works overseas is more problematic. For many years, the duration of copyright in most countries had been 50 years (more recently raised to 70 years in many countries) after the composer's death, which is now the law in the United States. Further, as noted above, many foreign works that had previously passed into the public domain in the United States have been revived by the United States's adherence to the terms of the North American Free Trade Agreement (NAFTA) and, more recently, the Uruguay Round of multilateral trade negotiations.[20] As it stands now, by virtue of the Uruguay Round Agreements Act of 1994, copyright protection now subsists in the United States for all works published within the last 75 years, as long as the original work was of foreign origin.

---

[18] See generally Chapter 9, *Duration of Copyright, Assignments of Copyright, and Licenses*.

[19] 17 U.S.C. Sec. 405.

[20] 17 U.S.C. Sec. 104A.

## D. Hidden Problems

Though the above considerations may be useful in ascertaining whether a work is in the public domain,[21] you should take care to exercise the appropriate diligence to be certain there are no hidden rights by virtue of which a license may still be required. The following are areas that may be traps for the unwary.

1. ***Territory***. As noted above, while you may be certain that a particular work has fallen into the public domain in the United States, the work may still be subject to protection outside the United States — where, for example, durations of copyright have been based upon when the author passed away, as opposed to a specified number of years. There are many works that have fallen into the public domain in the United States for one reason or another (e.g., failure to renew, publication without copyright notice, expiration of copyright), but whose copyright remains in force throughout the world. In that case, if your plans encompass distributing the work overseas, you must separately ascertain the copyright status in each relevant country.

2. ***Arrangements.*** Though many popular songs are clearly in the public domain, certain arrangements and orchestrations of those songs, created years after the original authorship of the song, may have been separately copyrighted as "derivative works," and to the extent the copyrights in the arrangements and orchestrations remain in effect, a license will be required to use them. If you plan to use a song in the public domain and you want to avoid having to license the use of a copyrighted arrangement, it is therefore advisable to obtain a copy of the sheet music dated prior to January 1, 1923. This will assure that the particular arrangement is also in the public domain, at least in the United States. Another approach is to gather as many arrangements and orchestrations as possible and copy only those portions that each version has in common with one or more of the others.

[21] The reader should consult a copyright treatise, such as Nimmer On Copyright, for further rules concerning the copyright status of works around the world.

3. ***Translations***. Similarly, copyright in translations of works in the public domain may have been secured separately from the underlying public domain work. If you are going to use a public domain song and you wish to use translations, you must separately ascertain the status of the copyrights in the translations.

4. ***Underlying Works.*** Care must be taken to carefully analyze the public domain work to be sure that no copyright in any work underlying the work being examined still subsists. For example, when the copyright in a motion picture expires at the end of a normal full term of copyright, the copyright on any underlying literary property on which the picture was based (e.g., novel, short story, play, screenplay) will normally have expired as well. However, should the copyright in the picture terminate before its full potential term of copyright (e.g., for failure to file a copyright renewal application), the underlying literary property, and many musical works used in the film, may still be subject to copyright protection. In such event, if you wish to reproduce or distribute the public domain film, a license would still be required from the owner of the copyright in the underlying literary work, as well as from the owner of the songs in the film. Though rarely is this applicable in the music field, one could well imagine a song's lyric having been derived from a copyrighted short story. If the song fell into the public domain early, permission from the owner of copyright in the underlying short story would be required for continued use of the lyric.

## VIII. DERIVING INCOME FROM MUSIC

The law provides three basic ways for you to derive income from your musical copyright:

A. You may *sell* your copyright or portions of it (i.e., assign all or a portion of your interest in the "undivided copyright");

B. You may carve up your copyright and sell to others one or more *exclusive rights under the copyright*; or

C. You may *license* (i.e., permit) others to use your music on a *non-exclusive* basis.

The remainder of this book primarily concerns this third and most common means of exploiting music copyrights: giving others permission to use the music on a non-exclusive basis, commonly known as *licensing*. Nevertheless, it is essential to understand the meaning of the first and second means of deriving income from music copyrights before delving into the concept of licensing.

## A. Sale of Copyright

Copyright, like other property rights, may be bought and sold, given away, taken away, bequeathed, or otherwise transferred. The transfer of copyright may occur in three basic ways:

(1) upon the copyright owner's death by his will or, when no will is left, by the operation of state law (i.e., intestate succession),

(2) by voluntary transfer or assignment, and

(3) by involuntary transfer, as in the course of a bankruptcy proceeding.

By far the most important of these means of copyright transfer is by *assignment*. As has been noted above, assignment is the first basic means by which an owner of a copyright can exploit his property — he can sell it.

A copyright may be assigned, or sold, in exchange for legal *consideration*, meaning something of value — for example, money or a promise to pay money or to perform certain obligations. An unusual story of consideration paid for an undivided interest in a song involved the famous big band orchestra leader, Abe Lyman, who collaborated as a writer of such famous songs as *Mary Lou* and *After I Say I'm Sorry*. The story goes that Abe was waving his baton on the bandstand of the Cocoanut Grove nightclub in Los Angeles in his usual fashion — with his back to the band and his face grinning at the couples on the dance floor — when suddenly he motioned to his pianist to carry on while he stepped off the platform. With typical Lyman brashness, he tapped one of the dancing patrons on the shoulder and explained he had a problem: he had recently purchased a luxury car and needed a few quick bucks to make his payment the next day or lose the car. "If you give me the necessary three C-notes and fifty," he said, "I'll give you a piece of my share of the profits on a song I just wrote with Arthur Freed." The stranger took the proposition in stride and asked to hear the song. Lyman jumped back on the bandstand, played the song, and a few minutes later completed the deal. The impromptu investor was later to be astounded with his first royalty check in the amount of $7,000. The song turned out to be *I Cried For You*, one of the great torch songs[22] of all time.

Money is not the only thing of value that may be given in exchange for a copyright. Copyrights have been known to be assigned in exchange for physical objects of either economic or sentimental value. For example, Judy Garland's Transcona Company, producers of the Warner Bros. Pictures release, A *Star is Born*, employed Roger Edens and Leonard Gersh to write the *Born in a Trunk* sequence used in the film. Gersh admired a certain chest of drawers that had been moved from Judy Garland's bedroom to her hallway. He asked for the chest in exchange for the copyright and in lieu of any future royalties, and Judy gave it to him.

If money or furniture will not do, then promises to pay or do something will be sufficient. When a songwriter signs a songwriter agreement with a music publisher, the publisher is promising to pay to the songwriter the royalties set forth in the contract based upon the publishing revenues from the song. The publisher's various obligations under the agreement — together with an implied obligation to use good faith efforts to promote the song — are considered sufficient legal consideration.

When a copyright is assigned in exchange for a promise, the assignment is said to be made *by contract*, which is the most common way copyrights are assigned or transferred. An assignment of copyright, however, does not require that legal consideration be given in exchange for it; a copyright may be given away as a gift.

As mentioned above, when a composer writes a song, a single copyright is said to *subsist* in the composer the moment he fixes the song in tangible form, such as on paper or recording tape. From that moment, the composer is the copyright owner and is considered to own

[22] The term *torch song*, adapted from the colloquial expression, "to carry a torch for" a loved one, became the phrase for a slow, sad, melancholy ballad.

a 100% *undivided* interest in the copyright of the song. The composer may transfer to another his 100% undivided interest in the copyright. If he does, he will then retain no part of the copyright and his *assignee* (i.e., the recipient in the assignment) will become the owner of the entire 100% interest in the copyright.

The composer is not limited to assigning 100% of his undivided interest in the copyright; he may assign a lesser percentage, such as 50% or 33⅓% of his undivided interest. Upon assigning his 50% interest, for example, the composer and the assignee will then each own a 50% undivided interest in the copyright.

When a songwriter signs a standard songwriter contract, he is generally assigning to the music publisher all of his 100% undivided interest in his songs. Where a songwriter signs a *co-publishing* agreement or *participation* deal, he is generally agreeing to assign only 75% or 50% of his undivided interest in the songs, reserving the remaining percentage to himself, which in turn the publisher may agree to *administer* on his or her behalf for a standard or negotiated administration fee. Examples of co-publishing and administration agreements are set forth in the appendix to Chapter 4, on *Co-Publishing and Administration.*

## B. Divisibility of Copyright and Sale of Exclusive Rights Under Copyright

Any or all of the exclusive rights under copyright, or any subdivision of those rights, may be assigned. This concept is known as the *divisibility* of copyright, and is one of the more important, but frequently misunderstood, features of the copyright law.

Because copyright is "divisible," a copyright owner is not limited to assigning just some percentage of his undivided interest in his copyright. He may also transfer any of an endless number of exclusive rights that comprise the copyright. Under Section 106 of the Copyright Act,[23] the owner of copyright has the exclusive rights to do and to authorize any of the following:

(1) to reproduce the copyrighted work in copies or phonorecords;

(2) to prepare derivative works based upon the copyrighted work;

[23] 17 U.S.C Sec. 106.

(3) to distribute copies or phonorecords of the copyrighted work to the public by sale or other transfer of ownership, or by rental, lease, or lending;

(4) in the case of literary, musical, dramatic, and choreographic works, pantomimes, and motion pictures and other audiovisual works, to perform the copyrighted work publicly;

(5) in the case of literary, musical, dramatic, and choreographic works, pantomimes, and pictorial, graphic, or sculptural works, including the individual images of a motion picture or other audiovisual work, to display the copyrighted work publicly; and

(6) in the case of sound recordings, to perform the copyrighted work publicly by means of a digital audio transmission.

Thus, for example, a copyright owner may assign to another the exclusive right to perform the work publicly, reserving all other exclusive rights, such as the right to reproduce the copyrighted work in copies or phonorecords and the right to prepare derivative works. This was at one time what songwriters and music publishers did when they became members of performing rights societies, such as ASCAP or BMI. In exchange for the copyright owner's assignment of performing rights from the songwriters and publishers, the performing rights society agreed to perform certain tasks, such as surveying performances, collecting performance fees, and distributing royalties to the songwriter and publisher members.[24]

The type of exclusive right that may be assigned, however, is not limited to the several listed in the Copyright Act. The Copyright Act provides that any subdivision of any of the rights specified in Section 106 may be transferred and owned separately.[25] Thus, a work may be

[24] Under certain consent decrees negotiated with the U.S. government, the performing rights societies were required to convert the agreements with their writer and publisher members from an exclusive to a non-exclusive basis, but as a practical matter the societies today exercise their licenses to sublicense music performances virtually on an exclusive basis.

[25] 17 U.S.C. Sec. 201(d)(2).

exclusively licensed in particular markets, in particular forms, in particular territories, and over particular periods of time.

For example, the owner of a copyright in a song may assign any or all of the following exclusive rights: the exclusive right to print sheet music throughout the world; the exclusive right to publish the song in songbooks in the United States and Canada; the exclusive right to publish the song in songbooks in all countries except the United States and Canada; the exclusive right to record the song and distribute phonorecords throughout the world for a period of five years; the exclusive right to record the song and distribute phonorecords in the United States only beginning in five years; the exclusive right to perform the song throughout the world; the exclusive right to record the song in synchronization with audiovisual images for theatrical distribution in the European Common Market countries for three years and in all other countries for ten years, etc. As the foregoing may suggest, the potential number of exclusive rights comprised in copyright would appear to be, if not unlimited, then limited only by the business practices and imaginations of the buyers and sellers of exclusive rights under copyright.

When a copyright owner assigns any of the many possible exclusive rights under the copyright, he reserves to himself all other rights that comprise and remain with the copyright. Using any or all of the examples mentioned above, the owner of the full *undivided* copyright, after having assigned the several exclusive rights mentioned, would still remain the owner of the undivided copyright, which would, of course, become subject to the rights of the new owners of the exclusive rights. That is, the copyright owner would be able to exercise all of his rights and privileges as owner of the copyright in the song except that he cannot do or authorize any of the things in which he has assigned to others the exclusive rights to do or authorize others to do. It is important to note that the interest in the copyright remaining with the owner would still be considered "undivided," even though certain exclusive rights have been carved out or "divided" and separately assigned to others, because the interest in all of the unassigned exclusive rights remaining under the copyright (infinite in number) is still undivided.

As we have seen, the copyright owner may then transfer 100%, or any lesser percentage, of that "undivided" copyright interest in what remains of the copyright. His assignee would become the owner of all or a lesser percentage of the "undivided" copyright, subject, of course, to the rights of the owners of any exclusive rights previously assigned to others.

A songwriter signing a standard music publishing agreement should be aware that he is promising (i.e., look for the words "warranting and representing") to the publisher that he has not previously assigned to anyone else any of the exclusive rights under the copyrights he is transferring to the music publisher (with the exception of the writer's share in performance rights, which are routinely licensed to the writer's performing rights society, such as ASCAP or BMI). Publishers may sometimes refuse to take anything less than full rights, particularly in the case of new, previously unpublished material for which the publisher may be taking a measure of financial risk to promote. Songwriters should therefore consider carefully any decision to transfer any of the exclusive rights under copyrights, giving particular attention to the potential effect such a decision may have on the value of the copyright. The value of the whole copyright may be greater than the value of the sum of its parts.

### C. Deriving Income by Licensing Use on a Non-Exclusive Basis

The most common means of deriving income from music copyrights arises from granting to others permission to use the music on a non-exclusive basis. This is commonly known as *issuing* or *granting* licenses, or merely, *licensing*. Nearly all licenses for the use of music involve the exercise of one of the four following exclusive rights under copyright:

1. the exclusive right to make copies: the *reproduction right*,
2. the exclusive right to perform the work publicly: the *public performance right*,
3. the exclusive right to prepare derivative works: the *adaptation right*,
4. the exclusive right to distribute copies: the *distribution* right, and
5. the exclusive right to display the work publicly: the *public display* right.

Each of these rights will be discussed in more detail in connection with the type of music license with which they are associated.

## IX. TYPES OF LICENSES FOR MUSIC

As we have seen, the copyright law gives the owner of copyright the exclusive rights to do and authorize various uses of the copyrighted work: such as to make and distribute copies of the copyrighted work, to make other versions, such as recordings of the work, and to perform the work in public. As we have said, these exclusive rights involve, by definition, the right to exclude others, through the power of the legal system, from performing those acts. It is this *right to exclude* that forms the basis of the *right to license* or, in other words, *right to give permission*. The various types of licenses that a copyright owner may grant are defined by *the use* for which permission is sought.

The following are the primary forms of licenses customarily used in the music industry:

### A. Print Licenses and Digital Print Licenses

A *print license* is a permission that authorizes one to make printed copies of music, such as the reproduction of musical notation in sheet music and printed music folios and reprints of lyrics in books, magazines, and print advertising. A print license typically invokes the copyright owner's exclusive rights of reproduction and distribution. With the advent of technologies that enable the digitization of musical notation, tablatures, and lyrics, new forms of print licenses, so-called *digital print licenses*, have emerged. Licenses of print and digital print are discussed in Chapter 12.

### B. Mechanical Licenses

A *mechanical license* is the form of permission that authorizes one to make audio-only mechanical reproductions of a musical composition that are not accompanied by a motion picture or other audiovisual work and that are made for the purpose of distributing them to the public for private use. Examples of such mechanical reproductions include music embodied in piano rolls, record albums, audiocassettes, digital audio tapes, compact optical discs, computer chips, and digital downloads. Motion picture films, videotapes, and audiovisual laser discs that contain music accompanied by motion pictures or other audiovisual works are never the subject of mechanical licenses. Mechanical licenses are discussed at length in Chapter 13, on *Licensing Music in Sound Recordings*.

## C. Electrical Transcription Licenses

An *electrical transcription license* is the form of permission that authorizes one to make mechanical reproductions of a musical composition that are not accompanied by a motion picture or other audiovisual work and that are made for radio broadcast or for purposes other than distribution to the public for private use. Mechanical reproductions of music for radio broadcast are called, "electrical transcriptions," or simply "transcriptions," the term "electrical" being a holdover from the days before magnetic tape. Examples of transcriptions include recordings of radio theme music, musical introductions, and background music for commercial advertising made specifically for radio broadcast, as well as recordings compiled for use in syndicated radio programs. Electrical Transcription licenses are discussed at length in Chapter 14.

## D. Synchronization Licenses

A *synchronization license* is the form of permission that authorizes one to make mechanical reproductions of a musical composition, that are accompanied by a motion picture or other audiovisual work, for use in connection with motion picture theatrical performance and television broadcast. Examples of such reproductions include motion pictures, television programs, and music videos, embodied in any form, such as film, tape, and optical laser disc. Technically, the music is not always "synchronized" or recorded, as some licenses say, "in timed-relation with" the motion picture, but these terms convey the notion that the permission to make reproductions of the music is strictly limited to copies embodying the specified motion picture together with the music. Most synchronization licenses contain a further restriction relating to how the copies of a motion picture that embodies a recording of the licensed music may be distributed: these licenses limit the distribution of the motion picture to only those copies that are directly related to effecting the performance of the picture in motion picture theaters and on television. These licenses may impliedly or explicitly restrict any other form of distribution, including distribution on videocassette laser discs for the home video market. Synchronization licenses are discussed at length in Chapter 15.

### E. Videogram Licenses

A *videogram license* is the form of permission that authorizes one to make mechanical reproductions of a musical composition that are accompanied by a motion picture or other audiovisual work and that may be distributed on videocassette, optical laser disc, or other home video device for distribution into the home video market. Videogram licenses are discussed at length in Chapter 15.

### F. Commercial Synchronization Licenses

A *commercial synchronization license* is the form of synchronization license that authorizes one to make reproductions of and broadcast performances of a musical composition in connection with the promotion or advertising of a commercial product. *See* Chapter 20 for a more detailed discussion of licenses for the use of music in commercial advertising.

### G. Musical Product Licenses

A *musical product license* or *merchandise license* is the form of permission that authorizes one to make mechanical reproductions of a musical composition in connection with the distribution of a commercial product, such as wind-up music boxes, singing dolls, and musical greeting cards.

This form of license may resemble either a mechanical license or a videogram license, depending on whether the use of music in the product is accompanied by audiovisual images. *See* Chapter 21 for a more detailed discussion of musical product licenses.

### H. Multimedia or "New Media" License

A *multimedia license* or *new media license* is a "catch-all" term for the form of permission that authorizes one to make reproductions of a musical composition in connection with the distribution of multimedia compact discs, computer software, karaoke, videogames, and other new media devices. *See* Chapter 22 for a more detailed discussion of these emerging forms of licenses.

### I. Digital Transmission Licenses and Digital Reproduction Licenses

The forms of licenses that authorize one to digitally transmit musical works and to reproduce them by means of digital transmissions have only recently acquired generally accepted names — such as digital phonorecord delivery license, a form of mechanical license. These licenses are generally described in Chapter 13, on *Licensing Music in Sound Recordings*, but some forms of these licenses are discussed elsewhere, as in Chapter 15, *Licensing Music in Audiovisual Works.*

### J. Performance Licenses

A *performance license* is a permission that authorizes one to perform a work publicly. These performances include live performances, such as those that occur in nightclubs and rock concerts, and performances of recorded music, such as radio and television broadcasts and certain kinds of transmissions over the Internet. Performance licenses are discussed in Chapter 18.

### K. Dramatic Performance Licenses and Grand Performance Licenses

A *dramatic performance license* is a permission that authorizes the performance of a song dramatically — that is, when the song is used to carry forward the plot or story of a dramatic work, such as a motion picture, television program, or theatrical play. A *grand performance license* is not a license in music at all; it is a license to perform a grand opera, or grand musical play, or portion thereof. The rights that form the basis of these types of licenses are discussed at length in Chapter 19.

### L. Dramatic Adaptation Licenses

A *dramatic adaptation license* is a permission that authorizes one to make a dramatization of a musical composition, or more accurately, its lyrics. Just as a motion picture can be a dramatic adaptation of a novel, a motion picture or television program may be a dramatic adaptation of the lyrics of a song. Although a motion picture adaptation of a song may include a performance of the song, a dramatic adaptation license does not authorize one to render a dramatic performance of the song, a license for which must be acquired separately. This type of license is discussed in Chapter 19.

## X. DIFFERENCES IN THE RIGHTS AND PRIVILEGES OF HOLDERS OF EXCLUSIVE RIGHTS AND NON-EXCLUSIVE LICENSES

The copyright law entitles the owner of any exclusive right, to the extent of that right, "all of the protection and remedies accorded to the copyright owner."[26] This means, for example, that a person holding an exclusive right to do something, such as perform a particular composition on television, may sue in his own name anyone who infringes that particular right, even though the undivided copyright remains in the hands of someone else. By contrast, a non-exclusive licensee of a similar right of performance would not be able to sue in his own name to stop others who perform the song without permission.

Similarly, an owner of exclusive rights under copyright, unlike a licensee, may file an application for copyright registration for his exclusive claim. (Though the exclusive rights owner may file the application, he must still identify the owner of the "undivided" copyright as the "claimant" on the copyright application.)

As will be noted in Chapter 8, the formalities required to effectuate an assignment of exclusive rights and a grant of non-exclusive licenses differ significantly. An assignment of exclusive rights must be in writing; a non-exclusive license may be effectuated orally.

Thus, the owner of an exclusive right, to the extent of his exclusive right, is treated much the same as the owner of the "undivided" copyright. By contrast, the non-exclusive licensee of a right under the copyright is not treated at all like an "owner"; he merely has permission to do an act that, without such permission, would constitute copyright infringement.

---

[26] 17 U.S.C. Sec. 201(d)(2).

As we have pointed out, the potential number and variety of exclusive rights comprised in copyright, and the potential number and variety of non-exclusive licenses, would appear to be limited only by the imaginations of the owners and users of music. Interestingly enough, as the precision with which exclusive rights are defined increases, the distinction between exclusive rights and non-exclusive rights becomes rather nebulous.

Consider, for example, the "exclusive right to perform a song on a certain television program to be broadcast in the United States next Tuesday evening between the hours of 7:00 and 9:00 PM EST." Would the owner of such an exclusive right have fewer privileges if the equivalent grant were made instead on a non-exclusive basis? The exclusivity being rather ephemeral, it becomes difficult to distinguish such an exclusive right from a non-exclusive license covering the same use.

We have listed above several differences between the rights of owners of exclusive rights and the privileges of non-exclusive licensees. An owner of an exclusive right under copyright, unlike a non-exclusive licensee, may sue in his own name anyone who infringes his exclusive right; an owner of exclusive rights under copyright, unlike a licensee, may file an application for copyright registration; and an assignment of exclusive rights must be in writing, while a non-exclusive license may be effected orally.

Though the foregoing suggests that there are some legal differences between transferring a narrowly defined exclusive license and granting an equivalent license on a non-exclusive basis, it is likely that the differences will have little or no practical significance, if for no other reason than that virtually all narrowly defined licenses are formulated on a non-exclusive basis.

## XI. AVOIDING CONFUSION — EXCLUSIVE RIGHT VERSUS NON-EXCLUSIVE LICENSE

At the outset of this chapter, we explained the difference between a *right* and a *license*, saying that a right is a *claim* — the ability, enforceable by law, to exclude others from exercising the privilege of possessing, using, or disposing of an object — and a license is a *permission* to do something with the object that, by reason of another's claim in it, one would not otherwise have the privilege to do.

Because the terms *right* and *license* refer to two completely different concepts, they should not be used interchangeably. For example, you should never use the term "exclusive license," a term that at best contradicts itself. The proper term is "exclusive right." If the "right" is not exclusive (i.e., no intent is present to give the licensee the legal authority to exclude others from doing the same thing), then it probably is a license (i.e., merely permission). If a license purports to be exclusive, then it is actually a right.

A phrase that is commonly used in contracts regarding intellectual property is "exclusive right and license." The use of this phrase may be proper depending upon the context. The only context in which such a use would be proper is if you consider the terms "exclusive right" and "license" separately. When you grant a license, you are granting a permission to another to exercise a privilege to do something. In addition to granting to another a license to do something, you may grant an exclusive right — that is, the right to exclude others from doing the same thing. Correctly construed, the phrase "A hereby grants to B the exclusive right and license to" do something means that (i) A grants to B the privilege to do something that otherwise B would not be able to do and (ii) A grants to B the right to exclude others from doing the same thing.

It might therefore be helpful if practitioners replaced the phrase "exclusive right and license" (which may be improperly construed as "exclusive right and exclusive license") with "license and exclusive right."

As will be noted in greater detail in Chapters 8 and 9, the distinction between a grant of an "exclusive right" and a grant of a "non-exclusive license" is significant in at least two respects: (1) the formalities necessary to effectuate assignments and licenses and (2) the duration of assignments and licenses.

## XII. AVOIDING CONFUSION — UNDERSTANDING OWNERSHIP OF THE "UNDIVIDED" COPYRIGHT

The understanding of the foregoing definitions and principles, and the solving of many day-to-day copyright problems, can be facilitated by considering one point: there is always just one copyright for each work — we call this the *undivided* copyright.

The undivided copyright may be owned by one or more individuals, each with equal or varying shares of a 100% total. Even though the copyright may be "divided" into numerous exclusive rights and even though some of those rights may be transferred away and owned by others, remember that each separately assigned exclusive right always relates back to that "undivided" copyright.

When this is understood, common legal questions relating to copyright, such as determining the proper copyright "claimant" in an application for copyright registration or the proper name to include in the "copyright notice," become simple: in each case it is always the owner or owners of the "undivided" copyright.

## XIII. AVOIDING CONFUSION — SELLING, ASSIGNING, GRANTING, AND LICENSING

Many of the formal terms used in copyright transfers and licenses are also misunderstood and may become the source of some confusion.

When you transfer (e.g., sell or give away) an interest in your undivided copyright, or in any exclusive rights under the copyright, the document effecting the transfer will typically state that you *grant*, *transfer*, *sell*, or *assign* such interest to the person receiving the interest. Any one of these words, alone or in combination, will be sufficient. If you are the buyer or assignee of a copyright or exclusive right, you would be advised to use the words "sells and assigns," which should make it absolutely certain that you are receiving an ownership claim, rather than merely a license.

If the instrument is intended to effectuate a non-exclusive license, then it would be improper for the instrument to use the words "assign," "transfer," or "sell." Non-exclusive licenses, unlike interests in the undivided copyright or exclusive rights under it, are not "rights."As we have pointed out, a right is a *claim* to ownership. A license is not a claim to ownership; it is merely a *permission* to do something that you would not otherwise have the privilege to do. People *grant* permission; they do not *transfer* or *assign* permission. Likewise, you do not transfer or assign a license; you *grant* a license. (Arguably, you can "sell" your permission and, accordingly, sell a license, but it is recommended that the word sell be used solely in the context of an actual transfer of rights.)

By the same token, to say "Publisher grants a non-exclusive right to . . ." is incorrect, because only a permission is being conferred, not a claim to ownership, or *right*, in any portion of either the undivided copyright or in any of the exclusive rights under the copyright. It is better, therefore, to say "Publisher grants a non-exclusive license to . . . ," in the sense that a permission or privilege to do something (i.e., to use the music in a certain way) is being allowed or granted, but not a claim of ownership (i.e., the legal ability to exclude others from doing the same thing).

Finally, the phrase "Publisher grants the right and license to . . ." is redundant in the context of a non-exclusive license, because only a permission is being conferred, not a claim to ownership, or *right*, and, in that context, the word "right" can only have been meant to be synonymous with "license."

## XIV. THE LANGUAGE OF THE ART

The language of music licensing is the lifeblood of the music business. The business of music, more than any other, is inextricably intertwined with the laws and contracts that define the legal relationships among owners and the users of the "objects" produced. These laws and contracts are comprised of words that express important concepts relating to the structure of legal relationships — but merely words, nothing more.

An art that is so reliant upon the use of words requires precision in the use of those words to perform the art well. For this reason, words that refer to completely different concepts should not be confounded or used indiscriminately. On the contrary, terms of art should be treated as such. When so much rests upon how and when these words are used, it behooves those who wish to succeed to use them well.

We mean no pedantry. On the contrary, it is fervently hoped that this be genuinely viewed as an aid to understanding. Clarity of thought about an art should increase one's understanding and appreciation of it and should make one's reaction to it more certain. If the precision suggested in this book aids the reader in understanding and finding solutions to practical problems in the business of music licensing, then it has served its purpose.

Chapter 8

# Formalities of Music Licensing

## Summary

# CHAPTER 8

# FORMALITIES OF MUSIC LICENSING

This chapter reviews the formalities necessary to effectuate grants of copyright, exclusive rights under copyright, and licenses.

As noted in the preceding chapter, only interests in undivided *copyrights* and *exclusive rights under copyright* may be *assigned* (i.e., sold or otherwise transferred from one person to another). Permission to use music on a non-exclusive basis is the subject of a *license*, and licenses are not proper subjects for "assignments," "transfers," or "sales" of rights.[1] A grant of license, or permission, does not require that any particular formalities be followed, but there are good reasons to comply with certain formalities when granting or clearing licenses, and these are discussed later in this chapter.

Certain formalities, however, are necessary conditions for effecting assignments of copyright and exclusive rights under copyright, and these will be discussed in the following section.

## I. FORMALITIES OF ASSIGNMENT

To *assign* a copyright means to transfer ownership of that copyright from one person to another. The ownership of copyright may be transferred in whole or in part by any means of conveyance or by operation of law and may be bequeathed by will or pass as personal property by the applicable laws of intestate succession.[2] In recognition of the

[1] "A 'transfer of copyright ownership' is an assignment, mortgage, exclusive license, or any other conveyance, alienation, or hypothecation of a copyright or any of the exclusive rights under copyright, whether or not it is limited in time or in place of effect, *but not including a nonexclusive license*." 17 U.S.C. Sec. 101 (emphasis added).

[2] 17 U.S.C. Sec. 201(d)(1).

divisibility of copyright, the law provides that any of the exclusive rights comprised in a copyright maybe also transferred and owned separately.[3]

## A. Assignment Must Be in Writing

A transfer of copyright, or any exclusive rights under copyright, other than by operation of law is not valid unless an instrument of conveyance, or a note or memorandum of the transfer, is in writing and signed by the owner of the rights or such owner's duly authorized agent.[4]

Legal *consideration* is not required for an assignment to be valid. This means the *assignee* (i.e., person receiving the assignment of rights) does not need to give something of value (e.g., money, promise to pay royalties, etc.) in return for the rights, unless, of course, the assignment was conditioned upon the receipt of such consideration. Thus, an assignment of rights may be a gift.

An assignment of copyright in a composition may be executed even when the song is not yet in existence; in such cases, the assignment will be deemed effective upon the song's creation. An example of such an assignment appears in any exclusive term songwriter agreement under which the songwriter promises to the music publisher the copyrights in all of the songs that the songwriter creates during the term of the contract.

The assignment form need not be notarized or witnessed to be valid. Nevertheless, a procedural advantage, though slight, in possible future court actions may be gained by a notarial acknowledgment.[5]

It is important to note that ownership of copyright in a work, or any of the exclusive rights under the copyright, is distinct from ownership of any material object in which the work may be embodied.[6] Accordingly, transfer of ownership of any material object, including the copy or phonorecord in which the work is first fixed (e.g., the original lead sheet or audiocassette recording), does not of itself convey any rights in the copyrighted work embodied in the object.

---

[3] 17 U.S.C. Sec. 201(d)(2).

[4] 17 U.S.C. Sec. 204(a).

[5] A properly executed certificate of acknowledgment is prima facie evidence of the execution of the transfer. 17 U.S.C. Sec. 204(b).

[6] 17 U.S.C. Sec. 202.

Nor, for that matter, does an assignment of the copyright convey property rights in any material object, even if that object contains the only existing copy or recording of the work. Further, the physical transfer of a certificate of copyright registration will not constitute an assignment of copyright. Transfer of ownership in copyrights and exclusive rights under copyright may be effected only by the express terms of written legal instruments, such as contracts, assignment forms, and the like.

## B. Recordation of Assignments

Although the Copyright Office does not supply any forms for transfers of copyright, the law does provide for the recordation in the Copyright Office of transfers of copyright.[7] Although recordation is not required to make a valid transfer as between parties, it does provide certain legal advantages and may be required to validate the transfer against third parties. For example, as between two conflicting transfers of the same copyright, the one executed first will be recognized and given legal effect if it is recorded in the Copyright Office within one month after its execution or at any time before the recordation of the later transfer. (Otherwise, the later transfer prevails if it is recorded and was received in good faith, for consideration, and without notice of the earlier transfer.) It is therefore good practice for assignees to record all assignments within 30 days after the execution of the assignment.

In addition to resolving conflicting assignments, another good practical reason for promptly recording all assignments is to maintain a complete and independent record of the copyright's *chain of title*. Maintaining a record of the important documents pertaining to a copyright in a safe, central location, such as the Copyright Office of the Library of Congress, will enable the copyright owner to reconstruct his copyright records in the event of a natural disaster or fire.

## C. Short-Form Assignment Document

Most assignments of copyrights in musical compositions are effected by contract, usually a music publishing contract. Several forms of agreements containing assignments of copyright, portions of

---

[7] 17 U.S.C. Sec. 205.

copyright, and exclusive rights under copyright are included in this book. For example, a standard form single-song music publishing agreement assigning the entire undivided copyright in an individual composition is set forth as Form 8.1 on the CD-ROM. Examples of co-publishing agreements that assign an undivided 50% interest in a copyright are set forth on the CD-ROM as Form 4.1. An exclusive print agreement, assigning certain exclusive rights under copyright, is set forth as Form 12.1 on the CD-ROM.

Each of these agreements involves an assignment of copyright, portion of copyright, or exclusive right under copyright, and each may be recorded in the Copyright Office. As previously discussed, there are a number of good reasons for recording assignments of copyrights. Nevertheless, there is good reason not to record these or any other kind of detailed music publishing agreement: it may be undesirable for the parties to allow the terms of their contract to become a matter of public knowledge. The problem is that a publishing agreement may contain (i) the detailed terms of the relationship that the parties desire to maintain in confidence, but, at the same time, (ii) a clear assignment of rights, the existence of which the parties desire to disclose to the world.

Custom and practice in the music industry, however, has provided a solution that apprises the public of the existence of the assignment without disclosing the terms of the contract. When a songwriter, or other assignor of copyright, signs a contract setting forth the full terms of the assignment of copyright (e.g., royalty rates, advances), he will usually be asked to simultaneously sign a second, often one page, document that describes the rights assigned, but omits all other information about what the assignee may have paid for, or agreed to perform, in exchange for the rights assigned. This document is known as a *short-form copyright assignment.*

The assignee records with the Copyright Office only the *short-form assignment document* and the parties maintain in confidence the details of the agreement contained in their *long-form* contract. The short-form assignment should not refer by its terms to any long-form contract covering the relationship between the parties, because the Copyright Office has been known to require that a copy of any document referred to in the assignment form also be recorded, which would defeat the purpose of using the short form. If the assignee is uncomfortable having a document that does not state the consideration being given in exchange for the assignment, he can include a provision in the short form that the assignment was made "for good and valuable consideration" or "for and in consideration of One Dollar ($1)." A sample short-form copyright assignment is set forth as Form 8.1 on the CD-ROM.[8]

## II. FORMALITIES OF LICENSING

In contrast to what is required to effect an assignment of copyright, or exclusive rights under copyright, the grant of a license on a non-exclusive basis is not required to be in writing. Licenses can be conferred in a number of ways: (1) in writing, (2) orally, (3) implied from the acts of the parties, or (4) created by operation of law.

### A. Written Licenses

The most common form of license is a formal written document setting forth precisely the scope of the permission. A *written license* may be in the form of a contract signed by the licensor and the licensee or merely by a letter granting permission signed by the licensor.

### B. Oral Licenses

*Oral licenses* are licenses spoken in person or over the telephone. Oral licenses are sometimes referred to as *verbal licenses*, but such use of the word verbal constitutes poor diction, as the word "verbal" refers to that which contains or concerns words, and certainly both oral and written licenses fit comfortably within that definition.

---

[8] *Kohn On Music Licensing* (3d Edition, 2002) was cited by the U.S. Supreme Court in *Eldred v. Ashcroft*, 537 U.S. 186, fn 21 (2003), because Form 8.1 contained evidence that the music industry anticipated that the duration of copyright could be extended by Congress from time to time. The assignment of copyright effected by the form included "the copyright in any and all versions of said musical composition(s), *and any renewals and extensions thereof* (whether presently available *or subsequently available as a result of intervening legislation*) in the United States of America and elsewhere throughout the world" (emphasis added).

Oral licenses are uncommon for a variety of reasons, which are discussed below. An apt observation that has been ascribed to movie producer Samuel Goldwyn is that "Oral agreements are not worth the paper they're written on."

## C. Implied Licenses

An *implied license* is a license that is not expressed in verbal (i.e., oral or written) form. A license may be *implied* when a person could reasonably infer from the conduct of the copyright owner that permission was granted.[9]

For example, a record company could be deemed to have an implied license to distribute an album containing a song written by the album's recording artist who, by recording the song under the terms of a separate agreement for purposes of putting on the album, lead the record company to reasonably believe that it had permission to distribute copies of the song on that album, notwithstanding the absence of a written mechanical license to do so. The scope of the permission would be determined by the conduct of the parties. In the above example, the record company's license would probably be limited to distribution of the song on the album, but would not include a synchronization license in the absence of evidence showing that the uses implied from the circumstances would go beyond that of use in the form of mechanical reproductions of the album (e.g., circumstances may imply that the song also was to be used by the record company in connection with some audiovisual work, such as a music video, but not in a motion picture unrelated to the artist's obligations or performance under his recording agreement).

---

[9] See *Effects Associates, Inc. v. Cohen*, 908 F.2d 555 (9th Cir. 1990) (Expressing its dismay at the parties' failing to memorialize a license in writing — "Movie-makers do lunch, not contracts" — the court nevertheless found a license was implied by the conduct of the parties); *Johnson v. Jones*, 885 F. Supp 1008, 1014 (E.D. Mich. 1995) ("[A]ll of the circumstances surrounding the negotiations made between the parties must be considered to determine if and to what extent an implied license was granted."). See also *McLean v. Wm. M. Mercer-Meidinger-Hanson*, 952 F.2d 769, 779 (3d Cir. 1991) ("Since a non-exclusive license does not transfer ownership of the copyright from the licensor to the licensee, the licensor can still bring suit for copyright infringement if the licensee's use goes beyond the scope of the nonexclusive license." [Citing *Effects Association*, 908 F.2d at 558 n.5]).

Licenses that are implied may be revoked at any time, but in certain instances the copyright owner's right to revoke may be limited or *estopped*, particularly when the licensee can show that he acted in justifiable reliance upon the owner's conduct and would be damaged by an unreasonable or untimely revocation of the license.

### D. Operation of Law

Licenses can also be created by *operation of law*. For example, licenses may be bequeathed by will or pass as personal property by the applicable laws of intestate succession. Licenses may also be conferred by operation of the compulsory license provision of the copyright law.[10]

## III. GET IT IN WRITING

All transactions discussed in this book should be reduced to writing. It is not a matter of having or showing a trust or distrust in another or even trust in an otherwise honest person's memory. Having a license in writing may protect you from a conflicting license or transfer of the copyright. A non-exclusive license, whether recorded with the Copyright Office or not, will be effective even if there exists a transfer of copyright ownership in conflict with it, as long as the license was *in writing* and was either granted before the transfer of copyright was executed or was received in good faith before the recordation of the transfer of copyright and taken without notice of the transfer.

A producer of a work that contains copyrighted works of others would be prudent to maintain a written record showing the contractual basis demonstrating that the producer has all the rights and licenses necessary to effect the intended use of the work. Having a good record of rights and licenses will become useful, and often essential, when the producer considers signing an important agreement for the distribution of the work or selling the work to another. Upon a sale of copyright, or important exclusive rights under copyright, the buyer is likely to

[10] 17 U.S.C. Sec. 115.

perform an extensive *due diligence* investigation to confirm whether the seller, indeed, has all of the rights and licenses necessary to support the warranties and representations that he is making in the sale contract. Keeping good files of contracts with, and licenses from, all the contributors of intellectual property to the final work will avoid unnecessary delay and unanticipated costs when it comes time to exploit or dispose of the work.

Even licensors are advised to memorialize all licenses in writing. If a copyright owner takes action leading a producer to believe that he had a license to synchronize music in a motion picture, a license may be *implied* from the circumstances. In any dispute with the producer regarding the scope of the license, the terms of the implied license would become a matter for the courts to decide. Because of the high costs of litigation, it may be uneconomical to file a lawsuit to have the courts circumscribe the scope of the license, thereby making it difficult to assert the right to collect additional fees for other uses, such as, for example, a royalty on the distribution of videogram copies of the work.

## IV. LETTER FORM VERSUS CONTRACT FORM

A common question in music licensing is: what is the difference between a license in *letter* form and a license in standard *contract* form, or long-form? Under what circumstances should one form be used over the other? An example of a "letter agreement" is set forth as Form 12.6 and an example of a "long-form contract" is set forth as Form 12.2 on the CD-ROM.

Letter agreements are generally shorter, omitting much of the usual boilerplate contained in longer form contracts. Used for simpler licenses, such as letters permitting the reprint of a song lyric, the letter form is clearly a more informal way of reducing an agreement to writing. Letter agreements are also used, however, to memorialize longer, more sophisticated agreements. Sometimes it is felt that, because of the long-standing relationship and previous dealings between the parties, the informality of the letter agreement is more appropriate. Some feel that letter forms should always be used in lieu of long-form contracts because, if the agreement ever became the subject of litigation, the letter form would be more approachable[11] by the courts and juries.

In answer to the question when to use a letter agreement or long-form contract, we offer the following suggestion: all licenses should be issued using an informal letter agreement; all grant of copyrights, or exclusive rights under copyright, should be effected by the more formal standard contract form. Following this procedure would properly reflect the fundamental difference between granting permission to exercise a privilege, which is the subject of a *license*, and granting a property right, which is the subject of an *assignment* of copyright or exclusive rights under copyright. Granting permission, or license, is a less formal event than assigning a property right, and the form used to effect each should reflect their relative formality. Accordingly, the license form that is most appropriate to the circumstances of the deal will always be used.

A common observation about contracts in the entertainment industry is that the more money that is involved in a transaction, the longer the contract. Motion picture distribution contracts, often involving hundreds of millions of dollars, tend to be longer and more complex than contracts used in the music recording industry, which usually involve only millions of dollars, and in turn tend to be longer and more complex than contracts used in the relatively smaller music publishing industry. Mere licenses for the use of music should be placed at the appropriate point along the scale of complexity. In today's world of word processing machines, it is a wonder how even the simplest permission letters have not become the subject of multiple page tomes that can now be generated at the touch of a button. It is hoped that people responsible for drafting or generating licenses from word processing software will continue to use the license form that is most appropriate to the circumstances of the deal.

## V. REFERENCE TO THE PARTIES

Sometimes the letter form goes one step further to become informal, more readable, or user-friendly: discarding terms such as "licensor"

[11] In computer software parlance, more "user-friendly."

and "publisher" and "licensee" and "producer," the letter refers to the parties as "we" and "us" and "you" and "your." Though this approach can be confusing when used in longer agreements, it is often quite appropriate and even welcomed in short letter agreements of one or two pages. An example of a letter agreement that uses this approach is set forth as Form 12.9 on the CD-ROM.

By contrast, the use of the formal terms "Licensor" and "Licensee," "Grantor" and "Grantee," or "Assignee" and "Assignor" in longer contracts, each of which pair differ only by two letters, can make longer agreements quite tedious to read and can even create some confusion in shorter contracts or letter agreements. It is therefore recommended that, when selecting terms with which to refer to the parties, the drafter should choose a pair of words that is dissimilar and less likely to cause confusion. For example, the music copyright owner — the party granting the license or transferring the rights — may be referred to as the "Owner" or "Publisher." The licensee may be referred to as "Licensee," "Producer," or some other term that best describes the party requiring the clearance.

If, in addition to the privilege to do something with respect to the music, the contract grants an assignment of exclusive rights (i.e., the right to exclude others from doing the same thing), then neither "Licensor" nor "Licensee" may be the most appropriate means of referring to a party. The "Licensor" is doing more than granting a license and, therefore, should be called something else, such as "Owner" or "Publisher." Because the grantee is receiving more than a mere permission to do something, he should be called something other than "Licensee," such as "Producer."

## VI. STANDARD TERMS AND CONDITIONS

An increasingly popular compromise between the informality of the letter agreement and the benefits of long-form license agreements is the use of a letter agreement that incorporates by reference a standard set of terms and conditions that is often applicable to several kinds of licenses. An example of such an agreement is set forth as Form 3.8 on the CD-ROM.

## VII. FORMS USED IN THIS BOOK

The forms used in this book, and its accompanying CD, do not consistently reflect the principals discussed above. They certainly do not always reflect the best principals of drafting, and their inclusion here should *not* be construed as their representing some form of ideal. On the contrary, the forms selected are representative of those customarily used in the music publishing industry today and are included primarily for the purpose of illustrating the practical guidance outlined in this book for both copyright owners and persons seeking to clear licenses.[12]

Accordingly, the forms should be used primarily to improve the reader's understanding and appreciation of that guidance. They should not be used without further consideration about how they should be applied to the transaction at hand and should not be used by laymen without seeking the advice of an attorney experienced in the field of licensing or music publishing.

[12] Form 8.1, a typical short-form copyright assignment, was cited by the U.S. Supreme Court in *Eldred v. Ashcroft*, 537 U.S. 186, n. 21 (2003), as evidence that copyright owners have had an expectation that the duration of copyright could be extended by legislation.

# Appendix to Chapter 8
# Formalities of Music Licensing

**Forms (On CD-Rom Only)**

| | |
|---|---|
| **Form 8.1** | **Short Form Copyright Assignment** |
| **Form 8.2** | **Multi-Purpose Work for Hire Agreement** |
| **Form 8.3** | **Musical Arrangement Work for Hire Agreement** |
| **Form 8.4** | **Lyric Translation Work for Hire Agreement** |

## Chapter 9

# Duration of Copyright, Assignments of Copyright, and Licenses

## Summary

CHAPTER 9

# DURATION OF COPYRIGHT, ASSIGNMENTS OF COPYRIGHT, AND LICENSES

This chapter is about the life of copyrights, including their creation, their expiration, and their renewal. This chapter also outlines the duration of transfers of copyright, transfers of renewal copyrights, and grants of licenses under copyright, and their termination.

Each of these subjects is discussed in the sections that follow. The reader should be forewarned, however, that topics such as the *duration of copyright*, *renewal of copyright*, and *termination of grants* are among the most complex provisions of the copyright law. Although a great deal of thought has been devoted to organizing these materials in a way that should be understandable to anyone willing to invest in them a thoughtful reading, intricate materials such as these, as good poetry, should not be expected to blossom forth enlightenment in the reader's mind upon a first reading.

A thorough understanding of these subjects is *not*, however, a requisite to understanding the practical licensing guidance and other advice offered in this book. Nevertheless, certain licensing problems cannot be resolved without some understanding of one or more of the topics covered in this chapter.

Moreover, the subject of *termination of grants* may, for some authors and their heirs, be one of the most important areas of copyright with which they or their advisors should become familiar. Termination has enabled some very well-known songwriters, or their heirs and estates, to recapture their copyrights decades after they thought they sold those copyrights forever. Even the threat of termination has enabled these songwriters and heirs to renegotiate lucrative deals that greatly improved upon the terms of songwriter agreements entered into decades ago.[1] Thus, everyone with a stake in copyrights — songwriters, heirs of songwriters, executors, trustees, attorneys, and music publishers — should become familiar with fundamental principles of termination of grants.

## I. INTRODUCTION

The duration of copyright protection is prescribed by law — in the United States, by the Copyright Act. The duration of assignments of copyright, and licenses under copyright, is governed by the applicable *term* provisions of agreements that effect assignments and licenses, but may also be subject to certain provisions of the copyright law that allow previously granted assignments and licenses to be terminated. Thus, the sale of a copyright may not necessarily endure for the life of the copyright and a grant of license may not necessarily endure for the term stated in the license agreement.

The discussion that follows is divided into five primary sections:

1. Duration of Copyright;
2. Renewal of Copyright;
3. Duration of Assignments of Copyright, and Exclusive Rights Under Copyright;
4. Duration of Assignments of Interests in Renewal Copyrights; and
5. Duration of Licenses.

It should be noted that readers using the following materials to help analyze a particular duration of copyright, assignment of copyright, or termination of grant problem in the United States should bear in mind that there is a significant difference in the way the problem is approached depending upon whether the work was created before or

[1] See, e.g., *Mills Music, Inc. v. Snyder*, 469 U.S. 153 (1985); *Fred Ahlert Music Corp. v. Warner/Chappell Music, Inc.*, 155 F.3d 17 (2d Cir. 1998); *Steinbeck v. McIntosh & Otis, Inc.*, 433 F. Supp. 2d 295 (S.D.N.Y. 2006); *Milne v. Stephen Slesinger, Inc.*, 430 F.3d 1036 (9th Cir. 2005).

after January 1, 1978. Accordingly, the reader should try to determine the applicable category in which the work falls before attempting to analyze the impact of any circumstances that may affect ownership questions. In addition, the duration of copyright differs overseas.

## II. DURATION OF COPYRIGHT

### A. Life

As life itself, copyright protection does not last forever. In fact, the limitation on the duration of copyright protection is a restriction that is prescribed by *the people* under the U.S. Constitution, which states:

> Congress shall have the power . . . To promote the progress of science and useful arts, by securing *for limited times* to authors and inventors the exclusive right to their respective writings and discoveries.[2]

The *duration* of copyright (i.e., how long the copyright protection lasts) is often referred to as the *life of the copyright*. When the life of a copyright expires, the work is said to fall into the public domain. Works in the *public domain* are works for which copyright protection was never secured or works that were protected by a copyright that has expired.[3]

### B. Creation

And, as in life, according to certain philosophers, the duration of copyright begins upon *creation*. Copyright subsists (i.e., is secured automatically) when the work is created, and a work is *created* when it is fixed in a tangible medium of expression for the first time.

The Copyright Act recognizes two types of *tangible media of expression*: copies and phonorecords. A *copy* is a material object from which a work can be read or visually perceived either directly or with the aid of a machine or device, such as a book, manuscript, piece

[2] U.S. Const. Art. I, Sec. 8.

[3] For a further discussion of public domain, see Chapter 7, on *The Language of Music Licensing*.

of sheet music, film, videotape, or microfilm. A *phonorecord* is a material object that embodies fixations of sounds (other than those sounds that are accompanied by a motion picture or other audiovisual work), such as audio tapes, phonograph records, and compact audio disks. Thus, for example, a song (i.e., a *work*) can be fixed in sheet music (i.e., a *copy*) or, when embodied in a sound recording, in a CD, hard disk, or flash memory device (i.e., a *phonorecord*).[4]

A work is *fixed* in a tangible medium of expression when its embodiment in a copy or a phonorecord is "sufficiently permanent or stable to permit it to be perceived, reproduced, or otherwise communicated for a period of more than transitory duration."[5] A work consisting of sounds, images, or both, that are being transmitted, is fixed if a fixation of the work is being made simultaneously with its transmission.[6] If a work is prepared over a period of time, the part of the work existing in fixed form on a particular date constitutes the created work as of that date.

While a work may be fixed in a copy or a phonorecord, the ownership of copyright in the work, or any of the exclusive rights under the copyright, is distinct from ownership of any material object in which the work is embodied.[7]

## C. History

Anglo-American copyright legislation began in England with the Statute of Anne, enacted in 1709. The Statute gave authors the protection of copyright for 14 years from publication, and at the expiration of the 14 years, if the author was living, the copyright could be renewed for another 14 years. The statute stated in part:

> Whereas *printers, booksellers, and other persons have of late frequently taken the liberty of printing, reprinting and publishing, or causing to be printed, reprinted, and published, books and other writings, without the consent of the authors or proprietors of such books and writings, to their very great detriment, and too often to the*

[4] 17 U.S.C. Sec. 101.

[5] *Id.*

[6] *Id.*

[7] 17 U.S.C. Sec. 202.

> *ruin of them and their families*: for preventing therefor such practices for the future and for the encouragement of learned men to compose and write useful books; may it please your Majesty, that it may be enacted, and be it enacted by the Queen's most excellent majesty, by and with the advice and consent of the lords spiritual and temporal, and commons, in this present parliament assembled, and by the authority of the same, . . . that the author of any book or books already composed, and not printed and published, or that shall hereafter be composed, and his assignee or assigns, shall have the sole liberty of printing and reprinting such book and books for the term of fourteen years, to commence from the day of the first publishing the same, and no longer;
>
> . . . Provided, always, That after the expiration of the said term of fourteen years, the sole right of printing or disposing of copies shall return to the authors thereof, if they are then living, for another term of fourteen years.

In this country, the copyright laws governing the original 13 states were based largely upon the Statute of Anne. On May 31, 1790, the Congress of the United States enacted this nation's first copyright statute, which reflected its historical antecedents. Under the Copyright Act of 1790, the author was afforded copyright protection for 14 years and "if, at the expiration of said term, the author or authors, or any of them, be living, and a citizen or citizens of these United States, or resident therein, the same exclusive right shall be continued to him or them, his or their executors, administrators or assigns, for the further term of fourteen years."

The U.S. copyright law has undergone three major changes since 1790. The Copyright Act of 1831 amended the 1790 Act in two respects: the original term was increased to 28 years, and the renewal term, though still only 14 years long, could pass to the author's widow or children if he did not survive the original term. The Copyright Act of 1909 maintained the original term of 28 years, but extended the length of the renewal term from 14 years to 28 years, and provided additional changes as to who may apply for renewal.[8] Finally, the copyright law underwent a complete overhaul with the Copyright Act of 1976, which

[8] Act of March 4, 1909, chap. 320, 35 Stat. 1075 (the "1909 Act").

took effect on January 1, 1978. Provisions of the law regarding the duration of certain copyrights created prior to January 1, 1978, was amended in 1992 and 1998. The provisions of the 1976 Act and its recent changes are discussed below.

## D. The Appropriate Duration of Copyright Protection

Before moving on to answering the question of how long *do* copyrights last under the law, it may be interesting to first take a moment to ask the question: how long *should* copyright protection last? While the question is interesting to ask, it is not one that can be easily answered, if it can be answered at all.

The purpose of copyright is to secure the general benefits derived by the public from the labors of authors. To this end, the copyright law seeks "to motivate the creative activity of authors . . . by the provision of a special reward."[9] That special reward is the recognition of the exclusive right of copyright, a limited *monopoly* on the exercise of privileges that others would otherwise have but for the author's exclusive rights.

It is generally agreed that, for the most part, monopolies are bad. The owner of a monopoly has the ability to charge monopoly pricing, and economists call the resulting loss to society a loss of economic welfare. If the market economy was a *static* place, there could be no justification for the monopoly of copyright. But the market economy is not static — it is quite, to the contrary, *dynamic*. The special incentive provided to authors serves to motivate the creative activity of authors *over time*. Thus, in contrast to the negative effects of monopolies under a static analysis, the monopoly of copyright in a dynamic world provides positive benefits to society.

The question, then, is whether and to what extent do the *dynamic benefits* to society of copyright outweigh the *static losses* to society resulting from the exercise of that monopoly by authors. Only to the extent that such benefits outweigh such losses should copyright be enforced. This principal of modern economic analysis was recognized over a century and a half ago by Lord Macaulay in a speech delivered to the British House of Commons:

---

[9] *Sony Corp. v. Universal City Studios, Inc.*, 464 U.S. 417 (1984).

> It is good that authors should be remunerated; and the least exceptionable way of remunerating them is by a monopoly. Yet monopoly is evil. For the sake of good we must submit to evil; but the evil ought not to last a day longer than is necessary for the purpose of securing the good.[10]

If the net effect of copyright protection is good for society, then why shouldn't copyright protection last forever? In 1908, Justice Oliver Wendell Holmes suggested one reason:

> The notion of property starts, I suppose, from confirmed possession of a tangible object and consists in the right to exclude others from interference with the more or less free doing with it as one wills. But in copyright property has reached a more abstract expression. The right to exclude is not directed to an object in possession or owned, but is *in vacuo*, so to speak. It restrains the spontaneity of men where but for it there would be nothing of any kind to hinder their doing as they saw fit. It is a prohibition of conduct remote from the persons or tangibles of the party having the right. It may be infringed a thousand miles from the owner and without his ever becoming aware of the wrong. It is a right which could not be recognized or endured for more than a limited time.[11]

Modern scholars have pointed to more specific grounds. As Professor Nimmer instructs:

> It may be questioned why literary property should be treated differently from other forms of property? If I may own Blackacre in perpetuity, why not also *Black Beauty*? The answer lies in the First Amendment. There is no countervailing speech interest which must be balanced against perpetual ownership of tangible real and personal property. There is such a speech interest with respect to literary property, or copyright.[12]

---

[10] Speech by Lord Macaulay in the British House of Commons, *The Works of Lord Macaulay* (1866).

[11] *White-Smith Music Publishing Co. v. Apollo Co.*, 209 U.S. 1, 19 (1907).

[12] Nimmer On Copyright, Sec. 1.10 (1991).

The issues regarding the appropriate duration of copyright protection were framed long ago by legal jurists, well before they were even taken up in the United States. For example, in 1785, Lord Mansfield said,

> [W]e must take care to guard against two extremes equally prejudicial; the one, that men of ability, who have employed their time for the service of the community, may not be deprived of their just merits, and the reward of their ingenuity, and labour; the other, that the world may not be deprived of improvements, nor the progress of the arts be retarded.[13]

No doubt Lord Mansfield was familiar with the works of Aristotle.[14]

The debate on the appropriate duration of copyright heated up when Congress passed the Sonny Bono Copyright Term Extension Act of 1998. The Bono Act brought the duration of copyright in the United States in conformity with copyright duration in many other countries by increasing the duration from life of the author plus 50 years to life of the author plus 70 years. The proponents of the Bono Act argued that the longer duration is justified by the increasing life expectancy of humans. In addition, by 1995, all member countries of the European Union had increased the term of copyright protection of all musical works originating in the EU to the life of author plus 70 years. Had the United States not brought U.S. copyright law in line with that of the EU, works of U.S. authors would fall subject to the Berne Convention's "rule of the shorter term,"' a policy of reciprocity under which a Berne member state with a longer copyright term can limit copyright protection for foreign nationals to the foreign country's shorter term. Thus, a work whose copyright expired in the United States would no longer enjoy protection in the EU.

Shortly after the passage of the Bono Act, the law was challenged as unconstitutional on the grounds that Congress exceeded its authority under the Constitution, which provides Congress with the power to secure for authors the exclusive rights in their respective writings,

[13] *Sayre v. Moore*, 1 East 361, 362, 102 Eng. Rep. 139, 140 (K.B. 1785).

[14] See generally Aristotle, *Nicomachean Ethics*, on "the rule of the mean."

but only "for limited times." Since the Constitution does not define "limited times," Congress has had, and has exercised, some leeway in setting the boundaries of copyright duration, increasing it, as we have seen, several times — in 1831, 1909, and again in 1976. Certainly, 70 years after an author's death is a "limited time" and it would seem the framers of the Constitution left it to Congress to determine the appropriate balance that Lord Macaulay would later articulate.

But the Constitution places a second limit on Congress's ability to act: its copyright power must "*promote* science and the useful arts." If the purpose of copyright is to provide authors with an incentive to create works of authorship, what incentive for creation would an increased term of copyright for a work provide an author, or the heirs of an author, who has already created that work? Certainly, Congress's ability to increase the duration of copyright is on stronger grounds when they are increasing the duration of works that have not yet been created.

These issues came to a head when a lawsuit challenging the Bono Act reached the U.S. Supreme Court. In *Eldred v. Ashcroft,* 537 U.S. 186 (2003),[15] the Court upheld all the extensions of copyright duration in the Bono Act, including the extensions to existing copyrights, but suggested that Congress's authority on the matter is not boundless and the Court may not take kindly to further extension, at least with respect to existing works. (In support of the Court's majority ruling, Judge Ginsberg cites the Second Edition of *Kohn On Music Licensing* in footnote 20 of the decision.)

With that, and without answering the question precisely how long is enough protection, we shall proceed by answering the question we began with: how long *do* copyrights last under the law.

## E. Duration of Copyright in Works Created After January 1, 1978

Under the Copyright Act of 1976, as amended by the Sonny Bono Copyright Term Extension Act of 1998, the term of copyright protection of works created (i.e., fixed in tangible form for the first time) after January 1, 1978 starts at the moment of creation and lasts for the author's life, plus an additional 70 years after the author's death.

[15] Citing the 2d Edition of *Kohn On Music Licensing* at 537 U.S. 186, fn. 21.

In the case of a *joint work* prepared by two or more authors, the term of protection lasts for 70 years after the last surviving author's death.

The above terms will not apply if the work was a work for hire, an anonymous work, or a pseudonymous work. A *work for hire* is (a) a work prepared by an employee within the scope of his employment or (b) a work that is specially ordered or commissioned in a writing that says the work is made for hire and that falls within one of several categories enumerated in the copyright law.[16] (*See* Chapters 3 and 7.) An *anonymous work* is a work on the copies or phonorecords of which no natural person is identified as author. A *pseudonymous work* is a work on copies or phonorecords of which the author is identified under a fictitious name. The term of protection for works made for hire, and for anonymous and pseudonymous works (unless the author's identity is revealed in Copyright Office records), the duration of copyright is 95 years from publication or 120 years from creation, whichever is shorter.[17]

## F. Duration of Copyright in Works Created Before January 1, 1978

Under the copyright law in effect before 1978, copyright was secured either on the date a work was published or on the date of registration if the work was registered in unpublished form.

Works that had been created before the new law came into effect but had neither been published nor registered for copyright before January 1, 1978, have been automatically brought under the new law and are now given federal copyright protection. The duration of copyright in these works generally is computed in the same way as for new works: the life-plus-70 or 95/120-year terms. However, all works in this category are guaranteed at least 45 years of statutory protection; the law specifies that in no case will copyright in a work of this sort expire before December 31, 2002, and if the work is published before that date the term may be extended by another 45 years, through the end of 2047.[18]

---

[16] 17 U.S.C. Sec. 101.

[17] See 17 U.S.C. Sec. 302(c).

[18] 17 U.S.C. Sec. 303.

For works in which statutory copyright protection had been secured before January 1, 1978, the new law retains the old system for computing the duration of protection, but with some changes. The law provides for a first term of 28 years, measured from the date protection originally was secured by publication or registration, with a right to a renewal term of 67 years. Renewal of copyright is discussed at length in the next section.

Copyrights that were in their renewal terms (i.e., second 28-year term) during the time spanning December 31, 1965 to December 31, 1977 were automatically extended an additional 39 years (thereby extending the total copyright duration for such works up to a maximum of 95 years), without the need for further renewal. This is now referred to as the *39-year extended term.*[19]

Until 1992, copyrights that were in their first term during the time spanning December 31, 1965 to December 31, 1977 were still required to be renewed to receive the full new maximum term of 75 years. After the Copyright Renewal Act of 1992 was signed into law, copyrights first published in 1964 or later are considered automatically renewed. The 1992 Act only applies to copyrights that still had to be renewed in the calendar year 1992 or later. Copyrights that have previously fallen into the public domain as a result of failure to file a renewal registration are not affected (i.e., they remain in the public domain).

The copyright law also provides that all terms of copyright will run through the end of the calendar year in which they would otherwise expire. This not only affects the duration of copyrights, but also the time limits for renewal registrations, discussed below.

## III. RENEWAL OF COPYRIGHT

As may be evident from the historical background noted above, the concept of renewal dates back to the earliest legislative enactments on copyright law. Under a renewal system, the duration of copyright is divided into two consecutive terms. The second term normally is conditioned upon the copyright owner filing a registration, within strict time limits, to secure copyright protection for the second term.

---

[19] 17 U.S.C. Sec. 304(b).

However, under a subsequent amendment to the U.S. copyright law, registration is no longer a condition for renewal of copyright under the copyright law. The Copyright Term Extension Act of 1998 extended the renewal term from 47 to 67 years.

### A. Permissive Registration

As noted, registration of renewal is no longer a condition for extending copyright protection through the renewal term (i.e., an additional 67 years beyond the original 28-year term) under U.S. copyright law. By the amendment to the copyright law signed into law on June 26, 1992, renewal is now automatic. Nevertheless, the law retains a permissive procedure of renewal registration that (a) provides a slight procedural incentive for claimants who file a renewal registration and (b) has a potential impact on determining who primarily benefits from the renewal.

If the application for renewal is filed within one year of expiration of the original term of copyright, the registration certificate would constitute *prima facie* evidence of validity of the copyright during its renewed and extended term and of the facts stated in the certificate of renewal registration.[20] It has always been the case that an original copyright registration, if filed within certain time limits, would constitute *prima facie* evidence of validity of the copyright and of the facts stated in the certificate of registration,[21] but, until the Copyright Renewal Act of 1992, renewal certificates never enjoyed the same recognition. The advantage is a slight one, but it does afford some convenience to copyright owners seeking to enforce their copyrights; in lawsuits for copyright infringement, the copyright owner with a certificate that constitutes evidence of validity of the copyright and of the facts stated in the certificate may avoid having to call to the stand witnesses to prove all of the facts in the certificate. This is a useful convenience in copyright piracy cases filed in jurisdictions that are a great distance away from the witnesses who could testify as to these facts.

Renewal registration may have an enormous, though hidden, impact on the determination of who primarily benefits from the renewal term. If the author of the work had previously granted his expectancy

[20] 17 U.S.C. Sec. 304(a)(4)(A).

[21] 17 U.S.C. Sec. 410(c).

interest in the renewal copyright to his music publisher, then under certain circumstances, renewal registration may affect whether the renewal copyright will vest in the author's music publisher or the heirs to the author's estate. This important subject will be discussed further below with respect to assignments of renewal interests.

## B. When May Renewal Registration Be Submitted

In accordance with the Copyright Renewal Act of 1992, an application to register a claim to the renewed and extended term of copyright in a work created during the time spanning the calendar years 1964 through 1977, inclusive, may be made to the Copyright Office (a) within one year before the expiration of the original term of copyright and (b) at any time during the renewed and extended term.[22] For all works created prior to 1964, the renewal application and fee must have been received in the Copyright Office within one year prior to the expiration of the original term; otherwise, the duration of the copyright expired at the end of the 28th year, and the work fell into the public domain.

Note, all terms of copyright run through the end of the year in which they would otherwise expire. Thus, all copyright terms will expire on December 31st of their year of expiration. Accordingly, all periods for renewal registration will run from January 1 of the 28th year of the original term of the copyright and will end on December 31 of the 28th year.

To determine the proper year in which to file a renewal application, follow these steps:

1. Find out the date of original copyright for the work.

   In the case of works originally registered in unpublished form prior to publication, the date of copyright is the date of its registration in the Copyright Office. Otherwise, the date of copyright is the date of first publication of a copy or phonorecord of a work bearing a valid copyright notice. *Publication* is the distribution of copies or phonorecords of a work to the public by sale or other transfer of ownership, or by rental, lease, or lending.[23] In one limited exception, the

[22] 17 U.S.C. Sec. 304(a)(3)(A).

[23] 17 U.S.C. Sec. 101.

date of copyright may be other than above: In any case when the year date in the copyright notice on copies distributed by authority of the copyright owner is earlier than the year of first publication, the date of copyright is considered to be the year contained in the notice.

2. Add 28 years to the date of copyright.

   The answer will be in the calendar year during which the copyright will be eligible for renewal registration, and December 31 of that year will be the renewal deadline.

The following table may be used to determine the time limits for filing a renewal application:

| | | | | |
|---|---|---|---|---|
| Mandatory Renewal | | | | |
| | 1950 | 1-1-78 | 12-31-78 | 12-31-2045 |
| | 1951 | 1-1-79 | 12-31-79 | 12-31-2046 |
| | 1952 | 1-1-80 | 12-31-80 | 12-31-2047 |
| | 1953 | 1-1-81 | 12-31-81 | 12-31-2048 |
| | 1954 | 1-1-82 | 12-31-82 | 12-31-2049 |
| | 1955 | 1-1-83 | 12-31-83 | 12-31-2050 |
| | 1956 | 1-1-84 | 12-31-84 | 12-31-2051 |
| | 1957 | 1-1-85 | 12-31-85 | 12-31-2052 |
| | 1958 | 1-1-86 | 12-31-86 | 12-31-2053 |
| | 1959 | 1-1-87 | 12-31-87 | 12-31-2054 |
| | 1960 | 1-1-88 | 12-31-88 | 12-31-2055 |
| | 1961 | 1-1-89 | 12-31-89 | 12-31-2056 |
| | 1962 | 1-1-90 | 12-31-90 | 12-31-2057 |
| | 1963 | 1-1-91 | 21-31-91 | 12-31-2058 |
| Permissive Renewal | | | | |
| | 1964 | 1-1-92 | 12-31-92 | 12-31-2059 |
| | 1965 | 1-1-93 | 12-31-93 | 12-31-2060 |
| | 1966 | 1-1-94 | 12-31-94 | 12-31-2061 |

| | | | |
|---|---|---|---|
| 1967 | 1-1-95 | 12-31-95 | 12-31-2062 |
| 1968 | 1-1-96 | 12-31-96 | 12-31-2063 |
| 1969 | 1-1-97 | 12-31-97 | 12-31-2064 |
| 1970 | 1-1-98 | 12-31-98 | 12-31-2065 |
| 1971 | 1-1-99 | 12-31-99 | 12-31-2066 |
| 1972 | 1-1-00 | 12-31-00 | 12-31-2067 |
| 1973 | 1-1-01 | 12-31-01 | 12-31-2068 |
| 1974 | 1-1-02 | 12-31-02 | 12-31-2069 |
| 1975 | 1-1-03 | 12-31-03 | 12-31-2070 |
| 1976 | 1-1-04 | 12-31-04 | 12-31-2071 |
| 1977 | 1-1-05 | 21-31-05 | 12-31-2072 |

*If the application for renewal for a work created prior to January 1, 1964 was not filed by the deadline, then the work fell into the public domain. This would not be the result for works created on or after January 1, 1964; renewal for such works is now automatic and the only consequence of failing to file a renewal application during the 28th year is the loss of certain procedural advantages in litigation and possibly an effect on who will own the renewal copyright upon its vesting.

Renewal registration is effective upon the Copyright Office's receipt of a completed application and the appropriate fee. Being unable to supply all of the information requested in the form should not deter the applicant from submitting the application, even if it is incomplete. The Copyright Office will consider a renewal application to be "acceptable" if it identifies the work by title and contains a correct statement of either the claimant or basis of claim. All other information supplied in the form will be considered minor and may be supplied later, even after the deadline for renewal, by a supplementary registration on Form CA. Whenever an applicant has cause to believe a formal application for renewal (Form RE), if sent by mail, might not be received in the Copyright Office before the renewal deadline, the application for renewal may be made by telephone, telegram, or other method of communication. However, the renewal fee was also required to be received by the Copyright Office by the deadline. Fortunately, as a result of the Copyright Renewal Act of 1992, the practice of getting a friend who lives in the vicinity of Washington, D.C. to brave the cold on New Year's

Eve to run down to the Copyright Office with your check or money order is now history.

Note, in the event the last day for filing the renewal falls on a Saturday, Sunday, holiday, or other non-business day within the District of Columbia or the Federal Government, the application may be filed on the next succeeding business day, and is effective as of the date when the period expired. Further, in any case in which the Register of Copyrights determines the application fee, or any other material to be delivered to the Copyright Office by the renewal deadline, would have been received in the Copyright Office in due time except for a general disruption or suspension of postal or other transportation or communications services, the actual receipt of such material in the Copyright Office within one month after the date on which the Register makes such determination, shall be considered timely.

The Copyright Office has no discretion to extend the renewal time limits. If an acceptable application and fee for works created prior to 1964 was not received within the strict time limits, copyright protection is lost permanently and the work falls into the public domain. Should that happen, the copyright cannot be revived.

## C. Renewal Copyright Claimants

This section summarizes who under the law is entitled to claim a renewal copyright. Crucial to the understanding of renewal registration is the understanding of the difference between who may *claim* a renewal, who may *submit* an application for renewal, and who ultimately gets to *own* the renewal copyright. The answer is not necessarily the same for each, depending on the circumstances.

Renewal copyright may be *claimed* only by those persons specified in the copyright law. (The statutory provisions on this point are essentially the same in the 1992 Act as those contained in the 1976 Act and 1909 Act.) Under the Copyright Renewal Act of 1992, an application to register a claim for renewal of copyright may be made (1) within one year before the expiration of the original term by any person entitled to claim the renewal (see below) or (2) at any time after expiration of the original term by any person in whom such further term vested, or by any successor or assign of such person, if the application is made in the name of such person.

In general, the law gives the right to *claim* renewal to the individual author of the work, regardless of who owned the copyright during the original term. If the author is deceased at the time for renewal, the statute gives the right to claim renewal to certain of the author's heirs in a particular order of preference, listed below.

In the case of the following three types of works, however, the person or entity entitled to claim renewal is not necessarily the individual creator of the work (or his heirs), but the copyright proprietor (i.e., owner of the copyright at the time application is made for renewal):

1. *Posthumous Works*. The owner of a posthumous work may claim renewal in such work. A *posthumous* work is a work as to which no copyright assignment or other contract for exploitation has occurred during the author's lifetime.

2. *Collective Work*. The owner of a collective work (e.g., periodical, encyclopedia, anthology, etc.) may claim renewal in all material in which he originally secured copyright, including the collective work as a whole, as well as any contributions to the collective work in which the owner originally claimed copyright. The author of any contribution to a collective work may claim renewal in his own name with respect to his contribution, if he originally secured a separate copyright in the contribution (i.e., he separately registered the contribution in unpublished form, or, upon publication, copies of the work contained a separate copyright notice in the name of the author).

3. *Works Made For Hire*. The owner of a work-made-for-hire may claim renewal in such work. Renewal rights may not be claimed by an employee-for-hire. To determine whether the relationship between the individual who actually created the work and the person for whom the work was created was a work-for-hire, *see* Chapter 7.

The persons in the following order of preference may claim renewal in all types of works except those three enumerated above:

1. The author, if living.
2. The widow (or widower) and children of the author.

If the author is not living, the author's widow (or widower), and children are entitled to claim renewal. All members of this class share the renewal interest equally. For example, if the deceased author leaves a widow and two children, the widow and each child shall receive a one-third interest in the right to claim renewal copyright.

An author's "children" are his or her immediate offspring, whether legitimate or not, and any children legally adopted by the author. The author's widow (or widower) is the author's surviving spouse, as determined under the law of the author's domicile at the time of his or her death, whether or not the spouse has later remarried. If the author and spouse were divorced, the former spouse does not constitute a "widow" upon the author's death.

3. The executor(s) named in the author's will.

   If there is no surviving widow (or widower) or children, then the executor(s) named in the author's will are entitled to claim the renewal copyright. This will be the case even if the author leaves surviving grandchildren.

   An *executor* is one who has been designated in a will as the person to carry out the directions and provisions designated in the will by the deceased author. When the renewal rights are claimed by the executors, they are not claimed for their personal benefit, but rather in trust for the benefit of those named in the will to receive the renewals or the residuary assets of the estate of the author. When the author dies leaving a will, but an executor is not named in the will, the courts will appoint an "administrator" to perform the duties of an executor. For renewal purposes, an administrator is the equivalent of an executor.

4. The next of kin of the deceased author.

   If there is no surviving widow (or widower) or children, and the author left no will, then the next of kin of the deceased author are entitled to claim the renewal copyright. Who comprises *next of kin* is determined by the intestate succession laws of the state of the author's domicile at the time of his or her death.

In summary, a person may not be a renewal *claimant* unless he is a member of the appropriate class set forth in the copyright law: a proprietor of the copyright (in the case of a posthumous work, collective work, or work made for hire); the author of the work; the widow (or widower) of the author; a child of the deceased author; or, where none of the foregoing are living, the executor under the author's will; or then, in the event no will is left, the next of kin of the deceased author.

One need not, however, be a member of one of the above classes to be entitled to submit an application for renewal on behalf of a proper renewal claimant. A discussion of who is entitled to submit an application for renewal is the subject of a section set forth below.

### D. Proper Claimants for Renewal of Arrangements, Translations, Compilations and Other Collective Works, and Derivative Works

In the case of the renewal of copyright in a new version of a previous work, such as an arrangement, translation, dramatization, compilation or work published with new material, a further consideration must be made in determining the proper claimant.

Generally, the copyright secured in a new version of a work is independent of any protection in the material published earlier. In other words, the copyright in the new version covers only the additions, changes, or other new material appearing for the first time in that version, and not to the underlying preexisting material. Thus, for renewal purposes, the "authors" of the new version are only those persons who contributed the new copyrightable matter to it; the person who wrote the original version on which the new work is based cannot be regarded as an "author" of the new version, unless that person also contributed to the new matter.

In the context of music publishing, arrangements, translations, and compilations are usually prepared by employees-for-hire of the publishing company. Therefore, the proper renewal claimant for such works will usually be the music publishing company, claiming as "proprietor of the copyright," not the composer of the song (or his statutory heirs).

Music publishers may ask whether it is desirable to file renewal registrations for their copyrighted arrangements, particularly where a renewal copyright has already been claimed in the underlying composition. The best policy is to file renewal registrations for all copyrighted arrangements of musical compositions. Some arrangements may continue to have sale and performance value well after the copyright in the underlying song has expired. In many instances, arrangements originally prepared for publication in the form of sheet music that was once discontinued were later reprinted, either as part of a folio, or when a decision is made to reprint the song and no replacement for the discontinued arrangement was readily available. Renewal should certainly be claimed if the arrangement was of a work in the public domain to begin with or when the arranger is entitled to a royalty on sales of the arrangement.

### E. Renewal Copyright Owners

Determining who the proper claimant of the renewal copyright is does not definitively lead to the determination of who will become the *owner* of the renewal copyright upon the expiration of the initial term of copyright. If the author never assigned to another his or her rights in his renewal copyright during the original term, then the claimant(s) will become the owner(s) of the renewal copyright upon the expiration of the initial term.

If the author did assign to another his or her rights in his renewal copyright during the original term, then the claimant(s) will not necessarily become the owner(s) of the renewal copyright. The effect of an assignment of a renewal prior to the expiration of the original copyright term on the claimant's potential right to own the renewal copyright is discussed below.

## IV. Duration of Assignments of Copyright

An *assignment* of copyright, or an assignment of any of the exclusive rights under copyright (e.g., assignment of reproduction rights), is a transfer of property, as in a gift or sale of property. An assignment of copyright, or assignment of any of the exclusive rights under copyright, may be limited in duration. The duration of an assignment may be limited (1) by the assignment itself, or (2) by the terms of the copyright law.

## A. Duration Limited by the Terms of the Assignment

The duration of an assignment may be limited by the terms of the assignment or contract relating to the assignment. For example, a songwriter may assign to a music publisher his copyright in a song for a period of 10 years; at the expiration of the 10 years, the copyright reverts to the songwriter. Such reversion may or may not be automatic, depending on the terms of the assignment. For example, the copyright may revert only if the publisher fails to have a commercial recording of the song distributed or if certain income levels are not achieved. Sometimes, specific action is required on the part of the songwriter to effect reversion. For example, under the terms of the AGAC Uniform Popular Songwriter's Contract of 1948 (Paragraph 8), the writer is entitled to be re-vested with all rights and copyrights outside the United States and Canada. To cause such re-vesting of foreign rights, the writer must send a notice to the publisher within six months of the writer's grant of such rights to another music publisher.

## B. Duration Limited by the Terms of the Copyright Law

In the event the assignment document does not expressly indicate the term of its duration, it will be deemed effective for the remainder of the copyright term existing at that time. However, certain provisions of the new copyright law, which went into effect on January 1, 1978, affect the duration of certain assignments.

### *1. Grants Executed by the Author After January 1, 1978*

The congressional purpose, in enacting the 1909 Act, in granting an author two consecutive 28-year terms was to guarantee him the enjoyment of the fruits of his creation after the initial 28-year term during which his work was exploited by his assignee. Under the 1909 Act, after the first term of 28 years, the renewal copyright was supposed to revert to the author or other specified beneficiaries. In the words of the Register of Copyrights, the renewal term was intended to remedy the situation "where the author actually turns out to have sold his birthright for a mess of pottage."[24] To a certain extent, however, this remedy was

[24] Register of Copyrights, Copyright Law Revision Pt. 3, Preliminary Draft for Revised U.S. Copyright Law and Discussions and Comments on the Draft, 88th Cong., 2d Sess. (Comm. Print 1964).

thwarted by a ruling of the Supreme Court in 1943, discussed below.[25] In enacting the 1976 Act, Congress dropped the renewal feature, except for works already in their first term of statutory protection when the new law took effect, but included several new provisions clearly intended to reinstate the right of the author to enjoy the fruits of his authorship years after his initial assignment of the copyright.

An assignment of copyright subject to the 1976 Act, or exclusive rights under such copyright, which is silent about its *term* (i.e., how long it will remain in effect) or *reversion* (i.e., circumstances under which rights will revert to the assignor), will endure for the life of the copyright. Under the 1976 Act, however, any assignment by an author after January 1, 1978, regardless of the term stated in the agreement effecting the transfer, is subject to being terminated 35 years after the date of the grant.[26] This power to terminate a transfer of copyright or exclusive rights under copyright (and, for that matter, non-exclusive licenses, discussed below) is sometimes referred to as the *35-year termination rule.*

Specifically, for transfers of rights made by an author on or after January 1, 1978, the copyright law permits the author or certain heirs of the author (of a work other than a work made for hire) to terminate a transfer during a 5-year period beginning at the end of 35 years from the date of the grant, or if the grant covers the right of publication, 35 years from the date of publication or 40 years from the date of the grant, whichever is shorter.

To terminate a grant, a written notice must be served on the transferee within the time limits specified by the copyright law.[27] The grant may be terminated at any time during the period spanning 5 years after 35 years from the year of publication, provided that a notice of termination is sent to the music publisher between a period spanning 10 years before the first possible effective date of termination and 2 years before the last possible effective date of termination.

Suppose the copyright in a song was granted to a music publisher in 1984 and it was published during the same year. Thus, in this example,

---

[25] See discussion below concerning *Fred Fisher Co. v. M. Witmark & Sons*, 318 U.S. 643 (1943).

[26] 17 U.S.C. Sec. 203.

[27] 17 U.S.C. Sec. 203 (a)(3), (4). A form for such termination is included on the CD-ROM.

the grant may be terminated at any time between 2019 (the first year in which termination can become effective) and 2024 (the last year in which termination can become effective), provided, however, that a notice of termination is sent to the music publisher between 2009 (the first possible effective date of termination) and 2022 (the last year that notice can be sent).

To effect the congressional purpose of the rule, certain key provisions were included to prevent the author from prematurely waiving or contracting away his right of termination. For example, termination of the grant may be effected notwithstanding any agreement to the contrary, including an agreement to make a will or to make any further grant.[28] Also, the rule provides that a re-grant of rights that revert after termination is valid only if it is executed after the effective date of termination.[29] An exception, however, was provided in favor of the current grantee: A further grant of a reverted right may be made to the original grantee or his successor in title, after the service of notice has been made.[30] Thus, for example, an author who serves notice of termination on his current music publisher may enter into a contract granting rights covering the remainder of the life of the copyright with that music publisher beginning the date the publisher is served with the notice. This in effect gives the current publisher a right of first refusal, affording him a two to ten year lead time over other publishers in dealing for the reverted rights.

An author may overcome the competitive advantage of his current publisher by merely waiting until the termination actually takes effect before accepting any offer from the publisher. Some clever publishers have conceived interesting ways of increasing their leverage in the negotiation for these reverted rights. The following is a rather innovative provision that may be found in some music publishing contracts drafted since the passage of the 1976 Act:

> Writer and Publisher hereby acknowledge that the copyrights and certain other rights in the Compositions granted to Publisher hereunder may be terminated by Writer or his successors (hereinafter,

[28] 17 U.S.C. Sec. 203 (a)(5).

[29] 17 U.S.C. Sec. 203 (b)(4).

[30] *Id.*

individually and collectively, "Writer") in accordance with the provisions of the Copyright Act. Writer and Publisher further acknowledge that it is their intention that, in the event that any such grants of copyright or other rights are terminated by Writer, Publisher shall have the exclusive right of first refusal with respect thereto, which right of first refusal shall be exercised as follows:

Until the expiration of a period of sixty (60) days following the Publisher's receipt of a valid notice of termination with respect to any such copyrights and other rights, Writer shall not negotiate with any third party with respect to the grant, sale, assignment, license, or other transfer thereof. During said sixty (60) day period, Writer agrees to negotiate in good faith and to exert best efforts to reach an agreement with Publisher for Publisher's acquisition of such copyrights and other rights. In the event that Publisher and Writer fail to reach agreement by the end of said sixty (60) day period, Writer shall be free to negotiate with third parties for the grant, sale, assignment license or other transfer of such copyrights and other rights, only for terms and conditions more favorable to Writer than those last offered by Publisher. If Writer receives such an offer from a bona fide third party, which offer Writer wishes to accept, Writer shall notify Publisher of the terms thereof in writing and Publisher shall have ten (10) days from its receipt thereof to notify Writer in writing that it desires to acquire the copyrights and other rights subject to the terms of such offer on the terms and conditions contained therein. In the event that Publisher so notifies Writer, said copyrights and other rights shall automatically vest in Publisher, and Writer shall enter into a written agreement with Publisher reflecting such terms and conditions promptly after Writer's receipt of such notice. In the event that Publisher does not so notify Writer and Writer does not accept such third party offer, the foregoing procedures shall apply to any future offers which Writer receives and wishes to accept, including any offer containing identical terms and conditions previously rejected by Writer, whether received by Writer from the same or from a different third party.

It is not clear whether such a provision will be enforceable. Arguably, it may be enforceable because it does not preclude the grant from being terminated. On the other hand, although the clause will not directly affect the right of termination, it does interfere with the free exploitation or re-sale of the copyright after termination becomes effective, and, on that ground, may be held unenforceable. Because the rights of termination for songs created under the 1976 Act will not begin to be exercised until 35 years has passed after the execution of the applicable grants, it will be a long time before the enforceability of such a provision is tested in court.

### *2. Grants Covering the Initial Term of Copyright*

An assignment of a copyright in a song created before January 1, 1978, in its original (i.e., first 28-year) term of copyright, which does not provide for any term or reversion, and *did not* provide for an assignment of renewal rights, will endure until the expiration of the original term of copyright only.

### *3. Grants Covering the Renewal Term of Copyright*

The duration of assignment of a copyright in a song created before January 1, 1978, in its original (i.e., first 28-year) term of copyright, which does not provide for any term or reversion, but *did* provide for an assignment of the author's interest in renewal rights will depend on the circumstances discussed in the section below on Duration of Assignment of Renewal Copyright.

### *4. Grants Covering the Extended (39-Year) Term of Copyright*

For works created before January 1, 1978, and in their first term of copyright as of December 31, 1977, a similar right of termination is provided with respect to transfers covering the newly added years extending the maximum term of copyright by 39 years, from 56 to 95 years.[31]

The assignment of a copyright in a song created before January 1, 1978, in its original term or its renewal term of copyright will endure until the expiration of the copyright (i.e., the 95th, and final year of the life of the copyright), unless otherwise provided by the terms of the assignment agreement or unless the author (or certain statutory beneficiaries) exercises a statutory right of termination that may be effective

[31] 17 U.S.C. Sec. 304 (c).

as early as 39 years prior to the final year of the copyright. Within certain time limits, an author or specified heirs of the author (or the author's estate), are generally entitled to file a notice terminating the author's transfers covering any part of the 39-year period that has now been added to the end of the second term of copyright in a work.

The same procedures provided for regarding the 35-year termination rule discussed above are applicable to terminations of grants covering the 39-year extended term. A termination of the grant may be effected notwithstanding any agreement to the contrary, including an agreement to make a will or to make any further grant.[32] Further, a regrant of rights that revert after termination is valid only if it is executed after the effective date of termination, and an exception was provided in favor of the current grantee.[33] While the procedures for such termination resemble those for termination under the 35-year termination rule, there are important differences. For example, while the 35-year termination rule provides for the recapture of only those rights that the *author* has transferred after January 1, 1978, grants by *either the author or his statutory successors* covering the 39-year extended term may be terminated, which effectively allows successors to terminate transfers of renewal expectancies, discussed below, and benefit fully from the 39-year extended term of copyright.

In addition, when under the Bono Act, the 19-year extended term became the 39-year extended term, Congress gave some authors, and their heirs and estates, a second chance to reclaim their copyrights if they failed to do so the first time around. If the right to terminate the grant came up before October 27, 1998, and the grant was not terminated by the deadline, the grant can still be terminated at any time within 5 years after the expiration of the first 75 years (giving the author, or his heirs or estate, control over the copyright for the final 20 years of its life).

[32] 17 U.S.C. Sec. 304 (c)(5). A form for such termination is included on the CD-ROM.

[33] 17 U.S.C. Sec. 304 (c)(6)(D).

## V. DURATION OF AN ASSIGNMENT OF RENEWAL COPYRIGHT

As noted above, an author's assignment of his renewal interest to another prior to the expiration of the original copyright term may affect a renewal claimant's potential right to own the renewal copyright. The person to whom the author assigned his renewal interest (or that person's successors or assigns) may become the owner of the renewal copyright under certain circumstances. Those circumstances, which involve the unfortunate subject of death, are discussed in this section.

### A. Limited Relevancy

Before proceeding into this gravely important topic, it is useful to note what this discussion does and does not concern. This discussion only concerns those works that were created before January 1, 1978, *and* that were in their original term of copyright as of January 1, 1978. Thus, this discussion concerns primarily the generation of musical compositions written and published during the mid-1950s to the end of 1977. Further, this discussion only concerns those compositions in which the author assigned to another during the original term of copyright his or her interest in the renewal copyright. If the author never assigned his or her rights in his renewal copyright or assigned such interest during the renewal term, then this discussion is not relevant to the ownership interests in the copyright.

If the author did assign to another his or her rights in his interest in the renewal copyright during the original term, then, under certain circumstances, the claimant(s) will not become the owner(s) of the renewal copyright.

### B. Renewal Copyright versus Renewal Expectancy

Under the 1909 Act, a copyright was secured by publication of the work with the proper copyright notice. The initial 28-year term was said to have *vested* immediately upon such securing. Though the law provided that the author of the work had the right, upon the expiration of the initial term, to *renew* the copyright for an additional 28-year term, the author's right to renew was not considered *vested* until the renewal period. Until then, the author had a mere *expectancy* in the renewal copyright.

In other words, upon the securing of copyright protection in a work created before January 1, 1978, a copyright owner possesses two things: (1) a right in the initial 28-year term of copyright, and (2) an expectancy interest in the 28-year (now, 67-year) renewal. A *right* is not the same as an *expectancy interest*, and the difference may have an impact upon who is entitled to *own* the renewal copyright.

## C. Transfer of Renewal Expectancy

The assignment of the *right* in the initial 28-year term of copyright operates the same as the assignment of any other type of property right: the assignee becomes the owner of the right, and may immediately exercise any or all of the incidents of ownership. The assignment of the *expectancy* in the renewal term before the actual commencement of the renewal term (i.e., before the renewal *vests*), does not operate to convey any legal *right* (over which the assignee may exercise as an owner), only the mere *expectancy* in the renewal copyright.

The distinction between *rights* and *expectancies* formed the basis of the following fundamental rule of copyright law concerning claims in renewal copyright announced by the U.S. Supreme Court:

> An assignment of a renewal expectancy will, upon its vesting, be binding upon the author so that if the author is living at the time of renewal, the assignee, not the author, will be entitled to own such renewal; if the author is not living at the time of renewal, then those persons who, as specified in the copyright law, are entitled to claim the renewal copyright (i.e., the statutory renewal claimants) are not bound by any assignment executed by the author, so that the assignee of the renewal expectancy takes nothing and the statutory renewal claimants take legal title to the renewal.[34]

[34] *Fred Fisher Co. v. M. Witmark & Sons*, 318 U.S. 643 (1943); *Miller Music Corp. v. Charles N. Daniels, Inc.*, 362 U.S. 373 (1960); *Stewart v. Abend*, 495 U.S. 207 (1990), hereinafter called, the "Rear Window" decision. The subject of the case was the 1954 film, "Rear Window," starring Grace Kelly and James Stewart, and directed by Alfred Hitchcock.

## D. Operation of the Rule of Renewal Expectancy

In other words, an assignment by an author of his or her interest in the renewal copyright before the initial copyright term expires is valid against the world, if the author lives until the commencement of the renewal period. For convenience, this rule will be called the *rule of renewal expectancy*.

Suppose, for example, a songwriter composed a song and assigned his copyright, including the renewal copyright, to his music publisher in 1967 and the original 28-year term of copyright in the song was expected to expire on December 31, 1995. Even though the music publishing contract may have included an assignment of "any and all renewal copyrights," the law only recognizes an assignment of the author's renewal "expectancy," which will not *vest* (i.e., become a renewal "right") until the renewal period. Accordingly, the rule of renewal expectancy will operate as follows: If the songwriter is living at the time the renewal copyright vests, then the legal title in the renewal right will automatically become the property of the music publisher. If the songwriter is not living when the renewal copyright vests, then the legal title will become the property of the author's beneficiaries (in a particular order of preference as specified in the copyright law).

The result in the foregoing example may differ if the author's statutory beneficiaries have previously transferred their own renewal expectancies. Suppose, for example, at the time the songwriter assigned his copyright and renewal expectancy in 1967, the songwriter's wife and children (as statutory beneficiaries) also signed documents assigning to the music publisher their own renewal expectancies in the song. In that event, even when the author is not living at the time the renewal vests, the music publisher would still take legal title to the renewal copyright. This, of course, assumes the author's wife and children or other statutory beneficiaries were living at the time the renewal copyright vested, because the renewal expectancies assigned by them to the music publisher also are subject to the rule of renewal expectancies. Thus, if the wife and children were not living when the renewal copyright vested, then the legal title in the renewal copyrights would become the property of the next order of beneficiaries under the statute, not the music publisher.

A music publisher's attempt to secure renewal rights by obtaining assignments of expectancies from as many potential beneficiaries as possible is not foolproof. The effort may be defeated by the songwriter's divorce and subsequent remarriage before death. In that case, his second wife, and widow, assuming she did not subsequently assign to the publisher her expectancy, will take title to her share of the renewal copyright at the commencement of the renewal term. A similar result would occur in the event the songwriter, subsequent to his wife's and children's assignment of their renewal expectancies, has additional children, by either birth or adoption; in that case, the children who did not join in the assignment of renewal expectancies will share in the renewal copyright upon its vesting if the songwriter is not living at the time the renewal copyright vests.

It appears a music publisher may never be absolutely certain about whether it will acquire the entire renewal copyright at the time it receives an assignment of copyright and renewal expectancies. The publisher can only attempt to obtain as many assignments of renewal expectancies as possible from every known member of the class of possible successors to the renewal copyright. For example, the songwriter, his spouse, all of his children, and all known next of kin of the songwriter. The music publisher may also seek agreement from the songwriter to write a will bequeathing to the publisher renewal rights. These attempts are often impractical and not worth the expense, but remain standard in the contracts of some music publishers.

The rule of renewal expectancy only applies to works created before January 1, 1978, and that were in their initial 28-year term of copyright. Works created before that date, but which are already in their renewal term, of course, are not subject to the rule, as the renewal copyrights in those works have vested in their owners. Works created after January 1, 1978 also are not subject to the rule, because under the new copyright law there will never be a renewal term of copyright (or renewal expectancies) in these works.

## E. Formalities of Assigning Renewal Expectancies

Virtually all of the normal formalities and other aspects of assigning copyrights discussed previously in Chapter 8 apply equally to the assignment of renewal expectancies. Note, however, that it appears assignments of renewal expectancies will be binding against their assignors only if the assignment was supported by sufficient legal consideration (e.g., something of value).[35] Note, further, that renewal expectancies may not pass as personal property under a will or by the operation of state law in the absence of a will, because the federal copyright law, by specifying the particular classes of individuals entitled to claim renewal upon the author's death, preempts any state law regarding wills and inheritances.

The courts have ruled on the contractual language necessary to effect an assignment of a renewal expectancy. Briefly, an assignment of "renewal copyright" or just "renewals" will be sufficient to effect an assignment of renewal expectancies. Also, "extensions of copyright" will suffice. In the absence of such relatively express language, the courts are hesitant to construe an assignment of "copyright" to include renewal copyright, without some other evidence the parties intended an assignment of renewal. A transfer of "all, right, title and interest" has been held not sufficient to cover renewals, but an assignment of rights "forever" has.

## F. Renewal Copyright Vesting

As indicated above, the copyright law gives the author the right to claim renewal if he is living at the time the renewal copyright vests. Gone unanswered throughout the discussion has been the question, at what time must one be living for a renewal claimed in his name to be effective? In other words, when do rights in the renewal copyright *vest*?

Prior to the Copyright Renewal Act of 1992, there were two possibilities: (1) the date on which the renewal application was filed or duly registered with the Copyright Office, or (2) the commencement of the renewal term. Until as recently as 1991, the question was the subject of a split of authority, with a court in the Southern District of New York holding that rights in a renewal copyright vested on the date on which the renewal application was filed with the Copyright Office[36] and the

[35] *Fisher v. Morris & Co.*, 113 U.S.P.Q. 251 (S.D.N.Y. 1957).

[36] *Frederick Music Company v. Sickler*, 708 F. Supp. 587 (S.D.N.Y. 1989).

Ninth Circuit Court of Appeals in California holding that rights in a renewal copyright do not vest until the actual commencement of the renewal term.[37]

The consequence of the rule suggested by the Ninth Circuit is that it may become impossible to determine with any degree of certainty who will be the proper copyright claimant until it becomes too late to file the claim. For example, the author is alive at the beginning of the 28th year of the original term and shortly thereafter files an application for renewal naming himself as renewal claimant. Shortly before the end of the same year, before the actual commencement of the renewal term, the author dies. Upon the author's death, the proper renewal claimants would be those in the appropriate successor class as listed above. Unless one of the members of the successor class is able to file a timely application for renewal, the renewal claim would fail, resulting in the work's falling into the public domain. Requiring members of the successor renewal class to file renewal claims in their name as an act of insurance against the possibility of the author's dying before the year is up often would result in redundant applications, and it is not clear whether the Copyright Office will even accept this practice.

Further, if you were an assignee of a renewal expectancy, you will want to know upon the commencement of the renewal term of copyright whether the copyright is vested in you or in the author or his heirs. The best way to determine this would be to perform a search of the records of the copyright office (*see* Circular R22 set forth at the end of Chapter 1) to discover whether the author was alive at the time of renewal. If the rule announced by the Ninth Circuit were followed, then an author could file a renewal application during the 28th year, die subsequent to the filing, but before the end of the year, and the records of the copyright office would not reflect the true ownership status of the renewal copyright. Unless the holder of the renewal expectancy had some separate way of confirming whether the author survived the expiration of the original term of copyright, it might take some investigation to determine, in fact, whether the holder is actually the owner of the copyright, or whether, if he continues to exploit the work, he is liable for copyright infringement. Similarly, as will be discussed at length later in this chapter, if you are a *derivative work licensee* (i.e., owner of a

---

[37] *Marascalco v. Fantasy, Inc.*, 953 F.2d 469 (9th Cir. 1991).

derivative work based on an underlying work of another under license from the author of the underlying work), you will want to know if, under the ruling in the *Rear Window* decision, you have the right to continue distributing your derivative work without further license from the author or his heirs.

## G. Renewal Vesting Under Copyright Renewal Act of 1992

It is the better view that, as long as the author survives until the date the renewal application is registered in the Copyright Office, a renewal claimed in the name of an author will be effective, even if he should die subsequent to the registration but before the end of the 28th year. This is in fact the rule adopted by Congress in the 1992 Act.

> (B) At the expiration of the original copyright term of copyright in a work specified in paragraph (1)(C) of this subsection, the copyright shall endure for a renewed and extended further term of 67 years, which —
>
> (i) if an application to register a claim to such further term has been made to the Copyright Office within 1 year before the expiration of the original term of copyright and the claim is registered, shall vest, upon the beginning of such further term, in any person who is entitled under paragraph (1)(C) [i.e., the statutory beneficiaries, such as author, widow, widower, children, etc.] to the renewal and extension of the copyright at the time the application is made; or
>
> (ii) if no such application is made or the claim pursuant to such application is not registered, shall vest, upon the beginning of such further term, in any person entitled under paragraph (1)(C), as of the last day of the original term of copyright, to the renewal and extension of the copyright.

The new law clearly indicates that the renewal copyright always *vests* upon the commencement date of the renewal term (i.e., "the copyright shall endure for a renewed and extended further term . . . *which . . . shall vest . . . upon the beginning of such further term . . .*"). However, it is also clear that the person or persons in whom the renewal copyright will actually vest may directly depend on whether a permissive renewal application is filed with the Copyright Office and when during the 28th year of the original term that application was filed.

If an application to register the renewal is filed within one year before the expiration of the original term of copyright, then the renewal copyright will vest in the person(s) entitled to claim the renewal *living at the time the application is made*. If, however, an application to register the renewal was not filed within one year before the expiration of the original term, then the renewal copyright will vest in the person(s) entitled to claim the renewal *living as of the last day of the original term of the copyright*.

## H. Effect of 1992 Act on Assignments of Rule of Renewal Expectancies

The 1992 Act has no effect on the rule of renewal expectancies itself, which remains the law of the land. Depending on the circumstances, however, the new law may have important consequences on the application of the rule in particular cases.

Taking a previous example, suppose a songwriter composed a song and assigned his copyright, including the renewal copyright, to his music publisher in 1967 and the original 28-year term of copyright in the song is expected to expire on December 31, 1995. Suppose further that the publisher did not receive any assignments of renewal expectancies from the songwriter's family, other than the songwriter's own renewal expectancy granted in 1967 under the terms of the music publishing agreement with the songwriter.

If an application to register the renewal is filed on December 1, 1995 (i.e., within one year before the expiration of the original term of copyright), then the renewal copyright will vest in the person entitled to claim the renewal living on December 1, 1995 (i.e., living at the time the application is made). If the songwriter is alive as of December 1, 1995, and the renewal application was filed in the name of the songwriter, then the songwriter's assignee (i.e., music publisher) will own the renewal copyright when it vests on January 1, 1996. If the songwriter died before December 1, 1995, and the renewal application was filed in the name of the songwriter's widow, then the widow will own the renewal copyright when it vests on January 1, 1996.

If no application to register the renewal is made during the calendar year 1995, then the renewal copyright will vest in the person entitled to claim the renewal living on December 31, 1995 (i.e., living as of the last day of the original term of copyright). If the songwriter is alive as of December 31, 1995, then the songwriter's assignee (i.e., music publisher) will own the renewal copyright when it vests on January 1, 1996. If the songwriter had died in a car accident driving home from a Christmas party on December 26, 1995, then the songwriter's widow will own the renewal copyright when it vests on January 1, 1996.

Accordingly, it appears that the determination of who will *own* the renewal copyright may depend on whether a renewal application has been filed and the timing of the author's death in relation to the time the renewal application is filed. This suggests that, even though registration is no longer a condition to claiming renewal copyrights, music publishers and songwriters should give serious consideration as to whether and when to file applications for renewal registration. Some of the issues to be considered by songwriters and publishers in this regard will be discussed below in the context of advice for music publishers and songwriters.

## I. Persons Entitled to Submit Renewal Applications

As noted, a registration for renewal of copyright will be valid only if it is claimed in the name of the person or persons who are among the statutory class of individuals entitled to such renewal. This does not mean, however, the person entitled to *claim* renewal must himself *submit* the application for renewal registration.

Generally, as long as the renewal application is filed in the name of the persons entitled to claim renewal the application may be filed by any person authorized by the proper claimant to do so. A person is considered authorized to file a renewal claim when (1) he is expressly authorized by a proper renewal claimant to do so, or (2) he has an express power of attorney to act generally, or with respect to copyright and renewal copyright matters, on behalf of the renewal claimant.

Of course, anyone who is specifically requested by a claimant to file a renewal application may do so. To remove any doubt about his agent's authority to file renewal applications on his behalf, the claimant should execute a power of attorney. A *power of attorney* is simply a written instrument authorizing another to act as one's agent or "attorney-in-fact." An attorney-in-fact, under a written power of attorney, need only have general powers to act on a person's behalf to be authorized to file renewal applications. Usually, however, copyright owners grant powers of attorney that are limited to the specific actions required by the attorney-in-fact to handle the copyright affairs of the copyright owner. For example, a copyright owner may grant a power of attorney to another for the purpose of filing renewal applications and notices of termination with respect to the 19-year extended term. An example of a power of attorney relating to an assignment of copyrights, including any renewals and extensions, is set forth as part of Form 8.1 found on the CD-ROM. An attorney licensed to practice law ("attorney-at-law") will always be considered authorized to file renewal applications on behalf of his clients whether or not expressed in writing.

It also has been commonly understood that a person is authorized to file a renewal claim when (1) he himself has a beneficial interest in the renewal copyright; or (2) by virtue of special circumstances, he is considered to have an implied power of attorney to file the renewal application on behalf of the claimant.

Because the failure to file a timely application for renewal registration for pre-1964 works had such drastic consequences, wide latitude was given to persons filing renewal applications in the names of others. For example, it has been thought that, even in the absence of a specific request, anyone who generally is entrusted to conduct the music or copyright affairs of the renewal claimant may probably file an application on the claimant's behalf. Similarly, one who has a beneficial interest in the renewal copyright may file an application for renewal on behalf of the renewal claimants. For example, in the case of a deceased author and no living widow or children, a person who is named in the will to receive the renewal rights will have a beneficial interest in the renewal copyright. (Recall, however, that under these circumstances, the renewal must be claimed in the name of the executor of the will, who will hold legal title in the renewal in trust for the beneficiaries named in the will. Though the renewal must be filed *in the name of* the executor, a beneficiary may nevertheless *submit* the renewal application, by virtue of his beneficial interest in the renewal copyright.)

One who has been granted a renewal expectancy interest (i.e., one who will be entitled to own the renewal once it vests) has also been entitled to submit applications for renewal on behalf of claimants. As previously noted, if the author has interest in the renewal copyright to a music publisher, then, depending on the circumstances, the ownership of the renewal copyright may vest in the music publisher, not in the author or his heirs, in accordance with the rule of expectancies. Though the renewal application must still be filed in the name of the author, not the publisher, the publisher may nevertheless file the application for renewal. He does so either by virtue of a power of attorney granted to him in the original music publishing contract with the author, or, in the absence of such a power, by virtue of the publisher's beneficial interest in the renewal (obtaining ownership upon its vesting).

However, because of the 1992 Act, the publisher's privilege to submit a renewal application may be subject to challenge if the publisher does not have a written power of attorney authorizing him to submit the application. This will be discussed further below.

### J. Advice for Music Publishers

As noted above, the determination of who will *own* the renewal copyright may depend on whether a renewal application has been filed and the timing of the author's death in relation to the time the renewal application is filed. This suggests that, to the extent music publishers have a right to file renewal applications in the name of songwriters, a strategy may be available for increasing the likelihood that a publisher's renewal expectancy will mature into a renewal copyright vested in the music publisher, rather than in the songwriter or the songwriter's heirs.

The strategy would be as follows: Music publishers who hold assignments of renewal expectancies should attempt to file renewal claims (on behalf of and in the name of each of the authors, as soon into the beginning of the final (i.e., 28th) year of the original term of copyright as possible. The following should illuminate the benefits of this strategy.

Using the previous example, should a music publisher file a renewal application on January 2, 1995 (i.e., the first business day of the 28th and final year of the original term of copyright of a song created in 1967), then the renewal copyright will vest in the person entitled to claim the renewal living on January 2, 1995 (i.e., living at the time the application is made). If the songwriter dies any time during the year 1995 after January 2, then the music publisher (i.e., the assignee of the songwriter's renewal expectancy) will own the renewal copyright when it vests on January 1, 1996. If the publisher waits until December 1, 1995 to file the renewal application and the songwriter dies prior to that date, then the songwriter's statutory beneficiaries at the time the application was filed will own the renewal copyright when it vests on January 1, 1996. If the music publisher and the songwriter's statutory beneficiaries fail to file the renewal application at all during the calendar year 1995, and the songwriter dies at any time during the year prior to December 31, 1995, then the songwriter's statutory beneficiaries as of December 31, 1995 will own the renewal copyright when it vests on January 1, 1996.

If the music publisher does not have a power of attorney from the songwriter to file renewal applications, can the music publisher nevertheless file the application in connection with implementing the strategy suggested above? As noted, even in the absence of a specific request, anyone who generally has been entrusted to conduct the music or copyright affairs of the renewal claimant has been allowed to file an application on the claimant's behalf. The Copyright Office has liberally allowed persons other than the claimant to file renewal applications, because failing to file had such drastic consequences (i.e., the work falling into the public domain). However, a question arises as to the effect of the Copyright Renewal Act of 1992, which has made renewal automatic, on the scope of the class of persons permitted to *submit* a renewal application to the Copyright Office.

The Act clearly does not affect the ability of the claimant's agent or one with a valid power of attorney to file renewal applications in the name of renewal claimants. Thus, if a music publisher had a power of attorney covering the filing of renewal applications, it could probably implement such a strategy without serious challenge. Suppose, however, the music publisher does not have a power of attorney or some other express authorization by the claimants to file the renewal application. Absent a power of attorney or some agency relationship between the claimant and the person submitting the application, may a music publisher who desires to submit the application do so solely on the basis of his beneficial interest in the renewal expectancy? Under the law prior to 1992, the answer clearly would have been yes, because it was in both the claimant's interest and the claimant's music publisher's interest that the renewal application be filed (otherwise the term of copyright would expire at the end of the 28th year). Under the 1992 Act, however, the interests of the music publisher and those of the claimants may be in conflict and such a conflict may suggest another conclusion. In fact, the music publisher's authority to file an application on the claimant's behalf may be subject to some doubt if the claimant specifically asked the publisher not to file a renewal application.

## K. Advice for Songwriters

Just as there is a strategy for music publishers, there is a strategy for songwriters and their heirs for increasing the likelihood that ownership in the renewal copyright will vest in them over a publisher's renewal expectancy.

The songwriter's strategy might be as follows: If you previously assigned your interest in the renewal copyright and there is a chance you might not live through the end of the original term, don't file an application for renewal registration. If you file and you die before the expiration of the original term of copyright, then, while you will be entitled to *claim* the renewal, the person who will be entitled to *own* the renewal is the person to whom you previously assigned your expectancy interest (e.g., the music publisher).

If you have retained (e.g., never assigned to another) your renewal expectancy interest, then your decision whether to file a renewal registration will depend on the chances of your not surviving the expiration of the original term of copyright, and whether you wish your renewal copyright to pass to your beneficiaries either (1) as defined under the copyright law or (2) as specified in your will. Assuming you wish the copyright to be bequeathed in accordance with your will, then you should file the renewal registration as soon into the final year of the original copyright term as possible. Remember, too, the slight legal advantages of filing a renewal application within one year prior to the expiration of the original term of copyright (i.e., renewal certificate becomes prima facie evidence of validity of the renewal copyright in infringement actions).

Each person who is entitled to claim renewal may file or cause to be filed a renewal application in his or her own name. This may be the case, for example, when a song was written by the collaboration of a composer and a lyricist. Though several persons may be entitled to file a renewal application, the filing of only one application, even if it is submitted in the name of only one of several proper renewal claimants, is required to effect renewal registration. The filing co-claimant and any non-filing co-claimants are considered to be in precisely the same position as though they had all properly filed applications. It would therefore appear that as long as one co-claimant files an application for renewal, it is not necessary for the other co-claimants to file separate, additional renewal applications. Though more than one renewal claimant may wish to file claims, it may be more economical for them to do so on the same form, rather than in separate applications. A renewal application contains room for three claimants, yet the same renewal registration fee will cover all three claims. In the event a question arises as to who will prove to be the proper claimant(s), the registration of competing renewal applications should be made. The Copyright Office will issue competing renewal certificates if, for example, it is not known whether an author, who has been missing for some time, is living or deceased, or there is a question as to the status of an illegitimate child. However, before filing an application for renewal registration, the songwriters or their survivors should carefully consider the potential effects on the vesting of the ultimate ownership interest in the renewal copyright.

Should the author specifically decide not to file an application for renewal registration, and it is thought that a music publisher who was previously assigned a renewal expectancy might file an application as a precaution against the author dying during the 28th year of the initial term of copyright, the author should send a letter to the publisher advising that he does not wish the publisher to file the application. If the author should die during the 28th year, this action may provide his heirs with some grounds for claiming the renewal copyright should vest in their name and not in the name of the music publisher.

## VI. Duration of Licenses

### A. By Terms of the License

A license normally lasts for as long as it says it lasts, usually in a provision called the *term* of license. For example, a license having a term of "five (5) years" will last five years. If the license does not state any limit on its term and if there is no evidence the parties intended the term to be limited, it normally will be deemed to continue effective for the life of the copyright. Non-exclusive licenses for which there is no stated term and for which there was no legal consideration (e.g., payment in exchange for the license) are revocable by the licensor at any time, unless circumstances are present that would make it unreasonable to allow the licensor to revoke permission.

A music copyright owner may grant licenses only for a term covering the time during which it has a right to grant licenses. For example, if a music publisher were granted rights only with respect to the original term of copyright, he could not grant licenses that purport to extend beyond the original term. An example of contracts containing such a songwriter provision are those that were entered using the form Uniform Popular Songwriter's Contract published in 1947 by the American Guild of Authors & Composers (now known as The Songwriter's Guild). Paragraph 8 of that form provides in part:

> 8. Terms of Contract. All rights in and to the composition and any copyrights thereon throughout the world, shall revert to the Writer upon the expiration of the original term of the United States copyright or at the end of twenty-eight (28) years from the date of publication in the United States, which ever period shall be shorter.

The AGAC contract provided, however, that if the songwriter failed to give to the publisher at least six months notice of any sale of the writer's U.S. renewal copyright to anyone other than the publisher, then the publisher shall be entitled to retain its rights under the contract for the renewal term in all countries outside the United States and Canada.

Further, paragraph 13 of the AGAC contract provided:

> 13. Termination of Contract. Upon the termination of this contract, all rights of any and every nature in and to the composition and

> in and to any and all copyrights secured thereon in the United States and throughout the world, shall re-vest in and become the property of the Writer, and shall be re-assigned to the Writer by the Publisher free of any and all encumbrances of any nature whatsoever, provided that: . . . (b) If the Publisher, prior to such termination, shall have granted a domestic license for the use of the composition, not inconsistent with the terms and provisions of this contract, the re-assignment may be subject to the terms of such license.

Accordingly, licenses issued by publishers during the original term of copyright and providing for a term that extended into the renewal term remain effective into the renewal term to the extent their territory is limited to the United States. As a practical matter, many licenses typically granted by music publishers have been made on a worldwide basis. Accordingly, if producers and other users of music cannot acquire from the music publisher a license of sufficient duration to meet his requirements, at least options to extend the term for additional periods of time, then producers will choose to use substitute songs for which such terms are available. Accordingly, the parties to an AGAC form contract have an incentive to alleviate any impediments to producers' licensing songs that revert to writers under the AGAC form. Music publisher and songwriters can alleviate the problem by entering into an agreement allowing the music publisher to continue actively issuing licenses that go beyond the original term of copyright, such as will be required for the issuance of synchronization licenses to exploit the songwriter's compositions in motion pictures, television productions, commercials, and videograms. An example of such an agreement is set forth as Form 14.6 found on the CD-ROM. Arrangements such as these should improve the licensing prospects of songs covered by these agreements. However, the problem is only partially alleviated with respect to certain songs. It was once thought that licenses granted during the original term of copyright purporting to cover the renewal term would continue in effect through the renewal term even though the renewal copyright reverted to a deceased author's survivors.[38] However, under the *Rear Window* decision, discussed below, it is

[38] *Rohauer v. Killiam Shows, Inc.*, 551 F.2d 484 (2d Cir. 1977); overturned by the U.S. Supreme Court in *Steward v. Abend*, 495 U.S. 207 (1990) (the *Rear Window* decision).

now the law that such licenses may expire at the end of the original term if the renewal copyright reverted to the author's beneficiaries.

## B. By Terms of the Copyright Law

Certain provisions of the copyright law affect the duration of certain licenses.

### *1. Termination of Licenses Granted by Authors After January 1, 1978*

Any license that is silent about its *term* (i.e., how long it will remain in effect) will endure for the life of the copyright. However, any license granted by an author after January 1, 1978, regardless of the term stated in the license agreement, is subject to being terminated 35 years after the date of the grant of license.[39] This power to terminate a license is sometimes referred to as the *35-year termination rule* (which also is applicable to the termination of assignment of copyright or exclusive right under copyright made by an author after January 1, 1978).

Specifically, licenses made by an author (of a work other than a work made for hire) on or after January 1, 1978, may be terminated by the author or certain heirs during a 5-year period beginning at the end of 35 years from the date of the grant, or if the grant covers the right of publication, 35 years from the date of publication or 40 years from the date of the grant, whichever is shorter. To terminate a grant, a written notice must be served on the transferee within the time limits specified by the copyright law.[40]

If termination is not effected under the terms of the rule, then the grant of license will continue in effect for the life of the copyright or will expire sooner in accordance with any applicable provisions of the agreement effecting the grant. If the termination is properly effected under the rule, then the grant of license terminates, provided that:

> A derivative work prepared under the authority of the grant before its termination may continue to be utilized under the terms of the grant after its termination, but this privilege does not extend to

---

[39] 17 U.S.C. Sec. 203.

[40] 17 U.S.C. Sec. 203 (a)(3),(4). A form for such termination is included on the CD-ROM.

> the preparation after the termination of other derivative works based upon the copyrighted work covered by the terminated grant.[41]

This is an important limitation on the rights of a copyright owner of a terminated grant. For example, a synchronization license to use music in a motion picture granted before termination would continue in effect for as long as provided in the license, but the licensee would not be able to use the music in other derivative works without a new license from the terminated rights owner. In other words, a motion picture producer could continue to distribute the motion picture without requiring a further license from the owner of the terminated rights, but, unless the terms of the original license permitted it, he could not use the music in a "remake" of the motion picture (i.e., "preparation after termination of other derivative works") without a new license.

When a music publisher created derivative works under the terms of its music publishing agreement with a songwriter who has terminated the grant of rights under that agreement, the terminated rights will be subject to the music publisher's right to continue to exploit any derivative works. Such derivative works may include arrangements, translations, compilations, and sound recordings created during the term of agreement.

The right of an original publisher of a composition that subsequently reverted to a songwriter (under the songwriter's statutory right of termination) to continue collecting revenue from licenses previously issued by the original publisher to use the song in derivative works was confirmed in the Supreme Court case of *Mills Music v. Snyder.*[42] Mills Music was the publisher of the song *Who's Sorry Now*, written by Ted Snyder and lyrics by Bert Kalmar and Harry Ruby. The heirs of Ted Snyder properly terminated the songwriter's assignment of copyright to Mills Music, and expected to enjoy all future revenues of ownership of the copyright for the remainder of its 19-year, now 39-year, duration. But Mills Music, during the time it controlled the copyright, had issued a number of mechanical licenses for the creation of sound recordings. Mills claimed that, despite the termination of assignment, it continued to have the right to the revenues from such

---

[41] 17 U.S.C. Sec. 203 (b)(1).

[42] *Mills Music v. Snyder*, 470 U.S. 1065 (1985).

recordings. In a 5-4 decision, the Supreme Court agreed with Mills, holding that the recordings were derivative works of the song and the money generated by the mechanical licenses issued to create them went to Mills Music.

Two other cases, however, have had the effect of refining the Mills Music case in favor of the terminating songwriter. In *Woods v. Bourne*,[43] Bourne Music took the position that every piece of printed music was a derivative work of the original lead sheet and, therefore, Bourne, not the songwriter was entitled to collect the income from all sheet music and folios containing the composition. The Second Circuit court of appeals disagreed, holding that sheet music is not a derivative work of the lead sheet.

In *Fred Ahlert Music Corp. v. Warner/Chappell Music, Inc.*,[44] the song *Bye Bye Blackbird* was owned by the music publisher, Warner/Chappell. After the passing of the 1976 Act, the heirs of the songwriters exercised their right of statutory termination and the copyright reverted back to them. While it controlled the copyright, Warner issued a mechanical license to A&M Records for a recording of the song by Joe Cocker. After the copyright later reverted to the heirs of the songwriter, the producer of the movie, *Sleepless In Seattle*, desired to license the Cocker recording for use in its movie soundtrack and on a soundtrack album of the movie. Warner claimed that it, not the heirs of the songwriters, had the right to receive the royalties derived from the Cocker recordings under the derivative works exception to the heir's right of termination. The court ruled otherwise, holding that the mechanical license granting A&M the right to use *Bye Bye Blackbird* was narrowly limited to the purpose of recording the Cocker derivative and releasing it as "Record No. SP 4182." Because the grant was limited to the record number, it did not authorize any additional releases of the Cocker derivative, much less its inclusion on a movie soundtrack. Thus, the heirs of the songwriters (or their new music publisher), not Warner, were entitled to receive the royalties on the use of the Cocker recording in the movie's soundtrack and soundtrack album. This case is also discussed in the chapter on mechanical licenses.

---

[43] *Woods v. Bourne*, 603 F.2d 978 (2d Cir. 1995).

[44] *Fred Ahlert Music Corp. v. Warner/Chappell Music, Inc.*, 155 F.3d 17 (2d Cir. 1998).

### 2. *Licenses Covering the Initial Term of Copyright*

A license to use a work created before January 1, 1978, in its original (i.e., first 28-year) term of copyright, which does not purport to cover the renewal term of copyright, will endure until the expiration of the original term of copyright only. As a practical matter, very few licenses, other than those that contain a fixed limitation on its term (e.g., five years), would fall into this category. A license "under the copyright" would probably expire at the end of the first term. A license granted during the first term of copyright, however, whose term is "in perpetuity" would be construed as covering the renewal term.

### 3. *Licensing Purporting to Cover the Renewal Term of Copyright*

Under a decision handed down by the U.S. Supreme Court in 1990 that has been described as "macabre," the duration of license, for the use of a song created before January 1, 1978, in its original (i.e., first 28-year) term of copyright, purporting to cover the renewal term would remain effective during the renewal term only if the author was living at the time of commencement of the renewal term.[45] Thus, it is an infringement of copyright to distribute a derivative work that is based on or incorporates a pre-1978 underlying work to which a license was obtained during its initial term if the author dies before the commencement of the renewal term, even though the author granted the producer of the derivative work a license to use the underlying work for its full term of copyright "including renewals and extensions."

The *Rear Window* decision does not affect (1) derivative works that were based on underlying works that were created or published for the first time since January 1, 1978; (2) derivative works that were based on underlying works that were in their renewal terms of copyright when the license to use the underlying work was granted; (3) derivative works that were based on underlying works that were works-made-for-hire of the owner of the derivative work; (4) derivative works that were based on underlying works that were in their initial term of copyright when the

---

[45] *Stewart v. Abend,* 110 S. Ct. 1750 (1990); see generally Lionel S. Sobel, View from the "Rear Window": A Practical Look at the Consequences of the Supreme Court's Decision in *Stewart vs. Abend*, 12/1 Entertainment Law Reporter 3 (June, 1990).

license to use the underlying work was granted, provided that the author of the underlying work lives until the time the renewal copyright may be claimed (i.e., 28th year of the original term of copyright) and an application to register the renewal copyright was actually filed while the author was alive;[46] and (5) derivative works that were based on underlying works created prior to 1964 that fell into the public domain because a claim for renewal was not filed by the applicable deadline.

The rule only affects derivative works created before January 1, 1978, that were based on underlying works of others that were in their initial terms of copyright when the license to use the underlying work was granted, provided that the author of the underlying work died prior to the renewal copyright could be claimed in his name [or the renewal otherwise vested in the author by contract] and the derivative licensee did not receive licenses from the author's statutory beneficiaries under their renewal expectancy interests. Nevertheless, because of the number of works that it does affect, the *Rear Window* decision has had far-reaching consequences.

#### *4. Effects of Rear Window on Music Licensing*

##### *a. Effect on Which Songs Will Be Used in New Derivative Works*

As noted in Chapters 10 and 14, producers of derivative works, such as motion pictures, television programs, and other audiovisual works, generally desire to obtain licenses that last as long as possible. Because of the possibility that a license subject to the *Rear Window* rule may have its term prematurely terminated by the untimely death of the songwriter, *derivative works licensees* (i.e., producers of derivative works obtaining licenses to use underlying works, such as music, in their productions) might wish to avoid using music that may be subject to a *Rear Window* termination.

Producers desiring to obtain licenses for the use of songs should ask the music copyright owner whether the song sought to be licensed is *safe* from the *Rear Window* decision or *tainted* by it. For example, works created or first published since 1978 are "safe" from the effects

[46] Except in the Ninth Circuit: Under *Marascalco v. Fantasy, Inc.*, 953 F.2d 469 (9th Cir. 1991), the rule as stated in this clause should read, "provided that the author of the underlying work lives until the commencement of the renewal term."

of the *Rear Window* decision. Also safe are works in their renewal terms (e.g., songs first published prior to 1964 are in their renewal term as of 1992). Works potentially "tainted" by the *Rear Window* decision, as of 2000, are works published between 1972 and 1977. The initial year of the tainted period will become 1973 in 2001, 1974 in 2002, 1975 in 2003, and 1977 will always be the final year of this period.

A song that would otherwise be tainted because it falls inside the tainted period may have become safe if the songwriters have already died before an application for renewal registration could be filed, because a license for the renewal term can then be obtained directly from the surviving spouses and children. However, there remain many unanswered legal questions that may affect whether or not a particular song is safe from the effects of the *Rear Window* decision. If the work falls within the tainted period, the producer may wish to consider a substitute song that is safe, such as songs falling in the safe periods or songs commissioned on a works for hire basis.

Music publishers and songwriters controlling rights in songs affected by the *Rear Window* decision may actually begin to find their licensing revenue from these songs decrease as expiration of the original term of copyright approaches. With respect to songs still in their original term, where it is clear the publisher will not have the right to issue licenses covering the renewal term, music publishers find themselves unable to issue licenses that have terms that go beyond the expiration of the original copyright term. As discussed in Chapter 9, many producers are now requiring licenses that have a term of perpetuity, or at least include options to extend the term by providing notice and additional payment. If the publisher is unable to provide these terms, producers will choose to use substitutes for which such terms are available. Accordingly, music publishers and songwriters have an incentive to alleviate any impediments to producers licensing their songs affected by the *Rear Window* decision.

As noted above, when renewal copyrights revert to songwriters under the provisions of a music publishing agreement, such as under the AGAC form contract, unless the writer and the publisher enter into an arrangement allowing the publisher to issue licenses during the original term whose term may extend into the renewal term, publishing income for songs whose protection is nearing the end of the original term may decline, because producers will avoid licensing compositions for which long-term licenses are not available. It is interesting to note that, under *Rear Window*, songwriters and music publishers have no similar ability to avoid a similar decline in their publishing income arising from producers choosing to avoid licensing songs tainted by the *Rear Window* problem, because, under *Rear Window*, any such agreement would be unenforceable against the beneficiaries of the renewal copyright in the event the author should die prior to the commencement of the renewal term. Accordingly, there is some reason to doubt whether the intent of the ruling in *Rear Window* actually serves to further its purported purpose.

### b. *Effect on the Terms, If Any, Upon Which Previously Produced Derivative Works May Continue to Be Exploited*

Not all is doom and gloom for producers and other owners of derivative works containing songs whose licenses are affected by the *Rear Window* decision. It appears that the distribution of such derivative works during the renewal term probably will not be subject to court injunction. The Ninth Circuit in deciding the *Rear Window* case specifically refused to grant an injunction and the Supreme Court did not upset the lower court's ruling in that regard.[47] The issue, then, probably will be limited to how much of the proceeds from the exploitation of the derivative work will have to be paid to the author's heirs during the term of the renewal copyright.

Discussion of the variety of works affected by the *Rear Window* decision is beyond the scope of this book. Indeed, some of the most dramatic effects caused by the *Rear Window* decision have been on agreements between producers of motion pictures and television programs and the authors of the literary works that underlie them and perhaps mainframe and minicomputer software not created on a work-for-hire basis that has become contributions to other computer programs. The following section sketches some of the effects of the *Rear Window* decision on existing music licenses.

#### (1) Licenses Granted to Music Publishers

Music publishers create a variety of derivative works during the term of music publishing contracts. Such derivative works may include

---

[47] See 110 S. Ct. at 1757, 1768.

arrangements, translations, compilations, and sound recordings. Under the *Rear Window* decision, the use of music in all such derivative works will require new licenses from the renewal copyright owner.

### (2) Mechanical Licenses Granted to Record Companies

Rights reverting to renewal copyright claimants under *Rear Window* also have the effect of terminating all mechanical licenses issued during the original term of copyright. This should have no practical effect, however, to the extent the original mechanical license provided that mechanical fees were payable at the statutory rate in effect at the time phonorecords were made and distributed. If the renewal copyright owner decided to terminate the mechanical license, the derivative licensee would simply enter into a new one under the same statutory terms, or if the copyright owner refused, the derivative licensee could compel the renewal owner to issue a mechanical license at the statutory rate. However, if the mechanical license was originally issued at a *rate* (*see* Chapter 13) or otherwise provided that the fee be set at the statutory rate in effect at the time the license was entered (i.e., without the benefit of subsequent increases), then the renewal owner could obtain more favorable terms by terminating the license and renegotiating the new license at the more favorable statutory rate.

### (3) Synchronization Licenses Granted to Producers

To the extent that producers of motion pictures and television programs have used music in the soundtracks of their derivative works that is tainted by the *Rear Window* decision, new licenses for the use of such music will be required from the renewal copyright owners. To the extent that the music is replaceable (e.g., recorded on a separate track or not materially featured in the picture), the producer has increased leverage in the negotiations over obtaining the license required.

### (4) Master Licenses Granted to Producers to Use Sound Recordings

Producers of motion pictures and television programs, who have licensed sound recordings from record companies for use in their derivative works, probably do not have much to be concerned about with respect to the continued use of those recordings. This is because virtually all sound recordings are produced under work for hire contracts. Because the recording company is considered the *author* of works it commissioned on a work-for-hire basis, the recording company's license to the producer for the full term of copyright "including any renewals and extensions" will remain in full force and effect.

#### (5) Owners of Copies or Phonorecords Containing Affected Works

If a licensee whose license has been terminated upon the expiration of the original term of copyright is the lawful owner of copies (or phonorecords) of works affected by *Rear Window*, then he may still distribute or otherwise dispose of such copies. Of course, he may not produce any new copies without a license covering the renewal term.

### 5. *Effect of 1992 Act*

For works created on or after January 1, 1964, the rule of the *Rear Window* case will not apply if a renewal application is not made within one year before the expiration of the original term of copyright in such works. The Copyright Renewal Act of 1992 states:

> If an application to register a claim to the renewed and extended term of copyright in a work is not made within 1 year before the expiration of the original term of copyright in a work, or if the claim pursuant to such application is not registered, then a derivative work prepared under the authority of a grant of a transfer or license of the copyright that is made before the expiration of the original term of copyright may continue to be used under the terms of the grant during the renewed and extended term of copyright without infringing the copyright, except that such use does not extend to the preparation during such renewed and extended term of other derivative works based upon the copyrighted work covered by such grant.[48]

Thus, if the songwriter or his survivors fail to file within one year before the expiration of the original term of copyright for a work created between January 1, 1964 and December 31, 1977, then a producer's

[48] 17 U.S.C. Sec. 304 (a)(4)(B).

previous license covering the term of copyright "including any renewals or extensions thereof" will be effective during the renewal term.

### *6. Advice for Derivative Licensees*

The cost of identifying the thousands of songs tainted with the *Rear Window* problem that may be contained in previously produced motion pictures and television programs may be exorbitant. Accordingly, the producer's only practical alternative may be to simply continue distributing the pictures until a demand letter is received from a songwriter or his estate.

Leaving that alternative aside, a producer who has identified a song affected by *Rear Window* has to choose another path, such as developing a strategy for negotiating with the songwriters, or their applicable statutory beneficiaries or survivors. If the song's copyright is already in its renewal term, the producer can withdraw the picture from distribution and begin negotiating with the songwriter's survivors or executor. If the author died before his statutory beneficiaries are entitled to file a claim for renewal (i.e., before the beginning of the 28th year of the original copyright term), the producer may continue distributing the motion picture under his license for the original term while commencing negotiations with the writer's survivors or executor for a license covering the renewal term. If the author has not died yet, the producer may seek to obtain licenses covering the renewal term from the songwriter's current spouse, children, or other beneficiaries; this strategy will be effective only if the author does not subsequently remarry or have any more children before dying.

The problem with the strategies in the foregoing paragraph is that they alert the author's beneficiaries of their rights concerning renewal. As noted above, under the 1992 Act, if a renewal application is not timely made (i.e., within one year before the expiration of the original term of copyright) for a work created between January 1, 1964 and December 31, 1977, then a derivative work prepared under the authority of a grant of a license made before the expiration of the original term of copyright may continue to be used under the terms of the grant during the renewed and extended term of copyright without infringing the copyright. If the songwriter or his survivors fail to file a renewal application, then a producer's previous license covering the term of copyright "including any renewals or extensions thereof" will be effective during the renewal term.

However, if the author has not died yet, and the original license agreement gives the producer the authority to renew the author's underlying copyright, the producer should file a renewal application as soon as possible after January 1 of the 28th year of the initial term. If the author is alive when the renewal application is registered, the renewal application is effective (under the 1992 Act) even if the author dies before the 29th year copyright protection begins.

### *7. Advice for Music Publishers*

Because licensing music is the life blood of a music publisher's business, music publishers should take whatever measures are available to facilitate the licensing of music in their catalogs. Music publishers should try to identify those songs in its catalog that have been affected by the *Rear Window* decision and that previously were licensed in derivative works, such as motion pictures and television programs. If it appears that the song may revert to the author or his survivors, the publisher should attempt to attain the renewal copyright from the estate of the author, entering into contracts giving the publisher renewal expectancy interests if necessary, or obtaining exclusive administration rights to the music for the renewal term. With control of the renewal rights, the publisher can then issue the necessary licenses for the use of music in derivative works that cover the renewal term.

Barring the ability to control the renewal copyright, there is not much else the music publisher can do to alleviate the problems caused by *Rear Window*.

### *8. Advice for Songwriters*

Nor is there much songwriters can do to alleviate the adverse effect *Rear Window* may have on pre-renewal licensing revenue for songs tainted by the decision.

With respect to filing renewal applications, it has been noted that under the Renewal Copyright Act of 1992, if a renewal application is not made within one year before the expiration of the original term of copyright, then "a derivative work prepared under the authority of a grant of a transfer or license of the copyright that is made before the expiration of the original term of copyright may continue to be used under the terms of the grant during the renewed and extended term of copyright without infringing the copyright, except that such use does not extend to the preparation during such renewed and extended term of other derivative works based on the copyrighted work covered by such grant."[49] This might lead a songwriter to file a registration within the prescribed time period. However, as noted above, if filing the renewal application could cause the renewal copyright to vest in the music publisher, rather than the heirs of the songwriter, it might be best not to file the application within one year before the expiration of the original term. However, should the songwriter die during the 28th year, then his beneficiaries should strongly consider filing a renewal application subsequent to his death in order to avoid the effect of Section 304(a)(4)(B) and preserve the ability to renegotiate licenses for the use of the song in derivative works during the renewal term. When the songwriter or his beneficiaries are in a position to renegotiate licenses for use of music in derivative works during the renewal term, they should not overlook the importance of coming to an agreement to license the song in derivative works. Remember that it is unlikely that you will be able to obtain an injunction stopping the exploitation of the derivative work during the renewal term and any litigation will boil down to just determining what is a reasonable license fee. Under these circumstances, litigation will rarely be worth the costs. Further, regardless of how unreasonably low the fee being offered may seem to be in relation to what the producer may stand to gain by exploiting the derivative work (or stand to cost him if you proceed to litigation), in the long run, you will tend to make up more than the difference between what is being offered and what you think you deserve by collecting important performance royalties from exhibition on television or otherwise from maintaining an active relationship between the song and the listening public.

### *9. Licenses Covering the Extended (39-Year) Term of Copyright*

For works created before January 1, 1978, and in their first term of copyright as of December 31, 1977, a right of termination, similar to

[49] 17 U.S.C. Sec. 304 (a)(4)(B).

that provided to authors of works created after January 1, 1978 (discussed above), is provided with respect to transfers covering the newly added years extending the maximum term of copyright by 19 years, from 56 to 75 years (now, 39 years, from 56 to 95 years).[50]

The assignment of a copyright in a song created before January 1, 1978, in its original term or its renewal term of copyright, will endure until the expiration of the copyright (i.e., the 95th and final year of the life of the copyright), unless otherwise provided by the terms of the assignment agreement or unless the author (or certain statutory beneficiaries) exercises a statutory right of termination that may be effective as early as 39 years prior to the final year of the copyright. Within certain time limits, an author or specified heirs of the author are generally entitled to file a notice terminating the author's transfers covering any part of the 39-year period that has now been added to the end of the second term of copyright in a work.

If termination is not effected under the terms of the rule, then the grant of license will continue in effect for the life of the copyright or will expire sooner in accordance with any applicable provisions of the agreement effecting the grant. If the termination is properly effected, then the grant of license terminates, provided that:

> A derivative work prepared under the authority of the grant before its termination may continue to be utilized under the terms of the grant after its termination, but this privilege does not extend to the preparation after the termination of other derivative works based upon the copyrighted work covered by the terminated grant.[51] The principles established in the *Mills Music*, *Bourne*, and *Warner/Chappell* cases discussed above would all apply to refine the scope of this exception to the right of termination.

This provision is worded identically to the similar provision concerning termination of terminated grants by authors made after January 1, 1978, and has the same legal and practical effects.

[50] 17 U.S.C. Sec. 304 (c). A form for such termination is included on the CD-ROM.

[51] 17 U.S.C. Sec. 304 (c)(6)(A).

## VII. AFTER LIFE

The Sonny Bono Copyright Term Extension Act of 1998 effectively pushed back by 20 years the date on which songs were scheduled to fall into the public domain in the United States.[52] For example, songs initially published in the year 1923 that were scheduled to fall into the public domain on January 1, 1999, will now retain their copyright until January 1, 2019. To give the reader some idea of what is happening, the appendix to this chapter includes a short list of songs that are now in the public domain in the United States. Persons involved in music licensing, whether granting licenses or clearing them, should take note that an ever-increasing number of songs will be available free of charge as substitutes to be used for those purposes for which music is used.

Yes, there is life after copyright. The continuing popularity of songs that will soon enter the public domain will demonstrate that musical works are destined to maintain an active relationship with the listening public, long after the life of their copyright has expired.

[52] Note the fact that a work has fallen into the public domain in the United States does not necessarily mean that it has fallen into the public domain in other countries. Each country has its own laws regarding the duration of copyright. For example, many countries follow the "rule of the shorter term." In such a country, the duration of copyright protection will last the shorter of (i) the term of protection accorded to nationals of that country or (ii) the term of protection accorded to the work in the home country of the work's author. Thus, if the copyright in a work has expired in the United States, it will not be protected in a country that follows the rule of the shorter term, even if that country provides a longer term of protection for its own citizens. However, because several significant countries (including the United Kingdom and Canada) do not follow the rule of the shorter term, an independent analysis must be made of the status of copyright for each country in which a user desires to exploit the work.

# Appendix to Chapter 9
# Duration of Copyright, Assignments of Copyright, and Licenses

## Laws and Regulations



## Lists



## Forms (On CD-Rom Only)

# LAW 9.1

## U.S. COPYRIGHT ACT — SECTION 203 TERMINATION OF TRANSFERS AND LICENSES GRANTED BY AUTHOR

## Chapter 2

## Copyright Ownership and Transfer

## §201 · Ownership of copyright[1]

(a) INITIAL OWNERSHIP.—Copyright in a work protected under this title vests initially in the author or authors of the work. The authors of a joint work are coowners of copyright in the work.

(b) WORKS MADE FOR HIRE.—In the case of a work made for hire, the employer or other person for whom the work was prepared is considered the author for purposes of this title, and, unless the parties have expressly agreed otherwise in a written instrument signed by them, owns all of the rights comprised in the copyright.

(c) CONTRIBUTIONS TO COLLECTIVE WORKS.—Copyright in each separate contribution to a collective work is distinct from copyright in the collective work as a whole, and vests initially in the author of the contribution. In the absence of an express transfer of the copyright or of any rights under it, the owner of copyright in the collective work is presumed to have acquired only the privilege of reproducing and distributing the contribution as part of that particular collective work, any revision of that collective work, and any later collective work in the same series.

(d) TRANSFER OF OWNERSHIP.—

(1) The ownership of a copyright may be transferred in whole or in part by any means of conveyance or by operation of law, and may be bequeathed by will or pass as personal property by the applicable laws of intestate succession.

(2) Any of the exclusive rights comprised in a copyright, including any subdivision of any of the rights specified by section 106, may be transferred as provided by clause (1) and owned separately. The owner of any particular exclusive right is entitled, to the extent of that right, to all of the protection and remedies accorded to the copyright owner by this title.

(e) INVOLUNTARY TRANSFER.—When an individual author's ownership of a copyright, or of any of the exclusive rights under a copyright, has not previously been transferred voluntarily by that individual author, no action by any governmental body or other official or organization purporting to seize, expropriate, transfer, or exercise rights of ownership with respect to the copyright, or any of the exclusive rights under a copyright, shall be given effect under this title, except as provided under title 11.[2]

## §202 · Ownership of copyright as distinct from ownership of material object

Ownership of a copyright, or of any of the exclusive rights under a copyright, is distinct from ownership of any material object in which the work is embodied. Transfer of ownership of any material object, including the copy or phonorecord in which the work is first fixed, does not of itself convey any rights in the copyrighted work embodied in the object; nor, in the absence of an agreement, does transfer of ownership of a copyright or of any exclusive rights under a copyright convey property rights in any material object.

### § 203 · Termination of transfers and licenses granted by the author[3]

(a) CONDITIONS FOR TERMINATION.—In the case of any work other than a work made for hire, the exclusive or nonexclusive grant of a transfer or license of copyright or of any right under a copyright, executed by the author on or after January 1, 1978, otherwise than by will, is subject to termination under the following conditions:

(1) In the case of a grant executed by one author, termination of the grant may be effected by that author or, if the author is dead, by the person or persons who, under clause (2) of this subsection, own and are entitled to exercise a total of more than one-half of that author's termination interest. In the case of a grant executed by two or more authors of a joint work, termination of the grant may be effected by a majority of the authors who executed it; if any of such authors is dead, the termination interest of any such author may be exercised as a unit by the person or persons who, under clause (2) of this subsection, own and are entitled to exercise a total of more than one-half of that author's interest.

(2) Where an author is dead, his or her termination interest is owned, and may be exercised, as follows:

(A) The widow or widower owns the author's entire termination interest unless there are any surviving children or grandchildren of the author, in which case the widow or widower owns one-half of the author's interest.

(B) The author's surviving children, and the surviving children of any dead child of the author, own the author's entire termination interest unless there is a widow or widower, in which case the ownership of one-half of the author's interest is divided among them.

(C) The rights of the author's children and grandchildren are in all cases divided among them and exercised on a per stirpes basis according to the number of such author's children represented; the share of the children of a dead child in a termination interest can be exercised only by the action of a majority of them.

(D) In the event that the author's widow or widower, children, and grandchildren are not living, the author's executor, administrator, personal representative, or trustee shall own the author's entire termination interest.

(3) Termination of the grant may be effected at any time during a period of five years beginning at the end of thirty-five years from the date of execution

of the grant; or, if the grant covers the right of publication of the work, the period begins at the end of thirty-five years from the date of publication of the work under the grant or at the end of forty years from the date of execution of the grant, whichever term ends earlier.

(4) The termination shall be effected by serving an advance notice in writing, signed by the number and proportion of owners of termination interests required under clauses (1) and (2) of this subsection, or by their duly authorized agents, upon the grantee or the grantee's successor in title.

(A) The notice shall state the effective date of the termination, which shall fall within the five-year period specified by clause (3) of this subsection, and the notice shall be served not less than two or more than ten years before that date. A copy of the notice shall be recorded in the Copyright Office before the effective date of termination, as a condition to its taking effect.

(B) The notice shall comply, in form, content, and manner of service, with requirements that the Register of Copyrights shall prescribe by regulation.

(5) Termination of the grant may be effected notwithstanding any agreement to the contrary, including an agreement to make a will or to make any future grant.

(b) EFFECT OF TERMINATION.—Upon the effective date of termination, all rights under this title that were covered by the terminated grants revert to the author, authors, and other persons owning termination interests under clauses (1) and (2) of subsection (a), including those owners who did not join in signing the notice of termination under clause (4) of subsection (a), but with the following limitations:

(1) A derivative work prepared under authority of the grant before its termination may continue to be utilized under the terms of the grant after its termination, but this privilege does not extend to the preparation after the termination of other derivative works based upon the copyrighted work covered by the terminated grant.

(2) The future rights that will revert upon termination of the grant become vested on the date the notice of termination has been served as provided by clause (4) of subsection (a). The rights vest in the author, authors, and other persons named in, and in the proportionate shares provided by, clauses (1) and (2) of subsection (a).

(3) Subject to the provisions of clause (4) of this subsection, a further grant, or agreement to make a further grant, of any right covered by a terminated grant is valid only if it is signed by the same number and proportion of the owners, in whom the right has vested under clause (2) of this subsection, as are required to terminate the grant under clauses (1) and (2) of subsection (a). Such further grant or agreement is effective with respect to all of the persons in whom the right it covers has vested under clause (2) of this subsection, including those who did not join in signing it. If any person dies after rights under a

terminated grant have vested in him or her, that person's legal representatives, legatees, or heirs at law represent him or her for purposes of this clause.

(4) A further grant, or agreement to make a further grant, of any right covered by a terminated grant is valid only if it is made after the effective date of the termination. As an exception, however, an agreement for such a further grant may be made between the persons provided by clause (3) of this subsection and the original grantee or such grantee's successor in title, after the notice of termination has been served as provided by clause (4) of subsection (a).

(5) Termination of a grant under this section affects only those rights covered by the grants that arise under this title, and in no way affects rights arising under any other Federal, State, or foreign laws.

(6) Unless and until termination is effected under this section, the grant, if it does not provide otherwise, continues in effect for the term of copyright provided by this title.

## § 204 · Execution of transfers of copyright ownership

(a) A transfer of copyright ownership, other than by operation of law, is not valid unless an instrument of conveyance, or a note or memorandum of the transfer, is in writing and signed by the owner of the rights conveyed or such owner's duly authorized agent.

(b) A certificate of acknowledgment is not required for the validity of a transfer, but is prima facie evidence of the execution of the transfer if—

(1) in the case of a transfer executed in the United States, the certificate is issued by a person authorized to administer oaths within the United States; or

(2) in the case of a transfer executed in a foreign country, the certificate is issued by a diplomatic or consular officer of the United States, or by a person authorized to administer oaths whose authority is proved by a certificate of such an officer.

## § 205 · Recordation of transfers and other documents[4]

(a) CONDITIONS FOR RECORDATION.—Any transfer of copyright ownership or other document pertaining to a copyright may be recorded in the Copyright Office if the document filed for recordation bears the actual signature of the person who executed it, or if it is accompanied by a sworn or official certification that it is a true copy of the original, signed document.

(b) CERTIFICATE OF RECORDATION.—The Register of Copyrights shall, upon receipt of a document as provided by subsection (a) and of the fee provided by section 708, record the document and return it with a certificate of recordation.

(c) RECORDATION AS CONSTRUCTIVE NOTICE.—Recordation of a document in the Copyright Office gives all persons constructive notice of the facts stated in the recorded document, but only if—

(1) the document, or material attached to it, specifically identifies the work to which it pertains so that, after the document is indexed by the Register of Copyrights, it would be revealed by a reasonable search under the title or registration number of the work; and

(2) registration has been made for the work.

(d) PRIORITY BETWEEN CONFLICTING TRANSFERS.—As between two conflicting transfers, the one executed first prevails if it is recorded, in the manner required to give constructive notice under subsection (c), within one month after its execution in the United States or within two months after its execution outside the United States, or at any time before recordation in such manner of the later transfer. Otherwise the later transfer prevails if recorded first in such manner, and if taken in good faith, for valuable consideration or on the basis of a binding promise to pay royalties, and without notice of the earlier transfer.

(e) PRIORITY BETWEEN CONFLICTING TRANSFER OF OWNERSHIP AND NONEXCLUSIVE LICENSE.—A nonexclusive license, whether recorded or not, prevails over a conflicting transfer of copyright ownership if the license is evidenced by a written instrument signed by the owner of the rights licensed or such owner's duly authorized agent, and if

(1) the license was taken before execution of the transfer; or

(2) the license was taken in good faith before recordation of the transfer and without notice of it.

## Chapter 2 · Endnotes

1. In 1978, section 201(e) was amended by deleting the period at the end and adding ", except as provided under title 11."

2. Title 11 of the *United States Code* is entitled "Bankruptcy."

3. In 1998, the Sonny Bono Copyright Term Extension Act amended section 203 by deleting "by his widow or her widower and his or her grandchildren" from the first sentence in paragraph (2) of subsection (a) and by adding subparagraph (D) to paragraph (2). Pub. L. No. 105-298, 112 Stat. 2827, 2829.

4. The Berne Convention Implementation Act of 1988 amended section 205 by deleting subsection (d) and redesignating subsections (e) and (f) as subsections (d) and (e), respectively. Pub. L. No. 100-568, 102 Stat. 2853, 2857.

# LAW 9.2

## U.S. COPYRIGHT ACT — SECTION 304 DURATION OF COPYRIGHT: SUBSISTING COPYRIGHT

## Chapter 3[1]

## Duration of Copyright

SECTION

## §301 · Preemption with respect to other laws[2]

(a) On and after January 1, 1978, all legal or equitable rights that are equivalent to any of the exclusive rights within the general scope of copyright as specified by section 106 in works of authorship that are fixed in a tangible medium of expression and come within the subject matter of copyright as specified by sections 102 and 103, whether created before or after that date and whether published or unpublished, are governed exclusively by this title. Thereafter, no person is entitled to any such right or equivalent right in any such work under the common law or statutes of any State.

(b) Nothing in this title annuls or limits any rights or remedies under the common law or statutes of any State with respect to—

(1) subject matter that does not come within the subject matter of copyright as specified by sections 102 and 103, including works of authorship not fixed in any tangible medium of expression; or

(2) any cause of action arising from undertakings commenced before January 1, 1978;

(3) activities violating legal or equitable rights that are not equivalent to any of the exclusive rights within the general scope of copyright as specified by section 106; or

(4) State and local landmarks, historic preservation, zoning, or building codes, relating to architectural works protected under section 102(a)(8).

(c) With respect to sound recordings fixed before February 15, 1972, any rights or remedies under the common law or statutes of any State shall not be annulled or limited by this title until February 15, 2067. The preemptive provisions of subsection (a) shall apply to any such rights and remedies pertaining to any cause of action arising from undertakings commenced on and after February 15, 2067. Notwithstanding the provisions of section 303, no sound recording fixed before February 15, 1972, shall be subject to copyright under this title before, on, or after February 15, 2067.

(d) Nothing in this title annuls or limits any rights or remedies under any other Federal statute.

(e) The scope of Federal preemption under this section is not affected by the adherence of the United States to the Berne Convention or the satisfaction of obligations of the United States thereunder.

(f)(1) On or after the effective date set forth in section 610(a) of the Visual Artists Rights Act of 1990, all legal or equitable rights that are equivalent to any of the rights conferred by section 106A with respect to works of visual art to which the rights conferred by section 106A apply are governed exclusively by section 106A and section 113(d) and the provisions of this title relating to such sections. Thereafter, no person is entitled to any such right or equivalent right in any work of visual art under the common law or statutes of any State.[3]

(2) Nothing in paragraph (1) annuls or limits any rights or remedies under the common law or statutes of any State with respect to—

(A) any cause of action from undertakings commenced before the effective date set forth in section 610(a) of the Visual Artists Rights Act of 1990;

(B) activities violating legal or equitable rights that are not equivalent to any of the rights conferred by section 106A with respect to works of visual art; or

(C) activities violating legal or equitable rights which extend beyond the life of the author.

## §302 · Duration of copyright: Works created on or after January 1, 1978[4]

(a) IN GENERAL.—Copyright in a work created on or after January 1, 1978, subsists from its creation and, except as provided by the following subsections, endures for a term consisting of the life of the author and 70 years after the author's death.

(b) JOINT WORKS.—In the case of a joint work prepared by two or more authors who did not work for hire, the copyright endures for a term consisting of the life of the last surviving author and 70 years after such last surviving author's death.

(c) ANONYMOUS WORKS, PSEUDONYMOUS WORKS, AND WORKS MADE FOR HIRE.—In the case of an anonymous work, a pseudonymous work, or a work made for hire, the copyright endures for a term of 95 years from the year of its first publication, or a term of 120 years from the year of its creation, whichever expires first. If, before the end of such term, the identity of one or more of the authors of an anonymous or pseudonymous work is revealed in the records of a registration made for that work under subsections (a) or (d) of section 408, or in the records provided by this subsection, the copyright in the work endures for the term specified by subsection (a) or (b), based on the life of the author or authors whose identity has been revealed. Any person having an interest in the copyright in an anonymous or pseudonymous work may at any time record, in records to be maintained by the Copyright Office for that purpose, a statement identifying one or more authors of the work; the statement shall also identify the person filing it, the nature of that person's interest, the source of the information recorded, and the particular work affected, and shall comply in form and content with requirements that the Register of Copyrights shall prescribe by regulation.

(d) RECORDS RELATING TO DEATH OF AUTHORS.—Any person having an interest in a copyright may at any time record in the Copyright Office a statement of the date of death of the author of the copyrighted work, or a statement that the author is still living on a particular date. The statement shall identify the person filing it, the nature of that person's interest, and the source of the information recorded, and shall comply in form and content with requirements that the Register of Copyrights shall prescribe by regulation. The Register shall maintain current records of information relating to the death of authors of copyrighted works, based on such recorded statements and, to the extent the Register considers practicable, on data contained in any of the records of the Copyright Office or in other reference sources.

(e) PRESUMPTION AS TO AUTHOR'S DEATH.—After a period of 95 years from the year of first publication of a work, or a period of 120 years from the year of its creation, whichever expires first, any person who obtains from the Copyright Office a certified report that the records provided by subsection (d) disclose nothing to indicate that the author of the work is living, or died less than 70 years before, is entitled to the benefit of a presumption that the author has been dead for at least 70 years. Reliance in good faith upon this presumption shall be a complete defense to any action for infringement under this title.

## §303 · Duration of copyright: Works created but not published or copyrighted before January 1, 1978[5]

(a) Copyright in a work created before January 1, 1978, but not theretofore in the public domain or copyrighted, subsists from January 1, 1978, and endures for the term provided by section 302. In no case, however, shall the term of copyright in such a work expire before December 31, 2002; and, if the work is published on or before December 31, 2002, the term of copyright shall not expire before December 31, 2047.

(b) The distribution before January 1, 1978, of a phonorecord shall not for any purpose constitute a publication of the musical work embodied therein.

## §304 · Duration of copyright: Subsisting copyrights[6]

(a) COPYRIGHTS IN THEIR FIRST TERM ON JANUARY 1, 1978.—

(1)(A) Any copyright, in the first term of which is subsisting on January 1, 1978, shall endure for 28 years from the date it was originally secured.

(B) In the case of—

(i) any posthumous work or of any periodical, cyclopedic, or other composite work upon which the copyright was originally secured by the proprietor thereof, or

(ii) any work copyrighted by a corporate body (otherwise than as assignee or licensee of the individual author) or by an employer for whom such work is made for hire, the proprietor of such copyright shall be entitled to a renewal and extension of the copyright in such work for the further term of 67 years.

(C) In the case of any other copyrighted work, including a contribution by an individual author to a periodical or to a cyclopedic or other composite work—

(i) the author of such work, if the author is still living,

(ii) the widow, widower, or children of the author, if the author is not living,

(iii) the author's executors, if such author, widow, widower, or children are not living, or

(iv) the author's next of kin, in the absence of a will of the author, shall be entitled to a renewal and extension of the copyright in such work for a further term of 67 years.

(2)(A) At the expiration of the original term of copyright in a work specified in paragraph (1)(B) of this subsection, the copyright shall endure for a renewed and extended further term of 67 years, which—

(i) if an application to register a claim to such further term has been made to the Copyright Office within 1 year before the expiration of the original term of copyright, and the claim is registered, shall vest, upon the beginning of such further term, in the proprietor of the copyright who is entitled to claim the renewal of copyright at the time the application is made; or

(ii) if no such application is made or the claim pursuant to such application is not registered, shall vest, upon the beginning of such further term, in the person or entity that was the proprietor of the copyright as of the last day of the original term of copyright.

(B) At the expiration of the original term of copyright in a work specified in paragraph (1)(C) of this subsection, the copyright shall endure for a renewed and extended further term of 67 years, which—

(i) if an application to register a claim to such further term has been made to the Copyright Office within 1 year before the expiration of the original term of copyright, and the claim is registered, shall vest, upon the beginning of such further term, in any person who is entitled under paragraph (1)(C) to the renewal and extension of the copyright at the time the application is made; or

(ii) if no such application is made or the claim pursuant to such application is not registered, shall vest, upon the beginning of such further term, in any person entitled under paragraph (1)(C), as of the last day of the original term of copyright, to the renewal and extension of the copyright.

(3)(A) An application to register a claim to the renewed and extended term of copyright in a work may be made to the Copyright Office—

(i) within 1 year before the expiration of the original term of copyright by any person entitled under paragraph (1)(B) or (C) to such further term of 67 years; and

(ii) at any time during the renewed and extended term by any person in whom such further term vested, under paragraph (2)(A) or (B), or by any successor or assign of such person, if the application is made in the name of such person.

(B) Such an application is not a condition of the renewal and extension of the copyright in a work for a further term of 67 years.

(4)(A) If an application to register a claim to the renewed and extended term of copyright in a work is not made within 1 year before the expiration of the original term of copyright in a work, or if the claim pursuant to such application is not registered, then a derivative work prepared under authority of a grant of a transfer or license of the copyright that is made before the expiration of the original term of copyright may continue to be used under the terms of the grant during the renewed and extended term of copyright without infringing the copyright, except that such use does not extend to the preparation during such renewed and extended term of other derivative works based upon the copyrighted work covered by such grant.

(B) If an application to register a claim to the renewed and extended term of copyright in a work is made within 1 year before its expiration, and the claim is registered, the certificate of such registration shall constitute prima facie evidence as to the validity of the copyright during its renewed and extended term and of the facts stated in the certificate. The evidentiary weight to be accorded the certificates of a registration of a renewed and extended term of copyright made after the end of that 1-year period shall be within the discretion of the court.

(b) COPYRIGHTS IN THEIR RENEWAL TERM AT THE TIME OF THE EFFECTIVE DATE OF THE SONNY BONO COPYRIGHT TERM EXTENSION ACT[7]—Any copyright still in its renewal term at the time that the Sonny Bono Copyright Term Extension Act becomes effective shall have a copyright term of 95 years from the date copyright was originally secured.[8]

(c) TERMINATION OF TRANSFERS AND LICENSES COVERING EXTENDED RENEWAL TERM.—In the case of any copyright subsisting in either its first or renewal term on January 1, 1978, other than a copyright in a work made for hire, the exclusive or nonexclusive grant of a transfer or license of the renewal copyright or any right under it, executed before January 1, 1978, by any of the persons designated by subsection (a)(1)(C) of this section, otherwise than by will, is subject to termination under the following conditions:

(1) In the case of a grant executed by a person or persons other than the author, termination of the grant may be effected by the surviving person or persons who executed it. In the case of a grant executed by one or more of the

authors of the work, termination of the grant may be effected, to the extent of a particular author's share in the ownership of the renewal copyright, by the author who executed it or, if such author is dead, by the person or persons who, under clause (2) of this subsection, own and are entitled to exercise a total of more than one-half of that author's termination interest.

(2) Where an author is dead, his or her termination interest is owned, and may be exercised, as follows:

(A) The widow or widower owns the author's entire termination interest unless there are any surviving children or grandchildren of the author, in which case the widow or widower owns one-half of the author's interest.

(B) The author's surviving children, and the surviving children of any dead child of the author, own the author's entire termination interest unless there is a widow or widower, in which case the ownership of one-half of the author's interest is divided among them.

(C) The rights of the author's children and grandchildren are in all cases divided among them and exercised on a per stirpes basis according to the number of such author's children represented; the share of the children of a dead child in a termination interest can be exercised only by the action of a majority of them.

(D) In the event that the author's widow or widower, children, and grandchildren are not living, the author's executor, administrator, personal representative, or trustee shall own the author's entire termination interest.

(3) Termination of the grant may be effected at any time during a period of five years beginning at the end of fifty-six years from the date copyright was originally secured, or beginning on January 1, 1978, whichever is later.

(4) The termination shall be effected by serving an advance notice in writing upon the grantee or the grantee's successor in title. In the case of a grant executed by a person or persons other than the author, the notice shall be signed by all of those entitled to terminate the grant under clause (1) of this subsection, or by their duly authorized agents. In the case of a grant executed by one or more of the authors of the work, the notice as to any one author's share shall be signed by that author or his or her duly authorized agent or, if that author is dead, by the number and proportion of the owners of his or her termination interest required under clauses (1) and (2) of this subsection, or by their duly authorized agents.

(A) The notice shall state the effective date of the termination, which shall fall within the five-year period specified by clause (3) of this subsection, or, in the case of a termination under subsection (d), within the five-year period specified by subsection (d)(2), and the notice shall be served not less than two or more than ten years before that date. A copy of the notice shall be recorded in the Copyright Office before the effective date of termination, as a condition to its taking effect.

(B) The notice shall comply, in form, content, and manner of service, with requirements that the Register of Copyrights shall prescribe by regulation.

(5) Termination of the grant may be effected notwithstanding any agreement to the contrary, including an agreement to make a will or to make any future grant.

(6) In the case of a grant executed by a person or persons other than the author, all rights under this title that were covered by the terminated grant revert, upon the effective date of termination, to all of those entitled to terminate the grant under clause (1) of this subsection. In the case of a grant executed by one or more of the authors of the work, all of a particular author's rights under this title that were covered by the terminated grant revert, upon the effective date of termination, to that author or, if that author is dead, to the persons owning his or her termination interest under clause (2) of this subsection, including those owners who did not join in signing the notice of termination under clause (4) of this subsection. In all cases the reversion of rights is subject to the following limitations:

(A) A derivative work prepared under authority of the grant before its termination may continue to be utilized under the terms of the grant after its termination, but this privilege does not extend to the preparation after the termination of other derivative works based upon the copyrighted work covered by the terminated grant.

(B) The future rights that will revert upon termination of the grant become vested on the date the notice of termination has been served as provided by clause (4) of this subsection.

(C) Where the author's rights revert to two or more persons under clause (2) of this subsection, they shall vest in those persons in the proportionate shares provided by that clause. In such a case, and subject to the provisions of subclause (D) of this clause, a further grant, or agreement to make a further grant, of a particular author's share with respect to any right covered by a terminated grant is valid only if it is signed by the same number and proportion of the owners, in whom the right has vested under this clause, as are required to terminate the grant under clause (2) of this subsection. Such further grant or agreement is effective with respect to all of the persons in whom the right it covers has vested under this subclause, including those who did not join in signing it. If any person dies after rights under a terminated grant have vested in him or her, that person's legal representatives, legatees, or heirs at law represent him or her for purposes of this subclause.

(D) A further grant, or agreement to make a further grant, of any right covered by a terminated grant is valid only if it is made after the effective date of the termination. As an exception, however, an agreement for such a further grant may be made between the author or any of the persons provided by the first sentence of clause (6) of this subsection, or between the persons provided by subclause (C) of this clause, and the original grantee or such grantee's successor in title, after the notice of termination has been served as provided by clause (4) of this subsection.

(E) Termination of a grant under this subsection affects only those rights covered by the grant that arise under this title, and in no way affects rights arising under any other Federal, State, or foreign laws.

(F) Unless and until termination is effected under this subsection, the grant, if it does not provide otherwise, continues in effect for the remainder of the extended renewal term.

(d) TERMINATION RIGHTS PROVIDED IN SUBSECTION (c) WHICH HAVE EXPIRED ON OR BEFORE THE EFFECTIVE DATE OF THE SONNY BONO COPYRIGHT TERM EXTENSION ACT.—In the case of any copyright other than a work made for hire, subsisting in its renewal term on the effective date of the Sonny Bono Copyright Term Extension Act[9] for which the termination right provided in subsection (c) has expired by such date, where the author or owner of the termination right has not previously exercised such termination right, the exclusive or nonexclusive grant of a transfer or license of the renewal copyright or any right under it, executed before January 1, 1978, by any of the persons designated in subsection (a)(1)(C) of this section, other than by will, is subject to termination under the following conditions:

(1) The conditions specified in subsections (c) (1), (2), (4), (5), and (6) of this section apply to terminations of the last 20 years of copyright term as provided by the amendments made by the Sonny Bono Copyright Term Extension Act.

(2) Termination of the grant may be effected at any time during a period of 5 years beginning at the end of 75 years from the date copyright was originally secured.

## §305 · Duration of copyright: Terminal date

All terms of copyright provided by sections 302 through 304 run to the end of the calendar year in which they would otherwise expire.

## Chapter 3 · Endnotes

1. Private Law 92-60, 85 Stat. 857, effective December 15, 1971, states that:

[A]ny provision of law to the contrary notwithstanding, copyright is hereby granted to the trustees under the will of Mary Baker Eddy, their successors, and assigns, in the work "Science and Health with Key to the Scriptures" (entitled also in some editions "Science and Health" or "Science and Health; with a Key to the Scriptures"), by Mary Baker Eddy, including all editions thereof in English and translation heretofore published, or hereafter published by or on behalf of said trustees, their successors or assigns, for a term of seventy-five years from the effective date of this Act or from the date of first publication, whichever is later.

But *cf. United Christian Scientists* v. *Christian Science Board of Directors, First Church of Christ, Scientist*, 829 F.2d 1152, 4 USPQ2d 1177 (D.C. Cir. 1987) (holding Priv. L. 92-60, 85 Stat. 857, to be unconstitutional because it violates the Establishment Clause).

2. The Berne Convention Implementation Act of 1988 amended section 301 by adding at the end thereof subsection (e). Pub. L. No. 100-568, 102 Stat. 2853, 2857. In 1990, the Architectural Works Copyright Protection Act amended section 301(b) by adding at the end thereof paragraph (4). Pub. L. No. 101-650, 104 Stat. 5133, 5134. The Visual Artists Rights Act of 1990 amended section 301 by adding at the end thereof subsection (f). Pub. L. No. 101-650, 104 Stat. 5089, 5131. In 1998, the Sonny Bono Copyright Term Extension Act amended section 301 by changing "February 15, 2047" to "February 15, 2067" each place it appeared in subsection (c). Pub. L. No. 105-298, 112 Stat. 2827.

3. The Visual Artists Rights Act of 1990, which added subsection (f), states, "Subject to subsection (b) and except as provided in subsection (c), this title and the amendments made by this title take effect 6 months after the date of the enactment of this Act," that is, 6 months after December 1, 1990. Pub. L. No. 101-650, 104 Stat. 5089, 5132. See also endnote 39, chapter 1.

4. In 1998, the Sonny Bono Copyright Term Extension Act amended section 302 by substituting "70" for "fifty," "95" for "seventy-five," and "120" for "one hundred" each place they appeared. Pub. L. No. 105-298, 112 Stat. 2827. This change was effective October 27, 1998. *Id.*

5. In 1997, section 303 was amended by adding subsection (b). Pub. L. No. 105-80, 111 Stat. 1529, 1534. In 1998, the Sonny Bono Copyright Term Extension Act amended section 303 by substituting "December 31, 2047" for "December 31, 2027." Pub. L. No. 105-298, 112 Stat. 2827.

6. The Copyright Renewal Act of 1992 amended section 304 by substituting a new subsection (a) and by making a conforming amendment in the matter preceding paragraph (1) of subsection (c). Pub. L. No. 102-307, 106 Stat. 264. The Act, as amended by the Sonny Bono Copyright Term Extension Act, states that the renewal and extension of a copyright for a further term of 67 years "shall have the same effect with respect to any grant, before the effective date of the Sonny Bono Copyright Term Extension Act [October 27, 1998], of a transfer or license of the further term as did the renewal of a copyright before the effective date of the Sonny Bono Copyright Term Extension Act [October 27, 1998] under the law in effect at the time of such grant." The Act also states that the 1992 amendments "shall apply only to those copyrights secured between January 1, 1964, and December 31, 1977. Copyrights secured before January 1, 1964, shall be governed by the provisions of section 304(a) of title 17, United States Code, as in effect on the day before … [enactment on June 26, 1992], except each reference to forty-seven years in such provisions shall be deemed to be 67 years." Pub. L. No. 102-307, 106 Stat. 264, 266, as amended by the Sonny Bono Copyright Term Extension Act, Pub. L. No. 105-298, 112 Stat. 2827, 2828.

In 1998, the Sonny Bono Copyright Term Extension Act amended section 304 by substituting "67" for "47" wherever it appeared in subsection (a), by substituting a new subsection (b), and by adding subsection (d) at the end thereof. Pub. L. No. 105-298, 112 Stat. 2827. That

Act also amended subsection 304(c) by deleting "by his widow or her widower and his or her children or grandchildren" from the first sentence of paragraph (2), by adding subparagraph (D) at the end of paragraph (2), and by inserting "or, in the case of a termination under subsection (d), within the five-year period specified by subsection (d)(2)," into the first sentence of subparagraph (4)(A). *Id.*

7. In 1998, the Sonny Bono Copyright Term Extension Act amendment to subsection 304(b) completely deleted the previous language that was originally part of the 1976 Copyright Act. Pub. L. No. 105-298, 112 Stat. 2827. That earlier statutory language continues to be relevant for calculating the term of protection for copyrights commencing between September 19, 1906, and December 31, 1949. The 1976 Copyright Act extended the terms for those copyrights by 20 years, provided they were in their renewal term between December 31, 1976, and December 31, 1977. The deleted language states:

The duration of any copyright, the renewal term of which is subsisting at any time between December 31, 1976, and December 31, 1977, inclusive, or for which renewal registration is made between December 31, 1976, and December 31, 1977, inclusive, is extended to endure for a term of seventy-five years from the date copyright was originally secured.

The effective date of this provision was October 19, 1976. That effective date provision is contained in Appendix A, herein, as section 102 of the Transitional and Supplementary Provisions of the Copyright Act of 1976. Copyright Act of 1976, Pub. L. No. 94-553, 90 Stat. 2541, 2598.

In addition, prior to the 1976 Copyright Act, Congress enacted a series of nine interim extensions for works whose copyright protection began between September 19, 1906, and December 31, 1918, if they were in their renewal terms. Without these interim extensions, copyrights commencing during that time period would have otherwise expired after 56 years, at the end of their renewal terms, between September 19, 1962, and December 31, 1976. The nine Acts authorizing the interim extensions are as follows, in chronological order:

Pub. L. No. 87-668, 76 Stat. 555 (extending copyrights from September 19, 1962, to December 31, 1965)
Pub. L. No. 89-142, 79 Stat. 581 (extending copyrights to December 31, 1967)
Pub. L. No. 90-141, 81 Stat. 464 (extending copyrights to December 31, 1968)
Pub. L. No. 90-416, 82 Stat. 397 (extending copyrights to December 31, 1969)
Pub. L. No. 91-147, 83 Stat. 360 (extending copyrights to December 31, 1970)
Pub. L. No. 91-555, 84 Stat. 1441 (extending copyrights to December 31, 1971)
Pub. L. No. 92-170, 85 Stat. 490 (extending copyrights to December 31, 1972)
Pub. L. No. 92-566, 86 Stat. 1181 (extending copyrights to December 31, 1974)
Pub. L. No. 93-573, 88 Stat. 1873 (extending copyrights to December 31, 1976)

8. The effective date of the Sonny Bono Copyright Term Extension Act is October 27, 1998.
9. See endnote 8, *supra*.

# LAW 9.3

## U.S. COPYRIGHT OFFICE REGULATIONS ON NOTICES OF TERMINATION OF TRANSFERS AND LICENSES UNDER SECTIONS 203 AND 304 OF THE COPYRIGHT ACT

### § 201.10 Notices of Termination of Transfers and Licenses.

This section covers notices of termination of transfers and licenses under sections 203, 304(c) and 304(d) of title 17, of the United States Code. A termination under section 304(d) is possible only if no termination was made under section 304(c), and federal copyright was originally secured on or between January 1, 1923, and October 26, 1939.

(a) *Form.* The Copyright Office does not provide printed forms for the use of persons serving notices of termination.

(b) *Contents.*

(1) A notice of termination covering the extended renewal term under sections 304(c) and 304(d) of title 17, U.S.C., must include a clear identification of each of the following:

(i) Whether the termination is made under section 304(c) or under section 304(d);

(ii) The name of each grantee whose rights are being terminated, or the grantee's successor in title, and each address at which service of the notice is being made;

(iii) The title and the name of at least one author of, and the date copyright was originally secured in, each work to which the notice of termination applies; and, if possible and practicable, the original copyright registration number;

(iv) A brief statement reasonably identifying the grant to which the notice of termination applies;

(v) The effective date of termination;

(vi) If termination is made under section 304(d), a statement that termination of renewal term rights under section 304(c) has not been previously exercised; and

(vii) In the case of a termination of a grant executed by a person or persons other than the author, a listing of the surviving person or persons who executed the grant. In the case of a termination of a grant executed by one or more of the authors of the work where the termination is exercised by the successors of a deceased author, a listing of the names and relationships to that deceased author of all of the following, together with specific indication of the person or persons executing the notice who constitute more than one-half of that author's termination interest: That author's surviving widow or widower; and all of that author's surviving children; and, where any of that author's children are dead, all of the surviving children of any such deceased child of that author; however, instead of the information required by this paragraph (vii), the notice may contain both of the following:

(A) A statement of as much of such information as is currently available to the person or persons signing the notice, with a brief explanation of the reasons why full information is or may be lacking; together with

(B) A statement that, to the best knowledge and belief of the person or persons signing the notice, the notice has been signed by all persons whose signature is necessary to terminate the grant under section 304 of title 17, U.S.C., or by their duly authorized agents.

(2) A notice of termination of an exclusive or nonexclusive grant of a transfer or license of copyright or of any right under a copyright, executed by the author on or after January 1, 1978, under section 203 of title 17, U.S.C., must include a clear identification of each of the following:

(i) A statement that the termination is made under section 203;

(ii) The name of each grantee whose rights are being terminated, or the grantee's successor in title, and each address at which service of the notice is being made;

(iii) The date of execution of the grant being terminated and, if the grant covered the right of publication of a work, the date of publication of the work under the grant;

(iv) For each work to which the notice of termination applies, the title of the work and the name of the author or, in the case of a joint work, the authors who executed the grant being terminated; and, if possible and practicable, the original copyright registration number;

(v) A brief statement reasonably identifying the grant to which the notice of termination applies;

(vi) The effective date of termination; and

(vii) In the case of a termination of a grant executed by one or more of the authors of the work where the termination is exercised by the successors of a deceased author, a listing of the names and relationships to that deceased author of all of the following, together with specific indication of the person or persons executing the notice who constitute more than one-half of that author's termination interest: That author's surviving widow or widower; and all of that author's surviving children; and, where any of that author's children are dead, all of the surviving children of any such deceased child of that author; however, instead of the information required by this paragraph (b)(2)(vii), the notice may contain both of the following:

(A) A statement of as much of such information as is currently available to the person or persons signing the notice, with a brief explanation of the reasons why full information is or may be lacking; together with

(B) A statement that, to the best knowledge and belief of the person or persons signing the notice, the notice has been signed by all persons whose signature is necessary to terminate the grant under section 203 of title 17, U.S.C., or by their duly authorized agents.

(3) Clear identification of the information specified by paragraphs (b)(1) and (b)(2) of this section requires a complete and unambiguous statement of facts in the notice itself, without incorporation by reference of information in other documents or records.

(c) *Signature.*

(1) In the case of a termination of a grant under section 304(c) or section 304(d) executed by a person or persons other than

the author, the notice shall be signed by all of the surviving person or persons who executed the grant, or by their duly authorized agents.

(2) In the case of a termination of a grant under section 304(c) or section 304(d) executed by one or more of the authors of the work, the notice as to any one author's share shall be signed by that author or by his or her duly authorized agent. If that author is dead, the notice shall be signed by the number and proportion of the owners of that author's termination interest required under section 304(c) or section 304(d), whichever applies, of title 17, U.S.C., or by their duly authorized agents, and shall contain a brief statement of their relationship or relationships to that author.

(3) In the case of a termination of a grant under section 203 executed by one or more of the authors of the work, the notice shall be signed by each author who is terminating the grant or by his or her duly authorized agent. If that author is dead, the notice shall be signed by the number and proportion of the owners of that author's termination interest required under section 203 of title 17, U.S.C., or by their duly authorized agents, and shall contain a brief statement of their relationship or relationships to that author.

(4) Where a signature is by a duly authorized agent, it shall clearly identify the person or persons on whose behalf the agent is acting.

(5) The handwritten signature of each person effecting the termination shall either be accompanied by a statement of the full name and address of that person, typewritten or printed legibly by hand, or shall clearly correspond to such a statement elswhere in the notice.

(d) *Service.*

(1) The notice of termination shall be served upon each grantee whose rights are being terminated, or the grantee's successor in title, by personal service, or by first-class mail sent to an address which, after a reasonable investigation, is found to be the last known address of the grantee or successor in title.

(2) The service provision of section 203, section 304(c) or section 304(d) of title 17, U.S.C., whichever applies, will be satisfied if, before the notice of termination is served, a reasonable investigation is made by the person or persons executing the notice as to the current ownership of the rights being terminated, and based on such investigation:

(i) If there is no reason to believe that such rights have been transferred by the grantee to a successor in title, the notice is served on the grantee; or

(ii) If there is reason to believe that such rights have been transferred by the grantee to a particular successor in title, the notice is served on such successor in title.

(3) For purposes of paragraph (d)(2) of this section, a *reasonable investigation* includes, but is not limited to, a search of the records in the Copyright Office; in the case of a musical composition with respect to which performing rights are licensed by a performing rights society, a 'reasonable investigation' also includes a report from that performing rights society identifying the person or persons claiming current ownership of the rights being terminated.

(4) Compliance with the provisions of paragraphs (d)(2) and (d)(3) of this section will satisfy the service requirements of section 203, section 304(c), or section 304(d) of title 17, U.S.C., whichever applies. However, as long as the statutory requirements have been met, the failure to comply with the regulatory provisions of paragraph (d)(2) or (d)(3) of this section will not affect the validity of the service.

(e) *Harmless errors.*

(1) Harmless errors in a notice that do not materially affect the adequacy of the information required to serve the purposes of section 203, section 304(c), or section 304(d) of title 17, U.S.C., whichever applies, shall not render the notice invalid.

(2) Without prejudice to the general rule provided by paragraph (e)(1) of this section, errors made in giving the date or registration number referred to in paragraph (b)(1)(iii), (b)(2)(iii), or (b)(2)(iv) of this section, or in complying with the provisions of paragraph (b)(1)(vii) or (b)(2)(vii) of this section, or in describing the precise relationships under paragraph (c)(2) or (c)(3) of

this section, shall not affect the validity of the notice if the errors were made in good faith and without any intention to deceive, mislead, or conceal relevant information.

(f) *Recordation.*

(1) A copy of the notice of termination will be recorded in the Copyright Office upon payment of the fee prescribed by paragraph (2) of this paragraph (f) and upon compliance with the following provisions:

(i) The copy submitted for recordation shall be a complete and exact duplicate of the notice of termination as served and shall include the actual signature or signatures, or a reproduction of the actual signature or signatures, appearing on the notice; where separate copies of the same notice were served on more than one grantee or successor in title, only one copy need be submitted for recordation; and

(ii) The copy submitted for recordation shall be accompanied by a statement setting forth the date on which the notice was served and the manner of service, unless such information is contained in the notice. In instances where service is made by first-class mail, the date of service shall be the day the notice of termination was deposited with the United States Postal Service.

(iii) The copy submitted for recordation must be legible per the requirements of § 201.4(c)(3).

(2) The fee for recordation of a document is prescribed in § 201.3(c).

(3) The date of recordation is the date when all of the elements required for recordation, including the prescribed fee and, if required, the statement referred to in paragraph (f)(1)(ii) of this section, have been received in the Copyright Office. After recordation, the document, including any accompanying statement, is returned to the sender with a certificate of record.

(4) Notwithstanding anything to the contrary in this section, the Copyright Office reserves the right to refuse recordation of a notice of termination if, in the judgment of the Copyright Office, such notice of termination is untimely. If a document is submitted as a notice of termination after the statutory deadline has

expired, the Office will offer to record the document as a "document pertaining to copyright" pursuant to § 201.4(c)(3), but the Office will not index the document as a notice of termination. Whether a document so recorded is sufficient in any instance to effect termination as a matter of law shall be determined by a court of competent jurisdiction.

(5) A copy of the notice of termination shall be recorded in the Copyright Office before the effective date of termination, as a condition to its taking effect. However, the fact that the Office has recorded the notice does not mean that it is otherwise sufficient under the law. Recordation of a notice of termination by the Copyright Office is without prejudice to any party claiming that the legal and formal requirements for issuing a valid notice have not been met.

(6) Notices of termination should be submitted to the address specified in § 201.1(b)(2).

(Pub. L. 94–553; 17 U.S.C. 304(c), 702, 708(11))

[42 FR 45920, Sept. 13, 1977, as amended at 56 FR 59885, Nov. 26, 1991; 60 FR 34168, June 30, 1995; 64 FR 29521, June 1, 1999; 64 FR 36574, July 7, 1999; 66 FR 34372, June 28, 2001; 67 FR 69136, Nov. 15, 2002; 67 FR 78176, Dec. 23, 2002; 68 FR 16959, Apr. 8, 2003; 71 FR 36486, June 27, 2006; 74 FR 12556, Mar. 25, 2009]

# LIST 9.1

## DURATION OF COPYRIGHT IN MUSICAL WORKS AROUND THE WORLD

DURATION OF COPYRIGHT IN MUSICAL WORKS AROUND THE WORLD

Richard Green

Number of years after the death of the author (or last surviving coauthor):

|  |  |
|---|---|
| Afghanistan | Minimal – protection no term defined |
| Albania | 70 years |
| Algeria | 50 years |
| Andorra | 70 years |
| Angola | 50 years |
| Antigua and Barbuda | 50 years |
| Argentina | 70 years |
| Armenia | 50 years |
| Australia | 70 years |
| Austria | 70 years |
| Azerbaijan | 50 years |
| Bahrain | 50 years |
| Bangladesh | 50 years |
| Barbados | 50 years |
| Belarus | 50 years |
| Belgium | 70 years |
| Belize | 50 years |
| Benin | 50 years |
| Bhutan | 50 years |
| Bolivia | 50 years |
| Bosnia and Herzegovina | 70 years |
| Brazil | 70 years |
| Brunei Darussalam | 50 years |
| Bulgaria | 70 years |
| Burkina Faso | 50 years |
| Burundi | 50 years |
| Cambodia | 50 years |
| Cameroon | 50 years |
| Canada | 50 years |
| Chile | 50 years |
| China | 50 years |
| Colombia | 80 years |
| Cook Islands | New Zealand Law, but Not enforced |
| Costa Rica | 70 years |
| Croatia | 70 years |
| Cuba | 50 years |
| Cyprus | 50 years |
| Czech Republic | 70 years |
| Denmark | 70 years |
| Djibouti | 25 years |
| Dominica | 70 years |
| Dominican Republic | 50 years |
| Ecuador | 70 years |
| Egypt | 50 years |
| El Salvador | 50 years |
| Estonia | 70 years |
| Fiji | 50 years |
| Finland | 70 years |
| France | 70 years |
| (war extensions for works created after World War I, but before World War II by nationals from any EU country) | Approx. 79 years |
| (war extensions for works created before World War I by nationals from any EU country) | 85 years |
| Georgia | 70 years |
| Germany | 70 years |
| Ghana | 50 years |
| Greece | 70 years |
| Guatemala | 75 years |
| Honduras | 75 years |
| Hong Kong | 50 years |
| Hungary | 70 years |
| Iceland | 70 years |
| India | 60 years |
| Indonesia | 50 years |
| Iran | 30 years |
| Iraq | 50 years |
| Ireland | 70 years |
| Israel | 70 years |
| Italy | 70 years |
| Ivory Coast | 99 years |
| Jamaica | 50 years |
| Japan | 50 years |
| Jordan | 50 years |
| Kazakhstan | 50 years |
| Kenya | 50 years |
| Kuwait | 50 years |
| Kyrgyzstan | 50 years |
| Laos | No copyright law |
| Latvia | 70 years |
| Lebanon | 50 years |
| Libya | No copyright law |
| Liechtenstein | 70 years |
| Lithuania | 70 years |
| Luxembourg | 70 years |
| Macao | 50 years |
| Macedonia | 70 years |
| Madagascar | 50 years |
| Malawi | 50 years |
| Malaysia | 50 years |
| Maldives | No copyright law |
| Mali | 50 years |
| Malta | 70 years |
| Marshall Islands | No copyright law |
| Mauritius | 50 years |
| Mexico | 100 years |
| Mongolia | 50 years |
| Morocco | 50 years |
| Namibia | 50 years |
| Nepal | 50 years |
| Netherlands | 70 years |
| New Zealand | 50 years |
| Nicaragua | 70 years |
| Niger | 50 years |
| Nigeria | 70 years |
| Norway | 70 years |
| Oman | 50 years |
| Pakistan | 50 years |
| Palau | 50years |
| Panama | 50 years |
| Papua New Guinea | 50 years |
| Paraguay | 70 years |
| Peru | 70 years |
| Philippines | 50 years |
| Poland | 70 years |
| Portugal | 70 years |
| Qatar | 50 years |
| Republic of Korea | 50 years |
| Republic of Moldova | 50 years |
| Romania | 70 years |
| Russian Federation | 50 years |
| Saint Vincent and the Grenadines | 50 years |
| Samoa | 75 years |
| Saudi Arabia | 50 years |
| Serbia and Montenegro | 50 years |
| Seychelles | 25 years |
| Singapore | 70 years |
| Slovakia | 70 years |
| Slovenia | 70 years |
| South Africa | 50 years |
| Spain | 70 years |
| (works created before 1987 by nationals from any EU Country) | 80 years |
| Sri Lanka | 50 years |
| Sudan | 50 years |
| Swaziland | No copyright law |
| Sweden | 70 years |
| Switzerland | 70 years |
| Syria | 50 years |
| Taiwan | 50 years |
| Thailand | 50 years |
| Togo | 50 years |
| Trinidad and Tobago | 50 years |
| Tunisia | 50 years |
| Turkey | 70 years |
| Tuvalu | Minimal protection - no term defined |
| Ukraine | 50 years |
| United Arab Emirates | 50 years |
| United Kingdom | 70 years |
| United Republic of Tanzania | 50 year |
| United States | 70 years |
| Uruguay | 50 years |
| Uzbekistan | Minimal protection - no protection for pre-existing work |
| Vatican City | 70 years |
| Venezuela | 60 years |
| Vietnam | 50 years |
| Yemen | 30 years |
| Zambia | 50 years |

The chart above represents the standard term of copyright protection for musical works. The main change for 2005 is the extension to 70 years of protection in Australia which went into effect January 1.

| 100 years | Mexico |
|---|---|
| 99 years | Ivory Coast |
| 85 years | France (war extensions for works created before World War I by nationals from any EU country) |
| 80 years | Colombia, Spain (works created before 1987 by nationals from any EU country) |
| Approx. 79 years | France (war extensions for works created after World War I, but before World War II by nationals from any EU country) |
| 75 years | Guatemala, Honduras, Samoa |
| 70 years | Albania, Andorra, Argentina, Australia, Austria, Belgium, Bosnia and Herzegovina, Brazil, Bulgaria, Costa Rica, Croatia, Czech Republic, Denmark, Dominica, Ecuador, Estonia, Finland, France, Georgia, Germany, Greece, Hungary, Iceland, Ireland, Israel, Italy, Latvia, Liechtenstein, Lithuania, Luxembourg, Macedonia, Malta, Netherlands, Nicaragua, Nigeria, Norway, Paraguay, Peru, Poland, Portugal, Romania, Singapore, Slovakia, Slovenia, Spain, Sweden, Switzerland, Turkey, United Kingdom, United States, Vatican City |
| 60 years | India, Venezuela |
| 50 years | Algeria, Angola, Antigua and Barbuda, Armenia, Azerbaijan, Bahrain, Bangladesh, Barbados, Belarus, Belize, Benin, Bhutan, Bolivia, Brunei Darussalam, Burkina Faso, Burundi, Cambodia, Cameroon, Canada, Chile, China, Cuba, Cyprus, Dominican Republic, Egypt, El Salvador, Fiji, Ghana, Hong Kong, Indonesia, Iraq, Jamaica, Japan, Jordan, Kazakhstan, Kenya, Kuwait, Kyrgyzstan, Lebanon, Macao, Madagascar, Malawi, Malaysia, Mali, Mauritius, Mongolia, Morocco, Namibia, Nepal, New Zealand, Niger, Oman, Pakistan, Palau, Panama, Papua New Guinea, Philippines, Qatar, Republic of Korea, Republic of Moldova, Russian Federation, Saint Vincent and the Grenadines, Saudi Arabia, Serbia and Montenegro, South Africa, Sri Lanka, Sudan, Syria, Taiwan, Thailand, Togo, Trinidad and Tobago, Tunisia, Ukraine, United Arab Emirates, United Republic of Tanzania, Uruguay, Vietnam, Zambia |
| 30 years | Iran, Yemen |
| 25 years | Djibouti, Seychelles |
| No copyright law or minimal copyright protection | Afghanistan (minimal – no term defined), Cook Islands (New Zealand Law, but not enforced), Laos, Libya, Maldives, Marshall Islands , Swaziland, Tuvalu (minimal – no term defined), Uzbekistan (no protection for pre-existing works) |

# List 9.2

## Duration of Copyright in Sound Recordings Around the World*

### Term of Protection of Sound Recordings

| Country | Term | Calculation | Legislation |
|---|---|---|---|
| **A** | | | |
| Albania | **50** | Either from 1st of January of the consecutive year or from the day after the record had been made available to the public if this happens during the consecutive year. | The Law Nr. 9380, Date 28.4.2005 The Copyright and Other Rights Related to it, Article 62 |
| Algeria | **50** | 50 years from the fixation of the phonogram or from the beginning of the year following communication to the public whichever comes first. | Law No. 03-17 (9 Ramadhan 1424 (Art. 123) corresponding to November 4, 2003) approving Ordinance No. 03-05 (19 Joumada El Oula 1424 corresponding to July 19, 2003) on Copyright and Related Rights |

* The author would like to thank Paul John Birch, Managing Director of Revolver Records in the U.K., for providing this list.

| | | | |
|---|---|---|---|
| Andorra | **50** | From 1st of January of the consecutive year or 50 years from the day after the record has been made available to the public if this happens during the consecutive year. | Draft law on copyright and neighbouring rights 10/06/1999 (The draft law is what the copyright office lists as their legislation on copyright) |
| Antigua and Barbuda | **50** | From the end of the calendar year in which it was made, or where it is made available to the public or published before the end of the year from the end of the calendar year in which it is so made available or published whichever date is the latest. | Copyright Act 2002, Art. 11 |
| Argentina | **50** | From fixation. | Intellectual Property Law 28/09/1933 (14/10/1998) No. 11.723 (No. 25.036) and decree 41.2233 of 1934 and amended by Decree No. 1670 of 1974 |
| Armenia | **50** | From the date of fixation. If the phonogram was lawfully published or lawfully made available to the public within this period, the rights of a producer of a phonogram shall emanate from the date of first such publication or from the first such making available to the public (whichever occurred earlier). | Law on Copyright and Related Rights, as adopted by the National Assembly 15 June 2006, Art. 61(2) |

| Country | Term | Calculation | Legislation |
|---|---|---|---|
| Australia | **70** | From the end of 70 years after the end of the calendar year in which the recording is first published. | Australian Copyright Act Sec. 93 (US — AUSTRALIA FTA, 18/05/2004 Article 17.4) |
| Austria | **50** | From January 1st of the year following the first production/publication. | Copyright Act 1936 as amended 2006, Art. 76(5) |
| Azerbaijan | **50** | From first publication or from first recording if unpublished. | The Law of Azerbaijan Republic on "Copyright and Neighbouring Rights" 1996 art. 39(2) |
| **B** | | | |
| Bahamas | **70/ 100** | From the end of the period of seventy years from the year of its first publication or a term of one hundred years from the year of its creation, whichever expires first. | Copyright Act 1988, Section 10(2) |
| Bahrain | **70** | Seventy years commencing at the first calendar year following the first lawful publication of the fixed performance, or failing such publication within fifty years from the fixation of the performance, seventy years from the end of the year in which fixation of the performance took place. | Article (42) of the 2005 Copyright Law (US-BAHRAIN FTA, 14/03/2004 Article 14.4) |

| Bangladesh | **60** | Sixty years commencing from the calendar day preceded by the circulation of the recording. | Copyright Act, No. 28/2000 Art. 27. |
|---|---|---|---|
| Barbados | **50** | From 1st of January of the following year in which the phonogram was made or where it was made available to the public before the end of this period, 50 years from the 1st of January of the following year after it was made available to the public. | Copyright Act nr. 4 03/1998 S.11 |
| Belarus | **50** | From first publication or fixation of phonogram whichever is first. | Law of Copyright and Related Rights, 1998 S.38(2) |
| Belgium | **50** | From fixation or first lawful publication, whichever is first. | Law on Copyright and Neighbouring Rights of June 30, 1994, Art. 39 |
| Belize | **50** | From the end of the calendar year of the first lawful publication, broadcast or is included in a cable programme service. | Copyright Act Chapter 252 revised edition 2000, Art. 11 |
| Benin | **50** | From January 1st the following year of the first publication, or, if such publication does not take place in the year of fixation, 50 years from the end of the year of fixation. | Loi N 2005-30 DU 05 Avril 2006 Reletive a la protection du droit d'auteur et des droits voisins en republique du Benin |
| Bhutan | **50** | From the publication of the sound recording until the end of the fiftieth calendar year | Copyright Act of the Kingdom of Bhutan 2001 Art. 24(2) and 25 (3) |

| Country | Term | Calculation | Legislation |
|---|---|---|---|
| | | following the year of publication or, if the sound recording has not been published, from the fixation of the sound recording until the end of the fiftieth calendar year following the year of fixation. | |
| Bolivia | **50** | From first publication, or fixation, if no publication took place. | Law no. 1322 of 13 April 1992 on Authors' Rights |
| Bosnia and Herzegovina | **50** | From the end of the year in which the phonogram was published, and if it has not been published as of the end of the year in which the recording took place. | Law on Copyright and Related Rights in Bosnia and Herzegovina Art. 109(6) |
| Botswana | **50** | From first publication until the end of the calendar year following first publication and if not published, from the first fixation. | Copyright and Neighbouring Rights Act, nr. 8 of 2000, section 25(2) and 26(3) |
| Brazil | **70** | From the first of January of the year following fixation for phonograms, transmission for the broadcasts of broadcasting organization, and public performance in other cases. | Law No. 9.610 of February 19, 1998 Art. 96 |
| Brunei | **50** | From the end of the year of first fixation of release (meaning publication, broadcasting or inclusion in a cable programme service) | Law on Copyright and Neighbouring Rights ratified on February 13th 2003. |

| Bulgaria | **50** | From 1st of January of the following year of the first publication or from fixation if no publication was made. | Law on Copyright and Neighbouring Rights of 1st of August 1993 as amended up to 2000. Art. 89 |
|---|---|---|---|
| Burkina Faso | **70** | From the end of the year of fixation. | Copyright Act, No. 032/1999 Art. 86 |
| **C** | | | |
| Cambodia | **50** | From the following calendar year after publication and in the absence of publication, from the end of the year following the fixation | Law on Copyright and Related Rights ratified 13th of February 2003, Art. 53(2) |
| Cameroon | **50** | From 1st of January of the following year the declaration of the work to the professional organism was made | Law No. 90/010 of 10th of August 1990 on Authors' Rights Art. 78 |
| Canada | **50** | From the end of the year in which first fixation was made. | Copyright Act 1985 as last amended in 1997 s.23 |
| Cape Verde | **50** | From publication or fixation if no publication. | Ley no 101/III/90 de 29 de dezembro de 1990 Art. 23 |
| Chile | **70** | From the end of the calendar year of the first authorized publication of the performance or phonogram, or failing such authorized publication within 50 years from the fixation of the performance or phonogram, 70 years from the end of the calendar year of the fixation of the performance or phonogram. | Lay N° 17.336 Propiedad Intelectual, Article 70 (CHILE FTA, 6/06/2003 Article 17.6) |

| Country | Term | Calculation | Legislation |
|---|---|---|---|
| China | **50** | Expiring on 31st of December 50 years after the first publication. | Copyright Law of the People's Republic of China (Adopted at the 15th Session of the Standing Committee of the Seventh National People's Congress on September 7, 1990, and Amended According to the Decision on the Revision of the Copyright Law of the People's Republic of China, Adopted at the 24th Session of the Standing Committee of the Ninth National People's Congress on October 27, 2001) Art. 41 |
| Colombia | **70** | From January 1st of the year following the first publication of the phonogram. | Law No. 83, 1998 on Intellectual Property Art. |
| Congo, Democratic Republic of | **20** | From the end of the year during which the phonogram was published for the first time or, failing that, was initially made. | Copyright Act, No. 24/1982 Art. 89 |
| Costa Rica | **70** | From the end of the calendar year of the first authorized publication of the work, performance, or phonogram, or failing such authorized publication, within 50 years from the creation of the work, performance, or phonogram, not less than 70 years from the end of | Law no 6683 of 14th of October 1982 last amended by law no. 8039 of 12th of October 2000 Art. 87. (US — CAFTA FTA, 5/08/2004 Article 15.5) |

| | | | |
|---|---|---|---|
| | | the calendar year of the creation of the work, performance, or phonogram. | |
| Cote d'Ivoire/ Ivory Coast | **99** | Following the 1st of January of the calendar year following that of the first communication to the public of the performance of the work, of the production of the programs, even where the performances and the fixation occurred prior to the date of entry into force of this Law | Law No. 96-564 of July 25, 1996 on the Protection of Intellectual Works and the Rights of Authors, Performers and Phonogram and Videogram Producers Art. 89 |
| Croatia | **50** | From the date of fixation or, if published during this period from the date of publication or if not published but lawfully communicated to the public as from this date | Copyright Law 2003, Art. 137 |
| Cyprus | **50** | From the end of the year in which the recording was made | The Copyright Laws 1976 to 1993 (Law No. 59, of December 3, 1976, as last amended by Law No. 18(I), 1993), Art. 4(2)(iii) |
| Czech Republic | **50** | From the end of the year in which the recording was made or published. | Law nr. 121/2000 on Copyright and Related Rights Art. 77 |
| **D** | | | |
| Denmark | **50** | 50 years after the end of the year of first publication/recording. 50 years after the end of being made public in any other manner of not being published but made public in any other manner within 50 years. | Consolidated Act on Copyright 2006 no 763 of 30th of June 2006. Art. 66(1) |

| Country | Term | Calculation | Legislation |
|---|---|---|---|
| Dominica | **50** | Expire at the end of fifty years from the date of the calendar year in which it was made, or where it is made available to the public before the end of that period, at the end of fifty years from the end of the calendar year in which it is so made available. | COMMONWEALTH OF DOMINICA, Copyright Act 2003, Art. 12 |
| Dominican Republic | **70** | From the end of the calendar year of the first authorized publication of the work, performance, or phonogram, or failing such authorized publication within 50 years from the creation of the work, performance, or phonogram, not less than 70 years from the end of the calendar year of the creation of the work, performance, or phonogram. | LEY SOBRE DERECHO DE AUTOR, Art. 29(1) (US — CAFTA FTA, 5/08/2004 Article 15.5) |
| **E** | | | |
| Ecuador | **70** | From the 1st of January of the year following the date of first publication of the phonogram. | Law on Intellectual Property, No. 83/1998 Art. 96 |
| Egypt | **50** | From the succeeding year of first fixation or first publication. | Law no. 82 of 2002 Pertaining to the Protection of Intellectual Property Rights. Art. 167 |

| | | | |
|---|---|---|---|
| El Salvador | **70** | From the end of the calendar year of the first authorized publication of the work, performance, or phonogram, or failing such authorized publication within 50 years from the creation of the work, performance, or phonogram, not less than 70 years from the end of the calendar year of the creation of the work, performance, or phonogram. | Law on Promotion and Protection of Intellectual Property of 15th of July 1993 Art. 86(e) (US — CAFTA FTA, 5/08/2004 Article 15.5) |
| Estonia | **50** | From 1st of January of the year following that of fixation, first publication or communication to the public. | Copyright Law of 11th of November 1992, in force 12th of December 1992 as last amended in 2004 |
| **F** | | | |
| Fiji | **50** | From the end of the calendar year of first fixation, first making available or first publication, whichever is the latest. | Copyright Act No. 11 1999 sec. 23. |
| Finland | **50** | From the year in which the recording was made, or, if published, from the end of the year in which the recording was first published or disseminated. | Copyright Act 404/1961 of 8th of July 1961 as last amended 2006, Art. 46 |
| France | **50** | From 1st of January of the calendar year following that of the first communication to the public. | Law No. 92-957 of 1st of July 1992 as last amended in 2006, Art. L211-4 |

| Country | Term | Calculation | Legislation |
|---|---|---|---|
| **G** | | | |
| Gabon | **20** | From the end of the year in which they were first effected. | Copyright Law, No. 1/1987 Art. 84 |
| Georgia | **50** | From the first disclosure of the phonogram. If within this term the phonogram was lawfully disclosed or displayed publicly, this term is continued from the first disclosure during 50 years. | Law on Copyright and Neighbouring Rights of Georgia 22/06/1999 Art. 48 |
| Germany | **50** | From the end of the calendar year of the first publication. If no publication took place 50 years after the communication to the public. If no publication or communication to the public, 50 years from fixation. | Law on Authors' Rights if 1965 amended last by Law of 10/09/2003, Art. 85(3) |
| Ghana | **70** | From the publication of the sound recording until the expiration of 70 years after the year of publication or, if the sound recording has not been published from the fixation of the sound recording, until the expiration of 70 years after the year of fixation | Ghana Copyright Act, No. 690/2005, Art. 16 |
| Greece | **50** | From the date of first fixation or first lawful publication to the public within that period. | Law on Intellectual Property and Neighbouring Rights of 04/03/1999 as last amended by Law 3057/2002, Art. 52 |

| | | | |
|---|---|---|---|
| Grenada | **50** | From the end of the calendar year in which the recording is first published | Copyright Act 1989, Section 12 |
| Guatemala | **75** | From the first fixation. | Copyright Act No. 33/1998 Art. 51 (US — CAFTA FTA, 5/08/2004 Article 15.5) |
| Guinea | **40** | From the end of the year of the first publication or fixation of no publication was made. | Law No. 043/APN/CP/80, August 1980 regulating Copyright and Neighboring Rights Protection. Art. 40 |
| | | **H** | |
| Honduras | **75** | From the first end of the year of first publication. | Law on Copyright and Related Rights, as enacted on December 13, 1999 Art. 120 (US — CAFTA FTA, 5/08/2004 Article 15.5) |
| Hong Kong | **50** | From the end of the year in which the recording was made or first released. | Copyright Ordinance 1997, Sec. 18 |
| Holy See | **50** | | Law of 12th of January 1960 applying Italian Law No. 633 of 22nd of April 1941 as last amended in 1996, Art. 75 |
| Hungary | **50** | From the end of the year of the first distribution to the public or the fixation. | Copyright Act 1999 as last amended in 2004. Art. 84(1) (a) |

| Country | Term | Calculation | Legislation |
|---|---|---|---|
| **I** | | | |
| Iceland | **50** | From the end of the year in which the recording was made or first distributed. | Copyright Act 1972 as last amended in 1998 Sec. 46. |
| India | **60** | From the beginning of the calendar year next following the year in which the sound recording is published. | Copyright Act 1957, as amended in 2000, Art. 27 |
| Indonesia | **50** | After the beginning of the calendar year following that of fixation. | Law on Copyright and Neighbouring Rights. 2002, Art. 50(1)(b)(2) |
| Iran | **30** | From the date of publication or public presentation. | Copyright Act, 1970, Art. 16 |
| Iraq | **50** | From fixation or publication. | Copyright Law no. 3 for the year 1971 for the protection of copyright as last amended April 2004. Art. 34bis(5) |
| Ireland | **50** | From the end of the year of the first publication or fixation. | COPYRIGHT AND RELATED RIGHTS ACT, 2000 Number 28 of 2000 Last amended 2004. Sec. 26 |
| Israel | **50** | From the making of the plate. | UK Copyright Act 1911 as modified by Copyright Ordinance 1924, by Law No. 5748/1988 of 27th of July 1988 and as amended last in 1996 and by the Copyright Amendment Bill in 2006. |

| Italy | **50** | From fixation or publication/communication to the public. | Law for the protection of Copyright and Neighbouring Rights (Law nr. 633 of 22nd of April 1941) and Law. No. 93 of 5th of February 1992 both as last amended on 28th of March 2003 |
|---|---|---|---|
| **J** | | | |
| Jamaica | **50** | From the end of the calendar year in which it was made or where it was made available to the public within this period, 50 years from the end of the calendar year in which it was made available. | The Copyright Act 1993 as last amended in September 1999. Sec. 11 |
| Japan | **50** | Expire at the end of a period of fifty years from the year when the publishing was made or when the first fixation of sounds was made if the publishing has not been made within a period of fifty years following the first fixation of sounds. | Copyright Law 1970 as last amended in June 2004. Art. 101 |
| Jordan | **50** | From the end of the year of publication or fixation. | Copyright Law 1992 as amended in 2003 and 2005 Art. 23(e)(2) |

| Country | Term | Calculation | Legislation |
|---|---|---|---|
| **K** | | | |
| Kazakhstan | **50** | 50 years from 1st of January of the year following that of first publication or fixation if no publication was made within this period. | Law on Authors' Rights and Neighbouring Rights of 10th of June 1996 |
| Kenya | **50** | From the end of the year in which the recording was made. | Copyright Act 2001 s. 23(2) |
| Korea, South | **50** | From the year following first fixation. | Law No. 3916 of 31st of December 1986 a last amended in July 2003. Art. 70 |
| Kyrgyzstan | **50** | From first publication or fixation. | Law on Copyright and Neighbouring Rights 1998 Art. 43(2) |
| **L** | | | |
| Latvia | **50** | From the end of the year of fixation or first publication. | Copyright Law 2000, Art. 55(2) |
| Lebanon | **50** | From the end of the year of first fixation. | Protection of Copyright and Artistic Property Act 1999 Art. 55 |
| Lesotho | **20** | From the end of the year of first publication or fixation if no publication was made. | Copyright Order 1989 Art. 26 |
| Liechtenstein | **50** | From December 31 of the year of fixation or communication to the public. | Law on Copyright And Related Rights of 23rd of July 1999 Art. 44 |

| | | | |
|---|---|---|---|
| Lithuania | **50** | From fixation or publication/lawful communication to the public within that period. | Law on Copyright and Related Rights 1999 as last amended on 5th of March 2003 Art. 59(2) |
| Luxembourg | **50** | From January 1st following the year of first fixation or publication. | Law No. 4431 of 18th of April 2001 as last amended on 29th of April 2004. Art. 45(1) |
| **M** | | | |
| Macao | **50** | From the end of the year of first fixation. | Copyright Act, 1999 Art. 188 |
| Macedonia | **50** | From fixation or first disclosure. | Law on Copyright and Related Rights of 20th of September 1996 as last amended in 1988. Art. 120 |
| Malawi | **20** | From the end of the year in which the sound recording was published for the first time. | Copyright Act, No. 9/1989 Art. 34 (4) |
| Malaysia | **50** | From the beginning of the calendar year following that of the first publication or fixation. | Copyright Act 1987 as last amended by Copyright Amendment Act 2000 Sec. 19 |
| Malta | **50** | From the end of the year of the first fixation or publication. | Copyright Act 2000 sec.16 |
| Mauritius | **50** | From the end of the year of publication or fixation. | Copyright Act 1997, sec. 26(2) and 29(3) |

| Country | Term | Calculation | Legislation |
|---|---|---|---|
| Myanmar | **50** | From making of original plate. | UK Copyright Act 1911 as amended by the Union of Burma (Adaptation of Laws) Order 1948, Art. 19 |
| Mexico | **75** | From the first fixation of the sound recording on the phonogram. | Federal Law on Copyright, as amended on July 23, 2003 Art. 134 |
| Micronesia | **75 or 100** | 75 years from the year of its first publication, or 100 years from the year of its creation, whichever expires first. | Federal State of Micronesia Copyright Act, TITLE 35. COPYRIGHT, PATENTS & TRADEMARKS s. 131 |
| Moldova | **50** | From 1st of January of the year following that of first publication or fixation. | Law on Copyright and Neighbouring Rights No. 293XIII of 23rd of November 1994. Art. 33 |
| Montenegro | **50** | From the production of the phonogram. If it has been lawfully published or communicated to the public within this period of 50 years, the term expires 50 years from the date of the first publication or communication to the public, whichever date is earlier. | The law on copyright and related rights. Art. 144 (2) |
| Morocco | **70** | From the end of the year when the phonogram was published or, failing such publication, from the fixation of the phonogram, starting from the end of the year of the fixation. | Copyright Law, No. 2 of 15 February 2000 Sec. 58 (US-Morocco FTA, 15/06/2004, Art. 15.5) |

| Mozambique | **50** | From the end of the year of fixation. | Copyright Act 2001 Art. 52 |
|---|---|---|---|
| **N** | | | |
| Nauru | **50** | From the end of the calendar year which in the recording was first published. | Customs and Adopted Laws 1971. UK Copyright Act 1956. Art. 12 |
| Nepal | **50** | As for musical works. | Copyright Act 1966, Art. 8 |
| The Netherlands | **50** | From 1st of January of the year following that in which the recording was made, or following publication if the recording was published within such period of time. | Law of 18th of March 1993 on Neighbouring Rights as amended up to 1933, Art 12 |
| New Zealand | **50** | From the end of the calendar year in which the recording was made or if made available to the public, before the end of that date, 50 years from the end of the calendar year in which it is made available. | Copyright Act 1994 s.23 |
| Nicaragua | **70** | From January 1 of the year following the year of publication of the phonograms or, failing that, from its fixation. | Copyright Law No. 312/1999 Art. 93 (US — CAFTA FTA, 5/08/2004 Article 15.5) |
| Nigeria | **50** | From the end of the year of recording. | Copyright Decree 1988 as last amended up to 1999. Schedule 1, Sec. 2(3) |

| Country | Term | Calculation | Legislation |
|---|---|---|---|
| Norway | **50** | From the end of the year in which the recording was made or from publication if the recording is released within that period. | Copyright Act 1961 as last amended on 30th of June 1995. Art. 45 |
| | | **O** | |
| Oman | **95 or 120** | 95 years from the end of the calendar year of the first authorized publication of the work, performance, or phonogram, or failing such authorized publication within 25 years from the creation of the work, performance, or phonogram, not less than 120 years from the end of the calendar year of the creation of the work, performance, or phonogram. | US — OMAN FTA, 19/01/2006 Article 15.4 |
| | | **P** | |
| Pakistan | **50** | From the end of the calendar year of first fixation or first performance. | Copyright Ordinance 1962 as last amended by Copyright Ordinance 2000. S. 24A (3) |
| Palau | **75 or 100** | Phonograms are protected as authorial works 75 years from publication or if not published, 100 years from creation. | Republic of Palau Copyright Act of 2003. S. 16(a) and (c) |
| Panama | **50** | From 1st of January of the year following that of first publication. | Law No. 15 of 8th of August 1994 on Copyright and Neighbouring Rights, and enacting other provisions, Art. 94 |

| Papua New Guinea | **50** | From the end of the year in which the sound recording was published or the fixation was made. | Copyright and Neighbouring Rights Act 2000 (No. 21 of 2000) Sec. 22(2) |
|---|---|---|---|
| Paraguay | **50** | From the 1st of January of the year following the first publication. | Copyright Law 1998, Art. 130 |
| Peru | **70** | From the 1st of January of the year following that of the first publication of the phonograph. | Copyright Act — Legislative Decree No. 822 of April 23, 1996 Art. 139 |
| Philippines | **50** | From the end of the year in which the recording took place. | Intellectual Property Code 1998 Sec. 215(1)(b) |
| Poland | **50** | From the end of the year in which the phonogram was made. | Law on Copyright and Neighbouring Rights of 4th of February 1994 as last amended on 1st of January 2003 |
| Portugal | **50** | From the beginning of the year following that of fixation. | Law No. 45/85 of 17th of September 1985 as last amended on 3rd of September 1991. Art. 186 |
| **Q** | | | |
| Qatar | **50** | From the beginning of the year following the year of publication or fixation if no publication was made. | Law No. 7 of 2002 Law on the Protection of Copyright and Neighbouring Rights. Art. 41 |

| Country | Term | Calculation | Legislation |
|---|---|---|---|
| **R** | | | |
| Romania | **50** | From 1st of January of the year following that of first fixation or publication if the recording was released within that period. | Law on Copyright and Neighbouring Rights of 20th of February 1996. Art. 106 |
| Russian Federation | **50** | From 1st of January of the year following that of publication or of fixation if no publication was made. | Law on Copyright and Neighbouring Rights of 9th of July 1993 as last amended in July 2004, Sec.43(2) |
| Rwanda | **25** | From the date on which the phonogram was published for the first time or was initially made. | Copyright Act, 1983 Art. 100 |
| **S** | | | |
| Saint Lucia | **50** | From the end of the calendar year in which it was made, or where it is made available to the public before the end of that period, at the end of the period of fifty years from the end of the calendar year in which it is so made available. | Copyright Act 1995 Art. 11. |
| Saint Vincent and the Grenadines | **50** | From 1st of January of the year following the year in which the phonogram was first lawfully made available to the public in St. V. and the G. or if not, from 1st of January of the year | Copyright Act No. 53 of December 1989, Sec. 31 |

| | | | |
|---|---|---|---|
| | | following in which the sound recording was made in St. V and G. | |
| Samoa | **75** | From the date of which the work was first published, or failing such an event within 75 years from the making of the work, from its making. | Copyright Act, No. 25/1998 Art. 16 |
| San Marino | **50** | | Law on Authors' Rights of 25th of January 1991 Art. 36 |
| Saudi Arabia | **50** | From the date of first performance of first fixation. | Copyright Law of 2003, Art. 19(2)2 |
| Serbia & Montenegro | **50** | From 1st of January of the year following that of first publication or fixation if no publication was made. | Law on Copyright and Related Rights 2004, Art. 138, Art. 99. |
| Seychelles | **25** | From the end of the year in which the recording was made. | Copyright Act, No. 25/1982 Art. 9 |
| Sierra Leone | **50** | From the end of the calendar year in which the recording was first published. | Copyright Act 1965, Art. 14 iii |
| Singapore | **70** | From the expiration of the calendar year in which the recording is first published. | Copyright Act of 1987, as amended in 1999 Art. 92 (US — SINGAPORE FTA, 6/05/2003) |
| Slovakia | **50** | From the end of the year of fixation or publication. | Copyright Act 1997 as last amended in 2000. Art. 47(5) |

| Country | Term | Calculation | Legislation |
|---|---|---|---|
| Slovenia | **50** | From 1st of January of the year following that of fixation/first publication/first communication. | Copyright and Related Rights Act of 1995 as last amended on 26th of January 2001. Art. 132 |
| Solomon Islands | **50** | From the end of the calendar year in which the recording was first published. | Copyright Act 1987, Art. 11(3) |
| South Africa | **50** | From the end of the year of first publication | Copyright Act No. 98. of 1978 as last amended in 2001. Sec. 3(2)(c) |
| Spain | **50** | From 1st of January of the year following that of publication or fixation. | Royal Decree Law I/1996 of 12th of April 1996, Law 11/1987 of 11th of November 1987. Art. 119. |
| Sri Lanka | **50** | From first publication until the end of the year in which the protection expires. | Code of Intellectual Property Act, No. 52 of 1979, Sec. 20(1). |
| St. Vincent and the Renadines | **50 or 75** | 50 years from the end of the calendar year in which it was made or, where it is made available to the public before the end of that period, or 75 years from the end of the calendar year in which it is so made available. | Copyright Act, 2003 Art. 9 |
| Sudan | **50** | From 1st of January of the year following that of fixation. | The Copyright and Neighbouring Rights Protection Act 1996, Art. 39(2) |
| Sweden | **50** | From the year in which the recording was made or published. | Act on Copyright in Literary and Artistic Works No 729 of 30th of |

| | | | |
|---|---|---|---|
| | | | December 1960 as last amended in 1999, Art. 46. |
| Switzerland | **50** | From 31st of December of the year of the first fixation. | Law on Authors' Rights and Neighbouring Rights of 9th of October 1992 as amended by Law of 16th of December 1994 Amended on 22nd of September 1926. Art. 39 |
| | | **T** | |
| Tajikistan | **40** | From first publication or fixation. | Law on Copyright and Neighbouring Rights, 1988, Art. 42(2) |
| Tanzania | **50** | From the end of the year of publication or fixation. | The Copyright and Neighbouring Rights Act 1999, Sec. 32(2) |
| Thailand | **50** | From first publication until 31st of December of the 50th year. | Copyright Act B.E. 2537 (1994) Sec. 21. |
| Togo | **25** | From the end of the year in which the phonogram was originally made. | Copyright Act, 1991 Art. 105 |
| Trinidad and Tobago | **50** | From the end of the calendar year of first publication or fixation. | The Copyright Act 1997. The Copyright Customs Regulations, 2000. Sex. 22(2) and 23(4). |
| Turkey | **70** | From the date of the initial broadcast of the sound carrying devices. | Copyright Act, No. 5846/1951, as amended |

| Country | Term | Calculation | Legislation |
|---|---|---|---|
| **U** | | | |
| Uganda | **50** | From the end of the year of recording if unpublished or 45 years from the end of the year of publication for recordings published within 50 years from recording. | Copyright Act 1964 Art. 2. (Schedule 3) |
| Ukraine | **50** | From 1st of January of the year following that of first publication or fixation. | Law on Copyright and Related Rights of 23rd of December 1993 as last amended on 11th of July 2001, Art. 44 |
| United Arab Emirates | **50** | From the beginning of the year following that of publication or fixation. | Law. No. 7 of 2002 for Copyright and Neighbouring Rights, Art. 20(8) |
| United Kingdom | **50** | 50 years from the beginning of the year following that of publication or fixation. | Copyright, Designs and Patents Act 1988 sec. 13A. 50 |
| United States | **95 or 120** | Works Made for Hire: 95 years from the year of its first publication, or a term of 120 years from the year of its creation, whichever expires first | Copyright Law of the United States s. 302 |
| Uruguay | **50** | From the 1st of January following the year of publication. | Law. No. 9739 concerning Literary and Artistic Copyright as amended by Law No. 17.616 of January 2003. Art. 18 |

| | | | |
|---|---|---|---|
| Uzbekistan | **50** | From the making of the recording. | Law on Copyright and Neighbouring Rights 1996 |
| | | **V** | |
| Vatican City | **50** | From fixation or publication/communication to the public. | Legge sill diritto di autore. 12 gennaio. 1960 GIOVANNI PP. XXIII Applying Italian Law. Law for the protection of Copyright and Neighbouring Rights (Law nr. 633 of 22nd of April 1941) and Law. No. 93 of 5th of February 1992 both as last amended on 28th of March 2003 |
| Venezuela | **60** | From January 1 of the year following the first publication of the phonogram | Law on Copyright of August 14, 1993 Art. 100 |
| Vietnam | **50** | From the date of first dissemination. | Intellectual Property Provisions in Civil Code and Implementing Decree of 29th of November 1996 Art. 744(2) |
| | | **Z** | |
| Zaire | **20** | From January 1 following the calendar year during which the phonogram or videogram or the copies thereof were made. | Copyright Act, 1987 Art. 95 |

| Country | Term | Calculation | Legislation |
|---|---|---|---|
| Zambia | **50** | From the end of the year of making or publication of sound recording. | Copyright and Performance Rights Act 1994 Sec. 13 |
| Zimbabwe | **50** | From the end of the year in which the recording was made. | Copyright Act 1967 Sec. 16 |

# LIST 9.3

## SOME POPULAR SONGS IN THE PUBLIC DOMAIN IN THE UNITED STATES

**1814**
STAR SPANGLED BANNER, THE
*Francis Scott Key*
*John Stafford Smith*

**1823**
HOME SWEET HOME
*John Howard Payne*

**1832**
AMERICA (My Country 'tis of Thee)
*Samuel Francis Smith*

**1837**
WOODMAN, SPARE THAT TREE
*Henry Russell*
*George P. Morris*

**1843**
OPEN THY LATTICE, LOVE
*Stephen Collins Foster*

**1848**
OH! SUSANNAH
*Stephen Collins Foster*

**1851**
OLD FOLKS AT HOME
*Stephen Collins Foster*

**1852**
MASSA'S IN DE COLD, COLD GROUND
*Stephen Collins Foster*

**1853**
MY OLD KENTUCKY HOME
*Stephen Collins Foster*

**1854**
JEANNIE WITH THE LIGHT BROWN HAIR
*Stephen Collins Foster*

**1855**
COME WHERE MY LOVE LIES DREAMING
*Stephen Collins Foster*

**1860**
DIXIE
*Daniel Emmett*
OLD BLACK JOE
*Stephen Collins Foster*

**1861**
MARYLAND, MY MARYLAND
*James Ryder Randall*

**1862**
BATTLE HYMN OF THE REPUBLIC, THE
*Julia Ward Howe*
*William Steffe*

**1864**
BEAUTIFUL DREAMER
*Stephen Collins Foster*

**1869**
SWEET GENEVIEVE
*George Cooper*
*Henry Tucker*

**1876**
I'LL TAKE YOU HOME AGAIN KATHLEEN
*Thomas P. Westendorf*

**1878**
CARRY ME BACK TO OL' VIRGINNY
*James A. Bland*
IN THE EVENING BY THE MOONLIGHT
*James A. Bland*

**1879**
OH, DEM GOLDEN SLIPPERS
*James A. Bland*

**1880**
HAND ME DOWN MY WALKING CANE
*James A. Bland*

**1885**
AMERICAN PATROL
*F. W. Meacham*

**1888**
SEMPER FIDELIS
*John Philip Sousa*

**1889**
WASHINGTON POST MARCH
*John Philip Sousa*

**1890**
OH PROMISE ME
*Reginald DeKoven*

**1891**
PICTURE THAT'S TURNED TOWARDS THE WALL, THE
*Charles Graham*
TA-RA-RA BOOM-DER-E'
*Henry J. Sayers*

**1892**
AFTER THE BALL
*Charles K. Harris*
DAISY BELL
*Harry Dacre*
BOWERY, THE
*Charles H. Hoyt*
*Percy Gaunt*

**1894**
FORGOTTEN
*Flora Wulschner*
*Eugene Cowles*

I DON'T WANT TO PLAY IN YOUR YARD
*Philip Wingate*
*H. W. Petrie*
SHE IS MORE TO BE PITIED THAN CENSURED
*William B. Gray*
SHE MAY HAVE SEEN BETTER DAYS
*James Thornton*
SIDEWALKS OF NEW YORK
*James W. Blake & Charles B. Lawlor*

**1895**
AMERICA THE BEAUTIFUL
*Catherine Lee Bates*
*Samuel A. Ward*
BAND PLAYED ON, THE
*John F. Palmer*
*Charles B. Ward*
EL CAPITAN
*John Philip Sousa*
KING COTTON
*John Philip Sousa*

**1896**
MOTHER WAS A LADY
*Edward B. Marks*
*Joseph W. Stern*
SWEET ROSIE O'GRADY
*Maude Nugent Jerome*
THERE'LL BE A HOT TIME IN THE OLD TOWN TONIGHT
*Theodore Metz*
*Joe Hayden*

**1897**
BREAK THE NEWS TO MOTHER
*Charles K. Harris*
ON THE BANKS OF THE WABASH
*Paul Dresser*
STARS AND STRIPES FOREVER
*John Philip Sousa*

**1898**
GYPSY LOVE SONG
*Victor Herbert & Harry B. Smith*
MY OLD NEW HAMPSHIRE HOME
*Andrew B. Sterling*
*Harry Von Tilzer*
ROSARY, THE
*Ethelbert Nevin & Robert Cameron Rodgers*
WHEN GOOD FELLOWS GET TOGETHER
*Richard Hovey*
*Frederick Field Bullard*

**1899**
HEARTS AND FLOWERS
*T. M. Tobani*
*Mary D. Brine*
HELLO MA BABY
*Joe E. Howard*
*Ida Emerson*
MAPLE LEAF RAG
*Scott Joplin*
MY WILD IRISH ROSE
*Chauncey Olcott*

YOU TELL ME YOUR DREAMS
*Seymour Rice*
*Albert H. Brown*
*Charles N. Daniels*

**1900**

BIRD IN A GILDED CAGE, A
*Arthur J. Lamb & Harry Von Tilzer*

**1901**

I LOVE YOU TRULY
*Carrie Jacobs Bond*
JUST A-WEARYIN' FOR YOU
*Carrie Jacobs Bond & Frank Stanton*
MIGHTY LAK' A ROSE
*Ethelbert Nevin & Frank Stanton*

**1902**

BECAUSE
*Guy D'Hardelot*
*Edward Teschemacher*
BILL BAILEY WON'T YOU PLEASE COME HOME
*Hughie Cannon*
DOWN WHERE THE WURZBURGER FLOWS
*Vincent P. Bryan*
*Harry Von Tilzer*
GLOW WORM, THE
*Paul Lincke*
*Lilla C. Robinson*
IN THE GOOD OLD SUMMER TIME
*Ren Shields*
*George Evans*
ON A SUNDAY AFTERNOON
*Harry Von Tilzer*
*Andrew B. Sterling*
OH! DIDN'T HE RAMBLE
*Bob Cole*
*Billy Johnson*
*J. Rosimond Johnson*

**1903**

BEDELIA
*William Jerome & Jean Schwartz*
DEAR OLD GIRL
*Theodore Morse*
*Richard Henry Buck*
ENTERTAINER, THE
*Scott Joplin*
IDA, SWEET AS APPLE CIDER
*Eddie Leonard*
*Eddie Munson*
KASHMIRI LOVE SONG
*Lawrence Hope & Amy Woodforde-Finden*
MARCH OF THE TOYS
*Victor Herbert*
TOYLAND
*Victor Herbert & Glen MacDonough*
YOU'RE THE FLOWER OF MY HEART, SWEET ADELINE
*Harry Armstrong & Richard H. Gerard*

**1904**

FASCINATION
(Valse Tzigane)
*F. D. Marchetti*

GIVE MY REGARDS TO BROADWAY
*George M. Cohan*
MEET ME IN ST. LOUIS, LOUIS
*Kerry Mills & Andrew B. Sterling*
PLEASE COME AND PLAY IN MY YARD
*Edward Madden*
*Theodore F. Morse*
YANKEE DOODLE BOY
*George M. Cohan*

**1905**
I DON'T CARE
*Jean Lenox*
*Harry O. Sutton*
IN MY MERRY OLDSMOBILE
*Vincent Bryan & Gus Edwards*
IN THE SHADE OF THE OLD APPLE TREE
*Egbert Van Alstyne & Harry Williams*
KISS ME AGAIN
*Henry Blossom & Victor Herbert*
MARY'S A GRAND OLD NAME
*George M. Cohan*
MY GAL SAL
*Paul Dresser*
PARADE OF THE WOODEN SOLDIERS
*Ballard MacDonald*
*Leon Jessel*
SO LONG MARY
*George M. Cohan*
TAMMANY
*Vincent P. Bryan*
*Gus Edwards*
WAIT TILL THE SUN SHINES NELLIE
*Andrew B. Sterling & Harry Von Tilzer*
WHERE THE RIVER SHANNON FLOWS
*James I. Russell*
WHISTLER AND HIS DOG, THE
*Arthur Pryor*
WILL YOU LOVE ME IN DECEMBER (AS YOU DO IN MAY)
*James J. Walker*
*Ernest R. Ball*
WON'T YOU COME OVER TO MY HOUSE
*Harry Williams*
*Egbert Van Alstyne*

**1906**
BECAUSE YOU'RE YOU
*Victor Herbert*
*Henry Blossom*
DILL PICKLES
*Charles L. Johnson*
EVERY DAY IS LADIES' DAY WITH ME
*Henry Blossom & Victor Herbert*
I LOVE YOU TRULY
*Carrie Jacobs Bond*

LOVE ME AND THE WORLD IS MINE
*Ernest R. Ball & David Reed, Jr.*

MOONBEAMS
*Henry Blossom & Victor Herbert*

NATIONAL EMBLEM
*E. E. Bagley*

SCHOOL DAYS
*Will D. Cobb & Gus Edwards*

WAITING AT THE CHURCH
*F. W. Leigh & Henry E. Pether*

YOU'RE A GRAND OLD FLAG
*George M. Cohan*

**1907**

ANCHORS AWEIGH
*George D. Lottman, A. H. Milies, Domenico Savino & Charles A. Zimmerman*

HARRIGAN
*George M. Cohan*

ON THE ROAD TO MANDALAY
*Rudyard Kipling & Oley Speaks*

RED WING
*Thurland Chattaway & Kerry Mills*

**1908**

CUDDLE UP A LITTLE CLOSER, LOVEY MINE
*Otto Harbach & Karl Hoschna*

DEAR LITTLE BOY OF MINE
*J. Keirn Brennan*
*Ernest R. Ball*

DOWN IN JUNGLE TOWN
*Edward Madden*
*Theodore Morse*

I WISH I HAD A GIRL
*Grace LeBoy Kahn & Gus Kahn*

SHINE ON HARVEST MOON
*Nora Bayes & Jack Norworth*

SUNBONNET SUE
*Will D. Cobb & Gus Edwards*

SWEET VIOLETS
*W. C. Powell*

TAKE ME OUT TO THE BALL GAME
*Jack Norworth & Albert Von Tilzer*

**1909**

BY THE LIGHT OF THE SILVERY MOON
*Gus Edwards & Edward Madden*

CASEY JONES
*Eddie Newton*
*T. Lawrence Seibert*

FROM THE LAND OF THE SKY BLUE WATER
*Charles Wakefield Cadman & Nelle Richmond Eberhart*

HAS ANYBODY HERE SEEN KELLY?
*C. W. Murphy*
*Will Letters*
*William J. McKenna*

I WONDER WHO'S KISSING HER NOW
*Frank R. Adams, Will M. Hough & Joseph E. Howard*
I'VE GOT RINGS ON MY FINGERS
*F. P. Barnes, Maurice Scott & R. P. Weston*
MEET ME TONIGHT IN DREAMLAND
*Leo Friedman & Beth Slater Whitson*
MY HERO
*Stanislaus Stange & Oscar Straus*
ON WISCONSIN
*Carl Beck & W. T. Purdy*
PUT ON YOUR OLD GREY BONNET
*Stanley Murphy & Percy Wenrich*
THAT'S A PLENTY
*Henry Creamer*
*Bert A. Williams*
WHEN YOU AND I WERE YOUNG, MAGGIE
*George W. Johnson*
*J. A. Butterfield*

**1910**
AH! SWEET MYSTERY OF LIFE
*Victor Herbert & Rida Johnson Young*
ALL ABOARD FOR BLANKET BAY
*Andrew B. Sterling*
*Harry Von Tilzer*
BIRTH OF PASSION
*Otto Harbach*
*Karl Hoschna*
CAPRICE VIENNOIS
*Fritz Kreisler*
CHINATOWN MY CHINATOWN
*William Jerome & Jean Schwartz*
COME JOSEPHINE IN MY FLYING MACHINE
*Fred Fisher*
*Alfred Bryan*
DOWN BY THE OLD MILL STREAM
*Tell Taylor*
EVERY LITTLE MOVEMENT
*Otto Harbach & Karl Hoschna*
I'D LOVE TO LIVE IN LOVELAND (WITH A GIRL LIKE YOU)
*W. R. Williams*
I'M FALLING IN LOVE WITH SOMEONE
*Victor Herbert & Rida Johnson Young*
ITALIAN STREET SONG
*Victor Herbert & Rida Johnson Young*
LET ME CALL YOU SWEETHEART
*Leo Friedman & Beth Slater Whitson*
LIEBESFREUD
*Fritz Kreisler*
LIEBESLIED
*Fritz Kreisler*

MOTHER MACHREE
*Ernest R. Ball, Chauncey Olcott & Rida Johnson Young*
PERFECT DAY, A
*Carrie Jacobs Bond*
PUT YOUR ARMS AROUND ME, HONEY
*Junie McCree & Albert Von Tilzer*
SOME OF THESE DAYS
*Shelton Brooks*
STEIN SONG
*Lincoln Colcord & E. A. Fenstad*

**1911**
ALEXANDER'S RAGTIME BAND
*Irving Berlin*
EVERYBODY'S DOIN' IT NOW
*Irving Berlin*
GOODNIGHT LADIES
*Harry Williams*
*Egbert Van Alstyne*
I WANT A GIRL (JUST LIKE THE GIRL THAT MARRIED DEAR OLD DAD)
*William Dilton & Harry Von Tilzer*
LITTLE GREY HOME IN THE WEST
*Hermann Lohr & D. Eardley Wilmot*
LITTLE LOVE, A LITTLE KISS, A
*A. Nilson Fysher, Adrian Ross & Lao Silesu*
OH YOU BEAUTIFUL DOLL
*Nat D. Ayer & A. Seymour Brown*
ROAMIN' IN THE GLOAMIN'
*Sir Harry Lauder*
SOMEWHERE A VOICE IS CALLING
*Eileen Newton & Arthur P. Tate*

**1912**
BE MY LITTLE BABY BUMBLE BEE
*Henry Marshall & Stanley Murphy*
GIANNINA MIA
*Rudolf Friml & Otto Harbach*
IT'S A LONG, LONG WAY TO TIPPERARY
*Jack Judge & Harry Williams*
MOONLIGHT BAY
*Edward Madden & Percy Wenrich*
MY MELANCHOLY BABY
*Ernie Burnett & George A. Norton*
RAGTIME COWBOY JOE
*Maurice Abrahams. Grant Clarke & Lewis F. Muir*
ROW, ROW, ROW
*William Jerome & James V. Monaco*
SWEETHEART OF SIGMA CHI
*Byron D. Stokes & F. Dudleigh Vernor*
SYMPATHY
*Rudolf Friml & Otto Harbach*

WAITING FOR THE ROBERT E. LEE
*L. Wolfe Gilbert & Lewis F. Muir*
WHEN I GET YOU ALONE TONIGHT
*Fred Fisher*
*Joe McCarthy*
*Joe Goodwin*
WHEN I LOST YOU
*Irving Berlin*
WHEN IRISH EYES ARE SMILING
*Ernest R. Ball,*
*George Graff, Jr. &*
*Chauncey Olcott*
WHEN THE MIDNIGHT CHOO CHOO LEAVES FOR ALABAM'
*Irving Berlin*
PEG O' MY HEART
*Alfred Bryan & Fred Fisher*
SWEETHEARTS
*Victor Herbert & Robert B. Smith*
TOO-RA-LOO-RA-LOO-RAL, THAT'S AN IRISH LULLABY
*James Royce Shannon*
TRAIL OF THE LONESOME PINE, THE
*Harry Carroll & Ballard MacDonald*
YOU MADE ME LOVE YOU, I DIDN'T WANT TO DO IT
*Joseph McCarthy & James V. Monaco*
WHERE DID YOU GET THAT GIRL?
*Bert Kalmar*
*Harry Puck*

**1913**
CURSE OF AN ACHING HEART, THE
*Al Piantadosi*
DANNY BOY
*Fred E. Weatherly (old Irish Air)*
GET OUT AND GET UNDER
*Grant Clarke, Edgar Leslie & Maurice Abrahams*
IF I HAD MY WAY
*James Kendis & Lou Klein*
MARCHETA
*Victor Schertzinger*
MY WIFE'S GONE TO THE COUNTRY
*Irving Berlin*

**1914**
ABA DABA HONEYMOON, THE
*Walter Donovan & Arthur Fields*
BALLIN' THE JACK
*Chris Smith & James H. Burris*
BY THE BEAUTIFUL SEA
*Harold Atteridge & Harry Carroll*
BY THE WATERS OF MINNETONKA
*Thurlow Lieurance*
CAN'T YOU HEAR ME CALLIN' CAROLINE
*William H. Gardner & Caro Roma*

DOWN AMONG THE SHELTERING PALMS
*James Brockman & Abe Olman*
GOOD-BYE, GIRLS, I'M THROUGH
*Ivan Caryll & John Golden*
HE'S A DEVIL IN HIS OWN HOME TOWN
*Irving Berlin & Grant Clarke*
I WANT TO GO BACK TO MICHIGAN, DOWN ON THE FARM
*Irving Berlin*
IF YOU DON'T WANT MY PEACHES, YOU'D BETTER STOP SHAKING MY TREE
*Irving Berlin*
KEEP THE HOME-FIRES BURNING, TILL THE BOYS COME HOME
*Lena G. Ford & Ivor Novello*
LITTLE BIT OF HEAVEN, SHURE THEY CALL IT IRELAND, A
*Ernest R. Ball & J. Keirn Brennan*
MISSOURI WALTZ
*Frederick Knight Logan & James R. Shannon*
ON THE 5:15
*Henry I. Marshall & Stanley Murphy*
ST. LOUIS BLUES
*W. C. Handy*
SIMPLE MELODY
*Irving Berlin*
SISTER SUSIE'S SEWING SHIRTS FOR SOLDIERS
*Hermann E. Darewski & R. P. Weston*
SYLVIA
*Clinton Scollard & Oley Speaks*
THAT'S A PLENTY
*Lew Pollack*
THERE'S A LONG, LONG TRAIL
*Zo Elliott & Stoddard King*
THEY DIDN'T BELIEVE ME
*Jerome Kern & M. E. Rourke*
TWELFTH STREET RAG
*Euday L. Bowman*
WHEN YOU WORE A TULIP AND I WORE A BIG RED ROSE
*Jack Mahoney & Percy Wenrich*
WHEN YOU'RE AWAY
*Henry Blossom & Victor Herbert*
WHEN YOU'RE A LONG, LONG WAY FROM HOME
*Sam M. Lewis & George W. Meyer*
YOU PLANTED A ROSE IN THE GARDEN OF LOVE
*Ernest R. Ball & J. Will Callahan*

**1915**

ALABAMA JUBILEE
*George L. Cobb & Jack Yellen*
ALONG THE ROCKY ROAD TO DUBLIN

*Bert Grant & Joe Young*
ARE YOU FROM DIXIE
*Jack Yellen*
*George L. Cobb*
AUF WIEDERSEHN
*Herbert Reynolds & Sigmund Romberg*
BABES IN THE WOOD
*Schuyler Greene & Jerome Kern*
BEATRICE FAIRFAX, TELL ME WHAT TO DO
*Grant Clarke, Joe McCarthy & James V. Monaco*
BY HECK
*S. R. Henry*
CANADIAN CAPERS
*Earl Burtnett, Gus Chandler, Henry Cohen & Bert White*
FASCINATION
*Harold Atteridge & Sigmund Romberg*
GIRL ON THE MAGAZINE COVER
*Irving Berlin*
HELLO, FRISCO!
*Gene Buck & Louis A. Hirsch*
HELLO, HAWAII, HOW ARE YOU
*Bert Kalmar, Edgar Leslie & Jean Schwartz*
I DIDN'T RAISE MY BOY TO BE A SOLDIER
*Alfred Bryan & Al Piantadosi*
IF WE CAN'T BE THE SAME OLD SWEETHEARTS, WE'LL JUST BE THE SAME OLD FRIENDS
*Joe McCarthy & James V. Monaco*
I LOVE A PIANO
*Irving Berlin*
IN A MONASTERY GARDEN
*Albert W. Ketelbey*
IRELAND IS IRELAND TO ME
*Ernest R. Ball, J. Keirn Brennan & Fiske O'Hara*
IT'S TULIP TIME IN HOLLAND
*Dave Redford & Richard A. Whiting*
JELLY ROLL BLUES
*Ferd (Jelly Roll) Morton*
JUST TRY TO PICTURE ME DOWN HOME IN TENNESSEE
*Walter Donaldson & William Jerome*
LOVE IS THE BEST OF ALL
*Henry Blossom & Victor Herbert*
MEMORIES
*Egbert Van Alstyne & Gus Kahn*
M-O-T-H-E-R, A WORD THAT MEANS THE WORLD TO ME
*Howard Johnson & Theodore Morse*
MY LITTLE GIRL
*Will Dillon, Sam M. Lewis & Albert Von Tilzer*
MY MOTHER'S ROSARY
*Sam M. Lewis & George W. Meyer*

NEAPOLITAN LOVE SONG
*Henry Blossom & Victor Herbert*
PACK UP YOUR TROUBLES IN YOUR OLD KIT-BAG
*George Asaf & Felix Powell*
PUT ME TO SLEEP WITH AN OLD-FASHIONED MELODY
*Dick Howard, Harry Jentes & Sam M. Lewis*
RAGGING THE SCALE
*Edward B. Claypoole*
SIAM
*Fred Fisher & Howard Johnson*
SO LONG LETTY
*Earl Carroll*
SOME LITLE BUG IS GOING TO FIND YOU
*Burt & Roy Atwell, Benjamin Hapgood, & Silvio Hein*
SUNSHINE OF YOUR SMILE, THE
*Leonard Cooke & Lillian Ray*
THERE'S A BROKEN HEART FOR EVERY LIGHT ON BROADWAY
*Fred Fisher & Howard Johnson*
THERE'S A LITTLE LANE WITHOUT A TURNING ON THE WAY TO HOME SWEET HOME
*Sam M. Lewis & George W. Meyer*
UNDERNEATH THE STARS
*Fleta Jan Brown & Herbert Spencer*
WE'LL HAVE A JUBILEE IN MY OLD KENTUCKY HOME
*Walter Donaldson & Coleman Goetz*
WHEN THE BOYS COME HOME
*John Hays & Oley Speaks*
WHEN I LEAVE THE WORLD BEHIND
*Irving Berlin*
WHEN YOU'RE IN LOVE WITH SOMEONE WHO IS NOT IN LOVE WITH YOU
*Grant Clarke & Al Piantadosi*
YOU KNOW AND I KNOW AND WE BOTH UNDER-STAND
*Schuyler Greene & Jerome Kern*
YOU'LL ALWAYS BE THE SAME SWEET GIRL
*Andrew B. Sterling & Harry Von Tilzer*

**1916**

ALLAH'S HOLIDAY
*Rudolf Friml & Otto Harbach*
ARRAH GO ON, I'M GONNA GO BACK TO OREGON
*Bert Grant, Sam M. Lewis & Joe Young*
BABY SHOES
*Joe Goodwin, Al Piantadosi & Ed Rose*
BEALE STREET BLUES
*W. C. Handy*
BOY SCOUTS OF AMERICA
*John Philip Sousa*

DOWN IN HONKY TONKY TOWN
*Charles McCarran & Chris Smith*
GIVE A LITTLE CREDIT TO YOUR DAD
*William Tracey & Nat Vincent*
GOOD-BYE, GOOD LUCK, GOD BLESS YOU
*Ernest R. Ball & J. Keirn Brennan*
HAVE A HEART
*Jerome Kern & P. G. Wodehouse*
HOW'S EVERY LITTLE THING IN DIXIE
*Albert Gumble & Jack Yellen*
I AIN'T GOT NOBODY
*Rogert Graham & Spencer Williams*
I CAN DANCE WITH EVERYBODY BUT MY WIFE
*Joseph Cawthorn & John L. Golden*
IF I KNOCK THE "L" OUT OF KELLY
*Bert Grant, Sam M. Lewis & Joe Young*
IF YOU HAD ALL THE WORLD AND ITS GOLD
*Bartley Costello, Harry Edelheit & Al Piantadosi*
IF YOU WERE THE ONLY GIRL IN THE WORLD
*Nat D. Ayer & Clifford Grey*
I'M SORRY I MADE YOU CRY
*N. J. Clesi*
IRELAND MUST BE HEAVEN, FOR MY MOTHER CAME FROM THERE
*Fred Fisher, Howard Johnson & Joe McCarthy*
KATINKA
*Rudolf Friml & Otto Harbach*
LI'L LIZA JANE
*Ada De Lachau*
MAMMY'S LITTLE COAL BLACK ROSE
*Raymond Egan & Richard A. Whiting*
M-I-S-S-I-S-S-I-P-P-I
*Bert Hanlon, Benny Ryan & Harry Tierney*
NAT'AN, NAT'AN, NAT'AN, TELL ME FOR WHAT ARE YOU WAITIN', NAT'AN
*James Kendis*
NOLA
*Felix Arndt*
OH! HOW SHE COULD YACKI, HACKI, WICKI, WACKI, WOO
*Charlene McCarron, Stanley Murphy & Albert Von Tilzer*
POOR BUTTERFLY
*Raymond Hubbell & John L. Golden*
PRETTY BABY
*Egbert Van Alstyne, Tony Jackson & Gus Kahn*
ROSES OF PICARDY
*Frederick E. Weatherly & Haydn Wood*

SINCE MAGGIE DOOLEY LEARNED THE HOOLEY HOOLEY
*Bert Kalmar, Edgar Leslie & George W. Meyer*
THERE'S A LITTLE BIT OF BAD IN EVERY GOOD LITTLE GIRL
*Grant Clarke & Fred Fisher*
THERE'S A QUAKER DOWN IN QUAKER TOWN
*David Berg & Alfred Solman*
THEY MADE IT TWICE AS NICE AS PARADISE (AND THEY CALLED IT DIXIELAND)
*Raymond Egan & Richard A. Whiting*
THEY'RE WEARING 'EM HIGHER IN HAWAII
*Joe Goodwin & Halsey K. Mohr*
THROW ME A ROSE
*Emmerich Kalman, Herbert Reynolds & P. G. Wodehouse*
TURN BACK THE UNIVERSE AND GIVE ME YESTERDAY
*Ernest R. Ball & J. Keirn Brennan*
WAY DOWN IN IOWA I'M GOING TO HIDE AWAY
*Sam M. Lewis, George W. Meyers & Joe Young*
WHAT DO YOU WANT TO MAKE THOSE EYES AT ME FOR
*Howard Johnson, Joe McCarthy & James V. Monaco*
YAAKA HULA HICKEY DULA
*E. Ray Goetz, Joe Young & Pete Wendling*
YOU CAN'T GET ALONG WITH 'EM OR WITHOUT 'EM
*Grant Clarke & Fred Fisher*

**1917**

ALL THE WORLD WILL BE JEALOUS OF ME
*Ernest R. Ball & Al Dubin*
BEALE STREET BLUES
*W. C. Handy*
BELLS OF ST. MARY'S, THE
*Emmett Adams & Douglas Furber*
BRING BACK MY DADDY TO ME
*Howard Johnson, George Meyer & William Tracey*
DARKTOWN STRUTTER'S BALL
*Shelton Brooks*
EILEEN (ALLANINA ASTH-ORE)
*Henry Blossom & Victor Herbert*
EVERYBODY OUGHT TO KNOW HOW TO DO THE TICKLE TOE
*Otto Harbach & Louis A. Hirsch*

FOR ME AND MY GAL
*E. Ray Goetz, Edgar Leslie & George W. Meyer*
GIVE A MAN A HORSE HE CAN RIDE
*Geoffrey O'Hara & James Thomson*
GIVE ME THE MOONLIGHT, GIVE ME THE GIRL
*Lew Brown & Albert Von Tilzer*
GOING UP
*Otto Harbach & Louis A. Hirsch*
GOOD-BYE BROADWAY, HELLO FRANCE
*Billy Baskette, Benny Davis & C. Francis Riesner*
HAIL, HAIL, THE GANGS ALL HERE
*Theodore Morse*
*Sir Arthur Sullivan*
HOMING
*Teresa Del Riego & Arthur L. Salmon*
I'D LOVE TO BE A MONKEY IN THE ZOO
*Bert Hanlon & Willie White*
I DON'T KNOW WHERE I'M GOING BUT I'M ON MY WAY
*George Fairman*
I DON'T WANT TO GET WELL
*Harry Jentes, Howard Johnson & Harry Pease*
I'M ALL BOUND 'ROUND WITH THE MASON DIXON LINE
*Sam M. Lewis, Jean Schwartz & Joe Young*
INDIANA
*James F. Hanely & Ballard MacDonald*
IRISH HAVE A GREAT DAY TONIGHT, THE
*Henry Blossom & Victor Herbert*
JOAN OF ARC, THEY ARE CALLING YOU
*Alfred Bryan, Willie Weston & Jack Wells*
JOHNSON RAG
*Henry Kleinkauf & Guy Hall*
JUMP JIM CROW
*Sigmund Romberg & Rida Johnson Young*
LEAVE IT TO JANE
*Jerome Kern & P. G. Wodehouse*
LITTLE MOTHER OF MINE
*Walter H. Brown & Harry T. Burleigh*
LORRAINE, MY BEAUTIFUL ALSACE LORRAINE
*Alfred Bryan & Fred Fisher*
LOVE WILL FIND A WAY
*Harry Graham & Harold Fraser- Simson*
NEAPOLITAN NIGHTS
*Harry D. Kerr & J. S. Zamecnik*

OH JOHNNY, OH JOHNNY, OH!
*Abe Olman & Ed Rose*
OUT WHERE THE WEST BEGINS
*Arthur Chapman & Estelle Philleo*
OVER THERE
*George M. Cohan*
RIALTO RIPPLES
*George Gershwin*
SAILIN' AWAY ON THE HENRY CLAY
*Egbert Van Alstyne & Gus Kahn*
SEND ME AWAY WITH A SMILE
*Al Piantadosi & Louis Weslyn*
SMILES
*J. Will Callahan & Lee S. Roberts*
SOME SUNDAY MORNING
*Raymond Egan, Gus Kahn & Richard A. Whiting*
THEY GO WILD, SIMPLY WILD OVER ME
*Fred Fisher & Joe McCarthy*
THINE ALONE
*Henry Blossom & Victor Herbert*
TIGER RAG
*Harry DeCosta & The Original Dixieland Jazz Band*
TILL THE CLOUDS ROLL BY
*Jerome Kern & P. G. Wodehouse*
WAIT TILL THE COWS COME HOME
*Anne Caldwell & Ivan Caryll*
WHEN YANKEE DOODLE LEARNS TO PARLEZ VOUS FRANCAIS
*William Hart & Ed Nelson*
WHERE DO WE GO FROM HERE?
*Howard Johnson & Percy Wenrich*
WHERE THE BLACK-EYED SUSANS GROW
*Dave Radford & Richard A. Whiting*
WHERE THE MORNING GLORIES GROW
*Raymond Egan, Gus Kahn & Richard A. Whiting*
WILL YOU REMEMBER
*Sigmund Romberg & Rida Johnson Young*

**1918**

AFTER YOU'VE GONE
*Henry Creamer & Turner Layton*
BEAUTIFUL OHIO
*Mary Earl & Ballard MacDonald*
CHONG
*Harold Weeks*
CLARINET MARMALADE
*H. W. Ragas*
*Larry Shields*

DAUGHTER OF ROSIE O'GRADY, THE
*Monty C. Brice & Walter Donaldson*
DEAR LITTLE BOY OF MINE
*Ernest R. Ball & J. Keirn Brennan*
DEAR OLD PAL OF MINE
*Gitz Rice & Harold Robe*
EVERYTHING IS PEACHES DOWN IN GEORGIA
*Milton Ager, Grant Clarke, & George W. Meyer*
GARDEN OF MY DREAMS
*Gene Buck & Dave Stamper*
GOOD MAN IS HARD TO FIND, A
*Eddie Green*
GOOD-MORNING, MR. ZIPZIP- ZIP
*Robert Lloyd*
HAVE A SMILE (FOR EVERYONE YOU MEET)
*J. Keirn Brennan, Paul Cunningham & Bert Rule*
HELLO, CENTRAL, GIVE ME NO MAN'S LAND
*Sam M. Levin, Jean Schwartz & Joe Young*
HINDUSTAN
*Oliver G. Wallace & Harold Weeks*
I FOUND THE END OF THE RAINBOW
*Joseph McCarthy, John Mears, & Harry Tierney*
I HATE TO LOSE YOU
*Grant Clarke & Archie Gottler*
I'M ALWAYS CHASING RAINBOWS
*Harry Carroll & Joseph McCarthy*
JA-DA
*Bob Carleton*
JUST A BABY'S PRAYER AT TWILIGHT
*M. K. Jerome, Sam Lewis & Joe Young*
K-K-K-KATY
*Geoffrey O'Hara*
LONESOME - THAT'S ALL
*Lee S. Roberts & Ben J. Bradley*
MADELON
*L. Bousquet, Alfred Bryan & Camille Robert*
MICKEY
*Neil Moret & Harry Williams*
OH! FRENCHY
*Con Conrad & Sam Ehrlich*
OH! HOW I HATE TO GET UP IN THE MORNING
*Irving Berlin*
OUI, OUI, MARIE
*Alfred Bryan, Fred Fisher & Joe McCarthy*
ROCK-A-BYE YOUR BABY WITH A DIXIE MELODY
*Sam M. Lewis, Jean Schwartz & Joe Young*
ROSE OF NO MAN'S LAND
*James A. Brennan & Jack Caddigan*

ROSE ROOM
*Art Hickman*
*Harry H. Williams*
SMILIN' THROUGH
*Arthur Penn*
SOMEBODY STOLE MY GAL
*Leo Wood*
SOMETIMES I FEEL LIKE A MOTHERLESS CHILD
*H. T. Burleigh*
SUNRISE AND YOU
*Arthur Penn*
THAT TUMBLE-DOWN SHACK IN ATHLONE
*Monte Carlo, Richard W. Pascoe & Alma Sanders*
THAT WONDERFUL MOTHER OF MINE
*Walter Goodwin & Clyde Hager*
THEY WERE ALL OUT OF STEP BUT JIM
*Irving Berlin*
TILL WE MEET AGAIN
*Raymond B. Egan & Richard A. Whiting*
WHEN YOU LOOK IN THE HEART OF A ROSE
*Marian Gillespie & Florence Methven*
WOULD YOU RATHER BE A COLONEL WITH AN EAGLE ON YOUR SHOULDER, OR A PRIVATE WITH A CHICKEN ON YOUR KNEE?
*Archie Gottler & Sidney D. Mitchell*

**1919**
ALICE BLUE GOWN
*Joseph McCarthy & Harry Tierney*
ALL THE QUAKERS ARE SHOULDER SHAKERS, DOWN IN QUAKER TOWN
*Bert Kalmar, Edgar Leslie & Pete Wendling*
AND HE'D SAY OO-LA LA! WEE WEE
*George Jessel & Harry Ruby*
BABY WON'T YOU PLEASE COME HOME
*Charles Warfield & Clarence Williams*
CHINESE LULLABY
*Robert Hood Bowers*
DADDY LONG LEGS
*Sam M. Lewis, Harry Ruby & Joe Young*
DARDANELLA
*Felix Bernard, Johnny S. Black & Fred Fisher*
HOW YA GONNA KEEP 'EM DOWN ON THE FARM AFTER THEY'VE SEEN PAREE?
*Walter Donaldson, Sam M. Lewis & Joe Young*
I MIGHT BE YOUR "ONCE-IN-A-WHILE"
*Victor Herbert & Robert B. Smith*
I WISH I COULD SHIMMY LIKE MY SISTER KATE
*Armand J. Piron*

I'M FOREVER BLOWING BUBBLES
*John W. Kellette & Jean Kenbrovin*
INDIAN SUMMER
*Al Dubin & Victor Herbert*
IRENE
*Harry Tierney*
*Joseph McCarthy*
JUST LIKE A GYPSY
*Nora Bayes & Seymour B. Simons*
LET THE REST OF THE WORLD GO BY
*Ernest R. Ball & J. Keirn Brennan*
LOVE SENDS A LITTLE GIFT OF ROSES
*Leslie Cooke & John Openshaw*
MAMMY O'MINE
*Maceo Pinkard & William Tracey*
MANDY
*Irving Berlin*
MY HOME TOWN IS A ONE HORSE TOWN, BUT IT'S BIG ENOUGH FOR ME
*Alex Gerber & Abner Silver*
MY ISLE OF GOLDEN DREAMS
*Walter Blaufuss & Gus Kahn*
NOBODY KNOWS AND NOBODY SEEMS TO CARE
*Irving Berlin*
OH BY JINGO, OH BY GEE, YOU'RE THE ONLY GIRL FOR ME
*Lew Brown & Albert Von Tilzer*
OH HOW I LAUGH WHEN I THINK HOW I CRIED ABOUT YOU
*George Jessel, Roy Turk & Willy White*
OH! WHAT A PAL WAS MARY
*Bert Kalmar, Edgar Leslie & Pete Wendling*
OLD FASHION GARDEN
*Cole Porter*
ON MIAMI SHORE
*Victor Jacobi & William LeBaron*
PEGGY
*Neil Moret & Harry Williams*
PRETTY GIRL IS LIKE A MELODY, A
*Irving Berlin*
ROSE OF WASHINGTON SQUARE
*James F. Hanley & Ballard MacDonald*
ROYAL GARDEN BLUES
*Clarence & Spencer Williams*
SUGAR BLUES
*Lucy Fletcher & Clarence Williams*
SWANEE
*Irving Caesar & George Gershwin*
TAKE YOUR GIRLIE TO THE MOVIES IF YOU CAN'T MAKE LOVE AT HOME
*Bert Kalmar, Edgar Leslie & Peter Wendling*

TELL ME
*J. Will Callahan & Max Kortlander*
THAT NAUGHTY WALTZ
*Sol P. Levy & Edwin Stanley*
TULIP TIME
*Gene Buck & Dave Stamper*
WAIT TILL YOU GET THEM UP IN THE AIR, BOYS
*Lew Brown & Albert Von Tilzer*
WHAT'LL WE DO ON A SATURDAY NIGHT, WHEN THE TOWN GOES DRY
*Harry Ruby*
WHIP-POOR-WILL
*Bud DeSylva & Jerome Kern*
WORLD IS WAITING FOR THE SUNRISE, THE
*Eugene Lockhart & Ernest Seitz*
YOU ARE FREE
*Victor Jacobi & William LeBaron*
YOUR EYES HAVE TOLD ME SO
*Egbert Van Alstyne, Walter Blaufuss & Gus Kahn*
YOU'RE A MILLION MILES FROM NOWHERE WHEN YOU'RE ONE LITTLE MILE FROM HOME
*Walter Donaldson, Sam M. Lewis & Joe Young*

**1920**

ALL SHE'D SAY WAS UMH HUM
*Mac Emery, Van & Schenck, King Zany*
ALT-WEIN
*Leopold Godowsky*
AVALON
*B. G. DeSylva, Al Jolson & Vincent Rose*
BEAUTIFUL ANNA BELL LEE
*Alfred Bryan, Artie Mehlinger & George W. Meyer*
BRIGHT EYES
*M. K. Jerome, Otto Motzan & Harry B. Smith*
BROADWAY ROSE
*Martin Fried, Otis Spencer & Eugene West*
CHILE BEAN
*Lew Brown & Albert Von Tilzer*
DADDY, YOU'VE BEEN A MOTHER TO ME
*Fred Fisher*
DO YOU EVER THINK OF ME
*Earl Burtnett*
DOWN BY THE O-HI-O
*Abe Olman & Jack Yellen*
FEATHER YOUR NEST
*James Brockman, James Kendis & Howard Johnson*
I LOST THE BEST PAL THAT I HAD
*Dick Thomas*
I NEVER KNEW I COULD LOVE ANYBODY LIKE I'M LOVING YOU
*Ray Egan, Roy K. Marsh & Tom Pitts*

I USED TO LOVE YOU BUT IT'S ALL OVER NOW
*Lew Brown & Albert Von Tilzer*

I'D LOVE TO FALL ASLEEP AND WAKE UP IN MY MAMMY'S ARMS
*Fred E. Ahlert, Sam M. Lewis & Joe Young*

IF YOU COULD CARE
*Herman Darewski & Arthur Wimperis*

I'LL BE WITH YOU IN APPLE BLOSSOM TIME
*Neville Fleeson & Albert Von Tilzer*

JAPANESE SANDMAN, THE
*Raymond B. Egan & Richard A. Whiting*

LEFT ALL ALONE AGAIN BLUES
*Anne Caldwell & Jerome Kern*

LILAC TREE (Perspicacity)
*George H. Gartlan*

LITTLE TOWN IN THE OULD COUNTY DOWN
*Monte Carlo, Richard W. Tilzer*
*Pascoe & Alma Sanders*

LOOK FOR THE SILVER LINING
*Bud DeSylva & Jerome Kern*

LOVE NEST
*Otto Harbach & Louis A. Hirsch*

MAH LINDY LOU
*Lily Strickland*

MARGIE
*Con Conrad, Benny Davis & J. Russel Robinson*

MY MAMMY
*Walter Donaldson, Sam Lewis*

WHISPERING
*Joe Young*

OLD PAL WHY DON'T YOU ANSWER ME
*M. K. Jerome, Sam M. Lewis & Joe Young*

PALE MOON
*Jesse G. M. Glick & Frederick Knight Logan*

PRETTY KITTY KELLY
*Edward G. Nelson & Harry Pease*

SAN
*Lindsay McPhail & Walter Michels*

SO LONG OO-LONG, HOW LONG YOU GONNA BE GONE
*Bert Kalmar & Harry Ruby*

TELL ME LITTLE GYPSY
*Irving Berlin*

THAT OLD IRISH MOTHER OF MINE
*William Jerome & Harry Von Tilzer*

TRIPOLI (On the Shores of Tripoli)
*Paul Cunningham, Al Dubin & Irving Weill*

WHEN BIG PROFUNDO SANG LOW C

*Marion T. Bohannon & George Botsford*
WHEN MY BABY SMILES AT ME
*Ted Lewis, Billy Munro, Andrew B. Sterling & Harry Von Tilzer*
WHISPERING
*Richard Coburn, John Schonberger & Vincent Rose*
WHOSE BABY ARE YOU
*Anne Caldwell & Jerome Kern*
WILD ROSE
*Clifford Grey & Jerome Kern*
YOUNG MAN'S FANCY, A
*Milton Ager, John Murray Anderson & Jack Yellen*

**1921**

AIN'T WE GOT FUN
*Raymond B. Egan, Gus Kahn & Richard A. Whiting*
ALL BY MYSELF
*Irving Berlin*
APRIL SHOWERS
*B. G. DeSylva & Louis Silvers*
BANDANA DAYS
*Eubie Blake & Noble Sissle*
BIMINI BAY
*Raymond B. Egan, Gus Kahn & Richard Whiting*
DAPPER DAN
*Lew Brown & Albert Von Tilzer*
DEAR OLD SOUTHLAND
*Henry Creamer & Turner Layton*
I AIN'T NOBODY'S DARLING
*Elmer Hughes & Robert A. King*
I FOUND A ROSE IN THE DEVIL'S GARDEN
*Fred Fisher & Willie Raskin*
I'LL FORGET YOU
*Ernest R. Ball & Annelu Burns*
I'M JUST WILD ABOUT HARRY
*Eubie Blake & Noble Sissle*
I'M NOBODY'S BABY
*Benny Davis & Milton Ager Lester Santley*
KA-LU-A
*Anne Caldwell & Jerome Kern*
KITTEN ON THE KEYS
*Zez Confrey & Sam Coslow*
LEARN TO SMILE
*Otto Harbach & Louis A. Hirsch*
LEAVE ME WITH A SMILE
*Earl Burtnett & Charles Koehler*
LOVE WILL FIND A WAY
*Eubie Blake & Noble Sissle*
MA, HE'S MAKING EYES AT ME
*Sidney Clare & Con Conrad*
MAKE BELIEVE
*Bennie Davis & Jack Shilkret*
MY MAN
*Jacques Charles, Channing Pollack, Albert Willemetz & Maurice Yvain*

PEGGY O'NEIL
*Gilbert Dodge, Ed G. Nelson & Harry Pease*
SALLY
*Clifford Grey & Jerome Kern*
SAY IT WITH MUSIC
*Irving Berlin*
SECOND HAND ROSE
*Grant Clarke & James F. Hanley*
SHEIK OF ARABY, THE
*Harry B. Smith, Ted Snyder & Francis Wheeler*
SHE'S MINE, ALL MINE
*Bert Kalmar & Harry Ruby*
SHUFFLE ALONG
*Eubie Blake & Noble Sissle*
SONG OF LOVE
*Dorothy Donnelly, adapted from melodies of H. Berte & F. Schubert by Sigmund Romberg*
SWANEE RIVER MOON
*H. Pitman Clarke*
SWEET LADY
*Frank Crumit, Howard Johnson & Dave Zoob*
TEN LITTLE FINGERS AND TEN LITTLE TOES, DOWN IN TENNESSEE
*Ed. G. Nelson, Harry Pease, Ira Schuster & Johnny White*
THERE'LL BE SOME CHANGES MADE
*W. Benton Overstreet & Bill Higgins*
THREE O'CLOCK IN THE MORNING
*Julian Robledo & Dorothy Terriss*
TUCK ME TO SLEEP IN MY OLD 'TUCKY HOME
*Sam Lewis, George W. Meyer & Joe Young*
WABASH BLUES
*Fred Meinken & Dave Ringle*
WANG-WANG BLUES
*Henry Busse, Buster Johnson, Gus Mueller & Leo Wood*
WHEN BUDDHA SMILES
*Nacio Herb Brown, Arthur Freed & King Zany*
WHEN FRANCIS DANCES WITH ME
*Benny Ryan & Violinsky*
WYOMING
*Gene Williams*
YOO-HOO
*B. G. DeSylva & Al Jolson*

**1922**

AGGRAVATIN' PAPA DON'T YOU TRY TO TWO-TIME ME
*Addy Britt, J. Russel Robinson & Roy Turk*
ALL OVER NOTHING AT ALL
*J. Keirn Brennan, Paul Cunningham & James S. Rule*
ANGEL CHILD
*Benny Davis, George E. Price & Abner Silver*

BLUE (AND BROKEN HEARTED)
*Lou Handman*
CAROLINA IN THE MORNING
*Walter Donaldson & Gus Kahn*
CHICAGO, THAT TODDLING TOWN
*Fred Fisher*
CHINA BOY
*Phil Boutelje & Dick Winfree*
CRINOLINE DAYS
*Irving Berlin*
DANCING FOOL
*Harry B. Smith, Ted Snyder & Francis Wheeler*
DO IT AGAIN
*B. G. DeSylva & George Gershwin*
DREAMY MELODY
*Ted Koehler*
*Frank Magine*
*Charlest Nast*
GEORGIA
*Walter Donaldson & Howard Johnson*
HOT LIPS
*Henry Busse, Lou Davis & Henry Lange*
I'LL BUILD A STAIRWAY TO PARADISE
*B. G. DeSylva, George Gershwin & Ira Gershwin*
KISS IN THE DARK, A
*B. G. DeSylva & Victor Herbert*
LADY OF THE EVENING
*Irving Berlin*
L'AMOUR TOUJOUR L'AMOUR
*Catherine C. Cushing & Rudolf Friml*
LIMEHOUSE BLUES
*Philip Braham & Doulgas Furber*
LOVESICK BLUES
*Cliff Friend & Irving Mills*
LOVIN' SAM, THE SHEIK OF ALABAM'
*Milton Ager & Jack Yellen*
MARY, DEAR, SOME DAY WE WILL MEET AGAIN
*Harry De Costa & M. J. Jerome*
MY BUDDY
*Walter Donaldson & Gus Kahn*
MY HONEY'S LOVIN' ARMS
*Joseph Meyer & Herman Ruby*
'NEATH THE SOUTH SEA MOON
*Gene Buck, Louis A. Hirsch, & Dave Stamper*
NOBODY LIED (When They Said That I Cried Over You)
*Hyatt Berry, Karyl Norman & Edwin J. Weber*
ON THE ALAMO
*Isham Jones, Gilbert Keyes & Joe Lyons*
O-OO ERNEST, ARE YOU EARNEST WITH ME

*Sidney Clare, Cliff Friend & Harry Tobias*
ROSE OF THE RIO GRANDE
*Ross Gorman, Edgar Leslie & Harry Warren*
RUNNIN' WILD
*A. Harrington Gibbs, Joe Grey & Leo Wood*
SAY IT WHILE DANCING
*Benny Davis & Abner Silver*
STUMBLING
*Zez Confrey*
TOOT, TOOT, TOOTSIE (GOO'BYE)
*Ernie Erdman, Ted Fiorito, Gus Kahn & Robert A. King*
TREES
*Joyce Kilmer & Oscar Rasbach*
'WAY DOWN YONDER IN NEW ORLEANS
*Henry Creamer & J. Turner Layton*
WHEN HEARTS ARE YOUNG
*Alfred Goodman, Sigmund Romberg & Cyrus Wood*
WHY SHOULD I CRY OVER YOU
*Ferde Grofe, Dorothy Terriss Ned Miller & Paul Whiteman Chester Conn*
YOU TELL HER I STUTTER
WONDERFUL ONE
*Cliff Friend & Billy Rose*

# CHAPTER 10

# BASIC CONSIDERATIONS IN MUSIC LICENSING

## SUMMARY

## III. COMMONLY USED BOILERPLATE TERMS AND CONDITIONS

A. Representations and Warranties
B. Indemnification
C. Assignment Clauses
D. Benefit of Successors and Assigns
E. Exclusion of All Other Express or Implied Warranties
F. Exclusion of Consequential Damages
G. Limitation of Liability
H. Severability
I. Cure Period
J. Entire Agreement or Integration Provision
K. Modifications and Amendments
L. Waiver
M. No Partnership or Agency
N. No Third-Party Beneficiaries
O. Choice of Law
P. Choice of Forum
Q. Arbitration
R. Confidentiality of Agreement
S. Notice
T. Advice of Legal Counsel
U. Attorneys' Fees
V. Recitals
W. Counterparts
X. Captions
Y. Gender
Z. Effective Date

## IV. AFFILIATED COMPANY PROBLEM

## V. GENERAL ADVICE TO MUSIC COPYRIGHT OWNER — ALWAYS ENCOURAGE ACTIVITY IN THE SONG

## VI. GENERAL ADVICE TO PERSONS SEEKING TO CLEAR LICENSES — FULLY DISCLOSE ALL THE USES YOU MIGHT CONCEIVABLY MAKE OF THE MUSIC

# CHAPTER 10

# BASIC CONSIDERATIONS IN MUSIC LICENSING

This chapter provides an outline of the basic considerations relevant in granting and clearing the several forms of licenses discussed in this book. It also provides a review of some of the basic terms and conditions commonly found in many music licenses, followed by some practical advice to both music copyright owners and persons seeking to clear a license to use music.

## I. Basic Music Licensing Factors

The basic considerations or factors in determining the provisions of most music licenses are:

A. The fee structure, whether it is established by custom, negotiation, or statute;

B. The value of the song, taking into consideration its popularity, historical significance, and overall quality;

C. The importance of the song in relation to its intended use; and

D. The scope of the intended use.

Each of these factors will be discussed generally in this chapter and then in more detail, and as they relate specifically to the various forms of licenses discussed, in the chapters that follow.

### A. Fee Structure

License fees are structured in various ways. Ideally, copyright owners would like to negotiate a fee each time their music is played, taking into consideration all the factors relevant to determining the fee structure and the appropriate fee to be charged, but certain practical and legal circumstances require that certain customary or compulsory fee structures be employed.

### *1. Practical Constraints*

For certain kinds of uses, such as the public performance of music in restaurants, theaters, concert halls, and nightclubs, and broadcast on radio and television, it would be impractical for music publishers to negotiate a separate license for each and every performance that occurs every day throughout the year. The transaction costs would be prohibitive.

The arrangement that has evolved for structuring and collecting fees for public performances is the *blanket license*, discussed more fully in Chapter 18. Every year, the performance rights societies issue a blanket license to each concert hall, restaurant, and other venue where the music in their repertoires is likely to be played, whether live or by use of a recording, and to every radio and television station that broadcasts programs containing copyrighted music. The fees collected under blanket licenses are then divided up by the performance rights society and distributed to their music publisher and songwriter members in accordance with a formula that attempts to allocate the funds on the basis of how much each song was performed during the year. Though they have the opportunity, owners of restaurants and nightclubs rarely negotiate the fees established by the performance rights societies for public performance licenses. But, considering the blanket nature of the license — permitting the performance of one or more of any of the hundreds of thousands of compositions in a performance rights society's repertoire as often as the user desires to perform them during the year — the fees charged are reasonable and it is generally not worth the effort to negotiate them.

ASCAP and BMI are each subject to court judgments, called *consent decrees*, which arose out of antitrust actions initiated by the U.S. Department of Justice many years ago. Where a licensee believes that the fees quoted by ASCAP or BMI are not reasonable, they may initiate a legal action, called a *rate hearing*, in a federal court for a determination of a reasonable fee for the use proposed by the licensee. Rate hearings are often lengthy and expensive and are usually initiated by radio and television broadcasters and large users of music on the Internet.

### *2. Legal Constraints*

In addition to practical constraints, various legal constraints dictate the types of fees and fee structures that are employed in licensing music. For example, a section of the U.S. copyright law commonly called the compulsory license provision,[1] which is more fully described in Chapter 13, compels a music copyright owner to license his music for use in certain audio recordings at a specific per copy fee that is established under the auspices of the U.S. Copyright Office. Where the law establishes a maximum fee, as it does here, there is little room for creativity and negotiation in granting and clearing licenses.

Also, certain court judgments, called *consent decrees*, agreed upon between performance rights societies and the U.S. government, require that permission to perform music in U.S. movie theatres be granted to film producers at the time the producers receive authorization to record the music in the film. This effectively requires licenses that would otherwise be negotiated by performance rights societies on a blanket basis with motion picture theaters to be licensed to the motion picture producers directly by the music copyright owners on a one time flat fee basis. Consent decrees also provide a mechanism to protect licensees from license fees they believe are exorbitant or the result of monopoly power. When a licensee believes a performance rights society subject to a consent decree is charging such fees, it may apply for relief in federal court in what is known as a *rate hearing.*

In some cases, copyright owners simply do not have the *right* upon which a license may be based. For example, though the copyright law confers upon the copyright owner an exclusive right of *public* performance, it does not confer an exclusive right of *private* performance. Accordingly, the copyright owner cannot require that a fee be paid every time you play a compact disc in your home, insert an audiocassette of copyrighted music in your car stereo, or sing a song in the shower. Instead, the fees derived from the use of music in recordings

---

[1] 17 U.S.C. Sec. 115.

are based on the number of copies of the recording that are made and distributed and the fees are charged to the record manufacturers at the time the recordings are made, rather than when a recording purchased by a consumer is played privately.

Thus, the particular structure used for a particular form of license can be influenced by one or more legal or practical considerations. In certain cases, the fee structure is determined merely by industry custom, which can be varied by negotiation. Fees are customarily structured on a flat fee, per copy fee, percentage of revenue, or blanket fee basis. Each of these fee structures will be discussed in the context in which they arise under the several forms of licenses discussed in the following chapters.

## B. Value of the Song

Whatever the fee structure, songs with higher inherent values can generally command higher fees for their use. A music copyright owner's ability to determine the value of a particular song will vary depending on his experience and access to information about the value of other musical compositions. The value of a song has both quantitative and qualitative factors, both adding up to the present value of the licensing revenue the song is expected to generate during the remainder of the life of the copyright.

### *1. Quantitative Factors Affecting Value*

The quantitative factors include how much the song has earned in licensing revenues in the past and how much others might be presently willing to pay for the copyright. It also includes the earnings potential of the song in relation to the earnings potential of other songs, particularly those in its genre. A music publisher with thousands of songs in its catalog and with years of experience in licensing music is likely to have access to much of the information necessary to adequately evaluate these factors. Because of its access to such information, a large music publisher is in a much better position than a typical licensee, songwriter, practicing lawyer, or small-scale music publisher to determine the quantitative value of a song for purposes of determining the appropriate license fee for a given use.

### 2. *Qualitative Factors Affecting Value*

The qualitative factors include the popularity of the song, the demographics of the listeners who are responsible for the song's popularity, the historical significance of the song, and overall quality of the song. Characteristics that help one understand these qualitative factors include, (1) a sound knowledge of music, whether in its writing, arranging or recording, (2) a person's experience with the song, either as having been "on the scene," either as a listener or as one working directly in the music business, when the song first became popular, and (3) a person's experience in having seen numerous examples of music of the same genre applied to a variety of uses. An appreciation of these qualitative factors is significant in determining the importance of the song in relation to its intended use. A large music publisher may have no special advantages over persons seeking to clear a license or others in evaluating these qualitative factors.

## C. The Importance of the Song in Relation to Its Intended Use

The more important the song is in relation to its intended use, the more money the copyright owner can charge in exchange for the license. Determining the importance of the song in relation to its intended use depends on a variety of factors. Before quoting a license fee, the music copyright owner should ask many questions of the potential licensee about the intended use of the song, and the person seeking to clear the license should be prepared with as many answers as possible.

### 1. *Why Is the Song Being Used?*

One question is whether the use will be primarily for a theatrical purpose or a promotional purpose. The purpose of the use may be purely to enhance the entertainment values of another work, such as when the use is in a motion picture, television program, television series, or musical play. By contrast, the purpose may be promotional in the sense of promoting some product, service, or the image of a particular company. There are special cases where the purpose of the audiovisual work is to feature the whole song itself, as is the case of a music video, in which case the purpose may be both theatrical (i.e., to entertain) and promotional, in the sense of promoting the recording artist or the song.

### *2. How Will the Song Be Rendered?*

Another issue is whether the use will include a vocal rendition or whether the use will be merely instrumental. Other questions include whether the music will be used as background music, foreground music, or music to help tell a story.

### *3. Will Any Changes Be Made?*

Still another question is whether the user intends to make any changes in the musical work. A licensee might ask for several kinds of changes, including:

a. A change in lyrics, for either purposes of parody, drama, or product endorsement;

b. A change in the fundamental character of the music, such as when a full-length version is edited down to suit special needs;

c. A translation of the lyrics into a foreign language.

Under most standard songwriter music publishing contracts, the songwriter grants to the publisher the right to change the lyrics and the right to authorize others to do so. However, some songwriters have negotiated provisions that give the songwriter the right to approve any changes to the work. Even if the contract does not contain such a provision, it is still good practice for the music publisher to consult with the songwriter before authorizing any changes in lyrics, particularly when the changes may be in the nature of a product endorsement or have some political significance, such as use in a political campaign.

The publisher and the songwriter should weigh the advantages of the license fee, performance credits, and general activity the use provides for the song against the possible damage to the long-term value of the song from an unsavory use. If changes to lyrics are approved, the exact nature of the new lyrics should be specified in the license; otherwise final approval should be withheld until the exact lyrics are determined.

#### *4. Will the Song's Title Be Used for a Special Purpose?*

Another question may be whether the song's title will be used for any special purpose. For example, the licensee may be intending to use the title as the title of his motion picture, television show, or product, such as a new brand of perfume. Note that song titles are not copyrightable; nor are they protectable as trademarks. However, there are some court decisions that indicate some recognition of rights in song titles akin to trademark protection, where the courts are trying to prevent unfair competition or someone from "palming off" their movie or product as somehow being associated with or endorsed by the writers or owners of the musical composition.[2]

Use of the title should be indicative of the importance of the song in relation to its intended use and some consideration should be given to charging an additional fee for its use. Specific examples of each of the foregoing considerations will be explored in the chapters that follow.

### D. The Scope of the Intended Use

Music copyright owners should avoid issuing a license that allows the licensee to do more with the song than the licensee originally intends. It is therefore important for the copyright owner to determine, before terms are quoted, just what the licensee intends to do with the song, where he intends to do it, and for how long. The license should be limited appropriately in all these respects.

Persons seeking to clear a license should attempt to obtain a license having as broad a scope as possible. Where this is not possible, the licensee should attempt to negotiate up front a series of options for additional uses that would otherwise require an additional license at a later time. It is therefore important for the licensee to tell the copyright owner up front everything he intends to do with the song. Factors that comprise the scope of a music license include:

1. the media in which the music will be embodied,

2. the term of the license,

---

[2] *Tomlin v. Walt Disney Productions*, 18 Cal. App. 3d 226, 235, 96 Cal. Rptr. 118 (1971).

3. the territory in which the use will be exercised,
4. the exclusivity required, if any,
5. other terms and conditions.

Each of these factors will be discussed in general terms below and at greater length in succeeding chapters.

### 1. What Media Will the License Cover?

The form of license (e.g., mechanical license, synchronization license, print license, etc.) that is appropriate for the requested use will depend upon the *media* for which the use is intended.

The media is often described with reference to the particular kind of physical copy in which the music is embodied and the compilation of materials with which the music is included. Examples of media include sheet music, songbooks or music folios, phonograph recordings, such as audiocassettes, long-playing albums and compact disks, motion pictures, television programs, videocassettes, laser video disks, music videos, television commercials, radio commercials, syndicated radio programs, published books, consumer products, such as music boxes, dolls, and other items, computer programs, audiovisual educational programs, and other media "now known or hereafter devised."

### 2. Through What Distribution Channels Will the Media Be Distributed?

Determining the media to be covered by the license involves a consideration of not only the physical media in which the music is to be embodied and any accompanying materials, but also the means by which the music is distributed, exhibited, or communicated to the public.

For example, the media may be broadly defined as "motion pictures." But motion pictures may be distributed through exhibition in movie theatres, broadcast on television, on videocassettes and laser discs intended for home distribution, and via the Internet, either downloaded for permanent use or streamed on-demand.

Television programs may be broadcast on local television stations, over television networks, by cable, by direct broadcast satellite, or by other forms of televised or broadcast distribution. Distribution may also be categorized by the manner in which television station operators are compensated — e.g., free TV, subscription channels, or pay-per-view channels. Music, of course, may also be the subject of live performances, such as those rendered in a nightclub, Broadway, or other stage production, or live performance that is broadcast on radio or television.

As we shall see in Chapter 15, on *Licensing of Music in Audiovisual Works*, the terms of the licenses for the same motion picture or television production will vary considerably, depending upon the means of distribution.

### *3. How Long Will the Use Be Permitted by the License?*

How long a use is permitted by the license is referred to as the *term*, or duration, of the license. The term of the license will often depend upon the type of license being granted. The music copyright owner should almost always prefer to restrict the license's duration to the shortest possible time, although the term of the license will normally be dictated by the custom and practice normally associated with similar licenses. Restricting the term of the license will allow the copyright owner to collect an additional fee upon its expiration if renewal of the license is desired by the licensee.

Persons seeking to clear a license should attempt to obtain a license having as long a term as possible. Where the copyright owner insists upon limiting the term, the licensee should attempt to negotiate, up front, a series of options to renew the term of the license, offering an additional fee payable upon the exercise of each renewal period. Even if the renewal fees, considered at the time the license is entered into, appear unreasonably high, by obtaining options to renew, the licensee will at least be assured that a license to extend the term will be readily available.

### *4. Where Will the Use Be Permitted?*

Music licenses typically contain a restriction on countries, or regions within countries, in which the licensee may perform, exhibit, broadcast or distribute copies of the music. This restriction is referred to as the *territory* of the license.

The territory in which the licensee may exercise his rights under the license is normally something less than *worldwide.* As with restricting how long the license lasts, the music copyright owner will generally prefer to restrict the territory of the license to the smallest geographic area consistent with the licensee's actual needs. Each additional territory will command an additional fee. Restricting the territory of the license will allow the music copyright owner to collect an additional fee if the licensee later determines that he would like to extend his use to other territories. The music copyright owner's leverage to charge a premium fee increases after the licensee has gone to great expense to incorporate his music into a work, particularly where it would be expensive, inconvenient, or impossible to replace the music with a less expensive alternative.

In many cases, the licensee will not require a license for other territories, such as, for example, where a license to use music in a radio advertisement for a local drugstore limits the territory to the region in which the drugstore finds all its customers. However, a licensee may wish to negotiate options to expand the territory to those areas in which it is likely the work will be used. For example, where a company desires to test a commercial advertisement for one of its national brands in a limited region of the country, the company may wish to pay only for the use of the music in the test region, while at the same time negotiating an option to expand the territory to the rest of the country for eventual network broadcast. The licensee's leverage is at its height before he commits to use the music or makes any substantial expenditure toward that end. A licensee, therefore, is advised to obtain options for additional territories wherever it is known that such licenses might be required. It is probably a good idea to obtain such options even when the likelihood of expanding the territory is remote.

The territory may be restricted to specific countries, such as "the United States," and "the United States and Canada." Licenses may be unrestricted in territory, as what is intended by the use of the term "worldwide," although it has been suggested the word "worldwide" would not cover use on space stations. With this in mind, a licensee might consider whether the term "universe" should be used in its place, or whether — with tongue in cheek — the term, "solar system" would be sufficient for most licenses. (We have seen licenses that employ the terms "universe" and "universe-wide" in place of "worldwide," so the reader should not think this idea is far-fetched.) To avoid ambiguities, names of actual countries should be used — Africa, Asia, and the Caribbean are not countries.

Certain contractual and organizational considerations may affect how a music publisher determines the territory of the license. Large music publishers may have policies with respect to the ability of its U.S. headquarters to negotiate on behalf of its international affiliates and subsidiaries for the licensing of use in territories outside the United States. These policies may actually be formally governed by the terms and conditions of the subpublication agreements between a United States publisher and its international affiliates or subsidiaries. Such policies and contractual terms may vary depending on the type of license. For example, motion picture synchronization licenses are generally negotiated centrally for worldwide use, but licenses for use in connection with product advertising may require negotiation on a country-by-country basis with local publishing affiliates.

Certain legal considerations may also affect how you define the territory. For example, European Union (EU) regulations that prohibit contracts that restrict the free flow of goods among member countries may invalidate licenses that attempt to provide exclusivity with respect to specified countries within the EU. The solution may be to simply define the territory as "member countries of the European Community." (A publisher might consider problems arising with respect to existing licenses and exclusive publishing arrangements as the membership in the EU changes over time.)

The license may also be limited to certain areas within the United States, such as "the State of New York." This, however, might not be acceptable to a licensee who intends to use the song in television or radio broadcasts. Radio waves don't normally respect state lines. Accordingly, the territory can be defined by some regional designation, such as "the greater New York City area," "Southern California," or "the mid-Atlantic states."

### 5. *Who Else May Exercise a Similar Privilege to Use the Work?*

*Exclusivity*, as we have seen, is a right to exclude or prevent others from doing some act. Granting exclusivity, therefore, is something more than merely granting permission, or a license, to another to do something he or she would not otherwise have the privilege of doing without your permission; it involves granting to another a claim or right under the copyright, an actual piece of property, which is a form of subdivision of the copyright.

Exclusive rights are, of course, granted in connection with a grant of an entire copyright (in which case all exclusive rights under the copyright are granted at one time, less any exclusive rights that are reserved to the original owner). Leaving aside that special circumstance, exclusivity is rarely granted in music revenue transactions, except in connection with the grant of exclusive print rights for printed sheet music or in certain cases where the publisher agrees, in connection with a license to use the music in commercial advertising, to a restriction on licensing the song for limited periods of time in connection with works or products that compete with the products of the licensee. For example, a music publisher may license the use of the song, *Hooray for Hollywood* for a one-year period in connection with television advertising of the Bank of Hollywood and may agree not to license the same song to another bank for advertising banking services in the Los Angeles area for the one-year period of the license.

Other than for such limited commercial uses, or other extraordinary uses, such as use of the song's title or story line, music publishers should generally avoid granting exclusivity, because earnings from other sources can be significantly curtailed by broadly applied exclusivity provisions. If exclusivity is granted in the appropriate cases, the operative language should be very carefully defined.

## II. Common Terms and Conditions Regarding Fees and Payment

Each particular kind of license will often require special provisions depending upon the nature of the distribution involved, the type of payment method agreed upon, or other provisions negotiated by the parties.

### A. Advances

An *advance* is a lump-sum payment received in consideration for a grant of rights or license that is *recoupable* (i.e., deductible), by the person who paid the advance, from future royalties that would otherwise be payable to the person who received the advance. Advances are often paid *up front*, such as upon signing of the agreement, but also may be paid on a periodic basis, regardless of whether sufficient royalties have been earned during the period in which the advance is paid.

Some advances are due when an agreed upon milestone is reached, sometimes referred to as a *roll-over advance.* For example, should a royalty statement indicate that an advance has been fully recouped, the agreement may require a further advance be paid in an amount agreed upon in advance, typically one that is the same size as the original advance. Another example of roll-over advance is when a certain pre-specified number of copies of an item under license have been sold an additional advance will be due.

Advances may be paid for a variety of reasons. A publisher often pays an advance to make sure the person receiving it, such as a songwriter, does not "starve" while he is performing services for the publisher. A songwriter may insist upon receiving an advance to make sure the publisher is making an investment sufficient to provide an incentive for the publisher to recoup that investment by making the proper efforts to promote the songwriter's works. A music publisher may insist upon an advance to make sure the licensee has sufficient incentive to market the products containing copies of the song licensed.

Advances are usually not *returnable*, meaning that if the advances turn out to be greater than the amount of royalties ever earned from sales, the person who received the advance never has to pay the unearned balance of the advance back to the person who paid it; in other words, an advance is not like a loan. Such advances are generally referred to as "non-returnable, recoupable advances." However, advances may be returnable if the person who receives the advance fails to perform material provisions of the agreement under which he has received the advance.

## B. Cross-Collateralization

Music publishers, recording companies, and other types of publishers who customarily have royalty obligations to artists and writers will nearly always be certain to *cross-collateralize* all contracts under which they pay advances to a particular artist. Contracts that are cross-collateralized are those under which royalties earned pursuant to one contract are used to recoup advances earned under another contract. You can spot cross-collateralization by looking for the following *Three Little Words*: "or any other." For example, the concept of cross-collateralization is contained in the following provision:

> Advances paid hereunder may be recouped from royalties earned under this *or any other* agreement between the parties.

Under certain circumstances, cross-collateralization will defeat one of the primary reasons artists seek advances. If the purpose of the advance is to give the person paying the advance the proper incentive to promote a particular song, allowing the cross-collateralization of that advance against royalties payable under a contract for another song, which by reason of its popularity might sell itself, will defeat the purpose of the original advance. Accordingly, a party might reasonably insist that the cross-collateralization provision be stricken from the agreement.

### C. Bonus

A *bonus* is a lump-sum payment that is not recoupable from royalties or any other payments earned under an agreement or other agreements. Bonuses are rare, with publishers almost always insisting on recouping lump-sum payments from royalties, even where the potential recoupment is remote. However, a publisher may offer a "signing" bonus to an artist whose business he is trying to attract.

### D. Payment and Accounting

Licenses that call for a flat fee payable by the licensee upon signing of the license will not require extensive provisions regarding the means of payment and accounting procedures. However, the person clearing a license requiring payment *upon signing* or *upon execution*, should negotiate a change to the payment provision to allow the licensee a reasonable period of time, such as seven days after execution, to remit payment.

Licenses that contain provisions for the payment of a royalty, such as a percentage of net revenues from sales of copies of the music, will contain sophisticated provisions relating to how and when the copyright owner will be paid the royalties. For example, payments are usually expected on a quarterly basis, within some reasonable period after the end of each calendar quarter in which there are revenues derived from the work. A written royalty statement detailing the sources of the revenues upon which the royalty is based commonly accompanies the payment.

A payment provision drafted in favor of a licensee required to pay royalties might be drafted as follows:

> Licensee will compute the total composite royalties earned by Owner pursuant to this agreement quarterly within forty five (45) days after the end of each quarter, and will deliver to Owner a royalty statement for each such period together with the net amount of royalties computed in accordance with this section, if any, which shall be payable after deducting any and all unrecouped advances and chargeable costs under this agreement or any other agreement between Owner and Licensee. No statement will be rendered to Owner for any quarterly period for which the cumulative balance due Owner is less than $50.00.

### E. Audit Privileges

In any contract providing for the payment of royalties based upon the number of units of a work sold or the gross or net revenues derived from sales of a work, the copyright owner will typically require an *audit privilege*, which is the privilege to inspect the books and records of the licensee relating to the revenues derived from the licensed work.

A licensee should negotiate some reasonable limitations on these privileges, such as a provision requiring advance notice of an audit, and requiring that the audit be conducted during normal business hours, only once a year, and at the expense of the copyright owner. The copyright owner will normally insist that if the audit reveals that the licensee underpaid the required license fee by more than 5–10%, then the licensee will pay for the costs of the audit. All licenses that contain audit provisions should also contain a provision that obligates the licensee to maintain accurate books and records in the first place. A number of accounting firms specialize in performing audits of such records, and a publisher should consider having its licensees audited on a periodic basis to, as the saying goes, "keep them honest."

An audit provision drafted in favor of a licensee whose books and records may potentially be made subject to inspection might be drafted as follows:

> Upon at least fifteen (15) days prior written notice to Licensee and at Owner's sole cost and expense, Owner, or a nationally recognized certified public accountant on Owner's behalf, shall have the right once each year to inspect and audit such of Licensee's business books and records as may reasonably be necessary for Owner to verify the accuracy of any royalty statement rendered by Licensee within the twelve (12) month period immediately preceding the date of the inspection. The information contained in a royalty statement shall be conclusively deemed correct and binding upon Owner, resulting in the loss of all further audit privileges with respect to such statement, unless specifically challenged by written notice from Owner within twelve (12) months from the date such royalty statement was delivered by Licensee. Any inspection of Licensee's books and records pursuant to this section shall be conducted by Owner at Licensee's premises, only during Licensee's normal business hours, under Licensee's supervision and in a manner which does not interfere with Licensee's business operations. Owner shall specify, at least fifteen (15) days in advance of any inspection, the list of items that Owner desires to inspect. Owner shall keep all information learned as a result of such inspection in strict confidence.

## F. Reserves Against Returns

A licensee obligated to pay royalties on physical copies sold to the public should attempt to negotiate the ability to hold a *reserve against returns.* When a licensee makes sales of copies of a work containing licensed music, such as a recording or a videogram, the licensee may expect that some of the sales during a quarter will be returned during a subsequent quarter. (Alluding to the customary designation of *gold*, as a record that sells a million copies, and *platinum*, as a record that sells two million, there circulates an old joke in the record business that a certain artist's album "shipped gold and returned platinum!") When a licensee holds a reserve against returns, he deducts a certain percentage (e.g.,

25%) from the royalties he would otherwise be required to pay for sales of the work for a particular quarter, and holds on to that deduction in anticipation that there might later be a return of 25% of the records sold during that quarter.

A provision permitting a licensee to hold a reserve against returns might look like this:

> Licensee may retain as a reserve against subsequent charges, credits or returns, a reasonable portion of payable royalties.

The importance of holding a reserve may depend on the licensee's feeling about the copyright owner's willingness and ability to reimburse the licensee in the event of an overpayment due to a subsequent return of sales. The copyright owner, if he is willing to accept this provision at all, would be wise to negotiate a limitation on the provision, requiring that any such reserve will be liquidated within some reasonable period of time after the quarter in which it is withheld. For example, a licensee might be required to liquidate, or pay reserves previously held, to the copyright owner in the quarter immediately following the quarter in which they were held. The copyright owner would also be advised to limit the percentage of the amount to be reserved to an amount that is reasonably related to the amount of sales returns the licensee actually tends to experience for similar kinds of works. For example, the amount of reserves against returns withheld in any one quarter could be limited to 15% or 25%.

Limitations on a licensee's right to hold a reserve against returns might be drafted as follows:

> Licensee may retain as a reserve against subsequent charges, credits or returns, a reasonable portion of payable royalties; provided, however, that such reserve shall be limited to 25% of royalties payable during a quarter and shall be liquidated in the quarterly accounting period immediately following that in which it was retained.

## G. Most Favored Nations

A copyright owner, unsure of what fee to charge, or even how to structure the fee, will sometimes ask that he be paid a license fee that is "no less favorable than" the fee received for the use of any other song featured in the licensee's work. Such a provision is commonly called a *most favored nations* clause. Most favored nations clauses are often used as a crutch by those who don't know how to analyze a use, don't have any experience with licensing for the particular use (and therefore have a fear of making a bad deal), or don't want to make the effort to analyze the particular use.

A person seeking to clear the license who is reluctant to agree to such a provision should be prepared to argue that the song for which he seeks a license has significantly less importance than other songs in the work. In other words, it makes no sense to compare *apples* and *oranges* when setting the terms of the license. If a licensee does agree to a most favored nations clause, a favorite negotiating technique may present itself to the licensee when clearing permission to use other songs in the same work: "I can't give you a higher fee, Mr. Copyright Owner, because giving you a higher fee would require me, under the most favored nations clauses that I've signed with other copyright owners, to raise all the other fees, and that I just cannot afford to do!"

## III. COMMONLY USED BOILERPLATE TERMS AND CONDITIONS

This section will summarize some of the standard provisions, sometimes referred to as *legal boilerplate* provisions, contained in many long-form license agreements.

### A. Representations and Warranties

Most long-form license agreements will contain a series of representations or warranties intended to give the licensee some comfort that he will be able to exercise without hindrance the privilege for which he is receiving permission.

A *representation* is a statement as to the existence or nonexistence of a fact or a state of mind that another relies upon in entering into a contract. For example, a copyright owner may represent "that it has the right to grant this license" and "that the work does not infringe any copyrights of another." A copyright owner may also make a representation as to his state of mind, such as when he represents "that, to the best of my knowledge, the work does not infringe any copyrights of another." A *best of knowledge* representation is significantly less meaningful than a representation as to the existence of a fact and will not always be acceptable to assignees or licensees.

A *warranty* is an assurance that certain facts or conditions exist and will continue to exist during the term of the license. A person negotiating a license on behalf of a licensee should request that the term "warrant" be added to provisions containing representations of the licensor. For example, the copyright owner should "represent *and warrant* that the work does not infringe any copyrights of another." The addition of the word "warrant" would enable the licensee to add, in an action for a breach of contract arising from a misrepresentation, a cause of action for *breach of warranty*, which could provide the licensee with some additional remedies and advantages in any litigation arising out of the licensor's breach of the agreement.

Note, however, music licensors are generally reluctant to modify their boilerplate language without legal advice, and where the cost of such legal advice may approach or exceed the license fee being charged for the license, it is unlikely that any change would even be considered. Should a licensee find some resistance in making changes, the licensee should weigh the business risks involved. Normally, it is not worth expending much time or expense to negotiate for these changes and being unable to negotiate such a change is certainly not worth walking away from a license unless you are aware of some specific facts that may justify having a strong set of warranties and representations.

Music licensors typically want to give as few warranties and representations as possible. Warranty provisions providing only minimal comfort are quite common and the following is a good example:

> Publisher warrants only that it has the right to grant this license and this license is given and accepted without any other representations, warranty or recourse, express or implied, except for Publisher's agreement to repay the consideration for this license if said warranty shall be breached with respect thereto. In no event shall the total liability of Publisher in any case exceed the amount of consideration received by it hereunder.

Licensees typically desire a little more than that and typically request warranties and representations sufficient to assure that the work will not infringe copyrights or other rights of another. Those who are receiving a full transfer of copyright might desire certain additional warranties, such as those contained in the following provision:

> Owner hereby warrants and represents to Company that Owner has the right to enter into this agreement and to grant to Company all of the rights granted herein, and that the exercise by Company of any and all of the rights granted to Company in this agreement will not violate or infringe upon any common law or statutory rights of any person, firm or corporation including, without limitation, contractual rights, copyrights, and rights of privacy. Owner further warrants that the rights granted herein are free and clear of any claims, demands, liens or encumbrances.

When the person who is transferring a copyright in a newly created work was the one who authored the work, the following set of warranties and representations may be required:

> Composer hereby warrants and represents that the Composition is an original work, that neither the Composition nor any part thereof infringes upon the title, literary or musical property or copyright of any other work nor the statutory, common law or other rights (including rights of privacy or publicity) of any person, firm or corporation or violates any applicable criminal statute, that he is the sole writer and composer and the sole owner of the Composition and of all the rights therein, that he has not sold, assigned, transferred, hypothecated or mortgaged any right, title or interest in or to the Composition or any part thereof or any of the rights herein conveyed, that he has not made or entered into any agreement with any other person, firm or corporation affecting the Composition or any right, title or interest therein or in the copyright thereof, that no person, firm or corporation other than Composer has or has had claims or has claimed any right, title or interest in or to the Composition or any part thereof, any use thereof or any copyright therein, that the Composition has never been published, and that Composer has full right, power and authority to make this present instrument of sale and transfer.

Music publishing agreements will also require the songwriter to warrant that he or she is the "sole author," providing an assurance that no one will come forth to claim to be the author or co-author of the work, and that the work was "original," meaning it was original with the songwriter and not copied from the work of another or from a work in the public domain.

If the copyright owner is assigning an exclusive right under the copyright, the assignee will want additional warranties such as the following:

> Owner shall not during the term of this Agreement do any act or authorize, license or knowingly permit any third party (other than a party authorized or licensed by Company) to do any act which would in any way derogate from or violate the exclusive right, license and privilege granted to Company by this Agreement. The parties expressly acknowledge that the Compositions and all rights granted and to be granted to Company hereunder are of a special, unique and intellectual character which gives them peculiar value, and that in the event of a breach by Owner of any term, condition, warranty, representation or agreement hereunder, Company will be caused irreparable injury. Owner expressly agrees that in the event of any such breach, Company shall be entitled to injunctive and other equitable relief or damages, in addition to any other rights and remedies available to it, and Company shall have the right to recoup any damages from any sums which may thereafter become due and payable to Owner hereunder.

## B. Indemnification

Representations and warranties are generally given additional force by an indemnification provision. The indemnification provision makes it clear that the entire financial burden incurred as a result of a breach of any representation or warranty set forth in the agreement will fall on the person making those representations and warranties.

The following is an example of a short, but comprehensive indemnification provision:

> Owner agrees to indemnify and hold Licensee harmless from any claim, demand, suit, action, proceeding, prosecution, damage, expense (including reasonable attorneys' fees), liability or loss of any kind or nature arising from or out of any claim asserted against Licensee which is inconsistent with any of the warranties, covenants or representations made by Owner herein.

A promise to *hold harmless* another against claims made and actions filed by third parties means that the person making the promise will bear all the expenses of defending the claim or lawsuit, but will also mean he or she will control the defense of the matter, unless contrary terms are specifically provided. Often, an assignee or licensee will not feel comfortable with the assignor or licensor maintaining control over the handling of the claim or lawsuit, particularly where the assignor or licensor is not wealthy or financially stable. Accordingly, publishing and licensing agreements will often clarify the rights and obligations of the parties with respect to any lawsuits filed concerning those matters covered by representations and warranties. For example, a standard publishing agreement between a songwriter and a music publisher may provide that the music publisher has (i) the privilege to defend itself against any claim or lawsuit, (ii) the privilege to choose its own legal counsel to do so, (iii) the privilege to settle any such claim or lawsuit on such terms as it deems appropriate, (iv) the right to reimbursement from the songwriter for any payments made as a result of a settlement or final judgment entered against the publisher, (v) the right to reimbursement of attorneys' fees and litigation costs incurred to defend the matter, whether or not such defense is successful, and (vi) the privilege to withhold any royalties and apply them to cover any obligations of the writer with respect to the claim or lawsuit.

A songwriter who has the bargaining leverage to vary such terms should attempt to eliminate any responsibility for mere "claims" and limit the indemnity to "final judgments." Because of their size, music publishers often attract lawsuits merely because of their "deep pockets," and songwriters should not be responsible for nuisance suits. If the publisher has a license from the writer to make derivative works, as they often do, the indemnity should not apply to the extent publisher added material or edited the work. In fact, the songwriter should require the publisher to provide an indemnity regarding any materials supplied to the writer or any materials added over which the writer had no control. For example, the following might be added to the writer's indemnification provision:

> Publisher similarly indemnifies and holds Writer harmless as to material furnished by Publisher for use by Writer hereunder or material added or changes made by Publisher.

A songwriter with a great degree of bargaining leverage may request that he be given the option to defend any lawsuits with counsel of his own choosing, at his own expense, provided that if he does, publisher may participate in the defense with counsel of its choosing and at its expense. The contours of "participating in the defense" can be problematic; generally, it is the person who "controls" the defense who makes the decisions in litigation.

Because any settlement will eventually come out of the songwriter's pocket, a songwriter may request that any settlements be made only with his consent, to make sure the publisher does not settle upon unreasonable terms. Publishers will not normally permit this, because it has the deep pockets and may not be able to collect from the songwriter for many years, if at all. A possible compromise to make sure the publisher has a good incentive to settle upon reasonable terms is to concede that the publisher has the sole right to settle, but require that the publisher be responsible for paying some percentage, perhaps 50%, of any settlement.

Publishers will want to withhold any payments due to the writer during the pendency of any claim or litigation. The writer should seek to curtail the amount that may be withheld to a percentage, place a dollar ceiling on the amount, or limit length of time during which moneys may be withheld with respect to any particular claim. If the publisher withholds any money, the money should go into escrow; this is to protect the writer's money in the event the publisher goes bankrupt.

## C. Assignment Clauses

A copyright owner will generally require that any assignment of the license be subject to the copyright owners consent. The following is a typical provision governing restricting the assignment of a license:

> This license is personal to Licensee and may not be assigned or transferred without Owner's prior written consent. No such transfer or assignment shall become effective unless and until the transferee or assignee shall deliver to Owner a written agreement assuming the further performance of Licensee's obligations hereunder, and no such transfer or assignment shall relieve Licensee of any obligation hereunder. However, Licensee may enter into sublicenses within the Territory to the extent necessary to permit the uses authorized by this license.

The following provision is a stronger, more complete restriction on a party's ability to assign its rights or delegate its obligations under an agreement:

> Licensee may not assign this Agreement or any of its rights or obligations hereunder (including without limitation rights and duties of performance) to any third party or entity, and this Agreement may not be involuntarily assigned or assigned by operation of law, without the prior written consent of Owner, which consent shall be given or withheld by Owner in the sole exercise of its discretion.

The restriction on assignments *by operation of law* is intended to require permission even when two corporations combine by *merger* — a circumstance that does not necessarily involve the transfer of an agreement from one party to another. In a merger, the parties combine to form one entity.[3]

A music publisher engaged in the merger or acquisition of another publisher should, in connection with its due diligence investigation prior to the closing of the transaction, consider the assignment provisions of all material songwriter agreements of the publisher being acquired. For example, the acquiring publisher may come across an assignment provision such as the following, which was excerpted from the 1978 version of the standard Songwriter's Guild Agreement (formerly, AGAC) between songwriters and publishers:

> 18. Except to the extent herein otherwise expressly provided, the Publisher shall not sell, transfer, assign, convey, encumber or otherwise dispose of the composition or the copyright or copyrights secured thereon without the prior written consent of the Writer. The Writer has been induced to enter into this contract in reliance upon the value to him of the personal service and ability of the Publisher in the exploitation of the composition, and by reason thereof it is the intention of the parties and the essence of the relationship between them that the rights herein granted to the Publisher shall remain with the Publisher and that the same shall not pass to any other person

[3] Despite our experience with mergers and an apparently sound etymological basis to support the suggestion, the word merger, as a friend of ours has suggested, is not a portmanteau or combination of the words "marriage" and "murder."

> including, without limitations, successors to or receivers or trustees of the property of the Publisher, either by act or deed of the Publisher or by operation of law, and in the event of the voluntary or involuntary bankruptcy of the Publisher, this contract shall terminate, provided, however, that the composition may be included by the Publisher in a bona fide voluntary sale of its music business or its entire catalog of musical compositions, or in a merger or consolidation of the Publisher with another corporation, in which event the Publisher shall immediately give written notice thereof to the Writer, and provided further that the composition and the copyright therein may be assigned by the Publisher to a subsidiary or affiliated company generally engaged in the music publishing business. If the Publisher is an individual, the composition may pass to a legatee or distributee as part of the inheritance of the Publisher's music business and entire catalog of musical compositions. Any such transfer or assignment, shall, however, be conditioned upon the execution and delivery by the transferee or assignee to the Writer of an agreement to be bound by and to perform all of the terms and conditions of this contract to be performed on the part of the Publisher.

While the foregoing assignment provision should not normally impose an obstacle to an acquisition or merger, the last sentence of the provision does impose the requirement that the publisher gives immediate written notice of the acquisition to the writer and deliver an agreement to be bound by the terms of the writer's contract. The assignment provision of the standard AGAC Songwriter's Agreement varies slightly depending upon the year the form was printed. Where the question of assignment is relevant, the applicable form should be consulted.

## D. Benefit of Successors and Assigns

If an agreement contains a restriction on the right of one party or other to assign the agreement to others, then the following provision, which is typically found in many license agreements, should have the word "permitted" included as the penultimate word as follows:

> This Agreement shall be binding upon and inure to the benefit of each of the parties hereto, and except as otherwise provided herein, their respective legal successors and permitted assigns.

### E. Exclusion of All Other Express or Implied Warranties

If a license agreement provides that any physical materials be transferred or loaned to, or services to be provided for, a licensee in connection with the licensee's exercise of the license, the license agreement may exclude, for the protection of the copyright owner, all warranties that are not expressly set forth in the license agreement, including certain warranties that may be implied by the law in the absence of such an exclusion.

The following is an example of such a provision:

> OTHER THAN THE REPRESENTATIONS AND WARRANTIES SPECIFICALLY SET FORTH IN THIS AGREEMENT, OWNER DOES NOT MAKE TO LICENSEE BY VIRTUE OF THIS AGREEMENT ANY REPRESENTATION OR WARRANTY, EXPRESS OR IMPLIED, AND HEREBY EXPRESSLY DISCLAIMS, ANY REPRESENTATION OR WARRANTY OF ANY KIND WITH RESPECT TO THE LICENSED WORK, INCLUDING WITHOUT LIMITATION ANY IMPLIED WARRANTIES OF MERCHANTABILITY AND FITNESS FOR A PARTICULAR PURPOSE. LICENSEE SHALL NOT MAKE OR PASS ON TO ITS CUSTOMERS OR LICENSEES ON BEHALF OF OWNER ANY WARRANTIES EXCLUDED HEREUNDER.

A copyright owner may desire such a provision if the physical materials being supplied with the license may cause damage to any property of the licensee. For example, music licensed in conjunction with MIDI software embodying the music may cause damage to other computer software or work product of the licensee's to the extent the MIDI software contains "bugs" (i.e., programming errors).

Clauses providing for the exclusion of warranties and other limitations on liability are required, under the Uniform Commercial Code, and under the Restatement of Contracts, to be *conspicuous.* It has been common practice to place all provisions that legally require conspicuity in all capital letters. It may be asked whether language in all capital letters is really more conspicuous than text printed in standard upper and lower case. Many people would agree that text printed in all caps can be most difficult to read. Being that we are on the verge of the release of low cost color laser printers and photocopy machines (and, soon to follow, color-capable fax machines), perhaps a better solution would be to print provisions that are required to be conspicuous in some conspicuous color, such as red.

## F. Exclusion of Consequential Damages

Consequential damages are damages incurred by a licensee for lost profits, lost data, lost time, or lost opportunities. A copyright owner may feel that the licensee is in a better position to assume the risk or obtain insurance to cover the risk of lost business income for losses resulting from breaches of the agreement or warranties by the copyright owner. The parties would transfer the risk of such losses to the licensee with the following provision:

> NOTWITHSTANDING ANYTHING TO THE CONTRARY CONTAINED HEREIN, OWNER SHALL NOT, UNDER ANY CIRCUMSTANCES, BE LIABLE TO LICENSEE FOR CONSEQUENTIAL, INCIDENTAL OR SPECIAL DAMAGES, EVEN IF OWNER HAS BEEN APPRISED OF THE LIKELIHOOD OF SUCH DAMAGES OCCURRING.

An alert licensee would quickly realize that such a provision would render meaningless any warranties by the copyright owner that the latter has the right to enter into the agreement and that the licensed work does not infringe upon the rights of others. Accordingly, a licensee who comes across such a provision, if he is unable to have it stricken from the agreement altogether, would be reasonable in demanding that the express warranties contained in the agreement, such as a warranty of non-infringement, be excluded from the applicability of this provision.

## G. Limitation of Liability

For the same reason, a copyright owner would wish to limit consequential damages, the copyright owner would wish to limit all other damages to the price paid for the license, and such a provision may be effected as follows:

> IN NO EVENT SHALL OWNER'S LIABILITY (WHETHER BASED ON AN ACTION OR CLAIM IN CONTRACT, TORT OR OTHERWISE) TO LICENSEE ARISING OUT OF OR RELATED

TO THIS AGREEMENT OR THE TRANSACTIONS CONTEMPLATED HEREUNDER AND NOT WITH THE SCOPE OF THE SECTION ABOVE ENTITLED "EXCLUSION OF CONSEQUENTIAL DAMAGES" EXCEED THE LICENSE FEE PAID BY LICENSEE HEREUNDER.

Again, a licensee should be able to have all express warranties, or at least the warranty of non-infringement, contained in the agreement excluded from the applicability of this provision, as well.

## H. Severability

Agreements that contain provisions for the exclusive services of an individual have come under close scrutiny by the courts. Examples include exclusive songwriter agreements typically entered into between music publishers and their "staff" songwriters, which afford the publisher the right to exclude the songwriter from providing his songwriting services to another. Often these agreements combine a right for the exclusive services of the songwriter with provisions for the assignment of copyrights in compositions developed by the songwriter during the term of the agreement. Should a court hold that a music publisher is unable to enforce the exclusivity provision, the publisher would not wish to risk losing all the copyrights acquired under an exclusive publishing agreement.

Accordingly, where there is a possibility that one part of an agreement may be held unenforceable, a copyright owner may wish to make sure that other portions of the agreement are not affected. Such a provision is called a severability clause, which might take the following form:

In the event that any provision hereof is found invalid or unenforceable pursuant to judicial decree or decision, the remainder of this Agreement shall remain valid and enforceable according to its terms.

If the agreement contains a provision excluding warranties or otherwise limiting the liability of the copyright owner, the copyright owner might add the following sentence to the severability provision:

WITHOUT LIMITING THE FOREGOING, IT IS EXPRESSLY UNDERSTOOD AND AGREED THAT EACH AND EVERY

> PROVISION OF THIS AGREEMENT WHICH PROVIDES FOR A LIMITATION OF LIABILITY, DISCLAIMER OR WARRANTIES OR EXCLUSION OF DAMAGES IS INTENDED BY THE PARTIES TO BE SEVERABLE AND INDEPENDENT OF ANY OTHER PROVISION AND TO BE ENFORCED AS SUCH. FURTHER, IT IS EXPRESSLY UNDERSTOOD AND AGREED THAT IN THE EVENT ANY REMEDY HEREUNDER IS DETERMINED TO HAVE FAILED OF ITS ESSENTIAL PURPOSE, ALL LIMITATIONS OF LIABILITY AND EXCLUSION OF DAMAGES SET FORTH HEREIN SHALL REMAIN IN FULL FORCE AND EFFECT.

## I. Cure Period

Copyright owners granting rights or licenses should always include, at least in long-form licenses, a provision that affords a period within which to cure any breach of contract alleged by the licensee.

> Owner shall not be deemed to be in breach of any of its obligations hereunder unless and until you shall have given Owner written notice by certified or registered mail, return receipt requested, specifying the nature of such breach and Owner shall have failed to cure such breach within thirty (30) days after Owner's receipt of such written notice.

Licensees should request to make this provision mutual:

> Neither party shall be deemed to be in breach of any of its obligations hereunder unless and until the party claiming a breach shall have given the other written notice by certified or registered mail, return receipt requested, specifying the nature of such breach and such other party shall have failed to cure such breach within thirty (30) days after receipt of such written notice.

## J. Entire Agreement or Integration Provision

When the parties have reduced their agreement to writing, and it is clear the parties intended that the agreement reflect their entire understanding and agreement or that all understandings and agreements regarding the subject matter were intended to be "integrated" or "merged" into the written agreement, then evidence of any other agreements, discussions, representations, or warranties may not be admissible as evidence to contradict or modify the terms of the agreement. In other words, unless there is some ambiguity in the terms of the agreement, the courts will look only to the "four corners" of the written contract to determine the scope of the agreement and the intent of the parties. Accordingly, the parties will often reflect their intent that a written agreement reflects their entire agreement or that all agreements are merged into the written agreement in a clause such as the following:

> This Agreement constitutes the entire understanding and contract between the parties and supersedes any and all prior and contemporaneous, oral or written representations, communications, understandings and agreements between the parties with respect to the subject matter hereof, all of which representations, communications, understandings and agreements are hereby canceled to the extent they are not specifically merged herein. The parties acknowledge and agree that neither of the parties is entering into this Agreement on the basis of any representations or promises not expressly contained herein. This is an integrated agreement.

## K. Modifications and Amendments

To avoid disputes about whether or how the terms of a written agreement were subsequently modified, the parties will often agree as follows:

> This Agreement shall not be modified, amended, canceled or in any way altered, nor may it be modified by custom and usage of trade or course of dealing, except by an instrument in writing and signed by both of the parties hereto. All amendments or modifications of this Agreement shall be binding upon the parties despite any lack of consideration so long as the same shall be in writing and executed by the parties hereto.

## L. Waiver

To avoid disputes about whether or under what terms a party's duty to perform an obligation of the contract was waived by the other party, the parties may agree as follows:

> Performance of any obligation required of a party hereunder may be waived only by a written waiver signed by the other party, which waiver shall be effective only with respect to the specific obligation described therein. The waiver by either party hereto of a breach of any provision of this Agreement by the other shall not operate or be construed as a waiver of any subsequent breach of the same provision or any other provision of this Agreement.

## M. No Partnership or Agency

An agreement between a buyer and seller or a licensor and licensee should make it clear that no other relationship between the parties is established unless otherwise specifically agreed:

> Nothing in this Agreement shall be construed as creating a joint venture, partnership, agency, employment relationship, franchise relationship or taxable entity between the parties, nor shall either party have the right, power or authority to create any obligations or duty, express or implied, on behalf of the other party hereto, it being understood that the parties are independent contractors vis-a-vis one another.

## N. No Third-Party Beneficiaries

An agreement intended solely to affect the rights and privileges of the parties signing the agreement might state that no rights or privileges are meant to be conferred on any third parties unless specifically provided:

> Nothing contained in this Agreement, express or implied, shall be deemed to confer any rights or remedies upon, nor obligate any of the parties hereto, to any person or entity other than such parties, unless so stated to the contrary.

## O. Choice of Law

The person drafting the license will generally try to insist that if any disputes arise under the agreement, the law of the state where that party is located should apply to the transaction.

> This Agreement shall be construed and enforced in accordance with the laws of the State of California applicable to agreements between residents of California wholly executed and wholly performed therein.

Where the parties reside in the same state, there should be little debate about the laws of which state should govern the agreement. Where the parties cannot agree upon whether to use the laws of the state of one party or the other, the parties should consider including either the state of New York or the state of California, because each of these states have developed a substantial body of case law concerning contracts in the entertainment industry.

Where one party is located in California and one in New York, the following compromise may be reached (where the Licensor is located in New York and the Licensee in California):

> Should the Owner bring any action or proceeding hereunder against the Licensee, this Agreement shall be construed and enforced in accordance with the laws of the State of California applicable to agreements between residents of California wholly executed and wholly performed therein. Should the Licensee bring any action or proceeding hereunder against the Owner, this Agreement shall be construed and enforced in accordance with the laws of the State of New York applicable to agreements between residents of New York wholly executed and wholly performed therein.

The prospect of litigating an action under the laws in effect of the state of the other party may provide an incentive to settle disputes in lieu of extensive litigation.

## P. Choice of Forum

Perhaps more significant than the choice of law provision is the provision that dictates the forum in which a lawsuit arising out of any dispute concerning the agreement must be filed. Unless otherwise agreed, a lawsuit may be brought in any state where the court has jurisdiction over the defendant, such as a state where the defendant is doing business. The costs of a party's litigating an action in a state other than the state in which his principal place of business, and that of his normal legal counsel, is located can be significantly more expensive than litigating in the courts of another state. Further, litigating in an unfamiliar state may induce, whether justified or not, a fear of the unknown or fear of a "home court" advantage.

To alleviate these fears and to minimize the potential costs of litigation, a party may negotiate a provision that identifies the state and county in which lawsuits arising under the agreement are to be brought. The courts will usually respect the agreement of the parties on the matter. Of course, where both parties are located in the same state and county, there is little reason to negotiate the issue of forum, unless one of the parties expects to move its operations to another state or county. Similarly, when both parties are major multi-national corporations, who do business in nearly all the states, this provision may not become an issue, unless a party can identify specific laws in a particular state that favor or disfavor one of the parties to the transaction.

While many license agreements contain a choice of law provision, the same agreements often neglect to include a choice of forum provision. Including a choice of law provision, but leaving the choice of forum silent may produce the anomalous result of a court in one state having to apply the laws of another state to resolve the dispute. It will therefore serve to remember that a choice of law provision is not the same as a choice of forum provision, and if the intent is to require that lawsuits be brought in a particular state, the agreement should contain, in addition to a choice of law provision, a provision such as the following:

> Any action or proceeding brought by either party against the other arising out of or related to this Agreement shall be brought only in a state or federal court of competent jurisdiction located in the County of Los Angeles, California, and the parties hereby consent to the *in personam* jurisdiction of said courts.

As with the choice of law, a compromise may be reached that provides an incentive to settle disputes:

> Any action or proceeding brought by the Owner against the Licensee arising out of or related to this Agreement shall be brought only in a state or federal court of competent jurisdiction located in the County of Los Angeles, California, and the parties hereby consent to the *in personam* jurisdiction of said courts. Any action or proceeding brought by the Licensee against the Owner arising out of or related to this Agreement shall be brought only in a state or federal court of competent jurisdiction located in the County of New York, New York, and the parties hereby consent to the *in personam* jurisdiction of said courts.

## Q. Arbitration

Where the parties agree to resolve disputes by arbitration, they may wish to enter into the following kind of provision:

> Any dispute or controversy arising out of, relating to, or concerning any interpretation, construction, performance, or breach of this Agreement, will be settled by arbitration to be held in New York, New York, in accordance with the rules then in effect of the American Arbitration Association. The arbitrator may grant injunctions or other relief in the dispute or controversy. The decision of the arbitrator will be final, conclusive, and binding on the parties to the arbitration. Judgment may be entered on the arbitrator's decision in any court having jurisdiction. Owner and Licensee will each pay one-half of the costs and expenses of the arbitration and each will separately pay their own counsel fees and expenses. This arbitration clause constitutes a waiver of each party's right to a jury trial for all disputes relating to all aspects of this Agreement or any and all dealings between the parties, including, but not limited to, the following: claims, both express and implied, for breach of contract, breach of the covenant of good faith and fair dealing, negligent or intentional misrepresentation, negligent or intentional interference with contract or prospective economic advantage, and defamation, any and all claims for violation of any federal, state, or municipal statute. The parties may apply to any court of competent jurisdiction for a temporary restraining order, preliminary injunction, or other

> interim or conservatory relief, as necessary, without breach of this Agreement and without abridgement of the powers of the arbitrator. Each party's promise to resolve claims by arbitration in accordance with the provisions of this Agreement, rather than through the courts, is consideration for the other party's like promise.

## R. Confidentiality of Agreement

A party may desire, for one reason or another, to maintain the confidentiality of the terms of the agreement. The following provision effects such confidentiality, recognizing the need for certain standard exceptions:

> Each of the parties to this Agreement warrants and agrees that neither it nor its counsel will disclose, disseminate, or cause to be disclosed the terms of this Agreement, except: (a) Insofar as disclosure is reasonably necessary to carry out and effectuate the terms of this Agreement; (b) Insofar as a party hereto is required by law to respond to any demand for information from any court, governmental entity, or governmental agency; (c) Insofar as disclosure is necessary to be made to a party's independent accountants for tax or audit purposes; and (d) Insofar as the parties may mutually agree in writing upon language to be contained in one or more press release.

## S. Notice

Notices that may be required or permitted under license agreements, for example, notices of exercise of any option provisions in the agreement, should always be in writing. Further, every long-form contract should have a provision clarifying just how such notices must be effected. This is to avoid any misunderstanding about whether notice was timely made and to make sure the notice actually gets to the appropriate person or department within each firm responsible for effecting or enforcing the performance of the agreement. The following notice provision recognizes the global nature of modern business and the new media of business communications that have become common during the past several years.

Unless otherwise specifically provided, all notices required or permitted by this Agreement shall be in writing and in English and may be delivered personally, or may be sent by cable, telex, facsimile or certified mail, return receipt requested, to the following, unless the parties are subsequently notified of any change of address in accordance with this section:

If to Owner:

Big Music Publishing Corp.
1000 Sunset Boulevard
Hollywood, California 90000
Attention: Legal Department
Telex: 123456 BIGPUB
Facsimile: (213) 555-1212

If to Licensee:

Attention:
Telex:
Facsimile:

Any notice shall be deemed to have been received as follows: (i) personal delivery, upon receipt; (ii) telex, cable or facsimile, twenty-four (24) hours after transmission or dispatch; (iii) certified mail, three (3) business days after delivery to the United States postal authorities by the party serving notice. If notice is sent by telex, facsimile or cable, a confirming copy of the same shall be sent by mail to the same address.

It is not uncommon for agreements to provide that copies of any notices to be provided under the agreement be sent to the outside counsel of the party upon which notice is to be served. This could help bring to the attention of the party entitled to the notice an important notice that might have otherwise gone unnoticed.

## T. Advice of Legal Counsel

When one of the parties is known to be unsophisticated in the ways of business, or is among a class of persons considered stereotypically to be "exploited" — such as artists and songwriters — the more sophisticated party should include the following provision in the agreement:

> Each party acknowledges and represents that, in executing this Agreement, it has received advice as to its legal rights from legal counsel and that the person signing on its behalf has read and understood all of the terms and provisions of this Agreement. Further, each party and their counsel have cooperated in the drafting and preparation of this Agreement. It shall be deemed their joint work product and may not be construed against any party by reason of its preparation or word processing.

## U. Attorneys' Fees

Under the American Rule of law, unless an award of attorneys' fees is provided by statute or by the express terms of a written agreement between the parties, a court will not award attorneys' fees to the prevailing party in litigation. To deter frivolous litigation, the parties may wish to include a specific provision in the agreement providing the prevailing party in any litigation over the agreement with an opportunity to collect its reasonable attorney fees and costs incurred during the course of the litigation.

> In any litigation between the parties regarding the terms or performance of this agreement, the prevailing party shall be entitled to recover its reasonable attorneys' fees and court costs.

## V. Recitals

Many agreements contain recitals of fact intended to provide the reader with some background information about the parties or the transaction. Recitals of fact may sometimes be identified by their being preceded by the word, *Whereas.* The parties to an agreement should be certain that the recitals accurately reflect the facts they purport to recite. California Evidence Code Section 622 states that facts recited in a written instrument (other than recitals of consideration) are conclusively presumed true as between the parties. Recitals, therefore, can serve to reduce the number of facts that can be placed into dispute in any litigation relating to the agreement.

If California Law does not govern the agreement, or the law of the state that governs the agreement does not have a law similar to the California provision concerning recitals, the parties may wish to give strong legal effect to the recitals by including the following provision:

> The recitals above set forth are incorporated into this agreement by reference. Each recital of fact concerning a party shall be conclusive as between the parties hereto. Such fact shall be incontestable in the event of any dispute between the parties regarding such fact and each party agrees not to introduce any evidence which would in any way serve to dispute such recited fact.

## W. Counterparts

It is our practice to always have one "original" copy signed for each party to the contract. For example, where there are two parties to the contract, each party will sign two agreements, with each receiving a fully executed original bearing the original signatures of both parties. Where the parties are signing an agreement in different locations or at different times, circumstances will require that each sign separate signature pages, which will later be attached to the original agreement. Though not necessary, agreements executed in such fashion should contain a provision such as the following:

> This Agreement may be executed in one or more counterparts, each of which shall be deemed an original, but all of which together shall constitute one and the same instrument.

## X. Captions

To prevent an unintended result caused by a poorly worded section heading or caption:

> The section headings and captions contained herein are for reference purposes and convenience only and shall not in any way affect the meaning or interpretation of this Agreement.

## Y. Gender

A favorite provision of ours which never fails to evoke reaction in negotiators who bother to explore the depths of the legal boilerplate typically found in many licenses:

> Where the context so requires, the masculine gender shall include the feminine or neuter, and the singular shall include the plural and the plural the singular.

## Z. Effective Date

When you send an agreement to another for signature, it could be construed as an "offer" for a contract, which the other party may "accept" by returning the agreement signed.

Most simple permission letters are sent with the understanding that they may be accepted by the licensee's signing and returning the letter to the music copyright owner. As a precaution, and as an incentive for the licensee to pay promptly, the copyright owner should specify that the license does not take effect until the owner receives payment of the license fee.

More formal license agreements will contain signature lines for both parties to sign and are not intended to be binding until the copyright owner counter-signs the agreement. A copyright owner would be prudent to first obtain the signature of the licensee before signing the contract himself. If there is a significant delay between the time you send an agreement and receive it signed, circumstances may change significantly during that time. For example, you may send a license to an advertising agency for the non-exclusive use of a musical composition in a television commercial, and while you are waiting for the license to be reviewed and returned, another advertiser offers a significantly higher license fee for the exclusive use of the song. In such circumstances, you would ideally want to be in a position to cease the negotiations with the first advertiser and accept the terms offered by the new advertiser. To have that ability, you would need to be certain that the first advertiser does not consider the license you sent to him binding upon you. If you had not signed the agreements before you sent them, then it should be an easy matter to be certain that no binding agreement was consummated.

If you had signed the agreements before having sent them, then you would have no assurance that the first advertiser considers that agreement not to have been entered until you actually receive written confirmation to that effect from the first advertiser, which may not always be easy.

Accordingly, other than the case of a simple permission letter for minor non-exclusive licenses where some risk can be assumed for the sake of administrative convenience, a copyright owner is advised to always counter-sign agreements after they have first been signed by the licensee. Further, the license agreement should contain the following provision:

> This Agreement shall become effective only after it has been signed by Licensee and has been accepted by Owner at its principal place of business, and its effective date shall be the date on which it is signed by Owner.

Finally, to avoid any misunderstanding as to the Effective Date of the agreement, which is often the start date of licenses whose term is based on loosely specified time periods (e.g., ". . . a term of one year commencing the Effective Date hereof"), the agreement should indicate the Effective Date directly below the signature block of the copyright owner, as follows:

| LICENSEE | OWNER |
|---|---|
| Signature:____________________ | Signature:____________________ |
| Printed Name:_________________ | Printed Name:_________________ |
| Title:_________________________ | Title:_________________________ |
| Dated:________________________ | Dated:________________________ |
| | (This is the effective date of the Agreement) |

## IV. AFFILIATED COMPANY PROBLEM

Certain problems arise when a music publisher is affiliated with a motion picture studio, which is the case when both entities are subsidiaries of a parent entertainment company or other conglomerate.

Under standard music publishing agreements, the songwriter is generally entitled to receive 50% of any and all sums actually received by the music publisher from the licensing uses of the music in motion pictures, television programs, videograms, and other media. Where the music publisher is affiliated with, for example, a motion picture studio or television network, who desires to license the music in a theatrical motion picture or television program, a conflict of interest may arise which may influence the publisher to enter into a deal that does not serve the best interests of the songwriter.

Because an obligation of good faith is implied by the relationship between the songwriter and publisher, the music publisher, in considering the terms of a license with an affiliated company, is required to negotiate "at arm's length." This means that publisher must treat the affiliated company as it would any other third party in similar circumstances in establishing the terms and conditions of the license. In the case of synchronization licenses, where synchronization fees have become relatively standardized, this is a fairly simple matter. However, in the area of home video licenses, where there are still few standards,[4] and often heated disputes as to whether original synchronization licenses covered home video uses of music,[5] the resolution of conflicts of interest is more difficult.

How a music publisher resolves this conflict will have an impact upon the publisher's legal relationships with its songwriters, the publisher's ability to acquire additional song catalogues, and the publisher's ability to recruit and contract with new songwriters. The senior management of the entertainment company or the conglomerate is not generally in the best position to resolve such conflicts, and the music publisher faced with this situation should come to grips with the question well before disputes arise with the songwriters they represent.

---

[4] See the discussion of videogram licenses in Chapter 15.

[5] See the discussion of the extent to which old synchronization licenses apply to new uses in Chapter 17.

## V. General Advice to Music Copyright Owner — Always Encourage Activity in the Song

Before exploring the foregoing factors in relation to the various customary forms of music licenses, we would like to admonish music copyright owners against making the fundamental errors that can lead a great song to obscurity.

Do not get too mired in the details. For example, do not let a negotiation over the wording of legal boilerplate obscure your vision of the forest through the trees. Do not let your perception of the value of the copyright go to your head. Remember that no matter how small the license fee you receive, in the long run, you will tend to make up more than the difference from maintaining a continuing active relationship between the song and the listening public. Do not let fear and uncertainty rule the day. Recognize that life is decision-making, and don't be afraid to make a decision. A good rule to follow is, when in doubt, license.

The music copyright owner's primary interest should always be to encourage as much activity in the song as possible.

## VI. General Advice to Persons Seeking to Clear Licenses — Fully Disclose All the Uses You Might Conceivably Make of the Music

There is nothing worse in business than a surprise. Too often, persons seeking to clear licenses think they are being clever by understating the nature or scope of the intended use in an effort to minimize the fee quoted by the copyright owner. This kind of attitude is inimical to the licensee's best interests. If, as a result of understating the nature of your use, you receive a license that does not adequately cover your requirements, you may find yourself being accused of infringement of copyright, subject to a serious threat of injunction at an inopportune time. You should not have to experience the high cost and ugly embarrassment of a lawsuit to learn the lesson that intentionally understating the nature and scope of your intended use for the purpose of minimizing your costs makes no business sense.

Music copyright owners will require a lot of information about your potential use of the music before quoting a license fee. While the copyright owner uses this information to quote a fee that reflects the importance of the use, it is also to your benefit to fully disclose all the uses you might conceivably make of the music. Usually, the music copyright owner will be more than happy to quote you a fee for all the uses that you can foresee. If the fees are reasonable, you would be advised to pick up as much a scope and duration as offered to you. If you are on a tight budget, you should ask for options which will give you important flexibility later on and may save you money in the long run.

CHAPTER 11

# THE ART OF GRANTING AND CLEARING MUSIC LICENSES

## SUMMARY

# CHAPTER 11

# THE ART OF GRANTING AND CLEARING MUSIC LICENSES

This book on music licensing is really about two distinct, yet related, arts: (1) the art of *granting* licenses for the purpose of earning a living from one's music copyrights, and (2) the art of obtaining licenses, or *clearing* permission, to commercially use music owned by another.

The ancient Greeks used the term "art" to refer to the technique, skill, or know-how for making things, such as a chair, a statue, or a house. They also recognized that art refers to the accomplishment of anything that requires human skill or know-how to render well, such as the art of cultivating crops, the art of making wine, and the art of singing a song.

We are living in a world today in which an increasing number of things that individuals desire to consume are not really *things* at all, in a material sense. In the pursuit of the good life, people are desiring the *intangible* — that which they cannot touch, but can feel or experience in an intellectual or emotional sense, such as reading a good story, identifying with a virtuous character, listening to good music, and receiving information (and, with the last-mentioned, one would hope, gaining some knowledge, understanding, and, ultimately, some wisdom).

What we are grappling with in this book may best be illustrated by a gag Victor Borge had used to tease his audience. The comedian asks, "Would you like a bit of music now?" Upon hearing the audience applauding their assent, he reaches into his piano bench, grabs a handful of sheet music, and passes it out. The joke invariably earns a good laugh. The point is that if the music the audience came to enjoy were really those bits of paper, few would have laughed. Clearly, what we are talking about is that which the audience has come to *hear* — something diffuse, something intangible.

The practice of an art is particularly complex when the product of the activity is so intangible. This is because the building blocks used to create intangible goods, such as a play or a movie, comprise a vast variety of other intangibles that are easily transportable and combinable. For example, consider a video clip and the intangible nature of the intellectual property of which it can be composed: a few bars of a melody, a few seconds of a sound recording, a short clip from a movie or a television program, a few steps from a choreographed dance routine or ballet, the plot of a novel or short story, the virtue or vice of a lead character, a biographical sketch, a scene from an opera, an animated character, a line of poetry, a still photograph, the cadence of a well-known distinctive voice, the likeness of a rock star. One simple work of art may comprise one or all of these intangible ingredients in some form or to some degree.

The complexity of the law governing transactions in intangible works of authorship seems to have inherited the complexity involved in creating these works, and the complexity of the questions concerning their ownership, transfer, use, and distribution are compounded by the fact that any one intangible work may be comprised of a multitude of other works. This makes the distillation, disposition, and exploitation of the ownership rights in intangible products an extremely complex activity. Fortunately, the skill or art of performing this activity may be acquired with cooperative effort and some practical experience.

When an art is performed well, it is the result of something the ancient Greeks called *arete*, which, translated into English means having a quality that is something between *virtuous* and *excellent.* To have virtue or excellence in performing an art is to have practical wisdom about the art. The goal of this book, in these noblest of terms, is to impart to the reader some practical wisdom about granting licenses and obtaining clearances for the use of music. We hope this book, together with some practical experience of your own, will help you acquire the art of music licensing.

## I. THE ART OF GRANTING LICENSES

Music has been defined as the art of organizing sounds and silences into meaningful patterns. Music publishing can be similarly defined: the art of organizing sounds and silences into meaningful revenue.

Certainly, the goal of the music copyright owner is to maximize the revenues generated by the musical composition. Maximizing revenue, however, involves more than merely how much money you can negotiate in exchange for granting licenses. It involves appraising the value of the song and recognizing that a variety of subtle factors dynamically affect the value of the song over time, including the types of uses, the number of uses, and the scope of uses that you permit over time. Maximizing revenue generated by a musical composition depends more on how you approach the exploitation of your music in the long run than how much money you demand in exchange for each license in the short run.

*Arete* in granting licenses to use music, accordingly, is achieved by putting the *long-term* interests of the song and the songwriter first. Recognizing that maximizing a song's revenue is a dynamic process — with the earnings potential of the music changing depending upon licensing decisions made over a period of time — is the first step in acquiring excellence in music licensing. With that in mind, we suggest that anyone who is responsible for maximizing the revenues of a song or a song catalog acquire the following three key habits:

A. Share in the economic success of the work in which the music is going to be used;

B. Maximize the long-term value of the work and avoid shortsightedness; and,

C. Maintain an active relationship between the song and the listening public.

We will explore each of these in turn.

## A. Share in the Economic Success of the Work in Which the Music Is Going to Be Used

The compensation one can collect in exchange for granting permission to use copyrighted music in another's work can be structured in a variety of ways. For example, one can receive a one-time *flat fee* (e.g., $1000 payable upon signing the license) for perpetual use, a flat fee for a limited period of use (e.g., $100 for a three-year license), or a flat fee for a limited period of use with options to renew the term of use (e.g., $100 for a three-year license and options to renew for additional one-year periods at a rate of $100 per year). However, flat fee arrangements, even if payable over a period of time, do not take into consideration the economic success of the work in which the music is used. Under a flat fee arrangement, whether a record album in which the music is used sells 100 copies or 1 million copies, the fee for the use of the music is the same.

Music copyright owners prefer to share the risk of success or failure of works that embody their music in exchange for receiving the potential rewards of having their music associated with *hit* records, motion pictures, and other works. Producers and other users of music will assert that music copyright owners do not deserve to participate in the success of the user's work, because the copyright owner does not bear any of the financial risks associated with the production of the work. In other words, how can the music licensor fail? What does he have at risk that justifies the reward from the success of the work he seeks?

Music copyright owners respond that the producers are undervaluing the importance of their music to the producer's work. For example, a major motion picture may cost $20 million to make and perhaps an equal amount to market. Music is often an extremely important element in these movies, yet the music owners only receive a few thousand dollars at most for the use of the music. An artist performing a song in the movie might command a fee of $1 million for his work in the picture, but only a tiny fraction of that amount is paid to the songwriter who wrote the very song the artist may be performing in the film. From the music copyright owner's perspective, he is taking a risk by accepting a low fee up front in the hope that he can make up for the value the music is adding to the film by sharing in additional revenues from television performances and videocassette sales should the motion picture become successful. Music copyright owners can also point to the profit participation percentages paid to actors, writers, and directors, who are taking no more "risk" in making their contributions than the music copyright owners.

Whatever its justification, this sharing in the economic success (and failure) of works is important and is accomplished by structuring the compensation payable for music licenses in the form of a *royalty.*

Royalties are generally calculated on the basis of the number of copies of the work distributed or the revenues received from the sale or performance of the work. For example, one can receive a royalty of 5 cents for each copy of the work distributed or a royalty of 5% of the net revenues derived from the sale or licensing of the work.

Few music licenses do not provide some form of royalty or other compensation based on the economic success of the work in which the music is included. Where the license does not explicitly provide for royalty payments, some other mechanism usually exists that implicitly provides the music copyright owner with the upside earnings potential that a successful work may provide.

For example, when music licensed for use in a television program is broadcast on television, the music copyright owner will receive payments derived from the collection of performance royalties from the television stations that broadcast the program, through separate fees charged to the stations. The mechanisms involved in the collection of performance royalties are explained in some detail in Chapter 18, on *Licensing Music in Live and Recorded Public Performances*. Suffice it to say here, that the license granted to the producer of the television program to include the music in the program is, as a matter of practice, granted in exchange for a flat fee. However, the music copyright owner knows that his share in the economic success of the television program is assured from the separate license fees charged for the performance of the television program in which his music is included. If the television program becomes popular and enjoys years of broadcast in syndication, the music copyright owner will similarly enjoy continuing performance royalty credit as long as the television program remains on the air in reruns and exploitation in other markets.

For this reason, music copyright owners should not lose sight of the performance royalty earnings when considering what license fee to charge for the initial inclusion of the song in works such as television programs. If, for example, a television producer is only willing to pay a certain flat fee for permission to use your song and you insist on a fee that is double what the producer is willing to pay, the producer will often find and use a substitute for your song. Ironically, more often than not, the performance royalties earned from the broadcast of the television program would have more than compensated for the difference between the flat fee you were quoting and the fee last offered by the producer.

If the television program becomes a hit and enjoys lengthy rerun exhibitions, the music copyright owner will have lost substantial performance revenues. The potential upside from having the song associated with a hit program is substantial, while the downside for accepting a lower up front fee is slight.

Of course, where there is no potential for receiving performance royalties, the music copyright owner should find alternative means of sharing in the economic success in the work. This, for example, is the case with respect to the sale of videocassettes, DVDs, and other home video devices containing copyrighted music; royalty structures used in licenses for home video device use are discussed at length in Chapter 15.

## B. Maximize the Long-Term Value of the Work

We have just seen in the preceding section an example of the folly of placing too much emphasis on the short term in negotiating the compensation of a license fee. In failing to resolve the difference between what the music copyright owner is willing to accept and what the music user is willing to pay in exchange for a license, the music copyright owner often overlooks the additional flow of revenue that could be earned from performance royalties.

The causes of such shortsightedness can be generally identified. It is difficult or perhaps impossible to measure the marginal performance royalties earned in connection with any one license because performance rights societies do not calculate performance royalties on the basis of every single performance. Further, the increase in performance royalties occurs over time, and usually not in the same quarter in which the license was granted. Thus, it is usually difficult to tie the issuance of one specific license to a specific dollar increase in performance royalties.

Sometimes the shortsightedness is due to inexperience or misunderstanding of the dynamics of music publishing revenues. A songwriter or small music publisher might be represented by a personal manager or attorney who, because he or she may only physically see the checks for the flat fee licenses he negotiates and not the performance royalty statements, only appreciates the short-term maximization of the size of these flat fee payments. Such representatives often fail to appreciate the dynamic effect that entering into licenses has on performance royalties. In other cases, representatives get mired in the details of the specific language of the license, agonizing over, for example, the inadequacies of a "warranties and representation" clause, losing sight of what's really important to the publishing company or songwriter he or she is representing.

Whatever the reason for this short-term thinking, though the marginal performance royalties earned in connection with any one license may not be measurable, they are real and this additional revenue from the collection of performance royalties is a tangible benefit not to be ignored while negotiating many flat fee licenses. More subtle benefits, such as those discussed in the section that immediately follows, should also encourage the copyright owner to come to resolution on negotiating license fees, even if it means taking less than the going rate on some up-front fees.

### C. Maintain an Active Relationship Between the Song and the Listening Public

As we have pointed out, maximizing a song's revenue is a dynamic process: the earnings potential of the music changes depending upon licensing decisions made over a period of time. One of the most important, but often ignored, factors that affect the value of the song over the life of the copyright is the *quantity* of licenses issued and the number of uses made of the song. The more often a song is used in other works, the greater the value of the copyright.

The essence of what you are doing when you license the use of the song is helping to maintain the relationship between the song and the listening public. Entering into licenses provides the song with a means of continual exposure to the listening public, including those who select music for use in television programs, motion pictures, commercial advertising, and other works that offer alternative licensing revenues. By encouraging use, you therefore increase the likelihood that future requests for licenses of the song will continue. The listening public is surprisingly fickle and will easily forget a tune. You should never let a song fall into a state of such disuse that no one will remember it. Accordingly, the first principal of *arete* in granting music licenses is this: *Encourage as much activity in the song as possible.* For this reason, a music copyright owner should not allow short-term thinking, fear, or uncertainty to creep into the negotiating of fees and get in the way of concluding a license. A music copyright owner should not be afraid to make a decision. Life is decision-making, and if you remember that the goal is to encourage as much use of the song as possible, you will inevitably make decisions that are in the long-term interest of the song and its songwriter, and *arete* in granting licenses will be achieved.

## II. THE ART OF CLEARING LICENSES

The counterpart to the art of granting licenses is the art of obtaining permission, or "clearing the rights," to commercially use music owned by another. *Arete* in obtaining clearance, or permission, to use music may best be achieved by establishing a good relationship with the music copyright owners from whom you seek to obtain permission. We suggest that the best way to accomplish that is to acquire the following habits:

A. Understand the license required for your use;

B. Know what music you wish to license;

C. Develop a licensing strategy;

D. Make the license request;

E. Understand the needs and fears of the copyright owner;

F. Allow enough time to complete the process.

We will explore each of these in turn.

### A. Understanding Your Use and the Nature of the License Required

The importance of understanding the rights involved in your use and the kinds of licenses you require is best illustrated by a common mistake made by many who are new to the music clearance process: thinking first of a popular recording of the desired song, a person seeking to clear a license to use the recording might overlook the fact that getting permission to do so involves not one, but two copyrights: (1) the copyright in the sound recording and (2) the copyright in the underlying song. While you may properly obtain permission to use the recording, clearance to use the underlying song is sometimes entirely overlooked. (Just as often, persons obtaining clearance to use the music will overlook the need to clear permission to use the recording.)

Understanding the rights you need to clear begins with (1) identifying the kind of copyrighted work your need to clear and (2) identifying the rights under the copyright in that work that you need to clear.

### *1. Identifying the Kind of Copyrighted Work You Need to Clear*

The Copyright Act lists several kinds of works of authorship. They include:

(1) *literary works* (such as books, essays, poems and other fiction and non-fiction works), as well as computer programs (i.e., a set of instructions intended to bring about a certain result with the aid of a device or machine);

(2) *musical works*, including any accompanying words;

(3) *dramatic works* (such as theatrical plays, operas, musicals), including any accompanying music;

(4) *pantomimes* and *choreographic works*;

(5) *pictorial, graphic, and sculptural works*;

(6) *motion pictures, television programs, music videos, and other audiovisual works*;

(7) *sound recordings*; and

(8) *architectural works.*

The two kinds of works about which this book is primarily focused are *musical works* and *sound recordings.* Though not defined in the Copyright Act, a *musical work* is either a song (i.e., a short musical composition, usually comprising a melody or other music and accompanying lyrics) or a full length musical composition (such as an orchestral work). A *sound recording* is a work that results from the fixation of a series of musical, spoken, or other sounds, regardless of the nature of the material objects, such as disks, tapes, or other phonorecords, in which they are embodied.

Musical works and sound recordings are separate works and should not be confused. The copyright in a sound recording is completely separate from the copyright in the underlying song that may be featured in the sound recording. For example, there exists a valid copyright in the song *I've Got You Under My Skin* by Cole Porter and the copyright is owned by Warner/Chappell Music, Inc., a music publishing company. At the same time, several records of *I've Got You Under My Skin* have been recorded by numerous recording artists over the years. A completely separate copyright exists for each particular recording — the sequence of sounds that make up the performance of the song by a singer and orchestra. These recordings are owned by the respective record companies that commissioned their creation. For example, Frank Sinatra's recording of *I've Got You Under My Skin*, arranged by Nelson Riddle, is owned by Reprise Records.

Thus, if you wished to obtain permission to use Sinatra's recording of *I've Got You Under My Skin*, you would require the permission (for the use of the sound recording) of one of the record companies who owns a version of Sinatra's recording of the song (e.g. Capitol Records or Reprise) *and* the permission (for the use of the musical work) of the music publisher who owns or controls the underlying song (e.g., Warner/Chappell). You could not use the recording without permission from both companies.

Most record companies have special divisions, often called *special products* departments, dedicated to granting licenses to use sound recordings in their catalog. Licenses for the use of such recordings are sometimes effected by what is called a *master use license*, derived from the term record "master" — a final, mixed recording used in the manufacture of other copies, such as albums, cassette tapes, or compact discs. If you have trouble obtaining approval to use a particular artist's recording of the song, the record company, or other record companies, may have substitute recordings that may meet your needs. You can, of course, always create your own original recording, in which event permission from a record company would not be necessary — the only permission required would be that sought from the copyright owner of the underlying song.

Suppose you wished to use a recording of a song from a dramatic work, such as a musical play. Would it be sufficient to acquire the license you need from the owner of the sound recording, underlying musical work? Or would you require a license from the owner of the musical play? The answer may depend upon the nature of your use. This rather interesting subject is covered at length in Chapter 19, *The Grand Rights Controversy.* Suffice it to say that you have identified not two, but three distinct works from which rights may need to be cleared for your particular use.

Imagine that you wanted to use a short clip from a particular dance scene in the motion picture, *West Side Story.* Not only would you require a license from the studio who owned the film, (i.e., an audio-visual work) you would require a license from the record company who owned the soundtrack recording (i.e., sound recording), a license from the music publisher of the song performed in the scene (i.e., musical work), a license from the authors who owned the "grand rights" to the Broadway play of the same name (i.e., dramatic work). You may also require permission from the representatives of the estate of Jerome Robbins, who reserved by his contract with the producers of the movie the right to approve uses of the film's choreography that were not performed in conjunction with the exhibition of the entire motion picture!

Of course, not all clearances will be so complicated. However, it is good practice to first carefully analyze the work you wish to license and break it down into its component parts. In complex works — i.e., works that contain multiple copyrights and other rights — the break down may result in one or more of the following separate rights:

- a copyright in the underlying song,
- a copyright in the recording of the song,
- a copyright in the video aspects of the work (motion picture, television program, etc.),
- a copyright in any choreography appearing in the work,
- a copyright in a literary work (where the work is based upon a novel, non-fiction book, newspaper article, biography, autobiography, etc.),

- a copyright in a theatrical production (such as a musical play, opera, or ballet),
- a copyright in an animated character,
- a copyright in a still photograph drawing or other pictorial work appearing in the work,
- a copyright of a translation or arrangement of a work in the public domain,
- a trademark or service mark associated with a product or service,
- the right of privacy (i.e., the right one has "to be left alone") of one or more individuals, or
- the right of publicity (i.e., the right an individual has to exclude others from using his or her name, voice, photograph, and likeness) of one or more individuals.

### *2. Identifying the Rights Under the Copyright You Need to Clear*

If all you want to do is reproduce and distribute CD of a single audio-only recording of a song, the type of right you need to clear — a mechanical reproduction license — is relatively straightforward. The same is true if all you intend to do is quote a song lyric in a book or use a song in a television commercial. In each case, you are dealing with one work, one copyright — the copyright in the song you are seeking permission to use. But sometimes identifying the particular work under copyright isn't enough. Sometimes, even if you are dealing with only one copyright, you may need to clear two separate licenses under the copyright to engage in the activity you wish.

In analyzing the rights you need cleared, you must also take into consideration the implications of a concept known as *divisibility of copyright.* The Copyright Act provides to the owner of copyright in a work an exclusive ownership over the work. That ownership is expressed as a certain set of carefully defined *exclusive rights* under copyright. These include the exclusive rights to do and authorize any of the following:

(1) to reproduce the copyrighted work in copies or phonorecords;

(2) to prepare derivative works based upon the copyrighted work;

(3) to distribute copies or phonorecords of the copyrighted work to the public by sale or other transfer of ownership, or by rental, lease, or lending;

(4) in the case of literary, musical, dramatic, and choreographic works, pantomimes, and motion pictures and other audiovisual works, to perform the copyrighted work publicly;

(5) in the case of literary, musical, dramatic, and choreographic works, pantomimes, and pictorial, graphic, or sculptural works, including the individual images of a motion picture or other audiovisual work, to display the copyrighted work publicly; and

(6) in the case of sound recordings, to perform the copyrighted work publicly by means of a digital audio transmission.

In a sense, a copyright is divided up into these exclusive rights — hence, the divisibility of copyright — and it is important to understand what kind of works each apply to and which of these rights needs to be cleared for a particular use. As will become clear, in many instances, a particular use may require the clearance of two distinct rights under the copyright (e.g., reproduction right and performance right) in the same work (e.g., musical work) and often, in the context of the music industry, the applicable rights need to be cleared from two separate entities. Let's first explore each of these exclusive rights under copyright, together with certain other important copyright concepts, and then apply them to several examples.

*a. The Reproduction Right*

One of the most important exclusive rights provided by the Copyright Act to the owner of a copyright is the exclusive right "to *reproduce* the copyrighted work in *copies* or *phonorecord*."

The Copyright Act defines a *copy* as follows:

> A *copy* is a material object from which a work can be read or visually perceived either directly or with the aid of a machine or device, such as a book, manuscript, piece of sheet music, film, videotape, or microfilm.

Thus, for example, the reproduction of (i.e., the act of reproducing) copies of *sheet music* requires the permission of the copyright owner of the musical work. It is important not to confuse the term *copy*, which is a material object, such as a piece of sheet music, with the *musical work* printed on the sheet music. Further, while a musical work may be fixed in a copy, the ownership of copyright in the musical work, or any of the exclusive rights under the copyright, is distinct from ownership of any material object in which the work is embodied. Thus, a person may own the copy of sheet music, but not own the copyright in the musical work it contains, and *vice versa.*

The Copyright Act defines a *phonorecord* as follows:

> A *phonorecord* is a material object that embodies fixations of sounds (other than those sounds accompanied by a motion picture or other audiovisual work), such as audio tapes, phonograph records, and compact audio disks.

A *phonorecord* can be viewed as a special kind of *copy*: one that contains a sound recording, but only if the sound recording is not accompanied by a motion picture or other audiovisual work. Thus, a compact disc (CD) containing a recording of *I've Got You Under My Skin* is a phonorecord. The CD may be accompanied by a photograph or drawing of Frank Sinatra, but such a visual image is not a motion picture or audiovisual work. If, however, the song *I've Got You Under My Skin* is recorded as part of a motion picture, such as the movie *Innocent Blood*, then a material object embodying the recording of the song, such as a DVD copy of the movie, would be considered a *copy*, not a phonorecord, because the recording is accompanied by a motion picture.

Like the reproduction of copies of *sheet music* or *audiovisual works* containing copyrighted music, the reproduction of *phonorecords* requires the permission of the copyright owner of the musical work.

The curious term *fixation*, used in the above definition of *phonorecord*, is also defined in the Copyright Act:

> A work is *fixed* in a tangible medium of expression when its embodiment in a copy or a phonorecord . . . is sufficiently permanent or stable to permit it to be perceived, reproduced, or otherwise communicated for a period of more than transitory duration. A work consisting of sounds, images, or both, that are being transmitted, is "fixed" for purposes of this [Act] if a fixation of the work is being made simultaneously with its transmission.

The way recordings are embodied on CDs is by the impression of microscopic pits on a metallic surface, which is covered with plastic for protection. These pits, though not indestructible, are clearly *permanent* as that term is used in the above definition. The way recordings are embodied on reel-to-reel magnetic tapes and audiocassettes is somewhat different. As you know, recordings embodied on tape are fixed by means of magnetic impulses placed on the tape-by-tape recording devices. Nevertheless, the realignment of molecules on the surface of the magnetic tape is considered "sufficiently permanent or stable to permit it to be perceived . . . for a period of more than transitory duration," as any owner of an audiocassette and tape player is aware. Finally, the placement of copyrighted material into a computer's memory, such as RAM (i.e., random access memory), for more than a very brief period has also been considered a fixing of that material,[1] though the temporary *buffering* of a recording in RAM for purposes facilitating a performance is believed by some not to involve the reproduction of a copy.[2]

Again, the term *phonorecord*, which is a material object, such as an audiocassette tape or compact audio laserdisc, should not be confused with the *sound recording* or *musical work* which may happen to have been embodied in the physical phonorecord. Most important, neither the

---

[1] See *MAI Systems Corp. v. Peak Computer, Inc.*, 991 F.2d 511, 519 (9th Cir. 1993) (holding that loading of operating system software into the random access memory of a computer constitutes making a "copy" under the Copyright Act); see also *Agee v. Paramount Communication, Inc.*, 59 F.3d 317 (2d Cir. 1995) (recognizing that the distribution right involves the distribution of material copies).

[2] See *Cartoon Network LP v. CSC Holdings, Inc.*, 536 F.3d 121 (2d Cir. 2008).

term *copy* nor *phonorecord* should be confused with the term *reproduction*, the former each denoting material objects and the later denoting the act of fixing or embodying musical works or sound recordings in the material objects.

In addition to reproducing a musical work in copies of sheet music and phonorecords of sound recordings, a musical work may be reproduced in copies containing audiovisual works. The license required to reproduce copies in sheet music is referred to as a *print license*; the license required to reproduce music in sound recordings (i.e., audio-only recordings) is called a *mechanical license*; and the license required to reproduce music in audiovisual works is called a *synchronization license.*

### *b. The Adaptation Right (or Right to Prepare Derivative Works)*

The copyright owner of a musical work also has the exclusive right to prepare adaptations or *derivative works.* The Copyright Act defines the term as follows:

> A "derivative work" is a work based upon one or more pre-existing works, such as a translation, musical arrangement, dramatization, fictionalization, motion picture version, sound recording, art reproduction, abridgment, condensation, or any other form in which a work may be recast, transformed, or adapted.

A piano arrangement used in a sheet music version of the song is a derivative work of the song. A sound recording that embodies a song is a derivative work of the song. A motion picture is a derivative work of the screenplay or novel upon which it is based. Any change in lyrics of a song would constitute a derivative work of the song. If you are creating a work in which a song is recorded, arranged, modified, or any form in which it may be recast, transformed, or adapted, you would be invoking the copyright owner's exclusive right of adaptation (or right to prepare derivative works).

### *c. The Distribution Right*

A copyright owner has the exclusive right "to distribute copies or phonorecords of the copyrighted work to the public by sale or other transfer of ownership, or by rental, lease, or lending." Thus, by definition, a *distribution* is the transfer of possession of a copy or phonorecord from one person to another.

The Copyright Act provides the copyright owner of a musical work the exclusive right "to *distribute* copies or phonorecords of the copyrighted work *to the public* by sale or other transfer of ownership, or by rental, lease, or lending."[3] Thus, by virtue of Section 106(3) of the Copyright Act, the distribution of copies and phonorecords of a copyrighted work to the public may only occur with the consent of the copyright owner. Accordingly, the public distribution of copies of sheet music, CDs containing recordings of copyrighted music, and DVD copies of motion pictures containing music, each requires the permission of the copyright owner.

Note that the Section 106(3) refers to the distribution of *copies or phonorecords* of a copyrighted work, not the copyrighted work itself. This is consistent with the notion that the term *distribute* has traditionally denoted the changing of possession of tangible copies of the work.[4] Thus, it is clear that under the Copyright Act, a distribution does not encompass the transmission of a work to a place beyond from which it is sent, because no tangible copy (or phonorecord) changes hands in connection with such a transmission.

For this reason, the digital delivery of a musical work or sound recording does not invoke the distribution right, only the reproduction right. (You cannot distribute a phonorecord — defined under the Copyright Act as "a material object" — by digital transmission any more than you can a bowling ball.) If a right separate from the reproduction right were deemed necessary to account for digital deliveries, then, we submit, such right should be characterized as "the exclusive right to reproduce a work in copies and phonorecords by means of a digital transmission."

Note further that a distribution includes the changing of possession of a copy from one person to another, and that not all distributions of a copyrighted work require the permission of the copyright owner.

---

[3] 17 U.S.C. Sec. 106(3).

[4] For example, see 17 U.S.C. Sec. 115(c)(2). ("For this purpose, a phonorecord is considered 'distributed' if the person exercising the compulsory license has voluntarily and permanently parted with its possession.")

The exclusive distribution right of the copyright owner only extends to distributions to the public, and the scope of the right is limited by the *first sale doctrine*:

> Notwithstanding the provisions of section 106(3) [i.e., the distribution right], the owner of a particular copy or phonorecord lawfully made under this title, or any person authorized by such owner, is entitled, without the authority of the copyright owner, to sell or otherwise dispose of the possession of that copy or phonorecord.[5]

Thus, for example, when you buy a compact disc containing tunes by your favorite recording artist, you may do whatever you want with that disc — you may throw it away, or give it away, lend it or sell it to a friend, just about anything but rent it for commercial advantage.[6] It is also important to understand, however, that the distribution of an *unlawfully* made (i.e., infringing) copy will subject any distributor to liability for infringement.

Note also that, by properly circumscribing the definition of distribution, one will avoid the mistake of applying the first sale doctrine to digital transmissions. The first sale doctrine only applies to the transfer of copies or phonorecords, both defined as material objects. When one person transmits a recording to another, thereby reproducing a second copy by digital transmission, no distribution is taking place — i.e., no material object changes hands. Thus, the person engaged in the transmission may not invoke the first sale doctrine to such transmission and reproduction, even if the person possessing the original phonorecord offers to delete the file immediately after the transmission.

*d. The Performance Right*

One of the exclusive rights provided by the Copyright Act to the owner of a copyright (in a literary, musical, dramatic, or audiovisual work — but not to the owner of a sound recording) is the exclusive right

---

[5] 17 U.S.C. Sec. 109(a).

[6] Section 109 of the Copyright Act contains special limitations concerning the right to rent copies and phonorecords of computer programs and sound recordings.

to *publicly perform* the copyrighted work. The Copyright Act defines a *performance* as follows:

> To *perform* a work means to recite, render, play, dance, or act it, either directly or by means of any device or process or, in the case of a motion picture or audiovisual work, to show its images in any sequence or to make the sounds accompanying it audible.[7]

For example, when Frank Sinatra sings the song, *I've Got You Under My Skin* in a nightclub, he is rendering a *performance.* When you sing the song in your living room or in your shower, you too are rendering a performance. When you play Sinatra's recording of the song *I've Got You Under My Skin* on a CD using your home stereo system, or from an MP3 file on your personal computer, you are *performing* the recording, both the *sound recording* by Sinatra and the underlying *musical composition* written by Cole Porter. In each of these instances, the performer or the device rendering the performance is transmitting sounds audible to the human ear. But the term performance, under the copyright law, is not so limited.

When you hear the same recording of *I've Got You Under My Skin* on the radio, the radio station is rendering a performance of both the song and the recording, but the transmission by the station is not comprised of sounds directly audible by the human ear, but of electromagnetic waves sent through space, which are converted to audible sounds by a radio receiver. The copyright law makes it clear that these transmissions, or broadcasts, also constitute performances:

> To "transmit" a performance or display is to communicate it by any device or process whereby images or sounds are received beyond the place from which they are sent.[8]

*Public v. Private Performances.* As noted above, the owner of a copyright in a musical work has an exclusive right to perform and authorize others to perform the work, but that right is limited to those performances that are *to the public.* A copyright owner has no right to control performances that occur *in private.*

---

[7] 17 U.S.C. Sec. 101.

[8] *Id.*

The Copyright Act defines a *public* performance as follows:

> To perform or display a work *publicly* means —
>
> (1) to perform or display it at a place open to the public or at any place where a substantial number of persons outside of a normal circle of a family and its social acquaintances is gathered; or
>
> (2) to transmit or otherwise communicate a performance or display of the work to a place specified by clause (1) or to the public, by means of any device or process, whether the members of the public capable of receiving the performance or display receive it in the same place or in separate places and at the same time or at different times.

Thus, when Frank Sinatra sings the song, *I've Got You Under My Skin* in a nightclub — clearly "a place open to the public or at any place where a substantial number of persons outside of a normal circle of a family and its social acquaintances is gathered" — he is rendering a *public* performance of the song.

By contrast, when you sing the song in your living room or in your shower, you are clearly rendering a *private* performance. Similarly, when you play Sinatra's recording of the song *I've Got You Under My Skin* on a CD or from an MP3 file using your personal computer or home stereo system, you are rendering a *private* performance. Because the Copyright Act limits the copyright owner's exclusive performance rights to those rendered *publicly*, you may perform a musical composition in your home without the need for a performance license from the copyright owner.

When a radio station broadcasts Sinatra's recording of *I've Got You Under My Skin*, the station is rendering a *public* performance of the composition. Even if the broadcast is made, instead of over the airwaves, over cable lines, sometimes called *narrowcasting* or *cablecasting* over the new medium of *cable radio*, the cablecast constitutes a public performance. The same is true when the broadcast is of a motion picture, television program, or other audiovisual work containing copyrighted music. The television station or cable system operator is rendering a public performance of both the audiovisual work and the underlying musical composition. Further, when a song is performed over the telephone — when you are *All Alone by the Telephone* (Irving Berlin) — waiting *on hold*, the performance is a *public* performance requiring a license from the performance rights society representing the owner of the musical composition telephonically transmitted.

It is by virtue of the public performance right that writers and publishers of musical works are able to collect public performance royalties when their musical compositions are broadcast on the radio, television, or cable. They collect those royalties through a performance rights society, which they appoint to represent them for such purpose, and the societies issue *blanket licenses* to those who engage in public performances of the music (e.g., concert halls, restaurants, and radio and television stations).

*Communication Right.* Upon the advent of digital transmissions over the Internet, a controversy has emerged over whether a permanent download of a sound recording or audiovisual work — without a simultaneous playing or rendering of the work — constitutes a performance of the musical work embodied in the work. One court has held that a permanent download of a sound recording, while invoking the reproduction right, does not invoke the public performance right in the song.[9] As of the time of this writing, the performance right societies continue to take the position, at least with respect to audiovisual works, a download of an audiovisual work requires a public performance license.

Under the copyright laws of Canada and most European countries, however, the copyright owner has, in addition to a public performance right, an exclusive right to *communicate* the work to the public. The act of communicating a work to the public is a broader activity than performing a work publicly. As mentioned above, to perform a work means to "recite, play, dance, or act it." To communicate a work would seem to include all those things, plus any form of transmission of the work, including a permanent download transmission of a file containing the work to the public.

*Performances of Sound Recordings.* Note that a radio broadcast or "music on hold" broadcast of the Sinatra recording of *I've Got You Under My Skin* each constitutes a public performance of both the *sound recording* by Sinatra and the underlying *musical composition* written by Cole Porter. The *sound recording* and the underlying *musical work* are separate works each of which are protected by their own copyright.

---

[9] *United States v. ASCAP in re: Application of RealNetworks, AOL, Yahoo, Inc.*, No. 41-1395 (S.D.N.Y. April 25, 2007).

However, in the United States, only the owner of the copyright in the musical work enjoys a public performance right; owners of *sound recordings* do not have an exclusive right to publicly perform their recordings. Thus, for many years, radio stations have had to pay the music publishers, through their performance rights societies, a license fee for public performances of songs, but have never had to pay the record companies for the public performances of their copyright sound recordings.

While the U.S. Congress has for some time been considering a general right of public performance for sound recordings, such a general right is not yet recognized in the United States, and owners of sound recordings are not entitled to royalties for the radio broadcasts, music on hold broadcasts, and many other public performances of their recordings. However, certain kinds of public performances of sound recordings — those that qualify as *digital audio transmissions* — are now protected under the U.S. Copyright Act by virtue of the *Digital Performance Rights in Sound Recordings Act of 1995*, the scope of which is discussed at length below. Nevertheless, as for now, there is no general public performance right in sound recordings in the United States.

Overseas, record companies do enjoy a public performance right in sound recordings, often referred to as a *neighboring right.* Given recent declines in revenues from the sale of physical recordings (e.g., CDs), the record industry has been lobbying hard for the same rights afforded recordings when broadcast overseas.

*e. The Display Right*

One of the other exclusive rights provided by the Copyright Act to the owner of copyright in a musical work is the exclusive right to *publicly display* the copyrighted musical work. The Copyright Act defines a *display* as follows:

> To *display* a work means to show a copy of it, either directly or by means of a film, slide, television image, or any other device or process or, in the case of a motion picture or audiovisual work, to show individual images nonsequentially.

The copyright owner's exclusive right to publicly display his work has rarely been the source of any significant income to music copyright owners. However, it is useful to understand how the right could be exercised. When you show a printed copy of a composition's musical notation or lyric, such as a copy of *sheet music*, to another person in your home, you are displaying the musical work *privately.* As with private performances, private displays of copyrighted works do not require the permission of copyright owners. However, should a copy of the sheet music be copied onto a transparency for display, for example, by an overhead projector, the display of the sheet music transparency by that means at a public seminar would constitute a public display requiring consent of the copyright owner.[10]

Moreover, the advent of digitization of sheet music and transmissions over the Internet now makes it possible for widespread *public displays* of musical notation and lyrics. For example, today, you can access a website that will transmit to you on command either the full text of the lyrics of many popular songs or the *bitmaps* (i.e., a format for storing electronic pictures) of the musical notation of those songs. Licensing considerations for these public displays of digital sheet music are discussed in Chapter 12, on *Licensing Music in Print and Digital Print.*

### *f. The Transmission Right*

When Congress passed the Digital Performance Rights in Sound Recordings Act of 1995, it added a new right under copyright for owners of sound recordings: the exclusive right to publicly perform sound recordings by means of a *digital audio transmission.* This new right does not extend to all transmissions of sound recordings — the transmissions must be *digital* (i.e., not analog) and they must be *audio-only.*

---

[10] Under the Copyright Act, if the sheet music itself (i.e., not the transparency copy) were publicly displayed, permission from the copyright owner would not be necessary for the public projection. "Notwithstanding the provisions of Section 106(5), the owner of a particular copy lawfully made under this title, or any person authorized by such owner, is entitled, without the authority of the copyright owner, to display that copy publicly, either directly or by the projection of no more than one image at a time, to viewers present at the place where the copy is located." 17 U.S.C. Sec. 109(c). Of course, permission would not be required for the making of even the transparency of the original copy made for the purpose of such projection if the making of the copy could be defended under the doctrine of fair use. For a discussion of fair use, see Chapter 25, on *The Fair Use Controversy.*

Sound recordings made part of audiovisual works are protected by the public performance right enjoyed by the owner of the audiovisual work.

Since this new right is framed as a public performance right, it would also seem to require that the work be played or rendered in the course of the transmission. Thus, a digital delivery of a sound recording, without a simultaneous playing or rendering, would not constitute an exercise of this right, but rather the exercise of the copyright owner's reproduction right. As suggested above, if a right separate from the reproduction right were deemed necessary to account for digital deliveries, then, such right should be characterized as "the exclusive right to reproduce a work in copies and phonorecords by means of a digital transmission."

For the same reason, the term *reproduction* (i.e., the act of fixing a work in a copy or phonorecord) should not be confused with the term *distribution* (i.e., the transfer of a physical copy or phonorecord of a work from one person to another), the term *transmission* should not be confused with the term *distribution.* The latter involves the movement of copies and phonorecords, which are each defined as *material objects.* At least until the invention of a transporter device, such as the fictional device featured in the television program, *Star Trek,* a copy or phonorecord, each being material objects, are not capable of being transmitted.

Thus, the term *distribute* (or *distribution)* denotes the changing of possession of a material object, such as a copy or phonorecord; the term *transmission* denotes the communication of a performance or display.[11] The term *reproduction* is the act of embodying or fixing in a copy or a phonorecord a musical work, sound recording or other copyrighted subject matter; it is neither a copy nor a phonorecord, though a reproduction may be effected by a transmission.

## B. Know What Music You Wish to License

### *1. Determine the Title of the Song*

In a project in which you are trying to clear a license to use a particular popular song, it would be helpful if you first — before

[11] See definition of publication: "A public performance or display of a work does not of itself constitute a publication." "A publication is a distribution of copies or phonorecords of a work . . ." 17 U.S.C. Sec. 101.

approaching a music publisher — tried to identify the title of the song for which you are seeking a license. Humming a few bars over the phone might not be adequate or helpful, especially in recent years, as many popular tunes, such as heavy metal and rap songs, are not particularly recognizable when you hum them. Even old standards, many of which have melodies that are quite hummable, might not be recognized by younger staff members of major music publishers who were raised exclusively on popular music of the past 10 to 20 years.

It might help to know a few important lines of lyrics, particularly with very old tunes, such as those published by Robbins Music Corp. early in the twentieth century. To the great consternation of many a lyrical artist, Jack Robbins insisted that the title of virtually all songs published by his company comprise the first few words of the lyrics. Examples include, *I'm in the Mood for Love*, *Blue Moon*, *Don't Blame Me*, *Sweet and Lovely*, and *You'll Never Know.* As opprobrious as the practice might seem to many songwriters, Jack Robbins knew his business and his idea is one that should be seriously considered today. Many contemporary songwriters attach bizarre titles to their songs, which often have no resemblance to any of the lyrics contained in the song. Where the song's title is not readily apparent from reading the lyrics, the clearance of a license for the use of the song can become very difficult. Accordingly, the use of such titles may adversely impact a songwriter's earnings.

If you know the lyrics, but not the title, you might try typing the lyrics into a lyric search engine, such as *I'm in the Mood for Love* or simply Google a couple of lines of the lyric. The first few results are likely to include a link to the full lyrics, with the song's title.

If the music was originally featured in a well-known motion picture, then knowing the name of the film might help. For example, if you asked for the music in the movie starring Humphrey Bogart, *Casablanca*, or the Woody Allen film, *Play it Again, Sam*, the publisher is likely to know that you are referring to the song, *As Time Goes By.* You might ask for the love theme from the movie *Superman*, without knowing the title *Can You Read My Mind.*

If you don't know the name of the song, but somehow know the name of the songwriter, you can go to ASCAP.com, BMI.com, or SESAC.com, the respective websites of the three performance rights societies in the United States, and perform a search for the name of the songwriter. The result of the search should be a list of titles of the songs he or she wrote.

If you have heard a recording of the song, and you can locate a copy of an LP or CD album containing the recording, you should have no trouble determining the name of the song, as it should be written on the album cover or in the CD booklet.

### *2. Looking for a Type of Composition*

If you don't even have a particular song in mind, but are looking for music from a particular genre or era, major publishing firms that have vast music catalogs should be of service in helping you identify songs that meet your requirements. For example, if you were looking for music that was popular during the 1920s, a publisher might recommend, *Baby Face*, *Ain't She Sweet*, and *Ain't We Got Fun*.

Note, however, that many of today's publishing firms are staffed by younger people who are not familiar with many of the older popular tunes. To address this problem, several years ago I helped compile a list of standard songs controlled by Warner Bros. Music, arranged in categories, such as 1920s music, 1930s music, 1940s music, western music, popular music, etc.[12] Warner/Chappell, for example, has prepared a compact disk containing hundreds of short recordings of many of the songs they have available for license.

The bottom line, however, is that unless you know the name of a specific song you are interested in, you might run into some serious problems finding what you are looking for.

### *3. Maybe You Just Need a Needledrop*

If you don't know what specific song you wish to license, but you know the kind of music you require, or if you do know the song you want, but you either can't find the copyright owner (or, if you found him, you wish you hadn't, because he refuses to budge from the exorbitant fee he quoted you), perhaps you should consider turning to what is known as a *production music library*.

---

[12] Throughout this book, references to "I" means co-author, Al Kohn, unless otherwise indicated.

A *production music library* is a special kind of music publishing company that licenses what is commonly referred to by any of the following names: *production music, library music, canned music*, or *needledrops* — i.e., music that has been pre-recorded over the years for various production purposes and is now available as part of a vast library of music, organized by genre (e.g., pop, swing, jazz, classical, electronic), mood (e.g., blues, dixie, comedy), and even by instrument (e.g., piano, violin, saxophone, symphony orchestra) from which a producer may select.

The term, *needledrop*, originated from the vinyl record era when recordings were played by dropping the arm of a record player equipped with a diamond stylus needle onto the grooves of a vinyl record revolving on a turntable (groovy, man!). Production music was traditionally licensed for each cue or segment of music that began when the needle was dropped onto the record and ended when the needle was lifted.

The great advantage of using production music is that the music library typically owns both the sound recording and the underlying musical composition. Accordingly, often for one flat fee, you can get a license to use both a song and a production quality sound recording of the song, on tape, ready for incorporation into your project, without the need to account for royalties.

Although a production music library will not contain the latest Michael Jackson hits or Frank Sinatra standards, producers of television programs rely quite heavily on these libraries for many music needs. For example, a particular scene of a television program or motion picture may depict a juke box, radio, or phonograph in the background. When a director or producer requires music to be added to the motion picture soundtrack so that it appears to be playing from one of these sources, the music is called *source music*. Often, in these circumstances, any music will suffice, and the producer will turn to a music library for the appropriate canned music to add to the soundtrack. Sometimes a band will be depicted performing on camera. In these circumstances, a producer on a low budget can save considerably by using canned music rather than renting a recording studio and hiring a small band to make the necessary recording.

If the project calls for classical music, even a producer with a substantial production budget will consider saving the cost of engaging a large symphony orchestra by instead using production music from a music library. Producers will often prefer newly composed and recorded music for important foreground purposes, but turn to production music licensed from a music library to fulfill the incidental or source music needs of the film. When a producer is looking for that standard song sound, he might consider choosing among the many soundalike songs — e.g., songs that sound like *As Time Goes By* or *Over the Rainbow* also available from music libraries. When only the original standard song will do, the producer can clear the music license from the music publisher and license the appropriate sound recording desired from a music library. Finally, many production music libraries also carry a large variety of sound effects, such as glass breaking or a toilet flushing, and these may be licensed on a basis similar to canned music (i.e., a canned flush for the can scene).

One disadvantage of using music libraries is that a producer may have to sift through much of the music library's catalog to find precisely the music for which he is seeking. For this purpose, many music libraries are beginning to offer samples of their catalogs on compact discs and on the Internet, but this still requires the producer to spend hours listening to alternatives, often without a natural ear for the task before him.

A good music library will have a staff that knows its catalog and can help you find and compile the appropriate source music. Roy Kohn, the manager and marketing director of one of the largest production music libraries, the Southern Library of Recorded Music,[13] provides substantial assistance to producers, often using his library's music to score an entire show or film, complete with an open and close, main title theme and incidental music of every type called for by the production. This service can save the producer thousands of dollars, and also offers the producer the advantage of hearing the melodies before paying for the music, unlike where a composer is contracted to deliver a score.

Producers of videogames who run into difficulties getting incidental or bumper music, or software publishers looking for music to

[13] Southern Library of Recorded Music, 39 Via san Marco, Rancho Mirage, CA 92270. Phone: 760-202-2357, Fax: 760 202 2327, E-mail: roykohn53@msn.com, Ralph Peer II, President; Roy Kohn, Manager. Other production music libraries include Getty Images, De Wolfe Music, APM, Extreme Music, FirstCom Music, Groove Addicts, Killer Tracks, Manhattan, Musicsupervisor.com, Non-Stop, 5 Alarm, Master Source, Megatrax, and Wild Whirled, all of which can be found through a search on Google.

include in product demonstrations, often turn to production music libraries for these purposes. Getting a license for both the song and the recording, royalty and hassle free, is a major advantage to a producer with a low budget and little time or patience to seek complex music clearances.

Production music is licensed either by *cue* or on a *blanket* basis. A cue is a single cut of music, often referred to as a *needledrop* — the segment of music that began when the needle was dropped onto the record and ended when the needle was lifted. Production music is also licensed on a blanket basis, with the producer paying a yearly fee to the music library for a license to use an unlimited number of cues from the library, but typically the music used must still be reported to the production library and separate licenses will be issued for each use.

A form license agreement used by one production music library is set forth as Form 22.10 on the CD-ROM. The fees typically charged by production music libraries are set forth in Chapter 26, on *Typical License Fees.*

#### *4. Maybe You Don't Need a License*

You may not always require a license to use a particular musical work. Besides getting a license (i.e., getting permission to use the music owned by another in your work), you may acquire or already possess the necessary legal privilege to use a copyrighted work by any of the following means: (a) using a work that is in the *public domain* (i.e., taking steps to assure the music is not subject to any legal rights of another); (b) *originating* the work (i.e., creating the music yourself); (c) *purchasing* the work (i.e., buying from another all the rights in the music); and (d) making a *fair use* of another's copyrighted work.

##### *a. Using Music in the Public Domain*

No permission is required to use a musical composition if it is in the public domain. A work in the *public domain* is a work (1) for which copyright protection was never available; (2) for which copyright protection was never properly secured; or (3) for which copyright protection, though it may have once existed, has expired or otherwise has been lost.

Prior to the effective date of the Copyright Act of 1976 (i.e., January 1, 1978), copyright protection in work was secured by publishing the work (i.e., distributing copies beyond a limited distribution) and making sure that such copies bore a proper copyright notice. Failure to include a copyright notice in published copies would cause the work to fall into the public domain. In addition, failure to timely file a renewal registration for a copyrighted work could also cause the work to fall into the public domain. A work whose copyright protection has expired (e.g., all works published in the United States prior to 1923) are in the public domain.

Note, however, the fact that a work has fallen into the public domain in the United States does not necessarily mean that it has fallen into the public domain in other countries. Each country has its own laws regarding the duration of copyright. For example, many countries follow the "rule of the shorter term." In such a country, the duration of copyright protection will last the shorter of (i) the term of protection accorded to nationals of that country or (ii) the term of protection accorded to the work in the home country of the work's author. Thus, if the copyright in a work has expired in the United States, it will not be protected in a country that follows the rule of the shorter term, even if that country provides a longer term of protection for its own citizens. However, because several significant countries (including the United Kingdom and Canada) do not follow the rule of the shorter term, an independent analysis must be made of the status of copyright for each country in which a user desires to exploit the work.

Determining whether a particular work is in the public domain (or "PD") is discussed more fully in Chapter 7, on *The Language of Music Licensing*, as well as in the context of the duration of copyright and in Chapter 9.

### *b. Originating Your Own Music*

Of course, to the extent you create your own work, and you own the work, free and clear of any obligation to pay royalties to anyone, you won't require a license to use it in another work. Creating your own work is known as *originating* the work. You may originate a work by either creating a completely original work, by making an original adaptation of a work in the public domain, or by combining a completely original work with content taken from the public domain. Examples of origination include composing a new musical composition yourself or writing an original arrangement of the *Star Spangled Banner*.

Under certain circumstances, you do not have to take any special action to secure the privileges required to use content that you originate yourself. As noted in Chapters 7 and 9, ownership of copyright subsists in the author the moment the work is fixed in a tangible medium of expression — e.g., the moment a song is written down or recorded. Under the law, an author has, at that moment, all the rights and privileges he requires to use his own work.

In practice, however, the circumstances under which no action is required to secure the appropriate privilege to use originated content are limited to those situations in which you are doing the origination, either personally or in direct collaboration with another. If, for example, you are a member of a partnership or corporation, or you are obtaining contributions from others to create the work, some formality may be required to properly evidence your procurement of the necessary privilege to use the work created, such as the execution of a written copyright assignment or work for hire agreement.

While the process of acquiring the privileges necessary to use content that you or your firm originates is considerably less complex than that of acquiring what you need to use content owned by another, some diligence is still required to secure the necessary privileges you will require. The necessary formalities are discussed in Chapter 8, on the *Formalities of Music Licensing.*

### c. Purchasing All Rights in the Work You Desire to Use

The preceding section sketched one basic way of acquiring permission to use music: originating it yourself. Of course, it is not always possible or practical for you to originate a work, and in some cases you may be unable to use the "work for hire" status in dealing with your contractors. More likely, the music you wish to use already exists, in which event you may clear your use either by obtaining permission or purchasing ownership rights in the content. The formalities necessary to effect a purchase or sale of a copyrighted composition are discussed in Chapter 8, on the *Formalities of Music Licensing.*

### d. Making a Fair Use of Another's Copyrighted Work

No permission is required to use a musical composition if the use is considered a *fair use.* However, the determination of whether a particular use falls within the fair use doctrine is often not an easy one, and should not be made lightly, and certainly not without the advice of competent legal counsel. The consequences of being wrong may be a costly lawsuit for copyright infringement. Determining whether a particular use would be considered a fair use is discussed in Chapter 25, on *The Fair Use Controversy.*

### C. Develop a Licensing Strategy

Before making your first phone call, develop a licensing strategy. The basic decision to make at this point is whether you *do it yourself* or whether you *hire a specialist.* The answer will often depend on the complexity of the project involved. Thus, you should, at the outset, get a feel for the complexity of the project.

Music clearance projects can be categorized into the simple and the complex. A simple project would be, for example, obtaining clearance to use one or two songs in a traditional kind of work, such as a novel, record album, or motion picture. A complex project would be obtaining clearance to use many songs for use in a traditional work or in a new form of media, such as an on-demand music subscription service. The approach you might use in obtaining music licenses for a simple project is likely to be significantly different from that of a complex project.

Whether a clearance project is simple or complex will often be a factor of the kind of music you require. If you can get by with what is commonly called *canned music*, your licensing strategy can be greatly simplified. In some cases, you may find that you don't require a license at all, as when the song you want to use is in the *public domain* or your use of the song is a *fair use* under the copyright law. But, even in these instances, some licensing strategy is still required, as determining whether a song is public domain or whether your use would be considered a fair use, may require the assistance of an attorney.

#### *1. Approaching the Simple Project*

You can probably clear licenses for simple projects yourself. If you know you are facing a complex project, or if, after a few attempts, your simple project turns out to be more complex than you originally anticipated, consider hiring a specialist.

### *a. Finding Out Who Owns the Song*

If you know the name of the song, or you managed to discover it without too much trouble, the next thing you need to know is who controls the rights to the song. In other words, with whom do you need to deal to obtain a license? This is not as easy a question to answer as you might expect. If you already know the answer, you are way ahead of the game. If you don't, you may be in for a rude awakening.

Even if you have a copy of another work in which the music originally appeared, such as a record album or a DVD of a motion picture, it is not likely that it will contain any useful information about where to find the person who controls the rights to the music. This is because credit in these works is rarely given to the music publishers or even to the songwriters on the packaging of record albums, motion pictures, and television programs. Few recording artists follow the fine tradition of performers like Frank Sinatra. Mr. Sinatra not only endeavored to give credit to songwriters but to the arrangers of the particular orchestrations he used on records and in public performances.

When working at Warner/Chappell, I often received calls directly from film companies, television producers, advertising agencies and others who seek permission to use a particular song. When I'm forced to regretfully inform the caller that the song is not among those in the catalog I represent, I am usually asked the next logical question: "Who *does* own the rights?" Quite often, I happen to be familiar with the song in question and would know off the top of my head the name of the music publisher who controlled the rights. Sad to say, the days of music publishers who have staffs familiar with the songs in their catalogs is nearing an end. Yet, even if licensing staffs were to become familiar with the songs contained in the major catalogs, it is becoming more difficult for anyone to know who owns or controls what song, as publishing interests of an increasing number of songs are being retained by songwriters and an increasing number of songs are becoming the subject of *split copyrights*, a problem discussed at length in Chapter 6.

### *b. Getting Help on the Internet*

While unfortunately there is no good, single database that you can access to help you find the owner or administrator of a particular song, there are some resources on the Internet to which you can turn.

*Performance Right Societies.* If you do not know who the copyright owner is, the best place to start is with the performance rights societies. There was a time when you could call the "index" department of ASCAP[14] or BMI[15] whose staff could help you determine the names of the music publisher who controlled any particular composition in their repertoire. Today, you can simply go to the respective websites of these societies — ASCAP.com or BMI.com — and search for the song titles you are seeking to clear; the results will show the title and the address of the music publisher(s) who control the administration rights to the songs you are seeking to clear.

If you don't know the society with which a particular song is affiliated, or if you don't know the name of any of the writers of the song, you might take a look at the liner notes on your audiocassette or the little booklet that comes with your CD; nearly all records will list the name of the songs on the album and many records will also list the performance rights society (i.e., ASCAP, BMI, or SESAC) with which the song is registered. If you can't determine which performance rights society to search, you're in luck — the performance rights societies that control performance rights for nearly all the music performed in the United States are only two in number. To determine whether to start at ASCAP.com or BMI.com, flip a coin. (If the coin should land on its edge, you might try calling SESAC,[16] the third, albeit the smallest of the performance rights societies in the United States.)[17]

*Harry Fox.* The Harry Fox Agency (www.harryfox.com) represents over 30,000 music publishers, or over 60% of all music publishers in the United States to facilitate the issuance and administration of mechanical licenses for the use of music in sound recordings. Before issuing a license, however, the Agency will require certain basic information

---

[14] ASCAP (American Society of Composers, Authors & Publishers), 1 Lincoln Plaza, New York, New York 10023, Phone: 212-621-6000, Fax: 212-787-1381, www.ascap.com.

[15] BMI (Broadcast Music, Inc.), 320 West 57th Street, New York, New York 10019, Phone: 212-586-2000, Fax 212-489-2368, www.bmi.com.

[16] SESAC, Inc., 421 West 54th Street, New York, New York 10019, Phone: 212-586-3450, Fax: 212-489-5699. Also, 55 Music Square East, Nashville, TN 37203, Phone: 615-320-0055, Fax: 615-329-9627, www.sesac.com.

[17] For a discussion of performance rights societies, see Chapter 18.

about the music you wish to use, including the title and the names of the writers of the composition, and the name of the publisher(s), if known.

To assist potential licensees in assembling this information, the Agency offers its eMechanical system, a web-based program intended for use by middle-market labels planning to produce more than 2,500 copies of each recorded song. In eMechanical, labels can search, request, and sign their mechanical licenses using the same online application. Users of eMechanical, however, must first sign up with the Harry Fox Agency. A more readily available system to those not having a relationship with HFA is Songfile, a web-based program intended for the licensing of a limited quantity of recordings (25-2,500 units), available to anyone with a web browser at songfile.com.

*U.S. Copyright Office.* If the records of the performing rights societies or the Harry Fox Agency are unable to help you, you might try searching the records of the U.S. Copyright Office of the U.S. Library of Congress at www.copyright.gov. For more difficult searches, you may consider commissioning a search of the records of the Copyright Office.

*Thomson & Thomson.* Thomson & Thomson is a provider of copyright research reports for the music industry. The firm routinely conducts research for major music publishers, record companies, and many independent music publishers, musicians, and songwriters. They also provide extensive research services for the motion picture, television, publishing, and computer industries. Research reports include information from the Library of Congress and Copyright Office records, from 1870 to the present, as well as information from online sources, Thomson & Thomson's own private databases, library and files (www.thomson-thomson.com). An example of a Thomson & Thomson research report of a copyright search is included in the appendix to this chapter.[18]

---

[18] Further intellectual property information may be found at the page maintained by the U.S. Patent & Trademark Office: http://www.uspto.gov and the U.S. Congress's THOMAS Legislative Information: http://thomas.loc.gov/. Links to these and other Internet resources may be found at Kohn On Music Licensing located on the Web at http://www.kohnmusic.com.

*c. A Last Resort*

If you cannot find the music publisher, copyright owner, songwriter, heirs of the songwriter, or someone authorized to grant licenses for use of a song, there is one last resort, if you still want to use the song and are prepared to take some risk. You can attempt to document the fact that you made good faith efforts to locate the licensing source. Perhaps the best way of doing so is to send a registered letter containing your request to clear a license to the name and address found in the Copyright Office files relating to the song you desire to use. If the letter is returned undelivered, you can use it as evidence some later time to show, perhaps to a federal judge if you must, that you used good faith to locate and obtain permission from the copyright owner.

Before relying on this procedure, however, you should be certain that you have used every commercially reasonable effort to discover the identity and location of the copyright owner. This may entail engaging a specialist to make sure that you have exhausted all possibilities.

Legislation has been introduced in the U.S. Congress that would limit the amount of damages a copyright holder could collect from an infringer of an orphan work. An orphan work is a copyrighted work of authorship whose owner has proven difficult to identify or reach for purposes of obtaining a license. The owner may be difficult to identify or reach because the work was published anonymously, the work may have been unpublished or self-published, the work is owned by the heirs of deceased author who are difficult to track down.

The proposed bill would limit damages for copyright infringement if the infringer performed a diligent search for the copyright holder before using the work. The goal of the legislation is to free up for reuse copyrighted works whose holders cannot be found. It would also set up a process for the Copyright Office to certify commercially produced visual registries to help people locate the holder of a copyright and prevent the orphaning of works in the future. As of the time of this printing, such legislation has not been passed.

*d. Using the Publisher's Website*

Some publisher websites permit you to search their repertoire by a variety of parameters (e.g., genre, moods, topics, vocal gender, tempo, etc.) and submit license requests online. Search results may also include whether the publisher controls 100% of the composition, thereby avoiding the problem of split copyright discussed in Chapter 6, and whether the publisher controls a master recording of the song, which might be available for licensing with the composition. The Cherry Lane Music website at www.cherrylane.com is a particularly good example of such a site.

*e. Contacting the Music Publisher*

When, and if, you finally obtain the name of the music publisher who controls the rights to the song, you must speak to the appropriate person at the publisher. When calling a music publisher, ask for the "director of licensing" or "licensing department."

Most large music publishing houses have large staffs to handle licensing of their copyrights, and are able to assign individuals who specialize in granting licenses for the various kinds of uses, such as record albums, motion pictures, and television advertising. Knowing the standard terminology employed for these uses (e.g., mechanical, synchronization) can help you get to the right person more quickly. So, if you successfully learn the jargon, you should feel free to use it.

Before getting in touch with the music publisher or administrator who controls the rights to the song you are seeking to clear, be sure to first compile the basic information you'll be asked to provide — summarized in the section below on *Making the License Request.*

### *2. Approaching the Complex Project*

As you can see from the preceding section, even a project that looks simple can turn out to be complex if the search for the music copyright owner becomes problematic. But some projects are complex from the start.

Many years ago, most music used in motion pictures was acquired by commissioning a composer to write an original score for the film's soundtrack. Obtaining the appropriate license to use the music in the motion picture was merely a matter of entering a standard composer's agreement with the composer.[19] All that changed in the mid-1970s with

[19] An example of a standard Composer's Agreement is set forth as Form 3.8 on the CD-ROM.

the release of the movie *Saturday Night Fever*, the music soundtrack of which comprised a series of disco tunes that were popular hits at that time. That event spawned a series of song-driven motion pictures, such as *Fast Times at Ridgemont High, Footloose*, *Top Gun*, and others.

The process of obtaining clearance to use several popular music songs in a motion picture will always be complex. This is because the producer should be thinking that he needs permission to use the songs not only in the motion picture but also on the soundtrack album for the picture. Once you begin thinking about soundtrack albums, you need to think about resolving any conflicts with exclusive record contracts, rights of approval from recording artists to *couple* their recordings on compilation albums, and songwriter agreements to which the performing artists are likely to be bound. Further, the music publishing interests of songs composed by members of rock groups are often divided among the members of the group and you may find the need to obtain permission from more than one publishing source for each song in the picture.

Clearing music for use on the Internet is often fraught with complexity. These new media works or Internet sites may contain recordings of hundreds of thousands of songs each of which will require separate clearance. The clearance of a few songs for use in a motion picture might look like child's play to one who might wish, for example, to clear several thousand songs for use on an on-demand music subscription service. Accordingly, for any work that involves the clearance of more than several songs, particularly recent recordings, you should consider getting professional assistance to clear your licenses.

#### *a. Getting Help from a Professional Music Supervisor*

A music supervisor, traditionally defined, is one who helps producers of motion pictures and television programs select the right music for their films and programs. Music supervision now extends to the production of videogames, television commercials, and other projects that involve an intensive use of music selected for a particular context. Music supervisors may be employed on a full-time basis, but more typically are engaged on a project-by-project basis by film and television producers, studios, videogame companies, and advertising agencies.

Music supervision is primarily a creative job, one that focuses on *spotting* the right music for each particular scene and overseeing the recording and assembly of the songs and recordings used in the project. Supervisors tend to be composers or musicians, but they often play an important administrative role. They can provide immense help not only in selecting the music and recordings to use in a project but also in budgeting, scheduling, administering *cue sheets* (i.e., a list of all the music used in a production in the order it is used, including timings; they are used by performance rights organizations to monitor the performance of music of their members), preparing the *credits* for featured music and recordings (that will appear on the rolling credits at the end of a film), overseeing the clearance process, and even negotiating the licenses required.

The music supervisor may either oversee the process of clearing the licenses necessary for the music used or work closely with music clearance people charged with that task. A good music supervisor understands that a smooth clearance process is equally as important as the selection of the right music for a particular project — he or she would not even suggest a song or a recording without first getting some idea as to whether the works are licensable at a reasonable price. This may be as simple as taking the time to determine who the publisher is and knowing from experience whether that publisher is someone they know, or at least has a reputation for facilitating the licensing of music at a reasonable cost. If a supervisor suggests a *temp track* (i.e., a piece of music used as a placeholder in the viewing of the film by the director in the pre-production process), a director may become accustomed seeing the film with the track and insist on its use, forcing the supervisor or the music clearance people to license the song at any cost.

### *b. Getting Help from Licensing Companies*

It always helps to developing a relationship with the synch clearance people at the major and independent music publishers, but there are also a number of companies that specialize in helping music publishers and record labels get their music used in film and television projects.

Several of the better known firms in this field include: Sugaroo (www.sugeroo.com), Broadjam.com, Optic Noise (www.optic-noise.com), Indyhits (www.indyhits.com), BFM Digital (bfmdigital.com),

Natural Energy Lab (www.naturalenergylab.com), Shelly Bay Music (www.shellybay.com), Ocean Park Music (www.oceanparkmusic.com), Big Sounds International (www.bigsoundsintl.com), Position Music (www.positionmusic.com), Love Cat Music (www.lovecatmusic.com), and Record Play (www.record-play.net), Konsonant (www.konsonant.com), Rock River Music Supervision and Licensing (www.rockrivermusic.com).

### c. *Music Clearing Houses and Other Professional Assistance*

A number of organizations specialize in providing professional assistance for the clearance of music licenses. These include Clear This Entertainment (www.clearthisent.com), EMG Music Clearance (www.clearance.com), Winogradsky/Sobel (www.winogradsky.com), BZ Rights and Permissions, Inc. (www.bzrights.com), Music Rightz (suzcoffman@earthlink.net), The Music Bridge (www.themusicbridge.com), Music Reports (www.musicreports.com), Diamond Time (www.diamondtime.net), Signature Sound (www.signature-sound.com), and The Rights Workshop (www.rightsworkshop.com).

These organizations typically charge a flat fee per clearance or set of clearances, which varies by project. These organizations cannot promise to actually obtain clearances for all the music you want to license, but because of their long-established relationships with most of the major music publishers and substantial experience in dealing with the problem of split copyrights, they will have a significantly better chance of succeeding than someone approaching the problem of clearance for the first time. You might consider hiring an attorney to clear your rights, but you will find the use of clearance companies less expensive, generally more effective, and often staffed or operated by trained attorneys experienced in the field.

The consulting fees charged by these companies are in addition to the cost of the licenses they may obtain for you. Accordingly, if you're responsible for a budget, don't just budget for the license fee. Be sure to budget for consulting fees for clearing rights and any additional research fees that may be required to obtain copies of the music you need.

*d. Finding the Recording or Orchestration*

The rights to use all this wonderful music is not worth anything if you can't find a copy of the music. Often, your particular use might call for having a copy of a recording of the song, a lead sheet, or a full orchestration. You should be prepared to do your own researching for any tangible copies of the music you seek. Don't expect a music publisher to help you find a recording. Many publishers, especially older and larger firms, might not have files with complete listings of recordings of particular copyrights, such as very old standard songs. The publisher might be able to get you a lead sheet, but don't count on it. The Copyright Act of 1978 allows a publisher or composer to register their song with a tape recording in lieu of creating and filing lead sheets; therefore, if a lead sheet is required for the use intended, the user might have to be satisfied with a lyric sheet and an audio tape of the song.

If the music you require originally appeared in a motion picture, and you are seeking a copy of the complete score, you may need to get in touch with the appropriate film music library. A listing of public libraries, motion picture studios, university libraries, libraries of historical societies, art museums, and private collections that contain original film score manuscripts can be obtained by writing for the *Directory of Film Music Collections in the United States* published by the Film Music Society (www.filmmusicsociety.org). You might also try the *Film Composer's Guide*, published by The Lone Eagle Publishing Company.

Even if you find the original orchestrations, you may find the studios who own them highly reluctant to license them. Scores for some film music, however, are available from Warner Bros. through special archive services provided by a major university.[20] Silent film soundtracks were compiled from many separately published pieces (rather than commissioned from one composer). Scores from silent films were compiled in so-called, *conductor books*. Even if you are able to find the conductor book you are looking for, the studio that possesses it may not have the right to license it. A studio might issue a quitclaim license for the use of the score (a license from them without any warranty or representation that they own the proper rights), but you would still

[20] Warner Bros. Archive, USC School of Cinema Television, University of Southern California, Los Angeles, California 90089.

need to obtain licenses from the copyright owners of the underlying music.

*e. Making the License Request*

After you find the person authorized to grant the license you require, you should be prepared to educate that person about precisely how you intend to use the music. Ideally, the person calling a music publisher for a license will know the language of music licensing as described in this book. Understanding the language will go a long way to facilitate the communication between the parties and the result should be a fruitful and efficient experience for all concerned.

In any negotiation, however, there are often hidden assumptions that can be the cause of some misunderstanding. Publishers are likely to test those assumptions, because of the precision they strive to achieve in fashioning the scope of the licenses they grant. You should therefore expect the music publisher to ferret out the precise scope of the permission you need in an effort to limit the scope of the permission to be granted solely to the uses that you intend, and no more. Further, the publisher will also attempt to determine the importance of the song in relation to its intended use or any other information that would be helpful in establishing the appropriate licensee fee structure and license fee.

Most publishers now require that you complete a form containing basic information about your request. Some publishers post these forms on their website; others will fax them to you upon request. Depending upon the type of license you are seeking (e.g., print, lyric, mechanical, synchronization, commercial advertising), these forms may ask for the kind of information set forth below. Accordingly, you should be prepared to answer some or all of the following questions, either on the phone or by completing the form provided by the publisher:

- The name of your company, address, your telephone number and email address;
- The title of the song you are seeking to license
- The names of the writers of the song
- The name of one or more of the artists who may have recorded the song

- Whether you seek to also license an existing master, or re-record the song
- What is the nature of the work in which the music will appear?
  - Commercial advertisement
  - Theatrical film
  - Theatrical film trailer
  - Television
  - In-house or corporate video
  - Karaoke
  - Merchandise
  - Website
- How will the music be rendered in the work? For example, if for use in an audiovisual work, whether your use would be a background use or visual (e.g., performed on the screen) and whether the use would be instrumental or vocal.
- Will the music comprise all or any part of the work?
- Will it be used once or multiple times?
- What is the duration in minutes and seconds of the use?
- Do you intend to use other songs in the work?
- Will you use non-music components, such as motion pictures, animation, text, photographs, dialogue, or other visual or audio elements?
- Will the music or lyrics be changed or edited?
- Will the title of the song be used in a special way, such as in the title of the film?
- Will the work be a dramatic adaptation of the song's lyrics?
- Will the song be performed dramatically?
- In what markets will the work be distributed?
- Will the song be used to promote a product?

- Will the song be made part of a product or other item of merchandise?
- Will the work be transmitted over the Internet?

In inquiring about the use of a song, be prepared to specify the type of use you seek. If the use is in a recording, you should specify whether the recording will be audio-only, or combined with motion pictures or other audiovisual materials. If the use is for television, you should distinguish between *free* television and *pay/cable* television. If the use is in a motion picture, you should specify if it will be in a film for normal theatrical release or whether it will be in a nontheatrical motion picture, such as a corporate training film or student documentary. Presenting this information correctly will assist the publisher in quoting the proper fees.

Some works may defy description. Perhaps the producer of the work can describe the work using the special jargon of a particular field, such as computers, but he should not assume that music publishers are even remotely familiar with the latest developments in technology or new Internet business models. For example, if you require a license to use a song "online," you might need to spend a little time explaining just what that means. Even if the music copyright owner begins to understand the work or service in which you intend to use the song, he may be entirely unprepared to determine just what kind of license would be appropriate for the use. The fear of making a bad deal (see below) suddenly takes center stage, and your project gets delayed while the publisher takes the matter to his lawyers, who are likely to know little more than the publisher about the media for which a license is sought.

Upon the advent of the home videocassette tape market for motion pictures, it took years for standard business practices to evolve that addressed how music copyright owners would be compensated for the use of their music in these tapes. It may not take as long for practices to emerge that resolve issues in licensing music for use in Internet transmission services, but producers of these new programs and services will find that they will not be able to ignore the established business practices of the music publishing business when negotiating the appropriate licenses for these uses.

If you have a work that is unusual or complex, you might be asked to provide a demonstration of your product or service, or provide access to similar services, or send copies of similar products or any marketing materials that would help the publisher understand how the music will be used in the context of the work.

Many songwriter contracts restrict the publisher's ability to permit others to make changes to lyrics of a song or make fundamental changes to the character of the music. For example, while Ira Gershwin was alive, he would never permit the rendition of his brother, George's composition *Rhapsody in Blue*, unless it was performed in its entirety. (He made the first exception when I persuaded him to allow Woody Allen to use a substantial excerpt in the film, *Manhattan*). A user should never consider making any substantial changes to lyrics or the music without first obtaining a license with special provisions permitting such changes.

## D. Negotiating the License

### *1. Arriving at the Appropriate License Fee and Terms*

Having gained some understanding of the rights involved, having developed some strategy for obtaining the license you need, and having learned where to contact the music copyright owner, you are ready to negotiate the terms of the license. The balance of this book is devoted to helping both the licensee and the licensor get a better understanding of the ranges of license fees and parameters of license terms for each of the different kinds of licenses touched upon to this point.

### *2. Understanding the Needs and Fears of the Music Copyright Owner*

If you are the potential licensee, it would be helpful during the negotiation process to remain mindful of the basic needs and fears of the music copyright owner.

Music copyright owners have three basic fears:

a. Fear of piracy

b. Fear of making a bad deal

c. Fear of getting sued

Each of these fears is discussed in turn.

### a. *Fear of Piracy*

Copyright means what the word implies — the right to copy. It is the right to exclude others from copying unless they have the right holder's permission to do so. But this right is violated as often as it is respected. Copyright owners lose billions of dollars a year to copyright *piracy*, the unauthorized use of copyrighted works. Ironically, the problem of copyright piracy stems from the very intangibility that gives music its value to mankind: The intangible nature of music renders copying easy to perform and unauthorized copying difficult to discover. Piracy has always been an insidious backdrop to the daily exercise of a music copyright owner's rights. However, recent developments have hurled a new challenge to those who rely on the exercise of copyrights to earn a living: The advent of the new technologies — such as the digital technology that forms the basis of computers, digital tape and laser discs — has made the process of copying faster, cheaper, easier, and more accurate than ever before. At the same time, few strides have been made to render unauthorized copying less difficult to discover. The recent emergence of these new capabilities has caused music copyright owners to have a heightened perspective on some old fears.

It should therefore be no surprise when you approach a music publisher for a license to use music, especially in new media works, to discover in the copyright owner an immediate resistance to license. The resistance will generally stem from the copyright owner's unwillingness to enter into any arrangement that might have unknown consequences on the value of his work. As far as the copyright owner is concerned, anything that he does not understand may, in fact, result in unforeseen adverse consequences.

The antidote to this fear, of course, is some combination of education and trust. The importance of educating the copyright owner is discussed later in this chapter. Establishing trust is often a function of the relationship between the copyright owner and the licensee or, quite often, the licensee's representative. The use of a reputable music clearing house that has had prior dealings with the music publisher may prove the decisive factor in closing a license to new or esoteric uses.

### *b. Fear of Making a Bad Deal*

One of a copyright owner's worst fears is entering into a deal he will later regret having made. For example, a music copyright owner may regret having quoted too low a fee for the use of his music in a low-budget movie that unexpectedly became a *blockbuster.* Also, if the copyright owner is dealing with a studio, a clearing house, or other person with whom he deals often, the copyright owner will be concerned about setting a precedent of which he will no doubt be reminded in future deals.

More important, because of the nature of copyright (i.e., intangible) and the means by which they may be exploited (i.e., granting permission to use), a bad deal may involve significantly more than failing to obtain a sufficiently high fee. If the copyright owner is not careful, he may find himself on the wrong end of a deal that has serious adverse consequences on the value of his copyright.

For example, a copyright owner may be persuaded to provide a license to use his music in computer software for a flat fee using a written license that grants permission to use the music "in digital form." Notwithstanding the copyright owner's rudimentary understanding of the phrase "in digital form" at the time the license was granted, the license may well have the effect of reducing the value of the copyright to virtually nothing if later virtually all distribution and performance of music is made "in digital form."

The fear of making a bad deal is more pronounced in owners of copyright than in owners of other kinds of assets. The owner of an asset, such as a car, can fairly predict the limited consequences of leasing the asset at an unprofitable rate; the risk of leasing the asset to one who would negligently destroy it may be covered by insurance and, in any event, the loss may be measured precisely and in advance. The value of a copyright, however, may vary over time and is directly affected by the nature and scope of the licenses granted by its owner. The copyright owner will be very concerned about limiting the scope of the license and to do so, he will be required to understand exactly what the nature of the use is.

Thus, the copyright owner's unwillingness to enter into any arrangement that might have unknown consequences on the value of his work — stemming from a lack of understanding of the use and its consequences — manifests itself in the fear of making a bad deal. Again, the best remedy is education and establishing a relationship with the copyright owner. In the end, you should find that copyright owners are actually quite eager to benefit from the opportunities afforded by the new technologies and most do not wish to be left behind.

### *c. Fear of Getting Sued*

This is of the same genre as making a deal that the copyright owner may regret, but the remorse has another cause. Getting sued is high on the list of a copyright owner's fears. The uncertainty of damage awards, the high costs of litigation, and the immeasurable damage to important long-term contractual relationships and business reputation all tend to make a copyright owner extremely conservative in making decisions that involve any risk that he may become embroiled in a lawsuit.

The latitude a copyright owner has in granting licenses is often limited by the terms of the contracts he may have with the songwriters and co-owners of the copyright. For example, as noted in Chapter 3, on *Songwriter Agreements*, a common provision of many songwriter contracts requires the music publisher to obtain the permission of the songwriter before authorizing anyone to alter or make any changes to the copyrighted work. Thus, if your use involves changing the lyrics of a song, the music publisher may require the written consent of the songwriter before issuing the license. Songwriter contracts may also restrict the music publisher's authority to grant licenses for the use of music in radio, television, and print advertising. Some artists are very sensitive about this and will deny consent for all kinds of uses, except recordings that are subject to the compulsory license provisions of the copyright law, discussed in Chapter 13, on *Licensing Music in Sound Recordings.*

You should not expect that a publisher will be able to give you a definitive answer right away. The publisher may wish to first review a contract to determine whether any consent is required for the use. The publisher might seek a legal opinion on the scope of his ability to grant to you the license you require. All of this will take time, and, where there is a possibility that an ambiguity could be decided against the publisher, there is no assurance that he will want to take any risk to help you.

The fear a publisher has of taking any action that may result in a legal dispute is coupled with a certain amount of frustration; the publisher often desires to issue a license, but may be forced to acquiesce to the shortsightedness of the artist or the artist's representative who insists on arbitrarily invoking a contractual right of approval. Thus, when faced with a situation in which the publisher's hands are tied, you should be aware that inability, not unwillingness, is at the root of the matter and you should keep communication with the publisher open in the hope that together you can find an alternative solution to your music clearance problem.

## E. Allow Enough Time to Complete the Process

Licensing music may sound as simple as knowing the name of the song you want, calling the performance rights society to find out who controls the rights, and obtaining the proper license. It sounds easy, but it's rarely that simple in practice.

Any number of things may come up that will delay the completion of a project that contains copyrighted music. For example, music publishers are well aware of the frustrations that producers experience when trying to track down copyright owners. A music publisher on the other side of a phone call will hear a producer express a long sigh of relief when, after nine or ten phone calls, he learns that he finally located the publisher. That's the good news. Then the producer learns the bad news, that the song is also controlled by three other publishers. When he finally finds all the publishers, he discovers that he also requires a print license to clear his particular use and then gets hit with the news that none of them control the print rights!

Allow yourself enough time to do the research and complete the negotiations necessary to obtain a license. You should always attempt to obtain your clearance *before* you begin integrating the music into your work. If you use the music before you receive a license and the copyright owner discovers it, you do two things: (i) you create a bad impression that may anger the publisher, who thinks you are trying to pressure him into giving you a license, and, perhaps more important, (ii) you greatly increase the publisher's leverage in the negotiation for the license.

After you've already spent the time and money recording the song or taping the performance, the publisher knows that it will cost you a fortune to find another song and re-record or retape the performance. While most professional publishers would not unreasonably "hold you up," you could find that any persuasive reason you may have had to support a lower fee will fall on deaf ears. Further, remember that these rights are often split up and you just don't know whether you can even obtain the license you require *at all.* If you can't obtain clearance, and you've recorded the song, you are a copyright infringer, subject to civil action and possible criminal penalties. In this situation, impatience can cost you, as the song goes, *More Than You Know.*

## III. SUMMARY

Excellence in the art of granting licenses for the purpose of earning a living from one's copyrighted music involves:

A. Sharing in the economic success of the work in which the music is going to be used;

B. Maximizing the long-term value of the work; and,

C. Maintaining an active relationship between the song and the listening public.

Excellence in obtaining licenses to use copyrighted music of others for commercial purposes involves:

A. Understanding the nature of the rights involved;

B. Knowing what music you wish to license;

C. Developing a licensing strategy;

D. Understanding the needs and fears of the copyright owner;

E. Spending time educating the copyright owner, particularly when licensing for high tech use; and

F. Allowing enough time (and budget) to complete the process.

# Appendix to Chapter 11
# The Art of Granting and Clearing Music Licenses

**Reports**

# REPORT 11.1

## THOMSON & THOMSON'S SEARCH OF THE COPYRIGHT OFFICE ON THE NAME, "ALBERT JOSEPH KOHN."

**SAMPLE REPORT**
July 20, 1995

**Author/Claimant Search - ALBERT JOSEPH KOHN**

A search of the records of the Copyright Office reveals the following copyright registrations and subsequent renewal information in connection with **ALBERT JOSEPH KOHN, ALBERT KOHN, AL KOHN** and/or **AL KOHN MUSIC** as the author and/or copyright claimant.

Our search reveals the following copyright registrations and subsequent renewals identifying **ALBERT JOSEPH KOHN** as the author and/or copyright claimant:

ONE LONELY NIGHT
Alternate Title:
Description: Unpublished musical composition
Author: Music by Albert Joseph Kohn
Application Author:
Copyright Claimant: Albert Joseph Kohn
Date of Publication:
Date of Registration (if unpublished): May 16, 1934
Registration Number: EU: 87617
New Matter:
Notes: With Pf. acc.
Renewal Claimant: No record of renewal is found

Our search reveals the following copyright registrations and subsequent renewals identifying **ALBERT KOHN** as the author and/or copyright claimant:

ACCIDENTS
Alternate Title:
Description: Musical composition
Author: Words and music by John Keen, arrangement by Albert Kohn
Application Author: Track Music, Inc., employer for hire of Albert Kohn
Copyright Claimant: Fabulous Music, Ltd.
Date of Publication: January 25, 1971
Date of Registration (if unpublished):
Registration Number: EP: 282175
New Matter: Arrangement for piano
Notes: Application states previously registered July 30, 1970, under entry No. EU: 197941. In Tunderclap Newman--Hollywood Dream.
Renewal Claimant: N/A

HOLLYWOOD DREAM
Alternate Title:
Description: Musical composition
Author: Music by Jimmy McCulloch, arrangement by Albert Kohn
Application Author: Track Music, Inc., employer for hire of Albert Kohn
Copyright Claimant: Fabulous Music, Ltd.
Date of Publication: January 25, 1971
Date of Registration (if unpublished):
Registration Number: EP: 282176
New Matter: Arrangement for piano
Notes: Application states previously registered July 30, 1970, under entry No. EU: 197943. In Tunderclap Newman--Hollywood Dream.
Renewal Claimant: N/A

HOLLYWOOD 1
Alternate Title:
Description: Musical composition
Author: Words and music by John Keen, arrangement by Albert Kohn
Application Author: Track Music, Inc., employer for hire of Albert Kohn
Copyright Claimant: Fabulous Music, Ltd.
Date of Publication: January 25, 1971
Date of Registration (if unpublished):
Registration Number: EP: 282180
New Matter: Arrangement for piano
Notes: Application states previously registered July 30, 1970, under entry No. EU: 197946. In Tunderclap Newman--Hollywood Dream.
Renewal Claimant: N/A

HOLLYWOOD 2
Alternate Title:
Description: Musical composition
Author: Words and music by John Keen, arrangement by Albert Kohn
Application Author: Track Music, Inc., employer for hire of Albert Kohn
Copyright Claimant: Fabulous Music, Ltd.
Date of Publication: January 25, 1971
Date of Registration (if unpublished):
Registration Number: EP: 282181
New Matter: Arrangement for piano
Notes: Application states previously registered July 30, 1970, under entry No. EU: 197947. In Tunderclap Newman--Hollywood Dream.
Renewal Claimant: N/A

I DON'T KNOW
Alternate Title:
Description: Musical composition
Author: Words and music by John Keen, arrangement by Albert Kohn

Author/Claimant Search - ALBERT JOSEPH KOHN

Application Author: Track Music, Inc., employer for hire of Albert Kohn
Copyright Claimant: Fabulous Music, Ltd.
Date of Publication: January 25, 1971
Date of Registration (if unpublished):
Registration Number: EP: 282182
New Matter: Arrangement for piano
Notes: Application states previously registered July 30, 1970, under entry No. EU: 197940. In Tunderclap Newman--Hollywood Dream.
Renewal Claimant: N/A

IT'S TIME FOR A CHANGE
Alternate Title:
Description: Unpublished musical composition
Author: Kevin Beverly and Albert Kohn
Application Author: Lyrics and music arranged by Kevin A. Beverly, lyrics by Albert Kohn
Copyright Claimant: Kevin A. Beverly and Albert Kohn
Date of Creation: 1980
Date of Publication:
Date of Registration (if unpublished): November 17, 1980
Registration Number: PAU: 248-662
New Matter:
Notes:
Renewal Claimant: N/A

KOLAN KOLOZALZ
Alternate Title:
Description: Unpublished musical composition
Author: Al Kohn and Mike Lanni
Application Author: Music and words to 1 song by Albert Kohn, words by Michael Lanni
Copyright Claimant: Albert Kohn and Michael Lanni
Date of Creation: 1984
Date of Publication:
Date of Registration (if unpublished): March 13, 1984
Registration Number: PAU: 596-861
New Matter:
Notes: Collection of songs
Renewal Claimant: N/A

LOOK AROUND
Alternate Title:
Description: Musical composition
Author: Words and music by John Keen, arrangement by Albert Kohn
Application Author: Track Music, Inc., employer for hire of Albert Kohn
Copyright Claimant: Fabulous Music, Ltd.

**Author/Claimant Search - ALBERT JOSEPH KOHN**

Date of Publication: January 25, 1971
Date of Registration (if unpublished):
Registration Number: EP: 282178
New Matter: Arrangement for piano
Notes: Application states previously registered July 30, 1970, under entry No. EU: 197949. In Tunderclap Newman--Hollywood Dream.
Renewal Claimant: N/A

OLD CORNMILL
Alternate Title:
Description: Musical composition
Author: Words and music by John Keen, arrangement by Albert Kohn
Application Author: Track Music, Inc., employer for hire of Albert Kohn
Copyright Claimant: Fabulous Music, Ltd.
Date of Publication: January 25, 1971
Date of Registration (if unpublished):
Registration Number: EP: 282184
New Matter: Arrangement for piano
Notes: Application states previously registered July 30, 1970, under entry No. EU: 197945. In Tunderclap Newman--Hollywood Dream.
Renewal Claimant: N/A

REASON
Alternate Title:
Description: Musical composition
Author: Words and music by John Keen, arrangement by Albert Kohn
Application Author: Track Music, Inc., employer for hire of Albert Kohn
Copyright Claimant: Fabulous Music, Ltd.
Date of Publication: January 25, 1971
Date of Registration (if unpublished):
Registration Number: EP: 282183
New Matter: Arrangement for piano
Notes: Application states previously registered July 30, 1970, under entry No. EU: 197948. In Tunderclap Newman--Hollywood Dream.
Renewal Claimant: N/A

THESE DAYS
Alternate Title: Application title: I'VE BEEN OUT WALKING
Description: Musical composition
Author: Words and music by Jackson Browne, arrangement by Albert Kohn
Application Author: Warner Tamerland Publishing Corporation, employer for hire of Albert Kohn

**Author/Claimant Search - ALBERT JOSEPH KOHN**

Copyright Claimant: Warner Tamerlane Publishing Corporation
Date of Publication: May 17, 1971
Date of Registration (if unpublished):
Registration Number: EP: 314354
New Matter: Piano accompaniment with guitar chords
Notes: In Tom Rush/Wrong End of the Tainbow. Previously registered Jnauary 12, 1967, under entry No. EU: 974715.
Renewal Claimant: N/A

WEDDING WALTZ
Alternate Title:
Description: Musical composition
Author: Music by Nick D'Amico, Gil Mills and Billy Faber, arrangement by Albert Kohn
Application Author:
Copyright Claimant: Leeds Music Corp.
Date of Publication: June 16, 1947
Date of Registration (if unpublished):
Registration Number: EP: 15091
New Matter:
Notes: Piano-conductor score (orchestra) and parts
Renewal Claimant: No record of renewal is found

WHEN I THINK
Alternate Title:
Description: Musical composition
Author: Words and music by John Keen, arrangement by Albert Kohn
Application Author: Track Music, Inc., employer for hire of Albert Kohn
Copyright Claimant: Fabulous Music, Ltd.
Date of Publication: January 25, 1971
Date of Registration (if unpublished):
Registration Number: EP: 282177
New Matter: Arrangement for piano
Notes: Application states previously registered July 30, 1970, under entry No. EU: 197944. In Tunderclap Newman--Hollywood Dream.
Renewal Claimant: N/A

WHEN THE SAINTS GO MARCHING ON
Alternate Title:
Description: Musical composition
Author: Traditional arrangement by Albert Kohn
Application Author:
Copyright Claimant: Kohn Music Corp.
Date of Publication: October 1, 1964
Date of Registration (if unpublished):
Registration Number: EP: 192778
New Matter: Piano arrangement

**Author/Claimant Search - ALBERT JOSEPH KOHN**

Notes: With words
Renewal Claimant: MCA Music, a division of MCA, Inc.
Capacity: Proprietor of copyright in a work made for hire
Date of Renewal: March 6, 1975
Renewal No.: R: 599676

WILD COUNTRY
Alternate Title:
Description: Musical composition
Author: Words and music by John Keen, arrangement by Albert Kohn
Application Author: Track Music, Inc., employer for hire of Albert Kohn
Copyright Claimant: Fabulous Music, Ltd.
Date of Publication: January 25, 1971
Date of Registration (if unpublished):
Registration Number: EP: 282179
New Matter: Arrangement for piano
Notes: Application states previously registered July 30, 1970, under entry No. EU: 197950. In Tunderclap Newman--Hollywood Dream.
Renewal Claimant: N/A

In addition, we also find the following books listing **ALBERT KOHN** as the author and/or claimant:

CREATION LITTERAIRE ER CONNAISSANCE ESSAIS EDITION ET INTRODUCTION (DICHTEN UND ERKENNEN)
Alternate Title:
Description: Book
Author: Hannah Arendt, translated from German by Albert Kohn
Application Author:
Copyright Claimant: Editions Gallimard
Date of Publication: November 25, 1966
Date of Registration (if unpublished):
Registration Number: AFO: 50214
New Matter:
Notes: Copyright is claimed on translation
Renewal Claimant: No record of renewal is found

GRANDEUR INCONNUE; BOOK BY JEUNESSE, LETTRES A WILLA MUIR (DIE UNBEKANNTE GROSSE), LA
Alternate Title:
Description: Book, Du monde entier
Author: Edition er introd. by Ernst Schonwiese, translated from German by Albert Kohn
Application Author:
Copyright Claimant: Editions Gallimard
Date of Publication: March 20, 1968
Date of Registration (if unpublished):

**Author/Claimant Search - ALBERT JOSEPH KOHN**

Registration Number: AFO: 54333
New Matter:
Notes: Copyright is claimed on translation
Renewal Claimant: N/A

MONTE DE VIRGILE (DER TOD DES VERGIL), LA
Alternate Title:
Description: Musical composition
Author: Translated from German by Albert Kohn
Application Author:
Copyright Claimant: Librairie Gallimard
Date of Publication: February 25, 1955
Date of Registration (if unpublished):
Registration Number: AFO: 17201
New Matter:
Notes:
Renewal Claimant: No record of renewal is found

ROMAN D'NEHRI IV (LA GUERRIER PACIFIQUE), LE
Alternate Title: Original title: DIE VOLLENDUNG DES KOENIGS HENRI QUATRE
Description: Book
Author: Translated from German by Albert Kohn
Application Author:
Copyright Claimant: Editions Gallimard
Date of Publication: May 20, 1972
Date of Registration (if unpublished):
Registration Number: AFO: 69664
New Matter:
Notes: Copyright is claimed on translation
Renewal Claimant: N/A

ROMAN D'NEHRI IV (LA JEUNESSE DU ROI), LE
Alternate Title: Original title: DIE JUGEND DES KOENIGS HENRI QUATRE
Description: Book
Author: Translated from German by Albert Kohn
Application Author:
Copyright Claimant: Editions Gallimard
Date of Publication: January 1, 1972
Date of Registration (if unpublished):
Registration Number: AFO: 67821
New Matter:
Notes: Copyright is claimed on translation
Renewal Claimant: N/A

ROMAN D'NEHRI IV (LE METIER DE ROI), LE
Alternate Title: Original title: DIE VOLLENDUNG DES KOENIGS HENRI QUATRE
Description: Book

**Author/Claimant Search - ALBERT JOSEPH KOHN**

Author: Translated from German by Albert Kohn
Application Author:
Copyright Claimant: Editions Gallimard
Date of Publication: March 30, 1972
Date of Registration (if unpublished):
Registration Number: AFO: 69253
New Matter:
Notes: Copyright is claimed on translation
Renewal Claimant: N/A

SOMNAMBULES (DIE SCHLAFWANDLER) 3: HUGUENAU ON LE REALISME, LES
Alternate Title:
Description: Book
Author: Translated from German by Albert Kohn
Application Author:
Copyright Claimant: Librairie Gallimard
Date of Publication: January 15, 1957
Date of Registration (if unpublished):
Registration Number: AFO: 22145
New Matter:
Notes:
Renewal Claimant: No record of renewal is found

VIE COMBATIVE (STREITBAUS LEBER), UNE
Alternate Title:
Description: Book, Connaissance de soi
Author: Translated from German by Albert Kohn
Application Author:
Copyright Claimant: Editions Gallimard
Date of Publication: March 30, 1964
Date of Registration (if unpublished):
Registration Number: AFO: 41993
New Matter:
Notes:
Renewal Claimant: No record of renewal is found

VIES POLIQUESTI
Alternate Title: Original title: MEN IN DARK TIMES
Description: Book
Author: Hanna Arendt, translated from German by Eric Adda, Jacques Bontemps, Barbara Cassin, Didier Don, Albert Kohn, Patrick Levy and Agnes Oppenheimer-Faure
Application Author:
Copyright Claimant: Editions Gallimard
Date of Publication: October 30, 1974
Date of Registration (if unpublished):
Registration Number: AFO: 79399

**Author/Claimant Search - ALBERT JOSEPH KOHN**

New Matter:
Notes: Copyright is claimed on translation.
Renewal Claimant: N/A

Our search reveals the following copyright registrations and subsequent renewals identifying **AL KOHN** as the author and/or copyright claimant:

ART OF MUSIC
Alternate Title:
Description: Textual work
Author: Al Kohn and Bob Kohn
Application Author:
Copyright Claimant: Al Kohn and Bob Kohn
Date of Creation: 1992
Date of Publication: October 27, 1992
Date of Registration (if unpublished): March 23, 1993
Registration Number: TX: 3-507-365
New Matter: Additions, compilation
Notes:
Renewal Claimant: N/A

AT THE ZOO
Alternate Title:
Description: Unpublished musical composition
Author: Words and music by Paul Simon, piano-vocal arrangement by Al Kohn
Application Author: Paul Simon, employer for hire
Copyright Claimant: Paul Simon
Date of Publication: May 31, 1967
Date of Registration (if unpublished):
Registration Number: EP: 232807
New Matter: Arrangement
Notes: Application states previously registered February 28, 1967, under entry No. EU: 983206. In "Songs by Paul Simon."
Renewal Claimant: This registration is up for renewal this year, however, no application has been filed as yet

AUCTION FROLIC
Alternate Title:
Description: Musical composition
Author: Al Kohn
Application Author:
Copyright Claimant: Al Kohn Music
Date of Publication: February 14, 1953
Date of Registration (if unpublished):
Registration Number: EP: 69786
New Matter:
Notes: For piano
Renewal Claimant: No record of renewal is found

**Author/Claimant Search - ALBERT JOSEPH KOHN**

AWAKEN LOVE
Alternate Title:
Description: Unpublished musical composition
Author: Words and music by Bob Jaxon and Al Kohn
Application Author:
Copyright Claimant: Leo Feist, Inc.
Date of Publication:
Date of Registration (if unpublished): August 5, 1957
Registration Number: EU: 488382
New Matter:
Notes:
Renewal Claimant: Bob Jaxon
Capacity: Author
Date of Renewal: January 3, 1985
Renewal No.: RE: 248-147

BIG, BRIGHT GREEN PLEASURE MACHINE
Alternate Title:
Description: Musical composition
Author: Words and music by Paul Simon, piano-vocal arrangement by Al Kohn
Application Author: Paul Simon, employer for hire
Copyright Claimant: Paul Simon
Date of Publication: May 31, 1967
Date of Registration (if unpublished):
Registration Number: EP: 232817
New Matter:
Notes: Copyright is claimed on arrangement. Application states previously registered October 4, 1966, under entry No. EU: 961603. In "Songs by Paul Simon."
Renewal Claimant: This registration is up for renewal this year, however, no application has been filed as yet

BIG YELLOW TAXI
Alternate Title:
Description: Musical composition
Author: Words and music by Joni Mitchell, arrangement by Al Kohn
Application Author: WB Music Corp., employer for hire of Al Kohn
Copyright Claimant: Siquomb Pub. Corp.
Date of Publication: May 5, 1970
Date of Registration (if unpublished):
Registration Number: EP: 296797
New Matter: Piano accompaniment and guitar chords
Notes: Application states previously registered January 7, 1970, under entry No. EU: 155770
Renewal Claimant: N/A

**Author/Claimant Search - ALBERT JOSEPH KOHN**

CLASS OF '63
Alternate Title:
Description: Musical composition
Author: Words and music by mark Charron, arrangement by Al Kohn
Application Author: Viva Music, Inc., employer for hire of Al Kohn
Copyright Claimant: Viva Music, Inc.
Date of Publication: April 21, 1969
Date of Registration (if unpublished):
Registration Number: EP: 354672
New Matter: Piano/vocal arrangement with guitar chords
Notes: Previously registered January 14, 1969, under entry No. EU: 93342
Renewal Claimant: N/A

CLOUDY
Alternate Title:
Description: Musical composition
Author: Words and music by Paul Simon, piano-vocal arrangement by Al Kohn
Application Author: Paul Simon, employer for hire
Copyright Claimant: Paul Simon
Date of Publication: May 31, 1967
Date of Registration (if unpublished):
Registration Number: EP: 232808
New Matter:
Notes: Copyright is claimed on arrangement. Application states previously registered October 4, 1966, under entry No. EU: 961604. In "Songs by Paul Simon."
Renewal Claimant: This registration is up for renewal this year, however, no application has been filed as yet

DAY GIG
Alternate Title:
Description: Musical composition
Author: Words and music by Sonny Curtis and Jerry Allison, arrangement by Al Kohn
Application Author: Viva Music, Inc., employer for hire of Al Kohn
Copyright Claimant: Viva Music, Inc.
Date of Publication: April 21, 1969
Date of Registration (if unpublished):
Registration Number: EP: 354674
New Matter: Piano/vocal arrangement with guitar chords
Notes: in "Songs for all Seasons." Previously registered January 14, 1969, under entry No. EU: 93341
Renewal Claimant: N/A

**Author/Claimant Search - ALBERT JOSEPH KOHN**

DAYS
Alternate Title:
Description: Musical composition
Author: Words and music by Anthony Paul Byrne, arrangement by Al Kohn
Application Author: Viva Music, Inc., employer for hire of Al Kohn
Copyright Claimant: Viva Music, Inc.
Date of Publication: April 21, 1969
Date of Registration (if unpublished):
Registration Number: EP: 354673
New Matter: Piano/vocal arrangement with guitar chords
Notes: Previously registered November 21, 1968, under entry No. EU: 86264. In "Songs for all Seasons, Book No. 01."
Renewal Claimant: N/A

FAKIN' IT
Alternate Title:
Description: Musical composition
Author: Words and music by Paul Simon, arrangement by Al Kohn
Application Author: Paul Simon, employer for hire
Copyright Claimant: Paul Simon
Date of Publication: August 14, 1967
Date of Registration (if unpublished):
Registration Number: EP: 237967
New Matter: Complete piano part
Notes: Application states previously registered July 7, 1967, under entry No. EU: 3352.
Renewal Claimant: This registration is up for renewal this year, however, no application has been filed as yet

59TH STREET BRIDGE SONG (FEELIN' GROOVY)
Alternate Title:
Description: Musical composition
Author: Words and music by Paul Simon, arrangement by Al Kohn
Application Author: Paul Simon, employer for hire
Copyright Claimant: Paul Simon
Date of Publication: March 17, 1967
Date of Registration (if unpublished):
Registration Number: EP: 229687
New Matter:
Notes: Copyright is claimed on arrangement. Application states previously registered October 4, 1966, under entry No. EU: 961605
Renewal Claimant: This registration is up for renewal this year, however, no application has been filed as yet

FOR EMILY, WHENEVER I MAY FIND HER
Alternate Title:
Description: Musical composition

**Author/Claimant Search - ALBERT JOSEPH KOHN**

Author: Words and music by Paul Simon, piano-vocal arrangement by Al Kohn
Application Author: Paul Simon, employer for hire
Copyright Claimant: Paul Simon
Date of Publication: May 31, 1967
Date of Registration (if unpublished):
Registration Number: EP: 232812
New Matter:
Notes: Copyright is claimed on arrangement. Application states previously registered October 4, 1966, under entry No. EU: 961606. In "Songs by Paul Simon."
Renewal Claimant: This registration is up for renewal this year, however, no application has been filed as yet

FOR TOMORROW
Alternate Title:
Description: Musical composition
Author: Al Kohn
Application Author:
Copyright Claimant: Al Kohn Music
Date of Publication: May 20, 1952
Date of Registration (if unpublished):
Registration Number: EP: 62781
New Matter:
Notes: For piano
Renewal Claimant: Al Kohn
Capacity: Author
Date of Renewal: December 29, 1980
Renewal No.: RE: 85-151

GIVE IN
Alternate Title:
Description: Musical composition
Author: Words and music by Jerry Fuller, arrangement by Al Kohn
Application Author: Viva Music, Inc., employer for hire of Al Kohn
Copyright Claimant: Viva Music, Inc.
Date of Publication: April 21, 1969
Date of Registration (if unpublished):
Registration Number: EP: 354665
New Matter: Piano/vocal arrangement with guitar chords
Notes: Previously registered October 30, 1968, under entry No. EU: 81992. In "Songs for all Seasons, Book 01."
Renewal Claimant: N/A

HAZY SHADE OF WINTER
Alternate Title:
Description: Musical composition

**Author/Claimant Search - ALBERT JOSEPH KOHN**

Author: Words and music by Paul Simon, piano-vocal arrangement by Al Kohn
Application Author: Paul Simon, employer for hire
Copyright Claimant: Paul Simon
Date of Publication: November 25, 1966
Date of Registration (if unpublished):
Registration Number: EP: 225928
New Matter: Arrangement, new musical notations
Notes: Application states previously registered October 10, 1966, under entry No. EU: 961602
Renewal Claimant: Paul Simon
Capacity: Claiming as author
Date of Renewal: January 21, 1994
Renewal No.: RE: 681-213

HEAVEN BELOW
Alternate Title:
Description: Musical composition
Author: Words and music by Jerry Fuller, arrangement by Al Kohn
Application Author: Viva Music, Inc., employer for hire of Al Kohn
Copyright Claimant: Viva Music, Inc.
Date of Publication: April 21, 1969
Date of Registration (if unpublished):
Registration Number: EP: 354666
New Matter: Piano/vocal arrangement with guitar chords
Notes: Previously registered April 10, 1969, under entry No. EU: 109697
Renewal Claimant: N/A

HOT FUN IN THE SUMMERTIME
Alternate Title:
Description: Musical composition
Author: Words and music by Sylvester Stewart, arranged by Al Kohn
Application Author: Stone Flower Music, employer for hire of Al Kohn
Copyright Claimant: Stone Flower Music
Date of Publication: October 14, 1969
Date of Registration (if unpublished):
Registration Number: EP: 300215
New Matter:
Notes: Copyright is claimed on arrangement. Application states previously registered August 21, 1969, under entry No. EU: 146667
Renewal Claimant: N/A

HOW LITTLE MEN CARE
Alternate Title:

**Author/Claimant Search - ALBERT JOSEPH KOHN**

Description: Musical composition
Author: Words and music by Sonny Curtis, arrangement by Al Kohn
Application Author: Viva Music, Inc., employer for hire of Al Kohn
Copyright Claimant: Viva Music, Inc.
Date of Publication: April 21, 1969
Date of Registration (if unpublished):
Registration Number: EP: 354667
New Matter: Piano/vocal arrangement with guitar chords
Notes: Previously registered January 15, 1968, under entry No. EU: 32678. In "Song for all Seasons, Book 01."
Renewal Claimant: N/A

I NEED YOU
Alternate Title:
Description: Musical composition
Author: Words and music by Gerry Beckley, arrangement by Al Kohn
Application Author: WB Music Corp., employer for hire of Al Kohn
Copyright Claimant: Kinney Music, Ltd.
Date of Publication: May 9, 1972
Date of Registration (if unpublished):
Registration Number: EP: 300216
New Matter: Piano accompaniment
Notes: Application states previously registered February 4, 1972, under entry No. EU: 314658.
Renewal Claimant: N/A

I WISH YOU COULD BE HERE
Alternate Title:
Description: Musical composition
Author: Words and music by Paul Simon and Bruce Woodley, piano-vocal arrangement by Al Kohn
Application Author: Lorna Music Co., Ltd., employer for hire of Al Kohn
Copyright Claimant: Lorna Music Co., Ltd.
Date of Publication: May 31, 1967
Date of Registration (if unpublished):
Registration Number: EP: 232810
New Matter: Arrangement
Notes: Application states previously registered January 18, 1967, under entry No. EU: 978970. In "Songs by Paul Simon."
Renewal Claimant: This registration is up for renewal this year, however, no application has been filed as yet

LITTLE TEA ROOM
Alternate Title:
Description: Musical composition

**Author/Claimant Search - ALBERT JOSEPH KOHN**

Author: Music by Al Kohn
Application Author:
Copyright Claimant: Al Kohn Music
Date of Publication: May 20, 1952
Date of Registration (if unpublished):
Registration Number: EP: 62780
New Matter:
Notes: For piano
Renewal Claimant: Al Kohn
Capacity: Author
Date of Renewal: December 29, 1980
Renewal No.: RE: 85-152

MAIN STREET
Alternate Title:
Description: Musical composition
Author: Words and music by Jimmy Griffin and Mike Gordon, arrangement by Al Kohn
Application Author: Stone Canyon Music, Inc., employer for hire of Al Kohn
Copyright Claimant: Stone Canyon Music, Inc.
Date of Publication: April 21, 1969
Date of Registration (if unpublished):
Registration Number: EP: 354668
New Matter: Piano/vocal arrangement with guitar chords
Notes: Previously published November 15, 1968, under entry No. EP: 324567. In "Songs for all Seasons, Book 01."
Renewal Claimant: N/A

MAIN STREET
Alternate Title:
Description: Musical composition
Author: Words and music by Jimmy Griffith and Mark Gordon, arrangement by Al Kohn
Application Author: Stone Canyon Music, Inc., employer for hire of Al Kohn
Copyright Claimant: Stone Canyon Music, Inc.
Date of Publication: November 15, 1968 (in notice 1966 and 1968)
Date of Registration (if unpublished):
Registration Number: EP: 324567
New Matter: Piano with guitar chords, easy piano easy organ arrangements
Notes: Previously registered July 11, 1966, under entry No. EU: 947514
Renewal Claimant: N/A

MARRAKESH EXPRESS
Alternate Title:
Description: Musical composition

**Author/Claimant Search - ALBERT JOSEPH KOHN**

Author: Words and music by Graham Nash, arrangement by Al Kohn
Application Author: WB Music Corp., employer for hire of Al Kohn
Copyright Claimant: Siquomb Pub. Corp.
Date of Publication: September 10, 1969
Date of Registration (if unpublished):
Registration Number: EP: 300214
New Matter: Piano accompaniment
Notes: Application states previously registered June 5, 1969, under entry No. EU: 119528
Renewal Claimant: N/A

MELODEE
Alternate Title:
Description: Musical composition
Author: Words and music by Jerry Fuller, arrangement by Al Kohn
Application Author: Viva Music, Inc., employer for hire of Al Kohn
Copyright Claimant: Viva Music, Inc.
Date of Publication: April 21, 1969
Date of Registration (if unpublished):
Registration Number: EP: 354675
New Matter: Piano/vocal arrangement with guitar chords
Notes: Previously registered February 19, 1969, under entry No. EU: 100634. In "Songs for all Seasons, Book 01."
Renewal Claimant: N/A

MEMPHIS
Alternate Title:
Description: Musical composition
Author: Music by Chuck Berry, arrangement by Al Kohn
Application Author:
Copyright Claimant: Arc Music Corp.
Date of Publication: July 12, 1963
Date of Registration (if unpublished):
Registration Number: EP: 177732
New Matter: New arrangement with chords and harmony added
Notes: Guitar and piano solo. Application states previously registered as MEMPHIS, TENN.
Renewal Claimant: No record of renewal is found

MISTER MEMORY
Alternate Title:
Description: Musical composition
Author: Words and music by Christopher Quinn and Michael Laurence, arrangement by Al Kohn
Application Author:
Copyright Claimant: Gringo Music Company

**Author/Claimant Search - ALBERT JOSEPH KOHN**

Date of Publication: April 21, 1969
Date of Registration (if unpublished):
Registration Number: EP: 354676
New Matter: Piano/vocal arrangement with guitar chords
Notes: Previously registered December 2, 1969, under entry No. 87646. In "Songs for all Seasons, Book 01."
Renewal Claimant: N/A

MORE THAN I CAN SAY
Alternate Title:
Description: Musical composition
Author: Words and music by Sonny Curtis and Jerry Allison, arrangement by Al Kohn
Application Author: Viva Music, Inc., employer for hire of Al Kohn
Copyright Claimant: Viva Music, Inc.
Date of Publication: April 21, 1969
Date of Registration (if unpublished):
Registration Number: EP: 354669
New Matter: Piano/vocal arrangement with guitar chords
Notes: Previously registered March 22, 1960, under entry No. EU: 617637, previously published March 23, 1961, under entry No. EP: 327863. In "Songs for all Seasons, Book 01."
Renewal Claimant: N/A

PATTERNS
Alternate Title:
Description: Musical composition
Author: Words and music by Paul Simon, piano-vocal arrangement by Al Kohn
Application Author: Charing Cross Music, employer for hire of Al Kohn
Copyright Claimant: Charing Cross Music
Date of Publication: May 31, 1967
Date of Registration (if unpublished):
Registration Number: EP: 232814
New Matter:
Notes: Copyright is claimed on arrangement. Application states previously registered September 24, 1965, under entry No. EP: 210630. In "Songs by Paul Simon."
Renewal Claimant: This registration is up for renewal this year, however, no application has been filed as yet

POEM ON THE UNDERGROUND WALL
Alternate Title:
Description: Musical composition
Author: Words and music by Paul Simon, piano-vocal arrangement by Al Kohn
Application Author: Paul Simon, employer for hire
Copyright Claimant: Paul Simon

**Author/Claimant Search - ALBERT JOSEPH KOHN**

Date of Publication: May 31, 1967
Date of Registration (if unpublished):
Registration Number: EP: 232813
New Matter:
Notes: Copyright is claimed on arrangement. Application states previously registered October 4, 1966, under entry No. EU: 961607. In "Songs by Paul Simon."
Renewal Claimant: This registration is up for renewal this year, however, no application has been filed as yet

SCARBOROUGH FAIR/CANTICLE
Alternate Title:
Description: Musical composition
Author: Words and music by Paul Simon and Art Garfunkel, piano-vocal arrangement by Al Kohn
Application Author:
Copyright Claimant: Paul Simon
Date of Publication: May 31, 1967
Date of Registration (if unpublished):
Registration Number: EP: 232809
New Matter:
Notes: Copyright is claimed on arrangement. Application states previously registered October 4, 1966, under entry No. EU: 961608. In "Songs by Paul Simon."
Renewal Claimant: This registration is up for renewal this year, however, no application has been filed as yet

7 O'CLOCK NEWS/SILENT NIGHT
Alternate Title:
Description: Musical composition
Author: Narration by Paul Simon, piano-vocal arrangement by Al Kohn
Application Author: Paul Simon, employer for hire
Copyright Claimant: Paul Simon
Date of Publication: November 25, 1966
Date of Registration (if unpublished):
Registration Number: EP: 227325
New Matter: Arrangement, new musical notations and narration
Notes:
Renewal Claimant: Paul Simon
Capacity: Claiming as author
Date of Renewal: January 21, 1994
Renewal No.: RE: 660-893

SOMEDAY, ONE DAY
Alternate Title:
Description: Musical composition
Author: Words and music by Paul Simon, piano-vocal arrangement by Al Kohn

Author/Claimant Search - ALBERT JOSEPH KOHN

Application Author: Charing Cross Music, employer for hire of Al Kohn
Copyright Claimant: Charing Cross Music
Date of Publication: May 31, 1967
Date of Registration (if unpublished):
Registration Number: EP: 232816
New Matter:
Notes: Copyright is claimed on the arrangement. Application states previously registered March 11, 1966, under entry No. EP: 215473. In "Songs by Paul Simon."
Renewal Claimant: This registration is up for renewal this year, however, no application has been filed as yet

TEACH YOUR CHILDREN
Alternate Title:
Description: Musical composition
Author: Words and music by Graham Nash, arrangement of piano accompaniment and guitar chords by Al Kohn
Application Author: Giving Room Music, Inc., employer for hire of Al Kohn
Copyright Claimant: Giving Room Music, Inc.
Date of Publication: June 11, 1970
Date of Registration (if unpublished):
Registration Number: EP: 296799
New Matter: Piano accompaniment with guitar chords
Notes: Application states previously registered 1970, under entry No. EU: 162978.
Renewal Claimant: N/A

THREE TEARS FOR THE SAD, HURT AND BLUE
Alternate Title:
Description: Musical composition
Author: Words and music by Jerry Fuller, arrangement by Al Kohn
Application Author: Viva Music, Inc., employer for hire of Al Kohn
Copyright Claimant: Viva Music, Inc.
Date of Publication: April 21, 1969
Date of Registration (if unpublished):
Registration Number: EP: 354670
New Matter: Piano/vocal arrangement with guitar chords
Notes: Previously registered November 21, 1968, under entry No. EU: 86263. In "Songs for all Seasons, Book 01."
Renewal Claimant: N/A

TRAIN OF THOUGHT
Alternate Title:
Description: Musical composition
Author: Words and music by Jerry Fuller, arrangement by Al Kohn

**Author/Claimant Search - ALBERT JOSEPH KOHN**

Application Author: Viva Music, Inc., employer for hire of Al Kohn
Copyright Claimant: Viva Music, Inc.
Date of Publication: April 21, 1969
Date of Registration (if unpublished):
Registration Number: EP: 354677
New Matter: Piano/vocal arrangement with guitar chords
Notes: Previously registered June 25, 1968, under entry No. EU: 60176. In "Songs for all Seasons, Book 01."
Renewal Claimant: N/A

WALK RIGHT BACK
Alternate Title:
Description: Musical composition
Author: Words and music by Sonny Curtisarrangement by Al Kohn
Application Author: Viva Music, Inc., employer for hire of Al Kohn
Copyright Claimant: Viva Music, Inc.
Date of Publication: April 21, 1969
Date of Registration (if unpublished):
Registration Number: EP: 354678
New Matter: Piano/vocal arrangement with guitar chords
Notes: Previously registered 1960, under entry No. EU: 652642. In "Songs for all Seasons, Book 01."
Renewal Claimant: N/A

WEDNESDAY MORNING, 3 A.M.
Alternate Title:
Description: Musical composition
Author: Words and music by Paul Simon, piano-vocal arrangement by Al Kohn
Application Author: Charing Cross Music, employer for hire of Al Kohn
Copyright Claimant: Charing Cross Music
Date of Publication: May 31, 1967
Date of Registration (if unpublished):
Registration Number: EP: 232811
New Matter:
Notes: Copyright is claimed on arrangement. Application states previously registered November 7, 1966, under entry No. EU: 966034. In "Songs by Paul Simon."
Renewal Claimant: This registration is up for renewal this year, however, no application has been filed as yet

Author/Claimant Search - ALBERT JOSEPH KOHN

WOMAN HELPING MAN
Alternate Title:
Description: Musical composition
Author: Words and music by Mark Charron, arrangement by Al Kohn
Application Author: Viva Music, Inc., employer for hire of Al Kohn
Copyright Claimant: Viva Music, Inc.
Date of Publication: April 21, 1969
Date of Registration (if unpublished):
Registration Number: EP: 354671
New Matter: Piano/vocal arrangement with guitar chords
Notes: Previously registered October 28, 1968, under entry No. EU: 81668. In "Songs for all Seasons, Book 01."
Renewal Claimant: N/A

WOODSTOCK
Alternate Title:
Description: Musical composition
Author: Words and music by Joni Mitchell, arrangement by Al Kohn
Application Author: WB Music Corp., employer for hire of Al Kohn
Copyright Claimant: Siquomb Pub. Corp.
Date of Publication: May 9, 1970 (in notice: 1969)
Date of Registration (if unpublished):
Registration Number: EP: 296798
New Matter: Piano accompaniment and guitar chords
Notes: Application states previously registered October 22, 1969, under entry No. EU: 144626.
Renewal Claimant: N/A

YOU DON'T KNOW WHERE YOUR INTEREST LIES
Alternate Title:
Description: Musical composition
Author: Words and music by Paul Simon, piano-vocal arrangement by Al Kohn
Application Author: Paul Simon, employer for hire
Copyright Claimant: Paul Simon
Date of Publication: May 31, 1967
Date of Registration (if unpublished):
Registration Number: EP: 232815
New Matter: Arrangement
Notes: Application states previously registered January 18, 1967, under entry No. EU: 978969. In "Songs by Paul Simon."
Renewal Claimant: This registration is up for renewal this year, however, no application has been filed as yet

**Author/Claimant Search - ALBERT JOSEPH KOHN**

A search of the assignment files of the Copyright Office reveals the following documents identifying the above as a party thereto:

**DOCUMENT DESCRIPTION:** Instrument executed June 30, 1971
ASSIGNOR: Kohn Music Corp.
ASSIGNEE: Creston Music Co.
DATE OF RECORDATION: July 14, 1971
VOLUME/PAGE: Vol. 1422, pages 33-35
WORK(S): A GLISS TO REMEMBER and 39 others. A photocopy of the pertinent pages listing additional titles is attached for your reference.

**DOCUMENT DESCRIPTION:** Instrument executed July 1, 1979
ASSIGNOR: Danny O'Keffe by Al Kohn (Atty)
ASSIGNEE: Warner-Tamerlane Publishing Corporation and Road Cannon Music, Inc.
DATE OF RECORDATION: September 11, 1979
VOLUME/PAGE: Vol. 1748, pages 321-322
WORK(S): FLYING; GIVE ME THE MEDICINE; HAIR OF THE DOG; IT'S AN OLD SONG; RIDE, RIDE, RIDE; SEX AND MONEY; and YOU DON'T HAVE TO BE RIGHT

**DOCUMENT DESCRIPTION:** Assignment executed October 10, 1979
ASSIGNOR: Warner-Tamerlane Publishing Corporation by Al Kohn
ASSIGNEE: W B Music Corporation
DATE OF RECORDATION: October 22, 1979
VOLUME/PAGE: Vol. 1752, page 186
WORK(S): No titles given

The in-process records of the Copyright Office failed to reveal any pending applications or documents in connection with the above.

If we may be of any further assistance, or if you have any questions regarding this report, please do not hesitate to call me at 1-800-356-8630.

Sincerely yours,

Debra A. Paeth

DAP
Enclosures

# REPORT 11.2

## COPYRIGHT OFFICE CIRCULAR 22 — HOW TO INVESTIGATE THE COPYRIGHT STATUS OF A WORK

Copyright
United States Copyright Office

# How to Investigate the Copyright Status of a Work

### In General

*Methods of Approaching a Copyright Investigation*

There are several ways to investigate whether a work is under copyright protection and, if so, the facts of the copyright. These are the main ones:

1 Examine a copy of the work for such elements as a copyright notice, place and date of publication, author and publisher. If the work is a sound recording, examine the disk, tape cartridge, or cassette in which the recorded sound is fixed, or the album cover, sleeve, or container in which the recording is sold;

2 Make a search of the Copyright Office catalogs and other records; *or*

3 Have the Copyright Office make a search for you.

### A Few Words of Caution About Copyright Investigations

Copyright investigations often involve more than one of these methods. Even if you follow all three approaches, the results may not be conclusive. Moreover, as explained in this circular, the changes brought about under the Copyright Act of 1976, the Berne Convention Implementation Act of 1988, the Copyright Renewal Act of 1992, and the Sonny Bono Copyright Term Extension Act of 1998 must be considered when investigating the copyright status of a work.

This circular offers some practical guidance on what to look for if you are making a copyright investigation. It is important to realize, however, that this circular contains only general information and that there are a number of exceptions to the principles outlined here. In many cases it is important to consult with a copyright attorney before reaching any conclusions regarding the copyright status of a work.

### How to Search Copyright Office Catalogs and Records

*Catalog of Copyright Entries*

The Copyright Office published the *Catalog of Copyright Entries* (*CCE*) in printed format from 1891 through 1978. From 1979 through 1982 the CCE was issued in microfiche format. The catalog was divided into parts according to the classes of works registered. Each CCE segment covered all registrations made during a particular period of time. Renewal registrations made from 1979 through 1982 are found in Section 8 of the catalog. Renewals prior to that time were generally listed at the end of the volume containing the class of work to which they pertained.

A number of libraries throughout the U.S. maintain copies of the *Catalog*, and this may provide a good starting point if you wish to make a search yourself. There are some cases, however, in which a search of the *Catalog* alone will not be sufficient to provide the needed information. For example:

- Because the *Catalog* does not include entries for assignments or other recorded documents, it cannot be used for searches involving the ownership of rights.
- The *Catalog* entry contains the essential facts concerning a registration, but it is not a verbatim transcript of the registration record. It does not contain the address of the copyright claimant.

Effective with registrations made since 1982 when the CCE was discontinued, the only method of searching outside the Library of Congress is by using the Internet to access the automated catalog. The automated catalog contains entries from 1978 to the present. Information on accessing the catalog via the Internet is provided below.

## Individual Searches of Copyright Records

The Copyright Office is located in the Library of Congress James Madison Memorial Building, 101 Independence Avenue SE, Washington, DC 20559-6000.

Most Copyright Office records are open to public inspection and searching from 8:30 AM to 5:00 PM, eastern time, Monday through Friday, except federal holidays. An exception is the area containing copyright applications from 1870 to the present, which is open from 9:00 AM to 4:30 PM. The various records freely available to the public include an extensive card catalog, an automated catalog containing records from 1978 forward, record books, and microfilm records of assignments and related documents. Other records, including correspondence files and deposit copies, are not open to the public for searching. However, they may be inspected upon request and payment of a search fee.*

***NOTE: Copyright Office fees are subject to change. For current fees, please check the Copyright Office website at *www.copyright.gov*, write the Copyright Office, or call (202) 707-3000.**

If you wish to do your own searching in the Copyright Office files open to the public, you will be given assistance in locating the records you need and in learning procedures for searching. If the Copyright Office staff actually makes the search for you, a search fee must be charged. The search will not be done while you wait.

In addition, Copyright Office records in machine-readable form cataloged from January 1, 1978, to the present, including registration and renewal information and recorded documents, are available for searching from the Copyright Office website at *www.copyright.gov*.

The Copyright Office does not offer search assistance to users on the Internet.

## Searching by the Copyright Office

### *In General*

Upon request, and at the statutory rate for each hour or fraction of an hour consumed, the Copyright Office staff will search its records covering the records of registrations and other recorded documents concerning ownership of copyrights and will provide a written report. If desired, an estimate can be provided. Estimates for searches are based on the information furnished and are provided for a set fee that is applied toward the cost of the search and report. Fees for estimates are nonrefundable and are good for up to one year. Requests must include an address and telephone number where you may be reached during business hours and an email address if available.

Certification of a search report is available for an additional fee. Certified searches are frequently requested to meet the evidentiary requirements of litigation.

Preferred payment is by personal check or credit card. Contact the Copyright Office for information regarding payment with money orders or by overseas banking institutions.

For information, correspondence, or payment, contact:

*Library of Congress*
*Copyright Office, Mail Stop 6306*
*101 Independence Avenue SE*
*Washington, DC 20559-6000*
PHONE: (202) 707-6850 (M–F, 8:30–5:00 eastern time)
FAX: (202) 252-3485
TTY: (202) 707-6737
EMAIL: *copysearch@loc.gov*

### *What the Fee Does Not Cover*

The search fee does *not* include the cost of additional certificates, photocopies of deposits, or copies of other Office records. For information concerning these services, request Circular 6, *Obtaining Access to and Copies of Copyright Office Records and Deposits.*

#### *Information Needed*

The more detailed information you can furnish with your request, the less expensive the search will be. Please provide as much of the following information as possible:

- the title of the work, with any possible variants
- the names of the authors, including possible pseudonyms
- the name of the probable copyright owner, which may be the publisher or producer
- the approximate year when the work was published or registered
- the type of work involved (book, play, musical composition, sound recording, photograph, etc.)
- for a work originally published as a part of a periodical or collection, the title of that publication and any other information, such as the volume or issue number, to help identify it
- the registration number or any other copyright data

Motion pictures are often based on other works such as books or serialized contributions to periodicals or other composite works. *If you desire a search for an underlying work or for music from a motion picture, you must specifically request such a search. You must also identify the underlying works and music and furnish the specific titles, authors, and approximate dates of these works.*

#### *Searches Involving Assignments and Other Documents Affecting Copyright Ownership*

For the standard hourly search fee, the Copyright Office staff will search its indexes covering the records of assignments and other recorded documents concerning ownership of copyrights. The reports of searches in these cases will state the facts shown in the Office's indexes of the recorded documents but will offer no interpretation of the content of the documents or their legal effect.

### Limitations on Searches

In determining whether or not to have a search made, you should keep the following points in mind:

**No Special Lists** · The Copyright Office does not maintain any listings of works by subject or any lists of works that are in the public domain.

**Contributions Not Listed Separately in Copyright Office Records** · Individual works such as stories, poems, articles, or musical compositions that were published as contributions to a copyrighted periodical or collection are usually not listed separately by title in our records.

**No Comparisons** · The Copyright Office does not search or compare copies of works to determine questions of possible infringement or to determine how much two or more versions of a work have in common.

**Titles and Names Not Copyrightable** · Copyright does not protect names and titles, and our records list many different works identified by the same or similar titles. Some brand names, trade names, slogans, and phrases may be entitled to protection under the general rules of law relating to unfair competition. They may also be entitled to registration under the provisions of the trademark laws. Questions about the trademark laws should be addressed to: *Commissioner of Patents and Trademarks, U.S. Patent and Trademark Office, PO Box 1450, Alexandria, VA 22313-1450*. Possible protection of names and titles under common law principles of unfair competition is a question of state law.

**No Legal Advice** · The Copyright Office cannot express any opinion as to the legal significance or effect of the facts included in a search report.

### Some Words of Caution

#### *Searches Not Always Conclusive*

Searches of the Copyright Office catalogs and records are useful in helping to determine the copyright status of a work, but they cannot be regarded as conclusive in all cases. The complete absence of any information about a work in the Office records does not mean that the work is unprotected. The following are examples of cases in which information about a particular work may be incomplete or lacking entirely in the Copyright Office:

- Before 1978, unpublished works were entitled to protection under common law without the need of registration.
- Works published with notice prior to 1978 may be registered at *any* time within the first 28-year term.
- Works copyrighted between January 1, 1964, and December 31, 1977, are affected by the Copyright Renewal Act of 1992, which automatically extends the copyright term and makes renewal registrations optional.
- For works under copyright protection on or after January 1, 1978, registration may be made at any time during the term of protection. Although registration is not required as a condition of copyright protection, there are certain

definite advantages to registration. For further information, request Circular 1, *Copyright Basics.*

- Since searches are ordinarily limited to registrations that have already been cataloged, a search report may not cover recent registrations for which catalog records are not yet available.
- The information in the search request may not have been complete or specific enough to identify the work.
- The work may have been registered under a different title or as part of a larger work.

#### *Protection in Foreign Countries*

Even if you conclude that a work is in the public domain in the United States, this does not necessarily mean that you are free to use it in other countries. Every nation has its own laws governing the length and scope of copyright protection, and these are applicable to uses of the work within that nation's borders. Thus, the expiration or loss of copyright protection in the United States may still leave the work fully protected against unauthorized use in other countries.

### Other Circulars

For further information, request Circular 6; Circular 15, *Renewal of Copyright*; Circular 15A, *Duration of Copyright*; and Circular 15T, *Extension of Copyright Terms*, from:

> *Library of Congress*
> *Copyright Office*
> *Publications Section*
> *101 Independence Avenue SE*
> *Washington, DC 20559-6000*

You may call the Forms and Publications Hotline at (202) 707-9100 at any time, day or night, to leave a recorded request for forms or circulars. Requests are filled and mailed promptly.

### Impact of the Copyright Act on Copyright Investigations

On October 19, 1976, the President signed into law a complete revision of the copyright law of the United States (title 17 of the *United States Code*). Most provisions of this statute came into force on January 1, 1978, superseding the copyright act of 1909. These provisions made significant changes in the copyright law. Further important changes resulted from the Berne Convention Implementation Act of 1988, which took effect March 1, 1989; the Copyright Renewal Act of 1992 (P.L. 102-307) enacted June 26, 1992, which amended the renewal provisions of the copyright law; and the Sonny Bono Copyright Term Extension Act of 1998 (P.L. 105-298) enacted October 27, 1998, which extended the term of copyrights for an additional 20 years.

If you need more information about the provisions of either the 1909 or the 1976 law, write or call the Copyright Office. For information about renewals, request Circular 15. For information about the Sonny Bono Copyright Term Extension Act, request SL-15, *New Terms for Copyright Protection*. For copies of the law, request Circular 92, *Copyright Law of the United States* (stock number is changed to 030-002-00197-7), from:

> *Superintendent of Documents*
> *PO Box 371954*
> *Pittsburgh, PA 15250-7954*
> PHONE: (202) 512-1800 [toll free: (866) 512-1800]
> FAX: (202) 512-2104

Or go to the Copyright Office website at *www.copyright.gov/title17*.

For copyright investigations, the following points about the impact of the Copyright Act of 1976, the Berne Convention Implementation Act of 1988, and the Copyright Renewal Act of 1992 should be considered.

#### *A Changed System of Copyright Formalities*

Some of the most sweeping changes under the 1976 Copyright Act involve copyright formalities, that is, the procedural requirements for securing and maintaining full copyright protection. The old system of formalities involved copyright notice, deposit and registration, recordation of transfers and licenses of copyright ownership, and U.S. manufacture, among other things. In general, while retaining formalities, the 1976 law reduced the chances of mistakes, softened the consequences of errors and omissions, and allowed for the correction of errors.

The Berne Convention Implementation Act of 1988 reduced formalities, most notably making the addition of the previously mandatory copyright notice optional. It should be noted that the amended notice requirements are not retroactive.

The Copyright Renewal Act of 1992, enacted June 26, 1992, automatically extends the term of copyrights secured between January 1, 1964, and December 31, 1977, making renewal registration optional. Consult Circular 15 for details. For additional information, you may contact the Copyright Office by phone at (202) 707-8180 or by fax at (202) 707-3849.

#### *Automatic Copyright*

Under the present copyright law, copyright exists in original works of authorship created and fixed in any tangible medium of expression, now known or later developed, from which they can be perceived, reproduced, or otherwise communicated, either directly, or indirectly with the aid of a machine or device. In other words, copyright is an incident of creative authorship not dependent on statutory formalities. Thus, registration with the Copyright Office generally is not required, but there are certain advantages that arise from a timely registration. For further information on the advantages of registration, write or call the Copyright Office and request Circular 1.

#### *Copyright Notice*

The 1909 Copyright Act and the 1976 Copyright Act as originally enacted required a notice of copyright on published works. For most works, a copyright notice consisted of the symbol ©, the word "Copyright" or the abbreviation "Copr.," together with the name of the owner of copyright and the year of first publication. For example: "© Joan Crane 2004" or "Copyright 2004 by Abraham Adams."

For sound recordings published on or after February 15, 1972, a copyright notice might read "℗ 1994 XYZ Records, Inc." See below for more information about sound recordings.

For mask works, a copyright notice might read "Ⓜ SDR Industries." Request Circular 100, *Federal Statutory Protection for Mask Works*, for more information.

As originally enacted, the 1976 law prescribed that all visually perceptible published copies of a work, or published phonorecords of a sound recording, should bear a proper copyright notice. This applies to such works published before March 1, 1989. After March 1, 1989, notice of copyright on these works is optional. Adding the notice, however, is strongly encouraged and if litigation involving the copyright occurs, certain advantages exist for publishing a work with notice.

Prior to March 1, 1989, the requirement for the notice applied equally whether the work was published in the United States or elsewhere by authority of the copyright owner. Compliance with the statutory notice requirements was the responsibility of the copyright owner. Unauthorized publication without the copyright notice, or with a defective notice, does not affect the validity of the copyright in the work.

Advance permission from, or registration with, the Copyright Office is not required before placing a copyright notice on copies of the work or on phonorecords of a sound recording. Moreover, for works first published on or after January 1, 1978, through February 28, 1989, omission of the required notice, or use of a defective notice, did not result in forfeiture or outright loss of copyright protection. Certain omissions of, or defects in, the notice of copyright, however, could have led to loss of copyright protection if steps were not taken to correct or cure the omissions or defects. The Copyright Office has issued a final regulation (37 *CFR* 201.20) that suggests various acceptable positions for the notice of copyright. For further information, write to the Copyright Office and request Circular 3, *Copyright Notice*. This regulation is available on the Copyright Office website at *www.copyright.gov/title37/201/index.html*.

#### *Works Already in the Public Domain*

No law will restore protection to works that fell into the public domain before the passage of the law. However, the North American Free Trade Agreement Implementation Act (NAFTA) and the Uruguay Round Agreements Act (URAA) may restore copyright in certain works of foreign origin that were in the public domain in the United States. Under the copyright law in effect prior to January 1, 1978, copyright could be lost in several situations. The most common were publication without the required notice of copyright, expiration of the first 28-year term without renewal, or final expiration of the second copyright term. The Copyright Renewal Act of 1992 automatically renews first term copyrights secured between January 1, 1964, and December 31, 1977.

#### *Scope of Exclusive Rights Under Copyright*

The present law has changed and enlarged in some cases the scope of the copyright owner's rights. The new rights apply to all uses of a work subject to protection by copyright after January 1, 1978, regardless of when the work was created.

### Duration of Copyright Protection

#### *Works Originally Copyrighted On or After January 1, 1978*

A work that is created and fixed in tangible form for the first time on or after January 1, 1978, is automatically protected from the moment of its creation and is ordinarily given a term enduring for the author's life plus an additional 70 years after the author's death. In the case of "a joint work prepared by two or more authors who did not work for hire," the term lasts for 70 years after the last surviving author's death. For works made for hire and for anonymous and pseudonymous works (unless the author's identity is revealed in the Copyright Office records), the duration of copyright will be 95 years from publication or 120 years from creation, whichever is less.

Works created before the 1976 law came into effect but neither published nor registered for copyright before January 1, 1978, have been automatically brought under the statute and are now given federal copyright protection. The duration of copyright in these works will generally be computed in the same way as for new works: the life-plus-70 or 95/120-year terms will apply. However, all works in this category are guaranteed at least 25 years of statutory protection.

### *Works Copyrighted Before January 1, 1978*

Under the law in effect before 1978, copyright was secured either on the date a work was published with notice of copyright or on the date of registration if the work was registered in unpublished form. In either case, copyright endured for a first term of 28 years from the date on which it was secured. During the last (28th) year of the first term, the copyright was eligible for renewal. The copyright law extends the renewal term from 28 to 67 years for copyrights in existence on January 1, 1978.

However, for works copyrighted prior to January 1, 1964, the copyright still must have been renewed in the 28th calendar year to receive the 67-year period of added protection. The amending legislation enacted June 26, 1992, automatically extends this second term for works first copyrighted between January 1, 1964, and December 31, 1977. For more detailed information on the copyright term, write or call the Copyright Office and request Circular 15A.

## Works First Published Before 1978: the Copyright Notice

### *General Information About the Copyright Notice*

In investigating the copyright status of works first published before January 1, 1978, the most important thing to look for is the notice of copyright. As a general rule under the previous law, copyright protection was lost permanently if the notice was omitted from the first authorized published edition of a work or if it appeared in the wrong form or position. The form and position of the copyright notice for various types of works were specified in the copyright statute. Some courts were liberal in overlooking relatively minor departures from the statutory requirements, but a basic failure to comply with the notice provisions forfeited copyright protection and put the work into the public domain in this country.

### *Absence of Copyright Notice*

For works first published before 1978, the complete absence of a copyright notice from a published copy generally indicates that the work is not protected by copyright. For works first published before March 1, 1989, the copyright notice is mandatory, but omission could have been cured by registration before or within 5 years of publication and by adding the notice to copies published in the United States after discovery of the omission. Some works may contain a notice, others may not. The absence of a notice in works published on or after March 1, 1989, does not necessarily indicate that the work is in the public domain.

**Unpublished Works** · No notice of copyright was required on the copies of any unpublished work. The concept of "publication" is very technical, and it was possible for a number of copies lacking a copyright notice to be reproduced and distributed without affecting copyright protection.

**Foreign Editions** · In the case of works seeking ad interim copyright,* copies of a copyrighted work were exempted from the notice requirements if they were first published outside the United States. Some copies of these foreign editions could find their way into the United States without impairing the copyright.

***NOTE: "Ad interim copyright" refers to a special short term of copyright available to certain pre-1978 books and periodicals. For further information on ad interim copyright, see page 8.**

**Accidental Omission** · The 1909 statute preserved copyright protection if the notice was omitted by accident or mistake from a "particular copy or copies."

**Unauthorized Publication** · A valid copyright was not secured if someone deleted the notice and/or published the work without authorization from the copyright owner.

**Sound Recordings** · Reproductions of sound recordings usually contain two different types of creative works: the underlying musical, dramatic, or literary work that is being performed or read and the fixation of the actual sounds embodying the performance or reading. For protection of the underlying musical or literary work embodied in a recording, it is not necessary that a copyright notice covering this material appear on the phonograph records or tapes on which the recording is reproduced. As noted above, a special notice is required for protection of the recording of a series of musical, spoken, or other sounds that were fixed on or after February 15, 1972. Sound recordings fixed before February 15, 1972, are not eligible for federal copyright protection. The Sound Recording Act of 1971, the present copyright law, and the Berne Convention Implementation Act of 1988 cannot be applied or be construed to provide any retroactive protection for sound recordings fixed before February 15, 1972. Such works, however, may be protected by various state laws or doctrines of common law.

### *The Date in the Copyright Notice*

If you find a copyright notice, the date it contains may be important in determining the copyright status of the work. In general, the notice on works published before 1978 must include the year in which copyright was secured by publication or, if the work was first registered for copyright in unpublished form, the year in which registration was made. There are two main exceptions to this rule.

1 For pictorial, graphic, or sculptural works (Classes F through K under the 1909 law), the law permitted omission of the year date in the notice.

2 For "new versions" of previously published or copyrighted works, the notice was not usually required to include more than the year of first publication of the new version itself. This is explained further under "Derivative Works" below.

The year in the notice usually (though not always) indicated when the copyright began. It is, therefore, significant in determining whether a copyright is still in effect; or, if the copyright has not yet run its course, the year date will help in deciding when the copyright is scheduled to expire. For further information about the duration of copyright, request Circular 15A.

In evaluating the meaning of the date in a notice, you should keep the following points in mind:

**Works Published and Copyrighted Before January 1, 1978** · A work published before January 1, 1978, and copyrighted within the past 75 years may still be protected by copyright in the United States if a valid renewal registration was made during the 28th year of the first term of the copyright. If renewed by registration or under the Copyright Renewal Act of 1992 and if still valid under the other provisions of the law, the copyright will expire 95 years from the end of the year in which it was first secured.

Therefore, the U.S. copyright in any work published or copyrighted prior to January 1, 1923, has expired by operation of law, and the work has permanently fallen into the public domain in the United States. For example, on January 1, 1997, copyrights in works first published or copyrighted before January 1, 1922, have expired; on January 1, 1998, copyrights in works first published or copyrighted before January 1, 1923, have expired. Unless the copyright law is changed again, no works under protection on January 1, 1999, will fall into the public domain in the United States until January 1, 2019.

**Works First Published or Copyrighted Between January 1, 1923, and December 31, 1949, But Not Renewed** · If a work was first published or copyrighted between January 1, 1923, and December 31, 1949, it is important to determine whether the copyright was renewed during the last (28th) year of the first term of the copyright. This can be done by searching the Copyright Office records or catalogs as explained previously. If no renewal registration was made, copyright protection expired permanently at the end of the 28th year of the year date it was first secured.

**Works First Published or Copyrighted Between January 1, 1923, and December 31, 1949, and Registered for Renewal** · When a valid renewal registration was made and copyright in the work was in its second term on December 31, 1977, the renewal copyright term was extended under the latest act to 67 years. In these cases, copyright will last for a total of 95 years from the end of the year in which copyright was originally secured. Example: Copyright in a work first published in 1925 and renewed in 1953 will expire on December 31, 2020.

**Works First Published or Copyrighted Between January 1, 1950, and December 31, 1963** · If a work was in its first 28-year term of copyright protection on January 1, 1978, it must have been renewed in a timely fashion to have secured the maximum term of copyright protection. If renewal registration was made during the 28th calendar year of its first term, copyright would endure for 95 years from the end of the year copyright was originally secured. If not renewed, the copyright expired at the end of its 28th calendar year.

**Works First Published or Copyrighted Between January 1, 1964, and December 31, 1977** · If a work was in its first 28-year term of copyright protection on June 26, 1992, renewal registration is now optional. The term of copyright for works published or copyrighted during this time period has been extended to 95 years by the Copyright Renewal Act of 1992 and the Sonny Bono Term Extension Act of 1998. There is no need to make the renewal filing to extend the original 28-year copyright term to the full 95 years.

However, there are several advantages to making a renewal registration during the 28th year of the original term of copyright. If renewal registration is made during the 28th year of the original term of copyright, the renewal copyright vests in the name of the renewal claimant on the effective date of the renewal registration; the renewal certificate constitutes prima facie evidence as to the validity of the copyright during the renewed and extended term and of the facts stated in the certificate; and, the right to use the derivative work in the extended term may be affected. Request Circular 15 for further information.

**Unpublished, Unregistered Works** · Before 1978, if a work had been neither "published" in the legal sense nor registered in the Copyright Office, it was subject to perpetual protection under the common law. On January 1, 1978, all works of this kind, subject to protection by copyright, were automatically brought under the federal copyright statute. The duration of copyright for these works can vary, but none of them expired before December 31, 2002.

### *Derivative Works*

In examining a copy (or a record, disc, or tape) for copyright information, it is important to determine whether that particular version of the work is an original edition of the work or a "new version." New versions include musical arrangements, adaptations, revised or newly edited editions, translations, dramatizations, abridgments, compilations, and works republished with new matter added. The law provides that derivative works, published or unpublished, are independently copyrightable and that the copyright in such a work does not affect or extend the protection, if any, in the underlying work. Under the 1909 law, courts have also held that the notice of copyright on a derivative work ordinarily need not include the dates or other information pertaining to the earlier works incorporated in it. This principle is specifically preserved in the present copyright law. Thus, if the copy (or the record, disc, or tape) constitutes a derivative version of the work, these points should be kept in mind:

- The date in the copyright notice is not necessarily an indication of when copyright in all the material in the work will expire. Some of the material may already be in the public domain, and some parts of the work may expire sooner than others.
- Even if some of the material in the derivative work is in the public domain and free for use, this does not mean that the "new" material added to it can be used without permission from the owner of copyright in the derivative work. It may be necessary to compare editions to determine what is free to use and what is not.
- Ownership of rights in the material included in a derivative work and in the preexisting work upon which it may be based may differ, and permission obtained from the owners of certain parts of the work may not authorize the use of other parts.

### *The Name in the Copyright Notice*

Under the copyright statute in effect before 1978, the notice was required to include "the name of the copyright proprietor." The present act requires that the notice include "the name of the owner of copyright in the work, or an abbreviation by which the name can be recognized, or a generally known alternative designation of the owner." The name in the notice (sometimes in combination with the other statements on the copy, records, disk, tape, container, or label) often gives persons wishing to use the work the information needed to identify the owner from whom licenses or permission can be sought. In other cases, the name provides a starting point for a search in the Copyright Office records or catalogs, as explained at the beginning of this circular.

In the case of works published before 1978, copyright registration is made in the name of the individual person or the entity identified as the copyright owner in the notice. For works published on or after January 1, 1978, registration is made in the name of the person or entity owning all the rights on the date the registration is made. This may or may not be the name appearing in the notice. In addition to its records of copyright registration, the Copyright Office maintains extensive records of assignments, exclusive licenses, and other documents dealing with copyright ownership.

### *Ad Interim*

Ad interim copyright was a special short-term copyright that applied to certain books and periodicals in the English language that were first manufactured and published outside the United States. It was a partial exception to the manufacturing requirements of the previous U.S. copyright law. Its purpose was to secure temporary U.S. protection for a work, pending the manufacture of an edition in the United States. The ad interim requirements changed several times over the years and were subject to a number of exceptions and qualifications.

The manufacturing provisions of the copyright act expired on July 1, 1986, and are no longer a part of the copyright law. The transitional and supplementary provisions of the act provide that for any work in which ad interim copyright was subsisting or capable of being secured on December 31, 1977, copyright protection would be extended for a term compatible with the other works in which copyright was subsisting on the effective date of the new act. Consequently, if the work was first published on or after July

1, 1977, and was eligible for ad interim copyright protection, the provisions of the present copyright act will be applicable to the protection of these works. Anyone investigating the copyright status of an English-language book or periodical first published outside the United States before July 1, 1977, should check carefully to determine:

- Whether the manufacturing requirements were applicable to the work; and
- If so, whether the ad interim requirements were met.

## For Further Information

***Information via the Internet***

Circulars, announcements, regulations, other related materials, and all copyright application forms are available from the Copyright Office website at *www.copyright.gov*.

***Information by telephone***

For general information about copyright, call the Copyright Public Information Office at (202) 707-3000. The TTY number is (202) 707-6737. Staff members are on duty from 8:30 AM to 5:00 PM, eastern time, Monday through Friday, except federal holidays. Recorded information is available 24 hours a day. Or, if you know which application forms and circulars you want, request them 24 hours a day from the Forms and Publications Hotline at (202) 707-9100. Leave a recorded message.

***Information by regular mail***

Write to:

*Library of Congress*
*Copyright Office*
*Publications Section*
*101 Independence Avenue SE*
*Washington, DC 20559-6000*

# Search Request Form

Library of Congress
Copyright Office
101 Independence Avenue SE
Washington, DC 20559-6000

Reference & Bibliography Section
8:30 AM to 5:00 PM eastern
Monday through Friday,
Phone: (202) 707-6850
Fax: (202) 252-3485

**TYPE OF WORK**

☐ Book ☐ Music ☐ Motion picture ☐ Drama ☐ Sound recording ☐ Computer program
☐ Photograph/artwork ☐ Map ☐ Periodical ☐ Contribution ☐ Architectural work ☐ Mask work

**SEARCH INFORMATION YOU REQUIRE**

☐ Registration ☐ Renewal ☐ Assignment ☐ Address

**SPECIFICS OF WORK TO BE SEARCHED**

Title ____________________

Author ____________________

Copyright claimant ____________________
(Name in © notice)

Approximate year date of publication/creation ____________________

Registration number (if known) ____________________

CUT HERE

*If you need more space please attach additional pages.*

The fee for a search report is based on a set statutory fee* for the hour(s) or fraction of an hour consumed. The more information you furnish as a basis for the search, the better service we can provide. The time between the date of receipt of your fee for the search and your receiving a report will vary, depending on the method of payment (personal check, money order, or credit card) and on the workload. If you desire an estimate for the cost of the search and report, indicate your preference by checking the box below. There is a separate fee for an estimate.

*Names, titles, and short phrases are not copyrightable.*

Please read Circular 22 for more information on copyright searches.

Your name ____________________ Date ____________________

Address ____________________

Daytime telephone ____________________ Email ____________________

Convey results of estimate/search by telephone? ☐ Yes ☐ No

Fee enclosed? ☐ Yes: AMOUNT: $ ____________________ ☐ No

***NOTE:** Copyright Office fees are subject to change. For current fees for estimates or searches, check the Copyright Office website at *www.copyright.gov*, write the Copyright Office, or call the Reference & Bibliography Section at (202) 707-6850.



CIRCULAR 22 REV: 07/2006 PRINT: 07/2006—••,000 Printed on recycled paper U.S. GOVERNMENT PRINTING OFFICE: 2006-•••-•••/••,•••

Chapter 12

# Licensing Music in Print and Digital Print (Print Licenses)

## Summary

E. Online Digital Tablature Sites

F. Online Karaoke Sites

### V. LEGAL BACKGROUND

A. Printed Music

1. Reproduction Right
2. Adaptation Right
3. Distribution Right
4. Display Right

B. Digital Print

1. Lyrics in Karaoke Discs
2. Online Reproduction and Display

C. Who Has the Right to License Digital Print?

### VI. CONSIDERATIONS IN GRANTING EXCLUSIVE PRINT RIGHTS

A. Granting Exclusive Print Rights

1. Grants by Songwriters to Music Publishers
2. Grants by Music Publishers to Print Music Distributors

### VII. CONSIDERATIONS IN GRANTING PHYSICAL PRINT LICENSES

A. Granting Non-Exclusive Licenses to Print Music in Folios

B. Granting and Clearing Licenses to Print Lyrics

1. Books
2. Record Albums
3. Lyric Magazines
4. Print Advertising

### VIII. CONSIDERATIONS IN GRANTING DIGITAL PRINT LICENSES

A. Granting Licenses for Digital Sheet Music

B. Granting Licenses for Digital Guitar Tabs

C. Granting Licenses for Digital Lyric Database Websites

D. Granting Licenses for Digital Lyrics in Karaoke Discs

E. Granting Licenses for Digital Lyrics in Karaoke and Online Karaoke

# CHAPTER 12

# LICENSING MUSIC IN PRINT AND DIGITAL PRINT (PRINT LICENSES)

Before digital downloads and records, before motion pictures and television programs, before AM & FM radio, before even player pianos and music boxes, the music business was composed of live performances and the creation and distribution of printed music to facilitate those performances — better known as, *sheet music*. In the 1890, when the modern music industry first emerged, the music business was essentially the sheet music business, with sheet music, like that of the popular song, *After The Ball*, selling in the millions of copies. While during the twentieth century the music industry saw its revenues shift from the sale of printed music to the licensing of public performances and mechanical reproductions, printed music in the twenty-first century is beginning to make a comeback.

With the advent of the digitization of music, the term *print* has also begun to encompass the concept of *digital print* — a term used to refer to the reproduction of musical notation or lyrics in electronic form, such as they may be embodied in displays of Internet websites or as part of information retrieval services, or "search-based" sites, where they may be looked up and viewed. They may also be embodied in downloadable files — comprising full orchestrations, specialized arrangements, or guitar tablatures — which may be made available for display or printing, and may also be capable of being played or rendered with the aid of specialized software.

A *print license* is a form of permission that authorizes one to make printed copies of musical notation or lyrics, or both, such as sheet music, printed music folios, concert arrangements, and reprints of lyrics in books, magazines, and print advertising. A *digital print license* permits the making of reproductions, transitions, and public displays of musical notation and lyrics in digital formats. The print license is derived from one of the most basic rights of a copyright owner: the exclusive right to make copies. The digital print license involves not only the reproduction right, but may also involve the exclusive right to publicly display the musical work.

This chapter sketches the historical and legal background of printed music and provides an outline of some of the common terms and conditions contained in customary print licenses and emerging licenses for digital print.

## I. HISTORICAL BACKGROUND

### A. Origins of Musical Notation

Music would seem to be a part of human nature. What man fails to express through gesturing, speaking, writing, painting, and sculpting, he expresses through making music. If music can be defined as the art of organizing sounds and silences into meaningful patterns, then it clearly had very early origins. Early songs probably developed from hunting calls and other vocal signals. As soon as these calls were used for the pleasure expressed or emotions evoked, apart from any useful purpose, they became music. Archeologists have unearthed evidence dating back to the dawn of antiquity of man's creating music throughout Asia, Europe, Africa, the Americas, and other parts of the globe. The ancient Egyptians, Persians, Africans, and Chinese all used musical instruments of one kind or another.

It was, however, the ancient Greeks who laid the foundations of modern music. In ancient Greece, poetry and music were treated as one art, and music became an integral part of Greek drama, including the theatrical works of Aeschylus, Sophocles, Euripides, and Aristophanes.

Most common among the Greek instruments was the lyre, a u-shaped instrument with a cross bar that supported four strings. The invention of the lyre, according to Greek mythology, occurred when Herme's foot came in contact with the tendons of a dead tortoise, which had dried and tightened on the animal's shell. The philosopher, Terpander, born about 676 B.C., is said to have added three strings to the lyre, and later, Pythagoras, born about 582 B.C., is said to have added the eighth string. Pythagoras, the first to give music a scientific basis, also invented a system of four tones, known as the *tetrachord*, which later evolved into the first scale of one *octave*.

Early in the fourth century A.D., a school of *chant* was established in Rome. For generations the melodies were handed down aurally from master to pupil. The learning of the growing repertory of melodies by heart was arduous and there eventually evolved a form of musical notation. This notation was called *neumes* from the Greek word *neuma* meaning nod or sign. While the system gradually included combinations of dashes, curves, and dots, the neumes notation did not indicate musical pitch. Although there are no official accounts of neume notation before the eighth century, it has been said that Pope Gregory the Great, in the sixth century, collected the sacred music of the Church. *Gregorian* music is the name given to a collection of over 600 songs connected with the Roman Catholic services of that age.

By the eighth century, Charlemagne was sending emissaries to Rome to get full and accurate details on the methods of Gregorian singing. During the tenth century, an anonymous theorist brought order and progress to musical notation with a single stroke of his pen. Most historians credit Guido d'Arezzo, a monk, c. 1000 A.D., with creating the modern notation system. With some red ink and a ruler, he drew a line across the page and marked it "F." This was the beginning of the musical staff and clef. The neumes were now written on the line and higher and lower pitch was indicated above or below the line. They served as a guide to memory and indicated whether the voice should go up or down, but not how far up or down it should go. The idea worked so well that soon another line was added; later, two more lines were added until, finally, another line was added, giving us the five line staff we use today.

There soon came a need for the notation to indicate an exact time value, and, in the thirteenth century, three devices were invented: the dot, the coloration of notes, and time signatures. Circles, broken circles, and circles with dots in them corresponded to beats and rhythms of varying length. These later evolved to form the notes, bars, measures, and the other features of musical notation with which we are familiar today.

Throughout this period, music remained closely associated with the Roman Catholic Church. The seat of the Church was first located in Rome, then in Constantinople, later returning to Rome. With the fall of Constantinople in 1204, its scholars, with their knowledge of Greek and

Latin classics, traveled to Rome and Western Europe bringing with them the Hellenic alliance between music and drama. The Italian influence has left its mark on many of the musical terms we use today, including *allegro, andante*, and *legato*.

## B. The Art of Printing

Prior to the sixteenth century, musical manuscripts were arduously drafted and illuminated by hand, usually in monasteries and other places of learning. The diffusion of music received great aid from the art of printing, which commenced upon Gutenberg's invention of movable type in 1451. About a quarter of a century after the first bible came off Gutenberg's printing press, Ulrich Hahn, a German working in Rome at the time, became the first to print music. But it wasn't until 1501 that a serious business of printing music began in earnest when Ottavanio Petrucci, working in Venice, secured a monopoly for printing music in that city and became the first to print and distribute music on a full time basis. Other music printing concerns were soon established throughout Europe.

In the early sixteenth century, Winking de Worde published the first English songbook. In the mid-seventeenth century, John Playford, a London publisher of several important books on musical theory, began to specialize in compiling, publishing, promoting, and distributing nearly all the important songs composed in England during his time, and in doing so, became the forerunner to modern music publishing businesses.

In 1745, Johann Gottlob Immanuel Breitkopf labored to improve the methods of printing music. By introducing separate movable music type, he brought about a revolution in music printing by 1750. Johann Breitkopf's son, Christoph Gottlob, eventually inherited the publishing house, and transferred the business to his friend Gottfried Christoph Hartel. Hartel worked the business under the name Breitkopf and Hartel, publishing the works of Bach, Haydn, Mozart, Beethoven, Chopin and others, and becoming the world's largest publisher of orchestral music. Years later, Breitkopf and Hartel employed a French music publisher, Paul Heineke, sending him to the United States in 1917 to establish a New York office. Paul Heineke later established SESAC, the second performance rights society in the United States.

## C. Printed Music Publishing in America

During most of the colonial era in America after 1607, the music used by colonists was imported from England. For many years, music was forbidden as a trade altogether in New England. The first book printed in the United States that contained musical notation was the ninth edition of *The Bay Psalm Book*, which contained 13 songs borrowed from Playford's *Whole Book of Psalms* published in 1677. In 1712, *The Art of Singing* by John Tufts, the first music instruction book published in America, was distributed throughout the colonies. Containing 37 songs, the Tuft's book was printed in many editions from its date of first publication through 1744.

In 1793, Benjamin Carr moved his family from England and established the first music publishing firm in the United States, printing chiefly music that had become popular in England. Other music publishers were established in many of the major cities on the eastern seaboard. With the development and increasing popularity of the piano, singing became a popular form of entertainment, and sales of printed sheet music began to flourish. It is estimated that, during the first 25 years of the nineteenth century, over 10,000 popular songs were published in the United States. By the end of the century, *After the Ball*, written and published by Charles K. Harris in 1893, became the first song to sell a million copies.

In 1880, after winning a toy printing press from school, Isadore, Julius, and J. Witmark opened a printing business in their home on West 40th Street in New York City. They earned a modest living printing Christmas cards. To augment his earnings, Jay became a performer of ballads in minstrel and variety shows. After achieving some success, it suddenly occurred to Jay, if it were possible for him to establish hit songs for others, why couldn't he publish his own music? After all, Isadore could write songs, and they had a printing press on which to print the music. Since the brothers were still minors, they had their father, Marcus, become director of the company, and thus, M. Witmark & Sons was established in 1885 as a publisher and printer of sheet music.

Other music publishing firms soon opened their doors, and music publishers quickly developed innovative ways to increase the sale of their sheet music. A part-time songwriter, Edward B. Marks, established a publishing firm under that name. Marks discovered a way to promote his songs by performing them during the intermissions at variety houses while illustrated slides were flashed onto a white sheet screen. Tom Harms of T.B. Harms Music Publishing Company became the first music publisher to discover the profitability in printing sheet music of songs appearing in successful Broadway shows. M. Witmark & Sons was the first music publisher in America to pay singers to perform their songs. Shapiro-Remick & Company employed Jerome Kern to demonstrate their songs. Kern was soon hired by Max Dreyfus of T.B. Harms as a staff pianist to *plug* (i.e., promote) songs at various department stores.

Sales of sheet music soared. In the days before the advent of sound motion pictures, radio, and television, it was not unusual for a popular song to sell upwards of 2,000,000 copies in sheet music. The sale of sheet music was the primary income of a music publisher, unless the publisher enjoyed other income from operating a musical instrument store, producing musical productions, or managing artists. When sales of single copies of sheet music would slow down, publishers and songwriters looked for successful ways to promote their songs. Sometimes a song would become a hit as a result of a combination of fortuitous circumstances.

In 1919, while dining at Dinty Moore's, a fashionable restaurant on Broadway, Irving Caesar suggested to his dinner partner, George Gershwin, they collaborate on a "two-step" type song that was the trend in dancing at the time. George was enthusiastic and suggested they take a bus to his apartment and try their luck. George played a few notes on the piano and, as Irving told me, "The words rushed out at me with inspired spontaneity." The song was first introduced in a Ned Wayburn revue at the Capitol Theatre in New York. In the lobby of the theatre, George and Irving shouted to the departing audience, "Here it is, *Swanee*, get your copies, *Swanee*." They did this night after night, but not one copy was sold. George and Irving having confidence in their creation begged their publisher, Max Dreyfus of T.B. Harms, to promote the song by other means. Max told them he loved the song, but it was not "commercial" enough to sell sheet music. A few weeks later, Buddy DeSylva — songwriter discovered by Al Jolson — invited George and Irving to a post-midnight party. When George was playing the piano, and Buddy his ukulele, Buddy started to sing *Swanee*. Al Jolson quickly turned to his musical director and told him to arrange the song and put it in his new show. The song became a smash hit. Max Dreyfus finally published the song and orders for sheet music began pouring in. When George and Irving asked Dreyfus how much royalties they had earned, Max told them about $10,000, a huge sum at the time. A little embarrassed, Dreyfus offered the two an advance against prospective royalties from sheet music sales in England. Max bought George the baby grand piano he wanted and Irving settled for cash.

### D. Print Music Publishing Today — The Emergence of Digital

At the turn of the twentieth century, most music publishing revenue was derived from the sale of printed music. With the increasing popularity of the phonograph, the advent of radio, sound motion pictures, or "talkies," and later the introduction of television, recordings of music replaced printed music notation as the primary source of music publishing revenue. Income from licensing the mechanical reproduction of music and performance of the resulting recordings soon eclipsed revenues from printed music to the point that, today, printed music represents only a small portion of a music publisher's income.

Traditionally, most printed music was sold in the form of *sheet* music, which contained the musical notation of a single song, and any accompanying lyrics. As the sales of printed music became a declining portion of music publishing income, modern music publishers continued to seek innovative ways to increase sales of printed music. This led to the development of new forms of "packaging" of sheet music, such as in *personality folios* and *educational editions*, which are described below.

More recently, however, digital technology has allowed creators and publishers of music to find new means of exploiting musical notation and lyrics — a means that has further diminished the importance of physical printed matter and has cross-pollinated musical notation and mechanical reproductions to create what can be considered an entirely new medium.

Creators and publishers can now take a transcription of a musical work — such as the musical notation in a typical "piano part" or other sheet music — put it into digital form, and deliver the resulting data file electronically, as a form of *digital sheet music*. Where this digital sheet music can be made to play itself (with the aid of software, such as Sibelius), a form of mechanical reproduction is involved. As discussed further below, the *digital guitar tablature* is a form of digital print that involves a special form of musical notation that facilitates the rendering of a song using a guitar. These, too, when digitally prepared with the right software, are typically capable of playing the song with the aid of a device or computer.

Most important, forms of digital print, such as digital sheet music and digital guitar tabs, are capable of being stored on computer servers, searched by title or creator, and transmitted over the Internet. As a result, new markets for musical notation have emerged, and along with it, new legal challenges regarding who controls the rights to these new uses, particularly where long-term contracts, or those limited by territory, used definitions of rights that did not fully anticipate the new applications of technology.

## II. TYPES OF PRINTED MUSIC

Today, printed music is available in various forms, each suited to the particular needs of musical artists.

### A. Sheet Music

The traditional form of printed music is *sheet music*. Sheet music is generally one song printed on unbound sheets of paper, containing music and any accompanying lyrics. Sheet music is generally arranged for piano, vocal, and guitar. Many piano arrangements include suggested guitar tablatures, discussed in more detail below.

### B. Folio

A *folio* is a compilation or anthology of sheet music bound into one, usually a soft cover volume. The songs may be written by various writers and recorded by various artists, but they are usually linked by a common theme, such as songs from the roaring twenties, famous movie themes, or songs of romance. Folios, sometimes referred to as *songbooks*, might contain editorial notes regarding the songs in the compilation or the theme of the anthology, related photographs, and similar materials. A songbook that contains a compilation of songs by various artists is called a *mixed folio*.

### C. Personality Folio

A *personality folio* is a folio consisting of songs written, recorded, or performed by the same artist or recording group, or written by the same songwriter. A personality folio may contain biographical material about the featured artist or group, as well as photographs. Such editions make the folio attractive even to fans who do not play an instrument, as many non-performing fans would purchase a personality folio just to obtain the photographs of their favorite artist or group. A personality folio that contains only the songs appearing on a particular record album is called a *companion folio*, or sometimes a *matching folio*.

### D. Instrument Folio

An *instrument folio* is a folio of compositions specially arranged for a particular musical instrument, such as a cello, harp, clarinet, oboe, recorder, tenor saxophone, alto saxophone, or violin.

### E. Music Instruction or "Method" Books

A *music instruction book*, sometimes called a *method book*, is a book designed to provide instruction on a particular musical instrument. An instruction book may be designed for beginners, intermediate, or advanced players. For example, an instruction book for novices may be used by someone learning to play the clarinet for the first time. Another may be used by an accomplished musician desiring to learn advanced techniques in, or a certain style of, playing the saxophone.

### F. Concert and Educational Editions

Sheet music and folios containing special arrangements for professional orchestras and other music groups are published in special editions called *concert editions*. These editions comprise one or more arrangements of popular music, symphonic music, chamber music, and music from Broadway shows, operas, and ballets. Concert editions are sometimes made available for sale, but for major orchestral works and operas, specialized print rental companies, such as Boosey & Hawkes, make these editions, called *performance materials*, available on a rental basis.

With the growth of school orchestras and marching bands, music publishers discovered a ready-made market for their sheet music. Special arrangements, called *educational editions*, were developed to accommodate various grades of young musicians from easy to play arrangements to the professional orchestrations prepared specifically for use by marching bands, jazz bands, and orchestras.

## G. Fakebook

A *fakebook* is a folio containing hundreds of songs presented in very short arrangements. These books enabled a professional musician, who might not be familiar with a particular "request" from his audience, to *fake* the performance (i.e., improvise and render it as though the song was familiar) using merely the melody line presented in the fake book. Early fakebooks were illegal or *bootleg*, meaning they were compiled without the permission of the copyright owners. Fakebooks were compiled by musicians over the years and handed down, copied, or sold on an informal basis. In recent years, music publishers, recognizing the demand for fakebooks, compiled and arranged "legal" fakebooks for commercial sale.

## H. Lyric Reprints

A *lyric* — a word that comes from the Greek word, *lyricos*, meaning "singing to the lyre" — is a set of words that make up a song, either by speaking or singing. Lyrics, or lines from popular lyrics, have often found their way into print and licensing these uses can be a welcome, though relatively small, source of income for a music publisher.

From time to time, a music publisher will receive a request from a book publisher to include a quote from a lyric for use in a commercial book or from an advertising agency to include a quote from a lyric in a print advertisement. In addition, the public's general interest in lyrics has spawned magazines specializing in printing the lyrics of popular songs. Entire books comprising a compilation of a songwriter's lyrics have been published, such as the lyric books of Ira Gershwin, Johnny Mercer, Bob Dylan, Paul Simon, and Sting.

In the 1980, when lyrics contained in many popular recordings — particularly *rap* and *punk rock* recordings — began to include words that many would consider indecent, radio stations became concerned that the broadcast of these recordings might jeopardize their broadcast licenses. As a result, the stations began requiring that, when record companies provide them with promotional copies of new releases, they include copies of the lyrics of those recordings for review. Since the print rights of lyrics are owned by music publishers, not the record companies, the latter began asking publishers for permission to reprint the lyrics, which they often provided in the interior booklets packaged with the CDs of the recordings.

## III. TYPES OF DIGITAL PRINT

In recent years, digital technologies have enabled the digitization of printed matter in to digital files that can be displayed on computer screens and handheld devices and distributed to the devices via the Internet and wireless networks. With the advent of these new technologies, a host of new applications for the commercialization of musical notation and lyrics has emerged.

### A. Digital Sheet Music

*Digital sheet music* is a digital data file, in one format or another (e.g., PDF or proprietary format), containing the musical notation and lyrics of a musical work. These files can be stored on a computer, server, or other electronic device, transmitted via the Internet (or by some other digital media like a CD-ROM or DVD) or otherwise accessed by an Internet user via their browser or other client software in which it may be viewed and/or downloaded to their device and then printed in hard-copy form. Some forms of digital sheet music contain instructions (e.g., MIDI or other proprietary language) that permit the playing of the song on the user's computer or device.

### B. Digital Lyrics

Perhaps the first practical exploitation of lyrics in digital form arose with the advent of karaoke discs — laser discs originally distributed to karaoke bars, first made popular in Japan. Karaoke devices enable the performance of custom-made, purely instrumental (i.e., without vocal renditions of the lyrics) recordings of popular songs while displaying the song's lyrics on a television monitor. The result enables individuals, usually amateurs, to sing along with the recordings. Karaoke recordings are now distributed to the public for use with home karaoke devices and are also used in online karaoke applications, such as MySpace Karaoke (formerly, Ksolo.com).

### C. Digital Lyric Databases

Search the word "lyrics" on Google and you will retrieve hundreds of websites that make lyrics available for free or on a subscription basis. Some of these sites are fully licensed by music publishers; many are not.

Licensed entities include Gracenote (which powers a number of lyric sites, such as MetroLyrics and LyricFind). Gracenote, now a subsidiary of Sony, has licensed large catalogs of music lyrics directly from over 80 music publishers, including all the major publishers, and uses its lyric database to power a number of lyric search websites, mobile, and other consumer electronic devices. Gracenote uses CMRRA, the Canadian Mechanical Reproduction Rights Agency, to calculate royalties and produce statements to its music publisher licensors on a quarterly basis.

One of the most ambitious projects affecting the exploitation of lyrics is LyricWiki, self-described as a "lyrical database-oriented website." As of mid-2009, it claimed to be the fifth largest wiki with over 870,000 pages. Users on the site can view, edit, and discuss the lyrics of songs, which are also available for purchase from links on the site. According to the website, "Users are told to be mindful of copyright while contributing, and copyright violations are removed upon request."

Perhaps most interesting, is LyricWiki's ability to allow programmatic access to its growing database of lyrics. Through its application programming interface (API), users have created plug-ins for many media players including iTunes, Winamp, and Windows Media Player. Thus, while you are listening to a song on your PC or iPhone, the lyrics can be displayed on your screen. LyricWiki has also released a Facebook application called "LyricWiki Challenge," a social, competitive game based on identifying lyrics from popular songs in several genres. According to the LyricWiki website, "As of August 2, 2009, however, lyrics themselves can no longer be supplied through the API, due to licensing issues."

### D. Digital Guitar Tabs

A *guitar tablature* is a special form of musical notation used by guitarists, consisting of a staff of 6 horizontal lines, each one representing a string of the guitar, containing numbers representing the fret to be played.

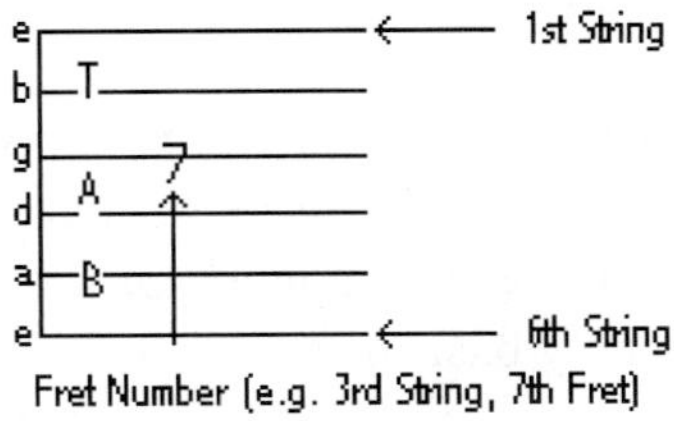


For example, the bottom line of the staff represents the lowest "E" string tab, the second line from the bottom the "A" string, etc. In the above example, the fret is telling you to play the third, or "G," string, holding the seventh fret.

Sheet music will typically include the appropriate guitar tablature required for a guitar accompaniment for the playing or singing of the music, and many guitar instruction books contain guitar tabs of popular music. The world of guitar tabs, in a commercial sense, were a mere footnote to music publishers until the development by a French firm in 1977 of computer software called, Guitar Pro, which facilitated the digitization of guitar tablatures.

A tab, as they have become known, generated in Guitar Pro software is far more advanced than a mere text tab: with the Guitar Pro software installed, you can listen to the tab to determine whether the tab is right for your purpose. Over the years, the Guitar Pro software has been greatly enhanced, offering options such as listening, printing, transposing and transcribing a score in standard notation, and importing and exporting MIDI and ASCII formats, which has greatly facilitated their sharing over the Internet.

## IV. PREPARATION AND DISTRIBUTION OF PRINTED MUSIC

In the first half of the twentieth century, when a songwriter submitted a tune to his publisher, it was assumed that the composer would prepare his own lead sheet of the music. A *lead sheet* is one or two pages of lined music paper consisting of the notes of the melody on a single staff with chord indications written above and lyrics written below the notes. The music publisher would use the lead sheet to register the copyright in the song with the U.S. Copyright Office. The lead sheet was then used by the music publisher's professional staff as the basis for preparing a piano/vocal arrangement of the song to be used in the printing of sheet music.

In addition to using staff arrangers, publishers frequently engaged freelance arrangers to prepare these arrangements. Staff and freelance arrangers are normally engaged on a *work for hire* basis, meaning they are paid wages on a weekly basis or paid a flat fee per arrangement for their work and do not acquire any ownership interest in their work. Staff and freelance arrangers do not normally participate in any form of royalty payment, unless the arranger is engaged to add some substantial material to the composition, or the work performed includes special arrangements of compositions in the public domain, such as the works of Beethoven and Mozart.

At one time, I was one of such freelancers, and had the privilege of creating piano arrangements for the works of artists such as Paul Simon & Art Garfunkel and groups such as Jefferson Airplane. The preparation of piano/vocal arrangements for rock songs is no easy task.[1]

---

[1] (The Arranger)

He sits in his corner with pencil in hand,
Arranging the music for concertos grand;
  Near-sighted, meek, but with songs in his heart,
  He lays out his work like a mariner's chart.
He never gets write ups, he never gets praise,
But works there unknown to the end of his days!
  Composers will give him but ten bars or more,
  And he must sit down and develop the score.
His arrangements may click, folks acclaim it as "hot"!
But does he get credit? Most certainly not!
  Composers will swagger and band-leaders strut,
  Accepting the praise for the work of this nut!
Alas, for the musical heydays of yore,
When composers of music arranged their own score;
  Arrangers today lead a life that is sad,
  They get naught if it's good, but catch h —
  if it's bad.

— Nick Kenny, songwriter (Nick & Charles Kenny, *There's a Gold Mine in the Sky*) and columnist for the *N. Y. Daily Mirror.*

I used to call upon my sons when they were young boys to help me discern virtually inaudible lyrics from rock recordings for which I was engaged to prepare piano arrangements. It was Paul Simon's desire that his compositions be arranged for sheet music publication as they were performed on his recordings. This I accomplished to his satisfaction by transposing the "sound" of his guitar to paper. While at that time one would need to play these arrangements on a harpsichord to get the feeling of a guitar sound, today all one would need to use is an electronic keyboard.

While sheet music sales have declined over the years, many teachers of music have demanded copies of editions specially arranged for "beginners." The recent work of several talented arrangers, who have become known for their simplified editions, have breathed new life into the market for sheet music. Nevertheless, some rock and contemporary music artists unreasonably insist upon having their sheet music arranged exactly as it was recorded; the resulting arrangements are often difficult for the average home musician to play. These artists forget that, while the professional musician can use any musical notation to fake a performance in his own style, the amateur enthusiast has to play the music as it is printed. Both professional and amateur would be served if all sheet music were arranged in a simplified fashion.

Eminent composers, such as Vincent Youmans, Jerome Kern, and George Gershwin, and master film music composers, such as Max Steiner, Alfred Newman, and Erich Wolfgang Korngold, prepared their own piano arrangements and orchestrations, often with the help of talented arrangers such as Hugo Friedhofer, but it is now extremely rare for a popular song composer to transcribe his music to paper. With the rock era, many artists and groups have emerged from the recording studio with hit records created by improvising the arrangement along the way, without the benefit of written material. Consequently, beginning about the 1950, nearly all songs were submitted to publishers on records or audiotape and many publishers found it necessary to prepare their own lead sheets just to fulfill the requirements of copyright registration. Through the lobbying efforts of representatives of artists and composers, Congress was made aware that many contemporary artists were not able to write out their compositions in musical notation, and the copyright law they enacted in 1976 finally allowed songwriters to submit audiotape recordings to fulfill copyright deposit requirements.[2]

Not all songs, however, are adaptable to the medium of printed music. Stripped of the production values in the recording, many contemporary songs simply don't have enough melody to carry a useful piano/vocal arrangement. Even if a song has a melody or lyrics sufficiently meaningful to be rendered in printed form, sheet music would not normally be published unless the song has attained a certain "hit" status or is published with other songs, by the same artist, that have become well-known hits.

## A. Independent Print Distributors

Today, of the thousands of independent music publishing companies only a handful engage in the expensive business of printing, selling, and distributing printed music. Even some of the largest music publishers enter into special relationships with print publisher/distributors that specialize in printing and distributing music, such as Hal Leonard and Alfred Music Publishing.

These print distributors distribute printed music through a network of wholesalers called *rack jobbers*, retail print music dealers, educational dealers, retail stores where musical instruments are sold, booksellers, and other retail establishments. They also publish digital sheet music on their own websites and those of online digital print retailers, such as MusicNotes, Lifeway, and WorshipKitchen.

Some music publishers enter into exclusive arrangements with these print distributors for the printed publication of some or all of the songs in the publisher's catalog for a limited time. Under these arrangements, the publisher receives a royalty on the basis of the print distributor's sales. Similar arrangements are also made on a song-by-song basis. Rather than granting exclusive print rights or a non-exclusive license to print music in return for a royalty, a music publisher may prefer to exercise its print rights through the use of a selling agent. Under this arrangement, the selling agent, usually a print publisher acting in an agency capacity, charges all printing, production, and distribution costs to the copyright

[2] 17. U.S.C. Sec. 407(a)(2).

owner, and pays over all its sales receipts directly to the copyright owner, deducting only a commission of about 25%.

The consolidation in the business of printed music has resulted from the decline in demand for printed music. But some advantages have resulted from this consolidation. For example, a print publisher who has relationships with several music publishers has the opportunity to cherry pick, from among the several catalogs for which it has print licenses, popular "hit" songs for inclusion in folios designed for maximum appeal.

## B. Rental of Performance Materials for Orchestral and Operatic Works

Not all copies of printed works are distributed for sale to the public. A major category of printed music is orchestral scores and parts for large-scale works, such as symphonies, concerti, and operas. Boosey & Hawkes and Music Sales Group rent full orchestrations of much of their repertoire, and arrangements of public domain works (usually classical) to orchestras and educational institutions around the world.

These *performance materials* are prepared by the music publisher and are licensed to the performing organization, such as major symphony and community orchestras, on a rental basis. Musical theater works are also licensed in this manner. Because the score and parts to a full-length opera, with soloists, chorus and orchestra can easily fill a bookshelf, it is not cost-effective for the publisher to make these works available for sale.

Another reason for making these works available on a rental basis has to do with how contemporary "classical" works are created. Contemporary classical composers such as Pulitzer Prize winners John Adams, John Corigliano, and David Lang are commissioned by one or more organizations, such as a consortium of symphony orchestras or opera companies. In exchange for commissioning the work, the commissioner(s) will generally be entitled to certain "exclusivities," such as the right to present the world or some territorial premiere of the work and often the exclusive right to perform the work within the "exclusive" territory for a certain period of time, such as one year. The commissioning agreement for the work will often have a provision to pay for the cost of preparing the score and parts. This fee is in addition to the composer's commission fee for writing the work. For large-scale orchestral works, these costs can easily exceed $10,000 and operatic works often cost several times that.

The need to honor commissioners' exclusivities for newly composed works is another reason why publishers do not want to have too many sets of performance materials of new works in circulation. Another is that composers will often revise the work after hearing it at the world premiere and the publisher wants to ensure that the most recent performance materials are the ones available for rental.

For older works in the standard repertory but that are still under copyright (Bernstein, Copland and Ives, for example), orchestras often request a set of performance materials that have been marked up (with bowings, for example) by a famous conductor and some conductors will try to request their "own" set of performance materials that they have previously used.

Considerations and fees for the rental of performance materials are set forth below.

### C. Online Digital Sheet Music Retailers

Music publishers and print publishers will also make arrangements with one or more online digital print retailers for the publication of digital sheet music. Such retailers include MusicNotes, Lifeway, WorshipKitchen, and others.

Digital sheet music is delivered in a number of ways under a number of different revenue models. Though the technical options for delivery and viewing are still evolving, most digital sheet music is either delivered in an Adobe Acrobat PDF file, or in one or more of a number of other popular proprietary formats, including Sibelius (Scorch format), Freehand (Solero format), or the fully interactive formats offered by Sibelius software and Finale software. These formats employ varying levels of *digital rights management (DRM)*, which are technical means of controlling how you view the digital sheet music, how many copies you may print, and whether (and how) you may save the file on your computer.

Using one or more of the technical delivery methods noted above, digital sheet music is commercially offered in several ways. The most common is by *a-la-carte sale* (or the sale of digital sheet music of a song by *permanent download*). You search for the song you want, choose among the several arrangements offered, and purchase the right to receive a download of a file that you may view on your computer and print on your printer.

Another increasingly common form is through a *subscription service*, where a user buys monthly or yearly access to an archive of digital sheet music. Some subscription services limit the number of songs or downloads a user can obtain in a given period, some will also allow group access, and some will grant a further license to make additional copies for a specified purpose (e.g., allowing you to make a limited number of photocopies of the sheet music for use by your band members). Subscription service prices vary by type of arrangement, the number of users that can access the archives, the type of sub-license granted, and the number of downloads allowed for a given period.

In addition to permanent (*a la carte*) download sales and subscription services, some music services are experimenting with an advertising-based model, where the service offers content to online users for free and pays the content owners a share of the revenue generated from the sale of advertising space on the website (pro-rated based on the number of times each song is accessed on the site by visitors). An example of this is Ultimate Guitar Archive, discussed below.

### D. Online Digital Lyric Sites

As mentioned above, music publishers and print publishers will also make arrangements with one or more digital lyric aggregators, such as GraceNote, and independent operators of websites that offer access to digital lyric databases. Unfortunately, the vast majority of digital lyric sites are unauthorized, which has presented a challenge to both music publishers seeking to rightfully exercise their exclusive rights and those who are trying to operate online businesses with legal authorization from the publishers. The ambitious LyricWiki, discussed above, will be an important project to watch as this subject evolves.

### E. Online Digital Tablature Sites

About a year after the introduction of Guitar Pro, Eugeny Naidenov, a student of economic faculty of Kaliningrad State University, Russia, started a website that has since grown to become one of the most popular music sites on the Internet. Starting in 1998 with guitar tabs of just 10 artists, Ultimate Guitar Archive has grown to contain a library of over 20,000 guitar tablatures.

The tabs were created and uploaded to the Ultimate Guitar website primarily by users of Guitar Pro who became members of the Ultimate Guitar website. Registered users of the site could not only upload their own digital tabs, they could search for tabs of their favorite songs and download them for free, rate them, and organize them by difficulty. The phenomenon that has come to be known as *user generated content.*

Though the content uploaded to Ultimate Guitar is user-generated, it is not all user-owned — that is, the user may create tabs, but the tabs typically contain copyrighted musical works of others. While a user may create a tab of another's copyrighted song for his own edification — and do so, at least in the United States, without the song owner's consent under the theory that the user is making "fair use" of the copyrighted material — the uploading of such a tab to the Ultimate Guitar website (and the further distribution of the tab to others by the Ultimate Guitar website) is an entirely different matter, as these are acts that require the permission of the song's copyright owner.

Here is an example of a typical guitar tab uploaded to the Ultimate Guitar website:

```
When You Wish Upon a Star[3]

e---3-1-0------5|---7-5-3-2-3-8|
B-1-------2-3--6|-3-------1----|
G-0---2--------7|-0------------|
D-2------------0|-0------------|
A-3-------------|-2------------|
E---------------|-------------8|

e-10-8-7-5---------|-5--7---|
B----------8--6-5-3|-6--7--0|
G------------------|-7-----0|
D------------------|-0--0--2|
A------6-----------|-------3|
E------------------|--------|
```

Ultimate Guitar gives the user the option to print the tab out or use the site to e-mail it to a friend. The revenue model for Ultimate Guitar has been primarily advertising-based. Like YouTube, Ultimate Guitar

[3] Copyright © Bourne Co. 1940.

believes it is shielded from immediate claims of U.S. copyright infringement under terms of the safe harbor afforded by Section 512 of the Copyright Act.[4] While the Ultimate Guitar website has been operating for years without formal licenses in place, the operators of the site and music publishers are working on commercial relationships that would formally legitimize its operation on a worldwide basis and generate a share of the potential revenues to music publishers and the print publishers (such as Alfred Music Publishing and Hal Leonard Music) who control the digital rights to guitar tabs for many catalogs. New models, including paid permanent downloads and subscription fees are beginning to emerge from these discussions.

### F. Online Karaoke Sites

As mentioned above, karaoke devices enable the performance of recordings of instrumental versions of popular songs while the songs' lyrics are displayed on a television monitor. These recordings have been licensed by online karaoke applications, such as MySpace Karaoke (formerly, Ksolo.com, a venture founded by Israeli entrepreneur, Nimrod Lev). With these websites, a user may listen to a recording while reading the lyrics displayed on the screen to create his or her own recording, which combines the instrumental version played over the Internet and their own voice track singing the lyrics. The resulting recording is uploaded to the karaoke website where others may listen to the recordings and cast votes for their favorite recordings.

## V. LEGAL BACKGROUND

### A. Printed Music

Under the Copyright Act[5], owners of copyrights of musical works have, in addition to the exclusive right to perform their works publicly, the following exclusive rights:

- to reproduce the copyrighted work in copies or phonorecords (i.e., the *reproduction right*);

[4] See Chapter 16, regarding *The User Generated Content Phenomenon.*

[5] 17 U.S.C. Sec. 106.

- to prepare derivative works based upon the copyrighted work (i.e., the *adaptation right*);
- to distribute copies or phonorecords of the copyrighted work to the public by sale or other transfer of ownership, or by rental, lease, or lending (i.e., the *distribution right*); and
- to display the copyrighted work publicly (i.e., the *display right*).

### *1. Reproduction Right*

A music publisher's right to license the printing of the musical notation or lyrics of a song stems from its exclusive right of reproduction, which provides the copyright owner with essentially the exclusive right to make copies of a song's notation and lyrics.

There are few limitations on the copyright owner's reproduction right. One that comes to mind is "fair use" of copyright, but, as discussed in Chapter 25, this affords a user a right to make copies without the copyright owner's permission only under very limited circumstances — such as for purposes of "criticism, comment, news reporting, teaching (including multiple copies for classroom use), scholarship, or research."[6] Thus, a news article, such as an obituary of a songwriter, or a review of an album or concert, could include a reprint of a lyric without permission of the copyright owner.

The use of a lyric, even a single line of a lyric, in a commercial book, such as a trade book or textbook, would normally require permission from the music publisher, though music publishers are typically open to granting such permission on a gratis basis or for a small fee plus a couple of copies of the book's first printing. A book comprising a compilation of album or concert reviews typically would not require permission, as the context is clear that the lyrics are being used for purposes of criticism — otherwise, a publisher or songwriter could withhold permission to reprint the lyric in a review critical of the musical work or performance.

[6] 17 U.S.C. Sec. 107.

### 2. Adaptation Right

The copyright owner of a musical work also has the exclusive right to prepare adaptations or *derivative works*. The Copyright Act defines the term as follows:

> A "derivative work" is a work based upon one or more preexisting works, such as a translation, musical arrangement, dramatization, fictionalization, motion picture version, sound recording, art reproduction, abridgment, condensation, or any other form in which a work may be recast, transformed, or adapted.

A musical arrangement — such as a piano arrangement that makes up a sheet music version of the song — is a derivative work of the song. The adaptation right typically arises in the context of the creation and preparation of particular arrangements of the song for use in sheet music and folios, discussed below.

### 3. Distribution Right

A right that is separate from the reproduction of the work in copies (e.g., sheet music) is the distribution right — the exclusive right "to distribute copies . . . of the copyrighted work to the public by sale or other transfer of ownership, or by rental, lease, or lending."[7]

Generally, when a music publisher grants to another a license to reproduce a musical work in copies, it simultaneously grants the right to distribute those copies. When a print music publisher rents copies of orchestrations to symphony orchestras or smaller community orchestras to facilitate the performance of the musical works embodied in such copies, it is invoking only its exclusive right of distribution by rental, not its exclusive right of reproduction.

It is important to note that, since the distribution right involves the right to distribute *copies* — and copies are physical objects, the distribution right has no bearing on the digital delivery of copies over the Internet. When a work, such as the musical notation or lyrics of a song, is digitally delivered over the Internet — whether by means of a

---

[7] 17 U.S.C. Sec. 106(3).

download or display — a copy is being reproduced, but *not distributed.* The reproduction is being made *by transmission, not by distribution.*

### *4. Display Right*

A copyright owner also has the exclusive right to display the work publicly. Under the Copyright Act,

> To "display" a work means to show a copy of it, either directly or by means of a film, slide, television image, or any other device or process or, in the case of a motion picture or other audiovisual work, to show individual images non-sequentially.[8]
>
> To display a work "publicly" means —
>
> (1) to . . . display it at a place open to the public or at any place where a substantial number of persons outside of a normal circle of a family and its social acquaintances is gathered; or
>
> (2) to transmit or otherwise communicate a . . . display of the work to
>
> - a place specified by clause (1) or
> - to the public, by means of any device or process, whether the members of the public capable of receiving the . . . display receive it in the same place or in separate places and at the same time or at different times.[9]

The display right usually comes up in the context of the visual arts — the owner of a copyright in a painting or sculpture has the right to control where and when the original or copies of the work are displayed publicly, such as in museums and art galleries.

The display right, in the context of *printed* musical notation and lyrics, does not generally arise in the commercial context, as there appears to be no distinct commercial market for the public display of, for example, printed sheet music. A public display of a printed advertisement containing a line from a song lyric, such as on a commercial billboard along a highway or in Times Square, would

---

[8] 17 U.S.C. Sec. 101.

[9] *Id.*

invoke the musical copyright owner's display right, but such right would normally be licensed as part of the license for the use of the lyric in the advertisement. (If any reader knows of other public display uses of notation or lyrics, please let your authors know about it.)

As discussed below, however, the emergence of digital print has given the public display right in musical works a life that perhaps never existed before.

## B. Digital Print

### *1. Lyrics in Karaoke Discs*

When karaoke discs first became popular in Japan, there was some confusion about just what specific rights were invoked by the use of musical works in these devices. Clearly, when the recordings of the songs were performed in a karaoke club, the public performance right was invoked and the club was responsible for obtaining the necessary blanket license from the appropriate performance right society (such as JASRAC, ASCAP, or BMI).

But it became clear that a performance license was not enough. When copies of the songs were fixed in the laser discs, the reproduction right is invoked. Thus, the makers of the disc required a reproduction license. Device makers first turned to the compulsory mechanical license provision of the U.S Copyright Act,[10] but there are two problems with this. If the devices were merely distributed to karaoke clubs for use in facilitating public performances, such use would arguably not fall within the terms of the compulsory license statute, which requires that the primary purpose is to distribute the copies "to the public for private use."[11] Since the karaoke club is a public or commercial use, the compulsory license provision would not apply.

But even if the discs were distributed to the public for private use, the compulsory license provision would not apply. The compulsory license provision only applies to the distribution of *phonorecords* of the licensed music — in other words, the recordings must be audio-only sound recordings. Since the lyrics of the song are displayed on a

[10] See 17 U.S.C. Sec. 115 and Chapter 13, on *Licensing Music in Sound Recordings*.

[11] 17 U.S.C. Sec. 115(a)(1).

screen, the recordings are *audiovisual*, not audio-only works, and thus the compulsory license may not be invoked for this use.[12] The fact that the visual images comprise only the lyrics does not preclude a finding that the recording is audiovisual.

When asked for a license to use musical works in karaoke discs, music publishers issue licenses that include a *synchronization* license to record the song in timed-relation with the audiovisual work (i.e., display of lyrics on the screen) combined with a *digital print license* to include a digital version of the lyrics in the device.

### *2. Online Reproduction and Display*

When karaoke recordings are rendered over the Internet, copies of the recordings are made on the website's servers and the audiovisual works are streamed to the end user. These uses invoke the copyright owner's reproduction right in the song and lyrics, the public display right in the lyrics, and the public performance right in the song. (The distribution right is not involved, because that right concerns the distribution — the movement from one person or place to another — of physical copies.) When asked for a license to use musical works in online karaoke, music publishers issue licenses that include a *synchronization* license to record the song in timed-relation with the audiovisual work (i.e., display of lyrics on the screen) and a *digital print license* to include a digital version of the lyrics in the device, conditioned upon a public performance license being obtained by the applicable performance rights society.

The digital delivery of musical notation (including guitar tabs) and lyrics over the Internet may invoke the copyright owner's *reproduction right* and *public display right*, and perhaps the *right to prepare derivative works*. (Again, the distribution right is not invoked.) When a work, such as the musical notation or lyrics of a song (assuming the data files that contain them do not have the ability to render a performance of the song), is digitally delivered over the Internet two rights may be invoked: the *reproduction right*, the *public display right*, or *both*. It would seem, for example, that when a copy of sheet music is either downloaded as a data file (e.g., PDF file) directly to the user's

---

[12] *Leadsinger, Inc. v. BMG Music Publishing*, 429 F. Supp. 2d 1190 (9th Cir. 2008).

hard disk, only the reproduction right is being invoked. Should the contents of the file (i.e., musical notation or lyrics) be displayed on the user's screen, the public display right is being invoked. (Recall that to display a work publicly includes the transmission of the work "to the public, by means of any device or process, whether the members of the public capable of receiving the . . . display receive it in the same place or in separate places and at the same time or at different times".)

It is suggested that those responsible for drafting licenses for digital print, keep in mind this distinction between the reproduction right and public display right, and for that matter, the derivative work right, as circumstances may arise where proper drafting could avoid later misunderstanding and disputes. One example should illustrate the point.

Suppose someone develops an iPhone or Palm Pre application that enables the playing of streamed music from any source, such as an MP3 file on the user's device, or from another source, such as Sirius satellite radio, Pandora, Rhapsody, Live 365 or other source of recordings. In addition, the application has the ability to identify the song being played, automatically search for the song at a popular online lyrics database, and then retrieve and display the lyrics on the user's screen in synchronization with the performance of the song, like a karaoke recording would.

It's not clear whether the ephemeral display of the lyrics on the user's device, line by line, as the recording is being played, would be considered a reproduction of a copy of the lyric. Certainly, an argument can be made that the lyrics are not "sufficiently permanent or stable to permit it to be perceived, reproduced, or otherwise communicated for a period of more than a transitory duration."[13] In other words, they are not fixed in a tangible medium of expression, and therefore, no reproduction of a copy is occurring with the transmission.

However, the lyrics are clearly being displayed publicly — in that the copy of the lyrics on the lyric database are being shown "by means of any device or process, whether the members of the public capable of

[13] 17 U.S.C. Sec. 101. (A work is "fixed" in a tangible medium of expression when its embodiment in a copy or phonorecord, by or under the authority of the author, is sufficiently permanent or stable to permit it to be perceived, reproduced, or otherwise communicated for a period of more than transitory duration. A work consisting of sounds, images, or both, that are being transmitted, is "fixed" for purposes of this title if a fixation of the work is being made simultaneously with its transmission.)

receiving the . . . display receive it in the same place or in separate places and at the same time or at different times." Thus, the music copyright owner could take the position that its, or its exclusive licensee's, exclusive right to publicly display the lyrics are being infringed.

In addition, the resulting combination of the lyrics being displayed in synchronization with a performance of a recording may itself be a derivative work — and it may be a derivative work of the song lyric and also of the sound recording. To infringe a copyright owner's exclusive right to derivative works does not require that a copy be made in the process of creating the derivative work.[14] Thus, perhaps both the owner of the song and the owner of the recording have a complaint for infringement of their respective exclusive rights to make derivative works.

A further question arises as to whether the *user* is infringing the lyric owner's exclusive right of public display and whether the developer of the iPhone application that performs the feat is liable for contributory infringement, under the reasoning of the *Grokster* case.[15]

In any event, the point should be clear that the distinction between a copyright owner's exclusive right of reproduction, exclusive right to make derivative works, and exclusive right to publicly display its works has become increasingly important in the context of digital print.

## C. Who Has the Right to License Digital Print?

In the Third Edition of this book, published in 2002, we stated that the transmission from a Web server to individual computers on the Internet of musical notation or lyrics constitutes both a reproduction of the work and, to the extent displayed on the user's screen, a public display of the work, and, unless the song was being played or rendered in connection with the download or display, none of the performance rights societies have the right to license the transmission. Online music

[14] 1976 House Report 62.

[15] *MGM v. Grokster*, 545 U.S. 913 (2005) (holding that "one who distributes a device with the object of promoting its use to infringe copyrights as shown by clear expression or other affirmative steps take to foster infringement, is liable for the resulting acts of infringement by third parties").

services who wished to make these transmissions would, therefore, have to acquire the necessary licenses directly from the music publishers. In 2002, no licensing standards as to these transmissions had yet emerged.

We hinted, however, as to a potential conflict arising when a music publisher grants exclusive print rights to a print publisher, such as Hal Leonard Corp. or Alfred Music Publishing, and then later desires to directly license to another the right to create MIDI files, which, if created in the right software, gives the user the ability to print the musical notation of the song. Did the prior grant of exclusive print rights to Hal Leonard give the licensee the right to make and grant to others the making of digital print editions of the song? The answer depends upon the wording of the contract. Consider the wording used in Form 12.1:

> Owner hereby grants to Publisher, its successors, assigns, affiliates, subsidiaries and licensees the sole and exclusive right during the term hereof, **to print, sell and distribute in bound or unbound editions or forms**, singly or together with such other compositions and contents as may be selected by Publisher, at Publisher's sole cost and expense, the copyrighted musical composition entitled:
>
> > Title: "I'LL LOVE YOU TILL YOU LEAVE ME"
> > Composer(s): Jennifer Aniston & Brad Pitt
> > Copyright Notice: Copyright © 1980 LITTLE MUSIC PUBLISHING CO.
>
> (which composition is for convenience hereinafter referred to as the "Subject Composition") **in any and all arrangements and adaptations thereof as Publisher may elect,** throughout the world (hereinafter referred to as the "Licensed Territory"), **and to sell the same at such prices and on whatever terms, conditions and discounts as Publisher may in its sole discretion** determine from time to time. (emphasis added)

When a user buys a display of digital sheet music with the right to print out a copy, does that printed copy constitute a violation of the print publisher's "exclusive right . . . to print"? If the answer to that question is yes, then an online music retailer who desires to offer digital sheet music must obtain at least the permission of the print publisher. But the transmission involves more than merely printing — the making of a digital server copy, the public display of the musical notation on the user's screen prior to printing, etc., acts, it would appear that may not be granted under the exclusive grant of print rights above. It would appear, therefore, that the original publisher also has a say in the matter, and may prevent the print publisher from asserting the exclusive right to grant all the licenses necessary for the intended use.

Accordingly, licensees who desire to engage in the online retailing of digital sheet music may find themselves having to obtain licenses from both the original music publisher and the print publisher to engage in the desired activity. This is not always the case, as previously granted exclusive print rights may have reverted to the original publisher and increasingly sophisticated contracts between original publishers and print publishers have addressed the changed circumstances brought about by the new technologies.

As a practical matter, print publishers like Hal Leonard need to maintain good relations with the original publishers from whom they license print rights. Accordingly, even where there is some ambiguity as to whether an exclusive print agreement includes the exclusive right to grant digital print licenses, the print publisher will acquiesce to the position of the original publishers.

Recent print licenses will now directly address whether the print publisher has been granted the exclusive digital print rights. In some instances, the original publisher has consciously granted to the print publisher the exclusive right to grant digital print licenses. Many may do so in exchange for a substantial advance. Consider the wording used in Form 12.3 found on the CD-ROM:

> In addition, Licensor agrees that PUBLISHER shall have the non-exclusive right to manufacture, publish, advertise, distribute and sell digital editions of the Composition(s) and other editions of the Composition(s) via any other such commonly exploited electronic media now known or hereafter devised, throughout the Territory.

When digital print rights are granted to a print publisher, the arrangement may be (a) exclusive, (b) non-exclusive, with the print publisher requiring prior consent from the original publisher before entering into a digital license, or (c) non-exclusive with no permission needed from original publisher prior to entering into a digital license. (Given that a print publisher may have to obtain permission from the original publisher before granting the print license, a digital print licensee may need to consider the additional time that may be required to license certain catalogs).

It may be worth asking why a music publisher would use a print publisher to handle the licensing for digital uses rather than cutting direct deals with the online sheet music retailers, lyric search sites, and other digital print platforms. The world of digital print is moving quickly, with many online retailers, search sites, and subscription services entering the market, each having varying degrees of reputation in the market, some surviving some thriving. In addition, many of these retailers provide large digital revenue reports indicating the amount of transactions or "hits" the pro ration provided to each song. Print publishers add value by staying abreast of the market, negotiating the deals, and helping music publishers aggregate these transaction reports.

## VI. CONSIDERATIONS IN GRANTING EXCLUSIVE PRINT RIGHTS

This section will address the exercise of a copyright owner's exclusive reproduction right with respect to printed music, including exclusive grants by songwriters to music publishers and exclusive grants by music publishers to printed music publishers.

### A. Granting Exclusive Print Rights

Exclusive print rights are generally granted in only the following limited contexts: (1) when a songwriter signs a publishing agreement in which he assigns his copyrights, and all rights under copyright, to a music publisher, and (2) when a music publisher grants to a printed music publisher the exclusive right to print sheet music and/or printed folios.

#### *1. Grants by Songwriters to Music Publishers*

The terms and conditions under which songwriters contract with music publishers are fairly standard, subject to some negotiation depending upon the leverage or the star status of the writer. Standard songwriter publishing contracts provide that the songwriter assign his copyrights in the music, including exclusive print rights and all other rights under copyright, to the music publisher and sets forth royalty rates for each of the various categories of printed editions. The various techniques of negotiating these songwriter agreements on behalf of the songwriter are covered in Chapter 3, on *Songwriter Agreements* and in several excellent books on the music industry.[16]

With respect to print rights, writers customarily receive 5 to 7 cents per copy of sheet music sold in the United States and Canada and 50% of the sheet music royalties received by the music publisher for sales in other countries. The royalty for the use of music in folios is generally 10 to 15% of the wholesale selling price, pro rated among the various songs in the folio. Songwriters are advised to make certain that their contract requires that only *copyrighted royalty-bearing* works in the folio are used in computing his pro rata share. This is to prevent the royalty from being reduced by the inclusion in the folio of music in the public domain, such as the Star Spangled Banner and classical music from prior centuries. It would be reasonable, however, for a music publisher to insist that copyrighted arrangements of public domain songs upon which it must pay royalties should also be included in computing the writer's pro rata share.

Further, where the music publisher does not engage in the business of printing music and distributing printed music itself, choosing instead to grant rights or licenses to independent print publishers who carry on this business under a royalty arrangement with the publisher, the writer should carefully negotiate provisions that assure that a fair portion of the income derived by the music publisher flows through to the writer.

In general, songwriters should not expect much result from hard line negotiations on terms regarding print rights and royalties. Sales of printed music no longer have the financial significance they once enjoyed, and songwriters, rather than struggle over meaningless royalty percentages, should instead devote their energies toward encouraging the music publisher to effect the printing of at least a sheet music edition

---

[16] For example, see, S. Shemel & M. Krasilovsky, *This Business of Music* 8th Ed. (Watson-Guptill 2007); Passman, *All You Need to Know About the Music Business* (Simon & Schuster, 2009); and Brabec & Brabec, *Music, Money and Success* (Schirmer Books 2008).

of their musical compositions. Leaving aside the sentimental value to the songwriter's posterity, printed music can be quite useful in promoting the song to orchestras, bands, and perhaps other artists who might be persuaded to make further recordings of the song. The late songwriter Ben Oakland (*Java Jive*, *If I Love Again*) once befriended and supplied sheet music to the person who played the organ at a professional ballpark. Sure enough, every once in a while one of Ben's songs could be heard on national television during the broadcast of a baseball game, making the song eligible for important performance credits.

Certain agreements between composers of film music and motion picture companies require that the main theme be printed in order for the elected publisher to claim any publishing rights to the composer's music.

### 2. Grants by Music Publishers to Print Music Distributors

As the revenues music publishers derived from printed music declined to a small fraction of total revenues, publishers who once printed their own sheet music and folios, such as Warner/Chappell Music, have long since shut down or sold those operations. In lieu of operating their own printed music divisions, most publishers license the print rights to publishers who specialize in marketing and distributing printed music, such as Hal Leonard Music and Alfred Music Publishing.

Traditionally, music publishers rarely granted print rights to print publishers on an exclusive basis. However, it is now becoming increasingly common for publishers, particularly the majors, to do so. Several years ago, Universal Music granted to Hal Leonard Music the exclusive rights to handle the print and digital print rights of Universal's vast catalog of songs. This was a multi-year exclusive agreement for which Hal Leonard purported to pay in the millions of dollars.

In the few cases that exclusivity is granted, it is normally limited to the printing of sheet music. Permission to print single songs in folios have almost always been on a non-exclusive basis, as publishers desire to remain free to negotiate the use of major songs in folios published by competing print publishers.

Print publishers might require some form of exclusivity in the case of personality folios. For example, a print publisher might acquire a license from a rock star and his publishing company to publish a folio of the star's greatest hits (e.g., "The Elton John Songbook") or may acquire a license to publish a companion folio, a folio of all the songs written and recorded by the artist for a particular album. In such cases, the print publisher would normally insist that the copyright owner not license the same songs for inclusion in a similar songbook or songbook having a confusingly similar title (e.g., "Elton John's Greatest Hits").

Where exclusivity is granted, the music publisher should be certain to reserve (i.e., exclude from the exclusivity) the right to license printed versions of the lyrics, a subject discussed in more detail later in this chapter, and the right to license materials akin to printed music, such as MIDI files, discussed in Chapter 22.

In exchange for granting the exclusive rights to print sheet music, the copyright owner will normally receive from the print publisher a royalty of some fixed number of cents per copy. To participate in price increases, the owner should consider requiring a percentage of the suggested retail or wholesale price in lieu of a fixed amount per copy. The print publisher assumes the costs of production, printing and distribution. The copyright owner usually receives an *advance* against royalties upon the signing of the contract. Should a copyright owner grant print rights to various songs under separate contracts that each provide for an advance against royalties, the owner should consider making sure that these advances are not *cross-collateralized*.[17]

The territory of exclusive sheet music contracts is generally limited to the United States and Canada. Music copyright owners will enter into separate arrangements with subpublishers overseas for the publication of printed editions. These arrangements are discussed in Chapter 5, on *International Subpublishing*. Nevertheless, print deals are beginning to reflect the challenges arising from a changing world marketplace, where the actual printing occurs in one country in multiple languages for shipment worldwide.

The term of these agreements is generally from three to five years. With respect to agreements with a longer term, a copyright owner would be prudent to include in the agreement minimum sales or royalty performance levels. If the print publisher does not achieve the prescribed level in any given year, the original publisher should have the option to convert the agreement to a non-exclusive basis or terminate the

[17] The concepts of advances and cross-collateralization are discussed in Chapter 10.

agreement altogether. Upon termination, the print publisher is generally given, on a non-exclusive basis, a period of six to twelve months to sell off its existing inventory. The agreement should provide, however, that the print publisher may only print enough copies to meet reasonably anticipated demand. This is to prevent the printer from manufacturing a large inventory just prior to termination for the purpose of "stuffing the channel" during the sell-off period.

The copyright owner granting exclusive print rights should also require the print publisher to print regular sheet music copies of the composition during the term of the agreement and to pay all cost of preparation, production, art work, arranging, and engraving.

## VII. Considerations in Granting Physical Print Licenses

### A. Granting Non-Exclusive Licenses to Print Music in Folios

As previously noted, print publishers who have relationships with several music copyright owner/publishers have taken the opportunity to cherry pick popular "hit" songs for inclusion in folios designed for maximum appeal. Many print publishers have increased the sale of slow selling or older standard songs by programming material in specialized compilations such as Music of the Roaring Twenties, Hit Songs of 1950, and compilations of well-known country and western songs. For this reason, it would be prudent for music copyright owners to reserve to themselves their exclusive rights to authorize the printing of music in folios in order to take advantage of the opportunity to license its compositions in these forms of compilations, on a non-exclusive basis, to as many print publishers and selling agents as possible.

Music copyright owners considering a license to permit the use of a song in a folio or songbook should attempt to limit the scope of the license to the specific use requested. For example, if a print publisher desires to clear the license to use a single song in a particular folio, the license should identify the folio by name or description and should expressly state that the song may be used solely in the particular folio named or described. Many standard form agreements for the licensing of a single song in folios will contain a broad grant to use the music in any kind of folio during the term of the license. Of course, the licensee would strongly desire the flexibility afforded by this broader form of license.

The royalty for including a song in a folio is customarily 12.5% of the suggested retail selling price of the songbook, *pro-rated* based upon the number of copyrighted songs in the folio. For example, if there are 10 songs in the folio and the suggested retail price of the folio is $10, a publisher that licensed 2 songs for the folio would receive one-fifth of $10 multiplied by 12.5%, or 25 cents per copy sold, less returns. The copyright owner should be certain that the *pro rata* share is calculated only on the basis of the number of *copyrighted, royalty-bearing* songs in the folio, which would prevent the inclusion of public domain works in the folio from reducing the royalty payable. The print publisher should make certain it is clear that copyrighted arrangements of public domain works upon which it must pay royalties should be included in the pro ration.

Personality folios will probably require the permission of the artist featured in the folio, particularly if biographical material or the artist's likeness or photograph is depicted in the folio. Artists typically demand a royalty of an additional 5% of the suggested retail price for such uses. Many contemporary artists refuse to grant permission for the publication of personality folios. Some artists, who have extensive consent provisions in their music publishing contracts, flatly refuse to allow the licensing of their songs in folios of any form. Artists who place such restrictions on the use of their music are being shortsighted and will someday regret making decisions that tend to sever the important relationship between the song and the listening public.

## B. Granting and Clearing Licenses to Print Lyrics

### *1. Books*

Quoting a song lyric in a book, such as a novel, biography, or other work, typically requires permission from the copyright owner of the song. The use of a lyric is not, as some may believe, automatically a *fair use* of copyright, which is a use that would not require permission of the copyright owner. Fair use is limited to some fairly specific circumstances defined in the copyright law,[18] such as commentary, criticism, news reporting, teaching, or research. Quotation of a lyric, or a portion of

[18] 17 U.S.C. Sec. 107; see also the discussion of the Fair Use doctrine in Chapter 25.

a lyric, in a book or magazine for commercial sale would not typically qualify for the fair use exception. If you have any doubt whether the fair use exception applies, then you should seek a license.

Music publishers will frequently receive calls for permission to use or quote a song lyric, and, if he controls the rights, will usually have no reluctance to granting such a license. Music publishers should not overlook the earnings potential of licensing lyrics of a song. The fees may be small, but they add up, and more important, it is a good way of keeping the song alive. Requests are often received for permission to use lyrics in text books, particularly History and English books, many of which take the opportunity to print an entire lyric by Bob Dylan or Joni Mitchell to illustrate a modern form of poetry or the mood of the country during the 1960.

Music publishers generally grant these licenses using a short-form permission letter. An example of such a letter is included as Form 12.7 on the CD-ROM. Book publishers sometimes make release forms available to its authors to facilitate the clearance of permission to use quotes. Whatever the form used to effect them, such licenses are generally not expensive. The copyright owner will normally charge a small flat fee for the use of a lyric in a book and may require two copies of the book upon publication. For the current fees typically charged for such uses, *see* Chapter 26.

The license is usually limited to using the lyric in one single hard cover edition of the book and its reprints, with additional payments required for paperback editions, translations, abridgments, and editions published by other firms. Fees are normally a one-time, flat fee, which is sometimes limited to the first 100,000 copies or some such negotiated arrangement. The territory is usually worldwide; remember, however, additional permission is required for translated versions. The privilege to use the lyric in other editions would require additional permission and fees. Persons seeking to clear these licenses who expect that permission for use in paperback editions, translations, abridgments, and other editions will be required should attempt to negotiate, in advance, options to pick up permission for these other editions or otherwise ask whether a license for all editions can be paid in advance. The publisher would be reluctant to issue such a license because of the ambiguity of the term "editions," but language such as "edition in book form" might be suggested to provide the comfort required by both parties.

An option arrangement may be more difficult to attain with respect to foreign language editions. Music publishers generally require that licenses for editions printed overseas be sought directly from its affiliated overseas subpublishing company.

### 2. Record Albums

Since the turbulent 1960, with its new forms of rock and psychedelic music, a disturbing number of rock, hard rock, heavy metal and rap songs have been released with lyrics containing offensive, indecent, or violent language. Unsuspecting disc jockeys, after programming and broadcasting these recordings, would became inundated with telephone calls from angry listeners protesting their broadcast. As a result, radio station program directors began requesting that record companies furnish a copy of the lyrics for each new single or album recording submitted for broadcast. Record companies, in turn, began asking music publishers to grant licenses or permission for these lyric reprints.

Many record albums recorded by popular contemporary artists now include a printed set of the lyrics of all the songs on the album, and it has become a standard practice for music publishers to grant permission for this use either for a small royalty or on a *gratis* (i.e., no charge) basis. An example of a permission letter used for this purpose is set forth as Form 12.9 on the CD-ROM.

In cases where the lyrics are not printed on the album, publishers will grant a gratis license to record companies permitting them to distribute printed copies of the lyrics in conjunction with the distribution of promotional copies of the album. An example of a permission letter used for this purpose is set forth as Form 12.10 on the CD-ROM. Many recording companies now request such permission when they submit requests for mechanical licenses, discussed in the next chapter.

### 3. Lyric Magazines

Permission to print entire lyrics is sought by publishers of magazines specially devoted to printing song lyrics. Examples of licenses permitting such use are set forth as Forms 12.11, 12.12, and 12.13 on the CD-ROM.

#### *4. Print Advertising*

Licensing lyrics for use in print advertising involves many of the same considerations in licensing music in connection with advertising in general, which is discussed in great detail in Chapter 20. A form for the license of lyrics for use in print advertising is included as Form 20.3 on the CD-ROM.

## VIII. CONSIDERATIONS IN GRANTING DIGITAL PRINT LICENSES

### A. Granting Licenses for Digital Sheet Music

Once the new digital print delivery platforms were established and users started to experience the convenience of on-demand, at-home access to sheet music, digital delivery of sheet music started to proliferate. Old and new companies started building websites to sell and deliver digital print.

Almost instantly, the industry standard print rate of 12.5% of suggested retail was doubled to 25% for digital sheet music licenses (or 50% of gross receipts).

Form 12.3 found on the CD-ROM, which grants to the print publisher the right to sublicense digital sheet music, provides:

> Based on your ownership/administrative share in each Composition(s), we shall pay you your pro-rata share of the higher amount of either Twenty-Five percent (25%) of the United States marked or suggested retail list price ("MSRP") or Fifty percent (50%) of our Gross Receipts (hereinafter defined) for such digital editions. As used herein, the term "Gross Receipts" means the gross amount of monies actually received by us, or credited to our account in respect of such sales, less any taxes, discounts, returns, and credits.

The duration of these licenses range from one to five years, three years being most typical.

When a music publisher or a print publisher licenses to a digital sheet music retailer the right to sell digital sheet music, the publisher receives an advance, the size of which varies with the size of the catalog, against 50% of gross receipts.

## B. Granting Licenses for Digital Guitar Tabs

Digital guitar tab sites, especially the ones relying on user-generated content (e.g., Ultimate Guitar), are trying to gain legitimacy by entering into the licenses they require to engage in their activity. Print publishers with digital print rights, and music publishers who have reserved their digital print rights, have recently begun granting digital licenses to Ultimate Guitar and other guitar tab sites, such as MXTabs.net.

These arrangements typically involve an advance against a royalty of 50% of gross receipts (including any subscription fees, advertising revenues, etc.). The sites provide reports to the publisher showing the amount of "hits" or "views" of the guitar tabs and pro rate the license fees among the songs and their respective owners accordingly. Some deals require the online retailer to pay a penny rate for each hit or view of the guitar tab. The term of these deals is typically three years.

Recall that a guitar tab, like any musical arrangement, is a derivative work of the song. Where these derivative works are *user-generated*, a question arises about the ownership status of user's tab. Since the publisher has the exclusive right to make derivative works, it could (and should) assert ownership of these derivative works. The guitar tab websites, however, do not want to see the music publisher download all the user-generated tabs and create their own guitar tab websites, or license others, with the repertoire the guitar website has painstakingly collected and organized on the basis of its relationship with their users. To address this problem, the parties typically agree that the music publisher owns the user-generated guitar tabs, but the publisher agrees not to exploit them other than in the context of the license to the guitar tab site. This seems to be a workable solution to the problem.

## C. Granting Licenses for Digital Lyric Database Websites

The vast majority of digital lyric search sites operate illegally. In recent years, several lyric sites that operate legitimately have emerged, and most publishers are happy to work with them, as they provide a regulated source of revenues and provide a hope that, if successful, these legitimate sites will expand and displace the illegal sites by offering a superior user experience. These include Gracenote (which powers a number of lyric sites such as MetroLyrics) and LyricFind.

Print licenses to legitimate lyric search sites work very much the same way as licenses to the guitar tab sites: an advance royalty of 50% of gross receipts (including any subscription fees, advertising revenues, etc.). The sites provide reports to the publisher showing the amount of "hits" or "views" of the lyrics and pro rate the license fees among the songs and their owners accordingly. The term is typically for three years.

Gracenote, now a subsidiary of Sony, has licensed large catalogs of music lyrics directly from music publishers and uses its lyric database to power a number of lyric search websites. Websites that offer lyrics supplied by Gracenote display the following terms of use:

Lyrics Terms of Service

USE OF LYRICS REQUIRES ACCEPTANCE OF THE TERMS BELOW. IF YOU DO NOT AGREE TO THESE TERMS, YOU MUST NOT USE LYRICS.

Lyrics Terms of Use

You may use lyrics ("Lyrics") supplied by Gracenote, Inc. of Emeryville, California ("Gracenote") only for search and display. You agree that you will use Lyrics only for your own personal non-commercial use. You agree not to assign, copy, transfer, or transmit any Lyrics to any third party. YOU AGREE NOT TO USE OR EXPLOIT LYRICS EXCEPT AS EXPRESSLY PERMITTED HEREIN.

You agree that your license to search and display Lyrics will terminate if you violate any of these restrictions. If your license terminates, you agree to cease any and all use of Lyrics. Gracenote and its suppliers reserve all rights in Lyrics, including all ownership rights. You agree that Gracenote, Inc. may enforce its rights under this Agreement against you directly in its own name.

YOU AGREE TO NOT TO USE ANY COPYRIGHTED WORKS SUPPLIED OTHER THAN AS LICENSED. YOU AGREE NOT TO DEFEAT, EVADE OR CIRCUMVENT ANY SYSTEM DESIGNED TO PROTECT LYRICS FROM UNAUTHORIZED USES.

Each Lyric is licensed to you "AS IS." Gracenote, MetroLyrics, and its suppliers make no representations or warranties, express or implied, regarding the accuracy of any Lyric. Gracenote and/or MetroLyrics reserves the right to remove Lyrics for any cause that Gracenote and/or MetroLyrics deems sufficient.

GRACENOTE, METROLYRICS AND THEIR SUPPLIERS DISCLAIM ALL WARRANTIES EXPRESS OR IMPLIED, INCLUDING, BUT NOT LIMITED TO, IMPLIED WARRANTIES OF

MERCHANTABILITY, FITNESS FOR A PARTICULAR PURPOSE, TITLE, AND NON-INFRINGEMENT. IN NO CASE WILL GRACENOTE, METROLYRICS OR THEIR SUPPLIERS BE LIABLE FOR ANY CONSEQUENTIAL OR INCIDENTAL DAMAGES OR FOR ANY LOST PROFITS OR LOST REVENUES.



### D. Granting Licenses for Digital Lyrics in Karaoke Discs

When asked for a license to use musical works in karaoke discs, music publishers issue licenses that include a *synchronization* license to record the song in timed-relation with the audiovisual work (i.e., display of lyrics on the screen) combined with a *digital print license* to include a digital version of the lyrics in the device. Music publishers typically demand an advance against either a flat penny rate per copy or a percentage of revenues (which usually contains a minimum penny rate per copy). A further discussion of licensing music in karaoke discs is set forth in Chapter 22.

### E. Granting Licenses for Digital Lyrics in Karaoke and Online Karaoke

When asked for a license to use musical works in online karaoke, music publishers issue licenses that include a *synchronization* license to record the song in timed-relation with the audiovisual work (i.e., display of lyrics on the screen) and a *digital print license* to include a digital version of the lyrics in the device, conditioned upon a public performance license being obtained by the applicable performance rights society. Music publishers typically demand an advance against a percentage of revenues, typically in the 12% to 15% range. A further discussion of licensing music in online karaoke sites is set forth in Chapter 22.

## IX. CONSIDERATIONS IN GRANTING RENTAL FEES FOR PERFORMANCE MATERIALS

### A. Rental Fee Structure

Rental fees for orchestral works are typically based off a publisher's rate card, taking into account the duration of the work and the level of the orchestra. For example, the New York or Los Angeles Philharmonic would expect to pay more to rent the score and parts for a particular symphony than a community orchestra. Rental fees for performances by major symphony orchestras may be in the range of \$300–\$500 per performance for a relatively brief orchestral work such as an overture and full-length symphonies and concerti will often cost in excess of \$1000 per performance.

### B. Performance License Aspects

Rental fees for performance materials of non-dramatic works, such as symphonies and concerti do not include public performance license fees, which are covered by the ASCAP or BMI license of the venue where the work is to be performed. Accordingly, the rental agreement will generally require that the performance take place in a licensed venue and that the program for the performance is submitted to both the publisher and directly to ASCAP or BMI, as applicable.

Note that, in the case where the performance materials embody an opera, ballet or other dramatico-musical work (as opposed to a standard orchestral musical composition), the ASCAP or BMI license will not cover the performance. *See generally* Chapter 19, on Grand Rights. Accordingly, a separate license to publicly perform the opera or dramatico-musical work will be required. Grand performing rights fees for operas and choreographic works will be licensed by the publisher for a fee in addition to that of the rental of performance materials. Fees for the grand performances of these works are typically done on a percentage of box office while those for choreographic works are more commonly done on a flat-fee basis, often in the \$100 to \$500 range per performance.

## X. Conclusion

At the beginning of the twentieth century, printed music was the body and soul of the music industry, but with the advent of new technologies like the phonograph, radio, and television during the first half of that century, it quickly became an afterthought while performance, mechanical, and synchronization income took an increasing share of music publishing attention. But the Internet has rekindled interest in printed music and music copyright owners are discovering revenue sources for musical notation and lyrics that never before existed. Successful publishers will keep current on these new technologies as they maximize revenues for themselves and the songwriters they represent.

# Appendix to Chapter 12
# Licensing Music in Print and Digital Print (Print Licenses)

Forms (On CD-Rom Only)

| | |
|---|---|
| **Form 12.1** | **Exclusive Print Rights Agreement for All Printed Editions of a Single Song** |
| **Form 12.2** | **Non-Exclusive Print Rights Agreement for Use of a Single Song in a Particular Portfolio** |
| **Form 12.3** | **Alternative Non-Exclusive Print Rights Agreement for Use of a Song or in a Particular Portfolio** |
| **Form 12.4** | **Exclusive Print Rights Agreement for Use of All Compositions of a Musical Group** |
| **Form 12.5** | **Non-Exclusive Print & Digital Print Rights Agreement for Music Publisher's Catalog (Form Used by a Print Publisher)** |
| **Form 12.6** | **Print License for Use of Lyrics in a Book** |
| **Form 12.7** | **Letter Agreement to Extend Lyric Print License for Use in New Edition of a Book** |
| **Form 12.8** | **Print License for Use of Lyrics in a Book** |
| **Form 12.9** | **License for Use of Lyrics in Connection with Commercial Distribution of a Recording** |
| **Form 12.10** | **Print License for Use of Lyrics in Connection with Promotional Distribution of a Recording** |
| **Form 12.11** | **Exclusive License to Print Lyrics in Lyric Magazine for Single Song(s)** |
| **Form 12.12** | **Exclusive License to Print Lyrics in Lyric Magazine for Entire Catalog** |
| **Form 12.13** | **Non-Exclusive License to Print Lyrics in Lyric Magazine for Entire Catalog with Special Payment Provisions** |
| **Form 12.14** | **Rental Agreement for Use of Orchestrations in Live Public Performances** |

# CHAPTER 13

# LICENSING MUSIC IN SOUND RECORDINGS (MECHANICAL LICENSES)

## SUMMARY

6. Copies of the Recording
7. Other Ringtone Terms

## IV. ANALYSIS OF STANDARD U.S. MECHANICAL LICENSE TERMS

## V. CLEARING THE MECHANICAL LICENSE IN THE UNITED STATES

A. Clearing a Song for Use on an Album
B. Bulk Clearances
C. Notice of Compulsory License

## VI. MECHANICAL RIGHTS AGENCIES IN THE UNITED STATES

## VII. INTERNATIONAL MECHANICAL RIGHTS ADMINISTRATION

A. Overview
B. Mechanical License Administration in Canada
   1. Mechanical Royalties Payable by Record Companies
   2. Mechanical Royalties Payable by Online Services
      a. Overview
      b. Role of Record Labels in Administering Online Licensing
      c. Rates Established by the CSI Tariff
         (1) Permanent Music Downloads
         (2) Limited Downloads
         (3) On-Demand Streams
      d. Musical Works Not in the CMRRA or SODRAQ Repertoire
      e. Reproductions Covered
      f. Reporting Requirements
      g. Audit Rights
      h. Late Fees
C. Mechanical License Administration in the United Kingdom
   1. Mechanical Royalties Payable by Record Companies
      a. AP1 Accounting
      b. AP2 Accounting

# CHAPTER 13

# LICENSING MUSIC IN SOUND RECORDINGS (MECHANICAL LICENSES)

In the preceding chapter, we explored the licensing of musical notation and lyrics for use in printed materials (e.g., sheet music and songbooks) and digital print (e.g., downloadable sheet music and electronic guitar tabs). In this chapter, we will explore the licensing of music for use in sound recordings — but only when made and distributed to the public for private use, a use traditionally permitted under what is known as a *mechanical license*.

A *sound recording* is an audio-only work of authorship that results from a fixation of a series of sounds. A sound recording is a completely separate copyrighted work from a musical work embodied in the sound recording. In fact, a musical sound recording is considered a *derivative work* of the song that is the subject of the recording. Because the Copyright Act gives the owner of the song the exclusive right to make derivative works of the song, anyone wishing to make a recording of a song requires the song owner's permission.

A *mechanical license* is a license that permits (i) the audio-only reproduction of music in copies that may be heard with the aid of a "mechanical" device — such as a player piano, a phonograph record, a CD player, personal computers, and digital music players, such as the MP3 players and the Apple iPod — and (ii) the distribution of such copies to the public for private use. Where the making of audio-only copies is not for distribution to the public for private use, but is for some other purpose, such as to facilitate another use, such as a broadcast or other kind of performance or transmission, the license required is called an *electrical transcription license* (which is discussed in the next chapter).

By definition, a mechanical license permits the reproduction of a musical work in *audio-only* form. As mentioned above, when a song is reproduced in audio-only form, the resulting derivative work is called a *sound recording*. The physical media on which sound recordings are embodied are called, *phonorecords.* If you wished to license a song for use in a work that is not an audio-only recording — such as a motion picture, television program, or other audiovisual work, then you would use a *synchronization license* or other form of applicable license, not a mechanical license. Likewise, if you wished to license a song for use in phonorecords that are not intended for distribution to the public for private use, you would use an electrical transcription license, not a mechanical license.

Like the print license, the mechanical license is derived from the copyright owner's exclusive right to reproduce work in copies and phonorecords. Traditionally, mechanical licenses were issued to permit the reproduction of music in "single" records (i.e., the "45" RPM record) long-playing record "albums" (i.e., the 33⅓ RPM record), and piano rolls used in "player" pianos. With the advent of the laser compact disc (CD) in the early 1980s, mechanical reproduction licenses for the reproduction of music in CDs far eclipsed those for analog media. The popularity of musical works distributed in CDs has, however, given way to a new form of delivery, which began in the late 1990s with pioneering streaming services from Real Networks and the first MP3 download service from eMusic. A decade after the launch of these and online music services like them, revenue from mechanical reproduction licenses for the use of music in downloadable and streaming music services will soon eclipse revenue from the sale of CDs. It is estimated that by the end of 2010, over 50% of the revenues from the mechanical reproduction of music will be derived from digital sources.

This chapter sketches the historical and legal background of music recorded on mechanical devices and provides an outline of some of the terms and conditions contained in customary mechanical licenses.

## I. HISTORICAL BACKGROUND

### A. Music Boxes

The first mechanical device designed to perform music was the *music box*, a mechanical instrument whose sounds are produced by a metal comb, the teeth of which are tuned to specific pitches, plucked by pins protruding from a cylinder that is rotated by a wound spring. Originally placed in snuff boxes, watches, and various ornamental objects and commonly used today in jewel boxes, figurines, and children's toys, the music box was invented in 1796 by Antoine Favre, a Swiss watchmaker. In the 1820s, as they became popular in homes, music boxes were mass produced to fulfill demand. By the mid-nineteenth century, several developments in the technology lead to music boxes that could play a wider selection of music for a longer period of time. Sophisticated music boxes, housed in massive pieces of furniture, could provide hours of listening pleasure. In 1885, a box was invented using metal discs instead of cylinders. Costing much less than the earlier box, it sold in vast quantities.

### B. Player Piano Rolls

As music boxes gained popularity, a new form of music box, affording a more familiar quality of performed music, emerged: the *player piano.* A player piano is a piano equipped with a mechanical attachment that depresses the piano's keys by air pressure, reproducing notes that are represented by perforations on a paper roll. Player *piano rolls* are special perforated paper rolls manufactured in large quantity for use in player pianos, and represented the second major form of "mechanical" reproduction of music. From the late 1800s to the late 1920s, the popularity of player pianos reached their height, and millions of player piano rolls, embodying the most popular piano music of that time, were sold annually.

### C. Phonograph Records

Nevertheless, both the music box and player piano industries were soon dealt a major blow by a new technological development: the record player. In 1877, Thomas Edison first reproduced recorded sound by using cylinders made of tin foil, an invention that he called the *phonograph.* The first phonograph was a hand-turned, metal cylinder covered with tin foil. A stylus resting on the tin foil was attached to a diaphragm, which was caused to vibrate as sound was applied. The vibrating diaphragm pressed the stylus onto the surface of the tinfoil, embossing it with a groove *analogous* to the sound that produced the vibrations in the diaphragm (hence, the name *analog* recording, as contrasted with *digital* recording, discussed below). After the groove was complete, the sounds could be "played back," by applying the stylus to the cylinder and rotating the cylinder at the same speed at which the sounds were originally recorded. Later, other inventors substituted a wax-covered cardboard cylinder for the tinfoil, which facilitated the mass production of this new form of mechanical reproduction of music.

The age of cylinders ended in 1912 with the advent of the *78 RPM record*, which was recorded and played back at a speed of 78 *revolutions per minute* (RPM). 78-RPM remained the basic phonograph record speed until 1948, when Columbia Records introduced the *long-playing record* (*LP*), which operated at 33⅓ RPM. Shortly thereafter, RCA Victor introduced a smaller 45-RPM record, which eventually became the medium for popular *single* recordings. For those readers who may be too young to remember, the LP was a vinyl platter, about the same size as a movie laser disc, which was placed onto a *turntable* that rotates at the speed of 33⅓ revolutions per minute; the tone arm, mounted next to the turntable, which contained a diamond stylus, or record *needle*, would be moved on its pivot so that the stylus would come to gently rest in the *groove* etched into the vinyl record (hence, the 60s' slang, *groovy*). As the record revolved, the stylus followed the grooves, spiraling in toward the center of the record, vibrating in response to the variations in the grooves. The vibration was converted into an analogous electrical signal, which, when strengthened by your amplifier, drove your speakers, where the signal was converted back into acoustic vibrations, which could be heard by an ear and understood by the human mind.

### D. Compact Discs

For those readers who may be too old to realize, the LP record has become virtually extinct (though it is now making a comeback among a circle of enthusiasts), having been replaced during the past 20 years by the popular optical *compact disc* (*CD*). Instead of a tone arm, the compact disc player uses a laser beam and a photoelectric cell to read the sound pattern imprinted on the disc as a series of microscopic pits.

During the 1970s, a new recording technique was developed, called *pulse code modulation* (*PCM*), to reduce the noise and distortion unavoidable in earlier recording methods. In PCM, the frequencies and amplitudes, or *analog* vibrations, of the original sound are analyzed and converted into *digital* pulses by the recording device. These digital pulses share the same basic components of the software that run modern computers: 1s and 0s, representing the *on* and *off* signals of the binary code. These "on" and "off" pulses are then processed and reconverted to ordinary sound signals when the record is cut. Upon the advent of the compact disc in the early 1980s, it was discovered that improved sound reproduction could be obtained by maintaining the digital character of the PCM recording in the process of mastering the CD. Thus, in the production of modern CDs, a digital, rather than analog, tape recorder is used during the sessions in which the sounds are (i) *recorded*, (ii) *mixed* or edited, and (iii) *mastered* for mass production.

## E. Computer Chips, Disks, and Other Memory Devices

Upon the advent of the digital computer, there have emerged new forms of mechanical devices upon which music may be stored and played. The microchips, a device that can pack hundreds of thousands of "transistors" onto a sliver of silicon the size of a thumbnail, may embody recorded music. Thus, when you open a greeting card, the song *Happy Birthday* is performed.

The kinds of storage platforms in which sound recordings may be stored have proliferated wildly since the advent of the computer "floppy disks" of the early 1980s. Now, removable computer hard disks, CD-ROMs, and flash memory chips can store music in a variety of formats, such as MIDI, .wav, and MP3 files.

## F. MIDI Files and Digitization

An important step in the development of sound recordings that could be manipulated in the recording production process and later played back on a variety of synthesized musical instruments and other computer devices was the development of the *musical instrument digital interface* (*MIDI*).

MIDI was the first standard computer format or protocol for transmitting music data electronically. With MIDI, instead of being recorded on tape or computer disks and played back via conventional audio tape, record album or CD, the musical sound recording is recorded and played back via computer as a MIDI file, or sequence. A *sequence* is generated in real time by using a MIDI *controller* (typically, a musical instrument keyboard) and a MIDI *sequencer*. The sequencer allows the MIDI data stream to be captured, stored, edited, and replayed. The controller can emulate the sound of nearly any instrument. MIDI files, or sequences, were first typically fixed on floppy diskettes, and then later in CDs, flash memory devices and other media upon which digital information may be stored and retrieved by a computer. They may be replayed in their entirety as recorded or in a number of other ways by replaying only certain instrument parts, by changing the pitch, the tempo or other variables made possible by the nature of the MIDI format and the capabilities of MIDI playback devices (e.g., electronic synthesizers). Most electronic instruments today, such as electronic piano keyboards and synthesizers, are MIDI equipped. Even sounds from acoustic instruments (including the human voice) can be converted to MIDI with special hardware and software. Compared to digitized audio, MIDI data is significantly more compact and more easily manipulated without loss of sound quality.

There are two main advantages to generating sound in MIDI rather than using audio stored in the traditional manner. The first is reduced file size, which reduces the computer memory needed to store the music and the time it takes to transmit a performance electronically. Data files used to store digitally sampled audio in PCM format (such as WAV files) tend to be quite large in comparison to those of regular audio files. For example, files containing high quality stereo sampled audio require about 10 megabytes of data per minute of sound; a typical MIDI sequence might consume less than 10 kilobytes of data per minute of sound. This is because the MIDI file only contains the instructions necessary for a sequencer to render the sounds, not the sounds themselves. The instructions tell the sequencer which notes to play, how to play them, in what pitch to play them, etc., and the sequencer actually creates sounds.

The other main advantage of MIDI involves the ease with which MIDI sequences may be edited or changed when they are played back. Thus, a MIDI sequence may be modified at the time of playback to suit the particular needs or tastes of the listener, such as the tempo or particular key desired by a user of karaoke equipment.

MIDI data is stored in a standardized format, which is compatible with different computer-based sequencers operating on a variety of computer hardware and operating system platforms. The format allows for the inclusion of information such as song name, tempo, time signatures, lyrics, and copyright information.

Since the development of the MIDI standard, far more sophisticated ways of manipulating sound recording have been developed. For example, computer software such as DigiDesign's ProTools allows the user to directly manipulate sound recordings (such as a commercially produced recording in a studio) that have been recorded and transferred to digital form. This enables recording artists and producers to add sophisticated effects, mixing sounds in creative ways, and even incorporating into one recording digital samples of sounds contained in another recording — a practice that has become known as *digital sampling*, discussed at length in Chapter 24.

### G. Downloadable Music Files

Sometime in late 1996, college students, purely on a grass roots basis, began what we now know as the MP3 phenomenon. It began with the simultaneous developments in personal computer hardware and software: the introduction of low cost CD-ROM drives for personal computers, and the development of three small utility software programs: *ripper* software, *MP3 encoder* software, and *MP3 decoder* software.

As personal computer enthusiasts discovered, CD-ROM drives not only allowed you to play interactive CD-ROM software and games, such as electronic encyclopedias and arcade games, it allowed you to use your computer to play compact discs (CDs) containing musical recordings. By downloading from the Internet and installing ripper software on your CD-ROM drive equipped personal computer, you could pop your favorite music CD into your CD-ROM drive, run the ripper software, and within minutes copy all of the tracks from your CD onto your computer's hard drive. The ripper software would actually read each digitally encoded track on your CD, recognize the 0s and 1s comprising the musical recording, and copy the track in digital form to your computer, which would appear as a .wav file on your hard disk.

The average musical recording today is about 3.5 minutes, and 3.5 minutes of musical data, in the form of 0s and 1s, is about 40 megabytes large. Given the average hard disk space at the time, about 2 to

4 gigabytes, it wouldn't take too many of these files to fill up your hard disk. In addition, if you wanted to e-mail the file to a friend, it would take, using a 28bps modem, nearly three hours to upload the file to an e-mail server and the same three hours for the recipient to download the file to his personal computer. At this rate, the sharing of musical files were not very practical. Even on a network, such as the computer network of a college or university, while file transfer rates among students is considerably faster, there's still the problem of the limited storage space on the students' hard disks.

In the 1990s, a group called the Motion Pictures Experts Group (MPEG) working group developed in association with the Fraunhofer-Gesellschaft group a set of standards for compressing audio and video files. MPEG 1, layer 3, later shortened to MP3, is simply a standard set of mathematical algorithms used for compressing sound files into an attractive format for downloading or streaming across the Internet. When the MP3 algorithms are run through a set of musical data, such as a digitally encoded recording, it eliminates virtually all of the 0s and 1s the human ear can't reasonably discern, leaving only those 0s and 1s that are recognizable. Because about 90% of the data in a typical digitally encoded musical recording are not essential to the reasonable listening experience, that 90% could be removed, leaving a greatly compressed file having only a slight reduction in sound quality. Though an audiophile or sound engineer could determine the difference between the original .wav file containing all the data of the recording and the compressed MP3 version of the recording, the latter, although degraded, still provides a quite acceptable listening experience for the average person.

As a result, a musical recording compressed with MP3 encoding software now comprised a file that was 11 times smaller than the original raw data file. In other words, the 40 megabyte file was now compressible to about 3.5 megabytes without a noticeable degradation in sound quality to most listeners. Now, a 1 gigabyte hard disk could contain over 10 times as many musical recordings, and while the raw data file took nearly 3 hours to transfer by modem, the file encoded in MP3 could be transferred in less than 15 minutes.

During the late 1990s, it was estimated that 60% of all college students had access to the Internet using high speed bandwidth. In other words, they were connected to the Internet at speeds offered by

T1 lines. Thus, a 3.5 megabyte MP3 file could be transferred over a school's network in less than 30 seconds.

A file encoded in MP3 is only useful if you can play it, and to play an MP3 file all you needed was MP3 decoding software. In the late 1990s, the Fraunhoffer institute posted on the Internet an example piece of MP3 encoding and decoding software, and actively encouraged its use. Software developers quickly developed various improvements in MP3 encoding software, and then a 19-year-old computer programmer in Sedona, Arizona developed what soon became the most popular MP3 software player, WinAMP. AOL later purchased this software for a reported $70 million.

In late 1997, two software executives working at software startup Pretty Good Privacy, Inc., conceived a business plan based on the notion that a vast number of people were beginning to learn the convenience and joys of *downloadable music* and that there would soon be a demand for legally licensed MP3 files offered at an affordable price. GoodNoise Corporation was formed by Bob Kohn, your coauthor, and Gene Hoffman. In July 1998, the company began offering MP3 files for 99¢ per track and the downloadable music era was born.[1] GoodNoise later changed its name to EMusic.com, Inc. After the company was taken public (NASDAQ: EMUS), it purchased the rights to operate Rollingstone.com. It was later purchased by Vivendi/Universal, almost two years before the launch of Apple's iTunes.

eMusic was the first of a series of websites dedicated to the commercial sale and "download" of music files and today remains the second most popular music download service after the industry leader, iTunes, which is operated by Apple Computer.

There were three primary factors that contributed to the rapid growth of market for these downloadable music files: (1) the availability of high bandwidth networks (to increase the speed at which the files could be reliably transmitted over the Internet), (2) portability (to allow people to take the music with them while they were exercising, riding on the train, or relaxing in a park), and (3) ease of use (to reach people who are not particularly adept at using computers).

---

[1] See Forbes magazine, http://www.forbes.com/forbes/1998/1116/6211051a.html (Nov. 16, 1998) and http://www.forbes.com/1999/02/04/mu5.html (Feb. 4, 1999)

Access to the Internet using high-speed bandwidth has grown to a point where virtually everyone with access to cable television in the home may subscribe to high-speed Internet access. It is estimated that as of January 2005, 48% of those with Internet access at home had a high-speed or broadband connection.[2]

The portability of these downloadable music files took a giant leap forward with development of the Apple iPod, a portable device that fits in the palm of your hand, but that contains (a) a hard disk capable of storing thousands of song titles (b) decoding software that allows the playback of music files stored on the hard disk, and (c) output to earphones. The iPod, which can contain a person's entire music collection, is small enough to fit in a user's shirt pocket and may provide the user with uninterrupted, stereo quality sound while jogging or engaging on other vigorous activity.

With the introduction of the iPod, Apple made significant strides in making the process of purchasing downloadable music files and loading them on to your iPod significantly easier than past systems, but to this day the downloadable music experience does not approach the ease of simply turning on a radio.

## H. Streaming Music

At about the time when entrepreneurs were experimenting with the downloadable music model, others were developing systems that enable a more radio-like experience to the delivery of music over the Internet — the transmission of music by "streaming."

Streaming transmissions are akin to radio broadcasts over the Internet, whether to the public at large or directly to individuals upon request. There are two basic kinds of streaming transmissions: (1) webcasting and (2) "on-demand" or "interactive" transmissions. A webcast is a stream of a series of separate recordings, such as one you might hear over the radio. An on-demand stream is the transmission of a specific recording selected by the user.

Streaming transmissions are effected much like music downloads — to a point. The process starts with "ripping" the recordings off a CD and copying them onto a hard disk. But rather than a user's computer hard

---

[2] Arbitron, *Internet and Multimedia 2005* at 2 (Apr. 19, 2005).

disk, the music files are loaded onto computer "servers" that are associated with a particular Internet website. Users either download a player application or "surf" a website where he or she is typically presented with one or more "playlists" from which to choose, often sorted by particular genres of music (e.g., jazz, pop, rock, etc.). By clicking on the playlist, the series of recordings that makeup the playlist are then transmitted to the user in the order pre-determined by the person who programmed the playlist. The user then enjoys the ensuing webcast in an experience that is very much like listening to a radio station.

In 1995, entrepreneur Mark Cuban started a company called Audionet, which was one of the first music streaming services on the Internet. (At the time, Mr. Cuban frequently posted legal questions on the bulletin board at kohnmusic.com.) Users would surf the Audionet website and could choose to listen to webcasts selected from a list of playlists. In 1998, Audionet changed its name to Broadcast.com, which was later purchased by Yahoo. Since then, others began offering webcasts by similar means, including AOL, RealNetworks' Launchcast, and thousands of other websites.

Alternatively, in lieu of being presented with a list of playlists, a user may visit a website, or download player software, and select from a list of recordings, enabling them to listen to what they want to hear, when they want to hear it, in the order they want to hear it. These are known as on demand or interactive streams. Services such as Real Network's Rhapsody offer these forms of interactive streaming transmissions of recorded music.

### I. Ringtones

A *ringtone* is a sound recording, packaged and often transmitted in the form of a downloadable music file, intended for use in telephones for the purpose of announcing incoming phone calls and text messages. (Technically, a "ring tone" is the sound made by a mobile phone to indicate the incoming communication, but the term, as used by the music industry, more commonly refers to the sound recording file residing on, and engaged by, the phone to render the audible performance of the sounds.) A mobile phone "rings" when the network to which it is associated wirelessly alerts the phone of an incoming call and the phone in turn audibly alerts the user.

The term "ring" originated from the fact that early telephones contained a mechanism consisting of a bell and an electromagnetically driven hammer, which, when stimulated by an electrical signal, produced a ringing sound. The electrical signal powered an electromagnet in the phone, which rapidly moved and released the hammer, striking the bell. The "ring" of modern mobile phones are now electronically produced with the sounds that vary as much as ringtone files can be made to reproduce them.

Commercial mobile phones equipped with ringtone capability — a few preset songs in the MIDI format — were first used in Japan in May 1996, with the release of a phone made by NEC for use on the NTT DoCoMo wireless network. Later that year, a competitor released a mobile phone that could be programmed to render popular melodies. In 1998, a Finnish wireless operator released a service called Harmonium, which contained both tools for individuals to create monophonic ring tones and a mechanism to deliver them over-the-air (OTA) via SMS (i.e., text messaging system) to a mobile handset.

Because of the popularity of personalized ringtones and the technical control wireless service providers maintained over how ringtones were delivered to and operated on the mobile phones they distributed, the mobile providers were able to charge over $3 per ringtone, significantly more than what a typical single download of a popular recording could command in the market. As a result, the concept not only spread quickly, it also developed into a multi-billion dollar industry.

Ringtones range in quality based upon the extent to which they contain the melody, harmony, or more complex mixtures of sounds that embody a musical work or, in some cases, literary work. The most rudimentary form is the *monophonic* ringtone, which merely contains a song's melody (or portion of the melody). A higher form of ringtone is the *polyphonic*, one that contains a song's melody, together with accompanying harmony (or portion thereof). The most complex form of ringtone is known as the *mastertone* (sometimes called, *realtones* or *truetones*), which is usually a pre-existing commercially released sound recording (or portion thereof), played either sequentially or looped in a pre-specified sequence. A mastertone may also contain a portion of a sound recording (and underlying musical work) with a message from the recording artist designed specifically for the ringtone user.

Non-musical mastertones include sound effects (e.g., the sound of a communicator from the original Star Trek series), audio clips from television programs or comedy recordings (e.g., George Carlin's *Seven Words You Can Never Say On Television*), or announcements of baseball plays (e.g., "It's going, going, gone"). Specific ringtones on many phones can be associated with particular callers or kinds of callers (e.g., when my son calls, my phone rings the Beatles hit, *Here Comes the Sun*).

### J. Ring-Backs

An *audible ringing tone* is the ringing sound that a calling party hears while on the telephone after dialing a call, but prior to the call being answered. In recent years, telephone carriers have offered their subscribers the ability to personalize these tones with *caller ring-back tones*, or *ring-backs*. A *ring-back* is an audio-only transmission of a sound recording, which the calling party hears while waiting for the recipient of the call to answer the phone. The ring-back is personalized by the recipient of the call, so that anyone who calls the recipient's number will hear, in lieu of the standard ringing tone of the phone network, a popular sound recording or special greeting selected by the recipient.

The file containing the sound recording comprising the ring-back is hosted on servers maintained by the telecommunications carrier and equipment at the back office of the carrier enables subscribers to replace the standard ringing tone with a personalized audio selection.

Ring-backs do not include *music-on-hold* services — where the sound recording is heard after the user has connected the call, but prior to the user speaking to the caller.

Ring-backs invoke both the reproduction right and the public performance right of the music copyright owner. Because the ring-back copy is not intended for distribution to the public for private user, but rather used to facilitate a performance of the ring-back, the proper reproduction license is an *electrical transcription license*, typically issued by the music publisher or its agent. Because the rendering of the ring-back constitutes a public performance, licenses for such performances are issued by performance rights societies.

## II. LEGAL BACKGROUND

As we have seen in the chapter on *International Subpublishing*, there are significant differences between how mechanical reproductions of musical works are administered in the United States and how they are administered in other countries. These differences stem from provisions in the U.S. Copyright Act that intervene in the markets for these licenses and from industry customs and practices that have evolved relating to how music publishers exploit mechanical reproductions and performances of their musical works.

The greater part of this chapter will focus on how music publishers exploit mechanical reproductions in the United States and how the changing economic landscape brought about by the advent of digital transmissions of music are stressing the traditional regimes for music rights management. Later in the chapter, we will touch on how other countries, such as Canada and the United Kingdom administer mechanical reproductions and how their traditional regimes are being affected by the increasing importance of digital distribution.

### A. U.S. Copyright Law

Even though far removed from the mechanical reproduction of music by piano rolls and music boxes, recordings of music in records, tapes, compact discs, and digital downloads continue to be referred to as *mechanical reproductions.* Likewise, the term used to describe permission to record a copyrighted song on a phonograph record, tape, compact disc, or digital downloads is called a *mechanical license.* Examples of mechanical license agreements are set forth as Forms 13.1 through 13.5 on the CD-ROM.

As noted in Chapter 7, licenses owe their existence to rights. The right to reproduce copyrighted music in mechanical devices, such as phonograph records, piano rolls, and music boxes, is one of the exclusive rights of reproduction held by the copyright owner. This, however, was not always so. In 1908, the United States Supreme Court startled the music industry by deciding that piano rolls and phonograph records were not "copies" of musical compositions and, therefore, not an infringement of the rights in the compositions, but merely part of the mechanism for their reproduction in sound.[3]

With the Copyright Act of 1909,[4] the U.S. Congress quickly overturned the effect of this decision by specifically recognizing the exclusive right of the copyright owner to make mechanical reproductions of music.

## B. Compulsory Licensing

### *1. In General*

In taking this step, however, Congress had more in mind than merely providing rights to the composer. Congress was concerned about certain developments in the piano roll industry that threatened to create a monopoly in the hands of The Aeolian Co., a leading manufacturer of piano rolls. In anticipation of the legal recognition of mechanical reproduction rights, Aeolian had entered into exclusive contracts with many of the major music publishers of that time for the right to make mechanical reproductions of the works in the repertoires of the publishers. With Aeolian having the exclusive mechanical reproduction rights to a vast majority of popular music, few other manufacturers of piano rolls could acquire the licenses they required to compete in the piano roll business.

To thwart this potential monopoly, Congress provided in the 1909 Copyright Act that if the copyright owner used or permitted the use of a copyrighted song for mechanical reproduction, then anyone else could *compel* the copyright owner of a song to permit the making and distribution of mechanical reproductions of that song by payment of a royalty of 2¢ per unit. In other words, if the copyright owner licenses the song for mechanical reproduction at least once, then he could be forced to license it for mechanical reproduction to anyone else thereafter for a fee set by the copyright law.

The provisions of the 1909 Act, and later the 1976 Copyright Act, that *compel* copyright owners to issue mechanical licenses became

---

[3] *White-Smith Music Pub. Co. v. Apollo Co.*, 209 U.S. 1 (1908).

[4] Act of March 19, 1909, ch. 320, 35 Stat. 1075, as thereafter codified in 17 U.S.C. Sec. 1 *et seq.*, and as amended.

known as the *compulsory license* provision.[5] The compulsory license provision applied to other forms of mechanical reproductions of music, such as Edison's cylindrical records, 78-RMP records, 45-RPM records, and 33-RPM records (also known as, LPs, for "long playing" records). These mechanical reproductions of music, including compact discs (CDs), are now called *phonorecords* under the 1976 Copyright Act.

### *2. The Section 115 Compulsory License Provision*

Recall that two of the exclusive rights under copyright enjoyed by an owner of copyright are (1) the reproduction right and (2) the distribution right. Section 115 of the 1976 Copyright Act serves as a limitation on those two exclusive rights by holders of copyrights in nondramatic musical works (i.e., songs and other musical compositions that are not part of a dramatic work, such as a story, opera, or musical). The compulsory license does not pose a restriction on dramatic works, literary works, or other nondramatic literary works. Accordingly, comedy, poetry readings, and other spoken-word works, to the extent they do not constitute musical works, are not subject to the compulsory license.

> *When phonorecords of a nondramatic musical work have been distributed to the public in the United States under the authority of the copyright owner*, any other person, including those who make phonorecords or digital phonorecord deliveries, may, by complying with the provisions of this section, obtain a compulsory license to make and distribute phonorecords of the work.

Thus, the compulsory license only applies *after* the musical work has been *distributed* in the United States. Thus, if you write a song, and own the copyright in that song, you may not be compelled to license it for use in sound recordings unless and until you have authorized the making of a sound recording of your song. Further, you can keep another from making a sound recording of your song until phonorecords of the first recording have been *distributed* to the public.

---

[5] 17 U.S.C. Sec. 115. Legislation enacted in 1995 amended Sec. 115 making the digital delivery of music files, or "digital phonorecord deliveries," subject to the compulsory license provision.

> A person may obtain a compulsory license only if his or her primary purpose in making phonorecords is to distribute them to the public for private use.

If your purpose is to make a phonorecord primarily for the purpose of facilitating a broadcast, you may not avail yourself of the compulsory license; you will need to obtain a license — often called an electrical transcription license — on terms negotiated with the song's copyright owner. To use the compulsory license, your manufacture and distribution of the phonorecords must be made with the permission of the owner of the sound recording in which the song is embodied.

> Any person who wishes to obtain a compulsory license under this section shall, before or within thirty days after making, and before distributing any phonorecords of the work, serve notice of intention to do so on the copyright owner. If the registration or other public records of the Copyright Office do not identify the copyright owner and include an address at which notice can be served, it shall be sufficient to file the notice of intention in the Copyright Office. The notice shall comply, in form, content, and manner of service, with requirements that the Register of Copyrights shall prescribe by regulation.

The practice of following the above procedure to obtain a mechanical license is rare. Because the requirements of strict compliance with the statute and its regulations are burdensome (e.g., filing of notice, monthly accounting), most mechanical licenses are obtained by voluntary means — through an application to a music publisher or its licensing representative and the issuance by the publisher of a form mechanical license agreement.

Nevertheless, the terms of voluntary licenses — subject to certain typical exceptions to be discussed below — tend to be very closely aligned with the terms of the compulsory license provision. Failure to either obtain a voluntary license or serve the required notice forecloses the possibility of a compulsory license and, in the absence of a negotiated license, renders the making and distribution of phonorecords actionable as acts of copyright infringement.

> To be entitled to receive royalties under a compulsory license, the copyright owner must be identified in the registration or other public

> records of the Copyright Office. The owner is entitled to royalties for phonorecords made and distributed after being so identified, but is not entitled to recover for any phonorecords previously made and distributed.

It thus behooves copyright owners of musical works to regularly register their copyrights with the U.S. Copyright Office. Upon the advent of online music subscription services, which engage in the deliveries of limited downloads and on-demand streams (discussed below), new online services find themselves in a position of having to clear potentially millions of mechanical licenses. Rather than attempting to obtain voluntarily licenses, which can be time-consuming, these services frequently avail themselves of the compulsory license provision itself, filing the requisite notices and proceeding to comply with the provision in accordance with the statute and its related regulations. In this environment, it is more important than ever that owners of musical works register their copyrights, lest they lose the privilege of collecting mechanical royalties from these services for uses occurring prior to copyright registration.

Section 115 established the royalty rate to be applied to every phonorecord made pursuant to a valid compulsory license.

> [T]he royalty under a compulsory license shall be payable for every phonorecord made and distributed in accordance with the license. . . . With respect to each work embodied in the phonorecord, the royalty shall be either two and three-fourths cents, or one-half of one cent per minute of playing time or fraction thereof, whichever amount is larger.

The second sentence of the above section set forth the mechanical royalty rate that existed at the time the 1976 Act was passed. It has since been increased many times.

### *3. Statutory Rate and Its History*

The prescribed mechanical royalty set forth in, or otherwise established pursuant to, the compulsory license provision of the U.S. Copyright Act is referred to as the *statutory rate.*

When Congress created the compulsory license as part of the 1909 Act, it set the statutory rate for the making and distributing of mechanical reproductions (e.g., piano rolls) at 2¢ for each musical work embodied in the reproduction. This rate remained in effect until Congress revised the copyright laws in 1978, with the passage of the 1976 Copyright Act.

In the 1976 Act, Congress codified the mechanical compulsory license as Section 115 and raised the statutory rate to 2.75¢ per phonorecord or .6¢ per minute of playing time or fraction thereof, whichever amount was larger. Congress also determined that future adjustments to the statutory rate would not be set by statute but rather would be made by the newly established Copyright Royalty Tribunal, an administrative body created by Congress in the 1976 Act to administer the compulsory license, among other things.

In 1980, the Tribunal conducted the first, contested proceeding to set rates for the Section 115 compulsory license. The copyright owners were represented by, among others, National Music Publishers Association (NMPA) and the Nashville Songwriters Association International, while the licensees were represented primarily by Recording Industry Association of America (RIAA). After taking 46 days of testimony from 35 witnesses, which comprised over 6,000 pages of transcripts, the Tribunal issued a lengthy decision in which it substantially increased the existing 2.75¢ rate per phonorecord made and distributed to 4¢ per phonorecord, or three quarters of 1¢ per minute of paying time or fraction thereof, whichever amount was larger. The Tribunal also adopted a series of automatic adjustments to occur in 1983, 1984, and 1986. By 1986, the rate had been increased to the larger of 5¢ per musical work or .95¢ per minute of playing time or fraction thereof.

The next adjustment of the statutory rate was scheduled to begin in 1987 when, on March 18, 1987, the Tribunal received a joint proposal from the NMPA and the Songwriters Guild of America (SGA), on behalf of the copyright owners, and the RIAA, on behalf of licensees, seeking adoption of rates voluntarily negotiated by the parties. The settlement, which was ultimately adopted by the Tribunal, set the rate at 5.25¢ per track beginning on January 1, 1988, and established a schedule of rate increases based on the percentage change in the consumer price index (CPI) every two years over the next 10 years, except that the rates would remain the same when the CPI declined and could not be increased in any single adjustment by more than 25%. Over the ensuing decade, the rate increased until 1996, when the rate was 6.95¢ per track or 1.3¢ per minute of playing time or fraction thereof.

In 1993, Congress abolished the Copyright Royalty Tribunal and replaced it with the Copyright Arbitration Royalty Panel (CARP) system. The CARPs were to set reasonable rates and, for the first time, terms for the Section 115 compulsory license, subject to review by the Librarian of Congress (Librarian). Because the rates set by the Tribunal pursuant to the 1987 settlement were set to expire on December 31, 1997, the year 1997 was a window year for adjusting the statutory rate. The first step in the process of adjusting rates under the CARP system was for the Librarian to initiate a voluntary negotiation period to allow copyright owners and users to negotiate terms and rates of the license. The Librarian set the negotiation period to run from July 17, 1996, through December 31, 1996. The second step of the process was to convene a CARP to determine reasonable terms and rates for parties not subject to a negotiated agreement.

The convening of a CARP was not necessary because NMPA, SGA, and RIAA were able, after lengthy negotiations, to reach an agreement regarding the adjustment of the physical phonorecord and digital phonorecord delivery royalty rates. Under the settlement, which was ultimately adopted by the Librarian, the rate for physical phonorecords was set at 7.1¢ per track beginning on January 1, 1998, and a schedule was established for fixed rate increases every two years over the next 10-year period with the rate beginning on January 1, 2006, being the larger of 9.1¢ per track or 1.75¢ per minute of playing time or fraction thereof.

The rates adopted for digital phonorecord deliveries for the 10-year period were the same as those set for physical phonorecords, and the rates for incidental DPDs were deferred until the next scheduled rate proceeding. Those rates for physical and digital phonorecords remained in effect until March 1, 2009, the effective date of regulations for a new statutory rate set by the newly established Copyright Royalty Board. Such new rates are discussed below.

### *4. Applicability of the Compulsory License to Digital Music Downloads*

On November 1, 1995, Section 115, the compulsory mechanical license provision, of the U.S. Copyright Law was amended to cover the delivery of sound recordings of musical works by digital transmission. This amendment, which became effective on February 1, 1996, was part of the *Digital Performance Right in Sound Recordings Act of 1995*, discussed further in Chapter 23, on *Licensing of Sound Recordings*.

The Digital Performance Rights in Sound Recordings Act of 1995 (the "1995 Act") was enacted to specifically address the concerns raised by copyright owners of musical works and sound recordings. This important legislation made two significant, but distinct, changes affecting the licensing of musical works and sound recordings under U.S. copyright law: (1) to address the questions raised by *webcasting*, it created a new, but limited, digital public performance right for sound recordings, and (2) to address the questions raised by *downloadable music* files, it broadened the Copyright Act's existing compulsory mechanical license provision to include the reproduction and delivery of musical works in sound recordings by digital transmission.

The operative portion of the compulsory license provision was amended by the addition of the following italicized words in the first two sentences of Section 115(a)(1):

> When phonorecords of a nondramatic musical work have been distributed to the public in the United States under the authority of the copyright owner, any other person, *including those who make phonorecords or digital phonorecord deliveries*, may, by complying with the provisions of this section, obtain a compulsory license to make and distribute phonorecords of the work. A person may obtain a compulsory license only if his or her primary purpose in making phonorecords is to distribute them to the public for private use, *including by means of a digital phonorecord delivery.*

Thus, the 1995 Act created a new term of art under the U.S. Copyright law: the *digital phonorecord delivery*.

> A digital phonorecord delivery is each individual delivery of a phonorecord by digital transmission of a sound recording which results in a specifically identifiable reproduction by or for any transmission recipient of a phonorecord of that sound recording, regardless of whether the digital transmission is also a public performance of the sound recording or any nondramatic musical work embodied therein.

Equally as important, the 1995 Act made it clear that:

> A compulsory license under this section includes the right of the compulsory licensee to distribute *or authorize* the distribution of a phonorecord of a nondramatic musical work by means of a digital transmission which constitutes a digital phonorecord delivery . . .

In other words, anyone who has obtained a compulsory license, or a voluntary license following the terms of the compulsory license provision, for the making of phonorecords containing a sound recording of the licensed musical work, need not seek an additional mechanical license to make digital phonorecord deliveries of such sound recording. Moreover, since the licensee has the right to *authorize* the distribution of the sound recording (and the song it embodies) by means of digital phonorecord deliveries, the record company licensee could authorize eMusic, iTunes, and other download music services to do so.

The resulting license to the download service has become known as a *pass-through* mechanical license — because the mechanical license was not issued directly from the music publisher to the download service, but rather passed through the record company under the authority of its existing mechanical license. Music publishers claim that not all mechanical licenses issued may be passed through. Some mechanical licenses (see below) were limited to a certain configuration — phonorecords manufactured in LP, cassette, or CD form — deviating from the terms of the compulsory license provision. The major record companies, however, often relied on the mechanical licenses issued as part of controlled composition clauses contained in their contracts with artists; whether or not the rate limitation in those clauses could be enforced under the 1995 Act, the mechanical licenses were not limited to any particular configuration.

Music publishers object to the pass-through license, because it gives them much less visibility into the making of phonorecords of their musical works. While they have the right to audit the record company to whom they issue mechanical licenses, there is no such right to audit iTunes (which is actually making the DPDs), because the music publisher has no direct relationship with iTunes. Moreover, while record labels are obliged to report mechanical royalties due on DPDs made by services such as iTunes, they are not obliged to report where such DPDs were made (e.g., iTunes, eMusic, or other download services). Thus, even if the publishers were to have audit rights vis-à-vis the download services, without the relevant information from the record labels, productive audits would be problematic.

Record labels prefer the pass-through license, because it gives them greater flexibility in the licensing of their recordings online, allows them to take advantage of any applicable controlled composition clauses in their artist contracts (see below), and gives them the benefit of the "float," the time value of money from the time they receive it from the download service until the time they have to pay it to the music publishers.

In February 1999, the Harry Fox Agency (HFA) and eMusic announced an agreement under which HFA would license their musical works directly to eMusic for the digital phonorecord deliveries they made of sound recordings licensed from independent record companies. (The major labels refused to license their repertoire to eMusic, because eMusic insisted on using the MP3 format.) eMusic was willing to do this because it was concerned that, if independent record labels did not have the proper mechanical licenses it required to engage in DPDs or did not properly pay the music publishers mechanical royalties due on DPDs made, eMusic, as the one doing the reproduction, could be liable for copyright infringement. eMusic was also concerned that good relations with the music publishers would be key factor in its success. A major lawsuit at such an early stage of eMusic's life could threaten its ability to raise financing and ultimately its very existence. Thus, eMusic paid mechanical royalties directly to the music publishers and HFA had a direct audit right.

Years later, when the major record companies entered their first agreements with Apple's iTunes store, they insisted on invoking their right under Section 115 and issued pass-through mechanical licenses to iTunes and Apple insisted that all labels submitting sound recording for digital download on iTunes issue similar pass-through licenses. eMusic later began requiring that their labels do the same.

In 2006, legislation was introduced to reform Section 115, which would have, among other things, eliminated the pass-through license, forcing iTunes and other download services to pay mechanical royalties on DPDs directly to music publishers and their representatives.[6] The legislation was never voted on by the full House or Senate, but music

[6] Section 115 Reform Act (SIRA), H.R. 5553 in the 109th Congress.

publishers are likely to revive the concept as soon as it looks likely that Congress would be receptive.

In 2003, the Copyright Act was amended to replace the CARP system of adjudicating statutory rates with a Copyright Royalty Board (CRB) consisting of three judges appointed by the Librarian of Congress.[7] In addition to setting the statutory rate, the CRB is authorized to adopt as a basis for statutory terms and rates an agreement concerning such matters reached among some or all of the participants in a rate proceeding.

On January 6, 2006, the CRB issued a notice announcing the commencement of a proceeding to determine a new statutory rate for both physical reproductions, as well as for digital downloads. Following nearly three years of reviewing briefs submitted, discovery taken, and testimony offered by virtually every corner of the music industry, the CRB published a decision that not only established a new statutory rate for physical mechanical reproductions and digital downloads, but also adopted an industry settlement regarding the statutory rates for so-called, "incidental downloads," covering mechanical license fees payable by services engaging in on-demand streams and tethered downloads, either on a subscription basis or under an advertising-based revenue model.

Effective March 1, 2009, the statutory rates to be paid to music publishers for the mechanical reproduction and distribution of their musical works in physical and permanent digital downloads is the larger of 9.1¢ or 1.75¢ per minute of playing time (or fraction thereof). The statutory rate for ringtones was set at 24¢. The CRB also established, for the first time, a late payment fee of 1.5% per month measured from the date the payment was due.

Details of the statutory rates for incidental downloads are described below.

### 5. *Applicability of the Compulsory License to Server Copies Used to Facilitate Digital Downloads*

It may be recalled that the compulsory license provision only applies to phonorecords and digital phonorecord deliveries that are *intended for distribution to the public for private use*. Copies reproduced for other purposes, such as facilitating broadcasts or other public performances, are not subject to the provision. Under what authority does an online music

[7] 17 U.S.C. Sec. 801 *et. seq.*

download service have to make copies of musical works on servers for the purpose of facilitating the making of digital phonorecord deliveries? The Copyright Office provided an answer to that question in an interim regulation that became effective on December 8, 2008. The interim regulation clarifies that whenever a transmission results in a digital phonorecord delivery, all reproductions of the musical work made for the purpose of making the DPD are also included as part of the DPD. Thus, any server copies made for the purpose of facilitating a digital phonorecord delivery is covered by the license that authorized the making of the digital phonorecord deliveries.

The Copyright Office recognized that the compulsory license provision has traditionally provided coverage beyond those phonorecords made and distributed to the public for private use, so long as such phonorecords were used to achieve the primary purpose of making and distributing the phonorecords under the compulsory license provision. When it enacted the 1976 Act, Congress stated that it intended for the license to cover "every possible manufacturing or other process capable of reproducing a sound recording in phonorecords." H. Rep. No. 94-1476 at 110. The right to make "masters" used in the manufacture of records for public distribution have long been understood to be included in the compulsory license to make the records. Similarly, server copies, as well as all intermediate copies used to make and distribute DPDs under the compulsory license, perform a function in the world of DPDs that is parallel to master recordings and manufacturing equipment in the physical world.

Accordingly, the Copyright Office issued an interim rule that confirms that server copies and intermediate reproductions may come within the scope of the compulsory license:

> A digital phonorecord delivery includes all phonorecords that are made for the purpose of making the digital phonorecord delivery.

Amending 37 C.F.R. Section 201.18 (effective December 8, 2008).

### *6. To What Extent Is a Performance License Required to Make a Digital Phonorecord Delivery?*

With a proper mechanical license in hand to make digital phonorecord deliveries, one would think that it would be safe to proceed in making digital phonorecord deliveries. Not so fast. The performance rights societies (e.g., ASCAP, BMI, and SESAC) have been taking the position that a *performance* license is required to effect a digital phonorecord delivery, even though a statutory mechanical reproduction license has already been obtained for the same delivery. In their view, all transmissions of songs constitute performances of songs, whether or not they result in a specifically identifiable phonorecord made by or for the transmission recipient, and therefore, they say, one must pay a public performance fee for these download transmissions, even after the statutory rate for the mechanical reproduction has been paid.

In the late 1990s, when digital downloading began, the performance rights societies offered to enter into "stand-still" agreements with online download services, under which neither the society nor the service conceded the point in controversy. eMusic, for example, conceded that on-demand streams of 30-second samples of recordings constituted a performance of the underlying musical work, but rejected the notion that a performance license was required for a permanent download.

eMusic, and services like it, asked: if you are paying 9.1¢ for a digital phonorecord delivery, why must you also pay for its performance, particularly if the phonorecord is not truly performed or in any way rendered during the transmission? Those who have answered that question in the negative take the position that, since no performance occurs in the download process, then no performance license should be required. To charge both a reproduction and a performance fee for a transmission, the purpose of which is a mere delivery of a phonorecord to the consumer — not unlike the delivery of a CD — constitutes a form of "double-dipping" by the music publishers.

The performance rights societies, in support of the contrary position, have pointed to the definition of "digital phonorecord delivery":

> A "digital phonorecord delivery" is each individual delivery of a phonorecord by digital transmission of a sound recording which results in a specifically identifiable reproduction by or for any transmission recipient of a phonorecord of that sound recording, *regardless of whether the digital transmission is also a public performance of* the sound recording or *any nondramatic musical work embodied therein*. (emphasis added).

The italicized language suggests, they say, that a digital phonorecord delivery *may* involve the public performance of the musical work embodied in the sound recording. Yet, only that it *may* do so is the best you can say about the language. It does *not* say that a download *does* constitute a performance. If Congress intended to definitively answer the question, it certainly could have done so in unambiguous terms, such as, "A digital transmission containing a sound recording that results in a digital phonorecord delivery constitutes a performance of any musical work embodied in that sound recording." But it didn't. Quite possibly, Congress recognized that some digital phonorecord deliveries may be performed or "streamed" for listening by the user while it is being downloaded; hence, the italicized language may have been needed to make certain that a digital phonorecord delivery will still be deemed such, even if the digital transmission happens also to constitute a public performance.

The performance rights societies could also point to the definition of *public performance* under the Copyright Act:

> To perform . . . a work *publicly* means —
>
> (1) to perform or display it at a place open to the public or at any place where a substantial number of persons outside of a normal circle of a family and its social acquaintances is gathered; or
>
> (2) to transmit or otherwise communicate a performance or display
>
> of the work to a place specified by clause (1) or to the public, by means of any device or process, whether the members of the public capable of receiving the performance or display receive it *in the same place* or *in separate places* and *at the same time* or *at different times*. (emphasis added).

It appears, from the italicized language, that it does not matter whether you hear the performance at the same time as you download the file. Certainly, when a recording is being streamed to you, it is first *buffered* in your computer's temporary memory, before the recording is actually played so that you can hear it. What is the difference between storing the recording in temporary memory and storing it on your hard disk (which is typically the case with a digital phonorecord delivery) prior to your hearing the recording?

The problem with these arguments is that the above definition concerns not what a *performance* is, but what it means to perform a work *publicly*, in contradistinction to performing a work *privately*. Even if the transmission of a work is considered a public one, it may still not constitute a *performance*. According to the Copyright Act:

> "To *perform* a work means to recite, render, play, dance, or act it, either directly or by means of any device or process. . . ."

It may well be asked, where, for purposes of the definition of "perform," is the "rendering" or the "playing" of the work in the transmission of a downloaded music file?

Clearly, a transmission need not be initially audible to constitute a performance. A radio broadcaster is not transmitting "sounds," but rather electromagnetic waves that the end-user converts into sounds with a radio receiver. Nevertheless, there is no question that such a broadcast is a performance. A transmission may reach the public in "any form" and qualify as a public performance.

The requirement of a presence in a transmission of a "capability of simultaneous rendering or showing of the work" is nowhere to be found in the legislative or case law history of the public performance right. More important, given the emergence of greater bandwidth of transmission media and improved data compression techniques, it would be hard to imagine any transmission of a work that does not have the *capability* of a simultaneous rendering or showing of the work. Any compilation of digital data capable of rendering a performance or display could be interpreted on-the-fly to render that performance or display perceivable at the time of the transmission at the election of the recipient. In other words, a recipient should be in a position to decide whether a receipt of a musical work by transmission is rendered audibly at the time of the transmission. But why should the user's decision to listen to the work as it is being transmitted have a bearing on whether the transmission itself is a public performance? The legislative history clearly states that for a transmission to constitute a performance there is no requirement that any potential audience member actually tune-in to the transmission. Even if a radio receiver is tuned into a broadcast, radio equipment is fully capable of receiving radio signals and recording them on tape even if the loud speakers attached to the radio receiver are not turned on and no user is around to "listen" to the transmission. Thus, whether or not a receiver is tuned in, or is tuned in and the speakers are turned off, the transmission constitutes a performance of the song. In other words, the fact that the performance is not perceived when it is transmitted does not make the transmission any less of a public performance. A transmission is complete once it is sent, and it constitutes a performance (or display) whether or not it is ultimately heard (or viewed) by an audience.

Any other result could cause perverse practical problems. For example, suppose a particular transmission initiates a simultaneous audible rendition, but, because the transmission of the work occurs at a speed that is much faster than the time it takes the user to perceive the work audibly, the entire file is fully downloaded before the audible rendering is completed. Does this constitute the simultaneous rendering or showing of the work necessary for the transmission to constitute a public performance?

Would not a sender or recipient of the work have the ability to avoid having a particular transmission constitute a public performance by merely avoiding an on-the-fly audible perception of the work as it is being transmitted? Could not a cable television operator avoid having to pay public performance royalties by transmitting a motion picture to the video tape recorders of its home subscribers under an agreement with its subscribers that the motion picture will not be viewed by the subscriber until after the transmission is complete, or after it has begun?

More realistically, could not a passive second carrier of a television transmission pick up a television transmission from an initial transmitter and turn around and retransmit the signal to a cable system (which then retransmits the signal to the public), avoiding liability for infringement of the public performance? The answer is yes, but not on the basis that his reception and retransmission did not involve an audible or visual rendering of the signal: The secondary transmission is exempt under Section 111 of the Copyright Act. If the inaudibility of the signal at the time of the retransmission meant that the retransmission was not a public performance, there would be no need for such an exemption.[8]

---

[8] *WGN Continental Broadcasting Co. v. United Video, Inc.*, 693 F.2d 622, 625 (7th Cir. 1982) (holding that "the Copyright Act defines 'perform or display . . . publicly' " broadly enough to encompass indirect transmission to the ultimate public); see also *Hubbard Broadcasting, Inc. v. Southern Satellite Sys, Inc.*, 593 F. Supp. 808, 813 (D. Minn. 1984) (stating that "under the broad definitions found in Section 101 of the Copyright Act, a transmission is a public performance whether made directly or indirectly to the public and whether the transmitter originates, concludes, or simply carries the signal"), *aff'd*, 777 F.2d 393 (8th Cir. 1985), *cert. denied*, 479 U.S. 1005 (1986).

The performance rights societies could take the position that a sound recording of a work is itself a "rendering" (i.e. a performance, albeit a recorded one) of the work. This is as opposed to sheet music where the musical notations only are listed. When one digitally transmits the sound file, one is engaged in a transmission of the recorded performance, as hence, it may be said, the requisite "rendering" is taking place. This argument would be plausible but not for the definition of "sound recordings," which is defined in the Copyright Act as "works that result from the fixation of a series of sounds." Thus, by definition, a sound recording is a *fixation* of sounds, not a *rendering* of sounds. Arguably, then, by transmitting a sound recording you are transmitting a fixation of sounds, not a performance or rendering of them.

A better argument, from the performance rights societies' perspective, would be to assert that the downloading of a digital file is part of a *process* that results in a rendering or playing of the work at the recipient's end. Recall that to perform a work means to render or play the work, "either directly or *by means of a device or process*." Thus, arguably, the process of transmitting the bits constituting a digital sound recording file, the recipient's buffering those bits or saving them to his hard disk or other storage media, and his playing of the bits, either as the bits are being downloaded or later, even after the entire file has been saved to disk, constitutes a playing or rendering of the sound recording, "either directly or by means of a device or process." Because technology now permits the playing of the bits either as the bits are being downloaded or after all the bits in the file have been received, the distinction between a digital phonorecord delivery (DPD) and a non-DPD (i.e., a purely "streaming" digital audio transmission) is being blurred.

The difference between a technologic step that involves a rendering or showing and one that does not is analogous to the distinction computer scientists make between the use of an *interpreter* program broad enough to encompass indirect transmission to the ultimate public[9] and

[9] *See also Hubbard Broadcasting, Inc. v. Southern Satellite Systems, Inc.*, 593 F. Supp. 808, 813 (D. Minn. 1984) (stating that "under the broad definitions found in Section 101 of the Copyright Act, a transmission is a public performance whether made directly or indirectly to the public and whether the transmitter originates, concludes, or simply carries the signal"), *aff'd*, 777 F.2d 393 (8th Cir. 1985), *cert. denied*, 479 U.S. 1005 (1986).

a *compiler* program. Both interpreters and compilers are used to allow a computer program — "a set of statements or instructions to be used directly or indirectly in a computer to bring about a certain result" to execute or operate — in other words, be rendered or shown — on a computer. Both interpreters and compilers translate the set of statements, written in a language that human beings can easily understand, into a set of statements that the computer can understand — basically, a series of 0s and 1s.

In computer parlance, an *interpreter* program translates the set of statements *one statement at a time* — in effect, translating the statements "on-the-fly" into something the computer can understand. The computer follows those instructions concurrent with the translation or interpretation process. By contrast, a *compiler* program translates the set of statements in "batch mode" — that is, all at one time, in advance — and, only after the entire translation is completed, is the result, a copy of the program in a different form (known as an executable file), ready to run on the computer. Thus, a rendering or showing concurrent with the transmission would be analogous to using an *interpreter* to render or show the performance or display; a rendering or showing after the transmission would be analogous to using a *compiler* to render or show the performance or display.

Computer scientists generally view the choice between using an interpreter or a compiler in a given situation a matter of design choice, depending upon what operation he wants to optimize when running the program. Will users make a similar choice when deciding whether to experience a rendering in *real-time* as the transmission is being downloaded or to receive the work in *compressed* form for subsequent viewing or listening? It should be clear that, whether a user chooses to employ an *interpreter* (i.e., for real-time rendering or showing) or a *compiler* (i.e., for compressed time and subsequent rendering or showing), each constitutes an act by which the work is shown or rendered to the public "whether members of the public are capable of receiving the performance or display receive it in the same place or in separate places or in separate places and at the same time or at different times."

As pointed out elsewhere in this book, however, given increasing bandwidth, the user will nearly always download first, that is, cache the file, and then render it, but conceivably the rendering will begin when the first bit is saved by the user. The performance rights societies may argue that all of these transmissions should be considered performances, merely because it is too impractical, on a case-by-case basis, to make a distinction between which download transmissions are simultaneously rendered and which are not.

In addition, the performance rights societies have argued that a digital phonorecord delivery provides an added value to the consumer — that is, with the advent of digital deliveries, the consumer no longer has to schlep down to a record store to buy a CD; he or she can just order it online and receive it in minutes. Consequently, that added value should be paid for. This argument, however, was first made before the success of companies like Amazon.com, from whom you can now order a CD and have it sent to you by overnight courier. What practical difference does it make whether the tracks constituting a record album come to you overnight or several minutes or hours after you have requested them to be downloaded?

The question of whether the downloading of a digital music file embodying a particular song constitutes a public performance of that song within the meaning of the U.S. Copyright Act was first officially taken up by the U.S. Department of Commerce:

> A distinction must be made between transmissions of *copies* of works and transmissions of *performances* or *displays* of works. When a copy of a work is transmitted over the wires, fiber optics, satellite signals or other modes of digital form so that it may be captured in a user's computer without the capability of simultaneous "rendering" or "showing," it has rather clearly not been performed. *U.S. Department of Commerce, Information Infrastructure Task Force, the Report of the Working Group on Intellectual Property Rights at 71 (September, 1995).*

In 2001, the U.S. Copyright Office agreed:

> Although we recognize that it is an unsettled point of law that is subject to debate, we do not endorse the proposition that a digital download constitutes a public performance even when no contemporaneous performance takes place. . . . [T]o the extent that such a download can be considered a public performance, the performance is merely a technical by-product of the transmission process that has no value separate from the value of the download. . . . [I]t is our view

that no liability should result under U.S. law from a technical "performance" that takes place in the course of a download. *U.S. Copyright Office, Digital Millennium Copyright Act Section 104 Report to the United States Congress (Marybeth Peters, Register of Copyrights), at xxvii-xxviii (August 29, 2001).*

Shortly thereafter, the performance rights societies arguably conceded the point in comments filed with the Copyright Office in early 2002:

> We appreciate that different uses of different rights may be valued differently in the marketplace. At opposite ends of the spectrum, it can be argued that 'pure' audio-only downloads should not require payment for the public performance right and that 'pure' audio-only webcast should not require payment for the mechanical right. But in between those poles lies many uses for which . . . both mechanical and performance rights are implicated. . . . For example, a 'pure' audio-only download could be one that met all these requirements: (1) the musical work could not be perceived (i.e., heard) while the transmission was taking place; (2) the sole purpose of the transmission was to deliver a phonorecord of the music work to the home user; (3) the resulting phonorecord received by the home user was permanent, capable of further non-commercial duplication by the home user, and not limited by time, usage, further payment, or any other factor; and (4) the transmission of the musical work was made on demand. *Comments of ASCAP, BMI, and SESAC Regarding the Interpretation and Application of the Mechanical and Digital Phonorecord Compulsory License to Certain Digital Music Services (January 28, 2002).*

The question was finally taken up by a federal court in 2007. Senior Federal District Court Judge Conner, in the course of a rate proceeding filed against ASCAP by AOL, Real Networks, and Yahoo, concluded that a permanent download, while being a reproduction, does not also necessarily constitute a performance. *United States v. ASCAP*, 485 F. Supp. 2d 438 (S.D.N.Y. 2007).

In that case, the court regarded the issue as "purely one of statutory construction." Referring to the definition of "perform" under the Copyright Act, the court noted that the terms "recite," "render" and "play" are not defined within the Copyright Act. Pointed to dictionary definitions of the words, the court concluded that,

> All three terms require contemporaneous perceptibility. We can conceive of no construction that extends it to the copying of a digital file from one computer to another in the absence of any perceptible rendition. Rather, the downloading of a music file is more accurately characterized as a method of *reproducing* that file . . . for it is not the availability of prompt replay but the simultaneous perceptible nature of a transmission that renders it a performance under the Act.

In reaching its conclusion that a download of a digital music file embodying a song does not constitute a performance of the song under the U.S. Copyright Act, the court did not foreclose the possibility that "a transmission might, under certain circumstances, constitute both a stream *and* a download, each of which implicates a different right." Nevertheless, the fact that it is theoretically possible for the same transmission to constitute both a public performance and a reproduction does not mean that all download transmissions constitute a performance.

Even if a digital phonorecord delivery involves the simultaneous rendering (and therefore performance) of the musical work, does not Section 115, by its compulsory nature, preclude the copyright owner from exacting a performance fee for the transmission? Note that the plain language of Section 115 makes it clear that, as long as the licensee complies with the statute, the licensee has the right to make digital phonorecord deliveries, "regardless of whether the digital transmission is also a public performance of . . . any musical work embodied therein." It would therefore appear that as long as the licensee complies with the compulsory license provision and pays the statutory rate, the licensee may make digital phonorecord deliveries without having to pay any more than statutory rate, *even if* the digital transmission happens also to constitute a public performance. Performance rights societies may argue that Section 115 only applies to mechanical reproductions, and therefore the performance right of the copyright owner may be separately invoked. Arguably, however, Section 115 applies to more than mere mechanical reproductions: it applies those reproductions that also constitute "digital phonorecord deliveries," which are, by definition, reproductions "regardless" of whether they are also public performances.

Thus, it could be argued that the payment of the statutory fee for a mechanical license would cover the sale of a copy (i.e., a physical phonorecord or a digital phonorecord delivery) and, theoretically, all *private* performances of the song arising from the use of such copy, as well as the first public performance or rendering that occurs concurrently with the transmission of the digital phonorecord delivery.

The conclusion of the U.S. Copyright Office and, now, at least one federal district court, would appear to have settled the matter — at least in the United States.[10] Overseas, the matter has long been settled, but to a result that is completely to the contrary. The conclusion that a digital download of a music file does not, without a simultaneous rendition, constitute a public performance has no relevancy in most countries outside the United States. This is because copyright laws in most countries outside the United States provide to copyright owners, in addition to the exclusive right of public performance, the exclusive right to communicate a work to the public. This communication right makes it irrelevant whether the song, in the course of a digital download, is contemporaneously perceptible. Overseas performance rights societies, therefore, collect from download services fees for the exercise of the communication right in addition to fees for exercise of the reproduction right.

### *7. The Applicability of the Compulsory License to On-Demand Streams and Limited Downloads*

The question discussed in the previous section — whether a pure digital phonorecord delivery (i.e., permanent download of a recording) constituted a public performance of the musical work underlying the recording — persisted for over ten years, ending, we hope, with the ASCAP rate court decision cited above. During the same period, a parallel controversy persisted over the flip side of the question: whether an on-demand stream (clearly, a public performance of the underlying musical work) also constituted a mechanical reproduction of the musical work. If the answer to that question is yes, then on-demand

[10] The NMPA and the performance rights societies have recently begun a lobbying effort for legislation to require the payment of performance fees on downloads of musical works contained in sound recordings and audiovisual works.

streams would require, in addition to a public performance license, the clearing of a mechanical license and payment of an associated mechanical license fee to the music publishers (in addition to a public performance fee payable to the publishers through their performance rights societies).

In the Third Edition of this book, the authors made the following prediction:

> It is our view that a compromise is likely to be reached which will allow the music publishers to collect both a performance fee and a mechanical reproduction on these on-demand streaming transmissions, but a lower mechanical reproduction rate will be applied for the incidental reproductions. Most important from the transmitter's perspective is that the mechanical rate for incidental digital phonorecord deliveries be established on the basis of a *percentage* of revenues, rather than on a cents per stream basis.

Kohn on Music Licensing (3d ed. 2002). We are pleased to report that this is exactly what happened — but not without "the law's delay," including nearly seven years of administrative proceedings and litigation, hundreds of hours of hearings, and millions of dollars in legal fees and the management time of all concerned.

The question whether an on-demand stream constitutes a mechanical reproduction has a long, storied history — one that was finally settled toward the end of 2008 by a landmark agreement among the trio of industry stakeholders in the controversy: the music publishers, represented by the National Music Publishers Association (NMPA); the record companies, represented by the Recording Industry Association of America (RIAA); and the online music service providers, represented by the Digital Media Association (DiMA).

Music publishers have long feared that on-demand streaming services threaten to replace the sale of copies — both physical and digital downloads. If you can listen to any recording on demand at any time, why purchase and store copies of them anymore? Should the market for digital downloads of recordings shift to on-demand streaming services, revenues that music publishers receive from mechanical licenses (over $500 million in the United States) would decline dramatically, with no assurance that such revenues would be replaced by the increase in public performance fees.

Largely on the basis that on-demand streams effectively replace the sale of a recording, the music publishers, acting through their trade association the NMPA, took the position that a digital audio transmission of a musical work that is effected by means of an "interactive service" (i.e., not a radio station-like webcast under Section 114) constitutes a digital phonorecord delivery, even though the recipient may not end up with a reusable copy of the recording. Under this view, interactive or on-demand streaming transmissions of musical works would require payment of the statutory fee under the Section 115 compulsory license (in addition to the payment of a public performance fee).

The music publishers' economic argument was compounded by a technological fear: The technology used to facilitate the listening of streaming transmissions may permit the listener — legally or not — to convert the stream into a download. The stream in question is not like a stream of a traditional radio broadcast, consisting of a series of tracks in some random or programmed order, which listeners are not likely to copy, but an *interactive* transmission where the listener may know *in advance* exactly what will be streamed to his or her computer and can prepare for it (i.e., prepare to download or save it to his or her hard drive).

Moreover, not only would on-demand streams of musical works completely displace sales of CDs and digital phonorecord deliveries, eliminating the mechanical license fee they would have otherwise earned, on-demand streams could threaten their public performance income, as well. The saving of an on-demand stream to one's hard disk as a downloaded file eliminates the need for further public performances of the work, because when a listener listens to the rendering of a file that has been downloaded to his or her computer, as opposed to listening to a stream from a website, the rendering is a *private* performance. Since music publishers have no exclusive right of *private* performance under the copyright law, only *public* performances, no further public performance royalties will be collected on performances rendered after the file has been downloaded (i.e., you only have to stream the file once and save the stream to get an infinite amount of performances from it).

The threat to both their mechanical license revenue and their public performance revenue, say the publishers, is untenable. The publishers maintain when Congress passed the Digital Performance Right in Sound Recording Act in 1995, an important provision was added to the Section 115 compulsory license provision to specifically address the issue:

> The provisions of this section concerning digital phonorecord deliveries shall not apply to any exempt transmissions or retransmissions under section 114(d)(1).

Section 115(c)(3)(L).

According to the music publishers, the above language *implies* that the provisions concerning digital phonorecord deliveries, while not applying to any exempt transmissions under Section 114(d)(1) does, in fact, apply to those transmissions that are *not* exempt under Section 114, which would include all transmissions made as part of interactive services.

Thus, according to the argument, the transmitter must pay a mechanical reproduction fee, subject to Section 115's compulsory license, for each interactive digital audio transmission, whether or not a copy results from the transmission. A potential problem with this last argument is exposed when you ask what does it mean for Section 115 to apply to a transmission? It means that any mechanical reproduction licenses that *may* be required for the transmission would be subject to the compulsory license provision; it does not automatically mean that the transmission itself is a mechanical reproduction. Nevertheless, if that were the case, Section 115(c)(3)(L) would appear to be entirely meaningless.

Opponents of the music publishers' view on the matter of on-demand streams included an unusual alliance between the record companies (represented by the RIAA) and the online music service providers (represented by DiMA) who suggested that any attempt to extract both a mechanical license fee and a public performance fee for the same transmission amounts to "double-dipping" by the music publishers. If a performance royalty is required to be paid to ASCAP and BMI for the stream, why, they say, should a reproduction royalty *also* need to be paid?

The controversy over on-demand streams is complicated by the problem of what has become known as "limited downloads" — typically defined as, "on-demand transmissions of a time-limited (i.e., non-permanent) download to a local storage device (e.g., the hard drive of a user's computer), using technology that causes the downloaded file to be available for listening only either during a limited time (e.g., a time certain or a time tied to ongoing subscription payments) or for a limited number of times."

Initially, the RIAA suggested that limited downloads may either be (1) incidental DPDs or (2) more in the nature of record rentals, leases, or lendings. The latter approach was based on the provision in the Section 115 compulsory license, which authorizes the maker of phonorecord to rent, lease, or lend it, provided that a royalty fee is paid. In any event, there was never a controversy about whether the compulsory license provision covered limited downloads. The only question was whether the full statutory rate for permanent downloads — presently, 9.1¢ — or something less than the full statutory rate would apply to these DPDs.

Meanwhile, the technology behind both limited downloads and on-demand streams spawned two potential business models that seemed to be preferable to the permanent download model: subscription music services and advertising-based music services. The major record labels, fearing the potential widespread piracy problem that appeared to be associated with the permanent download model, greatly favored a model under which a consumer would pay a monthly subscription fee for access to as many on-demand streams or limited downloads as they wished. To support these new models, the major record companies invested in two joint venture companies to effect this new model: Pressplay and MusicNet.

The problem, however, was how to charge a consumer $10 per month for unlimited streaming or limited downloads when each download, and if the music publishers get their way, each on-demand stream and limited download could cost, potentially, the full statutory rate under the compulsory license provision? The music publishers recognized that limited downloads could warrant a rate lower than the full statutory rate for permanent digital phonorecord deliveries. Moreover, the Copyright Act itself, as modified by the 1995 Amendment, contemplated a two-tier rate structure to address just this kind of problem. According to Section 115, the terms and rates established under the compulsory provision shall distinguish between:

> (i) digital phonorecord deliveries where the reproduction or distribution of a phonorecord is incidental to the transmission which constitutes a digital phonorecord delivery, and
> (ii) digital phonorecord deliveries in general.

Section 115(b)(3)(C).

Digital phonorecord deliveries "in general" have come to mean pure or permanent downloads and digital phonorecord deliveries "where the reproduction of a phonorecord is incidental to the transmission" have come to be called "incidental DPDs." With little guidance from the Copyright Act, no one had a clear handle on what kinds of transmissions would be covered by the term "incidental DPDs." The record companies took the position that limited downloads are just the kind of transmissions contemplated by incidental download subset and attempted to negotiate a reduced rate from the music publishers. At the same time, the record companies firmly held the view that an on-demand stream does not invoke the compulsory license provision, because if any reproduction was involved in the process (e.g., buffer copy), it did not meet the definition of DPD (which requires, among other things, that the copy be "specifically identifiable").

The music publishers, while conceding that limited downloads are covered by the compulsory license, feared that limited downloads could be "unlocked," such that users could end up with a permanent download — if that could happen, then the publishers wanted the full statutory rate paid on limited downloads. Moreover, the publishers maintained, if the term "incidental DPD" stood for anything, it stood for the proposition that an on-demand stream — which for all practical purposes involved the creation of a server copy at the transmitter's end and a "buffer" copy at the recipient's end, during the course of the transmission — was a transmission that involved the reproduction of a phonorecord, where such reproduction was merely incidental to the transmission.

Frustrated that negotiations with music publishers were not proceeding at the pace of the new technology and the prospects of the music subscription services the labels were eager to promote, the RIAA, on November 22, 2000, petitioned the U.S. Copyright Office to conduct a proceeding to resolve the question of which types of digital transmissions of recorded music constitute a general DPD and which types should be considered an incidental DPD. Specifically, the RIAA asked the Copyright Office to determine (1) whether on-demand streams are incidental DPDs covered by the compulsory license, (2) whether the compulsory license includes the right to make server copies or other copies necessary to transmit on-demand streams and limited downloads, and (3) the royalty rate applicable to on-demand streams (if they are covered by the compulsory license) and limited downloads.

The incentive for compromise gained impetus on March 9, 2001, the date the U.S. Copyright Office initiated a rulemaking proceeding in response to the RIAA request. See 66 Federal Register 14099 (March 9, 2001). The newly formed Digital Media Association (DiMA), together with a number of technology companies, including Napster and MP3.com, filed responses to the RIAA petition. DiMA expressed a particular concern with the status of copies of musical works made in the course of streaming. It was the position of their members — including several on-demand streaming services, including Real Networks — that on-demand streaming did not involve the making of digital phonorecord deliveries; accordingly, the only license required from music publishers would be a public performance license easily obtainable from the performance rights societies — no mechanical reproduction license, whether covered by the compulsory license or not, would be required.

With a new set of industry players — the technology companies — entering the scene, the music publishers felt it was time to settle. Thus, on October 5, 2001, the NMPA (with the Harry Fox Agency) and the RIAA reached an agreement concerning the mechanical licensing of musical works for the new subscription services that involved on-demand streams and limited downloads. The agreement provided a license covering all reproduction rights for the delivery of on-demand streams and limited downloads, and included the rights to make server copies, buffer copies, and other related intermediate copies used in the operation of an online music service covered by the agreement. The agreement also provided, at no additional cost, for on-demand streams of promotional excerpts, defined as a stream consisting of no more than 30 seconds of playing time of the sound recording of a musical work (or no more than the lesser of 10% or 60 seconds of playing time of a sound recording of a musical work longer than 5 minutes).

On December 14, 2001, the Copyright Office published a follow-up notice seeking comments on its previous March 9 hearing in light of the agreement negotiated by the RIAA and the NMPA. No actions were taken by the Copyright Office at that time.

Subsequently, Congress passed the Copyright Royalty and Distribution Reform Act of 2003. This Act altered the administrative structure for determining rates and terms for various compulsory licenses under the Copyright Act, replacing the previous CARP regime. The Reform Act established a tribunal of three Copyright Royalty Judges (also known as, the Copyright Royalty Board), who assumed authority for determining rates and terms for the statutory licenses, including the Section 115 compulsory license.

Meanwhile, the market for subscription services hadn't been meeting the lofty expectations of the record labels. Within a few years, the record companies began selling off their interests in Pressplay and MediaNet, and several technology companies entered the market to take on the challenge of subscription services. Real Networks acquire Listen.com, an on-demand streaming service, and re-launched the service under Rhapsody brand. Roxio bought the assets of Pressplay and of then-defunct Napster and launched a legal Napster, a subscription service that offered on-demand streams and limited downloads. MusicNet was purchased by Baker Capital, a private equity firm, and continued to power subscription services for a number of partners including Virgin Music, HMV, and later Microsoft Zune.

These technology companies were not parties to the agreement between the NMPA and the RIAA and some of them, through their trade association, DiMA, continued to express a vehement opposition to the notion that a purely on-demand streaming service required a mechanical reproduction license. In time, the Copyright Office became somewhat sympathetic to their position. On March 11, 2004, at a hearing held by the Subcommittee on Courts, the Internet, and Intellectual Property of the House Judiciary Committee, the Register of Copyright, referred to the agreement between the NMPA and RIAA:

> Of course, the parties' interpretation with respect to the scope of the Section 115 license is not binding on the Copyright Office or the courts. It merely represents their mutual understanding of the scope of

> the Section 115 license as a term of their privately negotiated license, an understanding I believe is not shared by everyone in the world of online services. This is an issue I will address in the rulemaking proceeding concerning digital phonorecord deliveries, and it is quite possible that I will reach a different interpretation as to what falls within the scope of the license, especially with respect to on-demand streams.

At the conclusion of that hearing, which was entitled, "Section 115 of the Copyright Act: In Need of an Update," the chairman of the subcommittee asked the Register of Copyrights to meet with the parties to explore a legislative solution to modernizing the Section 115 compulsory license to be more responsive to the emerging technologies.

The Register's discussions with the parties made limited progress, and legislative options were again explored at a hearing of the subcommittee on June 21, 2005, followed by a hearing by the Senate Judiciary Committee held on July 12, 2005. Following those hearings, the interested parties continued to discuss legislative reform leading to the introduction of the proposed Section 115 Reform Act (SIRA), H.R. 5553, in the 109th Congress, and a further hearing in the House subcommittee on May 16, 2006.

SIRA would have amended Section 115 to make clear that the compulsory license for DPDs would have covered "the making and distribution of general and incidental digital phonorecord deliveries in the form of full downloads, limited downloads, interactive streams, and any other form constituting a digital phonorecord delivery or hybrid offering" and it would have covered "all reproduction and distribution rights necessary to engage in" those activities. The proposed bill would also have granted a royalty-free license "for the making of server and incidental reproductions to facilitate noninteractive streaming." Although SIRA was approved by the House Subcommittee, the 109th Congress adjourned without further action on the proposed legislation.

On January 9, 2006, the Copyright Royalty Board (CRB) issued a notice announcing a proceeding to determine the rates and terms of royalty payments for the making and distribution of phonorecords, including digital phonorecord deliveries, under the Section 115 compulsory license. The announcement was followed by a period of unsuccessful voluntary negotiations among the music publishers, record companies, and online music services over the rates and terms for these mechanical reproductions.

A major obstruction to a negotiated voluntary settlement was a fundamental disagreement over whether a mechanical reproduction license was required at all for some of the activities involved in operating certain kinds of online music services. In addition, the market for permanent downloads was changing some of the basic economics under which records companies were operating their businesses. Previous negotiated statutory rates no longer reflected these changes. After an unsuccessful negotiation period, the interested parties were asked to file written statements by November 30, 2006.

Meanwhile, on March 22, 2007, the House subcommittee held another hearing, which explored legislative reform of the Section 115 compulsory license, but no legislation resulted.

Because of the lack of progress on legislative reform, the Copyright Office conducted a public roundtable "to refresh the record in order to ascertain the scope of the Section 115 license in relation to certain music services." Over 20 representatives, including one of the authors of this work, participated in the roundtable, which was held on June 15, 2007.

The Copyright Royalty Board proceeded with its hearing on new statutory rates under the Section 115 compulsory license. After a lengthy discovery period, live testimony was taken from January 28, 2008, through February 26, 2008, and rebuttal testimony taken from May 6 through May 21, 2008. Closing arguments were heard on July 24, 2008.

Before the conclusion of the hearing, the parties (through their representatives at the RIAA, DiMA, and the NMPA) informed the CRB on May 15, 2008, that they had reached a settlement regarding the rates and terms for limited downloads and interactive streaming, including all known incidental digital phonorecord deliveries. The specifics of the settlement were filed on September 22, 2008, and were published in the Federal Register on October 1, 2008. 73 F.R. 57033.

Congress's inaction on legislation to clarify the open questions relating to the operation of online music services and their obligations to music publishers threatened to put the Copyright Royalty Board in a difficult position. While the CRB has the authority to establish rates and terms of the statutory fees under the Section 115 compulsory license, its authority to resolve some of the basic issues of copyright under dispute — e.g., the extent to which on-demand streams require a mechanical reproduction license or the extent to which server or intermediate copies made to effect digital phonorecord deliveries are covered by a compulsory license — is another matter.

As a result, from time to time, the CRB has the authority to turn to the Copyright Office for "consultation" or for a decision on "novel questions of law." 17 U.S.C. Section 802(f(1)(B)-(E). Although the Copyright Office does not have the authority to reform the Copyright Act — something only Congress can do through legislation — it does have the authority to promulgate regulations that interpret the statute.

In response to a need to resolve these open issues, and perhaps to make the regulatory framework consistent with the resolution of these issues reached in the industry's negotiated settlement, the Copyright Office initiated a Notice of Proposed Rulemaking on July 16, 2008. Based on input it received from interested parties at previous hearings and the refresh of the record it received at roundtable held earlier in the year, the Copyright Office proposed to amend its regulations "in a way that would enable digital music services to utilize the compulsory license to clear all reproduction and distribution rights in musical works that may be necessary in order to engage in activities such as the making of full downloads, Limited Downloads, On-Demand Streams and non-interactive streams."

Specifically, the regulations proposed allowed online music services to employ the Section 115 license to cover all musical works embodied in phonorecords made and distributed to the public for private use including those phonorecords made on the end-users' RAM or hard drive, on transmission service's servers, and all intermediate reproductions on the networks through which transmission occurs. The Copyright Office received comments on the proposed regulations and took into consideration the Second Circuit Court of Appeal's decision in *Cartoon Network LP v. CSC Holdings, Inc.*, 536 F.3d 121 (2d Cir. 2008), which reversed the decision in *Twentieth Century Fox Film Corp. v. Cablevision Sys. Corp.*, 478 F. Supp. 2d 607 (S.D.N.Y. 2007), upon which the Copyright Office had partially relied.

On November 7, 2008, the Copyright Office issued an interim rule that revised its earlier proposed rule. While, in light of the *Cartoon Network* case, the Copyright Office refrained from taking a position as to whether a "buffer" copy constitutes a phonorecord, the interim rule does clarify that (1) whenever there is transmission that results in a DPD, all reproductions made for the purpose of making the DPD are also included as part of the DPD, and (2) limited downloads qualify as DPDs.

Thus, a service that offers permanent downloads (or limited downloads) who is making digital phonorecord deliveries under the authority of a compulsory license may make any server or other intermediary copies necessary to facilitate the making of such DPDs — and since such copies are not distributed to the public, such copies may be made royalty-free.

Whether on-demand streams constitute DPDs, in light of the decision in the *Cartoon Network* case, will have to be resolved another day. For all practical purposes, the issue is resolved with respect to musical works by virtue of the industry agreement relating to the payment of mechanical reproduction fees for both limited downloads and on-demand streams. That agreement was adopted by the CRB, which published in the Federal Register its decision in its Mechanical and Digital Phonorecord Delivery Rate Determination Proceeding on January 26, 2008. 37 C.F.R. Section 385. The effective date of that decision and the rates established by it was March 1, 2009. Such rates are discussed later in this chapter.

### 8. *The Applicability of the Compulsory License Provision to Ringtones*

The distribution of ringtone-capable mobile phones, which began in the late 1990s in Japan, has spawned a multi-billion dollar industry in the sale of downloadable ringtones — both polyphonic ringtones and more recently, mastertones. As mentioned above, wireless service providers have been able to maintain strict technical control over how ringtones were delivered to and operated on the mobile phones that operated on their wireless networks. That combined with the great popularity of the personalization afforded by ringtones to mobile phone users, mobile providers were able to charge over $3 per ringtone.

Since monophonic and polyphonic ringtones do not involve a license to the original popular recordings of the songs, the only license required for the distribution of such ringtones would be a license from the copyright owner of the song embodied in the ringtone. For some time after ringtones were in widespread use in the United States, there remained a question as to whether ringtones would be treated like any other digital phonorecord delivery under the Section 115 compulsory license provision. If that were the case, it would seem that the mechanical license required by the wireless provider would carry an effective maximum license fee of the statutory rate (e.g., 9.1¢). With a $3 price to the consumer and a royalty cost of only 9.1¢, the carriers who sold ringtones to their subscribers were in a position to make a profit margin that approached 96%! (The carrier's marginal cost of using their own network to deliver the small MIDI files to the mobile phone was virtually zero.)

It did not take too long for music publishers to formulate a legal strategy that attempted to place MIDI files and ringtones on a different legal plane from normal sound recordings — thereby taking the position that MIDI files and ringtones are not subject to the compulsory license and enabling them to charge far greater than the 9.1¢ per copy statutory rate.

The Harry Fox Agency, representing publishers in the United States, began using a special MIDI license form (*see* Form 22.4 on the CD-ROM), which sought royalty rates that exceeded the statutory rate and other terms more favorable than those provided by the compulsory license provision. Later, a special ringtone license was drafted, which attempted to yield a percentage of revenue (e.g., from 10% to 12% of retail), with a minimum of 10 to 12¢ per ringtone, and a one-time fixing fee of $25. Given a retail price of $2.95 per ringtone, a license fee of 10% of the retail selling price would mean a royalty of nearly 30¢ per ringtone, more than three times that which the compulsory license provision would afford the music publisher. Some ringtone license agreements even attempted to exact a percentage of any advertising revenue derived from web pages on which the ringtones were made available for sale.

With the advent of mobile phones that could support mastertones, the record labels now began to eye this new market for their recordings. And they could do so unfettered by the compulsory license provision, as they could demand whatever the market would bear for a license to their recordings for use in ringtones. But whatever the market would bear was subject to a simple restraint: the music publishers were demanding rates far exceeding the statutory rate for mechanical reproductions and would not permit the record labels from using their existing mechanical licenses in connection with the licensing of their recordings to the ringtone distributors.

The record companies thereupon engaged in a two-pronged strategy. First, when the major record companies began licensing their sound recordings for use in ringtones, they attempted to include a clause requiring the licensee to cease distributing monophonic and polyphonic ringtones that contained the same underlying song (so that monophonic and polyphonic ringtones of songs that did not contain the record companies' sound recordings of those songs would not compete with the mastertones that did). Second, to reduce the relative share that the music publishers receive out of the ringtone's earnings, as well as giving the record companies the freedom to license the songs under the mechanical licenses they already received in connection with their recordings, the record companies began engaging in legal maneuvers to have ringtones declared no different from any other sound recording, making them subject to the Section 115 compulsory license provision.

Thus, on August 1, 2006, as a new rate proceeding (to determine the new statutory rates for mechanical reproductions) by the Copyright Review Board was well under way, the RIAA requested that the CRB refer the question of whether mastertones are eligible for statutory licensing under the Section 115 compulsory license to the Copyright Office. After overcoming an objection by the NMPA, the question was finally referred to the Copyright Office on September 14, 2006.

On October 16, 2006, the Copyright Office issued a decision that sided with the RIAA:

> We believe that ringtones (including monophonic and polyphonic ringtones, as well as mastertones) qualify as digital phonorecord deliveries (DPDs) as defined in 17 U.S.C. § 115.[11]

Music publishers asserted that all ringtones are excluded from the Section 115 compulsory license for the following reasons: (1) the compulsory license is narrow in scope and does not encompass ringtones, (2) ringtones involve only a portion of the underlying composition, not

---

[11] *In the Matter of Mechanical and Digital Phonorecord Delivery Rate Adjustment Proceeding (Marybeth Peters, Register of Copyrights, October 16, 2006).*

the entire musical work, (3) ringtones are derivative works and therefore fall outside the express language of the compulsory license provision, (4) ringtones cannot be considered "arrangements," as that term is used in the music industry and, in any event, ringtones change the basic melody and fundamental character of the musical work, and (5) ringtones do not satisfy Section 115's requirement that the phonorecords be distributed for private use.

The Copyright Office determined that ringtones, even those that constitute mere excerpts of a preexisting sound recording, fall squarely within the scope of the statutory license. The compulsory license is not limited to entire works and the Act does not expressly exclude "portions of works." While agreeing with the music publishers that the compulsory license does not apply to derivative works, the Copyright Office pointed out that a ringtone, to be considered a derivative work, must exhibit a degree of originality sufficient enough to be copyrightable.

> Whether one would be considered a derivative work depends upon the nature of the ringtone. At one end of the spectrum are those ringtones that are simple excerpts of larger musical works. This type of ringtone is not a derivative work. At the other end of the spectrum are ringtones that contain additional original authorship. These would be considered derivative works if there was a sufficient amount of creative authorship in the new material. In between are ringtones that may include some new material (spoken words or music) in addition to the excerpt. Those ringtones cannot be properly analyzed in a factual vacuum and their status as derivative works need not be determined in this proceeding, but more appropriately determined on a case-by-case basis by the courts.

The compulsory license provision states that the "compulsory license includes the privilege of making a *musical arrangement* of the work to the extent necessary to conform it to the style or manner of interpretation of the performance involved, but the arrangement shall not change the *basic melody or fundamental character of the work*, and shall not be subject to protection as a derivative work under this title, except with the express consent of the copyright owner." 17 U.S.C. Section 115(a)(2). According to the Act's legislative history, the purpose of this limited "arrangement privilege" was to prevent the musical work from being "perverted, distorted, or travestied."

In analyzing the arrangement privilege, the Copyright Office turned to the definition of arrangement found in the New Encyclopedia of Music and Musicians (NEMM), which defined an *arrangement* as "the process or result of readjusting a work for performance by different artistic means from that originally intended. Also, a relatively close or literal rendering of the substance and form of a work with only those modifications demanded by the limitations or peculiarities of the medium in view." With that in view, the Copyright Office made three general observations on the subject: (1) the user's right to make a melodic arrangement should be limited so that the basic character of the musical work is preserved, (2) a mastertone that merely shortens the full length work to conform it to the physical limitations of the cellphone does not affect the musical work's arrangement, and (3) a ringtone that makes minor changes to lyrics of the underlying musical work generally does not affect its arrangement. As to the music publisher's response that ringtones are abridgements, not arrangements, the Copyright Office pointed out that it had already determined that such abridgements are not derivative works and therefore are not outside the scope of the compulsory license provision.

The music publishers asserted that even if ringtones qualify as arrangements, the compulsory license provision should not cover them, because they change the basic melody and fundamental character of the musical work — because ringtones delete large portions of the underlying works, including much of the melody, verses, bridges, codas, and instrumental interludes, the resulting reduction of the work to a short refrain excludes all of the other elements that make up the overall character of the work. Moreover, assert the publishers, that ringtones transform artistic works into utilitarian substitutes, fundamentally changing the "original artistic vision" expressed by the work into "a new purpose of serving a thirty second mobile phone ringer." This, they say, departs from the integrity of original composition, a result they say Congress intended to avoid by excluding such uses from the compulsory license provision.

The Copyright Office summarily dismissed this last argument to the extent it referred to mastertones. It should be assumed that the "basic melody" or "fundamental character" of the song was not changed when an existing commercial release of its sound recording, properly licensed either by means of a voluntary or compulsory license, was converted for use as a ringtone. As to the other forms of ringtones, the Copyright Office emphasized that in limiting the arrangement privilege, Congress intended to prevent the music from being "perverted, distorted, or travestied." The Copyright Office concluded that the reduction of a work to a short excerpt does not fundamentally change the overall character of the work or impugn the integrity of the work. "A typical monophonic or polyphonic ringtone," concluded the Copyright Office, "would be considered a mere 'stylized version' of the original musical work with no changes to the melody, but perhaps some changes to the tempo."

The compulsory license provision is applicable only if the licensee's "primary purpose in making the phonorecords is to distribute them to the public for private use including by means of a digital phonorecord delivery." The music publishers asserted that ringtones fail to satisfy the requirement that the phonorecords be distributed for "private use" — which, they assert includes only listening use for private enjoyment of music, not the public function that ringtones serve (e.g., a means for a user to publicly identify and express themselves to their friends, colleagues, and the public at large).

The Copyright Office rejected that argument using a couple of common examples of public uses of recordings: in boom boxes in public parks, in a car stereo while the automobile is driving down the street, etc. Use of phonorecords in public does not disqualify them from the compulsory license by violating their primary purpose of being for private use. The legislative history made it clear that the compulsory license "does not extend to manufacturers of phonorecords that are intended primarily for commercial use, including not only broadcasters and jukebox operators but also background music services." Section 115, however, does not impose any limitations on the use of a phonorecord once it is purchased by the consumer.

### 9. The Applicability of the Compulsory License Provision to MIDI Files

MIDI, the *musical instrument digital interface*, is briefly described above in section I.F. of this chapter. The storing of musical works in MIDI format raises some interesting music copyright and licensing questions. For example, is a MIDI computer file a mechanical reproduction, the distribution of which requires a mechanical license, subject to the compulsory license statute, or is it an audiovisual work, the distribution of which may be negotiated, such as the terms of a synchronization or videogram license, or is it akin to printed music, which requires the equivalent of a print license?

According to the U.S. Copyright Office, a standard MIDI file is a work of authorship copyrightable as a *sound recording*. This is because the information in the file causes a sound device to render the pitch, timbre, speed, duration, and volume of the musical notes in a certain order, as does a player piano in conjunction with a piano roll, or a compact disc player in conjunction with a compact disc. Thus, the media upon which a standard MIDI file is recorded is a *phonorecord* (as compared with a *copy*). Accordingly, a standard MIDI file is subject to the compulsory license provision under Section 115 of the Copyright Act.

It is important to note, however, that if the MIDI file includes instructions for generating motion pictures or other audiovisual works, the file would not be a sound recording, but rather an audiovisual work. As such, the compulsory license provision would not apply. The Harry Fox Agency has considered the fixation of music in MIDI files and, to deal with the increasing number of requests for this new form of license, has developed a special form MIDI license, a copy of which is set forth as Form 22.4 found on the CD-ROM.

What if the MIDI file contains the ability to display music notation on the screen of a personal computer or to print out the notation on a computer printer the equivalent of printed sheet music? Is it a combination of sheet music and mechanical reproduction of a sound recording, or is it an audiovisual work? The question becomes significant, because many music copyright owners have granted to print publishers the rights to distribute their music in printed form, such as sheet music and folios, on an exclusive basis. If the music copyright owner grants permission for the reproduction of MIDI files, and those files have the capability of printing out musical notation on laser printers, a print publisher who holds exclusive print rights in the music might take the position that the granting of the license was a breach of its exclusive print rights contract.

The Harry Fox license (Form 22.4) states that the license does not grant permission to the licensee "to program into the MIDI sequence [file] the capability of making any other use of the Composition not expressly authorized" by the license. One of the permissions not granted to the licensee is the license to print the licensed composition in sheet music form. Further, the license requires that a warning notice be placed conspicuously on each copy of the MIDI file stating that it is a violation of copyright law to print the file in the form of standard music notation without the permission of the copyright owner.

### *10. The Practical Effect of the Compulsory License Provision*

Oddly enough, because of the burdensome procedures required by the compulsory license provision — such as the requirement of monthly, rather than quarterly accounting to copyright owners and notice conforming to strict regulation — the compulsory license is hardly used. The vast majority of mechanical licenses issued today are negotiated or *voluntary licenses*, not true compulsory licenses. The terms of these voluntary mechanical licenses are given effect, regardless of whether those licenses strictly reflect the terms of the compulsory license provision of the Copyright Act.

In its decision published on January 26, 2009, the Copyright Royalty Board reflected on the seeming contradiction:

> In describing this history and structure of the section 115 license, the Judges note how extensive and detailed is its operation, particularly with respect to the regulations adopted by the Copyright Office. The complexity of compliance, and the associated transactions costs, create a curious anomaly: virtually no one uses section 115 to license reproductions of musical works, yet the parties in this proceeding are willing to expend considerable time and expense to litigate its royalty rates and terms. The Judges are, therefore, seemingly tasked with setting rates and terms for a useless license. The testimony in this proceeding makes clear, however, that despite its disuse, the section 115 license exerts a ghost-in-the-attic like effect on all those who live below it. [citation omitted]. Thus, the rates and terms that we set today will have considerable impact on the private agreements that enable copyright users to clear the rights for reproduction and distribution of musical works.

As the CRB recognized, even though the compulsory license provision is rarely invoked directly, its terms generally provide an outline for those of negotiated licenses. As a practical matter, the statutory rate effectively becomes the maximum limit on the mechanical license fees charged by copyright owners under negotiated licenses. The terms of these voluntary or compulsory licenses are discussed below in Section III.

### *11. The Rationale for the Compulsory License*

Some debate continues over whether it is time for the compulsory license provision to be repealed. Detractors say that the monopoly against which the provision was enacted to combat went out with high button shoes, and there is no reason today why mechanical licenses should not be as freely negotiable as licenses for other kinds of uses. Others say that the compulsory license has served to simplify the process of obtaining mechanical licenses and has reduced a significant amount of unnecessary transaction costs.

In 2004, the head of the U.S. Copyright Office unambiguously weighed-in against the compulsory license system, stating flatly, "I believe that the Section 115 should be repealed and that the licensing of right should be left to the marketplace, most likely by means of collective administration." The Register of Copyrights pointed out that the rest of the world manages to function without a compulsory solution and, in the United States, there is already a very successful model for collective administration of similar rights: the performance rights organizations (i.e., ASCAP, BMI, SESAC). Nevertheless, the Register acknowledged that "many parties with stakes in the current system will resist the proposal and that there would be many practical difficulties in implementing it." *Statement of Marybeth Peters, The Register of Copyrights before the Subcommittee on Courts, The Internet and Intellectual Property of the House Committee on the Judiciary (March 11, 2004).*

Perhaps the best reason, in our view, for maintaining the compulsory license is that it may be the most effective solution to the problem of split copyrights, discussed in Chapter 6. Split copyright does not become an issue when all the co-owners are required to accept no more than the statutory rate. Further, when the person seeking to clear a mechanical license cannot identify or locate the owner of the copyright, the compulsory license provision provides a safe harbor: if the public records of the Copyright Office do not identify the copyright owner and include an address at which notice under the provision can be served, it is sufficient to file the required notice with the Copyright Office.[12] By properly following the procedure and paying the statutory rate set forth in the compulsory license provision, a person seeking to clear permission will be assured a license without taking any risk of liability for copyright infringement. Thus, the music will become available to the public and a mechanism is in place to assure that, eventually, the rightsholders get paid for the use.

## III. CONSIDERATIONS IN GRANTING AND CLEARING MECHANICAL LICENSES IN THE UNITED STATES

As noted in the preceding section, the compulsory license provision has the effect of limiting the flexibility the copyright owner has in setting the terms of the mechanical license. As a result, two of the four primary factors in considering the terms of most music licenses — the value of the song and the importance of the song in relation to its intended use (*see* Chapter 10) — do not come much into play in the negotiation of mechanical licenses (with one notable exception: granting and clearing mechanical licenses for digital samples containing copyrighted music, a topic discussed at length in Chapter 24). Nevertheless, though the clearance of mechanical licenses is generally an administrative process in which very little negotiation takes place, there remains some degree of flexibility that deserves some discussion.

### A. Fee Structure

The fee structures of mechanical reproduction licenses in this section concern those reproductions that are made and distributed in the United States. A brief survey of how mechanical license fees are structured outside of the United States is set forth at the end of this chapter.

[12] 17 U.S.C. Sec. 115(b)(1).

### *1. The Statutory Rate*

The statutory rate payable for a mechanical reproduction of a musical work under the compulsory license provision depends upon the means by which the mechanical reproduction is made.

From 1909 through 1977, the statutory rate, as established by the Copyright Act of 1909, was 2¢. The Copyright Act of 1976 not only raised the rate to 2.75¢, but established a higher mechanical license fee when the song is used in recordings that are longer than 5.5 minutes of playing time. Thus, as of January 1, 1977, the statutory rate became 2.75¢ or .5¢ per minute of playing time, whichever was greater. The cent rate (e.g., 2.75¢) is known as *minimum statutory rate*. The alternative rate based on the "per minute of playing time," is often referred to as the *long-song* rate. If, by contract — e.g. a compulsory license provision (discussed below) — a mechanical license fee is calculated at the *minimum statutory rate*, the statutory cent rate (2.75¢) would apply, regardless of whether the fee would be higher if it were calculated at the long-song rate.

Since 1977, the statutory rate has been increased 16 times (see chart below). Until March 1, 2009, there was only one statutory rate — one that applied to both phonorecords that were made and distributed by traditional physical means and digital phonorecord deliveries.

Today, the applicable statutory rate depends upon the nature of mechanical reproductions being made and distributed. The four primary means by which mechanical reproductions are typically made and distributed today are (1) by the making of physical phonorecords and distributing them by traditional means (i.e. CDs, LPs, cassettes, etc.), (2) by the making of digital phonorecord deliveries in the form of permanent digital downloads, (3) by the making of digital phonorecord deliveries in the form of permanent downloads that are intended to be used as ringtones, and (4) by the making of digital phonorecord deliveries in connection with the making of limited downloads or on-demand streams. The statutory rates for each will be discussed in turn.

#### *a. Physical*

The statutory rate to be paid for each physical phonorecord (e.g., CDs, LPs, cassettes, etc.) made and distributed, during the period beginning March 1, 2009 and ending until modified by the CRB in a future rate proceeding, is the larger of 9.1¢ or 1.75¢ per minute of playing time (or fraction thereof). (For rates applicable during prior periods, see below.)

*b. Permanent Digital Downloads*

The statutory rate to be paid for each digital phonorecord delivery constituting a permanent download made during the period beginning March 1, 2009 and ending until modified by the CRB in a future rate proceeding is also the larger of 9.1¢ or 1.75¢ per minute of playing time (or fraction thereof). A *permanent digital download* is defined as "a digital phonorecord delivery that is distributed in the form of a download that may be retained and played on a permanent basis." 37 C.F.R. Section 385.2.

*c. Ringtones*

The statutory rate to be paid for each digital phonorecord delivery constituting a ringtone made during the period beginning March 1, 2009 and ending until modified by the CRB in a future rate proceeding is 24¢. A *ringtone* is defined as "a phonorecord of a partial musical work distributed as a digital phonorecord delivery in a format to be made resident on a telecommunications device for use to announce the reception of an incoming telephone call or other communication or message or to alert the receiver to the fact that there is a communication or message." 37 C.F.R. Section 385.2.

As noted above, prior to the Copyright Office's ruling in October 2006 and the Copyright Royalty Board's establishment of a special ringtone rate effective March 1, 2009, many music publishers, including their agents like the Harry Fox Agency, took the position that ringtones were excluded from the Section 115 compulsory license; therefore, they asserted, they could establish their own licensing regime for use of their music in ringtones.

As a result, they drafted special ringtone licenses, which typically charged a percentage of a ringtone's gross revenue (e.g., from 10% to 12% of retail), with a minimum "floor" of 10 to 12¢ per ringtone, and a one-time fixation fee of $25 or more. Given a retail price of $2.95 per ringtone, a license fee of 10% of the retail selling price would mean a royalty of nearly 30¢ per ringtone, more than three times that which the compulsory license provision at that time would afford the music publisher (i.e., 9.1¢). Some ringtone agreements used a simpler formula, such as two times statutory or a fixed amount anywhere from 20 to 40¢ per copy. Some ringtone license agreements were even far more complex, attempting to include a percentage of any advertising revenue derived from web pages on which the ringtones were made available for sale.

*d. Limited Downloads and On-Demand Streams*

The statutory rate payable for making mechanical reproductions of musical works in connection with services that conduct limited downloads and on-demand streams is, for the most part, 10.5% of service revenue less the amount of licensee fees paid for the public performances of such musical works in connection with such services, subject to certain minimum royalties depending upon the licensed activity, subject to subscriber minimums varying between 14.53% to 22% (depending upon several factors) of the royalties payable to owners of sound recordings for the streaming activity.

The means of calculating the royalty owed by a particular service comprises several pages of regulations — definitions, details, methodologies, and exceptions — for the calculation for the statutory fees, and minimum fees, for reproductions a service makes in connection with limited downloads and on-demand streams of musical works, and provisions for promotional use. Only a handful of music streaming services will be required to use them to calculate fees and only a handful of auditors will be required to check their accuracy. Set forth below is a summary of the rather complex and precise terms and conditions of regulations, they are rather set forth in full in the appendix to this chapter. 37 C.F.R. Section 385 Subpart B — Interactive Streaming, Other Incidental Digital Phonorecord Deliveries and Limited Downloads.

**Step 1 — Determine the Applicable "All in Royalty" Rate**

The All in Royalty is the greater of (i) 10.5% of the total service revenue (8.5% for streaming prior to December 31, 2007) or (ii) the applicable floor below, according to service type.

An online service desiring to engage in on-demand streaming or limited downloading should first expect to determine which of the following five kinds of *licensed activity* it intends to provide:

(1) a *standalone non-portable subscription, streaming only, service* is a service through which an end user can listen to

sound recordings only in the form of interactive streams and only from a non-portable device to which such streams are originally transmitted while the device has a live network connection;

(2) a *standalone non-portable subscription mixed service* is a service through which an end user can listen to sound recordings either in the form of interactive streams or limited downloads, but only from a non-portable device to which such streams or downloads are originally transmitted;

(3) a *standalone portable subscription service* is a service through which an end user can listen to sound recordings in the form of interactive streams or limited downloads from a portable device;

(4) a *bundled subscription service* is a service in which a subscription service made available to end users with one or more other products or services as part of a single transaction without pricing for the subscription service separate from the product or service with which it is made available (e.g., a case in which a user can buy a portable device and one-year access to a subscription service for a single price);

(5) a *free nonsubscription/ad-supported service* is a service offering a licensed activity free of any charge to the end user.

The computation of the minimum royalties to which the service will be subject will vary based upon the category of licensed activity under which a service falls:

| *Service Type* | *Minimum Royalty* |
|---|---|
| Standalone, non-portable subscriptions, streaming only | Lesser of 50¢ per subscriber per month and Subminimum 2 (see below) |
| Standalone, non-portable subscriptions, mixed streaming and limited download | Lesser of 50¢ per subscriber per month and Subminimum 1 (see below) |

| *Service Type* | *Minimum Royalty* |
|---|---|
| Standalone, portable subscriptions, mixed streaming and limited download | Lesser of 80¢ per subscriber per month and Subminimum 1 |
| Bundled subscription services (where subscription music services are bundled with other products and not separately priced | Subminimum 1 |
| Free nonsubscription or ad supported services | Subminimum 2 |

Note, this new royalty regime contemplates that some services may obtain their incidental mechanical licenses for the use of musical works *passed through* from record labels. Where this is the case, it is contemplated that the streaming service would report and pay these royalties to the labels through Step 3 below and the label would calculate Step 4 and generate reports. As of the time of this writing, all major streaming services in the United States intend to report and pay these royalties directly to music publishers, rather than to the record labels for pass-through to the publishers.

| *Subminimum 1* | *Subminimum 2* |
|---|---|
| A percentage of the royalties expensed by the Service for sound recordings related to interactive streams or limited downloads, as follows: | A percentage of the royalties expensed by the Service for sound recordings related to interactive streams or limited downloads, as follows: |
| Where Service pays incidental mechanical royalties directly to the music publishers or its agent (not passed through the label):<br>• After December 31, 2007: 21% of the royalties expensed by the Service | Where Service pays incidental mechanical royalties directly to the music publishers or its agent (not passed through the label):<br>• After December 31, 2007: 22% of the royalties expensed by the Service |

| *Subminimum 1* | *Subminimum 2* |
|---|---|
| • Before December 31, 2007: 17% of the royalties expensed by the Service | • Before December 31, 2007: 17% of the royalties expensed by the Service |
| Where Service pays incidental mechanical royalties to the label:<br>• After December 31, 2007: 17.36% of the royalties expensed by the Service<br>• Before December 31, 2007: 14.53% of the royalties expensed by the Service | Where Service pays incidental mechanical royalties to the label:<br>• After December 31, 2007: 18% of the royalties expensed by the Service<br>• Before December 31, 2007: 14.53% of the royalties expensed by the Service |

**Step 2 — Calculate the "Adjusted All In Royalty"**

Multiply the All In Royalty Rate by the applicable revenues of the Service. From that, subtract the public performance royalties paid to ASCAP, BMI, or SESAC.

**Step 3 — Determine the "Payable Royalty Pool"**

The Payable Royalty Pool is the greater of the Adjusted All In Royalty (calculated in accordance with Step 2) and the per subscriber floor as determined below:

| *Service Type* | *Per Subscriber Floor* |
|---|---|
| Standalone, non-portable subscriptions, streaming only | 15¢ per subscriber per month |
| Standalone, non-portable subscriptions, mixed streaming, and limited download | 30¢ per subscriber per month |
| Standalone, portable subscriptions, mixed streaming, and limited download | 50¢ per subscriber per month |

| *Service Type* | *Per Subscriber Floor* |
|---|---|
| Bundled subscription services (where subscription music services are bundled with other products and not separately priced) | 25¢ per subscriber per month |
| Free nonsubscription or ad supported services | No per subscriber floor |

**Step 4 — Define a Per Play Rate and Calculate Per Work Royalties**

Divide the Payable Royalty Pool (as determined in accordance with Step 3) by the total number of plays to calculate a Per Play Royalty. Multiply the Per Play Royalty by the total number of plays received by each work during the period to determine a Per Work Royalty.

After October 1, 2010, plays of recordings that are over 5 minutes in length will be adjusted so that 0.2 plays is added for each minute of playing time, or fraction thereof, exceeding 5 minutes. Thus, a recording that is 5 minutes and 25 seconds long will count at 1.2 plays.

***2. Fixation Fee***

The compulsory license provision set forth in Section 115 of the Copyright Act provides a licensee with the right to manufacture copies of the musical work and to distribute them to the public for private use. But not all copies made in the process are actually distributed to the public; some are *master* copies, tapes and later versions used for printing vinyl recordings and CDs and often stored for archive or later use in manufacturing. Since the compulsory license provision does not apply to such master or archive copies, it would seem that music publishers could charge whatever they want for the reproduction of such copies.

As one of the authors of this book explained to the Copyright Office at a Roundtable,[13] it has been the custom and practice of the music industry not to charge a separate fixation fee to record companies or

[13] 72 F.R. 30039-30042 (May 30, 2007) at http://www.copyright.gov/fedreg/2007/72fr30039.pdf.

manufacturers of recordings properly licensed under a mechanical reproduction license. If you had a mechanical license to make and distribute sound recordings of a song, it was implied that you also had a license to make copies necessary to facilitate the manufacturing process.

This custom was not applied upon the advent of ringtones, which publishers took the position did not fall under the compulsory license provision. Thus, in addition to charging a percentage of ringtone revenues, the publishers charged anywhere from $25 to $50 for each "server" copy the ringtone supplier made in connection with its reproduction and distribution of ringtones.

It may be recalled that, on December 8, 2008, the U.S. Copyright Office addressed the question in relation to server copies used to facilitate the making of digital phonorecord deliveries when it declared, "A digital phonorecord delivery includes all phonorecords that are made for the purpose of making the digital phonorecord delivery." Thus, any server copies made for the purpose of facilitating a digital phonorecord delivery is covered by the license that authorized the making of the digital phonorecord deliveries. Accordingly, makers of ringtones (and, for that matter, digital phonorecord deliveries) operating under a compulsory mechanical license, or its equivalent, do not need to pay a separate fixation fee for master or server copies.

### 3. *Giving or Getting "a Rate"*

A copyright owner will occasionally receive a request that a mechanical license be issued for a fee that is below the statutory rate. This is known as asking for *a rate.* To *give a rate* refers to charging a mechanical license fee that is below the statutory rate set by the compulsory license statute.

When a "rate" is offered, it is usually quoted at either 50% or 75% *of statutory.* Thus, assuming, for simplicity, the statutory rate were 8¢ per copy, then a "half of statutory" rate would, of course, be 4¢ per copy.

Under the appropriate circumstances, a person seeking to clear a mechanical license should ask for a rate, and a copyright owner should, when the circumstances are justified, grant a rate. For example, record companies seeking to exploit older recordings will use creative marketing techniques or lower prices, such as the sale of older recordings through record clubs or the packaging of recordings of older artists in an inexpensive album or series of albums, sometimes called a *budget line* record. For budget line and record club releases, most music publishers would consent to a fee of 75% of the statutory rate per song.

Some music publishers are willing to accept a reduced rate in exchange for an advance against royalties (e.g., an advance guaranteeing mechanical royalties on at least 20,000 units). Another justification for granting a rate is when, in the case of a split copyright, your co-publisher requests it. Acquiescing to a reduced rate in such circumstances may avoid the awkward situation of one co-writer getting a larger share than the other.

If a music publisher accepts a rate lower than statutory, it might wish to grant the reduced rate on a *most favored nations* basis — in other words, coupled with the written assurance that, if the licensee grants "more favorable terms" to any other mechanical licensor of songs on the album, such terms will apply to (i.e., supersede) the terms of the music publisher's license.

While it is unlikely that online service providers will ask the music publishing community for a reduced rate for making digital phonorecord deliveries, it is even less likely that music publishers would grant a rate that is less than statutory. Nonetheless, this does not mean that there is no precedent for such a rate.

In 2000, eMusic, the pioneering download service, which until then had been selling MP3 music files for 99¢ per track, embarked upon a subscription service, offering consumers an unlimited number of downloads for a monthly fee of $9.99 (for a 12-month commitment) or $14.99 (for a 3-month commitment). eMusic had conducted some experiments that concluded that consumers would download many files in the first month of a subscription, but then reduce their downloads in later months. Because the mechanical rate was set at a penny rate, there was a potential for mechanical fees to take a large portion of the download revenue. The risk, of course, could have been eliminated if the publishers were willing to take a percentage fee, rather than a mechanical rate based on a cent-rate. But eMusic was unable to persuade the publishers to take such a dramatic step.

Nevertheless, risk could be reduced if the publishers were willing to take a rate less than statutory. Because eMusic's model was to deduct the mechanical fee prior to calculating the label's share of download revenue, there was room for error. In addition, eMusic could always fall back on reducing the "unlimited" nature of the downloads to a maximum amount of downloads per month.

In addition, music publishers at the time were eager to find a way to increase their relative share of the revenue from a digital download. They reasoned that, if the record companies no longer had to incur the costs of packaging a physical product and no longer had to assume the risk of manufacturing and distributing more copies than demand warranted, their risk of taking the product to market is reduced. Hence, the share of the revenues of the sale of a download to the record company should be reduced relative to the share received by the music publishers.

Recognizing that publishers were eager to find a formula that increased their share of the download pie, eMusic ingeniously offered the publishers an upside in exchange for a reduced statutory rate: the publishers would be guaranteed the greater of 75% of the statutory rate or 10% of gross revenues. Thus, 10% of 99¢ was 9.9¢. Since the statutory rate at that time was 8¢, theoretically, the publishers would be getting an increase of 2.9¢ per download, or nearly 25% more than otherwise. Of course, the actual result assumed that a consumer under a 12-month subscription commitment only downloaded 120 tracks by the end of the year. Downloading more tracks would reduce the publishers' percentage. Nevertheless, it was an important step in the right direction as far as the publishers were concerned and an interesting experiment worth taking.

As it turned out, consumers tended to download more than 120 tracks per year and some enterprising hackers actually built software that attempted to automate the downloading of tracks from eMusic. eMusic quickly detected these cheaters and was able to technically thwart automated use of the unlimited download model. Even so, the music publishers could not consider these cheaters to be costing them real mechanical revenue, as these same people were just as likely to use the illegal Napster software (at its height of its notoriety at that time) to steal music as abuse the eMusic subscription model. Later, eMusic introduced a maximum number of copies per month that could be downloaded under the terms of the subscription service.

In 2003, after eMusic became a wholly-owned subsidiary of Universal Music Group, the Harry Fox Agency renewed the agreement with eMusic under even more innovative terms, finally approaching the percentage model that eMusic needed to make the subscription service economical. Under the new agreement, for each sound recording embodying non-major-label content downloaded through eMusic's subscription service (during the first 14 months of the agreement, or until such time as 40 million subscription downloads are made, whichever is sooner), eMusic agreed to pay the greater of (a) $.067 per end user subscriber per day during the applicable quarterly period (the equivalent of about $2 per month per subscriber) and (b) 17% of eMusic's adjusted gross subscription revenue for the applicable quarterly reporting period (total subscription fees less any affiliate and/or agency commissions). Such amount was then to be prorated to reflect the ownership percentage of download songs represented by the Harry Fox Agency. eMusic agree to pay an advance, recoupable from royalties, of as much as $1 million (depending upon publisher participation established through an opt-out process). The initial term of the agreement lasted until the end of 2004, subject to annual renewal, terminable by either eMusic or Harry Fox.

Thus, the music publishers for the first time set their sights on a model that would bring them 17% of gross revenue, using $2 per month per subscriber (over 20% of subscription revenue) as a floor.

The subscription model, and the Harry Fox agreement, was retained by the new owners of eMusic after its sale by Universal to a New York private equity firm. (Ironically, at about the same time eMusic was being sold, Universal Music Group started Fontana, a distributor dedicated to serving independent record companies. eMusic had by then amassed exclusive and non-exclusive digital distribution relationships with over 1,000 independent record labels. That asset was apparently not easily discernable to the group within Universal who started Fontana or to those charged with selling off eMusic for a figure purported to be about $3 million).

### *4. Applicability of Changes in the Statutory Rate*

Many mechanical licenses identify the fee being charged using the words, "statutory rate," rather than using the appropriate denomination of cents per copy in effect. For example, a license may state, "The royalty under this license shall be the statutory rate" or "The royalty under this license shall be one-half the statutory rate." The wording of this provision should be considered carefully.

If the license goes no further than to say the royalty shall be the statutory rate, then the license may be construed as meaning the copyright owner is entitled to only receive the statutory rate in effect at the time the license was executed. This would completely deprive the copyright owner of the benefit of any later increases in the statutory rate.

Accordingly, mechanical licenses that refer to the statutory rate in this way should make it clear that the rate to be applied is the statutory rate "in effect at the time the phonorecords are made."

An alternative means of dealing with rate changes is to draft the license to provide that the initial stated fee shall increase in proportion to increases in the statutory rate made by the Copyright Royalty Board. The mechanical license form set forth as Form 13.1 on the CD-ROM contains an example of this means of reflecting rate increases.

Persons seeking to clear mechanical licenses might attempt to limit the fee to the statutory rate in effect at the time the mechanical license is executed, regardless of when the copies of the licensed recording are made and distributed. The mechanical license form set forth as Form 12.3 on the CD-ROM contains an example of a provision that effects such terms. An alternative way of limiting the fee to the statutory rate is simply to have the mechanical license specify a particular penny rate (e.g., 8.5¢) with no provision specifying a higher amount should the statutory rate be increased.

From 1909 through 1977, the statutory rate was 2¢. The Copyright Act of 1976 authorized the first increase in the statutory rate in nearly 70 years when it established a rate of 2.75¢ per copy or .5¢ per minute of playing time, or fraction thereof, whichever amount is greater. Since then the rate has been increased 16 times. Where a statutory rate is "locked in," with no provision for increases, the following chart may be used to calculate the applicable mechanical rate in effect at the time of the lock-in date (e.g., time the mechanical license was entered, the time the master recording of the song commenced, etc.):

| *Effective Date of New Rate* | *Cents Per Copy* | *Cents Per Minute of Playing Time* |
|---|---|---|
| January 1, 1978 | 2.75 | .5 |
| July 1, 1981 | 4 | .75 |
| January 1, 1983 | 4.25 | .8 |
| July 1, 1984 | 4.5 | .85 |
| January 1, 1986 | 5 | .95 |
| January 1, 1988 | 5.25 | 1 |
| January 1, 1990 | 5.7 | 1.1 |
| January 1, 1992 | 6.25 | 1.2 |
| January 1, 1994 | 6.6 | 1.25 |
| January 1, 1996 | 6.95 | 1.3 |
| January 1, 1998 | 7.1 | 1.35 |
| January 1, 2000 | 7.55 | 1.45 |
| January 1, 2002 | 8 | 1.55 |
| January 1, 2004 | 8.5 | 1.65 |
| January 1, 2006 | 9.1 | 1.75 |
| March 1, 2009 | 9.1 | 1.75 |

### *5. Controlled Composition Clauses*

Compared with other forms of music licensing, the licensing of mechanical reproductions, by virtue of the compulsory license provision, is simple and straightforward. These licenses may be obtained without the permission of the copyright owner, are almost never the subject of negotiation, and bear fees that are effectively capped at the statutory rate. As discussed in the previous section, music publishers are often willing to provide a mechanical license at a rate below statutory, but record companies seeking a lower rate are obliged to justify their request (e.g., the songs would be used on a budget line CD).

Because of the significant savings a reduced mechanical rate can afford a release, record companies have found creative ways to use their bargaining leverage to reduce their mechanical royalty obligations on recordings they release. The time when a record company's leverage is strongest is when they are negotiating to sign a new act to an exclusive recording contract.

Because many recording artists now tend to write most of the songs they record, record companies take the opportunity to address the issue of mechanical licensing directly in the artist's recording contract. These contracts invariably contain a provision, called a *controlled composition* clause, which effectively limits the amount of money the record company is required to pay in mechanical royalties for each album produced by the artist under the contract. Because the terms of these clauses are often extremely complex, we will explore a sample controlled composition clause, from a typical record contract, one section at a time:

> All musical compositions or material recorded pursuant to this Agreement which are written or composed, in whole or in part, or owned or controlled, directly or indirectly, by Artist or any individual of Artist or any producer of the masters subject hereto (herein called "Controlled Compositions") shall be and are hereby licensed to Company for the United States, at a royalty per selection equal to seventy-five (75%) percent of the minimum statutory per selection rate (inclusive of playing time formula, if any) effective on the date of commencement of recording of the masters concerned. The aforesaid seventy-five (75%) percent per selection rate, but exclusive of any playing time, shall hereinafter sometimes be referred to as the "Per Selection Rate."

The above provision defines the term "controlled composition" about as broadly as such a term can be defined. It covers songs written by any member of the band or any producer of any of the masters on the albums covered by the recording contract. Some clauses add, "or anyone associated and/or affiliated with the Artist or Producer." The controlled compositions need only be controlled *in part* by any of these individuals to be covered by the provision. Thus, the clause covers songs that were co-written or co-owned by songwriters who are not members of or related to the band.

The clause then limits the mechanical rate payable by the record company for each controlled composition to 75% of the statutory rate. In other words, with respect to compositions written by the artist, or those over which the artist has some control, the record company is acquiring *a rate*. As noted above, a music publisher would usually quote a rate below statutory for recordings sold in a budget line or record club operation, but certainly not for first run popular recordings. Thus, the controlled composition clause is providing the record company with reduced mechanical licensing terms it would not otherwise be able to obtain from the music publisher.

Notice, moreover, that the rate is the statutory rate *effective on the date of commencement of recording of the masters concerned*, meaning that the rate is frozen and will not be subject to any increases over time, even if Congress or an administrative body were to increase the statutory rate. Again, a music publisher would normally require that the rate be no less than the statutory rate *in effect at the time the phonorecords are made*. To prevent the delay in the delivery of a master to cause an increase in applicable statutory rate, some clauses may lock the statutory rate in effect "on the date that is the earlier of (i) the commencement of the recording of the masters concerned, (ii) the date the master is delivered, or (iii) the date master was required to be delivered" under the terms of the recording agreement.

Note further that the statutory rate to which the provision refers is the *minimum* statutory rate, meaning that regardless of the duration of the recording, the rate used assumes the duration is 5 minutes or less. The controlled composition clause continues,

> Notwithstanding the foregoing, the maximum aggregate mechanical royalty rate which Company shall be required to pay in respect to any Single, Maxi-single or LP hereunder, regardless of the total number of all compositions contained therein, shall not exceed two (2) times, two (2) times, and ten (10) times the Per Selection Rate, respectively.

Thus, the controlled composition clause effectively limits the total mechanical fees payable for an entire record album to *ten times* 75% of the minimum statutory rate in effect at the time the masters were originally recorded. A popular recording artist with a great degree of commercial leverage may be able to negotiate a raise from 75% to 100% of full statutory. That negotiated change might have been sufficient to protect the artist at a time when vinyl records commonly included between 8 and 10 songs per album, but many record companies today are taking advantage of the greater capacity of compact discs and are including 11 or 12 songs per CD to enhance sales. Because the provision establishes a maximum mechanical fee the record company will pay for all music on an album, any liability above the negotiated maximum will come out of the pocket of the recording artist. This is important, because an artist's income from music publishing is, more often than not, going to be the only money the artist will ever see as a result of his efforts. Accordingly, a recording artist negotiating his recording contract should review this provision very carefully.

An artist with some bargaining power should be able to change the limit on the total mechanical fees payable from 10 times 75% of statutory to 10 times 100% of statutory, at least for the first album (perhaps 80% for future albums). An artist with strong bargaining power should be able to change the provision to 11 or 12 times statutory, and perhaps require that the rate be based upon the statutory rate in effect at the time copies of the records are made and distributed. In addition, an artist might be able to strike the part that requires payment to be based on the *minimum* statutory rate, regardless of the playing time. An artist is more likely to negotiate changes to a controlled composition clause if he agrees to enter into a publishing agreement with a music publisher who is affiliated with the record label. Of course, an artist with little or no bargaining power will generally be unable to negotiate any changes to this provision in his recording contract.

As noted above, record companies will seek a rate on budget line or record club sales, and a music publisher would typically grant a rate, such as 75% of the statutory rate, for such uses. Yet the way controlled composition clauses are structured, the record company often gives itself a double dip on a normally acceptable rate. For example, the clause may state that mechanical royalties payable with respect to record club or budget line releases are limited to "seventy five (75%) of the otherwise applicable Per Selection Rate," meaning the actual rate payable for such uses, assuming the Per Selection Rate is seventy-five (75%) percent, is actually just 56¼% (i.e., 75% of 75%). But the clause doesn't always stop there:

> Controlled Compositions which are arranged versions of any musical compositions in the public domain, when furnished by Artist for recordings hereunder, shall be royalty free.

An artist with some leverage, however, may be able to persuade the record company to pay mechanical royalties for public domain arrangements, but only to the extent that ASCAP or BMI pay performance royalties on such arrangements. Such a provision would look like this,

> Mechanical royalties for Controlled Compositions which are arranged versions of any musical compositions in the public domain, when furnished by Artist for recordings hereunder, shall be paid in the same proportion as the appropriate performing rights society grants performance credits to the publisher of such composition, provided Artist has furnished Company with a copy of the letter from such performing rights society setting forth the percentage of the otherwise applicable credit which the publisher will receive.

Finally, to prevent the artist from double-dipping by including a reprise of a song, or multiple remixes, on the same album:

> Notwithstanding anything in the foregoing to the contrary, if a particular selection recorded hereunder is embodied more than once on a particular record, Company shall pay mechanical royalties in connection therewith at the applicable rate for such composition as though the selection was embodied thereon only once.

Because of the terms imposed upon the artist in his recording agreement, a songwriter may be advised to negotiate in his music publishing or co-publishing agreement a provision requiring the publisher or co-publisher to comply with the terms of any controlled composition clause to which he may be bound. Publishers who are under no such obligation, of course, may charge the full statutory rate for the use of its music on an album, but should note that the presence of a controlled composition clause may cause a recording artist to reconsider the use of material, the cost of which may be charged as a direct reduction of his record royalties.

*Affect of Controlled Composition Clause on Mechanical Royalties for Digital Downloads*

The changes in Section 115, the compulsory mechanical license provision, made by the *Digital Performance Right in Sound Recordings*

*Act of 1995*, included a provision that will limit the effect of many controlled composition clauses. As mentioned above, the terms of mechanical licenses that are arrived at through voluntary negotiations will normally be given effect. However, with respect to digital phonorecord deliveries, the controlled composition clause may not always be enforceable, even though it was the subject of voluntary negotiations between a recording artist and his or her record company.

Except under the two circumstances discussed below, the copyright owner of the musical work is entitled to be paid at the full statutory rate for digital phonorecord deliveries, regardless of the royalty rates specified under a controlled composition clause in a record contract. The two circumstances under which the statutory rate will *not* supersede such a controlled composition clause are:

> (i) where the contract containing the controlled composition clause was entered into on or before June 22, 1995.
>
> (ii) where the contract containing the controlled composition clause is (a) entered into by an artist/songwriter who retains his music publishing rights (i.e., the right to grant licenses for the use of his songs) and (b) entered after the songs have been recorded.

## B. Importance of the Song in Relation to Its Intended Use

Because of the applicability of the compulsory license provision to mechanical licensing, considerations of the importance of the song in relation to its intended use rarely come into play in the negotiation of mechanical licenses. Nevertheless, not all uses of music on recordings intended for distribution to the general public will be governed by the compulsory license statute.

### *1. Arrangements and Changes*

In drafting the Copyright Act of 1976, Congress considered the extent to which someone making a recording under the compulsory license provision may depart from the musical work as originally written or recorded without violating the copyright owner's exclusive right to make an arrangement or other derivative work.

Congress recognized the practical need for a limited privilege to make arrangements of music being used under a compulsory license, but without allowing the music to be "perverted, distorted, or travestied."[14] Accordingly, the compulsory license provision includes the following balance of interests:

> "A compulsory license includes the privilege of making a musical arrangement of the work to the extent necessary to conform it to the style or manner of interpretation of the performance involved, but the arrangement shall not change the basic melody or fundamental character of the work, and shall not be subject to protection as a derivative work under this title, except with the express consent of the copyright owner."[15]

Nearly all mechanical licenses include a similar limitation or incorporate this provision directly by reference.

Interestingly, this provision would seem to make it clear that a mechanical license under the compulsory license provision of the copyright law would not be available to a person seeking to use a digital sample of another's copyrighted work in a way that would change the basic melody or fundamental character of the song from which the sample was taken. The problem of *digital sampling* is discussed at length in Chapter 24.

Accordingly, if the intended use would depart from the basic melody or change the fundamental character of the work, the copyright owner would be free to negotiate the terms of the mechanical license without regard to the restrictions normally imposed by the compulsory license provision.

Note, however, limitation on the arrangement privilege may not necessarily restrict the right of an artist to create a parody or satirical work embodying a musical work without permission of the song's copyright owner. This problem is discussed at length in Chapter 25, regarding *Fair Use of Copyright*.

### *2. First Use*

The compulsory license provision only applies to a composition after a recording of it has been made and copies of it have been

[14] House Report of the Copyright Act of 1976, No. 94-1476, at page 109 (Sept. 3, 1976).
[15] 17 U.S.C. Sec. 115(a)(2).

distributed to the public.[16] In other words, the compulsory license provision does not apply to the initial recording, or "first use," of a song. Accordingly, it is within the sole discretion of the copyright owner to decide whether, and under what terms, it wishes to grant permission to another to make a first mechanical recording of a composition.

When, however, a publisher agrees to grant a license to make the first recording, the license is typically issued at the prevailing statutory rate. As noted in Chapter 3, on *Songwriter Agreements*, a songwriter who is also a recording artist may contractually require in his songwriter agreement that neither the publisher, nor its subpublishers, issue a mechanical license for a cover record for a specified period after the artist's own recording of the composition has been released. By virtue of the compulsory license provision, however, the publisher's ability to deny the issuance of a mechanical license for other recordings distributed in the United States will end upon the public distribution of the artist's first recording of the song.

## C. Scope of the License

The form for a voluntary mechanical license is typically prepared and completed by the music copyright owner or its agent. Though it is primarily an administrative procedure, care should still be taken to draft the form to suit the intent of the parties.

### *1. Type of Media*

When issuing a mechanical license, a music publisher or its agent will typically try to narrow the scope of the license as much as possible. This generally preserves for the publisher the flexibility to take advantage of changing circumstances.

For example, the mechanical license might specify precisely what kind of media, or configuration (e.g., LP, cassette), the mechanical license covers. In this way, if a publisher grants a rate that is lower than the statutory rate, the reduced rate would only apply to the use of the musical work on the particular configuration specified. Thus, if a

---

[16] "*When phonorecords of a nondramatic musical work have been distributed to the public in the United States under the authority of the copyright owner,* any other person may, by complying with the provisions of this section, obtain a compulsory license to make and distribute phonorecords of the work." 17 U.S.C. Sec. 115(a)(1).

rate was granted for the use of a song on an album, but the mechanical license was limited to the LP configuration, then upon the advent of a new technology, such as CDs, the record company would be required to obtain a new license to reproduce the song in CDs. At that point, the publisher could demand the full statutory rate.

For some time, the form mechanical license used by the Harry Fox Agency limited the use to a particular configuration. Recently, the Harry Fox Agency has been issuing to record labels new mechanical licenses to cover distribution of recordings previously licensed in that way to cover digital phonorecord deliveries. For larger labels, these licenses will be issued in bulk.

Persons seeking to clear mechanical licenses should try to obtain a license to reproduce the recording in any format, or at least negotiate options to add additional formats at rates and other terms established at the time of the execution of the license.

### *2. Record Number vs. Master Number*

If the mechanical license did not limit the license to a particular configuration, but simply noted the *master number*, which is the number established at the recording studio for identification and filing purposes when the recording master is completed, then the mechanical license would apply to any configuration on which the recording identified by that master number was produced. To avoid granting such a broad license, a publisher might, instead, specify in the license the *record number*, the number that identifies the particular release made from that master (often, the catalog number assigned to the release). (Note, the record number may not necessarily be the same as the *tape number* or the *CD number* — i.e., the number identifying audiocassette tape or compact disc versions of the recording.)

By using the record number, rather than the master number, the publisher will have narrowed the scope of the license to permission to make reproductions of the particular album on which the song was intended to initially appear, rather than any record made from recordings appearing in the master.[17] If the master is later used, as, for

[17] See the district court opinion in *Fred Ahlert Music Corp. v. Warner/Chappell Music, Inc.*, 155 F.3d 17 (2d Cir. 1998), wherein the court's view was consistent with this author's view on the subject.

example, in making a remix of the original recording or in using recordings from the master in other record albums, the recording company would then be required to obtain an additional license from the copyright owner to use the recording for the new use.[18]

Accordingly, if the form of a previously executed mechanical license did not specify the type of media on which use of the recording is limited, then the use of the record number in the mechanical license may have effectively limited the use to the original configuration (e.g., LPs, CDs, etc.), but not digital phonorecord deliveries (DPD) or so-called "incidental" DPDs.[19]

Narrowing the scope of the license in this way may be quite advantageous, as the terms of the new license will reflect circumstances existing at the time the new use is made, rather than that existing at the time a license was issued for the use of the original master recording. Whenever a copyright owner narrows the scope of the license he is in effect requiring the licensee to ask additional permission for a new use[20] and, by doing so, he is preserving the ability to determine the terms of the license at a time when he can better assess the value of the use for which permission is being sought. For example, if a mechanical license were carefully limited to cover the specific recording originally made from the master (i.e., by use of the record number in identifying the recording licensed rather than the master number), then any new copies made from a remix of the master, or recordings made from the master, placed into other albums (such as a soundtrack album), would be subject to a new license, which could then be negotiated to reflect better terms for the copyright owner.

Though narrowing the scope of the license has its advantages, it also has its pitfalls. In *Fred Ahlert Music v. Warner/Chappell*,[21] the song

---

[18] See *Encore Entertainment LLC v. KidDesign, Inc.*, 2005 U.S. Dist. LEXIS 44386 (M.D. Tenn. Sept. 14, 2005), wherein the court quoted this paragraph in nearly its entirety.

[19] *Rogers & Hammerstein v. UMG Recordings, Inc.*, 2001 U.S. Dist. LEXIS 16111 (S.D.N.Y. Sept. 26, 2001) (mechanical licenses setting forth record numbers did not authorize the Internet streaming of sound recordings containing the copyrighted songs).

[20] The use of a copyrighted work in a way that is outside the scope of a license constitutes copyright infringement. *Bourne v. Walt Disney Co.*, 68 F.3d 621, 631 (2d Cir. 1995), citing *Gilliam v. American Broadcasting Cos.*, 538 F.2d 14, 20 (2d Cir. 1976).

[21] *Fred Ahlert Music Corp. v. Warner/Chappell Music, Inc.*, 155 F.3d 17 (2d Cir. 1998).

"Bye Bye Blackbird" was owned by the music publisher, Warner/ Chappell. After the passing of the 1976 Act, the heirs of the songwriters exercised their right of statutory termination and the copyright reverted back to them. For a discussion of how the termination provision works, *see* Chapter 9. Under an exception to the heir's right of termination, however, Warner retained the right to continue receiving royalties from any licenses it issued for the use of the song in derivative works, such as in recordings of the song distributed under the authority of any mechanical licenses issued by Warner. In fact, while it controlled the copyright, Warner issued a mechanical license to A&M Records for a recording of the song by Joe Cocker. After the copyright later reverted to the heirs of the songwriter, the producer of the movie, "Sleepless In Seattle," desired to license the Cocker recording for use in its movie soundtrack and on a soundtrack album of the movie. Warner claimed that it, not the heirs of the songwriters, had the right to receive the royalties derived from the Cocker recordings under the derivative works exception to the heir's right of termination. The court ruled otherwise, holding that in the mechanical license granting A&M the right to use "Bye Bye Blackbird" was narrowly limited to the purpose of recording the Cocker derivative and releasing it as "Record No. SP 4182." Because the grant was limited to the record number, it did not authorize any additional releases of the Cocker derivative, much less its inclusion on a movie soundtrack. Thus, the heirs of the songwriters, not Warner, were entitled to receive the royalties on the use of the Cocker recording in the movie's soundtrack and soundtrack album.

The lesson of the *Ahlert* case is that, before a publisher decides whether to issue mechanical licenses that are limited narrowly to a particular record number, the publisher should consider the likelihood of losing the copyright due to a termination of transfer. Since the publisher will continue, after the termination, to benefit from mechanical licenses before termination, some thought should be given as to whether to grant licenses that may be broadly applied.

### *3. Distribution Channels*

The compulsory license provision of the copyright law provides that "a person may obtain a compulsory license only if his or her primary purpose in making phonorecords is to distribute them to the public for private use."[22] All mechanical licenses reflect the same limitation. If, for example, the primary purpose of making the recordings is for use in the facilitation of commercial broadcasts of the recording, then a compulsory license is not available and the use is outside the scope of the mechanical license. The type of license required for such use is an *electrical transcription license*, which is discussed in detail in Chapter 14.

### *4. Term*

The term of a mechanical license is often not stated on the face of the license. It is assumed that the term is for the life of the copyright, because the compulsory license provision does not limit the term of mechanical licenses obtained under the statute. The license may be terminated, however, typically upon 30 days notice, if the licensee fails to pay the mechanical license fee.

### *5. Territory*

The territory of the mechanical license is usually limited. For example, most mechanical licenses issued in the United States limit the territory to the United States, including its territories and possessions. The mechanics of mechanical licensing outside the United States are discussed briefly below and in more detail in Chapter 5, on *International Subpublishing.*

Some older ringtone agreements afforded the telephone carrier the right to offer ringtones on a worldwide basis, but this is rare, with most ringtone providers now required to obtain licenses in each jurisdiction from the local mechanical collection society under the local license fee regime for ringtones and other mechanical reproductions.

### *6. Exclusivity*

A mechanical license is never granted on an exclusive basis. To grant exclusive mechanical rights would be in contradiction to the compulsory license provision, which requires that, once recordings of the

[22] 17 U.S.C. Sec. 115 (a)(1).

work have been distributed to the public, mechanical licenses are available to anyone upon the licensee's fulfillment of certain conditions.

Of course, since compulsory license provision only applies to a composition after a recording of it has been made and copies of it have been distributed to the public, the song's owner could refuse to grant a license for the first recording made of the song. This effectively allows the copyright owner to provide to a particular recording artist the exclusive right to make and distribute recordings of the song before anyone else can.

## D. Other Provisions

### *1. Late Fee*

Up until the new statutory rate went into effect on March 1, 2009, the compulsory license under Section 115 did not provide for a late fee. Being frustrated with delayed accounting with many record companies and other licensees, many publishers have long tried to include a late fee in their standard form mechanical license agreements. Such a provision might take this form:

> Licensee shall pay a late fee of 1.5% per month, or the highest lawful rate, whichever is lower, for any payment received by the licensor after the due date set forth in accordance with the terms of this license.

### *2. Reserves for Returns*

The compulsory license provision, at Section 115(c)(2), states the following:

> [T]he royalty under a compulsory license shall be payable for every phonorecord made and distributed in accordance with the license. For this purpose . . . a phonorecord is considered "distributed" if the person exercising the compulsory license has voluntarily and permanently parted with its possession.

The word "voluntary" was used to make it clear the licensee would not be required to pay a mechanical royalty on copies that were destroyed by accident, stolen, or otherwise disposed of involuntarily. The phrase "permanently parted with its possession" was an explicit recognition of the problem of returns — copies that had been distributed, but later returned by retail outlets as unsold.

The statute itself, however, did not directly provide that a licensee may hold a "reserve for returns," which would allow them to hold back a portion of the payment of mechanical royalties on copies that had been distributed in anticipation that some number of them would eventually be returned. To allow for this common industry practice, the statute provides at Section 115(c)(4) the following:

> . . . The Register [of Copyrights] shall also prescribe regulations under which detailed cumulative annual statements of account, certified by a certified public accountant, shall be filed for every compulsory license under this section. The regulations covering both the monthly and the annual statements of account shall prescribe the form, content, and manner of certification with respect to the number of records made and the number of records distributed.

By November, 1980, the Copyright Office published a complex set of regulations (since revised) governing the accounting procedures to be followed by mechanical licensees, including regulations concerning the maintenance and liquidation of reserves for returns. The regulations promulgated by the Copyright Office, set forth in the Appendix to this chapter, take into account the practice of holding such reserves and work an intricate compromise between the interest of music publishers wishing to get paid for the use of their musical works in recordings and record companies only wishing to pay a royalty based on net revenues associated with the sale of their recordings.

Most mechanical licenses are silent on the issue of returns, leaving the regulations to determine the extent to which publishers will get paid on returns, if at all. Some mechanical licenses attempt to limit the amount of reserves that may be retained for returns (e.g., 25%) and the time period within which the reserve must be liquidated (e.g., 9 months).

Music publishers and their representatives may negotiate with certain record companies a reserve policy that differs from those set forth in the regulations. In such a case, as when a record company and the Harry Fox Agency have come to an understanding on reserves, the following provision may be included in the mechanical license:

> Reasonable reserves may be withheld in the same manner as Licensee withholds and liquidates reserves in accordance with its current arrangement with The Harry Fox Agency, Inc.

### *3. Free Goods*

"Free goods" are copies of CDs that are provided to stores as part of a promotional incentive. A store may be considering the order of 85 CDs, and then be provided an extra 15 copies as an incentive to complete the order. Even though, technically, these CDs are provided for free, this does not mean that mechanical royalties are not due. Under the compulsory license provision, any and all phonorecords that are "made and distributed" (and not returned within a period specified by the regulations) are entitled to a royalty under the law.

As a practical matter, however, many free goods are actually bona fide promotional copies that are sent to radio stations, reviewers, DJs, and others instrumental in the promotion of the album. Music publishers, as a matter of custom and practice, allow these promotional copies to be exempt from mechanical license fees. In such cases, a licensee might wish to include the exemption in the mechanical license, which would typically take the following form:

> No royalty shall be payable hereunder with respect to promotional phonorecords sent to disc jockeys, reviewers, and the like, which are clearly marked "Promotional Records Not For Sale" and which are not being distributed by Licensee for resale.

Some publishers may add a provision that specifically limits the number of free goods or promotional copies that are exempt from royalties. Such provisions might limit free goods to 15% of the phonorecords distributed. Licensees would prefer a loser limitation, such as "a reasonable number of free goods."

### *4. Audit*

A mechanical license may typically require that the licensee allow the music publisher to conduct periodic audits of the licensee's books and records to verify the accuracy of the licensee's mechanical royalty reports. Such a provision may be added to a standard mechanical license in the following form:

> Upon written request and during Licensee's regular business hours, Licensee agrees to make its books and records relating to the subject matter hereof available for audit by Licensor and Licensor shall have the right to make copies thereof.

### *5. Credit*

Some mechanical licenses require that the songwriters and publishers be given credit on copies of the records distributed under the mechanical license. Such a provision may be added to a standard mechanical license in the following form:

> In regard to all phonorecords, manufactured, distributed and/or sold hereunder, you shall include in the label copy of all such phonorecords, or on the permanent containers of all such phonorecords, printed writer/publisher credit in the form of the names of the writer(s) and the publisher(s) of the copyrighted work.

### *6. Copies of the Recording*

A few mechanical licenses require that the licensee send to the publisher two copies of the album in which the licensed recording is included upon its first distribution.

### *7. Other Ringtone Terms*

In addition to the fee structure described above, ringtone licenses have often contained additional terms and conditions. For example, many of them included a limitation on the timing-length of the ringtone to 30 to 45 seconds. Some licenses are conditioned upon the telephone carrier's having a performance license from the applicable performance rights society. Although all ringtone reproduction licenses are non-exclusive, some restrict the music to use in polyphonic ringtones, as opposed to *mastertones* or realtones (i.e., those incorporating a popular recording of the song).

Many ringtone licenses issued by record companies actually preclude the licensee from making and distributing polyphonic ringtones embodying the same underlying song — on the grounds that it would serve as competition, and therefore detract from sales, of the mastertone version, which would be the only version the record company makes money from.

Ringtones tied to visual materials are known as *videotones*. Because audiovisual works are not subject to the compulsory license provision, music publishers may charge whatever the market will bear for the use of their music in them. Typically, they are seeking the same kinds of fees and fee structures they used to before the Copyright Office declared audio ringtones to be subject to Section 115 and the Copyright Royalty Board set a 24¢ rate for ringtone deliveries. Thus, for videotones, many publishers are adopting the model they originally devised for audio ringtones, and in some cases are seeking a higher percentage or a higher floor, such as 15¢ to 20¢ (rather than 10¢ to 12¢).

## IV. ANALYSIS OF STANDARD U.S. MECHANICAL LICENSE TERMS

The following is a brief annotated analysis of a typical mechanical license agreement voluntarily entered into between a music publisher and one desiring to make mechanical reproductions of a musical work.

MECHANICAL LICENSE AGREEMENT

A) TITLE:

In entering the song's title, you should be precise. Many titles are similar and you should be consistent in how you identify the song in your files, databases, and licenses. It is good practice to use the internal song code you use to identify the song in your royalty system. If you have an internationally recognized identifier, such as an ISWC code, for the song, you should use it.

DATE:

This refers to the date of the license. The release date of the phonorecord is requested below.

WRITER(S):

You should list all writers of the song, including composers and lyricists. You don't need to include their relative ownership shares.

B) PUBLISHER(S):

List each copyright owner, or publisher, of the song.

C) RECORD NUMBER

If you wish to narrow the license as much as possible, use the record number (rather than the master) to be used in connection with the physical distribution of the recording. If this were a mechanical license allowing distribution of the song by means of digital phonorecord deliveries, you would be asked for the ISRC code of the particular recording. This will help the music publisher track income from digital download and subscription services.

CONFIGURATION:

This is the type of format to be used in the distribution of copies. For example, "CD-Compact Disc"

ARTIST

This is the recording artist performing on the sound recording released by the licensee, not an artist who may have recorded an existing release of the song.

LABEL

This is the name of label under which the recording will be released.

PLAYING TIME

This is the length, in minutes and seconds, of the recording. As discussed above, if the recording is longer than approximately 5.5 minutes, the mechanical license fee will be based on the long-song rate, rather than the minimum statutory rate.

ROYALTY RATE

The music publisher should be careful to check just how this blank is completed. If a 75% rate were given, it would say, "75% of the statutory rate." A licensee may wish to fix the rate at the "statutory rate effective on the date of commencement of recording of the master licensed hereunder" or at specific penny rate. To avoid any misunderstandings, the publisher may wish to state, "Statutory rate in effect at the time the phonorecords are made."

RELEASE DATE:

This would be the date the recording has been planned for release.

> You have advised us as [in our capacity as Agent for] the Publisher(s) referred to in (B) supra, that you wish to obtain a compulsory license to make and distribute phonorecords of the copyrighted work

> referred to in (A) supra, under the compulsory license provision of Section 115 of the Copyright Act.
>
> Upon doing so, you shall have all rights which are granted to, and all the obligations which are imposed upon, users of said copyrighted work under the compulsory license provision of the Copyright Act, after phonorecords of the copyrighted work have been distributed to the public in the United States under the authority of the copyright owner by another person, except that with respect to phonorecords thereof made and distributed hereunder:

This language says that all of the terms of the Section 115 compulsory license, including the regulations promulgated by the Copyright Office concerning the license, are incorporated by reference, except that the following terms alter the terms of the statutory license.

> 1) You shall pay royalties and account to us as Publisher(s) quarterly, within forty-five days after the end of each calendar quarter, on the basis of phonorecords made and distributed;

Under the statutory compulsory license, royalties and accountings would have been due monthly within 20 days after the end of the month in which the phonorecords were distributed. The voluntary license relaxes this requirement, providing that accountings be made quarterly within 45 days after the end of the quarter. Mechanical license fee reporting is almost always done on a quarterly basis, but some record companies, especially if the publisher is controlled by the label's recording artist, may ask that they report on a bi-annual basis, consistent with the payment schedule under the artist's contract.

> 2) For such phonorecords made and distributed, the royalty shall be the Statutory rate in effect at the time the phonorecord is made, except as otherwise stated in (C) supra;

The above makes it clear that, if the royalty rate set forth in (C) above simply said, "75% of the statutory rate," then the rate would be calculated on the basis of the statutory rate in effect at the time the phonorecords are made, not at the time the mechanical license was entered into or any other time.

> 3) This compulsory license covers and is limited to one particular recording of said copyrighted work as performed by the artist and on

> the phonorecord number identified in (C) supra; and this compulsory license does not supersede nor in any way affect any prior agreements now in effect respecting phonorecords of said copyrighted work;

This makes it clear that if there are multiple recordings of the same song, this license only applies to one of them; a separate license would be required for other recordings of the song on the album. It also limits the license to the use of the song on the record number identified in the license. See the prior section of this chapter on the relative advantages and disadvantages of using the record number in a mechanical license. Finally, as noted, sometimes a reduced rate is provided for the use of a recording in budget line or lower cost albums; this section makes it clear that this mechanical license only applies to the particular record licensed, making it clear that this mechanical license will not affect or modify any existing mechanical license agreements in effect, especially those licensed at a higher mechanical rate, concerning the licensed song. In addition, if you received an advance on fees under an existing mechanical license, this provision makes it clear that such advance is not recoupable from any royalties payable under this license.

> 4) In the event you fail to account to us and pay royalties as herein provided for, said Publisher(s) may give written notice to you that, unless the default is remedied within 30 days of your receipt of the notice, this compulsory license will be automatically terminated. Such termination shall render either the making or the distribution, or both, of all phonorecords for which royalties have not been paid, actionable as acts of infringement under, and fully subject to the remedies provided by, the Copyright Act;

The above provision makes it clear that upon breach of the mechanical license, the music publisher will have all of the remedies under the Copyright Act for infringement of copyright. Such remedies are more advantageous than those that would otherwise be afforded in a mere action for breach of contract.

> 5) You need not serve or file the notice of intention to obtain a compulsory license required by the Copyright Act;

One of the requirements of the compulsory license provision is that the compulsory licensee provide a specific statutory notice to the music publisher prior to engaging in the reproduction and distribution of the phonorecords under the license. The entry into a voluntary mechanical license takes the place of such notice and the above provision makes that clear.

> 6) This agreement is limited to the United States, its territories and possessions.

If you wish to make and distribute copies outside the United States, or export the copies you make in the United States under the license, you are still subject to the copyright laws of other countries, which may either require you to pay a separate mechanical license fee for the manufacture and distribution of the recording overseas or an additional mechanical license fee for the import of the phonorecords manufactured in the United States, even if you paid a mechanical license fee in the United States for such manufacture.

## V. CLEARING THE MECHANICAL LICENSE IN THE UNITED STATES

The mechanical license is one of the easiest forms of music licenses to clear — provided you know who controls the rights to the song.

### A. Clearing a Song for Use on an Album

To clear a song, or several songs, for use on a record album, you would start by compiling some of the basic information that a music publisher or administrator would require to complete the license form. The following information, from a form posted by The Harry Fox Agency on their website, is typical of the kind of information you should be prepared to provide a publisher:

- Name, address and phone number of the Individual or Company responsible for payment of royalties:
- Exact Title of the Song:

  (When requesting "Selections From . . ." or "Medley" usage, please indicate **INDIVIDUAL SONG TITLES USED**, as well as the number of selections used. Each title must be licensed separately.)

- Composer:

  (Include arranger's name if the original version of the song is in the Public Domain.)

- Publisher Name(s):

  (i.e., the copyright owners of the song). If you need assistance in finding publishing information, Harry Fox suggests you contact either **ASCAP** (www.ascap.com or 212-621-6160) or **BMI** (www.bmi.com or 212-586-2000).

- Configuration & Product Number:

  (Place the number you are assigning to your product on the appropriate line (LP, Cassette, CD). If you do not have a product number, place an "X" on the appropriate line. Be sure to enter information regarding **YOUR** recording, not for the artist who originally recorded the song.

- Playing Time:

  (The exact timing of each selection.)

- Release Date:

  (The month and year of intended release of your recording.)

- Artist:

  (For your recording.)

- Title of the Album:

  (For your recording.)

## B. Bulk Clearances

There are certain instances where clearing one license at a time would not be economical. You may be a record company with a repertoire of recordings, long available on vinyl LPs or CDs under mechanical licenses limited to such configurations, for which you now require mechanical licenses to make digital phonorecord deliveries. Or you may be an online subscription music service desiring to engage in limited downloads or on-demand streams of thousands of recordings, each requiring a mechanical license to be cleared. In such cases, music publishers, or their representative agencies or administrators, are generally willing to provide the mechanical licenses required covering the entire catalogs they represent. Approaching the publishers with information about the kinds of services in which you intend to engage will generally result in your obtaining a license to engage in such activities in accordance with the applicable statutory rates.

### C. Notice of Compulsory License

As noted in Chapter 5, on *International Subpublishing*, online music services in Europe face as much as a "30-stop shop" to license the music publishing rights they require to operate a music download or on-demand service. In the United States, it's far worse. The U.S. mechanical collection agency, the Harry Fox Agency, is purported to represent only about 65% of the copyrights required by the typical on-demand music service. Anyone setting up such a service may have to obtain a license from as many as 10,000 to 20,000 separate music publishers, in addition to a license to the repertoire represented by the Harry Fox Agency.

Obtaining a voluntary mechanical reproduction license from so many entities is a daunting task. As a result, some of these services have turned to clearance consultants who, rather than seek voluntary licenses from these publishers, send out instead a formal "notice of compulsory license," an example of which is set forth as Form 13.6 on the CD-ROM.

Music publishers have not taken a liking to receiving these notices and it is yet to be seen what the ultimate reaction will be — that is, whether publishers will take a more aggressive stand against these online services should they use copyrights that have not been properly cleared or when it comes time to perform an audit on these services.

## VI. MECHANICAL RIGHTS AGENCIES IN THE UNITED STATES

Thousands of recording companies seek licenses to record potentially hundreds of thousands of copyrighted compositions. Because it would be economically prohibitive for copyright owners to negotiate with the great number of potential licensees, many copyright owners and music publishers engage the services of a special representative for the purpose of licensing their compositions to be used in sound recordings. In the United States, The Harry Fox Agency, Inc.,[23] The Songwriter's Guild of America (formerly, the American Guild of Authors and Composers, or AGAC),[24] SESAC, Inc.,[25] and AMRA[26] are among the organizations that issue mechanical licenses.

The Harry Fox Agency, established in 1927 by the National Music Publishers Association (NMPA), is by far the largest of these, representing over 27,000 music publishers. In addition to issuing mechanical licenses, the Harry Fox Agency also grants, on behalf of many of its member publishers, licenses for synchronization music with motion pictures and television programs, licenses for the creation of electrical transcriptions, and licenses for the use of music in commercial advertising. It also engages in the auditing of books and records of the licensees, such as record companies, using music under licenses issued by the Agency. The NMPA also provides mediation services to those member publishers who require an alternative to litigation as a means of settling a dispute between or among them. The information required by the Harry Fox Agency for the issuance of a mechanical license includes: (1) the name of the person to whom the license is to be issued, (2) the title and writers of the composition, and, if known, the publisher(s), (3) the record number, (4) the performing artist, (5) the playing time in minutes and seconds of the composition, and (6) the release date of the record.

The Harry Fox Agency will not issue a mechanical license for less than the statutory rate without permission from the copyright owner of the song, to whom all such requests are promptly referred. For its services in issuing mechanical licenses, collecting royalties and distributing to publishers, as well as for the periodic audits of record manufacturers, the Harry Fox Agency charges a small fee based on a percentage of mechanical license fees collected. As of the time of this writing, the commission rate charged by the agency to its music publishing clients, or *principals*, for administering a mechanical license

[23] The Harry Fox Agency, Inc., 601 W. 26th St., Suite 500, New York, NY 10001, Phone: 212-834-0100, Fax: 646-487-6779; www.harryfox.com.

[24] The Songwriters Guild of America, 209 10th Avenue South, Suite 321, Nashville, TN 37203; Phone: 615-742-9945; Fax: 615-742-9948, www.songwriters.org.

[25] See Chapter 18, on *Licensing Music in Live and Recorded Public Performances*.

[26] Information on AMRA may be found at www.amermechrights.com.

was 7.75%. This commission rate has increased substantially in recent years up from 2.75% in 1995. As of January 1, 2002, it was increased to 6%. In 1994, the Harry Fox Agency collected $357.9 million in royalties on behalf of music publishers.

Mechanical reproduction rights in music are recognized by law throughout the world. Though mechanical license fees vary from country to country, there is a mechanical right society in nearly every country that recognizes these rights. Further information on international mechanical rights societies affiliated with the Harry Fox Agency may be obtained from the Harry Fox Agency.

An alternative to Harry Fox in the United States is the American Mechanical Rights Agency, Inc. (AMRA), which provided a number of services to music publishers. Many music publishers perform mechanical clearance and collection in-house or use music publishing administrators for these services.

## VII. International Mechanical Rights Administration

As discussed in Chapter 5, on *International Subpublishing*, mechanical rights administration overseas differs significantly from the way mechanical licensing is conducted in the United States. In addition, recent developments in European antitrust law are significantly affecting the way both mechanical and performance licenses are administered in connection with the digital delivery of music. These developments are discussed at length in the chapter on *International Subpublishing* with some of the practical effects discussed below.

In this section, we will provide an overview of how mechanical licensing is generally administered overseas, followed by some detail about how mechanical licenses are administered in Canada, the United Kingdom, and on a pan-European basis.

### A. Overview

By contrast with the way mechanical licenses are administered in the United States — with thousands of individual music publishers, as well as The Harry Fox Agency, the Songwriter's Guild, and organizations specializing in the administration of music publishing catalogs, who each issue licenses to record companies and others for the mechanical reproduction of music under the regime established by the compulsory license provision of the U.S. Copyright Act — the collection of mechanical royalties overseas is typically conducted through a single mechanical rights agency or collection society in each territory.

The mechanical rights societies who operate in this way include PRS for Music, formerly, MCPS (U.K.), SDRM (France), GEMA (Germany), JASRAC (Japan), SIAE (Italy), SGAE (Spain), among others. The mechanical rights administration in Canada operates somewhat like the way it works in the United States, except that there is no compulsory license statute and rates are either negotiated or set by a governmental tariff that applies to the Canadian mechanical rights agencies, CMRRA, the *Canadian Musical Reproduction Rights Agency Limited*, and its French Canadian counterpart, SODRAC, discussed in more detail below.

Moreover, in most territories, licensing from the local mechanical rights society is *mandatory*. This means that all mechanical licenses in the territory are issued by the collection society, not by the individual music publishers; in other words, all record companies in the territory are required to pay mechanical royalties to the collection society, not to the individual publishers. In addition, the *pass-through* mechanical licenses that permit mechanical licenses obtained from music publishers by record labels to be passed through to allow online music services to make permanent downloads, does not, for the most part, exist overseas. The download services, such as iTunes Europe, iTunes Japan, and iTunes Australia, pay mechanical royalties for the music downloads they make, not to the record labels from whom they have licensed the sound recordings, but directly to the local collection society.

Further, rather than being set by statute, mechanical rates overseas are generally set by some form of collective bargaining agreement between the mandatory mechanical rights organizations and the record companies, or an organization representing them. From time to time, a confederation of mechanical rights organizations from 30 countries called BIEM, the *Bureau International des Societes Gerant les Droits d'Enregistrement et de Reproduction Mecanique*, gets together with IFPI, *the International Federation of Phonogram Industries*, representing the record companies, and these two organizations negotiate a collective bargaining agreement setting forth the terms and conditions for the licensing of mechanical reproductions. The terms of these agreements are then administered by the member mechanical rights societies on a country-by-country basis. The mechanical fees in some territories, however, are set by the local government, which is the case in Japan and India.

As noted above, mechanical royalties in the United States are effectively determined by the statutory rate, which is expressed as a number of cents per song for each copy made and distributed. Mechanical royalties overseas, whether established by a mechanical licensing society, the local government, or collective bargaining arrangement, are usually expressed as a *percentage* of either the retail selling price (RSP) or the published price to the dealer (PPD) of the compact disc or audiocassette recordings in which the composition is embodied. Further, the license is not issued on a per song basis, but this license is issued and the fee is collected on the entire album, regardless of the number of songs it contains. The percentage fees vary from about 6% to over 10% of PPD for the entire album. These rates are generally higher than those charged for mechanical reproduction in the United States and Canada.

The means by which the publishers get paid the mechanical royalties to which they are entitled is through a *claims* process — each local publisher registers with the collection society its claim to mechanical royalties with respect to each of its compositions, indicating its interest in the entire song or, in the case of split copyright ownership, its percentage interest in the composition. Subpublishers are often required to prove their claim by filing a copy of their subpublishing agreement with the collection society. In many countries, unclaimed mechanical royalties go into what is referred to metaphorically as, a *black box*, which, after a period of time, gets distributed to local subpublishing companies under procedures that vary from country to country. Black box moneys and what a U.S. subpublisher can do about them are discussed further in Chapter 5, on *International Subpublishing*.

## B. Mechanical License Administration in Canada

Canada is among the top 10 music markets in the world and represents about 2% of worldwide music publishing royalties. In Canada, as in other countries, if you sell, import, or distribute sound recordings containing copyrighted musical works, you must obtain a mechanical reproduction license. Mechanical royalties may be payable by record companies and others who manufacture recordings in Canada or import them into Canada or by online music services, which offer digital downloads, limited downloads, or on-demand streams from locations in Canada.

### *1. Mechanical Royalties Payable by Record Companies*

Unlike the United States, there is no compulsory license provision under the Canadian copyright law for the traditional manufacturing or importation of musical works in Canada. Until 1988, Canada's copyright law provided for a fixed price for each copy manufactured, but since then, the rates for mechanical licenses issued in Canada are, with some exceptions, established by industry negotiation (between representatives of the record industry and representatives of the music publishers).

Most mechanical licenses issued in Canada are issued by one of two mechanical rights collection agencies: CMRRA, the *Canadian Musical Reproduction Rights Agency Limited*, and its French Canadian counterpart, SODRAC. As of 2007, CMRRA represented approximately 38,240 music publishing catalogs. SODRAC represents over 4,100 songwriters and 1,600 music publishers, as well as others through their reciprocal agreements with foreign societies. In 2002, CMRRA and SODRAC formed CMRRA/SODRAC, Inc., also known as CSI, for the purpose of collecting royalties on their behalf for the reproduction of musical works in their respective repertoires by commercial radio stations. Later, CSI received an exclusive mandate from CMRRA and SODRAC to license the reproduction of musical works by online music services.

The following table shows the negotiated mechanical royalty rates in effect since 1988, expressed in Canadian dollars. Though no one is bound to these rates, they are considered "usual and customary" and have been used by CMRRA.

| *Effective Date of New Rate* | *Cents Per Copy* | *Cents Per Minute of Playing Time* |
|---|---|---|
| 1988 | 5.25 | 1.05 |
| 1990 | 5.9 | 1.18 |
| 1992 | 6.25 | 1.25 |
| 1994 | 6.47 | 1.294 |
| 1998 | 6.6 | 1.32 |
| 2000 | 7.1 | 1.42 |
| 2001 | 7.4 | 1.48 |
| 2002 | 7.7 | 1.54 |
| Current | 8.1 | 1.62 |

Currently, CMRRA issues mechanical licenses for 8.1¢ (Canadian) per copy for up to 5 minutes of playing time; for each additional minute (or part thereof) 1.62¢ is added to this rate. Like the Harry Fox Agency, CMRRA does not have a monopoly over mechanical licenses issued for copies made or imported to its country. Some music publishers who are not members of CMRRA charge a rate that is higher than the industry norm. Some U.S.-based publishers prefer to issue mechanical licenses to Canadian record companies. When they do, they typically use the Canadian rate. Under NAFTA, there is no tax on Canadian royalties paid to a U.S. company.

When a mechanical license is issued by CMRRA for traditional manufacturing or importing of copies, they do so under one of two kinds of licenses: (1) "pay-as-you-press" or (2) a "mechanical license agreement."

*Pay-As-You-Press.* If the record company plans to manufacture or import copies in very small quantities, or is releasing a sound recording on a "one-shot" basis, CMRRA will issue a Pay-As-You-Press License. Under this method, the licensee pays the appropriate license fee, at the standard royalty rate (e.g., $.081 per person, per copy for up to 5 minutes), at the time the license application is made. Canadian residents must add tax (e.g., 5% GST). Applications for this form of license may be obtained from the CMRRA website.

*Mechanical License Agreement.* If the licensee plans to manufacture or import recordings on a continual basis, CMRAA may require that it enter into their standard CMRAA Mechanical License Agreement. Under this form of agreement, mechanical royalties are payable on a quarterly basis, no later than 45 days after the end of each calendar quarter in which the copies are made. Royalty payments must be accompanies by formal royalty statements conforming to CMRAA's requirements.

### 2. Mechanical Royalties Payable by Online Services

#### a. Overview

On March 16, 2007, the Copyright Board of Canada changed the way mechanical reproduction licenses were administered with respect to copies made by online music services. Until that time, the online services and record companies took the same position as they did in the United States: sound recordings permanently downloaded to consumers by online music services were authorized under the terms of the existing mechanical licenses the labels obtained for physical CD manufacturing. In other words, the mechanical reproduction license was *passed through* from the record companies to the online services just as they were in the United States. In addition, the mechanical license rate used for physical sales were customarily applied to permanent downloads. The rates for limited downloads and on-demand streams were somewhat less clear, with the online services taking the position that on-demand streams did not require a reproduction license at all.

In 2004, CSI — acting on behalf of the interests of the members of CMRRA and SODRAC — filed a formal statement in accordance with the Canadian Copyright Act, regarding the royalty fees they proposed to charge for the use of the musical works they represent by online music services. A long list of potential users, including representatives for the record companies and online music services, filed their objections to CSI's proposed terms and conditions. In 2006, hearings were held by the Copyright Board of Canada to address the rates proposed and other aspects of the administration of mechanical reproductions of musical works in connection with permanent music downloads, limited downloads, and on-demand streams. Their decision, published on March 16, 2007, took the form of the *CSI Online Music Services Tariff, 2005-2007*

(CSI Tariff), a copy of which is contained in Appendix Law 13.4 at the end of this chapter.

*b. Role of Record Labels in Administering Online Licensing*

The most significant aspect of the Board's decision was to eliminate the role of record labels in the administration of reproduction licenses for musical works used in online music services — that is, they eliminated the pass-through license for works licensed under the tariff. The Board determined that allowing labels to license the use of CSI's repertoire under the tariff would add an unnecessary layer of communication between the collection societies and the online services, overly complicating the way in which CSI would obtain the information to which it is entitled. In addition, the entities ultimately responsible for paying the royalties are the online services; being that the online services bear the ultimate burden for any errors, they are least likely to commit them.

It is important to note that the CSI Tariff is only legally binding on the mechanical rates to be charged by CSI (i.e., CMRRA and SODRAQ). Any music publishers who are not members of either society, or who prefer to issue their own mechanical licenses, are not bound by the tariff, enabling them to charge what they wish for the required mechanical licenses. It is expected that the rates set forth in the tariff will become the "usual and customary rate" charged by music publishers who don't use CMRRA or SODRAQ for the administration of their online mechanical licensing.

Because there is no compulsory license in Canada, music publishers could even demand that sound recordings containing their music be taken down from online music services operating in Canada until their permission is obtained. By the same token, any online music service, such as iTunes, who engages in the distribution of musical works online without a license from CMRRA or SODRAQ — or if the work is not represented by either, without a license from the appropriate music publisher — could be committing copyright infringement.

There remains a question, however, the extent to which pass-through licenses may still be used to license works not represented by CSI. Whether the online service could rely on such a license would depend upon the language of the mechanical license issued by the music publisher. But relying on traditional mechanical licenses may be problematic. It is not likely that music publishers ever issued mechanical licenses authorizing on-demand streams or limited downloads at less than the full usual and customary rate applied to physical manufacturing. Where they issued mechanical licenses for physical reproduction, they typically restricted the reproduction to a specified configuration (e.g., LP, CD, cassette), in which case digital downloading would not have been authorized and would therefore not be subject to pass-through by the record labels.

The Copyright Board seemed to recognize that, in certifying a tariff that contemplates that online music services could be making copies of musical works not licensed by CSI, it "entrenches the systematic violation of the rights of those whom CSI does not represent." The Board, for a variety of practical reasons — e.g., "no one wishes to expend resources to determine who owns rights in something that generates no royalties" — concluded that this would simply have to be re-examined in subsequent proceedings.

#### c. *Rates Established by the CSI Tariff*

##### (1) Permanent Music Downloads

The rate payable to CSI under the tariff for each permanent download of musical works in their repertoire is 8.8% of the amount paid by a consumer for the download, subject to a minimum of 4.5¢ per file in a bundle and 5.9¢ per file in all other cases.

A *bundle* is defined as "two or more digital files offered as a single product, if at least one file is a permanent download." A *permanent download* is defined as "a download other than a limited download and a *limited download* is defined as 'a download that uses technology that causes the file to become unusable when a subscription ends.' "

For downloads occurring prior to January 1, 2008, the Board provided a 10% discount. Thus, the rate for permanent downloads occurring prior to January 1, 2008 is 7.9% of the amount paid by a consumer for the download, subject to a minimum of 4.1¢ per file in a bundle and 5.3¢ per file in all other cases.

### (2) Limited Downloads

The rate payable to CSI under the tariff for an online music service that offers limited downloads with or without on-demand streams is as follows: (A × B)/C — where A is 5.9% of the amounts paid by subscribers for the service during the month, B is the number of limited downloads requiring a CSI license during the month, and C is the total number of limited downloads during the month; subject to a minimum of 57¢ per subscriber if portable limited downloads are allowed and 37.4¢ per subscriber if they are not.

A *portable limited download* is "a limited download that uses technology that allows the subscriber to reproduce the file on a device other than a device to which an online music service delivered the file."

For limited downloads occurring prior to January 1, 2008, the Board provided a 10% discount. Thus, the rate payable for limited downloads with or without on-demand streams occurring prior to January 1, 2008 was as follows: (A × B)/C — where A is 5.3% of the amounts paid by subscribers for the service during the month, B is the number of limited downloads requiring a CSI license during the month, and C is the total number of limited downloads during the month; subject to a minimum of 51.3¢ per subscriber if portable limited downloads are allowed and 33.7¢ per subscriber if they are not.

### (3) On-Demand Streams

The rate payable to CSI under the tariff for an online music service that offers only on-demand streams of musical works in the CSI repertoire is as follows: (A × B)/C — where A is 4.6% of the amounts paid by subscribers for the service during the month, B is the number of plays of files requiring a CSI license during the month, and C is the total number of plays of all files during the month; subject to a minimum of 29.2¢ per subscriber.

An *on-demand stream* is defined as "a stream selected by its recipient." A *stream* means "a file that is intended to be copied onto a local storage device only to the extent required to allow listening to the file at substantially the same time as when the file is transmitted."

For limited downloads occurring prior to January 1, 2008, the Board provided a 10% discount. Thus, the rate payable to CSI for services that offers only on-demand streams occurring prior to January 1, 2008 was as follows: (A × B)/C — where A is 4.1% of the amounts paid by subscribers for the service during the month, B is the number of plays of files requiring a CSI license during the month, and C is the total number of plays of all files during the month; subject to a minimum of 26.3¢ per subscriber.

*d. Musical Works Not in the CMRRA or SODRAQ Repertoire*

Where CSI does not hold all the rights in a musical work, with respect to on-demand streams or limited downloads, only the share that CSI holds shall be included in "B" in the numerator of royalty formula; with respect to permanent downloads, the applicable rate shall be the relevant rate multiplied by CSI's share in the musical work.

To the extent a musical work is not licensed by CSI, under what authority may the online service engage in permanent downloads, limited downloads, or on-demand streams of the work? As noted above, the CSI Tariff is only legally binding on the mechanical rates to be charged by CSI (i.e., CMRRA and SODRAQ). Any music publishers who are not members of either society, or who prefer to issue their own mechanical licenses, are not bound by the tariff. Because there is no compulsory license in Canada, the online music service who engages in the distribution of musical works not licensed from CMRRA or SODRAQ, and not licensed by the work's music publisher, could well be committing copyright infringement.

Again, the Copyright Board recognized that, in certifying a tariff, it "entrenches the systematic violation of the rights of those whom CSI does not represent." For practical reasons, the Board concluded it would have to re-examine the matter in subsequent proceedings.

*e. Reproductions Covered*

The tariff allows an online music service and its authorized distributors to make all reproductions required in connection with the operation of the service, including server and any intermediary copies made to facilitate the service. It also allows the service to provide 30-second promotional and other previews without incurring any liability or reporting obligations.

*f. Reporting Requirements*

According to the CSI Tariff, each month the online services are expected to report to CSI basic information about the files it posts on its servers and other information necessary for CSI to calculate the royalties owed. CSI will then determine which files use CSI's repertoire, calculate the royalties owed to it, and invoice the services for royalties due.

Specifically, the online music services must provide CSI with information identifying the person or entity who operates the online music service, including the identity of the corporation, officers, any trade names it operates under, the address of its principal place of business, the name and address of any authorized distributor, and the URL of each Internet website at or through which the service is or will be offered.

In addition, with respect to each file that was reproduced, the service must provide CSI:

- its identifier,
- the title of the musical work,
- the name of each performer or group to whom the sound recording is credited,
- the name of the person who released the sound recording;
- if the file is being offered as part of a bundle, the name and identifier of the bundle,
- if the service believes that a CSI license is not required, an indication to that effect;
- if the sound recording was released in physical format as part of an album, the name, identifier, product catalog number and Universal Product Code (UPC) assigned to the album, together with the associated disc and track numbers,
- the Global Release Identifier (Grid) assigned to the file and, if applicable, the Grid of the album or bundle in which the file was released,
- the running time of the file, in minutes and seconds; and
- any alternative title used to designate the musical work or sound recording.

Basic music publishing information, however, need only be supplied to the extent the information is available to the online music service. Thus, with respect to each file that was reproduced, the service must provide to CSI, *if the information is available*:

i. the name of each author of the musical work,

ii. the ISRC code assigned to the sound recording,

iii. the name of the music publisher associated with the musical work, and

iv. the ISWC code assigned to the musical work.

The above information must be updated periodically. Within 20 days after receiving any such report from the online music service, CSI must send to the online music service a note indicating:

(a) which files contain a work that it then knows to be in the repertoire;

(b) which files contain a work that it then knows not to be in the repertoire;

(c) which files contain a work that it then knows to be in the repertoire only as to a fraction of the rights, with an indication of that fraction; and

(d) with respect to all other files, an indication of the reason for which CSI is unable to provide an answer pursuant to paragraph (*a*), (*b*) or (*c*).

No later than 20 days after receiving such a report from CSI, the online music service that disputes the indication that a file contains a work in the repertoire or requires a CSI license, shall provide to CSI information that establishes why the license is not required, unless the information was provided earlier.

Within 20 days after the end of each month, an online music service shall provide to CSI a sales report reflecting the number of plays or downloads, as applicable, for files requiring a CSI license, including the appropriate identifying information for those files.

Within 20 days after the last month in each quarter in which CSI has received such sales reports, CSI shall provide the online music service with a detailed calculation of the royalties payable in that quarter for each file and an invoice for such royalties. Royalties shall be due no later than 30 days after an online music service receives such invoice.

*g. Audit Rights*

The online service must maintain the information used as the basis of the royalty calculations for a period of 6 years after the end of the month to which they relate. CSI may audit such records during such a 6-year period. If an audit discloses that royalties due have been understated (not due to errors by CSI) in any quarter by more than 10%, the online music service must pay the reasonable costs of the audit.

*h. Late Fees*

Any amount not received by the due date shall bear interest at a rate equal to 1% above the Bank Rate on the last day of the preceding month (as published by the Bank of Canada).

## C. Mechanical License Administration in the United Kingdom

The United Kingdom is among the top five music markets in the world, representing about 10% of worldwide music publishing income. In the United Kingdom, as in nearly all countries outside the United States, record labels need only pay mechanical royalties for the sales songs embodied in physical copies (e.g., CDs, LPs, etc.) of their recordings; for copies sold by means of digital download, the online services pay mechanical royalties to the collection societies directly.

We will first explain how mechanical royalties are administered when they are payable by record companies, followed by how mechanical royalties are administered when payable by online music services.

### *1. Mechanical Royalties Payable by Record Companies*

Mechanical reproduction rights are administered in the United Kingdom very much like they are administered in Canada. The mechanical collection society in the United Kingdom is PRS for

Music (formerly, MCPS). Like CMRRA in Canada, PRS provides two basic methods for labels to report mechanicals on physical sales of audio-only recordings in physical formats (e.g., CDs, LPs, cassettes):

**AP1 Accounting** — where sales for all physical products are reported to MCPS on a quarterly basis, and,

**AP2 Accounting** — where royalties are paid in advance for the creation of physical products.

Entities that only expect to engage in a one-off pressing, or infrequent manufacture, of CDs that are not intended for distribution by a third party may apply for a Limited Manufacture License (LM). LM licenses are not available to record companies.

*a. AP1 Accounting*

Nearly all labels of substantial size or credibility use AP1 Accounting, which enables them to report their sales each quarter *after* the copies are sold and distributed, rather than *before* they are shipped out of the place of manufacture.

*Application.* Under the AP1 Accounting scheme, PRS requires that a record company follows a specific process for qualifying for the scheme, obtaining licenses, and reporting their sales. Inclusion in the AP1 Accounting scheme involves an application process involving a demonstration of a label's creditworthiness and administrative capability. A deposit of 50% of the royalties estimated during the first year may be required; the deposit will normally be refunded (with interest) after a year of fully satisfactory accounting. A label may apply for AP1 Accounting by completing the forms available on the PRS website.

*License Clearance.* Once admitted, the label applies for individual product licenses. A label obtains a clearance for each audio product it intends to ship by either completing an Excel spreadsheet provided by PRS for this purpose or, if the label is a member of PPL, the label may apply for clearance via Catco, which will forward the product details to PRS. Otherwise, a label may use a Notification of Intended Release (NIR) Form available on the PRS website. Upon receipt of a Notice of Intended Release, by any of the methods above, PRS will promptly issue a mechanical license.

*Sales Reporting*. A royalty becomes payable to PRS when an AP1 product is shipped from the label's distribution center. The net figure is calculated by taking the gross quantity shipped less returns within the same quarter, and less other adjustments, such as promotional copies and any negative balance brought forward from a previous quarter on the same catalog number and format. This information is supplied via a Statement of Shipments (SOS), which is due within 21 days after the end of each accounting quarter. SOS must be submitted electronically by either a PRS-approved Excel spreadsheet format or a format produced by either a commercially available software package (e.g., RoyaltyShare, Musicalc, Record Maestro) or the label's own proprietary software.

*Invoicing by PRS*. Upon receipt of an SOS, PRS's Royalty Operations department matches each line in the report to royalty information held in its system and applies the specified royalty rate (see below). PRS sends this information, 38 days after the end of the quarter, back to the label in the form of an invoice, noting the amount of the mechanical royalties due. Any unmatched items will be investigated further, and as soon as they are identified, another invoice will be generated. Payment is due by the 45th day after the end of the quarter.

*Rate*. The rate applied to albums sold is currently (2008) 8.5% of the published dealer price (plus VAT). Different rates may be applicable under certain circumstances; for example, where the published dealer price is not available the rate is 6.5% (plus VAT). The charges are reduced proportionately if music on the product (e.g., CD, LP) is in the public domain or is not in the PRS repertoire. Where timings are not available, tracks will be treated as of equal duration.

*Royalty Calculation*. The precise way PRS calculates the amount of mechanicals due to a label is quite complex, taking into account several factors including the status of the product (whether it is *deleted* or not), the sales channel, the country of sale, and the net units (i.e., gross units shipped, less units returned and promotional units). Mechanicals due for product shipped outside of the United Kingdom may differ depending upon the territory.

*Retentions*. For the first four periods of a product's life, a label is allowed but not required to hold *retentions* (same as *reserves* against returns) against this product for United Kingdom based sales only. Retention rates are set by PRS and are based on a variety of factors, including whether the product is being advertised on TV — because albums advertised on TV have a potentially higher rate of return, MCPS allows labels to hold extra retentions on them. On the fifth period, after the four retention periods, retentions are fully released.

*Promotional Copies*. Labels may make up to 1,500 copies of albums and 3,000 copies of singles used for promotional purposes without mechanical royalty obligation, provided that (i) the notice, "PROMOTIONAL COPY — NOT FOR SALE" is displayed on the product packaging as either a non-removable sticker or non-erasable notice and (ii) the copies are provided free of charge to broadcasters, DJs, critics, or other relevant parties for promotional use only (e.g., review or broadcast). The number of promotional copies manufactured must be set forth in the SOS.

*Territory*. Any U.K.-based label may manufacture a product in the United Kingdom and pay mechanical royalties under the U.K. rate and ship the product throughout the European Union without further mechanical royalty obligation.

*Administrative Assessment*. PRS may conduct an assessment visit to discuss requirements of AP1 Accounting and to examine the administrative arrangements for compliance. New labels can expect a full audit within 12 months of the start of the agreement. In addition, a stock check must be performed and provided to PRS prior to the commencement of the agreement. The quantities of stock for each item must be entered on the first SOS in the Prior Negative Quarter column to prevent paying royalties twice on these items.

*Copyright Control*. Labels must also establish a special bank account for royalties due on musical works where the current copyright ownership is in dispute or is designated "Copyright Control" (i.e., ownership unidentified). Written confirmation of these accounts must be made with PRS in advance of the commencement date of the agreement. When PRS identifies that a musical work is in either category, the relevant royalty sum should be placed in the appropriate account until the dispute is resolved or the owner is identified.

*Compliance*. Failure to comply with the terms of AP1 Accounting may be grounds for termination, which may result in the label's moving back to AP2 Accounting, requiring payment of mechanical royalties in advance of manufacture.

#### *b. AP2 Accounting*

Under AP2 Accounting, the label is charged based on the copies of products to be manufactured in advance of the actual manufacture. (Amateur music users who do not intend to distribute products in retail channels or through other third parties may be eligible for the PRS Limited Manufacture License.) The forms required to engage in AP2 Accounting are available on the PRS website.

The rates charged are the same as under AP1 Accounting and products manufactured may be distributed throughout the European Union with no further mechanical royalty obligation. The label must apply for a license for each product to be manufactured through the PRS website or, if the label is a member of PPL, through the PPL Repertoire database. Once the label tells how many products it intends to reproduce, PRS generates an invoice for mechanical royalties due. Once PRS receives the label's payment in advance for the pressing, PRS will grant clearance for pressing to the manufacturer.

To manufacture additional copies, the label completes a re-press form and returns it to PRS. PRS will return a license to press and provide a clearance to the manufacturer.

Promotional copies must follow the same guidelines as under AP1 Accounting, but where the label is applying for a first pressing of 500 copies or more, only up to 25% may be cleared as promotional copies, with a limit of 400 per format for a single and 250 per format for an album.

### *2. Mechanical Royalties Payable by Online Services*

Unlike the way mechanical royalties are administered for some uses of music by online services in the United States, where such royalties may be passed through the owners of the sound recordings before being paid to the music publishers, the mechanical license regime followed in most of the world, including the United Kingdom, places the obligation to pay mechanical royalties on the online music services, who must calculate and pay the mechanical royalties to the music publishing collection societies, rather than to the record companies.

In addition, the licensing regime in the United States draws a sharp line between performance licenses issued by the performance rights societies, and mechanical reproduction licenses issued by music publishers and their agents, such as the Harry Fox Agency. Licensees whose music uses invoke the music publisher's public performance (or public communication) and reproduction rights must negotiate with several organizations for the licenses they require. A sharp line also divides the regime for obtaining licenses for audio-only uses of music (often obtainable from the Harry Fox Agency) and licenses for audiovisual uses, which the licensee must almost always need to obtain directly from the music publisher or administrator of each individual copyright or copyright interest involved.

By contrast, in the United Kingdom, the mechanical collection society (MCPS) has been combined with the performance rights society (PRS) to form a single organization (PRS for Music) now responsible for licensing both the performance licenses (as well as *public communication licenses*) and the reproduction licenses necessary for the use of music online — the so-called, *joint online license* (JOL). In addition, PRS for Music is authorized to issue certain kinds of synchronization licenses for online use where music in their repertoire is used in music videos downloaded and streamed over the Internet.

By being able to represent the interests of songwriters in the licensing of public performances and mechanical reproductions, as well as certain kinds of audiovisual synchronization uses, PRS for Music, and similar counterparts in other countries, have been able to establish a more coherent regime for the licensing of music online. It also makes moot questions such as whether a permanent download constitutes a performance or whether an on-demand stream invokes the reproduction right. PRS for Music is in a position to provide all the clearance the licensee requires for the covered use.

The terms of the JOL were first established after unsuccessful negotiations between PRS for Music and the representatives of the online music services to agree on rates. The failure to negotiate a rate led to a hearing before the U.K. Copyright Tribunal which, in 2007, established rates for various online uses of music that remained in effect until June, 2009. Negotiations for rates to take effect upon the expiration of the JOL began in November, 2008, resulting in a series of new online music license rates (OML), which took effect on July 1, 2009.

The remainder of this section will summarize the basic license terms offered by PRS for Music for the various uses of the music in their repertoire online. Except where indicated below, these terms have been in effect since July 1, 2009 and shall run through June 30, 2012, though they may be subject to change as market circumstances warrant or as may be changed by appeal to U.K. Copyright Tribunal. In addition, the following is merely a summary of the applicable licenses. For the full details, the latest license terms, as set forth on the PRS website, should be consulted.[27]

Finally, it is important to note that the JOL and OML only apply to compositions represented by PRS for Music for online licensing. As of the time of this writing, all four major record companies have pulled their Anglo-American repertoires out of PRS for Music, and placed them in the care of one or more of the organizations described in the next section for pan-European licensing. This effectively left PRS for Music with less than 20% of its former repertoire available for online licensing in the United Kingdom.

In addition, the JOL and OML licenses only apply to compositions represented by PRS for Music for *national* licensing — that is, the licensing of online music services that deliver or transmit compositions to users located in the United Kingdom. Thus, any online music service delivering musical works only to U.K. users (i.e., a *national service*) can get a single license, in a single document (i.e., the OML), from PRS for Music for all mechanical reproductions and performances made to users in the United Kingdom. Should the service wish to deliver the music to users in other countries, it must enter into a pan-European license with each entity that offers it with respect to their respective repertoires. (Pan-European licensing is discussed in the next section). No one said this was easy.

*a. Music Download License (permanent downloads)*

*Coverage.* This license provides the public performance (or communication) and reproduction rights in musical works for use in

[27] www.prsformusic.com

permanent download services. It also covers the following types of audiovisual uses: (a) promotional music videos, (b) live concert performances, (c) combination of a musical work with images relating to the performer or composer of the work, and (d) the use of a musical work with an interview with an artist, composer, producer, or other person involved in the creation of music, where the work used is associated with the interviewee.

The license does not include the following:

- Moral rights,
- Graphic rights,
- The right to "adapt" a musical work,
- The "synchronization" of musical works with images (e.g., the filming of a music concert) for the purpose of online or mobile exploitation,
- The use of unauthorized arrangements, adaptations, parodies, burlesques and dramatico-musical works,
- The use of commercial musical works in contexts in which the licensee ought reasonably to consider as being prejudicial to the public standing of the composer, artist featured, or relevant copyright owners,
- The rights in sound recordings of musical work,
- Use of music with advertising or sponsorship of any product or service,
- Use of music in any audiovisual material other than that mentioned above,
- Mobile ringtones,
- Podcasting services, and
- "Simulcasting" of traditional scheduled broadcast services.

To engage in any such uses, permission must be cleared directly with the music publisher or appropriate rightsholder.

*Royalty Rate.* The royalty rate payable for permanent downloads containing the covered uses of musical works is 8% of gross revenue, subject to the following minimums:

| *Number of musical works in bundle* | *Royalty per musical work downloaded* |
|---|---|
| 1-7 | 4p |
| 8-12 | 3.5p |
| 13-17 | 3p |
| 18-29 | 2.5p |
| 30 or more | 2p |

*Gross Revenue.* Gross revenue means all revenue received by the licensee either directly from its users (via subscription fees or paid for activities) or other revenue streams, including, but not limited to, advertising, sponsorship, and commissions.

*Territory.* The territory is limited to delivering compositions to users located in the United Kingdom.

*Accounting and Reporting.* Online services generating up to £500,000 of gross revenue may report quarterly, within one month after the quarter's end, while services whose gross revenue exceeds that amount must report monthly, within one week of the month's end.

*Advertising.* Advertising revenue should be included as part of the total Gross Revenue where:

- An audio or audiovisual (or sponsorship message) is included within a stream or download or plays before or while a file is downloaded;
- Only music is offered; or
- Music contributes 75% or more of the area of the page. The space taken up by the advertising is ignored when carrying out the calculation;
- Revenue generated from sponsored searches, including click-through revenue from such searches is excluded.

*Discounts Applied to Gross Revenue.* Royalties are also subject to the following discounts and are applied against revenue only, not the minimums:

- 5% to be deducted from advertising revenue to reflect the cost of obtaining advertising or sponsorship;
- 15% to be deducted from Gross Revenue where it relates to the provision of audiovisual material.

The above reductions apply until retail prices for audiovisual material converge with audio-only material.

*Discounts for mobile permanent downloads and other mobile devices.* Rates and minimums are as for the services above, except that:

- For mobile permanent downloads, the Gross Revenue is reduced by 15%;
- For all other mobile services, the applicable revenue is reduced by 7.5%;
- The above reductions apply until prices converge with non-mobile prices.

*b. Music On Demand (Non-Subscription) License*

*Coverage.* This license covers both the performance and mechanical rights in musical works for on-demand streaming and limited/tethered download services where the service is not funded by subscription. It also covers the following types of audiovisual uses: (a) promotional music videos, (b) live concert performances, (c) combination of a musical work with images relating to the performer or composer of the work, and (d) the use of a musical work with an interview with an artist, composer, producer or other person involved in the creation of music, where the work used is associated with the interviewee.

As with the permanent download license, the music on demand license does not include the following: moral rights; graphic rights; the right to "adapt" a musical work; the synchronization of musical works with images (e.g., the filming of a music concert) for the purpose of online or mobile exploitation; the use of unauthorized arrangements, adaptations, parodies, burlesques, and dramatico-musical works; the use of commercial musical works in contexts in which the licensee ought reasonably to consider as being prejudicial to the public standing of the composer, artist featured or relevant copyright owners; the rights in sound recordings of musical work; use of music with advertising or sponsorship of any product or service; use of music in any audiovisual material other than that mentioned above; mobile ringtones; podcasting services; and simulcasting of traditional scheduled broadcast services. To engage in any such uses, permission must be cleared directly with the music publisher or appropriate rightsholder.

*Royalty Rate.* The royalty rate payable for on-demand streaming and limited downloads not offered on a subscription basis is 10.5% of gross revenue, subject to a minimum of .085p per track streamed. "Gross revenue" means all revenue received by the licensee either directly from its users (via subscription fees or paid for activities) or other revenue streams, including, but not limited to, advertising, sponsorship and commissions.

*Territory.* The territory is limited to delivering compositions to users located in the United Kingdom.

*Accounting and Reporting.* Online services generating up to £500,000 of gross revenue may report quarterly, within one month after the quarter's end, while services whose gross revenue exceeds that amount must report monthly, within one week of the month's end.

*Discounts.* The terms outlined in the previous section (relating to permanent downloads) for advertising, discounts applied to gross revenue, and discounts for mobile permanent downloads and other mobile devices, also apply to the music on-demand license.

### c. *Music On Demand (Subscription) License*

*Coverage.* This license covers both the performance and mechanical rights in musical works for on-demand streaming and limited/tethered download services where the service is funded by subscription. As with the basic Music On Demand License, this license also covers the several types of audiovisual uses listed in the previous section, and the same coverage exclusions outlined in the previous section apply here.

*Royalty Rate.* The royalty rate payable for on-demand streaming and limited downloads offered on a subscription basis is 8% of gross revenue, subject to the following minimums:

| *Type of Access* | *Per subscriber per month* |
|---|---|
| Duel Platform | 60p |
| Single Platform | 40p |
| Limited Service (<20,000 tracks) | 20p |

*Gross Revenue.* Gross revenue means all revenue received by the licensee either directly from its users (via subscription fees or paid for activities) or other revenue streams, including, but not limited to, advertising, sponsorship, and commissions.

*Territory.* The territory is limited to delivering compositions to users located in the United Kingdom.

*Accounting and Reporting.* Online services generating up to £500,000 of gross revenue may report quarterly, within one month after the quarter's end, while services whose gross revenue exceeds that amount must report monthly, within one week of the month's end.

*Discounts.* The terms outlined in the previous section (relating to on-demand streams on a non-subscription basis) for advertising, discounts applied to gross revenue, and discounts for mobile permanent downloads and other mobile devices, also apply to the music on-demand license.

### d. *Interactive Webcast (Non-Subscription) License*

*Coverage.* This license covers both the performance and mechanical rights in musical works in interactive webcasting services, where the service is funded by any means other than subscription (e.g., advertising-based service). An interactive service is on where the user of the service can influence the music they hear (e.g., play, fast forward, skip tracks, etc.). As with the on-demand music licenses, this license also covers the several types of audiovisual uses listed in the previous section, and the same coverage exclusions outlined in the previous section apply here.

*Royalty Rate.* The royalty rate payable for on-demand streaming and limited downloads offered on a subscription basis is 8% of gross revenue, subject to a minimum of 0.65p per track streamed.

*Gross Revenue*. Gross revenue means all revenue received by the licensee either directly from its users (via subscription fees or paid for activities) or other revenue streams, including, but not limited to, advertising, sponsorship and commissions.

*Territory*. The territory is limited to delivering compositions to users located in the United Kingdom.

*Accounting and Reporting*. Online services generating up to £500,000 of gross revenue may report quarterly, within one month after the quarter's end, while services whose gross revenue exceeds that amount must report monthly, within one week of the month's end.

*Discounts*. The terms outlined in the previous section (relating to on-demand streams on a non-subscription basis) for advertising, discounts applied to gross revenue, and discounts for mobile permanent downloads and other mobile devices, also apply to the music on-demand license.

*e. Interactive Webcast (Subscription) License*

*Coverage*. This license covers both the performance and mechanical rights in musical works in interactive webcasting services, where the service is funded by subscription (rather than, for example, an advertising-based service). Again, an interactive service is on where the user of the service can influence the music they hear (e.g., play, fast forward, skip tracks, etc.). As with the on-demand music licenses, this license also covers the several types of audiovisual uses listed in the previous section, and the same coverage exclusions outlined in the previous section apply here.

*Royalty Rate*. The royalty rate payable for on-demand streaming and limited downloads offered on a subscription basis is 6.5% of gross revenue, subject to a minimum of 22p per subscriber, per month.

*Gross Revenue*. Gross revenue means all revenue received by the licensee either directly from its users (via subscription fees or paid for activities) or other revenue streams, including, but not limited to, advertising, sponsorship and commissions.

*Territory*. The territory is limited to delivering compositions to users located in the United Kingdom.

*Accounting and Reporting*. Online services generating up to £500,000 of gross revenue may report quarterly, within one month after the quarter's end, while services whose gross revenue exceeds that amount must report monthly, within one week of the month's end.

*Discounts.* The terms outlined in the previous section (relating to on-demand streams on a non-subscription basis) for advertising, discounts applied to gross revenue, and discounts for mobile permanent downloads and other mobile devices, also apply to the music on-demand license.

### *f. Webcast License*

*Coverage.* This license covers both the performance and mechanical rights in musical works in non-interactive webcasting services, where the service is not funded by subscription (e.g., advertising-based service). As with the on-demand music licenses, this license also covers the several types of audiovisual uses listed in the previous section, and the same coverage exclusions outlined in the previous section apply here.

*Royalty Rate.* The royalty rate payable for on-demand streaming and limited downloads offered on a subscription basis is 6.5% of gross revenue, subject to a minimum of 0.05p per track streamed.

*Gross Revenue.* Gross revenue means all revenue received by the licensee either directly from its users (via subscription fees or paid for activities) or other revenue streams, including, but not limited to, advertising, sponsorship, and commissions.

*Territory.* The territory is limited to delivering compositions to users located in the United Kingdom.

*Accounting and Reporting.* Online services generating up to £500,000 of gross revenue may report quarterly, within one month after the quarter's end, while services whose gross revenue exceeds that amount must report monthly, within one week of the month's end.

*Discounts.* The terms outlined in the previous section (relating to on-demand streams on a non-subscription basis) for advertising, discounts applied to gross revenue, and discounts for mobile permanent downloads and other mobile devices, also apply to the music on-demand license.

### *g. Single Artist Webcast (Non-Subscription) License*

*Coverage.* This license covers both the performance and mechanical rights in musical works in interactive and non-interactive webcasting services, where the service is not funded by subscription (e.g., advertising-based service). A single artist webcast is defined as a service where more than 50% of the music on the service is by a single artist. As with the on-demand music licenses, this license also covers the several types of audiovisual uses listed in the previous section, and the same coverage exclusions outlined in the previous section apply here.

*Royalty Rate.* The royalty rate payable for on-demand streaming and limited downloads offered on a subscription basis is 10.5% of gross revenue, subject to a minimum of 0.085p per track streamed.

*Gross Revenue.* Gross revenue means all revenue received by the licensee either directly from its users (via subscription fees or paid for activities) or other revenue streams, including, but not limited to, advertising, sponsorship, and commissions.

*Territory.* The territory is limited to delivering compositions to users located in the United Kingdom.

*Accounting and Reporting.* Online services generating up to £500,000 of gross revenue may report quarterly, within one month after the quarter's end, while services whose gross revenue exceeds that amount must report monthly, within one week of the month's end.

*Discounts.* The terms outlined in the previous section (relating to on-demand streams on a non-subscription basis) for advertising, discounts applied to gross revenue, and discounts for mobile permanent downloads and other mobile devices, also apply to the music on-demand license.

### *h. Single Artist Webcast (Subscription) License*

*Coverage.* This license covers both the performance and mechanical rights in musical works in interactive and non-interactive webcasting services, where the service is funded by subscription. Again, a single artist webcast is defined as a service where more than 50% of the music on the service is by a single artist. As with the on-demand music licenses, this license also covers the several types of audiovisual uses listed in the previous section, and the same coverage exclusions outlined in the previous section apply here.

*Royalty Rate.* The royalty rate payable for on-demand streaming and limited downloads offered on a subscription basis is 8% of gross revenue, subject to a minimum fee to be negotiated in good faith between the licensee and PRS for Music.

*Gross Revenue.* Gross revenue means all revenue received by the licensee either directly from its users (via subscription fees or paid for activities) or other revenue streams, including, but not limited to, advertising, sponsorship, and commissions.

*Territory.* The territory is limited to delivering compositions to users located in the United Kingdom.

*Accounting and Reporting.* Online services generating up to £500,000 of gross revenue may report quarterly, within one month after the quarter's end, while services whose gross revenue exceeds that amount must report monthly, within one week of the month's end.

*Discounts.* The terms outlined in the previous section (relating to on-demand streams on a non-subscription basis) for advertising, discounts applied to gross revenue, and discounts for mobile permanent downloads and other mobile devices, also apply to the music on-demand license.

*i. Ringtone License*

*Coverage.* This license covers both the performance and mechanical rights in musical works necessary to (a) create and store musical works as ringtones, (b) provide on-demand streamed previews to users of up to 30 seconds, and (c) deliver the ringtone to users' handsets in the United Kingdom.

Excluded from the ringtone license are ringtones that incorporate more than 1 minute of music, the use of music with advertising or sponsorship, as well as other rights typically excluded from the online licenses discussed in the immediately preceding sections.

*Royalty Rate.* The royalty rate payable for the reproduction and distribution of ringtones is as follows:

- 12% of revenue charged for realtones with a minimum of 10p per realtone;
- 15% for all other types of ringtones (including mono and polyphonic) with a minimum of 15p per mono or polyphonic ringtone.

*Gross Revenue.* Gross revenue means all revenue received by the licensee either directly from its users (via subscription fees or paid for activities) or other revenue streams, including, but not limited to, advertising, sponsorship, and commissions.

*Territory*. The territory is limited to delivering compositions to users located in the United Kingdom.

*Term*. The term of the above ringtone license was due to expire on December 31, 2009.

*Accounting and Reporting*. Accounting reports are due quarterly, within 31 days after the quarter's end.

#### *j. Ringback License*

*Coverage*. This license covers both the performance and reproduction rights in musical works necessary to (a) create and store musical works as ringbacks, (b) and to stream them to the public. The license does not cover the ability to download the music to the caller and it does not include "music-on-hold" — where the sound recording is heard after the user has connected the call, but prior to the user speaking to the caller.

*Royalty Rate*. The royalty rate payable for the reproduction and distribution of ringtones is as follows:

- 15% of gross revenue from the service (including any subscription or recurring charges for accessing the service),
- Subject to a minimum of 15p per ringback tone (and a non-refundable advance of £1,000 (+VAT).

*Gross Revenue*. Gross revenue means all revenue received by the licensee either directly from its users (via subscription fees or paid for activities) or other revenue streams, including, but not limited to, advertising, sponsorship, and commissions.

*Territory*. The territory is limited to delivering compositions to users located in the United Kingdom.

*Term*. The term of the above ringtone license was due to expire on December 31, 2009.

*Accounting and Reporting*. Accounting reports are due quarterly, within 31 days after the quarter's end.

## D. The State of Mechanical License Administration in Europe

As described in Chapter 5, on *International Subpublishing*, the administration of mechanical licenses in Europe is undergoing an upheaval. The implications of the European Union's 2005 Recommendation and 2008 CISAC decision has provided greater flexibility to music publishers to determine their own ways and means of mechanical licensing in Europe. Publishers may now choose among the societies, or determine new means of administration, for the licensing of their music online on a pan-European basis. Collection societies are now thrust into competition with each other for the first time.

As of the time of this writing in 2009, all four major publishers have withdrawn (or partially withdrawn) their exclusive digital distribution rights from the European societies and reassigned them to other societies or joint venture entities. EMI Music has granted, on an exclusive basis, the right to sublicense its Anglo-American works for digital purposes on a pan-European basis to CELAS, a joint venture among EMI, PRS for Music (U.K. society), and the GEMA (German society). EMI's intention was that other major publishers would join them in the venture, which would provide the "one-stop shop" for which European licensees of digital rights have been craving. But this did not happen. Each of the other major publishers has formed their pan-European licensing joint venture. Sony/ATV has, with GEMA, formed PAECOL; Universal has joined with SACEM (France) to form DEAL (for "Digital European Administration and Licensing"). Warner/Chappell has tried something a little different: joining forces with each of PRS for Music, SACEM, STIM (Sweden), and BUMA/SEMRA (Netherlands) to offer its own Anglo-American repertoire on a non-exclusive, pan-European basis through any of those partners, but under a venture called PEDL (Pan European Digital Licensing). Peer Music, the largest independent music publisher, has chosen to provide its Anglo-American catalog for pan-European digital licensing to PRS for Music, and its Hispanic catalog to SGAE (Spain).

In addition, with music publishers now enabled to become direct members of any society in Europe, the structure of *original* music publishers working with local *subpublishers* in each European country may soon be replaced by a model that bypasses the old subpublisher network. It is estimated that, in each European country, non-local catalogs represent over 40% of recorded music sales. Without the lucrative share of this revenue that European subpublishers have traditionally collected for representing foreign catalogs, subpublishers may find themselves with businesses that are no longer viable. However, many original publishers located outside Europe are not yet fully acquainted with the rapid changes occurring in Europe and may prefer to leave their repertoires with their current European subpublishers, who are in a better position to make the right decisions for the original publisher's catalog.

Online music services, who were opening to see emerge a "one-stop shop," where they can receive all the licenses they require to operate their music services on a pan-European basis, are now seeing matters going in the opposite direction. Not only do these services now need to license repertoire from each of the societies in each of the 27 countries of the EU to obtain the licenses they require from the four major publishers, they must also enter into licensing arrangements with the several joint ventures that have emerged from the publisher's newly found freedom. What was once a 27-stop shop, with the hope of becoming a one-stop shop, is now at least a 30-stop shop!

Meanwhile, rates still vary by country and a multi-territory license regime has yet to emerge. This has come as a disappointment to the EU administrators concerned with consumers who continue to shop for online content on the basis of prices offered on sites other than those located in their own countries.

The final effect of all these changes remains to be seen. It is hoped that new administration models emerge, which put a premium on fair multinational rates, efficient licensing, low administration costs, high service levels, and accounting to music publishers that is accurate, comprehensive, and transparent. Whether this can be done by existing relationships and infrastructure or by something new will be borne out by time and patience.

# Appendix to Chapter 13
# Licensing Music in Sound Recordings (Mechanical Licenses)

Laws and Regulations

| | |
|---|---|
| Law 13.1 | Compulsory License Provision — Section 115 of U.S. Copyright Act |
| Law 13.2 | Copyright Office Regulations under Compulsory License Provision — Code of Federal Regulations — Section 201.19 Act |
| Law 13.3 | U.S. Copyright Royalty Board — Statutory Rate Regulations (effective March 1, 2009) |
| Law 13.4 | Canadian Copyright Board Royalty Rate Tariff (2007) |
| Law 13.5 | Canadian Copyright Royalty Board Decision (2007) |
| Law 13.6 | U.K. Copyright Tribunal Decision (2007) |

Forms (On CD-Rom Only)

| | |
|---|---|
| Form 13.1 | Standard Mechanical License Agreement |
| Form 13.2 | Alternative Mechanical License Drafted in Favor of Licensor |
| Form 13.3 | Alternative Mechanical License Drafted in Favor of the Licensee |
| Form 13.4 | Harry Fox Agency Mechanical License for Digital Phonorecord Deliveries |
| Form 13.5 | Mechanical License For On-Demand Streaming Service |
| Form 13.6 | Notice of Intention to Obtain a Compulsory License Under Section 115 of the Copyright Act |

# LAW 13.1

## COMPULSORY LICENSE PROVISION — SECTION 115 OF U.S. COPYRIGHT ACT

### § 115. Scope of exclusive rights in nondramatic musical works: Compulsory license for making and distributing phonorecords

In the case of nondramatic musical works, the exclusive rights provided by clauses (1) and (3) of section 106, to make and to distribute phonorecords of such works, are subject to compulsory licensing under the conditions specified by this section.

(a) AVAILABILITY AND SCOPE OF COMPULSORY LICENSE. —

(1) When phonorecords of a nondramatic musical work have been distributed to the public in the United States under the authority of the copyright owner, any other person, including those who make phonorecords or digital phonorecord deliveries, may, by complying with the provisions of this section, obtain a compulsory license to make and distribute phonorecords of the work. A person may obtain a compulsory license only if his or her primary purpose in making phonorecords is to distribute them to the public for private use, including by means of a digital phonorecord delivery. A person may not obtain a compulsory license for use of the work in the making of phonorecords duplicating a sound recording fixed by another, unless:

(i) such sound recording was fixed lawfully; and

(ii) the making of the phonorecords was authorized by the owner of copyright in the sound recording or, if the sound recording was fixed before February 15, 1972, by any person who fixed the sound recording pursuant to an express license from the owner of the copyright in the musical work or pursuant to a valid compulsory license for use of such work in a sound recording.

(2) A compulsory license includes the privilege of making a musical arrangement of the work to the extent necessary to conform it to the style or manner of interpretation of the performance involved, but the arrangement shall not change the basic melody or fundamental character of the work, and shall not be subject to protection as a derivative work under this title, except with the express consent of the copyright owner.

(b) NOTICE OF INTENTION TO OBTAIN COMPULSORY LICENSE. —

(1) Any person who wishes to obtain a compulsory license under this section shall, before or within thirty days after making, and before distributing any phonorecords of the work, serve notice of intention to do so on the copyright owner. If the registration or other public records of the Copyright Office do not identify the copyright owner and include an address at which notice can be served, it shall be sufficient to file the notice of intention in the Copyright Office. The notice shall comply, in form, content, and manner of service, with requirements that the Register of Copyrights shall prescribe by regulation.

(2) Failure to serve or file the notice required by clause (1) forecloses the possibility of a compulsory license and, in the absence of a negotiated license, renders the making and distribution of phonorecords actionable as acts of infringement under section 501 and fully subject to the remedies provided by sections 502 through 506 and 509.

(c) ROYALTY PAYABLE UNDER COMPULSORY LICENSE. —

(1) To be entitled to receive royalties under a compulsory license, the copyright owner must be identified in the registration or other public records of the Copyright Office. The owner is entitled to royalties for phonorecords made and distributed after

being so identified, but is not entitled to recover for any phonorecords previously made and distributed.

(2) Except as provided by clause (1), the royalty under a compulsory license shall be payable for every phonorecord made and distributed in accordance with the license. For this purpose, and other than as provided in paragraph (3), a phonorecord is considered "distributed" if the person exercising the compulsory license has voluntarily and permanently parted with its possession. With respect to each work embodied in the phonorecord, the royalty shall be either two and three-fourths cents, or one-half of one cent per minute of playing time or fraction thereof, whichever amount is larger.

(3) (A) A compulsory license under this section includes the right of the compulsory licensee to distribute or authorize the distribution of a phonorecord of a nondramatic musical work by means of a digital transmission which constitutes a digital phonorecord delivery, regardless of whether the digital transmission is also a public performance of the sound recording under section 106(6) of this title or of any nondramatic musical work embodied therein under section 106(4) of this title. For every digital phonorecord delivery by or under the authority of the compulsory licensee —

(i) on or before December 31, 1997, the royalty payable by the compulsory licensee shall be the royalty prescribed under paragraph (2) and chapter 8 of this title; and

(ii) on or after January 1, 1998, the royalty payable by the compulsory licensee shall be the royalty prescribed under subparagraphs (B) through (E) and chapter 8 of this title.

(B) Notwithstanding any provision of the antitrust laws, any copyright owners of nondramatic musical works and any persons entitled to obtain a compulsory license under subsection (a)(1) may negotiate and agree upon the terms and rates of royalty payments this section and the proportionate division of fees paid among copyright owners, and may designate common agents to negotiate, agree to, pay or receive such royalty payments. Such authority to negotiate the terms and rates of royalty payments includes, but is not limited to, the authority to negotiate the year during which the royalty rates prescribed under this subparagraph and subparagraphs (C) through (E) and chapter 8 of this title shall next be determined.

(C) Proceedings under chapter 8 shall determine reasonable rates and terms of royalty payments for the activities specified by this section during the period beginning with the effective date of such rates and terms, but not earlier than January 1 of the second year following the year in which the petition requesting the proceeding is filed, and ending on the effective date of successor rates and terms, or such other period as the parties may agree. Such terms and rates shall distinguish between (i) digital phonorecord deliveries where the reproduction or distribution of a phonorecord is incidental to the transmission which constitutes the digital phonorecord delivery, and (ii) digital phonorecord deliveries in general. Any copyright owners of nondramatic musical works and any persons entitled to obtain a compulsory license under subsection (a)(1) may submit to the Copyright Royalty Judges licenses covering such activities. The parties to each proceeding shall bear their own costs.

(D) The schedule of reasonable rates and terms determined by the Copyright Royalty Judges shall, subject to subparagraph (E), be binding on all copyright owners of nondramatic musical works and persons entitled to obtain a compulsory license under subsection (a)(1) during the period specified in subparagraph (C), such other period as may be determined pursuant to subparagraphs (B) and (C), or such other period as the parties may agree. Such terms and rates shall distinguish between (i) digital phonorecord deliveries where the reproduction or distribution of a phonorecord is incidental to the transmission which constitutes the digital phonorecord delivery, and (ii) digital phonorecord deliveries in general. In addition to the objectives set forth in section 801(b)(1), in establishing such rates and terms, the Copyright Royalty Judges may consider rates and terms under voluntary license agreements described in subparagraphs (B) and (C). The royalty rates payable for a compulsory license for a digital phonorecord delivery under this section shall be established de novo and no precedential effect shall be given to the amount of the royalty payable by a compulsory licensee for digital phonorecord deliveries on or before December 31, 1997. The Copyright Royalty Judges shall also establish requirements by which copyright owners may receive reasonable notice of the use of their works under this section, and under which records of such use shall be kept and made available by persons making digital phonorecord deliveries.

(E) (i) License agreements voluntarily negotiated at any time between one or more copyright owners of nondramatic musical works and one or more persons entitled to obtain a compulsory license under subsection (a)(1) shall be given effect in lieu of any determination by the Librarian of Congress and Copyright Royalty Judges. Subject to clause (ii), the royalty rates determined pursuant to subparagraph (C) and (D) shall be given effect as to digital phonorecord deliveries in lieu of any contrary royalty rates specified in a contract pursuant to which a recording artist who is the author of a nondramatic musical work grants a license under that person's exclusive rights in the musical work under paragraphs (1) and (3) of section 106 or commits another person to grant a license in that musical work under paragraphs (1) and (3) of section 106, to a person desiring to fix in a tangible medium of expression a sound recording embodying the musical work.

(ii) The second sentence of clause (i) shall not apply to —

(I) a contract entered into on or before June 22, 1995 and not modified thereafter for the purpose of reducing the royalty rates determined pursuant to subparagraph (C) and (D) or of increasing the number of musical works within the scope of the contract covered by the reduced rates, except if a contract entered into on or before June 22, 1995, is modified thereafter for the purpose of increasing the number of musical works within the scope of the contract, any contrary royalty rates specified in the contract shall be given effect in lieu of royalty rates determined pursuant to subparagraph (C) and (D) for the number of musical works within the scope of the contract as of June 22, 1995; and

(II) a contract entered into after the date that the sound recording is fixed in a tangible medium of expression substantially in a form intended for commercial release, if at the time the contract is entered into, the recording artist retains the right to grant licenses as to the musical work under paragraphs (1) and (3) of section 106.

(F) Except as provided in section 1002(e) of this title, a digital phonorecord delivery licensed under this paragraph shall be accompanied by the information encoded in the sound recording, if any, by or under the authority of the copyright owner of that sound recording, that identifies the title of the sound recording, the featured recording artist who performs on the sound recording, and related information, including information concerning the underlying musical work and its writer.

(G) (i) A digital phonorecord delivery of a sound recording is actionable as an act of infringement under section 501, and is fully subject to the remedies provided by sections 502 through 506 and section 509, unless —

(I) the digital phonorecord delivery has been authorized by the copyright owner of the sound recording; and

(II) the owner of the copyright in the sound recording or the entity making the digital phonorecord delivery has obtained a compulsory license under this section or has otherwise been authorized by the copyright owner of the musical work to distribute or authorize the distribution, by means of a digital phonorecord delivery, of each musical work embodied in the sound recording.

(ii) Any cause of action under this subparagraph shall be in addition to those available to the owner of the copyright in the nondramatic musical work under subsection (c)(6) and section 106(4) and the owner of the copyright in the sound recording under section 106(6).

(H) The liability of the copyright owner of a sound recording for infringement of the copyright in a nondramatic musical work embodied in the sound recording shall be determined in accordance with applicable law, except that the owner of a copyright in a sound recording shall not be liable for a digital phonorecord delivery by a third party if the owner of the copyright in the sound recording does not license the distribution of a phonorecord of the nondramatic musical work.

(I) Nothing in section 1008 shall be construed to prevent the exercise of the rights and remedies allowed by this paragraph, paragraph (6), and chapter 5 in the event of a digital phonorecord delivery, except that no action alleging infringement of copyright may be brought under this title against a manufacturer, importer or distributor of a digital audio recording device, a digital audio recording medium, an analog recording device, or an analog recording medium, or against a consumer, based on the actions described in such section.

(J) Nothing in this section annuls or limits

(i) the exclusive right to publicly perform a sound recording or the musical work embodied therein, including by means of a digital transmission, under sections 106(4) and 106(6), (ii) except for compulsory licensing under the conditions specified by this section, the exclusive rights to reproduce and distribute the sound recording and the musical work embodied therein under sections 106(1) and 106(3), including by means of a digital phonorecord delivery, or (iii) any other rights under any other provision of section 106, or remedies available under this title, as such rights or remedies exist either before or after the date of enactment of the Digital Performance Right in Sound Recordings Act of 1995.

(K) The provisions of this section concerning digital phonorecord deliveries shall not apply to any exempt transmissions or retransmissions under section 114(d)(1). The exemptions created in section 114(d)(1) do not expand or reduce the rights of copyright owners under section 106(1) through (5) with respect to such transmissions and retransmissions.

(4) A compulsory license under this section includes the right of the maker of a phonorecord of a nondramatic musical work under subsection (a)(1) to distribute or authorize distribution of such phonorecord by rental, lease, or lending (or by acts or practices in the nature of rental, lease, or lending). In addition to any royalty payable under clause (2) and chapter 8 of this title, a royalty shall be payable by the compulsory licensee for every act of distribution of a phonorecord by or in the nature of rental, lease, or lending, by or under the authority of the compulsory licensee. With respect to each nondramatic musical work embodied in the phonorecord, the royalty shall be a proportion of the revenue received by the compulsory licensee from every such act of distribution of the phonorecord under this clause equal to the proportion of the revenue received by the compulsory licensee from distribution of the phonorecord under clause (2) that is payable by a compulsory licensee under that clause and under chapter 8. The Register of Copyrights shall issue regulations to carry out the purpose of this clause.

(5) Royalty payments shall be made on or before the twentieth day of each month and shall include all royalties for the month next preceding. Each monthly payment shall be made under oath and shall comply with requirements that the Register of Copyrights shall prescribe by regulation. The Register shall also prescribe regulations under which detailed cumulative annual

statements of account, certified by a certified public accountant, shall be filed for every compulsory license under this section. The regulations covering both the monthly and the annual statements of account shall prescribe the form, content, and manner of certification with respect to the number of records made and the number of records distributed.

(6) If the copyright owner does not receive the monthly payment and the monthly and annual statements of account when due, the owner may give written notice to the licensee that, unless the default is remedied within thirty days from the date of the notice, the compulsory license will be automatically terminated. Such termination renders either the making or the distribution, or both, of all phonorecords for which the royalty has not been paid, actionable as acts of infringement under section 501 and fully subject to the remedies provided by sections 502 through 506 and 509.

(d) DEFINITION. — As used in this section, the following term has the following meaning: A "digital phonorecord delivery" is each individual delivery of a phonorecord by digital transmission of a sound recording which results in a specifically identifiable reproduction by or for any transmission recipient of a phonorecord of that sound recording, regardless of whether the digital transmission is also a public performance of the sound recording or any nondramatic musical work embodied therein. A digital phonorecord delivery does not result from a real-time, non-interactive subscription transmission of a sound recording where no reproduction of the sound recording or the musical work embodied therein is made from the inception of the transmission through to its receipt by the transmission recipient in order to make the sound recording audible.

**SOURCE: http://www.copyright.gov/title17/92chap1.html#115**

# LAW 13.2

## COPYRIGHT OFFICE REGULATIONS UNDER COMPULSORY LICENSE PROVISION — CODE OF FEDERAL REGULATIONS — SECTION 201.19 ACT

### § 201.19 Royalties and statements of account under compulsory license for making and distributing phonorecords of nondramatic musical works.

(a) *Definitions.*

(1) A *Monthly Statement of Account* is a statement accompanying monthly royalty payments identified in section 115(c)(5) of title 17 of the United States Code, as amended by Pub. L. 94-553, and required by that section to be made under the compulsory license to make and distribute phonorecords of nondramatic musical works, including by means of a digital phonorecord delivery.

(2) An *Annual Statement of Account* is a statement identified in section 115(c)(5) of title 17 of the United States Code, as amended by Pub. L. 94-553, and required by that section to be filed for every compulsory license to make and distribute phonorecords of nondramatic musical works.

(3) For the purposes of this section, a "digital phonorecord delivery" is each individual delivery of a phonorecord by digital transmission of a sound recording which results in a specifically identifiable reproduction by or for any transmission recipient of a phonorecord of that sound recording, regardless of whether the digital transmission is also a public performance of the sound recording or any nondramatic musical work embodied therein. The reproduction of the phonorecord must be sufficiently permanent or stable to permit it to be perceived, reproduced, or otherwise communicated for a period of more

than transitory duration. Such a phonorecord may be permanent or it may be made available to the transmission recipient for a limited period of time or for a specified number of performances. A digital phonorecord delivery includes all phonorecords that are made for the purpose of making the digital phonorecord delivery.

(4) For the purposes of this section, the term *copyright owner*, in the case of any work having more than one copyright owner, means any one of the co-owners.

(5) For the purposes of this section, the service of a Statement of Account on a copyright owner under paragraph (e)(7) or (f)(7) of this section may be accomplished by means of service on either the copyright owner or an agent of the copyright owner with authority to receive Statements of Account on behalf of the copyright owner. In the case where the work has more than one copyright owner, the service of the Statement of Account on one co-owner or upon an agent of one of the co-owners shall be sufficient with respect to all co-owners.

(6) For the purposes of this section, a *compulsory licensee* is a person or entity exercising the compulsory license to make and distribute phonorecords of nondramatic musical works as provided under section 115 of title 17 of the United States Code.

(7) For the purposes of this section, a digital phonorecord delivery shall be treated as a type of phonorecord configuration, and a digital phonorecord delivery shall be treated as a phonorecord, with the following clarifications:

(i) A digital phonorecord delivery shall be treated as a phonorecord made and distributed on the date the phonorecord is digitally transmitted; and

(ii) A digital phonorecord delivery shall be treated as having been *voluntarily distributed* and *relinquished from possession*, and a compulsory licensee shall be treated as having *permanently parted with possession* of a digital phonorecord delivery, on the date that the phonorecord is digitally transmitted.

(8) Except as provided in paragraph (a)(6) of this section, a phonorecord is considered *voluntarily distributed* if the compulsory licensee has voluntarily and permanently parted with possession of the phonorecord. For this purpose, and subject to the provisions of paragraph (d) of this section, a compulsory licensee shall be considered to have "permanently parted with possession" of a phonorecord made under the license:

(i) In the case of phonorecords relinquished from possession for purposes other than sale, at the time at which the compulsory licensee actually first parts with possession;

(ii) In the case of phonorecords relinquished from possession for purposes of sale without a privilege of returning unsold phonorecords for credit or exchange, at the time at which the compulsory licensee actually first parts with possession;

(iii) In the case of phonorecords relinquished from possession for purposes of sale accompanied by a privilege of returning unsold phonorecords for credit or exchange:

(A) At the time when revenue from a sale of the phonorecord is "recognized" by the compulsory licensee; or

(B) Nine months from the month in which the compulsory licensee actually first parted with possession, whichever occurs first.

For these purposes, a compulsory licensee shall be considered to "recognize" revenue from the sale of a phonorecord when sales revenue would be recognized in accordance with generally accepted accounting principles as expressed by the American Institute of Certified Public Accountants or the

Financial Accounting Standards Board, whichever would cause sales revenue to be recognized first.

(9) To the extent that the terms *reserve, credit* and *return* appear in this section, such provisions shall not apply to digital phonorecord deliveries.

(10) A *phonorecord reserve* comprises the number of phonorecords, if any, that have been relinquished from possession for purposes of sale in a given month accompanied by a privilege of return, as described in paragraph (a)(5)(iii) of this section, and that have not been considered voluntarily distributed during the month in which the compulsory licensee actually first parted with their possession. The initial number of phonorecords comprising a phonorecord reserve shall be determined in accordance with generally accepted accounting principles as expressed by the American Institute of Certified Public Accountants or the Financial Accounting Standards Board.

(11) A *negative reserve balance* comprises the aggregate number of phonorecords, if any, that have been relinquished from possession for purposes of sale accompanied by a privilege of return, as described in paragraph (a)(5)(iii) of this section, and that have been returned to the compulsory licensee, but because all available phonorecord reserves have been eliminated, have not been used to reduce a phonorecord reserve.

(12) An *incomplete transmission* is any digital transmission of a sound recording which, as determined by means within the sole control of the distributor, does not result in a specifically identifiable reproduction of the entire sound recording by or for any transmission recipient.

(13) A *retransmission* is a subsequent digital transmission of the same sound recording initially transmitted to an identified recipient for the purpose of completing the delivery of a complete and usable reproduction of that sound recording to that recipient.

(b) *Accounting requirements where sales revenue is "recognized".* Where under paragraph (a)(5)(iii)(A) of this section, revenue from the sale of phonorecords is "recognized" during any month after the month in which the compulsory licensee actually first parted with their possession, said compulsory licensee shall reduce particular phonorecord reserves by the number of phonorecords for which revenue is being "recognized," as follows:

(1) If the number of phonorecords for which revenue is being "recognized" is smaller than the number of phonorecords comprising the earliest eligible phonorecord reserve, this phonorecord reserve shall be reduced by the number of phonorecords for which revenue is being "recognized." Subject to the time limitations of paragraph (a)(7)(iii)(B) of this section, the number of phonorecords remaining in this reserve shall be available for use in subsequent months.

(2) If the number of phonorecords for which revenue is being "recognized" is greater than the number of phonorecords comprising the earliest eligible phonorecord reserve but less than the total number of phonorecords comprising all eligible phonorecord reserves, the compulsory licensee shall first eliminate those phonorecord reserves, beginning with the earliest eligible phonorecord reserve and continuing to the next succeeding phonorecord reserves, that are completely offset by phonorecords for which revenue is being "recognized." Said licensee shall then reduce the next succeeding phonorecord reserve by the number of phonorecords for which revenue is being "recognized" that have not been used to eliminate a phonorecord reserve. Subject to the time limitations of paragraph (a)(7)(iii)(B) of this section, the number of phonorecords remaining in this reserve shall be available for use in subsequent months.

(3) If the number of phonorecords for which revenue is being "recognized" equals the number of phonorecords comprising all eligible phonorecord reserves, the person or entity exercising the compulsory license shall eliminate all of the phonorecord reserves.

(c) *Accounting requirements for offsetting phonorecord reserves with returned phonorecords.*

(1) In the case of a phonorecord that has been relinquished from possession for purposes of sale accompanied by a privilege of return, as described in paragraph (a)(5)(iii) of this section, where the phonorecord is returned to the compulsory licensee for credit or exchange before said compulsory licensee is considered to have "permanently parted with possession" of the phonorecord under paragraph (a)(5) of this section, the compulsory licensee may use such phonorecord to reduce a "phonorecord reserve," as defined in paragraph (a)(6) of this section.

(2) In such cases, the compulsory licensee shall reduce particular phonorecord reserves by the number of phonorecords that are returned during the month covered by the Monthly Statement of Account in the following manner:

(i) If the number of phonorecords that are returned during the month covered by the Monthly Statement is smaller than the number comprising the earliest eligible phonorecord reserve, the compulsory licensee shall reduce this phonorecord reserve by the total number of returned phonorecords. Subject to the time limitations of paragraph (B) of § 201.19(a)(5)(iii), the number of phonorecords remaining in this reserve shall be available for use in subsequent months.

(ii) If the number of phonorecords that are returned during the month covered by the Monthly Statement is greater than the number of phonorecords comprising the earliest eligible phonorecord reserve but less than the total number of phonorecords comprising all eligible phonorecord reserves, the compulsory licensee shall first eliminate those phonorecord reserves, beginning with the earliest eligible phonorecord reserve, and continuing to the next succeeding phonorecord reserves, that are completely offset by returned phonorecords. Said licensee shall then reduce the next succeeding phonorecord reserve by the number of returned phonorecords that have not been used to eliminate a phonorecord reserve. Subject to the time limitations of paragraph (B) of § 201.19(a)(5)(iii), the number of phonorecords remaining in this reserve shall be available for use in subsequent months.

(iii) If the number of phonorecords that are returned during the month covered by the Monthly Statement is equal to or is greater than the total number of phonorecords comprising all eligible phonorecord reserves, the compulsory licensee shall eliminate all eligible phonorecord reserves. Where said number is greater than the total number of phonorecords comprising all eligible phonorecord reserves, said compulsory licensee shall establish a "negative reserve balance," as defined in paragraph (a)(10) of this section.

(3) Except where a negative reserve balance exists, a separate and distinct phonorecord reserve shall be established for each month during which the compulsory licensee relinquishes phonorecords from possession for purposes of sale accompanied by a privilege of return, as described in paragraph (a)(5)(iii) of this section. In accordance with paragraph (B) of § 201.19(a)(5)(iii), any phonorecord remaining in a particular phonorecord reserve nine months from the month in which the particular reserve was established shall be considered "voluntarily distributed"; at that point, the particular monthly phonorecord reserve shall lapse and royalties for the phonorecords remaining in it shall be paid as provided in paragraph (e)(4)(ii) of this section.

(4) Where a negative reserve balance exists, the aggregate total of phonorecords comprising it shall be accumulated into a single balance rather than being separated into distinct monthly balances. Following the establishment of a negative reserve balance, any phonorecords relinquished from possession by the compulsory licensee for purposes of sale or otherwise, shall be credited against such negative balance, and the negative reserve balance shall be reduced accordingly. The nine-month limit provided by paragraph (B) of § 201.19(a)(5)(iii)

shall have no effect upon a negative reserve balance; where a negative reserve balance exists, relinquishment from possession of a phonorecord by the compulsory licensee at any time shall be used to reduce such balance, and shall not be considered a "voluntary distribution" within the meaning of paragraph (a)(5) of this section.

(5) In no case shall a phonorecord reserve be established while a negative reserve balance is in existence; conversely, in no case shall a negative reserve balance be established before all available phonorecord reserves have been eliminated.

(d) *Situations in which a compulsory licensee is barred from maintaining reserves.* Notwithstanding any other provisions of this section, in any case where, within three years before the phonorecord was relinquished from possession, the compulsory licensee has had final judgment entered against it for failure to pay royalties for the reproduction of copyrighted music on phonorecords, or within such period has been definitively found in any proceeding involving bankruptcy, insolvency, receivership, assignment for the benefit of creditors, or similar action, to have failed to pay such royalties, that compulsory licensee shall be considered to have "Permanently parted with possession" of a phonorecord made under the license at the time at which that licensee actually first parts with possession. For these purposes the "compulsory licensee," as defined in paragraph (a)(5) of this section, shall include:

(1) In the case of any corporation, the corporation or any director, officer, or beneficial owner of twenty-five percent (25%) or more of the outstanding securities of the corporation;

(2) In all other cases, any entity or individual owning a beneficial interest of twenty-five percent (25%) or more in the entity exercising the compulsory license.

(e) *Monthly statements of account —*

(1) *Forms.* The Copyright Office does not provide printed forms for the use of persons serving Monthly Statements of Account.

(2) *General content.* A Monthly Statement of Account shall be clearly and prominently identified as a "Monthly Statement of Account Under Compulsory License for Making and Distributing Phonorecords," and shall include a clear statement of the following information:

(i) The period (month and year) covered by the Monthly Statement;

(ii) The full legal name of the compulsory licensee, together with all fictitious or assumed names used by such person or entity for the purpose of conducting the business of making and distributing phonorecords;

(iii) The full address, including a specific number and street name or rural route, of the place of business of the compulsory licensee. A post office box or similar designation will not be sufficient for this purpose, except where it is the only address that can be used in that geographic location;

(iv) The title or titles of the nondramatic musical work or works embodied in phonorecords made under the compulsory license and owned by the copyright owner being served with the Monthly Statement and the name of the author or authors of such work or works, if known;

(v) For each nondramatic musical work that is owned by the same copyright owner being served with the Monthly Statement and that is embodied in phonorecords covered by the compulsory license, a detailed statement of all of the information called for in paragraph (e)(3) of this section;

(vi) The total royalty payable for the month covered by the Monthly Statement, computed in accordance with the requirements of this section and the formula specified in paragraph (e)(4) of this section, together with a statement of account showing in detail how the royalty was computed; and

(vii) In any case where the compulsory licensee falls within the provisions of paragraph (d) of this section, a clear description of the action or proceeding involved, including the date of the final judgment or definitive finding described in that paragraph.

(3) *Specific content of monthly statements: Identification and accounting of phonorecords.* (i) The information called for by paragraph (e)(2)(v) of this section shall, with respect to each nondramatic musical work, include a separate listing of each of the following items of information:

(A) The number of phonorecords, including digital phonorecord deliveries, made during the month covered by the Monthly Statement;

(B) The number of phonorecords that, during the month covered by the Monthly Statement and regardless of when made, were either:

Relinquished from possession for purposes other than sale;

Relinquished from possession for purposes of sale without any privilege of returning unsold phonorecords for credit or exchange;

Relinquished from possession for purposes of sale accompanied by a privilege of returning unsold phonorecords for credit or exchange;

Returned to the compulsory licensee for credit or exchange;

Placed in a phonorecord reserve (except that if a negative reserve balance exists give either the number of phonorecords added to the negative reserve balance, or the number of phonorecords relinquished from possession that have been used to reduce the negative reserve balance);

Never delivered due to a failed transmission; or

Digitally retransmitted in order to complete a digital phonorecord delivery.

(C) The number of phonorecords, regardless of when made, that were relinquished from possession during a month earlier than the month covered by the Monthly Statement but that, during the month covered by the Monthly Statement either have had revenue from their sale "recognized" under paragraph (a)(5)(iii) of this section, or were comprised in a phonorecord reserve that lapsed after nine months under paragraph (B) of § 201.19(a)(5)(iii).

(ii) Each of the items of information called for by paragraph (e)(3)(i) of this section shall also include, and if necessary shall be broken down to identify separately, the following:

(A) The catalog number or numbers and label name or names, used on the phonorecords;

(B) The names of the principal recording artist or group engaged in rendering the performances fixed on the phonorecords;

(C) The playing time on the phonorecords of each nondramatic musical work covered by the statement; and

(D) Each phonorecord configuration involved (for example: single disk, long-playing disk, cartridge, cassette, reel-to-reel, digital phonorecord delivery, or a combination of them).

(E) The date of and a reason for each incomplete transmission.

(4) *Royalty payment and accounting.* (i) The total royalty called for by paragraph (e)(2)(vi) of this section shall, as specified in section 115(c)(2) of title 17 of the United States Code, be payable for every phonorecord "voluntarily distributed" during the month covered by the Monthly Statement.

(ii) The amount of the royalty payment shall be calculated in accordance with the following formula:

*Step 1: Compute the number of phonorecords shipped for sale with a privilege of return.* This is the total of phonorecords that, during the month covered by the Monthly Statement, were relinquished from possession by the compulsory licensee, accompanied by the privilege of returning unsold phonorecords to the compulsory licensee for credit or exchange. This total does *not* include: (1) Any phonorecords relinquished from possession by the compulsory licensee for purposes of sale without the privilege of return; and (2) any phonorecords relinquished from possession for purposes other than sale.

*Step 2: Subtract the number of phonorecords reserved.* This involves deducting, from the subtotal arrived at in Step 1, the number of phonorecords that have been placed in the phonorecord reserve for the month covered by the Monthly Statement. The number of phonorecords reserved is determined by multiplying the subtotal from Step 1 by the percentage reserve level established under Generally Accepted Accounting Practices. This step should be skipped by a compulsory licensee barred from maintaining reserves under paragraph (d) of this section.

*Step 3: Add the total of all phonorecords that were shipped during the month and were not counted in Step 1.*

This total is the sum of two figures: (1) The number of phonorecords that, during the month covered by the Monthly Statement, were relinquished from possession by the compulsory licensee for purposes of sale, without the privilege of returning unsold phonorecords to the compulsory licensee for credit or exchange; and (2) the number of phonorecords relinquished from possession by the compulsory licensee, during the month covered by the Monthly Statement, for purposes other than sale.

*Step 4: Make any necessary adjustments for sales revenue "recognized," lapsed reserves, or reduction of negative reserve balance during the month.* If necessary, this step involves adding to or subtracting from the subtotal arrived at in Step 3 on the basis of three possible types of adjustments:

(*a*) *Sales revenue "recognized."* If, in the month covered by the Monthly Statement, the compulsory licensee "recognized" revenue from the sale of phonorecords that had been relinquished from possession in an earlier month, the number of such phonorecords is *added* to the Step 3 subtotal;

(*b*) *Lapsed reserves.* If, in the month covered by the Monthly Statement, there are any phonorecords remaining in the phonorecord reserve for the ninth previous month (that is, any phonorecord reserves from the ninth previous month that have not been offset under FOFI, the first-out-first-in accounting convention, by actual returns during the intervening months), the reserve lapses and the number of phonorecords in it is *added* to the Step 3 subtotal.

(*c*) *Reduction of negative reserve balance.* If, in the month covered by the Monthly Statement, the aggregate reserve balance for all previous months is a negative amount, the number of phonorecords relinquished from possession by the compulsory licensee during that month and used to reduce the negative reserve balance is *subtracted* from the Step 3 subtotal.

(*d*) *Incomplete transmissions.* If, in the month covered by the Monthly Statement, there are any digital transmissions of a sound recording which do not result in specifically identifiable reproductions of the entire sound recording by or for any transmission recipient, as determined by means within the sole control of the distributor, the number of such phonorecords is subtracted from the Step 3 subtotal.

(*e*) *Retransmitted digital phonorecords.* If, in the month covered by the Monthly Statement, there are retransmissions of a digital phonorecord to a recipient who did not receive a complete and usable phonorecord during an initial transmission, and such transmissions are made for the sole purpose of delivering a complete and usable reproduction of the initially requested sound recording to that recipient, the number of such retransmitted digital phonorecords is subtracted from the Step 3 subtotal.

*Step 5: Multiply by the statutory royalty rate.* The total monthly royalty payment is obtained by multiplying the subtotal from Step 3, as adjusted if necessary by Step 4, by the statutory royalty rate of 5.7 cents or 1.1 cents per minute or fraction of playing time, whichever is larger.

(iii) Each step in computing the monthly payment, including the arithmetical calculations involved in each step, shall be set out in detail in the Monthly Statement.

(5) *Clear statements.* The information required by paragraphs (e) (2) and (3) of this section involves intelligible, legible, and unambiguous statements in the Monthly Statements of Account itself and without incorporation of facts or information contained in other documents or records.

(6) *Oath and signature.* Each Monthly Statement of Account shall include the handwritten signature of the compulsory licensee. If that compulsory licensee is a corporation, the signature shall be that of a duly authorized officer of the

corporation; if that compulsory licensee is a partnership, the signature shall be that of a partner. The signature shall be accompanied by:

(i) The printed or typewritten name of the person signing the Monthly Statement of Account;

(ii) The date of signature;

(iii) If the compulsory licensee is a partnership or a corporation, by the title or official position held in the partnership or corporation by the person signing the Monthly Statement of Account;

(iv) A certification of the capacity of the person signing; and

(v) The following statement:

I certify that I have examined this Monthly Statement of Account and that all statements of fact contained herein are true, complete, and correct to the best of my knowledge, information, and belief, and are made in good faith.

(7) *Service.* (i) Each Monthly Statement of Account shall be served on the copyright owner or the agent with authority to receive Monthly Statements of Account on behalf of the copyright owner to whom or which it is directed, together with the total royalty for the month covered by the Monthly Statement, by mail or by reputable courier service on or before the 20th day of the immediately succeeding month. However, in the case where the licensee has served its Notice of Intention upon an agent of the copyright owner pursuant to § 201.18, the licensee is not required to serve Monthly Statements of Account or make any royalty payments until the licensee receives from the agent with authority to receive the Notice of Intention notice of the name and address of the copyright owner or its agent upon whom the licensee shall serve Monthly Statements of Account and the monthly royalty

fees. Upon receipt of this information, the licensee shall serve Monthly Statements of Account and all royalty fees covering the intervening period upon the person or entity identified by the agent with authority to receive the Notice of Intention by or before the 20th day of the month following receipt of the notification. It shall not be necessary to file a copy of the Monthly Statement in the Copyright Office.

(ii)

(A) In any case where a Monthly Statement of Account is sent by mail or reputable courier service and the Monthly Statement of Account is returned to the sender because the copyright owner or agent is no longer located at that address or has refused to accept delivery, or in any case where an address for the copyright owner is not known, the Monthly Statement of Account, together with any evidence of mailing or attempted delivery by courier service, may be filed in the Licensing Division of the Copyright Office. Any Monthly Statement of Account submitted for filing in the Copyright Office shall be accompanied by a brief statement of the reason why it was not served on the copyright owner. A written acknowledgment of receipt and filing will be provided to the sender.

(B) The Copyright Office will not accept any royalty fees submitted with Monthly Statements of Account under this paragraph (e)(7)(ii).

(C) Neither the filing of a Monthly Statement of Account in the Copyright Office, nor the failure to file such Monthly Statement, shall have effect other than that which may be attributed to it by a court of competent jurisdiction.

(D) No filing fee will be required in the case of Monthly Statements of Account submitted to the Copyright Office under this paragraph (e)(7)(ii). Upon request and payment of the fee specified in § 201.3(e), a Certificate of Filing will be provided to the sender.

(iii) A separate Monthly Statement of Account shall be served for each month during which there is any activity relevant to the payment of royalties under section 115 of Title 17, United States Code, and under this section. The Annual Statement of Account identified in paragraph (f) of this section does not replace any Monthly Statement of Account.

(iv) If a Monthly Statement of Account is sent by certified mail or registered mail, a mailing receipt shall be sufficient to prove that service was timely. If a Monthly Statement of Account is delivered by a reputable courier, documentation from the courier showing the first date of attempted delivery shall also be sufficient to prove that service was timely. In the absence of a receipt from the United States Postal Service showing the date of delivery or documentation showing the first date of attempted delivery by a reputable courier, the compulsory licensee shall bear the burden of proving that the Monthly Statement of Account was served in a timely manner.

(f) *Annual statements of account* —

(1) *Forms.* The Copyright Office does not provide printed forms for the use of persons serving Annual Statements of Account.

(2) *Annual period.* Any Annual Statement of Account shall cover the full fiscal year of the compulsory licensee.

(3) *General content.* An Annual Statement of Account shall be clearly and prominently identified as an "Annual Statement of Account Under Compulsory License for Making and Distributing Phonorecords," and shall include a clear statement of the following information:

(i) The fiscal year covered by the Annual Statement;

(ii) The full legal name of the compulsory licensee, together with all fictitious or assumed names used by such person or entity for the purpose of conducting the business of making and distributing phonorecords;

(iii) If the compulsory licensee is a business organization, the name and title of the chief executive officer, managing partner, sole proprietor or other person similarly responsible for the management of such entity.

(iv) The full address, including a specific number and street name or rural route, or the place of business of the compulsory licensee. A post office box or similar designation will not be sufficient for this purpose except where it is the only address that can be used in that geographic location;

(v) The title or titles of the nondramatic musical work or works embodied in phonorecords made under the compulsory license and owned by the copyright owner being served with the Annual Statement and the name of the author or authors of such work or works, if known;

(vi) The playing time of each nondramatic musical work on such phonorecords;

(vii) For each nondramatic musical work that is owned by the same copyright owner being served with the Annual Statement and that is embodied in phonorecords covered by the compulsory license, a detailed statement of all of the information called for in paragraph (f)(4) of this section;

(viii) The total royalty payable for the fiscal year covered by the Annual Statement computed in accordance with the requirements of this section, together with a statement of account showing in detail how the royalty was computed. For these purposes, the applicable royalty as specified in section 115(c)(2) of title 17 of the United States Code, shall be payable for every phonorecord "voluntarily distributed" during the fiscal year covered by the Annual Statement;

(ix) The total sum paid under Monthly Statements of Account by the compulsory licensee to the copyright owner being served with the Annual Statement during the fiscal year covered by the Annual Statement; and

(x) In any case where the compulsory license falls within the provisions of paragraph (d) of this section, a clear description of the action or proceeding involved, including the date of the final judgment or definitive finding described in that paragraph.

(4) *Specific content of annual statements: Identification and accounting of phonorecords.* (i) The information called for by paragraph (f)(3)(vii) of this section shall, with respect to each nondramatic musical work, include a separate listing of each of the following items of information separately stated and identified for each phonorecord configuration (for example, single disk, long playing disk, cartridge, cassette, or reel-to-reel) made:

(A) The number of phonorecords made through the end of the fiscal year covered by the Annual Statement, including any made during earlier years;

(B) The number of phonorecords which have never been relinquished from possession of the compulsory licensee through the end of the fiscal year covered by the Annual Statement;

(C) The number of phonorecords involuntarily relinquished from possession (as through fire or theft) of the compulsory licensee during the fiscal year covered by the Annual Statement and any earlier years, together with a description of the facts of such involuntary relinquishment;

(D) The number of phonorecords "voluntarily distributed" by the compulsory licensee during all years before the fiscal year covered by the Annual Statement;

(E) The number of phonorecords relinquished from possession of the compulsory licensee for purposes of sale during the fiscal year covered by the Annual Statement accompanied by a privilege of returning unsold records for credit or exchange, but not "voluntarily distributed" by the end of that year;

(F) The number of phonorecords "voluntarily distributed" by the compulsory licensee during the fiscal year covered by the Annual Statement, together with:

(*1*) The catalog number or numbers, and label name or names, used on such phonorecords; and

(*2*) The names of the principal recording artists or groups engaged in rendering the performances fixed on such phonorecords.

(ii) If the information given under paragraphs (f)(4)(i)(A) through (F) of this section does not reconcile, the Annual Statement shall also include a clear and detailed explanation of the difference. For these purposes, the information given under such paragraphs shall be considered not to reconcile if, after the number of phonorecords given under paragraphs (B), (C), (D), and (E) are added together and that sum is deducted from the number of phonorecords given under paragraph (A), the result is different from the amount given under paragraph (F).

(5) *Clear statement.* The information required by paragraph (f)(3) of this section involves intelligible, legible, and unambiguous statements in the Annual Statement of Account itself and without incorporation by reference of facts or information contained in other documents or records.

(6) *Signature and certification.* (i) Each Annual Statement of Account shall include the handwritten signature of the compulsory licensee. If that compulsory licensee is a corporation, the signature shall be that of a duly authorized officer of the corporation;

if that compulsory licensee is a partnership, the signature shall be that of a partner. The signature shall be accompanied by: (A) The printed or typewritten name of the person signing the Annual Statement of Account; (B) the date of signature; (C) if the compulsory licensee is a partnership or a corporation, by the title or official position held in the partnership or corporation by the person signing the Annual Statement of Account; and (D) a certification of the capacity of the person signing.

(ii)

(A) Each Annual Statement of Account shall also be certified by a licensed Certified Public Accountant. Such certification shall consist of the following statement:

We have examined the attached "Annual Statement of Account Under Compulsory License For Making and Distributing Phonorecords" for the fiscal year ended (date) of (name of the compulsory licensee) applicable to phonorecords embodying (title or titles of nondramatic musical works embodied in phonorecords made under the compulsory license) made under the provisions of section 115 of title 17 of the United States Code, as amended by Pub. L. 94-553, and applicable regulations of the United States Copyright Office. Our examination was made in accordance with generally accepted auditing standards and accordingly, included tests of the accounting records and such other auditing procedures as we considered necessary in the circumstances.

In our opinion the Annual Statement of Account referred to above presents fairly the number of phonorecords embodying each of the above-identified nondramatic musical works made under compulsory license and voluntarily distributed by (name of the compulsory licensee) during the fiscal year ending (date), and the amount of royalties applicable thereto under such compulsory license, on a consistent basis and in accordance with the above cited law and applicable regulations published thereunder. ______________________

(City and State of Execution) ____________________

(Signature of Certified Public Accountant or CPA Firm) ____________________

Certificate Number ____________________

Jurisdiction of Certificate ____________________

(Date of Opinion)

(B) The certificate shall be signed by an individual, or in the name of a partnership or a professional corporation with two or more shareholders. The certificate number and jurisdiction are not required if the certificate is signed in the name of a partnership or a professional corporation with two or more shareholders.

(7) *Service.* (i) Each Annual Statement of Account shall be served on the copyright owner or the agent with authority to receive Annual Statements of Account on behalf of the copyright owner to whom or which it is directed by mail or by reputable courier service on or before the 20th day of the third month following the end of the fiscal year covered by the Annual Statement. It shall not be necessary to file a copy of the Annual Statement in the Copyright Office. An Annual Statement of Account shall be served for each fiscal year during which at least one Monthly Statement of Account was required to have been served under paragraph (e)(7) of this section.

(ii) In any case where the amount required to be stated in the Annual Statement of Account under paragraph (f)(3)(viii) of this section is greater than the amount stated in that Annual Statement under paragraph (f)(3)(ix) of this section, the difference between such amounts shall be delivered to the copyright owner together with the service of the Annual Statement. The delivery of such sum does not require the copyright owner to accept such sum, or to forego any right, relief, or remedy which may be available under law.

(iii)

(A) In any case where an Annual Statement of Account is sent by mail or by reputable courier service and is returned to the sender because the copyright owner or agent is not located at that address or has refused to accept delivery, or in any case where an address for the copyright owner is not known, the Annual Statement of Account, together with any evidence of mailing or attempted delivery by courier service, may be filed in the Licensing Division of the Copyright Office. Any Annual Statement of Account submitted for filing shall be accompanied by a brief statement of the reason why it was not served on the copyright owner. A written acknowledgment of receipt and filing will be provided to the sender.

(B) The Copyright Office will not accept any royalty fees submitted with Annual Statements of Account under this paragraph (f)(7)(iii).

(C) Neither the filing of an Annual Statement of Account in the Copyright Office, nor the failure to file such Annual Statement, shall have any effect other than that which may be attributed to it by a court of competent jurisdiction.

(D) No filing fee will be required in the case of Annual Statements of Account submitted to the Copyright Office under this § 201.19(f)(7)(iii). Upon request and payment of the fee specified in § 201.3(e), a Certificate of Filing will be provided to the sender.

(iv) If an Annual Statement of Account is sent by certified mail or registered mail, a mailing receipt shall be sufficient to prove that service was timely. If an Annual Statement of Account is delivered by a reputable courier, documentation from the courier showing the first date of attempted delivery shall also be sufficient to prove that service was timely. In the absence of a receipt from the United States Postal Service showing the date of delivery or documentation showing the first date of attempted delivery by a reputable courier, the compulsory licensee shall bear the burden of proving that the Annual Statement of Account was served in a timely manner.

(g) *Documentation.* All compulsory licensees shall, for a period of at least three years from the date of service of an Annual Statement of Account, keep and retain in their possession all records and documents necessary and appropriate to support fully the information set forth in such Annual Statement and in Monthly Statements served during the fiscal year covered by such Annual Statement.

(17 U.S.C. 115, 702, 708)

[45 FR 79046, Nov. 28, 1980, as amended at 56 FR 7813, Feb. 26, 1991; 56 FR 59885, Nov. 26, 1991; 63 FR 30635, June 5, 1998; 64 FR 29521, June 1, 1999; 64 FR 36574, 36575, July 7, 1999; 64 FR 41289, July 30, 1999; 66 FR 34373, June 28, 2001; 69 FR 34584, June 22, 2004; 73 FR 66181, Nov. 7, 2008]

**SOURCE:** GPO Electronic Code of Federal Regulations (e-CFR) **http://www.copyright.gov/title37/201/index.html**

Data current as of **February 12, 2009.**

# LAW 13.3

## U.S. COPYRIGHT ROYALTY BOARD — STATUTORY RATE REGULATIONS (EFFECTIVE MARCH 1, 2009)

Part 385 to Chapter III of title 37 of the Code of Federal Regulations

## PART 385 — RATES AND TERMS FOR USE OF MUSICAL WORKS UNDER COMPULSORY LICENSE FOR MAKING AND DISTRIBUTING OF PHYSICAL AND DIGITAL PHONORECORDS

### Subpart A — Physical Phonorecord Deliveries, Permanent Digital Downloads and Ringtones

Sec.



### Subpart B — Interactive Streaming, Other Incidental Digital Phonorecord Deliveries and Limited Downloads

Sec.

**Authority:** 17 U.S.C. 115, 801(b)(1), 804(b)(4).

## Subpart A — Physical Phonorecord Deliveries, Permanent Digital Downloads and Ringtones

### § 385.1 General.

(a) *Scope.* This subpart establishes rates and terms of royalty payments for making and distributing phonorecords, including by means of digital phonorecord deliveries, in accordance with the provisions of 17 U.S.C. 115.

(b) *Legal compliance.* Licensees relying upon the compulsory license set forth in 17 U.S.C. 115 shall comply with the requirements of that section, the rates and terms of this subpart, and any other applicable regulations.

(c) *Relationship to voluntary agreements.* Notwithstanding the royalty rates and terms established in this subpart, the rates and terms of any license agreements entered into by Copyright Owners and Licensees shall apply in lieu of the rates and terms of this subpart to use of musical works within the scope of such agreements.

### § 385.2 Definitions.

For purposes of this subpart, the following definitions apply:

*Copyright Owners* are nondramatic musical work copyright owners who are entitled to royalty payments made under this subpart pursuant to the compulsory license under 17 U.S.C. 115.

*Digital phonorecord delivery* means a digital phonorecord delivery as defined in 17 U.S.C. 115(d).

*Licensee* is a person or entity that has obtained a compulsory license under 17 U.S.C. 115, and the implementing regulations, to make and distribute phonorecords of a nondramatic musical work, including by means of a digital phonorecord delivery.

*Permanent digital download* means a digital phonorecord delivery that is distributed in the form of a download that may be retained and played on a permanent basis.

*Ringtone* means a phonorecord of a partial musical work distributed as a digital phonorecord delivery in a format to be made resident on a telecommunications device for use to announce the reception of an incoming telephone call or other communication or message or to alert the receiver to the fact that there is a communication or message.

### § 385.3 Royalty rates for making and distributing phonorecords.

(a) *Physical phonorecord deliveries and permanent digital downloads.* For every physical phonorecord and permanent digital download made and distributed, the royalty rate payable for each work embodied in such phonorecord shall be either 9.1 cents or 1.75 cents per minute of playing time or fraction thereof, whichever amount is larger.

(b) *Ringtones.* For every ringtone made and distributed, the royalty rate payable for each work embodied therein shall be 24 cents.

### § 385.4 Late payments.

A Licensee shall pay a late fee of 1.5% per month, or the highest lawful rate, whichever is lower, for any payment received by the Copyright Owner after the due date set forth in (201.19(e)(7)(i) of this title. Late fees shall accrue from the due date until payment is received by the Copyright Owner.

## Subpart B — Interactive Streaming, Other Incidental Digital Phonorecord Deliveries and Limited Downloads

### § 385.10 General.

(a) *Scope.* This subpart establishes rates and terms of royalty payments for interactive streams and limited downloads of musical works by subscription and nonsubscription digital music services in accordance with the provisions of 17 U.S.C. 115.

(b) *Legal compliance.* A licensee that makes or authorizes interactive streams or limited downloads of musical works through subscription or nonsubscription digital music services pursuant to 17 U.S.C. 115 shall comply with the requirements of that section, the rates and terms of this subpart, and any other applicable regulations.

**§ 385.11 Definitions.**
For purposes of this subpart, the following definitions shall apply:

*Interactive stream* means a stream of a sound recording of a musical work, where the performance of the sound recording by means of the stream is not exempt under 17 U.S.C. 114(d)(1) and does not in itself or as a result of a program in which it is included qualify for statutory licensing under 17 U.S.C. 114(d)(2). An interactive stream is an incidental digital phonorecord delivery under 17 U.S.C. 115(c)(3)(C) and (D).

*Licensee* means a person that has obtained a compulsory license under 17 U.S.C. 115 and its implementing regulations.

*Licensed activity* means interactive streams or limited downloads of musical works, as applicable.

*Limited download* means a digital transmission of a sound recording of a musical work to an end user, other than a stream, that results in a specifically identifiable reproduction of that sound recording that is only accessible for listening for —

(1) An amount of time not to exceed 1 month from the time of the transmission (unless the service, in lieu of retransmitting the same sound recording as another limited download, separately and upon specific request of the end user made through a live network connection, reauthorizes use for another time period not to exceed 1 month), or in the

case of a subscription transmission, a period of time following the end of the applicable subscription no longer than a subscription renewal period or 3 months, whichever is shorter; or

(2) A specified number of times not to exceed 12 (unless the service, in lieu of retransmitting the same sound recording as another limited download, separately and upon specific request of the end user made through a live network connection, reauthorizes use of another series of 12 or fewer plays), or in the case of a subscription transmission, 12 times after the end of the applicable subscription.

(3) A limited download is a general digital phonorecord delivery under 17 U.S.C. 115(c)(3)(C) and (D). *Offering* means a service's offering of licensed activity that is subject to a particular rate set forth in § 385.13(a) (*e.g.*, a particular subscription plan available through the service).

*Promotional royalty rate* means the statutory royalty rate of zero in the case of certain promotional interactive streams and certain promotional limited downloads, as provided in § 385.14.

*Publication date* means January 26, 2009.

*Record company* means a person or entity that (1) Is a copyright owner of a sound recording of a musical work; (2) In the case of a sound recording of a musical work fixed before February 15, 1972, has rights to the sound recording, under the common law or statutes of any State, that are equivalent to the rights of a copyright owner of a sound recording of a musical work under title 17, United States Code; (3) Is an exclusive licensee of the rights to reproduce and distribute a sound recording of a musical work; or (4) Performs the functions of marketing and authorizing the distribution of a sound recording of a musical work under its own label, under the authority of the copyright owner of the sound recording.

*Relevant page* means a page (including a Web page, screen or display) from which licensed activity offered by a service is directly available to end users, but only where the offering of licensed activity and content that directly relates to the offering of licensed activity (*e.g.*, an image of the artist or artwork closely associated with such offering, artist or album information, reviews of such offering, credits and music player controls) comprises 75% or more of the space on that page, excluding any space occupied by advertising. A licensed activity is directly available to end users from a page if sound recordings of musical works can be accessed by end users for limited downloads or interactive streams from such page (in most cases this will be the page where the limited download or interactive stream takes place).

*Service* means that entity (which may or may not be the licensee) that, with respect to the licensed activity, (1) Contracts with or has a direct relationship with end users in a case where a contract or relationship exists, or otherwise controls the content made available to end users; (2) Is able to report fully on service revenue from the provision of the licensed activity to the public, and to the extent applicable, verify service revenue through an audit; and (3) Is able to report fully on usage of musical works by the service, or procure such reporting, and to the extent applicable, verify usage through an audit.

*Service revenue.* (1) Subject to paragraphs (2) through (5) of the definition of "Service revenue," and subject to U.S. Generally Accepted Accounting Principles, *service revenue* shall mean the following:

(i) All revenue recognized by the service from end users from the provision of licensed activity;

(ii) All revenue recognized by the service by way of sponsorship and commissions as a result of the inclusion of third-party "in-stream" or "indownload" advertising as part of licensed activity (*i.e.*, advertising placed immediately at the start, end or during the actual delivery, by way of interactive streaming or limited downloads, as applicable, of a musical work); and

(iii) All revenue recognized by the service, including by way of sponsorship and commissions, as a result of the placement of third-party advertising on a relevant page of the service or on any page that directly follows such relevant page leading up to and including the limited download or interactive streaming, as applicable, of a musical work; provided that, in the case where more than one service is actually available to end users from a relevant page, any advertising revenue shall be allocated between such services on the basis of the relative amounts of the page they occupy.

(2) In each of the cases identified in paragraph (1) of the definition of "Service revenue," such revenue shall, for the avoidance of doubt,

(i) Include any such revenue recognized by the service, or if not recognized by the service, by any associate, affiliate, agent or representative of such service in lieu of its being recognized by the service;

(ii) Include the value of any barter or other nonmonetary consideration;

(iii) Not be reduced by credit card commissions or similar payment process charges; and

(iv) Except as expressly set forth in this subpart, not be subject to any other deduction or set-off other than refunds to end users for licensed activity that they were unable to use due to technical faults in the licensed activity or other bona fide refunds or credits issued to end users in the ordinary course of business.

(3) In each of the cases identified in paragraph (1) of the definition of "Service revenue," such revenue shall, for the avoidance of doubt, exclude revenue derived solely in connection with

services and activities other than licensed activity, provided that advertising or sponsorship revenue shall be treated as provided in paragraphs (2) and (4) of the definition of "Service revenue." By way of example, the following kinds of revenue shall be excluded:

(i) Revenue derived from non-music voice, content and text services;

(ii) Revenue derived from other nonmusic products and services (including search services, sponsored searches and click-through commissions); and

(iii) Revenue derived from music or music-related products and services that are not or do not include licensed activity.

(4) For purposes of paragraph (1) of the definition of "Service revenue," advertising or sponsorship revenue shall be reduced by the actual cost of obtaining such revenue, not to exceed 15%.

(5) Where the licensed activity is provided to end users as part of the same transaction with one or more other products or services that are not a music service engaged in licensed activity, then the revenue deemed to be recognized from end users for the service for the purpose of the definition in paragraph (1) of the definition of "Service revenue" shall be the revenue recognized from end users for the bundle less the standalone published price for end users for each of the other component(s) of the bundle; provided that, if there is no such standalone published price for a component of the bundle, then the average standalone published price for end users for the most closely comparable product or service in the U.S. shall be used or, if more than one such comparable exists, the average of such standalone prices for such comparables shall be used. In connection with such a bundle, if a record company providing sound recording rights to the service

(i) Recognizes revenue (in accordance with U.S. Generally Accepted Accounting Principles, and including for the avoidance of doubt barter or nonmonetary consideration) from a person or entity other than the service providing the licensed activity and;

(ii) Such revenue is received, in the context of the transactions involved, as consideration for the ability to make interactive streams or limited downloads of sound recordings, then such revenue shall be added to the amounts expensed by the service for purposes of § 385.13(b). Where the service is the licensee, if the service provides the record company all information necessary for the record company to determine whether additional royalties are payable by the service hereunder as a result of revenue recognized from a person or entity other than the service as described in the immediately preceding sentence, then the record company shall provide such further information as necessary for the service to calculate the additional royalties and indemnify the service for such additional royalties. The sole obligation of the record company shall be to pay the licensee such additional royalties if actually payable as royalties hereunder; provided, however, that this shall not affect any otherwise existing right or remedy of the copyright owner nor diminish the licensee's obligations to the copyright owner.

*Stream* means the digital transmission of a sound recording of a musical work to an end user —

(1) To allow the end user to listen to the sound recording, while maintaining a live network connection to the transmitting service, substantially at the time of transmission, except to the extent that the sound recording remains accessible for future listening from a streaming cache reproduction;

(2) Using technology that is designed such that the sound recording does not remain accessible for future listening, except to the extent that the sound recording remains accessible for future listening from a streaming cache reproduction; and

(3) That is also subject to licensing as a public performance of the musical work.

*Streaming cache reproduction* means a reproduction of a sound recording of a musical work made on a computer or other receiving device by a service solely for the purpose of permitting an end user who has previously received a stream of such sound recording to play such sound recording again from local storage on such computer or other device rather than by means of a transmission; provided that the user is only able to do so while maintaining a live network connection to the service, and such reproduction is encrypted or otherwise protected consistent with prevailing industry standards to prevent it from being played in any other manner or on any device other than the computer or other device on which it was originally made.

*Subscription service* means a digital music service for which end users are required to pay a fee to access the service for defined subscription periods of 3 years or less (in contrast to, for example, a service where the basic charge to users is a payment per download or per play), whether such payment is made for access to the service on a standalone basis or as part of a bundle with one or more other products or services, and including any use of such a service on a trial basis without charge as described in § 385.14(b).

**§ 385.12 Calculation of royalty payments in general.**

(a) *Applicable royalty.* Licensees that make or authorize licensed activity pursuant to 17 U.S.C. 115 shall pay royalties therefor that are calculated as provided in this section, subject to the minimum royalties and subscriber based royalty floors for specific types of services provided in § 385.13, except as provided for certain promotional uses in § 385.14.

(b) *Rate calculation methodology.*

Royalty payments for licensed activity shall be calculated as provided in paragraph (b) of this section. If a service includes different offerings, royalties must be separately calculated with respect to each such offering. Uses subject to the promotional royalty rate shall be excluded from the calculation of royalties due, as further described in this section and the following § 385.13.

(1) *Step 1:* Calculate the All-In Royalty for the Service. For each accounting period, the all-in royalty for each offering of the service is the greater of (i) The applicable percentage of service revenue as set forth in paragraph (c) of this section (excluding any service revenue derived solely from licensed activity uses subject to the promotional royalty rate), and (ii) The minimum specified in § 385.13 of the offering involved.

(2) *Step 2:* Subtract Applicable Performance Royalties. From the amount determined in step 1 in paragraph (b)(1) of this section, for each offering of the service, subtract the total amount of royalties for public performance of musical works that has been or will be expensed by the service pursuant to public performance licenses in connection with uses of musical works through such offering during the accounting period that constitute licensed activity (other than licensed activity subject to the promotional royalty rate). While this amount may be the total of the service's payments for that offering for the accounting period under its agreements with performing rights societies as defined in 17 U.S.C. 101, it will be less than the total of such public performance payments if the service is also engaging in public performance of musical works that does not constitute licensed activity. In the latter case, the amount to be subtracted for public performance payments shall be the amount of such payments allocable to licensed activity uses (other than promotional royalty rate uses) through the relevant offering, as determined in relation to all uses of musical works for which the public performance payments are made for the accounting period. Such allocation shall be made on the basis of plays of musical works or, where per-play information is unavailable due to bona fide technical limitations as described in step 4 in paragraph (b)(4) of this section, using the same alternative methodology as provided in step 4.

(3) *Step 3:* Determine the Payable Royalty Pool. This is the amount payable for the reproduction and distribution of all musical works used by the service by virtue of its licensed activity for a particular offering during the accounting period. This

amount is the greater of (i) The result determined in step 2 in paragraph (b)(2) of this section, and (ii) The subscriber-based royalty floor resulting from the calculations described in § 385.13.

(4) *Step 4:* Calculate the Per-Work Royalty Allocation for Each Relevant Work. This is the amount payable for the reproduction and distribution of each musical work used by the service by virtue of its licensed activity through a particular offering during the accounting period. To determine this amount, the result determined in step 3 in paragraph (b)(3) of this section must be allocated to each musical work used through the offering. The allocation shall be accomplished by dividing the payable royalty pool determined in step 3 for such offering by the total number of plays of all musical works through such offering during the accounting period (other than promotional royalty rate plays) to yield a per-play allocation, and multiplying that result by the number of plays of each musical work (other than promotional royalty rate plays) through the offering during the accounting period. For purposes of determining the per-work royalty allocation in all calculations under this step 4 only (*i.e.*, after the payable royalty pool has been determined), for sound recordings of musical works with a playing time of over 5 minutes, each play on or after October 1, 2010 shall be counted as provided in paragraph (d) of this section. Notwithstanding the foregoing, if the service is not capable of tracking play information due to bona fide limitations of the available technology for services of that nature or of devices useable with the service, the per-work royalty allocation may instead be accomplished in a manner consistent with the methodology used by the service for making royalty payment allocations for the use of individual sound recordings.

(c) *Percentage of service revenue.* The percentage of service revenue applicable under paragraph (b) of this section is 10.5%, except that such percentage shall be discounted by 2% (*i.e.*, to 8.5%) in the case of licensed activity occurring on or before December 31, 2007.

(d) *Overtime adjustment.* For licensed activity on or after October 1, 2010, for purposes of the calculations in step 4 in paragraph (b)(4) of this section only, for sound recordings of musical works with a playing time of over 5 minutes, adjust the number of plays as follows:

(1) 5:01 to 6:00 minutes — Each play =1.2 plays

(2) 6:01 to 7:00 minutes — Each play =1.4 plays

(3) 7:01 to 8:00 minutes — Each play =1.6 plays

(4) 8:01 to 9:00 minutes — Each play =1.8 plays

(5) 9:01 to 10:00 minutes — Each play= 2.0 plays

(6) For playing times of greater than 10 minutes, continue to add .2 for each additional minute or fraction thereof.

(e) *Accounting.* The calculations required by paragraph (b) of this section shall be made in good faith and on the basis of the best knowledge, information and belief of the licensee at the time payment is due, and subject to the additional accounting and certification requirements of 17 U.S.C. 115(c)(5) and § 201.19 of this title. Without limitation, a licensee's statements of account shall set forth each step of its calculations with sufficient information to allow the copyright owner to assess the accuracy and manner in which the licensee determined the payable royalty pool and per-play allocations (including information sufficient to demonstrate whether and how a minimum royalty or subscriber-based royalty floor pursuant to § 385.13 does or does not apply) and, for each offering reported, also indicate the type of licensed activity involved and the number of plays of each musical work (including an indication of any overtime adjustment applied) that is the basis of the per-work royalty allocation being paid.

### § 385.13 Minimum royalty rates and subscriber-based royalty floors for specific types of services.

(a) *In general.* The following minimum royalty rates and subscriber based royalty floors shall apply to the following types of licensed activity:

(1) *Standalone non-portable subscription — streaming only.*

Except as provided in paragraph (a)(4) of this section, in the case of a subscription service through which an end user can listen to sound recordings only in the form of interactive streams and only from a non-portable device to which such streams are originally transmitted while the device has a live network connection, the minimum for use in step 1 of § 385.12(b)(1) is the lesser of subminimum II as described in paragraph (c) of this section for the accounting period and the aggregate amount of 50 cents per subscriber per month. The subscriber-based royalty floor for use in step 3 of § 385.12(b)(3) is the aggregate amount of 15 cents per subscriber per month.

(2) *Standalone non-portable subscription — mixed.*

Except as provided in paragraph (a)(4) of this section, in the case of a subscription service through which an end user can listen to sound recordings either in the form of interactive streams or limited downloads but only from a non-portable device to which such streams or downloads are originally transmitted, the minimum for use in step 1 of § 385.12(b)(1) is the lesser of the subminimum I as described in paragraph (b) of this section for the accounting period and the aggregate amount of 50 cents per subscriber per month. The subscriber-based royalty floor for use in step 3 of § 385.12(b)(3) is the aggregate amount of 30 cents per subscriber per month.

(3) *Standalone portable subscription service.* Except as provided in paragraph (a)(4) of this section, in the case of a subscription service through which an end user can listen to sound

recordings in the form of interactive streams or limited downloads from a portable device, the minimum for use in step 1 of § 385.12(b)(1) is the lesser of subminimum I as described in paragraph (b) of this section for the accounting period and the aggregate amount of 80 cents per subscriber per month. The subscriber-based royalty floor for use in step 3 of § 385.12(b)(3) is the aggregate amount of 50 cents per subscriber per month.

(4) *Bundled subscription services.* In the case of a subscription service made available to end users with one or more other products or services as part of a single transaction without pricing for the subscription service separate from the product(s) or service(s) with which it is made available (*e.g.*, a case in which a user can buy a portable device and one-year access to a subscription service for a single price), the minimum for use in step 1 of § 385.12(b)(1) is subminimum I as described in paragraph (b) of this section for the accounting period. The subscriber-based royalty floor for use in step 3 of § 385.12(b)(3) is the aggregate amount of 25 cents per month for each end user who has made at least one play of a licensed work during such month (each such end user to be considered an "active subscriber").

(5) *Free nonsubscription/adsupported services.* In the case of a service offering licensed activity free of any charge to the end user, the minimum for use in step 1 of § 385.12(b)(1) is subminimum II described in paragraph (c) of this section for the accounting period. There is no subscriber-based royalty floor for use in step 3 of § 385.12(b)(3).

(b) *Computation of subminimum I.*

For purposes of paragraphs (a)(2), (3) and (4) of this section, and with reference to paragraph (5) of the definition of "service revenue" in § 385.11 if applicable, subminimum I for an accounting period means the aggregate of the following with respect to all sound recordings of musical works used in the relevant offering of the service during the accounting period —

(1) In cases in which a record company is the licensee under 17 U.S.C. 115 and a third-party service has obtained from the record company the rights to make interactive streams or limited downloads of a sound recording together with the right to reproduce and distribute the musical work embodied therein, 17.36% of the total amount expensed by the service in accordance with U.S. Generally Accepted Accounting Principles, which for the avoidance of doubt shall include the value of any barter or other nonmonetary consideration provided by the service, for such rights for the accounting period, except that for licensed activity occurring on or before December 31, 2007, subminimum I for an accounting period shall be 14.53% of the amount expensed by the service for such rights for the accounting period.

(2) In cases in which the relevant service is the licensee under 17 U.S.C. 115 and the relevant service has obtained from a third-party record company the rights to make interactive streams or limited downloads of a sound recording without the right to reproduce and distribute the musical work embodied therein, 21% of the total amount expensed by the service in accordance with U.S. Generally Accepted Accounting Principles, which for the avoidance of doubt shall include the value of any barter or other nonmonetary consideration provided by the service, for such sound recording rights for the accounting period, except that for licensed activity occurring on or before December 31, 2007, subminimum I for an accounting period shall be 17% of the amount expensed by the service for such sound recording rights for the accounting period.

(c) *Computation of subminimum II.*

For purposes of paragraphs(a)(1) and (5) of this section, subminimum II for an accounting period means the aggregate of the following with respect to all sound recordings of musical works used by the relevant service during the accounting period —

(1) In cases in which a record company is the licensee under 17 U.S.C. 115 and a third-party service has

obtained from the record company the rights to make interactive streams and limited downloads of a sound recording together with the right to reproduce and distribute the musical work embodied therein, 18% of the total amount expensed by the service in accordance with U.S. Generally Accepted Accounting Principles, which for the avoidance of doubt shall include the value of any barter or other nonmonetary consideration provided by the service, for such rights for the accounting period, except that for licensed activity occurring on or before December 31, 2007, subminimum II for an accounting period shall be 14.53% of the amount expensed by the service for such rights for the accounting period.

(2) In cases in which the relevant service is the licensee under 17 U.S.C. 115 and the relevant service has obtained from a third-party record company the rights to make interactive streams or limited downloads of a sound recording without the right to reproduce and distribute the musical work embodied therein, 22% of the total amount expensed by the service in accordance with U.S. Generally Accepted Accounting Principles, which for the avoidance of doubt shall include the value of any barter or other nonmonetary consideration provided by the service, for such sound recording rights for the accounting period, except that for licensed activity occurring on or before December 31, 2007, subminimum II for an accounting period shall be 17% of the amount expensed by the service for such sound recording rights for the accounting period.

(d) *Computation of subscriber-based royalty rates.* For purposes of paragraph (a) of this section, to determine the minimum or subscriber-based royalty floor, as applicable to any particular offering, the service shall for the relevant offering calculate its total number of subscriber-months for the accounting period, taking into account all end users who were subscribers for complete calendar months, prorating in the case of end users who were subscribers for only part of a calendar month, and deducting on a prorated basis for end users covered by a free trial period subject to the promotional royalty rate as described in § 385.14(b)(2), except that in the case of a bundled subscription service, subscriber-months shall instead be determined with respect to active subscribers as defined in paragraph (a)(4) of this section. The product of the total number of subscriber-months for the accounting period and the specified number of cents per subscriber (or active subscriber, as the case may be) shall be used as the subscriber-based component of the minimum or subscriber-based royalty floor, as applicable, for the accounting period.

### § 385.14 Promotional royalty rate.

(a) *General provisions.* (1) This section establishes a royalty rate of zero in the case of certain promotional interactive streaming activities, and of certain promotional limited downloads offered in the context of a free trial period for a digital music subscription service under a license pursuant to 17 U.S.C. 115. Subject to the requirements of 17 U.S.C. 115 and the additional provisions of paragraphs (b) through (e) of this section, the promotional royalty rate shall apply to a musical work when a record company transmits or authorizes the transmission of interactive streams or limited downloads of a sound recording that embodies such musical work, only if —

(i) The primary purpose of the record company in making or authorizing the interactive streams or limited downloads is to promote the sale or other paid use of sound recordings by the relevant artists, including such sound recording, through established retail channels or the paid use of one or more established retail music services through which the sound recording is available, and not to promote any other good or service;

(ii) Either —

(A) The sound recording (or a different version of the sound recording embodying the same musical work) is being lawfully distributed and offered to consumers through the established retail channels or services described in paragraph (a)(1)(i) of this section; or (B) In the case of a sound recording of a musical work being prepared for commercial release but not yet released, the record company has a good faith intention of lawfully distributing and offering to consumers the sound recording (or a different version of the sound recording embodying the same musical work) through the established retail channels or services described in paragraph (a)(1)(i) of this section within 90 days after the commencement of the first promotional use authorized under this section (and in fact does so, unless it can demonstrate that notwithstanding its bona fide intention, it unexpectedly did not meet the scheduled release date);

(iii) In connection with authorizing the promotional interactive streams or limited downloads, the record company has obtained from the service it authorizes a written representation that —

A) In the case of a promotional use commencing on or after October 1, 2010, except interactive streaming subject to paragraph (d) of this section, the service agrees to maintain for a period of no less than 5 years from the conclusion of the promotional activity complete and accurate records of the relevant authorization and dates on which the promotion was conducted, and identifying each sound recording of a musical work made available through the promotion, the licensed activity involved, and the number of plays of such recording;

(B) The service is in all material respects operating with appropriate license authority with respect to the musical works it is using for promotional and other purposes; and (C) The representation is signed by a person authorized to make the representation on behalf of the service; (iv) Upon receipt by the record company of written notice from the copyright owner of a musical work or agent of the copyright owner stating in good faith that a particular service is in a material manner operating without appropriate license authority from such copyright owner, the record company shall within 5 business days withdraw by written notice its authorization of such uses of such copyright owner's musical works under the promotional royalty rate by that service;

(v) The interactive streams or limited downloads are offered free of any charge to the end user and, except in the case of interactive streaming subject to paragraph (d) of this section in the case of a free trial period for a digital music subscription service, no more than 5 sound recordings at a time are streamed in response to any individual request of an end user;

(vi) The interactive streams and limited downloads are offered in a manner such that the user is at the same time (*e.g.*, on the same Web page) presented with a purchase opportunity for the relevant sound recording or an opportunity to subscribe to a paid service offering the sound recording, or a link to such a purchase or subscription opportunity, except —

(A) In the case of interactive streaming of a sound recording being prepared for commercial release but not yet released, certain mobile applications or other circumstances in which the foregoing is impracticable in view of the current state of the relevant technology; and

(B) In the case of a free trial period for a digital music subscription service, if end users are periodically offered an opportunity to subscribe to the service during such free trial period; and (vii) The interactive streams and limited downloads are not provided in a manner that is likely to cause mistake, to confuse or to deceive, reasonable end users as to the endorsement or association of the author of the musical work with any product, service or activity other than the sale or paid use of sound recordings or paid use of a music service through which sound recordings are available. Without limiting the foregoing, upon receipt of written notice from the copyright owner of a musical work or agent of the copyright owner stating in good faith that a particular use of such work under this section violates the limitation set forth in this paragraph (a)(1)(vii), the record company shall promptly cease such use of that work, and within 5 business days withdraw by written notice its authorization of such use by all relevant third parties it has authorized under this section.

(2) To rely upon the promotional royalty rate, a record company making or authorizing interactive streams or limited downloads shall keep complete and accurate contemporaneous written records of such uses, including the sound recordings and musical works involved, the artists, the release dates of the sound recordings, a brief statement of the promotional activities authorized, the identity of the service or services where each promotion is authorized (including the Internet address if applicable), the beginning and end date of each period of promotional activity authorized, and the representation required by paragraph (a)(1)(iii) of this section; provided that, in the case of trial subscription uses, such records shall instead consist of the contractual terms that bear upon promotional uses by the particular digital music subscription services it authorizes; and further provided that, if the record company itself is conducting the promotion, it shall also maintain any additional records described in paragraph (a)(1)(iii)(A) of this section. The records required by this paragraph (a)(2) shall be maintained for no less time than the record company maintains records of usage of royalty-bearing uses involving the same type of licensed activity in the ordinary course of business, but in no event for less than 5 years from the conclusion of the promotional activity to which they pertain. If the copyright owner of a musical work or its agent requests a copy of the information to be maintained under this paragraph (a)(2) with respect to a specific promotion or relating to a particular sound recording of a musical work, the record company shall provide complete and accurate documentation within 10 business days, except for any information required under paragraph (a)(1)(iii)(A) of this section, which shall be provided within 20 business days, and provided that if the copyright owner or agent requests information concerning a large volume of promotions or sound recordings, the record company shall have a reasonable time, in view of the amount of information requested, to respond to any request of such copyright owner or agent. If the record company does not provide required information within the required time, and upon receipt of written notice citing such failure does not provide such information within a further 10 business days, the uses will be considered not to be subject to the

promotional royalty rate and the record company (but not any third-party service it has authorized) shall be liable for any payment due for such uses; provided, however, that all rights and remedies of the copyright owner with respect to unauthorized uses shall be preserved.

(3) If the copyright owner of a musical work or its agent requests a copy of the information to be maintained under paragraph (a)(1)(iii)(A) of this section by a service authorized by a record company with respect to a specific promotion, the service shall provide complete and accurate documentation within 20 business days, provided that if the copyright owner or agent requests information concerning a large volume of promotions or sound recordings, the service shall have a reasonable time, in view of the amount of information requested, to respond to any request of such copyright owner or agent. If the service does not provide required information within the required time, and upon receipt of written notice citing such failure does not provide such information within a further 10 business days, the uses will be considered not to be subject to the promotional royalty rate and the service (but not the record company) will be liable for any payment due for such uses; provided, however, that all rights and remedies of the copyright owner with respect to unauthorized uses shall be preserved.

(4) The promotional royalty rate is exclusively for audio-only interactive streaming and limited downloads of musical works subject to licensing under 17 U.S.C. 115. The promotional royalty rate does not apply to any other use under 17 U.S.C. 115; nor does it apply to public performances, audiovisual works, lyrics or other uses outside the scope of 17 U.S.C. 115. Without limitation, uses subject to licensing under 17 U.S.C. 115 that do not qualify for the promotional royalty rate (including without limitation interactive streaming or limited downloads of a musical work beyond the time limitations applicable to the promotional royalty rate) require payment of applicable royalties. This section is based on an understanding of industry practices and market conditions at the time of its

development, among other things. The terms of this section shall be subject to de novo review and consideration (or elimination altogether) in future proceedings before the Copyright Royalty Judges. Nothing in this section shall be interpreted or construed in such a manner as to nullify or diminish any limitation, requirement or obligation of 17 U.S.C. 115 or other protection for musical works afforded by the Copyright Act, 17 U.S.C. 101 *et seq.* For the avoidance of doubt, however, except as provided in paragraph (a) of this section, statements of account under 17 U.S.C. 115 need not reflect interactive streams or limited downloads subject to the promotional royalty rate.

(b) *Interactive streaming and limited downloads of full-length musical works through third-party services.* In addition to those of paragraph (a) of this section, the provisions of this paragraph (b) apply to interactive streaming, and limited downloads (in the context of a free trial period for a digital music subscription service), authorized by record companies under the promotional royalty rate through third party services (including Web sites) that is not subject to paragraphs (c) or (d) of and limited downloads may be made or authorized by a record company under the promotional royalty rate only if —

(1) No cash, other monetary payment, barter or other consideration for making or authorizing the relevant interactive streams or limited downloads is received by the record company, its parent company, any entity owned in whole or in part by or under common ownership with the record company, or any other person or entity acting on behalf of or in lieu of the record company, except for in-kind promotional consideration used to promote the sale or paid use of sound recordings or the paid use of music services through which sound recordings are available;

(2) In the case of interactive streaming and limited downloads offered in the context of a free trial period for a digital music subscription service, the free trial period does not exceed 30 consecutive days per subscriber per two-year period; and

(3) In contexts other than a free trial period for a digital music subscription service, interactive streaming subject to paragraph (b) of this section of a particular sound recording is authorized by the record company on no more than 60 days total for all services (*i.e.*, interactive streaming under paragraph (b) of this section of a particular sound recording may be authorized on no more than a total of 60 days, which need not be consecutive, and on any one such day, interactive streams may be offered on one or more services); provided, however, that an additional 60 days shall be available each time the sound recording is re-released by the record company in a remastered form or as a part of a compilation with a different set of sound recordings than the original release or any prior compilation including such sound recording. (4) In the event that a record company authorizes promotional uses in excess of the time limitations of paragraph (b) of this section, the record company, and not the third-party service it has authorized, shall be liable for any payment due for such uses; provided, however, that all rights and remedies of the copyright owner with respect to unauthorized uses shall be preserved. In the event that a third-party service exceeds the scope of any authorization by a record company, the service, and not the record company, shall be liable for any payment due for such uses; provided, however, that all rights and remedies of the copyright owner with respect to unauthorized uses shall be preserved.

(c) *Interactive streaming of full-length musical works through record company and artist services.* In addition to those of paragraph (a) of this section, the provisions of this paragraph (c) apply to interactive streaming conducted or authorized by record companies under the promotional royalty rate through a service (*e.g.*, a Web site) directly owned or operated by the record company, or directly owned or operated by a recording artist under the authorization of the record company, and that is not subject to paragraph (d) of this section. For the avoidance of doubt and without limitation, an artist page or site on a third-party service (*e.g.*, a social networking service) shall not be considered a service operated by the record company or artist. Such interactive streams may be made or authorized by a record company under the promotional royalty rate only if — (1) The interactive streaming subject to this paragraph (c) of a particular sound recording is offered or authorized by the record company on no more than 90 days total for all services (i.e., interactive streaming under this paragraph (c) of a particular sound recording may be authorized on no more than a total of 90 days, which need not be consecutive, and on any such day, interactive streams may be offered on one or more services operated by the record company or artist, subject to the provisions of paragraph (b)(2) of this section); provided, however, that an additional 90 days shall be available each time the sound recording is rereleased by the record company in a remastered form or as part of a compilation with a different set of sound recordings than prior compilations that include that sound recording; (2) In the case of interactive streaming through a service devoted to one featured artist, the interactive streams subject to this paragraph (c) of this section of a particular sound recording are made or authorized by the record company on no more than one official artist site per artist and are recordings of that artist; and (3) In the case of interactive streaming through a service that is not limited to a single featured artist, all interactive streaming on such service (whether eligible for the promotional royalty rate or not) is limited to sound recordings of a single record company and its affiliates and the service would not reasonably be considered to be a meaningful substitute for a paid music service.

(d) *Interactive streaming of clips.* In addition to those in paragraph (a) of this section, the provisions of this paragraph (d) apply to interactive streaming conducted or authorized by record companies under the promotional royalty rate of segments of sound recordings of musical works with a playing time that does not exceed the greater of:

(1) 30 seconds, or

(2) 10% of the playing time of the complete sound recording, but in no event in excess of 60 seconds. Such interactive streams may be made or authorized by a record company under the promotional royalty rate without any of the temporal

limitations set forth in paragraphs (b) and (c) of this section (but subject to the other conditions of paragraphs (b) and (c) of this section, as applicable). For clarity, this paragraph (d) is strictly limited to the uses described herein and shall not be construed as permitting the creation or use of an excerpt of a musical work in violation of 17 U.S.C. 106(2) or 115(a)(2) or any other right of a musical work owner.

(e) *Activities prior to the publication date.* Notwithstanding paragraphs (a) through (d) of this section, in the case of licensed activity prior to the publication date, the promotional royalty rate shall apply to promotional interactive streams, and to limited downloads offered in the context of a free trial period for a digital music subscription service, that in either case are authorized by the relevant record company, if the condition set forth in paragraph (a)(1)(i) of this section is satisfied, subject only to the additional condition in paragraph (b)(1) of this section, and provided that a free trial period for a digital music subscription service authorized by the relevant record company shall be considered to be of 30 days' duration. In the event of a dispute concerning the eligibility of licensed activity prior to the publication date for the promotional royalty rate, a service asserting that its licensed activity is eligible for the promotional royalty rate shall bear the burden of proving that its licensed activity was authorized by the relevant record company and shall certify that the condition in paragraph (b)(1) of this section was satisfied.

**§ 385.15 Timing of payments.**

Payment for any accounting period for which payment otherwise would be due more than 180 days after the publication date shall be due as otherwise provided under 17 U.S.C. 115 and its implementing regulations. Payment for any prior accounting period shall be due 180 days after the publication date.

**§ 385.16 Reproduction and distribution rights covered.**

A compulsory license under 17 U.S.C. 115 extends to all reproduction and distribution rights that may be necessary for the provision of the licensed activity, solely for the purpose of providing such licensed activity (and no other purpose).

### § 385.17 Effect of rates.

In any future proceedings under 17 U.S.C. 115(c)(3)(C) and (D), the royalty rates payable for a compulsory license shall be established de novo.

# LAW 13.4

## CANADIAN COPYRIGHT BOARD ROYALTY RATE TARIFF (2007)

Copyright Board Canada

CANADA

Commission du droit d'auteur Canada

## COPYRIGHT BOARD

## Statement of Royalties to Be Collected by CMRRA/SODRAC Inc. for the Reproduction of Musical Works, in Canada, by Online Music Services in 2005, 2006 and 2007

**STATEMENT OF ROYALTIES TO BE COLLECTED BY CMRRA/SODRAC INC. FOR THE REPRODUCTION OF MUSICAL WORKS, IN CANADA, BY ONLINE MUSIC SERVICES IN 2005, 2006 AND 2007**

*Short Title*

1. This tariff may be cited as the *CSI Online Music Services Tariff, 2005-2007.*

*Definitions*

2. In this tariff

"bundle" means two or more digital files offered as a single product, if at least one file is a permanent download; (« *ensemble* »)

"CSI" means CMRRA/SODRAC Inc.; (« *CSI* »)

"download" means a file intended to be copied onto a consumer's local storage device; (« *téléchargement* »)

"file" except in the definition of "bundle", means a digital file of a sound recording of a musical work; (« *fichier* »)

"identifier" means the unique identifier an online music service assigns to a file or bundle; (« *identificateur* »)

"limited download" means a download that uses technology that causes the file to become unusable when a subscription ends; (« *téléchargement limité* »)

"on-demand stream" means a stream selected by its recipient; (« *transmission sur demande* »)

"online music service" means a service that delivers streams or limited downloads to subscribers or permanent downloads to consumers, other than a service that offers only streams in which the file is selected by the service, which can only be listened to at a time chosen by the service and for which no advance play list is published; (« *service de musique en ligne* »)

"permanent download" means a download other than a limited download; (« *téléchargement permanent* »)

"play" means the single performance of an on-demand stream; (« *écoute* »)

"portable limited download" means a limited download that uses technology that allows the subscriber to reproduce the file on a device other than a device to which an online music service delivered the file; (« *téléchargement limité portable* »)

"quarter" means from January to March, from April to June, from July to September and from October to December; (« *trimestre* »)

"repertoire" means the musical works for which CSI is entitled to grant a licence pursuant to section 3; (« *répertoire* ») "stream" means a file that is intended to be copied onto a local storage device only to the extent required to allow listening to the file at substantially the same time as when the file is transmitted; (« *transmission* »)

*Application*

3. (1) This tariff entitles an online music service and its authorized distributors

(*a*) to reproduce all or part of a musical work in the repertoire for the purpose of transmitting it in a file to consumers in Canada via the Internet or another similar computer network, including by wireless transmission,

(*b*) to authorize a person to reproduce the musical work for the purpose of delivering to the service a file that can then be reproduced and transmitted pursuant to paragraph (*a*), and

(*c*) to authorize consumers in Canada to further reproduce the musical work for their own private use,

in connection with the operation of the service.

(2) An online music service who complies with this tariff does not incur any obligation pursuant to sections 5, 6 or 8 in relation to streams of 30 seconds or less offered to promote the service or to allow consumers to preview a file.

4. (1) This tariff does not authorize the reproduction of a work in a medley, for the purpose of creating a mashup, for use as a sample or, subject to subsection 3(2), in association with a product, service, cause or institution.

(2) This tariff does not entitle the owner of the copyright in a sound recording of a musical work to authorize the reproduction of that work.

*Royalties*

5. (1) Subject to paragraph (4)(*a*), the royalties payable in a month for an online music service that offers only on-demand streams shall be:

$$\frac{A \times B}{C}$$

where

(A) is 4.1 per cent of the amounts paid by subscribers for the service during the month,

(B) is the number of plays of files requiring a CSI licence during the month, and

(C) is the number of plays of all files during the month,

subject to a minimum of 26.3¢ per subscriber.

(2) Subject to paragraph (4)(*a*), the royalties payable in a month for an online music service that offers limited downloads with or without on-demand streams shall be:

$$\frac{A \times B}{C}$$

where

(A) is 5.3 per cent of the amounts paid by subscribers for the service during the month,

(B) is the number of limited downloads requiring a CSI licence during the month, and

(C) is the total number of limited downloads during the month,

subject to a minimum of 51.3¢ per subscriber if portable limited downloads are allowed, and 33.7¢ per subscriber if they are not.

(3) Subject to paragraph (4)(*b*), the royalty payable for a permanent download requiring a CSI licence shall be 7.9 per cent of the amount paid by a consumer for the download, subject to a minimum of 4.1¢ per file in a bundle and 5.3¢ per file in all other cases.

(4) Where CSI does not hold all the rights in a musical work,

(*a*) for the purposes of subsections (1) and (2), only the share that CSI holds shall be included in (B), and

(*b*) for the purposes of subsection (3), the applicable rate shall be the relevant rate multiplied by CSI's share in the musical work.

(5) All royalties payable under this tariff are exclusive of any federal, provincial or other governmental taxes or levies of any kind.

ADMINISTRATIVE PROVISIONS

*Reporting Requirements*

6. (1) No later than 20 days after the end of the first month during which an online music service reproduces a file requiring a CSI licence, the service shall provide to CSI the following information:

(*a*) the name of the person who operates the service, including:

(i) the name of a corporation and a mention of its jurisdiction of incorporation,

(ii) the name of the proprietor of an individual proprietorship, or

(iii) the names of the principal officers of any other service,

together with any other trade name under which the service carries on business;

(*b*) the address of its principal place of business;

(*c*) its address (including email) for the purposes of notice;

(*d*) the name and address of any authorized distributor;

(*e*) the Uniform Resource Locator (URL) of each Internet website at or through which the service is or will be offered;

(*f*) with respect to each file that was reproduced:

(i) its identifier;

(ii) the title of the musical work;

(iii) the name of each performer or group to whom the sound recording is credited;

(iv) the name of the person who released the sound recording;

(v) if the file is being offered as part of a bundle, the name and identifier of the bundle as well as the identifier of each file in the bundle;

(vi) if the service believes that a CSI licence is not required, an indication to that effect; and

(*g*) with respect to each file that was reproduced, if the information is available:

(i) the name of each author of the musical work;

(ii) the International Standard Recording Code (ISRC) assigned to the sound recording;

(iii) the name of the music publisher associated with the musical work;

(iv) the International Standard Musical Work Code (ISWC) assigned to the musical work;

(v) if the sound recording was released in physical format as part of an album, the name, identifier, product catalogue number and Universal Product Code (UPC) assigned to the album, together with the associated disc and track numbers;

(vi) the Global Release Identifier (GRid) assigned to the file and, if applicable, the GRid of the album or bundle in which the file was released;

(vii) the running time of the file, in minutes and seconds; and

(viii) any alternative title used to designate the musical work or sound recording.

(2) No later than 20 days after the end of each subsequent month, an online music service shall provide to CSI the following information:

(*a*) any change to the information previously reported pursuant to paragraphs (1)(*a*) to (*g*) as well as any information set out in paragraph (1)(*g*) that became available during the month;

(*b*) with respect to each file that the service first made available during the month, the information set out in paragraphs (1)(*f*) and (*g*); and

(*c*) with respect to each file that the service ceased to make available during the month, its identifier.

7. (1) No later than 20 days after receiving a report pursuant to section 6, CSI shall send to the online music service a notice indicating:

(*a*) which files contain a work that it then knows to be in the repertoire;

(*b*) which files contain a work that it then knows not to be in the repertoire;

(*c*) which files contain a work that it then knows to be in the repertoire only as to a fraction of the rights, with an indication of that fraction; and

(*d*) with respect to all other files, an indication of the reason for which CSI is unable to provide an answer pursuant to paragraph (*a*), (*b*) or (*c*).

(2) No later than 20 days after the end of each month, CSI shall update the information provided pursuant to subsection (1).

(3) No later than 20 days after receiving a report pursuant to subsection (1) or (2), the online music service that disputes the indication that a file contains a work in the repertoire or requires a CSI licence, shall provide to CSI information that establishes why the licence is not required, unless the information was provided earlier.

*Sales Reports*

8. (1) No later than 20 days after the end of each month, an online music service that offers only on-demand streams shall provide to CSI a report setting out, for that month:

(*a*) the identifier and number of plays of each file requiring a CSI licence;

(*b*) the total number of plays of files requiring a CSI licence;

(*c*) the total number of plays of all files; and

(*d*) the number of subscribers to the service and the total amounts paid by them.

(2) No later than 20 days after the end of each month, an online music service that offers limited downloads shall provide to CSI a report setting out, for that month:

(*a*) the identifier, number of portable limited downloads and number of other limited downloads of each file requiring a CSI licence;

(*b*) the total number of portable limited downloads and other limited downloads requiring a CSI licence;

(*c*) the total number of portable limited downloads and other limited downloads; and

(*d*) the number of subscribers entitled to receive portable limited downloads, the number of other subscribers and the total amounts paid by all subscribers.

(3) No later than 20 days after the end of each month, an online music service that offers permanent downloads shall provide to CSI a report setting out, for that month:

(*a*) the identifier and number of times each file requiring a CSI licence was downloaded as part of a bundle, the amount paid by consumers for each bundle and a description of the manner in which the service assigned a share of that amount to the file; and

(*b*) the identifier and number of other downloads of each file requiring a CSI licence and the amount paid by consumers for the file.

(4) No later than 20 days after the end of the month during which an online music service is notified, in an update provided pursuant to subsection 7(2), that a file contains a work now known to be in the repertoire, the service shall provide to CSI the information set out in subsections (1) to (3) in relation to that file for each month during which the work was in the repertoire.

*Calculation and Payment of Royalties*

9. No later than 20 days after receiving a report pursuant to section 8 for the last month in a quarter, CSI shall provide the online music service with a detailed calculation of the royalties payable in that quarter for each file.

10. Royalties shall be due no later than 30 days after an online music service receives a report pursuant to section 9.

*Adjustments*

11. (1) Subject to subsection (2), adjustments in the amount of royalties owed, including excess payments, as a result of the discovery of an error or otherwise, shall be made on the date the next royalty payment is due.

(2) Any excess payment resulting from an online music service providing incorrect or incomplete information about a file shall be deducted from future amounts owed for the use of works owned by the same person as the work in that file.

(3) Adjustments in any information provided pursuant to section 8 or 9 shall be provided with the next report dealing with such information.

*Records and Audits*

12. (1) An online music service shall keep and preserve, for a period of six years after the end of the month

to which they relate, records from which the information set out in section 6, subsection 7(3) and section 8 can be readily ascertained.

(2) CSI may audit these records at any time during the period set out in subsection (1) on reasonable notice and during normal business hours.

(3) Subject to subsection (4), if an audit discloses that royalties due have been understated in any quarter by more than 10 per cent, the online music service shall pay the reasonable costs of the audit within 30 days of the demand for such payment.

(4) For the purposes of subsection (3), any amount owing as a result of an error or omission on the part of CSI shall not be taken into account.

*Breach and Termination*

13. (1) An online music service who fails to pay royalties within five business days of the date on which the royalties are due is not entitled to do any of the acts described in section 3 as of the first day of the quarter in respect of which the royalties should have been paid and until the royalties and any accrued interest are paid.

(2) An online music service who fails to comply with any other provision of this tariff is not entitled to do any of the acts described in section 3 five business days after CSI has notified the service in writing of that failure and until the service remedies that failure.

(3) An online music service who becomes insolvent, commits an act of bankruptcy, makes an assignment for the benefit of its creditors, files for protection under the *Companies Creditors Arrangement Act* or other comparable legislation in another jurisdiction, winds up its affairs, ceases to carry on business, or has a receiver/manager appointed for it or for a substantial part of its property, is not entitled to do any of the acts described in section 3 as of the day immediately preceding the day of the relevant occurrence.

*Confidentiality*

14. (1) Subject to subsections (2) and (3), CSI, SODRAC and CMRRA shall treat in confidence information received pursuant to this tariff, unless the online music service consents in writing to the information being treated otherwise.

(2) Information referred to in subsection (1) may be shared

(*a*) amongst CSI, SODRAC and CMRRA;

(*b*) with the Copyright Board;

(*c*) in connection with proceedings before the Board, once the online music service had a reasonable opportunity to request a confidentiality order;

(*d*) with any person who knows or is presumed to know the information;

(*e*) to the extent required to effect the distribution of royalties, with royalty claimants; and

(*f*) if ordered by law or by a court of law.

(3) Subsection (1) does not apply to information that is publicly available, or to information obtained from someone other than an online music service and who is not under an apparent duty of confidentiality to the service.

*Interest on Late Payments*

15. (1) Subject to subsection (3), any amount not received by the due date shall bear interest from that date until the date the amount is received.

(2) Any overpayment resulting from an error or omission on the part of CSI shall bear interest from the date of the overpayment until the overpayment is refunded.

(3) Any amount owing as a result of an error or omission on the part of CSI shall not bear interest until 30 days after CSI has corrected the error or omission.

(4) Interest shall be calculated daily at a rate equal to one per cent above the Bank Rate effective on the last day of the previous month (as published by the Bank of Canada). Interest shall not compound.

*Addresses for Notices, etc.*

16. (1) Anything that an online music service sends to CSI shall be sent to 759 Carré Victoria, Suite 420, Montréal, QC H2Y 2J7, email: csi@cmrrasodrac.ca, fax: 514-845-3401, or to any other address of which the service has been notified in writing.

(2) Anything that CSI sends to an online music service shall be sent to the last address of which CSI has been notified in writing.

*Delivery of Notices and Payments*

17. (1) Subject to subsection (2), a notice may be delivered by hand, by postage paid mail, by fax, by email or by file transfer protocol (FTP).

(2) Information provided pursuant to sections 6 to 9 and to subsection 11(2) shall be delivered electronically, in plain text format or in any other format agreed upon by CSI and the online music service.

(3) A notice or payment mailed in Canada shall be presumed to have been received three business days after the day it was mailed.

(4) A notice sent by fax, by email or by file transfer protocol (FTP) shall be presumed to have been received the day it is transmitted.

*Transitional Provisions*

18. (1) An online music service shall provide to CSI the information set out in sections 6 and 8 pertaining to January 2005 to March 2007 no later than on May 31, 2007.

(2) CSI shall provide the information set out in sections 7 and 9 pertaining to January 2005 to March 2007 no later than 60 days after receiving the information mentioned in subsection (1).

(3) Royalties payable for every quarter from January 2005 to March 2007 shall be due no later than 30 days after CSI sends the information mentioned in subsection (2).

# LAW 13.5

## CANADIAN COPYRIGHT ROYALTY BOARD DECISION (2007)

Copyright Board Canada

Commission du droit d'auteur Canada

CANADA

**Collective Administration in Relation to Rights Under Sections 3, 15, 18 and 21**

***Copyright Act*, subsection 70.15(1)**

File: Reproduction of Musical Works

STATEMENT OF ROYALTIES TO BE COLLECTED BY CMRRA/SODRAC INC. FOR THE REPRODUCTION OF MUSICAL WORKS, IN CANADA, BY ONLINE MUSIC SERVICES IN 2005, 2006 AND 2007

**DECISION OF THE BOARD**

*Reasons delivered by:*

Mr. Justice William J. Vancise
Mr. Stephen J. Callary
Mrs. Francine Bertrand-Venne

*Date of Decision*

March 16, 2007

**Gestion collective relative aux droits visés aux articles 3, 15, 18 et 21**

***Loi sur le droit d'auteur*, paragraphe 70.15(1)**

Dossier : Reproduction d'œuvres musicales

TARIF DES REDEVANCES À PERCEVOIR PAR CMRRA/SODRAC INC. POUR LA REPRODUCTION D'ŒUVRES MUSICALES, AU CANADA, PAR LES SERVICES DE MUSIQUE EN LIGNE EN 2005, 2006 ET 2007

**DÉCISION DE LA COMMISSION**

*Motifs exprimés par :*

M. le juge William J. Vancise
M. Stephen J. Callary
M[e] Francine Bertrand-Venne

*Date de la décision*

Le 16 mars 2007

Ottawa, March 16, 2007

**File: Reproduction of Musical Works**

**Reproduction of Musical Works by Online Music Services (2005-2007)**

**Reasons for the decision**

**I. INTRODUCTION**

[1] Online services are changing the way we listen to and use music. More than ever, music listening is moving from the home or car to the street, to the metro, to the jogging track or to the office. Everywhere one looks, young people, old people and people in-between are going about their business hooked up by ear buds to iPods or MP3 players.

[2] Online services are also changing the way people buy music. CDs still hold the lion's share of the market, but paid downloads are growing at an exponential rate. In 2005, permanent downloads represented $28.6 million or 3.6 per cent of Canadian retail music sales; this more than doubled in 2006. Apple sold more than 20 million iPods over the 2006 holiday season. One market research firm predicts that worldwide revenues from mobile full-track downloads will increase by more than 600 per cent between 2006 and 2011.[1]

[3] On March 31, 2004, CMRRA/SODRAC Inc. (CSI) filed, pursuant to subsection 70.13 of the *Copyright Act* (the "*Act*"), a statement of the royalties it proposes to collect for the reproduction, in Canada, by online music services in 2005, 2006 and 2007, of musical works in the combined repertoires of the Canadian Musical Reproduction Rights Agency (CMRRA) on the one hand, and of the *Société du droit de reproduction des auteurs, compositeurs et éditeurs au Canada* and SODRAC 2003 Inc. (SODRAC) on the other. The statement was

Ottawa, le 16 mars 2007

**Dossier : Reproduction d'œuvres musicales**

**Reproduction d'œuvres musicales par les services de musique en ligne (2005-2007)**

**Motifs de la décision**

**I. INTRODUCTION**

[1] Les services en ligne modifient notre façon d'écouter et d'utiliser la musique. L'écoute se fait de moins en moins chez soi ou en voiture et de plus en plus sur la rue, dans le métro, en joggant ou au bureau. Partout, jeunes, vieux ou entre deux, vaquent à leurs occupations, écouteurs aux oreilles, branchés à un iPod ou à un lecteur MP3.

[2] Les services en ligne influencent tout autant la façon d'acheter la musique. Les CD dominent toujours le marché mais le nombre de téléchargements payants croît à une vitesse exponentielle. En 2005, les Canadiens ont acheté pour 28,6 millions de dollars de téléchargements permanents; c'est 3,6 pour cent des ventes au détail de musique. En 2006, ce montant a plus que doublé. Apple a vendu plus de 20 millions d'iPod durant les fêtes de fin d'année 2006. D'après une entreprise spécialisée en études de marché, les revenus mondiaux provenant des téléchargements sans fil de musique pleine piste augmenteront de plus de 600 pour cent entre 2006 et 2011.[1]

[3] Le 31 mars 2004, CMRRA/SODRAC inc. (CSI) déposait, conformément à l'article 70.13 de la *Loi sur le droit d'auteur* (la « *Loi* »), un tarif des redevances qu'elle propose de percevoir pour la reproduction, au Canada, par les services de musique en ligne en 2005, 2006 et 2007, d'œuvres musicales faisant partie des répertoires combinés de l'Agence canadienne des droits de reproduction musicaux (CMRRA) d'une part, et de la Société du droit de reproduction des auteurs, compositeurs et éditeurs au Canada et SODRAC 2003 inc. (SODRAC) d'autre part. Le

published in the *Canada Gazette* on May 1, 2004. Potential users and their representatives were notified of their right to file an objection no later than June 30, 2004.

[4] Apple Canada Inc. (Apple), Napster LLC (Napster), Bell Canada (Bell), the Canadian Association of Broadcasters (CAB), the Canadian Broadcasting Corporation (CBC), the Canadian Cable Telecommunications Association (CCTA), the Canadian Recording Industry Association (CRIA), CHUM Ltd., EMI Music Canada (EMI), Archambault Group Inc., Moontaxi Media Inc., MusicNet Inc., RealNetworks Inc., Sirius Canada, Sony BMG Music Canada (Sony), TELUS, Universal Music Canada (Universal), Warner Music Canada (Warner) and Yahoo! Canada filed timely objections. *L'Association québécoise de l'industrie du disque, du spectacle et de la vidéo* (ADISQ) and Rogers Communications Inc./Rogers Wireless Partnership (Rogers) were granted leave to intervene. Before the hearings started, ADISQ, Archambault Group Inc., CCTA, CHUM Ltd., Moontaxi Media Inc., MusicNet Inc., RealNetworks Inc., Sirius Canada and Yahoo! Canada withdrew from the proceedings, while CBC and TELUS withdrew their objections but applied for leave to intervene; these applications were denied.

[5] The hearings started on September 6, 2006 and extended over ten days. Those who participated in the hearings were CSI on the one hand, and Apple, Bell, Rogers, CRIA and its Class A members (EMI, Sony, Universal and Warner), as well as CAB (collectively "the Objectors") on the other. The record of the proceedings was closed on September 29, 2006, when CSI and the Objectors filed their written arguments.

## II. BACKGROUND

### *A. The Target of the Tariff*

[6] The development of the technology used to store sounds in a digital format began in the late

tarif a été publié dans la *Gazette du Canada* le 1er mai 2004. Les utilisateurs potentiels et leurs représentants ont été informés de leur droit de s'opposer au projet au plus tard le 30 juin 2004.

[4] Apple Canada Inc. (Apple), Napster LLC (Napster), Bell Canada (Bell), l'Association canadienne des radiodiffuseurs (ACR), la Société Radio-Canada (SRC), l'Association canadienne de télécommunications par câble (ACTC), l'Association de l'industrie canadienne de l'enregistrement (CRIA), CHUM Ltée., EMI Music Canada (EMI), Groupe Archambault inc., Moontaxi Media Inc., MusicNet Inc., RealNetworks Inc., Sirius Canada, Sony BMG Music Canada (Sony), TELUS, Universal Music Canada (Universal), Warner Music Canada (Warner) et Yahoo! Canada ont déposé en temps opportun des avis d'opposition. L'Association québécoise de l'industrie du disque, du spectacle et de la vidéo (ADISQ) et les sociétés Rogers Communications Inc. et Rogers Wireless Partnership (Rogers) ont obtenu l'autorisation d'intervenir. Avant le début des audiences, l'ADISQ, Groupe Archambault inc., l'ACTC, CHUM Ltée, Moontaxi Media Inc., MusicNet Inc., RealNetworks Inc., Sirius Canada et Yahoo! Canada se sont désistés. La SRC et TELUS ont retiré leurs oppositions et demandé l'autorisation d'intervenir; ces demandes ont été rejetées.

[5] Les audiences ont débuté le 6 septembre 2006 et ont duré dix jours. Ont participé aux audiences CSI d'une part, et de l'autre, Apple, Bell, Rogers, la CRIA et ses membres de la classe A (EMI, Sony, Universal et Warner), de même que l'ACR (collectivement « les opposantes »). Le dossier a été complété le 29 septembre 2006, lorsque CSI et les opposantes ont déposé leur argumentation écrite.

## II. CONTEXTE

### *A. L'objet du tarif*

[6] Le développement de la technologie de stockage des sons sous forme numérique a débuté

1970s. The first digital musical product, the prerecorded CD, was launched in 1983. Over the next decade or so, it radically changed the music business. We are now in the midst of experiencing the next radical change: the authorized download over the Internet of digital files containing sound recordings of musical works. These reasons deal with three types of online music offerings: permanent downloads, limited downloads and on-demand streaming.

à la fin des années 70. Le premier produit musical numérique, le CD préenregistré, a été lancé en 1983. Il a radicalement modifié le marché de la musique au cours de la décennie qui a suivi. Nous assistons maintenant au prochain changement radical : le téléchargement autorisé sur Internet de fichiers numériques d'enregistrements sonores d'œuvres musicales. Les présents motifs visent trois types de produits musicaux offerts en ligne : les téléchargements permanents, les téléchargements limités et les transmissions sur demande.

[7] A permanent music download is a file that contains a sound recording of a musical work. That file is generally sent to and stored on the device (computer, cell phone) used to purchase it. The purchaser is then authorized to copy the recording onto MP3 players or other devices, such as a computer or digital audio recorder, or onto a blank CD. The number and kind of copies that can be made is determined by the terms of purchase and controlled through the digital rights management (DRM) software attached to the file.

[7] Un téléchargement permanent de musique est un fichier renfermant l'enregistrement sonore d'une œuvre musicale. En général, ce fichier est reçu et stocké sur l'appareil (ordinateur, téléphone cellulaire) utilisé pour l'acheter. L'acheteur peut ensuite copier l'enregistrement sur un lecteur MP3 ou un autre appareil, comme un ordinateur ou un enregistreur audionumérique, ou sur un CD vierge. Le nombre et le genre de copies autorisées sont déterminés par les modalités d'achat et contrôlés par le logiciel de gestion des droits numériques (GDN) joint au fichier.

[8] Limited downloads are generally offered with on-demand streams, as part of a subscription service. From a technical point of view, limited and permanent downloads are identical. The difference lies in what the DRM software allows the user to do. The subscriber may copy the recording onto other computers, sometimes even onto a portable music player. The DRM software allows the use of the original file and copies as long as the subscription is maintained; if it expires, the user will retain the file and copies but the DRM will prevent the user from listening to the recording or from making further copies of it. The DRM also prevents the user from putting the recording onto a blank CD at any time, since that would thwart the limited nature of the download.

[8] On offre généralement les téléchargements limités avec les transmissions sur demande dans le cadre d'un même abonnement. Sur le plan technique, les téléchargements limités et permanents sont identiques. La différence se situe au niveau de ce que le logiciel de GDN permet de faire. L'abonné peut copier l'enregistrement sur d'autres ordinateurs, parfois même sur un lecteur portatif de musique. Le logiciel de GDN permet d'utiliser le fichier original et les copies aussi longtemps que dure l'abonnement; si ce dernier prend fin, l'utilisateur conserve le fichier et les copies, mais le logiciel empêche qu'on écoute l'enregistrement ou qu'on en fasse d'autres copies. Le logiciel empêche aussi l'utilisateur de transférer en tout temps l'enregistrement sur un CD vierge, ce qui irait à l'encontre du caractère limité du téléchargement.

[9] On-demand streams are not downloads. The service's server never sends the complete file

[9] Les transmissions sur demande ne sont pas des téléchargements. Le serveur du service

containing the sound recording. It only transmits or streams enough data to allow the user to listen to the recording seamlessly at the time of transmission; that data is erased from the device used to receive it as the recording is played. The DRM software prevents the user from copying the recording onto a recording medium or device.

n'envoie jamais le fichier complet renfermant l'enregistrement sonore. Il ne transmet que suffisamment de données pour permettre à l'utilisateur d'écouter l'enregistrement sans interruption à ce moment-là; les données sont effacées de l'appareil qui les reçoit au fur et à mesure de l'écoute. Le logiciel de GDN empêche l'utilisateur de copier l'enregistrement sur un support ou un appareil.

***B. The Canadian and American Online Music Markets***

[10] Online music services developed in the United States much earlier than in Canada and in most other countries. MusicNet was founded in 1999 and launched two years later, with investment from EMI, BMG, Real Networks and AOL Time Warner. Pressplay was launched as a joint venture of Sony and Vivendi Universal. It was subsequently purchased by Roxio Inc. and is the vehicle that launched Napster as a legitimate online supplier of music.

[11] The American market did not expand rapidly until Apple launched its *iTunes Music Store* in 2003 (iTunes). Until then, online services focused on offering subscription packages that provided on-demand streams and limited downloads. iTunes changed the landscape in at least three ways. It offered permanent downloads, as single tracks for 99¢ or as albums for $9.99. The number of titles it made available was much larger and it made possible the use of downloads in many more ways.

[12] In Canada, PureTracks launched its online music service in October 2003, offering permanent downloads of sound recordings from the major record companies (or "labels") as well as a number of independent Canadian labels. It is currently the second largest player in the Canadian market. In January 2004, Archambault Group Inc. launched *Archambaultzik*; this Quebec-based online service offers a wide range of French language and Quebec sound

***B. Les marchés canadien et américain de la musique en ligne***

[10] Les services de musique en ligne se sont développés beaucoup plus tôt aux États-Unis qu'au Canada ou dans la plupart des autres pays. MusicNet a été fondé en 1999 et lancé deux ans plus tard; EMI, BMG, Real Networks et AOL Time Warner y ont investi. Pressplay, coentreprise de Sony et de Vivendi Universal, a été achetée ultérieurement par Roxio Inc. et est le véhicule qui a lancé Napster en tant que fournisseur légitime de musique en ligne.

[11] C'est lorsque Apple a lancé son *iTunes Music Store* en 2003 (iTunes) que le marché américain s'est vraiment développé. Jusque-là, les services en ligne proposaient surtout des abonnements offrant des transmissions sur demande et des téléchargements limités. iTunes a changé la donne d'au moins trois façons. Il a offert des téléchargements permanents de pistes individuelles pour 99 ¢ ou d'albums pour 9,99 $. Il a offert un bien plus large éventail de titres et a rendu possible une utilisation beaucoup plus variée des téléchargements.

[12] Au Canada, PureTracks a lancé son service de musique en ligne en octobre 2003, en offrant des téléchargements permanents d'enregistrements sonores des grandes maisons de disques et de plusieurs maisons canadiennes indépendantes. C'est actuellement le deuxième acteur en importance sur le marché canadien. En janvier 2004, Groupe Archambault inc. a lancé *Archambaultzik*, service en ligne québécois qui offre une vaste gamme d'enregistrements sonores

recordings. Napster began operating in Canada in May 2004. iTunes followed in December of that year and quickly came to dominate the Canadian market.

en français et du Québec. Napster est devenu actif au Canada en mai 2004. iTunes a suivi en décembre de la même année et a réussi en peu de temps à dominer le marché canadien.

[13] Subscription services, offering only limited downloads and on-demand streams, have not grown as rapidly as services that offer permanent downloads. The fact that originally, it was not possible to transfer music to portable players no doubt contributed to this lack of success. Those restrictions disappeared with the introduction of *Yahoo! Music Unlimited To Go* and *Napster To Go*. Time will tell how this market will grow.

[13] Les services d'abonnement, en n'offrant que des téléchargements limités et des transmissions sur demande, n'ont pas connu une expansion aussi rapide que les services offrant des téléchargements permanents. Le fait qu'au départ, il était impossible de transférer de la musique à des lecteurs portatifs a sans nul doute contribué à ce moindre succès. Cette restriction a disparu avec l'entrée en scène de *Yahoo! Music Unlimited To Go* et de *Napster To Go*. Le temps dira si ce marché se développera.

[14] Most online services, including those offered through the Internet service providers or wireless carriers of Bell, TELUS and Rogers, rely on technology operated by others such as PureTracks or MusicNet for a number of back-room operations that must be performed in order to offer music to consumers. These include software management, maintenance of digital track libraries, digital rights management and reporting issues. These "white label" services may also perform other functions, such as clearing the right to use the record labels' master recordings or to communicate and reproduce the musical works embedded in the recording. Bell, TELUS and AOL use PureTracks while Rogers-Yahoo! relies on MusicNet.

[14] La plupart des services en ligne, y compris ceux qui sont offerts par l'entremise des fournisseurs de service Internet ou des entreprises de télécommunications sans fil de Bell, de TELUS et de Rogers, comptent sur une technologie exploitée par d'autres, comme PureTracks ou MusicNet, pour un certain nombre d'opérations d'appoint nécessaires pour offrir de la musique aux consommateurs. Ces opérations incluent la gestion de logiciels, la maintenance de bibliothèques de pistes numériques, la gestion des droits numériques et la production de rapports. Ces services « sans nom » peuvent remplir d'autres fonctions, comme l'obtention de licences pour utiliser les enregistrements sonores des maisons de disques ou pour communiquer et reproduire les œuvres musicales qu'ils contiennent. Bell, TELUS et AOL ont recours à PureTracks, tandis que Rogers-Yahoo! utilise MusicNet.

## III. THE PARTIES

[15] CMRRA sometimes refers to itself as a music reproduction licencing agency but it is a collective society as defined in the *Act*. CMRRA only acts for publishers. Those publishers who wish to be represented by it sign an affiliation agreement appointing CMRRA as their licencing agent for some or all of various types of

## III. LES PARTIES

[15] La CMRRA se décrit parfois comme une agence autorisant la reproduction d'œuvres musicales; aux termes de la *Loi*, c'est une société de gestion. Elle ne représente que des éditeurs. Ceux qui lui demandent d'agir pour leur compte signent un contrat d'affiliation la désignant à titre d'agent pour autoriser une partie ou la totalité de

reproduction activities, including those targeted in the tariff under examination. Other publishers have signed "stand-alone" agreements dealing specifically with online licensing. In these proceedings, CMRRA represents all or part of 38,240 publishing catalogues. In approximately 80 per cent of instances, CMRRA acts as exclusive agent.[2]

[16] SODRAC is a collective society whose objects include the collective administration of the right to reproduce musical works. SODRAC 2003 Inc. has been progressively taking over the rights, assets and activities of SODRAC since 2003. Authors and publishers represented by SODRAC assign to it the right to authorize or prohibit all forms of reproduction of their musical works throughout the world. SODRAC currently acts for more than 4,100 authors and 1,600 publishers. It also represents in Canada the interests of a vast number of foreign authors and publishers, through its reciprocal agreements with a number of foreign collective societies.

[17] CSI is a corporation created in 2002 by CMRRA and SODRAC for the purpose of collecting royalties on their behalf for the reproduction of musical works by commercial radio stations. CSI now has an exclusive mandate from CMRRA and SODRAC to licence the reproduction of musical works in their respective repertoires for uses targeted in the tariff under examination.

[18] CSI has entered into licencing agreements with all the online services currently operating in Canada as well as a number of those who are contemplating to do so. CSI requires a tariff because the agreements only provide for interim payments. The final royalties are to be set by the Board, in the tariff.

[19] Apple, Bell, CAB, CRIA, EMI, Rogers, Sony, Universal and Warner are, or represent,

divers types d'activités de reproduction, y compris celles qui sont visées dans le tarif à l'étude. D'autres éditeurs ont signé des ententes autonomes portant expressément sur la concession de licences pour les droits en ligne. Dans la présente affaire, la CMRRA représente en tout ou en partie 38 240 catalogues d'édition. Elle agit à titre exclusif dans environ 80 pour cent des cas.[2]

[16] La SODRAC est une société de gestion qui s'occupe notamment de gérer collectivement le droit de reproduire des œuvres musicales. SODRAC 2003 inc. prend progressivement à sa charge les droits, actifs et activités de la SODRAC depuis 2003. Les auteurs et éditeurs que la SODRAC représente lui cèdent le droit d'autoriser ou d'interdire partout dans le monde toute forme de reproduction de leurs œuvres musicales. La SODRAC agit actuellement pour le compte de plus de 4100 auteurs et 1600 éditeurs. Elle représente également au Canada les intérêts d'un grand nombre d'auteurs et d'éditeurs étrangers, en vertu d'ententes de réciprocité avec plusieurs sociétés de gestion étrangères.

[17] CSI est une société créée en 2002 par la CMRRA et la SODRAC, afin de percevoir en leur nom des redevances pour la reproduction d'œuvres musicales par les stations de radio commerciales. La CMRRA et la SODRAC lui ont confié le mandat exclusif d'autoriser la reproduction d'œuvres musicales de leurs répertoires aux fins d'utilisations visées par le présent tarif.

[18] CSI a conclu des ententes de licence avec tous les services en ligne faisant actuellement affaire au Canada et avec certains autres qui envisagent de le faire. Elle a besoin d'un tarif parce que les ententes ne prévoient que des versements provisoires. La Commission doit fixer les redevances finales, par voie de tarif.

[19] Apple, Bell, l'ACR, la CRIA, EMI, Rogers, Sony, Universal et Warner sont, ou représentent,

corporations that offer, purport to offer or intend to offer some form of online music service. As such, all require a licence to reproduce musical works onto their servers and to authorize their customers to make their own reproductions onto personal computers, portable music players and recordable CDs.[3]

des sociétés qui offrent, disent offrir ou entendent offrir une forme quelconque de service de musique en ligne. Toutes ont donc besoin d'une licence pour reproduire des œuvres musicales sur leurs serveurs et pour autoriser leurs clients à faire eux-mêmes des reproductions sur des ordinateurs personnels, des lecteurs portatifs de musique et des CD enregistrables.[3]

## IV. POSITIONS AND EVIDENCE

### A. *CSI*

[20] CSI's original proposal asked for the greater of: (a) 7.5 per cent of gross revenue or 75¢ per month per subscriber for services that only offer on-demand streams; (b) 10 per cent of gross revenue or one dollar per month per subscriber for services that offer limited downloads, with or without on-demand streams; and (c) 15 per cent of gross revenue or 10¢ per permanent download of a single musical work.

[21] In its statement of case, CSI modified its proposal in two respects. For category (a), CSI asked for 5.8 per cent of gross revenue or 45¢ per month per subscriber. For category (b), it asked for 8 per cent of gross revenue or 60¢ per month per subscriber if the service does not allow reproductions onto portable devices and $1.40 if it does. Originally, category (b) targeted only limited downloads that could not be reproduced further on other readable media. Some subscription services now allow subscribers to make "portable limited downloads", that is to copy music tracks onto portable devices. CSI proposed to amend the definition of limited downloads to reflect this. In final argument, CSI again modified its proposals to 6.7 per cent and 45¢ for category (a), and to 9.8 per cent, 72¢ and $1.75 for category (b), to reflect a change in the way to account for the use of works that are not in CSI's repertoire.

## IV. POSITIONS ET PREUVE

### A. *CSI*

[20] Au départ, CSI demandait le plus élevé de : a) 7,5 pour cent des revenus bruts ou 75 ¢ par mois par abonné pour un service n'offrant que des transmissions sur demande; b) 10 pour cent des revenus bruts ou un dollar par mois par abonné pour un service offrant des téléchargements limités, avec ou sans transmissions sur demande; c) 15 pour cent des revenus bruts ou 10 ¢ par téléchargement permanent d'une seule œuvre musicale.

[21] Dans son énoncé de cause, CSI a modifié deux aspects de sa proposition. Pour la catégorie a), elle a demandé 5,8 pour cent des revenus bruts ou 45 ¢ par mois par abonné. Pour la catégorie b), elle a demandé 8 pour cent des revenus bruts ou 60 ¢ par mois par abonné si le service n'autorise pas de reproductions sur des appareils portatifs et 1,40 $ s'il les autorise. Au départ, la catégorie b) ne visait que les téléchargements limités ne pouvant être reproduits par la suite sur d'autres supports lisibles. Certains services d'abonnement permettent maintenant aux abonnés d'effectuer des « téléchargements limités portables », c'est-à-dire de copier une piste musicale sur un appareil portatif. CSI a proposé de modifier la définition de téléchargement limité pour refléter cette nouvelle réalité. Dans son argumentation finale, CSI a encore une fois modifié ses propositions à 6,7 pour cent et 45 ¢ pour la catégorie a), et 9,8 pour cent, 72 ¢ et 1,75 $ pour la catégorie b), pour refléter un changement dans la façon de rendre compte de l'utilisation d'œuvres qui ne font pas partie de son répertoire.

[22] CSI called several persons involved with CMRRA and SODRAC as well as a number of experts to support its proposed tariff.

[22] CSI a fait appel à plusieurs personnes associées à la CMRRA et à la SODRAC ainsi qu'à certains experts pour appuyer le tarif qu'elle a proposé.

[23] Mrs. Claudette Fortier, President of CSI, described its corporate structure and that of its shareholders. She explained the differences in the way CMRRA and SODRAC secure their repertoire generally, and for the purposes of the tariff under examination specifically. She emphasized that the licences they grant to record labels do not allow them to use their repertoire in connection with the operation of an online music service. She also explained the practical reasons behind the collectives' practice to mostly deal with the person who actually uses a musical work, and not with an intermediary.

[23] M[me] Claudette Fortier, présidente de CSI, a décrit la structure organisationnelle de la société et celle de ses actionnaires. Elle a expliqué les différences entre les façons dont la CMRRA et la SODRAC acquièrent leur répertoire en général, et aux fins du tarif à l'étude en particulier. Elle a souligné que les droits que concèdent ces sociétés aux maisons de disques ne permettent pas à ces dernières d'utiliser leur répertoire dans le cadre de l'exploitation d'un service de musique en ligne. Elle a aussi expliqué les raisons pratiques qui sous-tendent l'habitude des sociétés de gestion de traiter principalement avec la personne qui utilise réellement une œuvre musicale, et non pas avec un intermédiaire.

[24] Mr. David Basskin, President of CMRRA and Vice-President of CSI, described Canadian online services and the ways in which they offer music to consumers. He dealt at some length with the terms of the Mechanical Licencing Agreement (MLA) entered into between CMRRA and CRIA, which licences record labels to reproduce musical works onto prerecorded CDs; in particular, he discussed the various discounts the agreement allows in respect of promotional products, budget goods and the like.

[24] M. David Basskin, président de la CMRRA et vice-président de CSI, a décrit les services en ligne canadiens et leurs façons d'offrir de la musique aux consommateurs. Il a traité longuement des modalités de l'entente de licence de reproduction mécanique (MLA) conclue entre la CMRRA et la CRIA, qui autorise les maisons de disques à reproduire des œuvres musicales sur des CD préenregistrés. Il a parlé, en particulier, des divers escomptes que l'entente accorde pour les produits promotionnels, articles bon marché et autres produits du genre.

[25] Mr. Basskin and Mrs. Fortier testified on the operation of the so-called controlled composition clause (CCC) in the music industry. The CCC originated in the United States in the 1970s, and is more prevalent there than in Canada. This clause is found in agreements between a record label and a performing artist. It allows the label to obtain a mechanical licence at a reduced rate when the artist owns or controls some or all of the copyright in the works the artist records. Typically, it reduces the rate per track by 25 per cent, freezes royalties at the rate in effect at the time of entering into a contract,

[25] M. Basskin et M[me] Fortier ont témoigné au sujet de l'application de ce qui est communément appelé la clause de composition contrôlée (CCC) dans l'industrie de la musique. La CCC a pris naissance aux États-Unis dans les années 70 et y est plus répandue qu'au Canada. On la trouve dans des ententes entre maisons de disques et interprètes. Elle permet à la maison d'obtenir une licence de reproduction mécanique à un taux réduit lorsque l'artiste possède ou contrôle tout ou partie des droits sur les œuvres qu'il enregistre. La clause réduit habituellement le taux par piste de 25 pour cent, gèle les

caps the number of tracks for which royalties must be paid and treats up to 15 per cent of CDs as "free goods" for which no royalties are payable.

redevances au taux en vigueur au moment de la conclusion du contrat, plafonne le nombre de pistes pour lesquelles il faut verser des redevances et traite jusqu'à 15 pour cent des CD comme des « biens gratuits » pour lesquels aucune redevance n'est exigible.

[26] The MLA limits the impact of the CCC in Canada through a number of mechanisms. Its influence with respect to SODRAC's repertoire is much less significant. SODRAC has never included the CCC in its agreements with Quebec independent record producers and has refused since 1995 to renew its contract with CRIA precisely to avoid the application of such a clause.

[26] La MLA limite les répercussions de la CCC au Canada au moyen d'un certain nombre de mécanismes. L'impact de la CCC sur le répertoire de la SODRAC est beaucoup moins important. Cette dernière n'a jamais inclus cette disposition dans ses ententes avec des producteurs de disques indépendants du Québec et refuse depuis 1995 de renouveler son contrat avec la CRIA précisément pour éviter l'application d'une telle clause.

[27] A panel representing the Canadian music publishing industry consisted of Messrs. Mark Jowett of Nettwerk One, Daniel Lafrance of *Éditorial Avenue* and Jodie Ferneyhough of Universal Music Publishing Canada. They provided an overview of the industry and of the role it plays in talent development.

[27] Le panel représentant l'industrie de l'édition de musique canadienne se composait de MM. Mark Jowett de Nettwerk One, Daniel Lafrance d'Éditorial Avenue et Jodie Ferneyhough de Universal Music Publishing Canada. Ils ont offert un survol de l'industrie et du rôle qu'elle joue dans le développement des artistes.

[28] Mr. Paul Audley, President, Paul Audley and Associates Ltd., reviewed a study he prepared with others regarding the Canadian music publishing industry. The study documented, among other things, that sales of prerecorded albums declined by 25 per cent between 1998 and 2003 and that revenues decreased by 24 per cent over the same period.

[28] M. Paul Audley, président de Paul Audley and Associates Ltd., a passé en revue un rapport qu'il a préparé avec d'autres sur l'industrie de l'édition de musique canadienne. Ce rapport indique entre autres que les ventes d'albums préenregistrés ont diminué de 25 pour cent entre 1998 et 2003 et que les revenus en découlant ont baissé de 24 pour cent au cours de la même période.

[29] Mr. Audley also prepared with Professor Douglas Hyatt of the Rotman School of Management, Centre for Industrial Relations, at the University of Toronto and Division of Management, University of Toronto at Scarborough, a report that proposed a method to determine the royalties payable for the uses targeted in the tariff under examination. They testified that the market for mastertones[4] was in effect part of the same digital market as online

[29] De concert avec le professeur Douglas Hyatt de la *Rotman School of Management, Centre for Industrial Relations* de l'Université de Toronto et de la *Division of Management* de l'Université de Toronto à Scarborough, M. Audley a aussi préparé un rapport proposant une façon d'établir les redevances exigibles pour les utilisations visées dans le tarif à l'étude. Les auteurs ont conclu que, dans les faits, le marché des sonneries authentiques[4] fait partie du même

music and proposed to derive a rate for permanent downloads by comparing the prices paid for copyright protected inputs in both markets. Their fundamental assumption was that, given the similarities between mastertones and permanent downloads, the ratio between the royalties paid for the reproduction of musical works and of sound recordings should be the same for both. The New Digital Media Agreements (or NDMAs) between American record labels and American music publishers set the price to be paid to reproduce the musical work and the sound recording into a mastertone.[5] The witnesses applied the ratio between those prices to what online services pay to labels for the use of their sound recordings, to arrive at a rate to be paid for the reproduction of musical works. The resulting rate is higher than what CSI is seeking. Messrs. Audley and Hyatt then used the rate they developed for permanent downloads to derive the royalties to be paid for limited downloads and on-demand streams.

marché numérique que la musique en ligne et ont proposé d'établir le tarif pour les téléchargements permanents en comparant les prix payés pour les intrants protégés par le droit d'auteur dans les deux marchés. Suivant leur hypothèse de base, compte tenu des similarités entre les sonneries authentiques et les téléchargements permanents, le rapport entre les redevances versées pour la reproduction d'œuvres musicales et celles payées pour la reproduction d'enregistrements sonores devrait être le même pour les deux. Les *New Digital Media Agreements* (NDMA ou ententes sur les nouveaux médias numériques) entre les maisons de disques américaines et les éditeurs de musique américains fixent le prix à payer pour reproduire l'œuvre musicale et l'enregistrement sonore dans une sonnerie authentique.[5] Les témoins ont appliqué le rapport entre ces prix à ce que les services en ligne paient aux maisons de disques pour l'utilisation de leurs enregistrements sonores, afin d'en arriver à un taux à verser pour la reproduction d'œuvres musicales. Le taux obtenu est plus élevé que ce que CSI demande. MM. Audley et Hyatt ont ensuite utilisé le taux qu'ils ont mis au point pour les téléchargements permanents afin de calculer les redevances à verser pour les téléchargements limités et les transmissions sur demande.

[30] In their reply evidence, Messrs. Audley and Hyatt looked at three other ways of deriving a tariff for permanent downloads. The first was based on information provided by CRIA on the breakdown of the cost of a CD purchased in Canada, the second on information on the breakdown of revenues from CD sales in Quebec and the third on the income record labels receive from pressing and distribution agreements. All started from the existing mechanical royalty rate for the reproduction of musical works onto a physical medium. All were based on comparing the percentage of retail price that record labels receive in a variety of transactions involving prerecorded CDs to the equivalent percentage that labels receive in the online market. The fundamental assumption in those instances was that if the remuneration of labels increases in the

[30] Dans leur contre-preuve, MM. Audley et Hyatt ont examiné trois autres façons d'en arriver à un tarif pour les téléchargements permanents. La première reposait sur des renseignements fournis par la CRIA au sujet de la ventilation du coût d'un CD acheté au Canada, la deuxième, sur des données relatives à la ventilation des revenus découlant des ventes de CD au Québec et la troisième, sur les revenus que les maisons de disques touchent dans le cadre des ententes de pressage et de distribution. Toutes avaient pour point de départ le taux actuel de redevance pour la reproduction mécanique d'œuvres musicales sur un support matériel. Toutes reposaient également sur une comparaison du pourcentage du prix de détail que les maisons de disques touchent dans le cadre de diverses opérations concernant des CD

online market, the remuneration of authors should increase at the same rate. These alternative approaches resulted in rates between 13 and 15 per cent.

[31] Mr. Marcel Boyer is Bell Canada Professor of industrial economics, Department of Economics, *Université de Montréal* and Fellow of the Centre for Interuniversity Research and Analysis on Organizations, of the *Centre interuniversitaire de recherche en économie quantitative* and of the C.D. Howe Institute. He reviewed the valuation evidence offered by CSI and the Objectors. He discussed issues such as the notion of option value, patent pools and sharing of benefits. He testified that the relative value of the reproduction rights of labels and authors should be similar between mastertones and permanent downloads and that, since the music market seems to be expanding, this should result in equal pressure to increase the cost of all of these input prices in the permanent download market.

[32] Mr. Clark Miller, General Counsel Worldwide, EMI Publishing and Mr. Frank P. Scibilia, Partner at Pryor Cashman Sherman & Flynn LLP testified about the content and impact of various agreements that license the use of EMI's repertoire of musical works, including the NDMAs that allow the use of that repertoire in mastertones. They described section 115 of the U.S. Copyright Act, which provides for a compulsory licence for the mechanical reproduction of music onto sound recordings and explained in detail the operation of CCCs in the United States.

[33] Ms. Caroline Rioux, Vice-President Operations, CMRRA, testified on the extent of

préenregistrés au pourcentage équivalent que ces maisons touchent sur le marché en ligne. L'hypothèse de base dans ces cas est que si les revenus des maisons augmentent sur le marché en ligne, ceux des auteurs devraient augmenter au même rythme. Ces différentes méthodes donnaient des taux variant entre 13 et 15 pour cent.

[31] M. Marcel Boyer est titulaire de la Chaire Bell Canada en économie industrielle au Département de sciences économiques de l'Université de Montréal et *fellow* du Centre interuniversitaire de recherche en analyse des organisations, du Centre interuniversitaire de recherche en économie quantitative et de l'Institut C.D. Howe. Il a examiné la preuve sur l'évaluation présentée par CSI et les opposantes. Il a traité de questions comme la notion de valeur d'option, les communautés de brevets et le partage des bénéfices. Il a déclaré que la valeur relative des droits de reproduction des maisons de disques et des auteurs devrait être la même pour les sonneries authentiques et les téléchargements permanents et que cela, étant donné que le marché de la musique semble en pleine expansion, devrait entraîner des pressions égales en faveur d'une augmentation de tous les prix de ces intrants sur le marché des téléchargements permanents.

[32] M. Clark Miller, conseiller juridique international chez EMI Publishing, et M. Frank P. Scibilia, associé chez Pryor Cashman Sherman & Flynn LLP, ont parlé du contenu et des répercussions de diverses ententes qui autorisent l'utilisation du répertoire d'œuvres musicales d'EMI, y compris les NDMA qui permettent l'emploi de ce répertoire pour les sonneries authentiques. Ils ont décrit l'article 115 de la loi américaine sur le droit d'auteur, qui prévoit une licence obligatoire pour la reproduction mécanique de musique dans un enregistrement sonore et expliqué en détail l'application des CCC aux États-Unis.

[33] M[me] Caroline Rioux, vice-présidente aux opérations de la CMRRA, a témoigné à propos

the CSI repertoire, the extent of its use and the challenges created by the delivery of musical works in the digital environment generally, and through online services particularly. The CMRRA and SODRAC databases, which were consolidated in 2005, list approximately 1.1 million musical works. The consolidated database is updated daily, to add new compositions and to reflect the fact that publishers' catalogues are regularly bought and sold. In 2005, CSI began issuing licences to eight online services. Ms. Rioux described the licensing process, noting that CSI has invested over a million dollars to design and implement a computerized system to expeditiously assess the applications of services and to grant them licences. She stated that in the first 18 months of operations, 1.5 million licences were issued, which is more than the total number of licences issued for prerecorded media (vinyl, cassettes and CDs) since the creation of CMRRA some 30 years ago. At the time of the hearings, online services had filed some 5.7 million applications.

de l'étendue du répertoire de CSI, de l'ampleur de son utilisation et des défis que pose la distribution d'œuvres musicales dans l'environnement numérique en général et par l'intermédiaire des services en ligne en particulier. Les bases de données de la CMRRA et de la SODRAC, qui ont été groupées en 2005, comptent environ 1,1 million d'œuvres musicales. Une mise à jour quotidienne est effectuée pour y intégrer de nouvelles compositions et pour rendre compte du fait qu'on transige régulièrement les catalogues d'éditeurs. CSI a entrepris en 2005 de délivrer des licences à huit services en ligne. M[me] Rioux a décrit le mécanisme de délivrance de licences et souligné que CSI a investi jusqu'ici plus d'un million de dollars pour la conception et la mise en œuvre d'un système informatisé permettant d'évaluer rapidement les demandes des services et de leur délivrer des licences. Elle a déclaré qu'au cours des 18 premiers mois d'activité, CSI a délivré 1,5 million de licences, ce qui est plus que le nombre total de licences délivrées pour des supports préenregistrés (vinyles, cassettes et CD) depuis la création de la CMRRA il y a une trentaine d'années. Au moment des audiences, les services en ligne avaient déposé quelque 5,7 millions de demandes.

[34] A panel consisting of Ms. Rioux, Mr. Joël Martin, Project Manager, SODRAC and Mr. Benoît Gauthier, President, *Réseau Circum*, explained the analysis that was performed to determine the relative share of Canadian air play of the CSI repertoire. For reasons that will become clear, this analysis is now irrelevant and as a result, there is no need to set out the evidence in detail.

[34] Un panel composé de M[me] Rioux, de M. Joël Martin, chef de projet, SODRAC, et de M. Benoît Gauthier, président de Réseau Circum, a expliqué l'analyse effectuée pour déterminer le temps d'antenne que le répertoire de CSI occupe sur les ondes canadiennes. Pour des raisons qui deviendront évidentes, cette analyse n'est plus pertinente. Il n'est donc pas nécessaire d'exposer en détail la preuve s'y rattachant.

[35] CSI contends that the offering of music on line increases the value of its repertoire and that right holders are entitled to a share in the value of this new economic activity. The right to reproduce musical works and to authorize subscribers to make their own copies is essential to online services. Indeed, without it, they could not operate. The use made of the reproduction right is much more extensive here than in the

[35] CSI prétend qu'offrir de la musique en ligne accroît la valeur de son répertoire et que les titulaires ont droit à une part de la valeur de cette nouvelle activité économique. Les services en ligne ont absolument besoin du droit de reproduire des œuvres musicales et d'autoriser leurs abonnés à en faire eux-mêmes des copies. En effet, sans ce droit, les services ne pourraient fonctionner. L'utilisation qu'on fait du droit de

market for prerecorded CDs. For example, online services allow subscribers to make multiple copies. That ability to make additional copies gives services a competitive edge and provides added value to consumers. Rights holders should benefit from that added value.

reproduction est beaucoup plus étendue dans ce cas que sur le marché des CD préenregistrés. Les services en ligne autorisent, par exemple, leurs abonnés à faire plusieurs copies. Cette faculté de faire des copies additionnelles donne aux services un avantage concurrentiel et fournit aux consommateurs une valeur ajoutée dont les titulaires de droits devraient tirer profit.

[36] CSI proposes: that the tariff set minimum rates; that the rate for limited downloads be one-third lower than for permanent downloads; and that the rate for on-demand streams be somewhere between what is set for limited downloads and what pay audio services have agreed to. Finally, it proposes that the licences be issued only to online services and opposes the possibility of allowing record labels to obtain a licence from CSI and then sub-licence the use of CSI's repertoire by those services.

[36] CSI propose qu'on fixe des taux de redevances minimales, que le taux pour les téléchargements limités soit inférieur d'un tiers à celui pour les téléchargements permanents et que le taux pour les transmissions sur demande se situe entre les taux établis pour les téléchargements limités et ceux de l'entente avec les services sonores payants. Enfin, CSI propose de délivrer la licence uniquement aux services en ligne et s'oppose à ce qu'on permette aux maisons de disques d'obtenir une licence de CSI pour ensuite autoriser les services, au moyen d'une sous-licence, à utiliser son répertoire.

***B. Objectors***

[37] The Objectors filed a joint statement of case. They propose royalties of 5.3 per cent for permanent downloads, 3.5 per cent for limited downloads and 0.5 per cent for on-demand streaming. They ask that the rate base be what subscribers pay, not gross income. They propose minimum rates of 3.85¢ for permanent downloads; for services that allow limited downloads and on-demand streaming, they propose a minimum of 21¢ per month per subscriber if a service does not authorize reproductions onto portable devices and 33¢ if it does. They propose either that no minimum be applied to downloads of albums or that the minimum price be reduced so as to avoid excessive royalties in the case of albums containing a large number of tracks. Finally, they seek the right for record labels to be allowed to apply for the licence so as to then sub-licence the right to reproduce the musical work to online services.

***B. Les opposantes***

[37] Les opposantes ont déposé un énoncé de cause conjoint. Elles proposent des redevances de 5,3 pour cent pour les téléchargements permanents, de 3,5 pour cent pour les téléchargements limités et de 0,5 pour cent pour les transmissions sur demande. Elles demandent que la base tarifaire corresponde à ce que paient les consommateurs et non pas au revenu brut. Elles proposent un minimum de 3,85 ¢ pour les téléchargements permanents, de 21 ¢ par mois par abonné pour les services qui permettent les téléchargements limités et les transmissions sur demande si la reproduction sur un appareil portatif est interdite et de 33 ¢ si elle est permise. Elles proposent également de n'appliquer aucun minimum aux téléchargements d'albums ou de réduire ce minimum de façon à éviter des redevances excessives dans le cas des albums renfermant une grande quantité de pistes. Enfin, elles cherchent à ce que les maisons de disques puissent demander la licence pour ensuite délivrer aux services en ligne une sous-licence de reproduction des œuvres musicales.

[38] The Objectors called several witnesses in support of their proposed approach.

[38] Les opposantes ont fait appel à plusieurs témoins pour appuyer leur approche.

[39] Mr. Alistair Mitchell, CEO and co-founder of PureTracks, described the development of this, the first online music service in Canada. He testified that PureTracks used the traditional physical music market as its business model, and considers online music as simply an extension of that market. In his opinion, there is a lack of understanding about the resources required to operate an online service. It requires a very costly infrastructure, which must be updated continually. It also involves the (sometimes costly) need to deal with a large number of credit card micro-transactions.

[39] M. Alistair Mitchell, président-directeur général et co-fondateur de PureTracks, a décrit le développement de ce premier service de musique en ligne au Canada. Il a déclaré que PureTracks a utilisé le marché matériel traditionnel de la musique comme modèle d'entreprise et considère la musique en ligne simplement comme un prolongement de ce marché. À son avis, on connaît mal les ressources nécessaires à l'exploitation d'un service en ligne. Cela exige une infrastructure très coûteuse, qu'il faut continuellement moderniser, ainsi que l'obligation (parfois onéreuse) de traiter un grand nombre de micro-opérations par carte de crédit.

[40] Mr. Graham Henderson, President of CRIA, Mr. Mark Jones, Vice-President, Finance and Information Technology, Universal Music, and Ms. Christine Prudham, Vice-President, Legal and Regulatory Affairs, SONY BMG Music (Canada) Inc., testified on behalf of CRIA. They outlined the difficulties of growing the online music market in Canada, which they attribute to the negative effect of unauthorized downloads. They quoted figures according to which as few as 6 per cent of Canadians who download music obtain it from authorized services and that there are 14 unauthorized downloads for every authorized one.

[40] M. Graham Henderson, président de la CRIA, M. Mark Jones, vice-président aux finances et à la technologie de l'information chez Universal Music, et M[me] Christine Prudham, vice-présidente aux affaires juridiques et réglementaires chez SONY BMG Music (Canada) Inc., ont témoigné au nom de la CRIA. Ils ont fourni un aperçu des problèmes de croissance du marché de la musique en ligne au Canada, qu'ils attribuent à l'effet négatif des téléchargements non autorisés. Ils ont cité des chiffres selon lesquels à peine 6 pour cent des Canadiens qui téléchargent de la musique l'obtiennent de services autorisés et qu'il y a 14 téléchargements non autorisés pour chaque téléchargement autorisé.

[41] The panel outlined the significant costs that record labels have incurred to enter the digital market. These include not only the development of infrastructures and systems to manage the information, but also the digitization of the back catalogue, which requires re-mastering hundreds of thousands of sound recordings made before the advent of digital technology. It is also necessary in most instances to transform those recordings into the various formats adopted by those who retail mastertones and full-track downloads.

[41] Le panel a fourni un aperçu des coûts substantiels qu'encourent les maisons de disques pour entrer sur le marché numérique. Ces coûts incluent non seulement le développement d'infrastructures et de systèmes pour gérer l'information, mais également la numérisation du catalogue existant, qui exige le rematriçage de centaines de milliers d'enregistrements sonores réalisés avant l'avènement de la technologie numérique. Dans la plupart des cas, il faut aussi convertir ces enregistrements selon les divers formats adoptés par les détaillants de sonneries authentiques et de téléchargements pleine piste.

[42] The panel also testified about the money and resources that record labels expend on finding and developing artists and producing master recordings that can then be marketed as prerecorded CDs and music downloads. These costs are not expected to drop simply because recordings will now be offered online. The panel contrasted the role of publishers and labels, arguing that labels spend far more than publishers on finding and developing new talent.

[42] Le panel a aussi parlé des sommes d'argent et autres ressources que les maisons de disques consacrent à la découverte et à la mise en valeur d'artistes et à la production d'enregistrements originaux qu'on peut ensuite commercialiser sous forme de CD préenregistrés et de téléchargements. Ces coûts ne devraient pas chuter simplement parce qu'on offrira désormais des enregistrements en ligne. Le panel a comparé le rôle des éditeurs à celui des maisons de disques et soutenu que ces dernières dépensent beaucoup plus que les premiers pour découvrir et pour développer de nouveaux talents.

[43] The CRIA panel outlined what they believe to be the distinctions between mastertones and online music. Mastertones are fashion statements; downloads are not. Differences in buying patterns are significant: consumers tend to buy less than two mastertones per month, as opposed to more than twenty downloads of music per month.

[43] Le panel de la CRIA a fourni un aperçu de ce qu'ils croient être les distinctions entre les sonneries authentiques et la musique en ligne. Contrairement aux téléchargements, les sonneries authentiques sont des formes d'expression à la mode. Les différences sur le plan des habitudes d'achat sont importantes : les consommateurs ont tendance à acheter moins de deux sonneries authentiques par mois, comparativement à plus de vingt téléchargements de musique.

[44] Finally, the panel explained why it wished that record labels be allowed to purchase the licence from CSI and then deal with the online services. This would be both cost effective and administratively more efficient, and would take into account the fact that CSI does not represent all of the repertoire offered by the labels.

[44] Enfin, le panel a expliqué pourquoi il faudrait qu'on permette aux maisons de disques d'acheter la licence de CSI, puis de traiter avec les services en ligne. Cela serait à la fois rentable et plus efficace, sur le plan administratif, et tiendrait compte du fait que CSI ne représente pas l'ensemble du répertoire qu'offrent les maisons de disques.

[45] Mr. Steven Globerman is Kaiser Professor of International Business, Western Washington University, College of Business and Economics and Adjunct Professor at the Faculty of Business Administration, Simon Fraser University. He was asked to assess which, of the mastertone and prerecorded CD markets, constitutes a better proxy for permanent downloads. He was not asked to suggest an appropriate price or rate.

[45] M. Steven Globerman est professeur titulaire de la Chaire Kaiser de commerce international au *College of Business and Economics* à l'Université Western Washington et professeur adjoint à la Faculté d'administration des affaires de l'Université Simon Fraser. On lui a demandé d'évaluer quel marché, celui des sonneries authentiques ou celui des CD préenregistrés, représente une meilleure référence pour les téléchargements permanents. On ne lui a pas demandé de suggérer un prix ou un taux approprié.

[46] Professor Globerman began by examining what makes the price paid for a factor of production fair and equitable. That price should be equal to the value of the input's marginal product, which is the marginal productivity of the input weighted by the price of the product.[6] He then stated that intellectual property has characteristics that make it difficult, if not impossible, to apply to it notions that are valid when dealing with ordinary goods. For example, contrary to what Professor Boyer stated, it is difficult, if not impossible, to conceive of such a thing as marginal consumption of intellectual property. When using a divisible capital asset, it is possible to influence the end result by increasing the use of the input: thus, for example, one can use more fertilizer to increase the yield of a crop. Intellectual property is an indivisible capital asset. Either one uses it or one does not. As a result, the notion that one can use a little more or a little less of intellectual property in order to determine its value is not realistic. However, assimilating the reproduction right to a capital asset makes it possible to define a fair and equitable input price in a similar way as for ordinary goods.

[46] Le professeur Globerman a d'abord examiné ce qui fait que le prix payé pour un facteur de production est juste et équitable. Ce prix devrait être égal à la valeur du produit marginal d'un intrant, qui est la productivité marginale de l'intrant pondérée par le prix du produit.[6] Il a ensuite précisé que la propriété intellectuelle a des caractéristiques rendant difficile, sinon impossible, d'y appliquer des notions qui sont valables lorsqu'on a affaire à des biens ordinaires. Par exemple, contrairement à ce que le professeur Boyer a déclaré, il est difficile, sinon impossible, de parler en termes de consommation marginale de la propriété intellectuelle. Lorsqu'on utilise un actif immobilisé divisible, on peut influencer le résultat final en accroissant l'utilisation de l'intrant : on peut, par exemple, répandre plus d'engrais pour accroître le rendement d'une récolte. La propriété intellectuelle est un actif immobilisé indivisible, dont on se sert ou pas. La notion suivant laquelle on peut utiliser un peu plus ou un peu moins de propriété intellectuelle afin d'en déterminer la valeur est donc irréaliste. Cependant, en assimilant le droit de reproduction à un actif immobilisé, il est possible de définir le prix d'intrant juste et équitable de la même façon que pour des biens ordinaires.

[47] Professor Globerman then explained how he compared permanent downloads to other potential proxy markets. Based on his notion of a fair and equitable input price, he identified three characteristics he considered helpful to determine whether a market constitutes an appropriate proxy. Those are the price for which the good is sold (output price), the costs incurred to produce and offer the good (input prices), and the seller's discount rate. Since no information was available to determine the discount rate, Professor Globerman chose to ignore that factor, adding that this did not affect his analysis.

[47] Le professeur Globerman a ensuite expliqué comment il a comparé les téléchargements permanents à d'autres marchés de référence potentiels. En se fondant sur sa notion du prix juste et équitable d'un intrant, il a identifié trois caractéristiques qu'il juge utiles pour déterminer si un marché représente une référence appropriée. Ces caractéristiques sont le prix auquel le bien est vendu (le prix de l'extrant), les coûts encourus pour produire et offrir le bien (les prix des intrants) et le taux d'escompte du vendeur. En l'absence de toute information permettant de déterminer ce taux d'escompte, le professeur Globerman a décidé de ne pas en tenir compte, ajoutant que cela n'influençait pas son analyse.

[48] With respect to the first characteristic, Professor Globerman stated that the closer the

[48] En ce qui concerne la première caractéristique, le professeur Globerman a

output prices are in two markets, the more likely one is to constitute an appropriate proxy for the other. Conversely, when prices in two markets differ significantly, one probably does not constitute an appropriate proxy for the other. He then observed that the retail price for mastertones is three times that for permanent downloads. By contrast, the per-track retail price of a prerecorded CD is more or less the same as the price of a single permanent download. Using data provided in Messrs. Audley and Hyatt's reply evidence, Professor Globerman calculated the average price per track for both CDs and permanent downloads. He concluded that the per unit price was more similar between CDs and permanent downloads than between mastertones and permanent downloads.

précisé que plus le prix d'extrants sur deux marchés se rapprochent, plus il est probable que l'un constitue une référence appropriée pour l'autre. Le contraire est vrai lorsque les prix sur deux marchés diffèrent énormément. Il a ensuite observé que le prix de détail des sonneries authentiques est le triple de celui des téléchargements permanents. À l'opposé, le prix de détail par piste d'un CD préenregistré est plus ou moins le même que le prix du téléchargement permanent d'une piste simple. À l'aide de données fournies dans la contre-preuve de MM. Audley et Hyatt, le professeur Globerman a calculé le prix moyen par piste pour les CD et les téléchargements permanents. Il a conclu que le prix à l'unité était plus similaire entre les CD et les téléchargements permanents qu'entre les sonneries authentiques et les téléchargements permanents.

[49] Professor Globerman then described the notion of "value chain", which is a set of activities carried out by a business to create a commercially valuable output. It is typically comprised of primary activities (logistics, operations, marketing, sales and customer services) and support activities (planning, research, human resources management). Using that notion, he disagreed with the conclusion of Messrs. Audley and Hyatt to the effect that input costs are very different between the prerecorded CD and permanent download markets. He stated that, once costs were properly accounted for, they were closely comparable.

[49] Le professeur Globerman a ensuite décrit la notion de « chaîne de valeur », soit l'ensemble d'activités que réalise une entreprise pour créer un extrant ayant une valeur commerciale. Cette chaîne se compose habituellement d'activités principales (logistique, opérations, commercialisation, ventes et services aux clients) et d'activités de soutien (planification, recherche, gestion des ressources humaines). Invoquant cette notion, il s'est déclaré en désaccord avec la conclusion de MM. Audley et Hyatt selon laquelle il y avait une très grande différence, sur le plan des coûts des intrants, entre les marchés des CD préenregistrés et celui des téléchargements permanents. Il a précisé que ces marchés étaient étroitement comparables une fois les coûts correctement comptabilisés.

[50] Professor Globerman's overall conclusion was that these similarities between the input and output prices of prerecorded CDs and permanent downloads confirm that the former probably constitute the best available proxy to set the tariff for the latter.

[50] Le professeur Globerman a conclu globalement que ces similarités entre les prix des intrants et ceux des extrants des CD préenregistrés et des téléchargements permanents confirment que les premiers représentent probablement la meilleure référence disponible pour fixer le tarif des seconds.

[51] Mr. Ted Cohen, former Senior Vice-President, Digital Development and Distribution

[51] M. Ted Cohen, ex-premier vice-président au développement numérique et à la distribution

for EMI Music, has played a key role in the development of a number of online services. He described the costs associated with the delivery of a sound recording as a prerecorded CD and as a download. He admitted that there may be significant differences between the value chains in the physical and digital environments, but maintained that the business model used to market prerecorded CDs remains the closest to digital downloads. In his opinion, mastertones will cease to exist as a stand-alone business within two years and will be bundled with permanent downloads. If only for that reason, he considers that the mastertone market is not an appropriate business model to use as a proxy. Mastertones, in his opinion, are personalization products, not music products.

chez EMI Music, a joué un rôle clé dans la mise sur pied d'un certain nombre de services en ligne. Il a décrit les coûts se rattachant à la distribution d'un enregistrement sonore sous forme de CD préenregistré et de téléchargement. Il a reconnu qu'il peut exister d'importantes différences entre les chaînes de valeur d'un environnement matériel et d'un environnement numérique, mais a soutenu que le modèle d'entreprise utilisé pour commercialiser les CD préenregistrés reste celui qui se rapproche le plus de celui des téléchargements numériques. À son avis, d'ici deux ans, les sonneries authentiques ne constitueront plus une branche d'activité indépendante et seront vendues avec les téléchargements permanents. Ne serait-ce que pour cette raison, il considère que le marché des sonneries authentiques ne représente pas un modèle d'entreprise approprié à utiliser comme référence. Les sonneries authentiques sont, à son avis, des produits de personnalisation, pas des produits musicaux.

[52] Mr. Stephen Stohn, Partner at Stohn Hay Cafazzo Dembroski Richmond LLP and expert in the music business, was commissioned to summarize the typical contractual provisions and agreements in the music industry relevant to the reproduction right and to suggest the most appropriate proxy in the Canadian music market to determine an appropriate royalty rate.

[52] M. Stephen Stohn, associé chez Stohn Hay Cafazzo Dembroski Richmond LLP et spécialiste de l'industrie de la musique, a été engagé pour résumer les dispositions et les ententes contractuelles types dans l'industrie portant sur le droit de reproduction et pour suggérer la référence la plus appropriée sur le marché canadien de la musique afin de déterminer un taux de redevance convenable.

[53] Mr. Joseph Salvo, special counsel, Weil, Gotshal & Manges LLP, and as former counsel for SONY, one of the negotiators of the NDMAs, testified about the genesis, content and impact of the NDMAs and on the relevance of the mechanical compulsory licence and of CCCs in the digital environment in the United States.

[53] M. Joseph Salvo, conseiller spécial chez Weil, Gotshal & Manges LLP et ex-conseiller pour SONY, l'un des négociateurs des NDMA, a témoigné au sujet de la genèse, du contenu et des répercussions de ces ententes et de la pertinence de la licence obligatoire de reproduction mécanique et des CCC dans l'environnement numérique aux États-Unis.

[54] Messrs. Terry Canning, Vice-President and General Manager of the Rogers Hi-Speed Internet Service, Patrick McLean, General Manager of Consumer Internet Services at Bell Canada, and Kerry Munro, General Manager of Yahoo! Canada, described the development and

[54] MM. Terry Canning, vice-président et directeur général des services Internet haute vitesse de Rogers, Patrick McLean, directeur général des services Internet aux consommateurs chez Bell Canada, et Kerry Munro, directeur général de Yahoo! Canada, ont décrit le

operations of the online music services provided by their companies. They testified to the precarious financial environment in which they currently operate and to the time that it is expected to take before these businesses can show a profit.

développement et le fonctionnement des services de musique en ligne fournis par leurs sociétés. Ils ont fait état du cadre financier précaire dans lequel ces sociétés font actuellement des affaires et traité du temps qu'il faudra, d'après les prévisions, avant que ces entreprises ne puissent déclarer des bénéfices.

[55] Mr. Eddy Cue, Vice-President of Apple's iTunes, was responsible for the development and implementation of the *iTunes Music Stores*, which now operate in 22 countries. He described the development of the *iTunes Music Store*, which offers over 2 million tracks in Canada and over 3.4 million in the United States, and now include audio books, videos, movies and television shows.

[55] M. Eddy Cue, vice-président d'iTunes chez Apple, a piloté le développement et la mise sur pied des *iTunes Music Stores*, qui sont maintenant actifs dans 22 pays. Il a décrit la mise sur pied du magasin, qui offre plus de 2 millions de pistes au Canada et plus de 3,4 millions aux États-Unis, y compris des livres parlés, des vidéos, des films et des émissions de télévision.

[56] Mr. Cue testified that Apple established its 99¢ price point in the United States having regard to its competition, which it viewed as coming from two sources: free, unauthorized downloads and prerecorded CDs. The CD market was important in determining a price and business model because most people purchase their music on CDs and that creates an expectation of what an album is worth. When Apple opened its Canadian online music service, it looked at all those factors, as well as considering the added advantage of not having to change the North American price, and maintained the 99¢ price.

[56] M. Cue a déclaré que la société Apple a établi son niveau de prix à 99 ¢ aux États-Unis eu égard à la concurrence, qui, selon elle, venait de deux sources : les téléchargements gratuits, non autorisés et les CD préenregistrés. Le marché des CD était important pour déterminer un prix et un modèle d'entreprise, parce que la plupart des gens achètent leur musique sur ces supports, ce qui crée des attentes vis-à-vis de la valeur d'un album. Lorsqu'elle a inauguré son service canadien de musique en ligne, Apple a examiné ces facteurs et tenu compte de l'avantage supplémentaire de ne pas avoir à modifier le prix établi pour l'Amérique du Nord, et a maintenu son prix de 99 ¢.

[57] Mr. Cue acknowledged that some of the costs incurred in delivering prerecorded CDs are not incurred in delivering music online, but added that the online delivery of music involves other costs that make the overall expense of delivering a sound recording as significant in one as in the other. He rejected comparisons between mastertones and permanent downloads. In his opinion, mastertones are a different product that uses music in a different way and targets a different market.

[57] M. Cue a reconnu que pour la distribution de la musique en ligne, on ne supporte pas certains des coûts encourus pour assurer la distribution de CD préenregistrés. Il a cependant ajouté que distribuer de la musique en ligne entraîne d'autres coûts qui font que les dépenses globales de distribution d'un enregistrement sonore sont aussi importantes dans un cas que dans l'autre. Il a rejeté les comparaisons entre les sonneries authentiques et les téléchargements permanents. Les sonneries authentiques constituent, à son avis, un produit différent qui fait appel à la musique de façon différente et qui vise un marché différent.

[58] Mr. Cue compared the way in which iTunes clears rights in Canada, the United States and Europe. In the United States, record labels generally provide all necessary rights for one fee, having secured the right to reproduce the musical work. In Europe, iTunes must purchase the rights for the sound recording and for the musical work separately, but is able to purchase the right to reproduce and communicate the work in a single transaction. In Canada, iTunes must licence separately the right to reproduce the musical work, the right to communicate the musical work and the right to reproduce the sound recording.

[58] M. Cue a comparé la façon dont iTunes affranchit les droits au Canada, aux États-Unis, et en Europe. Aux États-Unis, les maisons de disques offrent généralement tous les droits nécessaires pour un même prix, ayant obtenu le droit de reproduire l'œuvre musicale. En Europe, iTunes doit acheter les droits pour l'enregistrement sonore et pour l'œuvre musicale séparément, mais peut acheter le droit de reproduire et de communiquer l'œuvre dans le cadre d'une seule opération. Au Canada, iTunes doit acheter séparément le droit de reproduire l'œuvre musicale, le droit de la communiquer et le droit de reproduire l'enregistrement sonore.

[59] The final panel consisted of Messrs. Upinder Saini, Vice-President, New Products and Content Development, Rogers Wireless, Andrew Wright, Director of Business Development, Bell Mobility, and Nauby Jacob, Director, Browser and Messaging Services, TELUS. Rogers, Bell and TELUS offer both mastertones and permanent music downloads to their subscribers. In Canada, ringtone services were launched in 2001 and mastertones were first offered in 2003. Permanent music downloads only became available in 2005. In their opinion, mastertones and downloads are separate products and are marketed differently. Mastertones are not a music product, but a personalization tool.

[59] Le dernier panel se composait de MM. Upinder Saini, vice-président aux nouveaux produits et au développement de leur contenu chez Rogers Wireless, Andrew Wright, directeur du développement des entreprises chez Bell Mobilité, et Nauby Jacob, directeur des services de navigation et de messagerie chez TELUS. Rogers, Bell et TELUS offrent des sonneries authentiques et des téléchargements permanents de musique à leurs abonnés. Au Canada, les services de sonneries ont été lancés en 2001 et les sonneries authentiques ont fait leur apparition en 2003. Les téléchargements permanents de musique n'ont été offerts qu'en 2005. Les sonneries authentiques et les téléchargements sont, d'après eux, des produits séparés et sont commercialisés différemment. Les sonneries authentiques ne sont pas tant des produits musicaux que des outils de personnalisation.

[60] The Objectors contend that prerecorded CDs are the appropriate proxy for permanent downloads and, all things being equal, the price paid for the right to reproduce a musical work should be the same for both. In their submission, CDs and downloads are simply different delivery mechanisms for the same product – sound recordings of musical works. In Canada, the price paid to copy musical works onto a prerecorded medium has varied over time, but has always been the same whether the format was vinyl, cassette or CD. In the Objectors'

[60] Les opposantes prétendent que les CD préenregistrés représentent le marché de référence approprié pour les téléchargements permanents et que, toutes choses égales, le prix payé pour le droit de reproduire une œuvre musicale devrait être le même dans les deux cas. Elles soutiennent que les CD et les téléchargements sont simplement des mécanismes différents de distribution du même produit : l'enregistrement sonore d'une œuvre musicale. Au Canada, le prix payé pour copier une œuvre musicale sur un support préenregistré a varié au fil du temps,

submission, there is no reason for this to change in the digital environment.

mais a toujours été le même, indépendamment du format : vinyle, cassette ou CD. Les opposantes soutiennent qu'il n'y a aucune raison pour que cela change dans l'environnement numérique.

[61] Consequently, the Objectors submit that the appropriate way to derive a rate for permanent downloads is to start from the MLA and then adjust it so as to determine the average net compensation paid in Canada for the reproduction of a single track onto a prerecorded CD. They then ask that this amount be converted into a percentage of the price of a download. The Objectors disagree with CSI's argument that the value of the reproduction right has increased simply because it is now possible to copy music to a hard drive or portable music player.

[61] Par conséquent, les opposantes sont d'avis que la bonne façon d'établir un taux pour les téléchargements permanents consiste à se fonder sur la MLA, puis à l'ajuster de façon à déterminer la rémunération nette moyenne payée au Canada pour la reproduction d'une piste individuelle sur un CD préenregistré. Elles demandent ensuite qu'on convertisse ce montant en un pourcentage du prix d'un téléchargement. Les opposantes sont en désaccord avec l'argument de CSI, selon lequel la valeur du droit de reproduction a augmenté simplement parce qu'il est maintenant possible de copier de la musique sur un disque dur ou un lecteur portatif de musique.

### *C. Observations*

[62] Pursuant to the Board's directive on procedure, the *Union des artistes* and ArtistI filed written observations dealing primarily with the nature of, and limits to, the rights of performers to authorize the reproduction of their performances generally and in a digital environment. The remarks outlined the difficulties that may arise if record labels are allowed to act as intermediaries for the licensing of performers' rights. The letter also argued for the importance, where performers' rights do exist, of ensuring that fixed performances are not used "for a purpose other than that for which the performer's authorization was given" as is provided in subparagraph 15(1)(*b*)(ii) of the *Act*.

### *C. Observations*

[62] Conformément à la directive sur la procédure de la Commission, l'Union des artistes et ArtistI ont déposé des observations écrites portant principalement sur la nature et les limites des droits qu'ont les artistes-interprètes d'autoriser la reproduction de leurs prestations en général et dans un environnement numérique en particulier. Leurs remarques esquissent les difficultés qui pourraient survenir si l'on permettait aux maisons de disques de jouer le rôle d'intermédiaires pour l'utilisation des droits de ces artistes. Elles soutenaient également dans leur lettre qu'il est important, lorsqu'un artiste-interprète a des droits, de s'assurer que les exécutions fixées ne servent pas à une fin autre que celle pour laquelle l'artiste-interprète a donné son autorisation, comme il est prévu au sous-alinéa 15(1)*b*)(ii) de la *Loi*.

## V. ANALYSIS

[63] To set a tariff in this instance, we must perform the following tasks. The first is to determine the proxy that will be used to establish

## V. ANALYSE

[63] Pour établir le présent tarif, nous devons effectuer cinq tâches : déterminer le prix de référence qui servira à établir le tarif pour les

the tariff for permanent downloads. The second is to adapt that proxy to the online music market and establish the tariff for permanent downloads. The third is to determine the tariff for limited downloads and on-demand streams. The fourth is to select the rate base that will be used to calculate royalties. Finally, it will be necessary to examine what role, if any, the record labels can and should play in the context of the tariff we are certifying.

téléchargements permanents; adapter ce prix au marché de la musique en ligne et établir le tarif; déterminer le tarif pour les téléchargements limités et les transmissions sur demande; choisir la base tarifaire servant au calcul des redevances; enfin, examiner la nature du rôle que les maisons de disques pourraient et devraient jouer dans le contexte du tarif que nous homologuons.

***A. The Appropriate Proxy***

***A. Le prix de référence approprié***

[64] Throughout this process, CSI and the Objectors adopted the same approach. First, they both contended that there is a readily available proxy that should be used to set the tariff. Second, the proxy selected should be used to set a price for permanent downloads and that price can then be used to determine royalties for limited downloads and on-demand streams. We agree with this approach.

[64] Pendant tout ce processus, CSI et les opposantes ont adopté la même approche. Elles affirment qu'il existe un prix de référence évident à utiliser pour fixer le tarif. Elles avancent que ce prix devrait servir à fixer un tarif pour les téléchargements permanents. Elles estiment que ce tarif peut ensuite servir à établir les redevances pour les téléchargements limités et les transmissions sur demande. Nous partageons leur point de vue.

[65] While CSI and the Objectors agree on the approach, they differ on what the appropriate proxy should be. CSI favours mastertones, but also offered some alternatives. The Objectors argue that the price paid in the online market should be derived from what record labels pay to reproduce music on prerecorded CDs.

[65] Même si elles s'entendent sur l'approche, CSI et les opposantes divergent d'opinion au sujet du choix d'un prix de référence. La première préfère les sonneries authentiques, tout en offrant d'autres solutions. Les secondes soutiennent qu'il faut établir le prix pour la musique en ligne à partir du montant que les maisons de disques versent pour reproduire de la musique sur des CD préenregistrés.

*1. The Mastertone Market*

*1. Le marché des sonneries authentiques*

[66] CSI argues that the mastertone market is the appropriate starting point. Mastertones and permanent downloads form part of the same, broad digital market. Both involve the sale of digital files of music that are delivered electronically to consumers. Though they are not substitutes for each other, the business models are very similar. We disagree, for the following reasons.

[66] CSI affirme que le marché des sonneries authentiques constitue le point de départ approprié. Ces sonneries et les téléchargements permanents font partie du même vaste marché numérique. Les unes et les autres impliquent la vente de fichiers numériques de musique distribués par voie électronique aux consommateurs. Les modèles d'entreprise sont très similaires, même s'ils ne constituent pas des substituts les uns pour les autres. Nous ne sommes pas d'accord, pour les motifs suivants.

[67] First, mastertones are not a substitute for permanent downloads. Downloads compete with CDs, not mastertones. Mastertones are not priced as a function of downloads, or vice-versa. Both products may be delivered through similar modes, but that hardly is sufficient to justify a choice of proxy. We agree with the many witnesses who testified that mastertones are a different product that serves a different purpose. They are a personal identification medium, a fashion statement. Consumers purchase permanent downloads to listen to them; no one purchases a mastertone to listen to it on a computer or an iPod.

[67] Premièrement, une sonnerie authentique n'est pas un substitut pour un téléchargement permanent. Les téléchargements font concurrence aux CD, pas aux sonneries. Le prix d'une sonnerie authentique n'est pas fonction des téléchargements, ni vice-versa. Le fait que les deux produits sont distribués par des moyens similaires ne suffit pas à justifier le choix d'un prix de référence. Nous sommes d'accord avec les nombreux témoins qui ont déclaré qu'une sonnerie authentique constitue un produit différent servant à une fin différente. C'est un moyen d'identification personnelle, une forme d'expression à la mode. Le consommateur achète un téléchargement permanent pour l'écouter; personne n'achète une sonnerie authentique pour l'écouter sur un ordinateur ou sur un iPod.

[68] Second, we agree with Professor Globerman that mastertones do not have the required characteristics of a good proxy for permanent downloads. Simply put, the input and output prices in these markets are too different for one to be helpful in the other. Permanent downloads sell for as little as one-third of the price of mastertones. This is a strong signal that each product may exhibit different characteristics. CSI simply failed to account for that difference.

[68] Deuxièmement, nous sommes d'accord avec l'affirmation du professeur Globerman selon laquelle les sonneries authentiques ne possèdent pas les caractéristiques requises d'un bon prix de référence pour les téléchargements permanents. Tout simplement, les prix des intrants et des extrants sur ces marchés sont trop différents pour que l'un soit utile pour l'autre. Un téléchargement permanent se vend pour aussi peu que le tiers du prix d'une sonnerie authentique, ce qui indique bien que chaque produit peut afficher des caractéristiques différentes. CSI n'a simplement pas tenu compte de cette différence.

[69] Finally, in our opinion, the mastertone market is not mature enough, and its future too uncertain, for it to serve as a reliable proxy. The industry's revenues and expenses have not yet reached a stable level of growth. Mastertones may not last as a stand-alone business. It would be inappropriate to establish a tariff using a proxy based on such uncertain grounds.

[69] Enfin, à notre avis, le marché des sonneries authentiques n'est pas suffisamment établi et son avenir est trop incertain pour qu'il serve de référence fiable. Les revenus et les dépenses de l'industrie n'ont pas encore atteint un niveau stable de croissance. Ce marché risque de ne pas survivre en tant que branche d'activité indépendante sur Internet. Il serait inapproprié d'établir un tarif à l'aide d'un prix de référence reposant sur des fondements aussi incertains.

*2. Other Proxies Proposed by CSI*

*2. Autres prix de référence proposés par CSI*

[70] The three alternative proposals offered in the reply evidence of Messrs. Audley and Hyatt

[70] Les trois propositions de rechange soumises dans la contre-preuve de MM. Audley et Hyatt

suffer from a number of common problems. All are based on approximations; at best, they can only be used as validation measures. All compare percentages, when comparisons of actual amounts seem preferable. Finally, we agree with Professor Globerman that when the actual net amounts received by a record label are compared, all seem to confirm, not contradict, his conclusions.

comportent un certain nombre de problèmes communs. Toutes reposent sur des approximations. Au mieux, elles pourraient servir de mesures de validation. Toutes ont pour point de comparaison des pourcentages, alors que des comparaisons de montants réels paraissent préférables. Enfin, nous sommes d'accord avec l'affirmation du professeur Globerman, qui indique que lorsque l'on compare les montants nets réels que touche une maison de disques, tous paraissent confirmer, non pas contredire, ses conclusions.

*3. The Prerecorded CD Market*

*3. Le marché des CD préenregistrés*

[71] The Objectors offer four reasons to argue that the amount paid for the right to reproduce a musical work onto a prerecorded CD is a good starting point. First, permanent downloads compete with prerecorded CDs and are priced accordingly. Second, as Professor Globerman demonstrated, the value chains for the two products, as well as their input and output prices, are sufficiently close to justify using one to set the amount for the other. Third, permanent downloads are just another form of sound recording. The media onto which a recording is reproduced has changed over time, but the price paid to reproduce a musical work has always been the same at any given time irrespective of the type of medium onto which the work has been put.[7] Fourth, online services view physical CDs as a substitute product, and CD retailers as their competitors. We agree with the Objectors.

[71] Les opposantes soutiennent que le montant payé pour le droit de reproduire une œuvre musicale sur un CD préenregistré constitue un bon point de départ, et ce, pour quatre raisons. Premièrement, les téléchargements permanents font concurrence aux CD préenregistrés et leurs prix sont établis en conséquence. Deuxièmement, comme le professeur Globerman l'a démontré, les chaînes de valeur pour les deux produits, de même que les prix de leurs intrants et extrants, se rapprochent suffisamment pour justifier qu'on en utilise un afin de fixer la valeur de l'autre. Troisièmement, le téléchargement permanent est simplement une autre forme d'enregistrement sonore. Le support auquel on l'incorpore a changé au fil du temps, mais le prix payé pour reproduire l'œuvre musicale a toujours été le même, indépendamment du type de support sur lequel elle est copiée.[7] Quatrièmement, les services en ligne considèrent que le CD matériel est un produit de substitution et que les vendeurs au détail de CD sont leurs concurrents. Nous sommes d'accord avec les opposantes.

[72] CSI puts forth three main arguments to support its submission that the prerecorded CD market is not an appropriate starting point. We are not persuaded by these arguments.

[72] CSI avance trois arguments principaux pour expliquer pourquoi elle considère que le marché des CD préenregistrés ne constitue pas un point de départ approprié. Ces arguments ne nous convainquent pas.

[73] CSI argues that the use made of the reproduction right in the online market is very

[73] CSI soutient que l'utilisation qu'on fait du droit de reproduction sur le marché en ligne est

different, and much more extensive, than in the prerecorded CD market. The delivery of a prerecorded CD involves only two copies: the master recording and the CD itself. The delivery of a permanent download involves at least the creation of a digital master file and its reproduction onto the online service's server, in addition to the downstream copies made by the service's customers on any number of media and devices. Insofar as this is either correct[8] or relevant, this can be taken into account through an adjustment in the rate and therefore, does not reduce the usefulness of the MLA as a proxy.

très différente, et beaucoup plus importante, que celle qu'on en fait sur le marché des CD préenregistrés. La distribution d'un CD préenregistré ne nécessite que deux copies : la bande maîtresse et le disque compact lui-même. La distribution d'un téléchargement permanent nécessite au moins la création d'un fichier maître numérique et sa reproduction sur le serveur du service en ligne, en plus des copies en aval faites par le client du service sur un certain nombre de supports et d'appareils. Dans la mesure où cela est exact[8] ou pertinent, on peut en tenir compte en ajustant le taux, ce qui ne réduit donc pas l'utilité de la MLA en tant que référence.

[74] CSI also argues that online music services use the reproduction right in a manner that allows them to create a consumer experience that differs substantially from what occurs when a consumer purchases and uses a prerecorded CD. For example, online consumers enjoy a greater variety and choice of music, the ability to purchase individual tracks, to create their own playlists, to sample excerpts before making a purchase and to research their purchases at their leisure, much more effectively and thoroughly than in a record store. Again, be that as it may, it does not deter from the usefulness of the MLA as a proxy. Over the years, record stores have changed the way they sell sound recordings. Many times, the industry has even changed the format in which sound recordings are offered: singles have come and gone, and now appear poised to make a comeback in the digital world. And yet, the MLA has always set the same price for a track, whether sold as a single or as part of an album.

[74] CSI affirme aussi que les services de musique en ligne utilisent le droit de reproduction d'une façon qui leur permet d'offrir au consommateur une expérience très différente de ce qui se passe quand on achète et utilise un CD préenregistré. Les consommateurs en ligne, par exemple, ont accès à une plus grande variété et un plus grand choix de musique, peuvent acheter des pistes individuelles, créer leurs propres listes d'écoute, écouter des extraits avant d'acheter et effectuer des recherches pour leurs achats quand bon leur semble, et ce, beaucoup plus efficacement et minutieusement que chez un disquaire. Encore une fois, quoi qu'il en soit, cette affirmation ne réduit pas l'utilité de la MLA comme référence. Au fil des ans, les disquaires ont modifié leur façon de vendre des enregistrements sonores. L'industrie a même souvent modifié le format sous lequel elle offre ses enregistrements; le disque simple, qui a connu ses heures de gloire, semble maintenant prêt à resurgir dans l'univers numérique. Et pourtant, on a toujours fixé dans la MLA le même prix pour une piste, qu'elle soit vendue individuellement ou qu'elle fasse partie d'un album.

[75] Finally, CSI points out that record labels do not play the same role in the digital and physical worlds. Labels no longer manufacture or distribute finished goods. Instead, they licence their sound recordings to online services, who

[75] Enfin, CSI fait remarquer que la maison de disques ne joue pas le même rôle dans les univers numérique et matériel. Elle ne fabrique plus et ne distribue plus de produits finis. Elle octroie des licences pour ses enregistrements sonores à des

then reproduce them for distribution and authorize their subscribers to make further copies. This is not relevant. From an economic perspective, prerecorded CDs and permanent downloads simply are different ways of marketing sound recordings that are meant to be listened to by the same consumer in the same manner.[9] The price paid to reproduce a musical work embedded onto a sound recording should be the same, irrespective of the way in which that recording is marketed.

services en ligne, qui ensuite les reproduisent afin de les distribuer et autorisent leurs abonnés à en faire d'autres copies. Cela n'est pas pertinent. D'un point de vue économique, les CD préenregistrés et les téléchargements permanents sont simplement des moyens différents de commercialiser des enregistrements sonores destinés à être écoutés de la même façon par les mêmes consommateurs.[9] Le prix payé pour reproduire l'œuvre musicale incorporée à un enregistrement sonore devrait être le même, indépendamment du moyen de commercialisation de cet enregistrement.

[76] On a related point, we reject the position developed by CSI on the differences in the respective value chains. When the Internet is used to deliver recorded music, it remains necessary to carry out important stages of the value chain such as production, distribution and inventorying. Though the input mixes may be different, marketing the product still requires performing every specific stage. For example, inventory costs will involve renting or buying server space rather than warehouse space, while distribution will require bandwidth instead of trucks.

[76] Dans le même ordre d'idées, nous rejetons la position de CSI au sujet des différences à l'intérieur de chacune des chaînes de valeur. Lorsqu'on utilise Internet pour distribuer de la musique enregistrée, il faut quand même passer par les étapes importantes de la chaîne de valeur comme la production, la distribution et l'établissement de l'inventaire. Même si les combinaisons d'intrants peuvent être différentes, la commercialisation du produit exige encore la réalisation de chacune des étapes. Par exemple, les coûts de stockage impliqueront la location ou l'achat d'un espace sur un serveur, plutôt que d'un espace dans un entrepôt, tandis que la distribution exigera de la bande passante plutôt que des camions.

[77] We therefore find that the price for permanent downloads should be determined using the price currently paid to reproduce a musical work onto a prerecorded CD. This rate has been set at 7.7¢ per track, plus 1.54¢ per minute or fraction thereof over 5 minutes, since 2002. Even though the latest MLA expired at the end of June 2006, that rate continues to be used while the parties renegotiate the agreement. We will therefore use that rate as a starting point even though the effective rate may be slightly higher due to the existence of sound recordings lasting more than 5 minutes. We do not see the need to make the correction, which would probably be marginal at best.

[77] Nous concluons donc qu'il faut déterminer le prix des téléchargements permanents à partir du prix actuellement payé pour reproduire une œuvre musicale sur un CD préenregistré. Ce taux est fixé depuis 2002 à 7,7 ¢ la piste, plus 1,54 ¢ la minute ou fraction de minute au-delà de 5 minutes. Même si la plus récente MLA a pris fin à la fin de juin 2006, ce taux continue d'être utilisé pendant que les parties renégocient le contrat. Nous utiliserons donc ce taux comme point de départ, bien que le taux effectif puisse être légèrement supérieur en raison de l'existence d'enregistrements durant plus de 5 minutes. Nous ne voyons pas la nécessité d'effectuer la correction, qui serait probablement minime dans le meilleur des cas.

***B. Deriving a Rate for Permanent Downloads***

*1. A Percentage Rate*

[78] In Canada, the price paid to reproduce musical works onto sound recordings has always been expressed as a number of cents per track. Attempts were made recently to harmonize Canadian practice with that of most foreign jurisdictions and set the rate as a percentage of wholesale or retail. This has not occurred to date.

[79] In these proceedings, both sides request that the rate be expressed as a percentage. The Board has alluded to the merits of this approach many times over the years. Setting the rate as a percentage permits the royalty to vary according to the value the market attributes to the final product and to the business cycles of an industry. It also avoids the need for repeated adjustments to take into account the effect of inflation.

[80] Several agreements between record labels and online services contain rates expressed in cents. Setting a rate in percentage for the use of musical works will result in variations in the relative remuneration of authors, performers and makers as the price of online music varies. This could eventually become an issue the parties will have to deal with. It does not, however, take away from the inherent merits of using a percentage in this tariff.

*2. Adjusting the MLA Rate*

[81] Before deriving a rate, it is necessary to examine the various adjustments to the MLA rate proposed by CSI and the Objectors.

[82] The Objectors proposed two adjustments that are based on Mr. Stohn's analysis. His stated objective was to ensure that the rate for

***B. Calcul d'un taux pour les téléchargements permanents***

*1. Établissement d'un pourcentage*

[78] Au Canada, le prix payé pour reproduire une œuvre musicale sur un enregistrement sonore a toujours été exprimé en cents par piste. On a récemment tenté d'harmoniser la pratique en usage au Canada avec celle de la plupart des marchés étrangers et de fixer le taux sous forme de pourcentage du prix de gros ou de détail, mais jusqu'ici sans succès.

[79] Dans la présente affaire, tous demandent d'exprimer le taux sous forme de pourcentage. Au fil des ans, la Commission a souvent fait allusion aux mérites de cette méthode. Fixer le taux sous forme de pourcentage permet à la redevance de varier suivant la valeur que le marché attribue au produit final et les cycles économiques d'une industrie. Cette façon de procéder évite également d'avoir à faire des ajustements à répétition pour tenir compte de l'effet de l'inflation.

[80] Plusieurs ententes entre maisons de disques et services en ligne renferment des taux exprimés en cents. Le fait de fixer un taux en pourcentage pour l'utilisation d'œuvres musicales entraînera des variations de la rémunération relative des auteurs, artistes-interprètes et producteurs, en fonction des fluctuations de prix de la musique en ligne. Cela pourrait devenir un enjeu que les parties auront à régler, mais n'enlève rien aux mérites inhérents de l'utilisation d'un pourcentage dans le présent tarif.

*2. Ajustement du taux de la MLA*

[81] Avant de calculer un taux, il faut examiner les divers ajustements que CSI et les opposantes proposent d'apporter au taux de la MLA.

[82] Les opposantes ont proposé deux ajustements reposant sur l'analyse de M. Stohn. L'objectif déclaré de ce dernier consistait à

permanent downloads correspond to the effective average rate being paid for the reproduction of musical works onto prerecorded CDs. Both adjustments seek to account for discounts that result from the application of CCCs. Their combined effect would be to reduce the rate by approximately 32 per cent.

[83] These adjustments are either unnecessary or irrelevant. First, Mr. Stohn admitted that not all sound recordings are subject to CCCs and that no available information would allow him to estimate the proportion of those that are. Second, though the evidence was contradictory in this respect, it would appear that the impact of CCCs in the market for permanent downloads is significantly less than in the prerecorded CD market. For example, in the United States, where CCCs originated, provisions in a record deal signed after June 22, 1995 that purport to allow a record label to obtain a mechanical licence at a reduced rate for a "digital phonorecord delivery" are in effect inoperative.[10] Third, CCCs are designed first and foremost for the physical world: it is difficult to conceive of "free goods", as this expression is used in CCCs, on iTunes. Finally, and most importantly, CCCs exist because labels designed them and ask for them. As a result, they are most able to lead cogent and convincing evidence about the relevance and role of these provisions in the digital environment. They did not. Absent such evidence, the prudent course is simply to ignore CCCs.

[84] The Objectors submit that the tariff, for the reproduction of musical works, should be discounted to reflect the value of the right to communicate these same works. The submission is based on two false assumptions. The first is that this decision will establish the price for all rights. This is simply not the case.[11] The second

veiller à ce que le taux pour les téléchargements permanents corresponde au taux moyen en vigueur payé pour la reproduction d'une œuvre musicale sur un CD préenregistré. Les deux ajustements visent à prendre en considération des escomptes qui découlent de l'application de la CCC. Combinés, ils auraient pour effet de réduire le taux d'environ 32 pour cent.

[83] Ces deux ajustements sont inutiles ou hors de propos. Premièrement, M. Stohn a admis que tous les enregistrements sonores ne sont pas assujettis à des CCC et qu'aucun renseignement disponible ne lui permettait d'estimer la proportion de ceux qui le sont. Deuxièmement, même si la preuve était contradictoire sous ce rapport, il semblerait que les répercussions de la CCC sur le marché des téléchargements permanents soient bien moindres que sur le marché des CD préenregistrés. Par exemple, aux États-Unis, où la CCC a pris naissance, les dispositions d'un contrat signé après le 22 juin 1995 censées permettre à une maison de disques d'obtenir des droits de reproduction mécanique à un taux réduit pour la distribution d'un enregistrement sonore numérique sont dans les faits inopérantes.[10] Troisièmement, la CCC est conçue d'abord et avant tout pour le monde matériel : il est difficile d'associer des « biens gratuits », tels qu'on en parle dans les CCC, à iTunes. Enfin et surtout, si les CCC existent, c'est que les maisons de disques les ont inventées et qu'elles les demandent. Elles sont donc le plus en mesure de fournir une preuve forte et convaincante quant à la pertinence et au rôle de telles dispositions dans le monde numérique. Elles ne l'ont pas fait. En l'absence d'une telle preuve, la voie de la prudence consiste simplement à ne pas les prendre en considération.

[84] Les opposantes estiment qu'on devrait prévoir un escompte dans le présent tarif, qui vise la reproduction d'œuvres musicales, afin de refléter la valeur du droit de communiquer ces œuvres. Cette prétention repose sur deux hypothèses erronées. La première, c'est que la présente décision établira le prix pour tous les

is that the price should be the same whether one or two rights are required to deliver a product. The Board has rejected that argument more than once.[12] In addition, the proxy that we have adopted is the one proposed by the Objectors. It involves only the reproduction right.

droits, ce qui n'est simplement pas le cas.[11] La seconde, c'est que le prix devrait être le même, qu'il faille un ou deux droits pour distribuer un produit. La Commission a rejeté cet argument plus d'une fois.[12] Le prix de référence que nous avons adopté est, en outre, celui proposé par les opposantes. Il n'englobe que le droit de reproduction.

[85] For its part, CSI proposed two adjustments.

[85] CSI a, pour sa part, proposé deux ajustements.

[86] The first would account for the fact that members of ADISQ currently pay SODRAC mechanical royalties of 8.9¢. Messrs. Audley and Hyatt proposed an adjustment based on the assumption that the SODRAC-ADISQ agreement applies to 15 per cent of the Canadian market. The Objectors argue this number is too high; in their opinion, SODRAC's overall share of the Canadian market is 15 per cent and ADISQ accounts for only one third of SODRAC's business, or 5 per cent of the total market. The rest would be governed by SODRAC's agreement with CRIA, which uses the 7.7¢ rate. In our opinion, CSI could have provided information allowing us to determine precisely the importance of the SODRAC-ADISQ agreement in the Canadian market; it did not do so. We find the figures advanced by the Objectors inherently more credible, given what the Board has learned over the years of the Canadian market for prerecorded CDs. In any event, even if we accepted CSI's submissions, it would only have a marginal impact on the result. The correction to account for the SODRAC-ADISQ agreement yields an adjusted rate of 7.8¢.

[86] Le premier tiendrait compte du fait que les membres de l'ADISQ paient actuellement à la SODRAC des droits mécaniques de 8,9 ¢. MM. Audley et Hyatt ont proposé un ajustement fondé sur l'hypothèse selon laquelle l'entente entre la SODRAC et l'ADISQ s'applique à 15 pour cent du marché canadien. Les opposantes soutiennent que ce pourcentage est trop élevé; la SODRAC détient globalement, à leur avis, 15 pour cent du marché canadien et l'ADISQ ne représente que le tiers des affaires de la SODRAC, ou 5 pour cent du marché total. Le reste serait régi par l'entente conclue avec la CRIA, qui utilise le taux de 7,7 ¢. À notre avis, CSI aurait pu fournir de l'information permettant de déterminer précisément l'importance de l'entente entre la SODRAC et l'ADISQ sur le marché canadien; elle ne l'a pas fait. Nous considérons les chiffres présentés par les opposantes comme étant plus crédibles, compte tenu de ce que la Commission a appris au fil des ans du marché canadien des CD préenregistrés. De toute façon, même si nous acceptions les arguments de CSI, cela n'aurait que des répercussions minimes sur le résultat. La correction permettant de tenir compte de l'entente entre la SODRAC et l'ADISQ donne un taux ajusté de 7,8 ¢.

[87] The second proposed adjustment would take into account that online services expressly grant consumers the right to make several copies of a download onto any number of devices or media. Some of these copies may be private copies; others are not and therefore, require the

[87] Le second ajustement proposé tiendrait compte du fait que les services en ligne accordent expressément aux consommateurs le droit de faire plusieurs copies d'un téléchargement sur un éventail d'appareils ou de supports. Certaines de ces copies peuvent être des copies privées;

rightsholder's permission. At first glance, one would expect that consumers get added value from being able to make more than one copy, even when that option is not being exercised.[13] It could also be argued that being able to authorize their subscribers to make more than one copy gives online services a competitive advantage over retailers of prerecorded CDs. If so, the MLA rate should be adjusted to take into account the value of these additional rights. There is evidence to the effect that the right to make extra copies is worth something in at least the wireless services market, where consumers pay less when music is downloaded only onto a PC than when it is downloaded onto both a cell phone and a PC.

[88] That being said, this is not the occasion to determine whether, or by how much, the price should be increased on this account. First, there is not enough evidence of what the right to make extra copies might be worth. Second, there may be factors that tend to considerably reduce this added value. For example, the fact that prerecorded and downloaded tracks sell at approximately the same price may indicate that the right to make additional copies is actually being given away to clinch the sale; nothing else seems important. Existing agreements between record labels and online services tend to show that labels have come to this conclusion. Third, expressing the rate as a percentage of the retail price will allow the market to implicitly attribute the value these additional rights may have, as is the case with wireless downloads.

[89] However, we reject the argument of the Objectors that it is unnecessary to account for these extra copies. To say that the MLA already takes into account that consumers are able in

d'autres ne le sont pas. Il faut donc la permission du titulaire de droits pour les faire. Au premier coup d'œil, on s'attendrait à ce que les consommateurs tirent une valeur ajoutée de la possibilité pour eux de faire plus d'une copie, même lorsqu'ils n'exercent pas cette option.[13] On pourrait aussi soutenir qu'en pouvant autoriser leurs abonnés à faire plus d'une copie, les services en ligne détiennent un avantage concurrentiel par rapport aux détaillants de CD préenregistrés. Si c'est le cas, il faudrait ajuster le taux de la MLA pour tenir compte de la valeur de ces droits additionnels. La preuve démontre que le droit de faire des copies additionnelles a une certaine valeur, du moins sur le marché des services sans fil, où le consommateur paie moins lorsqu'il télécharge de la musique uniquement sur un ordinateur personnel que lorsqu'il la télécharge aussi sur son téléphone cellulaire.

[88] Cela dit, ce n'est pas le moment de déterminer si le prix devrait être majoré pour cette raison, et de combien, le cas échéant. Tout d'abord, il n'y a pas suffisamment de données concluantes permettant de déterminer ce que le droit de faire des copies additionnelles pourrait valoir. Deuxièmement, il peut exister des facteurs qui contribueraient à réduire considérablement cette valeur ajoutée. Le fait, par exemple, que les pistes préenregistrées et téléchargées se vendent environ au même prix pourrait signifier que dans les faits, on donne gratuitement le droit de faire des copies additionnelles pour conclure la vente; rien d'autre ne paraît avoir d'importance. Les ententes actuelles entre les services en ligne et les maisons de disques ont tendance à montrer que ces dernières en sont venues à cette conclusion. Troisièmement, exprimer le taux sous forme de pourcentage du prix de détail permettra au marché d'attribuer implicitement la valeur que peuvent avoir ces droits additionnels, comme dans le cas des téléchargements sans fil.

[89] Nous rejetons cependant l'argument des opposantes selon lequel il n'est pas nécessaire de tenir compte de la possibilité de faire des copies additionnelles. Dire que la MLA tient déjà

practice to make an unlimited number of copies is to argue that the MLA factors in a largely illegal activity. In addition, to argue that the private copying regime already takes care of these copies is to look at the issue from the wrong end of the telescope. CSI's suggestion that section 80 of the *Act* applies only to copies that have not otherwise been authorized is incorrect. A private copy is a private copy, whether or not it was authorized. However, some of the copies online services authorize clearly are not private copies. More importantly, the private copying regime exists to compensate the effects of a market failure, without being contingent on the extent of that failure. Confronted with this conundrum, and with a view to reinforcing the nexus that must exist between the regime and its stated objectives in order for the regime to remain constitutionally valid, the Board decided early on that it would discount authorized private copies from the calculation of the levy and leave it to the market to set the price for such copies.

compte de la capacité pratique des consommateurs de faire un nombre illimité de copies, c'est affirmer que cette entente prend en compte une activité en grande partie illégale. En outre, avancer que le régime de copie privée voit déjà à ces copies, c'est envisager la question par le mauvais bout de la lunette. CSI fait erreur lorsqu'elle suggère que l'article 80 de la *Loi* ne s'applique qu'aux copies qu'on n'a pas par ailleurs autorisées. Une copie privée, autorisée ou non, est une copie privée. Cela dit, certaines des copies que les services en ligne autorisent de faire sont manifestement autre chose que des copies privées. Plus important encore, le régime de copie privée a été créé pour contrebalancer les effets d'un échec de marché, sans le subordonner à l'ampleur de l'échec. Confrontée à ce problème épineux et désireuse de renforcer le lien qui doit exister entre le régime et ses objectifs déclarés pour que ce régime demeure constitutionnellement valide, la Commission a décidé très tôt qu'elle soustrairait les copies privées autorisées lors du calcul des redevances et laisserait le marché déterminer le prix de ces copies.

*3. The Average Retail Price of a Downloaded Track; the Resulting Rate*

*3. Prix de détail moyen d'une piste téléchargée et taux applicable*

[90] The numerator that we will use to set the rate for permanent downloads, as indicated in paragraph 86, is 7.8¢. In order to derive a percentage rate, we now need to determine the average retail price of a downloaded track.

[90] Le numérateur que nous utiliserons pour établir le taux applicable aux téléchargements permanents, tel qu'il est indiqué au paragraphe 86, est 7,8 ¢. Nous devons maintenant déterminer le prix de détail moyen d'une piste téléchargée afin de calculer un pourcentage.

[91] The predominant retail price for single track permanent downloads appears to be 99¢. iTunes sells virtually all of its single tracks for that price. Some competitors sell tracks for more and sometimes offer promotions for less. Even in the unlikely scenario that 10 per cent of tracks were sold at $1.19, the average price of a track would increase by only 2¢. We find that 99¢ is a reliable estimate of the average price of a single-track permanent download in Canada.

[91] Le prix de détail prédominant pour le téléchargement permanent d'une piste individuelle semble être de 99 ¢. iTunes vend pratiquement toutes ses pistes individuelles à ce prix. Certains concurrents vendent des pistes plus cher et offrent parfois des promotions à prix réduit. Même dans le scénario improbable où l'on aurait vendu 10 pour cent des pistes à 1,19 $, le prix moyen d'une piste n'augmenterait que de 2 ¢. Nous concluons que 99 ¢ est une estimation fiable du prix moyen au Canada d'un téléchargement permanent d'une piste.

[92] In the physical world, a reproduction triggers the same amount of remuneration whether it is sold as a single or as part of an album. On the other hand, the average price of a track is not the same when it is sold as part of an album. This price must be factored into our calculations. iTunes sells most of its albums for $9.99.[14] According to Mr. Cue, the average number of tracks on an album downloaded from iTunes is 13.[15] The average price per track on an album is then 77¢. According to numbers on sales of permanent downloads provided by CSI,[16] 55 per cent of all tracks sold as permanent downloads are singles, and 45 per cent are part of an album. Using these weighted figures yields an average price per track sold as a permanent download, either as a single or included on an album, of 89¢, resulting in a rate of 8.8 per cent [7.8¢ ÷ 89¢].

[92] Dans le monde matériel, une reproduction enclenche le versement d'un même montant, qu'elle soit vendue à la pièce ou fasse partie d'un album. Par contre, le prix moyen d'une piste individuelle n'est pas le même lorsqu'elle est vendue en tant que partie d'un album. Nous devons prendre en compte ce prix dans nos calculs. iTunes vend la plupart de ses albums 9,99 $.[14] D'après M. Cue, un album téléchargé à partir d'iTunes renferme en moyenne 13 pistes.[15] Le prix moyen par piste sur un album est donc 77 ¢. Selon les chiffres sur les ventes de téléchargements permanents fournis par CSI,[16] 55 pour cent de toutes les pistes vendues sous forme de téléchargements permanents sont individuelles et 45 pour cent font partie d'un album. Ces chiffres pondérés donnent un prix moyen de 89 ¢ par piste vendue sous forme de téléchargement permanent, qu'il s'agisse d'une piste individuelle ou faisant partie d'un album, ce qui se traduit par un taux de 8,8 pour cent [7,8 ¢ ÷ 89 ¢].

[93] Subject to an adjustment discussed later, we certify that rate. We want the tariff to generate the same amount of royalties as if online music services paid 7.8¢ per track. The following Table 1 shows that, if the relative share of album and single-track sales remains relatively stable, that result will be achieved.

[93] Nous homologuons ce taux sous réserve d'un ajustement dont nous traiterons plus loin. Nous voulons que le tarif produise le même montant de redevances que si les services de musique en ligne payaient 7,8 ¢ la piste. Le Tableau 1 qui suit montre qu'on atteindra ce résultat si la part relative des ventes d'albums et de pistes individuelles reste relativement stable.

**TABLE 1**
**ROYALTY FLOW AT 8.8 PER CENT OF RETAIL**

| | Units | Price per unit | Total number of tracks | Sales | Royalties at 8.8% of retail price | Effective penny rate |
|---|---|---|---|---|---|---|
| **Singles** | 7,258,100 | 99¢ | 7,258,100 | $7,185,519 | $632,326 | 8.7¢ |
| **Albums** | 464,600 | $9.99 | 6,039,800 | $4,641,354 | $408,439 | 6.8¢ |
| **Total** | | | 13,297,900 | $11,826,873 | $1,040,765 | 7.8¢ |

Based on Exhibit CSI-27.A, Table 1, page 3. The number of units of singles and albums are for year-to-date sales for July 23, 2006. A similar result was achieved using data recently released by Nielsen SoundScan Canada on downloads of tracks and albums in 2005 and 2006.

**TABLEAU 1**
**FLUX DE REDEVANCES À 8,8 POUR CENT DU PRIX DE DÉTAIL**

| | Unités | Prix unitaire | Nombre total de pistes | Ventes | Redevances à 8,8 % du prix de détail | Taux effectif en cents |
|---|---|---|---|---|---|---|
| **Pistes individuelles** | 7 258 100 | 99 ¢ | 7 258 100 | 7 185 519 $ | 632 326 $ | 8,7 ¢ |
| **Albums** | 464 600 | 9,99 $ | 6 039 800 | 4 641 354 $ | 408 439 $ | 6,8 ¢ |
| **Total** | | | 13 297 900 | 11 826 873 $ | 1 040 765 $ | 7,8 ¢ |

Basé sur la pièce CSI-27.A, Tableau 1, page 3. Le nombre d'unités de pistes individuelles et d'albums correspond aux ventes depuis le début de l'année 2006 jusqu'au 23 juillet 2006. Des résultats semblables ont été obtenus en utilisant les données publiées récemment par *Nielsen SoundScan Canada* portant sur les téléchargements de pistes et d'albums en 2005 et 2006.

*4. Setting a Minimum Price*

[94] Both sides agree that the tariff should set a minimum fee that is two-thirds of the royalties generated by the full rate at the average price of a track when sold as a single. We agree. The minimum fee per track for permanent download is set at 5.9¢.

[95] The Objectors argue that the application of a per-track minimum fee to albums would hurt emerging artists whose albums they say tend to be priced lower than $9.99, and would result in an unintended and unfair increase in the rate. With the increasing number of tracks on an album, the sum of the individual minimum fees would eventually surpass the amount that the application of the full rate to the price of the album would generate. To prevent this from happening, the Objectors proposed either that there be no minimum fee on albums or to replicate the approach followed in the United Kingdom, where minimum fees decrease as the number of tracks in a bundle increases. CSI argues on the other hand that if there is no minimum fee, bundles with a very large number of tracks could be sold at a price that would

*4. Établissement d'un minimum*

[94] Tous conviennent que le tarif devrait prévoir un prix minimum correspondant aux deux tiers des redevances que rapporte le plein taux au prix moyen d'une piste simple. Nous sommes d'accord. Le prix minimum par piste pour un téléchargement permanent est fixé à 5,9 ¢.

[95] Les opposantes soutiennent que l'imposition d'une redevance minimale par piste aux albums nuirait aux artistes de la relève, dont les prix des albums ont tendance, selon eux, à être établis à moins de 9,99 $, et entraînerait une augmentation non délibérée et injuste du taux. Avec le nombre croissant de pistes sur un album, la somme des minimums dépasserait finalement le montant que rapporterait l'application du plein taux au prix de l'album. Pour éviter que cela ne se produise, les opposantes ont proposé qu'il n'y ait aucune redevance minimale sur les albums ou que soit adoptée la méthode qu'on suit au Royaume-Uni, où le minimum diminue à mesure que le nombre de pistes dans un ensemble (« *bundle* ») augmente. CSI affirme par contre que, s'il n'y a aucune redevance minimale, des ensembles renfermant un très grand nombre de pistes

result in an inappropriately low payment of royalties.

[96] The evidence the Objectors offered in this respect is rather thin. In fact, there is no evidence on which we could find that emerging artists' albums are being sold for less. Also, as we already noted, there is evidence that the average number of tracks on a downloaded album is 13, not 15.

[97] We are willing however to set minimum fees that will allow online services to test new business models in this emerging market while ensuring fair compensation for rights owners. Applying the single track minimum fee to a bundle priced at $9.99 would result in royalties that are higher than the rate we set if the bundle contains more than 15 tracks. In our opinion, as for single tracks, the minimum fee for albums should be set at two-thirds of the royalties generated when the rate is applied to the average price of an album containing an average number of tracks. Consequently, we set the minimum fee for bundles at 4.5¢ per track [9.99 × 8.8% ÷ 13 × 0.67]. In this way, the payment of the minimum fee will be triggered only when a bundle selling at $9.99 contains 20 tracks or more. The Board will no doubt expect to be provided information about the impact of this measure in future proceedings dealing with this tariff.

***C. The Rate for Limited Downloads and On-Demand Streaming***

*1. Limited Downloads*

[98] We adopt the position agreed upon by the parties, to the effect that the rate for limited downloads should be two-thirds of the rate for

pourraient être vendus à un prix qui entraînerait le versement d'un montant de redevances trop peu élevé.

[96] La preuve que les opposantes ont présentée à ce sujet est plutôt mince. En fait, il n'y a aucune preuve permettant de conclure que les albums des artistes de la relève se vendent actuellement meilleur marché. Également, comme nous l'avons déjà noté, la preuve démontre qu'il y a sur un album téléchargé en moyenne 13 pistes, et non pas 15.

[97] Nous sommes prêts cependant à fixer des redevances minimales qui permettront aux services en ligne de mettre à l'essai de nouveaux modèles d'entreprise sur ce marché naissant, tout en assurant une rémunération juste pour les titulaires des droits. L'application de la redevance minimale par piste à un ensemble dont le prix est établi à 9,99 $ entraînerait des redevances qui seraient plus élevées que le taux que nous fixons si l'ensemble renferme plus de 15 pistes. Comme pour les pistes individuelles, on devrait, à notre avis, fixer la redevance minimale pour les ensembles aux deux tiers des redevances que rapporte l'application du taux au prix moyen d'un album renfermant un nombre moyen de pistes. Nous fixons, par conséquent, la redevance minimale par piste d'un ensemble à 4,5 ¢ [9,99 × 8,8 % ÷ 13 × 0,67]. De cette façon, il n'y aura enclenchement du versement du minimum que lorsqu'un ensemble vendu à 9,99 $ renferme 20 pistes ou plus. La Commission s'attendra sûrement à ce qu'on lui fournisse de l'information sur les répercussions de cette mesure à l'occasion des prochaines audiences portant sur le présent tarif.

***C. Taux pour les téléchargements limités et les transmissions sur demande***

*1. Téléchargements limités*

[98] Nous adoptons la position dont les parties ont convenu selon laquelle le taux pour les téléchargements limités devrait correspondre aux

permanent downloads. We certify a rate of 5.9 per cent. We remain concerned with the possibility that this approach may lead to some level of double discounting. The lower price charged for limited downloads already reflects a lower value, compared with permanent downloads. A lower royalty rate, intended to reflect a lower value for the right, might be an additional reduction to account for the same lower value.

deux tiers du taux pour les téléchargements permanents. Nous homologuons un taux de 5,9 pour cent. Nous craignons la possibilité que cette approche n'entraîne, dans une certaine mesure, un double escompte. Le prix moins élevé facturé pour les téléchargements limités reflète déjà une valeur inférieure par rapport aux téléchargements permanents. Un taux de redevance moins élevé, destiné à refléter une valeur inférieure pour le droit, pourrait constituer une réduction additionnelle qui tient compte de la même valeur inférieure.

[99] CSI's original proposal provided only one minimum fee for limited downloads. CSI now asks that different minimum fees apply according to whether or not a subscriber is authorized to copy the file onto a portable device. The Objectors first debated whether setting separate rates for portable limited downloads would go beyond the gazetted proposal. CSI's original proposal treated portable limited downloads as permanent downloads; moving them with limited downloads will result in lower rates. CSI's new proposal also has the merit of rationally accounting for the emergence of a business model that could not have been anticipated at the time of filing the tariff.

[99] Au départ, CSI ne prévoyait qu'une seule redevance minimale pour les téléchargements limités. Elle demande maintenant de moduler la redevance minimale suivant qu'un abonné est ou non autorisé à copier le fichier sur un appareil portatif. Les opposantes ont d'abord discuté de la question à savoir si le fait de fixer des taux séparés pour les téléchargements limités portables irait plus loin que la proposition publiée dans la *Gazette du Canada*. Dans sa proposition originale, CSI traitait les téléchargements limités portables comme des téléchargements permanents; les englober avec les téléchargements limités entraîne des taux moins élevés. La nouvelle proposition de CSI a également le mérite de tenir compte logiquement de la création d'un modèle d'entreprise qui n'aurait pas pu être prévu au moment du dépôt du tarif.

[100] CSI proposes that the ratio between the minimum fee payable when a subscriber can and cannot copy a file to a portable device be the same as for the amounts paid to record labels under the same circumstances. The Objectors would prefer that the ratio used be the one that exists between the average price paid for non-portable and portable limited downloads subscriptions. We agree with the Objectors' methodology, if only because it is more consistent with the approach we have used in setting the rate for permanent downloads. However, we would use the average between what Napster and MusicNet charge for such

[100] CSI propose que le rapport entre la redevance minimale exigible selon qu'un abonné peut ou non copier un fichier sur un appareil portatif soit le même que pour les montants versés aux maisons de disques dans ces cas. Les opposantes préféreraient que le rapport utilisé soit celui qui existe entre le prix moyen payé pour l'abonnement qui permet de copier un fichier sur un appareil portatif et celui qui ne le permet pas. Nous sommes d'accord avec la méthodologie des opposantes, ne serait-ce que parce qu'elle est plus conforme à l'approche que nous avons adoptée en fixant le taux pour les téléchargements permanents. Nous utiliserons

subscription as the average monthly subscription fees. These numbers are $9.50 when further reproduction on a portable device is not allowed, and $14.50 when it is. The resulting minimum fees that we certify are 37.4¢ and 57.0¢ per month respectively.

toutefois comme moyenne des frais d'abonnements mensuels la moyenne entre ce que facturent *Napster* et *MusicNet* pour un tel abonnement. Ces montants sont de 9,50 $ lorsque la reproduction sur un appareil portatif n'est pas permise et de 14,50 $ quand elle l'est. Les redevances minimales en découlant et que nous homologuons sont respectivement de 37,4 ¢ et de 57,0 ¢ par mois.

*2. On-Demand Streaming*

[101] CSI requested a tariff for services that only offer on-demand streaming, even though no such service currently exists. The Objectors suggest that we should not certify a tariff for non-existent services. This suggestion misses one important point. Tariffs are in essence prospective and can well target uses of which little is known. CSI has asked for a tariff that ostensibly targets a possible, protected use of its repertoire, and should be allowed to have a tariff certified for that use.

[102] CSI asked that the rate for on-demand streaming be set somewhere between the rate set for limited downloads and the rate pay audio services (Galaxie and Max Trax) have agreed to pay to CSI. Its assumption is that on-demand streams are worth less than limited downloads but more than pay audio, since on-demand streaming allows customers to select the tracks they listen to while pay audio services are non-interactive streaming. For their part, the Objectors proposed that the royalties be based on what commercial radio stations pay for the right to use CSI's repertoire, and proposed a rate of 0.5 per cent.

[103] We reject the Objectors' proposal for two reasons. First, music is worth more to on-demand streaming than to commercial radio, if only because listeners choose commercial radio for a variety of reasons, one of which is music, while

*2. Transmissions sur demande*

[101] CSI a demandé un tarif pour les services qui n'offrent que des transmissions sur demande, même s'il n'en existe actuellement aucun. Les opposantes prétendent que nous ne devrions pas homologuer un tarif pour des services qui n'existent pas. Cette prétention ne tient pas compte d'un point important. Les tarifs sont essentiellement prospectifs et peuvent viser des utilisations dont on sait peu de choses. CSI a demandé un tarif qui vise une possible utilisation protégée de son répertoire, et devrait pouvoir faire homologuer un tarif à cette fin.

[102] CSI veut que le taux pour les transmissions sur demande se situe entre le taux établi pour les téléchargements limités et ce que les services sonores payants (Galaxie et Max Trax) ont accepté de lui verser. Cela suppose que les transmissions sur demande valent moins que les téléchargements limités, mais davantage que les services sonores payants; les transmissions sur demande permettent aux consommateurs de choisir les pistes qu'ils écoutent, tandis que les services sonores payants sont des transmissions non interactives. Pour leur part, les opposantes ont proposé que les redevances reflètent ce que paient les stations de radio commerciales pour leur utilisation du répertoire de CSI, et ont proposé un taux de 0,5 pour cent.

[103] Nous rejetons la proposition des opposantes pour deux motifs. Premièrement, la musique a plus de valeur pour les transmissions sur demande que pour la radio commerciale, ne serait-ce que parce que les auditeurs choisissent

those who listen to on-demand streams do so exclusively for the music. Second, a radio station has the option of operating without making reproductions of musical works; a streaming service does not have that option. That makes the right to reproduce more valuable in a stream than over the radio.[17]

la radio pour diverses raisons, dont la musique, tandis que ceux qui écoutent une transmission sur demande le font exclusivement pour la musique. Deuxièmement, une station de radio peut fonctionner sans faire de reproduction d'œuvres musicales; un service de transmissions n'a pas cette possibilité, ce qui rend le droit de reproduire plus précieux pour le second que pour la première.[17]

[104] Once again, we are concerned with the possibility that CSI's approach may lead to some level of double discounting, if the retail price of a service offering only on-demand streams is lower than for one that also offers limited downloads. Notwithstanding this, we adopt CSI's methodology. This results in a rate of 4.6 per cent.

[104] Encore une fois, nous craignons que l'approche de CSI puisse entraîner, dans une certaine mesure, un double escompte, si le prix de détail d'un service n'offrant que des transmissions sur demande est inférieur à celui d'un service qui offre également des téléchargements limités. Nous adoptons néanmoins la méthodologie de CSI, ce qui donne un taux de 4,6 pour cent.

[105] CSI requested that the minimum fee for on-demand streaming be set as a function of the ratio between the percentage rate for on-demand streaming and limited downloads. The Objectors did not propose a minimum rate for this category. Applying CSI's methodology to the rates yields a minimum fee of 29.2¢ [4.6 ÷ 5.9 × 37.4].

[105] CSI a demandé que la redevance minimale pour les transmissions sur demande soit fixée en fonction du rapport entre le taux pour ces transmissions et le taux pour les téléchargements limités. Les opposantes n'ont pas proposé de taux minimum pour cette catégorie. L'application de la méthodologie de CSI aux taux donne une redevance minimale de 29,2 ¢ [4,6 ÷ 5,9 × 37,4].

*3. Adjusting the Rates to Account for the Use of Music not in CSI's Repertoire*

*3. Ajustement des taux pour tenir compte de l'utilisation de musique non incluse dans le répertoire de CSI*

[106] CSI initially proposed that the rates for limited downloads and on-demand streams be adjusted to reflect the fact that not all works an online service uses are in CSI's repertoire. During the hearings, it became clear that there was no need to do so. The Services know of every instance in which a track is downloaded or streamed; indeed, the DRMs they use with limited downloads report the number of times a download was played when the consumer's device "reports" to the service. CSI is therefore able to segregate tracks that use its repertoire from those that do not and to calculate royalties accordingly.

[106] CSI proposait au départ un ajustement des taux pour les téléchargements limités et les transmissions sur demande afin de rendre compte du fait que son répertoire n'inclut pas toutes les œuvres qu'utilise un service en ligne. Durant les audiences, il est devenu évident qu'un tel ajustement n'était pas nécessaire. Les services sont au courant de chaque téléchargement et de chaque transmission; les GDM dont ils se servent signalent même le nombre de fois qu'un téléchargement a été joué lorsque l'appareil du consommateur « communique » avec le service. CSI peut donc distinguer les pistes faisant appel à son répertoire de celles qui ne le font pas et calculer en conséquence les redevances.

[107] Both sides agree that royalties for services that offer only on-demand streams be calculated according to the number of individual streams. As for services that offer both on-demand streams and limited downloads, CSI asked that the royalties be calculated according to the number of plays, while the Objectors asked that they be calculated according to the number of downloads. The Objectors' main argument in this regard is that since this is a reproduction tariff, reproductions, not plays, should be used whenever possible to calculate the royalties. We disagree. When practical, reproduction royalties (and their distribution) should be a function of consumption. Recorded music is consumed by listening to it. The *CMRRA/SODRAC Inc. Commercial Radio Tariff, 2007* reflects this: a low-use station pays less than other stations not because it makes fewer copies, but because it airs the repertoire less. In this instance, however, we agree with Rogers that using plays to calculate royalties for limited downloads would create significant practical problems. Moreover, at least for the time being, there is little to gain in accuracy by using both plays and downloads to calculate royalties for services that offer both on-demand streams and limited downloads. Consequently, royalties for these services will be calculated using only downloads.

[107] Tous s'entendent pour dire que les redevances pour les services n'offrant que des transmissions sur demande soient fonction du nombre de transmissions. Pour les services offrant des transmissions sur demande et des téléchargements limités, CSI demande que les redevances soient fonction du nombre d'écoutes; selon les opposantes, c'est le nombre de téléchargements qui, lorsque c'est possible, devrait servir à ce calcul, au motif principal que les copies, non les écoutes, devraient servir à calculer les redevances dans un tarif portant sur la reproduction. Nous ne sommes pas d'accord. Lorsque cela est pratique, les redevances pour la reproduction devraient être établies (et réparties) en fonction de la consommation. La musique enregistrée se consomme en l'écoutant. Le *Tarif CMRRA/SODRAC inc. pour la radio commerciale, 2007* reflète ce principe : une station à faible utilisation paie moins qu'une autre station non pas parce qu'elle fait moins de copies, mais parce qu'elle diffuse moins le répertoire. Dans la présente affaire, toutefois, nous sommes d'accord avec Rogers. Le fait de calculer les redevances pour les téléchargements limités en fonction de l'écoute entraînerait des problèmes pratiques importants. Qui plus est, du moins pour l'instant, le résultat obtenu en utilisant tant l'écoute que le téléchargement pour établir les redevances des services qui offrent à la fois des transmissions sur demande et des téléchargements limités ne serait pas vraiment plus précis. Par conséquent, les redevances de ces services seront fonction uniquement du nombre de téléchargements.

### *D. The Rate Base*

[108] CSI requested that royalties be calculated using all revenues received in connection with the products and services that are subject to the licence covered by the tariff, including advertising revenues. The Objectors, on the other hand, argue that royalties should be based on what consumers pay to use the online service. They purport that CSI's proposed approach is

### *D. Base tarifaire*

[108] CSI a demandé qu'on calcule les redevances en fonction de tous les revenus découlant des produits et services assujettis à la licence visée par le tarif, y compris les revenus de publicité. Les opposantes, pour leur part, soutiennent que les redevances devraient reposer sur ce que paient les consommateurs pour utiliser le service en ligne. Selon elles, l'approche

contrary to what it has agreed to with services on the one hand, and with record labels on the other.

proposée par CSI est contraire à ce dont cette dernière a convenu avec les services d'une part, et avec les maisons de disques d'autre part.

[109] We agree with the Objectors' proposed approach, but for different reasons. First, online music services do not earn much more than what consumers pay. Second, we need to know whether, and to what extent, these other revenue streams are attributable to the use of CSI's repertoire. There was some evidence that advertising-based services may start offering music for free on the Internet. We think that these new services will remain relatively marginal, at least for the life of the current tariff. In the meantime, the minimum fees that we have set should generate sufficient royalties from those services. For these reasons, the tariff will use what consumers pay to the services as the rate base.

[109] Nous sommes d'accord avec l'approche proposée par les opposantes, mais pour des raisons différentes. Premièrement, les services de musique en ligne ne touchent pas beaucoup plus que ce que les consommateurs paient. Deuxièmement, nous devons savoir si, et dans quelle mesure, ces autres sources de revenus découlent de l'utilisation du répertoire de CSI. Certains éléments de preuve montrent que les services fondés sur la publicité pourraient commencer à offrir gratuitement de la musique sur Internet. Nous pensons que ces nouveaux services demeureront relativement marginaux, du moins pendant la durée de validité du présent tarif. Entre-temps, les redevances minimales que nous avons fixées devraient rapporter suffisamment de redevances de ces services. Pour ces raisons, le tarif aura comme base tarifaire ce que les consommateurs versent aux services.

### *E. The Role of Record Labels*

### *E. Le rôle des maisons de disques*

[110] CRIA's Class A members were allowed to object to the proposed tariff because they operate or intend to operate their own online services. Their interest goes beyond this, however. They wish to be able to act as intermediaries between CSI and the online services, presumably only with respect to the musical works that are embedded onto sound recordings that each of them owns. In order to achieve this, they ask that the tariff not specify who can apply for a licence.

[110] Les membres de la classe A de la CRIA ont pu s'opposer au tarif proposé parce qu'ils exploitent ou ont l'intention d'exploiter leurs propres services en ligne. Leur intérêt ne s'arrête cependant pas là. Ils désirent pouvoir jouer le rôle d'intermédiaires entre CSI et les services en ligne, probablement uniquement pour les œuvres musicales incorporées à des enregistrements sonores que possède chacun d'eux. Ils demandent, pour y arriver, que le tarif ne précise pas qui peut demander une licence.

[111] CRIA's members argue that the systems currently in place to clear rights for prerecorded CDs can easily be put to use in the online market, allowing them to provide fully cleared products here as in the physical world. They point to certain difficulties which online services have encountered in obtaining licences from CSI, all of which they argue can be overcome if record

[111] Les membres de la CRIA soutiennent qu'on peut facilement avoir recours, sur le marché en ligne, aux systèmes actuellement établis pour affranchir les droits relatifs aux CD préenregistrés, ce qui leur permettrait d'y offrir des produits entièrement affranchis, comme dans un environnement matériel. Ils font mention de certaines difficultés que les services en ligne ont

labels are allowed to sub-licence CSI's repertoire to the services.

éprouvées pour obtenir des licences de CSI, difficultés qui, selon eux, peuvent toutes être surmontées si les maisons de disques sont autorisées à octroyer des sous-licences aux services pour le répertoire de CSI.

[112] CSI opposes this request. It notes that the request does not come from the online music services themselves, who all have agreements with CSI. It submits that there are no valid legal or practical reasons to allow the record labels to step into the shoes of the actual users of the repertoire and that there is no precedent for such action. CSI acknowledges that there have been difficulties in processing the applications of online services. It points out that given the sheer numbers involved, it was to be expected that setting up the required systems would take some time. CSI has hired additional staff to address the problem. It mentions the labels' allegedly less than stellar record of compliance with the MLA as an indication that they should not be allowed to interpose themselves in the relationship between user and collective. Finally, CSI insists that it must be able to maintain a direct relationship with the users in order to properly monitor the actual use of its repertoire.

[112] CSI s'oppose à cette demande. Elle souligne que la demande ne provient pas des services, qui ont tous des ententes avec CSI. Elle fait valoir qu'il n'existe aucune raison valable, sur le plan juridique ou pratique, de permettre aux maisons de disques de se substituer aux utilisateurs réels du répertoire et qu'il n'existe aucun précédent pour une telle mesure. CSI reconnaît que le traitement des demandes des services en ligne a soulevé des difficultés. Elle fait remarquer qu'étant donné l'énormité du nombre de demandes, il fallait s'attendre à ce que la mise en place des systèmes nécessaires prenne un certain temps. On a commencé à embaucher du personnel additionnel pour s'attaquer au problème. CSI signale qu'en raison des antécédents de conformité à la MLA des maisons de disques, qui n'auraient rien d'admirable, celles-ci ne devraient pas être autorisées à s'interposer dans la relation entre l'utilisateur et la société de gestion. Enfin, CSI soutient qu'elle doit pouvoir maintenir un rapport direct avec les utilisateurs afin de surveiller adéquatement l'usage réel de son répertoire.

[113] We are convinced that the tariff should not allow the record labels to interpose themselves between CSI and the online music service, for the following reasons.

[113] Nous sommes convaincus que le tarif ne devrait pas permettre aux maisons de disques de s'interposer entre CSI et le service de musique en ligne, pour les motifs suivants.

[114] First, allowing the record labels to licence the use of CSI's repertoire pursuant to this tariff would add an unnecessary layer of communication between the collective and the actual user of its repertoire. As Mrs. Fortier explained, this has not been common practice in the past; it should not become common practice in this case.[18]

[114] Premièrement, permettre aux maisons de disques d'octroyer une licence d'utilisation du répertoire de CSI en vertu du présent tarif ajouterait inutilement un niveau de communication entre la société de gestion et l'utilisateur réel de son répertoire. Comme M<sup>me</sup> Fortier l'a expliqué, ce n'était pas la pratique courante dans le passé; il ne faudrait pas que cela le devienne dans ce cas.[18]

[115] Second, to allow the record labels to interpose themselves would overly complicate the

[115] Deuxièmement, permettre aux maisons de disques de s'interposer compliquerait trop la

way in which CSI would obtain the information to which it is entitled. If all four major labels were to avail themselves of the tariff, CSI would receive, in each reporting period, at least five reports with respect to each service: one from the service and one from each label. Allowing independent labels to enter the fray would further complicate these relationships.

façon dont CSI obtiendrait l'information à laquelle elle a droit. Si les quatre grandes maisons se prévalaient du tarif, CSI recevrait, pour chaque période de déclaration, au moins cinq rapports pour chaque service : un du service et un de chaque maison. Permettre à des maisons indépendantes d'entrer en lice compliquerait ces relations encore davantage.

[116] Third, CSI has already established direct relationships with all the services that operate in Canada. There seems to be no need to disrupt those relationships.

[116] Troisièmement, CSI a déjà établi des relations directes avec tous les services faisant affaire au Canada. Il n'y a aucune raison de perturber ces relations.

[117] Fourth, the person who is ultimately liable for the royalties pursuant to the tariff remains the actual user of the repertoire. Providing unreliable information can result in increased liability. Thus, it is probable that the person who bears the ultimate burden for an error is least likely to commit that error.

[117] Quatrièmement, la personne devant payer, en fin de compte, les redevances prévues au tarif demeure l'utilisateur réel du répertoire. Fournir des renseignements peu fiables risque d'entraîner une responsabilité accrue. Il est donc probable que la personne qui supporte en dernière analyse le fardeau d'une erreur est la moins susceptible de commettre cette erreur.

[118] Fifth, the efficiencies that the record labels contend can be achieved by dealing through them are far from certain. No one knows whether it would be more efficient for labels to report on part of the sales of several online services or for each service to report on its total sales from a number of overlapping catalogues of sound recordings. Nothing prevents the labels from convincing CSI and the services that they can help to make reporting under the tariff more efficient. Nothing prevents CSI from rearranging its reporting channels; we will not force it to do so.

[118] Cinquièmement, les gains d'efficacité que les maisons de disques prétendent qu'il est possible de réaliser en traitant par leur entremise sont loin d'être certains. Nul ne sait s'il serait plus efficace pour les maisons de faire rapport d'une partie des ventes de plusieurs services en ligne ou pour chaque service de faire rapport de son chiffre d'affaires global à partir d'un certain nombre de catalogues d'enregistrements sonores qui se recoupent. Rien n'empêche les maisons de persuader CSI et les services qu'elles peuvent contribuer à faire rapport plus efficacement aux termes du tarif. Rien n'empêche non plus CSI de remanier sa filière de communication de rapports; nous ne l'obligerons pas à le faire.

[119] In the past, the Board has stated that generally speaking, a tariff should target uses, not users.[19] The *Act*, not the Board, determines who is liable to pay for a protected use. A tariff can neither impose liability where the *Act* does not nor remove liability where it exists.

[119] La Commission a déclaré dans le passé qu'en règle générale, un tarif devrait viser les utilisations, non pas les utilisateurs.[19] C'est la *Loi*, non pas la Commission, qui détermine qui est tenu de payer pour une utilisation protégée. Un tarif ne peut ni imposer une responsabilité lorsque la *Loi* ne le fait pas, ni dégager une responsabilité lorsque celle-ci existe.

[120] The Board has also stated that generally speaking, a tariff should target both the right to do and the right to authorize. When administered collectively, the right to authorize an act is subject to the same regime as the act itself. Furthermore, the authorization right, though separate, co-exists with the right to do.[20]

[121] We agree with both propositions. We do not consider that proscribing record labels from availing themselves of this tariff contradicts either proposition.

[122] Thus, many of the tariffs that do not mention whom it can be collected from involve persons who are jointly liable for a single act. This is the case, for example, of the non-broadcast television service and the cable operator for the single communication that occurs when a program is transmitted from the service, to the operator and then on to the operator's subscriber. Simply put, it is not possible to split a single act. Here, as we pointed out, the record labels cannot claim to be the actual users, though they may carry some liability for that use if they purport to authorize it. It is possible to segregate what the labels do from what the online music services do. The Board has already underlined that it is legally possible to assign the right to do to a collective and the right to authorize to another.[21]

[123] Also, almost all tariffs that deal with both the right to act and the right to authorize are SOCAN tariffs. If SOCAN did not file tariffs for both acts, subsection 67.1(4) of the *Act* would prevent it from seeking payment from those who authorize. Here, this is not the case; record labels will not be able to avail themselves of the tariff, but CSI will retain the option to license them if it wishes, and to sue them if they purport to authorize the unlicensed use of its repertoire.

[120] La Commission a aussi déclaré qu'en règle générale, un tarif devrait viser aussi bien le droit d'accomplir que le droit d'autoriser. Lorsqu'il est administré collectivement, le droit d'autoriser un acte est assujetti au même régime que l'acte lui-même. En outre, le droit d'autorisation, bien que distinct, existe de pair avec le droit d'accomplir.[20]

[121] Nous sommes d'accord avec les deux propositions. À notre avis, prescrire que les maisons de disques ne peuvent se prévaloir du présent tarif ne contredit pas l'une ou l'autre proposition.

[122] Ainsi, nombre de tarifs qui ne mentionnent pas de qui les redevances peuvent être perçues visent des personnes solidairement responsables d'un même acte. C'est le cas, par exemple, du service de télévision spécialisée et payante et du câblodistributeur, pour la communication unique qui se produit lorsqu'une émission est transmise à partir du service au câblodistributeur, puis de là à l'abonné de ce dernier. Il est tout simplement impossible de scinder un acte unique. Dans le cas présent, comme nous l'avons fait remarquer, les maisons de disques ne peuvent pas prétendre être les utilisateurs réels, même si elles peuvent assumer une certaine responsabilité pour cette utilisation si elles prétendent l'autoriser. Il est possible de séparer ce que font les maisons de ce que font les services de musique en ligne. La Commission a déjà souligné qu'il est légalement possible d'accorder le droit d'accomplir à une société de gestion et le droit d'autoriser à une autre.[21]

[123] Également, presque tous les tarifs qui portent sur le droit d'accomplir et le droit d'autoriser sont des tarifs de la SOCAN. Si la SOCAN n'a pas déposé de tarif pour les deux actes, le paragraphe 67.1(4) de la *Loi* l'empêche de demander un paiement à ceux qui autorisent. Ici, ce n'est pas le cas. Les maisons de disques ne pourront se prévaloir du tarif, mais CSI pourra toujours leur octroyer une licence si elle le désire ou les poursuivre en justice si elles prétendent autoriser l'utilisation sans licence de son répertoire.

[124] Other tariffs specifically provide that they do not apply to certain types of use. This is what we propose to do. The relevant provision prevents the record labels from interposing themselves only to the extent that a CSI licence is required. Labels will remain free to licence the use of musical works where they are already authorized to do so.

[124] D'autres tarifs prévoient expressément qu'ils ne s'appliquent pas à certains types d'utilisation. C'est ce que nous proposons de faire. La disposition pertinente empêche les maisons de disques de s'interposer uniquement dans la mesure où une licence de CSI est nécessaire. Les maisons de disques seront toujours en mesure de permettre l'utilisation d'une œuvre musicale lorsqu'elles sont déjà autorisées à le faire.

[125] Had we not been convinced that we are able to expressly prevent record labels to avail themselves of the tariff, we would have designed the administrative provisions so as to ensure that CSI would not be obliged to deal with multiple reporting channels. For example, we would have provided that unless CSI consented, one, and only one, report per service could be filed in a reporting period.

[125] Si nous n'avions pas été persuadés que nous pouvons expressément empêcher les maisons de disques de se prévaloir du tarif, nous aurions conçu des dispositions administratives qui auraient fait en sorte que CSI ne soit pas obligée de traiter avec plusieurs filières de communication de rapports. Par exemple, nous aurions prévu qu'à moins que CSI n'y consente, il y aurait dépôt d'un seul et unique rapport par service durant une période de déclaration.

### *F. Ability to Pay*

[126] The online music industry is in its infancy. It is small by any standard, with relatively low profit margins and long payouts. Still, we believe that online services can absorb the royalties we set without raising prices while at the same time remaining able to meet their mid- and long-term business objectives.

### *F. Capacité de payer*

[126] L'industrie de la musique en ligne en est encore à ses débuts. Selon tous les critères, elle est petite, sa marge bénéficiaire est relativement peu élevée et ses dépenses sont importantes. Nous croyons quand même que les services en ligne peuvent absorber les redevances que nous fixons sans avoir à hausser leurs prix, tout en conservant la capacité de respecter à moyen et à long terme leurs objectifs commerciaux.

[127] We think that it is appropriate to phase in this new tariff by applying a discount of 10 per cent to the rates we would set otherwise. This discount is the same that the Board granted when it first certified the Pay Audio Services Tariff. This discount is intended to apply only for the life of this tariff.

[127] Nous pensons qu'il y a lieu de faire entrer progressivement en vigueur le nouveau tarif en appliquant un escompte de 10 pour cent aux taux que nous fixerions autrement. Cet escompte est le même que celui que la Commission a accordé lorsqu'elle a pour la première fois homologué le tarif pour les services sonores payants. Il n'est destiné à s'appliquer que durant la durée de validité du présent tarif.

### *G. Validation Measures*

[128] There is evidence before us which permits us to compare the rates we certify with those in three major foreign markets.

### *G. Mesures de validation*

[128] Le preuve au dossier nous permet de comparer les taux que nous homologuons à ceux qui sont établis sur trois grands marchés étrangers.

[129] In the United States, for the reproduction of the musical work, permanent downloads currently are subject to the compulsory licence rate of 9.1¢ per track, which corresponds to 9.1 per cent of the retail price of a download from the *iTunes Music Store*.[22] That rate will be subject to review by the Copyright Royalty Board for the period starting January 1, 2008.

[129] Aux États-Unis, pour la reproduction des œuvres musicales, les téléchargements permanents sont actuellement assujettis au taux de la licence obligatoire de 9,1 ¢ la piste, ce qui correspond à 9,1 pour cent du prix de détail d'un téléchargement à partir du *iTunes Music Store*.[22] Ce taux sera soumis à un examen du *Copyright Royalty Board* pour la période débutant le 1er janvier 2008.

[130] In Germany, the *Gesellschaft für musikalische Aufführungs-und mechanische Vervielfältigungsrechte* (GEMA) intends to collect an effective rate of 12 per cent of gross revenues for the right to communicate and reproduce the musical work (not the sound recording) with respect to permanent and limited downloads. The German association representing producers of musical recordings has proposed a royalty of 6 per cent generally and 4.8 per cent for the downloading of music onto cell phones.

[130] En Allemagne, la *Gesellschaft für musikalische Aufführungs-und mechanische Vervielfältigungsrechte* (GEMA) veut percevoir un taux effectif de 12 pour cent des revenus bruts pour le droit de communiquer et de reproduire les œuvres musicales (non pas les enregistrements sonores) dans le cas des téléchargements permanents et limités. L'association allemande représentant les producteurs d'enregistrements musicaux a proposé une redevance de 6 pour cent en général et de 4,8 pour cent pour le téléchargement de musique sur un téléphone cellulaire.

[131] In the United Kingdom, the Mechanical Copyright Protection Society, the Performing Rights Society and the British Phonographic Industry settled on a rate of 8 per cent for the reproduction and communication of musical works in all downloads and on-demand streams. The rate base, however, continues to be the object of a dispute which will be settled by the Copyright Tribunal.

[131] Au Royaume-Uni, la *Mechanical Copyright Protection Society*, la *Performing Rights Society* et la *British Phonographic Industry* ont convenu d'un taux de 8 pour cent pour la reproduction et la communication d'œuvres musicales dans tous les téléchargements et toutes les transmissions sur demande. La base tarifaire continue cependant de faire l'objet d'un différend qui sera réglé par le *Copyright Tribunal*.

[132] The rates we are certifying would be 8.8, 5.9 and 4.6 per cent before discount. After discount, they are 7.9, 5.3 and 4.1 per cent. The simple average of these rates are 6.4 and 5.8 per cent. The weighted average rates, reflecting the relative importance of each type of download, would be much closer to the higher, permanent download rate.

[132] Les taux que nous homologuons seraient de 8,8, de 5,9 et de 4,6 pour cent avant escompte. Ils sont, après escompte, de 7,9, de 5,3 et de 4,1 pour cent. Les moyennes simples de ces taux sont 6,4 et 5,8 pour cent. Les taux moyens pondérés, qui reflètent l'importance relative de chaque type de téléchargement, se rapprocheraient beaucoup plus du taux plus élevé s'appliquant aux téléchargements permanents.

[133] The Board has often stated that caution must be exercised when comparing the rates it

[133] La Commission a souvent déclaré qu'il faut faire preuve de prudence lorsqu'il y a

certifies to those that apply in other jurisdictions. We nevertheless find that looking at the U.S., U.K. and German situations brings us some measure of comfort that the rates we set in this decision are fair to both copyright owners and copyright users.

comparaison des taux qu'elle homologue et de ceux qui s'appliquent dans d'autres ressorts. Nous concluons néanmoins que l'examen de ce qui se pratique aux États-Unis, au Royaume-Uni et en Allemagne confirme, dans une certaine mesure, que les taux que nous homologuons dans la présente décision sont justes à la fois pour les titulaires de droits et pour les utilisateurs de ces droits.

### VI. TARIFF WORDING

[134] Arriving at the wording of the tariff we certify proved to be a complicated task. Consultations started almost as soon as the hearings ended, when we addressed a series of questions on the structure of the tariff and what it ought to address. Over more than four months, parties, helped by Board counsel, exchanged several sets of correspondence. They met with our counsel for one full-day meeting. They received two drafts, the second being significantly different than the first. Consultations ended barely two weeks ago.

[135] The wording of the tariff we certify is very different from what was published in the *Canada Gazette* or what CSI proposed in the end. This explains why this section of our reasons is somewhat longer than usual.

*Definitions*

[136] We removed a number of unnecessary definitions. Of those that remain or were removed, some deserve comment.

[137] Section 3 lists what an online music service "and its authorized distributors" are allowed to do pursuant to the tariff. The parties proposed a definition of authorized distributor which we did not include in the tariff. The notion simply does not need to be defined.

### VI. LIBELLÉ DU TARIF

[134] Il a été difficile de finaliser le libellé du tarif que nous homologuons. Les consultations ont débuté très peu de temps après la fin des audiences, par une série de questions que nous avons adressées concernant la structure du tarif et ce dont il devrait traiter. Pendant plus de quatre mois, les parties, avec l'aide de notre conseiller juridique, ont procédé à plusieurs échanges. Elles se sont rencontrées avec notre conseiller pour une journée entière. Elles ont reçu deux projets, dont le deuxième différait substantiellement du premier. Les consultations se sont terminées il y a deux semaines à peine.

[135] Le libellé du tarif que nous homologuons est fort différent du projet publié dans la *Gazette du Canada* ou de ce que CSI proposait en bout de piste. Voilà pourquoi la présente section de nos motifs est passablement plus longue qu'à l'habitude.

*Définitions*

[136] Nous avons omis plusieurs définitions inutiles. Parmi celles qui restent ou que nous avons enlevées, certaines méritent qu'on les commente.

[137] L'article 3 décrit ce qu'un service de musique en ligne « et ses distributeurs autorisés » peuvent faire en vertu du tarif. Les parties ont proposé une définition de distributeur autorisé que nous n'avons pas retenue. Le concept peut fort bien se passer de définition.

[138] CSI asked that the tariff apply to on-demand streams and limited downloads only when they are offered for a fee. CSI and the Objectors agreed that to achieve this, a definition of subscriber was required. We believe that simply using the term without defining it is sufficient. The notion of subscription implies that a payment is made for what is the object of the subscription. Furthermore, in the longer term, we believe that it would probably be appropriate to include such services in the tariff even when they are financed through other means, such as advertising.

[138] CSI demandait que le tarif vise les transmissions sur demande et les téléchargements limités uniquement lorsqu'il faut payer pour les obtenir. CSI et les opposantes s'entendaient pour dire que pour y arriver, il fallait définir ce qu'est un abonné. Nous croyons qu'il suffit d'utiliser le terme sans le définir. La notion d'abonnement implique d'effectuer un paiement pour ce à quoi on s'abonne. Qui plus est, à plus long terme, nous croyons qu'il conviendrait sans doute que le tarif vise de tels services et ce, même s'ils sont financés autrement, au moyen de la publicité, par exemple.

[139] The definition of portable limited download was the subject of lengthy discussions. We agree with Rogers that portable limited downloads should be defined as copies that are made by the subscriber. When a service allows the file to be delivered by it to more than one device, as we described in paragraph 87, this should not be considered a portable download.

[139] La définition de téléchargement limité portable a fait l'objet de longs échanges. Nous sommes d'accord avec Rogers que le téléchargement limité portable devrait être une copie que fait l'abonné. Le service permettant à un fichier d'être livré à plus d'un appareil, comme celui que nous décrivons au paragraphe 87, ne devrait pas être considéré comme un téléchargement portable.

*Application*

[140] The tariff allows an online music service and its authorized distributors to make all reproductions required in connection with the operation of a service. It also allows the service to provide 30-second promotional and other previews without incurring any liability or reporting obligations.

*Application*

[140] Le tarif permet au service de musique en ligne et à ses distributeurs autorisés de faire toutes les reproductions nécessaires à l'exploitation du service. Il permet aussi au service de fournir des fichiers promotionnels et d'écoute préalable de 30 secondes sans que cela n'entraîne de paiement ou d'obligations de rapport.

[141] The tariff does not apply to medleys. In the physical market, these uses apparently are not licensed through the MLA; they are the subject of separate deals. It is no imposition on those who negotiate those deals to require them to also address uses in the online market.

[141] Le tarif ne vise pas les pots-pourris. Dans le marché physique, on n'utilise pas la MLA pour autoriser ces utilisations; elles font l'objet de licences distinctes. Ce n'est pas trop exiger de ceux qui négocient ces licences de tenir compte des utilisations dans le marché en ligne.

*Reporting Requirements*

[142] The information that an online music service is required to provide CSI is considerably less than what CSI was asking for. The following

*Exigences de rapport*

[142] L'information qu'un service de musique en ligne doit fournir à CSI est moindre, et de loin, que ce que CSI demandait. Les principes suivants

principles guided us in deciding what should and should not be provided.

nous ont guidés pour décider ce qui devrait ou non être fourni.

[143] First, CSI should get enough information to allow it to identify which files use its repertoire and which do not. For this reason, services must report descriptive information concerning files for which, according to the service, no licence is required.

[143] Premièrement, CSI devrait obtenir suffisamment de renseignements pour lui permettre de distinguer les fichiers qui utilisent son répertoire de ceux qui ne le font pas. Pour ce motif, les services doivent fournir des renseignements descriptifs sur les fichiers pour lesquels le service soutient qu'une licence n'est pas nécessaire.

[144] Some objectors fear that CSI may seek to use the information it gets on works that are not in its repertoire to recruit new members. We do not think it necessary to account for this possibility for two reasons. First, the reporting timelines are simply too tight for CSI to be able to gain any significant advantage in this respect. Second, there is no reason to believe that CSI has done this in the past or may be thinking of doing it in the future. Needless to say, any indication to the contrary would result in the Board changing the reporting requirements and imposing restrictions on what CSI may use the information for.

[144] Certaines opposantes craignent que CSI utilise les renseignements concernant les œuvres ne faisant pas partie de son répertoire pour recruter de nouveaux membres. Il ne nous semble pas nécessaire de tenir compte de ce scénario pour deux motifs. D'abord, les échéances de rapport sont bien trop courtes pour permettre à CSI d'obtenir un avantage important sous cet aspect. Ensuite, rien ne permet de croire que CSI a agi ainsi par le passé ou pourrait songer à agir ainsi à l'avenir. Rien ne sert d'ajouter qu'une indication à l'effet contraire entraînerait un resserrement considérable de l'information que CSI obtient en vertu du tarif et de l'usage qu'elle peut en faire.

[145] Second, given the way in which business has been conducted to date in related markets, CSI should obtain a certain amount of information that is otherwise redundant. CSI has convinced us that there is enough uncertainty in the information it gets pursuant to the MLA, for example, to justify providing a certain amount of alternative, additional information. That being said, redundancy should be limited to what is clearly informative and helpful. Asking for more information than necessary penalizes those who provide CSI with all the information it needs in the first place. Generally speaking, the best way to get correct information is to ask for it and to sanction those who do not comply.

[145] Deuxièmement, compte tenu de la façon dont les choses se passent dans des marchés connexes, CSI devrait obtenir certains renseignements qui sont par ailleurs redondants. CSI nous a convaincus, par exemple, que l'information qu'elle obtient en vertu de la MLA est suffisamment aléatoire pour justifier qu'on lui fournisse certains renseignements alternatifs, additionnels. Cela dit, la redondance devrait se limiter à ce qui est nettement instructif et utile. Demander plus d'information que nécessaire pénalise ceux qui fournissent déjà à CSI les renseignements dont elle a besoin. Règle générale, la meilleure façon d'obtenir la bonne information est de la demander puis de pénaliser ceux qui ne le font pas.

[146] Third, CSI should get not only the information it requires to calculate and distribute

[146] Troisièmement, CSI devrait obtenir non seulement l'information qu'il lui faut pour

royalties, but also other information that will allow it to develop a sense of overall compliance without having to resort to systematic audits. This is why we would have required services to provide information about their overall sales, had CSI not agreed in the end to abandon this request. On the other hand, financial information concerning files for which no licence is required ought to be kept to a minimum.

[147] Financial information concerning files using works whose status is uncertain is another matter. Thus, when CSI realized that we would probably not require services to provide it with detailed sales reports for all files, it asked to be provided with at least a list of all files that had been streamed or downloaded in a month. We would not have done so for files for which no licence is required. We thought of requiring some sales information regarding files using works whose status is uncertain but did not do so in the end. For this tariff, at least, it seems to us that CSI will be sufficiently busy dealing with files it knows to be in its repertoire. Moreover, some services already provide complete sales data to CSI simply because it is more convenient to do so. The matter should be reexamined when the time comes to certify the next tariff.

[148] Fourth, if information is essential, a service ought to provide it even if this means getting it from someone else. Music labels do not always provide online music services the name of the author of a musical work, the International Standard Recording Code assigned to a sound recording or a variety of information about the album on which a sound recording may have been released in physical format. This is not reason enough to relieve the service from providing the information. Services require a licence. They need CSI's help to determine what is in its repertoire and what is not. Basic

calculer et répartir les redevances, mais aussi celle lui permettant de se faire une idée du niveau de conformité sans devoir recourir à des vérifications systématiques. Nous aurions donc exigé des services qu'ils fassent part de leurs ventes totales si CSI n'avait pas en bout de piste abandonné sa demande à cet effet. Par contre, la fourniture de données financières portant sur les fichiers ne nécessitant pas de licence doit être ramenée au strict nécessaire.

[147] Il faut aborder autrement les données financières portant sur les fichiers utilisant des œuvres dont le statut est incertain. Ainsi, après avoir constaté que nous n'exigerions sans doute pas que les services lui fournissent des rapports de vente détaillés pour tous les fichiers, CSI a demandé de recevoir au moins la liste de tous ceux qui sont transmis ou téléchargés durant le mois. Nous ne l'aurions pas fait pour les fichiers ne nécessitant pas de licence. Nous avons songé à exiger la fourniture de certaines données concernant les fichiers utilisant des œuvres dont le statut est incertain, mais nous ne l'avons finalement pas fait. Aux fins du présent tarif à tout le moins, il nous semble que CSI en aura bien assez de traiter des fichiers qu'elle sait faire partie de son répertoire. Qui plus est, certains services fournissent déjà à CSI des rapports de vente complets tout simplement parce que cela leur simplifie la tâche. Il faudra réexaminer la question avant d'homologuer le prochain tarif.

[148] Quatrièmement, si un renseignement est essentiel, le service devrait le fournir même s'il doit se le procurer ailleurs. Les maisons de disque ne fournissent pas toujours aux services de musique en ligne le nom de l'auteur de l'œuvre musicale, le code international normalisé des enregistrements attribué à l'enregistrement sonore ou d'autres renseignements concernant l'album sur lequel un enregistrement a pu être publié sur support physique. Cela ne suffit pas à exempter le service de fournir ces renseignements. Les services ont besoin d'une licence. Ils ont besoin de l'aide de CSI pour

copyright information should therefore be provided. In other cases, where the information is helpful but not essential, the information ought to be provided only if available.

[149] In this tariff, however, we are willing to make an exception. This is a first tariff with significant retroactive effects. CSI's licences with the services do not oblige them to provide the information. Requiring the labels and the services to adjust their systems rapidly could prove unnecessarily costly. However, it appears that the worldwide reporting format currently being discussed contemplates including most if not all of that information. In any event, the services should expect to be required to supply this information in all cases in the near future.

*Information Flow*

[150] Upon starting operations, a service will report and update monthly basic information about itself and the files it posts on its server. CSI will then tell the service which files use CSI's repertoire. We are conscious that in so doing, we are certifying a tariff that entrenches the systematic violation of the rights of those whom CSI does not represent. For practical reasons, it would be difficult to act otherwise, at least for the time being. This may be due in large part to what could be seen as a variety of applications of the so-called long tail effect to this market. First, the market was originally structured around the compulsory licence that existed in Canada until 1989 and that still exists in the United States. Second, this market requires players to rapidly digitize and offer back catalogues whose owners may not always be easy to identify. Third, the quest to offer everything that is available means that a lot of what is offered may be consumed little, if at all; understandably, no one wishes to expend resources to determine who owns the rights in something that generates no royalties. This is a

établir ce qui est ou non dans son répertoire. Ils devraient donc fournir des renseignements de base concernant le droit d'auteur. Autrement, lorsque l'information recherchée est utile sans être essentielle, elle ne devrait être fournie que si elle est disponible.

[149] Dans le présent tarif, toutefois, nous sommes prêts à faire une exception. Il s'agit d'un premier tarif dont l'effet rétroactif est important. Les licences de CSI n'obligent pas les services à fournir ces renseignements. Exiger des maisons de disques et des services qu'ils ajustent leurs systèmes à courte échéance pourrait coûter fort cher inutilement. Cela dit, il semble que le format mondial de rapport dont on discute en ce moment pourrait inclure la plupart, sinon la totalité, des renseignements pertinents. À tout événement, les services devraient s'attendre à devoir bientôt fournir cette information dans tous les cas.

*Flux d'information*

[150] Dès que son exploitation débute, un service fournira et mettra à jour mensuellement des données de base sur le service et sur les fichiers qu'il offre sur son serveur. CSI indiquera ensuite au service les fichiers qui utilisent son répertoire. Nous sommes conscients qu'en agissant ainsi, nous homologuons un tarif qui enchâsse la violation systématique des droits de ceux que CSI ne représente pas. Pour des raisons pratiques, il serait difficile d'agir autrement, du moins pour l'instant. Cet état de fait pourrait être en grande partie imputable à ce qui pourrait être perçu comme diverses applications à ce marché du soi-disant effet de longue traîne. Premièrement, le marché a d'abord été structuré en fonction de la licence obligatoire qui existait au Canada jusqu'en 1989 et qui existe encore aux États-Unis. Deuxièmement, ce marché exige que les participants numérisent et offrent rapidement des catalogues existants dont les propriétaires pourraient ne pas toujours être faciles à identifier. Troisièmement, la tentative d'offrir tout ce qui est disponible signifie qu'on peut consommer peu, ou pas du tout, une large part de

matter that will have to be re-examined in subsequent proceedings.

ce qui est offert; personne ne désire, naturellement, consacrer des ressources pour déterminer qui possède les droits sur une piste qui ne rapporte aucune redevance. C'est là une question qu'il faudra réexaminer dans le cadre d'affaires subséquentes.

[151] Each month, a service will report to CSI the information required to calculate the royalties owing and CSI will do so, based on the reports each service files, and then invoice the service. The Objectors' request to have the option of calculating royalties themselves or asking CSI to do so would create unnecessary uncertainty and delays.

[151] Chaque mois, le service fournira à CSI les renseignements requis pour calculer les redevances payables, CSI effectuera ce calcul en utilisant ces renseignements puis fera parvenir un état de compte au service. La demande des opposantes d'avoir l'option de calculer les redevances elles-mêmes ou de demander à CSI de le faire engendrerait de l'incertitude et des délais inutiles.

[152] Reporting and payment dates have been set to allow CMRRA to continue to distribute royalties within 75 days of each quarter. This can be made easier by spreading the reporting burden over time. For this reason, information is to be exchanged every month even though payments are made only once per quarter.

[152] Nous avons établi les échéances de rapport et de paiement de façon à permettre à la CMRRA de continuer à répartir les redevances au plus tard 75 jours après la fin du trimestre. Il sera plus facile d'y arriver en étalant les obligations de rapport. Pour ce motif, l'échange de renseignements se fait à chaque mois même si les paiements sont effectués seulement une fois par trimestre.

[153] Involving CSI in the information chain has certain consequences. Since the system is not fully self-reporting, for example, it is possible that a service may pay an incorrect amount of royalties through no fault of its own. A service should not then be held liable for the consequences of CSI's errors. We have reworded the usual provisions dealing with payment adjustments, liability for audit costs and interests accordingly. We did not grant CSI's request that liability be shifted only where incorrect payments are the result "solely" of an error or omission on the part of CSI. We do not wish to put all the burden of a joint error on only one party.

[153] Certaines conséquences découlent du fait d'impliquer CSI dans l'échange de renseignements. Ainsi, comme le fardeau de rapport n'incombe pas uniquement à l'utilisateur, il est possible qu'un service verse un montant de redevances incorrect sans avoir lui-même commis d'erreur. Un service ne devrait pas faire les frais des erreurs que CSI commet. Nous avons réécrit en conséquence les dispositions usuelles traitant des ajustements de paiement, de la responsabilité pour les frais de vérification et des intérêts. Nous n'avons pas fait droit à la demande de CSI voulant que la responsabilité pour un paiement erroné ne lui incombe que s'il découle « uniquement » d'une erreur ou d'une omission de sa part. Nous ne souhaitons pas imposer le fardeau d'une erreur conjointe à une seule personne.

[154] On the other hand, we have not allowed the Objectors to audit CSI's books. CSI will provide

[154] Par contre, nous n'avons pas permis aux opposantes de vérifier les livres de CSI. Cette

detailed royalty calculations; these should be sufficient for a service to verify if the amount being asked of it is correct.

dernière fournira un calcul détaillé des redevances, ce qui devrait suffire au service pour vérifier si le montant qu'on lui demande est le bon.

*Termination of the Licence*

[155] CSI asks that the tariff provide for the termination of the licence if a service does not pay royalties, does not comply with the tariff or becomes bankrupt or insolvent. The only other tariffs to do so are the Canadian Broadcasters Rights Agency (CBRA) Media Monitoring Tariffs. The Objectors disagree. They point out, among other things, that certain provisions of the *Bankruptcy and Insolvency Act* (*BIA*) and of the *Companies' Creditors Arrangements Act* prevent the termination of agreements.

*Résiliation de la licence*

[155] CSI demande que le tarif prévoie la résiliation de la licence si un service ne verse pas ses redevances, ne se conforme pas au tarif, fait faillite ou devient insolvable. Les seuls autres tarifs dans lesquels on retrouve une telle disposition sont les tarifs de l'Agence des droits des radiodiffuseurs canadiens (CBRA) pour la veille médiatique. Les opposantes sont en désaccord. Elles soulignent, entre autres, que certaines dispositions de la *Loi sur la faillite et l'insolvabilité* (*LFI*) et de la *Loi sur les arrangements avec les créanciers des compagnies* empêchent qu'on mette fin à des ententes.

[156] Our understanding is that the *BIA* addresses copyright issues differently. It seems to us that if, as section 83 of the *BIA* provides, an assignment of copyright is terminated by operation of the law (that is, without the scenario having been provided for in the assignment contract), then *a fortiori*, a licence can provide that a bankrupt licensee shall not be entitled to avail itself of the licence. We see no reason why copyright owners should subsidize an insolvent operation. Furthermore, we would rather let the ordinary courts of law determine whether or not a provision such as section 13 of the tariff is or not effective.

[156] Selon nous, la *LFI* traite différemment les questions de droit d'auteur. Il nous semble que si son article 83 permet de mettre fin à une cession de droit d'auteur par opération de la loi (et donc, sans que le contrat de cession permette la résiliation), il faut, *a fortiori*, qu'une licence puisse stipuler que le licencié en faillite ne peut plus s'en prévaloir. Nous ne voyons pas pourquoi les titulaires de droits d'auteur devraient subventionner une exploitation insolvable. Qui plus est, nous préférons laisser aux tribunaux de droit commun le soin de décider si une disposition telle l'article 13 du tarif est efficace ou non.

[157] Subsections 65.1(1) and (2) of the *BIA* may prevent CSI from ending the licence for the sole reason that royalties are owing "in respect of" a period before the filing of a notice of intention or proposal. Apparently, this allows a trustee to use the licence as long as it is complied with from the date of the notice of intention or proposal. Subsection 65.1(4) also provides that a person is entitled to require immediate payment for the use of "licensed property" after the filing

[157] Les paragraphes 65.1(1) et (2) de la *LFI* pourraient empêcher CSI de mettre fin à la licence au seul motif que des redevances sont impayées « à l'égard » d'une période antérieure au dépôt de l'avis d'intention ou de la proposition. Cela semble permettre au syndic de se prévaloir de la licence pour autant qu'il s'y conforme à partir de la date de l'avis ou de la proposition. Le paragraphe 65.1(4) prévoit par ailleurs qu'une personne peut exiger d'être payée

of the notice or proposal, or to require the further advance of money or credit. In the longer term, a solution may be to provide that an insolvent service must pay royalties in advance. Again, analyzing this matter is better left to another time.

sur-le-champ pour l'utilisation de « biens ... faisant l'objet d'une licence » après le dépôt de l'avis ou de la proposition ou encore, d'exiger la prestation de nouvelles avances de fonds ou de nouveaux crédits. À plus long terme, il conviendrait peut-être de prévoir qu'un service insolvable doit verser des avances sur ses redevances. Encore une fois, il est préférable de remettre cette analyse à plus tard.

*Security, TPMs and Other Requirements*

[158] The tariff does not deal with minimum security requirements, the use of technological protection measures (TPMs), the nature and extent of the information regarding copyright that a service should provide to its customers or customer content usage rules. From the outset, it was agreed that at most, the tariff would require that the service comply with the same rules as those agreed upon with the music labels. As time went on, it became clear that such a provision would be redundant at best. Then recently, PureTracks announced that it had started offering some files without any attached DRM software. It is better to address this matter later, to the extent it is relevant.

*Sécurité, MPT et autres exigences*

[158] Le tarif ne traite pas de normes minimales de sécurité, de l'utilisation de mesures de protection technologiques (MPT), de la nature ou du contenu des renseignements concernant le droit d'auteur que le service devrait fournir à ses clients ou de normes d'utilisation du contenu par ces derniers. Dès le départ, on s'entendait pour dire que le tarif, tout au plus, prévoirait que le service se conforme aux règles convenues avec les maisons de disques. Avec le temps, il est devenu évident qu'une telle disposition serait au mieux redondante. Puis récemment, PureTracks a annoncé qu'elle offrait désormais certains fichiers libres de tout logiciel de GDN. Il vaut mieux remettre cette question à plus tard, si tant est qu'elle soit même pertinente.

*Transitional Provisions*

[159] We have allowed for extended delays to file reports that relate to periods before the tariff was certified. The agreements between CSI and the online services require the services to make interim payments until the Board certified the tariff. The discrepancies between these payments and what the final tariff sets, though not insignificant, are relatively modest. Furthermore, CSI has not yet provided many of the reports it must supply in order for the services to know what they ought to pay. Under the circumstances, we see no need to provide for the payment of interests on the difference.

*Dispositions transitoires*

[159] Nous avons allongé les délais d'échange des rapports visant des périodes écoulées avant que le tarif soit homologué. En vertu des ententes entre CSI et les services en ligne, ces derniers effectuent des versements provisoires jusqu'à ce que la Commission homologue un tarif. La différence entre ces paiements et ce que le tarif final établi, sans être insignifiante, est relativement modeste. Qui plus est, CSI n'a pas encore fourni plusieurs des rapports qui doivent être remis aux services pour leur permettre de savoir combien ils doivent payer. Dans les circonstances, nous ne croyons pas qu'il soit nécessaire de prévoir le versement d'intérêts sur la différence.

## VII. FINAL RATES

[160] The following Table 2 shows the rates we obtain before the application of the 10 per cent discount, and the ones we certify, after its application.

## VII. TAUX DÉFINITIFS

[160] Le Tableau 2 qui suit montre les taux que nous obtenons avant l'application de l'escompte de 10 pour cent, et ceux que nous homologuons, après son application.

**TABLE 2**

| Category | Rates before discount | Rates certified, after discount |
|---|---|---|
| **Permanent Download** | 8.8% of the amount paid by a consumer<br>Minimum fee:<br>4.5¢ per file in a bundle;<br>5.9¢ per file in all other cases | 7.9% of the amount paid by a consumer<br>Minimum fee:<br>4.1¢ per file in a bundle;<br>5.3¢ per file in all other cases |
| **Limited Download** | 5.9% of the amounts paid by subscribers<br>Minimum fee:<br>57.0¢ per month, per subscriber if portable limited downloads are allowed;<br>37.4¢ if not | 5.3% of the amounts paid by subscribers<br>Minimum fee:<br>51.3¢ per month, per subscriber if portable limited downloads are allowed;<br>33.7¢ if not |
| **On-demand Stream** | 4.6% of the amounts paid by subscribers<br>Minimum fee:<br>29.2¢ per month, per subscriber | 4.1% of the amounts paid by subscribers<br>Minimum fee:<br>26.3¢ per month, per subscriber |

**TABLEAU 2**

| Catégorie | Taux avant escompte | Taux homologués, après escompte |
|---|---|---|
| **Téléchargement permanent** | 8,8 % du montant payé par le consommateur<br>Redevance minimale :<br>4,5 ¢ par fichier faisant partie d'un ensemble;<br>5,9 ¢ pour tout autre fichier | 7,9 % du montant payé par le consommateur<br>Redevance minimale :<br>4,1 ¢ par fichier faisant partie d'un ensemble;<br>5,3 ¢ pour tout autre fichier |
| **Téléchargement limité** | 5,9 % des sommes payées par les abonnés<br>Redevance minimale :<br>57,0 ¢ par mois, par abonné si les téléchargements limités portables sont permis;<br>37,4 ¢ si ce n'est pas le cas | 5,3 % des sommes payées par les abonnés<br>Redevance minimale :<br>51,3 ¢ par mois, par abonné si les téléchargements limités portables sont permis;<br>33,7 ¢ si ce n'est pas le cas |
| **Transmission sur demande** | 4,6 % des sommes payées par les abonnés<br>Redevance minimale :<br>29,2 ¢ par mois, par abonné | 4,1 % des sommes payées par les abonnés<br>Redevance minimale :<br>26,3 ¢ par mois, par abonné |

[161] It is not possible to estimate with any reliability the total amount of royalties that this tariff will generate for CSI. However, based on numbers recently publicly released by Nielsen SoundScan Canada, it is possible to estimate that the tariff on permanent downloads would generate royalties close to $2 million in 2006, and slightly under $1 million in 2005.

[161] Il est impossible d'estimer avec quelque degré de fiabilité que ce soit le montant total des redevances que le présent tarif rapportera à CSI. D'après les chiffres récemment rendus publics par *Nielsen SoundScan Canada*, il est cependant possible d'évaluer que le tarif pour les téléchargements permanents rapporterait près de 2 millions de dollars de redevances en 2006 et un peu moins de 1 million de dollars en 2005.

Le secrétaire général,

Claude Majeau
Secretary General

**ENDNOTES**

1. Exhibit CSI-27.A, Tab C, *Mobile Music, Juniper Research*, at page 157.

2. When CMRRA is not a publisher's exclusive agent, it is possible to obtain a licence directly from the publisher.

3. At least to the extent that those are not private copies within the meaning of Part VIII of the *Act*.

4. Ringtones that use the original sound recording of a musical work. Throughout the hearings, parties referred to them as "ringtunes".

5. Though the parties to NDMAs are American, they do apply to Canadian transactions.

6. Professor Globerman defined the value of the marginal product as "the monetary value of the increased output associated with additional usage of the input holding usage of other inputs constant".

7. No one alluded to the fact that when the "decision" to charge the same price to reproduce a musical work on vinyl, cassette or CD was made, that price was regulated. It still is in the United States. This might have influenced the decision to continue charging a single price in Canada even after 1989, when free bargaining was allowed to occur. In our view, this is not sufficient to allow us to ignore the historical reality of the MLA, especially since the single price continued to prevail after deregulation, which occurred at a time when all three known prerecorded formats were still competing.

8. Making a prerecorded CD involves other copies that were not mentioned, including

**NOTES**

1. Pièce CSI-27.A, onglet C, *Mobile Music, Juniper Research*, à la page 157.

2. Lorsque la CMRRA n'est pas l'agent exclusif d'un éditeur, il est possible d'obtenir une licence directement de ce dernier.

3. Du moins dans la mesure où il ne s'agit pas de copies privées au sens de la Partie VIII de la *Loi*.

4. Les sonneries utilisant l'enregistrement sonore original d'une œuvre musicale. Pendant toute l'audience, les parties ont parlé de « *ringtunes* ».

5. Même si les parties aux NDMA sont américaines, les ententes s'appliquent à des opérations canadiennes.

6. Le professeur Globerman a défini la valeur du produit marginal comme étant [TRADUCTION] « la valeur monétaire de l'augmentation de l'extrant se rattachant à l'usage additionnel de l'intrant en maintenant l'utilisation des autres intrants constante ».

7. On a passé sous silence le fait que lorsque la « décision » de facturer le même prix pour reproduire une œuvre musicale sur un vinyle, une cassette ou un CD a été prise, ce prix était réglementé. Il l'est encore aux États-Unis. Cela a pu influencer la décision de continuer à facturer un seul prix au Canada même après 1989, moment où on a déréglementé le prix. Ce n'est pas suffisant, à notre avis, pour que nous ne tenions pas compte de la réalité historique de la MLA, étant donné surtout que le prix unique a continué à prévaloir après la déréglementation, qui est survenue à une époque où les trois formats préenregistrés connus se faisaient encore concurrence.

8. La fabrication d'un CD préenregistré nécessite des reproductions dont on n'a pas

those that are used to embed the musical work onto the CD; the master recording itself is not used for that purpose.

fait mention, y compris celles qui sont utilisées pour graver l'œuvre musicale sur le disque compact; on n'utilise pas la bande maîtresse à cette fin.

9. The legal perspective is altogether different however, as we point out in paragraph 84 below.

9. La perspective juridique est fort différente toutefois, comme nous le soulignons plus loin, au paragraphe 84.

10. See U.S. Copyright Act, 17 U.S.C. §115 (c) (3) (E) (ii) (II).

10. Voir la loi américaine sur le droit d'auteur, 17 U.S.C. §115 (c) (3) (E) (ii) (II).

11. The tariff allowing an online music service to communicate a musical work will be set following hearings into SOCAN Tariff 22, which are due to start on April 17, 2007.

11. Le tarif permettant à un service de musique en ligne de communiquer une œuvre musicale sera fixé après les audiences relatives au tarif 22 de la SOCAN qui doivent débuter le 17 avril 2007.

12. See, for example, decision of October 20, 2006 certifying the NRCC Background Music Tariff, 2003-2009, at paragraph 114.

12. Voir, entre autres, la décision du 20 octobre 2006 homologuant le Tarif SCGDV pour la musique de fond, 2003-2009, au paragraphe 114.

13. Decision of December 12, 2003 certifying the Private Copying Tariff, 2003-2004, at page 27.

13. Décision du 12 décembre 2003 homologuant le Tarif pour la copie privée, 2003-2004, à la page 27.

14. There are some sales at higher prices, but nothing indicates that they have a significant impact on the market.

14. On en vend certains à des prix plus élevés, mais rien n'indique que ces ventes ont des répercussions importantes sur le marché.

15. We prefer this figure to the one of 15, used by Messrs. Audley and Hyatt, which is based on data provided by SoundScan, for two reasons. First, the average number of tracks is increased by the availability of prerecorded compilation albums which are not generally available online. Second, the evidence offered by Mr. Cue as to what occurs at iTunes, the dominant player in the market, is the best evidence available.

15. Nous préférons ce chiffre à 15, utilisé par MM. Audley et Hyatt, qui est fondé sur des données fournies par *SoundScan*, et ce, pour deux raisons. Premièrement, les albums de compilation préenregistrés, qui ne sont généralement pas offerts en ligne, accroissent le nombre moyen de pistes. Deuxièmement, la preuve présentée par M. Cue au sujet de ce qui se passe chez iTunes, l'acteur dominant sur le marché, est la meilleure preuve disponible.

16. Exhibit CSI-27.A, at page 3, Table 1.

16. Pièce CSI-27.A, à la page 3, Tableau 1.

17. Decision of March 28, 2003 certifying the CMRRA/SODRAC Inc. Commercial Radio

17. Décision du 28 mars 2003 homologuant le Tarif de la CMRRA/SODRAC inc. pour la

Tariff, 2001-2004, at page 13; Decision of August 18, 2006 certifying SOCAN Tariff 24 (Ringtones), at paragraphs 93 to 99.

18. There are, of course, exceptions to this. Royalties for public performances in concert venues and reception rooms are mostly collected from the venues, not the performers. There are practical reasons for doing so, which are simply not present here, as we explain in the following paragraph.

19. Decision of March 15, 2002 certifying the SOCAN-NRCC Pay Audio Services Tariff, 1997-2002, at pages 27-28; Decision of March 19, 2004 certifying SOCAN Tariffs 2.A (Commercial Television) and 17 (Pay and Specialty Television), at pages 38-39.

20. See generally, decision of March 26, 2004 dealing with an issue of jurisdiction concerning SOCAN Tariff 4 (Concerts), at pages 8-9.

21. *Idem*, at page 11.

22. A "digital phonorecord delivery" does not trigger the equivalent of the Canadian communication right in the United States.

radio commerciale, 2001-2004, à la page 13; Décision du 18 août 2006 homologuant le Tarif 24 de la SOCAN (Sonneries), aux paragraphes 93 à 99.

18. Il existe évidemment des exceptions à ce principe. En règle générale, on perçoit les redevances pour l'exécution publique de musique dans les salles de concert ou de réceptions des exploitants de ces salles et non des interprètes. Il y a des motifs pratiques pour ce faire, motifs qui n'existent tout simplement pas en l'espèce, comme nous l'expliquons dans le paragraphe suivant.

19. Décision du 15 mars 2002 homologuant le Tarif SOCAN-SCGDV applicable aux services sonores payants, *1997-2002*, aux pages 27-28; Décision du 19 mars 2004 homologuant les tarifs 2.A (Télévision commerciale) et 17 (Télévision payante et spécialisée) de la SOCAN, aux pages 38-39.

20. Voir de façon générale, la décision du 26 mars 2004 disposant d'une question de compétence portant sur le tarif 4 de la SOCAN (Concerts), aux pages 8-9.

21. *Idem*, à la page 11.

22. La distribution d'un enregistrement sonore numérique n'enclenche pas le versement de l'équivalent du droit canadien de communication aux États-Unis.

# LAW 13.6

## U.K. COPYRIGHT TRIBUNAL DECISION (2007)

19/07/2007 **CT84-90/05**

**IN THE MATTER OF A REFERENCE UNDER THE COPYRIGHT, DESIGNS AND PATENTS ACT 1988 (as amended)**

**Before: His Honour Judge Fysh QC, SC (Chairman)**
**Rear-Admiral James Carine and**
**Colonel Roderick Arnold**

**BETWEEN:**

(1) THE BRITISH PHONOGRAPHIC INDUSTRY LIMITED
(2) MUSICNET (UK) LIMITED
(3) YAHOO ! UK LIMITED
(4) AOL (UK) LIMITED
(5) REALNETWORKS LIMITED
(6) NAPSTER LLC
(7) SONY UNITED KINGDOM LIMITED
(8) iTUNES S.a.r.l.
(9) O2 (UK) LIMITED
(10) T-MOBILE INTERNATIONAL (UK) LIMITED
(11) VODAFONE UK CONTENT SERVICES LIMITED
(12) ORANGE PERSONAL COMMUNICATIONS SERVICES LIMITED

**Applicants and Interveners**

**and**

(1) MECHANICAL-COPYRIGHT PROTECTION SOCIETY LIMITED
(2) PERFORMING RIGHT SOCIETY LIMITED
(3) BRITISH ACADEMY OF COMPOSERS AND SONGWRITERS

**Respondents and Intervener**

## INTERIM DECISION

## INDEX

Representation
A Glossary
Authorities cited in the Decision
Dates of hearing
Documentary citations in the Decision
Terminology: 'Online' and 'Offline', 'downloads' and 'streams'

I INTRODUCTION

Prologue
Miscellaneous preliminary matters

II THE TRIBUNAL'S APPROACH: GENERAL PRINCIPLES

The Statutory framework
General approach
Tribunal decisions considered

III THE NEW JOL

The eve of trial settlements: An overview
The New JOL
The Royalty Table
Permanent downloads
Limited downloads and on-demand services
Pure Webcasting
Special Webcasting

IV THE WITNESSES

Witnesses of fact
Expert witnesses

V COMPARATORS

Is the New JOL a proper 'comparator'?
The need for minima

VI THE MUSICAL OFFERINGS

Back to back music: Pure Webcasting
Is the CRCA Agreement: a proper comparator?

**Representation**:

***Applicants and Interveners***

28 September 2006 [ie prior to the partial settlement]

*Ian Mill QC* and *Mark Vinall* (instructed by *Olswang*) appeared on behalf of the British Phonographic Industry Limited.

*Kenneth Steinthal* (New York Bar), *Joe Salvo* (New York Bar) and *Kambiz Larizadeh* of *Weil, Gotshal & Manges* appeared on behalf of MusicNet UK Limited, Yahoo! UK Limited, AOL (UK) Limited, RealNetworks Ltd, Napster LLC and Sony United Kingdom Limited.

*Tom Weisselberg* (instructed by *Davenport Lyons*) appeared on behalf of iTunes S.a.r.l. (Interveners)

*Henry Carr QC* (instructed by Baker & Mackenzie) and *Ben Allgrove* of *Baker & McKenzie* appeared on behalf of O2 (UK) Limited, T-Mobile International (UK) Limited, Vodafone UK Content Services Limited and Orange Personal Communications Services Limited.

***Respondents and Intervener***

*Lawrence Rabinowitz QC, Robert Howe* and *Ben Jaffey* (instructed by *Denton Wilde Sapte*) appeared on behalf of the Mechanical-Copyright Protection Society Limited and the Performing Right Society Limited.

*Charles Aldous QC* and *Edmund Cullen* (instructed by *Denton Wilde Sapte*) appeared on behalf of the British Academy of Composers & Songwriters (Interveners).

15 November 2006 to 17 January 2007

***Applicants and Interveners***

*Kenneth Steinthal* (of the New York Bar), *Joe Salvo* (of the New York Bar) and *Kambiz Larizadeh* of *Weil, Gotshal & Manges*) appeared on behalf of Yahoo! UK Limited, AOL (UK) Limited and RealNetworks Ltd.

*Tom Weisselberg* (instructed by *Davenport Lyons*) appeared on behalf of iTunes S.a.r.l.(Interveners)

*Henry Carr QC* (instructed by Baker & Mackenzie)and *Ben Allgrove* of *Baker & McKenzie*) appeared on behalf of O2 (UK)

Limited, T-Mobile International (UK) Limited, Vodafone UK Content Services Limited and Orange Personal Communications Services Limited.

***Respondents and Intervener***

*Laurence Rabinowitz QC*, *Robert Howe* and *Ben Jaffey* (instructed by *Denton Wilde Sapte*) appeared on behalf of the Mechanical-Copyright Protection Society Limited and the Performing Right Society Limited.

*Charles Aldous QC* and *Edmund Cullen* (instructed by *Denton Wilde Sapte*) appeared on behalf of the British Academy of Composers & Songwriters (Interveners).

**A Glossary**[1]

**The Academy** or **BACS** : British Academy of Composers and Songwriters. Members of the Academy are generally also members of **PRS** and/or **MCPS**.

**The Act:** The Copyright, Designs and Patents Act 1988 (as amended), otherwise 'CDPA '88'.

**The Alliance: PRS** and **MCPS.** These are two collecting societies. Though separate legal entities, PRS and MCPS merged their operations in 1997. In order for any exploitation of music to take place online it is necessary both to make copies of musical works (see **MCPS** below) and to communicate them in public over the Internet or in the case of the MNOs, wirelessly over a mobile network (see **PRS** below). Hence the presence of the combination of the two in these Applications has been called 'the Alliance'.

**The Applicants:** Collectively (and in context), iTunes, the **MNOs** and the **Remaining MSPs.**

**BPI:** The British Phonographic Industry Limited. This is the UK record industry trade association and represents the interests of more than 300 record companies based in the UK.

**CRCA:** Commercial Radio Companies Association. The CRCA Agreement contains the Alliance's licence terms for commercial radio

**DRM:** Digital Rights Management. A technology applicable to downloads which requires the authorised user to obtain a licence to make use of protected material which he possesses.

**FTD:** Full track download. Approximately equivalent to a permanent download.

**iTunes:** iTunes s.a.r.l

**JOL:** A Joint Online Licence promulgated by **the Alliance.** There have been a number of these all of which have been proposed on an annual basis, the first having been promulgated in 2002. All of them have now been superseded.

[1] A glossary of technical and industry terms is to be found at Annex B to the Alliance's closing written submissions. By the time of writing this Decision, this glossary had been largely (but not completely) agreed between the parties.

**The New JOL:** The New Joint Online Licence. That is, the **JOL** as substantially amended as a result of a settlement with **BPI** (and others) on 28 September 2006 and which is in issue in these proceedings.

**LD/ODS:** Limited download/on - demand streaming

**MCPS**: Mechanical-Copyright Protection Society Limited. **MCPS** licences the mechanical right (i.e. the right to authorise or prohibit the making of copies of musical works)[2] on behalf of its members who are authors, composers and publishers.

**MNO:** Mobile Network Operator, being the following four[3] parties:

**O2:** O2 (UK) Limited
**T-Mobile**: T-Mobile International (UK) Limited
**Vodafone:** Vodafone UK Content Services Limited
**Orange:** Orange Personal Communications Services Limited.

The interest of the MNOs in these proceedings is both as retailers of online music ( and who therefore require a licence from the Alliance) and also as mobile internet service providers for third party retailers of online music.

**MSP:** Music Service Provider. The MSPs in these Applications are referred to as **'The Remaining MSPs',** also referred to as **'The Webcasters':**

**Yahoo !:** Yahoo ! UK Ltd ,
**AOL:** AOL (UK) Ltd, and
**RealNetworks** : RealNetworks Limited .

**PPL:** Phonographic Performance Ltd. PPL was formed by EMI and Decca in 1934.

**PRS**: Performing Right Society Limited. PRS licences the communication of works to the public together with the performing right for the benefit of a membership similar to that of MCPS[4]. Both PRS and MCPS are collecting societies and licensing bodies within the meaning of the Act, s 116(2)

**PRT**: Performing Right Tribunal. The predecessor to the **Copyright Tribunal.**

**Authorities cited in the Decision:**

*AIRC v PPL* [1993] EMLR 181
*AIRC v PPL* 16 January 1986 (unrep. Harman J)
*AEI v PPL* [1998] EMLR 240, [1998] RPC 335
*APRA v ABC* (1985) 5 IPR 449
*BPI v MCPS (no 2)* [1993] EMLR 86
*BSkyB v PRS* [1998] EMLR 193 *BACTA v PPL* [1992] RPC 149
*Cala Homes v McAlpine Ltd* [1995] FSR 818
*ITCA v PRS* (PRT 38/81, unrep. October 19 1983)
*Manx Radio v PPL* (unrep) PRT 18/64 29 May 1965
*PRS v BSkyB* [1998] EMLR 193
*PRS v BEDA* (PRT unrep, 1 August 1989), and Hoffmann J [1993] EMLR 325.

[2] The Act, ss. 17 and 18.
[3] Of the five mobile network operators in the UK
[4] The Act, ss 19 and 20.

*R v Chen* [2006] EWCA Crim. 2526
*Rockwater v Technip France SA* [2004] RPC 919
*SBC v PRS* [1991] FSR 573
*The Ikarian Reefer* [1993] FSR 563
*Universities UK Ltd v CLA* [2002] RPC 693
*Working Men's Club & Institute Union Ltd v PRS* [1992] RPC 227

**Dates of hearing**:

28 September, 14-17, 20-24 and 28 November,
5-8 December 2006, 15-17 January 2007 and 16- 17 July 2007.

**Documentary citations in the Decision**

Trial bundles will be referred to by binder number, tab and where appropriate, page number: e.g. A3/2/18.
Witness statements and Expert reports will be referred to by the surname of the witness or expert followed by the number of his/her statement/report and the paragraph number: e.g. Ferguson 1/ §6
Transcript evidence: will be referred to by day, page and where appropriate, line number: e.g. D11/187/5

**Terminology: 'online' and 'offline', 'downloads' and 'streams'.**

Since these terms are used throughout this Decision and in spite of the fact that many readers of it will be well aware of what they mean, we have nevertheless thought it best to record the ambit and context of our usage of these terms. This case is concerned only with digital recordings of music. It is possible to access and to download a digital music file via the Internet. It is also possible to access digital music using mobile telephone handsets, the latter being served via mobile telephone networks which in turn are operated by **MNOs**. Both possibilities are collectively referred to as **'online'** music access. On the other hand, the delivery of music via a physical medium, typically a CD, a DVD, a tape or a vinyl (or other) record, *or* via a radio or television broadcast *or* by cable, has been collectively included within the term **'offline'** music. A **download** means a file of recorded music intended to be copied onto a consumer's local storage device from a remote source such as a website server. On the other hand, a **stream** is a file of continuous music which may be listened to through a consumer's receiving computer or device but only to the extent required to allow listening to the file at substantially the same time as the file is transmitted i.e. no playable copy of the music remains.

# I INTRODUCTION

## *Prologue*

1. This Decision concerns a number of references to the Copyright Tribunal ('the Tribunal') relating to the terms of licences issued by two collecting societies, PRS and MCPS (collectively called 'the Alliance'), which enable music legitimately to be made available online to members of the public.

2. More than twenty years ago music first became available in digital form; the CD began to replace tapes and vinyl records as the standard carrier of music. The next major development in the music industry has already proved to be considerably more radical than the digital revolution. Everywhere one now sees people of all ages wired into MP3[5] players such as iPods. They are enjoying the ubiquitous benefits of music downloaded from the Internet. Perhaps even more members of the public enjoy such music by being in possession of mobile telephones with Internet access and of course, of personal computers.

3. Those disputing the terms of the Alliance's licences are most of the powerful protagonists of the online music industry. We are aware that much is at stake in these proceedings. Though there has been a measure of compromise among the parties, the issues remaining have proved difficult to resolve largely as a result of the complex and changing nature of the online music offerings involved. There are in fact three very broad types of such offerings: permanent downloads, limited downloads and on-demand streaming/webcasting. However, as we shall show, what is actually happening in the music industry is more complex.

4. Among the references to the Tribunal, this group of applications[6] must be unique.

   - In the first place, this has been the first reference which is concerned with valuing the use of copyright material (in this case, the work of composers, writers and publishers of music), which is available *online* for sourcing and consumption.

   - Secondly, these Applications originally involved more parties than any other before it of which we are aware, all of the parties being major players in various aspects of the online entertainment, communications and music industries.

   - Thirdly, this Application is concerned with what one expert called 'new phenomena'. The means by which online music is made available to users and the manner in which it can be manipulated for consumption is complex and sophisticated and seemed to grow as the case went on. This appears to be the

[5] MPEG-1 Audio Layer 3. A digital audio encoding and compression format.

[6] These were in fact both references and interventions (see Copyright Tribunal Rules 1989 ('CTR') rr. 3 and 7). For convenience we have used the word '**Applications**' to describe them collectively.

result of both rapidly advancing technology and innovative business models. Not surprisingly, this development has proved to be a lucrative forum for establishing all manner of advertising and subscription, thereby generating new revenue streams within the industry. The Tribunal is not therefore dealing with the traditional music exploitation such as by the sale of a physical product (such as a CD), by broadcasting or by making music available within a particular environment, say, a night club. We are now concerned with the availability of music embedded as it were, in a variety of electronic vehicles ('business models') devised by highly intelligent and motivated innovators for an increasingly sophisticated, user-led consumption[7].

- Before the hearing, a settlement of a major portion of the dispute occurred. The status of this very recent settlement as a relevant comparator for what remains to be adjudicated has been an important ongoing issue in the case.

- Finally, we believe that this reference must have been about the most costly ever to have been litigated in the Tribunal, the parties having spent (so we understand) some £12 million in costs by the date of the conclusion of the hearing [8]. We shall have more to say about this at the end of this Decision.

5. At the Tribunal's request, an agreed *dramatis personae* has been prepared (as **Annex 1** hereto[9]) which identifies (*inter alia*) the parties and epitomises their relevant commercial interests.

6. It is important at the outset to have an overview of the events leading to the Applications. We shall first identify the participants as they originally were when the Applications were initiated and then see how the position has changed. As may be seen from the title page of this Decision, the original Applicants were twelve in all. All were actively involved in one way or another in inter alia the online and mobile music industry[10]. They fell into three broad groups: the BPI, the MNOs and the MSPs.

7. Shortly before the hearing, a degree of settlement (both complete and qualified) reduced the number of Applicants - and also the number of contentious issues. The terms of the licensing schemes originally proposed by the Alliance for the use of online music which triggered these Applications ('the JOLs') were amended as a result of this settlement and became a new scheme, **'the New JOL.'**[11] This New JOL generated substantially amended (or supplemental) Statements of Case, all of which are to be found in Volume A6. We would add that all the licensing proposals which have been in issue have been 'schemes' within the meaning of the Act, s 116 (1).

[7] Not all forms of online exploitation of the Alliance repertoire are covered by existing and proposed licences. Ringtones for example (though mentioned from time to time) are without the present terms of reference.

[8] According to a statement which was posted on the Alliance's website in December 2006.

[9] **Annex 1** is actually a combined *dramatis personae*, witness list (containing abbreviated details of both witnesses of fact and expert witnesses) and a chronology. There was partial disagreement in the detail of one item of this document and in addition, some suggestion that such detail was confidential. We have considered these suggestions and do not believe either to be sustainable.

[10] The Academy was a late intervener –a *respondent* intervener.

[11] H/1/13.

8. **The Alliance** were represented by Mr Rabinowitz QC, Mr Robert Howe and Mr Jaffey. In the Glossary, we referred to why a Joint Online Licensing agreement is needed. There is in fact a technical reason (see '*Dubbing*' below) why online exploiters of music need licences from both the PRS and the MCPS in order to make their services available to the public online.

9. Prior to trial, on 10 November 2006, the Alliance and the MNOs agreed certain facts which have been included in (inter alia) the MNOs' Revised Opening Skeleton Argument as Annex 1. The record of the agreement is referred to as 'the **Agreed Facts**', the idea having been to reduce the scope of the evidence and argument to be advanced at trial. In correspondence with the Tribunal, iTunes also agreed facts 5 and 12. In what follows, we have made use of this document.

10. The **BPI** is the trade association of the principal record companies in this country and is responsible for over 90% of commercial sound and audio-visual recordings. The Agreed Facts (11) records the following:

> 'The BPI's members are most commonly content suppliers to music retailers, like the MNOs and the MSPs rather than music retailers themselves. In their capacity as content suppliers to music retailers, the BPI's members would not be licensed under the JOL, as they are not Music Service Providers.'

11. Shortly before the hearing (so shortly in fact, as to require an adjournment), a settlement was reached between BPI, iTunes and the MNO's on the one hand and the Alliance and the Academy on the other ('**the Settlement Agreements**'). Attached to the Settlement Agreements was the New JOL. BPI's settlement was comprehensive and it thereupon withdrew from *any* further participation in the proceedings. The settlement with iTunes and the MNOs however was conditional upon the resolution of an important item relating to the definition of 'Gross Revenue'. These were their so-called '**Disputed Contentions**' (see below).

12. Other parties[12] also settled but on the basis of a different definition of Gross Revenue ('the **Home Page Concession**'- see below) and with the benefit of any gains made by iTunes on the issue of Gross Revenue.

13. The **MNOs** offer a variety of items to the public via their content portals. This includes a broad mix of commercial products: games, audio and audio-visual downloads and streaming (music and non-music), news, sports, ringtones, 'wallpapers', audio-books mobile TV and probably by now, other services as well. Most of these have nothing at all to do with music or activities licensed under the New JOL and thus, what is essentially at stake in these Applications.

14. The New JOL provides for the payment of royalty to the Alliance in respect of identified revenue streams, being based on what is defined as '**Gross Revenue**'. The Disputed Contentions of the **MNOs** and **iTunes** were related and concerned the definition of Gross Revenue when music was offered (respectively) for free

[12] Napster, MusicNet and Sony

or at a subsidised rate, in either case as a result of advertising, sponsorship etc. The Home Page Concession on the other hand was part of a comprehensive settlement with the Alliance and hence there has been no further argument from the parties involved in that aspect of the definition.

15. That left the three **'Remaining MSPs[13]'**, sometimes called **'The Webcasters'**, whose online musical offerings primarily consist of webcasting services. They were represented by Mr Steinthal and did not participate in the Settlement Agreements[14]. Their submissions differed slightly from those of iTunes and the MNOs on the issue of Gross Revenue –and generally.

16. Mr Steinthal tended to distance the Remaining MSPs from most of the terms of the New JOL – in particular, those relating to webcasting. Looking ahead for a moment, the New JOL was not, he argued, a useful 'comparator' for the Tribunal principally because, so he submitted, those licensed thereunder had no present, practical interest in webcasting. Their core commercial interests were elsewhere. As far as its signatories were concerned, its webcasting terms had merely been part of a package – and, said Mr Steinthal, an unimportant part at that. Nonetheless, by the time of the hearing, Mr Steinthal did accept the propriety of some of its terms, including terms which prior to the Settlement Agreements, had been universally in contention.

### *Miscellaneous preliminary matters* [15]

17. **The PRS** The PRS was incorporated in 1914 as a non-profit company limited by guarantee. The members of the PRS comprise:

(a) composers of music
(b) authors of lyrics
(c) publishers of such music and lyrics, and
(d) successors in title of deceased composers and authors.

18. The PRS exists to administer the rights of public performance, broadcasting and diffusion by cable given by the copyright in those works. Virtually all composers, lyricists and music publishers in the UK have assigned their relevant public performance copyrights to the PRS which thus has an effective *de facto* monopoly on the grant of licences for copyright music in the UK. The PRS' income derives principally from its licensing activities. It deducts administration costs and then passes on royalties to its members in accordance with its own rules of distribution.

19. The PRS has reciprocal arrangements with similar collecting societies all in other countries.

---

[13] That is Yahoo !, AOL and RealNetworks
[14] Though Mr Steinthal had been involved in settlement discussions with other MSPs and the Alliance.
[15] In no particular order of importance.

20. The PRS' repertoire, which we refer to simply as 'the repertoire', comprises an enormous *corpus* of music and lyrics representing the collected output of many, many composers and lyricists over a very considerable time. There is of course some small amount of music which is not within the repertoire and in this case (as in numerous others), this fact has been raised to bolster arguments from would be licensees. In view however of the preponderance of material within the repertoire, we have taken no account of it. In doing so we have followed a long tradition of the Tribunal and of its predecessor.

21. ***The Academy*** The Academy entered these proceedings as late interveners and also participated in the Settlement Agreements. They instructed the same firm of solicitors as the Alliance (albeit using a different in-house team) and were separately represented by Mr Charles Aldous QC and Mr Edmund Cullen. Mr Aldous explained that many members of the Academy were self-employed freelance composers and writers who were also members of the Alliance. However, their interests, he said, were not always the same as those of the corporate members of the PRS - such as its influential publisher members. The Academy had therefore decided to intervene so as to ensure that the interests of writers and composers (whose works are after all, at the heart of these proceedings), were properly represented. Needless to say, the Academy endorsed the New JOL. We felt however that overall, the contribution of the Academy was inevitably a recapitulation of the Alliance's case. And where Mr Aldous made a submission which the Alliance had not made *expressis verbis*, it was endorsed by the Alliance. In fact (and despite the eloquence of Mr Aldous' presentation), we discerned no difference of substance between the Alliance's and the Academy's cases. Henceforth, when we refer (for example) to the submissions of the Alliance we intend to include those of the Academy – and *vice versa.*

22. ***Piracy*** This is a topic which we felt was more debated at the beginning of the proceedings than at the end. It is not in dispute (indeed it is notorious) that there is now a very high level of piracy in the music industry, online and offline[16]. There was a certain amount of evidence about how serious this is[17] and how it occurs. There was evidence (for example) of the use of filesharing technology to promote the distribution of music and of the unauthorised downloading of files containing music in the Alliance's repertoire via the Internet. We learnt of the practical problems associated with online liability and immunity and of the difficulty of pursuing the huge numbers of people who practice illegal filesharing and downloading.

23. We record that this is a matter which we (like many others) take most seriously; it is undoubtedly a huge problem for the music industry. Its relevance to these proceedings was twofold. First, it was said to be enough, to justify a '*New Format Discount*' which is still of concern to the remaining MSPs. This will be considered towards the end of the Decision. Secondly, iTunes (who have been pioneers in the downloading sector) regard piracy and the purchase of CDs (in that order) as their main competitors. In order to compete therefore, iTunes has

[16] For a recent example, see R v Chen [2006] EWCA Crim. 2526.
[17] See for example, the Alliance's expert Ms Enders, D11/117 and 122, the Applicants' second expert Mr Ridyard (Ridyard 1, §88) and the Alliance's second expert Mr Biro (Biro 2/61ff)

had to set up an attractive, easy to use, and *reasonably priced* online service in order to provide an alternative to piracy – which, said Mr Weisselberg, is ultimately to the benefit of the Alliance's members. It has thus had to shoulder *risks which the Alliance has not borne* and that the gravity of these risks was uncertain because of the uncertainty of the impact of piracy in the future - and thus upon its ability to offer attractive pricing in the future. As we shall show, whether there has been risk-sharing is indeed a relevant issue and piracy is (so it was argued) a factor for the Tribunal to take into account in what follows. Though we have much sympathy for the emotive argument that the Applicants are in truth the 'good guys' of the music industry and should be in a measure rewarded for being so, this is an appeal *ad hominem* which is rather more difficult to factor into the general principles within which our decision must be reached. Our conclusions have thus tended to be 'pirate neutral'.

24. ***Confidentiality of documents.*** A good deal of time was taken at the interlocutory stages of these Applications to devise means to prevent the disclosure, inadvertent or otherwise, of a considerable amount of disclosure material which the parties (particularly the Alliance) considered to be both relevant and confidential. The quality of such confidential information was categorised and its legitimate recipients were identified.

25. The principal order relating to confidentiality on disclosure is dated 10 February 2006 and was made by Mr Simon Thorley QC sitting as a Deputy Chairman of the Tribunal. First, two degrees of confidentiality were envisaged: Class 1 and Class 2 documents. The former was less sensitive, its disclosure being limited to the Tribunal, external legal advisers, experts and named individuals from the receiving party. Disclosure of Class 2 material was limited to the above persons except that there was to be a maximum of one recipient in the receiving party (if the receiving party elected to nominate a recipient at all)[18]. With the concurrence of the Tribunal, a 'confidentiality club' was therefore set up.

26. This régime seems to have worked well at trial. Nonetheless, the proliferation of confidential material during the course of this case has created for all those concerned a potential minefield. We have taken steps to exclude such material from this Decision though the narrative may have intermittently suffered as a result. We would add that Mr Rabinowitz sought to justify much of the lengthy evidence given by the Alliance's industry expert Ms Enders on the basis that without her synthesis of the mass of confidential and semi-confidential material filed, the Tribunal might never be able to form a reasonable picture of how the industry operated.

27. ***Factual Evidence*** As noted, the BPI withdrew all its factual evidence. Following the settlement, the Alliance has also withdrawn all its factual evidence, leaving only exhibited documents. The Academy has also withdrawn all its factual evidence. The MSPs on the other hand were busy filing supplementary evidence, factual and expert, right up to the time of the hearing – all of which has been admitted.

---

[18] The somewhat complex detail is to be found at A5/84.

28. ***Unanswered Evidence*** The evidence filed by the parties in this reference can with understatement be described as being voluminous – though it is fair to say that some of it pre-dates the Settlement Agreements. Not surprisingly therefore, there have been submissions by all the remaining parties that a number of items of written evidence remain 'unanswered' or 'unchallenged'. Whilst we have noted these matters, we have also taken into account part of an interlocutory order made on 9 November 2005 by Mr Thorley, QC which reads as follows:

> '15. It shall not be necessary for a witness to be cross-examined in order to challenge his evidence. This provision also applies to part of the statement of a witness who is cross-examined but not on those parts.'

29. Similar provisions are often to be found in interlocutory orders made by the Tribunal with a view to discouraging prolonged (and too often unprofitable) bouts of cross-examination at the hearing.

30. ***Demonstrations*** Another difficulty in preparing this Decision has been adequately to describe the many online services in issue. Sensing perhaps some unfamiliarity on the part of members of the Tribunal with the panoply of online services in question, the parties kindly arranged for a number of demonstrations to take place where the services could be demonstrated to us and more importantly, where we could access and use the services for ourselves. There were two principal demonstrations, the second having been arranged by the time the hearing was about mid-way. The demonstrations took place at the London offices of Mr Steinthal's firm, Messrs Weil, Gotshal & Manges in the City and there exists among the documents a short programme recording what we were shown. We record that we found these demonstrations to have been of immense assistance in the adjudication of this matter. They have however reinforced our view that no amount of prose can do justice to what we saw and heard and that for a proper appreciation of the issues in these Applications, there is no substitute for actually using the services for oneself.

31. ***Shifting positions.*** During the course of the hearing, much play was made by Messrs. Carr, Weisselberg and Steinthal on the fact that since the Applications had been made, the Alliance had substantially to moderate its demands on a number of major issues and continued to do so down to the time of closing speeches and even after[19]. In a word, it was said that they had been shifting their case from an outright attempt to obtain what Mr Weisselberg termed 'an unprincipled windfall', trying that is, to capture revenue streams to which they had no conceivable right, to demands of more modest proportion[20] . There may be some truth in this but we do not regard that as necessarily a bad thing –or indeed anything unusual in cases such as this. With technology and business models such as we are dealing with here, there must, we feel, be room for early ranging shots to be fired. The narrowing of issues in litigation is always to be

[19] After the conclusion of the evidence, the Alliance sent the parties a letter dated 4 December 2006 (**'the 4 Dec. Letter'**) purporting to elucidate certain issues in the light of the evidence and the observations of the Tribunal. The Alliance was given leave to make short post-hearing submissions in writing. This resulted in inter partes correspondence which concluded on 23 January 2007.

[20] In fact, Mr Carr argued that in some respects their most recent demands were subtly more covetous by being dressed in woolly language. Mr Weisselberg was also of the view that the Alliance's case had become more 'hardline' during the course of the hearing.

welcomed and is not necessarily symptomatic of (for example), a 'try on'. We would mention that many of the Applicants also modified their cases as proceedings progressed –as may be seen from the settlements. In other words, these manoeuvres have had no impact on our Decision.

32. ***Mr Kenneth Steinthal*** Mr Kenneth Steinthal (of the New York Bar) is a member of the law firm Weil, Gotshal & Manges whose London office instructs him on behalf of the Remaining MSPs as their trial lawyer. At a procedural stage before the hearing began, Mr Steinthal, together with his colleague from the same firm, Mr Joe Salvo, sought leave to address the Tribunal. There was no opposition to the application and audience was accordingly given to both gentlemen.

33. By the time of closing speeches however, both the Alliance and the Academy had launched a personal attack on Mr Steinthal on the basis that he had misled the Tribunal in a material respect. The matter was almost entirely argued by Mr Charles Aldous QC, but what he submitted was (as we understood it) endorsed by Mr Rabinowitz QC on behalf of the Alliance.

34. The attack arose in relation to a substantive argument on the relevance of proper comparators which Mr Steinthal had advanced in apparently similar proceedings before The US Copyright Royalty Board ('the Board') in Washington DC in December 2006. There he was representing the Digital Media Association and its member companies America On Line Inc and Yahoo! Inc, to which he referred as 'webcasters'. As we understand it, the latter companies are closely related to two of the three remaining MSPs for whom Mr Steinthal has appeared in London. Copies of the US webcasters' written Preliminary Statement and Conclusions of Law were produced by Mr Aldous to support the complaint that one of the arguments proposed by the Remaining MSPs before the Tribunal was precisely the opposite to that espoused by Mr Steinthal in Washington before the Board. He also suggested that had it not been for some astute research on behalf of the Alliance in Washington, the matter might never have come to light. The point essentially concerned the historic licensing for public performance on radio in the US of musical works and the suitability of such licensing arrangements as a comparator or 'benchmark' for the purposes of the assessment with which the Board was then concerned.

35. Mr Steinthal, who it should be said had no warning of this attack, spent over an hour of his closing speech explaining what in fact he had been arguing before the Board. He first said that the US proceedings, the existence of which the Alliance had at all material times been well aware, were conducted in open court; there was thus never any question of covert manoeuvre on his part. He next referred at length to various issues and details arising in the US proceedings, to relevant US copyright law on the public performance of sound recordings and to other matters as well. In this way he sought to explain and justify the allegedly contradictory position into which he was said to have fallen.

36. In view of the way Mr Steinthal met this accusation and to the manner in which we have reached our own conclusions, we do not find it either profitable or necessary to revisit the detail of this incident. We were certainly not misled.

37. ***Unfair Exclusion of the Remaining MSPs from negotiations?*** It was more than once suggested by Mr Steinthal that the remaining MSPs were somehow deliberately excluded from the negotiations which led to the settlements[21]. Since these Applicants were offered the same terms as those who did negotiate and moreover are major players in the online music world with impressive legal advice to hand, this appeal for sympathy rings hollow – particularly as Mr Steinthal represented certain MSPs who did settle.

38. Some account nevertheless needs to be taken of the fact that the Remaining MSPs were indeed absent from the Settlement Agreement. They were of course very important players in the business. The effect of their absence on the levels of royalty eventually reached for webcasting services by those who did settle, is we believe, a legitimate matter for consideration by the Tribunal.

## II THE TRIBUNAL'S APPROACH: GENERAL PRINCIPLES

### *The Statutory framework*

39. Chapter VII CDPA '88 is entitled 'Copyright Licensing'. Section 116(1) and (3) provide as follows:

> '(1) In this Part, a "licensing scheme" means a scheme setting out –
> (a) the classes of case in which the operator of the scheme or the person on whose behalf he acts, is willing to grant copyright licences, and
> (b) the terms on which the licences would be granted in those classes of case; and for this purpose a "scheme" includes anything in the nature of a scheme, whether described as a scheme or as a tariff or by any other name
> (2) …..
> (3) In this section "copyright licences" means licences to do or authorise the doing of any of the acts restricted by copyright.'

40. We highlight this section because a major issue raised by the Applicants is that 'Gross Revenue' as defined in the New JOL covers activities for which no copyright licence can conceivably be required at law; the classic 'copyright language' of sub-section (3) has, they say, been conveniently overlooked by the Alliance.

41. The Applications have been brought under ss. 119, 121 and 126 of the Act. The terms of these and other relevant sections of the Act are so well known as to make it unnecessary to set them out fully and they are therefore incorporated into this Decision by reference. The group of sections in the Act which touch upon the power of the Tribunal to make orders after a reference has been made, all end with the phrase '*as the Tribunal may determine to be* ***reasonable in the***

[21] This was said upon the evidence of e.g. Mr Gabriel Levy, General Manager of Label Relations at RealNetworks: see Levy 3,§ 8.2.

***circumstances***'- or variants of it. In the exercise of its powers, the Tribunal therefore has a discretion of the '*widest and most general form*'[22]. It has also been said that it is a determination which is '*notoriously difficult*' to arrive at[23], being at the end of the day 'a judgment call' taking into account a wide variety of factors.

42. Sections 129 and 135 offer some statutory guidance on the matters to be taken into account in the exercise of the discretion. Section 129 ('*General considerations Unreasonable Discrimination*') requires the Tribunal in coming to its decision, to have regard to the existence of 'other schemes or licences', a topic commonly referred to in this jurisdiction as 'comparators'. The section provides as follows:

> 'In determining what is reasonable in a reference or application under this Chapter relating to a licensing scheme or licence, the Copyright Tribunal shall have regard to –
>
> a) the availability of other schemes or the granting of other licences, to other persons in similar circumstances, and
>
> (b) the terms of those schemes or licences,
>
> and shall exercise its powers so as to secure that there is no unreasonable discrimination between licensees, or prospective licensees, under the scheme or licence to which the reference or application relates and licensees under other schemes operated by, or other licences granted by, the same person.'

43. Section 135 is in more general terms and confirms the breadth of the discretion:

> 'The mention in sections 129-134 of specific matters to which the Copyright Tribunal is to have regard in certain classes of case does not affect the Tribunal's general obligation in any case to have regard to all relevant considerations'.

### *General approach*

44. Before considering the relevant principles to be derived from past decisions, we should record that we are mindful of this general fact: that copyright (and thus the régime under which collecting societies operate), exists for the benefit of right holders – in this case, authors, musicians, performers etc. That benefit to the right holder is the primary policy of copyright has been present from the beginnings of modern copyright law[24]. Statutory 'users' rights' as such are quite limited: see for example, the Act, Chapter III ('*Acts permitted in Relation to Copyright Works*')[25].

---

[22] Per Harman J , AIRC v PPL (unreported) 16 January 1986.
[23] AEI v PPL [1998] EMLR 240 at 250.
[24] See for example, the Preamble to the Berne Convention ('BC') 1886, Art 9(1) and the use in the original of the phrase '*droit d'auteur*'. See also the WIPO Copyright Treaty Arts. 6-8 and the Infosoc Directive (2001/29/EC), recitals 9 and 10 and Art. 5(5).
[25] See also BC Art. 9(2) ('*Certain Special Cases*').

45. We mention this in the light of Mr Steinthal's broadest submission on behalf of the Remaining MSPs that certain of the terms (which he termed 'demands') proposed by the Alliance were 'outrageous' and that in the circumstances, his clients' response had had to be over-generous to a fault. The Alliance was, he suggested, exploiting a serendipitous right to participate in developments in information technology in which it had played no part and in which it had taken no risks. Moreover, he seemed disinclined even to acknowledge the practical (and mutual) benefits of collective licensing, benefits which have long been given universal statutory recognition. We consider this to be an unbalanced approach. The position is essentially this: the collecting societies have been accorded statutory (and indeed international) recognition in order to advance the proprietary (that is basically, the financial[26]) interests of the right holders who comprise their membership. But the effects of that responsibility may sometimes have to be tempered. An important purpose of the Tribunal (and indeed of its counterparts elsewhere) is therefore to curb any tendency to *unwarranted* gain as a result of the *de facto* monopoly position in which the collecting societies find themselves[27]. Overall however, the Tribunal's job as we see it is to favour neither side. It is to maintain a balance between copyright owners and users.

46. There is no presumption in favour of the referred scheme nor is there a presumption that a referred scheme should be varied [28]. As to the burden of proof this hardly featured in argument. On an application to the Tribunal, the burden of proof is on the applicant to show that the *particular* licence offered to him is *un*reasonable; but he does not have to show that the proposals of the licensing body are unreasonable on any footing[29].

### *Tribunal decisions considered*

47. A number of decisions of the Tribunal and of its predecessor[30] (and appeals to the High Court) were cited in argument. Save perhaps on the issue of Gross Revenue, there was no significant disagreement between the parties as to the general principles to be applied or as to the relevant law. The parties did however differ in the emphasis they laid on the relevance of certain of these decisions to the present case, particularly the relevance of some older decisions which were given at a time before the existence (let alone the availability) of online musical offerings. We have taken this into account and further record that we have not felt ourselves to be *bound* by any earlier decision of this Tribunal (or of the PRT).We record that three authorities assumed particular importance: BPI v MCPS (no 2), BSkyB v PRS and AIRC v PPL. We therefore turn to the guidance which is to be found from previous decisions taking these in no particular order.

---

[26] "*What counts is money in the end.*" The oft quoted words of Mr Nicholas Lowe a solicitor and former Director of Broadcasting at the PRS.
[27] BSkyB v PRS [1998] EMLR 193 at 214-215.
[28] BPI v MCPS (No 2) [1993] EMLR 556.
[29] Manx Radio Case (18/64) PRT unrep. 29 May 1965.
[30] The Performing Right Tribunal ('PRT').

48. **Fairness**. In the exercise of its discretion and in the light of the evidence, the Tribunal must determine whether the *legitimate financial expectations* of (in this case) the Alliance, acting on behalf of its right holders, are *reasonable* in all the relevant circumstances. The Tribunal performs a discretionary, balancing exercise wherein the result must be

> " both fair to the licensee in terms of the value to the licensee of having access to the copyright sound recordings, and also fair to the licensee in giving him a proper reward for the effort put into the exploitation of the licensees' intellectual property rights"[31]

49. **The willing buyer/willing seller test**. This is a classic test in this jurisdiction whose present applicability has been expressly endorsed by all concerned. In assessing a reasonable tariff, the Tribunal has frequently addressed the matter on the basis that the proper rate is that which would be negotiated between a willing licensee and a willing licensee of the copyright repertoire[32]. Before examination of the relevant circumstances to be taken into account in this notional exercise, it is however common practice to identify an existing tariff as a starting point. If such a licence exists (and particularly, if it is recent) and addresses comparable subject matter - and even better, if it was freely negotiated (rather than being as it were, 'imposed' by the Tribunal), that may be particularly relevant and helpful in determining the right tariff (and other terms) of a licence. Such an agreement it has been said, is the best record of the market value of the relevant rights at the time (see below '*Comparators*'). The Alliance submitted that this approach, though certainly not wrong, is simplistic since it often does not take into account the benefits to the licensee of collective bargaining. Nonetheless, our assessment of the centrality of this consideration and its relevance to this case, is undiminished.

50. **Comparators**[33] As noted above, s. 129 of the Act *requires* the Tribunal to take into account schemes and licences 'to other persons in similar circumstances.' Mr Richard Boulton, the Applicants' principal expert, put the position with admirable clarity in his first Report, thus[34]:

> *" The comparable royalties approach is often regarded as the best approach to use in circumstances where the parties do not agree on the level of royalty. Negotiations between a willing licensor and a willing licensee, in the circumstances, will provide, in theory, the best available information about the level of a reasonable royalty."*

51. In AIRC v PPL[35], the Tribunal stressed the importance of comparators:

> 'It is for the Tribunal in assessing the transactions cited as comparable to decide to what extent the rights licensed are of the same *or a similar kind*, whether the transactions were concluded at arm's length with neither side affected by stress, and whether they were affected by legal factors which do

[31] AEI v PPL [1998] RPC 335 at 343.
[32] See for example, Working Men's Club & Institute Union Ltd v PRS [1992] RPC 227 at 232.
[33] Also called 'a readily available or appropriate proxy' in some jurisdictions.
[34] B7/33/1442.
[35] [1993]EMLR 181 at 218.

> not apply in this case. It is then for the Tribunal to adapt any relevant comparators to the case under review.' [*Emphasis added*]

Thus, starting with a cited comparator, it is open to the Tribunal to take notice of it (or of parts of it) and to use it (or reject it entirely) as the case may require. The authorities show that whilst the utility of comparators has frequently occupied the Tribunal's time, in practice they appear to have been more of a legitimate quarry (or template) for particular terms and figures rather than as full precedents for a particular licence. In a few cases, comparators, particularly comparators from overseas, have proved to possess very little probative value whatever.

52. On the issue of royalty rates, comparators have featured strongly in the arguments of both the Alliance and of the Remaining MSPs, reliance being placed (by the Alliance) upon the licensing of the same rights (i.e. in the New JOL) and (by the Remaining MSPs) other rights alleged to be of a similar kind. Not surprisingly the Alliance characterised the New JOL as being 'a compelling comparator ' in all respects – a contention robustly challenged by Mr Steinthal. Rival comparators emerged during the course of the evidence and we shall have to consider them in due course.

53. When one is dealing with the licensing of 'similar' rights, some comparators may be more relevant than others. For example, in cases where the exploitation of music requires licences both from the owners of the rights in the composition (i.e. the Alliance representing composers and publishers of music) and that of the owners of the rights in the sound recordings (i.e. the record companies or the PPL), the Tribunal has held that (a) these two types of rights are legitimate comparators, and (b) there is no reason to treat one as being qualitatively superior to the other[36]. Therefore said the Alliance, since such licences do exist, it is relevant to compare the present proposals with what the record companies (or PPL) receive for exploitation of their rights.

54. Where there are sufficiently comparable licences, the Tribunal should adopt a similar rate "*absent any special circumstances*": AEI v PPL *supra* at 256.

55. What one usually finds in the authorities is evidence of a *degree* of comparability, ranging from the superficial to the more realistic. iTunes submitted that even where the comparability was rather inexact, one could nonetheless take the comparables into account "*but scale them down because of the differences.*"[37]

56. Finally, this must be said of comparables: though the Tribunal may impose different rates upon different parties in respect of essentially the same rights, it

[36] The Manx Radio case (supra); BEDA v PRS (1August 1989); AIRC v PPL (16 January 1986).There is no reason to assert , a priori, that either of the two forms of copyright has a higher or lower value than the other: see AIRC v PPL [1993] EMLR 181 where the Tribunal decided that the PRS and the PPL tariffs should be "*in the same general range*"
[37] Cf BPI v MCPS (no 2) supra at 116.

must not thereby discriminate between licensees (see above § 41) unless there is "a logical reason for it"[38]

57. **A simple and workable tariff** The tariff should be simple and workable having regard to the service being licensed – *"with a straightforward rate structure based on straightforward definitions"*. Most tariffs can be shown to produce anomalies in certain circumstances but a complex rate structure will be more likely to produce anomalies (and thus problems) particularly at the margins of its rates: AIRC v PPL [1993] EMLR 181 at 229. Simplicity of operation and clarity of expression should always be a *desideratum*. In Universities UK v CLA [2002] RPC 693, the Tribunal said:

> " Overall we have been seeking to achieve a simple, economic, universal system promoting good education for the benefit of staff and students whilst at the same time achieving fair and reasonable remuneration for the owners of the rights." (at p726)

58. In these Applications, the desiderata of simplicity and practicality present formidable problems in relation to the definition of 'Gross Revenue': see Part VII below. The difficulty arises partly as a result of an inherently changing and complex technology and partly because of the sudden viability of upgraded business models and new modes of delivery of the products to be licensed. We were told of additions to the business models available as the case went on. For example, a US downloading service called Spiral Frog® made its appearance during the hearing in this context. In fact, in our judgment, 'Gross Revenue' is more or less incapable of technically succinct definition without invoking a broad (and thus according to the Applicants, unacceptable) simplification favoured by the Alliance. Nonetheless, in reaching our decision on this aspect of the Applications, we have chosen what we believe to be reasonably simple and workable solutions to the problem of definition.

59. **The revenue-based approach to royalty.** The decision of the Tribunal in AIRC v PPL [1993] EMLR 181 at 229 *et seq* endorsed the use of a revenue-based approach to royalty. We say 'endorsed' because a revenue-based tariff had already been *agreed* between the parties. The Tribunal had been called upon to rule on what a reasonable royalty was for licensing sound recordings for use in commercial radio in the UK. The applicants had in fact proposed a royalty of 3.5% of net advertising revenue (subject to certain qualifications) whilst the PPL had proposed a royalty of 15% of 'relevant revenue' calculated by reference to usage. We note in particular the following observation of the Tribunal (at 229):

> "The revenue-based approach ...proceeds on the reasonable assumption that the stations will seek to maximise their revenue for sound commercial reasons. It is *an imperfect measure* of value because the revenue on which it is based is created by the station's entire broadcast output, its promotion of itself and its image as an advertising medium. PPL's music is only part of this.... Under the revenue-based system, the licensing body has the disadvantage that its royalty may become adversely affected by economic recession or by commercial misjudgements of the licensee. On the other hand

[38] BSkyB v PRS at 208.

> there is no direct connection between revenue and profit and under this system the licensing body shares in revenue whether or not the management skills of the station turn it into profit. While both sides accept the limitations of a revenue based system, they accept that there is a logic to it and that it should remain the basis upon which royalty should be assessed" [*Emphasis added*]

60. That, we believe, has relevance in these Applications where a revenue-based approach to royalty was also *agreed* at an early stage. Such agreement obviously makes practical sense. However, like the Tribunal in AIRC v PPL (and in BSkyB v PRS), we have been alive to the fact that this enquiry is at heart concerned with the licensing of copyright and not merely with the endorsement of sensible commercial arrangements[39]. The Tribunal said[40]:

> " However, although a revenue-based tariff is urged by both sides and has been adopted by us in the Decision, it is an over-simplification to see a *direct causal connection* between the use of the PPL repertoire and the achievement of advertising revenue. The playing of PPL repertoire would not result in the level of advertising revenue which the stations obtain without the stations' programming mix, their sales strategy and their marketing and promotional efforts." [*Emphasis added*]

61. Therefore within such *inter partes* consensus on a royalty-based approach there must be more; there must also be a *nexus* (or *'direct causal connection')* between use of the Alliance's repertoire and revenues earned by the Applicants- however 'imperfect' a measure that may appear.

62. **Free music and *'faute de mieux'***. We shall deal with this requirement in the paragraphs which follow but before doing so we must highlight an argument based on the AIRC v PPL which was at the forefront of Mr Carr's case on the MNO's Disputed Contention[41]: that in that case (unlike this) there was in truth *no other source of revenue on which to levy a royalty.* From the outset, commercial radio stations were fully funded by commercial advertising. AIRC v PPL was therefore, he said (borrowing words from the decision of the Tribunal in BSkyB), a '*faute de mieux*' situation; AIRC v PPL was not applicable when a consumer has fully paid for e.g. a permanent download or a stream of music – as in the normal case he would do here in the present case. It does not therefore arise *unless the music is offered free as a result of advertising*[42].

63. **'Adequate Nexus'** or **'Sufficient Connection'** The need for 'direct causal connection' was stated in AIRC v PPL (supra).This was a topic common to all the remaining parties after the Settlement Agreements; and in connection with the 'Disputed Contentions', it was in effect, the *only* issue.

64. In the past, the Tribunal and its predecessor have undoubtedly rejected as unreasonable a royalty based on a percentage of revenue. The several authorities cited under this head demonstrate the requirement that there must indeed be a

[39] What the Tribunal called '*a pleasing agreement*' in BSkyB v PRS (supra) at 218.
[40] At 207.
[41] And to a degree, Mr Weisselberg's as well on iTunes' Disputed Contention.
[42] Or logically, at a rate subsidised by. advertising.

*sufficiency of connection* between the licensee's revenue and the use of the Alliance's repertoire so as to make that revenue source 'commissionable'. Put another way, the Tribunal must always look for a 'sufficient connection' or 'close, direct relationship' between revenue and repertoire so as to make it *reasonable* to relate the royalty for use of the repertoire directly to that revenue. In the recent past, the Tribunal's attitude to revenue-based royalty has been palpably hostile:[43]

> " The Tribunal is unable to accept that there is any adequate correlation between the use of music from the PRS repertoire by the Companies and the [revenue] of those Companies.... The question is...whether the fact that the music is -or may be to a greater or lesser extent- part of the package which attracts the television audiences and accordingly generates [revenue], establishes or helps to establish a sufficient connection between music and revenue, to make it reasonable to relate the royalty for the music use directly to [revenue]. We are satisfied that it does not... First, the television programme or commercial is the product of a wide variety of artistic and technical skills of which music is only a part. and not we think, in general, the predominant part; the smaller the significance of the contribution of a part to the whole, the less certain can any attribution of a generative effect be. The contrast with sound radio and, say, grand opera, is we think, illuminating"

65. The principle has been re-stated in a number of Tribunal decisions[44] all of which, *on the facts*, reject the existence of a close correlation between the repertoire and the revenue of the users. For example, in PRS v BEDA (PRT, unrep. 1 August 1989) in order for royalty to accrue, the Tribunal required

> 'a close direct relationship between the value of the input and the value of the output[45].

66. The Tribunal's decision in BSkyB [1998] EMLR 193 affords particular assistance on this point even though in that case the Tribunal again *rejected* the submission of the PRS that the royalty should be calculated as a percentage of BSkyB's net revenue receipts[46].

> "What offends one's common sense is that a single component of a complex final product such as a television programme should be remunerated on a basis which rises and falls with the revenues obtained from the final product, when that component may have had nothing at all to do with those changes in revenue."

Nonetheless, the *possibility* of excise on revenue was, perhaps for the first time, positively acknowledged[47]

[43] ITCA v PRS ,(October 19 1983 PRT 38/81, pp 68-69). The Tribunal went on to give reasons which were specific to factors in that case.
[44] PRS v BEDA, BPI v MCPS, AIRC v PPL and BSkyB v PRS (supra).
[45] p. 6. The Tribunal held that there was no close connection between PRS' music and the total receipts of a discotheque. There was no risk-sharing and no incentive to perform in a mutually advantageous way. Symbiosis is not enough.
[46] At 217.
[47] At 219.

> "What the decided cases show is that, before one can ever use revenue as a measure of the value of the music to a broadcaster, one must be satisfied that there is an adequate nexus between the use of the music and revenues earned."

and:

> " We do not consider it correct to approach the issue before us as one of whether the revenue basis ... is correct 'in principle': if one adopted that approach one would be in danger of losing sight of the overall objective. What we are to endeavour to do is to determine what approach is most 'reasonable in the circumstances' i.e. the circumstances of this case."
>
> "The role music plays in a company's output can vary widely. At one extreme was an example discussed in argument of the music played in the lift of the offices of a bank....At the other extreme might be the sale of records or sheet music, where the music is the whole or at least a vast proportion of what the consumer pays for. At some point on this 'spectrum' it could become appropriate to adopt a revenue-based approach: the question we have to decide is whether it is appropriate to do so in the present case."[48]

67. The requirement for 'close causal connection' has also been considered in another offline case. In BPI v MCPS [1993] EMLR 86, under their CD licence, the MCPS does not get a share of any other revenue which might simply 'result from' or 'arise in relation to the provision of or be 'driven by' or even be 'derived from' music content. The royalty rate was expressed as a percentage of published price to dealers (PPD) even though the 'profits available' were a relevant consideration 'but should by no means be regarded as determinative.'

68. As noted, in this case it has been agreed that, with appropriate qualification, a revenue - based royalty *is* appropriate, the qualification being a matter of degree over which there is a dispute. This consensus was reached, it seems, on the basis that it has an established precedent in relation to offline music (physical product and radio – see above) which we were told, has worked well enough over many years. So much for the principle. What the authorities warn against however is the illegitimacy of over-broadening that revenue base; in the 'spectrum' referred to in BSkyB, there must be a defined *ne plus ultra*. If there were not, one runs the risk of undermining the legal justification for the 'royalty to revenue link' altogether.

69. We should record here that our attention was drawn to the fact that revenue - based royalty is a fact of life in collective licensing practice in overseas jurisdictions, even in those having a regime like our own: see: APRA v ABC (1985) 5 IPR 449 (Australia) and SBC v PRS [1991] FSR 573 (Singapore).

70. **Risk sharing** We shall next raise 'risk sharing' since it is quite clear (if it is not actually accepted) that the Alliance has borne no risk in delivering to the public any of the musical offerings with which we are here concerned.

---

[48] At 221.

71. The question of risk sharing has been a relevant issue in numerous cases before the Tribunal. In the extreme case where there is no risk-sharing, the Tribunal in BSkyB considered that the revenue basis was actually a poor approach to remuneration for the use of music.

> "But where revenues may be rising or falling rapidly for reasons connected with the introduction of new technology and entrepreneurial risk-taking and unconnected with music, we think the revenue basis may be less appropriate." [49]

So risk sharing is an issue we have to factor into our decision on what is 'reasonable in the circumstances'.

72. In addressing the relevance of this consideration, Tribunals have referred to the analogy with revenue sharing arrangements and partnerships where revenue *and* risk are usually shared. On the other hand, in situations in which the issue is the use of the repertoire by a licensee, the norm is that PRS does not share in the commercial risk associated with the viability of the delivery means in question. This is a factor which the Tribunal will take into account in striking a tariff. In ITCA v PRS[50] for example, the Tribunal said:

> "We make one general point at this stage which we think of importance. The point is that it is not....right to regard those whom the PRS represents as co-adventurers in the business of television with the Companies. They are not."

## III THE NEW JOL

### *The eve of trial settlements: An overview*

73. We shall now consider the pre-trial settlements in more detail.

74. On 28 September 2006, the **BPI,** the Alliance and the Academy resolved their differences, the outcome being recorded in the Settlement Agreement. The Settlement Agreement has appended to it (as Schedule 1) the New JOL. As a result of the settlement, BPI agreed to withdraw its reference, its written submissions and its witnesses of fact evidence, the only evidence remaining being that of the experts Mr Richard Boulton and Mr Derek Ridyard who now gave evidence on behalf of all the Applicants. The New JOL has been drafted to cover all the online music services in which the Applicants are likely to be interested.

75. On the same date, **iTunes and the MNOs** also settled all their differences with the Alliance on the basis of the same terms and conditions *save for*:

---

[49] At 216 and 219.
[50] Supra at § 6.4.

(a) in respect of iTunes, 'the iTunes **Disputed Contention'**, and
(b) in respect of the MNOs , 'the MNOs' **Disputed Contention'**.

As a result of the settlements, both iTunes and the MNOs no longer rely upon a good deal of their evidence. Both however rely upon parts of Mr Boulton's reports. The MNOs also rely upon Mr Bill's first witness statement. iTunes also relied on some of the existing evidence including sections of Mr Eddy Cue's first and second witness statements. iTunes was formerly a member of the MSP consortium but since partial settlement, it parted company with them and is now of course, separately represented

76. These Disputed Contentions (which are not identical) are defined[51] in the Settlement Agreement and relate to the definition of **'Gross Revenue'**. The Disputed Contentions have this in common however: both address a situation where the full price of the music consumed is not paid, the difference having been made up by 'advertising revenue'[52]. Gross Revenue is considered *in extenso* in Part VII of this decision,

77. The ***MNOs Disputed Contention*** allows them to continue as Applicants solely for the purpose of contending that:

> *"revenue derived from advertising, sponsorship and commissions on or in connection with a **Mobile** Licensed Service should only be included within Gross Revenue [as defined] where that revenue is earned as a result of an advertisement, sponsorship or a click-through link located on a page of a Licensed Service from which the **Mobile** Licensed Service is actually offered (subject to apportionment where other services not requiring a licence are offered from the same page) and only where that Mobile Licensed Service is offered to the User **for free**."*

78. The ***iTunes Disputed Contention*** allows them to continue as Applicants solely for the purpose of contending that

> *" revenue derived from advertising, sponsorship and commissions on or in connection with a Licensed Service should only be included within Gross Revenue [as defined] where that revenue is earned as a result of an advertisement, sponsorship or a click-through link located on a page of a Licensed Service from which the Licensed Service is actually offered (subject to apportionment where other services not requiring a licence are offered from the same page) and only where the Licensed Service is offered to the User **at a price which has been artificially depressed to reflect such revenue.***

79. The difference in wording between the two Disputed Contentions has been emboldened and will require separate consideration.

---

[51] H/1/3.

[52] Hereafter, advertising, sponsorship and commission revenue is most often collectively referred to as **'advertising revenue'**.

80. It is to be observed that:

(i) In both of the Disputed Contentions, the entrée for royalty to arise is advertising revenue generated from a page (that is, *any* page including the home page) from which a Licensed Service is 'actually offered'. The implications of music being 'actually offered' are discussed below under 'Gross Revenue'.

(ii) The possible need to apportion in order to calculate the revenue due is envisaged in both Disputed Contentions.

(iii) Neither of these Disputed Contentions formed part of the cases of either iTunes or the MNOs as originally pleaded.

(iv) iTunes and the MNOs agree that the approach to Gross Revenue adopted by the Alliance in the New JOL is both unreasonable and unacceptable.

(v) However, subject to these Disputed Contentions, iTunes and the MNO's fully endorse the New JOL. Thus, paragraph 12(d) of the Settlement Agreement reads:

> [subject to the two Disputed Contentions]
>
> *(vi) the Settlement Agreement including the [New JOL] is a package deal and taken in its entirety, its terms are fair and reasonable; and*
>
> *(vii) MCPS, PRS the Academy the BPI the MNOs and iTunes shall advance and defend the position in the Copyright Tribunal (or any appeal)....and shall contend that the [New JOL] represents the terms that should apply to all licensees for online and mobile music services within the scope of the Scheme for the purposes of the References",*

(iv) Thus, iTunes and the MNOs now accept (subject to their Disputed Contentions) that when viewed as a whole, the New JOL is 'fair and reasonable as applied to all licensees' (our emphasis). Looking ahead, this acknowledgement therefore puts considerable space between these Applicants and the Remaining MSPs who at any rate at the start of the hearing, seemed to be contesting just about everything of importance except rates and minima for *permanent and limited downloads* (see below).

81. **Napster and MusicNet** settled their dispute with the Alliance on 6 October 2006 (the **Napster Settlement'**[53]) and on 10 October 2006, **Sony**[54] also settled

[53] H/6/82.

[54] H/8/133.

with the Alliance (the **Sony Settlement**). By these settlements, the parties withdrew their Applications and evidence and agreed to be bound by the Tribunal's decision on all webcasting issues and on the outcome of iTunes' Disputed Contention.

82. The Napster and Sony Settlements imported a significant limitation into the definition of 'Gross Revenue' contained in the New JOL. This limitation, which has been referred to as the Home Page Concession, relates *only* to advertising on the 'home page'. It has been endorsed by iTunes and the MNOs as a step in the right direction – but, so they argue, it still does not go far enough. We shall return to the Home Page Concession under 'Gross Revenue' below.

83. We have mentioned that the Napster/MusicNet and Sony Settlements were all expressly made subject to the outcome of the *iTunes* Disputed Contention. For this reason, Mr Weisselberg contends (in our view reasonably) that the iTunes Disputed Contention appears to have 'a degree of support' from Napster, MusicNet and Sony.

84. The **Remaining MSPs** have not reached any settlement with the Alliance. They began by pursuing their cases on a broad range of pleaded issues[55]: royalty rates, revenue base and minima for everything except permanent downloads, Gross Revenue, audio-visual deductions, new format discounts, proper licensee and non-alliance repertoire. By the close of the hearing however, we concluded that at any rate, *some* of these matters were no longer in contention.

85. All the parties' settlement documents have been conveniently collected in Court Bundle H. The New JOL governs the licensing of the signatories' online services for three years only, that is, from 1 July 2006. However, as it appears to be a groundbreaking event, its effect may be felt well beyond its expiry date.

86. We would observe that in terms of market share, the Alliance has now largely settled its differences with the majority of the online music industry in this country. Looked at another way, out of twelve original Applicants, only three of the MSPs (hence 'the Remaining MSPs') have failed to come to any sort of settlement. There is no need to elaborate on the facts leading to these settlements other than to say that the parties involved are major players in the online music industry (both national and international) who (as it appears to us), were driven by commercial considerations to strike a mutually beneficial bargain. In so doing, in addition to their extensive in-house expertise, they were assisted by an abundance of specialist lawyers and also by experts in the industry.

87. The importance of the New JOL to this case can hardly be exaggerated. Not surprisingly, it is the Alliance's 'compelling' comparator upon which their case largely turns. We have already considered the Tribunal's jurisprudence in relation to comparators but Mr Rabinowitz submitted (rightly in our view) that in this Application, the following observation of the Tribunal was particularly apposite:

---

[55] A6/1.

> "It is for the Tribunal in assessing transactions cited as comparable to decide to what extent the rights licensed are of the same or a similar kind, whether the transactions were concluded at arm's length with neither side affected by stress, and whether they were affected by legal factors which do not apply in this case. It is then for the Tribunal to adopt any relevant comparators to the case under review."[56]

88. As for 'stress', in spite of a suggestion by Mr Steinthal[57] that the negotiations were conducted under pressure to achieve a deal quickly[58] and *were* therefore conducted under 'stress', we have found no evidence to justify that submission. According to Mr Geoff Taylor[59], a major factor which led to the settlement was in fact a commendable desire to save money by not undergoing a trial.

89. In the light of this and the circumstances leading to the New JOL, Mr Steinthal evidently had an uphill task in trying to persuade us to adopt other (for instance, offline) comparators as being more relevant. We shall assess the relevance of the New JOL and these other comparators later in this decision.

### *The New JOL[60]: The Royalty Table*

90. For the purposes of the hearing, the Alliance and the Academy made use of a synoptic summary of what had been agreed in the settlements regarding royalties for the services in issue. iTunes and the MNOs were also able to make use of this table without difficulty. We have referred to this as '**the Royalty Table**' and it is reproduced below.

---

[56] AIRC v PPL [1993] EMLR 181 at 218.
[57] And at one stage by the Applicants' expert Mr Boulton.
[58] "*Necessity*" said Mr Steinthal, "*never makes a good bargain.*"
[59] Formerly General Counsel to the BPI
[60] H/1/13.

| *Service* | *Rate* | *Minimum* |
|---|---|---|
| Permanent Download | 8% | **£0.04** per download<br>- reducing by degrees for larger bundles of tracks, or certain older tracks, to £0.02 (in respect of a bundle of thirty or more) |
| Limited Download or On Demand Service | 8% | - Mobile Subscription: **£0.60** per subscriber per month<br>- PC Subscription: **£0.40** per subscriber per month<br>- Limited Subscription: **£0.20** per subscriber per month<br>- All others: **£0.0022** per Musical Work communicated to the public |
| Special Webcasting<br>(which means a premium or interactive service where more than 50% of the content is by a single artist or band) | 8% | - **£0.0022** per Musical Work played (if not subscription)<br>- if the service is subscription, minimum is to be negotiated in good faith |
| Premium or Interactive Webcasting | 6.5% | - Subscription: **£0.22** per subscriber per month<br>- Otherwise, **£0.00085** per musical work communicated to the public |
| Pure Webcasting | 6.5% | - Subscription: **£0.22** per subscriber per month<br>- Otherwise, **£0.0006** per musical work communicated to the public |
| Mobile Permanent Downloads and other Mobile services | Rates and minima as for the services above, except that:<br>For Mobile Permanent Downloads, the applicable revenue is reduced by 15%<br>For all other Mobile Services, the applicable revenue is reduced by 7.5%<br>The above reductions apply until prices converge with non-mobile prices | |

91. The categories of licensed services identified in the Royalty Table correspond with those identified in the definition schedule (Schedule 1) to the New JOL[61]. The Remaining MSPs took issue primarily with the webcasting items in the Royalty Table but in our view made no important submissions regarding the other parts of it. They had no comment on the *rate* for the On Demand Service but they did object to the existence of a minimum in relation to that service. With regard to the remainder, they took issue with the way the webcasting services were identified with the webcasting rates, with the need for minima and with the rates thereof.

92. We shall next consider these services in more detail.

### *Permanent downloads.*

93. The Tribunal has often been concerned with determining rates for a spectrum of services and this case is no exception. In this case our task has been made easier since the settlements to which we have referred have at least yielded a highest rate (8%) which is not in dispute and which is undoubtedly relevant to what the appropriate level should be for other services[62] . This ceiling rate relates first to what are termed **Permanent Downloads**[63], that is, to transfers of music from a website to for example, a computer or mobile telephone for permanent retention and use whenever the purchaser wishes. We have regarded permanent downloads as the online analogue of a CD. A classic case of permanent download will be the purchase by a subscriber of an item offered for sale by say, iTunes' Store for use on an iPod[64]. Neither the need for a minimum royalty in this category of service nor its value have been questioned[65].

### *Limited downloads and on demand services*

94. A **Limited Download** (also referred to as an LD) is similar to a permanent download and the royalty rate for it was agreed to be the same. Limited downloads differ from permanent downloads in that the consumer's use of the copy is in some way restricted by associated technology. A limited download may be intentionally ephemeral in nature commonly, by means of a technology called 'digital rights management' or DRM. This makes a file unusable when a subscription ends. The minima here are however different to those for a permanent download. In the same category are **on demand services (or on demand streaming)**[66] where an offering is streamed to the listener to enable him to listen once, twice or a number of times during the period he subscribes to the service. 'On Demand Streaming' does not permit an offering to be downloaded for copying but the user has in many respects

[61] See 'Music Service' in H/1/35
[62] Mr Boulton D4/164
[63] As far as we can tell, this was said by counsel to be synonymous with an FTD.
[64] In fact, the iTunes service is funded through retail sales revenue and not at present as a result of advertising. But, said Mr Cue, Global Vice-President of iTunes, iTunes may well carry advertising in future - hence their interest in these Applications.
[65] Which will be of significance when we examine the Remaining MSPs' reluctance even to contemplate the propriety of minima as such in relation to other services.
[66] 'Streaming' is a technique for transferring music in a continuous stream for use once and without retention of a copy. ODS is thus very similar to an LD and the two are often associated.

the same access to and ability to enjoy a piece of music as the owner of a digital copy.

95. In either case, the user simply initiates the more limited service but does not realistically interact with what he gets, once he gets it. We need say little more about either permanent or limited downloads since the Remaining MSPs did not take issue with the New JOL in relation to these categories of service. A disagreement arose regarding minima (and only minima) with on demand streaming

96. LD/ODSs are offered by a number of the MSPs. Regarding on demand streaming, Napster, a signatory to the Settlements, offers a subscription-funded limited download and on demand streaming service.

97. The rates for permanent downloads and LD/ODS' were established as the result of classic negotiation and compromise: the Alliance came *down* (12% to 8%) whilst the Applicants went *up*, both as to the rate applicable to the service itself and to the presence of relevant minimum rates[67].

98. The present significance of the position of permanent and limited downloads in the Royalty Table is that it fixes one end of a spectrum of services which involves an incremental degree of control or interactivity by the user on the delivery (i.e. form, duration and timing) of the music. The points on this spectrum are to some degree, interrelated.

### *Pure webcasting*

99. At the other end of the spectrum is **Pure Webcasting.** Here the user receives a stream of back to back music, the stream consisting of pre-programmed music chosen *by the MSP*. It is in fact non-interactive and any potential for interactivity (including even pausing the stream of music or skipping and rating of tracks) is prohibited.

100. Mr Steinthal suggests that this is the online equivalent of a terrestrial commercial radio station broadcasting mainly music. Radio @ AOL, which has over a hundred channels available, is he says, an example of this kind of service. We were told that AOL's channels are largely 'genre specific'. Also in this category, RealNetworks apparently has an even larger mood -specific repertoire. In addition, with pure webcasting, there is no intrusion of the human voice. Since webcasting (or as he called it 'General Webcasting') formed the major part of Mr Steinthal's case, we shall return to it later in detail.

101. In between lie **Premium and Interactive Webcasting** - the so-called 'intermediate services'[68].This is webcasting which does not satisfy the pure webcasting prohibitions and includes such personalised services as LAUNCHcast and Pandora.

---

[67] Minima had hitherto been opposed as such.

[68] Also in Mr Steinthal's parlance, 'General Webcasting'.

### *Special webcasting*

102. This is a service where the user can choose a stream of music, the majority of which comprises works from one source – an artist, a group/ensemble or the record of a particular concert, for example. This enables a listener to enjoy an entire album of a particular artist or event. Though we have no recollection of it being demonstrated to us, it seems to be very similar to on demand streaming and attracts a royalty of 8%. In fact, there was little evidence about special webcasting. Mr Steinthal said[69]:

> *" Put aside Special Webcasting...it is not something you should worry about. We do not know of anybody doing it right now in this market."*

Though he promised to return the special webcasting 'later', we cannot find relevant further reference to it. Evidently it is not yet an important offering and we need say no more about it.

## IV THE WITNESSES

103. The names of those who gave evidence at the hearing together with a summary of their employment details are set out in **Annex I** to this Decision. The bulk of the evidence given at trial was expert evidence.

### *Witnesses of fact*

104. We have already identified some of the witnesses of fact in the foregoing narrative. We have no particular comment to make on the quality of any of them as witnesses; they were we believe, all trying to assist the Tribunal and in addition, no serious attack was made upon any of them. The evidence of some was no doubt of more relevance than that of others but there is no need separately to dwell upon the relative contribution made by each. Evidence was offered on behalf of each of the three Remaining MSPs. Also, three witnesses, Mr Geoff Taylor (ex-BPI and General Counsel), Mr Mark Mooradian (MusicNet Inc.) and Mr Andrew Lee (T-Mobile) were called by Mr Steinthal by means of witness summonses. Mr Taylor's evidence was, we felt, particularly fair, helpful and clear. Mr Jonathan Bill, the former head of advertising and industry at Vodafone Ltd gave evidence which we found most useful on a number of aspects of the case. Another witness, Mr Eddy Cue, Vice-President of Apple's iTunes gave evidence from the USA by video link, which was in fact hardly challenged. He had been responsible for the development and implementation of the iTunes Store. The latter offers millions of tracks of music, audio-books, videos, movies, and no doubt other things too.

105. We found the evidence of fact relating to the range of online music services which are (and may soon become) available to have been particularly illuminating – and largely uncontroversial. This evidence confirmed our initial impression that in these Applications we are concerned with a rapidly developing and commercially

---

[69] D1/23

exciting area of business . We consider that this must have been well in the minds of all the signatories to the New JOL – whatever might have been their commercial interests at the time. We say this in response to Mr Steinthal's frequent assertion[70] that the settling parties had no immediate commercial interest in the terms of the New JOL in so far as they related to webcasting, that such terms were part of a 'package' and that they were therefore unreliable as comparators. We consider it unrealistic to regard the music industry as being blinkered and compartmentalised as Mr Steinthal (and to some extent Mr Boulton) suggested. Quite apart from the evidence relating to the extant interests of Vodafone in webcasting (see below), these terms were, we consider, given adequate commercial consideration by the signatories who in truth had at least *an* interest in these matters[71].

### *Expert witnesses.*

106. Our assessment of the expert witnesses[72] cannot be summarised as we have done with the 'lay' witnesses - as Mr Rabinowitz has called them. In the first place, there was serious conflict as to how the Tribunal should treat some of the expert evidence, of what value it was (if any), and whether it was materially wrong. In essence:

(a) the Alliance devoted most of the cross-examination of Mr Boulton, the Applicants' main expert, to attacking his qualifications as a 'licensing expert', his credibility, his independence and the admissibility of some of his evidence - rather than going to his 'raw' evidence as such. With an expert of the calibre of Mr Boulton, this was a risky tactic.

(b) Ms Enders, one of the Alliance's experts, was said by Mr Carr to have misunderstood her role and to have spent inordinate time giving evidence which was in fact of little or no use to the Tribunal. Mr Weisselberg's criticism was that she was a 'poor and unimpressive witness'. Mr Steinthal's criticism of Ms Enders was even more radical.

We shall therefore have to go into the matter of the experts' evidence at some length.

107. **The expert's role** We shall first identify our approach to assessing the parties' contentions regarding the expert evidence. The general role of the expert is epitomised in CPR, r. 35 and the notes thereon. In the light of the massive quantity of expert evidence filed by both sides, we first reproduce the following words of CPR, Part 35.1[73]:

> 'Expert evidence shall be *restricted* to what is reasonably required to resolve the proceedings.'[Emphasis added].

108. In addition to the well-known observations of Creswell J in The Ikarian Reefer [1993] FSR 563, there are numerous other authorities relating to the role of expert

[70] See for example, his opening speech: D1/8.
[71] This was actually confirmed by Mr Taylor of BPI: D6/71.
[72] Whose names and provenance are also set out in **Annex I.**
[73] See also The Chancery Guide 2005 (" Expert Evidence") §§ 4.6-4.9 and 8.16-8.18.

witnesses. Though stated in relation to a patent action, we believe that in a case like this there is good sense in the further characterisation of the court expert given by Jacob LJ in Rockwater Ltd v Technip France SA and another [2004] RPC 919. He said:

> "...they come as teachers...What matters is how good they are at explaining things."

In Cala Homes (South) Ltd v McAlpine Ltd [1995] FSR 818 at 843, Laddie J said:

> "But in the case of an expert witness the court is likely to lower its guard. Of course the court will be aware that a party is likely to choose as its expert someone whose view is most sympathetic to its position. Subject to that caveat, the court is likely to assume that the expert witness is more interested in being honest and right than in ensuring that one side or another wins. An expert should not consider that it is his job to stand shoulder to shoulder through thick and thin with the side which is paying his bill."

In AEI v PPL (supra) at 357, the Tribunal said:

> "It is obviously difficult to draw a line between what is relevant evidence and what is either legal argument and comment on facts as to which the witnesses have no real relevant experience or expertise. Nevertheless for the future, we would suggest that it is a waste of time and money for the parties to file argument under the guise of accounting evidence."

109. Before considering the expert witnesses, we would record that:

(a) all such witnesses possessed both academic and professional qualifications appropriate to issues in these Applications. These are to be found in their witness statements and need not be set out here.
(b) most of the written evidence had been served before the time of the settlements and the relevance of much of it was in our view diminished if not overtaken by the appearance of the New JOL; and
(c) one of the Applicants' witnesses, a Mr Derek Ridyard of RBB, an economist, made two reports, largely dealing with permanent downloads. Since he was neither cross-examined nor hardly even mentioned at the hearing, we need say no more about him.

110. **The Experts' Fees** The principal expert witnesses were Ms Claire Enders of Enders Analysis for the Alliance and Mr Richard Boulton of LECG Ltd for the Applicants. Towards the end of the hearing, we became concerned with the value of much of the evidence of these experts and invited the parties to state in round figures the professional fees charged for preparing their reports (that is, excluding VAT and their charges for attendance at the hearing). Ms Enders informed us that her firm had charged the Alliance about £ 750,000[74] whereas Mr Boulton said that his firm had charged the Applicants a little less, some £685,000[75]. Mr MacGregor,

[74] D11/198.
[75] D12/85.

another expert called by the Alliance, booked fees of £810,000[76]. Add to these the fees of one other expert and the cost of their attendance at the hearing, one arrives at a very substantial sum of money.

111. Incurring expert fees of this order of magnitude (and even taking into account the existence of the Settlement and the substantial sums of money at stake), was in our view, seriously disproportionate. The blame for this, we feel, must fall on all the parties.

112. Finally mention was made by the Alliance of the need to disregard expert evidence which is directed to a question in issue for the court, since this may usurp the role of the court or tribunal. We detect however some slight change in the attitude of the courts to an expert opining on an 'ultimate question' which is not one of law (see for example, Rockwater, *supra*). However whilst such an opinion may now be admissible, the court need not of course accept it. It may nonetheless consider the underlying reasons for any relevant opinion to assess its cogency.

113. **Ms Claire Enders** Ms Enders is an 'industry expert' and is Chief Executive of Enders Analysis which analyses industry facts and compiles assessments on strategic issues facing the media and telecommunications industries[77]. She is thus (as Mr Carr said) a commentator or a 'highly-paid industry observer" (as Mr Steinthal said), rather than being a lively participant in any relevant field – such as for example, Mr Cue of iTunes. We do not however regard this as a damaging criticism of this witness; one hardly needs to be a member of a football team to have an informed view about its performance. Ms Enders told us that she had never before appeared in court as an expert witness. She was cross-examined, vigorously and at length, by Messrs Carr, Steinthal and Weisselberg during which she made it clear on a number of occasions (rightly, in Mr Rabinowitz's view) that unlike Mr Boulton, she was not a 'licensing expert'. This statement was characterised by the Applicants merely as an unhelpful avoidance tactic.

114. With an eye no doubt on comparables, Ms Enders gave evidence about trade practices in a large number of media businesses and in particular in the online, offline and telecoms industries - and indeed in certain satellite industries (such as the place of music in the commercial radio and entertainment industries). She also gave evidence on potentially comparable markets, products and services on which licences had been granted by collecting societies. In particular, she gave evidence to refute the suggestion that webcasting and commercial broadcast music should be regarded as comparable products.

115. The MNOs made no personal criticism of Ms Enders but said that she had misunderstood her role and thus that her evidence was of little assistance to the Tribunal. It was said by all the Applicants that her evidence was unreliable (because it had been largely collated from third party sources) and in relation to comparables, was of little assistance to the Tribunal.

---

[76] D12/83
[77] Her CV is to be found at E7/17/1770.

116. Even taking into account Ms Enders' inexperience in this jurisdiction, her performance as an expert was, we thought, rather uninspiring. Her reports (which comprised a fulsome lever arch file of evidence together with numerous lever arch volumes of exhibits thereto) consisted to a large extent of data which had indeed been sourced by others, sometimes by a team which she herself led and the reliability of whose work she (often unquestioningly) relied on - only to find it wanting on closer examination. We certainly sympathise with the impossibility of mastering everything within so large a corpus of material. Nonetheless, on a number of key issues she seemed confused, occasionally inaccurate[78] and, more importantly, sometimes unable to provide reasons for the assumptions upon which her evidence was based. Surprisingly, she had not actually read the New JOL but relied on a summary thereof. We do not wish to give the impression however that Ms Enders' evidence was misleading; it was not. But we were not greatly assisted by it.

117. **Mr Richard Boulton** is a director of LECG Ltd ('LECG') and had been an accountant with Arthur Anderson for some 20 years[79]. LECG is a global expert services firm which provides courts, lawyers, regulators and governments with independent advice and analysis on matters of economics, finance and strategy. Mr Boulton gave evidence as a forensic accountant and in addition (and to a greater extent), as what he called a 'licensing expert'. He had in fact a double advantage over Ms Enders: he has given evidence before the Tribunal (and to the courts) on the licensing of IP rights (and on other issues) on *many* previous occasions - and he is also a practising barrister. Generally speaking, he was a knowledgeable witness in the field of licensing IP rights and had ready answers to what was put to him. Moreover, he gave a polished and confident performance as an expert.

118. As will be seen, his status as a 'licensing expert' was nonetheless subject of particular criticism by the Alliance and a number of attacks were made on Mr Boulton personally [80]– all of which in our view, failed.

119. In his first report, Mr Boulton said that his instructions were to make a report[81]:

> *" based upon [his] experience in licensing negotiations, on the structure and level of a reasonable royalty for the supply of music content online."*

120. Our attention was however drawn by Mr Rabinowitz to the order of the Tribunal regarding experts (which is always made on such occasions)[82] and in particular to the fact that his role as expert on 'licensing' as such was neither suggested nor sanctioned therein. Both Mr Rabinowitz and Mr Aldous further submitted that this emerging yet unapproved expert *persona* enabled Mr Boulton to stray into impermissible territory in that (in particular) it was inappropriate for him to express opinions about what royalty rates or minima should prevail for particular services – or indeed what general terms should be present in a licensing agreement of the sort under consideration. The Alliance in fact recorded their objection to Mr

---

[78] For example in relation to Ofcom Reports
[79] His CV is at B7/33/1612-1619.
[80] Such as suggesting, that his present evidence was inconsistent with evidence given in other cases.
[81] B7/1383.
[82] A5/82/2.

Boulton's role at an early stage. In the result, said the Alliance, the parts of Mr Boulton's reports most relied on by the Applicants were little short of extended submissions, rephrased later by counsel as submissions. The confusion of roles on Mr Boulton's part demonstrated a serious lack of objectivity, so they submitted.

121. We have found the demarcation of expertise in this jurisdiction to be a rather grey area and have noted that other Tribunals have found likewise. As a forensic accountant, Mr Boulton was of course free to give evidence on matters such as costs, investments, revenue streams and their relevance etc and to provide comment and criticism of industry reports on topics such as statistics, revenue sources and similar technical matters. Indeed he did so. In our view he was also entitled to express an opinion about which comparable licence agreements (or parts thereof) might (or might not) be relevant comparables (see above). But in our view it was not helpful in this case for him to opine on what rates of royalty (or minima) were reasonable for a particular service, what deductions should apply and so on. Such evidence tends to become "*a mere bit of empty rhetoric*" Wigmore, *Evidence,* (Chadbourn rev) § 1920. These are core matters for the decision of the Tribunal in the light of the evidence. The Tribunal's function on terms and rates must not be usurped by the views of a 'licensing expert', however experienced. In reaching our decisions, we have in fact borne well in mind both Mr Boulton's considerable experience as an expert and our essential tasks as a Tribunal. We have not allowed his views as to the 'ultimate questions' to cloud our judgment – but neither have we as it were, struck them out. We have made frequent use of Mr Boulton's general expertise in the field of IP licensing, as will be seen.

122. Two other experts gave evidence for the Alliance, a forensic accountant, **Mr Gervase MacGregor** and an economist, **Mr Zoltan Biro**. Mr MacGregor was a practicing chartered accountant with the firm BDO Stoy Hayward LLP[83]. Mr MacGregor's evidence was largely directed to challenging Mr Boulton's facts and figures. He disagreed with Mr Boulton on a number of accountancy matters and complained (with justification in our view) of the limited extent of the Applicants' disclosure which he said, he needed in order to prepare his response. He said that he had no material adequately to challenge Mr Boulton's raw inputs. However, as many of these issues were of more significance before the Settlement Agreements, we need not now analyse these debates or their outcome. We were however to some extent assisted by his evidence.

123. **Mr Biro** leads a consultancy specialising in economic analysis: Frontier Economics Ltd[84]. Mr Biro gave evidence as to how different technologies might lead to different values being attributed to the music content of offerings to the public. He also considered that the Tribunal might gain assistance on royalty rates from consideration of the agreements made between the MSPs and the record companies/PPL. We found Mr Biro to be a most helpful witness, having a clear manner of delivery and explanation combined with confidence in what he said.

[83] His CV is at E6/15/1386

[84] His CV is at E6/13/1325

## V COMPARATORS

### *Is the New JOL a proper 'comparator'?*

124. We shall next consider whether the New JOL may be regarded as the nearest 'comparator' in enabling us to reach a view on the statutory test of 'reasonableness'. We have already set out the terms of s. 129 of the Act[85] which *inter alia* requires[86] consideration of comparators in reaching a conclusion as to whether the terms of a licensing scheme are '*reasonable in the circumstances*'. This issue concerned only the Remaining MSPs' licence, on whose behalf, Mr Steinthal submitted that the New JOL was not at all suitable in this respect[87].

125. **The Alliance's case.** This aspect of the case, said the Alliance, was clear. The New JOL was a classic example of the outcome of a balanced compromise between a willing licensor and a willing licensee; it is indeed a 'compelling' comparable. Moreover, it is recent, has involved most of the major players in the industry and was concluded after protracted negotiation with the benefit of ample legal and technical back up. As against the Remaining MSPs' proposals, it could hardly be more relevant, said both Mr Rabinowitz and Mr Aldous. In its entirety it articulates the proper 'going terms' and the Tribunal should have no qualms about applying them to the Remaining MSPs' licence. Moreover, the Remaining MSPs' did not even attempt to try and work out a compromise with the Alliance when they had the opportunity to do so.

126. **The Remaining MSPs' case.** The comparator pleaded by the MSPs was traditional commercial radio:

> 'The Webcasters maintain that the most appropriate comparator for determining a reasonable rate for General Webcasting[88] is traditional radio broadcasting.'[89]

127. Mr Steinthal was initially dismissive of even the general *relevance* of the New JOL. His submission was that as webcasting is "functionally identical to" terrestrial radio, the main agreement relating to the latter (an agreement referred to as 'the CRCA Agreement') was the best comparator. Furthermore, he submitted that those subscribing to the New JOL were not in reality commercially concerned with any form of webcasting. Thus, he said, those parts of the New JOL which were concerned with webcasting (in particular) were quite unreliable as comparators and should be disregarded: "*Plainly, no entity with a meaningful interest in webcasting was at the table*"[90]. Referring to the services available in the New JOL, his invitation to us was to disregard not only most of the categories of service identified

---

[85] Para 42 above

[86] '*shall have regard*'.

[87] The definition of 'Gross Revenue' in the New JOL (in either the BPI version or with the Home Page Concession) cannot of course be used as a comparator against iTunes and the MNOs as they deliberately excepted themselves from it.

[88] According to Mr Steinthal's submissions, this means all webcasting except perhaps, special webcasting.

[89] A6/1/11.5.5

[90] D1/28

but also the rates for anything 'below' that of on-demand streaming. The position of the Remaining MSPs was epitomised by Mr Gabriel Levy of RealNetworks[91]:

> *" ..the New JOL from our perspective, is nothing more than the Alliance's unilateral imposition of webcasting terms and conditions upon the Webcasters....I simply fail to see how a document negotiated by parties with little or no commercial interest in webcasting can purport to bind webcasters to its terms and conditions or be proffered as 'the result of arm's length negotiations between sophisticated commercial parties.'."*

Ms Shannon Ferguson, Managing Director of Yahoo Music Europe Ltd, was of a like view:

> *"..plainly there was no 'side' representing the interests of Webcasters in the negotiations leading to these settlements."*[92].

128. In our view, in adopting this approach, Mr Steinthal has had to overlook a number of important primary facts.

129. First, the parties' experts *all* regarded the New JOL as being a *relevant* comparator as a whole[93] . We do not regard this view as being conclusive since the assessment of comparables must be one for the Tribunal in the light of the evidence, particularly that touching Vodafone's Radio DJ Service - which is next considered; but it is certainly persuasive.

130. **Vodafone's Radio DJ Service** Secondly, a company within the Vodafone Group related to one of the MNOs (hereafter 'Vodafone'), has already actually launched a subscription-funded service called the Vodafone Radio DJ service. This is indisputably a webcasting service since it enables the user to influence the playlist. In addition, it runs an on demand music video streaming service. Evidence about these services was given by Mr Jonathan Bill, the former head of advertising and industry development at Vodafone Ltd both in his witness statement and in cross-examination[94]. Vodafone currently charges £7.50 per month for its Vodafone Radio DJ webcasting service. This supports § 8 of the MNOs' pre-Settlement Agreement written submissions, where Mr Carr QC wrote[95]:

> *" It should be noted, though, that one MNO, Vodafone, does presently offer a webcasting product charged for on a subscription basis......and so Vodafone and the MNOs generally, do have an interest in the treatment of webcasting under the 2006 Scheme"*[Emphasis added]

131. Furthermore, according to the evidence, Vodafone (and other MNOs) are already trialling advertising on various services.

---

[91] Levy 3, §§ 8.2, 8.4
[92] Ferguson 3, § 5.2
[93] Mr Boulton at first being cautious in so doing: Boulton 5, §§ 8,10 but later agreeing in answers to questions from the Tribunal, that the New JOL *as between the parties there present*, fulfilled the 'willing buyer, willing seller test'.: see B7/33/1385 quoted in § 133 below and D4/161-162.
[94] Bill 1,§ 13 and D5/14-15. We would add that we found Mr Bill to be a good witness.
[95] X1/5/4.

132. Thirdly, we do not believe that the interests of the record companies and the BPI must be seen as being *confined* to permanent or limited downloads; the Royalty Table covers services which are part of what has been called '*the music value chain*'. Mr Taylor gave helpful evidence in this connection. He had been General Counsel to BPI and was at the time he gave his evidence to us, General Counsel and Executive vice-president of IFPI. In our assessment, he was also a reliable witness. Though we accept that BPI had no current direct interest in webcasting in September 2006, in our view BPI (who represent over 300 record companies) had at least enough of *an* interest in webcasting to agree to parts of the New JOL which concerned webcasting. As a matter of common sense, a major player like BPI would we think, be most unlikely to have agreed to theoretical or let alone otiose terms in so important an agreement. Vodafone's position is of course even stronger. Their settlement with the Alliance was subject of a separate agreement; they were not, as Mr Steinthal would have us believe, swept into settlement by a tsunami created by BPI.

133. Before considering the Remaining MSPs' case, we were reminded that Mr Boulton correctly and succinctly epitomised the characteristics of a reasonable royalty when he said that it was an agreement[96] :

> " *between a willing licensor and a willing licensee acting at arm's length in a competitive market.* "

He then went on to identify the most common approaches used to determine a reasonable royalty one of which, the comparables approach, is that which has been used in this case.

134. Finally, we have several times drawn attention to the developing and shifting nature of the online music industry. In the light of this, when it came to negotiation, it seems to us inconceivable that the numerous signatories to the Settlement Agreement (and the New JOL), every one of them major players in the industry, were somehow blind or worse, unconcerned as to what developments might lie ahead. Existing business opportunities and substantial sums of money were involved. And judging from the witnesses we have seen, those involved were shrewd and experienced men of business.

135. In our view, as against the Remaining MSPs, the New JOL is indeed the most relevant comparator. It is not even the record of an agreement relating to some 'proxy' activity (such as an offline music service). Neither is it a record of say, an overseas experience, neither is it a commercially or technologically outdated agreement. Nor was it entered into under 'stress'. It was for the Remaining MSPs effectively to challenge the relevance of its terms. They have failed to do so; it is the nearest comparator.

## *The need for minima.*

136. This short topic may conveniently be addressed at this juncture. It has two limbs. First, there is a general issue: whether minima are appropriate in respect of

[96] Boulton 1[B7/33/1385.]

*any* category of webcasting (and on demand streaming). Secondly, if provision for minima is considered reasonable, the minimum royalty rates themselves will need to be determined.

137. In our view, the presence of minima in the New JOL provides a strong indication that in this field of licensing, the application of minima to each category of service is generally reasonable in the circumstances. Our view is strengthened by the fact that, as we shall show, minima provide a practical way of compensating the Alliance for any underpricing of music by licensees. Underpricing will assume particular importance in the second part of this Decision under the topic '*Gross Revenue'*.

138. The Alliance's statement of purpose in insisting on minima was one of the Agreed Facts (12):

> 'The Alliance's stated purpose for including minima in the JOL is to ensure the Alliance's members receive a minimum level of compensation for the exploitation of their rights, to protect the Alliance's members against extreme underpricing and to assist in resolving difficult unbundling issues.'

139. In their post-hearing written submissions[97], the Alliance elaborated their intentions thus:

> (a) The Alliance minima were agreed as part of the New JOL. That is where they 'came from'.- they are apparent on the face of the document, the outcome of the negotiations between the negotiations between the settling parties.
>
> (b) The minima are, further, closely comparable to the record company and PPL charges. They lie between the per stream sum in the PPL Webcasting scheme, and the charges which one principal webcaster has agreed to pay certain of the record companies.

140. The Remaining MSPs have continued to oppose the inclusion of minima (whether on a per stream or per subscriber basis) in relation to all forms of webcasting and in addition, in relation to on-demand streaming. It was Mr Steinthal's opening case that there was no need for minima in relation to any such category of service - save a minimum that was intended to cover the costs of licensing[98]. So minimalist a gesture, as Mr Rabinovoitch pointed out, would be cold comfort to songwriters and composers. By the time of his closing address however, we detected a more flexible tone in Mr Steinthal's approach; it seemed that he now accepted the propriety of the presence of minima in the licence *in principle* but challenged some of the levels stipulated in the New JOL quantum.

141. It was not in dispute that minimum royalties are frequently provided for in agreements relating to the licensing of intellectual property – as may be seen (for example) in the numerous reports of compulsory licence cases in the patent and design fields. Minima are required for the protection of the licensor in the event of say, an adventitious market change, in the event of giveaways by the licensee so as

[97] 19/1/07 §15.

[98] See D11/175-176.

to make neighbouring services more attractive, as a result of a deliberate policy of underpricing by the licensee, by the manoeuvres of an unscrupulous licensee - or for whatever reason.

142. In the present case, minima have been proposed to meet a variety of possible situations: they may be required for example, if for some commercial reason (e.g. the presence of advertising), the licensee underprices a service. Minima may also be required where the business model of the licensee is not structured so as to maximise revenues from exploitation of the repertoire; in which event, the provision of minima may have more bite than a 'best endeavours' clause. Minima may also be required to address the complex unbundling problems which arise where, as in this case, music content is sold bundled with other services and it is not possible easily to ascribe particular prices for separate elements in the bundle.

143. In our judgment, the New JOL provides a compelling comparable for the presence of minima in a licence of the kind presently under consideration. Originally all the Applicants opposed the introduction of minima on principle. The settling parties have, however, agreed that it is reasonable to make provision for the payment of minima, albeit at levels significantly below those originally proposed by the Alliance. This, in our view, amply demonstrates the reasonableness of the inclusion of minima in all categories of service.

144. Moreover, since the Remaining MSPs do not seem to oppose the provision of minima for *permanent* or *limited downloads* (or even the rates for such services), it seems illogical for them to oppose minima *in principle* in relation to the other online services.

145. We have no doubt that the provision of minima for all online services must be a feature of any licence from the Alliance and our findings on the definition of Gross Revenue in the latter part of this Decision require it. We also consider that (as with headline rates for permanent and limited downloads) the rates provided in the New JOL must be benchmark rates for such minima.

146. We shall next consider minimum rates for the several webcasting services in question but before doing so we must consider the nature of the services themselves.

## VI THE MUSICAL OFFERINGS

147. The Royalty Table provides a convenient summary of the musical offerings with which the New JOL is concerned. We should say at once that so far as the Remaining MSPs are concerned, the webcasting categories within the Royalty Table are in their view, improperly defined. As noted, the presentation in the Royalty Table is in the form of a spectrum, determined by the degree of control which the consumer has in relation to the music he receives. At one end are permanent downloads whilst at the other, is pure webcasting, the latter being the Remaining MSP's particular interest.

### *Back to back music: Pure Webcasting*

148. Though prior to this case, we were rather unfamiliar with the *arcana* of the online music world, as listeners we were familiar with commercial radio programmes. When Mr Steinthal first made submissions relating to the equivalence of the webcasters' service and that of commercial radio, we were frankly puzzled and, it must be said, at the end of the day we remain so. Though no doubt involving a degree of subjective impression, the two services strike us as being *quite different*. However in deference to the time (and evidence) devoted to the point, we shall shortly revisit what was urged. We shall do so in two parts, the first being to examine what was argued regarding the suggested comparability of online and offline services as such. We shall then consider Mr Steinthal's submissions regarding the allegedly comparable CRCA Agreement and reach an interim conclusion on such comparability.

149. Before doing so however we should briefly mention **'simulcasting'**. Simulcasting is the simultaneous re-transmission by a licensed radio (or television) station over the Internet (or via an MNO) of broadcast material. The person receiving the simulcast normally makes no permanent copy of it. It is like listening to the radio and is an offline service even though available via the Internet. In what follows, we shall place simulcasting in the offline category of services. Nevertheless, in recent times, traditional terrestrial broadcasters have begun to offer what Mr Steinthal described as 'side channels'. There was evidence for example of the opportunity to listen (or listen again) to programmes first broadcast earlier in the day, the opportunity to 'pause' a broadcast while answering the telephone and so on. We do not regard these activities as the equivalent to online offerings; they are qualitatively different.

150. The existence of 'nothing but music' services has in fact exercised the Tribunal on previous occasions in relation to offline references. In <u>AEI Rediffusion v PPL</u> [1998] RPC 335[99], for example, the Tribunal was of the view that independent commercial radio offered quite a different service to a 'music, music, music'[100] service and that different terms were necessary to reflect the increased use of music. A similar attitude to increased use of music in broadcasting has been adopted by PPL (see below). Mr Rabinowitz submitted that this philosophy is equally applicable to a webcasters' services.

151. The following struck us being the more relevant matters raised in evidence and argument relating to the differences between online and offline services – taken in no particular order:

(a) first and most importantly, in relation to pure webcasting, we have already referred to both the uninterrupted stream of musical output available online and to the large number of truly genre-specific offerings available. Though there may be broad differences in bias between commercial radio stations (jazz, classical, indie, 'golden oldies', easy

[99] See in particular at p 348

[100] See the Chairman's remarks: D7/13

listening, ethnic etc), these are simply not of the same order as the mood- specific channels offered by say, Radio@AOL[101]

(b) in pure webcasting therefore the music in an online 'music' service makes a *far* greater impact on the listener and thus has a greater connection with the revenues it generates.

(c) a terrestrial broadcaster in this country must have a licence from Ofcom and such a licence compels it to broadcast a substantial quantity of non-music material. In this connection, Mr Boulton has estimated that in a commercial broadcast from a 'music' station, a fair average music/speech mix is 70% music[102]. The webcaster does not add value to the output in the way a commercial radio station does – for example, through the voice of a popular disc jockey, the programme contents, the format etc.

(d) though Mr Steinthal made a number of observations about increased listener interactivity which commercial radio stations now make available and encourage (e.g. by phone-in or the e-mailing of requests), none in our view even approach the degree of interactivity which may be achieved through premium and interactive webcasting

(e) there was conflicting expert evidence concerning the costs of setting up and operating a webcasting service in comparison with that of even a modest terrestrial broadcasting service. We shall not go into this since the evidence was unnecessarily detailed and the upshot self-evident. The webcasters' music output is derived from a virtually automatic source[103] . Yahoo! for example, employs just two music programmers for this purpose and[104]

(f) some of the new options available to listeners of commercial radio in fact have nothing to do with the broadcasters at all: the pause and rewind facility availability on the latest Roberts® DAB Portable Radio is an example of this.

In this connection, it is well to bear in mind what the Tribunal had to say about commercial radio stations in AIRC v PPL [1993] EMLR 181 at 206-207:

> "It has been suggested to us that these stations are merely 'jukeboxes of the air'. Such a description ignores the contribution which the presentation and selection of the music makes to the success of a station and the considerable attraction of its talk and features.'

[101] Calling a service 'Radio@AOL' or 'Vodafone Radio DJ' does not of course make them a radio station.

[102] Boulton 1 § 12.34 [B7/33/1540]

[103] D729-30.

[104] Fergusson 2§16.8 [C1/11/210]

### *Is the CRCA[105] Agreement a proper comparator?*

152. The fragility of Mr Steinthal's 'comparison' becomes even more apparent when one considers the agreement upon which he principally relies: the CRCA Agreement with PRS[106]. Under this agreement, independent commercial radio broadcasters were charged a sliding scale of rates ranging from 3% to 25% for both broadcasts and simulcasts. Nevertheless, it was said by Mr Steinthal to cover activities 'functionally equivalent' to (at least) pure webcasting in the New JOL and thus, that the financial terms of the former could justifiably be extrapolated to the latter. We would add that though this view was espoused by Mr Boulton in the early stages of his evidence, by the time of his cross-examination we were far from sure that he still adhered to this view.

153. In answer, the first point made by Mr Rabinowitz is that the CRCA Agreement does not cover a number of the activities upon which Mr Steinthal relied. It grants a licensee to '*broadcast as part of its licence from the Radio Authority or to perform in public the PRS repertoire or any part thereof.*' Thus, the transmission in question has to be '*a broadcast*' within the definition in the Act[107] and must therefore be made simultaneously to members of the public or transmitted at a time solely determined by the broadcaster. Internet transmissions are actually excluded unless they fall within one of the exceptions in s 6(1)A of the Act: see also s. 19(2) of the Act. In our view, the only *online* activity which is unarguably licensed under the CRCA Agreement is simulcasting.

154. The Alliance also pointed out that there is an additional difference between what is licensed under the CRCA Agreement and the online music presently under discussion: the CRCA Agreement does not licence the MCPS' mechanical right, the exploitation of which ('dubbing') is important to the way in which webcasters (but not broadcasters) make their music available to users. In our view this is an important point which justifies a higher rate of royalty.

155. **'Dubbing' and the ephemeral right.** 'Dubbing' as we understand it, means simply making a copy of a track. Traditional radio broadcasters do not need a dubbing licence if ab to the extent that they can rely upon the 'ephemeral right' provisions under s 68 of the Act. Webcasters are however in a different position as they rely upon the use of a permanent (and enormous) database of tracks in order to provide their services through instant user selection, streaming etc. We believe that the Alliance is right when it submits that the Remaining MSPs must also pay the MCPS for the right to maintain millions of tracks of music in their immense databases.

---

[105] Commercial Radio Companies Association

[106] E3/8/755.

[107] I.e. '*transmitted for simultaneous reception*'.

156. At this point, we were also referred to current PPL policy on such matters. If a 'music,music,music' service wishes to be licensed by PPL, it would *not* be so licensed under the PPL/CRCA Agreement but rather, would seek to grant a licence under new terms recently published by PPL which require a *much higher* (20%) headline rate[108].

157. Our conclusion in the light of the foregoing is that neither terrestrial commercial radio broadcasts nor the CRCA Agreement to which it relates, are fit comparators when it comes to assessing the royalty rate for pure (or indeed any other sort of) webcasting. In our view, the CRCA Agreement is not the closest comparable. Moreover, our conclusion is for the same reasons, equally applicable to answer Mr Steinthal's suggestion that such a finding would result in '*unreasonable discrimination between licensees or prospective licensees*'[109]. In spite of Mr Steinthal's forceful submissions, in our view, the outstanding comparable in this part of the case, remains the New JOL.

158. Turning to royalty rates, Mr Boulton's initial view was that since the CRCA Agreement was the closest comparable, on that basis, he could justify a rate for pure webcasting of no more than 5%. In the light of the conclusion to which we have come, we need not go into the evidence by which he reached this figure nor his cross-examination on it[110]. In relation to a comparison with commercial radio alone, the reasonable royalty rate for pure webcasting *must* at least be greater than Mr Steinthal's 5%. In fact the mark-up must be even greater than that when one also takes 'dubbing' into account.

159. **Mr Boulton on comparables** Before leaving this section we should turn to some evidence from the cross-examination of Mr Boulton since it shows, we believe, an important qualification to the evidence he originally gave in relation to this issue of comparables. He agreed that

> *:"...what is in the New JOL is agreed between a willing licensor and a licensee; they are at arm's length. It is a competitive market....As I look at the New JOL, Sir, the places where I draw back from saying that [it] provides the right answer are where it does not appear that those with an economic interest [in] the outcome are part of the New JOL"*[111]

And later, in answer to questions from Mr Steinthal[112]:

> *" That is where I do not see the New JOL as being a reasonable royalty agreed between willing licensor and willing licensee, because it does not appear to me that the webcasters themselves were represented in the negotiation. It is not an agreement between a webcaster and the Alliance as to a webcasting rate.*
>
> *THE CHAIRMAN: Because they were not there.*

[108] See G2/23/557
[109] cf s.129 of the Act
[110] See for example D10/95-96
[111] D4/161
[112] D4/163.

> *A, Yes. And because the parties had agreed to it. Sir, if this was 'five webcasters were there and two were not', you would look at it and say: of course it is a relevant comparable because webcasters signed up to it and it becomes a product of willing licensor and licensee negotiations. If it is agreed by parties who do not webcast, it seems to me Sir, it cannot in itself be a comparable for webcasting*
>
> *THE CHAIRMAN: At all?*
>
> *A. I do not think it can, Sir. If webcasters are not represented in the negotiations they have had no say in what the rates could be. The rate might have been agreed at 50% if no webcasters were there...The fact that 8% has been agreed for downloads would of course be relevant to what the webcasting rate should be...It appears to be accepted that webcasting is a lower value product in terms of music use and it would be a lower royalty.." [Emphasis added]*

We accept that had more webcasters been present at the negotiations, that fact might well have led to a more favourable result from their point of view. But a webcaster of substance *was* of course present at the settlement negotiations: Vodafone.

### *Other online comparators*

160. The Alliance drew our attention to two online licence agreements with *recording companies* and submitted that they would be of far more assistance to the Tribunal as comparators than the CRCA Agreement. We agree. There are two aspects to the submission. First, on authority[113], the licences granted by the owner of the recording right are usually regarded as being relevant comparators for the licences granted by the owner of the publishing right. Secondly such licences must be doubly relevant if they are licences for an online activity.

161. The first such agreement was the PPL agreement for pure webcasting which may be found at G2/12/415. The second was in fact a group of agreements entered into by Yahoo! with certain record companies, the details of which remain confidential. Both agreements were the result of recent arm's length negotiation. We consider that Mr Biro's evidence in this area was particularly important. He thought that it would be 'interesting' first to compare the relative treatment of the sound recording copyrights in the offline environment with those in the online environment and did so: see D12/43ff. In the *offline* world the comparison revealed levels of PPL royalty comparable with that which the PPL receives in the CRCA Agreement which we have already considered. On the other hand in the *online* world, the licence fees were considerably greater. In fact, the per play rates in the New JOL and the PPL agreement for pure webcasting are approximately six times those which Mr Steinthal submitted could be derived from the royalties paid under the CRCA Agreement. As to that, Mr Biro had this to say[114]:

---

[113] See §66 above.

[114] D12/29.

> *"One would need to ask oneself why the same would not apply [for the Alliance] in a commercial negotiation in a competitive market."*

And later:

> *" What I can say is that the record companies are producing a sound recording, the composers are producing the composed work and as a matter of logic that same 1:6 ratio should apply equally. I cannot see a reason why it should not...The absolute levels that people could earn could differ because people make different contributions. But that ratio from commercial to webcasting if it applies to the record companies, I cannot see why it should not apply equally to the composers when they are in competitive negotiations."*

162. The upshot of this evidence is that subject to argument regarding the valuation of the categories of webcasting services, it confirms that the general royalty figures and minima reached in the New JOL Agreement may safely be taken as being approximately at the right level.

### *The categorisation of the licensed services.*

163. The Remaining MSPs also took issue with several of the *categories* of webcasting services provided for in the Royalty Table[115] . As they saw it, there should be but one category of webcasting : '*General Webcasting*'. Within that, so they submitted, all forms of webcasting could legitimately be subsumed. The core issue then is whether, considering the tariff for webcasting, one may ignore the categories of service provided for in the Royalty Table and replace them simply with 'General Webcasting'.

164. In addressing this issue, we must again consider comparators. Mr Rabinowitz, submitted that the categorisation of webcasting services established in the Royalty Table makes practical sense and *must* have been the subject of consideration and careful drafting by those who subscribed to it, all of whom were among the most knowledgeable about such matters in the Kingdom – and one of whom was in any event, a webcaster at the time. In addition, Mr Aldous argued that one may take into account the fact that the Remaining MSPs have not (for some reason) quibbled about the first four categories in the Royalty Table, so why should they do so over those remaining?

165. To buttress his submission on General Webcasting, Mr Steinthal had to import a notion from US copyright law: **'DMCA Compliance'**. 'DCMA' stands for the Digital Millennium Copyright Act of 1998 - which is of course, a US statute relating so we were told, to inter alia compulsory statutory webcasting licensing matters and the terms thereof. Mr Steinthal said that a webcasting service *in this country* should properly be so called only if it qualified the webcaster for a compulsory licence to webcast sound recordings under the US Copyright Act 1976 s. 114(d)(2)(C)(i) to (x) as amended by the DMCA. In other words, he was suggesting that it was reasonable (and likely) that negotiations in this country

[115] Save for special webcasting-see above.

for a licence in respect of any webcasting would be concluded on the basis of a definition of subject matter imported from a US statute. This was desirable he suggested on the basis of international understanding in relation to this novel and international area of economic activity. For reasons which are given below, we have not thought it necessary to go into the workings of the DMCA in any detail.

166. In response, the Alliance described these submissions as being hopeless. Whilst it was true that the DMCA definition included a number of interactive services, there was no compelling reason why parties negotiating for an online licence in this jurisdiction would ever want to invoke the rather complicated (and apparently controversial) provisions of a foreign statute to settle the important question of what exactly was being licensed in the UK. No doubt out of an abundance of caution, the Remaining MSPs also led some evidence, none of it conclusive, about the DMCA[116] and its effects. At a certain stage we felt that this sub-enquiry had become so off target that we indicated to counsel at the time that we were not impressed with it. Perhaps as a result, interest in the DMCA subsided - on both sides. We therefore need make no findings on the matter other than to re-iterate our belief that invoking the DMCA does not assist us in the resolution of the dispute on the identification of webcasting services. The best (and in truth, the only) comparator in the UK remains the New JOL and we shall therefore work to the categories of service set out in the Royalty Table

### *Conclusions on comparators and royalty*

167. In the light of the foregoing, our conclusions on this part of the case are as follows

- The categorisation of online services set out in the Royalty Table has been recognised by the relevant commercial interests in the UK, is apparently workable and should therefore remain unamended.

- We believe that the royalty rate and the minimum agreed by the parties in respect of premium or interactive webcasting (i.e. a royalty of 6.5%) are reasonable in the circumstances and should be carried over unamended into the licence with the Remaining MSPs.

- With regard to the pure webcasting service, the level must (as we have said) be higher than the offline PRS figure of 5.25 % but should not we think, be as high as the 6.5 % provided for in the New JOL. We feel that had the Remaining MSPs been present at the Settlement Negotiations, their collective bargaining power would have achieved a *slightly* more favourable outcome from their point of view within this category of service. We should say that this is not some notional adjustment driven more by charity than by fact; neither has it a mathematical basis. It is a value judgment based upon our

[116] Including evidence of extant litigation in the USA touching inter alia the scope of its definition of webcasting.

overall assessment of the evidence and the commercial circumstances. In addition, we have taken into account the fact that commercially speaking, more favourable results were achieved by the physical presence at the negotiations of iTunes and the MNOs (with their insistence on the Disputed Contentions) and Napster, MusicNet and Sony (with the Home Page Concession).

- We shall therefore fix the royalty figure for Pure Webcasting at **5.75%.**
- With regard to corresponding minima, we would reduce the subscription rate to **£0.20 per subscriber** per month and otherwise, to **£0.00055 per musical work** communicated to the public.

## VII GROSS REVENUE

### *The New JOL: 'Gross Revenue' defined*

168. In the New JOL, the parties are agreed that royalty should be based on a *percentage of revenue*. But what revenue? There are of course a number of possible revenue streams, in particular, revenue arising from the purchase of music together with revenue arising from advertising, subscription and in other ways. In this part of the Decision we address which revenue streams are in our view suitable for royalty excise in the light of authority and the evidence. With regard to revenue arising from the actual sale of music (at full price), only the Remaining MSPs have a problem, and that is an issue of wording rather than one of principle. As for the rest, we have found it to be a particularly difficult task adequately, simply and fairly to identify the revenue streams which should reasonably attract royalty.

169. The Alliance has invited us at this stage simply to identify the relevant revenue streams, to establish the 'general principles' to be applied and not to attempt to re-draft the definition of 'Gross Revenue'; that, they suggested, will come later.

> "Once the Tribunal has given its decision, formulating suitable expert determination clauses should not be controversial."[117]

170. The invitation is indeed tempting in the light of past events. There are two definitions of Gross Revenue in the New JOLs[118]. Then there are the two formulae proposed in the Disputed Contentions and another espoused by the Remaining MSPs. Finally, since the Settlement, the Alliance has come up with arguably, three further modifications[119]. Ironically perhaps, there seems to be no dispute about 'general legal principles', at least a broad level of generalisation.

---

[117] 4 December 2006 letter, final paragraph.
[118] Not to mention other definitions in antecedent JOLs
[119] Though this has been characterised by the Alliance as 'drafting improvements'.

The devil, it seems, is as ever, in the detail. We will accept the Alliance's suggestion and in what follows, avoid any attempts at drafting. Rather, the parties should collaborate in drafting a definition in the light of our interim decision. The outcome will then be reflected in our final Decision.

171. In the online world, revenue from music usage may be generated in several ways. First, it will most commonly arise from the direct purchase of music from a page by the consumer – usually by activating a tab, image, photograph or icon or by selection from a list which includes (for example) the word 'music'. As we understand it, such revenue is as yet hardly affected by the presence of advertising on a page or within a service. But this may soon change. A familiar site for such a transaction is iTunes' Store. Music and music-related services may also be paid for by means of customer subscription. Lastly, it is the Alliance's case that revenue relevant to these Applications will now increasingly arise from advertising and sponsorship *at or near* the point of access to and/or consumption of music. It is the definition of this last stream that is at the heart of the second principal aspect of these Applications.

172. Revenue streams likely to arise from advertising, sponsorship and commissions are recognised in the New JOL. The royalty base against which headline rates are to be applied is called the '**Gross Revenue'** and is defined in Schedule 3 of the New JOL as follows[120]:

> *"'Gross Revenue' means, subject to the provisions of the Schedule :*
>
> *(a) all revenue received (or receivable) by the Licensee from Users in relation to the provision of the Licensed Services:*
>
> *and*
>
> *(b all revenue received (or receivable) by the Licensee as a result of the placement of advertising on or within the Licensed Services.*
>
> *and*
>
> *(c) all revenue received (or receivable) by the Licensee as sponsorship fees in relation to the provision of the Licensed Services:*
>
> *and*
>
> *(d) all revenue received (or receivable) in the form of commissions from third parties as a result of the Users accessing and/or purchasing from a service of a third party via the Licensed Services:*
>
> *and*

[120] H/1/44.

> *(e) any other revenue received or receivable by the Licensee arising in relation to the provision to Users of the Licensed Services (including without limitation, such revenue received in relation to donations, barter or contra deals, such deals to be valued for these purposes);*
>
> *and in each of the above cases such revenue shall, for the avoidance of doubt, include any such revenue whether received or receivable by the Licensee or any associate, affiliate, agent or representative of such a party.*
>
> *Subject to the remainder of this Schedule 3, there shall be no other deduction or set-off from the above revenues other than refunds to Users for services that they were unable to use due to technical faults in the licensed services. "*

173. After the Settlement Agreement, the Alliance, the MNOs and iTunes agreed to amend the definition of Gross Revenue in relation to the home page (the so-called **'Home Page Concession'**) in the light of the Alliance's settlement with Napster, Sony and MusicNet – see below.

174. **'Licensed Services'** is defined to mean *'the **Music Services** set out in Schedule 6'*: New JOL, Appendix 1§1 *'Definitions'*. Schedule 6[121] contains 'boxes' to be filled in by the licensee, none of which actually refers to the 'Music Services'. There is however a box entitled 'Licensed Services'. Schedule 6 therefore seems to be tailor-made for each 'User'. Concerning Schedule 6, the Alliance hoped to clear up any confusion concerning the phrase 'Licensed Service' with the following explanation:

> 'rarely had any disputes with licensees over this in the five years or so that the JOL has been operating...The Alliance appreciates that the details of the Licensed Service are important to licensees as they are in effect key to the extent of the revenue base. The Alliance also appreciates that this mechanism might not be apparent to licensees on the face of the New JOL because it will actually involve a discussion with each potential licensee on a case-by-case basis. The Alliance does not believe it is possible to create hard and fast rules for this definition '.

We record that have not been much assisted by that explanation.

175. **'Music Service'**, which more or less corresponds to the items in the Royalty Table, is defined in Schedule 1[122] as being

> 'a service or the relevant part of a service which is:
>
> (a) a Permanent Download Service
> (b) an LD/ODS Service
> (c) a Premium and [*sic*] Interactive Webcasting Service
> (d) a Pure Webcasting Service; or
> (e) a combination of (a) to (d) above'

Items (a)-(d) are further defined in that Schedule.

[121] *'Licence Details'* see H/1/48
[122] H/1/35 *'Definition of Music Service'*

176. We have mentioned above the MNOs' **'Home Page Concession'.** This affects home pages (only) where the music content of a home page is '*insubstantial*' An example of a Yahoo! home page where music is said to be only an insubstantial part of the suite of services offered, is appended to the Alliance's Answer to the MNO's Supplemental Statement of Case as **Exhibit B**. The only relevant item in Exhibit B appears to be the word 'music' which occurs in a list of online offerings providing links to other (presently irrelevant) services. If actuated, the music service provides a sub-page from which it can actually be downloaded.

177. Paragraph 3.1.2 of the same pleading records the following 'common ground':

> *" (a) The parties are agreed that revenue from advertising on a home page is not within the scope of Gross Revenue where the home page offers a variety of services , of which music is only one, no music is actually offered from the home page and music is only an insubstantial part of the suite of services offered....*
>
> *(b) However, if music is actually offered from a home page, ....or if music is not an insubstantial part of the page, the Alliance should receive a royalty based on an appropriate proportion of the advertising revenue from that page.*
>
> *(c) Importantly, the Alliance does not and has never contended that it should receive a royalty based on all the advertising revenue, only a fair apportionment... "*

178. *A propos* the foregoing, we would mention that:

> (a) in the light of authority, sub-paragraph 3.1.2 (a) above seems more a statement of the obvious than a 'concession';
>
> (b) the words '*music...actually offered*' assume importance in relation to the conclusion we have reached later in this decision, and
>
> (c) the practical determination of what constitutes an 'insubstantial part' of music on the home pages of a number of parties whose home pages are in flux, changing perhaps at an hourly rate, struck us as having an element of unreality about it.

179. We have noted that the fact that the parties have agreed that royalty should be based on revenue has given rise to no great difficulty in relation to sub-paragraph (a) in the definition of Gross Revenue. This sub-paragraph may be thought of as covering FTDs and is akin to the sale of a digital CD recording. We would record here however that in sub-paragraph (a), we favour the use of the words 'consideration for' rather than 'relation to'[123]. The problems arise

[123] The phrase suggested by iTunes and the Alliance.

whenever advertising etc revenue crops up in the context of sub-paragraphs (b), (c) and (d) of the definition.

180. Sub-paragraph (e) was evidently intended to be a broad, unspecific omnibus clause and no doubt for this reason alone it was the subject of sustained objection by the Applicants. This did not surprise us. In our view, clause (e) should have no place in a licence of this character. Apart from classic legal objection on the basis of 'lack of nexus', the clause seems to us on its face to lack certainty and thus to be a recipe for contention in the future. In our view, it must go; it is simply too vague.

181. Schedule 3 para 1 ('*General*') contains some explanatory exclusions. For example revenue from non-music voice content, non-music products and text services are excluded.

182. Paragraph 2 (a), (b) and (c) of Schedule 3 of the New JOL *('Advertising and Sponsorship Revenue')* is also relevant to the Applicants' cases. These paragraphs read as follows:

> (a) Gross Revenue obtained in the form of advertising or sponsorship revenue shall be reduced by 5% to reflect the costs of obtaining it.
>
> (b) By way of clarification, advertising and sponsorship revenue shall be included in the definition of Gross Revenue if it is derived in relation to pages within the Licensed Service, including music related pages which do not contain or enable *direct access* to Repertoire Works (e.g. content consisting of concert or music reviews).
>
> (c) Where advertising or sponsorship revenue is derived from pages which include both music and non-music related services (e.g. on a home page or sub-home page of a service), then a reasonable proportion of such revenue shall be included in the Gross Revenue (such proportion to reflect the relative dominance of the music and non-music content).' [Emphasis added]

Mr Steinthal took issue with the propriety of all three paragraphs[124] whilst iTunes and the MNOs took issue with paragraphs (b) and (c) only.

## *Various forms of advertising*

183. We should next say something about the more common forms which online advertising may take. During the demonstrations, we were in fact shown a number of examples of online advertising.

184. The only advertising with which the definition of Gross Revenue is concerned is third party advertising. This should be spelt out in the definition.

[124] In relation to sub-paragraph (a), Mr Steinthal sought a deduction in the Gross Revenue base of 15%. We shall deal with this later in Part IX: '*A deduction for advertising costs*'

185. We shall first consider website pages and pages of MNO 'phone content portals' where advertising (if any) is at present mainly of two types[125]. First and most common is **banner advertising** which is a basic graphical Internet advertisement occurring on *any* page. This takes the form of rectangles (or sometimes squares or ovals) which contain advertising material (usually in colour) having both a literary and pictorial content. There may also be links to other web pages (or web sites) which have been selected *by the advertiser*. Such links are common examples of a 'click-through' – of which more later. 'Clicking' on the image may also lead to expansion of the advertisement itself. The examples of banner advertising which we saw featured some well known trade marks for goods and services. Banner advertising may be placed in different positions on a page and (as we also saw for ourselves) may be of different sizes thus striking the viewer with unequal degrees of prominence. In the same category is **skyscraper advertising** which also takes a tall rectangular form and runs vertically to the side of the main content of the page. Some advertisements may also have an audio content.

186. **In-stream advertising** (also referred to as 'in-download' advertising) is of considerable importance to this part of the Applications since it is the only mode of advertising which the parties all agree should fall within the definition of Gross Revenue. It may be visual, audio or audio-visual in form and as we understand it, it always occurs *after the consumer has initiated the downloading or streaming* operation. It is perhaps analogous to the advertising material. which is sometimes added to a purchased DVD, trailing a forthcoming film for example, and which the purchaser has to view. The nature of in-stream advertising was epitomised in the Alliance/MNOs' Agreed Facts (2(b))[126]. This states that (in relation of course to the provision of music) in-stream advertising is:

> '...advertising included within a webcasting stream or advertising immediately preceding or immediately after a particular content download or on-demand content stream so as to be part of the same content delivery.''

The MSPs provided the following definition[127]:

> " Audio or audio-visual advertising played before, during or between music tracks or streams and which either interrupts the music service or is played while a file is downloaded."

Mr Cue of iTunes put it in a similar way[128]:

> *"The placement of third party advertising at the start, end or during actual delivery of a Repertoire Work to a customer by way of a permanent download."*

[125] Pictures in colour of an MNO's **possible** 'phone content portal which well illustrate banner advertising are to be found in Annex B of the Agreed Facts (see Annex 1 to the MNOs' Revised Opening Skeleton).

[126] It is similarly defined in the Alliance's Answer to the MNOs' Supplemental Statement of Case;A6/5/109A where a simple example of it is annexed to the pleading as **Exhibit A**

[127] Annex B (**'***Draft Glossary'*) to the Alliance's closing skeleton of argument

[128] Cue 3: I/9/24.

187. Though there could be subtle differences between these records of what 'in-stream' advertising actually is (or may be), we felt that there was sufficient consensus of understanding for us safely to use the expression as a 'term of art' – and we shall henceforth do so.

188. We should also mention **sponsored search advertising** and **click-through commissions** which will be considered below. Revenue arising from these are essentially derivatives of advertising revenue and can arise at the same time as banner and in-stream advertising.

189. In view of the ingenuity which we have seen deployed in this area of the advertising business, there may well be other forms of advertising which we have not mentioned.

## *Music 'actually offered'*

190. We need next to consider some further threshold concepts in order to understand what follows. In this part of the case, much use was made by the parties, particularly by the Applicants, of the phrase '**music actually offered'** in relation to website pages. In our view, it is indeed a key phrase in the context of the definition of Gross Revenue and we have adopted it; it is the trigger for the operation of 'in-stream' advertising and also, of both the Disputed Contentions. It is important therefore to understand the concept of music being 'actually offered' from a page.

191. In what follows, by music **'actually offered'**, we refer to music which is enabled or is made directly available to the consumer for downloading or streaming from *any* page on an online service. In the language of the New JOL, it is where the Licensed Service can actually be consumed by a User and in most cases, where the music is purchased. Pages which identify music 'actually offered' may of course also carry advertising, and/or music-related material or indeed, other material as well.

192. The Alliance did not favour the use of the phrase music 'actually offered' in excepting advertising revenue from Gross Revenue; it was, they said, unfairly prescriptive –though it did make use of it from time to time. Two paragraphs from their Answer to the MNOs' Supplemental Statement of Case[129], under the rubric '*Actually Offered'*, sufficiently epitomise their position:

> '4.4 No good reason has been advanced for the contention that music must be actually and immediately accessible on a page in order for composers and songwriters to receive a fair share of advertising revenue. The mere fact that there is an intermediate page between identifying music and making the purchase is a matter of form, not substance, and not a good reason for depriving composers …of any share in advertising revenue. Where the music content provided by the Alliance's members is driving advertising revenues, it is fair and proper that composers….should share in that income.

[129] Though essentially the same point arises against the other Applicants as well.

> 4.5 The MNOs' proposal also provides an unhealthy incentive to the MNOs to structure their services so that Users have to pass through pages of adverts before making a making a final choice to download music. The MNOs would receive revenue from these adverts. Users would be watching the adverts solely because they wished to use the Licensed Services, yet composers would receive nothing.'

### *'Non-music' and 'Music-related' pages*

193. By contrast, there are pages which 'actually offer' no music but which mention 'music' or are concerned with music-related items - and which may of course also carry advertising[130]. We have already mentioned the MNOs' home pages as being examples of this. Such pages are unarguably without the scope of the Gross Revenue definition – even when they contain 'music-related' items. In this category we have in mind:

> (a) **'Non-music' items or pages**: pages offering items such as news, sport, games, mobile TV, audio books, travel, horoscopes, 'chat and community' and so on; and,
>
> (b) **'Music-related' items or pages;**. These will include such downloadable material as music and concert reviews[131], singers' biographies, ringtones, posters, T-shirts and other pop group paraphernalia, audio-books and suchlike, being material which falls outside the scope of the New JOL.

Music 'actually offered' may be found together with 'non-music' and 'music related' items on 'mixed pages' (see below) and such mixed pages are at the heart of the disagreement between the Applicants and the Alliance.

### *'Gross Revenue' further considered*

194. Put broadly, iTunes, the MNOs and the Remaining MSPs have a shared (but not a coincident[132]) interest in opposing what they believe to be an overly broad and unclear definition of Gross Revenue in the New JOL. They object to this definition as having the propensity to capture 'advertising revenue'[133] generated when there is no (or no sufficient) 'causal nexus' between the contribution of the Alliance's repertoire and the revenues of the licensee. Were the present definition of Gross Revenue (including the Home Page Concession) to be sanctioned, it would (they say), be in serious derogation of the standards laid

[130] See for example, Annex B (i) to the Agreed Facts.

[131] Even if such reviews contain illustrative excerpts of the music in question.

[132] It was suggested that the differences between the Applicants in the definition of Gross Revenue reflected their differing forecasts of how advertising was to feature in their products.

[133] In fact, revenues derived by licensees from advertising, sponsorship and commissions which are all referred to (as before) simply as **'advertising revenue'**.

down and applied by previous decisions of this Tribunal and those of its predecessor – particularly in BSkyB (supra).

195. On several occasions, we have referred to the core requirement (which derives from the Act itself) that in cases such as this, the relevant base revenues must be '*directly attributable*' to a licensee's use of the Alliance's repertoire -and that it is for the Alliance to show that this condition is met. In these Applications, the problem arises in relation to the Alliance's proposed imposition of royalty upon '*all revenue received ….in relation to the Provision of Licensed Services*" and was, we think, exacerbated by their reliance upon a construct of Mr Rabinowitz's which he called '*the Music Site*'. The Alliance based their submissions upon the 'draw' that the repertoire possessed; this they said resulted in a close connection between advertising revenue and accompanying music. The two were in a way, symbiotic. The Alliance's position was succinctly stated in their opening written submissions where[134] they asserted that Gross Revenue should include:

> (a) All advertising, sponsorship and commissions revenue generated by a page which is '*within the Licensed/Music Service*', and
>
> (b) an *apportionment* of revenue generated by pages '*outside the Licensed/Music Service*', if music is 'actually offered' from that page, unless the music content of the page is an *insubstantial* part of it[135].

196. iTunes and the MNOs have identified some practical examples where, it was said, the Gross Revenue definition in the New JOL is unduly overreaching and should not conceivably attract royalty – which they do (so *they* say[136]) under the present definition of 'Gross Revenue'. In this category, the more important examples seemed to be:

(i) Outstandingly, banner advertising on 'mixed' pages
(ii) Sponsored search and click-through' advertising, and
(iii) Advertising which enables or permits a 'double recovery', otherwise known as 'double dipping'.

The Remaining MSPs agreed with the MNOs' and iTunes' submissions and, if anything, were more radical in their objections. In support of their cases, the MNOs and iTunes also gave examples from the *offline* world of the limits of legitimate (and of illegitimate) royalty tribute to collecting societies and in particular, drew attention to the working of the CD licences which are promulgated by MCPS.

197. The Alliance, particularly in their 4 December 2006 letter, tried to allay the Applicants' fears of excessive royalty being demanded. This did not however satisfy the Applicants who saw it as a further example of 'creeping concession' on the part of the Alliance, of an even greater uncertainty in character and

[134] §§ 8.30.1 and 8.30.2
[135] The words in italics identify points of difficulty for the Applicants.
[136] The Alliance disagree in part at any rate with *their* construction of the definition.

generally, of the still unsatisfactory definition of 'Gross Revenue'. The ongoing concern of the Alliance was stated as follows in that letter:

> 'Encapsulating [the exploitation of their repertoire] in drafting a definition is far from easy, particularly because no two online and mobile services are the same. Furthermore, the Alliance does not know what business models are around the corner. Therefore, precise drafting is difficult. The Alliance has learned from experience as a licensing body that any attempt to draft the definition of Gross Revenue in too prescriptive a manner may lead to evasion of royalty payments and can result in inadvertent discrimination between licensees operating varying business models.'

The general problem facing all the parties (and indeed the Tribunal) was also well characterised by Mr Weisselberg in his opening address[137]:

> *"What the MNOs and the MSPs offer is a range of services; the services are provided in a number of ways. There are often multiple revenue streams, they are not always linked in a straightforward manner to any particular service."*

198. ***Evidence*** In our view, the Alliance's case on the scope of 'Gross Revenue' is built more on submission than on evidence. They *believe* that it is the presence of the music that so strongly draws consumers and subscribers to avail themselves of pages and that this is so whether the page is devoted entirely to music 'actually offered' or whether the page has non-music or music-related content as well i.e. within mixed pages. We are not in doubt about the sincerity of their belief, particularly in the light of evidence from a number of witnesses of the importance (sometimes, the centrality) of music offered within the mix of services. In the case of mixed pages however, the assessment must, they agree, be a question of degree when apportionment should yield a fair result. At trial, this was called the 'spillover effect'.

199. Nevertheless, the apparently unchallenged evidence of Yahoo![138] and AOL[139] is distinctly less enthusiastic about the power of music. Moreover, discussing the impact of music on online advertising, Mr Bill[140] of Vodafone drew our attention to the actual experience of Vodafone Live! He was of the view that whilst music was certainly an 'important component' in their mix of products and services, it was not at all a 'driver of traffic'.

> *" Of the mix of products and services ....in respect of Vodafone Live! Music is certainly an important component. However, I would say that the addition of advertising to the music elements of the Vodafone Live ! service has a downside in the sense that advertisements may distract customers from the purchase of music content which remains our core business in respect of music The inclusion of advertising on music pages is therefore something that Vodafone is approaching with caution.".*

137 D2/73
138 Ferguson I, C1/10/179-180.
139 Wolffe I C1/1/10-13.
140 I/8/19.

200. Mr Lee of T-Mobile said that the greater part of their revenue from music related services was actually from ringtones (which are not within the scope of the present enquiry) and not from FTDs[141].

201. We accept this evidence but note that these are early days. Like a number of other matters covered by evidence in these Applications, the witnesses were to a degree speculating as to the likely turn of events during the term of the licence.

202. In addition, having viewed for ourselves these mixed pages and assessed their impact overall, we are not persuaded that in many cases the availability of music (still less, music-related items) has the immediate, compulsive effect for which Mr Rabinowitz contends. In our view the placing of a few music 'buttons' (even if music is thereby 'actually offered') on a mixed page does not *ipso facto* come near to establishing the required 'nexus' with the Alliance's repertoire. The matter is, we feel, to be judged as being one of degree. Considered as the Tribunal did in BSkyB, there will exist a 'spectrum' of factual connection with the repertoire upon which the Tribunal must come to a value judgment in the manner of a jury[142]. If (as often happens) the sole or predominant part of a website page (excluding any advertising) is devoted to music 'actually offered', then it is obvious that the 'driver of traffic' on that page is likely to be the Alliance's repertoire. On the other hand, a page with say, a single 'button' for music downloading cannot be regarded as the *raison d'être* of the page from either the point of view of the proprietor or the consumer.

203. In the form of progressive questions, the basic issues appear to us to be these:

(a) Should Gross Revenue *ever* cover more than what consumers actually pay to purchase or use the Alliance's music in an online service and if (as seems to be agreed) should it cover more,
(b) Can it legitimately include associated advertising revenue and if (as also seems to be agreed) it can,
(c) Where in the kaleidoscopic world of online services does one 'draw the line' on legitimate royalty-attracting advertising revenue. As Mr Rabinowitz put it in the post-hearing written submissions:

> " The debate is as to where the nexus ceases to be sufficient."

Then there is the 'wild card' which so vexes the MNOs and iTunes,

(d) What should happen if the music service is paid for (in whole or in part) as a result of advertising revenue i.e. it is offered to the consumer, free or at a subsidised rate? Are these the unique cases where one is justified in looking 'outside in-stream advertising' ?

And overall

[141] D5/163.
[142] See § 65 above.

(e) How may the result be articulated in a simple yet practical manner?

204. Our chief problem in devising a fair, working definition of 'Gross Revenue' has of course been in the context of webcasting. We were invited to consider many actual examples of how advertising might appear when a consumer downloads music on a webcasting service. During the demonstration sessions, representatives of the Applicants put their clients' offerings through their paces. Similar illustrations were also provided at the hearing itself by means of an overhead projector, particularly by Mr Carr. On these occasions we were invited to view selected (and often, we suspect, selectively problematic) material to illustrate and bolster particular arguments of Counsel. A number of photographs of web pages were also put to the Alliance in correspondence accompanied by the question: "*Please tell us, is this 'in'?*" The Alliance's refusal to answer until a later stage (characterised by Mr Weisselberg as 'coyness') was the subject of sustained comment. In this connection, we have also been shown how for example, the home page of the iTunes Store is frequently changed.

205. To further complicate matters, there was evidence that the content on Vodafone's home page changes on a daily or even possibly on an hourly basis[143]. On some webcasting services, customers can actually 'personalise' their content; one consumer can choose pure music offerings for his homepage, whilst another may prefer news, sport or say, music videos.

206. ***The Alliance's Position***. As a practical matter, said Mr Rabinowitz, one should avoid formulae which are tailor-made for a particular music service. To do so might even require the definition to be construed before its *possible* application - in the manner of words in say, a contract or a patent claim. This would be most unsatisfactory. It would be unfair to composers and songwriters and would moreover be a recipe for future dispute and wasted money. That, said Mr Rabinowitz, was why a simply-worded formula for Gross Revenue had been chosen for the New JOL. Moreover, so he argues, unduly restrictive wording would encourage avoidance and become a temptation to 'game the system' [144]. It is all too easy, say the Alliance, to use music to sell advertising and to do so in such a way that the advertisement does not actually appear on the same page or at the same time as the music offered. We shall therefore consider the question of 'gaming the system' below.

207. ***The Applicants' positions***. The response of the Applicants was simple and predictable: the Alliance, they submitted, had no unqualified right to impose so broad a definition under the guise of simplicity so as to capture streams of revenue to which they were not entitled. They had no right to demand licences to make use of material in respect of which they do not own (or control) the copyright. This said Mr Weisselberg, would be an 'unprincipled windfall'. Only in the limited cases envisaged by the Disputed Contentions (and by in-stream

[143] 21/11/51 and 84

[144] See the example given in the Alliance's Answer to the Remaining MSPs' Statement of Case : A6/2/88 §6.15 – and see below.

advertising –see below) could a royalty possibly be justified. Difficult cases would undoubtedly arise (for example with 'bundled' material[145]) but these could be assessed *ad hoc* and if necessary, apportioned for liability by an **independent online assessor**. The present definition of Gross Revenue may indeed look simple, they said, but it was also open to so broad a construction as to enable the Alliance to benefit beyond their legal entitlement.

208. In a separate argument, the Applicants pointed out that the Alliance had contributed nothing to developing, implementing and launching either the music services in question or a fortiori, the mix of services in which it was embedded. It had no input into the basic technology and neither did it share in the considerable business risks involved in getting user-friendly and commercial online products to the public – and indeed, in promoting them once they were there.

> *"Significant to the success of Vodafone generating advertising revenue is its ability to secure subscribers to its network. This will be determined by the range of products and services offered by Vodafone including its voice and text services and pricing plans, its customer service, its content offerings ( both music and non-music), the handsets that it offers consumers, its marketing, its network coverage and its reliability."*[146]

An overgenerous definition of Gross Revenue would be manifestly unjust, they argued, in the light of the *rationale* of e.g. BSkyB .

209. The importance of **minima** to this discussion was stressed[147]. In the New JOL. minima had been agreed for the very purpose of addressing a suggestion by the Alliance of a possible policy of deliberate underpricing by a licensee in the future. Mr Weisselberg also reminded us that in cross-examination by Mr Carr, Mr Biro had agreed that the application of appropriate minima and not an extension of the definition of revenue base, was the appropriate answer to the possibility of underpricing: D12/8-9. He also regarded the use of minima for this purpose as being both fair and non-discriminatory. So, it was argued, the Alliance was in any event protected by the minima to which it had agreed.

210. We are impressed with Mr Biro's evidence on minima. We have therefore taken the view that the function of minima is indeed to provide a safety net to protect the Alliance from inter alia the vagaries of underpricing. Music could for instance be substantially subsidised (or given away) as a result of (for example) the availability of healthy advertising revenues. We shall return to the question of underpricing in the practical context of iTunes and the MNOs' Disputed Contentions below.

211. In connection with the Applicants' cases on Gross Revenue, we found helpful a synoptic chart of the parties' positions on the New JOL (as amended by the Home Page Concession), the original New JOL having been marked-up in different colours. This New JOL as 'amended' forms Annex 2 to iTunes' written

[145] See Kershaw I, §§26-30
[146] Bill I , I/8/§18
[147] See §§136-148 supra.

closing submissions and also incorporates the relevant parts of Mr Steinthal's proposed New JOL as 'amended'. The Alliance, so we were told, had declined to collaborate in the preparation of this document.

### *A pervading mutual mistrust: 'Gaming the System'*

212. Ms Enders explained what 'gaming the system' means[148].

> *"It is not cheating....Gaming the system is using whatever loophole there is in order to avoid doing something or other which involves paying copyright [royalty]. ...Gaming the system means using whatever advantage there is in order to do that and that can be creating a website that has infinite inventory or does various things. It is very easy to do with software. It is very hard to do in the offline world but it is very ,very easy to do with software."*

213. Whilst we have noted Ms Enders' opinion, there is no evidence of licensees actually indulging in gaming the system and in the context of the present Applications, we are unable to assess the potential magnitude of this activity. Moreover, we also believe that it would be in the commercial interest of users of the repertoire to maximise their additional revenues[149]. If music is the powerful draw the Alliance says it is, gaming the system might run counter to it. Lest it be thought otherwise, we record that we have not regarded 'gaming the system' as being in some way a dishonest activity.

214. We sensed on the part of the Alliance a near certitude that given the chance, the Applicants *would* 'game the system' whenever they could. The Applicants on the other hand, felt that with so broad a formula for Gross Revenue, the monopolistic opportunism of the Alliance would know no bounds and in addition, that the present formula would be a prescription for dispute – and that it would be likely also to be discriminatory. In other words, on the issue of Gross Revenue, a palpable degree of mutual mistrust suffused the parties' cases.

215. We record that as matters stand, we remain of the view that gaming the system is more a hypothetical problem than a real one. Time will no doubt tell.

### *Borderline cases*

216. In determining what is 'reasonable in the circumstances', the Tribunal has been faced with an unusually difficult task of fairly balancing the parties' interests. The existence of troublesome, borderline cases is not a new problem in this jurisdiction. We are aware that perfection in devising an acceptable definition of Gross Revenue even if desirable, will seldom if ever, be achieved. We are aware too that the experience of licensed use during the short period of operation of this licence may throw up unforeseen difficulties which may require subsequent cure. In the competition between the problems posed by

---

[148] D10/67-68.

[149] See Mr Cue 3,§29 , I/9.

borderline cases on the one hand and the danger of over generosity to the Alliance on the other, the need for a workable and simple outcome must we think be our foremost consideration

> " We approach this decision with a preference that the tariff should be as simple as possible with a straightforward rate structure based on straightforward definitions. Any tariff will produce anomalies. Whatever tariff is adopted, some situations will fare better than others; but in our view, a complex rate structure is more likely to produce anomalies, especially at the margins of its rates."[150]

Though expressed in terms of the tariff in the AIRC case, the principle is germane to the operative aspects of many a copyright licence. We therefore regard the need for clarity of expression and simplicity of operation in the formulation of the definition of Gross Revenue as being general *desiderata,* even if there may be some degree of quantitative inequity or anomaly at its limits. In the end, we have come to recognise that probably no definition of Gross Revenue will perfectly balance the interests of all concerned.

217. Before turning to the core aspects of this part of the Applications, we are fortunately in a position at this juncture to make two general findings: the first relates to the need for an independent online adjudicator and the other to in-stream advertising. Both issues seem to us to be clear cut – and by the conclusion of the hearing, both seemed to be common ground between the parties. We should nonetheless set them out.

## *An independent online adjudicator*

218. Our first proposal in attempting to resolve the problem of possible disputes as to the interpretation of the terms of the New JOL, arose out of what struck us as an obvious operational *lacuna.* We suggested to the parties during the course of the hearing that the New JOL should be amended to provide for a dispute resolution mechanism via the appointment of an online adjudicator, being a suitably qualified and independent person who would be the first port of call in the event of dispute on the interpretation of *any* clauses in the New JOL. A decision as to whether or not a particular offering fell within the definition of Gross Revenue in the New JOL would of course be well within his terms of reference.

219. At the time, this suggestion drew remarkably little interest from the Alliance, though it should be said that both iTunes and the MNOs proposed an independent adjudicator in their Statements of Case[151]. By the conclusion of the hearing however, the Alliance seemed to have accepted the sense of such a proposal. In the event of our insisting upon provision being made for the adjudicator, Mr Rabinowitz undertook to try to define his qualifications and role with his colleagues in a draft amendment to the New JOL. On 16 January 2007

[150] AIRC v PPL (supra) at 229.
[151] MNOs' Statement of Case A6/4/ii(b) and 16(c) and iTunes' Statement of Case A6/6/17. The independent adjudicator was also advocated by Mr Carr in his opening submissions.

Mr Rabinowitz handed up the Alliance's proposed drafting, which he informed us was agreed by the other parties. We *do* insist on provision being made for an adjudicator and we would now invite the parties to settle an appropriate form of wording to meet this requirement for incorporation in our final Decision.

220. We would expect the parties to summon the adjudicator only if negotiations between the parties failed. A period of say 14 days should be allowed for this

## *In-stream advertising with music fully paid for*

221. By the time of the hearing, a cautious compromise had been reached on the liability of at least one stream of advertising revenue to royalty. All the Applicants were agreed that revenue arising as a result of '*in-stream' (or in-download) advertising* is sufficiently linked to the delivery of the Alliance's repertoire as *arguably* to warrant the payment of royalty. The Alliance were not however satisfied with the inclusion merely of in-stream advertising; they argued that this 'concession' did not sufficiently compensate their members for the use of the repertoire online in either present or future offerings and in addition, was inconsistent with other features of their cases.

222. We have noted the word 'arguably' in the compromise but accept it as a *fait accompli*. For example, this is what Mr Bill of Vodafone said about this development:[152]

> *"While as a matter of principle, Vodafone thinks that in-stream advertising should not be included in the revenue base where consumers pay for a music service, it has, in a spirit of compromise, accepted the inclusion of revenue earned from such advertising in the revenue base. This is intended to give the Alliance and its members some comfort that they will benefit if any shift from paid music services to advertising funded music services materialises, without those music services going all the way to being offered for free."*

We have also assumed for present purposes that the compromise proceeds on the basis that the consumer has **fully paid** for the content he has downloaded for 'in-stream' consumption. On that basis, we accept this consensus as a practical and sensible way of dealing with the liability of at least one *locus* for online advertising royalty and we also consider that there exists here a sufficient nexus between the music and its consumption to justify a royalty. We shall also consider the position if a consumer has *not* paid (or has only partly paid) for what he has consumed because of the presence of advertising, when we come to consider the two Disputed Contentions.

223. We have already recorded our understanding of what in-stream advertising means: see § 183. It is understood to occur

> *immediately* before,
> during (such as in between tracks)or
> *immediately* after

[152] I/8/16

a download – which has already been initiated by the consumer[153]. Advertising '*immediately before*' a download would not however qualify for 'in-stream' status if it occurs on what is called a 'music home page[154]' – such as one sees for example in iTunes' Store – even though music is 'actually offered' there; that would be outside 'in-stream' advertising as we understand it – a topic dealt with in the following section.

224. As we understand it, such advertising could in principle arise as a result of the activation of most of the services identified in the Royalty Table -.but it must always be part of the same 'content delivery'. The MNOs provided schematic 'photograb' illustrations of possible in-stream advertising as Annex C to the Agreed Facts.

225. The Alliance suggested however that this 'concession' (as they called it) substantially eroded iTunes' and the MNOs' arguments on their Disputed Contentions since it disclosed

> 'No principled reason … as to why this type of advertising alone should be exempted from the revenue-narrowing proposals of the MNOs' Disputed Contention.'.

226. We disagree. Under in-stream conditions, it is our view that the 'close nexus' is clearly present. Music *is* actually being consumed as a result of selection of an offer from a web page and moreover, in visual and audio-visual terms the music and advertising are symbiotic. It therefore appears logical to treat these three potential locations for advertising equally *a propos* advertising revenue for inclusion in the definition of Gross Revenue. In BSkyB terms, this revenue is at the top end of the 'spectrum' of association with the repertoire.

227. In addition, since in-stream advertising is inextricably connected with the actual consumption of the music purchased, such consumption has to be recorded and accounted for by users in any event. So in practice, there should be no problems.

228. So much for 'in-stream' advertising as such. This is a justifiable revenue stream for royalty purposes and in our view, it must be spelt out in the definition of Gross Revenue. iTunes and the MNOs have proposed slightly different versions of wording on this point for inclusion in the revised Gross Revenue definition[155]. The Remaining MSPs cover this in different wording as follows:

> "..provided that such advertisement …appears at the same time as a Repertoire Work is being utilised by or served from the Licensed Service."

229. We prefer the MNOs' version which reads as follows:

---

[153] We have been shown relevant advertising immediately before and during download. We have not however seen advertising immediately *after* download.

[154] Or perhaps a music sub-home page.

[155] Annex 2 to iTunes' closing written submissions.

> (b) all revenue, including by way of sponsorship and commissions, received (or receivable) by the Licensee as a result of the inclusion of third party advertising "in-stream) as part of the Licensed Service, being advertising placed immediately at the start, end or during the actual delivery of a Repertoire Work to a User, ..."

### *Outside 'in-stream' advertising: 'Music only' pages and mixed pages*

230. The consensus on in-stream advertising assists us somewhat in establishing whether a nexus exists between music and advertising in outside in-stream situations and if it does, where the 'line of sufficient connection' should be drawn. The enquiry arises of course, only when music is 'actually offered' online

231. The MNOs' and iTune's positions were that in such circumstances, revenue can arise *only* in the circumstances envisaged by their respective Disputed Contentions i.e. full payment for the music downloaded exhausts all further tribute.

232. The Remaining MSPs (as we understood it) contended that in-stream advertising was the only revenue stream which the Alliance could legitimately lay claim to.

233. In our view however, there are three categories of pages which are outside 'in-stream' pages, all of which *ex hypothesi* may carry advertising. First, there are those pages which have no music or music-related content. These have already been considered and no further mention need be made of them.

234. Secondly there are pages where (the advertisement apart) the **entire operative content** of the page comprises 'music actually offered'. Choice of any item on such a page will lead to a music download and for this reason, such pages were sometimes referred to as '**music only pages**' or as '**music home pages**'. It seems to us that the association of such pages with the Alliance's repertoire must in real terms be about as close as it is with 'in-stream advertising' and may logically be considered to be part of it. All advertising revenue from such pages should therefore in our view, also be subject to royalty being paid – for the same reason. 'Music only pages' must now be specifically mentioned in the new definition of Gross Revenue.

235. Of greater importance to this case is the third category, the so-called '**mixed pages**'. By 'mixed pages' we mean web pages where non-music (and/or music-related[156]) services are simultaneously offered with music for direct downloading. As we understand it, mixed pages may occur virtually anywhere online but for the purposes of illustration, a home page was often cited for this purpose. In such cases, as both the Disputed Contentions and the Home Page Concession recognise, the relative 'contributions' of the music and non-music

[156] See § 190.

parts (again disregarding the advertising itself) may vary between the 'insubstantial' and the predominant.

236. Whereas the discussion at trial (and before it) focussed more upon the effect of the 'music offered' being *insubstantial* in relation to the whole, we consider it to be both realistic, more practical and in line with principle to look at the situation the other way around. The relevant question therefore is: Does the character of the **predominant part** of the page (disregarding the advertisement itself for this purpose) make it a royalty attracting page when advertising is present?

237. In our view, if ' music actually offered' comprises the predominant part of the entire content displayed on a web page (which *ex hypothesi* also carries advertising –which may be ignored for present purposes), then advertising revenue arising from it may legitimately be included in the definition of Gross Revenue. In practical terms, this conclusion thus disposes of the Disputed Contentions.

238. ***Apportionment***. This is a strategy which has been proposed on several occasions to tackle the revenue calculation on mixed pages in hopefully, a fair way. Both the Disputed Contentions, the Home Page Concession and the arguments of counsel on other related issues, have from time to time raised the spectre of trying to separate on a mixed page, services not requiring a licence from those that do, followed by an exercise in some sort of apportionment. It stands accepted that precision is unlikely ever to be achieved in practice and that once again, the assistance of the adjudicator is likely to be sought. In the light of what we saw at the demonstrations, we find the likelihood of repeated, detailed apportionment exercises as being something to be avoided if at all possible. Subject therefore to the paragraph following, we wish to avoid detailed apportionment exercises.

239. We would therefore add the following regarding our view of what the **'predominant part'** of the content of a mixed page should be. Here, the assessment must primarily be visual[157]. It will be the result of examining the *area* of a page actually occupied by the mixed offerings and establishing the 'relative dominance' of the music and non-music elements – the advertisement itself being disregarded for this purpose. For the avoidance of doubt, we record that by the **'predominant part'** of the entire content of a mixed page, we envisage the page to contain 75% or over of 'music actually offered'. Though this is another value judgement, we feel that this apportionment is relatively easy to carry out whilst at the same time serving the need for a close connection between the music and the revenue generated from advertising on that page.

240. Should there be difficulty about either what is to be regarded as being 'in-stream advertising' or whether the 'predominant part' of a mixed page is indeed related to 'music actually offered', this could, we feel, conveniently be left for the adjudicator's determination.

[157] We were not addressed at any length on how to deal with the assessment of 'audio only' advertising.

### *The Alliance's 'Music Site'*

241. Prior to trial, the Alliance often used the phrase *'within/outside the Licensed/Music Service'*[158] to identify the royalty-attracting 'zone': see for example § 192 above. However, during the trial, Mr Rabinowitz began to identify the Alliance's principal royalty-attracting revenue streams as arising at (and around) what he called a **'Music Site'.** The notion of the Music Site seemed to us to come to a head in the Alliance's 4 December 2006 letter (p. 3) where it was identified thus:

> 'What constitutes a 'music site' should *in most cases* be obvious to the casual observer. The music site will be that part of the MSPs' or the MNOs' offering which is *built around* the offering of the music licensed under the New JOL.' [*Emphasis added*]

242. We learned this much more about Music Sites (principally again, from the 4 December letter):

(a) Music Sites are separately branded and have their own 'look and feel'.

(b) They are in some way broader than a Music Service[159] since

> *" it is not limited to the Music Services as defined in Schedule 1 of the Scheme. If it were, Advertising Revenue qualifying as Gross Revenue would on Mr Carr's construction, only be generated from pages from which music is' actually offered'."* ,

(c) Music Sites are "*generally.. identified with the word 'music' or some related description*".

(d) "*Of course, under the New JOL it may be necessary to have a discussion with a potential licensee about the extent of its Music Site."*

243. The Alliance's position concerning their proposed 'Music Site' was this: Mr Rabinowitz said that all revenues earned thereabouts should 'in general' be within the royalty base. Nevertheless, the Alliance also laid claim to undefined territory outside the Music Site. Here however, Mr Rabinowitz recognised that a more complex situation prevailed and in fairness, an apportionment of revenues based on subjective assessment might be required – if necessary, with the intervention of the adjudicator. Since the foregoing still left us unenlightened as to where the line was to be drawn, we must evidently look more closely into the limits of the Alliance's 'Music Site'.

244. First, according to the Alliance, as the Music Site royalty-attracting advertising is evidently intended to include at least

(a) 'in-stream' advertising, and

---

[158] Or simply 'the music service'.
[159] Defined: see § 168.

(b) advertising which is present where there is provision for downloading music (i.e. 'music actually offered').

245. However we view the Alliance's idea of a Music Site with suspicion in so far as it lays claim to more than this. Like the Applicants, we question the use of the phrase '*built around*' the offering of the licensed repertoire; this is a relative term and if questioned, may inherently be prone to debate and misunderstanding. As we observed at trial: Where does the perimeter to what has been 'built around' lie? Mr Carr's response was in effect, that the perimeter was elastic[160]:

> *"There are not any limits because it is all in their discretion."*

246. This is obviously unsatisfactory. If (as it appears in view of the foregoing) the meaning of 'Music Site' is to a significant degree, indeterminate (or its application is capricious), its use in the definition of Gross Revenue would be likely to give rise to problems. It should not be used in our view.

## *Music fully paid for: Conclusions*

247. *When music is fully paid for* there are three situations where in our judgment, advertising revenue should attract royalty:

- when the advertising is 'in-stream',
- when the 'music actually offered' forms the sole content of a page on which advertising is also present (ie a 'music only' page), and
- when the 'music actually offered' forms the 'predominant' part of a page on which advertising is also present (i.e. a 'mixed page')

In the second and third cases, the part of the page in question occupied by the advertising itself will be disregarded for the purposes of estimation. In the third case, 'predominant' will be understood to mean that the music actually offered forms 75% or over of a mixed page. Mathematical precision is not envisaged and disagreement on any of the foregoing matters can be referred to the adjudicator. If music is not 'actually offered' on a page, the issue of royalty on advertising revenue does not of course arise.

## *Music not fully paid for: The 'Disputed Contentions' and minima*

248. So far, we have assumed that the consumer will be paying the *full price* for music downloads. But the full price may not always be required and in such a case, two possibilities will arise, both of which underpin the Disputed Contentions. First, there is the MNOs' Disputed Contention which envisages downloaded music being offered *free*, its cost having been entirely defrayed by

[160] D2/38.

concomitant advertising[161]. Secondly, there is iTunes' Disputed Contention where music is offered at an '*artificially depressed*' price, that is, by *subsidy* from concomitant advertising. The music for consumption must of course be 'actually offered'. In either situation, subject to the comfort of minima (see above), the Alliance considered that their members might lose out on royalty from the sale or use of the music – all because of the presence of the advertising associated in some way with it. That said the Alliance, would be unfair.

249. The Alliance's argument is however flawed in that it completely ignores the presence and negotiated purpose of minima: see §§ 138-139, supra. . Nonetheless, we shall examine the arguments.

250. The iTunes' proposal was, said Mr Weisselberg, a more 'nuanced' position than that taken by the MNOs. Indeed, iTunes' 'concession' was acknowledged by Mr Rabinowitz to represent the 'middle ground' and was thus more reasonable from the Alliance's point of view. However, it was one which still did not go far enough for the Alliance.

251. Whenever the full price *is* paid for music, the Applicants submit that ('in-stream advertising' apart), the Alliance's members will have been sufficiently rewarded for the use of the repertoire. No royalty is therefore due on advertising. On the other hand, the MNOs and iTunes *are* prepared to pay royalty when the music is free or is subsidised by advertising. When this occurs, royalty for use of the music can *only* be levied on the advertising revenue with which it is associated since there is nothing else to go on. In justifying this approach, Mr Carr drew support from the *faute de mieux* basis upon which the Tribunal had to act in the commercial radio case, AIRC v PPL [1993] EMLR 181 (supra). There, it will be recalled, there was also no alternative to a royalty based on advertising revenue, commercial radio being free to the consumer.

252. We have in effect rejected the word 'only' in the phrase '*should only be included within Gross Revenue*' which is to be found in both Disputed Contentions. We have thus rejected the premise on which the Disputed Contentions are based because, we believe, that even when the music is fully paid for, there are circumstances where royalty on advertising revenue should still be available to the Alliance; see the previous ***Conclusions.*** The situations envisaged in the Disputed Contentions are merely, *a fortiori*.

253. Pointing to an apparent illogicality in the positions of iTunes and the MNOs on this point, Mr Rabinowitz said that if free or subsidised music apparently creates a 'sufficient nexus', how could it be said that music offered at full price in the same situation did not? We understand that argument. We are not however sure that the *faute de mieux* order for royalty in AIRC is expressed to be based on the need for a 'sufficient nexus' between broadcasting of the music and its associated advertising. The award arose because compensation based on advertising royalty was the *only* solution which the Tribunal found 'reasonable in the circumstances'.

[161] Actually, in both cases, 'advertising, sponsorship and commissions'.

254. We shall certainly follow the AIRC approach in this part of our own decision without analyzing its *ratio*. We believe however that there is further justification for doing so. When music is free or subsidised, that very fact must also fuel an increased draw to the page whence the music is actually offered. For that reason, there, is a separate 'close connection' between music and advertising. Consumers are obviously attracted to free (and subsidised) offers; ask any pirate.

255. ***iTunes' calculations***. For all its engaging 'nuance', iTunes' proposal has an uncomfortable pinch about it. When online music is offered free there is, of course, unlikely to be a problem. But that is not the case when any degree of subsidy is present.

256. In our view, the iTunes Disputed Contention suffers from the seriously unattractive feature that it would be difficult to operate in practice. Part of the difficulty may be appreciated merely by looking at para (c) of the iTunes' proposals for amending the New JOL which are incorporated in the synoptic marked up version which is Annex 2 to their written closing submissions. Royalty revenue due on artificially depressed pricing is expressed in terms of a formula which requires an assessment of inter alia the number of underpriced Musical Works sold. The artificial depression could be determined as follows:

$$A \times \frac{UMV}{NUMW}, \quad \text{where}$$

A=Applicable royalty revenue received in respect of the period when an underpriced musical work is offered for sake

UMW = Number of underpriced Musical Works sold, and

NUMW = number of Musical Works sold

257. The above formula presupposes however that there will be antecedent agreement about when a Musical Work is 'underpriced'. But this appears to be no easy matter. For example, the evidence of Mr Bill of Vodafone, gives two real illustrations of disputes over whether the price for FTD was in truth 'underpriced'[162]. On this point, Mr Bill also described the iTunes proposal as being "*subjective and difficult*"[163]. We accept this evidence. In cross-examination, he also said[164]:

> "*..I am not suggesting that it would be impossible. I am saying it is convoluted and perhaps less black and white than the proposal that we put forward.*"

[162] I/8/§25.
[163] I/8/§25.
[164] D5/79-80.

258. iTunes tried to meet this difficulty in two ways. First, it proposed a practical mechanism whereby underpricing shall be *deemed* to have arisen[165]. The proposal reads as follows:

> " The price payable by the user shall be deemed to have been artificially depressed ...where 8% of the ex-VAT price to be paid to by the user for a Musical Work would have produced a royalty of less than half the applicable minimum payment".

259. Secondly, Mr Weisselberg having accepted that in practice it might not be easy to decide when the price paid by the User has in fact been subsidised by advertising revenue (and if so, to what degree), was therefore compelled to put forward the hard-pressed online adjudicator to resolve any dispute on the issue.

260. For the foregoing reasons, we have come to the conclusion that the iTunes Disputed Contention is in any event unacceptable. It would, we think, be a prescription for serious practical difficulty in the future. The *degree of subsidy* (which is its *raison d'être)* cannot be ignored. Other parties submitted that what was needed was a relatively simple, workable definition which on the authorities is always a *desideratum*. That, says Mr Carr, is a reason why the MNOs' proposal should be accepted.

261. We believe first that when *any* element of subsidy or underpricing is present in the sale or use of the repertoire online, that state of affairs should be presumed to be due to concomitant advertising. We further believe that the degree of subsidy should be ignored; free music and subsidised music should be treated in the same way.

262. Mr Steinthal's submission on this part of the case was again based on the criterion that for royalty to accrue, advertising must in all circumstances be '*directly attributable*' to the repertoire. That is of course correct. The Remaining MSPs' formula for triggering the operation of royalty accrual in respect of online advertising is, as we understand it, remarkably similar to the conclusion we have reached in relation to the downloading of fully paid music outside 'in stream' advertising. It reads thus[166]:

> "(b) All revenue received (or receivable) by the licensee in the Territory as a result of the placement of third party advertising on or within the Licensed Services, provided that such advertisement appears on the same webpage adjoining or immediately proximate to the use of Repertoire Works, or [in-stream – see above]"

## *Overall conclusions*

263. In summary, we accept on authority, that the Alliance is entitled to participate by royalty in some of the advertising revenue in limited circumstances outside

---

[165] Again from the 'marked-up' New JOL, being Annex 2 to iTunes closing submissions. We have assumed that this proposal will be workable within the industry.

[166] All three proposals for amendment of the New JOL definition of Gross Revenue at this juncture introduce the concept of 'the Territory'. We see no harm in retaining this.

in-stream advertising. We are minded to treat all the cases basically on an equal footing, that is, whether the music is fully paid for or whether it is either free or it is artificially depressed by advertising. When the sole or predominant part of a page relates to 'music actually offered', royalty is due. Furthermore, in relation to the 'sole or predominant' requirement, our view is that it should also be understood in the same way in all cases.

264. It is of course true that when music is not fully paid for, the Alliance may to some degree 'lose out' on the sale. But that is surely why minima are present in the Tariff.

### *Sponsored search advertising and 'click through' sales*

265. These days, various sorts of sponsored search are a common (and useful) feature of web pages. Sponsored search advertising is the return of links to advertisers on a search results page where the user uses a search facility on say, an MNO's content portal. Such advertising is akin to the 'sponsored links' that are often returned on an Internet search engine's results page. In Annex D to his closing written submissions, Mr Carr provided an illustration of sponsored search advertising by showing the results page of a Google search on 'Robbie Williams' . This showed 10 results, two of which (entitled 'Sponsored Links') enabled one to download Robbie Williams songs *via a third party website.* The remainder of the results page related to stories and articles of various kinds concerning the singer.

266. In our view, a search facility is a distinct non-music service offered to consumers who, in the case of customers of the MNOs, expect to search content wherever they are within the service. It may be regarded in the same way as the music button on a home page. It may be music-related or it may not be. More importantly, this form of advertising has in our view, only a tenuous a link with the use of the repertoire *by the MNO (or by iTunes) and* in our judgment sponsored search advertising cannot qualify for inclusion in the definition of Gross Revenue. The final licence should therefore explicitly spell out this exclusion.

267. Third party sales are in any event excluded from the Gross Revenue by the New JOL: H/1/44-45 § 1 (b)(ii).

### *Rearrangement of page content*

268. We have already mentioned this recent phenomenon but were not addressed on the topic at any length. In theory, rearrangement could possibly lead to advertisements being moved by the consumer into new positions relevant to this enquiry. Such re-arrangement is in our view, out of the hands of the MNOs or MSPs and is thus without the scope of the Gross Revenue provision. In addition, a general direction to the customer referring to the provision of a facility for rearranging the content of an offering is, we consider, also without the scope of the present enquiry. This is so on the basis of the narrow meaning given by the

courts to 'authorisation' in copyright cases: see for example CBS Songs Ltd v Amstrad Consumer Electronics plc [1988] AC 1013 at 1054[167].

## VIII 'DOUBLE DIPPING'

269. This was another 'quia timet' topic if we may so call it. The Alliance was from time to time accused of a desire to collect royalty on the same revenue stream twice and examples of this possibility were put forward. In response, the Alliance vehemently denied any wish (or indeed entitlement) to do so and sought to clarify their position in their letter of 4 December 2006. Double dipping is obviously objectionable in the present context but it is to be contrasted with two separate revenue streams generated from two separate acts of exploitation of music. That is not the same thing. We have considered the evidence regarding the possibility of double dipping and do not believe that the likelihood of its happening to be sufficient to require it to be addressed specifically in the definition of Gross Revenue.

## IX A DEDUCTION FOR ADVERTISING COSTS

270. The Remaining MSPs seek a deduction from the Gross Revenue base of 15% for the costs of securing advertising revenues. All the other parties have settled with the Alliance on the basis that there should merely be a 5% deduction under this head.

271. The basis for the Remaining MSPs' contention seems again to hark back to the position of the commercial radio broadcasters. In the case in question, AIRC v PPL [1993] EMLR 181 at [217], the Tribunal found as a fact that the cost of obtaining direct advertising was " *in many cases ...probably greater than 15% of sales revenue. In some cases it is as much as 30%"*. Nevertheless the Tribunal applied a 15% deduction.

272. Two points which are presently relevant may be gleaned from this decision. First, that these figures were based on actual evidence of advertising rates and costs. Secondly that the Tribunal applied a deduction which was intended to cover only a *proportion* of the costs of obtaining advertising.

273. In this case, the most important factor for us to take into account is undoubtedly the existence of the New JOL as a comparator. For the reasons upon which we have already elaborated, we are of the view that in this aspect of the case, the New JOL must indeed be regarded as a compelling comparator. We should therefore require cogent evidence to be persuaded that the settlement figure of 5% was *not* fair and reasonable in the circumstances.

274. In addition, the evidence touching the actual costs of advertising in this case falls far short of that standard in our view. Some relevant *estimates* were provided by Yahoo! and calculations were made by Mr Boulton on behalf of

---

[167] Not referred to by counsel.

AOL. The outcome struck us as derivative in character and in addition, was criticised by Mr MacGregor. On the other hand, the evidence of Mr Bill on behalf of the MNOs suggests that at the time of the settlement, they indeed had an ongoing commercial interest on this question of advertising costs.[168]. This also supports our view that the New JOL is the best comparator in this matter

275. We have reviewed the material under this head and find that the Remaining MSPs have failed to justify a deduction beyond that already agreed by the settling parties to the New JOL

## X A DEDUCTION FOR AUDIO VISUAL MATERIALS

276. A reduction in the *royalty rate* (but no reduction for *minima*) in respect of audio-visual materials of 15% was agreed between the Alliance and all the other settling parties (iTunes and the MNOs included) in the New JOL. However, the Remaining MSPs have argued for a 25% reduction in both the royalty rate and minima on the basis that the music provided by the Alliance only forms a relatively small part of a more valuable product.

277. Mr Boulton stated that the New JOL has "*some merit as a comparable*" on this point[169] . For the reasons already given, we regard the New JOL as being the best comparator under this head as well. This is an area where iTunes had a real interest, Mr Cue stating that audio-visual materials had a "*huge potential*" as far as his company was concerned. In fact his company is already offering audiovisual downloads (of various kinds) in a number of markets. He also confirmed in cross-examination that in September last year, his company's interest was as great as it is today in this business area[170]. Evidence on this topic was also given by Mr Bill and Mr Lee. These parties evidently well knew what they were doing when they signed the Settlement Agreements.

278. We have reviewed the material before us on this topic and have unhesitatingly reached the view that the position agreed by the settling parties in the New JOL is fair and reasonable – and should apply to all new licences. The Remaining MSPs case on this point is therefore rejected.

## XI A 'NEW FORMAT' DISCOUNT?

279. The Remaining MSPs were also seeking a 'new format' discount. Their proposal was that only one third of the rates determined by the Tribunal should apply to the 'nascent webcasting services market' for a period of at least 5 years: Supplemental Statement of Case § 18.1. It was said that 'the webcasting industry when compared to the commercial radio industry is 'underdeveloped and still in its infancy'. Relying on precedent (BPI v MCPS [1993] EMLR 86 at 115) it was submitted that in situations such as this, a 'new format' deduction

[168] I/8/10
[169] G1/6/32
[170] D7/99-101

was amply justified. Needless to say, this submission was strongly opposed by the Alliance.

280. There is no provision for a 'new format' discount in the New JOL. Moreover, though the Remaining MSPs' position on this issue was never abandoned, we gained the impression that this a was a topic which by the time of the closing speeches, Mr Steinthal was not pressing as strongly as he was in opening.

281. The evidence on this point comes first from Mr Boulton upon which he notably disagreed with the Remaining MSPs. Confirming our own view (and for the reasons previously given) he agreed that the New JOL was a valid comparator on this issue. Ms Enders firmly rejected the suggestion that webcasting was a 'nascent' industry. We accept this evidence. In addition, the Remaining MSPs' argument has a hollow ring when one considers that they themselves were the first to launch on the UK market and take licences from the Alliance[171] For these reasons, we are of the view that the Remaining MSPs have failed to establish their case that there should be provision for a 'new format' discount.

## XII COSTS IN THE COPYRIGHT TRIBUNAL

282. References to the Tribunal have become more frequent and so too has been the criticism by users and potential users (many of them of modest means) about the heavy cost of resolving disputes with the collecting societies. Invoking the assistance of the Tribunal to resolve disputes must not become the preserve of the powerful and the wealthy by reason of costs. It is, so we consider, the duty of users of the Tribunal, particularly the collecting societies, to ensure that these references are conducted in a thoroughly proportionate and economic manner, and overall, in accordance with the requirements of CPR, Rules 1.1-1.4, that is, the **Overriding Objective**.

283. In Universities UK v Copyright Licensing Agency Ltd [2002] RPC 36, the Tribunal said this[172]:

> "The written evidence is extensive and extremely detailed. No point, however irrelevant, is allowed to go unanswered with the result that the second round witness statements turned out in some cases to be longer than the original ones.....
>
> "To do its job effectively, the Copyright Tribunal must be accessible at reasonable cost. It exists at least in part, to prevent unreasonable terms being imposed on licensees who have little choice but to take a licence. Yet in the present case, we heard evidence from both sides that a reference to the Copyright Tribunal was regarded as a last resort: a failure of a most serious kind. The reason for this view is the perception that the proceedings are necessarily extremely costly, intolerably lengthy and highly complex. The danger that lurks in such a state of affairs is that the cost of a reference to the

[171] RealNetworks was licensed from July 2002 for example and Yahoo! and AOL a year later.

[172] § 16.

> Tribunal could be seen as an incentive to the acceptance of unreasonable terms, in conflict with the above objective".

284. Though the parties' presentation of court material has been excellent, we feel that more thought could and should have been given to trying to save costs on the way. In particular, in this case:

(a) The overkill on expert evidence has already been noted and commented upon, and
(b) The parties' unabated enthusiasm for the generation of long-winded *inter partes* correspondence seemed quite unstoppable – and to have been arguably unnecessary.

## XIII EPILOGUE

266. We have noted on several occasions that as far as we are aware, this Decision has been made in virtually uncharted waters[173]. In addition, our decision on a number of issues has been reached more by hypothesis than as a result of experience. Only time will tell whether the way a number of matters have been resolved proves to be fair and satisfactory. We therefore feel it appropriate to conclude with the following two observations, the first being a quotation from the judgment of Hoffmann J (as he was) in an appeal from the Tribunal in PRS v BEDA [1993] EMLR 325, which we believe to be particularly apposite to the present decision:

> "Thus the Tribunal found itself with very little guidance other than its own expertise and general impressions of the evidence, engaged in an exercise in which it is notoriously easier to be right than to explain why."

267. Secondly, the licences which become effective as a result of the final Decision will have a relatively short period to run. By the same token, the technology of delivery, the online offerings themselves, the advertising strategies and even the music are all in a state of development and flux which seems to be as rapid as it is unpredictable. Whilst we of course have confidence in the 'reasonableness' of the conclusions we have reached in this Decision, its effect and utility as a working prescription for the future will have to be tested by experience.

| **The Copyright Tribunal** | **Tribiwnlys Hawlfriant** |
|---|---|
| **The UK Intellectual Property Office** | **Swyddfa Eiddo Deallusol y DG** |
| **Newport NP 10 8QQ** | **Casnewydd NP10 8QQ** |

[173] We have however been sent (and have read) the decision of the Copyright Board of Canada relating to the tariff of royalties to be collected by CMRRA/SODRAC INC on online musical services, dated March 16 2007.

**Annex 1**

**DRAMATIS PERSONAE and CHRONOLOGY**

**PARTIES**

| **Current Parties** | | **Webcasters' position** |
|---|---|---|
| Yahoo! UK Limited | UK-subsidiary of Yahoo! Inc., a global internet company trading.<br><br>Yahoo! UK provides a range of internet-content services in the UK. Its online music services consist of:<br><br>1. "LAUNCHcast", a free advertising-supported webcasting service comprising:<br><br>(a) about 80 pre-programmed channels programmed by Yahoo! by way of genre, artist, era etc., and<br><br>(b) a user-customised channel which can be made available by the user to other users.<br><br>Each of these channels allows the user to rate artists, albums, songs and genres and, thus to influence the playlist generated by Yahoo! for the channel. Each channel also allows the user to pause the stream, to skip forward through an unlimited number of tracks, to turn off explicit lyrics and to see a list of recently listened to songs.<br><br>2. "LAUNCHcast Plus", an additional webcasting service comprising 11 extra channels made available only to subscribers to the BT Yahoo! Broadband service.<br><br>3. Free on-demand music video streams which will be followed by pre- | Each of these channels allows the user to rate artists, albums, songs and genres and thereby have some influence over the playlist generated by Yahoo! for the channel. Each channel also allows the user to pause the stream, to skip forward to the next (unidentified) song in the playlist, to turn off explicit lyrics and to see a list of recently listened to songs. Channels within the LAUNCHcast service allow only 5 skips forward per hour.<br><br>3. Free on-demand music video streams which will be followed by pre-programmed streams of further music videos selected by Yahoo! At any time, the User may choose |

| | | |
|---|---|---|
| | programmed streams of further music videos selected by Yahoo! If the User wishes, he may select another on-demand video at any time. | to restart this process by selecting another video on demand. |
| AOL (UK) Limited | UK-subsidiary of TimeWarner Inc (formerly AOL TimeWarner Inc.), a global media and entertainment company trading.<br><br>AOL (UK) provides a range of internet-content services and a broadband internet access subscription service (which is currently being sold to CarphoneWarehouse subject to regulatory approval). Its online music services consist of:<br><br>1. "Radio@AOL", a webcasting service comprising about 120 in-stream advertising-free channels currently made available only to AOL broadband internet subscribers. AOL (UK) intends to make this a free advertising-supported service available via its web portal in the near future.<br><br>2. "Sessions@AOL", free advertising-supported on-demand video streaming service comprising specially recorded sessions/concerts by selected artists.<br><br>3. Free advertising-supported on-demand music video streams.<br><br>4. "Listening Post", a free advertising-supported on-demand streaming service of a limited number of audio-only tracks. | UK-subsidiary of TimeWarner Inc (formerly AOL TimeWarner Inc.), a global media and entertainment trading company.<br><br>1. "Radio@AOL", a webcasting service comprising about 120 channels currently made available only to AOL broadband internet subscribers. These channels currently do not contain in-stream audio advertisements; but banner ads are sold on web pages associated with AOL's radio service. AOL (UK) intends to make this a fully free-to-the-consumer, advertising-supported service available via its web portal in the near future.<br><br>2. "Sessions@AOL", a free-to-the-consumer advertising-supported on-demand video streaming service comprising specially recorded sessions/concerts by selected artists.<br><br>3. Free-to-the-consumer advertising-supported on-demand music video streams.<br><br>4. "Listening Post", a free-to-the-consumer advertising-supported on-demand streaming service of a limited number of audio-only tracks. |
| RealNetworks Ltd | UK-subsidiary of RealNetworks Inc., a multi-national software and internet company.<br><br>RealNetworks Ltd provides media player software to internet users and its online | |

| | |
|---|---|
| | music services consist of:<br>1. RealMusic, a subscription webcasting service offering a selection of advertising-free webcasting and simulcasting channels and on-demand music video streams.<br>2. SuperPass, a subscription video service which includes music videos. |
| iTunes SARL | Luxembourg-incorporated subsidiary of Apple Inc. (formerly Apple Computer, Inc.), a global computer software and hardware company. Apple Inc. manufactures the personal music player, the iPod.<br>iTunes operates an online store for permanent downloads. It has music and non-music content. Its music content consists of both audio-only music downloads and music videos. Its non-music content currently includes audio book downloads, games and short animated films. It also provides a directory of podcasts available from third-party providers.<br>It is the largest provider of permanent music downloads in the UK. |
| O2 (UK) Limited | UK mobile network operator which is ultimately wholly-owned by Spanish telecommunication company, Telefonica SA.<br>O2 provides a range of mobile network access and content services in the UK. Its music service comprises offering its mobile network users a permanent download music service. In the past O2 has also, on a few occasions, streamed content from live music concerts. |
| T-Mobile International UK Limited | UK mobile network operator which is wholly owned by T-Mobile International AG & Co KG whose ultimate parent company is the German telecommunications company, Deutsche Telekom AG.<br>The T-Mobile group provides a range of mobile network access services in the |

| | |
|---|---|
| | UK. Its music service comprises offering its mobile network users permanent music download services. |
| Vodafone UK Content Services Limited | Content subsidiary of UK mobile network operator which is part of Vodafone Group plc.<br><br>Vodafone provides a range of mobile network access and content services in the UK. Its music service comprises offering its mobile network users permanent full track music downloads, music video streams and music video downloads and Vodafone Radio DJ, a subscription webcasting service. |
| Orange Personal Communications Services Limited | UK mobile network operator which is ultimately wholly-owned by French telecommunication company, France Telecom SA.<br><br>Orange provides a range of mobile network access and content services in the UK. Its music service comprises offering its mobile network users a permanent download music service. Its affiliate, Orange Home UK plc, offers a permanent download music service via the Internet. |
| Mechanical Copyright Protection Society | UK collecting society for the licensing of mechanical rights in musical works. It has approximately 14,000 individual composer and songwriter members and approximately 5,000 music publisher members. It distributed over £210m to its members in 2005. |
| Performing Rights Society | UK collecting society for the licensing of performing rights in musical works. It has approximately 38,000 individual composer and songwriter members and approximately 3,400 music publisher members. It distributed over £270m to its members in 2005. |
| British Academy for Composers and Songwriters | UK trade body for composers and songwriters. It has approximately 2,500 members. |

**Former Parties**

| | | |
|---|---|---|
| British Phonographic Industry Limited | UK trade association for producers and licensees of audio and audio-visual recordings of music. Over 300 members (including all the 4 major record companies, Universal, SonyBMG, EMI and Warner) together responsible for over 90% of commercial sound recordings. | |
| MusicNet UK Limited | UK-subsidiary of MusicNet Inc., a US-based "white-label" business-to-business, online music service provider which offers permanent download, on-demand and webcasting services to third parties.<br>MusicNet UK provides permanent download and on-demand music services to Virgin Digital and HMV Digital. | UK-subsidiary of MusicNet Inc., a US-based "white-label" business-to-business, online music service provider which offers permanent download and on-demand services to third parties. |
| Napster LLC | A multi-national online music service provider. In the UK, Napster SARL, a wholly-owned subsidiary of Napster LLC, offers consumers subscription limited download and on-demand streaming services. These services can be PC-based only (Napster PC Music Service) or for portable music players as well (Napster to Go). It also offers UK users a permanent download music service (Napster Light). | |
| Sony United Kingdom Limited | UK-subsidiary of Sony Corporation, a global computer hardware, communications and entertainment company.<br>In the UK, SonyConnect offers users a permanent download music service. | |

**FACTUAL WITNESSES (who gave oral evidence at trial)**

**For the MSPs**

| | |
|---|---|
| Gabriel Levy | General Manager Label Relations |

| | | |
|---|---|---|
| | (and formerly Head of Music, Europe) at RealNetworks | |
| Andrew Lee | Head of Legal Department at T-Mobile International UK Limited. Gave evidence under a witness summons. | |
| Paul Brown | European Managing Director of Pandora Media Inc. Pandora Inc. is a US-based free advertising-supported webcasting service which plans to launch its service in the UK.<br><br>Pandora's service allows the user to create his own personalised channel, to select an artist for the first track to be streamed, to pause the stream, to skip forward through up to 6 tracks per hour and to rate tracks, albums and artists thus influencing the playlist generated by Pandora for the channel. | European Managing Director of Pandora Media Inc. Pandora Inc. is a US-based free-to-the-consumer advertising-supported webcasting service which plans to launch its service in the UK.<br><br>Pandora's service allows the user to create his own personalised channel, to select an artist for the first track to be streamed and to rate tracks, albums and artists, and thereby to influence the playlist generated by Pandora for the channel. Pandora's service also allows the consumer to pause the stream and skip forward to the next (unidentified) song in the channel playlist up to six tracks per hour. |
| Geoff Taylor | General Counsel and Executive Vice-President of the International Federation of the Phonographic Industry (IFPI), the trade association of the international recording industry (and formerly General Counsel to the BPI). Gave evidence under a witness summons. | |
| Mark Mooradian | Vice-President Strategic Planning and Business Development for MusicNet Inc. Gave evidence under a witness summons. | |
| Christopher Johnstone | Head of Legal at Music Choice Ltd. Music Choice is a provider of digital music broadcasting services via TV and intends in the future to operate a video on-demand service. It operates a permanent download online music store and video on-demand service in the UK. | |

| | |
|---|---|
| David Wolffe | Chief Financial Officer and Senior Vice President of AOL (Europe) (and formerly CFO and Senior VP of AOL (UK)). |
| Christopher Hicks | Interim Manager and Director of Finance for UK Audience Business at AOL (UK). |
| Shannon Ferguson | Managing Director of Yahoo! Music Europe. |

**For iTunes**

| | |
|---|---|
| Eddy Cue | Global Vice-President of iTunes. |

**For the MNOs**

| | |
|---|---|
| Jonathan Bill | Former Head of Advertising and Industry Development at Vodafone Limited. |

**EXPERT WITNESSES**

**For the Applicants/Interveners**

| | |
|---|---|
| Richard Boulton | LECG. |
| Derek Ridyard | RBB (did not give oral evidence). |

**For the Alliance/BACS**

| | |
|---|---|
| Claire Enders | Enders Analysis. |
| Gervase MacGregor | BDO Stoy Hayward. |
| Zoltan Biro | Frontier Economics Ltd. |

**Chronology**

| | |
|---|---|
| --/10/1995 | MCPS trial licence of Cerberus – the first online MCPS licence: Porter 1 para 16 (E1/6) |
| 09/08/1996 | MCPS licence of Cerberus for music downloads service: E2/178 |
| --/--/1997 | RealNetworks UK operation incorporated: Levy 1 para 9 (C1/121) |
| 01/01/2002 | Commencement date for the first online scheme promulgated by the Alliance: E2/216 |
| 01/07/2002 | RealNetworks' music service launched: E2/520 |
| 24/03/2003 | Orange launched 7-week video trial: E3/578 |
| 14/04/2003 | O2 launched audio download trial service: Porter 1 para 35(h) (E1/16) |
| 06/05/2003 | Orange retrospectively agreed licence terms for its 7 week video trial: E3/581 |
| 19/05/2003 | O2 agreed online licence with the Alliance for its trial service: E3/585 |
| --/06/2003 | Yahoo!'s UK music services launched: Ferguson 1 para 12 (C1/176) |
| 25/06/2003 | AOL agreed online licence with the Alliance: E2/468. This agreement was subsequently extended on 24/10/03 (E2/472), 9/12/03 (E2/475) and 29/01/04 (E2/477) |
| --/08/2003 | AOL Sessions music service launched: Wolffe 1 para 23 (C1/9) |
| 09/09/2003 | Hutchinson 3G UK launched mobile music service: Porter 1 para 36 (E1/17) |
| --/10/2003 | Radio@AOL music service launched: Wolffe 1 para 23 (C1/9) |
| 19/11/2003 | O2's permanent download music service launched: E3/589 |
| --/--/2004 | Vodafone permanent download music service launched: Kershaw 1 para 9 (D1/3) |
| --/03/2004 | MusicNet UK formed: Mooradian 1 para 12 (C1/58) |
| 18/03/2004 | New AOL online music licence with the Alliance: E2/479. This agreement was subsequently extended on 14/12/04, 21/03/05 and 31/05/05: E2/486 |
| --/05/2004 | Napster launched UK music services: McAuliffe 1 para 12 (C1/91) |
| --/06/2004 | T-Mobile launched the Mobile Mix "jukebox" permanent download music service, which offered short remixes of audio tracks: Porter 1 para 40(a) |

| | |
|---|---|
| | (E1/18) |
| 07/06/2004 | Hutchinson 3G UK agreed online music licence with the Alliance with retrospective effect to 9/9/03: E3/595 |
| 11/06/2004 | Napster agreed online music licence with the Alliance: E2/489. This agreement was subsequently extended on 11/08/04, 17/09/04, 19/11/04, 21/01/05, 23/03/05, 01/06/05 and 02/11/05 (E2/492-505) |
| 14/06/2004 | iTunes agreed online music licence with the Alliance: E2/441 |
| 28/06/2004 | iTunes Music Store launched in the UK: Cue 1 para 8 (C1/30); Enders 1 para 93 (E7/1639) |
| 30/06/2004 | DVD1 licence settlement agreement between BPI and MCPS: B5/1089 |
| 05/07/2004 | Sony launched online music service: Ashcroft 1 para 9 (C1/158) |
| 07/07/2004 | Sony agreed online music licence with the Alliance expiring on 31/12/04: E3/539. From then until its settlement agreement in these references, Sony's download service was unlicensed. |
| 01/10/2004 | Orange launched audio music download service Musicplayer and video service: Porter 1 para 35(g) (E1/16) |
| 08/10/2004 | O2 agreed (under protest) online music licence with the Alliance for 2004 with retrospective effect to 19/11/03: E3/587 and 590 |
| 10/12/2004 | Yahoo! agreed online music licence with the Alliance: E2/506. This agreement was subsequently extended on 31/10/05: E2/516 |
| 14/12/2004 | RealNetworks agreed online licence with the Alliance (with retrospective effect to the launch of its service): E2/520. This agreement was subsequently extended on 31/10/05: E2/527 |
| --/03/2005 | Vodafone launched music video download and music video streaming services. |
| 28/06/2005 | BPI referred the Alliance's 2005 JOL (Joint Online Licence) to the Copyright Tribunal under section 119 of the CDPA<br>Napster, RealNetworks, AOL and Yahoo! served references under section 126 of the CDPA<br>MusicNet and Sony served references under section 119 of the CDPA<br>See Statements of Case at A1 tabs 1 and 3 to 8 |
| 28/06/2005 | iTunes served notice of intervention in each of the references and a Statement of Interest: A1 tab 2 |
| 05/08/2005 | MNOs served notices of intervention in each of the references |

| | |
|---|---|
| 26/08/2005 | MNOs' Statement of Case served: A1 tab 11 |
| 02/09/2005 | MusicNet's Amended Statement of Case served: A1 tab 7 |
| --/09/2005 | MusicNet UK concluded distribution agreements with HMV Digital and Virgin Digital for their UK permanent download and on-demand streaming services: Mooradian 1 para 12 (C1/58) |
| 03/11/2005 | Alliance served Requests for Information in relation to each of the Applicants'/Interveners' Statements of Case: A3 tabs 32-40 |
| 08/11/2005 | BACS served notice of intervention in each of the references |
| 09/11/2005 | Directions hearing before Mr Simon Thorley QC. For copies of the transcript of hearing and the order made see A5 tabs 81 & 82 respectively |
| 02/12/2005 | Alliance's Answers served: A2 tab 13 and A3 tabs 14-22 |
| 02/12/2005 | BPI, the MNOs, Napster, Sony, Yahoo!, AOL and RealNetworks served Preliminary Replies to the Alliance's Requests for Information: A3 tabs 41-42; A4 tabs 44-47 and 49 |
| 05/12/2005 | MusicNet and iTunes served Preliminary Replies to the Alliance's Requests for Information: A3 tab 43; A4 tab 48 |
| 09/12/2005 | BACS' Statement of Case served: A3 tab 22 |
| 02/02/2006 | Replies of the BPI, MSPs and MNOs served: A3 tabs 23-31 |
| 02/02/2006 | BPI, MSPs and MNOs served Replies to the Alliance's Requests for Information in relation to their Statements of Case: A4 tabs 50-58A |
| 02/02/2006 | BPI served Requests for Information in relation the Alliance's Answer: A4 tab 59 |
| 03/02/2006 | MSPs served Requests for Information in relation the Alliance's Answer: A4 tab 60 |
| 09/02/2006 &10/02/2006 | Directions hearing before Mr Simon Thorley QC. For copies of the transcript of hearing and the order made see A5 tabs 83 & 84 respectively |
| 23/02/2006 | Alliance served Preliminary Replies to the BPI's and the MSPs' Requests for Information: A4 tabs 61-62 |
| --/03/2006 | T-Mobile launched its full track download "jukebox" service. |
| 09/03/2006 | Alliance served Requests for Information in relation to each of the Applicants'/Interveners' Replies: A4 tabs 63-71 |
| 22/03/2006 | Directions hearing before Mr Simon Thorley QC. For copies of the transcript of hearing and the order made see A5 tabs 85 & 86 respectively |

| | |
|---|---|
| 29/03/2006 | Alliance served Replies to the BPI's and the MSPs' Requests for Information in relation to their Answers: A4 tabs 62A and 62B |
| 10/04/2006 | BPI, MSPs' and MNOs' served Replies to the Alliance's Requests for Information in relation to their Replies: A4 tabs 72-80 |
| 13/04/2006 | Alliance's Amended Answer to BPI Statement of Case served: A2 tab 13A |
| 28/04/2006 | Mutual Non-Disclosure Agreement concluded between all parties to the References for certain information to be classified as Class 1 and Class 2 Confidential Information and for each party to nominate Recipients of such information. |
| 26/05/2006 | 1st round exchange of witness evidence (factual and expert) and disclosure |
| 26/05/2006 | MNOs' Amended Statement of Case served: A1 tab 11A |
| 14/06/2006 | Directions hearing before HHJ Fysh. For copies of the transcript of hearing and the order made see A5 tabs 87 & 88 respectively |
| 28/06/2006 and following few days | Following an Order by the Tribunal made 14 June 2006, the Applicants/Interveners provided further disclosure relating to their sound recording licensing agreements with the record companies and certain financial information. |
| 01/07/2006 | Vodafone launched Vodafone Radio DJ subscription webcasting service in the UK. |
| 14/07/2006 | MSPs' served their Answer to the Alliance's case in relation to podcasting services: A3 tab 30A |
| 19/07/2006 | Without prejudice expert meeting took place between Mr Boulton (for the Applicants/Interveners) and Mr MacGregor (for the Respondents). |
| 26/07/2006 | 2nd round exchange of witness evidence (factual and expert) and further disclosure |
| 25/08/2006 | BPI's Amended Statement of Case served: A1 tab 1 |
| 12/09/2006 | Mr Boulton wrote a letter ("Boulton 3") to his instructing solicitors regarding the without prejudice meeting with Mr MacGregor held on 19 July 2006. This letter was sent to the Tribunal and the Respondents on 14 September 2006: B8 tab 34A. On the same date, the Respondents asked the Tribunal not to look at the letter: inter-solicitor correspondence bundle 2, page 614. |
| 12/09/2006 | Alliance served Claire Enders' third expert report: E7 tab 19 |
| 13/09/2006 | Directions hearing before HHJ Fysh. For copies of the transcript of hearing |

| | |
|---|---|
| | and the order made see A5 tabs 89 & 90 respectively |
| 14/09/2006 | BPI's Re-Amended Statement of Case served: A1 tab 1 |
| 20/09/2006 | Mr Boulton served his fourth report ("Boulton 4"): G tab 6 |
| 28/09/2006 | Mr MacGregor wrote a letter to his instructing solicitors (sent later that day to the Tribunal and other parties) in response to Mr Boulton's letter of 12 September 2006 regarding the without prejudice meeting between them on 19 July 2006: G tab 10 pages 164-169. This letter (plus the letter from Mr Boulton to which it referred) was attached to Mr MacGregor's third report served by the Respondents on 3 November 2006. |
| 28/09/2006 | Settlement agreement concluded between Alliance, BACS, BPI, MNOs and iTunes: H tab 1. From this point iTunes was represented separately from the other MSPs in relation to the References. |
| 28/09/2006 | Substantive hearing before HHJ Fysh, Colonel Arnold and Rear Admiral Carine starts and is adjourned. For a copy of the transcript of hearing see A5 tab 91 |
| 06/10/2006 | Settlement agreement concluded between Alliance, BACS, MusicNet and Napster: H tab 6 |
| 10/10/2006 | Settlement agreement concluded between Alliance, BACS and Sony: H tab 8 |
| 16/10/2006 | MNOs' and iTunes' Supplemental Statements of Case served: A6 tabs 4 and 6 |
| 20/10/2006 | AOL, Yahoo! and RealNetworks served their Supplemental Statement of Case: A6 tab 1 |
| 27/10/2006 | Alliance's Answers to the MNOs' and iTunes' Supplemental Statements of Case served: A6 tabs 5 and 7 |
| 30/10/2006 | Alliance's Answer to the Supplement Statement of Case of AOL, Yahoo! and RealNetworks served: A6 tab 2 |
| 03/11/2006 | 3rd round exchange of witness evidence |
| 15/11/2006 | 1st day of hearing |

CHAPTER 14

# LICENSING MUSIC IN BACKGROUND MUSIC SERVICES, DIGITAL JUKEBOXES, AND OTHER COMMERCIAL REPRODUCTIONS

## (ELECTRICAL TRANSCRIPTION LICENSES)

### SUMMARY

4. Territory
5. Exclusivity

**IV. TYPICAL LICENSE FEES FOR ELECTRICAL TRANSCRIPTION LICENSES**

A. Background Music Services
   1. Musical Works
   2. Sound Recordings
B. Digital Jukeboxes
   1. Musical Works
   2. Sound Recordings

**V. RIGHTS AGENCIES**

## APPENDICES

# CHAPTER 14

# LICENSING MUSIC IN BACKGROUND MUSIC SERVICES, DIGITAL JUKEBOXES, AND OTHER COMMERCIAL REPRODUCTIONS (ELECTRICAL TRANSCRIPTION LICENSES)

A background music service is the type of music performance described in the BMI public performance license as the "unobtrusive accompaniment to work, shopping, conversation, dining and relaxation," which has been humorously referred to as "elevator" music — the music you hear while standing in an elevator or the mood-setting accompaniment you may or may not notice while waiting in a hotel lobby, standing in line at the bank, having a meal in a restaurant, or even while waiting "on hold" during a telephone call. It has been said that background music isn't music to listen to, it's music to hear.

Background music services, as well as certain other forms of commercial reproductions, require a special form of reproduction license, historically called an *electrical transcription license.* This is a license that permits the reproduction of music in audio-only sound recordings that are made *for purposes other than distribution to the public for private use*, such as to facilitate a radio broadcast or Internet transmission, such as a ring-back. Like print licenses and mechanical licenses, electrical transcription licenses are derived from the copyright owner's exclusive right of reproduction.[1] Electrical transcription licenses are commonly used for the reproduction of music by radio stations, producers of syndicated radio programs, background music services, and music reproduced for in-flight use by commercial airlines.

[1] 17 U.S.C. Sec. 106(1).

This chapter provides an overview of the terms and conditions contained in customary electrical transcription licenses.

## I. Distinction Between Mechanical Licenses and Electrical Transcription Licenses

The distinction between mechanical recordings and electrical transcriptions inheres in the use for which the recording is intended: copies of *mechanical* recordings, such as record albums, audiocassettes, and compact discs, are primarily intended for distribution to the public *for private use*; copies of *electrical transcription* recordings are intended for distribution to radio stations, background music services, and special music services for public broadcasting purposes. This distinction is important because only mechanical recordings intended for distribution to the public for private use are subject to the compulsory licensing provision of the copyright law.[2] Accordingly, fees and other terms for licenses to make recordings intended for background music services and radio broadcast may be freely negotiated without regard to the limitations set forth in the compulsory licensing provision.

## II. Types of Electrical Transcriptions

Electrical transcription licenses are issued in connection with the following kinds of transcription recordings:

### A. Transcriptions for Radio Broadcast

The making of recordings of introductory musical themes, background music for radio commercials, and compilations of musical compositions distributed as part of syndicated radio shows, all require permission from the copyright owners of the music involved. The permission to make such recordings is entirely distinct from the permission required to perform the recordings. The latter is normally acquired from the

[2] Section 115 of the Copyright Act states, "A person may obtain a compulsory license only if his or her primary purpose in making phonorecords is to distribute them *to the public for private use.*" 17 U.S.C. Sec. 115(a)(1) (emphasis added).

performance rights society, such as ASCAP or BMI, but permission to create the recording itself and make copies of it is acquired directly from the copyright owner.

### *1. Themes and Introductions*

Radio programs, such as news programs and talk shows, often use some short familiar theme music as an introduction to the program or as background music for *segues* (i.e., transitions) to and from commercials or other breaks in the program. Music publishers often prepare electrical transcription recordings containing a variety of short themes and introductions for this purpose and distribute them to radio stations free of charge. A music publisher's incentive for providing this service, of course, is the performance fees it will receive from performance rights societies as a result of the airplay of these short pieces of music. Performance licenses are discussed at length in Chapter 18.

### *2. Syndicated Radio Programs*

A *syndicated radio program* is a series of pre-recorded, one- or two-hour radio programs of music, usually accompanied by introductory and background commentary delivered by an announcer. The pre-recorded tapes of these programs are licensed by their producers on an individual basis to local radio stations around the country. For example, a producer may prepare a series of syndicated radio programs of selected Frank Sinatra recordings, including short commentaries regarding each recording, identifying the songwriters, the arrangers, and any interesting circumstances related to the recording or the time during the artist's life when the recording was made. Short interviews with the artist may also be featured in some of these programs. Series such as these might be attractive to local radio stations that cater to the audience for which the program was designed.

The tapes containing these programs and recordings are not mechanical reproductions, in the strict sense of the term, because they are primarily intended for distribution to broadcast stations for further broadcast — not for distribution to the public for private use. The compulsory license provision would therefore not apply and the music copyright owner is free to negotiate fees for such recordings. The standard form used by the Harry Fox Agency for licensing electrical transcriptions for syndicated radio programs is set forth as Form 14.1 on the CD-ROM.

### *3. Commercial Advertisements Prepared for Radio Broadcast*

Recordings that contain commercial advertising, which include licensed music, are electrical transcriptions, and the licenses for the use of such music are electrical transcription licenses. Because the use of the music for commercial advertising purposes requires special consideration, the subject of licensing the use of music in radio commercials is discussed in Chapter 20.

Licenses to make electrical transcriptions for commercial radio broadcast generally do not contain a license to *perform* the music. The performance license will be covered by the radio station's license from the performance rights societies, such as BMI or ASCAP. Performance licenses are discussed in greater detail in Chapter 18.

## B. Transcriptions for Background Music Services

Background music services were once dominated by two organizations, Muzak and 3M. 3M's background music service no longer operates, but it has been replaced in the market by the fast growing, Austin-based, DMX. Muzak and DMX each serve the music needs of hundreds of thousands of business establishments, including most of the major retail chains, restaurants, hotels, and other public establishments and businesses.

### *1. Muzak and DMX*

Muzak and DMX each maintain professional music programming staffs each of which create and maintain over 100 programming "channels" of recorded music in a large variety of genres and sub-genres. A chain of fashion stores, for example, may choose a channel comprised of techno or "chill" music, approximating the music played during professional fashion shows. Supermarkets may choose an entirely different variety of music, and that variety may differ depending upon regional tastes.

Though some businesses have tried to create their own playlists, using an iPOD to maintain and perform the desired recordings, keeping a music channel programmed with a fresh variety of new music that fits within the desired genre is a specialty that no one store or chain of stores can practically manage themselves. Chain stores, hotels, and other establishments are also careful about how they maintain their brand image; accordingly, they often wish to control precisely the kinds of music played in their stores. These businesses will usually find it less expensive to use a shared service such as DMX or Muzak than to hire their own music programmers for this highly specialized task.

Muzak and DMX each offer their retail clients a choice between two delivery methods: on-premise or broadcast — that is, either by periodically sending hard disks containing the programmed music to each client's location (for playback on devices on the premises of the client) or via satellite transmission or other broadcast to each client location. Muzak currently derives over 75% of its revenues from on-premise distribution and DMX derives more than half of its revenues from on-premise distribution. Each charge a flat monthly subscription fee to its clients based on the number of locations to which the programming is delivered.

These activities may require two types of licenses: a public performance license (to transmit the performances by satellite and the performances that occur at the client's location) and a reproduction license (to make any hard disk or server copies that may be required to facilitate those transmissions).

### 2. Reproduction License Aspects

It is possible for a background music service to avoid the server copy fee by using the original CDs purchased at retail. By employing a form of jukebox of CDs from which the programmed channels obtain their recordings for satellite transmission, the background music service would only be responsible for obtaining the necessary public performance license for the transmissions made, avoiding the reproduction license altogether. While background music services employ this method, the equipment necessary to make it work is very costly to maintain.

The reproduction license, where it is necessary, is obtained through the issuance of an electrical transcription licenses, typically obtained from the music publisher or through the publisher's administrator or agent, such as the Harry Fox Agency. Because the terms of electrical transcription licenses are not subject to the compulsory license provisions of the copyright law, their terms and conditions are subject to negotiation. Nevertheless, the fees tend to follow standard patterns and generally do not vary from song to song. Accordingly, many of the basic considerations in granting licenses — determining the value of the song, the importance of the song in relation to its intended use, and the scope of the use — will not in practice apply to granting or clearing electrical transcription licenses for background music services.

Further, the terms and conditions for licensing music for background music services will vary depending upon the delivery method used by the particular background music service. Electrical transcription licenses issued for satellite transmission are for a fixed term of years, generally 1 or 3 years, with a single payment for all copies of the composition made during the term. A licensee is often given an option to renew for an additional fee payable upon renewal. Electrical transcription licenses issued for the hard disk delivery method amounts to more like a mechanical license fee, except that it is based on a percentage of subscription fee charged to the customer.

### *3. Performance License Aspects*

Background music services, whether provided by Muzak or DMX, entail not only the making of copies of music not intended for distribution to the public for private use, but also the performance of the music to the public. Accordingly, background music services require both an electrical transcription license to make any copies used in the process and a performance license to render the performances of the musical works to the public.

Electrical transcription licenses for background music services may or may not include the license necessary to perform the music recorded under the authorization of the transcription license. Where a transcription license does not include one, the performance license must be obtained by separate agreement from the applicable performance rights society. Performance licenses are handled differently, depending on the background music service and the performance rights society involved.

Muzak and DMX procure from the performance rights societies (e.g., ASCAP and BMI) the public performance licenses their clients will need to perform the music at their locations. This is so their clients won't have to — a useful feature of the service. While the background music service typically obtains their performance license from the performance rights society, a recent trend is for music publishers to issue the performance license together with the electrical transcription license — in effect, bypassing the performance license society.

## C. Transcriptions for Digital Jukebox Services

Jukeboxes have been around nearly as long as the phonorecord itself. The Copyright Act defines a jukebox in the following terms:

> A "coin-operated phonorecord player" is a machine or device that —
>
> (A) is employed solely for the performance of nondramatic musical works by means of phonorecords upon being activated by the insertion of coins, currency, tokens, or other monetary units or their equivalent;
>
> (B) is located in an establishment making no direct or indirect charge for admission;
>
> (C) is accompanied by a list which is comprised of the titles of all the musical works available for performance on it, and is affixed to the phonorecord player or posted in the establishment in a prominent position where it can be readily examined by the public; and
>
> (D) affords a choice of works available for performance and permits the choice to be made by the patrons of the establishment in which it is located.[3]

The licensing of music on jukeboxes is governed by Section 116 of the Copyright Act, which contemplates that jukebox owners negotiate voluntary licenses with music publishers acting on a collective basis, but where voluntary negotiations fail, rates may be determined by the Copyright Royalty Board.[4]

---

[3] 17 U.S.C. Sec. 116(d).

[4] 17 U.S.C. Sec. 116.

The advent of digital delivery of music led to more sophisticated forms of jukeboxes, which use MP3 or equivalent files rather than 45-RPM records or CDs as the source of the recordings. The digital format allows the centralized control and electronic delivery of recorded music to digital jukeboxes located in public places, but connected to the Internet. This reduces the cost of maintaining the jukeboxes and allows for more frequent updating of the repertoire available on the devices.

The leading supplier of digital jukeboxes is TouchTunes Music Corporation of Quebec, Canada. TouchTunes offers business establishments digital jukebox services under two basic models: (1) coin-operated digital jukeboxes and (2) background music service digital jukeboxes.

Coin-operated digital jukeboxes use the classic pay-per-play model, where patrons of the establishments where such jukeboxes are located select the specific recordings they want played in the order they want them played. Background music service digital jukeboxes, which operate under a subscription agreement with the digital jukebox owner (e.g., a restaurant or bowling alley), play recordings chosen and played by the jukebox on a random or programmed basis without payment by patrons.

Terms between TouchTunes and music publishers for the use of musical works is set forth below and forms agreements between TouchTunes and music publishers and record companies are set forth in Forms 14.4 and 14.5 on the CD-ROM.

## D. Transcriptions for In-Flight Use on Airlines

Special pre-recorded music programs compiled for use on passenger airlines are akin to both background music services and syndicated radio programs. However, unlike background music services, which are scientifically designed to promote a certain efficiency or relaxation in its listeners, programs designed for in-flight listening are specifically for the active entertainment of its audience. Airline music is programmed to be listened to. These programs, revised on a monthly basis, offer specific categories of music entertainment, such as easy listening, top rock 'n roll hits, country and western, jazz, classical, and international music, from which the passenger may choose. In this respect, they are more like syndicated radio programs, whose "broadcast" is really a closed-circuit "cablecast" distributed to an audience of passengers on board the flights of a particular airline during any given month.

Electrical transcription licenses for this purpose are similar to the license set forth as Form 14.1 on the CD-ROM for syndicated radio programs. Because the performance of music on an airplane or jet liner is a public performance requiring permission of the copyright owner, performance rights societies issue special performance licenses to the airlines for this purpose.

In recent years, some airlines have been licensing recorded programming from services such as XM/Sirius satellite radio.

## E. Transcriptions for Ringbacks

As discussed in the previous chapter, a *ringback* is an audio-only transmission of a sound recording, which the calling party hears while waiting for the recipient of the call to answer the phone. The ringback is personalized by the recipient of the call, so that anyone who calls the recipient's number will hear, in lieu of the standard ringing tone of the phone network, a popular sound recording or special greeting selected by the recipient. The file containing the sound recording comprising the ringback is hosted on servers maintained by the telecommunications carrier and equipment at the back office of the carrier and it enables subscribers to replace the standard ringing tone with a personalized audio selection.

Because ringbacks invoke both the reproduction right and the public performance right, carriers who wish to provide ringback services require two kinds of licenses: an electrical transcription license (for the server copy) and a public performance license (for the transmissions). Though you are not likely to find a license to make reproductions for ringback purposes called an electrical transcription license, that is technically what it is.

## F. Transcriptions for Other Internet Transmissions (i.e., Server Copies)

For that matter, any server copy of a musical work used to facilitate a transmission of the music by streaming or limited download requires an electrical transcription license (though the license to permit such use is typically called a *server license* or *ephemeral recording license*). As discussed in the previous chapter, server copies made to facilitate the making of digital phonorecord deliveries do not require a license in addition to a mechanical license because the license to make the server copy is implied (much like the right to make the master recording "stamper" was implied in a mechanical license to manufacture vinyl phonorecords).

## III. Considerations in Granting and Clearing Electrical Transcription Licenses

Because it does not apply to recordings made for purposes other than for distribution to the public for private use, the compulsory license provision does not limit the flexibility the copyright owner has in negotiating the terms of electrical transcription licenses.

### A. Fee Structure

Although there is room for negotiation in determining the appropriate fee to charge for an electrical transcription license, the fees are generally not high in comparison with other kinds of uses. Licenses to make transcriptions for background music for use by radio stations and syndicated radio program producers are commonly issued on a flat dollar amount per copy made. The same is true for transcriptions made for in-flight use by airlines. Background music services who deliver programming for use by businesses, such as retailers, will typically pay a percentage of their net subscription revenue for reproductions made and a flat per location fee for public performances. Typical fees charged for the making of transcription copies are set forth in Chapter 26.

It is important to remember that licenses for making transcription copies do not normally include the license to perform the music publicly; accordingly, separate fees for music performed publicly by the use of licensed transcriptions are collected on a blanket basis by performance rights societies from the broadcasters or other organizations rendering the performance.

### B. Value of the Song and Its Importance in Relation to the Intended Use

Because the fees for transcription licenses are generally not high in comparison with other kinds of uses, music copyright owners will not generally engage in the more extensive analysis given to the consideration of other forms of licenses, such as theatrical synchronization, videogram, and commercial advertising licenses. By the same token, copyright owners should not agonize over what fees to charge for these uses, because the ability to share in the economic success of the transcription is available through the collection of performance fees for the public performances of the transcriptions licensed.

#### *1. Arrangements and Changes*

Many of the provisions common in electrical transcription licenses are derived from standard mechanical license forms. For example, if new recordings are being made for the transcriptions, the license will provide that the arrangements made shall not change the basic melody or fundamental character of the work. These licenses will also provide that neither the title nor the lyrics of the music shall be changed, added to, or translated, without the further permission of the copyright owner.

### C. Scope of Use

#### *1. Type of Media*

The electrical transcription license will generally provide the licensee with some flexibility in using the various forms of recording media. The only important restraint is that the media is limited to audio devices only, and not those that include visual images.

#### *2. Distribution Channels*

The transcription license will generally limit the purpose of the recordings and distribution to the purpose stated in the license, such as for syndicated radio broadcasts. Accordingly, a license for syndicated radio broadcasts will not allow copies of the recording to be made for any other purpose, including distribution of copies to the public, distribution of copies for inclusion in juke boxes, distribution of copies for background music services, or distribution of copies for in-flight performance.

Even if the transcription license is limited to a specific use, such as syndicated radio programs, the music copyright owner should try to be as specific as possible, requiring the license to identify by name the specific syndicated radio program, programs, or series of programs for which the music is being licensed. This is particularly important if any form of exclusivity is being considered.

### *3. Term*

The term of an electrical transcription license will generally be from one to three years. Of course, the license may be terminated sooner if the licensee fails to pay the required fee.

### *4. Territory*

The territory of an electrical transcription license is usually limited to the United States and Canada. Most music publishers with overseas affiliates will require licenses for additional territories to be negotiated locally on a country-by-country basis.

### *5. Exclusivity*

Transcription licenses are rarely granted on an exclusive basis, but some form of exclusivity could be acceptable for an increased license fee, provided it is narrowly defined. Considerations for granting and clearing exclusivity provisions in connection with the use of music in commercial advertising is discussed more fully in Chapter 20.

## IV. TYPICAL LICENSE FEES FOR ELECTRICAL TRANSCRIPTION LICENSES

### A. Background Music Services

Background music services, such as Muzak and DMX, have to consider the rights of both music publishers and record companies when engaging in the reproduction of copies to facilitate their transmissions. The following will provide a general idea of what music publishers and record companies can expect to receive in connection with licensing their musical works and recordings to these services.

Recall that background music services may deliver recordings to their business customers in one of two ways: by a "broadcast" transmission or by "on-premise" delivery of a device containing copies of the recordings and musical works. The typical business subscriber to a background music service pays between $55 to $65 per month for background music services delivered via broadcast transmission and $65 to $75 per month for services delivered by devices used on premises.

### *1. Musical Works*

For the use of copies of *musical works* contained in the recordings offered by background music services, music publishers typically receive the following:

| | |
|---|---|
| On-premise: | 1% of net revenues derived from subscription fees received pro rated among the compositions used |
| Broadcast: | Where the broadcast is made from CDs playing by computer control on industrial jukeboxes, no payment is made for electrical transcriptions, because none are being made to facilitate the broadcast transmissions; otherwise, the publisher may receive an electrical transcription fee of $15 per year per song. |

In addition to the above reproduction fees, the background music service must also pay fees for the public performance of the musical works arising from the transmissions emanating from the service or on the premises at the business establishment subscribers. Such fees are typically $6.50 to $6.75 per month per location, regardless of whether the performances are from on-premise or broadcast transmissions.

### *2. Sound Recordings*

For the use of copies of *sound recordings* offered by background music services, record companies typically receive the following:

| | |
|---|---|
| On-premise: | 5% to 10% (or more) of net revenues derived from subscription fees received pro rated among the recordings used |
| Broadcast: | Where the broadcast is made from CDs playing by computer control on industrial jukeboxes, no payment is made for making copies of the recordings, because none |

> are being made to facilitate the broadcast transmissions; where tape or server copies are made, 5% to 10% (or more) of net revenues derived from subscription fees received pro rated among the recordings used.

The reason fees paid to record companies are substantially higher than those paid to music publishers is because the music publishers also get paid their share of public performance income, which the performance rights societies separately collect from the background music services (i.e., at $6.50 per month per location, the services are paying about 10-15% of their subscription revenue to the performance rights societies, in addition to the direct payments to music publishers).

Note, also, that owners of sound recordings do not have a general public performance right; the limited right granted to them under the 1995 Act was to make public performances of sound recordings by means of *digital* audio transmissions. Since both the on-premise transmissions and the broadcast transmissions of sound recordings are all *analog*, not digital, nothing is owed to the record companies for the public performances.

Some background music services broadcast their programming through subscription satellite services, such as EchoStar or the Dish Network. Since these broadcasts are digital audio transmissions, public performance payments for use of the sound recordings may be due. To the extent such programming is transmitted to the consumer for private use, the background music service, or its satellite service partner, must pay the statutory fees due to SoundExchange for such transmissions under Section 114 of the Copyright Act.[5] To the extent such transmissions are received by business establishments, and meet the sound recording performance complement, they are exempt under Section 114(d) and no public performance fees would be payable to SoundExchange.

### B. Digital Jukeboxes

Patrons wanting to hear a recording on a digital jukebox typically pay 25¢ per selection. The monthly subscription fee charged to owners of digital jukeboxes varies.

---

[5] See generally, Chapter 23, on *Licensing of Sound Recordings.*

### *1. Musical Works*

For the reproduction and distribution of musical works contained in the recordings offered by TouchTunes, music publishers receive the following:

| | |
|---|---|
| Coin-operated digital jukeboxes: | one-half cent ($.005) per performance of each composition. |
| Background music service digital jukebox: | ten percent (10%) of the monthly subscription fee received from licensees. |

With respect to both services, for the public performances made by jukeboxes under either service, TouchTunes pays performance license fees directly to the performing rights societies. A form agreement between music publishers and digital jukebox service operators is included on the CD-ROM.

### *2. Sound Recordings*

For reproduction and distribution of sound recordings offered by TouchTunes, record companies receive the following:

| | |
|---|---|
| Coin-operated digital jukeboxes: | one cent ($.01) per performance of each recording. |
| Background music service digital jukebox: | ten percent (10%) of the monthly subscription fee received from licensees. |

Because the public performances emanating from digital jukeboxes are analog, and since the public performance right in sound recordings is limited to audio transmissions that are *digital*,[6] there is no public performance fee payable to record companies for these performances. A form agreement between record companies and digital jukebox service operators is included on the CD-ROM.

---

[6] 17 U.S.C. Sec. 106(6).

## V. RIGHTS AGENCIES

Electronic transcription licenses are generally available directly from music publishers. However, the Harry Fox Agency does issue these licenses on behalf of many of its member publishers. For more information on the Harry Fox Agency, *see* Chapter 13. In many countries, licenses for background music services and other electronic transcriptions are issued by the local mechanical collection and performance rights societies.

# APPENDIX TO CHAPTER 14
# LICENSING MUSIC IN BACKGROUND MUSIC SERVICES, DIGITAL JUKEBOXES AND OTHER COMMERCIAL REPRODUCTIONS (ELECTRICAL TRANSCRIPTION LICENSES)

FORMS (ON CD-ROM ONLY)

| | |
|---|---|
| **Form 14.1** | **Electrical Transcription License for Syndicated Radio Broadcasts Used by the Harry Fox Agency** |
| **Form 14.2** | **Electrical Transcription License for Background Music Services Used by the Harry Fox Agency** |
| **Form 14.3** | **Electrical Transcription License for Background Music Services Used by 3M Company** |
| **Form 14.4** | **Digital Jukebox — Publisher License Agreement** |
| **Form 14.5** | **Digital Jukebox Sound Recording License Agreement** |

## CHAPTER 15

# LICENSING MUSIC IN AUDIOVISUAL WORKS (SYNCHRONIZATION LICENSES)

## SUMMARY

# CHAPTER 15

# LICENSING MUSIC IN AUDIOVISUAL WORKS (SYNCHRONIZATION LICENSES)

In previous chapters, we explored the licensing of music for use in printed materials (e.g., sheet music and songbooks), digital print (e.g., downloadable sheet music and electronic guitar tabs) and sound recordings (i.e., an audio-only work that results from a fixation of a series of sounds) — whether those copies of those recordings were intended for distribution to the public (under a *mechanical license*) or solely intended to facilitate another use, such as a broadcast (under an *electrical transcription license*). In this chapter, we will explore the licensing of music for use in audiovisual works, traditionally permitted under what is known as a *synchronization license.*

An *audiovisual work* is a work of authorship that consists of a series of related images, which are intrinsically intended to be shown by the use of machines or devices such as projectors, viewers, or electronic equipment, together with accompanying sounds, if any, regardless of the nature of the material objects, such as films or tapes, in which the works are embodied. Motion pictures, television programs, and music videos are examples of audiovisual works.

A *synchronization license* is a license that permits another to synchronize music with an audiovisual work, such as a motion picture or television program. The synchronization license also permits the making of copies of the audiovisual works that contain licensed music, but only permits the distribution of those copies for the specific purposes set forth in the license — traditionally, for the sole purpose of exhibiting the audiovisual work in motion picture theaters or broadcasting the work on television. Internet streaming is a new use that is now often added to a traditional synchronization license. The distribution of copies for any other purpose, such as in videocassettes, laser discs, permanent download and the like, for home use, requires an additional license. Many synchronization licenses, however, now include terms for the making and distribution of home video devices and delivery of permanent downloads.

The synchronization license is derived from the copyright owner's exclusive right of reproduction.[1] The synchronization license might properly be called an *audiovisual reproduction license*, but the word, "synchronization" continues to be commonly used, perhaps because, technically, synchronizing involves making a piece of music an integral part of the audiovisual work — by recording the music in "timed-relation" with the moving pictures in an audiovisual work. In addition, the permission granted under a synchronization license is traditionally limited to the making of a recording of a musical composition subject to the condition that (i) the recording only be used as part of the particular audiovisual work specified in the agreement, and (ii) any copies made of the recording only be used in a particular way — to facilitate exhibition or broadcast, but not for physical distribution to the public.

The synchronization license is distinguishable from a mechanical license in the sense that a mechanical license only permits the reproduction of a musical work as part of a *sound recording* — that is, an *audio-only* recording, not recordings that include visual materials (i.e., audiovisual works). The traditional synch license, however, is more akin to an electrical transcription license than a mechanical license. Recall that an electrical transcription license represents permission to make and distribute music embodied in audio-only recordings solely for the purpose of facilitating an audio-only performance of some kind (e.g., radio, Internet streaming); the copies made may not be distributed to the public for home use without the proper mechanical license. A synch license represents permission to make and distribute music embodied in audiovisual works solely for the purpose of facilitating an audiovisual performance of some kind (e.g., theatrical, television broadcast, Internet streaming); the copies made may not be distributed

[1] 17 U.S.C. Sec. 106(1).

to the public for home use without the proper videogram license or videogram terms added to the synch license.

The kind of audiovisual work into which music is licensed for synchronization is specified in each synchronization license agreement and is often reflected in the title of the license agreement. For example, permission to synchronize music in a motion picture for theatrical release was traditionally called a *theatrical* synchronization license; permission to synchronize music in a television program for television broadcast is usually called a *television* synchronization license; and permission to synchronize music in an audiovisual work for promotional music videos is called a *promotional music video* synchronization license. As the need to more precisely specify the uses to which synchronized recordings may be made, new classes of synchronization licenses have also emerged, such as synchronization licenses for cable television, direct satellite broadcast, and other forms of television program exhibition, and for use of motion pictures and television programs containing music in videograms, such as laser discs and videocassettes. Perhaps the most recent form of synch license that has emerged is the *Internet streaming synchronization license.*

Today, many theatrical synchronization licenses include terms for the exhibition of the film on television, in videograms distributed for home use, in Internet streaming and Internet downloading — in other words, all forms of uses "now known or hereafter devised." These "broad rights" under a synchronization license may be acquired either up front or as a series of options, as we shall explore below.

## I. HISTORICAL BACKGROUND

### A. Early Motion Picture Technology

When a person visually observes a succession of still images at a rate above 15 frames a second, he will perceive an illusion of continuous movement. Successive photography of actual movement was first achieved in 1877 by Eadweard Muybridge when he used 12 equally spaced cameras to demonstrate that at some time all four hooves of a galloping horse left the ground at once. The Muybridge photographs, and successive photographs like them, were soon used in a popular parlor device, known as a zoetrope, which created the illusion of movement from pictures mounted in a rotating drum.

Shortly thereafter, mechanisms were developed to enable a sequence of photographs to be taken within a single camera at regular, rapid intervals. Thomas Alva Edison, usually credited with the invention of the motion picture camera, actually combined several existing technologies to create the Kinetograph camera in 1889, the same year that the George Eastman company developed a photographic film sturdy and flexible enough to be transported within a camera for receiving a rapid succession of images. The version of the Kinetograph camera developed by the end of 1892 used essentially the same format in use today — a film 35 millimeters in width, with two rows of sprockets, four holes per frame, used to advance the film through the camera. The first motion pictures were not projected, but used in a parlor device known as the Kinetoscope, a cabinet in which a reel of film, illuminated by a light bulb, was advanced in a continuous loop at the rate of 40 frames per second in synchronization with a rotating shutter wheel. The viewer would "peep" into the cabinet to view the motion picture, or *peep show*.

In 1895, Thomas Armat employed several mechanical techniques developed in France to create a motion picture projector, which the following year he allowed Edison to produce and market as Edison Vitascopes. The art of projection was significantly advanced with the introduction of carbon arc lamps to improve the illumination of the projected image.

## B. The Emergence of the Motion Picture Industry

It was in France that early filmmakers began to make the important transition from using motion picture technology to convey mere animated photographs to using the same technology to convey narratives or tell stories. In 1902, French filmmaker Georges Méliés startled the world with his 30-scene, 14-minute film narrative, *Voyage to the Moon*, based on the novel by Jules Verne. Meanwhile, in the United States, Edwin S. Porter, a projectionist and engineer who joined the Edison Company in 1900, while serving as producer and director of many of the films produced by Edison, began experimenting with the techniques established by Méliés. In 1903, Porter shot *The Great Train*

*Robbery*, widely acknowledged to be the first narrative film to achieve true temporal continuity of action, combining 14 separate shots of non-continuous overlapping action. The film's spectacular success led to the establishment of the first permanent film theaters, or nickelodeons (Greek for "nickel theater").

In 1903, Adolph Zukor, a 30-year old furrier restless for new opportunities, and Mitchell Marks, an operator of penny arcades, established the Automatic Vaudeville Company, opening its first arcade on 14th Street in New York City. With an investment from another successful furrier, Marcus Loew, the outfit spread its operations to Boston, Philadelphia, and Newark. Loew established his own chain of arcades and within two years, they each converted their arcades into nickelodeons, giving their customers a peek at the short one-reel movies being churned out by Edison, Vitagraph, Biograph, and other film production companies of the day. The two rode the spectacular boom in popularity of the nickelodeon, which grew in number from a mere handful in 1904 to nearly 10,000 by 1908. In 1910, the two combined their efforts, forming Loew's Consolidated Enterprises.

Yet Zukor grew restless once again, selling his interest in Loews, and, with Marcus Loew's best wishes, Zukor formed a film production company called Famous Players In Famous Plays, hiring Edwin Porter as head of direction and photography. Within a few years, Famous Players was making 30 films a year, starring such notables as John Barrymore and Mary Pickford.

As narrative techniques matured, viewers of motion pictures were becoming increasingly sophisticated. Consequently, production companies began to produce high budget, multiple-reel "feature" films suitable to the tastes of this new audience. In 1913, Samuel Goldfish, Jesse Lasky, and Cecil B. DeMille formed a small film company, the Jesse L. Lasky Feature Play Company, one of the hundreds of small production companies springing up to meet the increasing demand for feature films.

At the same time, motion picture exhibitors began to accommodate the growing audience for motion pictures with large elegant theaters, known as "dream palaces." One of the first theaters of this kind, the 3,300-seat Strand Theater on Broadway, was built by Mitchell Marks in 1914.

By 1916, over 21,000 movie theaters dotted the country, and the nickelodeon era was over. But Zukor was not one to allow rapidly changing technology to leave him behind. In July 1916, he masterminded the consolidation of his Famous Players Company with Lasky's Feature Play Company. Two months later, Famous Players-Lasky bought out the Paramount Company, a film distribution company, later to become known as Paramount Pictures.

As part of the transaction, Zukor bought out Samuel Goldfish's share of Feature Play Company and Goldfish established his own company by forming a partnership with the Edgar Selwyn's Selwyn Theatrical Empire, calling the new company, The Goldwyn Company. Goldfish decided to change his name, combining *Gold* with *Wyn.* (Had he taken the first syllable of SELwyn and the second syllable of GoldFISH, he would have had SELFISH.)

Meanwhile, the demand for motion pictures made it necessary for film production companies to maintain a year-round schedule. Because of the need for light, most films were still being shot outdoors, but the east coast winter climate could not accommodate the continuous production schedules required. The temperate and sunny climate of Southern California, together with the topographic variety afforded by the greater Los Angeles area, proved to be the perfect place for movie making. By 1911, several major production companies established studios in Hollywood, and, by 1915, more than 60% of American film production was produced by 15,000 workers employed by the motion picture industry in Hollywood.

All of the major studios of the day established operations in Hollywood, including Zukor's Famous Players-Lasky Corporation; Samuel Goldfish's Goldwyn Picture Corporation; Universal Pictures, which was founded by Carl Laemmle in 1912 through a merger of five independent production companies of that time; Metro Picture Corporation and Louis B. Mayer Pictures, founded by Louis B. Mayer in 1915 and 1917, respectively; and the Fox Film Corporation (becoming 20th Century-Fox in 1935), founded by William Fox in 1915. In 1924, sensing the direction film production would be going, Marcus Loew, who owned about 140 theaters at the time, went to Hollywood and encouraged Samuel Goldwyn to sell out his Goldwyn Picture Corporation to Loews, Inc. Marcus Loew then merged Goldwyn's Goldwyn Picture Corporation with the Louis B. Mayer's Metro Picture Corporation. The merged company became Metro-Goldwyn-Mayer, a subsidiary of Loews, Inc. Loew asked both Louis B. Mayer and Samuel Goldwyn to join the new firm, but while Mayer accepted, Goldwyn decided to become an independent producer. When he was offered the position with MGM, Goldwyn was believed to have said, "Include me out." Another famous Goldwynism came to light when his secretary asked him if she could destroy files from years back. He replied, "Yes, but keep copies."

Other studios that opened operations in Hollywood included First National Pictures, Inc., a circuit of independent exhibitors who established their own production facilities at Burbank, Calif., in 1922; Warner Bros. Pictures, Inc., founded by Harry, Albert, Samuel, and Jack Warner in 1923; and Columbia Pictures, Inc., incorporated in 1924 by Harry and Jack Cohn.

### C. Talkies

With the increasing popularity of motion pictures at the turn of the century, it did not take long for inventors to seek a means by which motion pictures could be accompanied by sound. In 1907, Dr. Lee De Forest invented the Audion, a photoelectric vacuum tube that made it possible to amplify sound, enabling a sound recording to be presented in a full auditorium. De Forest then turned his attention to the problem of synchronizing the sound with the motion picture. He developed a process for photographing sound impulses, which could later be read by shining a light through the filmed sound image onto a photocell. This became known as his Phonofilm system. De Forest sold his basic *audion* tube patents to the Bell Telephone Company. By creating short feature films with vaudeville headliners at that time, such as Eddie Cantor and George Jessel, De Forest tried to stimulate interest in his short films by showing them at the Rivoli Theater in New York City on March 13, 1923. The sounds were reproduced through an electronic amplification system of his own design. From 1923 through 1927, De Forest was unsuccessful in his attempts to stimulate interest in his system.

About the same time, one of De Forest's former associates, Theodore Case, demonstrated his own sound-on-film system to William Fox. Fox accepted the system, calling it MovieTone. Like De Forest, Fox also began putting vaudeville headline acts on film, but Fox had more success applying the sound process to a very successful newsreel he had been producing. When he began adding sound to his "MovieTone

News," the audience not only saw famous people of their day, such as Babe Ruth and Charles Lindberg, but for the first time they heard their voices. MovieTone News recorded Lindberg's takeoff from Long Island on May 20, 1927, his arrival in France, and his subsequent ticker-tape parade in New York City.

Meanwhile, Bell Laboratories and its parent company Western Electric were making extensive studies on the nature of sounds and techniques for recording and reproducing such sounds, and continued to experiment with ways of adapting De Forest's audion tube for amplification of sound in theaters. One experiment resulted in a process of recording sound on a 16-inch phonographic disc rotated at 33⅓ revolutions per minute. Combining these recorded discs together with an improved system of amplification, Bell attracted the interest of Warner Bros. Pictures who acquired from Bell the necessary patent licenses to establish the Vitaphone Corporation to market the complete system. With the Vitaphone system, a motion picture producer was able to synchronize a phonograph recording of various sound effects, music, and voice with the action of the picture. For replay, the disc was placed on a phonograph turntable, rotating at a uniform speed in precise relation to the motion picture.

Jack Warner of Warner Bros. Pictures had just finished an elaborate and expensive film, John Barrymore's *Don Juan*, with Mary Astor. While filming was in progress, William Axt, David Mendoza, and Major Edward Bowes were working on a musical score. Warner decided to send the prints of the completed film to New York where the score could be recorded by the New York Philharmonic in synchronization with the film. Sound effects were added and Will Hayes, director of the *Motion Picture Producers and Distributors Association of America*, was invited to record a filmed speech about the future of sound-on-film.

On August 6, 1926, Warner Bros. Pictures presented the first All-Vitaphone program at their Warner Theater in New York City. With the showing of *Don Juan*, which had synchronized music and sound effects but no speech, together with a presentation of Will Haye's filmed remarks, "talking pictures," or "talkies," were born.

On October 6, 1927, an audience of notables at the Warner Theater in New York watched as the silent film, *The Jazz Singer*, was projected onto the screen. At one early point in the movie, then popular singing artist, Al Jolson was heard over the theater's sound system, singing in a night club scene. After a rendition of the song, "Dirty Hands, Dirty Face," Jolson ad libbed, "Wait a minute, wait a minute, you ain't heard nothin' yet. Wait a minute, I tell ya, you ain't heard nothin.' You wanna hear 'Toot Toot Tootsie'? "

With those words, the film business changed forever. Entertainment columnist Louella Parsons wrote in the December 29, 1927 issue of the *Los Angeles Examiner*, under the headline, " '*Jazz Singer*,' *with Vitaphone, Triumph for Jolson: Film at Criterion Rich in Pathos and Interest*,"

> The strong protests uttered against the Vitaphone as a destroyer of the peaceful silence of the motion picture, suffered a glorious defeat last night. Without the Vitaphone "The Jazz Singer" would not have completely won over the large audience at the Criterion Theater. "The Jazz Singer" and the Vitaphone are affinities that do not jangle out of tune. If there had been long conversations and more attempts at vocal comedy, the effect would not have been so satisfactory. But very wisely Warner Brothers, save for a single scene between Al Jolson and his mother, eliminated the spoken words. But the singing! Think of hearing Al Jolson sing the words of his songs as part of the screen play. The combination exceeded this reviewer's best expectations.
>
> I have been one who has lamented the encroachment of the voice in the silent drama. "The Jazz Singer," therefore, comes as an agreeable surprise. I must right here make it clear that there are few pictures that lend themselves so perfectly to the synchronization of music as "The Jazz Singer."

In 1927, Warner Bros. acquired First National Pictures Co., not for its film library, but to gain access to the hundreds of affiliated First National theaters across the country, which it began to wire for "sound." While other studios chose a "wait-and-see" policy, Warners went ahead and produced and released on July 7, 1928 the first all talking picture, *The Lights of New York.* The next month Warner released *The Terror*, in which actor, Conrad Nagel, dressed in white tie, tails, opera hat and mask even spoke the opening titles and credits. At the end of 1927, only about 150 theaters in the United States were wired for sound. By the end of 1929, there were over 8,000, which included every major motion picture theater in the nation. Though studio heads were initially skeptical of what they considered to be an expensive novelty, "talkies" became a novelty that the public could not get enough of.

When Paramount executives Adolph Zukor and Jesse Lasky had first seen demonstrations of Warner's Vitaphone and Fox's MovieTone systems, they were unimpressed. Paramount and the rest of the industry only began looking into the matter of sound when they learned how the money was pouring in at Warner Bros. from *The Jazz Singer, Don Juan*, and other Vitaphone productions. Early in 1928, at the annual production meetings held at Paramount Pictures's home office in New York City, Adolph Zucker and Jesse Lasky decided to adopt the MovieTone sound-on-film method, soon adopted by other studios. During the 15 months between late 1927 and the end of 1928, studio profits increased 600 percent. By that time, it became clear that "talking pictures" were here to stay.

### D. Talkies and Music Publishing

The popularity of talking pictures created an enormous demand for music by the Hollywood studios and this lead to studio buy-outs of many of the major music publishers.

In 1928, Warner Bros. Pictures acquired M. Witmark & Sons, which had the publishing rights to the big three of Broadway musical composers, Victor Herbert, Sigmund Romberg, and Rudolf Friml. In 1929, they purchased Remick Music Corporation, which held the rights to the works of Gus Kahn, Richard Whiting, Al Dubin, and Harry Warren. In the same year, Warners purchased Harms, Inc. from Max Dreyfus for $11 million, but with that purchase, Warner's acquired new Broadway musical writers such as George and Ira Gershwin, Vincent Youmans, Irving Caesar, Richard Rodgers, Larry Hart, Oscar Hammerstein, and Jerome Kern. Also in 1929, MGM entered into a publishing administration agreement with Robbins Music Corp. for the publishing of music written for use in MGM pictures. Paramount Pictures established their own music publishing firm, Famous Music. Perhaps the name was adapted from Famous Players, which was Adolph Zukor's former company.

As more and more theaters were being wired for sound, musicians became worried. Vitaphone and MovieTone systems were performing the required music without the need for live musicians. Many musicians began migrating to Hollywood, as the demand for the recording of thematic and background music for motion pictures increased. Soon, virtually all the studios were producing musicals and dancing extravaganzas, such as Busby Berkeley's *Gold Diggers of Broadway*, *Forty Second Street*, *Footlight Parade*, and *Dames*.

Meanwhile, independent music publishers began negotiating the licenses for the use of their popular songs in motion pictures, using what became known as a synchronization license — i.e., permission to synchronize music in timed-relation with a motion picture — and ASCAP began demanding performance royalties from studios as well as theaters that were projecting talking pictures containing copyrighted music. By 1926, movie theaters were required to have a license from ASCAP to perform any music in ASCAP's extensive repertoire. These performance licenses remained in effect until 1948, when the practice of ASCAP (and BMI) of licensing performances in theaters in the United States came to an end.

### E. Television

The first wireless signal was transmitted by Guglielmo Marconi, an Italian electrical engineer, in 1895. Marconi soon formed telegraph companies in England and opened the first wireless office in New York City. When, in 1901, Marconi telegraphed the letter "S" across the Atlantic Ocean, the U.S. Navy was so impressed that, for its ship-to-shore communications, it replaced a flock of carrier pigeons with the new "wireless" technology. On Good Friday, 1917, after German U-boats torpedoed and sank four American ships without warning, the United States declared war on Germany and President Wilson directed the Navy to take over all wireless stations during the emergency, including Marconi's ship-to-shore operations.

Shortly after the end of World War I, upon the urging of the U.S. government, the General Electric Corporation (GE) formed the Radio Corporation of America (RCA), which took over the assets of American Marconi. RCA also assumed responsibility for marketing the radio equipment produced by GE and Westinghouse. RCA's business from wireless and the sale of radio sets grew rapidly. Within days of receiving the first commercial broadcasting license in 1920, station KDKA went on the air with the returns of the Harding-Cox presidential election. By next summer, RCA was broadcasting the world heavyweight boxing championship, a marketing brainstorm of RCA General Manager David Sarnoff, who recognized the importance of offering compelling content to promote the sale of radio sets.

In the early 1920s, Sarnoff publicly speculated on the possibility of "every farmhouse equipped not only with a sound-receiving device but with a screen that would mirror the sights of life." In 1926, Sarnoff formed the National Broadcasting Company (NBC), the first major broadcast network in the United States.

On September 1, 1928, Philo T. Farnworth demonstrated to journalists the world's first working television system by televising a motion picture with electronic scanning by both the pickup and display devices. Ten years later, after several court battles over the ownership in several patents on the invention, Sarnoff managed to steal the spotlight from Farnsworth (if not more), and RCA introduced television at the 1939-40 New York World's Fair. On April 30, 1939, President Franklin Roosevelt appeared at the fair, before the NBC cameras, becoming the first U.S. president to appear on television. The next day, four models of RCA television sets were offered for sale.

Television's experimental period ended and full commercial telecasting began on July 1, 1941. NBC's New York station W2XBS received the first commercial license, adopting the call letters WNBT (later becoming, WNBC-TV). The first official, paid television commercial on that day broadcast by any station in the United States was for Bulova Watches, appearing just before the start of a telecast of a Brooklyn Dodgers game. Limited programming continued until the United States entered World War II. Telecasts were curtailed in the early years of the war. On V-E Day, May 8, 1945, WNBT broadcast hours of news coverage, and remotes from around New York City.

Television blossomed in the early 1950s when the medium's first big star, Milton Berle, drew large audiences to NBC with his antics on *The Texaco Star Theater.* (I was a musical arranger on the show.) It was said that Milton Berle sold more television sets than anyone in the country. The first radio and television simulcasts were made when conductor Arturo Toscanini, who had been conducting the NBC Symphony Orchestra on radio since 1937, conducted ten concerts on NBC television between 1948 and 1952.

Several companies, including CBS, began to develop color television systems, but the standards war was won by Sarnoff in December, 1953. The Rose Bowl Parade was broadcast in color on January 1, 1954, although few people had access to color receivers. The first RCA consumer color televisions were produced in March 1954. By 1960, a half million color TV sets were in use, and more than two-thirds of NBC's prime-time nightly broadcasts were "colorcast" during the 1962-63 season. It was no surprise that color programming proved to be the most important driver in the sale of color TV sets. The most popular show during most of the 1960s, and the first western televised in color, was NBC's "Bonanza."

Where reception of over-the-air transmissions was limited by mountainous terrain, large *community antennas* were constructed from which cables were run to individual households. Thus, in 1948, Community Antenna Television, or CATV (now, "Cable TV") was born. *Cable television* is a system of providing performances of audiovisual programs to viewers via radio frequency signals transmitted to televisions through fixed optical fibers or coaxial cables as opposed to the over-the-air method used in traditional television broadcasting (via radio waves) in which a television antenna is required.

In 1970, Ted Turner, the head of a successful Atlanta-based outdoor advertising firm, purchased WJRJ-Atlanta, Channel 17, a small, struggling ultra-high frequency (UHF) station, which he renamed WTCG, after his Turner Communications Group. In December 1976, Turner ingeniously conceived the idea of offering the programming of WTCG to CATV networks around the country. By transmitting WTCG's signal to cable systems via satellite he thus originated the first "superstation." Because of the high bandwidth of these cable networks, cable television providers began to offer far more television stations, often at far higher transmission quality, than could be made available over-the-air. Cable television has since become more common than over-the-air or "free" television, even in large cities where terrain does not pose an obstacle to quality reception. In addition, these cable networks are now also used to provide FM radio programming, high-speed Internet, telephony, and similar services.

*Direct broadcast satellite* (DBS) television refers to a means of transmitting performances of audiovisual (and audio-only) performances by means of broadcast transmission from satellites directly for reception into the home. The first DBS broadcast service was launched in the United Kingdom and Ireland by Sky Television in 1989. It was followed by Primestar, which, in 1991 began transmitting to North America and later, in 1994, by DirecTV, which acquired Primestar in 1999. In 1996, EchoStar's Dish Network went online in the United States, becoming DirecTV's primary competitor.

*Pay-per-view* (PPV) is a means of providing audiovisual programming into the home by a broadcast transmission that requires the home viewer to pay a specific fee for the privilege of viewing the particular broadcast. Programs available through pay-per-view are broadcast at pre-determined times and therefore shown at the same time to everyone paying for it, as opposed to video on demand (see below), which allows a viewer to see the program at the time of the viewer's choosing. Payment may be made by following instructions provided on-screen or by calling the cable or satellite TV provider. Many cable and satellite providers offer channels that are dedicated to providing pay-per-view programming. Such programming may be recorded by a DVR for later viewing.

*Video on demand* (VOD) is a means of providing audiovisual programming into the home in a way that allows a viewer to see the program at the time of his or her choosing. Video on demand is conducted by either streaming the program through a set-top box, allowing the viewing of the program in real time, or downloading the program to a device such as a computer or DVR for later viewing.

*Near video on demand* (NVOD) is a form of pay-per-view in which multiple copies of a program are broadcast at short time intervals (typically every 10 or 20 minutes). This allows the viewer to order a program and view it from the beginning within minutes.

## F. Home Video Devices

A *home video device* is a physical recording medium, such as a tape cassette or laserdisc, on which an audiovisual work is recorded for purposes of distributing it to consumers for home viewing with the aid of a video device player. Some of these devices may also be used to store audiovisual works taped off the air for later home viewing by the consumer, a practice that became known as "home taping."

*VCR.* The earliest home video devices were intended solely for home taping, which afforded the consumer the convenience of tape-recording a television program at the time it aired for later playback and viewing at a time more convenient for the consumer. Although professional reel-to-reel video tape recorders could be used for this purpose, their high cost made them uneconomical for commercial use in the home. That changed in 1972 upon the introduction by Philips Electronics of the first videocassette recorder (VCR). The Philips device, however, was relatively expensive and found a home with only a few early adopters. It wasn't until the release by Sony Corporation of the Betamax in 1975 did home video recording capture the imagination of the consuming public.

The practice of taping programs off the air using VCRs was legally challenged by Universal Studios when it filed a lawsuit against Sony in 1976, charging that the distribution of their Betamax VCRs in the United States constituted contributory copyright infringement of their television programs. The case went to the Supreme Court, which ruled that the making of copies of television programs by users of the Betamax machine for purposes of time-shifting constituted a fair use of copyright and, therefore, Sony was not liable for contributory copyright infringement. *Sony Corp. of America v. Universal City Studios, Inc.*, 464 U.S. 417 (1984).

The victory, however, came at a time when the Betamax format had already suffered a humiliating defeat in the marketplace. Despite early efforts by Sony to convince other Japanese electronics makers to adopt a single standard, that effort was thwarted by Victor Corporation of Japan (JVC), who introduced a competing VCR format called VHS (for "Video Home System"). A format war between Betamax and VHS ensued.

The early VCRs had a limited recording time, with Betamax able to record one hour of programming and the first VHS devices up to two hours. Thus, early VCRs were not ideal for the distribution of high quality audiovisual recordings of long-form entertainment, such as motion pictures, which often required more than two hours of playing time.

To fulfill the need for the home distribution of motion pictures, several record-style discs were introduced, such as RCA's Capacitance Electronic Disc, JVC's Video High Density disc, and Philips' LaserDisc. All these devices produced fairly high quality pictures of feature length films, but since none were capable of recording programs off the air, they failed to find significant markets outside a niche of movie collectors and videophiles.

Meanwhile, the format war between Betamax and VHS continued. In the early years, Betamax was widely perceived as the better format, because of its superior picture quality. But VHS had the advantage of a simpler tape transport mechanism, which allowed the early VHS machines to rewind and fast forward the tape faster than a Betamax. Eventually, VHS caught up in picture quality. But the primary factor that many attribute to the ultimate triumph of VHS over Betamax is recording length.

Sony believed that the one-hour length would be sufficient for home use, but fans of Monday Night Football thought otherwise. The four-hour "Long Play" VHS recorders offered by RCA and Panasonic in 1976 became popular with men who could afford the new devices and who were not concerned about the lower picture quality. The longer recording time of the VHS also accommodated pre-recorded movies. Thus, with a VHS machine at home, early adopters who could afford the new home video technology — typically middle-aged men — no longer had to visit the red-light district to view X-rated entertainment, as the pornographers quickly seized upon the opportunity to make their films available for the home video market.

The accommodation of full length feature films was also a factor that enabled the video rental business, which blossomed in the 1980s. Eventually, Betamax would support four hours of recording time, but the VHS could be extended to over nine hours, affording consumers who used VCRs mainly for recording broadcasts a significant cost savings on blank videocassette tapes.

While Betamax jumped to an early market share lead, by 1981, Betamax sales in the United States declined to only 25% of the VCR market. The economy of scale afforded by the success of VHS in North America permitted VHS devices to be introduced to the European market at a far lower cost than the Betamax. When, in 1988, Sony began to market VHS machines under the Sony brand, the war was declared over.

*DVD.* In 1995, after two years of negotiation among a consortium of electronics manufacturers to avoid a format war like the one a decade before between Betamax and VHS, the specification for the optical disc format known as, DVD (for "Digital Versatile Disc" or "Digital Video Disc") was born. DVD discs have the same dimensions as compact discs (CDs), but have the capacity to store far more data — as much as 6 times more, nearly 5 gigabytes — thereby accommodating full length feature films in a form that is both compact and affording far higher picture quality than videocassettes.

DVDs were released in the United States in 1997 and, by 2003, revenues from the rental of DVDs surpassed those from VHS rentals. Within a few years, most film studios ceased releasing new titles in the VHS format and, by 2008, the VCRs were declared dead.

*DVR.* Early on, DVDs were non-recordable and thus could not be used for the time-shifting of scheduled broadcasts. One would think, therefore, that the new format would have suffered the same fate as earlier non-recordable laser disc formats. But the DVD format benefited from the introduction in 1999 of the DVR (for Digital Video Recorder) — a device that digitally records audiovisual programming to a disk drive or other permanent form of storage.

That year, DVRs by TiVo and ReplayTV hit the market and introduced a form of time-shifting that was far more flexible and convenient than that afforded by the traditional VCR. Those old enough to remember them may recall how notoriously difficult VCRs were to use. A user had to know precisely the day, and the time of day, the television program was going to be aired and then typically had to refer to the documentation accompanying the device to learn how to properly record the broadcast. In addition, because of the linear nature of the tape, playback features were limited. When forwarding or rewinding a tape, the user often had to guess when to stop to find the portion of the tape they wished to view.

All this changed with the DVR. Using the TiVo remote control, you could scan through a graphical program listing, quickly point and click to the program you sought to record (or search for it by keying-in the first few letters of its title), and then simply press the record button. The program, when aired, would be recorded on a hard disk inside your TiVo or ReplayTV box hooked up to your cable or satellite receiver. Features such as instant replay, pausing the action, stepping through the action frame-by-frame, and the fast-forwarding through advertisements were among the marvels of the new device. New versions of these devices accommodated the recording of programs onto DVD, automatic skipping of television commercials, and remote programming over the Internet.

Some cable TV providers, such as Cablevision, have begun offering the features of a DVR, but instead of providing a DVR to consumers who would record programs onto the DVR's hard disk, the cable provider built the capability to receive DVR commands through its cable boxes and records the programs for the use on hard disk servers maintained at the cable provider's facilities. The practice was challenged in court, as a direct violation of copyright by the cable company, which had no authorization to make the copies on behalf of consumers and no authorization to make the buffer copies required to facilitate the process. In a decision that has been highly criticized by the copyright bar, the court ruled in favor of the cable company. *Cartoon Network LP v. CSC Holdings, Inc. and Cablevision Systems Corp.*, 536 F.3d 121 (2d Cir. 2008) (reversing *Twentieth Century Fox v. Cablevision*, 478 F. Supp. 2d 607 (S.D.N.Y. 2007)).

*Blu-ray.* With the introduction of high definition television screens (HDTV) in the late 1990s, which dramatically improved the picture quality of video programming in the home, a new generation of high-definition home video devices was developed to take advantage of the higher resolution screens.

Commercially released in 2006, Blu-ray is an optical disc storage medium that has the same physical dimensions as the DVD and CD, but has over 10 times the data storage capacity as the standard DVD disc (approximately 50 gigabytes). The greater data capacity was required to store the large data requirements of high definition recording. The device's name was derived from the blue-violet (short wave-length) laser used to read and write to the optical disc. A short format war was waged between Blu-ray and a competing technology backed by Toshiba, HD DVD, but when Warner Bros. announced in January 2008 that it would no longer release titles in the HD DVD format and Toshiba announced a month later that it would no longer make and distribute HD DVD devices, the brief war was over.

## G. Streaming Video

*Streaming video* is a means of delivering a performance of an audiovisual work to a viewer using a telecommunications network, such as the Internet, while the work is being viewed at the same time it is being transmitted. Streaming video may be *live* or *on demand.* On-demand streams are stored on a server and are available for transmission upon a viewer's request. Live streams are only available as they occur, as in a video stream of a live sporting event, unless it is later stored for eventual on-demand streaming.

Streaming video over the Internet is distinguished from *video on demand* (VOD) in that the latter allows a user upon request to select and watch a video program, either by stream or download (to a digital video recorder (DVR), typically through a set-top box connected to their television and a cable or satellite television provider. Conversely, video streaming could be considered a web-based video on demand service. Eventually, streaming video and VOD will converge — with set-top boxes being connected to the Internet or videogame players, such as the XBOX and Playstation devices, or personal computers serving the functions of the set-top boxes and/or DVRs.

Several advancements in computer technology emerged in the 1980s, and network technologies in the 1990s, converged to make streaming video commercially practical, including: the increasing power of central processing units (CPU) and computer chip "bus-bandwidth," both necessary to support the required data rates; low-latency interrupt paths in computer operating systems (OS) necessary to prevent buffer under-run; greater network bandwidth, especially in the last mile to the home or business; increasing access to networks, especially the Internet; the use of standard protocols and formats, such as TCP/IP, HTTP, and HTML; decreasing costs of storing and transmitting data; the advent of compression technologies, such as the MPEG standards; and the commercialization of the Internet, including various types of advertising (such as, banner ads, website and page sponsorships, search ads, and in-line advertisements).

Providers of video streaming services are growing quickly, but the best known include YouTube, Hulu, Joost, Netflix, Real Networks, and Google Video.

### H. Permanent Downloads of Video

The first commercial web-based video download service that offered content licensed from the motion picture studios was a service called, MovieLink, a joint venture of five major movie studios (Metro-Goldwyn-Mayer Studios, Paramount Pictures, Sony Pictures Entertainment, Universal Studios and Warner Bros. Studios). Initially, films downloaded from the service could only be viewed on a personal computer screen or a television connected to a personal computer. Later, the other devices, like the Xbox 360 and certain cable set-top boxes, could be used in lieu of a computer, allowing the viewing of the films on television screens. In 2007, MovieLink was acquired by Blockbuster.

CinemaNow was another early provider of web-based downloads of major motion pictures on other studio content. The company was acquired by Sonic Solutions in November 2008, and in January 2009, Sonic and Blockbuster, Inc. announced an alliance to offer a single service under the Blockbuster brand, essentially merging CinemaNow and Movielink.

Another video download service that has struggled is Vongo, which offered films for a fixed monthly subscription fee. Movies downloaded were viewed on personal computers using Adobe/Macromedia Flash software and were viewable during a fixed time after download, typically from 4-6 months or 12-24 months. Upon the expiration of the viewing period, the film was deleted from the user's hard drive. (Later, films could be viewed on Microsoft's Xbox 360.) The service changed its name to StarzPlay, after its parent company, Starz Entertainment, owned by Liberty Media.

In October 2005, Apple Computer started selling TV shows from ABC/Disney in its iTunes download store. It now offers a growing list of studio content, including movies, which are available in the store the same day they are released on DVD. Programs downloaded from the iTunes store may be viewed on personal computers and transferred to the Apple iPod for portable viewing.

## II. CONSIDERATIONS IN GRANTING AND CLEARING SYNCHRONIZATION LICENSES

What has been said with regard to music licensing in general (*see* Chapter 11) applies directly with regard to synchronization licensing. The primary factors are:

A. The fee structure;

B. The value of the song, taking into consideration its popularity, historical significance, and overall quality;

C. The importance of the song in relation to its intended use; and,

D. The scope of the intended use.

The following discussion begins where the general discussion in Chapter 11 left off, describing each of the foregoing factors in detail as applied to considerations in granting and clearing synchronization licenses.

## A. Fee Structure

The fee structure of nearly all synchronization licenses permitting the exhibition of licensed music in theaters or on television, or both, is a flat fee — the motion picture or television producer will pay a one-time, flat dollar amount for the term of the license, regardless of the number of copies of the film that is made or how many times the film is exhibited during the term.

Synchronization licenses, traditionally, permitted merely the exhibition of the motion picture or audiovisual work in which the music is recorded on television or in theaters. They did not permit videograms — i.e., the use of the music in videocassettes, DVDs, or other home video devices for home distribution; permission for such uses were typically provided under the terms of a separate videogram license, often included in the same form agreement as the synchronization license.

In recent years, producers and film studios have been increasingly demanding that the synchronization license include as many rights as possible. This is to reduce the business risks and transaction costs of repeatedly having to return to the publisher for a new license for each new means of exploiting their audiovisual work. In this case, the producer may ask for what is commonly called *broad rights.* This would be a license to use the song as part of the audiovisual work whether in theaters, on television, in home video devices, through Internet download or streaming, or in advertisements, promotional trailers, and similar uses. In addition, a broad rights license would be worldwide, rather than just for the United States, and will endure for the life of the copyright, not just a fixed set of years, such as 5 years.

The key constraint on these broad rights synch licenses is that the song is used by any of these means only *in context* — i.e., just as it appears as synchronized in the film. The use of the song *out of context* — e.g., using the song in an advertisement in a way that was not precisely how it was used in the film — would require a separate license, carrying an additional fee.

Note, the synchronization license permits merely the making of a *recording* of music in synchronization with an audiovisual work and the making of copies of that recording; it does not permit the *performance* of music even though the making of recordings was authorized by the synchronization license. With one exception (discussed below), a separate performance license is required whenever the audiovisual work (and the song embodied in it) is performed. Accordingly, if the film is exhibited on television, or in motion picture theaters located outside the United States (see below), the music copyright owner will still be entitled to collect fees for public performances of the picture from its performance rights society.

As mentioned previously, it is always to the music publisher's advantage to structure a license fee in a way that provides an economic upside whenever a work in which its song is used becomes successful. For example, the more copies a sound recording containing the publisher's song is sold, the higher the mechanical royalties the publisher will expect to receive. The problem with issuing a synchronization license on a flat fee basis would appear to preclude such an upside. Once the flat synch fee is paid, the publisher will not get a second bite at the apple should the film in which the song is used become a blockbuster.

But let's not forget the performance fee. Even though the synchronization license is issued on a flat fee basis, the music publisher, for the most part, will get to participate in the economic success of the film, because the performance fees collected are based generally upon how widely the audiovisual work is performed. Motion picture and television producers will assert that music copyright owners do not deserve to receive a chance to participate in the economic success of their theatrical and television works, because the music copyright owners are not taking any of the risks associated with the financing and development of such works. Nevertheless, it is the broadcasters and distributors of the producer's works who will eventually be responsible for performance and other music license fees associated with the distribution, exhibition, and broadcast of their works, and the producers are generally satisfied if they can obtain the necessary synchronization fees they require at a reasonable cost.

### *1. Performance License Aspects*

By court consent decrees entered into between the Department of Justice and the major performance rights societies, music copyright owners were required to issue public performance licenses to movie producers on a per-film basis, if requested. As a result, performance rights societies do not license performance rights in music in theaters located in the United States, and most synchronization licenses issued today include a provision that provides permission to the producer to publicly perform the music in U.S. theaters. Thus, for a motion picture to be released in theaters located in the United States, a producer obtains from music copyright owners two fundamental licenses in music: (1) a synchronization license to reproduce the music in *copies* of the motion picture and (2) a performance license to *perform* the music publicly in movie theaters in the United States.

In determining what to charge for the U.S. theatrical performances of the music, it has long been the custom of music publishers, when determining the total fee, to charge a fee on the same flat fee basis as the synchronization fee, often by merely doubling the synchronization fee. For example, if the synch fee was determined to be $1,000, the total fee for the synch license and the U.S. theatrical performance license would be $2,000. This was done for the sake of simplicity, and not necessarily derived from good publishing practices. Nevertheless, the practice is likely to continue, because no one has yet scientifically determined the reasonable value of a performance license in the United States for a motion picture playing in several thousand theaters for a normal series of theatrical runs.

Public performances in theaters in other countries are subject to local performance fees collected by local performance rights societies.

### *2. Step Deals*

Where, by virtue of a small production budget, a producer cannot afford to pay the fee necessary for a broad rights license, a publisher could offer what is known as a *step deal* — a license under which the producer pays a dramatically lower flat fee for a very limited set of uses (e.g., theatrical release with gross box office receipts of less than some pre-determined amount or a limited number of screens). The publisher gets additional flat fee payments as gross box office reaches certain additional milestones (e.g., additional gross box office receipts or increased number of screens) and when the producer releases the film by other means (e.g., television, home video, etc.) or in other territories (e.g., outside the United States). Gross box office receipts are typically defined as those reported by the film trade publication Daily Variety.

For example, a step deal might be structured this way: For the rights to distribute in theaters located in the United States over a term of 5 years, $5,000, payable upon execution of the license. In addition, producer shall pay an additional $5,000 upon the occurrence of each of the following events: upon achievement of gross box office receipts of $5 million (as reported in Daily Variety); upon achievement of each additional $5 million in gross box office receipts; upon the release of the film for any form of television exhibition; upon the release of the film on home video devices. The term may be extended to perpetuity upon the payment of an additional $5,000.

Some music publishers are wary of issuing too many step deals, as it may have the effect of overexposing the song. On the other hand, steps deals allow the publisher to maintain a relationship between the song and the listening public, while assuring that if the film is successful, the publisher will not have underpriced the license.

## B. The Value of the Song

The admonition made in Chapter 10 suggesting that copyright owners avoid maintaining inflated perceptions about the value of the musical composition and getting mired in the details of licensing terms is particularly applicable to synchronization licensing. Regardless of the popularity of the song, the scope of the use, or its importance to the licensee, the copyright owner's overall interest should always be getting as much activity in the song as possible.

Often a copyright owner's approach is to attempt to get all the market will bear. Such an attitude should be tempered by several important considerations. First, very few songs have no close substitutes. In other words, there will usually be a song in the same genre owned by someone else, which will suit the licensee just as well. A good music licensing executive who knows his catalog will always be able to find a song in the genre for which the licensee is seeking. Persons experienced in seeking to obtain clearances for the use of music will always be on the watch for close substitutes for the music he is seeking to clear.

Second, the music performance revenues a copyright owner receives when the audiovisual work is publicly performed (*see* Chapter 18) acts as a form of multiplier on the synchronization license fee collected. The music copyright owner will earn performance credits from its performance rights society (e.g., ASCAP, BMI) on public performances of the song on television worldwide and in theaters overseas, and these can be substantial when the picture in which the song is licensed becomes a box office success or is broadcast on network television and in television syndication. The fewer licenses you issue, the less performance activity the song receives, and the fewer performance credits and performance income you will receive. Particularly applicable here is the adage, "Penny wise, pound foolish." Accordingly, no music copyright owner, whether he is responsible for a single song or a large catalog of popular songs and standards, can afford to be "too difficult to deal with."

By the same token, if you are seeking to clear a license from a copyright owner who is being difficult, you might persuade him to quote you a more reasonable fee by reminding him of the performance fees he will be foregoing if you choose an alternative song from another publisher that will serve your purposes just as well. In addition, the producer may offer a step deal, as described above, which will assure the publisher of fair compensation in the event of a successful production, and assure the producer of the music rights he will need in case such success permits lucrative exploitation in other markets.

## C. The Importance of the Song in Relation to Its Intended Use

Sometimes one song will not serve the purpose just as well as another. Before quoting a synchronization license fee, the copyright owner should ask many questions of the potential licensee about the intended use of the song to find out just how important the song is in relation to its intended use.

To determine the importance of the song in relation to its intended use, it is sometimes useful to inquire in some detail what the motion picture is about and how the song is going to be used in the picture.

For example, the use of the song *Rhapsody in Blue* as purely background music in a comedy is significantly different than the use of the song in a biographical film on the life of George Gershwin; surely, a biography of George Gershwin would not be possible without a license to use several of the composer's most important compositions.

Thus, with respect to motion pictures and television programs, the central questions usually relate to the description of the work in which the music will be used:

- whether the use is a *vocal* rendition or merely *instrumental*;
- whether the music is used as *background* music or foreground music;
- whether the use relates to how the composition was *originally presented* to the public;
- whether an *original recording* is used;
- whether the lyrics of the song is used to help *tell the story*;
- whether the music will be used over the *title sequence* or *closing credits*; and
- whether the title of the song will be used as the *title* of the film.

*Vocal or Instrumental.* A *vocal* rendition is when someone is singing, or perhaps humming, the composition in the motion picture; an *instrumental* rendition is when the composition is played without a rendition of lyrics. Rarely does the fee vary merely because the song is rendered with or without the lyrics; however, information as to whether the lyrics are going to be used may lead to other information that assists a copyright owner in formulating the terms of the license.

*Background or Foreground.* If someone is rendering the composition in the motion picture — as, for example, when the protagonist of the picture plays or sings on screen a rendition of Bob Dylan's *Blowin' In the Wind* — it is called a visual or *foreground* use. If the composition is heard in the background and no one is seen performing the song, it is a *background* use. All other things being equal, a foreground use will generally command a higher license fee than a background use.

*Original Presentation.* The extent to which the intended use relates to how the composition was originally presented to the public may also be important. For example, the song *Blowin' In the Wind* was originally presented at a certain time in the 1960s that is usually associated with the "peace" movement or the "new generation" of young people of that time. A background use of the song *Blowin' In the Wind* for a scene in a movie set in the 1990s is different from the use of the same song in a movie about war protesters in the 1960s or otherwise in a movie set in the 1960s to provide the feeling of that decade. Though virtually any song could substitute for a random use of the song in the background of an average, unremarkable scene, the publisher could command a higher fee for uses that acutely relate to the setting of the film, as there are few substitutes that convey the particular feeling of the late 1960s that is best conveyed by the song *Blowin' In the Wind.*

*Original Recording.* Whether the original recording of the song is used in the motion picture or a new recording is made by the producer may also be a factor, though generally most music publishers do not vary the license fee on this basis. If the producer desires to use an original sound recording in the motion picture, he would be required to obtain a separate license to do so from the owner of the recording. The publisher should ask for most favored nations with any masters of the song licensed — i.e., that the synch fee paid for the use of the song be no less favorable than the fee paid for the use of a master recording of the song. If the songwriter recorded an original recording of the song, some consideration should be given to encourage the producer to use the songwriter's recording rather than a cover or new recording.

*Dramatic Use of Lyrics.* The movie may be a dramatic adaptation of the lyrics of a song, as was the case in the motion picture adaptation of the song, *Ode to Billie Joe* and the 1970s television series adaptation of the song *Harper Valley PTA.* In each of these cases, the absence of the music from the soundtrack would have been quite unnatural and conspicuous, and, accordingly, the copyright owner should recognize the opportunity to command a higher than average fee for synchronization licenses in these circumstances. A separate license and fee may be appropriate for permission to create the dramatic adaptation of the lyrics. *Dramatic adaptations* of song lyrics are discussed in Chapter 19.

*Title Sequence/Closing Credits.* A premium is warranted if the song will be used over the title sequence or, to a lesser degree, the closing credits of the motion picture.

*Use of Song Title.* If the song's title is used for a special purpose in the motion picture, such as the title of the motion picture, the importance of the song in relation to its intended use becomes obvious. Some additional consideration for the use of the music could be considered, as well as a separate fee for the use of the song in the title of the motion picture. In this regard, it might be wise for a copyright owner to make certain that his standard synchronization license agreement states specifically that the license does not include permission to use the title of the song as the title of the audiovisual work in which the music will be synchronized. A producer who intends to use the title of the song for a special purpose should be certain to clear any further permission that may be required.

The importance of the music to a promotional music video featuring the song is the extreme case of the importance of the song to the audiovisual work, but there are other considerations in setting the terms of music video licenses and these are touched upon in this chapter.

## D. Scope of the Use

### *1. Media and Distribution Channels*

For many years, synchronization licenses for motion pictures were carefully drawn to permit only a very narrow set of uses, such as the reproduction of copies for the purpose of normal theatrical exhibition and/or television broadcast.

Even the term "television" was often carefully defined, with distinctions among network, local, syndicated, cable, direct satellite broadcast, etc. being considered. The typical kinds of television uses today include: All Television, Free TV, Basic Cable TV, Pay/Subscription Cable TV, HDTV, and Industrial or Corporate (exhibition at trade shows, corporate sales meetings, etc.). If the motion picture was to be distributed in videograms, such as videocassettes and DVDs for home use, the terms and conditions under which these uses were permitted were separately negotiated, either in a separate license or in special provisions set forth in the synchronization license form.

But as new technologies, such as Internet streaming and permanent downloading of videos, emerged, the motion picture studios began a process of simplifying their music licensing process and began demanding *broad rights* to use the music they desired — in other words, the right to use the music in the film by any means of exhibition, broadcast, or means of distribution, now known or hereafter devised.

While music publishers continue to try to issue licenses that have as narrow a scope as possible, those seeking to clear synchronization licenses are increasingly seeking to obtain these broad rights — or at least an option or series of options, negotiated at the time the original synchronization license is issued (and preferably before a final decision to use that piece of music in the work is made), to distribute the work in all other types of media and means of distribution. These, as we have seen, are known as *step deals* — typical fee structures for which are provided below.

### *2. Term*

The term of a synchronization license will depend upon the specific use. Though it is preferable for a music publisher to restrict the license's duration to the shortest possible time, the term of synchronization licenses for motion pictures is generally in perpetuity. Since the music copyright owner will benefit from the performance of music on the radio, in international theaters, and on television, it is not entirely to his disadvantage to allow a long-term use in motion pictures with hopes that the picture becomes successful and is televised over a period of many years, perhaps in the footsteps of a classic film, such as *Casablanca.* The song, *As Time Goes By*, which was written and published many years before the picture was created, owes its *standard song* status to the synchronization license, which permitted its use in the film.

Though motion picture synchronization licenses are commonly granted in perpetuity, such term is generally confined to public performances of the film in theaters and, perhaps, on television; if the same motion picture is to be distributed in videograms, the duration of such use will normally be stated separately in another license, or in special provisions of the synchronization license, regarding distribution in videogram form.

Synchronization licenses for use of music in television programs are generally shorter in duration, tending normally to be for a three to five-year period, but this is often subject to negotiation. When television synchronization licenses are granted at the same time as a synchronization license for a theatrical motion picture release, the term of the license is normally in perpetuity. But even when the license is only for a program made for television, the recent trend, which has been at the insistence of those seeking to clear licenses, has been to grant the synchronization licenses for a perpetual term.

The term of a synch license typically commences upon the first exhibition, broadcast, Internet transmission or applicable use.

*a. Authority to Issue Long-Term Licenses*

While producers are increasingly demanding long-term licenses, the music copyright owner may not always have the authority to grant the license desired. A music copyright owner may grant licenses covering only the term for which it has authority to grant licenses; that authority may be limited by the terms of the copyright owner's contract with the songwriter. As noted in Chapter 9, on the *Duration of Copyright, Assignments of Copyright, and Licenses*, certain music publishing agreements between songwriters and publishers only granted rights with respect to the original term of copyright. An example of such a contract is any music publishing agreement based upon the Uniform Popular Songwriter's Contract published in 1947 by the American Guild of Authors & Composers (now known as The Songwriter's Guild). Under that agreement, the renewal copyright for U.S. rights, and under certain circumstances international rights as well, reverted to the songwriter at the expiration of the original term of copyright. If the Publisher granted any licenses for the use of the composition in the United States during the original term, then such licenses will continue in effect under their terms during the renewal term, despite the reversion of rights to the writer. However, this only applies to domestic licenses. In other words, the music publisher in such circumstance does not have the authority to issue licenses for use outside the United States covering the renewal term, unless it later turned out that the publisher retained international rights (due to the writer's failing to provide the proper notice).

To the extent a publisher cannot issue a worldwide license beyond the initial term of copyright, licensing opportunities will be lost. Virtually all motion picture and television synchronization licenses today are required to be issued on a worldwide basis and most require a term of perpetuity. If a producer cannot obtain a license having a sufficiently broad territory (i.e., worldwide) and a sufficiently long term (i.e., in perpetuity), he is likely to choose a substitute song. Thus, where renewal copyrights revert to songwriters under the provisions of a music publishing agreement, such as under the AGAC form contract, publishing income for songs whose protection is nearing the end of the original term may decline, because producers will avoid licensing compositions for which long-term, worldwide licenses are not available.

Songwriters can alleviate the problem by granting their interest in renewal rights to the song or by entering into an arrangement allowing the publisher during the original term to issue licenses that have terms extending beyond the original term and into the renewal term. An example of such an agreement is set forth as Form 15.7 on the CD-ROM.

#### b. *Affect of Rear Window Decision*

As discussed at length in Chapter 9, on the *Duration of Copyright, Assignments of Copyright, and Licenses*, granting renewal interests in copyright will not completely fulfill the need of producers to obtain long-term licenses and there is no agreement that a Publisher can reach with a songwriter that would absolutely assure producers that the license will cover the renewal term. Publishers can only assure producers that licenses for songs *tainted* by the *Rear Window* decision will last only until the expiration of the original term of copyright. The producers' options with respect to such songs are limited and are discussed in Chapter 9.

### 3. *Territory*

The territory of synchronization licenses for theatrical motion picture releases is generally worldwide. Network television, local television, and syndicated television were at one time granted on a per-country and regional basis, but the recent trend has been to extend the territory to throughout the world. Synchronization licenses are beginning to reflect recent economic changes toward a consolidating global marketplace.

### 4. Exclusivity

Synchronization licenses for motion pictures and television are nearly always granted on a non-exclusive basis. If the particular use is extraordinary, such as licensing a dramatic use of a song or using the song's title as the title of the motion picture or television program, and a substantial fee is offered, a copyright owner might agree to certain limitations on granting competing licenses for a limited period of time.

### 5. Credit

Unfortunately, motion picture producers rarely give on-screen credit to songs used in motion pictures. This is particularly true for background thematic music. Even more rarely will you find credit given to the artists who performed the material; rarer still is credit to songwriters, and we would offer our gratitude to anyone who can identify a motion picture that gives credit to the music publisher. It is time that music publishers consider requesting in their synchronization licenses for motion pictures and television programs, that the song, the composers, the music publishing company, and the performance rights society are given credit for the music used in such works. If nothing else, this would facilitate the task of licensing clearance for future uses of the motion picture, such as, perhaps, performance on television under a per-program performance license scheme (*see* Chapter 18).

### 6. Changes and Translations

The synchronization license should also state that no changes will be made in the lyrics or fundamental character of the music and that no translations will be made of the lyrics without the permission of the copyright owner. Any changes would be subject to additional fee and perhaps approval of the songwriter. If any translations are authorized, ownership in the translations should be retained by the music copyright owner; care should be taken so that the translation made by the licensee is of a good quality and not materially inconsistent with any translations that might have been previously done in international markets.

### 7. Screenings and Free Copies

Copyright owners should request an invitation to a pre-release screening of the motion picture to examine the use of the music and any credits required under the license. If a videogram of the picture is released, the copyright owner should request two copies for his files.

### *8. Most Favored Nations*

From time to time an artist's representative will ask for a *most favored nations* clause, a provision requiring that the fee to be charged will be on no less favorable terms than those offered for the use of any other song in the motion picture.

Requests for these clauses are often made by less experienced music publishers, who, not knowing what to charge, would offer some guess at an appropriate fee and require favored nations status to make sure his or her client does not receive a lower fee than anyone else who owns music being used in the picture. One problem with this approach, as we have seen, is that each song has a unique inherent value. Some are standard songs that are irreplaceable in the context of the use; others, like actors playing bit parts in the film, have many substitutes. Another problem is that each song is likely to have a different playing time in the motion picture, and some songs in the picture may be used for foreground music, some as background music. In such cases, how is a producer to determine whether the fee for the use of one song is on "more favorable terms" than the fee for the use of another?

Nevertheless, there are some instances where most favored nations clauses are justifiable, such as when both the song and a master recording of the song are used in the audiovisual work. Typically, a synch license for the song and a master use license for the recording command the same fee. Thus, a publisher may legitimately ask that the synch license fee paid for the song be no less favorable than the master use license fee paid for the song's recording.

In addition, if the song's copyright ownership is split among several co-publishers, it is not unusual for a publisher who quotes a fee for the synch use under his undivided share of the copyright on a most favored basis with the fee paid for any other share of the copyright. The fee quoted for a split copyright is typically based on 100% of the copyright, prorated for the share of the publisher making the quote. Suppose, for example, one co-publisher of a copyright owned or administered equally by two parties quotes $100,000 based on 100% of the copyright prorated for its share. If the other co-owner obtains a $60,000 for its share, then the first co-owner would be entitled to a $60,000 fee, rather than the $50,000 he originally agreed upon.

Because of the disputes that may potentially arise from such provisions, a producer would be advised to avoid most favored provisions or might consider paying a fee that is slightly higher than warranted rather than to get entangled in such an arrangement.

### *9. Out-of-Context Uses*

If the music publisher carefully limited uses of the music in the audiovisual work as only *in context*, then ancillary or *out-of-context* uses, such as the use of the song in promotional trailers, advertising, or as background music to a DVD menu, will be subject to the terms of a separate license. Depending upon the use, a music publisher could negotiate for the out-of-context use as much as 100% of what it received for the in-context use.

## III. THEATRICAL MOTION PICTURE TRAILERS

A *trailer* is a short film of several minutes length containing a tightly edited compilation or montage of clips from a motion picture created for the purpose of advertising the motion picture (i.e., "coming attraction"). The creation of good trailers is now considered an art form and certain artists specialize in this craft, such as the award winning producer, Lee Stein.

Music licensed for use in the motion picture are almost inevitably used in trailers that advertise them, and since the trailer is considered a work separate from the film, a separate synchronization license for the use of the music in the trailer is required. Such licenses are limited to use in the trailer for exhibition in movie theaters, and for additional fees, for inclusion in videocassettes and videodiscs that contain other motion pictures distributed to the home video market. The license is generally worldwide and limited to one year with options for renewal.

## IV. PROMOTIONAL MUSIC VIDEOS

A *promotional music video* is a short audiovisual work customarily created by a record company to promote the recording of a single song.

Promotional videos are broadcast on national cable television networks that are devoted to musical entertainment, such as MTV and VH1. The record company that creates a promotional video will be required to obtain a synchronization license to use the music in the video. The license will be limited to one rendition of the licensed song for a length that is not more than the duration of the original recording of the song.

Promotional music video synchronization licenses are generally worldwide and limited to two to five years with options for renewal normally available. The synchronization fee is usually quite nominal, set at an amount intended merely to cover the administrative costs of preparing the paperwork for the license grant. This is because the copyright owner stands to substantially benefit from the performance royalties resulting from the exhibition of the music video on cable television, and from the general benefit the video serves in helping the song become a "hit."

The license is limited to broadcast on television, and other uses, such as theatrical exhibition or the making and distribution of videograms containing the video performance are not permitted unless an additional license, and additional fees, are provided for. The license will not authorize the alteration of the lyric or any change in the fundamental character of the music or the use of the title, or any portion of the lyric of the composition, as the title of the video. Some licenses will prohibit the dramatization of the lyrical content of the licensed composition without further permission from the copyright owner.

## V. NON-THEATRICAL BUSINESS VIDEO PROGRAMS

A publisher will occasionally receive a request from a corporation to use a song in a video program produced for the purpose of training the corporation's employees or customers, or promoting a product or service. For the use of a song in such a work, the publisher will issue a special synchronization license for a flat fee. The term of such a license will be limited to three to five years and the use will generally be limited to the internal exhibition or broadcast of the program by the licensee. Permission may be obtained to make videogram copies of the program for an additional fee (*see* Section IV, below). Examples of non-theatrical film synchronization licenses are set forth as Forms 15.5 and 15.6 on the CD-ROM.

## VI. HOME VIDEO DEVICES

As noted above, when a music publisher issues a standard theatrical synchronization license, he is giving permission to the producer to make a recording of a song upon not only the condition that the recording only be used as part of the specified audiovisual work, but that it only be reproduced or performed in a particular way. That particular way is the exhibition of the motion picture in theaters, and other public places where motion pictures are customarily exhibited, and by television broadcast by entities that are licensed by performing rights societies to publicly perform the music embodied in those works. For example, the license set forth as Form 15.1 on the CD is limited to theatrical exhibition and television broadcast, and does not include permission to make copies of a motion picture embodying the licensed musical composition in devices like videocassettes, DVDs, and Blu-ray discs for home video distribution.

Upon the advent of the market for home video in the late 1970s, the distribution of films and television programs to the public on home video devices (e.g., at the time, videocassettes in the VHS or Betamax format) was a new use not contemplated by many theatrical or synchronization licenses previously issued. When producers approached music publishers to obtain the necessary permission to make copies of their music for home video distribution, a new form of synchronization license emerged: the *videogram* license. A videogram license is a license that permits the reproduction of music in recordings that are accompanied by moving pictures, such as motion pictures, television programs and other audiovisual works, and specifically allows such recordings to be distributed to the public in audiovisual devices, such as videocassettes or laser discs, primarily intended for use in the home on a videotape or optical-laser player and a television set. (The use of music in other kinds of programs, such as videogames, pre-packaged computer software, and multimedia works, such as CD-ROM and other optical disc devices are discussed in a subsequent chapter.)

The essential right involved in the licensing of music on home video devices is the reproduction right. Specifically, it is the exclusive right to reproduce, or *to fix*,[2] a musical composition on an audiovisual device, such as a videocassette or laser disc. The exercise of this right, however, is not subject to the compulsory licensing provision for mechanical reproductions set forth in Section 115 of the copyright law. The compulsory license provision only applies to fixing musical compositions in *phonorecords*, which the law defines as devices in which only sounds are fixed. If the sounds are accompanied by motion pictures or other audiovisual works, then the device is not a phonorecord (it is a *copy*) and the compulsory license provision does not apply. Accordingly, the copyright owner is free to negotiate the fees and other terms of licenses to fix their music in videogram devices, such as videocassettes and videodiscs.

Because these devices are primarily intended for use in the home, the right of *public performance* is not involved. The playing of a videocassette or videodisc of a motion picture, for example, in your home is merely a *private* performance. The copyright law does not afford copyright owners an exclusive right of private performance, which is why you may play a videocassette in your home as often as you wish without additional payment.

The business terms of videogram licenses evolved slowly. Early on, because of the lack of standards in negotiating license fees for the videogram licenses, music publishers approached the licensing of their music for inclusion in home video devices with great caution, quoting license fees that motion picture producers viewed as exorbitant. In many cases, music copyright owners refused to issue licenses altogether until they became further acquainted with all of the economic factors concerning the videogram device distribution of motion pictures.

At the heart of the matter was the question whether music copyright owners should receive from the producers of motion pictures some participation in the economic success of home video distribution. Indeed, from the perspective of the music publishers the question was not whether they would participate in the economic success of

[2] The copyright law at 17 U.S.C. Sec. 102(a) notes that a work of authorship is *fixed* in tangible medium of expression. The terms *to fix* and *fixation* are customarily found, in lieu of the terms to record and recording, in many videogram licenses.

home video distribution, but how they would do so. Despite the fact that copyright owners charged a flat fee for the synchronization of their music with motion pictures, they had an opportunity to participate in the success of motion pictures, because of the lucrative performance royalties they could receive from performing rights societies, such as ASCAP and BMI, arising from the exhibition of motion pictures on television and from the exhibition of motion pictures overseas in theaters. The more successful the motion picture in which their music was recorded, the greater their share in performance royalties collected in connection with the telecast and exhibition of motion pictures.

The problem with home videocassettes and videodiscs is that once copies are recorded and distributed, no *public* performance is involved in their exhibition. As noted above, the playing of a videocassette or videodisc in your home is merely a *private* performance. Accordingly, no performance royalties arise from the home viewing of videograms, and music copyright owners do not receive any compensation beyond the flat synchronization fee received upon the original recording of the music in the film.

The problem is compounded by the fact that home viewing of motion pictures by videocassette and laser disc, resulting in private performances, tends to reduce the audience for public performances of the work on broadcast television and overseas theatrical exhibition, which would generate performance royalties. Accordingly, music copyright owners insisted on a replacement for the participation in the economic success they were beginning to lose as a result of the trend away from broadcast television and theatrical performance to home viewing of videograms.

The solution insisted upon by the music copyright owners was to participate in the economic success of videogram distribution in much the same way as they participate in the success of record albums — by collecting a royalty for each unit sold. The problem they faced in implementing this system, however, was that motion picture producers were not accustomed to paying royalties on a per-copy basis. They simply did not have the administrative infrastructure to account for copies sold and were reluctant to agree upon these terms. For a while, there was a stalemate. Producers accustomed to paying flat fees for synchronization licenses, refused to accept videogram licenses on terms requiring royalties to be accounted for and paid. Synchronization licenses began to specifically address videograms, but only to expressly provide that separate permission, and some form of additional payment, would be required for the videogram uses.

Soon, however, music copyright owners and motion picture producers began to negotiate a variety of interim solutions. For example, some early synchronization licenses provided that the parties shall negotiate in good faith to establish an appropriate videogram license fee, and failing an agreement, the parties would agree to submit the question to arbitration. In other cases, the music copyright owner would grant the videogram license for a limited term, such as five years, after which the parties would negotiate a fee or have a permanent fee set by arbitration. The interim fee was sometimes a flat dollar amount and sometimes a fee based upon some multiple (e.g., 200%) of the compulsory mechanical royalties provided for in Section 115 of the copyright law.

Eventually, seeing the writing on the wall, some film producers established the administrative capability to compensate copyright owners for videogram licenses on a royalty basis and began accepting videogram licenses containing royalty provisions. Others, however, remained insistent on obtaining home video rights on a flat fee basis — either as part of a broad rights license or a step deal, which required a flat fee payment upon the release of the work in the home video market.

At the end of the day, a motion picture producer is likely to obtain the right to make and distribute home video copies in exchange for payment of a flat fee when it has the most leverage to do so. That is typically at a point in which it still has the option to choose a substitute song in the event it cannot negotiate the desired fee structure — in other words, before the soundtrack of the motion picture is completed and when it is offering the publisher a large license fee for theatrical exhibition, either paid up front or under a step deal.

A producer, obviously, has fewer options when the use is in the foreground of the film, such as when a song is being performed on the screen by a character as opposed to being source music, such as music being played on the car radio in a scene. The question will become whether it would be cheaper to reshoot the scene using a different song than to acquiesce to pay the fee demanded by the publisher. In addition, if a producer is seeking to clear the home video device rights to a song used in a film released years ago under a synchronization license that was limited to theatrical exhibition, replacing the song is rarely an option.

## VII. INTERNET VIDEO STREAMING

As described earlier, *streaming video* is a means of performing an audiovisual work *on demand* (i.e., at the time desired by the viewer) over the Internet such that the work is being viewed while it is being transmitted. It is much like *video on demand* (VOD), except that while a VOD transmission typically occurs through a cable or satellite TV operator's set-top box, *streaming video* is conducted via a typical Internet connection, usually through a personal computer. However, these technologies are converging and there would seem to be little to base a substantially different music licensing model for these varying forms of on-demand video streaming.

Thus, a license to allow the use of a song in an audiovisual work streamed over the Internet would be very much like a television synchronization license: one that is issued on a flat fee basis, but conditioned upon the organization doing the transmitting obtaining a public performance license from a performance rights society (e.g., ASCAP, BMI, or SESAC in the United States).

## VIII. INTERNET VIDEO DOWNLOADING

*Downloading video* over the Internet is much like *streaming video* in that they are both a means of delivering an audiovisual work *on demand* (i.e., at the time desired by the viewer), but downloading involves the fixation of a copy on a home video or other device controlled by the viewer, such as a personal computer, set-top box (e.g., Tivo) or videogame player (e.g., Xbox 360 or Playstation), such that the copy can be viewed at a later time by the viewer.

The downloaded file may either be *tethered*, in which case viewing may be limited (typically by some form of digital rights management, or DRM) in the number of times it may be viewed (e.g., 3 or 4 times) or in the timeframe during which it may be viewed (e.g., as many times as the viewer wishes in a 24-hour time frame of the viewer's choosing). Where the transmission is a *tethered download*, it is typically treated much like a *streaming video* — meaning that music synchronization licenses for tethered downloads have very similar terms as those issued for streaming video. Thus, they are generally issued on a flat fee basis and are conditioned upon the delivery or transmission being subject to the payment of a license fee for the public performance of the song.

Where the file is a permanent download, with no restriction on the number of times or time frame in which the consumer may view the file, then the economic transaction is quite different — being much more like the sale of a home video device than a television exhibition.

The essential right involved in the licensing of music in permanent downloads, like home video devices (e.g., videocassettes, DVDs), is the reproduction right. Specifically, it is the exclusive right to reproduce, or *to fix*, a musical composition (as part of a specific audiovisual work) on the recipient's memory device (e.g., hard disk or flash memory) by means of a digital delivery or transmission. Arguably, the right of *public performance* is not involved, because the playing of the downloaded video file in the home is merely a *private* performance. The copyright law does not afford copyright owners an exclusive right of private performance, which is why you may play a DVD or downloaded video in your home as often as you wish without additional payment to a performance rights society.

(Note, however, that the copyright law in Europe and in many other countries provides for, in addition to the copyright owner's exclusive right of public performance right, an exclusive right to communicate the work to the public. This *public communications* right is typically administered by public performance societies outside the United States — e.g., PRS for Music (U.K.), SACEM (France) and GEMA (Germany). Thus, a permanent download of a video would invoke both the reproduction right and the public communication right. In the United States, however, only the reproduction right would be involved in the download of a sound recording or audiovisual work.

Thus, when a music publisher issues a license to use a song in audiovisual works distributed by DVD on a flat fee basis, it is foregoing additional income that it may receive when many copies of the DVD are sold — no royalty is paid to the publisher on copies sold and no public performance income accrues to the publisher for the private performance of the DVD in the home. In this sense, permanent downloads of video are no different.

While music publishers have agreed to videogram licenses on a flat fee basis, either as part of a large upfront fee or option in a step deal, music publishers should think very carefully about applying the same terms to permanent downloads. Arguably, with the advent of on-demand streaming and permanent downloads of video, the technological life of DVDs and Blu-ray disc are limited. Home video devices may well go the way of audio-only CDs, which are rapidly being eclipsed by streaming and download services. We've already seen VHS devices being eclipsed by the superior DVD format, and it is only a matter of time before DVDs and even Blu-ray devices are replaced by digital transmission — both into the home and to portable devices.

If home video devices are going to become obsolete, music publishers are not foregoing much by licensing them on a flat fee basis. Nevertheless, to provide licenses for permanent downloads on anything other than some form of royalty basis — or, alternatively, on a flat fee basis combined with public performance or public communication rights income — would be to forever forego an economic stake in the success of the audiovisual work in which the song appeared.

Note also, of course, that even though permanent downloads of videos containing music invokes the reproduction right, the exercise of this right is not subject to the compulsory licensing provision for mechanical reproductions set forth in Section 115 of the copyright law. The compulsory license provision only applies to fixing musical compositions in *phonorecords*, which the law defines as devices in which only sounds are fixed. If the sounds are accompanied by motion pictures or other audiovisual works, then the device is not a phonorecord (it is a *copy*) and the compulsory license provision does not apply. Accordingly, the copyright owner is free to negotiate the fees and other terms of licenses to offer their music in permanent downloads.

## IX. USER-GENERATED CONTENT

Streaming and download video services can basically be divided into two camps: those whose content is primarily provided to the service under license from content owners, such as movie studios, television producers, and record companies, and those whose content is primarily uploaded by Internet users, a form of content that has become known as "user generated content." The leading example of the former is Hulu, a joint venture of NBC/Universal and of the latter, YouTube, a division of Google.

Hulu is largely comprised of television programs, movie trailers, and a few full length feature films licensed for streaming by the partners in the joint venture and others; the service does not appear yet to accept user-generated videos. The videos available on YouTube are largely user generated, but the service has entered into a number of arrangements with studios, record companies, and music publishers to offer professionally produced content under license. Both Hulu and YouTube are streaming services, but several technologies, such as Bitorrent, are being applied to enable the peer-to-peer sharing of user-generated content by permanent download.

The problem of licensing music in user-generated videos is discussed at length in the next chapter.

## X. Clearing the Synchronization License

In Chapter 11, on the Art of Clearing Licenses, we suggested that persons seeking to clear a license should be prepared to educate that music publisher about precisely how the music is intended to be used. It is now common practice for music publishers to require prospective licensees to complete a form containing the information they will need to fashion an appropriate quote for the use desired.

In this regard, producers should be prepared to answer some or all of the following questions, either on the phone or by completing a form provided by the publisher:

Your name:<br>
Company:<br>
Address:<br>
Phone:<br>
Fax:<br>
Email:<br>
Exact Title of the Song:<br>
Writer(s)<br>
Publishers(s)<br>
Artist(s) who recorded the song:<br>
Label(s) on which the recordings appeared:<br>
Will any of these recordings be used in the production?

Name of Your Production:
Prominent Cast Members:
Director:
Name of Production/Distribution Company:
Production Budget:
Music Budget:
Expected film rating (PG, R, X, etc.):
Brief synopsis of the plot:
Detailed description of the scene(s) in which the song would appear:
Nature of the use(s) (background/foreground, instrumental/vocal, opening credits, closing credits, repeated theme, etc.):
Duration of the use(s):
Media (theatrical release, television, Internet streaming, permanent download, etc.):
Ancillary uses (e.g., trailers, advertising, featurettes, such as "making of" documentary, sequels, soundtrack album, etc.):
Desired Term:
Desired Territory (U.S., North American, Worldwide, etc.):
Other:

A producer does not necessarily have to answer all the questions asked, but the more information he can provide, the smoother the process will be. Producers should be mindful that music publishers and administrators have very small licensing staffs that are often inundated with license requests. The information provided should be as complete as possible and follow-up will often be required to keep your request on top of the stack.

When a producer receives a quote, he will find that the publisher will typically put a time limit on how long the producer has to accept or respond to the quote — a typical expiration being 90 days. Publishers are advised to make any quote, often made by email, "subject to the entry of a definitive license agreement signed by both parties." Producers, however, have often been burned by publishers who provide an oral quote, but fail to provide a definitive license for signature until well after the producer has relied on the original quote. Because of changes in personnel at the publisher, or simply an unscrupulous publisher, a producer may see himself facing a dramatically increased license fee at a time when it is too late to switch to another song. Producers are therefore advised, when confirming their acceptance of a quote, to state that they are proceeding in reliance on the accepted quote, which strengthens their position, in case of later trouble, that binding license exists, even though no definitive agreement was signed by both parties.

## XI. TYPICAL FEES FOR THE SYNCHRONIZATION LICENSE

Having explored in general the various considerations involved in negotiating the terms of a typical synchronization license, we now turn to the license fees that are typically charged for the various uses of music in these kinds of licenses. This section provides some of the ranges within which synch fees have tended to fall at the time this edition went to print in early 2010.

It should be noted, at the outset, that the fee ranges set forth below are based upon some broad generalizations and assumptions. Consequently, many of the fees stated do not fully take into consideration some of the key factors discussed in this chapter, including the countervailing factors of (i) the importance of the song in relation to its intended use and (ii) the availability of close substitutes for the song.

For example, if a song is needed to merely establish the setting of a scene in the 1940s, the song *As Time Goes By* from the motion picture *Casablanca* might fulfill that need quite well. However, songs such as *Boogie Woogie Bugle Boy* and *I'll Be with You in Apple Blossom Time* (made popular by the Andrews Sisters) may serve that purpose just as well. If the licensor of *As Time Goes By* were to quote too high a license fee, the producer may choose one of the other ready alternatives. If, on the other hand, the song is required for a movie such as Woody Allen's *Play It Again, Sam,* virtually no close substitutes for the song, *As Time Goes By* will suffice, and it is more likely the producer would expect to pay a license fee in the high end of the range, if not above the range, for this particular use of that song.

Nevertheless, despite the generalizations made and the likelihood that these ranges will, *As Time Goes By*, begin to age, the fees provided below may still be useful for the information they provide about *relative* values — that is, the fees as they relate in proportion to each other — which is not likely to change significantly over time.

## A. Television Synchronization License Fees

The typical fees for background use of a song in a network television program, including certain options that may be negotiated as part of a step deal, are as follows:

| | *Term* | *Territory* | *Media* | *Fee* |
|---|---|---|---|---|
| Base license | 5 year | U.S. only | Free television | $2,000-2,500 |
| Option | 5-year renewal | | | +100% of base fee |
| Option | | Rest of World | | +50% of base fee |
| Base license | Life of copyright | U.S. only | Free television | $4,000-5,000 |
| Option | | | Pay TV | +30% of base fee |
| Base license | Life of copyright | Worldwide | All television | $8,000-12,000 |
| Option | Life of copyright | Worldwide | Home video devices | +10,000-$12,500 |
| Option | Life of copyright | Worldwide | Internet video streaming & download | +10,000-$15,000 |
| Option | Life of copyright | Worldwide | Airlines, etc. | +2,500-$5,000 |
| Option | Life of copyright | Worldwide | Foreign theatrical | +2,500-$5,000 |
| Base license | Life of copyright | Worldwide | All media, excluding U.S. theatrical | $20,000-50,000 |
| Base license | Life of copyright | Worldwide | Broad rights | $50,000-100,000 |

Note, the use assumed has been *background* — that is, where no one on the screen is seen performing the song, either instrumentally or vocally. If use is foreground (i.e., song performed on screen instrumentally or vocally), add 20% to the above amounts. If song is featured, such as used over the title of a particular episode or over the closing credits, add 25 to 50%.

Use of the title of the song as the title of the television series or an episode would warrant an additional 50-100%; however, music publishers typically reduce the above fees by 25% if the song is used in every episode of the series (thereby increasing the performance fees significantly). On the other hand, if the producer wishes to use an established hit song as the theme song for the series, the publisher must consider the detrimental effect the use may have on potential commercial uses of the song in the future. Unless the publisher doesn't think the song would otherwise have a lucrative commercial future, the publisher may ask for a significant premium for such a use. If the story of an episode is a dramatization of the song's lyrics, add anywhere from 100-200% and consider other uses, such as sequels, spin-offs, and the like.

Multiple uses of the song in the same episode, even if the total time performed on screen is less than an entire performance of the song, will warrant a premium of 10-25% of the base fee. Certain variety and award shows use an unusually high number of songs in the program; in such cases, a reduced fee may be warranted. Reduced fees are also warranted when the producer is reviving an old television series for television syndication, home video, or Internet downloading or streaming.

Where a producer desires to use the song in an advertising campaign, including spots on radio, television, and Internet advertising, a music publisher may typically charge between $1,000-5,000 per week, depending upon whether the use is *in context* or *out of context.* Adding theatrical use in the United States, or licensing so-called *broad rights* (i.e., all media, worldwide, for life of copyright) should be considered and negotiated, as though it were a theatrical synchronization license.

### B. Theatrical Motion Picture Synchronization License Fees — Major Studio

The typical fees for use of a song in a theatrical motion picture, including certain options that may be negotiated as part of a step deal, are as follows:

| *Term* | *Territory* | *Media* | *Background* | *Foreground — Visual/Vocal* | *Featured* |
|---|---|---|---|---|---|
| Life of copyright | Worldwide | Theatrical exhibition | $5,000-25,000 | $7,500-$50,000 | $15,000-$100,000 |
| Life of copyright | Worldwide | Television broadcast | + 5,000-25,000 | + 7,500-$50,000 | + 50,000-$100,000 |
| Life of copyright | Worldwide | Internet Streaming | + 5,000-25,000 | + 7,500-$50,000 | + 50,000-$100,000 |
| Life of copyright | Worldwide | Home video & Internet download royalty | + $.10-$.20 per copy against advance of $5,000-$10,000 | | |
| Life of copyright | Worldwide | Home video & Internet download Buy-out | + 10,000-25,000 | + 15,000-$50,000 | + 25,000-$250,000 |
| Life of copyright | Worldwide | Broad Rights Buy-out (includes all of above) | $15,000-100,000 | $25,000-$200,000 | $50,000-$500,000 |

*Duration and Territory.* The duration of theatrical synch licenses issued to films produced or distributed by the major studios are almost always life of copyright and the territory is almost always worldwide (or the "universe"). Where a shorter term is negotiated, such as a 5-year term, the term will commence upon the first commercial theatrical exhibition of the film.

*Featured Use.* A *featured use* is where the song performed over the opening title sequence or becomes an important part of the presentation of a character or turning point in the film's plot. A featured use could warrant double the usual synch fee. Use of the song over the closing credits will also command a premium, though not as high as for the opening title sequence.

*Lyric Changes.* Lyric changes will also command a premium, but the publisher should (i) carefully consider the long term effect on the song if the film becomes a hit or classic and (ii) obtain any permission that may be required from the songwriter(s).

*Use of Song Title.* Use of the title of the song as the title of the motion picture should bring an additional 50-100% over the fees above, or more if the song is a standard and its title fairly unique or closely identified with an important act.

*Multiple Uses.* Multiple uses of the song, even if the total time performed on screen is less than an entire performance of the song, will warrant a premium of 10-25% of the base fee.

*Broad rights.* Broad rights include use all media, including U.S. and overseas theatrical release, all television and home video devices, such as videocassettes and DVDs, and Internet download and streaming for *in context* use. Thus, because the synch fee includes a buy-out of the home video rights, no additional royalties would be payable for distribution of videocassettes, DVDs, or BluRay discs. Because Internet downloads could eventually replace home video devices, and perhaps threaten the classic television or theatrical performance itself, a music publisher would be wise to try to exclude Internet use (i.e., video streaming and download). A publisher might give up on getting a carve out for video streaming, provided that the performances inherent in such streams are subject to license by the appropriate performance rights society. Video downloads are another matter and publishers should be wary of issuing long term licenses until the market for downloads matures. A five or even ten year term for video download use, from the publisher's perspective, would be far better than life of copyright.

*Performance Fees.* To remain consistent with the antitrust consent decrees with performance rights societies in the U.S., the synch license will include a license component to permit performances in movie theaters in the United States. Unless the license specifies the synchronization component and performance component separately, the music publisher usually considers that 1/2 of the stated fee is allocated to U.S. performance rights. Nevertheless, public performances in theaters in other countries will be subject to theaters having appropriate performance licenses from their local performance rights societies.

The television exhibition component of the license will also be subject to broadcast on stations licensed by the appropriate U.S. performance rights society (e.g., ASCAP, BMI, SESAC), but some producers try to insist on obtaining the necessary performance licenses directly from the publisher as part of the synch license. A publisher might agree to this only to the extent a television station for some reason does have an ASCAP, BMI or SESAC license or those societies are legally prohibited from issuing television performance license.

*Trailers.* The above fees will also include use in trailers, even if used in an advertising campaign (including spots on radio, television, and Internet advertising), provided they are *in context*, as discussed above.

*Out of Context Use.* If the use is *out of context*, a music publisher may typically charge between $1,000-5,000 per week. If the song is not used in the motion picture, but the producer wishes to use the song in a trailer for publicizing the film, a music publisher may charge $1,000-5,000 per week (less, if only performed on radio) or anywhere from $10,000 to $100,000 for the life of copyright.

### C. Theatrical Motion Picture Synchronization License Fees — Independent, Low Budget, Non-Profit or Student Films

A low budget film is one with a production budget of between $500,000 and $5 million. Student films, of course, may have production budgets that are significantly lower. Because of the limited ability of the producer to fully pay the going rate for a song up front, music publishers will often agree to a step deal — one that closely approximates the one set forth in Section A above, except that the steps may be triggered by the number of screens to which the film is distributed (e.g., over 1,000) or certain levels of box office receipts (e.g., $5 million, $10 million, $25 million, etc.).

A true student film may warrant the granting of a license for a nominal fee, with step deal terms in the event the film eventually becomes successful. Alternatively, a license could be granted for free or for a nominal fee, but could be limited to exhibition at film festivals or a very limited theatrical engagement within a specified period of time. Music publishers should be encouraged to permit the use of their music in student films as a means of supporting budding filmmakers while taking the opportunity to educate them on the terms typically required for the use of music in motion pictures.

## D. Non-Theatrical Film Synchronization License Fees

The fee for the use of a musical composition in a corporate video to be used for in-house training or trade show convention use ranges from $3,000 to $5,000. The term is generally for one year. A quote should be dependent on the audience size, number of meetings, and size of the convention or show city. User is normally authorized to retain one copy of the video for archival purposes.

## E. Television Synchronization License for Music Videos

When a popular song video is to be televised purely for promotional purposes, a publisher will generally charge a handling fee of $100. However, one can expect these fees to increase as the broadcast of these videos are becoming less promotional and more for pure entertainment. This initial license should not include the distribution of the video in videocassettes, DVDs or Blu-ray discs for the home market.

## F. Synchronization License for Feature Film Trailers

For a well-known musical composition not originally used in the motion picture to be advertised (i.e., *out-of-context* use), a typical fee would be $25,000. Unless the producer obtained broad rights, which would include this use, for a musical composition used (perhaps as background) and not "featured" in the motion picture being advertised, a typical fee would be $15,000. For the use of a song on the radio to promote a motion picture, a typical fee may be $1,000 per week.

## G. Videogram Synchronization License Fees

*Motion Pictures.* Recently, it has been the practice of motion picture producers to ask for terms that would allow them to buy-out the videogram license for a one time flat fee payment. While music publishers have resisted this, a producer might typically pay, in addition to the standard synchronization license fee, a flat fee videogram license buy-out of $25,000 to $35,000. Since no public performance fees are collected on performances in the home, publishers will normally make every effort to avoid offering a buy-out provision and may suggest instead an advance that would cover 20,000 or more units, which should be more than sufficient to cover a normal home video release of the motion picture.

Where the publisher can negotiate a royalty per unit, the average per unit royalty for each song used in a videocassette, DVD, or other home video device is currently between 10¢ and 20¢. The actual per unit royalty would vary according to the considerations set forth above, such as whether the use is background, foreground, or special. A publisher will generally require an advance against royalties of about $5,000 to $10,000. Sometimes, a publisher may also negotiate a roll-over advance, in which case the producer must pay an additional advance (e.g., $12,500) when a certain number of copies are sold (e.g., 100,000).

*Music Videos.* Standards for licensing of music videos for home video distribution have still not yet fully emerged. Synchronization licenses will continue to provide a short-term, perhaps two years, license for a flat fee with additional negotiations at the end of the term, with a buy-out of between $10,000 and $25,000.

*Video Yearbooks.* There is a $50 buyout fee for high school, $100 for college, per song.

*Corporate Videos.* There is a fixing fee of $1,000; royalty of $.10 per unit; buy-out of royalty about $5,000. Term can be up to five years.

## H. Video Download Synchronization License Fees

As we discussed above, it is very important for music publishers to consider that, when it issues a license to use a song in audiovisual works distributed by home video devices (e.g., DVD, Blu-ray) on a flat fee basis, it is foregoing an opportunity to participate in the economic success of the audiovisual work in which it was embodied — no royalties are paid to the publisher on copies sold and no public performance income accrues to the publisher for the private performances of the work in the home. This is especially so when the duration of such a license is for the life of the copyright.

Providing a videogram license on a flat fee basis may be acceptable, home video devices are likely to become obsolete, replaced by streaming video and video downloads. But if streaming and downloading becomes the technological end of the road, then to provide licenses for permanent downloads on anything other than some form of royalty basis — or, alternatively, on a flat fee basis combined with public performance or public communication rights income — would be to forever forego an economic stake in the success of the audiovisual work in which the song appeared. The music publisher's only hope would be the exercise of the public communication right overseas and the passage of a new exclusive right of public communication in the United States.

Where a publisher has the leverage to demand and obtain a royalty, the royalty may well be very similar to that which is typically received upon the distribution and sale of home video devices: currently between 10¢ and 20¢. Again, the actual per unit royalty would vary according to the considerations set forth above, such as whether the use is background, foreground, or special. A publisher will generally require an advance against royalties of about $5,000 to $10,000. Sometimes, a publisher may also negotiate a roll-over advance, in which case the producer must pay an additional advance (e.g., $12,500) when a certain number of copies are downloaded (e.g., 100,000). Films that use a relatively high number of songs may command a lesser rate per song, and in such instances a publisher may provide a reduced rate with some form of most favored nations provision.

Where a producer is still insistent upon a full video download license on a flat fee basis, one solution would be to limit the term of the license to five or ten years, to preserve the right to charge some form of royalty or fee based upon the number of transmissions at some later date.

## XII. CONCLUSION

The synchronization of musical works with motion pictures, television programs, and other audiovisual works has become an important and lucrative source of revenue for the music copyright owner. With the emerging importance of delivering audiovisual content to the public via the Internet through streaming and download, music publishers face new licensing opportunities and challenges. The instant availability of previously hard to find works containing copyrighted music will provide new sources of revenue, but making sure publishers continue to benefit from the economic success of the works that contain their music will remain a challenge. In a world of user-generated content, where modifications of copyrighted content by amateur content producers become more widespread, music publishers will face challenges maintaining the integrity of their repertoire. It may be that some loss of control will be necessary to assure payment is made for the use of the music. The next chapter will explore some of the solutions to these problems that are emerging from negotiations between the content and high tech communities.

# Appendix to Chapter 15
# Licensing Music in Audiovisual Works (Synchronization Licenses)

Forms (On CD-Rom Only)

| | |
|---|---|
| **Form 15.1** | **Synchronization License for Motion Picture Theatrical and Television Exhibition (Includes No License for Home Use Videogram Distribution)** |
| **Form 15.2** | **Synchronization License for Theatrical Trailer** |
| **Form 15.3** | **Television Synchronization License** |
| **Form 15.4** | **Television Synchronization License for Promotional Music Videos** |
| **Form 15.5** | **Non-theatrical Film Synchronization License** |
| **Form 15.6** | **Non-theatrical Film Synchronization License with Options to Renew** |
| **Form 15.7** | **Arrangement with Songwriter that Permits Music Publisher to Grant Synchronization License Covering the Renewal Term** |
| **Form 15.8** | **Synchronization License for Motion Picture Theatrical and Television Exhibition with Videogram License on a Percentage Royalty Basis** |
| **Form 15.9** | **Videogram License Provisions on "Block of Copies" Basis** |
| **Form 15.10** | **Videogram License Provisions on "Flat Fee" Basis for Fixed Term with Arbitration Provision** |
| **Form 15.11** | **Videogram License Provisions on Twice "Statutory Rate" Basis with Arbitration Provision** |
| **Form 15.12** | **Audiovisual Work Synchronization and Videogram License (Includes No Theatrical or Television License Exhibition Provisions)** |
| **Form 15.13** | **Videogram Synchronization License Used by Harry Fox Agency** |

CHAPTER 16

# THE USER-GENERATED CONTENT PHENOMENON

## SUMMARY

CHAPTER **16**

# THE USER-GENERATED CONTENT PHENOMENON

## I. Introduction

The use of music we have explored in the previous chapters primarily involved the creation of new content — such as, sheet music, sound recordings, and audiovisual works — in which musical works are licensed as an underlying element. Copyright owners typically issue these licenses to institutional licensees who are in the business of creating professionally produced content, such as print publishers, record companies, and motion picture or television producers. New technologies, however, have opened up a vast new group of potential licensees, challenging the way music and other copyrighted content has been licensed in the past.

Upon the advent of easy access to the Internet in the mid-1990, virtually any individual who had the time and means of setting up a website could easily and inexpensively become a publisher of content. Initially, the content published by users was as simple as family photographs posted on a "home page" and Internet "links" to other favorite websites. Later, users turned to the production of more sophisticated content when "blogging" software allowed them to become "pajama" journalists, producing sophisticated cultural or political analysis and promoting the content through a network of links syndicated by other bloggers. This amateur or semi-professional content by non-institutional publishers became known as *user-generated content* (or UGC).

The variety and sophistication of user-generated content produced by these users took a giant leap forward when the cost of several complementary technologies dropped significantly — including the cost of hard disks, server storage, Internet bandwidth, home video cameras, and software for creating digital sheet music and guitar tablatures and for editing sound recordings and audiovisual works.

In 2005, a young startup called YouTube was founded, which exploited this convergence by allowing home users to take videos produced with their digital camcorders and upload them to the YouTube servers. Once uploaded to YouTube, the video content became then instantly available for free Internet streaming to anyone browsing or searching the YouTube site. Another start up, IMeem, allowed users to similarly upload sound recordings that became immediately available for listening by users, and still another, Ultimate Guitar, allowed users to upload digital guitar tabs, created in Guitar Pro software, which could be downloaded and played and modified by anyone else who had the Guitar Pro software.

When bloggers post their opinions on the web, they are creating original copyrighted content. When they incorporate into their own posts the writings of others, they either post a brief quote written by another blogger or a journalist in the print media, or they refer to original source with an Internet link. In either case, because the use of the material is in the context of commentary, the use is typically defended from charges of copyright infringement by the doctrine of "fair use."[1]

When users gained access to technology that easily enabled them to economically create *rich* content (e.g., sound recordings, audiovisual works, musical notation, and guitar tabs), it enabled them to simply copy the musical works, sound recordings, and videos of others, or embody the content of others, into their own creations. Unless the use of these copyrighted materials is in the context of commentary or satire, protectable by the fair use doctrine, the incorporation of copyrighted materials into user-generated videos without permission constitutes copyright infringement.

YouTube estimates that 15 hours of new video is uploaded to YouTube.com every minute of every day. The sheer volume of user-generated content that potentially infringes the copyrights of millions of copyright owners presents one of the most profound challenges to the licensing community. This chapter will summarize some of the basic legal issues arising from the user-generated content phenomenon and will touch upon an emerging licensing regime that one service provider, YouTube, has been using to address the challenges that stem from it.

---

[1] See Chapter 25, *The Fair Use Controversy.*

## II. LEGAL BACKGROUND

### A. The Types of Works and Rights Involved

User-generated content can embody a variety of copyrighted works of authorship, including musical works, sound recordings, audiovisual works, literary works (e.g., text on the screen or spoken word recordings of fiction or non-fiction text or comedy material), combinations of these, multiple works (e.g., two or more songs or recordings), and finally modifications (e.g., changed lyrics, remixed recordings, edited videos).

When a user fixes any of these works in a video, the user requires permission from the copyright owner to make the first copy under the copyright owner's exclusive right to make reproductions.[2] Should the user post the video on his own website for streaming by others, permission would then be required to publicly perform each of the copyrighted works (e.g., video, song) in the user-created video. Should the user post the video to the website of a service provider, such as YouTube, the service provider now has obligations vis-à-vis of the copyright owners whose works are contained in the video.

Given the volume of user-generated works being created, the limited economic value of each work, and the transactions costs of clearing the rights from so many copyright owners by so many unsophisticated users, the licensing challenge is daunting.

### B. U.S. Copyright Act — Safe Harbor of Section 512

On May 4, 2007, music publisher Bourne Co., together with the Football Association Premier League Ltd., filed a class action lawsuit[3] in U.S. District Court for the Southern District of New York, "to stop the unauthorized and uncompensated use of their creative works and those of all other similarly situated copyright holders whose works have been displayed without permission on the YouTube.com website." The complaint alleges that YouTube has been "pursuing a deliberate strategy of engaging in, permitting, encouraging, and facilitating massive copyright infringement on the YouTube website" in order to build

[2] 17 U.S.C. Sec. 106(a).

[3] *The Football Association Premier League Limited, et. al. v. YouTube, Inc., et al.*, 2009 U.S. Dist. LEXIS 57438 (S.D.N.Y. July 3, 2009).

traffic to the site. YouTube, according to the complaint, has long been aware of this pattern of massive infringement yet has purposefully refrained from employing readily available measures to curb the infringement, because YouTube believes that the popularity of YouTube.com (and its value as a platform for other uses) stems primarily from the ability of website visitors to access, view, and otherwise exploit copyrighted materials without having to pay the owners of those materials. It was this very business model, according to the complaint, that persuaded Google to pay $1.65 billion to purchase YouTube in November 2006.

In its answer to the complaint, YouTube alleges that the claims are barred because, among other defenses, it is protected by one or more of the DMCA Safe Harbors in Section 512 of the Copyright Act (set forth in full in the appendix to this chapter), which was added to the Act by the Digital Millennium Copyright Act of 2000.

Under Section 512(c), a service provider would not be liable for copyright infringement

> "by reason of the storage at the direction of a user of material that resides on a system or network controlled or operated by or for the service provider, if the service provider —
>
> (A) (i) does not have actual knowledge that the material or an activity using the material on the system or network is infringing;
>
> (ii) in the absence of such actual knowledge, is not aware of facts or circumstances from which infringing activity is apparent; or
>
> (iii) upon obtaining such knowledge or awareness, acts expeditiously to remove, or disable access to, the material;
>
> (B) does not receive a financial benefit directly attributable to the infringing activity, in a case in which the service provider has the right and ability to control such activity; and
>
> (C) upon notification of claimed infringement as described in paragraph (3), responds expeditiously to remove, or disable access to, the material that is claimed to be infringing or to be the subject of infringing activity.

Whether YouTube's handling the user-generated content available on its service and its response to copyright owners will provide it with immunity from charges of copyright infringement by virtue of the safe harbor of Section 512 will be for the courts to decide or for the parties to resolve by settlement.

One court recently opined on the extent to which a site may avail itself of the Copyright Act's Safe Harbor provision. In a case against Veoh Networks, which hosts user-provided videos similar to YouTube, a federal district court held that Veoh met its burden in establishing its entitlement to the safe harbor provisions.

> The ever expanding realm of the Internet provides many new ways for people to connect with one another. This court appreciates that these new opportunities also present challenges to the protection of copyright in the online world; and, the decision rendered here is confined to the particular combination of facts in this case and is not intended to push the bounds of the safe harbor so wide that less than scrupulous service providers may claim its protection. Nevertheless, the court does not find that the DMCA was intended to have Veoh shoulder the entire burden of policing third-party copyrights on its website (at the cost of losing its business if it cannot). Rather, the issue is whether Veoh takes appropriate steps to deal with copyright infringement that takes place. The record presented demonstrates that, far from encouraging copyright infringement, Veoh has a strong DMCA policy, take active steps to limit incidents of infringement on its website and works diligently to keep unauthorized works off its website.[4]

## III. CONSIDERATIONS IN GRANTING AND CLEARING LICENSES FOR USE OF MUSIC IN USER-GENERATED CONTENT — BY YOUTUBE

One licensing regime that has emerged to address the problem of user-generated content has been proposed by the legal department of YouTube. To understand what YouTube has proposed to owners of copyrighted music and sound recordings featured in user-generated

[4] *IO Group, Inc. v. Veoh Networks, Inc.*, 586 F. Supp. 2d 1132 (N.D. Cal. 2008). More recently, another federal district court reached a similar conclusion in *UMG Recordings, Inc. v. Veoh Networks, Inc.*, CV 07 5744 (AHM) (C.D. Cal. Sept. 14, 2009) (holding that the DMCS safe harbor provisions protected Veoh Networks from liability for hosting user-provided music videos owned by Universal Music Group).

videos uploaded to YouTube, it will be useful to summarize the kinds of music-related videos that are covered by the YouTube proposals:

A. Existing music videos created, owned and uploaded to YouTube by record companies;

B. Existing music videos created and owned by record companies, but uploaded to YouTube by users without permission;

C. Original videos created by users that include commercial, copyrighted sound recordings without permission;

D. Original videos created by users that include an original performance of a copyrighted song, known as a "cover video," without permission; and

E. Original videos created by users that include one or more sound recordings and songs, elements of which have been combined (e.g., sampled, remixed, mashed-up) or otherwise modified.

Each of these scenarios creates a set of licensing challenges, discussed in more detail below.

### A. Existing Music Videos Owned and Supplied by Record Companies

YouTube has entered into a number of license arrangements with several major and independent record companies to make their music videos available on a commercial basis. The details of these agreements are discussed below, but under these arrangements, the record labels are responsible for providing the rights to reproduce and publicly perform the sound recording and for clearing the synchronization rights in the underlying musical works. YouTube has licenses from the performance rights societies covering the public performances of the underlying musical works.

Once YouTube receives a fully rights-cleared music video, it releases that video with associated advertisements that generate revenues, a portion of which is paid to the record companies, and a portion paid to the performance rights societies. (The way this works outside the United States may vary, depending upon the extent to which the music performing rights societies control the licensing of audiovisual works containing copyrighted musical compositions.)

### B. Existing Music Videos Uploaded by Internet Users

Many of the copyrighted music videos uploaded to YouTube were not uploaded by their record label owners, but by users with accounts on YouTube, without authorization of the owners. These users are typically fans of the recording artists featured in the videos. As mentioned above, the users, having no license to make these copies, are clearly acting in violation of the exclusive reproduction rights of the record companies and would be liable for infringement of copyright.

As a practical matter, however, transaction costs of tracking down these users and initiating copyright infringement lawsuits to deter the activity is problematic. The record industry, for example, has had limited success in stopping piracy of their recordings by users using peer-to-peer services to facilitate their infringement. For redress, the copyright owners have thus turned to YouTube. But, as far as YouTube is concerned, the storage and use of the videos on its service is immune from copyright infringement under the safe harbor provisions of Section 512, the terms of which, they insist, they are in full compliance.

Nevertheless, it is far from clear whether the actions that have been taken by YouTube to comply with the safe harbor provisions have been sufficient to protect them from liability for infringement. As a result, YouTube is not only under constant pressure to expeditiously respond to notice and take down claims, but they have begun taking other actions to avoid the charge that it is intentionally engaging in an activity that induces copyright infringement.[5]

For example, YouTube has begun employing a content identification system that is aimed at facilitating the efficient removal of videos uploaded by users without authorization from copyright owners. Under the system, a copyright owner provides to YouTube reference files, or lists of recordings owned by the labels, together with their associated metadata information (e.g., track title, artist name, ISRC code, etc.). When a user uploads a video, the video is electronically scanned for copyrighted sound recordings. (Each recording has its own unique "fingerprint" which can be identified with content identification software).

[5] *MGM Studios Inc. v. Grokster, Ltd.*, 545 U.S. 913 (U.S. 2005).

The recording is then matched to the reference database supplied by the record company to determine what usage policy to apply: (1) remove the video, (2) permit streaming of the video with advertisements, paying a share to the label, or (3) permit streaming of the video and share usage metrics with the label (e.g., what search terms were used to get to the video, location and general demographics of the user, etc.).

The terms of the above arrangement are set forth in the Sound Recording and Audiovisual Content License set forth in the Appendix on the CD-ROM, and discussed below.

## C. Original Videos Created by Users that Include Commercial Sound Recordings

Users of YouTube frequently create their own videos, including their own original work, which could be as simple as a home movie, posted on YouTube for the benefit of friends and family, to a serious effort at making an entertaining or instructive video for wide public consumption. These videos often embody in them popular commercial sound recordings, sometimes unintentionally, as when a radio or stereo is playing in the background, or intentionally, as when a user records a video of their friends dancing to popular music.

When YouTube enters into licensing arrangements with labels for the use of their commercial music videos, they also include terms that provide YouTube with a license to use the label's sound recordings when they turn up in these original videos produced and uploaded by users. The license works much the same way as with user uploaded commercial videos: YouTube applies its content identification system, permits streaming of the video with advertisements, and shares a portion of the revenues with the label.

Clearing the music publishing rights in these circumstances, however, is a little more challenging. Since the video was not produced by a record label, no video synchronization license was obtained at the time the video was produced. Since the video was produced by an amateur user, the chances the user obtained a valid synch license from the appropriate music publisher(s) is remote. Again, the music publishers are looking to YouTube for redress for the unauthorized use of their copyrighted music in these user-created videos.

From YouTube's perspective, the process of working with the music publishers has proven a bit frustrating — especially given the fact that, as of this writing, they remain a defendant of a class action lawsuit for mass copyright infringement. As mentioned above, YouTube, to the extent they are not immune under the Section 512 safe harbor, must obtain both a reproduction license, for the copies of the songs that have been reproduced on their servers, and performance licenses, for the public performances of the copyrighted songs in connection with the streaming of the videos to their users.

YouTube has acquired the necessary performance licenses from ASCAP, BMI, and SESAC, but has initiated rate hearings to minimize the fees owed to the performance societies for these performances.

In addition to performance licenses for streaming videos that contain copyrighted music, YouTube would also be responsible for obtaining licenses for copies of such videos reproduced on its servers. Such licenses are typically provided by music publishers as part of a synchronization license. However, since the musical work is being fixed in the video by the user, not YouTube, it would seem the user, not YouTube, would be responsible for obtaining a synchronization license from the music publisher at the time the music was fixed in the video.

Obviously, it would be impractical for each user to contact and negotiate with music publishers for synch licenses prior to uploading these videos. Nevertheless, YouTube would still appear to require a license to make the server copies. Since the copies of the sound recordings are part of audiovisual works (i.e., the user generated video), they are not audio-only sound recordings and therefore not subject to the compulsory license provision under Section 115 of the Copyright Act. Accordingly, the mechanical license regime is unavailable to YouTube.

Though, under Section 512, the music publishers have the right to demand the expeditious removal of any videos in which their copyrighted music has been synchronized without their authorization, YouTube would prefer a system whereby its users could continue incorporating copyrighted music in their original videos and YouTube could continue making those videos available by streaming. But, under established licensing regimes in the music industry, YouTube or its users must obtain synchronization licenses on a case-by-case basis, song by song, publisher by publisher, dealing with all the split copyright and territorial issues that are inherent in traditional music industry models. With no publicly available database to determine who owns which song in which territory, such a task is highly impractical.

In an effort to start the process of licensing the music required for these videos, YouTube entered into licensing arrangements with several major music publishers under which YouTube received, for itself and on behalf of its users, the synchronization licenses they needed on a blanket basis (i.e., covering the entire catalog of the major music publisher). Nevertheless, the terms of these blanket licenses proved impractical.

As you may recall from Chapter 3, on *Songwriter Agreements*, songwriters with bargaining leverage should be able to obtain the right to approve synchronization licenses for the use of their music in audiovisual works. Sometimes such approval is limited to uses that involve an X-rating or exclude certain forms of commercial advertising. Thus, to the extent music publishers issue blanket synch licenses, it must reserve some right to deny a use if it runs against its own licensing policy or would run afoul of a songwriter's contractual approval rights. Accordingly, some music publishers required that when YouTube identified a video containing a song in the publisher's repertoire, YouTube was required to send the video to the publisher for approval. With 15 hours of video being uploaded to YouTube every minute, such an arrangement is obviously impractical. As a result, some agreement was reached to allow YouTube to publish the video, but the music publisher reserved the right to issue a "take-down" notice should it or the songwriter decide to deny the particular use.

While some of these agreements were reached, YouTube was left with the challenge of identifying which videos uploaded by end users contain the copyrighted songs of the music publisher. Recall that YouTube has developed technology to identify a sound recording by its unique digital "fingerprint." YouTube can then match the sound recording against a "metadata" list of recordings. But there is no comprehensive database that matches popular sound recordings to musical works and then, of course, to the owners of the musical works. We can imagine YouTube working to solve this problem, but until it is solved, there will be a practical challenge in identifying songs used in these videos and notifying the appropriate music publishers for approval.

## D. Original Videos Created by Users that Include Original Performances of Copyrighted Songs

Some user-generated videos do not contain popular sound recordings, but may contain a popular song, as when a user records a performance of himself or a friend singing a copyrighted song, such as *Happy Birthday.* Since the user's recording is original, YouTube would not have the fingerprint of the recording in its database. Thus, there is no known metadata record of the recording to which to match. A video containing a new recording of a musical work by a user is called a *cover video.*

YouTube has provided to music publishers certain online tools that are intended to facilitate the manual location of cover videos containing their songs. Music publishers, however, believe it should be YouTube's responsibility to police their own system for copyright infringement.

In the meantime, YouTube has begun offering independent music publishers a means to provide YouTube with blanket synchronization licenses in exchange for a share of the revenues generated by videos containing the publishers' copyrighted music. The terms of the YouTube Composition License are discussed below.

## E. Original Videos Created by Users that Combine Elements of Several Songs or Sound Recordings or Modifications of Such Works

Finally, it is important to mention that some user-generated videos contain substantial modifications of the copyrighted works they embody. These videos may contain one or more sound recordings or songs, elements of which have been combined (e.g., sampled, remixed, mashed-up) or otherwise changed. They may also contain other videos, portions of literary works, either verbatim or modified for some purpose, and other works of authorship.

One of the conditions of the Section 512 safe harbor is that "the material is transmitted through the system or network without modification of its content." But, while the user may modify the sound recordings and musical works it fixes in his or her original video, YouTube is not modifying the content of the videos it receives from the user. Thus, to the extent YouTube is protected from liability by the safe harbor, it would not be responsible for the modifications made by the end user.

Nevertheless, the practical problem of who needs to obtain the approval for modifications, or whether such approval should be necessary at all, will either have to be resolved by the legislature or by some institutional agreement.

## IV. SUMMARY OF YOUTUBE LICENSE TERMS

In its attempt to reach an agreement with record labels and music publishers to allow user-generated videos to flourish in an environment where copyrighted sound recordings and musical works will inevitably be embodied in these videos, YouTube has developed two forms of agreement: (1) Sound Recording and Audiovisual Content License and (2) Composition Rights License, the forms of which, existing as of 2009, are included in the appendix on the CD-ROM. This section will discuss the salient terms of each.

### A. YouTube Sound Recording and Audiovisual Content License

In this form, YouTube is attempting to acquire a license from a record label to its repertoire of music videos (called Provider Videos), as well as a license to use the label's sound recordings in user-generated videos (called User Videos).

The label is responsible for procuring and paying for the necessary synchronization licenses from the music publishers and for making any payments due to recording artists, actors, producers and all other royalty participants arising from YouTube's exploitations videos, except that YouTube will remain responsible for obtaining any public performance licenses from the applicable performance rights societies around the world (e.g., from ASCAP, BMI, PRS for Music, JASRAC, etc.).

The label provides to YouTube copies of its recordings and associated metadata. YouTube will provide the label with an account, providing access to a system to facilitate the removal of Provider Videos or User Videos in the YouTube service. YouTube may serve advertising on pages associated with the videos and agree to pay a portion of the net advertising revenues generated in connection with streams of the videos on a quarterly basis.

For Provider Videos (i.e., videos owned and produced by the label), YouTube will pay the label 50% of the net advertising revenues associated with use of the video in the United States and 40% with respect to uses outside the United States. For the labels sound recordings used in User Videos, YouTube will pay 30% of the net advertising revenues derived from exploitation anywhere in the world. Net advertising revenue includes gross ad revenues less VAT taxes, if any, and less 10% "to pay for, in part, operating costs including bandwidth and third party advertising fees." Net advertising revenue "specifically excludes any advertising, e-commerce and referral fees received by Google related to recorded music 'upsells'."

### B. YouTube Composition Right License

In this form, YouTube is attempting to acquire a license from music publisher to its repertoire of musical compositions that are used in User Videos, except a distinction is made between User Videos that contain commercial sound recordings and User Cover Videos, which involve an original performance of a composition in a user-generated video.

In exchange for the necessary reproduction licenses from the music publishers, YouTube will pay the publishers a royalty of 10% of net advertising revenues with respect to compositions used in Use Videos that contain Commercial Recordings and a royalty of 15% with respect to compositions used in User Cover Videos. With respect to co-published compositions, the royalties will be apportioned among the respective owners. In addition, YouTube will be responsible for obtaining and paying for any public performance licenses from the applicable performance rights societies.

The administration of removal of videos will work the same way as it does under the label agreement discussed above.

## V. CONCLUSION

With hundreds of hours of audio, video, and other forms of rich content being uploaded every day by amateur content creators to websites such as YouTube, Imeem, and Ultimate Guitar — much of it incorporating copyrighted content of others without permission — a new licensing paradigm is bound to emerge. Google's YouTube is trying to address these issues with innovative technology and agreements with content owners, but it is not yet clear whether technology or private agreements alone will solve the problem. With Congress hopelessly behind in creating legislative solutions to address the impact of technological developments upon copyright, and the incentives copyright are intended to foster, we may need to await settlement of these issues in court. The settlement between the book publishing industry and Google, we submit, may prove to be a useful model for resolving the licensing challenges presented by the user-generated content phenomenon.

# Appendix to Chapter 16
# The User-Generated Content Phenomenon

Laws and Regulations

**Law 16.1** Section 512 of the U.S. Copyright Act

Forms (On CD-Rom Only)

**Form 16.1** YouTube Sound Recording and Audiovisual Content License

**Form 16.2** YouTube Composition Rights License

# LAW 16.1

## SECTION 512 OF THE U.S. COPYRIGHT ACT

### § 512 · Limitations on liability relating to material online

(a) TRANSITORY DIGITAL NETWORK COMMUNICATIONS. — A service provider shall not be liable for monetary relief, or, except as provided in subsection (j), for injunctive or other equitable relief, for infringement of copyright by reason of the provider's transmitting, routing, or providing connections for, material through a system or network controlled or operated by or for the service provider, or by reason of the intermediate and transient storage of that material in the course of such transmitting, routing, or providing connections, if —

(1) the transmission of the material was initiated by or at the direction of a person other than the service provider;

(2) the transmission, routing, provision of connections, or storage is carried out through an automatic technical process without selection of the material by the service provider;

(3) the service provider does not select the recipients of the material except as an automatic response to the request of another person;

(4) no copy of the material made by the service provider in the course of such intermediate or transient storage is maintained on the system or network in a manner ordinarily accessible to anyone other than anticipated recipients, and no such copy is maintained on the system or network in a manner ordinarily accessible to such anticipated recipients for a longer period than is reasonably necessary for the transmission, routing, or provision of connections; and

(5) the material is transmitted through the system or network without modification of its content.

(b) SYSTEM CACHING. —

(1) LIMITATION ON LIABILITY. — A service provider shall not be liable for monetary relief, or, except as provided in subsection

(j), for injunctive or other equitable relief, for infringement of copyright by reason of the intermediate and temporary storage of material on a system or network controlled or operated by or for the service provider in a case in which —

(A) the material is made available online by a person other than the service provider;

(B) the material is transmitted from the person described in subparagraph (A) through the system or network to a person other than the person described in subparagraph (A) at the direction of that other person; and

(C) the storage is carried out through an automatic technical process for the purpose of making the material available to users of the system or network who, after the material is transmitted as described in subparagraph (B), request access to the material from the person described in subparagraph (A), if the conditions set forth in paragraph (2) are met.

(2) CONDITIONS. — The conditions referred to in paragraph (1) are that —

(A) the material described in paragraph (1) is transmitted to the subsequent users described in paragraph (1)(C) without modification to its content from the manner in which the material was transmitted from the person described in paragraph (1)(A);

(B) the service provider described in paragraph (1) complies with rules concerning the refreshing, reloading, or other updating of the material when specified by the person making the material available online in accordance with a generally accepted industry standard data communications protocol for the system or network through which that person makes the material available, except that this subparagraph applies only if those rules are not used by the person described in paragraph (1)(A) to prevent or unreasonably impair the intermediate storage to which this subsection applies;

(C) the service provider does not interfere with the ability of technology associated with the material to return to the person described in paragraph (1)(A) the information that would have been available to that person if the material had been obtained by the subsequent users described in paragraph (1)(C) directly from that person, except that this subparagraph applies only if that technology —

(i) does not significantly interfere with the performance of the provider's system or network or with the intermediate storage of the material;

(ii) is consistent with generally accepted industry standard communications protocols; and

(iii) does not extract information from the provider's system or network other than the information that would have been available to the person described in paragraph (1)(A) if the subsequent users had gained access to the material directly from that person;

(D) if the person described in paragraph (1)(A) has in effect a condition that a person must meet prior to having access to the material, such as a condition based on payment of a fee or provision of a password or other information, the service provider permits access to the stored material in significant part only to users of its system or network that have met those conditions and only in accordance with those conditions; and

(E) if the person described in paragraph (1)(A) makes that material available online without the authorization of the copyright owner of the material, the service provider responds expeditiously to remove, or disable access to, the material that is claimed to be infringing upon notification of claimed infringement as described in subsection (c)(3), except that this subparagraph applies only if —

(i) the material has previously been removed from the originating site or access to it has been disabled, or a court has ordered that the material be removed from the originating site or that access to the material on the originating site be disabled; and

(ii) the party giving the notification includes in the notification a statement confirming that the material has been removed from the originating site or access to it has been disabled or that a court has ordered that the material be removed from the originating site or that access to the material on the originating site be disabled.

(c) INFORMATION RESIDING ON SYSTEMS OR NETWORKS AT DIRECTION OF USERS. —

(1) IN GENERAL. — A service provider shall not be liable for monetary relief, or, except as provided in subsection (j), for injunctive or other equitable relief, for infringement of copyright by reason of the storage at the direction of a user of material that resides on a system or network controlled or operated by or for the service provider, if the service provider —

(A)(i) does not have actual knowledge that the material or an activity using the material on the system or network is infringing;

(ii) in the absence of such actual knowledge, is not aware of facts or circumstances from which infringing activity is apparent; or

(iii) upon obtaining such knowledge or awareness, acts expeditiously to remove, or disable access to, the material;

(B) does not receive a financial benefit directly attributable to the infringing activity, in a case in which the service provider has the right and ability to control such activity; and

(C) upon notification of claimed infringement as described in paragraph (3), responds expeditiously to remove, or disable access to, the material that is claimed to be infringing or to be the subject of infringing activity.

(2) DESIGNATED AGENT. — The limitations on liability established in this subsection apply to a service provider only if the service provider has designated an agent to receive notifications of claimed infringement described in paragraph (3), by making available through its service, including on its website in a location accessible to the public, and by providing to the Copyright Office, substantially the following information:

(A) the name, address, phone number, and electronic mail address of the agent.

(B) other contact information which the Register of Copyrights may deem appropriate.

The Register of Copyrights shall maintain a current directory of agents available to the public for inspection, including through the

Internet, in both electronic and hard copy formats, and may require payment of a fee by service providers to cover the costs of maintaining the directory.

(3) ELEMENTS OF NOTIFICATION. —

(A) To be effective under this subsection, a notification of claimed infringement must be a written communication provided to the designated agent of a service provider that includes substantially the following:

(i) A physical or electronic signature of a person authorized to act on behalf of the owner of an exclusive right that is allegedly infringed.

(ii) Identification of the copyrighted work claimed to have been infringed, or, if multiple copyrighted works at a single online site are covered by a single notification, a representative list of such works at that site.

(iii) Identification of the material that is claimed to be infringing or to be the subject of infringing activity and that is to be removed or access to which is to be disabled, and information reasonably sufficient to permit the service provider to locate the material.

(iv) Information reasonably sufficient to permit the service provider to contact the complaining party, such as an address, telephone number, and, if available, an electronic mail address at which the complaining party may be contacted.

(v) A statement that the complaining party has a good faith belief that use of the material in the manner complained of is not authorized by the copyright owner, its agent, or the law.

(vi) A statement that the information in the notification is accurate, and under penalty of perjury, that the complaining party is authorized to act on behalf of the owner of an exclusive right that is allegedly infringed.

(B)(i) Subject to clause (ii), a notification from a copyright owner or from a person authorized to act on behalf of the copyright owner that fails to comply substantially with the provisions of subparagraph (A) shall not be considered under paragraph (1)(A) in determining whether a service provider has actual knowledge or is aware of facts or circumstances from which infringing activity is apparent.

(ii) In a case in which the notification that is provided to the service provider's designated agent fails to comply substantially with all the provisions of subparagraph (A) but substantially complies with clauses (ii), (iii), and (iv) of subparagraph (A), clause (i) of this subparagraph applies only if the service provider promptly attempts to contact the person making the notification or takes other reasonable steps to assist in the receipt of notification that substantially complies with all the provisions of subparagraph (A).

(d) INFORMATION LOCATION TOOLS. — A service provider shall not be liable for monetary relief, or, except as provided in subsection (j), for injunctive or other equitable relief, for infringement of copyright by reason of the provider referring or linking users to an online location containing infringing material or infringing activity, by using information location tools, including a directory, index, reference, pointer, or hypertext link, if the service provider —

(1) (A) does not have actual knowledge that the material or activity is infringing;

(B) in the absence of such actual knowledge, is not aware of facts or circumstances from which infringing activity is apparent; or

(C) upon obtaining such knowledge or awareness, acts expeditiously to remove, or disable access to, the material;

(2) does not receive a financial benefit directly attributable to the infringing activity, in a case in which the service provider has the right and ability to control such activity; and

(3) upon notification of claimed infringement as described in subsection (c)(3), responds expeditiously to remove, or disable access to, the material that is claimed to be infringing or to be the subject of infringing activity, except that, for purposes of this paragraph, the information described in subsection (c)(3)(A)(iii) shall be identification of the reference or link, to material or activity claimed to be infringing, that is to be removed or access to which is to be disabled, and information reasonably sufficient to permit the service provider to locate that reference or link.

(e) LIMITATION ON LIABILITY OF NONPROFIT EDUCATIONAL INSTITUTIONS. — (1) When a public or other nonprofit institution of higher education is a service provider, and when a faculty member or graduate student who is an employee of such institution is performing a teaching or research function, for the purposes of subsections (a) and (b) such faculty member or graduate student shall be considered to be a person other than the institution, and for the purposes of subsections (c) and (d) such faculty member's or graduate student's knowledge or awareness of his or her infringing activities shall not be attributed to the institution, if —

(A) such faculty member's or graduate student's infringing activities do not involve the provision of online access to instructional materials that are or were required or recommended, within the preceding 3-year period, for a course taught at the institution by such faculty member or graduate student;

(B) the institution has not, within the preceding 3-year period, received more than 2 notifications described in subsection (c)(3) of claimed infringement by such faculty member or graduate student, and such notifications of claimed infringement were not actionable under subsection (f); and

(C) the institution provides to all users of its system or network informational materials that accurately describe, and promote compliance with, the laws of the United States relating to copyright.

(2) For the purposes of this subsection, the limitations on injunctive relief contained in subsections (j)(2) and (j)(3), but not those in (j)(1), shall apply.

(f) MISREPRESENTATIONS. — Any person who knowingly materially misrepresents under this section —

(1) that material or activity is infringing, or

(2) that material or activity was removed or disabled by mistake or misidentification,

shall be liable for any damages, including costs and attorneys' fees, incurred by the alleged infringer, by any copyright owner or copyright owner's authorized licensee, or by a service provider, who is injured by such misrepresentation, as the result of the service provider relying upon such misrepresentation in removing or disabling access to the material or activity claimed to be infringing, or in replacing the removed material or ceasing to disable access to it.

(g) REPLACEMENT OF REMOVED OR DISABLED MATERIAL AND LIMITATION ON OTHER LIABILITY. —

(1) NO LIABILITY FOR TAKING DOWN GENERALLY. — Subject to paragraph (2), a service provider shall not be liable to any person for any claim based on the service provider's good faith disabling of access to, or removal of, material or activity claimed to be infringing or based on facts or circumstances from which infringing activity is apparent, regardless of whether the material or activity is ultimately determined to be infringing.

(2) EXCEPTION. — Paragraph (1) shall not apply with respect to material residing at the direction of a subscriber of the service provider on a system or network controlled or operated by or for the service provider that is removed, or to which access is disabled by the service provider, pursuant to a notice provided under subsection (c)(1)(C), unless the service provider —

(A) takes reasonable steps promptly to notify the subscriber that it has removed or disabled access to the material;

(B) upon receipt of a counter notification described in paragraph (3), promptly provides the person who provided the notification under subsection (c)(1)(C) with a copy of the counter notification, and informs that person that it will replace the removed material or cease disabling access to it in 10 business days; and

(C) replaces the removed material and ceases disabling access to it not less than 10, nor more than 14, business days following receipt of the counter notice, unless its designated agent first receives notice from the person who submitted the notification under subsection (c)(1)(C) that such person has filed an action seeking a court order to restrain the subscriber from engaging in infringing activity relating to the material on the service provider's system or network.

(3) CONTENTS OF COUNTER NOTIFICATION. — To be effective under this subsection, a counter notification must be a written communication provided to the service provider's designated agent that includes substantially the following:

(A) A physical or electronic signature of the subscriber.

(B) Identification of the material that has been removed or to which access has been disabled and the location at which the material appeared before it was removed or access to it was disabled.

(C) A statement under penalty of perjury that the subscriber has a good faith belief that the material was removed or disabled as a result of mistake or misidentification of the material to be removed or disabled.

(D) The subscriber's name, address, and telephone number, and a statement that the subscriber consents to the jurisdiction of Federal District Court for the judicial district in which the address is located, or if the subscriber's address is outside of the United States, for any judicial district in which the service provider may be found, and that the subscriber will accept service of process from the person who provided notification under subsection (c)(1)(C) or an agent of such person.

(4) LIMITATION ON OTHER LIABILITY. — A service provider's compliance with paragraph (2) shall not subject the service provider to liability for copyright infringement with respect to the material identified in the notice provided under subsection (c)(1)(C).

(h) SUBPOENA TO IDENTIFY INFRINGER. —

(1) REQUEST. — A copyright owner or a person authorized to act on the owner's behalf may request the clerk of any United States district court to issue a subpoena to a service provider for identification of an alleged infringer in accordance with this subsection.

(2) CONTENTS OF REQUEST. — The request may be made by filing with the clerk —

(A) a copy of a notification described in subsection (c)(3)(A);

(B) a proposed subpoena; and

(C) a sworn declaration to the effect that the purpose for which the subpoena is sought is to obtain the identity of an alleged infringer and that such information will only be used for the purpose of protecting rights under this title.

(3) CONTENTS OF SUBPOENA. — The subpoena shall authorize and order the service provider receiving the notification and the

subpoena to expeditiously disclose to the copyright owner or person authorized by the copyright owner information sufficient to identify the alleged infringer of the material described in the notification to the extent such information is available to the service provider.

(4) BASIS FOR GRANTING SUBPOENA. — If the notification filed satisfies the provisions of subsection (c)(3)(A), the proposed subpoena is in proper form, and the accompanying declaration is properly executed, the clerk shall expeditiously issue and sign the proposed subpoena and return it to the requester for delivery to the service provider.

(5) ACTIONS OF SERVICE PROVIDER RECEIVING SUBPOENA. — Upon receipt of the issued subpoena, either accompanying or subsequent to the receipt of a notification described in subsection (c)(3)(A), the service provider shall expeditiously disclose to the copyright owner or person authorized by the copyright owner the information required by the subpoena, notwithstanding any other provision of law and regardless of whether the service provider responds to the notification.

(6) Rules applicable to subpoena. — Unless otherwise provided by this section or by applicable rules of the court, the procedure for issuance and delivery of the subpoena, and the remedies for noncompliance with the subpoena, shall be governed to the greatest extent practicable by those provisions of the Federal Rules of Civil Procedure governing the issuance, service, and enforcement of a subpoena duces tecum.

(i) CONDITIONS FOR ELIGIBILITY. —

(1) ACCOMMODATION OF TECHNOLOGY. — The limitations on liability established by this section shall apply to a service provider only if the service provider —

(A) has adopted and reasonably implemented, and informs subscribers and account holders of the service provider's system or network of, a policy that provides for the termination in appropriate circumstances of subscribers and account holders of the service provider's system or network who are repeat infringers; and

(B) accommodates and does not interfere with standard technical measures.

(2) DEFINITION. — As used in this subsection, the term "standard technical measures" means technical measures that are used by copyright owners to identify or protect copyrighted works and —

(A) have been developed pursuant to a broad consensus of copyright owners and service providers in an open, fair, voluntary, multiindustry standards process;

(B) are available to any person on reasonable and nondiscriminatory terms; and

(C) do not impose substantial costs on service providers or substantial burdens on their systems or networks.

(j) INJUNCTIONS. — The following rules shall apply in the case of any application for an injunction under section 502 against a service provider that is not subject to monetary remedies under this section:

(1) SCOPE OF RELIEF. — (A) With respect to conduct other than that which qualifies for the limitation on remedies set forth in subsection (a), the court may grant injunctive relief with respect to a service provider only in one or more of the following forms:

(i) An order restraining the service provider from providing access to infringing material or activity residing at a particular online site on the provider's system or network.

(ii) An order restraining the service provider from providing access to a subscriber or account holder of the service provider's system or network who is engaging in infringing activity and is identified in the order, by terminating the accounts of the subscriber or account holder that are specified in the order.

(iii) Such other injunctive relief as the court may consider necessary to prevent or restrain infringement of copyrighted material specified in the order of the court at a particular online location, if such relief is the least burdensome to the service provider among the forms of relief comparably effective for that purpose.

(B) If the service provider qualifies for the limitation on remedies described in subsection (a), the court may only grant injunctive relief in one or both of the following forms:

(i) An order restraining the service provider from providing access to a subscriber or account holder of the service provider's system or network who is using the provider's service to engage in infringing activity and is identified in the order, by terminating the accounts of the subscriber or account holder that are specified in the order.

(ii) An order restraining the service provider from providing access, by taking reasonable steps specified in the order to block access, to a specific, identified, online location outside the United States.

(2) CONSIDERATIONS. — The court, in considering the relevant criteria for injunctive relief under applicable law, shall consider —

(A) whether such an injunction, either alone or in combination with other such injunctions issued against the same service provider under this subsection, would significantly burden either the provider or the operation of the provider's system or network;

(B) the magnitude of the harm likely to be suffered by the copyright owner in the digital network environment if steps are not taken to prevent or restrain the infringement;

(C) whether implementation of such an injunction would be technically feasible and effective, and would not interfere with access to noninfringing material at other online locations; and

(D) whether other less burdensome and comparably effective means of preventing or restraining access to the infringing material are available.

(3) NOTICE AND EX PARTE ORDERS. — Injunctive relief under this subsection shall be available only after notice to the service provider and an opportunity for the service provider to appear are provided, except for orders ensuring the preservation of evidence or other orders having no material adverse effect on the operation of the service provider's communications network.

(k) DEFINITIONS. —

(1) SERVICE PROVIDER. — (A) As used in subsection (a), the term "service provider" means an entity offering the transmission, routing, or providing of connections for digital online communications, between or among points specified by a user, of material of the user's choosing, without modification to the content of the material as sent or received.

(B) As used in this section, other than subsection (a), the term "service provider" means a provider of online services or network access, or the operator of facilities therefor, and includes an entity described in sub-paragraph (A).

(2) MONETARY RELIEF. — As used in this section, the term "monetary relief" means damages, costs, attorneys' fees, and any other form of monetary payment.

(l) OTHER DEFENSES NOT AFFECTED. — The failure of a service provider's conduct to qualify for limitation of liability under this section shall not bear adversely upon the consideration of a defense by the service provider that the service provider's conduct is not infringing under this title or any other defense.

(m) PROTECTION OF PRIVACY. — Nothing in this section shall be construed to condition the applicability of subsections (a) through (d) on —

(1) a service provider monitoring its service or affirmatively seeking facts indicating infringing activity, except to the extent consistent with a standard technical measure complying with the provisions of subsection (i); or

(2) a service provider gaining access to, removing, or disabling access to material in cases in which such conduct is prohibited by law.

(n) CONSTRUCTION. — Subsections (a), (b), (c), and (d) describe separate and distinct functions for purposes of applying this section. Whether a service provider qualifies for the limitation on liability in any one of those subsections shall be based solely on the criteria in that subsection, and shall not affect a determination of whether that service provider qualifies for the limitations on liability under any other such subsection.

Chapter 17

# Old Licenses, New Uses

## Summary

v. Boosey & Hawkes v. Buena Vista Home Video (1998)

w. Batiste v. Island Records (1999)

x. Chambers v. Time Warner, Inc. (2000)

y. Greenfield v. Philles Records (2002)

z. Intersport, Inc. v. National Collegiate Athletic Association

aa. Reinhardt v. Wal-Mart Stores, Inc. (2008)

## II. DETERMINING THE SCOPE OF AMBIGUOUS LICENSES — A SUGGESTED APPROACH

A. The Type of Grant

1. Grant of Copyright

2. Grant of Exclusive Rights Under Copyright

3. Grant of a Non-Exclusive License

B. The Language of the Grant

C. Evidence of Specific Intent of the Parties

D. Where No Clear Specific Intent of the Parties Is Evident

1. Whether an Old Theatrical Synchronization License Permits Distribution in Videocassettes, DVDs and Other Home Video Devices?

a. Expectations of the Licensee/Motion Picture Producer — What would he have done?

(1) Would the Music Publisher's Exercise Its Exclusive Right to the New Use Impair the Studio's Use Under the Old License?

(2) Would the Studio's Exercise of the License Be Impaired by the Failure to Obtain a License for the New Use?

b. Expectations of the Music Publisher — What would he have done?

(1) Would the Producer's Exercise of Its License of the Song for the New Use Impair the Music Publisher's Exclusive Rights in the Song?

(2) Would the Producer's Exercise of the License Impair the Music Publisher's Expectations of Compensation from the Old License?

c. Analysis of Decision in *Boosey & Hawkes v. Disney* — What should the court have done?

2. Whether an Old Theatrical Synchronization License Permit Distribution in On-Demand Streaming or Download Over the Internet?

3. Whether a Grant of Exclusive Rights to Reproduce and Distribute a Book Includes the Right to Reproduce and Distribute EBooks?

## III. AVOIDING AMBIGUITY

## APPENDICES

# CHAPTER 17

# OLD LICENSES, NEW USES

In the early 1980s, as the local home video rental store was becoming as commonplace as the neighborhood bakery, the motion picture studios that produced the movies that made up the bread and butter of these stores found themselves in the middle of quite a fix: they began to realize they were not participating in the increasing amount of rental revenues derived from the rental of their videocassettes by the video rental stores. After receiving only one payment for the sale of a videocassette to a video rental store, the producer would watch that same videocassette be rented to home viewers over and over, as many times as the tape could physically endure being played and rewound, and replayed. In addition, the studios feared the availability of videocassettes for home viewing would mean a certain decline in the number of people who went out to movie theaters for their motion picture entertainment. (The subsequent success of DVDs proved these fears to be unfounded.) Making matters worse, the film studios began receiving notices from music publishers that their use of music in these videocassettes was not authorized by their synchronization licenses and required the payment of additional license fees.

By the time DVDs broadened the market for home video distribution, it became clear that virtually every film would eventually become available in the lucrative home video market. For films produced during the past 20 years or so, producers normally have been able to obtain, concurrent with their theatrical synchronization licenses, the videogram license necessary to permit them to reproduce their musical works in videocassettes, DVDs, and other forms of home video devices.

But what about motion pictures released many years ago, well before the advent of videocassettes, DVDs, and Blu-ray discs? Did not the old licenses for the use of music in these films cover the distribution of the films on these new devices in the home video market?

This is an important question, as it is well-established law that the use of a copyrighted work in a way that is outside the scope of a license constitutes copyright infringement.[1]

Music publishers reviewed these old synchronization licenses and the answer they came up with was, "no" — that the theatrical and television synch licenses they issued years ago did not permit the use of their songs in films distributed on home video devices. In many cases, this answer was clearly correct. Some of these old synchronization licenses either specifically identified home video use and expressly excluded it, or the license was otherwise clear with respect to what uses were granted — all other uses, including home video use, whether or not anticipated at the time, being reserved by implication. Other licenses were quite broad, covering all uses "in any form or medium, and in any manner, now known or hereafter devised."

In between those two extremes are synch licenses that were ambiguous as their scope, and the answer to the question, with respect to some of these licenses, was left for the courts to decide. Several decisions, discussed below, have provided some guidance on the scope of these ambiguous licenses.

But, as Yogi says, "It ain't over 'till it's over": Just as the question of whether these old theatrical synch licenses covered the distribution of the films in videocassettes was being settled, a new technology emerged only to reopen the issue: *whether these old synch licenses included the right to distribute the work by streaming or download over the Internet.* Producers and motion pictures studios, contemplating the emerging market for Internet streaming and download, are currently pouring over these old synch licenses to make just that determination and, where necessary, clearing the additional licenses they need for these uses.

This chapter will review language typically found in several old synchronization licenses, provide a survey of the prominent U.S. court decisions bearing on the subject, and will conclude with an analysis of those decisions and a recommended approach for determining whether an old license covers a new use.

---

[1] *Bourne v. Walt Disney Co.*, 68 F.3d 621, 631 (2d Cir. 1995), citing *Gilliam v. American Broadcasting Cos.*, 538 F.2d 14, 20 (2d Cir. 1976).

## I. TYPES OF OLD SYNCHRONIZATION LICENSES

Old synchronization licenses fall into three general classes:

A. Licenses that Clearly Included New Forms of Distribution

B. Licenses that Clearly Excluded New Forms of Distribution

C. Licenses Whose Scope Is Unclear

Each of these will be discussed in turn.

### A. Old Licenses that Clearly Included New Forms of Distribution

Before the advent of the home video market, some attorneys representing motion picture producers foresaw the possibility of new forms of distribution of motion pictures and negotiated synchronization licenses that reflected their prescience. Such licenses permitted the recording of the music in synchronism or timed-relation with the specified motion picture,

> "for use in any form or medium, and in any manner, now known or hereafter devised."

A license such as this would seem to clearly include the right of reproduction of the motion picture for home video distribution.[2] By the early 1980s, motion picture synchronization licenses were drafted to specifically include permission to reproduce copies of the motion picture for home video distribution. These license provisions are commonly called *videogram licenses* and have been discussed in detail in the preceding chapter. Early in the history of videogram licensing, when music publishers were reluctant to negotiate specific terms until some standards had begun to emerge, videogram licenses were granted for short duration and called for good faith negotiations and arbitration upon the expiration of their terms. Later, specific royalty provisions, with buyout options, became common.

[2] See *Brown v. Twentieth Century Fox Film Corp.*, 799 F. Supp. 166 (1992), discussed below.

The above license language would also clearly include the delivery of the motion picture via the Internet — whether by streaming or download technologies.[3]

## B. Old Licenses that Clearly Excluded New Forms of Distribution

At the other extreme are those synchronization licenses that clearly exclude any form of exhibition, broadcast, distribution, transmission, or other delivery, other than the means that is expressly identified in the license (e.g., theatrical exhibition, television broadcast).

Licenses that specifically refer to home video devices or Internet transmission, and specifically exclude their use, are relatively rare, as they are likely to have been issued just as awareness of the technology (i.e., home video market or the Internet) was emerging. For example, the following provision of a typical synchronization license issued in the early to mid-1970s makes it clear that the license does not include the use of copies made for home video distribution:

> Cassettes. Notwithstanding anything to the contrary hereinabove contained, this agreement does not grant to Producer the right to manufacture or duplicate said motion picture by means of audiotelevision devices or contrivances, such as cassettes, discs or other similar configurations (herein called "cassettes"), for the purpose of selling such cassettes to the public. The sale of cassettes of the motion picture to the public shall be governed by the applicable law and/or by future good faith negotiations of the parties with respect to the fees to be paid in connection with such sales to the public, giving due consideration to customary practices which may develop with respect thereto.

Most licenses that exclude new technologies, however, did so not by specifically calling out the new technology, but by carefully specifying just how the motion picture could be exploited. Consider the following license, in common use about 1927, which would also appear to clearly exclude the making of copies for home video distribution:

> You are hereby granted a license to manufacture devices serving to mechanically reproduce the same, in whole or in part, and to use such

[3] See *Reinhardt v. Wal-Mart Stores, Inc.*, 547 F. Supp. 356 (2008), discussed below.

> devices solely in conjunction with and as an integral part of the appliance or mechanism known as THE VITAPHONE, in the United States and Canada, subject to the following conditions:
>
> 1. This License is not exclusive, and applies solely to the above described mechanical recording and public reproduction of the above named composition.
>
> 2. This License extends to and includes public performances by means of records as aforesaid serving to reproduce mechanically such above described composition in conjunction with THE VITAPHONE.
>
> 3. This License is subject to the rights of the American Society of Composers, Authors, and Publishers in the said composition with respect to the public performance thereof for profit; and the public reproductions or performance thereof for profit shall take place only in establishments licensed by the said Society.

The above license appears to have been very narrowly drafted to cover the reproduction of the composition "solely in conjunction with and as an integral part of the appliance or mechanism known as THE VITAPHONE." A little history will make clear the reason for such precision.

Under a patent licensed from Western Electric, Vitaphone Corporation — a joint venture established by Warner Bros. and a talented inventor — developed the first practical synchronized recording system and became the first producer of motion pictures to enter the sound picture (i.e., *talkies*) market. Originally, the Vitaphone process employed separate records for the sound portion of the motion picture. In the case of very early talkies, the records contained only the musical scores. Later, the records contained music, dialogue, and sound effects. Since records containing the musical scores could easily be misused to compete with commercial sound recordings, it was necessary to make it very clear in the license that the use of music was confined to the Vitaphone process, which was a sound process used solely for the theatrical exhibition of motion pictures. This is precisely what was accomplished by the Vitaphone license set forth in part above. It seems clear, therefore, that any other device, such as mechanisms used today to reproduce works in home video devices, for use in the home, would be outside the scope of the old Vitaphone license.

As noted in Chapter 15, the essential right involved in the licensing of videograms is the reproduction right. Because the sounds reproduced on a videogram are accompanied by moving visual images, the reproduction of videograms does not involve a "mechanical" reproduction right under the United States copyright law and, therefore, is not subject to the copyright law's compulsory licensing provisions for mechanical reproductions. Thus, music copyright owners are free to negotiate videogram licenses under a variety of terms.

While the current copyright law is quite clear on this point, it was not always so. At the turn of the century, with the advent of motion pictures, it was thought that the process of integrating music with motion pictures was permissible under the compulsory license provision of the copyright law existing at that time.[4] In fact, because the sounds in the Vitaphone process that accompanied the motion pictures were originally recorded onto phonograph records, Vitaphone took the position that a compulsory license under the law was available to it for this purpose. Vitaphone quickly discovered, however, that a strong combination of music publishers, through an organization called the Music Publishers' Protective Association, would insist otherwise and began a determined and successful effort to require motion picture producers to buy licenses for negotiated fees.

Their strategy was simple: By 1926, a movie theater was required to have an ASCAP license if the theater wished to perform music in the extensive ASCAP repertoire; the music publishers threatened to withdraw their performing rights from ASCAP unless Vitaphone agreed to buy special synchronization licenses at rates much higher than the statutory rate, which at that time was two cents per composition per record. In October, 1926, Vitaphone finally capitulated and agreed to pay approximately $100,000.00 per year.

## C. Old Licenses Whose Scope Is Unclear

### 1. Analysis of Several Old Licenses

During the time that the carefully crafted Vitaphone license set forth above was in use, other licenses that were issued during this

[4] 17 U.S.C. Sec. 1(e) (1909 Act).

period were less sophisticated. For example, a license issued in 1927 stated simply:

> Gentlemen:
>
> We hereby grant you permission to record and reproduce publicly for profit, but only in association with the motion picture, entitled XYZ, the following named musical composition, upon which we own the copyright, to wit: ABC.
>
> Very truly yours,

To argue that such a seemingly broad license did not grant permission for home video use, the music copyright owner would have to take the position that by saying "reproduce publicly . . . with the motion picture" he was intending to refer solely to the means of performing motion pictures (e.g., theatrical exhibition) that existed at that time. Perhaps the phrase "reproduce publicly" would itself indicate that distribution for *private* viewing was not contemplated. The motion picture producer might assert that the license limited distribution of copies "only in association with the motion picture" and that if any other limitation were intended the copyright owner could have expressed it just as easily.

In 1932, a more sophisticated synchronization license began wide circulation and had been used for many years thereafter as the basis for countless synchronization licenses. Its salient provisions were as follows:

> In consideration of the sum of $xxx the undersigned does hereby give XYZ Pictures the non-exclusive, irrevocable right, license, privilege and authority to record in any manner, medium or form, in any country covered by this license, the musical composition hereinbelow set out, and to make copies of such recording and to import said copies of recordings into any country covered by this license, all in accordance with the terms, conditions, and limitations hereinafter set out.
>
> . . . The license hereinabove set out is limited to the use of the musical compositions in synchronism or timed-relation with the motion picture hereinabove specified.
>
> . . . The right to record the musical compositions as covered by this agreement is conditioned upon the performance of the musical work in theatres having valid licenses from the American Society of

> Composers, Authors, and Publishers, or any other performing rights society having jurisdiction in the territory in which the said musical compositions are performed.
>
> . . . Licensor reserves to itself all rights and uses in and to said musical compositions not herein specifically granted.

Was the above license intended to restrict the use of motion pictures containing the licensed music to exhibition in theaters or did it allow distribution by another medium, such as videograms distributed for home viewing or Internet streaming or download?

A producer might assert that the broad grant to record "in any manner, medium, or form" subject only to conditions set forth in the license should be broadly interpreted in favor of the licensee, and that the true intent of the agreement is to limit the use "in synchronism or timed-relation with the motion picture." As long as the recording is used only in connection with that motion picture or wherever the motion picture may be exploited, the producer would argue, the use is within the license. In other words, all uses were licensed, subject to clearing the performance rights by theaters. No reference to television or videocassettes being made, no restriction was intended.

The music copyright owner would, however, refer our attention to the provision in the license stating that "the right to record" the songs is "conditioned upon the performance of the musical work in theatres." While the intent of the paragraph containing this language appears to be to assure that performances were made only in theaters having valid performing licenses (e.g., from ASCAP or BMI), it would also appear to indicate that the performance of the motion picture was contemplated to take place in theaters and not elsewhere, such as in private homes.

The language in the above license underwent some modification by the mid-1950s:

> In consideration of the sum of $xxx, the receipt of which is hereby acknowledged, the undersigned does hereby give XYZ Pictures, its successors and assigns, the non-exclusive irrevocable right and license, privilege and authority to record, in any manner, medium, form or language, in any country within the territory covered by this license, the words and music of the musical composition hereinbelow set out, and to make copies of said recordings and to import said recordings and/or copies of said recordings into any country within the territory covered by this license, and to perform

> said musical composition everywhere, all in accordance with the terms, conditions, and limitations hereinafter set out.
>
> . . . The license hereinabove set out is limited to the use of the musical composition in synchronism or timed-relation with the motion picture hereinabove specified, and trailers thereof.
>
> . . . The right to *perform* said musical composition as covered by this agreement is conditioned upon the performance of said musical composition in theatres having valid licenses from any performing rights society having jurisdiction in the territory in which the said musical composition is performed.
>
> . . . Licensor reserves to itself all rights and uses in and to said musical compositions not herein specifically granted.

A producer might take heart in the fact that the third paragraph above was modified by the replacement of the word "record" with the word "perform." It would appear that the license to record was no longer conditioned upon the performance of the song in theaters having valid licenses; only the license to perform was. The music copyright owner would be quick to point out, however, that the first paragraph was modified so that the license was "to make copies of said recordings . . . and to perform said musical composition everywhere, all in accordance with the terms, conditions, and limitations hereinafter set out." It appears that the words "to perform" were used merely to make it clear at the outset that the license included both a recording license and a public performing license, and was not intended to expand or further restrict the uses permitted under the license. This is confirmed by the fact that the change in language coincided precisely with the entry of the consent decrees between the Department of Justice and the performance rights societies, which, among other things, required music copyright owners to grant performance licenses for U.S. theatrical distribution.[5]

Consider the following television synchronization licenses issued in the 1970s that attempted to narrowly define what use may be made of the synchronized recording:

> In consideration of the sum of $xxx, and upon agreement hereto and the acceptance hereof as indicated below and the payment of said consideration to the undersigned, the undersigned does hereby give and grant

[5] See Chapter 18, on *Licensing Music in Live and Recorded Public Performances.*

> unto, XYZ Pictures, the non-exclusive, irrevocable right and license to record the following copyrighted musical composition in synchronism or timed-relation with a picture made and produced solely for television purposes by the said licensee and known as: [The TV Movie].

The license was drafted with a view toward limiting the use to television, intending to exclude exhibition in motion picture theaters and like establishments. It may be questioned, however, whether the above language successfully excluded the privilege of reproducing videocassettes for home video distribution. The first paragraph limits the use "solely for television purposes." Is the making of videocassettes of the picture for home video distribution a "television purpose"? If "television purpose," as used here, is synonymous with "broadcast purpose," the answer to the question would be, "no," and therefore home video use would not be covered by the license.

### 2. *Survey of the Court Decisions*

The general question of whether an old synchronization license covers a new use of a licensed work in another medium generally focuses on whether the original license restricted the use to a particular medium or whether it allowed distribution by another means, either one that existed at the time the original license was entered into or was developed subsequently. In other words, is the scope of the original license sufficiently broad to cover new uses that became conceivable or practical only years after the license was issued?

This question has been addressed countless times by the courts since the turn of the twentieth century as new technologies emerged to confound the intent of businessmen and challenge their ability to foresee the consequences of the license provisions to which they agreed. This section will provide an overview of some of the more important cases bearing on the question. An analysis of these decisions will follow in the context of this author's recommended approach to resolving these seemingly irresolvable disputes.

#### *a. Harper Bros. v. Klaw (1916)*

In *Harper Bros. v. Klaw*,[6] the author of the novel, *Ben Hur*, published in 1899, and Harper Bros., his publisher, provided a license to

[6] *Harper Bros. v. Klaw*, 232 F. 609 (S.D.N.Y. 1916).

the defendant, Klaw & Erlanger, to produce "a dramatic version" of the novel. After 14 years of successfully producing their live, staged performances of *Ben Hur*, Klaw & Erlanger desired to produce a filmed version of the play and asserted that they alone had the exclusive rights to produce Ben Hur as a motion picture. To restrain them from doing so, the suit was brought by the author and publisher of the book.

The court conceded that, had the parties' agreement "granted the exclusive right of dramatizing Ben Hur, or producing any play or plays that might be made out of Ben Hur, there would be no doubt at all as to [defendant's] right to make a 'movie play,' as well as the kind of play that has heretofore been produced."[7] The court, however, found that the license under dispute to be far more limited.

The license conferred the right to produce one version of the play only, and only in a particular manner, and in places limited to cities of a certain size. It further prohibited any change in the manner or performance or text, and contained royalty provisions inconsistent with the means by which royalties could be produced by motion picture distribution. The whole arrangement between the parties, concluded the court, was "not only in consistent with, but repugnant to, the thought of making 'movies' out of Ben Hur."

Finding that the making of a motion picture version of the book exceeded the scope of the license, the court enjoined Klaw & Erlanger from making a motion picture version of *Ben Hur*. Yet, the court did not stop there and continued with the following remarkable holding:

> Plaintiffs assert, and almost assume, that since defendants cannot make a 'movie' out of Ben Hur, and such right must exist somewhere, it is in them, as being an unconveyed portion of the copyright estate wherefrom was carved defendants' limited license. In strictness of law I think this true; but it does not always follow that, because one owns a certain thing, he may use it to the detriment of another, especially if the owner is under contractual obligations to such other. The 'movie' right to Ben Hur undoubtedly existed in 1899, but *in nubibus*,

---

[7] Citing *Kalem Co. v. Harper Bros.*, 222 U.S. 55 (1911) (holding that an unauthorized motion picture that depicts the principle scenes of a novel as to tell a story constitutes a "dramatization" of the novel and therefore an infringement of the copyright in the novel).

> or (what is frequently the same thing) in contemplation of law only.[8] As matter of fact they are an accretion or unearned increment conferred of late years upon copyright owners by the ingenuity of many inventors and mechanicians.
>
> In my opinion there is an implied negative covenant on the part of the plaintiffs (grantors of defendants' restricted license) not to use the ungranted portion of the copyright estate to the detriment, if not destruction, of the licensee's estate. Admittedly, if Harper Bros. (or Klaw & Erlanger, for the matter of that) permitted photo-plays of Ben Hur to infest the country, the market for the spoken play would be greatly impaired, if not destroyed. This being the fact, the law is analogous to that which implies, from a covenant to make a certain use of property, a covenant negative against doing anything else with it. High on Injunctions (4th Ed.) § 1151A, and cases cited.
>
> The result is that plaintiffs may take the injunction prayed for against defendants, and the defendants may have the same relief against plaintiffs. The meaning of such double injunction is that, as long as the contract of 1899 exists, neither party thereto can product a photoplay of Ben Hur except by bargain with the other.

This last odd twist of the case must have come as a surprise to all concerned, and may seem surprising to today's practitioners of copyright law, but the ruling caught the attention of one of our most prominent jurists and may well have some relevancy to the resolution of similar problem on today's horizon.

*b. Manners v. Morosco (1920)*

In *Manners v. Morosco,*[9] the author of the play *Peg O' My Heart* granted to defendant Morosco "the sole and exclusive liberty to produce, perform and represent said play" subject to the terms and conditions of the contract. The author filed suit to restrain Morosco from producing a motion picture, which the defendant asserted was permitted under the terms of the license to produce the play.

---

[8] "When this contract was made the moving picture art was (in the trite phrase) in its infancy. There were moving pictures, but it was then completely beyond the known possibilities of the art to produce a series of picture representing such and so spectacular and elaborate play or performance as Ben Hur of Klaw & Erlanger." *Harper Bros. v. Klaw*, 232 F. 609 at 612 (S.D.N.Y. 1916).

[9] *Manners v. Morosco* 252 U.S. 317 (1920).

In a decision written by Justice Oliver Wendell Holmes, the U.S. Supreme Court held that the license to produce the play did not encompass a license to produce a motion picture, because every detail of the license — e.g., limitation on the number of performances over several seasons, presentation of the play only in first-class theaters with a competent company and with a certain person in the title role, and stipulations regarding rehearsals being under the direction of the author — pointed to "a spoken drama alone is provided for" by the license.

The lower court's ruling — that the license to produce the play included the license to produce a motion picture version of the play — was based on the impossibility of supposing that the author reserved the right to destroy the value of the right granted by retaining power to set up the same play in motion pictures a few doors off with a much smaller admission fee. "We agree with the premise," stated Justice Holmes, "but not with the conclusion." Quoting *Harper v. Klaw* with approval, the Supreme Court held,

> There is an implied negative covenant on the part of the plaintiffs (grantors of defendants' restricted license) not to use the ungranted portion of the copyright estate to the detriment, if not destruction, of the licensee's estate. Admittedly, if Harper Bros. (or Klaw & Erlanger, for the matter of that) permitted photo-plays of Ben Hur to infest the country, the market for the spoken play would be greatly impaired, if not destroyed.

The result is that the plaintiff is entitled to an injunction against the representation of the play in motion pictures but upon the terms that the plaintiff also shall abstain from presenting or authorize the presentation of the play in that form. Decree reversed. Injunction to issue upon the condition that the plaintiff shall neither represent nor authorize the representation of the play *Peg O' My Heart* in moving pictures while the contract with the defendant remains in force.[10]

*c. Cinema Corporation of America v. De Mille (1933)*

By 1929, a new technology was taking the entertainment business by storm — motion pictures accompanied by synchronized sound: the

[10] *Id.*

"talkie." And, again, the courts were asked to interpret an old license in the light of the new technology — in this case, whether a license to make a dramatization or motion picture, issued before the advent of talkies, permitted the licensee to make a sound motion picture.

In *Cinema Corporation of America v. DeMille*,[11] the court held that where the same person holds both the silent picture rights and the dramatic rights, equating the latter with dialogue rights, he owns everything necessary to the making of a talking motion picture.

*d. Kirk La Shelle Co. v. Paul Armstrong Co. (1933)*

A novel by O. Henry was dramatized by a playwright, Paul Armstrong, and the resulting play was produced on stage in 1914.[12] One of Armstrong's creditors later acquired an interest in one-half of the revenues from revivals of the play in an agreement under which Armstrong agreed that "all contracts . . . affecting title to the dramatic rights (exclusive of motion picture rights)" to the play would be subject to the approval of the creditor. Armstrong later assigned the motion picture rights to a predecessor of MGM, which began distributing silent films based upon the play. In 1928, MGM, under its contract with Armstrong, began distributing a "talkie" based upon the play. The question was whether the creditor was entitled to one-half of the profits resulting from the grant of the "talkie" rights to MGM.

The court held that that

> Since "talkies" were unknown at the time when the contract was entered into, it cannot be said that "talkie" rights were within the contemplation of the parties either as a subject of an interest therein to the [creditor] or as included in the motion picture rights specifically excepted.

Nevertheless, applying the principals of *Harper Bros. v. Klaw & Erlanger* and *Manners v. Morosco*, the court found that the contract providing MGM with rights to make and distribute "talkies" would have a commercial effect upon stage productions of the play and

---

[11] *Cinema Corporation of America v. De Mille*, 267 N.Y. Supp. 589 (1933).

[12] *Kirk La Shelle Co. v. Paul Armstrong Co.*, 263 N.Y. 79; 188 N.E. 163 (1933).

would therefore diminish the value and affect the title to the creditor's interest in the dramatic rights in the play.

> [I]n every contract there is an implied covenant that neither party shall do anything which will have the effect of destroying or injuring the right of the other party to received the fruits of the contract, which means that in every contract there exists an implied covenant of good faith and fair dealing.

The creditor was thus entitled to receive one-half of the profits from distribution of the talkies.

*e. L.C. Page & Co. v. Fox Film Corp. (1936)*

In this case, plaintiff L.C. Page & Co., a book publisher, acquired by contract from Laura Richards, the author of the novel, *Captain January*, the "exclusive moving picture rights" of all books of the author. Page later granted the silent film rights to Principal Pictures Corp. Desiring to make a talkie version of the novel, Fox Films, apparently believing that plaintiff did not have the talkie rights, ignored plaintiff, and sought the rights directly from the author and Principal Pictures.

The question was whether the grant of moving picture rights by the author to plaintiff was sufficient to constitute a grant of talkie motion picture rights. The Court of Appeals for the Second Circuit held in the affirmative, stating:

> The mere fact that the species "talkies" may have been unknown and not within the contemplation of the parties in their description of the generic "moving pictures" does not prevent the latter from comprehending the former.[13]

Though "talkies" were not commercially available at the time plaintiff acquired the motion picture rights from the author, and even though it did not appear the author contemplated sound motion pictures at that time, plaintiff clearly contemplated the development of sound motion pictures at that time. Shortly after plaintiff's agreement with the author,

[13] *L.C. Page & Co. v. Fox Film Corp.*, 83 F.2d 196, 199 (2d Cir. 1936).

plaintiff granted motion picture rights to Principal Pictures that were specifically limited to the production of silent film versions.

The court recognized that its holding may be in conflict with that of *Kirk La Shelle Co. v. Paul Armstrong Co.*, but felt constrained to follow the doctrine of the Supreme Court in *Kalem Co. v. Harper Bros.*

*f. Murphy v. Warner Bros. Pictures (1940)*

In *Murphy v. Warner Bros.*,[14] the author of the play, *The Nightmare*, granted to Warner Bros., on April 30, 1928, "the exclusive, complete and entire motion picture rights" in the play and "to adapt, change, transpose, and subtract from [the play] . . . to such extent as the purchaser may deem expedient." The Court of Appeals for the Ninth Circuit had no trouble ruling that such a broadly worded grant included the right to make talking motion pictures.

*g. G. Ricordi & Co. v. Paramount Pictures (1950)*

In *G. Ricordi & Co. v. Paramount Pictures*,[15] the author of the novel *Madame Butterfly* and the dramatist who, under license from the author, wrote a play based on the novel, each granted to G. Ricordi & Co. the "exclusive right for all countries of the world in all languages to make a Libretto for an opera" based on the play and the novel *Madame Butterfly*. G. Ricordi & Co. then engaged Giacomo Pucini and others to collaborate on the later-renowned, three-act opera, *Madam Butterfly*. About ten years later, Paramount acquired from the author the right to make a motion picture version of the novel, and later released the silent film, *Madame Butterfly*, starring Mary Pickford.

In 1932, Paramount acquired from the estate of the author, and the estate of the playwright, the exclusive rights to make a motion picture version of the novel and play, with sound and dialogue, songs and music, and musical accompaniment. Based on its assignments from the estates, Paramount claimed the exclusive right to make motion pictures based on the novel and the play, and, accordingly, G. Ricordi & Co. would not have the right to produce a motion picture version of Puccini's opera, *Madame Butterfly*. Subsequently, G. Ricordi & Co.

---

[14] *Murphy v. Warner Bros. Pictures*, 112 F.2d 746 (9th Cir. 1940).

[15] *G. Ricordi & Co. v. Paramount Pictures*, 92 F. Supp. 537 (1950).

filed an action for declaratory judgment that it, too, had the right to make a motion picture, one based on its opera, despite Paramount's exclusive rights obtained from the author and playwright.

The court, with little more to go on than the language of the G. Ricordi's agreements with the author and playwright, considered that the broad language of the grant: "The said Libretto and all rights therein dramatic and otherwise to be the exclusive property of Messrs. G. Ricordi & Co. for all countries of the world" and "further to have the exclusive dramatic rights of the said operatic version of the drama Madame Butterfly in any theatre of the world."

"I am convinced," said the court, "that the Opera Madame Butterfly finally created was a new work entirely separate in form at least from the drama and the novel, the theme being the feature in common."

Accordingly, the court concluded that the interests of the parties to make their respective films were not in conflict.

*h. Ettore v. Philco Television Broadcasting Corp. (1956)*

Enter television. Albert Ettore is not only remembered for having been knocked down in the first and fourth rounds, and finally knocked out in the fifth, by heavyweight champion, Joe Lewis, he was the plaintiff in a lawsuit[16] over the televising of motion pictures made of several rounds of his losing bout. Ettore contracted to be paid 20% of the proceeds derived from the sale of the motion picture rights of the contract. Ettore received payment, but 13 years later, films made of the fight were telecast as part of a series, "Greatest Fights of the Century."

The issue before the court was whether the picture could be performed both in theaters and on television, or only in theaters. The court held that the picture could only be performed in theaters, basing its decision on the fact that the televising of motion pictures was a "use not in existence" in 1936. Of course, the feasibility of television was contemplated as early as 1927 and, by 1929, a provision granting motion picture studios the license to televise motion pictures began appearing in standard motion picture rights acquisition contracts. By 1932, Warner Bros.'s Brunswick subsidiary was experimenting with

[16] *Ettore v. Philco Television Broadcasting Corp.*, 229 F.2d 481 (3d Cir. 1956).

color television. Thus, to say that television was "not in existence" in 1936 was a stretch.

### *i. Bartsch v. Metro-Goldwyn-Mayer*

*Bartsch v. Metro-Goldwyn-Mayer*[17] raised the question whether an assignee of exclusive motion picture rights to a musical play is entitled to authorize the television broadcast of the film based on the musical. In this case, the decision turned on the scope of the rather broad assignment of the right "to copyright, vend, License and exhibit such motion picture photoplays throughout the world."

Unlike the assignment in *Manners v. Morosco*, which was replete with references relating to stage presentations, and nothing more, the court here found that " 'Exhibit' means to 'display' or to 'show' by any method, and nothing in the rest of the grant sufficiently reveals a contrary intention."

The court also distinguished the facts here from those in *Kirk La Shelle*, in which "the new medium was completely unknown at the time when the contract was written."

> During the 1930 the future possibilities of television were recognized by knowledgeable people in the entertainment and motion picture industries, though surely not in the scope it attained. . . . [W]e have found no case holding that an experienced businessman like Bartsch is not bound by the natural implications of the language he accepted when he had reason to know of the new medium's potential.

The court also distinguished *Ettore v Philco Television*, saying "unlike Bartsch, the grantor, Ettore, was not an experienced businessman but a prize fighter, and the Court relied heavily on his lack of sophistication in determining whether it was fair to charge with him knowledge of the new medium."

The court noted the frustrations of trying to determine the intent of the parties with the plaintiff dead and the relevant lawyers having no recollection of the negotiations. "[A]ny effort to reconstruct what the parties actually intended nearly forty years ago is doomed to failure." Rather than attempting to distill decisive meaning out of language that

---

17 *Bartsch v. Metro-Goldwyn-Mayer, Inc.*, 391 F.2d 150 (2d Cir.), *cert. denied*, 393 U.S. 826 (1968).

very likely had none, the court turned to the discussion by Professor Nimmer on a choice between two basic approaches: (a) that a license of rights in a given medium (e.g., "motion picture rights") includes only such uses as fall within the unambiguous core meaning of the term (e.g., exhibition of motion picture film in motion picture theaters) and exclude any uses that lie within the ambiguous penumbra (e.g., exhibition of motion picture film on television) or (b) a licensee may properly pursue any uses that may reasonably be said to fall within the medium as described in the license.

Nimmer preferred the latter approach, and so did the court, which concluded, "If the words are broad enough to cover the new use, it seems fairer that the burden of framing and negotiating an exception would fall on the grantor."

> If the grantor desired to limit the exhibit of the motion picture to the convention method where light is carried from a projector to a screen directly beheld by a viewer, they could have said so. A further reason favoring the broader view in case like this is that it provides a single person who can make the copyrighted work available to the public over the penumbral medium, whereas the narrower one involves the risk that a deadlock between the grantor and the grantee might prevent the work's being shown over the new medium at all.

### *j. Hellman v. Samuel Goldwyn Productions (1970)*

The author Lillian Hellman objected[18] to the televising of a motion picture based on her play, *The Little Foxes*. In 1940, she granted to Goldwyn all motion picture rights in the play, including all sound, musical, and talking motion picture rights, and including the rights "to make, exhibit and market everywhere motion picture trailers sound records . . . using any methods or devices for such purposes whether now or hereafter known or used."

Although the author reserved "television rights direct from living actors," the contract also stated that the studio had the "right to televise (by broadcast, wire, or any other means or methods) motion pictures, sound or silent, based in whole or in part, on the property."

---

[18] *Hellman v. Samuel Goldwyn Productions*, 26b N.Y.2d 175 (1970).

The court had no trouble rejecting the author's claim, being that it was clear from the terms of the contract that the studio had the right to televise the films it made under the contract.

*k. Landon v. Twentieth Century-Fox Film Corp. (1974)*

In 1944, the author Margaret Landon granted to Twentieth Century-Fox motion picture rights to her book, *Anna and the King of Siam*. When in 1972 Fox produced 13 episodes of a weekly serial entitled, *Anna and the King*, she filed suit,[19] claiming her original contract with Fox only granted the right to produce feature length films intended for first exhibition in movie theaters, and not those intended for first exhibition on television.

The court analyzed the broad grant of rights in the contract that it concluded did "not contain or suggest the purported distinction between motion pictures for first exhibition on television and those made for theater presentation." While Landon reserved "the right to broadcast the literary property by television direct from living actors," the court only construed that as evidence that if the author intended to reserve the right make and exhibit filmed television versions, "she and her noted and experienced literary agents, the William Morris Agency, knew how to do so."

*l. Rooney v. Columbia Pictures Industries, Inc. (1982)*

Enter videocassettes. The question whether old licenses applied to new uses appeared in a class action lawsuit lead by the well-known entertainer, Mickey Rooney, against nearly all of the major motion picture studios, including Columbia Pictures, Metro-Goldwyn-Mayer, Paramount Pictures, RKO General, Twentieth Century Fox, United Artists, Universal City Studios, and Warner Bros.[20] The case involved the contracts between the studios and all performers appearing in motion pictures produced or distributed by the studios prior to 1960. The court ruled that the contracts between the performers and the studios, which granted rights to exhibit these films, also gave the studios

[19] *Landon v. Twentieth Century-Fox Film Corp.*, 384 F. Supp. 450 (1974).

[20] *Rooney v. Columbia Pictures Industries, Inc.*, 538 F. Supp. 211 (S.D.N.Y. 1982).

the right to sell videocassettes of the films, without further compensation to the performers.

The court's conclusion was based on the sweeping language of the contracts, which included, for example, the right to "record, reproduce, transmit, exhibit, distribute, and exploit" the films "by any present or future methods or means" and by "any other means now known or unknown." The court concluded that the contracts gave the studios extremely broad rights in the distribution and exhibition of the films, "plainly intending that such rights would be without limitation unless otherwise specified and further indicating that future technological advances in methods of reproduction, transmission, and exhibition would inure to the benefit of [the studios]."

*m. Platinum Record Co. v. Lucasfilm, Ltd. (1983)*

In 1973, Lucasfilm entered into *master use* agreements to acquire the right to use the master recordings of four popular songs (*Almost Grown* and *Johnny B. Goode*, recorded by Chuck Berry; *Book of Love*, recorded by the Monotones; and *Goodnight Sweetheart*, recorded by the Spaniels) for use in the sound track of the motion picture, *American Graffiti*. The licensor contended that the license under which the recordings were granted did not permit the use of the recordings in copies of the film distributed in videocassettes and videodiscs.[21]

The license agreement granted to Lucasfilm the "right to record, dub and synchronize the . . . master recordings, or portions thereof, into and with [the] motion picture and trailers therefor, and to exhibit, distribute, market and perform said motion picture, its air, screen and television trailers, perpetually throughout the world by any means or methods now or hereafter known."

The court ruled in favor of the Lucasfilm and the studio, reasoning that the language in the agreement was "extremely broad and completely unambiguous, and precludes any need in the Agreement for an exhaustive list of specific potential uses of the film. . . . It is obvious that the contract in question may 'fairly be read' to be including newly developed media, and the absence of any specific mention in the Agreement of videotapes and videocassettes is thus insignificant."

[21] *Platinum Record Company, Inc. v. Lucasfilm, Ltd.*, 566 F. Supp. 226 (D.N.J. 1983).

*n. Cohen v. Paramount Pictures Corp. (1988)*

The question whether a synch license permitting the use of music in a motion picture or television program, authorized the reproduction of copies of the music in connection with the distribution of videocassettes of the motion picture or television show, finally became the subject of a lawsuit that was concluded in the Federal Court of Appeals in 1988.[22] Paramount Pictures had just begun the reproduction of videocassettes of the motion picture, *Medium Cool*, when the copyright owner of the song *Merry-Go-Round*, one of the songs contained in the film's soundtrack, filed suit claiming that the old synchronization license to use the song in the motion picture did not grant a license to distribute copies of the song in videocassettes of the motion picture.

The court of appeals considered the scope of a synchronization license, which was not unlike the scope of the licenses described in the preceding section. That license granted to the Paramount:

> . . . the authority . . . to record, in any manner, medium, form or language, the words and music of the musical composition . . . with the motion picture . . . to make copies of such recordings and to perform said musical composition everywhere, all in accordance with the terms, conditions and limitations hereinafter set forth. . . .
>
> The . . . license herein granted to perform . . . said musical composition is granted for:
>
> (a) The exhibition of said motion picture . . . to audiences in motion picture theatres and other places of public entertainment where motion pictures are customarily exhibited . . .
>
> (b) The exhibition of said motion picture . . . by means of television . . . , including "pay television," "subscription television," and "closed circuit into homes' television". . . .

It was undisputed that category (a) of the preceding paragraph could not be construed as authorizing the distribution of videocassettes through the sale and rental to the general public for viewing in their homes. Paramount argued, however, that videogram distribution was covered by category (b), in that the distribution of videocassettes for

---

[22] *Cohen v. Paramount Pictures Corp.*, 845 F.2d 851 (9th Cir. 1988).

showing in private homes was the equivalent of "exhibition by means of television." The court disagreed and ruled that the license did *not* include the distribution of videocassettes for home viewing.

After going to great lengths to describe the technical differences between broadcast television and home videocassette viewing,[23] the court stated that the "primary reason" why the words "exhibition by means of television" in the license cannot be construed as including the distribution of videocassettes for home viewing is that "VCR's were not invented or known in 1969, when the license was executed."

Because videocassettes did not exist when the license was executed, the court reasoned, the licensor must have assumed television exhibition was to be effected by broadcast and the "licensee could not have bargained for, or paid for, the rights associated with videocassette reproduction."

This reasoning, of course, is flawed, because it is simply incorrect to say that the licensee could not have bargained for the rights of use that did not exist or were unknown at the time the license was executed. First, at a later point in its opinion, the court suggested that a party could bargain for a use that was not yet known at the time of the license, as long as the license specifically conferred the right to exhibit the films by methods yet to be invented.[24] This is precisely what the parties are doing when they enter into licenses that are specifically intended to cover uses unknown or not invented at the time the license is executed (e.g., a license for "use in any form or medium, and in any manner, now known or hereafter devised"). To enforce licenses for only those uses that were either known or invented at the time the license is executed would unduly limit the scope of licenses for which parties are otherwise free to bargain.

---

[23] Without concrete evidence of what the intent of the parties was at the time the license was signed, the court compared and contrasted the characteristics of broadcast television and home videocassette viewing in arriving at a meaning and usage of the term, "exhibition by television." Although the court was insightful in pointing to some important differences that would have affected a negotiation had the facts been known, a comparison of the characteristics of these two systems alone does not provide us with the answer to the salient question in these cases: what would the music publishers and producers have actually negotiated had this different use been known to the parties at the time of the license.

[24] See *Cohen*, 845 F.2d at 855.

Second, it is not clear, under the court's reasoning, whether the use must actually be invented or merely known or conceived at the time the license is entered. If the court would require the use to have been invented at the time the license was executed, then what legal doctrine would support the unenforceability of a bargain over a specific use that parties clearly contemplated? There seems to be no reason why a court should not enforce, for example, a license to use music in a holographic motion picture several years before the practicability of holographic movies. If the court would require the use to be "known" at the time the license was executed, who is to say whether a particular use is "known" generally or to a party at any particular point in time? Science fiction books, television shows, and motion pictures present hundreds of examples of uses commonly known long before their actual invention. Finally, contracts often try to cover what is not known and it is not unreasonable to enforce bargains struck between parties over the allocation of unknown or unforeseen risks or contingencies, such as the subsequent development of a new use.

*o. Tele-Pac, Inc. v. Grainger (1992)*

In this case, a state court held that a license to distribute certain motion pictures "broadcasting by television or any other similar device now known or hereafter to be made known" did not encompass the right to distribute the motion pictures by videocassette.[25]

> Transmission of sound and images from a point outside the home for reception by the general public . . . is implicit in the concept of "broadcasting by television." Conversely, while one may speak of "playing," "showing," "displaying," or even perhaps "exhibiting" a videotape, we are unaware of any usage of the term 'broadcasting' in that context.[26]

*p. Bourne Co. v. The Walt Disney Co. (1992)*

Bourne Co., a music publisher that owns the copyright to the song, "*When You Wish Upon A Star*," filed suit against Disney for using the

[25] *Tele-Pac, Inc. v. Grainger*, 168 A.D.2d 11, 570 N.Y.S.2d 521 (1991).
[26] *Id*, 570 N.Y.S.2d at 523.

song in trailer advertisements for the sale of videocassettes of films containing the song.[27]

The license provided to Disney in 1939 stated,

> We hereby grant to you . . . the non-exclusive right to mechanically and/or electrically record the said musical compositions and/or lyrics, if any, in synchronism with any and all of the motion pictures which may be made by you and the right to export such recordings to all of the countries of the world, and the right to give public performances of such recordings in connection with the exhibition of the motion pictures with which said recordings were synchronized. . . . Upon your request we will deliver to you a separate synchronization license duly executed by us in terms as broad as stated in this paragraph.

The court granted Bourne's motion for preliminary injunction on the grounds that Bourne's claim — that synchronized videocassette trailer advertisements are outside the scope of the license — raises at least sufficiently serious questions going to the merits to make them a fair ground for litigation. "Disney is producing videocassettes for home use, and private viewings of home videocassettes are not 'public performances.'"[28]

*q. Brown v. Twentieth Century Fox Film Corp.*

James Brown challenged the use in defendant's movie, "The Commitments," of a 27-second clip of Brown's performance on a television show broadcast in 1965.[29] Prior to performing on the television appearance, Brown signed a release under which he granted a license to use his "acts, poses, plays, and appearances" on the show, and "to exhibit,

---

[27] *Bourne Co. v. The Walt Disney Co.*, 1992 U.S. Dist. LEXIS 9853 (1992), *rev'd on other grounds, Bourne v. Walt Disney Co., v. Tower Records, Inc.*, 976 F.2d 99 (2d Cir. 1992) (holding that the district court gave insufficient weight to Bourne's delay in seeking relief. "Whatever the meaning of the contract, Disney exercised for decades its claimed rights without protest by Bourne.").

[28] See Sec. 17 U.S.C. Sec. 101; *Columbia Pictures Indus., Inc. v. Redd Horne, Inc.*, 749 F.2d 154, 158-160 (3d Cir. 1984) (distinguishing public showcasing of videocassettes from renting or selling videocassettes for home use on ground that only the former is a "public performance").

[29] *Brown v. Twentieth Century Fox Film Corp.*, 799 F. Supp. 166 (D.C. 1992).

transmit, reproduce, distribute, broadcast, and exploit, and license or permit others" to do the same "in connection with all or any portion" of the performance and "in and by all media and means whatsoever."

Brown contended that the above language was ambiguous with respect to whether the grant included the right to use his performances in films, film productions, and videocassettes. The court held that, as a matter of law, the agreement was not reasonably susceptible to Brown's limited interpretation. "The fact that the agreement expressly permits the reproduction and license of a 'portion' of the performance indicates that the contracting parties contemplated the later use of the performance as segments of other larger projects."

In addition, the language, "in and by all media and means whatever" may be fairly read to include release on videocassettes despite their non-existence at the time the agreement was made.

*r. Rey v. Lafferty (1993)*

Margaret Rey, who owned the copyright to the "Curious George" children's books, filed suit for a determination, among other things, that her grant of a license to a production company to produce animated films based on the Curious George character "for television viewing" did not include the right to permit the making and distribution of videocassettes of the films for home distribution.

After reciting the alternative approaches outlined by Nimmer, and referring to the outcomes in *Barscht, Cohen, Rooney, Platinum*, and *Tele-Pac*, discussed above, the court held that the grant of rights to the Curious George films "for television viewing" did *not* encompass the right to distribute the films in videocassettes.[30]

The license, opined the court, contained no general grant of rights in technologies to be developed, and no explicit reference to future methods of exhibition. Though it contained no specific limiting language, such limitation is reasonably inferable from the general tenor in which the "television in viewing" rights were granted. "Television viewing" and "videocassette" viewing are not coextensive terms. Further, the license was drafted by a professional investment firm accustomed to licensing agreements; because, Rey, an elderly woman, does not appear

[30] *Rey v. Lafferty*, 990 F.2d 1379 (1st Cir. 1993).

to have been represented by counsel during the larger part of the transaction, the ambiguities were resolved against the drafter.

While narrowly construing the license at hand, the court made the following observation that should provide licensees some solace:

> The problem becomes particularly acute when the analogous technology develops so rapidly as to supplant the originally contemplated application of the licensed work, rendering the parties' original bargain obsolete. Thus, for example, broad grants of "motion picture rights," made before technological advances permitted the combination of moving images with sound, later were held, typically, to encompass the rights to sound motion picture technology; a narrower holding would have left the original license virtually worthless, despite its broad language, and would have provided the licensor with an undeserved windfall. See, e.g., Murphy, 112 F.2d at 748; L.C. Page & Co. v. Fox Film Corp., 83 F.2d 196 (2d Cir.1936).[31]

*s. Abkco Music, Inc. v. Westminster Music*

In 1966, the U.S.-based music publisher, Abkco Music, copyright holder of certain songs by the Rolling Stones, granted to the U.K.-based music publisher Westminster Music "all rights" to the songs outside the United States and Canada.[32] The question in dispute was whether the "all rights" language conveyed to Westminster the right to issue licenses for the songs on videocassettes and other media that were not in existence when the contract was executed.

In the absence of intent of the parties, the question, said the court, becomes, "in the context of the particular agreement, which party should properly 'reap the . . . windfall associated with the new medium' " (quoting *Cohen v. Paramount Pictures*). The court adopted Nimmer's preferred view that "the licensee may properly pursue any uses which may reasonably said to fall within the medium as described in the license." The windfall would be the licensor's only where the new use was completely unforeseeable and therefore could not possibly have formed part of the bargain between the parties at the time of the original grant (citing *Bartsch*).

---

[31] *Id.* at note 7.

[32] *Abkco Music, Inc. v. Westminster Music*, 838 F. Supp. 153 (S.D.N.Y. 1993).

In this case, Abkco and Westminster were "obviously sophisticated music publishing companies who have issued hundreds if not thousands of licenses and who were fully conversant at the time of the Contract with the pace of technologic change in the music business." The contract, as opposed to the contract at issue in *Bourne*, does contain a grant, however disputed, of "all rights" in the songs.

*t. Bloom v. Hearst Entertainment, Inc. (1994)*

The question before the court in this case[33] was whether the following grant of rights provision included a grant of home video rights in a book:

> The authors hereby grant and assign solely and exclusively to the Publisher throughout the world during the full term of copyright and all renewals thereof on the terms set out in the Agreement, the book and volume publishing rights in the English language throughout the world in [Evidence of Love] along with the following rights: abridgement, syndication, radio broadcasting, television, mechanical recording and rendition, projection, Braille, microfilm, translation, dramatic, and motion pictures; ancillary commercial promotion rights, together with the right to grant licenses for the exercise of and/or to dispose of any or all of the rights granted.

The court held the provision was ambiguous, allowing the court to consider extrinsic evidence of the parties' intent, but found that such evidence overwhelmingly supported an intent to transfer the home video rights in the book.

*u. Maljack Productions, Inc. v. Goodtimes Home Videos (1996)*

In this case, decided by the Fifth Circuit Federal Court of Appeals,[34] a grant of all rights, including the copyrights, in "the music and musical compositions recorded or contained upon the soundtrack of" the motion picture *McLintock*, precluded a later claim by the grantor that a further

[33] *Bloom v. Hearst Entertainment, Inc.*, 33 F.3d 518 (5th Cir. 1994).

[34] *Maljack Productions, Inc. v. Goodtimes Home Video Corp.*, 81 F.3d 881 (5th Cir. 1996).

license was required for the manufacture and sale of videocassettes of the picture.

*v. Boosey & Hawkes v. Buena Vista Home Video (1998)*

In 1939, Igor Stravinsky licensed his orchestral work, *Rites of Spring* to Disney for use in the animated motion picture, "Fantasia."[35] Since the composition was in the public domain in the United States, Disney only needed permission to reproduce and copy the film in countries where the composition was still under copyright. Stravinsky issued a standard worldwide, theatrical synchronization license to Disney for a one-time, flat fee of $6,000. The agreement provided that:

> In consideration of the sum of Six Thousand ($6,000) Dollars, receipt of which is hereby acknowledged, [Stravinsky] does hereby give and grant unto Walt Disney Enterprises, a California corporation . . . the nonexclusive, irrevocable right, license, privilege and authority to record in any manner, medium or form, and to license the performance of, the musical composition hereinbelow set out.

Under the section of the license entitled, "type of use," the agreement specified:

> The music of said musical composition may be used in one motion picture throughout the length thereof or through such portion or portions thereof as the Purchaser shall desire. The said music may be used in whole or in part and may be adapted, changed, added to or subtracted from, all as shall appear desirable to the Purchaser in its uncontrolled discretion. . . . The title "Rites of Spring" or "Le Sacre de Printemps," or any other title, may be used as the title of said motion picture and the name of [Stravinsky] may be announced in or in connection with said motion picture.

The synch license provided further,

> The right to record the musical composition as covered by this agreement is conditioned upon the performance of the musical work

[35] *Boosey & Hawkes Music Publishers, Ltd. v. Buena Vista Home Video*, 145 F.3d 481 (2d Cir. 1998).

> in theatres having valid licenses from the American Society of Composers, Authors and Publishers, or any other performing rights society having jurisdiction in the territory in which the said musical composition is performed.

And finally, it provided,

> . . . the licensor reserves to himself all rights and uses in and to the said musical composition not herein specifically granted.

In 1991, Disney released *Fantasia* on videocassettes, generating within seven years more than $360 million. Stravinsky's successor to the copyright in the composition, music publisher Boosey & Hawkes, filed suit for a declaration that the synch license did not grant rights to Disney to use Rites of Spring in videocassettes for home distribution. The district court agreed with Boosey & Hawkes, but the Second Circuit Court of Appeals reversed. Though the Second Circuit cited *Kohn On Music Licensing* (Third Edition) with approval, we believe it did so for the wrong reason. We criticize the court's holding later in this chapter.

*w. Batiste v. Island Records (1999)*

In 1968, the brothers comprising the group, "David Batiste & the Gladiators," wrote a song called "Funky Soul" and recorded it with the assistance of Isaac Bolden, a music publisher and record producer. The group entered into (1) a recording agreement, under which the group granted to Bolden all rights to the sound recording of "Funky Soul," including the "exclusive, unlimited and perpetual right . . . to manufacture, advertise, sell, lease, license or otherwise dispose of, in any or all fields of use, by any method now or hereafter known, throughout the world, records embodying the performances," and (2) a songwriter agreement under which they granted to Bolton copyright in the song.

Fast forward to 1992, when the musical group, "P.M. Dawn," decided to sample six and one-half seconds of the recording and song, "Funky Soul" as part of the creation of a new recording called "So On and So On." P.M. Dawn's record company obtained permission from Bolton for the use of the sample of the song and recording. In 1995, the Batiste brothers filed suit, claiming that their songwriter and recording agreements did not anticipate nor authorize the digital sampling of the composition and recordings.[36] The court held the grant of the copyright in the composition was “sufficiently broad to include the licensing of a record containing a digital sample of ‘Funky Soul.’ ”

*x. Chambers v. Time Warner, Inc. (2000)*

Members of the groups, The Chambers Brothers, The Coasters, and the Drifters filed suit against their respective record companies, claiming that their original agreements did not include the right to authorize the digital distribution of their recordings and songs.[37] Judge Rakoff found that the language of the recording agreements in question were clear: without limitation, they convey all rights in the recordings to the record companies, including the right to exploit the recordings by any method whatsoever, whether known at the time or hereafter to become known. Having concluded the groups had contractually assigned to the record companies the uses they claimed to have retained, the court dismissed the claims.

*y. Greenfield v. Philles Records (2002)*

In a suit by the singing group, *The Ronettes*, against record producer Phil Spector, the question was whether the artists’ transfer of full ownership rights to the master recordings of their performances carried with it the unconditional right of the producer to distribute those recordings in any technological format. In the absence of an explicit contractual reservation of rights, the court concluded that it did.[38]

*z. Intersport, Inc. v. National Collegiate Athletic Association*

In this case, a state court found that a licensing to a trademark “to advertise, promote, and sell videos” of certain sports programming encompassed the right to distribute content to video-enabled wireless communication devices on demand.[39] Distinguishing *Cohen v.*

[36] *Batiste v. Island Records Inc.*, 179 F.3d 217 (1999).

[37] *Chambers v. Time Warner, Inc.*, 123 F. Supp. 2d 198 (2000).

[38] *Greenfield v. Philles Records, Inc.*, 98 N.Y.2d 562 (2002).

[39] *Intersport, Inc. v. National Collegiate Athletic Association*, 381 Ill. App. 3d 312; 885 N.E. 2d 532 (Ill. 2008).

*Paramount* and *Ray v. Lafferty*, the court determined that operative word used in those cases, "television," is a more specific term than "video."

*aa. Reinhardt v. Wal-Mart Stores, Inc. (2008)*

A member of the punk rock band, The Ramones, sued his record company, Ramones Productions, alleging that the use of the musical compositions he wrote did not include distribution by digital download.[40] Under the recording agreement, Reinhardt granted to Ramones Productions the right to use his compositions "to manufacture, advertise, sell, distribute, lease, license or otherwise use or dispose of the Masters and phonograph records embodying the Masters, in any or all fields of use, by any method now or hereafter known." The agreement defined "phonograph records," as including "all *forms of reproduction* including pre-recorded tapes and discs and electronic video recordings, *now or hereafter known*, manufactured or sold primarily for home use, school use, juke box use or use on means of transportation . . . ."

The court held that the language was clear and unambiguous, clearly authorizing the digital uses employed by the record company.

> The phrase "now or hereafter known," when referring to forms of reproduction, reveals that future technologies are covered by the agreement. This language creates an expansive rather than a restrictive conveyance of rights. It is not reasonable to construe the phrase "all forms" "now or hereafter known" to exclude Defendants' alleged digital download form, which now constitutes a form of reproduction. This unambiguous language forecloses other interpretations and the need to consider extrinsic evidence.

## II. DETERMINING THE SCOPE OF AMBIGUOUS LICENSES — A SUGGESTED APPROACH

All of the above controversies — whether a dramatic license included a license to make silent motion pictures, whether a motion picture license entered into during the silent film era included a license to make "talkies," whether a motion picture synch license included a

[40] *Reinhardt v. Wal-Mart Stores, Inc.*, 547 F. Supp. 346 (2008).

license to broadcast by means of television, whether a motion picture or television synchronization license included a license for home video distribution or Internet streaming or download — have two common basic characteristics: a grant of rights or license to make certain uses and the subsequent development of new uses.

The following approach is intended to provide a practical analysis for determining whether an old grant of a right or license covers a new use, whether or not the new use was contemplated or even conceivable by the parties at the time the grant of right or license was entered into. The first step in determining the scope of such a grant is to determine the type of grant involved: whether the grant was an assignment of copyright, a grant of divisible exclusive rights under copyright, or a grant of a non-exclusive license.

## A. The Type of Grant

The starting point for any analysis of the scope of a grant of rights or license — whether that scope includes any new uses or new technologies that came into being since the date of the grant — is the type of grant involved: (1) a grant of the entire copyright (or a co-owner's interest, or entire or partial percentage thereof, in the undivided copyright), (2) a grant of certain exclusive rights under the copyright, or (3) a grant of a non-exclusive license.

### *1. Grant of Copyright*

The owner of copyright in a work has the exclusive rights to do or authorize any of a number of acts with respect to the work: to reproduce the work in copies, to distribute copies of the work, to prepare derivative works, and to perform the work publicly, among other things.[41] The ownership of a copyright may be transferred to another in whole or in part.[42] A grant of copyright transfers all of the exclusive rights under copyright (i.e., the whole bundle of rights) that an owner of copyright may exercise in the copyright, unless certain exclusive rights under copyright are specifically reserved.

---

[41] 17 U.S.C. Sec. 106.

[42] 17 U.S.C. Sec. 201(d)(1).

Since the grantee of a copyright obtains all of the rights under copyright, except those specifically reserved by the grantor, the courts have taken an expansive view of how the grantee may exercise its rights in light of a later developed technology. Thus, in *Greenfield v. Philles Records*,[43] an artist's grant of full ownership rights in sound recordings under a standard record contract carried with it the unconditional right of the producer to redistribute those performances in any technological format. In *Chambers v. Time Warner*,[44] a grant of rights by an artist to his record company under an exclusive recording agreement permitted all uses, whether known or unknown, at the time the agreement was entered.

Similarly, a songwriter who enters into a standard songwriter agreement, under which he is assigning his copyright to the music publisher, could not restrain his publisher from exercising the publishing rights in later technological uses unless the agreement specifically reserved rights in the applicable uses. The same would be true if the songwriter assigned only a 50% interest in the copyright to the publisher under a standard co-publishing agreement, unless there were specific limitations in the agreement limiting the publisher's right to exercise its co-ownership interest in the copyright. Thus, in *Batiste v. Island Records*,[45] a grant of an entire musical composition, including the right to secure copyright, and all rights whatsoever relating to the copyright, included the right to license the use of the song in a record containing a digital sample of the song.

### *2. Grant of Exclusive Rights Under Copyright*

Not only may a copyright be transferred, in whole or in part, but any of the exclusive rights comprised in a copyright may also be transferred.[46] Thus, one may transfer "the exclusive right to reproduce the work in copies" or "the exclusive right to perform the work publicly." In addition, one may even transfer any subdivision of any of the copyright owner's exclusive rights: thus, for example, an owner may transfer to

[43] See *supra* at footnote 38.
[44] See *supra* at footnote 37.
[45] See *supra* at footnote 36.
[46] 17 U.S.C. Sec. 201(d)(2).

another "the exclusive rights to make copies in the United States," or "the exclusive rights to make copies in the form of videocassettes," or "the exclusive rights to make copies in the form of videocassettes which may be distributed only to public libraries," etc.

The owner of any particular exclusive right is entitled, to the extent of that right, to all of the protection and remedies accorded to the copyright owner by the Copyright Act.[46] This means, among other things, that the transferee of an exclusive right may file copyright infringement actions to stop others from doing what the transferee is entitled to do exclusively. By contrast, the grantee of a non-exclusive license has no right to stop others from engaging in infringement of copyright, a right reserved to the copyright owner or owner of exclusive rights under copyright.

Since the grant of exclusive rights under copyright does not convey the whole bundle of rights that conveyance of copyright instills in a grantee, the courts must proceed to another level of analysis to determine whether the grant of rights was sufficiently broad to cover the new use. The courts might be tempted to give weight to the fact that the grantee received the equivalent of an ownership interest in the copyright, but because exclusive rights under copyrights are infinitely divisible, at some point there is little difference between an exclusive right and a non-exclusive license. (Compare, for example, the exclusive license to broadcast by television a film on the NBC network on Wednesday, July 1, 2012, between the hours of 9pm and 11pm and a non-exclusive license to do the same.)

Thus, where the grant of exclusive rights was broadly worded, the courts had no trouble interpreting the scope of the grant to include the new use. In *L.C. Page & Co. v. Fox Film Corporation*,[47] a grant of "exclusive moving picture rights" in an author's book included both the right to make a silent film adaptation of the book, as well as a "talkie" film adaptation, even though talkies were not commercially available at the time the agreement was entered into. In *Hellman v. Samuel Goldwyn Productions*,[48] a grant of all motion picture rights in a play was construed to include the right to exhibit the resulting theatrical motion

---

[46] *Id.*

[47] 83 F.2d 196 (2d Cir. 1936), *supra* at footnote 13.

[48] 301 N.Y.S. 2d 165 (App. Div. 1969), *supra* at footnote 18.

picture on television. In *Murphy v. Warner Bros.*,[49] a grant of "the exclusive, complete and entire motion picture rights" in the play and "to adapt, change, transpose, and subtract from [the play] . . . to such extent as the purchaser may deem expedient" included the right to make talking motion pictures. In *Bartsch v. Metro-Goldwyn-Mayer, Inc.*,[50] a grant of exclusive motion picture rights to a musical play (i.e., the right "to copyright, vend, License and exhibit such motion picture photoplays throughout the world") entitled the grantee to televise a film based on the licensed musical.

Similarly, in *Landon*, a grant of all motion picture rights included the right to make a new motion picture for first exhibition on television. In *Maljack Prod. v. GoodTimes Home Video Corp.*,[51] an unconditional grant of motion picture music rights included the right to synchronize music in videocassette format.

In *Abkco v. Westminster*,[52] a grant of "all rights" to songs outside the United States and Canada was construed to convey to the grantee the right to issue licenses for the songs on videocassettes and other media that were not in existence when the contract was executed.

### *3. Grant of a Non-Exclusive License*

When a copyright owner grants a non-exclusive license, he is not granting any rights that are the equivalent of ownership rights, but is simply providing permission to the grantee to engage in an activity that would otherwise constitute an infringement of the owner's copyright. The considerations here are much the same as in the case of grants of exclusive rights.

Where the license was broadly worded, the courts are inclined to permit the licensee to engage in a use that was neither contemplated nor technologically feasible at the time the license was entered into. Thus, in *Rooney v. Columbia Pictures Industries, Inc.*,[53] an actor's agreement permitting a film studio to "record, reproduce, transmit,

---

[49] *Murphy v. Warner Bros. Pictures*, 112 F.2d 746 (9th Cir. 1940), *supra* at footnote 14.

[50] 391 F.2d 150 (2d Cir. 1968), *supra* at footnote 17.

[51] 81 F.3d 881 (9th Cir. 1996), *supra* at footnote 34.

[52] 538 F. Supp. 211 (S.D.N.Y. 1982), *aff'd*, 714 F.2d 117 (2d Cir. 1982), *supra* at footnote 20.

[53] *Supra* at foornote 32.

exhibit, distribute, and exploit" films, containing the actors performances, "by any present or future methods or means" and by "any other means now known or unknown" was deemed extremely broad, "plainly intending that such rights would be without limitation unless otherwise specified and further indicating that future technological advances in methods of reproduction, transmission, and exhibition would inure to the benefit of [the studios]."

In *Platinum Record Co.*,[54] a master use license to use four popular sound recordings for use in the sound track of the motion picture "and to exhibit, distribute, market and perform said motion picture, its air, screen and television trailers, perpetually throughout the world by any means or methods now or hereafter known," was deemed broad enough to permit the use of the recordings in copies of the film distributed in videocassettes and videodiscs.

In *Brown*,[55] a release under which an entertainer granted a license to use his "acts, poses, plays, and appearances" on a television program, and "to exhibit, transmit, reproduce, distribute, broadcast, and exploit, and license or permit others" to do the same "in connection with all or any portion" of the performance and "in and by all media and means whatsoever" was deemed fairly read to include release on videocassettes despite their non-existence at the time the agreement was made.

In the absence of broad, unambiguous language that would cover a use, whether the use was contemplated or even conceivable at the time the license was entered into, the court must step to the next level of analysis.

By the same token, since the copyright owner reserved to itself all of the exclusive rights under copyright not subject to the grant, some consideration might be given to the effect of the grantee's exercises of rights with respect to the new use on the rights retained by the copyright owner.

## B. The Language of the Grant

In determining the scope of an old license a court would first look to the language of the license itself. As was stated at the outset, some grants are clear and some are ambiguous. It is established law that a

[54] *Platinum Record Company, Inc. v. Lucasfilm, Ltd.*, 566 F. Supp. 226 (D.N.J. 1983), *supra* at footnote 21.

[55] *Brown v. Twentieth Century Fox Film Corp.*, 799 F. Supp. 166 (1992), *supra* at footnote 29.

written agreement that is complete, clear, and unambiguous on its face must be enforced according to the plain meaning of its terms. For example, we have shown a number of grants that clearly include new uses, new technologies, and new forms of distribution by virtue of the broad wording of the grant — either an assignment of copyright that does not expressly reserve the new use, a grant of exclusive rights, such as "all motion picture rights," or grants of licenses that include the right to use the work "in any form or medium, and in any manner, now known or hereafter devised."

Such broadly worded grants should not become the subject of hotly contested litigation. Thus, a license permitting the recording of the music in synchronism with a specified motion picture "for use in any form or medium, and in any manner, now known or hereafter devised" does not admit to much ambiguity, without some further qualification, would clearly include a license to reproduce the motion picture for distribution in home video devices[56] and in connection with on-demand streams and downloads over the Internet.[57] This would be true regardless of whether the technologies existed, or were not even conceived of, at the time the license was entered into.

As we have also seen, a license stating that it "does not grant to Producer the right to manufacture or duplicate said motion picture by means of audio-television devices or contrivances, such as cassettes, discs or other similar configurations (herein called 'cassettes'), for the purpose of selling such cassettes to the public" should not give rise to a dispute about home video distribution. The music publisher unambiguously reserved home video device rights.

Not all grants of rights have been so straightforward. Where a grant is ambiguous, the courts have preceded to the next step in the analysis: evidence of intent of the parties.

## C. Evidence of Specific Intent of the Parties

Where the terms of the agreement are ambiguous, courts will normally permit the parties to a lawsuit to introduce evidence that falls outside the "four corners" of the document to aid in the interpretation of

[56] See *Brown v. Twentieth Century Fox Film Corp.*, 799 F. Supp. 166 (1992), *supra* at footnote 29.

[57] See *Reinhardt v. Wal-Mart Stores, Inc.*, 547 F. Supp. 356 (2008), *supra* at footnote 40.

ambiguous provisions. Such evidence might include letters and testimony of the parties reflecting their intent at the time the license was entered into. However, evidence of the intent of the parties to a license entered 50 years ago might prove difficult to find, particularly as many old synchronization licenses were issued on standard forms and signed without negotiation of their terms with the possible exception of price and territory.

### D. Where No Clear Specific Intent of the Parties Is Evident

This is where the trouble begins. Where no clear intent of the parties is evident, the courts and commentators have struggled to find legal regime upon which to base the resolution of disputes over the scope of an old license in light of new technologies.

In the absence of specific intent of the parties, as evidenced by contemporary documents, letters, and testimony, one court suggested an enquiry "to identify any indicia of mutual *general* intent to apportion rights to 'new uses,' insofar as such general intent can be discerned from the language of the license, the surrounding circumstances, and trade usage."[58]

In *Abkco*, the court suggested that "Where such general intent cannot be discerned from the language of the contract, or from the surrounding circumstances and trade usage, courts have resorted, as the First Circuit notes, to either of the two approaches canvassed by *Nimmer.*"[59] In such cases, as the court noted in *Rey*:

> . . . the very fact that we are most often dealing with a later developed technological process . . . suggests that the parties' ambiguous phraseology masks an absence of intent rather than a hidden intent which the court simply must "find." *Nimmer* § 10.10[B] at 10-85 (quoted in *Rey*, 990 F.2d at 1387).
>
> . . . Given an absence of intent by the parties, it does not automatically follow, as a mechanical application of the *La Shelle* language would have it, that future uses should necessarily be precluded.

---

[58] *ABKCO Music, Inc. v. Westminster Music Ltd.*, 838 F. Supp. 153 (1993), quoting *Rey v. Lafferty*, 990 F.2d 1379, 1387-1391 (1st Cir. 1993), *cert. denied*, 126 L. Ed. 2d 61 (1993), and citing *Rooney v. Columbia Pictures Inds., supra*.

[59] See *Rey*, 990 F.2d at 1387-1388.

> Rather, the allocation of the risks and rewards of unforeseen "new uses" to one party or another becomes an issue of policy which it is the responsibility of the courts to decide. The question becomes: In the context of the particular agreement, which party should properly "reap the . . . windfall" associated with the new medium?

Nimmer proposed the issue as a choice between two basic approaches: (a) that a license of rights in a given medium (e.g., "motion picture rights") includes only such uses as fall within the unambiguous core meaning of the term (e.g., exhibition of motion picture film in motion picture theaters) and exclude any uses that lie within the ambiguous penumbra (e.g., exhibition of motion picture film on television) or (b) a licensee may properly pursue any uses that may reasonably be said to fall within the medium as described in the license. Nimmer preferred the latter approach and the courts have generally agreed. "If the words are broad enough to cover the new use, it seems fairer that the burden of framing and negotiating an exception would fall on the grantor."[60]

The problem with the Nimmer approach is what real help does it provide the parties or a court in determining the policy question of the "allocation of the risks and rewards of unforeseen 'new uses' to one party or another"? It doesn't. In fact, the application of the approach has been used to reach unfortunate conclusions, such as that in *Boosey*, discussed below. In *Bartsch*, the Nimmer approach led Judge Friendly to repeat the bizarre statement that Nimmer's narrow "rule" is appropriate only in cases in which the parties

> ". . . could not know of the invention's existence . . ." and in which, in addition, the possibility of such not-yet-developed uses "could not possibly have formed part of the bargain between the parties," citing *Rey*, 990 F.2d at 1388.

If non-existent uses could not possibly have formed part of the bargain between the parties, then how would he explain the courts' frequent inclusion of non-existent technologies in the scope of grant where, for example, the grant is of the entire copyright or a license that includes all uses "now known or hereafter devised"? Clearly,

---

[60] *Bartsch v. Metro-Goldwyn-Mayer*, 391 F.2d 150 (2d Cir. 1968).

non-existent, even inconceivable, uses have and can always become part of the bargain.

Judge Friendly in *Bartsch* and the First Circuit in *Rey*, however, did strike at the heart of the matter by at least referring to what could or could not have "formed part of the bargain" between the parties — because that is where the courts are most likely to find the answer they are looking for in these cases.

It is submitted, therefore, that the issue in these cases will be best approached, not by an empty rule as to whether a use may "reasonably be said to fall within the medium" described by the license, but by *an inquiry into the bargain originally reached by the parties*. As the courts have said, in the absence of intent of the parties, the court should attempt "to identify any indicia of mutual *general* intent to apportion rights to 'new uses,' insofar as such general intent can be discerned from the language of the license, the surrounding circumstances, and trade usage."[61]

Thus, in making this inquiry into the bargain, the court should seek to determine the following: What would the parties have likely bargained if they had foreseen the subsequent development of the new use at the time the license was entered into? In other words, how would they have allocated the risk of an unforeseen use, had they actually foreseen it at the time they made the original bargain?

By focusing on the bargain — and the parties expectations at the time of the grant — the courts will have a far better chance of justly determining who gets to "reap the windfall" of the unforeseen new use.

In the following section, we will look at three examples of whether the ambiguous language of an old grant covered a new use not specifically contemplated by the parties at the time of the grant.

### 1. Whether an Old Theatrical Synchronization License Permits Distribution in Videocassettes, DVDs, and Other Home Video Devices?

In determining whether an old synch license permits the distribution of a motion picture containing the licensed song in the form of

---

[61] *ABKCO Music, Inc. v. Westminster Music Ltd.*, 838 F. Supp. 153 (1993), quoting *Rey v. Lafferty*, 990 F.2d 1379, 1387-1391 (1st Cir. 1993), *cert. denied*, 126 L. Ed. 2d 61 (1993), and citing *Rooney v. Columbia Pictures Inds., supra*.

videocassettes or DVDs, the court should inquire what would the motion picture producer and the music publisher have done at the time they entered into the synch license, their bargain, had each known about the potential market for distributing films in home video devices.

### *a. Expectations of the Licensee/Motion Picture Producer — What would he have done?*

In determining what bargain the licensee would likely have struck had he foreseen the new use at the time the parties entered into the license, it may be well to ask (a) whether the licensor's unfettered exercise of its exclusive right to the new use would impair the licensee's use under the grant or (b) whether the licensee's exercise of the license would be impaired by the failure to obtain a license for the new use?

#### (1) Would the Music Publisher's Exercise of Its Exclusive Right to the New Use Impair the Studio's Use Under the Old License?

As a matter of custom and practice, theatrical synchronization licenses are nearly all issued on a non-exclusive basis. In other words, there is almost never a restriction on how a music publisher may license the same song in the future. They may issue other theatrical synch licenses and may even issue a synch license to the same song for use in two motion pictures on the same subject or to be released in the same time frame. Under these circumstances, it would be hard to imagine how a film producer's expectations would be thwarted by virtue of the licensor's exercise of its rights in the song, as the issuance of the old synch license did not likely impose any restriction on the music publisher's exercise of its rights in the song. By virtue of the non-exclusive nature of the license, the licensee fully expected that the music publisher could and would grant other licenses for similar uses to other potential licensees. Accordingly, no action by the publisher to grant permission to others to record the same music in other motion pictures, regardless of the media, such as videocassettes, should produce any unexpected result or unjust affect on the film producer's original use.

Thus, had both parties known and considered the new use at the time they were negotiating the license agreement, the fact that the music publisher retained unfettered right to issue licenses in the song for purpose of any new use (e.g., talkies, television, home video devices), would have had no bearing on what the licensee would have bargained for at the time, as it would have been extremely unlikely that the licensee would have been able to bargain for a limitation on the music publisher's exercise of its rights to license the song for new uses.

Contrast this with the grant of exclusive dramatization rights by the author of novel *Ben Hur* to a producer of stage plays, which the Supreme Court held did not by its terms grant the right to produce and distribute motion picture versions of the novel.[62] The retention by the author of the exclusive right to grant motion picture versions of the novel was considered a potential impairment of the exclusive license received by the licensee. The author, by retaining the ability to authorize the inexpensive exhibition of motion pictures based on the novel, could reduce the income of the producer of the stage version. Since the play producer was granted an exclusive right to produce the plays, Justice Oliver Wendell Holmes concluded that, under such circumstances, the licensor had an obligation not to impair the licensee's rights to produce the plays, which the court found that motion picture exhibition would do. Accordingly, the Supreme Court enjoined the defendant from producing motion picture versions of the novel, but also enjoined the plaintiff author from authorizing motion picture versions for the duration of the defendant's license to produce and exhibit the plays.

Suppose a music publisher's synchronization license granted a licensee the exclusive right to use a song (perhaps, *A Bicycle Built for Two*) in connection with advertisements of bicycles and, during the term of the license, the motorcycle was invented. Would the old license cover the licensee's use of the song to promote motorcycles? A court could go to great lengths to compare and contrast a bicycle and a motorcycle (see *Cohen*[63]), but at the end of the day, the grant by the publisher to the same song to a competitor of the licensee who manufactures and sells motorcycles — to the extent they are, or were in their day, competitive modes of travel — would clearly impair the first licensee's expectations under the license.

This would not be the end of the analysis, but it does have some bearing on the following question: had the licensee known about motorcycles at the time the old license was entered into, would he have

[62] *Kalem Co. v. Harper Bros.*, 222 U.S. 55 (1911).

[63] *Cohen v. Paramount Pictures Corp.*, 845 F. 2d 851 (981 Cir. 1988), *supra* at footnote 22.

bargained for an extension of the license to cover the new technology? The answer is probably, yes. Would the music publisher have denied extending the scope of the license to include motorcycles? Unless there were some extenuating circumstances (e.g., the publisher previously granted a license to use the song in advertisements for automobiles), the answer is probably, no.

Under such circumstances, a court would be within its authority, in the absence of specific intent of the parties, "to identify any indicia of mutual *general* intent to apportion rights to 'new uses,' insofar as such general intent can be discerned from the language of the license, the surrounding circumstances, and trade usage."[64] In this case, a ruling that the synchronization license for bicycles could rightly be construed as including motorcycles.

### (2) Would the Studio's Exercise of the License Be Impaired by the Failure to Obtain a License for the New Use?

Upon the advent of television, it was feared (briefly) that all movies in the future would be exhibited on television, rather than in theaters. History repeated itself when, upon the advent of home video devices, it was feared (briefly) that all movies would be delivered by videocassettes sold in or rented from retail stores — that is, they would replace both theatrical and television exhibition of movies. Under such circumstances, it could be said that motion picture producers faced the possibility that their films could not be distributed at all unless they expanded the scope of the license to include television, and later, home video devices.

As history has taught us, however, television did not cause the demise of theatrical exhibition and home video distribution has not caused the demise of either theatrical exhibition or television. But suppose, however, they did. Suppose home video distribution substantially cannibalized theatrical and television exhibition.

The music publisher would assert that, even though the old use, theatrical or television exhibition may no longer be lucrative, the producer still has the license to continue using the music for the originally licensed uses, however outmoded they may have become. The

[64] *ABKCO Music, Inc. v. Westminster Music Ltd.*, 838 F. Supp. 153 (1993), quoting *Rey v. Lafferty*, 990 F.2d 1379, 1387-1391 (1st Cir. 1993), *cert. denied*, 126 L. Ed. 2d 61 (1993), and citing *Rooney v. Columbia Pictures Inds., supra*.

unforeseen risk at the time the license was executed was not only that a particular new use may eventually come into existence, but that a new use would be devised that changes the economics of motion picture distribution. The question here is, who was in a better position to assume the risk that a new distribution medium would arise that affects the economics of motion picture distribution? A court could properly place that risk at the foot of the motion picture producers, and not music publishers or songwriters.

On the other hand, if the music publisher's expectations were otherwise being met by home video distribution, then why would the publisher have withheld the rights to home video distribution at the time it issued the synch license? As will be shown in the next section, the music publisher's expectations were not being met by home video distribution and would not likely have included home video distribution as part of the bargain.

### *b. Expectations of the Music Publisher — What would he have done?*

In determining what bargain would likely have been struck by the parties had they foreseen the new use at the time they entered into the license, it may be well to ask (a) whether the motion picture producer's exercise of its exclusive right to the new use would impair the music publisher's unfettered use of the song or (b) whether the music publisher's expectations of his bargain be impaired by the motion picture producer's new use?

#### (1) Would the Producer's Exercise of Its License of the Song for the New Use Impair the Music Publisher's Exclusive Rights in the Song?

In determining what the music publisher would likely have done had he foreseen the new use at the time he issued the license, it may be useful to ask whether the film producer's exercise of the new use (i.e., making and distributing videogram copies for home use) under the old license without paying additional compensation to the music publisher would impair the publisher's ability to exercise its exclusive right to the new use (i.e., to license to others the recording of his music in home video devices)?

Construing an old synchronization license as granting a license to make videocassette reproductions without further compensation would not impair the music publisher's ability to exercise his right to license his music for use on other videocassettes. It may impair the copyright owner's ability to grant a license to use the song in videocassettes on an *exclusive* basis, but rarely is a copyright owner inclined to grant such exclusivity.

#### (2) Would the Producer's Exercise of the License Impair the Music Publisher's Expectations of Compensation from the Old License?

If the music publisher did not contemplate the new use at the time the old license was executed, then it could be said he would not have had an expectation of deriving income from the producer for the new use. But this is not universally the case. It is probably true that the motion picture producers who procured synchronization licenses expected to pay a one-time flat fee and never expected to have to go back to the licensor again for a license to distribute his film by whatever means. But it is not equally true that the copyright owners had no expectations beyond the one time fees they received.

It appears from the face of the old synchronization licenses that a principal concern of the music copyright owners was that, for whatever use was to be permitted, there be some mechanism in place to collect performance fees (e.g., through ASCAP or BMI) on all exhibitions or broadcasts of the work containing the musical composition. This was the mechanism by which the music copyright owners could participate in the economic success of the works containing their music. The flat fee required under the synchronization license simply could not serve this purpose. The performance fees, collected on performances occurring at the time the film is exhibited in theaters or on television, were expected *in addition* to the flat synchronization fee required for the privilege to make the copies of the motion pictures necessary for distribution.

So important was the requirement that performance fees be collected on performances of works for which the synchronization of their music was licensed, it seems clear that if there were no mechanism for the collection of fees for the performance of the music, music copyright owners would not have granted the license to synchronize the music in copies — at least not without negotiating some mechanism to collect compensation based upon the success of the work in which the music appeared.

Because the distribution of motion pictures in videocassette form deprives the music copyright owner of his expected additional compensation from theatrical and television performances, synchronization licenses that are silent or ambiguous as to their coverage of such distribution should not be construed as including the distribution of the videocassettes and other devices used for home viewing.

The copyright law provides the copyright owner with the exclusive right of *public* performance and it is on *public* performances that performance rights societies collect license fees on behalf of copyright owners. The exhibition of a videocassette at home is a *private* performance. Since none of the distribution, sale, rental, or home performance of videocassettes involves a public performance, there is no public performance upon which a performance fee can be based. When the original synchronization licenses were issued for a flat fee, music copyright owners anticipated that fees to be later collected for the public performances of the works containing their music would afford a means by which the copyright owner could participate in the economic success of the work in which his music was included. The more popular the motion picture, the more it would be exhibited and the more performance royalties would accrue to the copyright owner of the music.

Prior to 1948, when performance rights societies in the United States, such as BMI and ASCAP, began to be made subject to court ordered consent decrees, music copyright owners were entitled to fees from the performance of their music in motion picture theaters located in the United States and overseas. The consent decrees changed this by requiring music copyright owners to issue licenses to permit producers and their distributors to perform their music in motion picture theaters located in the United States. This performance license was required to be issued at the same time the copyright owner issued the license to synchronize their music in copies for theatrical distribution. In practice, the license to perform the music in U.S. theaters was included in the same document as the synchronization license and the copyright owner typically charged the same one-time flat fee, in effect doubling the fee normally charged for the synchronization license. The consent decrees are still in effect today.

Despite the consent decrees' effectively eliminating the music copyright owner's ability to share in the success of U.S. theatrical performances of motion pictures containing their music, music copyright owners still expected the payment of performance fees for performances of music in theaters outside the United States (and the jurisdiction of the American courts which imposed the consent decree) as well as for performances that occurred on broadcast television. The requirement that copyright owners include a license (for a flat fee) for the public performance of music in motion picture U.S. theaters did not apply to television exhibition and exhibition in theaters outside the United States, for which the performing rights societies do collect performance fees to this day.

Not only is the music copyright owner unable to share in the success of motion pictures distributed by videocassette (because virtually all performances of videocassettes are private, not public, performances), but to the extent the home videocassette performances of motion pictures, for which no public performance payment is collected by ASCAP or BMI, replaces broadcast television performances and international theatrical exhibition, for which ASCAP and BMI fees are collected, the performance revenue that the copyright owner anticipated when he granted the old synchronization license actually decreases.

Accordingly, the advent of home video distribution on videocassettes and laserdiscs of motion pictures containing copyrighted music seriously affects the expectations that the copyright owner was likely to have had at the time of entering the old synchronization license. If the music copyright owner had known of this new development at the time the license was executed, an alternative to performance fees would probably have been developed to ensure the music copyright owner with some ability to share in the success of the motion pictures in which their music was used. The kinds of mechanisms that most likely would have evolved would probably have been like those that have recently emerged since the advent of the videogram market, such as royalties or additional buy-out fees, as are illustrated by the provisions contained at the end of Chapter 15, on *Licensing Music in Audiovisual Works.*

The one historical anomaly that producers can point to that would appear to belie the music copyright owners' expectations of a share in the economic success in the exploitation of motion pictures containing their music is that music publishers never objected when producers licensed non-theatrical 16mm rights to independent distributors. Either publishers expected that these films were primarily intended for performance in establishments licensed by ASCAP and BMI, such as non-exempt schools and libraries, or that the revenues from the sales of 16mm films to individuals for private performances were just too small to notice. It would seem unjust to construe a waiver — perhaps under estoppels or laches — of rights in fees not high enough to justify litigation as a waiver of rights to fees that do.

Another principal of contract interpretation is that an ambiguous document is interpreted against the party who drafted it. This is because the drafter was in a better position to avoid the ambiguity by being more precise in his employment of language in the document, thus providing an incentive for drafters to be precise. Since most of these old synchronization license forms were drafted by music publishers and their representatives, there is an argument that they were in a better position to prevent the ambiguity by being more precise in their use of terms such as "exhibition on television."

On the other hand, the music publishers could take the position that the producers of the motion pictures were in a better position to predict what potential forms of distribution could be made of their films and if they could have foreseen these new forms of distribution, they should have informed the music publishers of the potential new use at the time the license was entered into, which could have lead to a negotiated allocation based upon a full disclosure of information.

#### c. *Analysis of Decision in* **Boosey & Hawkes v. Disney** — *What should the court have done?*

When faced with precisely the question at hand, the Second Circuit Court of Appeals seems to have got it wrong.[65]

Recall that in *Boosey*, Igor Stravinsky in 1939 licensed his orchestral composition, *Rites of Spring* to Disney for use in the animated film, "Fantasia." Stravinsky issued a standard worldwide, theatrical synchronization license to Disney for a one-time, flat fee of $6,000.

In 1991, Disney released *Fantasia* on videocassettes, generating within seven years more than $360 million. Stravinsky's successor to the copyright in the composition, music publisher Boosey & Hawkes,

[65] *Boosey & Hawkes v. Buena Vista Home Video*, 145 F.3d 481 (2d Cir. 1998), *supra* at footnote 35.

filed suit for a declaration that the synch license did not grant rights to Disney to use *Rites of Spring* in videocassettes for home distribution. The district court agreed with Boosey & Hawkes, but the Second Circuit Court of Appeals reversed.

The Second Circuit's decision demonstrated precisely what could go wrong when the courts try to blindly follow a rule of construction rather than engage in a substantive analysis of the original bargain struck by the parties in the context of the new use. Thus, applying the rule suggested by Nimmer, and followed by *Bartsch*, the court reached the wrong result.

As the Second Circuit formulated the rule, "Bartsch holds that . . . when a license includes a grant of rights that is reasonably read to cover a new use (at least where the new use was foreseeable at the time of contracting), the burden of excluding the new use will rest with the grantor." The court then held that "The license 'to record in any manner, medium or form' doubtless extends to videocassette recording and we can see no reason why the grant of 'motion picture' reproduction rights should not include the video format, absent any indication in the Agreement to the contrary."

Acknowledging that its conclusion was not a happy one for an author-licensor who was being forced to be content with the $6,000 it collected in 1939, in face of ruling for a large media company who reaped over $360 million from sales of videocassettes to which the *Rites of Spring* was a substantial contribution, the court leaned on what it termed, "neutral principals of contract interpretation rather than solicitude for either party."

But in doing so, the court turned a blind eye to the intent of the parties:

> Although contract interpretation normally requires inquiry into the intent of the contracting parties, . . . intent is not likely to be helpful when the subject of the inquiry is something the parties weren't thinking about. See Nimmer, § 10.10[B] at 10-90 (noting that usually "there simply was no intent at all at the time of execution with respect to . . . whether the grant includes a new use developed at a later time.")

But it was simply not the case that the parties "weren't thinking about" the use in question. Granted, the parties may not have been thinking about the specific use of videocassettes for home distribution, but the parties clearly and unequivocally struck a bargain that contemplated just how they would have dealt with the use had they actually contemplated it at the time.

That intent was embodied in what the court referred to as the ASCAP Condition:

> The right to record the musical composition as covered by this agreement is conditioned upon the performance of the musical work in theatres having valid licenses from the American Society of Composers, Authors and Publishers, or any other performing rights society having jurisdiction in the territory in which the said musical composition is performed.

While the district court found this provision dispositive — holding that it prevented Disney from distributing the film by means other than to theaters having a performance license from ASCAP or other performing rights society, perhaps too strict an interpretation — the Second Circuit interpreted the provision in a way that defies custom and practice in the entertainment industry:

> Read literally, this language requires no more of Disney than that it expose the motion picture in two or more ASCAP-certified theaters, a condition long ago satisfied. Whatever may have been the interpretation, the ASCAP Condition does not unambiguously prohibit Disney from exhibiting the composition in non-ASCAP theaters, or from distributing the film directly to consumers.

"Whatever may have been the interpretation?" It's quite clear what the interpretation was to anyone familiar with synch licensing back in 1939 or today and the authors described that interpretation in the 2d Edition of *Kohn On Music Licensing*:

> It appears from the face of the old synchronization licenses that a principal concern of the music copyright owners was that, for whatever use was to be permitted, there be some mechanism in place to collect performance fees (e.g., through ASCAP or BMI) on all exhibitions or broadcasts of the work containing the musical composition. This was the mechanism by which the music copyright owners could participate in the economic success of the works containing their music. The flat fee required under the synchronization license simply could not serve this purpose. The performance fees, collected on performances occurring at the time the film is exhibited in theatres or on television, were expected *in addition* to the flat synchronization fee required for the privilege to make the copies of the motion pictures necessary for distribution.

The court quoted our treatise, but missed our point:

> Furthermore, we learn from a leading treatise on music licensing that this very clause was industry boilerplate that appeared in "countless synchronization licenses" for U.S. films. Al Kohn & Bob Kohn, *Kohn on Music Licensing*, 838-40, 857-58 (2d ed. 1996). If the clause meant what Boosey contents, studios whose films included copyrighted works licensed with this boilerplate provision would be completely prohibited from showing their films at all in the United States in the event that U.S. movie theaters ceased to employ ASCAP licenses.

The court's reasoning was based on the false premise that the lower court's ruling in fact would have gone so far as rescinding the bargain made by the studios — a $6,000 payment for the exhibition of the film in theaters. It didn't. The bargain was: "I'll grant you a synch fee on a flat fee basis, provided I participate in the economic success of Fantasia." The way Stravinsky and all publishers achieve that objective in their license agreements is either the collection of a performance fee whenever the recording or movie is performed or a royalty whenever a copy of the recording or movie is sold.

Thus, the bargain that Stravinsky entered into was to grant the right to synch the song with the movie for a one-time flat fee, on condition that he has the opportunity to participate in the success of the film by participating in a share of public performance fees the film generates. That was the clear meaning of the ASCAP Condition. When ASCAP lost the right under its consent decree to license motion picture theaters in the United States, *Disney would still have been able to exhibit its film in theaters*. Stravinsky, as a result of actions by his performance right society, lost the right to collect for such uses, but that has nothing to do with the bargain he reached with Disney in 1939.

As Boosey & Hawkes explained to the court, Disney's right to "record" — that is, to make copies of — the song, in whatever "manner, medium, or form," was specifically conditioned on the film being exhibited in theaters having a performance license — the customary means by which songwriters share in the commercial success of the films in which their compositions are licensed. To suggest that the ASCAP Condition was included to guarantee that the film was exhibited in at least two theaters licensed by a performance rights society is ludicrous; to ignore the clear intent of the provision was a miscarriage of justice.

Videocassette distribution circumvents the need for public performances and the public performance income that Stravinsky bargained for. But it was clear what the bargain was: a $6,000 one-time flat fee to record the song in any medium, plus a right to collect fees reflecting the economic success of the movie. In the case of videocassettes and DVDs, that intent would be fulfilled by a royalty on every copy sold. Either the videocassette use should not have been deemed included in the scope of the 1939 synch license or the courts should have recognized the intent of the ASCAP Condition and granted a reasonable royalty for each copy of the videocassette sold.

By the same token, should Disney have desired to broadcast the film on television, then Disney would have had to obtain a license to do so from Stravinsky, because the original synchronization license was clearly limited to exhibition in theaters. Disney certainly knew about television in 1939 and could have obtained a license at that time to televise the film. The fact that Disney produced evidence to the court that it, without seeking Stravinsky's permission, televised the film numerous times, is not, as the court found, evidence supporting Disneys' interpretation of the license.

On the contrary, the fact that Stravinsky made no objection to the television should have been viewed as direct evidence *supporting* Stravinsky's interpretation of the license, and specifically the intent of the ASCAP Condition. Why would Stravinsky object, and why would Disney think there would be a problem with televising the movie, when each knew that Stravinsky would be getting precisely what he bargained for in the license: performance royalty income whenever the film was televised — precisely what he bargained for in 1939. The court was grossly mistaken to confuse this with evidence that Stravinsky would have no objection to videocassette distribution, which the court knew would produce no additional revenue to Stravinsky, and perhaps reduce potential public performance fees from the televising of the film.

### 2. *Whether an Old Theatrical Synchronization License Permits Distribution in On-Demand Streaming or Download Over the Internet?*

Upon the advent of television, it was feared (for several years) that all movies in the future would be exhibited on television, rather than in theaters. History repeated itself when, upon the advent of home video devices, it was feared (for several years) that all movies would be delivered by videocassettes sold in or rented from retail stores — that is, they would replace both theatrical and television exhibition of movies. Under such circumstances, it could be said that motion picture producers faced the possibility that their films could not be distributed at all unless they expanded the scope of the license to include television, and later, home video devices. By the same token, if the old licenses were not broad enough for streaming and downloading on the Internet, the same fear that they had before would be repeated: without music licenses, the exercise of the license they thought they had received years ago would be impaired.

As history has taught us, television did not cause the demise of theatrical exhibition and home video distribution has not caused the demise of either theatrical exhibition or television. Nor is Internet downloading or streaming likely to cause the demise of any of these older means of entertainment delivery, but it could impair them.

As we have seen, when an old synch license is unambiguous — whether it provides a license to reproduce and distribute the work in any form or means now known or hereafter devised or clearly circumscribes or limits the use — little controversy as to the scope of the license should arise. But where a license is ambiguous, what can we say about the scope of the license and licensee's desire to effect on-demand streaming or downloading over the Internet?

In the absence of clear evidence of intent as to what the parties would have done had they foreseen the new use, it is suggested that the decision as to whether an old license covered a new use should depend upon an analysis of the likely expectations of the parties at the time the license was executed.

Thus, under its synch license from Stravinsky, does Disney have the right to authorize on-demand streams or digital downloads of *Fantasia* without further payment to Boosey & Hawkes? As before, Stravinsky's bargain was to provide a synch license for a flat fee on condition that there be a mechanism for him to participate in the economic success of the work — as evidenced by the ASCAP Condition. In the case of on-demand streaming, Stravinsky would have negotiated a condition that *Fantasia* be streamed only where public performance fees are collected by ASCAP. As for downloads, where the public performance right may not necessarily be involved, his bargain would have included a royalty as a means to participate in the success of the film.

### 3. *Whether a Grant of Exclusive Rights to Reproduce and Distribute a Book Includes the Right to Reproduce and Distribute eBooks?*

In 1967, Kurt Vonnegut, author of a number of literary works, granted to his publisher, Random House, the exclusive right to "print, publish and sell the work in book form."[66] In addition, he granted to Random House the "exclusive right to publish and license the Work for publication, after book publication . . . in anthologies, selections, digests, abridgements, magazines condensations, serializations, newspaper syndication, picture book versions, microfilming, Xerox and other forms of copying, either now in use or hereinafter developed." Vonnegut reserved for himself the "dramatic . . . motion picture (silent and sound) . . . radio broadcasting (including mechanical renditions and or recordings of the text) . . . [and] television rights."

In 2000, Vonnegut licensed to Rosetta Books the right to publish several of his books in digital format over the Internet, books that were the subject of his agreement with Random House. Thereupon, Random House filed a copyright infringement suit against Rosetta Books. A federal district court denied Random House's motion for preliminary injunction, finding that Random House's rights under its contract with Vonnegut "do not include the right to publish to works in the format that has become known as the ebook."

Relying on the legal principles set forth in *Boosey* and *Bartsch*, the court supported its findings as follows (accompanied by criticisms with which the book publishing community could be expected to respond):

First, the grant of exclusive rights "itself distinguishes between the pure content" — i.e., "the work" and the format of display — "in book form."

*Response*: The court did not provide a basis for its finding that "in book form" referred to "the format of display" and never considered the fact that the phrase "in book form" may be a way of distinguishing a linear text version of the work and a non-text derivative work such as a motion picture or television program based upon the work. Under standard publishing agreements, book publishers are granted the rights to publish the linear text version in a variety of forms and authors

---

[66] *Random House, Inc. v. Rosetta Books LLC*, 150 F. Supp. 2d 613 (S.D.N.Y 2001).

generally reserve the right to exploit the work in non-linear text versions, such as motion pictures and television programs.

Second, the court pointed out that the dictionary defines a "book" as "a written or printed work of fiction or nonfiction, usually on sheets of paper fastened or bound together within covers."

*Response*: The court did not comment on the phrase, "*written or* printed work," which suggests that the word "written" does not necessarily mean "printed," a word typically associated with stamping ink on physical paper. Nor did the court comment on the phrase, "*usually* on sheets of paper," which suggests that "books" may be written (not printed) on materials other than sheets of paper. It would seem, contrary to the court's conclusion, that the dictionary definition of the word "book" actually supports a finding that the word "book" includes "ebook."

Third, the court pointed out that the dictionary defines the word, "form" as "external appearance of a clearly defined area, as distinguished from color or material, the shape of a thing or person."

*Response*: The philosopher Aristotle would be surprised by such a limited view of the word, "form," which simply means the kind of thing something is as distinguished from something else. "Book form" could simply refer to the work being in textual form, as opposed to its dramatic elements and dialogue being embodied and performed in a motion picture. The very next paragraph of the grant clause, also referred to in court's opinion, refers to "abridged form," suggesting the word "form" is not being used to denote "external appearance," but to an abbreviated version, a kind of derivative work of the work.

Fourth, the court points out that, in the grant paragraph of the author's publishing contract, "separate language is used to convey the rights to publish book club editions, reprint editions, abridged forms, and editions in Braille." This language, said the court, "would not be necessary if the phrase "in book form" encompassed all types of books."

*Response*: This is not necessarily the case. It is not at all clear that a grant to publish the work "in book form" would allow the publisher to publish certain kinds of derivative works of the work even in printed form, such as abridged forms and Braille editions. In addition, the court failed to note standard entertainment industry practice that even where full rights are granted in an agreement, the agreement typically goes on to list certain specific rights. Though appearing redundant, this is often done to avoid misunderstanding as to what the grantee may do with the work. For example, if "abridged form" and Braille editions were not listed, it is not clear whether the publisher would have the right to create them under its grant to publish the work "in book form," because it begs the question whether the "work" includes derivative works, such as abbreviations or translations, such as Braille. Moreover, a redundant listing of rights often serves to indicate that a grant of broad rights, rather than narrow rights was intended.

Fifth, the court suggested its conclusion was supported by the fact that the author deleted certain exploitations and specifically reserved others.

*Response*: The fact is, none of the rights deleted or reserved had anything to do with the right to publish ebooks, digital downloads, electronic versions, etc. Where the author intended to reserve rights, the deletions that were done evidenced the author knew how to reserve rights when it intended that rights be reserved.

Sixth, the court rejected Random House's contention that the following provision had any bearing on the scope of the grant: a clause requiring Random House to "publish the work at its own expense and in such a style and manner and at such a price as Publisher deems suitable." The court interpreted this as simply meaning that the publisher retained "control over the appearance of the formats granted to Random House in the first paragraph; i.e., control over the style of the book."

*Response*: While the word "style" may connote appearance, this still leaves the phrase, "publish the work . . . in such a . . . *manner* . . . as Publisher deems suitable."

Seventh, the court dismissed the final phrase of the grant provision, which granted to Random House the right to "Xerox and other forms of copying, either now in use or hereafter developed." This "photocopy clause," said the court, "clearly refers only to new developments in xerography and other forms of photocopying."

*Response*: In 1967, when the publishing agreement was signed, Xerox was the poster child for new technology. It was not unlikely that the word Xerox was used not to limit what followed to photocopying, but to convey a broad inclusion of new means of reproducing the work in book form "either now in use or hereafter developed." Not long after Vonnegut signed his contract with Random House, Xerox established Xerox PARC (for "Palo Alto Research Center"), which became responsible for such developments as laser printing, the Ethernet, and the modern personal computer graphical user interface (GUI). There is little to no basis to read into the phrase "and other forms of copying, either now in use or hereafter developed" as limited to new forms of making photocopies.

Eighth, the court concluded that a reasonable person "cognizant of the customs, practices, usages and terminology as generally understood in the particular trade or business" would conclude that the grant language does not include ebooks. "To print, publish and sell the work in book form," concluded the court, "is understood in the publishing industry to be a limited grant."

*Response*: Few would disagree that it was a limited grant. People in the book business are quite familiar with the practice that authors reserve rights to exploit the work in motion pictures and other forms of derivative works, including foreign translations.

Finally, distinguishing the *Bartsch* and *Boosey* cases, the court suggested the language conveying rights in those cases were "far broader" than here. The court suggested that the new use in those cases — "i.e., display of a motion picture on television or videocassette — fell squarely in the same medium as the original grant." By contrast, the new use in this case, said the court, is "electronic digital signals sent over the Internet," which the court found to be "a separate medium from the original use — printed words on paper."

*Response*: First, the exhibition of a motion picture in a movie theater is hardly the same medium as a videocassette distributed to the home through the mail. Second, the court proceeded to list the physical differences between information stored digitally and information printed on paper, making the same mistake the *Cohen* court did by describing the physical differences between theatrical exhibition of films and distribution of film on videocassette. Such discussions are completely beside the point.

In the absence of clear evidence of intent as to what the parties would have done had they foreseen the new use, it is suggested that the decision as to whether an old license covered a new use should depend upon an analysis of the likely expectations of the parties at the time the license was executed.

Judge Friendly in *Bartsch*[67] got to the heart of the matter by asking what could or could not have "formed part of the bargain" between the

---

[67] 391 F.2d 150 (2d Cir. 1968), *supra* at footnote 17.

parties. That's how these cases should be decided: by *an inquiry into the bargain originally reached by the parties*. As the courts have said, in the absence of intent of the parties, the court should attempt "to identify any indicia of mutual *general* intent to apportion rights to 'new uses,' insofar as such general intent can be discerned from the language of the license, the surrounding circumstances, and trade usage."[68]

Again, in this inquiry into the bargain, the court should seek to determine what the parties would have likely bargained if they had foreseen the subsequent development of the new use at the time the license was entered into? In other words, how would they have allocated the risk of an unforeseen use, had they actually foreseen it at the time they made the original bargain?

In the context of ebooks, publishers would agree that use of the phrase "in book form" is meant to reflect the industry custom and practice of allocating the right to publish linear text versions of the work, while reserving to authors the right to authorize the creation of motion picture and other non-text derivative works based on the work. Because some derivative works are typically within the publisher's purview — abridged editions, foreign language translations, Braille versions — separate grant language is included to make it clear that these forms of derivative works are included in the grant of the right to publish the work in book form.

Ebooks is a new use that does not appear to be specifically contemplated by the contract. Arguably, the grant of rights to "Xerox and other forms of copying, either now in use or hereafter developed" fully encompassed ebooks, digital distribution, and new forms of distribution of books. A court clearly could stop there by determining this unambiguously included ebooks.

Were a court to determine the language was ambiguous, extrinsic evidence could be considered "to identify any indicia of mutual *general* intent to apportion rights to 'new uses,' insofar as such general intent can be discerned from the language of the license, the surrounding circumstances, and trade usage."[69] The objective would be, as Judge

[68] *ABKCO Music, Inc. v. Westminster Music Ltd.*, 838 F. Supp. 153 (1993), quoting *Rey v. Lafferty*, 990 F.2d 1379, 1387-91 (1st Cir. 1993), *cert. denied*, 126 L. Ed. 2d 61 (1993), and citing *Rooney v. Columbia Pictures Inds., supra.*

[69] *Id.*

Friendly suggested, to determine whether the new use "formed part of the bargain" and who should gain the "windfall" of ebook rights.

If the publisher gained the windfall, how would the author be affected? The publisher would control the style, manner, and price of distributing the ebook, but its exploitation of the right would be subject to paying the author the agreed upon royalty. Because the costs associated with digital distribution are arguably lower than physical distribution, perhaps the author would have negotiated a higher royalty rate. In any event, the fact that the publisher, rather than the author, gets to control the digital distribution has no effect on the author's exploitation of motion picture versions of the work, as rights in such derivative works (as well as, perhaps, foreign translations of the work) were reserved to the author.

If the author gained the windfall, how would the publisher be affected? Unlike the motion picture versions of the work, which when released generally increase sales of the work available in book form, the release of an ebook of the work would compete directly with publisher's sales of the work in printed form. Conceivably, the market for ebook versions could eclipse the market for printed editions (as the market for musical recordings in download form is quickly replacing the market for CDs). Under that scenario, the bargain the publisher reached with the author for the exclusive right to publish the work in book form for the life of copyright in the work would effectively be cut short by the advent of the new use.

Had Random House known about the potential for ebooks in 1967, what would they have done? Today, book publishers insist on the right to publish digital or electronic versions of books and do so for the very reason just mentioned: it would be an unacceptable bargain to pay an advance, provide editorial assistance, and spend marketing resources for the exclusive right to publish the work in printed form when the author could at the same time distribute the work in digital form at any price lower than the printed version, or even for free.

Such a bargain was likely to be as unacceptable in 1967 had the parties specifically considered it as it is now when the parties do specifically consider it. The court presiding over *Rey* seemed to foresee this possibility when it wrote:

> The problem becomes particularly acute when the analogous technology develops so rapidly as to supplant the originally

> contemplated application of the licensed work, rendering the parties' original bargain obsolete. Thus, for example, broad grants of "motion picture rights," made before technological advances permitted the combination of moving images with sound, later were held, typically, to encompass the rights to sound motion picture technology; a narrower holding would have left the original license virtually worthless, despite its broad language, and would have provided the licensor with an undeserved windfall. See, e.g., Murphy, 112 F.2d at 748; L.C. Page & Co. v. Fox Film Corp., 83 F.2d 196 (2d Cir. 1936).[70]

Perhaps it was just such circumstances that prompted Justice Oliver Wendell Holmes to find a negative covenant against the author who claimed that his grant of rights to present the play did not include motion picture rights. The Supreme Court held that it was clear the original grant was limited to a spoken drama performed on stage and not motion pictures, but because the court believed that the author's granting of motion picture rights would destroy the value of the stage rights granted, the court restricted the author's right to grant motion picture rights to third parties.

It is not suggested that the court consider reinstituting a long-ago abandoned theory of implied negative covenant, but simply recognize that what the courts have been grappling with in these cases, and should be grappling with, is not empty statements of law or long descriptions of alternative technologies, but a real effort to identify mutual general intent — insofar as such intent can be discerned from the language of the license, the surrounding circumstances, and trade usage — to determine how the new use would have affected the bargain reached by the parties had they considered the new use at the time. In that way, who should gain the windfall should become clear.

## III. AVOIDING AMBIGUITY

Music copyright owners should grant only the permission required to meet the known needs of those requesting the permission. The language effecting the owner's permission should be precise, should

[70] *Rey* at note 7.

include clear definitions of all the important terms used, and should always expressly reserve all other privileges not specifically granted. Producers, and others seeking to clear synchronization licenses, should attempt to obtain licenses that have as broad a scope as possible. Because of the availability of broad language that has been specifically confirmed by the courts, it is easier for a producer to draft language that will provide a license having an expansive scope than it is for music copyright owners to draft language that is tailored to the specific, immediately foreseeable needs of the producer. However, persuading a music copyright owner to accept such broad language may truly be the *Impossible Dream*.

# Appendix to Chapter 17
# Old Licenses, New Uses

**Form 17.1** **Old Motion Picture Synchronization License**

# FORM 17.1

## OLD MOTION PICTURE SYNCHRONIZATION LICENSE

New York, New York, October 12, 1933

In consideration of the sum of ONE HUNDRED AND FIFTY DOLLARS ($150), the undersigned does hereby give to Columbia Pictures Corporation, 729 Seventh Avenue, New York City, the non-exclusive, irrevocable right, license, privilege and authority to record in any manner, medium or form, in any country covered by this license, the musical compositions hereinbelow set out, and to make copies of such recordings and to import said copies of recordings into any country covered by this license, all in accordance with the terms, conditions and limitations hereinafter set out.

1. The Compositions covered by this license are:

Prisoner's Song Massey Shapiro Bernstein & Co. Inc.

2. The title of the motion picture with which said musical compositions are to be used is "Lady For a Day".

3. The type of use to be made of the musical composition is vocal visual — short whistling, and the amount of uses to be made is two.

4. The license hereinabove set out is limited to the use of the musical compositions in synchronism or timed-relation with the motion picture hereinabove specified.

5. The right to record the musical compositions as covered by this agreement is conditioned upon the performance of the musical work in theatres having valid licenses from the American Society of Composers, Authors and Publishers, or any other performing rights organization having jurisdiction in the territory in which the said musical compositions are performed.

6. The territory covered by this license is the entire world.

7. Except that the undersigned warrants that the principal for whom he is acting is the owner of the said musical compositions, this license is given without warranty or recourse, and the licensor reserves to itself all rights and uses in and to the said musical compositions not herein specifically granted.

____________________________

Agent and Trustee

Chapter 18

# Licensing Music in Live and Recorded Public Performances (Public Performance Licenses)

## Summary

## IV. Performance License Grants to Performance Rights Societies

A. Non-Exclusive

B. Equal Shares

C. Assignability of Writer's Share

D. Nondramatic Performances

## V. Considerations in Granting and Clearing Performance Licenses

A. Blanket Licenses

B. Source Licenses and Direct Licenses

C. Per Program Licenses

## VI. Collection of Performance Royalties from Music Users

A. Broadcast Licensing
   1. Radio
   2. Television

B. Internet and New Media Licensing
   1. Internet Radio and Websites
      a. ASCAP
         (1) ASCAP Experimental License Agreement for Non-Interactive Services
         (2) ASCAP Experimental License Agreement for Interactive Services
         (3) ASCAP Experimental License Agreement for Multiple Sites and Services
      b. BMI
         (1) BMI Website Music Performance Agreement
         (2) BMI Website Music Performance Agreement — Corporate Image License
         (3) BMI Non-Commercial Website Music Performance Agreement
         (4) BMI Live 365 Member Micro-Caster Music Performance Agreement
         (5) BMI Live 365 Member Mini-Caster Music Performance Agreement
         (6) BMI Klik-Thru Digital Licensing Center

# CHAPTER 18

# LICENSING MUSIC IN LIVE AND RECORDED PUBLIC PERFORMANCES (PUBLIC PERFORMANCE LICENSES)

Performance of music has become ubiquitous in our society. You hear performances of music while listening to the radio, dining in a restaurant, shopping at a mall, and standing in an elevator. Of all the forms of using music — making recordings, printing sheet music, synchronizing with motion pictures, etc. — clearly the most common use is its *performance*. Consequently, revenue from public performances of music represents nearly one-half of the total music publishing revenue from all sources.

A casual listener may often wonder how the songwriter gets paid for this performance. Does the shopping mall send a check to the estate of Sammy Cahn every time the song *My Kind of Town* is performed over its sound system? Does anyone have to get Mr. Cahn's permission before performing the song?

This chapter sketches the historical and legal background of performance rights and performance rights societies and provides an outline of the customs and practices in licensing public performances of music.

## I. Historical Background

### A. Performance Rights Societies

In October, 1913 at a dinner meeting held at the famous theatrical club, *The Lambs*, in New York City, a small group of songwriters were engaged in a serious discussion about these very questions. At that dinner, songwriter Victor Herbert told Irving Berlin, John Philip Sousa ("the march king"), Jay Witmark (successful writer and publisher), Nathan Burkan, Esq. (an attorney), Gene Buck (writer of the many Florenz Ziegfeld Broadway shows and later president of ASCAP) and others at this meeting, of his frustration at hearing a song of his performed at a nearby swank New York restaurant, but having no means of collecting a royalty for the performance.

The problem these songwriters faced was twofold. First, as Nathan Burkan, Esq. surely must have advised, it wasn't altogether clear whether songwriters had a right to collect for performances of their songs in restaurants, nightclubs, cabarets, and like establishments. Granted, the revision of the United States copyright act in 1897 established for the first time the copyright owner's exclusive right of public performance. The 1909 revision of the United States copyright law, however, placed a restriction on the right of performance, stating that a license from the copyright owner is required only if the performance was rendered "publicly for profit."[1] This provision was generally interpreted to mean that a license was required only if an admission fee was charged to hear the performance. If, for example, no admission fee was charged for entering a restaurant, performances of music at the restaurant would not be considered "for profit." Indeed, the common wisdom among music publishers at that time was that public performances of music stimulated the sales of sheet music. Accordingly, the publishers did not want to do anything that would discourage public performances, whether authorized or not. In those days, sheet music often bore a printed notice that granted the purchaser of the sheet music the right to perform the composition in public.

The second problem was the very practical problem of policing the performance of compositions in every nightclub, cabaret, music hall, theater, or any other place where music can be performed in public. It would be financially impractical for every individual songwriter to attempt to enforce his right of exclusive public performance in his work and for every nightclub, cabaret, music hall, and theater owner to clear permission to perform music by obtaining a separate license

[1] 17 U.S.C. Sec. 1(d) (1909 Act).

for each performance of a song from each individual songwriter or publisher.

## B. American Society of Composers, Authors & Publishers (ASCAP)

It was to address these problems that the American Society of Composers, Authors and Publishers (ASCAP) was established by this small group of songwriters and music publishers in 1914. The group immediately went to work by establishing a nationwide policing organization, which offered licenses to amusement establishments to perform the songs of its members.

The group then took the major step of filing a lawsuit against a restaurant located in Times Square in New York called *Shanley's* for the unauthorized public performance of the ASCAP musical composition, *Sweethearts*, by Victor Herbert. *Shanley's* argued, predictably, that since no specific charge was made for admission to the premises where the performances occurred, the music was not being performed "for profit." The case went all the way to the U.S. Supreme Court.[2] In rendering the majority decision in 1917, Chief Justice Oliver Wendell Holmes, himself a writer of poetry, said "If music did not pay, it would be given up. If it pays, it pays out of the public's pocket. Whether it pays or not, the purpose of employing it is for profit and that is enough." Thus, the business of a restaurant was to make a profit, and, because the music was part of the service that the restaurant rendered to make a profit, that is enough.

On the heels of this great victory, ASCAP quickly went on a licensing crusade, issuing music performance licenses to hotels, concert halls, cabarets, and other similar places where music was performed for profit under the Supreme Court's new interpretation of that term.

The advent of coast-to-coast radio broadcasting in 1926 brightened the economic interests of songwriters on a scale never before conceived. Here was a new opportunity to earn performance royalties from this new media and ASCAP was quick to recognize it. By that time, the U.S. Supreme Court, in another landmark decision,[3] had held that even

[2] *Herbert v. Shanley*, 242 U.S. 591 (1917).

[3] *M. Witmark & Sons v. L. Bamberger & Co.*, 291 F. 776 (D.N.J. 1923).

though a radio broadcast was disseminated free of charge, performances by radio broadcast were "for profit" and therefore required a license from the copyright owner.

At first, broadcasters resisted paying for performances, but publishers finally overcame their objections after winning several lengthy court battles. By 1932, ASCAP was able to negotiate a performance license for radio stations that established rates based upon a percentage of advertising. ASCAP was gaining strength and, with the backing of the courts, was able to raise the rates it charged. The broadcasters were becoming concerned that, with ASCAP's virtual monopoly in the field, rates could be increased to unreasonable levels. With each passing year, negotiations between ASCAP and the broadcasters became increasingly difficult. By the mid 1930s, radio stations had agreed to pay as much as 5% of their advertising revenues and from 1931 to 1939, ASCAP succeeded in increasing its fees from $960,000 to $4.3 million.

## C. Broadcast Music Incorporated (BMI)

In 1940, in anticipation of a breakdown in negotiations with ASCAP over the rates to be charged for the following year, a group of broadcasters, including the major radio networks and nearly 500 independent radio stations, established an organization called Broadcast Music Incorporated (BMI), opening offices in New York City on February 15, 1940. That spring, in anticipation of the expiration of its five-year agreement with the broadcasters, ASCAP was threatening to double its rates.

At that time, I was the producer and arranger of the popular national radio show, *Waltz Time*, broadcast over the NBC radio network, featuring Abe Lyman's orchestra with Frank Munn, "The Golden Voice of Radio." We were aware negotiations between ASCAP and the radio networks were not going too well. During the rehearsal of *Waltz Time* on Friday afternoon, December 27, 1940, I received a call from two executives of the newly formed BMI, Robert Burton and Robert Sour, who told me of "problems next week." Sure enough, the following week we were advised that the ASCAP repertoire would not be available for broadcast after Tuesday December 31, 1940, and we were to clear all music prior to our next broadcast with NBC's clearance department. Our next broadcast was scheduled for Friday, January 3, 1941. A new show was prepared overnight.

The first salvo was fired in the war between BMI and ASCAP when I became the first arranger to call upon "public domain" writer, Stephen Foster, in arranging and programming the song, *I Dream of Jeannie With the Light Brown Hair*, together with several waltzes by Waldteufel and Strauss. Our broadcast on the evening of January 3, 1941 had an unexpected "continental" sound. But what about next week? To my surprise, BMI was well prepared. During the previous year, BMI had been acquiring a catalog of popular songs for licensing in competition with ASCAP. That week, the BMI "song pluggers" furnished us with new popular songs from their newly compiled catalogue of works. Remarkably, BMI had been prepared with full orchestrations that had already been printed. ASCAP member George M. Cohan remarked during this period that of the hundreds of thousands of songs that BMI claimed to control, "Half are called *Turkey in the Straw* and the other half are about a girl called *Jeannie*."

In early January 1941, BMI became the new self-proclaimed "automatic performance royalty earning machine" for songwriters and publishers. New BMI affiliated publishers were established along with some older ASCAP affiliated firms such as Edward B. Marks Music and the Peer-Southern Music Organization. After having seen its songs off the air for about eight months, ASCAP finally settled with the networks and its repertoire was again available for broadcast by late 1941. BMI has remained ever since a strong competitive factor in performance rights licensing.

## D. Society of European State Authors and Composers (SESAC)

From 1914 to 1931, ASCAP was the sole organization engaged in the licensing of performing rights in the United States. In 1931, Paul Heineke, a European music publisher, established the second oldest music licensing organization in the United States. Originally known as the Society of European State Authors and Composers, it is presently known just as SESAC, Inc.

In the past, SESAC considered itself a publisher-oriented organization noted primarily for its activity in the Gospel and Country music fields. In 1973, SESAC began to affiliate writers directly and has since rapidly expanded its repertory in the areas of pop, rock, rhythm and blues, jazz, latin, and classical music. Recently, SESAC has undergone a change of ownership and the new owners may have some interesting long-term plans for the society. One indication of these plans could be the recent enrollment of Bob Dylan and Neil Diamond as writer members of the society.

### E. International Performance Rights Societies

Performance rights societies were operating overseas long before ASCAP was established in the United States. The first European performance rights society, Societe des Auteurs, Compositeurs et Editeurs de Musique (SACEM), was formed in France in 1851. ASCAP is said to have been modeled after SACEM. By the end of the nineteenth century, SACEM had established an office in London for the purpose of collecting fees for the public performance of French compositions in England even before the establishment of a performance rights society for British composers. This left the British in an awkward position: while British compositions could be freely performed without compensation, it was necessary for restaurants and concert halls in England to pay for a license if they wished to perform French compositions. In 1914, after a series of meetings between important British music publishers, authors, and composers, including David Day of Francis, Day and Hunter and William Boosey of Chappell & Co. Ltd., the English Performance Right Society was finally established. Around the turn of the century, other societies had been established in Europe, including the first German society, Genosenschaft Deutscher Tonsetzer (GDT), the predecessor to today's GEMA, which was founded in Berlin in 1903.

## II. LEGAL BACKGROUND

### A. Performances Under the Copyright Act Today

To *perform* music means to "recite, render, [or] play . . . it, either directly or by means of a device or process."[4] For example, a singer

---

[4] 17 U.S.C. Sec. 101.

is performing when he or she sings a song; a broadcaster is performing when it transmits the singer's performance (whether simultaneously or from records); a local broadcaster is performing when it re-transmits the network broadcast; a cable television system is performing when it re-transmits the broadcast to its subscribers; and any individual is performing when he or she plays a record album embodying the performance or communicates the performance by turning on a radio.[5]

The *performance right* in music is the exclusive right to perform or authorize the performance of the music "publicly."[6] To perform music *publicly* means (1) to "perform . . . it at a place open to the public or at any place where a substantial number of persons outside of a normal circle of family and its social acquaintances is gathered" or (2) "to transmit or otherwise communicate a performance. . . . of the work to a place specified by clause (1) or to the public, by means of any device or process, whether the members of the public capable of receiving the performance receive it in the same place or in separate places and at the same time or different times."[7] The term "family" in this context would include an individual living alone, so that a gathering confined to the individual's social acquaintances would normally be regarded as private. Performances of music at routine meetings of business and governmental personnel would not be considered public because they do not represent the gathering of a "substantial number of persons." However, performances in semi-public places, such as clubs, lodges, factories, summer camps, and schools are considered public performances.

The Copyright Act of 1976 specifically eliminated the requirement that performances be "for profit" and gave the owner of copyright the exclusive right to license the performance of a musical composition in public, whether it be for profit or otherwise.[8]

[5] House of Rep. Report No. 94-1476, 94th Cong., 2d Sess. (1976) at p. 63.

[6] 17 U.S.C. Sec. 106(4).

[7] 17 U.S.C. Sec. 101.

[8] 17 U.S.C. Sec. 106(4).

## B. Limitations on the Exclusive Right of Public Performance

In eliminating the "for profit" requirement, however, the new copyright law substituted in its place a series of limitations to the exclusive right of public performance.[9]

### *1. Non-Profit Performances*

These limitations include exemptions for four kinds of *non-profit* performances. The first exempts from the exclusive right of public performance those performances of music that are rendered in the course of the face-to-face teaching activities of non-profit educational institutions.[10] The second exempts certain governmental and non-profit educational broadcasts of music where the purpose is to further systematic instructional activities.[11] The third exempts performances of music of a religious nature rendered during the course of religious services; this exemption does not apply, however, to any religious broadcast, even when the broadcast originates at the place of worship.[12] The fourth exempts performances that lack any direct or indirect commercial advantage; for this exemption to apply, no direct or indirect admission may be charged for the performance and no payment of any fee or other compensation for the performance may be made to any of its performers, promoters, or organizers.[13]

### *2. Mom and Pop Stores, Restaurants, and Bars*

Other exemptions from the exclusive right of public performance include certain performances by small public establishments by means of radio broadcasts.[14] The exemption applies to public performances on "a single receiving apparatus of a kind commonly used in private homes." This exemption was intended only to apply to small commercial establishments (e.g., "mom & pop" stores) where the performances are made

---

[9] 17 U.S.C. Sec. 110.

[10] 17 U.S.C. Sec. 110(1).

[11] 17 U.S.C. Sec. 110(2).

[12] 17 U.S.C. Sec. 110(3).

[13] 17 U.S.C. Sec. 110(4).

[14] 17 U.S.C. Sec. 110(5), expanded by amendments made by the "Fairness in Music Licensing Act" (Pub. Law 105-298, 112 Stat. 2830 (Oct. 27, 1998)).

by using a small radio or home stereo receiver, with no more than four ordinary speakers grouped within a relatively narrow circumference from the receiving equipment.[15]

The exemption would not apply to broadcasts transmitted by speakers or similar devices in such establishments as bus terminals, supermarkets, factories and commercial offices, department and clothing stores, hotels, restaurants and fast-food or quick-service chain stores, or where the establishment makes use of any commercial sound equipment or conversion of a home-type receiver into its equivalent. However, businesses that perform music only from radio, television, cable and satellite sources, that do not re-transmit these performances beyond their establishments, and do not charge admission, are exempted if (a) their establishments are smaller than 2,000 gross square feet or (b) in the case of any restaurant, bar, grill or other food service or drinking establishment that are smaller than 3,750 gross square feet.

Businesses whose square footage exceeds these amounts also qualify for the exemption if they use 6 or fewer speakers with no more than 4 speakers in any one room or use audiovisual equipment consisting of no more than 4 televisions, with no more than 1 television in each room, and no television having a diagonal screen size greater than 55 inches, together with the same speaker restrictions.

### 3. Record Stores

The copyright law also exempts performances of music in record stores where the sole purpose of the performance is to demonstrate, and thereby promote the sales of the records offered for sale at the store.[16] For the exemption to apply, no charge may be made for admission to the store. Further, the exemption applies only if the performance is not transmitted beyond the place where the store is located and is limited to the immediate area where the sale is occurring. Accordingly, where record sales are made in one part of a large department store, the exemption does not apply to performances transmitted to other parts of the department store.

---

[15] House Report at pp. 86-87.

[16] 17 U.S.C. Sec. 110(7).

### 4. State Fairs

Also exempt are performances of music at state fairs by governmental bodies and non-profit organizations, and performances of music as part of programs designed for the blind, deaf, or handicapped, provided they are broadcast through the facilities of government, non-profit organizations, public broadcasting entities, and cable radio or television systems.

### 5. Public Broadcasting

Fearing the political pressure that the public broadcasting industry could apply to Congress at the time the copyright law of 1976 was being considered, Congress adopted a compulsory license for performances of music broadcast by public broadcasting entities. The provision encourages copyright owners, through their respective performance rights societies, and public broadcasters to negotiate in good faith and reach agreement on performance license fees. Should they fail to reach agreement, the compulsory fees would be established by the Copyright Royalty Board, appointed and convened by the Librarian of Congress.[17]

## III. PERFORMANCE RIGHTS SOCIETIES TODAY

Today, nearly all licensing of performances of music in the United States is conducted through the auspices of ASCAP, BMI, and SESAC, and through over 40 music license organizations operating throughout the world. Virtually all professional songwriters and music publishers are members of or affiliated with performance rights societies.

## A. ASCAP

ASCAP is owned and run by over 250,000 writers and music publishers, who are referred to as *members*.[18] Members have the opportunity to raise questions and express their views at four meetings each

[17] 17 U.S.C. Sec. 801-803.

[18] American Society of Composers, Authors & Publishers, 1 Lincoln Plaza, New York, New York 10023, Phone: 212-621-6000; Fax: 212-787-1381, www.ascap.com.

year, two in New York and two in Los Angeles. The society also holds meetings in Nashville, Tennessee. The Board of Directors of ASCAP is elected by its membership and is composed of composers, lyricists, and music publishers. The Board, which meets once a month to plan, review, set policy, and appoints officers, has 12 writer directors elected by the writer members and 12 publisher directors elected by the publisher members.

### B. BMI, Inc.

BMI is owned by about 500 radio and television stations who are successors to the radio stations who established BMI in 1940.[19] No dividends, however, have ever been paid to the shareholders of BMI; after the deduction of operating expenses, all amounts collected have been paid to the over 300,000 writers and publishers affiliated with BMI, called *affiliates*.

### C. SESAC, Inc.

SESAC, by far the smallest of the U.S. performance rights organizations, is a private company originally established by the Heineke family.[20] SESAC represents over 900 writers and 750 publishers with respect to over 150,000 musical compositions. Like ASCAP and BMI, SESAC makes its catalog available to the broadcast industry, airlines, auditoriums, nightclubs, hotels, restaurants. Unlike the other performance rights societies, however, SESAC promotes performance activity of the music in its writers' and publishers' catalogs. SESAC is also unique in that it provides its affiliates with consultation, legal advice on copyrights, and placement assistance with publishers and record labels.

### D. International Performance Rights Societies

Performance rights societies similar to ASCAP, BMI, and SESAC operate in many countries around the world. Under reciprocal

[19] Broadcast Music, Inc., 320 West 57th Street, New York, New York 10019, Phone: 212-586-2000; Fax: 212-489-2368, www.bmi.com.

[20] SESAC, Inc., 421 West 54th Street, New York, NY, 10019, Phone: 212-586-3450, Fax: 212-489-5966, www.sesac.com.

representation agreements, each society licenses performances and collects royalties in its local country on behalf of songwriter and publisher members of affiliated performance rights societies in other countries. Overseas performance rights societies generally divide performance royalties into equal publisher and writer shares. The writers' shares of performance fees are paid to the respective societies representing the writers; the publisher's shares are paid to the respective societies representing the publishers or, if the publisher instructs, to its local publisher representative located in the country in which the fees are collected.

A list of the major international performance rights societies is set forth at the end of this chapter, and a discussion of the international administration of public performance rights is discussed in Chapter 5, on *International Subpublishing*.

## E. Membership Requirements

Membership in the performance rights societies is fairly open. Applications for membership may be obtained by writing to or visiting any of their regional offices.

A songwriter desiring to become a member of ASCAP must show he or she has written a musical composition that has been (a) commercially recorded, (b) made available in the form of sheet music for sale in regular commercial outlets, or (c) performed in a media licensed by ASCAP, such as radio. To become a publisher member of ASCAP, you must be regularly engaged in the business of music publishing. If you do not meet the requirements for full membership, you may become an associate writer member if you have had at least one work written and registered with the U.S. Copyright Office. It does not cost anything to join ASCAP. Annual dues are fairly nominal.

Similarly, a songwriter is eligible to affiliate with BMI by showing he or she has written a musical composition that has been either commercially published or recorded or otherwise likely to be performed. BMI charges no fees or annual dues to writers. To affiliate with BMI as a publisher member, you must satisfy reasonable standards of literacy and integrity and should have some musical compositions being performed, or likely to be performed, by broadcasting stations or in other public performances. BMI does not charge publisher members any annual fees or dues. Instead, BMI charges publishers an initial charge of $25.00, made only at the time of affiliation, and intended only to help defray the administrative cost involved in affiliation. There is no fee for affiliation of either writers or publishers with SESAC, but SESAC is far more selective about who may become members.

### F. Choosing the Society with Which to Affiliate

A songwriter may only affiliate with one performance rights society, foreign or domestic, at any one time. However, a writer who belongs to one society may collaborate on the writing of a song with a writer who is affiliated with another society.

Songwriters and publishers frequently ask the question, "Which performing rights society should I join?" Large music publishers will belong to both ASCAP and BMI, establishing separate publishing subsidiaries for this purpose, but the question as to which performance society would be best for any particular song or catalog of songs remains.

It was once believed that the decision of which society to join depended on the type of music the songwriter composes or the type of music that comprises the catalog. A composer of rock, jazz, or country or western was said to be better off with BMI, because of the emphasis BMI placed on independent radio stations, rather than radio networks, in making its surveys; composers of music more likely to be performed on networks over a long period of time were advised to join ASCAP. However, these distinctions no longer apply, and songwriters and publishers are advised to meet with representatives of each society to determine which is better for them.

In the early 1970s, each of the performance rights societies began allowing what is known as "cross-registration." This facilitated the performance rights administration of songs written by a writer affiliated with one society working in collaboration with a writer affiliated with another. For example, performance royalties for a song co-written by an ASCAP writer and a BMI writer, each having a 50% interest in the writer's share, would be paid as follows: ASCAP would pay to the ASCAP writer 50% of the writer's share of ASCAP collections derived from performances of the song and BMI would pay to the BMI writer 50% of the writer's share of BMI collections derived from such performances, provided, however, that each of the respective publisher's share matches the respective writer's share — i.e., in this case, an ASCAP affiliated publisher must own a 50% interest in the publisher's share and a BMI affiliated publisher must own a 50% interest in the publisher's share.

The point of all this is that, because a series of performance royalty statements will be generated by each society with respect to the earnings arising from surveys of the same performances of the same song, one should be able to determine from comparing these statements over time, which society is "better." Unfortunately, publishers and writers who have had an opportunity to make the foregoing comparison report mixed results. In some cases, ASCAP paid more, and, in other cases, BMI paid more, and these comparisons suggest no particular guidelines about which society would better represent a writer or publisher with respect to certain genres of music or certain kinds of performances.

To attract new members and affiliates, ASCAP and BMI will, from time to time, offer certain writers and publishers advances against future performance royalties. The amount of advances offered by a society might seem a good reason to select one society over another, but if you are considering such an offer, you should remember that the advance being offered is really your money to begin with. The basis of your decision about which society to join should be made on longer term considerations as to which society is really best for you.

## G. Procedures upon Affiliation

It is the music publisher's responsibility to provide to the performance rights society the information necessary to collect and pay royalties for performances. After affiliation with a performance rights society, publishers should follow the following procedures:

1. Register your active musical compositions with your performance rights society immediately. You will not be credited for performances until your songs are registered with the society. Forms for registration are available from the performance rights society.

2. Register each new work promptly after it is created, preferably before its anticipated first recording or first performance.

3. When a music publisher in the United States signs a *subpublishing agreement* with a music publisher in another country, the procedures for the collection of performance royalties should be specified in the agreement. For example, the agreement should specify to which performance rights society (e.g., ASCAP, BMI, or SESAC) the U.S. publisher has granted performing rights and the percentage of the publisher's share of performance royalties it should receive. The agreement should also specify whether the publisher's share will be collected on its behalf by the foreign publisher or whether it is to be paid by the foreign society to the U.S. performance rights society for its account. The writers' shares of foreign performance fees collected by the overseas societies are transferred to the appropriate U.S. society who in turn pays these fees directly to writers.
4. Notify your performance rights society whenever you change your address.

## IV. PERFORMANCE LICENSE GRANTS TO PERFORMANCE RIGHTS SOCIETIES

### A. Non-Exclusive

Because of the impracticability of enforcing their exclusive right to public performances of the song, music copyright owners customarily become members of performance right societies. Upon affiliation with a society, songwriters and copyright owners grant to performance rights societies a license to sublicense the rendition of public performances of their musical works. In accordance with the court ordered consent decrees that govern the agreements between the performance rights societies and their members and affiliates, these licenses granted to the societies are made strictly on a non-exclusive basis.

### B. Equal Shares

In return, performance rights societies will pay 50% of the performance royalties earned by any particular composition to the copyright owner of the song — this is known as the *publisher's share* of performance royalties. The other 50% is paid directly to the songwriters, whether or not they own the copyright in the song — this is known as the *writer's share* of performance royalties. Both the songwriters and the publishers will each receive their respective 50% shares of performance royalties directly from the performance rights societies. Guidelines for the allocation of royalties within each of these groups are governed by the amended consent decree.[21]

As noted in Chapter 5, on *International Subpublishing*, overseas the division of shares between writers and publishers varies from society to society. For example, the division of publisher and writer shares for Dutch works is approximately 2/3 to writers and 1/3 to publishers.

## C. Assignability of Writer's Share

When a songwriter signs a standard music publishing agreement, he assigns to the publisher his copyright in his song, but reserves the rights necessary to grant to his performance rights society his writer's share of nondramatic public performance rights. Should a writer assign his writer's share of performance royalties to another, the performance rights society will not always recognize the assignment. The societies will do this as a matter of policy to protect writers from entering into unconscionable contracts. However, this policy is not universally applied and may be subject to overruling by a court. Accordingly, a writer should not rely upon it when considering making an assignment he is later likely to regret.

## D. Nondramatic Performances

Performance rights societies receive from their music publisher and songwriter members the right to license only *nondramatic* performances of their musical compositions, not *dramatic* performances. Accordingly, performance licenses issued by the societies to radio and television stations, nightclubs, concert halls, and like establishments, permit the rendition of performances of music in only a manner that is *nondramatic* in nature. The difference between dramatic and

[21] See *United States v. ASCAP*, 32 C.O. Bull. 601 (S.D.N.Y. 1960), and *United States v. ASCAP*, 442 F.2d 601 (2d Cir. 1971).

nondramatic performances is discussed at great length in Chapter 19, on the *Grand Rights Controversy.*

## V. CONSIDERATIONS IN GRANTING AND CLEARING PERFORMANCE LICENSES

Performance rights societies control virtually all administration of performance licenses. Accordingly, persons seeking permission to render nondramatic public performances of music usually must seek permission directly from one or more of the performance rights societies. Unless a music publisher is willing to grant a *direct license* (see below) for the public performance of its music, the publisher will generally have very little to say about the fees negotiated by ASCAP.

### A. Blanket Licenses

Persons or entities acquiring public performance licenses pay ASCAP and BMI an annual fee for the privilege to render an unlimited number of nondramatic performances of one or more of any of the hundreds of thousands of songs in their respective catalogs. Because of its extraordinarily broad coverage, this type of licensing arrangement is called a *blanket license.*

The fee charged for a blanket license, in the case of radio and television stations and certain other establishments, is based on the adjusted gross receipts of the station or establishment, approximating 2% to 2½%. For other businesses, such as restaurants, nightclubs, dancing schools, and the like, the fee for the blanket license may be an annual flat fee in accordance with various schedules established by the respective societies. Examples of several forms of blanket licenses are set forth at the end of this chapter.

If any music user believes the fees quoted by a performance rights society are unreasonable, he may apply for a ruling with the federal court under either of the respective consent decrees that govern the dealings of ASCAP and BMI.[22]

---

[22] See generally, Sobel, "The Music Business and the Sherman Act: An Analysis of the 'Economic Realities' of Blanket Licensing," 3 Loyola of Los Angeles Ent.L.J. 1 (1983).

## B. Source Licenses and Direct Licenses

Under the terms of the consent decrees entered into between ASCAP and the U.S. Department of Justice and between BMI and the U.S. Department of Justice, and the agreements between the societies and their members or affiliates, all members and affiliates of the performance rights societies are free to negotiate non-exclusive licenses directly with users, such as radio and television stations, on any mutually agreeable terms.

When members or affiliates negotiate performance licenses directly with users, they do so by entering into either a direct license or a source license. A *direct license* is a license to perform music on television that a television broadcaster obtains directly from the composers and/or publishers of the music it broadcasts. A *source license* is a license to perform music on television that a producer of a television program obtains directly from the composers and/or publishers of the music contained in the program. The difference between a *source license* and a *direct license* is that a source license is one that is obtained by the person who owns the work in which the song is used (e.g., motion picture, television program) and a direct license is a license that is obtained by one who broadcasts (e.g., television network or local television station), but does not necessarily own, the work being broadcast.

Over the years since the entry of the consent decrees very few nondramatic performance licenses have been issued by music copyright owners directly to broadcasters or other users of music. Most users, including the three national television networks, local television stations, local radio stations, have not sought source or direct licenses from copyright owners, but, instead have sought and obtained blanket licenses from the performance rights societies. Under their blanket licenses, these users have been entitled to perform some or all of the music in the repertories of the performance rights societies without the need to seek individual performance licenses from the individual members or affiliates.

From time to time, however, television and radio stations have sought to improve their leverage in bargaining with the performance license societies by either threatening to cease negotiating for blanket licenses or by filing lawsuits claiming that the arrangements under which performance rights societies operate violate the U.S. antitrust laws. In the early 1980s, a group of local television broadcasters filed a lawsuit against ASCAP and BMI charging just such violations.[23] Later, a group of local radio broadcasters filed a similar lawsuit against the societies.[24] After these lawsuits were filed, music publishers began receiving requests from broadcasters for direct licenses to perform music in their catalogs, intended, apparently, to elicit responses that could later be used as evidence in the pending litigation.

Even though music copyright owners are entirely free to enter into source or direct licenses under any terms that may be agreeable to them, few have any experience in issuing direct or source performance licenses. In considering the terms upon which to enter into a source or direct license, a music copyright owner should consider that, while a single lump sum payment may be attractive in the short-term, accepting such terms will mean foregoing any compensation from the performance rights society based upon the type and number of performances of the work that are rendered over time. It will be recalled that the performance revenues of a society are distributed under a system that awards performance fees on the basis of statistical surveys. Surveyed performances upon which these fees are based must necessarily exclude performances that are licensed directly by the member or affiliate; otherwise, the copyright owner would theoretically be paid twice for the same performance. Accordingly, members or affiliates of performance rights societies who enter into direct or source licenses are required to notify their performance rights society that a direct or source license has been issued, the title of the song licensed, the writer or writers of the song, the publisher or publishers of the song, the name of the licensee, and the term of the license.

In other words, unless the source or direct license is structured on some royalty basis, the music copyright owner entering into such licenses is giving up the important ability to benefit from the economic success of the work or broadcast for which the music is being licensed. While there may be economic circumstances under which it would make good business sense to license nondramatic performances of a song or catalog of songs directly, rather than through the performance

[23] *Buffalo Broadcasting Company, Inc. v. ASCAP and BMI*, 223 U.S.P.Q. 478 (2d Cir. 1984).

[24] *Alton Rainbow Corp. v. ASCAP*, 98 F.R.D. 299 (1983).

rights societies, those circumstances should be considered very carefully with the advice of skilled legal counsel and financial analysts.

### C. Per Program Licenses

The court's ruling in the *Buffalo Broadcasting* case resulted in a new form of license that is now available to television stations from the performance rights societies. Under the ruling, each television station has a choice between a traditional blanket license and a new *per program license*. A number of television stations are choosing to secure a per program license instead of the traditional blanket license. A per program license is often considered a modified blanket license, because it operates much the same way as the blanket license. Television stations that desire a per program license may broadcast any and all songs in the ASCAP and BMI catalogs, but instead of paying fees for a license to use all of the music in each society's catalog — whether they use them or not — stations pay each society only for television programs that contain music controlled by that society pursuant to a prescribed formula. Per program fee structures are negotiated between the performance rights societies and various representatives of the television industry, much the same way as blanket licenses are negotiated. As in the case of blanket licenses, if an agreement cannot be reached, a proceeding before the Federal District Court in New York will take place to establish a reasonable rate structure.

Stations electing the per program license option pays fees to ASCAP and BMI on a monthly basis. However, unlike the blanket license, a vast amount of record keeping attends the per program licensing scheme. For example, a station must report the episode titles of the television programs it broadcasts, together with records of what music is contained in each program and when each program is broadcast. The key document used to determine which composers and publishers are entitled to receive royalty distributions is the music cue sheet. A *cue sheet* is a document that lists all of the music in a program, the order of performance, the amount of time each performance runs, the names of the song's composers and music publishers, and performance rights affiliations. The television stations participating in the per program option are using the services of independent database management companies to assimilate all this information and prepare reports based on the cue sheets and the information furnished by the televisions stations who choose the per program option.

The per program license should not be confused with either the source license or the direct license. While source and direct licenses are issued to producers and broadcasters by music publishers and other music copyright owners, the *per program* license is issued by the performance rights society much the same as they issue blanket licenses.

## VI. COLLECTION OF PERFORMANCE ROYALTIES FROM MUSIC USERS

A *music user*, for purpose of performance rights collection, is any person, business, or other entity that publicly performs music. A music user may publicly perform music (i) by live performance in concert on stage with or without the aid of a loudspeaker, or (ii) by transmission of a live performance or a recorded performance by radio, television, cable, telephone or other form of broadcast or retransmission. Examples of music users include local and network radio stations, local and network television stations, cable television operators, theaters, concert halls, nightclubs, restaurants, discos, ballrooms, hotels and motels, sports arenas and stadiums, amusement parks, airlines, jukebox operators, retail stores, corporations who play music over the telephone to callers "on hold" and many others. In general, each society negotiates directly with radio and television networks, independent stations, and all other establishments where their respective music repertoires are performed publicly.

Traditionally, performance rights societies generally divided their collection operations into two divisions: broadcast licensing and general licensing. The broadcast licensing division engages in complex negotiations with radio and television stations to establish the annual rates and fees due with respect to the use of music in these media. The general licensing division collects fees from all licensees other than radio and television broadcasters, such as nightclubs, restaurants, sports arenas, and the like.

Since the advent of the Internet and wireless devices, such as mobile phones, the performance rights societies have created added "new media" divisions devoted to licensing performances on the Internet and in a variety of new media, services, and products.

## A. Broadcast Licensing

In the United States, by far the largest source of revenues for the public performances of music is derived from licensing performances to television and radio stations, including cable and satellite broadcasting. The U.S. performance rights societies license over 1,200 local television stations, as well as the large networks (e.g., ABC, CBS, NBC, PBS, Fox, and Univision), and over 9,000 cable systems for performances of music on their local origination channels.

As mentioned above, the broadcast licensing divisions of the major performance rights societies engage in complex negotiations with radio and television stations, and cable and satellite providers, to establish the annual rates and fees due with respect to the performance of music in connection with their broadcasts. The complexity of these negotiations have been magnified by a series of lawsuits brought against the performance rights societies by television broadcasters, including the major television networks, local television stations, and cable television operators.

Although these lawsuits have not significantly changed the way music is licensed to broadcasters, the use of alternatives to the blanket licenses offered by performance rights societies is becoming more practical. These alternatives include source licensing, direct licensing, and per program licensing, each of which are described in the previous section.

### *1. Radio*

Periodically, ASCAP and BMI each negotiate performance fees payable by FCC-licensed commercial radio stations with an organization called the Radio Music License Committee (RMLC), which is made up of representatives from local radio stations.

Current license terms for the use of the ASCAP repertoire on commercial radio stations have been in effect since January 1, 2001, which were approved by the late Judge William C. Conner of the United States District Court for the Southern District of New York on October 15, 2004. BMI and the RMLC agreed upon a three-year term extension to the previous ten-year performing right agreement retroactive to January 1, 2007. The agreement was submitted to Judge Louis J. Stanton in the Federal District Court of New York, who finalized the accord by order dated May 18, 2009.

### *2. Television*

ASCAP and BMI also periodically negotiate with the Television Music License Committee (TMLC), which is made up of representatives from local television stations. Currently, for the ASCAP repertoire, TMLC is subject to an industry-wide flat dollar annual performance fee that is adjusted annually based upon the number of licensed stations in the country and changes in the Consumer Price Index. The industry-wide fee is then allocated among individual stations, in accordance with a methodology devised by the Committee (and approved by the court) to produce each station's annual blanket license fee.

According to ASCAP, the TMLC's allocation formula has two steps: First, the industry-wide fee is divided among all the television or "ADI" (Areas of Dominant Influence) markets across the country — for example, Omaha is a market; Dallas-Fort Worth is a market — and the share of the total for each market is weighted according to size. The Dallas-Fort Worth market is weighted higher than Omaha, for example, because Dallas-Fort Worth has more stations and more viewers. The result is that total fees paid by all of the stations in the Dallas market are greater than the total fees paid by all of the stations in the Omaha market.

Once the total fee for a market has been calculated, it is allocated to the individual stations in that market. This allocation is based on verified ratings — i.e., the household viewership for each of the stations. Thus, a highly rated station in a market will pay a greater fee than a station with low viewer ratings; accordingly, a highly rated station in a large market will have a higher blanket fee than a highly rated station in a small market.

## B. Internet and New Media Licensing

### *1. Internet Radio and Websites*

A growing, but still unsettled area of performance revenue has been from the use of music on websites, Internet radio, and other transmissions of musical works over the Internet and by wireless. Licenses issued to "pureplay" web casters who perform music as part of radio-like audio transmissions over the Internet are fairly straightforward.

It is when a website, such as a portal, which offers a bundle of services, including radio, streamed audio and video ads, along with other services like news, sports, and culture information and entertainment that present licensing challenges. Each of the performance rights societies offer license agreements to websites which attempt to take into account the importance of music relative to the activity of the site. Though the performance rights societies have set rates and have started to receive substantial collections from Internet performances, these rates have been challenged in the courts for a variety of reasons.

For example, the importance of music and the way it is used on the website of one of the big three auto-makers is quite different than how and why music is used on a web portal such as Yahoo. Web portals and music services such as Yahoo, AOL, and RealNetworks have taken the position that rates should vary depending upon the nature of the stream. For example, they propose a multi-tiered approach under which they would pay 2.5% for on-demand audio, 1.7% for Internet radio, and .9% for music videos. Unable to reach agreement with ASCAP, Yahoo, AOL, and RealNetworks initiated a rate hearing in the U.S. District Court for the Southern District of New York. On April 30, 2008, the late District Judge Conner issued a decision setting a blanket license rate at 2.5% of revenues on a service-wide basis, regardless of whether the revenue was directly attributed to the music usage. [25] This ruling was being appealed at the time this edition went to print.

In another rate proceeding before the same court, Judge Conner set interim fees for a blanket license for the public performance of ASCAP's repertory on the streaming video service, YouTube.[26] The court saw no reason why the basic formula that ASCAP proposed and the Court adopted in *United States v. ASCAP in re AOL, RealNetworks and Yahoo! Inc.*, 562 F. Supp. 2d 413 (S.D.N.Y. 2008) was not equally appropriate in the present context. The court ordered YouTube to pay ASCAP the sum of $1,610,000 for interim fees accrued through March 31, 2009 and, within one week after the end of each calendar month thereafter the sum of $70,000 until the determination of final fees

---

[25] *United States v. ASCAP in re: Application of AOL, RealNetworks, and Yahoo, Inc.*, 559 F. Supp. 2d 332 (S.D.N.Y. 2008).

[26] *United States v. ASCAP in re: Application of YouTube LLC*, 616 F. Supp. 2d 447 (S.D.N.Y. 2009).

in the rate proceeding. The interim fees are subject to retroactive adjustment when final fees are determined.

*a. ASCAP*

Currently, ASCAP publicly offers three kinds of new media performance licenses:

**(1) ASCAP Experimental License Agreement for Non-Interactive Services**

The "Non-Interactive" license is intended for services that perform ASCAP music in a non-interactive manner, meaning performances of specific songs are not selected by users. For example, traditional radio-like webcasts, streaming of background music, and previews or samples (excerpts of songs that are 60 second or less in duration). ASCAP uses three alternative rate schedules from which the user can choose. This license is subject to a minimum annual fee of $288 regardless of the rate method chosen.

**(2) ASCAP Experimental License Agreement for Interactive Services**

The "Interactive" license is intended for services that perform music in an interactive manner, meaning performances of specific songs are selected by users. Examples include "on-demand" performances (e.g., on-demand streaming services, Internet jukeboxes, and music videos) and "custom radio" (e.g., user-determined play-lists). ASCAP uses three alternative rate schedules from which the user can choose. This license is subject to a minimum annual fee of $340 regardless of the rate method chosen.

**(3) ASCAP Experimental License Agreement for Multiple Sites and Services**

The Multi-Site license provides a license to cover all services on a website that perform music in various ways. ASCAP uses three alternative rate schedules from which the user can choose. This license is subject to a minimum annual fee of $288 regardless of the rate method chosen.

*b. BMI*

BMI offers at least the following performance licenses for new media uses:

**(1) BMI Website Music Performance Agreement**

This license covers any form of transmission of music from a commercial website. The fee is based on either the site's gross revenue or music revenue, which is at the user's option. If based on the former, the fee is 1.75% of gross revenue; if the latter, the fee is the greater of (a) 2.5% of music revenue or (b) music page impressions at 12 cents per 1,000. Either rate is subject to a $299 per year minimum license fee.

**(2) BMI Website Music Performance Agreement — Corporate Image License**

This license covers websites whose purpose is to promote a corporate image or brand name, such as the Coca-Cola corporate website. The fee is based on either a page impression calculation or a music page impression calculation, at the user's option. If the former, the fee is 40 cents per 1,000 impressions; if the latter, the fee is 60 cents per 1,000 music page impressions. Either rate is subject to a $299 per year minimum license fee.

**(3) BMI Non-Commercial Website Music Performance Agreement**

This license covers non-commercial websites. The fee is based on either a page impression calculation or a music page impression calculation, at the user's option. If the former, the fee is 8 cents per 1,000 impressions; if the latter, the fee is 12 cents per 1,000 music page impressions. Either rate is subject to a $299 per year minimum license fee.

**(4) BMI Live 365 Member Micro-Caster Music Performance Agreement**

BMI negotiated special license terms for those small webcasters using the Live 365 webcasting platform. Live 365 member webcasters whose revenues are less than $500 per month and allow a maximum of 25 simultaneous listeners qualify for the micro-caster license fee.

Qualifying members of Live 365 may apply for this license on the Live 365 website.

#### (5) BMI Live 365 Member Mini-Caster Music Performance Agreement

Live 365 member webcasters whose revenues are between $500 and $1,200 per month and allow a maximum of 500 simultaneous listeners qualify for the mini-caster license fee. Qualifying members of Live 365 may apply for this license on the Live 365 website.

#### (6) BMI Klik-Thru Digital Licensing Center

Webcasters whose estimate fees are less than $1,000 per year, may obtain their performance license through the completion of a web-form, called the Klik-Thru Digital Licensing Center that BMI has established for small accounts on its website.

### *2. Permanent Downloads and Ringtones*

While the performance rights societies are trying to maximize royalties from streams of music on the Internet, they are also leaving no stone unturned in their pursuit of revenues for their membership. For example, recall from Chapter 13, on *Licensing Music in Sound Recordings* that the performance rights societies have been taking the position that a *performance* license is required to effect a digital phonorecord delivery, even though a statutory mechanical reproduction license has already been obtained for the same delivery. In their view, all transmissions of songs constitute performances of songs, whether or not they result in a specifically identifiable phonorecord made by or for the transmission recipient, and therefore, they say, one must pay a public performance fee for these download transmissions, even after the statutory rate for the mechanical reproduction has been paid. During the course of the rate hearing initiated by AOL, Yahoo, and RealNetworks, the question was taken up by the late Senior Federal District Court Judge Conner, who concluded that a permanent download, while being a reproduction, does not also necessarily constitute a performance.[27]

[27] *United States v. ASCAP in re: Application of AOL, RealNetworks, and Yahoo, Inc.* 485 F. Supp. 2d 438 (S.D.N.Y. 2007).

On October 14, 2009, U.S. District Judge Denise Cote ruled that a ringtone does not involve a public performance that would require Verizon Wireless to pay public performance fees.[28] The court held that the "transmission of a ringtone to a cellular telephone customer does not constitute a performance of a musical work 'publicly.' " In addition, "when a ringtone plays on a cellular telephone, even when that occurs in public, the user is exempt from copyright liability, and [the carrier] is not liable either secondarily or directly." The court pointed to Section 110(4) of the Copyright Act, which exempts public performances undertaken "without any purpose of direct or indirect commercial advantage." According to the court, "customers do not play ringtones with any expectation of profit." We can expect this ruling to be appealed, as well.

### *3. Ring-Backs*

As mentioned in Chapter 13, on *Licensing Music in Sound Recordings*, an *audible ringing tone* is the ringing sound that a calling party hears while on the telephone after dialing a call, but prior to the call being answered. In recent years, telephone carriers have offered their subscribers the ability to personalize these tones with *caller ring-back tones*, or *ring-backs*. A *ring-back* is an audio-only transmission of a sound recording (and musical work), which the calling party hears after placing a call and while waiting for the call's intended recipient to answer the phone. The ring-back is personalized by the recipient of the call, so that anyone who calls the recipient's number will hear, in lieu of the standard ringing tone of the phone network, a popular sound recording or special greeting selected by the recipient.

The file containing the sound recording comprising the ring-back is hosted on servers maintained by the telecommunications carrier and equipment at the back office of the carrier enables subscribers to replace the standard ringing tone with a personalized audio selection. Ring-backs do not include *music-on-hold* services — where the sound recording is heard after the user has connected the call, but prior to the user speaking to the caller.

---

[28] *United States v. ASCAP in re: Application of Verizon Wireless*, 41 CIV 1395 (DLC) (S.D.N.Y. Oct. 14, 2009).

Ring-backs invoke both the reproduction right and the public performance right of the music copyright owner. Because the ring-back copy is not intended for distribution to the public for private use, but rather used to facilitate a performance of the ring-back, the proper reproduction license is an *electrical transcription license*, typically issued by the music publisher or its agent. Since the rendering of the ring-back constitutes a public performance, licenses for such performances are issued by performance rights societies.

According to BMI, revenue made by the phone carriers for selling ring-back services to mobile phone users will in 2009 surpass $235 million, up 15% from the prior year. BMI estimates that more than 10 million U.S. subscribers are signed up for ring-back tone services with their wireless carriers. It is estimated that about 4% of all mobile subscribers use ring-back services, with some carriers having as much as 9% of their subscribers use ring-backs.

The fee for a ring-back service ranges between $1.99 and $2.50 per tone, with the vast majority selling at $1.99, which allows the subscriber to use the ring-back for anywhere from 90 days to 12 months. With only one exception, all major carriers require a monthly recurring subscription fee to the service, which is required before a subscriber can purchase a tone. The monthly recurring charge ranges from $.99 to $5.00, although most only pay $.99 or less.

The performance license fees charged to the carriers by the performance rights societies in the United States is not public knowledge, but in the United Kingdom, PRS for Music provides a license that covers both the performance rights and the reproduction right necessary to (a) create and store musical works as ring-backs, (b) and to stream them to the public. The royalty rate payable for the reproduction and distribution of ringtones is: 15% of gross revenue from the service (including any subscription or recurring charges for accessing the service), subject to a minimum of 15p per ring-back tone (and a non-refundable advance of £1,000) (+VAT).

## C. General Licensing

The general licensing division of performance rights societies collects fees from all licensees other than radio and television broadcasters and Internet transmitters, such as nightclubs, restaurants, sports arenas, and the like. The performance rights societies have separate licenses and rate schedules for each major category of general users. The ASCAP website lists quite a few:

Airline Supplier

Airlines

Amusement Parks

Aquariums and Zoos Owned and Operated by Non-Profit Organizations

Arenas and Stadiums

Auto Racing Tracks

Background/Foreground Music Service

Baseball — Leagues and Teams

Basketball — Leagues and Teams

Body Building Contests

Bowl Games

Bowling Centers

Boxing

Buses

Camps

Campgrounds

Carnivals

Cheerleading Competition

Circuses

Clogging

Colleges and Universities

Competitions/Shows

Concerts and Recitals

Conventions, Expositions, Industrial Shows, Meeting and Trade Shows

Cruise Ships

Dance Clubs and Associations

Dance Schools — Individual and Chains

Direct Marketing/Distribution Companies

Dog Racing Tracks

Dog Shows and Competitions

Drag Boat Racing

Drive-in Movie Theatres — Recorded Music

Entertainment Facilities

Equestrian Events

Family Shows

Fashion Shows

Festivals

Fitness Weight Loss Centers

Football — Leagues and Teams

Football (College) Bowl Games

Funeral Establishments — Individual and Chain

Grand Prix Auto Racing

Gymnastics Competitions

Halls of Fame, Wax Museums and Similar Establishments

Helicopters

Hockey — Leagues and Teams

Horse and Harness Racing Tracks

Horse Competitions

Hotels and Motels

Ice Skating Rinks

Jai-Alai Frontons

Jewish Community Centers

Jukeboxes

Lacrosse — Indoor and Outdoor

Laser Shows

Local Governmental Entities

Marine Vessels with Overnight Accommodations for Passengers

Mechanical Music — Chain Stores with Audio and Audio Visual Uses

Motels

Motion Picture Theatres — Music Supplier

Motion Picture Theatres Individual and Chain

Motorcoaches

Motorcycle Racing/Motorcross

Multi-Media Film Program

Municipalities

Museums

Music-in-Business

Music-on-Hold — Individual and Chain

Music Supplier — Radio Over Speaker

Orchestras

Pay Per View Programming Services — Hotels

Polo Matches — Horse

Playgrounds (Indoor) — Individual and Chain

Private Clubs

Professional Photographers

Professional Speakers

Race Tracks

Radio-Over-Speaker Music Supplier

Resorts

Restaurants, Taverns, Nightclubs and Similar Establishments

Retail Stores — Individual and Chain

Rodeos

Roller Skating Rinks

Roller Games/Roller Derby

Shopping Centers and Shopping Malls

Shows/Competitions

Skateparks

Skating Competitions

Skating Rinks — Ice or Roller

Skiing Competitions

Soccer — Teams and Leagues

Speakers, Professional

Special Events

Square/Round Dancing

Stadiums and Arenas

Swimming Competitions

Symphony Orchestras

Television Chairs Audio-Visual Uses

Tennis Competitions

Theme and Amusement Parks

Tractor Pulls

Train Cars

Training and Development Sessions, Educational or Informational Seminars

Trucks, Vans, Trailers and Similar Vehicles

Universities and Colleges

Urban Transportation

Video Services

Volleyball — Indoor and Outdoor

Wind Ensembles

Wrestling

YMCA/YMHA/YWHA/YWCA

YoYo Competitions

Zoos and Aquariums Owned and Operated by Non-Profit Organizations

Examples of general licenses are set forth on the CD-ROM. The latest forms and information about current licensing terms and rates may be obtained by calling any of the regional offices of the societies.

## VII. Distribution of Performance Royalties to Publisher and Writer Members

ASCAP, BMI, and SESAC calculate and distribute performance royalties under different systems. These systems are exceedingly complex and, accordingly, no effort is made here to provide a comprehensive description of them. Readers interested in more information on this subject should confer directly with the performance rights societies.

### A. Statistical Sampling

ASCAP and BMI both employ elaborate systems of statistical sampling to determine which selections from their respective repertoires have been used and with what frequency. No effort is made to determine exactly the actual number of times each selection is performed during the year in the United States. Because of the vast numbers of musical performances that are rendered each year and locations at which music is performed publicly in this country, such an effort would require an expenditure that would far exceed the aggregate income of all the U.S. performance rights societies. Fortunately, statistical science has rendered such a complete survey unnecessary. By surveying a relatively few number of performances, the societies can establish a surprisingly accurate measurement of what songs are being performed during the year and with what relative frequency.

Most performance data is drawn from broadcast sources, under the assumption that the music being performed over radio and television is roughly the same as the music being performed in cafes, hotels, sports arenas, and restaurants, and nightclubs. ASCAP and BMI have different ways of sampling broadcast performances. ASCAP primarily relies upon tape recordings made by teams of surveyors sent to different parts of the country during the year. BMI primarily relies upon logs of all songs performed during a particular week by statistically selected broadcast stations. These logs are prepared by television and radio stations once every year or so as a condition of their performance license.

While the royalty distribution payments by ASCAP to its affiliated publisher and writer members are primarily based on a survey of users and BMI by a logging system prepared by users, SESAC payments to its affiliates begin when a recording of its product is released for sale to the public or otherwise begins to earn monies. SESAC does not have a formal logging procedure, but relies instead on performance of songs on industry standard "Top 100" charts, combined with spot checking of broadcast stations, to gage the relative performances of songs in its repertoire. Payments are determined by set rates based on industry hit chart activities.

## B. Credit Systems

Once the sample is taken, the resulting information is rolled into a complex formula that takes into consideration a number of factors, including the size of the broadcast stations sampled, the time of day of the performance, the type of program on which the music is performed, whether the performance is a feature performance or a background performance, etc. Each performance is assigned one or more credits, or fractions thereof, and the accumulated credits are used to allocate the fees collected from music users among the various writer and publisher members and affiliates of the society. After deductions of operating expenses, the funds collected from all sources are divided equally between writers and publishers in accordance with the credit formula.

## C. Grievance Procedures

ASCAP and BMI have each adopted a grievance procedure under which any of its writer or publisher members or affiliates may file formal complaints with the respective society. Complaints filed against ASCAP are reviewed by a special Board of Review. Disputes with BMI may be governed by arbitration under the rules of the American Arbitration Association. Complaints may ultimately be subject to the Federal Courts retaining jurisdiction of the consent decrees to which ASCAP and BMI remain respectively subject. SESAC is not subject to a consent decree.

# Appendix to Chapter 18
# Licensing Music in Live and Recorded Public Performances
# (Public Performance Licenses)

Lists

| | |
|---|---|
| **List 18-1** | **Major Overseas Performance Rights Societies** |

Forms (on CD-Rom Only)

| | |
|---|---|
| **Form 18-1** | **BMI Writer Agreement** |
| **Form 18-2** | **BMI Publisher Agreement** |
| **Form 18-3** | **ASCAP Membership Agreement** |
| **Form 18-4** | **BMI Music License for Eating and Drinking Establishments** |
| **Form 18-5** | **BMI Hotel/Motel License** |
| **Form 18-6** | **BMI Meetings, Conventions, Trade Shows and Expositions License** |
| **Form 18-7** | **BMI Athletic Clubs/Dance Classes License** |
| **Form 18-8** | **BMI Business Multiple Use License** |
| **Form 18-9** | **BMI Health Care Multiple Use License** |
| **Form 18-10** | **BMI College/University (Tier 1) License** |
| **Form 18-11** | **BMI College/University (Tier 2) License** |
| **Form 18-12** | **ASCAP Local Station Blanket Radio License (1990)** |
| **Form 18-13** | **ASCAP Local Station Per Program Radio License (1990)** |
| **Form 18-14** | **ASCAP General License (for Restaurants, Bars, Café's Clubs, etc.)** |
| **Form 18-15** | **ASCAP Hotels and Motels License** |
| **Form 18-16** | **ASCAP Music-on-Hold License** |
| **Form 18-17** | **ASCAP Concert and Recitals License (Blanket)** |
| **Form 18-18** | **ASCAP Concert and Recitals License (Per Concert)** |
| **Form 18-19** | **ASCAP Music-In-Business Blanket License** |

# LIST 18.1

## MAJOR OVERSEAS PERFORMANCE RIGHTS SOCIETIES

| | |
|---|---|
| SADAIC | Sociedad Argentina de Autores y Compositores de Musica<br>Argentina<br>Lavalle 1547<br>(1048) Buenos Aires, Capital Federal<br>ARGENTINA<br>www.sadaic.org.ar |
| A.P.R.A. | Australasian Performing Right Association<br>Australia – New Zealand<br>16 Mountain Street<br>Ultimo NSW 2007<br>AUSTRALIA<br>www.apra-amcos.com.au |
| AKM | Autoren, Komponisten, Musikverleger<br>Austria<br>1030 Wien<br>Baumannstraße 10<br>Postfach 259, 1031 Vienna<br>AUSTRIA<br>www.akm.co.at |
| S.A.B.A.M. | Societe Belge des Auteurs, Compositeurs et Editeurs<br>Belgium<br>75-77 Rue Arlon<br>1040 Brussels<br>BELGIUM<br>www.sabam.be |

| | |
|---|---|
| UBC | Uniao Brasileira de Compositores<br>Brazil<br>Rua Visconde de Inhauma 107<br>Rio de Janeiro<br>RJ<br>Cep 20091-007<br>BRAZIL<br>www.ubc.org.br |
| MUSCIAUTOR | Music author<br>Bulgaria<br>Sofia 1000<br>Budapest 17, fl 4<br>BULGARIA<br>www.musicautor.org |
| S.O.C.A.N. | Society of Composers, Authors and Music Publishers of Canada<br>Canada<br>41 Valleybrook Drive<br>Toronto, Ontario<br>M3B 2S6<br>www.socan.ca |
| SCD | Sociedad Chilena Del Derecho De Autor<br>Chile<br>Condell 346<br>Providencia, Santiago<br>CHILE<br>www.scd.cl |
| SAYCO | Sociedad de Autores y Compositttores de Colombia<br>Colombia<br>Calle 95 No. 11-31<br>Bogotá<br>COLOMBIA<br>www.sayco.org |

| | |
|---|---|
| ACAM | Asociación de Compositores de Autores Musicales de Costa Rica<br>Costa Rica<br>Apartado. Postal 234-2400<br>San José<br>COSTA RICA<br>www.acamcr.org |
| HDS | Croatian Composers Society<br>Croatia<br>www.hds.hr |
| OSA | Society for the Protection of the Rights of Music Authors and Publishers<br>Czech Republic<br>Čs. armády 20<br>160 56 Prague 6<br>CZECH REPUBLIC<br>www.osa.cz |
| KODA | Danske Sangskrivere og Komponister<br>Denmark<br>Landemærket 23-25<br>P O Box 2154<br>DK-1016 Copenhagen K<br>DENMARK<br>www.koda.dk |
| P.R.S. | The Performing Right Society (PRS for Music)<br>United Kingdom and Northern Ireland<br>Copyright House<br>29-33 Berners Street<br>London W1T 3AB<br>ENGLAND<br>www.prsformusic.com |
| EAU | Eesti Autorie Uhing<br>Estonia |

| | |
|---|---|
| | Registrikood 80004182<br>Lille 13 10614 Tallinn<br>ESTONIA<br>www.eauthors.ee |
| FPRA | Fiji Performing Right Association Ltd.<br>Fiji<br>Lynica House<br>3 Goodenough Street<br>GPO BOX 15061<br>Suva<br>FIJI<br>www.fpra.com.fj |
| TEOSTO | Finnish Composers' Copyright Society<br>Finland<br>Lauttasaarentie 1<br>FI-00200 Helsinki<br>FINLAND<br>www.teosto.fi |
| S.A.C.E.M. | Societe des Auteurs, Compositeurs et Editeurs de Musique<br>France<br>225 Avenue Charles de Gaulle<br>92528 Nevilly-Sur-Seine Cedex<br>FRANCE<br>www.sacem.fr |
| G.E.M.A. | Gesellschaft für musikalische Aufführungs- und mechanische Vervielfältigungsrechte.<br>Germany<br>Rosenheimer Str. 11<br>81667 München<br>GERMANY<br>www.gema.de |
| AEPI | Hellenic Society for the Protection of Intellectual Property Greece<br>Greece |

| | |
|---|---|
| | Fragoklisias and 51<br>Samou Str.<br>Polidroso Amarousiou<br>P.C. 151 25<br>GREECE<br>www.aepi.gr |
| CASH | Composers and Authors Society Of Hong Kong<br>Hong Kong<br>18/F<br>Universal Trade Centre<br>3 Arbuthnot Road<br>Central<br>HONG KONG<br>www.cash.org.hk |
| ARTISJUS | Society Artisjus Hungarian Bureau for the Protection of Authors' Rights<br>Hungary<br>1016 Budapest, Mészáros U. 15-17.<br>1539 Budapest 114. P.O.B. 593<br>HUNGARY<br>www.artisjus.hu |
| STEF | Samband Tonskalda og Eigenda Flutningsrettar<br>Iceland<br>Laufásvegi 40<br>IS-101 Reykjavík<br>ICELAND<br>www.stef.is |
| IPRS | Indian Performing Right Society<br>India<br>208, Golden Chambers<br>New Andheri Link Road<br>Andheri (W)<br>Mumbai 400 053<br>INDIA<br>www.iprs.org |

| | |
|---|---|
| IMRO | Irish Music Rights Association<br>Ireland<br>Copyright House<br>Pembroke Row<br>Lower Baggot Street<br>Dublin 2<br>IRELAND<br>www.imro.ie |
| ACUM | The Composers, Authors and Publishers Society of Israel<br>Israel<br>Tuval 9st. (Hilazon Corner)<br>P O Box 1704<br>Ramat Gan<br>52,117<br>ISRAEL<br>www.acum.org.il |
| SIAE | Soceita Italiano degli Autori ed Editori<br>Italy<br>Viale della Letteratura 30<br>00144 Rome<br>ITALY<br>www.siae.it |
| JASRAC | Japanese Society for Rights of Authors, Composers and Publishers<br>Japan<br>3-6-12 Uehara<br>Shibuya-Ku<br>Tokyo 151-8540<br>JAPAN<br>www.jasrac.or.jp |
| KOMCA | Korean Music Copyright Association<br>South Korea<br>KOMCA Building |

| | |
|---|---|
| | Naebalsan-dong 649<br>Kangseo-gu<br>Seoul 157-824<br>KOREA<br>www.komca.or.kr |
| AKKA–LAA | Latvia Authors Association<br>Latvia<br>A. Čaka iela 97<br>Rīga, LV-1011<br>LATVIA<br>www.akka-laa.lv |
| LATGA-A | Lithuanian Copyright Protection Association Agency<br>Lithuania<br>J. Basanavičiaus 4b<br>LT-01118 Vilnius<br>LITHUANIA<br>www.latga.lt |
| MACP | Music Authors' Copyright Protection<br>Malaysia<br>No: 6-3, Jalan 3/114<br>Kuchai Business Centre<br>Jalan Kuchai Lama<br>Kuala Lumpur 58200<br>MALAYSIA<br>www.macp.com.my |
| SACM | Sociedad de Autores y Composittores de Mexico<br>Mexico<br>Royal Mayorazgo 129<br>Col Xoco<br>C.P. 03330<br>MEXICO District Federales<br>www.sacm.org.mx |

| | |
|---|---|
| TONO | Norsk Komponistforenings Internasjonale Musikkbyra<br>Norway<br>Box 9171<br>Grønland<br>0134 Oslo<br>NORWAY<br>www.tono.no |
| APA | Autores Paraguayos Asociados<br>Paraguay<br>Direccion Postal Chile 850<br>Asuncion<br>PARAGUAY<br>www.apa.org.py |
| APDAYC | Asociacion Peruana de Autores y Compositores<br>Peru<br>Petit Thouars<br>5038 Miraflores<br>Lima<br>PERU<br>www.apdayc.org.pe |
| FILSCAP | Filipino Society of Composers Authors and Publishers<br>Philippines<br>140 Scout Rallos Street<br>Brgy. Sacred Heart<br>Quezon City<br>PHILIPPINES<br>www.filscap.com.ph |
| ZAiKS | Society of Authors ZAiKS<br>Poland<br>ul. Hipoteczna 2<br>00-092 Warsaw<br>POLAND<br>www.zaiks.org |

| | |
|---|---|
| SPA | Sociedade Portugesa de Autores<br>Portugal<br>Av. Duque de Loulé, 31<br>1069-153 Lisboa Codex<br>PORTUGAL<br>www.spautores.pt |
| RAO | Russian Authors Society<br>Russia<br>123995<br>GSP-5<br>Moscow<br>st. B. Bronnaya<br>6A<br>RUSSIA<br>www.rao.ru |
| SOKOJ | Serbian Music Authors' Association<br>Serbia<br>Misarska 12-14<br>11000 Belgrade<br>SERBIA<br>www.sokoj.rs |
| SOZA | Slovak Performing and Mechanical Rights Society<br>Slovakia<br>Rastislavova 3<br>821 08 Bratislava 2<br>SLOVAKIA<br>www.soza.sk |
| SAZAS | Society SAZAS<br>Slovenia<br>Združenje SAZAS<br>Špruha 19<br>1236 Trzin<br>SLOVENIA<br>www.sazas.org |

| | |
|---|---|
| SAMRO | Southern African Music Rights Organisation<br>South Africa<br>SAMRO Place<br>20 De Korte Street<br>Braamfontein<br>2001<br>SOUTH AFRICA<br>www.samro.org.za |
| SGAE | Sociedad General de Autores y Editores<br>Spain<br>Fernando VI<br>4 28004 Madrid<br>SPAIN<br>www.sgae.es |
| STIM | Svenska Tonsattares Internationella Musikbyra<br>Sweden<br>Sandhamsgatan 79<br>SE-102 54 Stockholm<br>SWEDEN<br>www.stim.se |
| SUISA | Cooperative Society of Music Authors and Publishers<br>Switzerland<br>Bellariastrasse 82<br>Postfach 782<br>CH-8038 Zürich<br>SWITZERLAND<br>www.suisa.ch |
| BUMA | Het Bureau voor Muziek-Auteursrecht<br>Netherlands<br>Siriusdreef 22-28<br>2132 WT Hoofddorp<br>THE NETHERLANDS<br>www.bumastemra.nl |

AGADU

Asociación General de Autores del Uruguay
Uruguay
Canelones 1122
CP. 11.100
Montevideo
URUGUAY
www.agadu.com.uy

SACVEN

Sociedad de Autores y Compositores de Venezuela
Venezuela
Av. Andrés Bello
Edif. VAM
Torre Oeste, Pisos 9 y 10
Caracas
Distrito Capital
VENEZUELA–1050
www.sacven.org

CHAPTER 19

# THE GRAND RIGHTS CONTROVERSY

## SUMMARY

1. A nondramatic rendition of a musical composition, that was not originally part of any opera, operetta, musical comedy, play, or like production, on stage in a theatre, nightclub, cabaret, concert hall, or like establishment.
2. A dramatic rendition of a musical composition, that was not originally part of an opera, operetta, musical comedy, play, or like production, on stage in a theatre, nightclub, cabaret, concert hall, or like establishment.
3. A nondramatic rendition of a musical composition that was originally part of an opera, operetta, musical comedy, play, or like production, on stage in a theatre, nightclub, cabaret, concert hall, or like establishment.
4. A dramatic rendition of a musical composition, that was originally part of an opera, operetta, musical comedy, play, or like production, on stage in a nightclub, cabaret, concert hall, or like establishment.
5. A nondramatic rendition of a musical composition, that was not originally part of an opera, operetta, musical comedy, play, or like production, in a television program, motion picture, videogram, or like work.
6. A dramatic rendition of a musical composition, that was not originally part of an opera, operetta, musical comedy, play, or like production, in a television program, motion picture, videogram, or like work.
7. A nondramatic rendition of a musical composition, that was originally part of any opera, operetta, musical comedy, play, or like production, in a television program, motion picture, videogram, or like work.
8. A dramatic rendition of a musical composition, that was originally part of an opera, operetta, musical comedy, play, or like production, in a television program, motion picture, videogram, or like work.

## VII. Recent Court Cases

A. Frank Music Corp. v. MGM Grand Hotel

B. Gershwin v. The Whole Thing Co.

## VIII. Grand Right in a Person's Life Story?

## IX. Broadcast of an Entire Album

A. Operas

B. Musical Plays

C. Other Albums

# CHAPTER 19

# THE GRAND RIGHTS CONTROVERSY

As noted in the preceding chapter, performance rights societies only provide licenses to render performances of music that are *nondramatic*. They do not grant licenses to render dramatic performances. This chapter will explore the distinction between dramatic and nondramatic performances and will suggest a framework for answering the question, from whom, if not the performance rights society, must one seek permission to render a *dramatic* performance of a musical composition? This chapter will also provide examples of dramatic and nondramatic uses and will analyze the type of license appropriate for each use.

A considerable amount of confusion among music publishers, songwriters, musical playwrights, producers, and their legal representatives has clouded the licensing of dramatic performances of music on stage, on television, and in motion pictures. Much of this confusion stems from a misunderstanding of the rights involved and, in particular, the frequent misuse of the term *grand rights*.

Before proceeding with our discussion of the meaning of dramatic, nondramatic, and grand rights, it will be useful to first survey the various ways music may be used in theatrical and non-theatrical productions.

## I. Overview of Theatrical Musical Productions

By theatrical production, we mean a production created for the living stage, which contains some literary or visual elements going beyond the mere physical appearance and rendition of music by singers and musicians. It should be noted that the kinds of theatrical productions described below should not be confused with the type of *venue* (e.g., nightclub, cabaret, concert hall, legitimate theater) at which these productions may be performed. Each kind of theatrical performance described below may be performed at any of the various kinds of venues.

The theatrical productions in which music may be used can be classified into four categories:

### A. Non-Musical Play with Incidental Music

A *non-musical play with incidental music* is what the term implies. The music is usually contracted for after the play is written and is not considered part of the play. An example might be Shakespeare's *Hamlet* with music performed merely incidental to the play.

### B. Play with Music

*Play with music* is the term reserved for a play that is essentially non-musical, but contains music, with or without lyrics. The music may be integral to the play, used to create atmosphere, indicate the time when the action is taking place, or to assist in evoking a mood or the expression of the mood or desires of a character in the play, but it does not have the effect of carrying the action ahead to the extent it does in a dramatico-musical work.

### C. Musical Revue

A *musical revue* is a stage presentation of skillfully arranged, separate musical numbers. Years ago, revues, such as Ziegfeld's *Follies*, Earl Carroll's *Vanities*, and George White's *Scandals*, contained a variety of acts, including singing, dancing, sketches, comedy bits, blackouts, and specialty performances of individuals, animal acts, and, of course, chorus girls. Today, revues usually consist entirely of musical numbers, with some sketches or improvisation. A recent example of a musical revue is *Ain't Misbehavin'*.

### D. Dramatico-Musical Work

A *dramatico-musical work* is a theatrical work in which the music is integral to the story told by the book in the sense that the music is used to carry the action of the story forward. Examples include operas, operettas, ballet, and musical plays. An *opera* — once commonly referred to as a *grand opera* — is a play with virtually the entire text of its book, or libretto, set to music or sung, with no or few spoken words. An *operetta* is the same as an opera except that a significant portion of the text of the book is spoken, rather than sung. A *ballet* is an elaborate dramatic dance set to music, often choreographed to render a narrative story. The *musical play*, or musical comedy, the modern successor to the operetta, is a play with music and lyrics that are used to carry forward the action of the story or book of the play, the text of which is rendered in spoken form. Musical plays were once commonly called *grand musical plays*, but today they are more commonly called, simply, *musicals*.

## II. Overview of Non-Theatrical Productions

The term *non-theatrical productions*, for purposes of this chapter, comprises all productions that are not live musical theatrical productions, but in which music may be used in dramatic and nondramatic ways.

### A. Motion Pictures, Television Programs, and Other Video Productions

Needless to say, motion pictures, television programs, music videos, and other forms of video productions, whether exhibited theatrically, broadcast on television, distributed in home video devices such as DVDs, or offered for download or streaming on the Internet, all employ a variety of musical works. A background and history of the use of music in motion pictures is set forth in Chapter 15, on *Licensing Music in Audiovisual Works*.

### B. Videogames

Videogames, whether distributed in home video devices for use in game consoles or made available for free or by subscription over the Internet, also employ a variety of musical works, often of genres such as alternative rock, classic rock, or urban music, suitable to the audience the game company wishes to attract to the game.

## C. Theme Park Rides and Attractions

Many major motion picture studios and entertainment conglomerates have established or purchased amusement or theme parks in the United States and abroad. Walt Disney pioneered the concept with his famous *Disneyland* theme park in Southern California and later established *Disney World* in Florida. Universal Pictures opened its studios to private and later public tours, and now the *Universal Studio Tour* is a major theme park in its own right. Time Warner acquired *Six Flags Magic Mountain.* Originally an amusement park, *Six Flags* now offers many theme attractions in its many locations. Thinking that it is a small world after all, Disney then opened versions of its *Disneyland* theme park in Japan and in Europe.

Each of these theme parks uses music, both generally and in its rides and attractions. Disneyland may perform a variety of recorded songs on its famous Main Street, throughout the day and during its popular evening parades and fireworks displays.

In addition, *Disneyland* offers a *Raiders of the Lost Ark* attraction featuring music from the soundtrack of the *Indiana Jones* movie series. Music from the Warner Bros. Pictures *Bugs Bunny* cartoons and *Superman* movies are being used in attractions in the theme parks operated by Time Warner. At Universal Studios in Hollywood, the Universal Pictures hit film *Jurassic Park* has become the theme of an attraction known as *Jurassic Park, the Ride*. Characters from Disney's *Beauty and the Beast* have also been combined with portions of the motion picture score in attractions, audioanimatronic shows, and live stage shows performed in each of the Disney theme parks.

## D. Non-Theatrical Live Performances

A musical concert of performances by a singer or recording artist, such as Tony Bennett or *The Police*, would be considered to be non-theatrical. A performance by a comedian, such as Jerry Seinfeld, would also be a non-theatrical production. As discussed below, it is possible that a musical concert or comedy performance may contain dramatic scenes or other dramatic elements, but whether a particular performance is theatrical depends upon whether the criteria for dramatic performances are met.

## III. LEGAL BACKGROUND

### A. Copyright

The copyright law identifies several categories of works of authorship, including literary works, dramatic works, musical works, choreographic works, pictorial works, sculptural works, and audiovisual works. A book, for example, is considered a *literary work*, as would a comedy routine to the extent the routine was fixed in some tangible medium of expression. A play is considered a *dramatic work*. A song, of course, is a *musical work*. *Plays with music* are considered dramatic works. *Musical revues* may be considered dramatic works, or merely compilations of musical works accompanied by incidental, literary material (e.g., monologue, dialogue, or narration). *Non-musical plays with incidental music*, as we have defined that term, are literary works accompanied by separate musical works.

Wherever the literary contribution to a work is separate from the musical contribution to a work, such as the literary and musical contributions to a non-musical play with incidental music, the copyright in the literary contribution is separate from the copyright in the musical contribution. By contrast, a *dramatico-musical work*, such as an opera or a musical play, is a work whose music is an integral part of the literary material, the music often carrying forward the action of the story. Although a copyright in each contribution to a dramatico-musical work (e.g., literary work, music, lyrics) may be claimed separately, a copyright in the dramatico-musical work as a whole may also be claimed as a single work. For example, the playwright, lyricist, and composer of a musical play can claim a copyright in the musical play in its entirety (including literary material, music, and lyrics), with each owning an undivided one-third interest in the copyright in the entire dramatico-musical work.

The owner of the copyright in a book, play, or song has the exclusive right of performance in the book, play, or song. In other words, public performances of these works require the permission of the copyright owner. Likewise, the owner of a dramatico-musical work, as a single work comprised of music, lyrics, and libretto, has the exclusive right of performance in the dramatico-musical work, and the public performance of an opera, musical play, or other dramatico-musical work requires the permission of the copyright owner of the opera or play.

## B. Licensing by Theatrical Production Companies and Theatrical Agencies

Public performances of operas, musical plays, and other dramatico-musical works, or portions of such works, at theaters, concert halls, and schools, are licensed by the copyright owners of such works, usually the play's producer or theatrical production company, but sometimes the playwrights themselves. These producers, companies, or playwrights are often represented by agencies specializing in the licensing of dramatico-musical works on their behalf. These agencies include the Tams-Witmark Music Library, Inc., Music Theatre, Inc., and Samuel French in New York, and Dramatic Publishing Co., in Chicago.[1]

## C. Licensing by Performance Rights Societies

As noted in the preceding chapter, performance rights societies license only those uses over which they have the authority or right to license. Performance rights societies do not receive any rights from theatrical production companies to license dramatico-musical works (works that comprise words, music, libretto, scenery, costumes, etc.). Further, performance rights societies receive from their music publisher and songwriter members the right to license only *nondramatic* renditions of their musical compositions, not *dramatic* renditions. Accordingly, performance licenses issued by the societies to radio and television stations, nightclubs, concert halls, and like establishments, permit the rendition of performances of music in only a manner that is *nondramatic* in nature and do not permit any performances of plays, musicals, and other dramatico-musical works. Distinguishing between dramatic and nondramatic renditions is discussed below.

---

[1] Samuel French, Inc., 25 West 45th Street, New York, NY 10036, Phone: 1-212-582-4700. www.samuelfrench.com; Tams-Witmark Music Library, Inc., 560 Lexington Avenue, New York, NY 10022, Phone: 800-221-7196, Fax: 212-688-3232; Dramatic Publishing Co., 311 Washington Street, Woodstock, IL 60098. Phone: 1-815-338-7170. www.dramaticpublishing.com.

### D. Licensing by Music Publishers

As noted above, theatrical producers, playwrights, or their agencies have the right to license performances of dramatico-musical works; performance rights societies have the right to license nondramatic performances of music in their repertoire (but they have no right to license dramatic performances and no right to license dramatico-musical works). The right to license *all other uses* of music is vested solely in the copyright owner of the music, usually a music publisher. For example, the owner of the copyright in a musical composition that was not originally part of a dramatico-musical work has the exclusive right to license *dramatic* performances of that musical composition. Nondramatic performances of that composition are licensed by the performance rights society to which a license to sublicense nondramatic performances has been granted. In some cases, a music publisher may require the consent of the songwriter to issue certain kinds of licenses, such as licenses to permit the dramatic performance of the composition, but the right to license these uses is vested exclusively in the copyright owner.

## IV. DISTINGUISHING BETWEEN DRAMATIC RIGHTS, NONDRAMATIC RIGHTS, AND GRAND RIGHTS

As the preceding sections suggest, the question of whether a particular performance is a dramatic performance, a nondramatic performance, or a performance of a dramatico-musical work is an important one, because its answer will determine who among the theatrical producers, music publishers, and songwriters have the right to license the use for which clearance is being sought. It is the question to which we now turn: the distinction between dramatic uses, nondramatic uses, and uses of dramatico-musical works — and the rights that form the basis for licensing such uses: dramatic performance rights, nondramatic performance rights, and grand rights, respectively.

### A. Dramatic Performance Defined

The essence of a dramatic performance is drama. The term *drama* implies the telling of a story or the involvement of human conflict.

Accordingly, the term *dramatic performance* has been best defined as a performance of a musical composition that is woven into and carries forward a definite plot and its accompanying action. Examples of dramatic performances are provided and discussed below.

### B. Nondramatic Performance Defined

Conversely, a *nondramatic performance* is a performance of a musical composition that is not woven into or does not carry forward a definite plot and its accompanying action. The mere singing of a song with its lyrics on stage and the broadcasting of a recording of a song on the radio would each constitute a nondramatic performance.

### C. Grand Rights Defined

A *grand right* is the exclusive right to license the reproduction, adaptation, performance or other use of a dramatico-musical work, or what was once known as a "grand opera" or "grand musical play." It is a right in all the contributions of the musical play *as a single work*. It is not a right in just the music or in any single song or other literary, musical, or other contribution to the play. The subject of the grand right is a collective work comprised of words, music, choreography, the *book* (i.e., the plot, story, or libretto), setting, scenery, costumes, and other visual representations. There is no grand right in any of the individual songs in the collective, grand musical play; as we have explained, the copyright in the grand play, including the accompanying music, is quite distinct from the copyrights in the individual compositions that comprise it.

## V. GRAND RIGHTS DISTINGUISHED FROM DRAMATIC RIGHTS

Accordingly, a *grand performance* is the performance of a grand opera, grand musical play, or other dramatico-musical work, or a substantial, recognizable portion of it. This is not the same as a *dramatic performance* of an individual composition, which is a rendition of a song (regardless of whether the song was originally part of a dramatico-musical work) that is woven into and carries forward a definite plot and its accompanying action.

The fact that there is a distinction between a *dramatic performance* and a *grand performance* may come as a surprise to many publishers and attorneys who have come to understand the terms as synonymous. Many understand the term *grand performance* to mean any dramatic performance of any musical composition and that all other performances are nondramatic, or *small performances.*[2] A careful analysis of the rights involved reveals that this is clearly not a proper usage of the terms.

## VI. ANALYSIS OF VARIOUS DRAMATIC AND NONDRAMATIC USES OF MUSIC

To illustrate what a *grand right* is, it is most useful to first examine what it is not. This section will explore the differences between dramatic and nondramatic performances by analyzing several examples of performances of music.

### A. Performance Rights Societies

As noted in Chapter 18, on *Licensing Music in Live and Recorded Public Performances*, songwriters and copyright owners grant to performance rights societies a license to sublicense the rendition of public performances of their musical works. These grants are limited solely to the rendition of performances in a *nondramatic* manner and solely to performances of their *music*. Songwriters and copyright owners do not grant to performance rights societies any right to perform music in a dramatic manner and do not grant to the societies any rights in their literary works, plays, operas, ballets, choreographic works, and other types of works of authorship.

For example, in the agreement between ASCAP and its writer and publisher members, the member may grant to ASCAP nondramatic performance rights in the separate compositions that may form part

[2] Compare, for example, *Nimmer On Copyright*, Sec. 10.10[E] (1995). If we may, in commenting upon the passage in Nimmer on the subject of grand rights, borrow a phrase that Nimmer himself used in criticism of a decision by Judge Friendly, which itself was a phrase borrowed from Horace by Judge Learned Hand to criticize a decision of Justice Oliver Wendell Holmes, "for once Homer nodded." See *Nimmer On Copyright*, Sec. 307 [A][2] (1995).

of a musical play authored by the songwriter member and owned by the publisher member, but the right to perform the musical play itself is reserved to the members.

The ASCAP agreement with each of its writer and publisher members states:

> The rights hereby granted [to ASCAP] shall include:
>
> . . . (b) The non-exclusive right of public performance of the separate numbers, songs, fragments or arrangements, melodies or selections forming part or parts of musical plays and dramatico-musical compositions, the Owner [i.e., writer or publisher] reserving and excepting from this grant the right of performance of musical plays and dramatico-musical compositions on the legitimate stage.

Thus, musical compositions that are part of dramatico-musical works may be licensed by ASCAP for public performance, provided that the performance does not include (a) the public performance of the musical play in which the song may have originally appeared or (b) the public performance of a musical composition that was originally part of a musical play on the legitimate stage. Thus, for example, ASCAP could license the song, *Tea For Two* (originally from the musical play, "No, No, Nanette") in any venue or forum, except "the legitimate stage."

The use of the term *legitimate stage* is interesting, because it is not defined in the ASCAP agreement. The term *legitimate theater* has been defined as a "live performance that relies entirely on diegetic elements, with actors performing through speech and natural movement." Diegetic elements are internal, or related to the imaginary world the characters of the play are depicting. Musical accompaniment that is done for effect on the audience, but not supposed to be part of the experience of the characters in the play, is a non-diegetic element; dancing by characters who are actually portrayed as attending a dance is diegetic; while dancing for the benefit of the audience, as in a revue or musical, is non-diegetic.[3]

[3] Babylon's Online Dictionary at http://dictionary.babylon.com. According to Wikipedia, the term *legitimate theater* "goes back to the Licensing Act of 1737 that restricted 'serious' theatre performances to the two patent theatres that had been licensed to perform "spoken drama" after the English Restoration in 1662. Other theatres were permitted to show comedy, pantomime or melodrama — and ranked as illegitimate theatre."

Thus, it would appear that, under the above provision, ASCAP could license the public performance of the song *Tea For Two* as part of a comedy performance by Jerry Seinfeld, whether the performance occurred in a comedy club or on Broadway, as the comedy performance would not be considered a "legitimate stage" performance. However, if the performance of the song were "woven into and carries forward a definite plot and its accompanying action" it would constitute a dramatic performance, which ASCAP is not authorized to license.

In its enumeration of the rights a writer or publisher member of ASCAP grants to the society, the ASCAP member agreement continues (in relevant part):

> (d) The non-exclusive right of public performance by television broadcasting; provided, however, that:
>
> (i) This grant does not extend to or include the right to license the public performance by television broadcasting or otherwise of any rendition or performance of
>
> (a) any opera, operetta, musical comedy, play or like production, as (whether or not such opera, operetta, musical comedy, play or like production was presented on the stage or motion picture form) in a manner which recreates the performance of such composition with substantially such distinctive scenery or costume as was used in the presentation of such opera, operetta, musical comedy, play or like production (whether or not such opera, operetta, musical comedy, play or like production was presented on the stage or in motion picture form): provided, however, that the rights hereby granted shall be deemed to include a grant of right to license nondramatic performances of compositions by television broadcasting of a motion picture containing such composition if the right in such motion picture other than those granted hereby have been obtained from the parties in interest . . .
>
> (e) The Owner may at any time and from time to time, in good faith, restrict the radio or television broadcasting of compositions from musical comedies, operas, operettas and motion pictures, or any other composition being excessively broadcast, only for the purpose of preventing harmful effect upon such musical comedies, operas, operettas, motion pictures, or compositions . . .

The BMI Agreement with the Writer states:

> 5. (a) The rights granted to us [hereunder] shall not include the right to perform or license the performance of more than one song or aria from an opera, operetta, or musical comedy or more than five minutes from a ballet if such performance is accompanied by the dramatic action, costumes or scenery of that opera, operetta, musical comedy or ballet. (b) You, together with the publisher and your collaborators, if any, of a work, shall have the right jointly, by written notice to us, to exclude from the grant made [hereunder] performances of more than thirty (30) minutes' duration of a work which is an opera, operetta or musical comedy, but this right shall not apply to a work which is the score of a film originally produced for exhibition in motion picture theaters when performed as incorporated in such film, or which is a score originally written for a radio or television program when performed as incorporated in such program.

Because the performance rights societies have no authority to grant licenses with respect to rights reserved by their members, blanket performance licenses issued by the societies to radio and television stations, nightclubs, concert halls, and like establishments, are careful to permit the rendition of only *nondramatic* performances of music. They do not permit *dramatic* performances and do not permit any performances of plays, musicals, and other dramatico-musical works. These limitations in the scope of licenses issued by performance rights societies are set forth in the nondramatic license forms issued to radio and television stations, nightclubs, concert halls, and other licensees. The specific language used in the several forms of performance license agreements, however, varies considerably. We will review the following three representative provisions and then apply them to specific examples of musical renditions to determine the nature of the use in each example.

## B. Performance License Provisions

The current ASCAP general license agreement for restaurants, taverns, nightclubs, and similar establishments states:

> This license is limited to nondramatic performances, and does not authorize any dramatic performances. For purposes of this agreement, a dramatic performance shall include, but not be limited to, the

> following: broadcast, only for the purpose of preventing harmful effect upon such musical comedies, operas, operettas, motion pictures, or compositions . . .

The BMI Agreement with the Writer states:

> 5. (a) The rights granted to us [hereunder] shall not include the right to perform or license the performance of more than one song or aria from an opera, operetta, or musical comedy or more than five minutes from a ballet if such performance is accompanied by the dramatic action, costumes or scenery of that opera, operetta, musical comedy or ballet.
>
> (b) You, together with the publisher and your collaborators, if any, of a work, shall have the right jointly, by written notice to us, to exclude from the grant made [hereunder] performances of more than thirty (30) minutes' duration of a work which is an opera, operetta or musical comedy, but this right shall not apply to a work which is the score of a film originally produced for exhibition in motion picture theaters when performed as incorporated in such film, or which is a score originally written for a radio or television program when performed as incorporated in such program.
>
> (i) performance of a "dramatico-musical work" (as hereinafter defined) in its entirety;
>
> (ii) performance of one or more musical compositions from a "dramatico-musical work" (as hereinafter defined) accompanied by dialogue, pantomime, dance, stage action, or visual representation of the work from which the music is taken;
>
> (iii) performance of one or more musical compositions as part of a story or plot, whether accompanied or unaccompanied by dialogue, pantomime, dance, stage action, or visual representation;
>
> (iv) performance of a concert version of a "dramatico-musical work" (as hereinafter defined).
>
> The term "dramatico-musical work" as used in this agreement, shall include, but not be limited to, a musical comedy, oratorio, choral work, opera, play with music, revue, or ballet.

The BMI general license agreement for restaurants, taverns, nightclubs, and similar establishments state:

> [This] license shall not include dramatic rights, the right to perform dramatico-musical works in whole or in substantial part, the right to present individual works in a dramatic setting or the right

to use the music licensed hereunder in any other context which may constitute an exercise of the "grand rights" therein.

The ASCAP license agreement under which television stations are licensed to perform music within ASCAP's repertoire contains the following definition of dramatic performance:

> [A] dramatic performance shall mean a performance of the musical composition on a television program in which there is a definite plot depicted by action and where the performance of the musical composition is woven into and carries forward the plot and its accompanying action. The use of dialogue to establish a mere program format or the use of any non-dramatic device merely to introduce a performance of a composition shall not be deemed to make such performance dramatic.

## C. Eight Examples of Performances of Music

The performance license provisions set forth in the preceding section appear to be a function of one or more of the following circumstances: (a) whether the nature of the performance is dramatic or non-dramatic; (b) whether the musical composition was originally part of a dramatico-musical work; and (c) whether the performance is rendered on stage or broadcast on television.

We have formulated from the above circumstances eight examples of performances of music helpful to a discussion of the scope of these performance licenses. We will analyze each of them to determine what type of license is appropriate in each case and then determine who is vested with the right to grant the license for the particular use. Finally, we will discuss the considerations used in establishing the terms of such licenses.

### *1. A nondramatic rendition of a musical composition that was not originally part of any opera, operetta, musical comedy, play, or like production, on stage in a theater, nightclub, cabaret, concert hall, or like establishment.*

Suppose Frank Sinatra sang the song, *Yesterday* (Lennon/ McCartney), as part of his popular nightclub act at a Las Vegas resort hotel.

His performance would fall within none of the four categories of dramatic performances set forth in the ASCAP general license. The song originated from a single release or record album recorded by *The Beatles* in the late 1960s. Because it did not originate from any opera, operetta, musical comedy, play, ballet, or like production, only subparagraph (iii) of the ASCAP definition might apply:

> (iii) performance of one or more musical compositions as part of a story or plot, whether accompanied or unaccompanied by dialogue, pantomime, dance, stage action, or visual representation;

Mr. Sinatra's act was composed of a series of vocal renditions of songs performed on stage with the aid of a microphone backed up by a swing orchestra, with no other significant visual representations — that is, no costume or stage props other than a well-cut tuxedo and an occasional glass of *Jack Daniels* — and as part of no story or plot, other than monologue or dialogue incidental to the introduction and performance of the song. This performance, while quite entertaining, would clearly be considered *nondramatic*.

Because the performance of *Yesterday* is nondramatic, the performance is covered by the hotel's blanket license with the performance rights society. No further permission for the use would be required.

### *2. A dramatic rendition of a musical composition that was not originally part of an opera, operetta, musical comedy, play, or like production, on stage in a theater, nightclub, cabaret, concert hall, or like establishment.*

Suppose the same song, *Yesterday*, was performed by the pop star, Madonna, as part of an elaborate performance that contained significant visual representations, making use of costume, settings, scenery, props, and other visual allusions to, for example, ancient Rome. Again, since the song is not a dramatico-musical work nor was it originally part of one, only the following category of the definition of dramatic performance in the ASCAP license might apply:

> (iii) performance of one or more musical compositions as part of a story or plot, whether accompanied or unaccompanied by dialogue, pantomime, dance, stage action, or visual representation;

Though the performance is accompanied by significant visual representations, it is not being rendered "as part of a story or plot," under the facts in this example. It is merely being performed by an artist in costume in front of scenery — no story or plot accompanies the presentation. It appears, therefore, that this performance would not be considered a dramatic rendition under the definition of dramatic performance set forth in the ASCAP license.

At this point, we will turn to the BMI general license (applying these facts as though the song were in the BMI repertoire):

> [This] license shall not include dramatic rights, . . . the right to present individual works in a dramatic setting or the right to use the music licensed hereunder in any other context which may constitute an exercise of the "grand rights" therein.

The phrase, "This license shall not include dramatic rights," is unfortunate. As noted in Chapter 7, a *license* is not a *right* — a right is a claim of ownership that allows you to exclude someone from doing something with respect to the subject of your property; a license is a permission or privilege to do something with respect to another's property that you would not otherwise have the privilege to do without the license. What the phrase beginning, "This license shall not include dramatic rights . . . ," probably means is, "This license does not include permission to render performances of music that are dramatic or to present individual songs in a dramatic setting . . ."

This still leaves us with the question whether this performance would be considered a *dramatic* performance or a presentation of the song *in a dramatic setting.* If not, then Madonna's performance in this example, like Mr. Sinatra's performance in the preceding example, would be covered by the BMI license, and no separate license would be required.

For help in determining whether a performance is dramatic or presented in a dramatic setting, most people look to the standard set forth in the definition of dramatic performance contained in the ASCAP television license, which states that a performance of a musical composition on a television program is dramatic if "the musical composition is woven into and carries forward [a definite] plot and its accompanying action."

Interestingly enough, the ASCAP general license is not precisely consistent with this language (saying instead, "performance of one or more compositions *as part of* a story or plot") and the BMI general license does not explicitly use language relating to stories or plots at all. Nevertheless, it is believed that the definition of dramatic performance that appears in the television performance license of ASCAP is most helpful in analyzing whether a performance is dramatic or nondramatic. This is the case regardless of where the performance may be rendered, even though the definition would appear by its terms to be limited to dramatic performances rendered *on television.*

A little history may shed some light on the origin of this useful definition. It is said to have been written by Oscar Hammerstein II in the 1940s. Mr. Hammerstein was concerned that television would have the potential of competing with and reducing receipts of live theatrical performances of musical plays. It is not difficult to understand why Mr. Hammerstein suggested this particular language. Musical compositions in successful musical plays are not just incorporated randomly between acts in the play; good musical playwrights consciously make use of songs to *carry forward the action* of the play, and the best use of music in a musical play is made when a composition is used to underscore a major turning point in the plot, such as a personal discovery of a principal character.[4]

The "woven into and carry forward the plot" language in Mr. Hammerstein's definition, however, seems to do more than protect the economic interests of owners of dramatico-musical works. As incorporated into the ASCAP license, it is not limited to compositions that were originally part of musical plays, operas and like productions; it appears to apply to other songs, as well, including songs such as *Yesterday*, which were not originally part of dramatico-musical works. Nevertheless, there is still good reason why publishers and writers of non-show music reserve the right to license dramatic performances from performance rights societies.

The main concern of a performing rights society is administering the collection and payment of sums generated by the performances of

[4] See Frankel, *Writing the Broadway Musical* at p. 29 (Drama Book Specialists, New York 1977).

compositions. While the value of certain performances is given greater weight than that of others (e.g., a use of a composition in a television commercial might be given more performance credits than the use of the same song as background music in a situation comedy), the importance of the song in relation to the intended use is not taken into consideration in compensating publishers and writers. A use of a particular song in a dramatic rendition (i.e., woven into and carrying forward a plot) is generally more important to the intended use than mere nondramatic renditions.

Though the differences in credits given for various kinds of performances are relatively small, the differences in the license fee charged for dramatic uses of compositions, as opposed to nondramatic uses, may vary greatly. They may vary greatly because the importance of the song in relation to the intended use varies greatly, depending, for example, upon how closely the music is woven into a dramatic plot. The more a song is woven into a plot, the more important it is to the use. The more important the song is in relation to the use desired, the higher the fee that can be commanded for its use.

Songwriters and music publishers reserve the right to issue dramatic performance licenses from their performing rights societies, because they are in a better position than the societies to determine the value of the musical composition in relation to its intended dramatic use and to price the license accordingly. Performing rights societies, who merely survey performances to roughly measure how often the songs in their repertory are performed, are not in the best position to perform this analysis. How a publisher determines the value of a license of a dramatic performance varies from song to song, and from use to use, but the publishers and writers are in a better position to reflect upon such factors and determine the value of the dramatic uses of their musical works. Thus, writers and publishers have more to gain by reserving the rights to grant licenses for the dramatic use of their music, rather than giving the performance rights society such rights. Determining when a musical composition performed on a television program is "woven into and carries forward the plot and its accompanying action" must obviously be done on a case-by-case basis. Reasonable minds may differ as to whether the facts presented would lead to a conclusion that any performance is dramatic or nondramatic. However, even though neither the general performance licenses of ASCAP or BMI mention it specifically, the standard proposed by Oscar Hammerstein II for determining the nature of performances rendered on television programs appears to be the best standard for determining whether any particular performance is dramatic or nondramatic.

If, in our example, Madonna's performance of *Yesterday* were preceded or followed by a dialogue performed on stage to establish the format of the act or if a nondramatic device were used merely to introduce her performance of the song, the performance would remain nondramatic, even if accompanied by significant visual representations, such as costumes and scenery of ancient Rome. However, any variation of facts might change the outcome. If Madonna's act carried a definite plot depicted by action and the performance of the song is woven into and carries forward the plot and its accompanying action, the performance would be dramatic. For example, the performance would probably be dramatic if her act was to some extent based upon the story of *Antony and Cleopatra* and the song *Yesterday* was woven into the act at a certain point to carry forward the idea that "all [her] troubles seemed so far away."

Assuming that the performance was deemed dramatic, then, because the performance is not covered by the ASCAP or BMI licenses (which cover only nondramatic performances), a dramatic performance license would be required before Madonna could proceed with the performance.

From whom would such a license be cleared? The license for the dramatic performance is not covered by the hotel's blanket performance license and is not available separately from the performance rights societies. The hotel, Madonna, or the producer of her act would require permission from the copyright owner of the song, which in most cases is the music publisher.

Some would suggest that the license to perform the song dramatically or in a dramatic setting must be cleared by the songwriter, because, they say, "a dramatic performance is an exercise of a grand right" and "grand rights are reserved to songwriters." However, because the song in this example was not originally part of a dramatico-musical work, *no grand right* is involved, and permission would be required from the copyright owner (i.e., the music publisher, not the songwriter — unless the songwriter's agreement with its publisher required his consent under these circumstances).

### 3. A nondramatic rendition of a musical composition that was originally part of an opera, operetta, musical comedy, play, or like production, on stage in a theater, nightclub, cabaret, concert hall, or like establishment.

An example of this use may be found in a true story and court trial in which I testified as a witness in early 1948.[5] The copyright owner of *The Student Prince* sued the owner of a cabaret in New York City called *The Harem* (owned, incidentally, at that time by Lou Walters, the father of newscaster Barbara Walters) for infringement based upon performances at the club of a medley of songs from *The Student Prince*. The nightclub owner claimed the performance was licensed under the club's standard blanket license from ASCAP. The court ruled, correctly in our view, that the performance was covered by the ASCAP license and that the medley did not infringe the musical play, *The Student Prince*. This decision has been criticized as too narrowly construing the scope of the term *dramatic performance*.[6] A close review of the facts reveals this criticism is misplaced.

The medley of songs from *The Student Prince* was performed by the choral group *Ben Yost and his Royal Guardsmen*, which was the ninth act in a ten-act nightclub show entitled, "The One Thousand and Second Night." The show was not connected by a story line or plot and the medley was just one of the numbers performed by the *Royal Guardsmen*, a small part of their act. The stage had no scenery and the act was performed in front of the nightclub stage curtain. The *Royal Guardsmen* did wear costumes — white outfits with fanciful short, red formal jackets. Nevertheless, neither the costumes nor the visual presentation bore any resemblance to the distinctive scenery or costume used in the presentation of the musical play, *The Student Prince*. Finally, the medley was truly a medley; no song from *The Student Prince* was sung in its entirety. I can confirm this because I worked for Ben Yost at the time and I personally arranged the medley that was the subject of this lawsuit.[7] I testified before the judge in the case that the medley comprised

---

[5] *April Productions, Inc. v. Strand Enterprises, Inc.*, 221 F.2d 292 (2d Cir. 1955).

[6] Nimmer On Copyright, Sec. 10.10[E] n.44 (1991) (stating that, "This decision, if followed, could mean the virtual extinction of dramatic (or grand) performing rights with respect to noninstrumental musical compositions.").

[7] A photograph of *Ben Yost and his Royal Guardsmen* in their costumes may be found at www.alkohn.com.

mostly the refrains of songs from the show connected by transitions that I composed.

The court was faced with the task of interpreting an older form of the ASCAP license for performances in nightclubs. The form, which the court was not reticent to criticize (observing, for example, "the form of the license is such that almost nothing is sure") granted to the Harem nightclub permission to render nondramatic performances of ASCAP music. The court determined that the language granting permission to render "nondramatic" renditions can best be construed in light of the other provisions of the license which describe what is not included in the license. One of those provisions prohibited the performance of compositions with "words, dialogue, costume accompanying dramatic action or scenery accessory" that was "of the work from which the music was taken."

The court observed that the form "on the one hand, describes the performance right granted as 'non-dramatic' but, on the other, in substance authorizes their exercise with 'words, dialogue, costume accompanying dramatic action or scenery accessory' " (as long as such elements were not of the work from which the music was taken). In other words, the ASCAP license permitted the rendition of musical compositions with costume, scenery, dialogue, dramatic actions, and other visual representations without their getting into the "dramatic" class. After closely examining the facts in the case, the court concluded that the performance was nondramatic. None of the costumes, scenery, dialogue or other visual representations present when the medley was performed bore any resemblance to those used in the presentation of the musical play, *The Student Prince*. Even if *The Harem* put on a dramatic performance, the court said, the selections from *The Student Prince* were not part of it.

If the court had before it the modern ASCAP nightclub performance license to construe, the result would have been no different. The performance of the medley falls within none of the four categories that comprise the definition of a dramatic performance: the performance of a medley of songs from *The Student Prince* is not (i) a performance of *the musical play* itself; (ii) the performance of one or more musical compositions from *The Student Prince* accompanied by dialogue, pantomime, dance, stage action, or visual representation *of the work from which the music is taken*; (iii) the performance of one or more musical compositions *as part of a story or plot*, whether accompanied or unaccompanied by dialogue, pantomime, dance, stage action, or visual representation; or (iv) the performance of *a concert version of* the musical play, *The Student Prince*.

Note that even the modern ASCAP license contemplates that a performance of a song originally from a dramatico-musical work may be nondramatic, even though the performance is accompanied by dialogue, pantomime, dance, stage action, or visual representation, as long as such elements are not *of the work from which the music is taken*.

Applying the facts of this case to the modern BMI general license, the same result would be reached. The BMI license does not provide permission to perform dramatico-musical works, in whole or in substantial part. The performance of a medley of songs from a musical play should not be construed as the performance of a substantial part of the musical play, unless something more is present that substantially evokes the drama inherent in the musical play. That something may be costumes, scenery, or other visual representations from the musical play or some dialogue from the play, other than that which may be part of the lyrics to the music.

The BMI general license also states that permission does not include, "the right to present individual works in a dramatic setting." Arguably, the medley from *The Student Prince* could be considered to have been presented in a dramatic setting, if the entire evening's performance at *The Harem* were considered a dramatic performance. But the court specifically held, and correctly, that the worst that could be said about the performance is that the medley was sung in an intermission between the acts of a dramatic performance, and that such a rendition was nondramatic within the meaning of the ASCAP license. A contrary holding would have the effect of rendering any simple stand-up performance of a song by an act in a variety show a dramatic performance merely because the variety show includes other acts that render dramatic performances.

Arguably, the medley could be considered to have been presented in a dramatic setting if the singers were in costume and the stage contained scenery. But the mere presence of costumes, scenery, or other visual representations should not by themselves render a setting dramatic. Something more must be present: something in the nature of drama. As noted above, the term *drama* implies the acting out or telling of a story, or the involvement of human conflict. For a setting to be dramatic, therefore, either (i) the song must be interwoven into a plot or story, or (ii) the lyrics of the song must be rendered with the presence of costumes, scenery, and visual representations from the musical play for which the song was originally written. Either of these elements, or perhaps others, such as dialogue from the musical play, would more strongly evoke the drama of the musical play than the mere performance of lyrics or instrumental arrangement. Accordingly, the performance of a medley of selections from *The Student Prince*, with little more than some fanciful costumes unrelated to the musical play, was not a rendition in a dramatic setting or a performance of the musical in whole or in substantial part.

#### *4. A dramatic rendition of a musical composition that was originally part of an opera, operetta, musical comedy, play, or like production, on stage in a nightclub, cabaret, concert hall, or like establishment.*

A concert performance of a substantial number of songs from the rock opera *Jesus Christ Superstar* is an example of a performance of music that was originally part of an opera or musical play that was held by a court to be dramatic.[8]

Timothy Rice wrote the opera's libretto and Andrew Lloyd Webber composed the score of the opera's overture and 23 songs, which depict the last seven days in the life of Jesus. The Robert Stigwood Group, the owner of the exclusive right to make stage and dramatic presentations of the rock opera, brought a lawsuit against a theatrical touring company, which produced a series of live stage performances that included 20 of the 23 musical compositions from the opera, all but one of which was rendered in identical sequence as in the original opera. As in the opera, the singers enter and exit, maintaining specific roles and occasionally making gestures, and preserving the story line of the original production. The theatrical company contended that its presentation was a *non-dramatic* performance of the compositions in *Jesus Christ Superstar*, which could be performed under the theater's license from ASCAP. Stigwood took the position that it is a dramatic performance of the

[8] *Robert Stigwood Group Limited v. Sperber*, 457 F.2d 50 (2d Cir. 1972).

songs, which is not covered by the ASCAP license. The court correctly concluded that the production was an infringement on Stigwood's rights in the opera *Jesus Christ Superstar*. However, even though the court pointed out that separate copyright registrations were obtained for the opera as a dramatico-musical work as a whole and for each of the individual musical compositions as musical works, it failed in its analysis to recognize the import of the distinction between the copyright in the opera and the copyrights in the individual compositions.

As a result, the court unnecessarily wrestled with the distinction between dramatic and nondramatic performances of the songs, when, in fact, it was not dealing with the issue of whether the performances of the songs were done in a dramatic fashion, but with the issue of whether the performance was an infringement of the rights in the dramatico-musical work *Jesus Christ Superstar*. In other words, the court held that the performance of the songs were *dramatic*, rather than holding that the performance constituted a *grand performance* of the grand opera *Jesus Christ Superstar*.

To its credit, the court recognized that it was "inescapable that the *story* of the last seven days in the life of Christ is portrayed in the [defendant's] performances substantially as in Superstar." We add emphasis to the word *story*, because the subject of the infringement was a performance of the dramatico-musical work, including its story or libretto, which is a substantial part of the dramatico-musical work. The lack of costumes or scenery did not prevent the story from being infringed. The rendition of 20 of the 23 songs in virtually the same order as they appeared in the opera, with or without costumes or scenery from the opera, is essentially a performance of the story. It should not make a difference that none of the costumes or scenery used in this performance was from the original opera presentation.

This case can be distinguished from *The Student Prince* case. In the latter, only a medley of a selection of songs from the musical was performed in a short act that was part of a variety show. For the performance of the medley to have been dramatic, something more than the rendition of the medley was required to make the performance tantamount to a performance of the musical play itself, or a substantial part of it — something like dialogue, costumes, scenery, or visual representations from the musical itself. In the *Superstar* case, the play was an opera in which most of the dialogue was comprised in the lyrics. By performing 20 of the 23 songs in order, you, in effect, render a performance of the opera, if not in whole, surely, in substantial part. No costumes, scenery, or other visual representations from the original opera need be present under these circumstances to evoke *Superstar's* drama, which was substantially comprised in the lyrics of the 20 songs selected for the performance.

Although ASCAP licensed the nondramatic performance of the individual musical compositions, ASCAP had no right to license the story, or any performance of the music that includes a substantial performance of the grand opera. The rights in the grand opera were infringed in this case. Since the ASCAP license did not permit this performance, a license would be required from Stigwood, the owners of the exclusive rights to present the opera. Note, that even if the music publishing rights to the musical compositions were granted by Stigwood to an independent music publishing company, a license to perform the opera would still be required from Stigwood, not the music publishing company. This is because the rights in the play are separate from the rights in the music, and the music publishing company would have no right to grant a license for this grand performance, unless it were given rights to the play, or some other authorization from the play's owner to do so.

### *5. A nondramatic rendition of a musical composition that was not originally part of an opera, operetta, musical comedy, play, or like production, in a television program, motion picture, videogram, or like work.*

As previously noted, the ASCAP license agreement under which television stations are licensed to perform music within ASCAP's repertoire contains a definition of dramatic performance that boils down to this: a performance of a musical composition on a television program is dramatic if the musical composition is woven into and carries forward a definite plot and its accompanying action. Determining when a musical composition performed on a television program is "woven into and carries forward the plot and its accompanying action" must be done on a case-by-case basis.

Taking the example of Frank Sinatra's singing the song *Yesterday* in his nightclub act, if we were to record Mr. Sinatra's performance on videotape and televise it, the answer to our question would be no different: the performance would not be considered dramatic. It would not be dramatic under the ASCAP license, because there is no definite plot or accompanying action into which the music can be woven or be used to carry forward. Nor would the performance be dramatic under the BMI license, inasmuch as the setting of Frank Sinatra's act would not be considered *dramatic*, in the absence of some plot and accompanying action.

Similarly, a song performed by a singer on a television variety show, such as the *Ed Sullivan Show*, would not be considered dramatic, even though portions of the variety show may contain scenes of a dramatic nature. This would be similar to the facts of *The Student Prince* case, discussed above, where the medley of songs from *The Student Prince* performed by a singing group was not deemed to be a dramatic performance, even though several other acts presented during the course of the evening at *The Harem* nightclub may have been of a dramatic nature.

Certainly, the performance of a musical composition by a band, such as the NBC band on the *Tonight Show*, is not a dramatic performance. Nor would the use of theme music over the main titles of a situation comedy, or the use of background music in a made-for-TV-movie, be considered a dramatic performance. The use of music under those circumstances could not be considered woven into and carrying forward the plot of the dramatic or comedic action.

Perhaps the music played in the background of a breathtaking car chase in a crime drama program might help carry forward the accompanying action, but it would hardly be considered woven into the plot, as nearly any action music could be substituted. The definition of dramatic performance requires, as it should, that the music be both *carrying forward* a definite plot *and* be *woven into* the plot and its accompanying action. Music that accompanies dramatic action just to vicariously enhance the action would not be considered a dramatic use.

### *6. A dramatic rendition of a musical composition that was not originally part of an opera, operetta, musical comedy, play, or like production, in a television program, motion picture, videogram, or like work.*

As we have suggested, the standard used by the ASCAP definition of dramatic performances on television programs — whether the music is woven into and carries forward a definite plot and its accompanying action — is useful for determining whether performances are dramatic, whether the performances are rendered on television, on stage, in motion pictures, or elsewhere.

Thus, the analysis of the example of Madonna's singing the song *Yesterday* in her nightclub act would be the same, whether the act were performed live, broadcast on television, or filmed for theatrical exhibition.

It may be asked whether a rock "music video" containing an audio performance of a song and a theatrical portrayal of the lyrics on screen is a dramatic performance of the song. If the song carries forward a definite plot and is woven into the plot and its accompanying action, then the performance would be dramatic. This might be the case if the story is an allegory, which the lyrics help carry forward. If the story had nothing to do with the lyrics, or if there were no story, merely some special effects or the band performing on a stage, then the use would be merely a nondramatic performance. Finally, if the story presented on the screen is actually a derivative work of the lyrics, then the use would be a *dramatic adaptation* of the lyrics, about which more is said later in this chapter.

### 7. A nondramatic rendition of a musical composition that was originally part of any opera, operetta, musical comedy, play, or like production, in a television program, motion picture, videogram, or like work.

It was sometime in the early 1960s, while working at Leo Feist, Inc., music publishing company, when I received a call requesting clearance to use the song *If I Only Had a Heart* from the MGM film production *The Wizard of Oz*, which was originally performed by Judy Garland, playing Dorothy, and Ray Bolger, as the Scarecrow. The producers of *The Garry Moore Show* wished to use the song as part of a dance number on the show, which was to be broadcast over the CBS television network. Naturally, I issued the appropriate synchronization license for the use. Unknown to the Garry Moore people or us at Leo Feist, CBS-TV had purchased the exclusive right to broadcast the motion picture, *The Wizard of Oz*, during the Christmas holiday that particular year.

A few days later, during a rehearsal of *The Garry Moore Show*, someone at CBS noticed that dancing girls were wearing scarecrow costumes somewhat similar to those worn by Ray Bolger in the motion picture. When the clearance department and legal staff of CBS heard about it, they raised hell, claiming that their grand rights in the motion picture would be infringed by the dance routine to be performed on *The Garry Moore Show* (infringed by their own network!).

As noted, the ASCAP license agreement under which television stations are licensed to perform music within ASCAP's repertoire contains the following definition of dramatic performance: a performance of a musical composition on a television program is dramatic if the musical composition is woven into and carries forward a definite plot and its accompanying action. It is clear that the mere performance on a variety television program of a single song by a group of dancers in costume does not carry forward a definite plot or story and accompanying action. Thus, the performance is not a dramatic performance. However, there is another provision in the television license that squarely governs this situation: The ASCAP television license, by its terms,

> "does not extend to or include the public performances by television broadcasting or otherwise of any rendition or performance of . . . any composition from any opera, operetta, musical comedy, play or like production (whether or not such opera, operetta, musical comedy, play *or like production* was presented on the stage or in motion picture form) in a manner which recreates the performance of such composition with substantially such distinctive scenery or costume as was used in the presentation of such opera, operetta, musical comedy, play *or like production* (whether or not such opera, operetta, musical comedy, play or like production was presented on the stage or in motion picture form)." (emphasis added)

The musical motion picture production *The Wizard of Oz* would certainly be considered a production that would fall within the scope of the above provision. Further, the performance of the song *If I Only Had a Heart* from the film *The Wizard of Oz* with scarecrow costumes by several dancers would probably be considered a manner that recreates the performance of the song, though not precisely, with substantially such distinctive costume as was used in the motion picture. Accordingly, the proposed performance would probably have constituted a grand performance in violation of CBS's exclusive rights to televise the motion picture.

To avoid the problem, the producers of *The Garry Moore Show* cleverly changed the routine: Instead of wearing the scarecrow costumes, the dancers performed the routine in their rehearsal clothes. Stories about the incident appeared in the entertainment sections of many newspapers across the country and, needless to say, the show enjoyed one of the best ratings that week.

The above incident carries several lessons for both licensors and licensees. The lesson for music copyright owners is that it is not your responsibility to guarantee that the licensee has all the rights he needs to effect the desired performance. It is the producer's responsibility to make sure he obtains a license to effect a grand performance, if that is what he will need. The producer is in a better position than you are to know just how he will be rendering the performance, and, thus, whether the performance would infringe a grand right, or some other right, such as the laws of defamation or invasion of privacy. All you can provide the producer is the license to do what you have the right to stop him from doing, such as synchronizing the song in an audio-visual work. By the same token, you should never warrant to a producer that you are giving him all the rights he needs to render the performance, as you can only license that over which you have the right to grant. If the producer renders a grand performance, he is going beyond the license you provide and is engaging in an area about which you have no responsibility.

The lesson for the person who needs to clear licenses is that it is your responsibility to clear all permissions that you require to proceed. Failure to do so will expose you to a claim for copyright infringement or some other violation of the law. Sometimes problems can be avoided by telling the music publisher precisely how you intend to use the music, and the publisher might be able to advise you that you require a license from another party to effect your use. But the copyright owner cannot guarantee that the license granted covers all the permissions that you'll require for your use, and it is not his responsibility to do so. Of course, sometimes you just can't predict a problem, as the publisher and producers didn't know that CBS acquired exclusive rights to broadcast the motion picture *The Wizard of Oz*.

In the case of *The Garry Moore Show*, the network executives probably over-reacted. The music and scarecrow costumes were going to be performed in the television studio without any scenery or background that could be associated with the film. At best, the use of the song promoted the later broadcast of the full-length motion picture on CBS. At worst, they would be in competition with themselves. If, however, it had been another network that acquired the exclusive rights, the situation could have gotten a lot worse for the producer. Finally, what should be noted by both licensors and licensees, is that while the performance of the song in scarecrow costumes would have been a *nondramatic performance* (because the routine, as rendered on *The Garry Moore Show*, would not have carried forward a definite plot and its accompanying action), it was still a performance that was not covered by the ASCAP television license. It is a *grand performance* of a song from a grand musical work, the motion picture *The Wizard of Oz*.

If the reader has followed this chapter through this point, it should have started to become apparent that a *dramatic performance* is not the same as a *grand performance*. Attempts at simplifying the complex subject of grand rights, have lead to a misuse of certain important terms. For example, the terms *small performing rights* and *grand performing rights* have been, but should not be, equated with the terms *nondramatic performing rights* and *dramatic performing rights*, respectively. We will revisit this point later in the chapter.

### *8. A dramatic rendition of a musical composition that was originally part of an opera, operetta, musical comedy, play, or like production, in a television program, motion picture, videogram, or like work.*

In a popular television series about the school life of a group of high school students, one episode called for the students to perform portions of the play *The Music Man*. The producers soon learned that television synchronization licenses to record the songs from the musical in the television program and the ASCAP licenses of the television stations to perform the songs were not going to be sufficient to clear the use, as the rendition of portions of the musical play constituted a grand performance of the musical, which required the additional permission of the owners of the musical play. Permission from the owners of *The Music Man* was required, not because the performance was dramatic, but because the use was being made of a substantial part of the musical, and permission was required to perform portions of the musical.

Many years ago, a special television program called *The Helen Morgan Story* was broadcast on the program *Playhouse '90* over the CBS Television networks. Helen Morgan was a popular entertainer in the 1920s and 1930s who became known for her singing of melancholy ballads and her gimmick of sitting on top of a piano while singing. Her most memorable role included starring in the Broadway musical *Show Boat* (1928). Over the years, she became identified with several of the songs from the musical *Show Boat*, especially the song *Bill*, which became her theme song. *The Helen Morgan Story* was the story of the entertainer's life, as told by Helen Morgan, sitting on a piano with her legs crossed. The only song featured in the program was her theme song, *Bill*.

What made the performance so unusual was that the song was the only song used in the program and was played throughout the program at various tempos, depending upon the period of the entertainer's life being presented. For example, while Morgan was describing a tranquil period of her life, the song was performed *adagio*; while she was describing a tempestuous period of her life, the song was performed *allegro*. The owners of the song sued CBS, claiming that the use was dramatic, and therefore outside the scope of the ASCAP performance license. The case was settled, but the issue as to whether CBS actually required an additional license is still an interesting one.

If the song *Bill* was performed with dialogue, costumes, scenery, or other visual representations from the musical *Show Boat*, then the performance would clearly have been a grand performance of the musical *Show Boat* (or a substantial part of it), which would have required permission from the owners of the show. This, however, was clearly not the case in *The Helen Morgan Story* television program. At most, she may have sung the song at a point in the show where she was describing the events surrounding her Broadway experiences, but this would not be a performance of the musical play *Show Boat*, without some material from the show, such as dialogue, costume, or scenery, in addition to the rendition of the lyrics of the song.

If the song was "interwoven and carrying forward a definite plot and its accompanying action," the performance would be *dramatic*, requiring a license from the copyright owner of the song, because the ASCAP license for nondramatic performance would not cover the use. Sometimes the answer to the question of whether a performance carries forward a definite plot is, "I know it when I see it," and the answer in this case may require an actual viewing of the program. If the lyrics of the song *Bill* somehow carried forward the story, then it is more likely that the use was dramatic. For example, if there were an actual person named Bill, who played a part in Helen Morgan's life, and the song *Bill* carried forward some action concerning Helen Morgan and the real-life person named Bill, then it could be said the song carried forward the story. If the use of the music was merely instrumental, or of the lyrics of the song *Bill* had no relation to any events in her life, then it is more likely that the song did not carry forward the story.

Even assuming the song did "carry forward" Helen Morgan's telling of the story of her life, the question remains, does a life story have a *plot*, as that term is used in the ASCAP license, or otherwise used in determining whether a performance is dramatic? There is a public policy, grounded in the First Amendment to the U.S. Constitution, favoring the free dissemination of ideas, which, among other things, affords creators of biographical and other historical works a higher degree of flexibility in incorporating into their works the works of others than is afforded creators of purely fictional works. Nevertheless, biographies when presented in television programs and motion pictures, other than pure documentary programs, tend to contain a substantial amount of fictional material. Called *docu-dramas*,[9] these programs, while purporting to be biographies, often contain more fiction than fact and are created more for their entertainment value than for their value as a contribution to historical knowledge.

In light of the foregoing considerations, it is believed that a performance of a song that carries forward the "plot" and accompanying action in a docu-drama would more likely constitute a dramatic use; a performance of a song that carries forward a life story in a pure documentary would be less likely to constitute dramatic use. The question whether *The Helen Morgan Story* would be considered more of the nature of a docu-drama or of the nature of a documentary, and whether the use of the song *Bill* in the Helen Morgan Story was a dramatic or nondramatic performance, we will leave for historians and legal scholars to ponder.

---

[9] See, generally, Lionel S. Sobel, *The Trials and Tribulations of Producing Docu-Dramas*, 5/3 Entertainment Law Reporter 3 (August 1983).

## VII. RECENT COURT CASES

### A. Frank Music Corp. v. MGM Grand Hotel

Probably the first court to recognize, at least implicitly, the distinction between a dramatic performance of individual songs and the exercise of a grand right, or *grand performance* of a play or musical, is the Ninth Circuit Court of Appeals in a case involving a harem of a different sort.[10]

In 1974, the MGM Grand Hotel in Las Vegas, Nevada, produced a musical revue called *Hallelujah Hollywood* in the hotel's lavish Ziegfeld Theatre. The show featured ten acts of singing, dancing, and variety performances. Of the ten acts, four were labeled as "tributes" to MGM motion pictures of the past and one was a tribute to the *Ziegfeld Follies*. The remaining acts were variety numbers, which included performances by a live tiger, a juggler, and the magicians, Siegfried and Roy. Act IV of *Hallelujah Hollywood* was entitled *Kismet*, which became the subject of the lawsuit.

The original version of *Kismet* was a dramatic play, written by Edward Knoblock in 1911, which entered the public domain in 1967. In 1952, Edwin Lester acquired the right to produce a musical stage production of the dramatic play *Kismet*. In 1953, Lester hired Luther David and Charles Lederer to write the libretto and Robert Wright and George Forrest to write the music and lyrics for the dramatico-musical adaptation. In 1953, Lederer and Davis copyrighted their dramatico-musical play *Kismet*, and Wright and Forrest assigned to Frank Music Corporation the right to copyright all portions of the musical score written for the musical. Frank Music subsequently obtained copyrights for the entire score and for each of the songs in the score. In 1954, Lederer, Wright, and Forrest entered into a license agreement with MGM, Inc. granting it the rights to produce a musical motion picture based on their dramatico-musical play. MGM released its motion picture version of *Kismet*, starring Howard Keel and Ann Blyth, in 1955.

The story presented in the MGM film and in the dramatico-musical play is essentially the same as that told in Knoblock's dramatic play.

---

[10] *Frank Music Corp. v. Metro-Goldwyn-Mayer, Inc.*, 772 F.2d 505 (9th Cir. 1985).

*Kismet* is the tale of a day in the life of a poetic beggar named Hajj and his daughter, Marsinah. The story is set in ancient Baghdad, with major scenes in the streets of Baghdad, the Wazir's palace, an enchanted garden, and the Wazir's harem.

Act IV of *Hallelujah Hollywood* presented at the MGM Grand Hotel, entitled *Kismet*, was billed as a tribute to the MGM movie of that name. Comprised of four scenes, the *Kismet* act was eleven and one-half minutes in length. It was set in ancient Baghdad, as was the dramatico-musical play, and the characters were called by the same or similar names to those used in the musical play. Five songs were taken in whole or in part from the musical. No dialogue was spoken during the act, and, in all, it contained 6 minutes of music taken directly from the musical play, and the songs were performed by singers identified as characters from the musical play, dressed in costumes designed to recreate *Kismet*. The performance made use of locale, settings, scenery, props, and dance style music of the type used in the musical play *Kismet*.

Within a few months after the premier of *Hallelujah Hollywood*, the MGM Grand was informed that it was infringing the *Kismet* musical play. MGM Grand responded that it believed its use of the music from the musical play was covered by its performance license from ASCAP.

The case went to court and the lower court held that the *Kismet* performances at the MGM Grand constituted copyright infringements, because the performance was outside the scope of the ASCAP license. The court addressed two clauses of the ASCAP license: (i) the clause that limits the performances by MGM Grand to "non-dramatic" renditions, and (ii) the clause that excludes from the license "dramatico-musical works, or songs [accompanied by] visual representations of the work from which the music is taken." The lower court ruled that, while the performances were nondramatic, they were outside the scope of the latter clause of the ASCAP license, because they contained visual representations from the musical play. (The court of appeals agreed with the result reached by the lower court, but stated that there was no need to consider whether Act IV was dramatic or nondramatic, because the clause excluding the performance of dramatico-musical work was sufficiently determinative.)

Both the lower court and the court of appeals seemed to recognize that the issue in the case was not whether the performance of the individual songs was dramatic in nature, but whether the hotel had a license to present a portion of the dramatico-musical play. In other words, whether the play producer's *grand right* in the play was infringed. In this case, the lower court ruled that the grand right was infringed, even though the performance was nondramatic! So much for the idea that grand performances are the equivalent of dramatic performances!

### B. Gershwin v. The Whole Thing Co.

A more complex example of a stage performance of music that was claimed to be unauthorized was the musical revue entitled *Let's Call the Whole Thing Gershwin.*[11]

The revue, created in 1978, consisted of theatrical performances of approximately forty songs, written entirely or largely by George and Ira Gershwin, and performed by a cast of eight actors and actresses wearing a variety of costumes and rendering some original dance routines and dance skits. The revue used some scenery such as photographs of the Gershwins and a limited amount of dialogue describing the Gershwins, their music, and the circumstances in which their works were created. The revue included an identifiable character, Ira Gershwin, who appears as a man struggling to write lyrics for his brother George's music.

After deciding to produce the revue, the producer sought to obtain licenses from certain music publishers. Having obtained "living stage" licenses from the music publishers, the producer then proceeded on the assumption that a license from Mr. Gershwin was not required. When Mr. Gershwin's attorneys became aware of the fact that the producer was to stage the revue, they informed the producer that a license was required from Mr. Gershwin because, they asserted, the music publishers did not possess sufficient rights of copyright for the dramatic stage production of the revue and because Mr. Gershwin's rights of publicity would be invaded by the contemplated production. The producer asserted that its living stage licenses from the music publishers were sufficient and a license from Mr. Gershwin was not required.

After some negotiation, the parties entered into a settlement agreement, which enabled the producer to stage the revue without a lawsuit.

---

[11] *Gershwin v. The Whole Thing Co.*, 208 U.S.P.Q. (C.D. Cal. 1980).

Nevertheless, after the production opened, a lawsuit ensued over extent of the rights granted under that agreement. The court granted a preliminary injunction halting the performance of the play beyond a certain date. It also ordered the producer not to engage in any further agreements for future presentations of the play beyond that date nor present the revue at any location other than at the theater at which the revue was then being presented.

The legal question explored here is whether, in addition to the license the producer had received from the music publishing companies, a license from the Gershwins was required to produce the revue. Though that question was not specifically resolved by the court, the court's opinion is notable, because it is one of the few cases that attempts to define the term *grand rights*.

What makes the analysis of this case so complex is the fact that, though some of the songs performed in the revue were originally part of a Gershwin musical or opera, such as *Lady Be Good*, and *Porgy and Bess*, others were not, such as the instrumental work, *Concerto in F*.

In our view, with respect to the compositions that were not originally part of a Gershwin musical play, the producer received all the licenses it needed under a living stage license that it received from the music publishers to use these songs in a musical revue on stage. Any nondramatic renditions of the songs were covered by the theater's performance licenses from ASCAP and BMI; any dramatic renditions (and any nondramatic renditions, to the extent the theater was not licensed by the appropriate performance rights societies) were covered by the living stage licenses obtained from the music publishers.

With respect to the compositions that were originally part of a Gershwin musical, the producer only needed a license to the extent the performance would constitute an infringement of the musical or opera in which the songs originally appeared — that is, whether they are performed "in a manner which recreates the performance of such composition with substantially such distinctive scenery or costume *as was used in the presentation of* such opera, operetta, musical comedy, play, or like production." To the extent the performances were not used in such manner, the producer could rely on the living stage license that it received from the music publishers.

It would not matter if the performers in the revue were wearing *any* kind of costumes or if the scenery used was *any* kind of scenery.

The producer could avoid infringing the *grand right* in the grand operas and grand musical plays as long as the costumes were not from the operas and musicals and the scenery and other visual presentations from the Gershwin musicals and operas. In other words, the libretto, scenery and costumes of the original Gershwin shows form the basis of the *grand rights* the Gershwins have in those shows, not any new plot or unrelated scenery or costumes that may have been created for the revue.

Having seen the musical revue in question, we do not believe that any of the performances in *Let's Call the Whole Thing Gershwin* amounted to a performance that was substantially similar to any of the Gershwin musicals, or any substantial portion of them, in which certain songs in the revue were originally a part. The revue was a series of musical compositions interwoven into an original story that had no resemblance to any of the original musical plays in which the songs originally appeared. The only resemblance was in the fact that the performances in the revue, like some of the songs in the original plays, were rendered live on stage, but the producer had already obtained the right to make such living stage performances of the music. Accordingly, no grand right was invaded, and if the producer would have prevailed on the theory that the libretto was a constitutionally protected biographical work, then, assuming there was nothing in the agreement between the music publishers and the Gershwins reserving to the Gershwins living stage rights to their compositions, the living stage licenses the producer received from the music publishers would have been sufficient to permit performances of the revue and no further rights from the Gershwins were necessary.

We said the case was interesting for the definition it offered for the term *grand rights*:

> There are two basic tests to determine whether grand rights are required. Grand Rights are required if (1) a song is used to tell a story . . . or (2) a song is performed with dialogue, scenery or costumes.

The errors in this over-simplified statement of the definition of *grand rights* should be obvious at this point, and it is hoped that courts would pass over it in favor of a more precise analysis, such as that rendered in the MGM Grand case discussed previously.

## VIII. GRAND RIGHT IN A PERSON'S LIFE STORY?

It may be recalled that one of the grounds that Ira Gershwin, by his attorneys, asserted to prevent the further performances of *Let's Call the Whole Thing Gershwin* is that the play infringed the right of publicity of George and Ira Gershwin. The *right of publicity* is the exclusive right a person has to exploit his or her name, likeness or photograph for commercial or advertising purposes.

A substantial body of law has evolved over the scope of one's right of publicity, including whether such a right survives a person's death and inures to the benefit of his estate. Over the past 50 years, the exclusive right of a person to commercially exploit his name and likeness has evolved through a number of court decisions, involving a number of well known celebrities, including Groucho Marx, Elvis Presley, and Nancy Sinatra. Initially, the courts recognized this commercial right as part of a person's *right to privacy*; later they began to separately identify a person's *right of publicity* and some states have since enacted legislation specifically governing the scope and duration of this right.[12]

A complete discussion of the right of publicity is beyond the scope of this book. Suffice it to say, however, that if you are seeking to clear permission to use a musical composition and you also desire to use the name, likeness, or photograph of the songwriter or artist who recorded the work, you may be required to obtain a separate clearance for that use directly from the songwriter or artist.

The Gershwin case presented some interesting issues that have not been completely decided by the courts. One intriguing issue is the extent to which the right of publicity allows a person to control the use of biographical information about himself. Gershwin claimed that the use of the pictorial and biographical material about him, including the use of the name "Gershwin" in the title of the revue, *Let's Call the Whole Thing Gershwin*, required his permission. The use of such materials, his attorneys asserted, infringed upon Gershwin's right of publicity. In effect, Ira Gershwin was seeking to establish a form of *grand right* in his life story.

---

[12] See, generally, J.T. McCarthy, *The Rights of Publicity and Privacy* (1995).

As previously noted, the courts have recognized a strong public policy interest in the free dissemination of ideas and information, a policy that finds its basis in the guarantee of free speech in the First Amendment of the U.S. Constitution. For this reason, public figures may not assert a *right of publicity* to prevent the publication of "unauthorized" biographies. It is possible, therefore, that the libretto of *Let's Call the Whole Thing Gershwin* would be deemed primarily biographical in nature and therefore, Gershwin's right of publicity would not have been an effective bar to allowing this information to be used as part of performances of the revue.

The line, however, between a person's name and likeness in a biographical work, the use of which does not require a license, and a person's name and likeness for commercial merchandising purposes, which does require a license, is not always an easy one to draw. Television or motion picture *docu-dramas*, which are based on biographical material, have been challenged as merchandising uses that require permission, on the basis that the fictional "pillow talk" dramatized in these productions does not even pretend to be historical fact, and is created not for historical or general interest, but merely for their entertainment value as fiction.

The issues relating to the right of publicity are complex, and your use of materials concerning celebrities or other public figures may also require a consideration of the law of libel and right of privacy. Accordingly, when treading this ground, you should seek counsel of an attorney experienced in these areas.

## IX. Broadcast of an Entire Album

### A. Operas

The *Jesus Christ Superstar* case discussed above — involving the stage performance of 20 of the 23 musical compositions from the opera, all but one rendered in identical sequence as in the original opera — raises another interesting question: Does a radio broadcast of an entire cast album of an opera involve more than the mere nondramatic performance of the musical compositions in the play? In other words, would an unauthorized broadcast of an entire cast album of an opera constitute an infringement of the opera? The outcome of the *Jesus Christ Superstar* case suggests that the answer is Yes.[13] The radio broadcast of an entire cast album of a grand opera would probably constitute a *grand performance* of the opera, requiring the permission of the owner of the *grand rights* in the opera. To be a grand performance, however, the broadcast would have to be of a substantial number of the songs in the opera in substantially the sequence that they appear in the opera.

## B. Musical Plays

A different result may be reached if the broadcast were of an album of a musical play, rather than of an opera. It may be recalled that an *opera* is a play with virtually the entire text of its book, or libretto, set to music or sung, with no or few spoken words. By contrast, a *musical play* is a play with music and lyrics with the text of the book rendered in spoken form. Cast albums of musical plays rarely include all of the spoken text of the book. Accordingly, the broadcast of a cast album of a musical play is less likely to be deemed a grand performance of the musical play than the broadcast of a recording of an opera, because two important parts of the work — the visual presentation and the book — are absent from the performance. A recording of an opera, broadcast in its entirety, includes every element of the opera, except the visual presentation.

Nevertheless, while the broadcast of the cast album of a musical play will not usually constitute an infringement of the musical play, it may be an infringement of another copyright, which is discussed in the following section.

## C. Other Albums

Owners of cast album recordings of musical plays, and, for that matter, owners of all other kinds of record albums — including pop, jazz, and rock recordings — may have an independent ground upon which to enforce an exclusive right to broadcast entire record albums. It has long been the position of the recording industry that the

[13] In fact, the court specifically suggested an affirmative answer to this question, but partly on the wrong basis: "Indeed, radio performances of operas are considered dramatic, because the story is told by the music and lyrics." 457 F.2d at 55 (1972).

unauthorized broadcast of an entire record album, or substantially all of a record album, with no or few commercial interruptions, constitutes an infringement of copyright. The copyright that forms the basis of such infringement would be the *compilation* of the songs included on the album.

Under the copyright law, a *compilation* is "a work formed by the collection and assembling of preexisting materials or of data that are selected, coordinated, or arranged in such a way that the resulting work as a whole constitutes an original work of authorship."[14] If the selection and sequential ordering of the recordings on a record album can be considered an original work of authorship, then the unauthorized public performance of the compilation, as a work separate and apart from the recordings that comprise the compilation, would constitute copyright infringement. Some record companies have filed copyright registrations to claim compilation copyrights in their selection and arrangement of recordings on the record albums they publish. Though a compilation copyright in a record album, as a whole, is not a *grand right*, it is akin to a grand right and a performance of an entire record album, or substantially all of a record album, is akin to a grand performance of a grand opera or grand musical play.

If the selection and sequential ordering of the recordings on a record album can be considered copyrightable compilation, then a question arises as to whether services used by Apple's iTunes software infringes that compilation by providing the ability to identify the recordings in a CD compilation and rip those CDs to a hard disk, together with the names of the tracks, in the order they were compiled by the compilation's copyright owner. No one has yet challenged such software on this basis.

## X. THEME PARK RIDES AND ATTRACTIONS

As discussed above, performance rights societies do not license music in performances that are anything other than nondramatic performances. To engage in the dramatic performance or to create a dramatic adaptation of a copyrighted song, you must obtain permission from the music publisher. To summarize briefly, a *nondramatic*

---

[14] 17 U.S.C. Sec. 101.

*performance* is a performance of a musical composition that is not woven into or does not carry forward a definite plot and its accompanying action. Conversely, a *dramatic performance* is a performance of a song that is woven into and carries forward a definite plot and its accompanying action.

The question that arises is: does the use of the musical title theme from the motion picture *Raiders of the Lost Ark* in a ride at *Disneyland* that employs the images, sounds, and effects of the motion picture of that name, become a dramatic performance of the song? As thin as the argument may be, the music publishers have taken the position that a theme park ride or attraction indeed has a plot, or at least the requisite element of drama, for the performance of the song to be considered dramatic. Similarly, the use of the music from the film *Jurassic Park* in *"Jurassic Park, the Ride,"* in which visitors are frightened with images of dinosaurs and their associated sounds and effects, are considered to be dramatic performances of the song.

Accordingly, the theme park, Disneyland and Universal Studios, in these examples, have not been able to rely merely on the blanket licenses they obtained from the performance rights societies, such as ASCAP and BMI in the United States, to cover these uses. In many cases, they have been required to obtain dramatic performance licenses directly from the music publishers of the songs.

The same would be true if the ride or attraction was a dramatic adaptation (e.g., creating an attraction out of the lyrics of a song) or the exercise of a grand right in a musical play (e.g., a ride or attraction that combines the performance of a song with the scenes of a play or similar work in which the song was originally an integral part). In either event, the important point is that if the use is not strictly a nondramatic performance, then engaging in the use may require something other than a blanket license from a performance rights society and that license must be obtained from the copyright owner of the song.

## XI. DRAMATIC ADAPTATION RIGHTS

### A. Legal Background

The copyright law grants to the owner of copyright certain exclusive rights in a musical composition, among which, we have noted, are the exclusive right to make copies of the song (called the *reproduction right*), the exclusive right to perform the song (the *performance right*), and the exclusive right to prepare derivative works of the song (often referred to as the *adaptation right*).

A copyright owner of a song may exercise his reproduction right by granting a license to allow another to reproduce the song in printed form (by a "print license") or on a record album (by a "mechanical license"). The copyright owner may exercise his performance right by allowing the rendition of the song in a nightclub or by broadcast on live television or radio. Both the reproduction right and the performance right involve the use of the musical composition verbatim — that is, the exercise of these rights involve permission to use the song word-for-word, note-for-note. By contrast, the *adaptation right* involves preparation of a different version of the song or the preparation of another work that is in some way derived from the song. A work that is derived from another work is called a *derivative work.* A copyright owner's exclusive right to prepare adaptations, or derivative works, is a most important right, because it defines the scope of the copyright protection. The copyright law contains a fairly precise definition of the term, derivative work:

> A 'derivative work' is a work based upon one or more preexisting works, such as a translation, musical arrangement, dramatization, fictionalization, motion picture version, sound recording, art reproduction, abridgment, condensation, or any other form in which a work may be recast, transformed, or adapted.

Thus, when the music copyright owner commissions the translation of the lyrics of a song into a foreign language or the arrangement of the music for certain instruments, such as a big band arrangement, he is exercising his adaptation right — permitting the preparation of an adaptation or derivative work of the song.

## B. Popular Songs

A music copyright owner is also exercising his adaptation right when he allows another to make a dramatization, or dramatic adaptation, of the lyrics of a song. For example, the screenplay and motion picture entitled *Ode to Billie Joe* was a dramatic adaptation of the song of the same title written and performed by country singer Bobbie

Gentry. Similarly, the 1970s television series *Harper Valley P. T. A.* was a dramatic adaptation of the lyrics of the song of the same name, written by Tom Hall and originally recorded by country singer Jeannie Riley.

The script of a motion picture that is derived from the lyrics of a song would be a "derivative" work of the song. The exclusive right *to prepare derivative works* is a right under copyright completely distinct from the right *to perform a work publicly*. While the singing of the song *Ode to Billie Joe* during the motion picture of that title is a *performance* and its licensing an exercise of the performance right in the song, the creation of the motion picture itself, which is *a dramatic adaptation* of the song, is an exercise of the adaptation right, not the performance right, in the song.

Therefore, neither the creation of the motion picture *Ode to Billie Joe* nor the script from which it is derived is a "performance" of the song. The performance of the movie involves a performance of the song only to the extent the song, as recorded in the soundtrack, is rendered during the performance of the movie. Thus, if one were to make a movie based upon the lyrics of a song — a dramatization or motion picture version of the song — without permission from the copyright owner of the song, the movie maker would be liable not for an unauthorized performance, but for violating the copyright owner's right to make derivative works of the song, that is, the copyright owner's dramatic adaptation right. The right of reproduction in the song would be violated if, and only if, a recording of the song were made part of the motion picture soundtrack without a license; the performance right in the song would be violated only if the sound track were performed in theaters without a license. The dramatization of the lyrics involves a separate exclusive right under the copyright — the adaptation right.

## C. Show Tunes

Suppose a producer wished to prepare a short movie dramatization of the song, *Tea For Two*, a song that was originally part of the Broadway musical *No, No, Nanette*. This movie might be a short love story about a young couple having tea together while discussing their desire to have a boy for her and a girl for him. As long as the movie dramatization of the lyrics did not use any elements of the show *No, No, Nanette* — such as dialogue, costumes, scenery or other visual representations from the musical — the grand rights in the musical would not be infringed. Accordingly, while the producer of the movie would require permission of the copyright owner of the song (i.e., the music publisher) to make the dramatic adaptation, no permission from the owners of the show *No, No, Nanette* would be required for this use. Of course, if the song *Tea For Two* were to be performed in the movie, either on screen or as background music, or if any of the lyrics were to be quoted as part of the dialogue in the action, then a synchronization license would also be required.

### D. Music Videos

It may be interesting to note that some "music videos" seen on television networks such as MTV may represent examples of dramatic adaptations. Though in many of these video programs, the featured musicians are seen performing the song on a stage or in the streets, some videos depict the performing artists visually portraying or acting out the story of the lyrics. If the visual scenario of the video is a direct dramatization of the song's lyrics, it would be considered a dramatic adaptation, or derivative work, of the song, the making of which, as we have said, requires separate permission from the song's copyright owner. If the artists are acting out a story, but the story is not the story told by the lyrics, the video would not be considered a derivative work, or dramatic adaptation of the song; however, if the song is otherwise interwoven into and carries forward some definite plot, the song is being performed dramatically, and the rendition of a dramatic performance also requires permission from the song's copyright owner.

### E. Separate Adaptation License Required

Whether or not a song was originally published as part of a dramatico-musical work, the performance licenses issued by performance rights societies would not cover the adaptation of the song *Ode to Billie Joe* or the song *Tea For Two* into a motion picture, or the song *Harper Valley P. T. A.* into a television series — not by virtue of the dramatic nature of the use, but by virtue of the fact that the uses are not performances. Since performance rights societies only license performances, and not the preparation of derivative works, performance licenses would not authorize the use.

Further, standard synchronization licenses permitting the producer to make reproductions of a recording of the song in timed-relation with audiovisual programs, such as motion pictures, television shows, and music videos, would not include permission to create a dramatic adaptation of the lyrics of the song. In fact, some carefully drafted synchronization licenses specifically exclude such uses by reference. Accordingly, wherever a license to dramatize a lyric is desired, a separate license under the copyright owner's exclusive adaptation right will be required. Producers should not think they are acquiring such a right by merely obtaining a synchronization license or a performance license.

### F. Dramatic Adaptation Right Is Not a Grand Right

Dramatic adaptations of song lyrics have often been mistakenly associated with the concept of the grand right. As we have stated, the grand right is a performance right — a right in grand operas and musical plays, not in individual songs. Further, it is a right to *perform*, not to adapt. A *dramatic adaptation* is a derivative work of the lyrics of a song, whether or not the song was originally part of a musical play. A derivative work is a *work* — a new version of a song — not a *performance* of the song. Accordingly, the script and motion picture *Ode to Billie Joe*, for example, does *not* involve the exercise of a *grand right*. It is a new work, not a performance (and not a performance of a part of a grand opera or musical play).

## XII. DETERMINING WHO HAS THE RIGHT TO LICENSE THESE USES

Who has the right to license a particular use of music depends upon (1) the proper identification of the rights on the basis of which licenses can be cleared for the use and (2) the provisions of the contracts governing those rights among those that have an interest (i.e., copyright or contractual) in the music.

Despite the widespread confusion on the subject, it is important to correctly draw a distinction among small dramatic performances, small nondramatic performances, grand performances, and dramatic adaptations. A proper distinction among these rights is often critical to determining what rights need to be cleared in order to render a dramatic or theatrical performance and who — among the performance rights societies, the songwriters, the playwrights, the music publishers, and the theatrical producers — has the right to license such uses.

## A. Nondramatic Performances

Under their respective agreements with performance rights societies, songwriters and music publishers grant to their respective performance rights societies a license to sublicense the rendition of nondramatic performances of musical works.

If a song is being performed on a radio station, in a television station, or in a nightclub, a concert hall, or other establishment licensed by the performance rights society, and the use is within the scope of the performance license, then no further license is required to render the performance. A use is outside the performance license if the performance is dramatic, if the performance is a grand performance of a dramatico-musical work, or if the performance infringes upon any number of other rights of individuals, such as, for example, the right of publicity, the right of privacy, or the right not to be defamed.

The performance rights society has no right to grant licenses for uses that are outside the scope of their standard performance licenses and, accordingly, clearance to make any other use requires permission of some other person or organization who owns the right involved.

## B. Dramatic Performances

A *dramatic performance* of an individual composition is a rendition of a song that is woven into and carries forward a definite plot and its accompanying action, regardless of whether the song was originally part of a dramatico-musical work.

Under most standard music publishing agreements, the songwriter grants to the music publisher the undivided copyright in the song. The grant includes a grant of all exclusive rights, including the exclusive right to grant dramatic performance licenses. The only licenses that the songwriter is authorized to grant are those that are specifically reserved to the songwriter in the music publishing contract. The exclusive right to license dramatic performances is not typically among the rights reserved to the writer. The only right typically reserved to the writer is the right to receive the writer's share of performance royalties directly from the writer's performance rights society (e.g., ASCAP or BMI), a right that the writer receives from his performance rights society when he becomes a member. Since the rights the writer retains is limited to the right to grant licenses for nondramatic performances, the rights to grant licenses to dramatic performances are vested in the music publisher under the broad grant of rights typically made in standard songwriter contracts. Consequently, with respect to most songs that were not originally part of musical plays or other dramatico-musical works, it is the music publisher who is exclusively entitled to grant permission for dramatic performances of the song.

Some songwriter contracts, however, require that the publisher obtain the writer's consent before granting dramatic performance licenses. Such a requirement appears in the standard form contract recommended by the Songwriter's Guild (formerly AGAC). The Songwriter's Guild agreement does not empower the writer to grant dramatic performance licenses; only the publisher has the power to grant such licenses, but the issuance of such licenses requires the consent of the songwriter.

Unless the agreement between the writer and his publisher specifically reserves to the writer the right to license dramatic performances of the composition, or reserves for the writer a right of approval over such dramatic uses, the publisher has the sole right as between the parties to license such rights.

## C. Dramatic Adaptations

As stated above, songwriters typically grant their undivided interest in the copyright in the song to their music publishers, reserving only the rights related to collecting the writer's share of performance fees for the rendition of nondramatic performances, which the writer receives from his performance right society. All other rights reside with the music publisher, subject, of course, to the payment of royalties to the writer arising from revenues associated with the exercise of the rights assigned to the music publisher. Thus, the music publisher is typically vested with the exclusive right to license dramatizations, or dramatic adaptations, and other derivative works.

Unless the songwriter's contract provided otherwise, the music publisher would have the sole right as between the songwriter and the music publisher to license dramatic adaptations of the writer's lyrics in any manner and by any means. It will be recalled that a dramatization is a derivative work, not a type of performance. Even if a songwriter contract specifically reserves to the writer the right to license dramatic performances, or reserves to the songwriter the right of consent to the publisher's granting of dramatic performances, this has no effect on the publisher's exclusive right to prepare or license the preparation by others of derivative works, such as dramatizations of lyrics.

Some music publishing agreements provide that the publisher's right to license dramatizations is subject to the consent of the songwriter. Again, such a provision would not give the writer the right to grant dramatic performance licenses; the publisher has the sole power to grant such licenses, but the issuance of such licenses requires the consent of the songwriter.

### D. Grand Performances

As we have said, the *grand right* is the exclusive right to license the reproduction, adaptation, performance, or other use of a dramatico-musical work, or what was once known as a "grand opera" or "grand musical play." It is a *right in the play, not in the music*, although the play may include music. The *grand right* rests with the owner of the play, not in the owner of the individual compositions in the play. Accordingly, if you intend to clear a license to render a *grand performance* of a musical play, or a substantial, recognizable portion of the play, then you require permission from the owner of the musical play. If you intend to clear a license to render a *dramatic performance* of an individual composition, which is a rendition of a song (regardless of whether the song was originally part of a dramatico-musical work) that is woven into and carries forward a definite plot and its accompanying action, then you will require permission from the copyright owner of the song.

## XIII. LICENSING CONSIDERATIONS

### A. Considerations in Granting and Clearing Dramatic Performance Licenses

A producer who desires to render a performance of music that is interwoven into and carries forward a definite plot and its accompanying action should take care to obtain the additional licenses necessary to effect the desired use. If the use was properly disclosed at the time the producer seeks a synchronization license, an alert music publisher will recognize that a dramatic performance will also be required for the use.

Because of the infinite variety of ways a song may be dramatically rendered in another work, there are no special standards for determining just how a music copyright owner might arrive at a fee in exchange for permitting the performance. However, copyright owners might use the same considerations for approaching grants of dramatic performance licenses as the considerations they might use relating to the licensing of reproductions of their musical compositions in similar works. These considerations are discussed in the previous chapters. By the same token, the producer might use the considerations for clearing licenses set forth in those same chapters.

The parties should analyze the use carefully to be sure the use does not fall within the scope of what might be considered a dramatic adaptation, some licensing considerations for which are discussed briefly below.

## B. Considerations in Granting and Clearing Adaptation Licenses

When a music copyright owner is asked to consider granting a license allowing another to prepare a dramatic adaptation of a song's lyrics (e.g., a motion picture adaptation of the lyrics of *Ode to Billie Joe* or a television adaptation of the lyrics of *Harper Valley P. T. A.*), the copyright owner should immediately do the following: view the lyrics as a literary work.

The considerations for licensing an audiovisual adaptation of a literary work should be viewed much the same way an author of a novel would consider the licensing of a motion picture or television adaptation of his work — through what is commonly referred to as a *literary rights acquisition agreement.* There are many issues the music copyright owner should thoughtfully consider, including the negotiations of payments for options that expire if the adaptation is not made within specified periods of time, the disposition of rights and revenues in the event that other adaptations or new versions are made subsequent to the release of the first (sequels, prequels, remakes, spin-offs, and the like), profit participations, credit for the songwriters, and other terms that are customarily negotiated in literary rights contracts. Producers of motion pictures and television programs are generally quite familiar with the issues relating to literary rights acquisitions.

A further analysis of the issues that should be considered in connection with these deals is beyond the scope of this book. The music copyright owner should consider obtaining the special assistance of a literary agent or an attorney who specializes in representing authors who frequently license their literary works for dramatic adaptations.

### C. Considerations in Granting and Clearing Grand Performances

The considerations in granting and clearing the right to perform musical plays, operas, and other dramatico-musical works in their entirety are beyond the scope of this book. Nevertheless, a few important comments relating to the licensing of *portions of* dramatico-musical works is in order.

When play producers and their agents are asked to consider granting a license to use a small portion of their works, such as a few moments of a musical play in a television program or multimedia work, they might use the same considerations in approaching such grants as those concerning the licensing of reproductions of music compositions set forth in the preceding chapters.

An owner of a musical play who has granted to a music publisher the music publishing rights in and to the individual musical compositions in the play should keep in mind that his right to license reproductions and performances of the musical play is limited to the dramatico-musical play itself and does not extend to the individual songs themselves. Musical play owners, or their agents, may grant, for example, grand performances of the play. This may include a performance of one or more musical compositions from the play, but only to the extent the performance contains elements taken directly from the musical play (e.g., dialogue, pantomime, dance, stage action, costumes, scenery, or other visual representations). If the performance of the music does not contain any such element taken from the musical play, then the right of performance is not controlled by the owner of the musical play, even if the performance contains other dramatic or visual elements.

Where the performance of the music does not contain dramatic elements from the musical play, then, unless there are provisions to the contrary in any agreement between the play owners and the music publisher, the right of performance is controlled by the owner of the music publishing rights. In other words, the music publisher has the sole right to license nondramatic performances through its performance rights society and dramatic performances directly, provided the performance does not contain any elements from the play that would render the performance a grand performance (the latter of which would require permission from the owner of the play).

### D. Considerations in Granting and Clearing the Use of Music in Theme Park Rides and Attractions

Music publishers generally charge a flat annual fee for the use of a song in a particular ride or attraction. Theme park operators, or a producer of a ride or attraction, often seek to avoid the annual fee and try to obtain as broad a license as possible. We have seen a request as broad as the following:

> to use the song in any Company-owned, Company-operated or Company-licensed theme park, including resorts, attractions, entertainment centers (including, without limitation, any so-called location based entertainment venues), restaurants, hotels, cruise ships, cruise ship ports and destinations, retail or other facility, as well as any advertising and promotion in connection therewith in perpetuity, throughout the universe.

The theme park operator might offer a one-time flat fee for perpetual use of the song in the attraction. He also might ask to have that fee cover the use of the music in any promotions for the attraction. For use in any live stage show at the theme park, the theme park operator might offer an additional one-time flat fee.

Because of the infinite variety of ways a song may be rendered in a ride or attraction, there are no special standards for determining just how a music copyright owner might arrive at a fee in exchange for permitting the performance. A copyright owner would use the same considerations for approaching grants of dramatic performance licenses as the considerations they might use in considering licensing of music in other reproductions.

Thus, a sophisticated music publisher would resist one time buy-out fees. However, it may be difficult to collect a royalty, as few theme parks charge separately for admission to specific attractions.

Thus, a good compromise might be to charge a flat fee payable on an annual basis for as long as the attraction is operating. A music publisher might charge separately for each venue of the attraction, and the theme park operator may wish to negotiate in advance an option to add new venues as required. For live stage shows, the copyright owner might ask for a flat amount per week for the run of the show. For details on current fees, please see Chapter 26, on *Typical License Fees*.

## XIV. RECOMMENDATIONS AND SUMMARY

As noted in Chapter 7, on *The Language of Music Licensing*, words that refer to completely different concepts should not be confused or used indiscriminately. Greater precision in the use of terms of art will promote clarity of thought and avoid costly legal disputes. It is important to correctly draw distinctions among grand rights, dramatic rights, and dramatic adaptation rights, so that all parties concerned can properly determine who has the right to license the proposed use.

To that end, the authors make the following recommendations:

1. Avoid using the term *dramatic right*, which leaves an ambiguity as to whether it denotes a performance right or an adaptation right. In its place, use phrases such as, *dramatic performance right* or *dramatic adaptation right*, as the situation warrants. Likewise, when granting a license under these rights, state, "a license to render a dramatic performance" or "a license to make a dramatic adaptation."

2. The industry should embrace the definition of *dramatic performance* found in the ASCAP Publisher/Writer agreement, with the following modification: strike the words "on a television program." Do not use the definition of dramatic performance in the ASCAP general license, which confounds the concepts of dramatic performances of music with grand performances of musical productions.

3. Use the term *grand right* only when the song was originally part of a dramatico-musical work (grand opera or grand musical play).
4. The next revision of ASCAP and BMI licenses should be redrafted to recognize the difference between dramatic performances of songs and grand performances of songs originally part of grand operas and grand musical plays.

Finally, it is not the practice of music publishers to represent or warrant that they are providing a license that is sufficient for the producer to render the desired performance. If the producer intends to render a grand performance, or a performance that infringes on another's right of publicity, invades someone's privacy, or defames someone's reputation, it is the producer's responsibility to properly clear all permissions that he requires to proceed with the performance. The producer is in a better position than the publisher to know just how the performance will be rendered, and, thus, whether the performance would infringe a grand right, or some other right, such as the laws of defamation or invasion of privacy. All the music publisher can do is provide the producer with the license to do what the publisher would otherwise have the right to stop the producer from doing, such as synchronizing the song in an audiovisual work.

Sometimes the producer can avoid problems by telling the music publisher precisely how he intends to use the music. The publisher might be able to provide additional information about other licenses the producer may require to effect the use, but the music publisher cannot be expected to guarantee that the license it grants covers all the permissions that are required for the use.

# Appendix to Chapter 19
# The Grand Rights Controversy

Forms (On CD-Rom Only)

| | |
|---|---|
| **Form 19.1** | **License to Perform Music in a Live Stage Production** |
| **Form 19.2** | **License to Perform Music in a Live Stage Performance of Choreography** |
| **Form 19.3** | **Collaboration Agreement Among Writers of a Musical Play** |

CHAPTER 20

# LICENSING MUSIC IN TELEVISION, RADIO, PRINT, AND INTERNET ADVERTISING

## SUMMARY

CHAPTER 20

# LICENSING MUSIC IN TELEVISION, RADIO, PRINT, AND INTERNET ADVERTISING

The convergence of radio and television with the commercial advertising industry has created one of the most lucrative markets for the licensing of music. In recent years, the Internet has been attracting an increasing portion of advertising dollars. This chapter will explore the considerations in licensing music in radio, television, print, and Internet advertising.

## I. Industry Background

### A. Importance of Music in Advertising

Advertisers and the advertising agencies that represent them both recognize and appreciate the great value that music adds to commercial advertising. Music plays an important role in setting the mood and enhancing the memorability of the commercial message. Advertising experts have shown that with short commercials — in 30-second and 15-second lengths — music becomes even more important, because of the music's ability to quickly set the mood and convey information about the product.

In producing a radio or television commercial, an advertising agency has several alternatives in considering the application of music to its client's commercial message. The agency may hire a composer to write a song specially created for the commercial, called a commercial *jingle*, or it may license an established, popular song. The agency might use music without lyrics, use an instrumental version of a song that originally had lyrics, modify a song's lyrics, or create new lyrics to suit the commercial message.

Increasingly, agencies and advertisers have been deciding to use established, popular songs, rather than having new ones custom made, to sell a product. Popular songs are already known to the audience, so the advertiser does not have to wait for the tunes to catch on with its audience, as he does with music created just for the advertising.

Also, advertisers have become increasingly sophisticated in directing their messages to specific target audiences. Hit music of the 1950 and early 1960, for example, can be quite effective in advertising that is targeted to reach the post World War II baby-boom generation. With an established song, an advertiser can capitalize on the customer's identification with a familiar song to improve the customer's continued recall of the product. Although creating a jingle or a new song tailored to an advertisement provides the advertiser with certain flexibility, it's hard to compete with a great, standard song, especially if the song already says a lot of things that the advertiser wants to say.

According to the Interactive Advertising Bureau (IAB), advertisers spent $296.8 billion in 2008 on commercial advertisements in the United States.[1] Of that, they spent:

- $60 billion (20% of total ad dollars) for direct mail
- $34.4 billion (12%) with newspapers
- $28.8 billion (10%) with TV program distributors
- $23.4 billion (8%) for the Internet
- $22.7 billion (7%) with consumer and trade magazines
- $21.4 billion (7%) for cable TV
- $18 billion (6%) for network TV
- $17.2 billion (6%) for radio
- $71 billion (24%) with other outlets

Given the importance of music in creating a mood or identity for the product and its potential audience, it would behoove music publishers and record companies to devote a fair amount of resources to garnering a fair share of these lucrative advertising expenditures.

[1] IAB Internet Ad Revenue Figures at http://www.iab.net (last visited Oct. 5, 2009).

## B. Advertising on the Internet

While music has been traditionally licensed for use in advertisements on television and radio, the Internet is becoming an increasingly important vehicle for advertising. Advertising on the Internet has grown more rapidly than any other category, from just $267 million in 1996 to $23.4 billion in 2008, far outpacing the growth in other traditional media.

Internet companies generate advertising revenues in a number of ways. These include:

- **Display advertising**, where advertisers pay for space on an online company's site or media players to display graphic advertisements. These graphics are often referred to as "banner" advertisements. Advertisers are paid for display advertising based on the number of "impressions" or views of that advertisement by users of the site where the advertising appears. Display, or banner, advertising make up about 21% of all advertising on the Internet.

- **Search**, where advertisers pay to provide text links to their sites in connection with a specific search word or phrase. Search advertising includes "paid listings," where text links appear at the top or side of results for searches run on the site that is selling the advertising, and "contextual search" results, where text links appear in connection with the context of the content on a webpage. Payment for sponsored search and contextual search occurs when a user clicks on the link. Search advertisements make up nearly 50% of all advertising on the Internet.

- **Rich media advertising**, also known as streaming advertising, where the advertising appearing on a site's page or media player consists of some form of streaming audio or video. For example, a video clip might be preceded by a 15- or 30-second video advertisement, sometimes known as "pre-roll" or "in-stream" advertising. Rich media advertising is also paid on the basis of impressions.

- **Sponsorships**, where an advertiser sponsors a portion of an online company's website. Pepsi Smash and Nissan Live Sets are examples of music sponsorships of portions of Yahoo!'s music sites.

All these forms of Internet advertising have a common element — the greater the audience, the greater the revenue. Therefore, any person or company that sells advertising has an incentive to build as large an audience as possible that will, in turn, generate revenue from impressions, click-throughs, sponsorships, and the like.

Internet advertising also has a number of advantages over advertising in other media. There is a well-known axiom in the advertising business that "half of all advertising expenditures are wasted, but you just never know which half." A television advertisement for a cosmetics product like mascara is a good example — as much as half the audience may never be inclined to purchase the product, yet the advertiser is forced to pay the same price as, say, the maker of a brand of aspirin, to reach the same audience. But the potential effectiveness of even a television advertisement for aspirin is difficult to measure. The problem is that there is no way to track whether a person viewing the ad actually goes to the store, as a direct result of the ad, to buy a bottle of the product.

If, however, an advertiser knew exactly what portion of an advertising expenditure resulted in a sale and what portion did not, would he not prefer to invest in that form of advertising as opposed to a form that did not? The Internet provides the answer to this question. Because of its interactive nature, the Internet provides a definitive way to track whether a person viewing the ad actually goes to the store, as a direct result of the ad, to buy the product.

When an advertisement appears on the screen, it carries a "link" to another website such that when the viewer of the ad clicks on the link, he or she is taken directly to the website where there is either more information about the product or where the product may be promptly purchased. This is commonly known as a *click-through.* Click-through rates used to average between 1½ to 3% (*i.e.*, for every 1000 impressions, 15 to 30 viewers would actually click on the ad). Today, the average has dropped to about 0.1% — that is, only 1 viewer would actually click through.

What makes click-through advertising so powerful is a special code embedded in the link, known as a "trackable link," which enables the advertiser to track what ad the user clicked on before being directed to its website. When the viewer lands on the website and buys a product, the advertiser can then figure out the precise rate of return on its advertising expenditure.

The two primary ways to buy advertisements on the Internet are: (1) pay per impression and (2) pay per click-through. An impression occurs each time the webpage that includes the ad is viewed. Impression ads are sold by the CPM — price per 1,000 impressions. Pay per click-through ads are sold by charging the advertiser a fee each time the viewer actually clicks on the advertisement. Pay per click-through ads are becoming the most popular means of Internet advertising.

Suppose an advertiser of widgets places an ad on the Internet and is charged 10 cents every time a viewer clicks on the advertisement. Assuming that 1 out of 10 people who view the ad click on it, then for every 100 viewers of the ad, 10 of them will click on the ad. When each viewer clicks on the ad, he or she is directed to a website where the advertiser offers the widgets for sale. Thus, for every 10 viewers who are directed to the advertiser's website by virtue of clicking on the ad, it costs the advertiser $1.00 (10 clicks × 10 cents). Suppose, only 1 out of the 10 viewers directed to the advertiser's website purchases a widget. Then the direct cost of advertising that widget is $1.00. That is, the advertiser had to pay $1.00 to attract 10 viewers to sell 1 widget. If the widget sold for $10.00, then the advertising expense as a percentage of revenue would be 10% (i.e., $1 divided by $10). In other words, the return on investment ("ROI") for each advertising dollar spent on the Internet ad is 10 times (10×). (If the cost of goods sold on the $10 product — e.g., the royalties payable on a download — were $2, then the true marginal ROI on the sale would be 8×).

To be sure, advertisers may calculate an ROI on advertisements they place in newspapers by trying to approximate how many widgets sold were attributable to the incremental advertising dollars spent on the ad, but the Internet offers advertisers a level of precision that no offline advertisement expenditure can match. For example, if the advertiser learns from experience that changing one word in their website will double the number of viewers who will purchase the product, then the ROI on the advertising dollar would double to 20×. By the same token, if by changing one word in the Internet ad the advertiser can double the amount of viewers likely to purchase the widget once they reach the website, then the ROI on each advertising dollar spent would double again.

Because of the interactive nature of the Internet, the ROI's of ads that draw large amounts of traffic can be tested almost immediately.

Slight variations in advertisements may be tested quickly, often within a matter of minutes, to maximize the ROI's of the ads.

This is but one example of the advantages of online advertising over traditional forms of advertising. But Internet advertising not only allows precise, after-the-fact tracking, it also facilitates effective delivery of advertisements to a target audience. For example, studies show young people are no longer watching television or listening to the radio as much as they used to; instead, they prefer surfing the net, managing their social network sites (e.g., Facebook, MySpace, or their own blog or Twitter page), and playing online games. Advertisers who wish to target their ads to young people can get precise demographic information regarding a website's viewership in advance of placing their ads.

Another important feature arising from the interactive nature of the Internet is the practice of monitoring "click-streams." A click-stream is the path, or sequence of mouse clicks, that a user has taken in navigating Internet sites. Online companies like Yahoo! have developed software to track users' click-streams. Using that information, these companies can serve up targeted advertisements based on the user's past behavior. For example, by analyzing "click streams" on its network, an Internet portal like Yahoo! can spot potential buyers at various stages of the user's surfing experience. For example, if the portal discovers a pattern of users who has viewed information about baseball, followed by information about movies, followed by a comparison of truck prices, it could then offer the auto companies this information so they can determine where best to place the advertisements for their trucks.

Such advertising is a far cry from the old days when half of all advertising expenditures were wasted. The Internet affords advertisers to effectively target their ads to the right consumers and precisely monitor the effectiveness of the campaigns, and that is an important reason why advertisers are devoting an increasing percentage of their advertising budget to Internet advertisements.

Because of music's special use in helping an advertiser connect with a certain targeted audience, we can expect to see a more scientific, numbers-oriented approach to licensing music in connection with advertisements on the Internet. It will be interesting to watch new business models for these licensing arrangements emerge from further research in this field.

## II. CONSIDERATIONS IN GRANTING AND CLEARING LICENSES TO USE MUSIC IN ADVERTISING

### A. Fee Structure

The fee structure of the typical commercial synchronization license is a one-time, flat fee for the term of the license, with additional fees payable on any extensions to the term or expansion of the territory. These fees vary greatly and are subject to negotiation. Typical fees charged at the time of this writing for the use of music in commercial advertising are set forth in Chapter 26.

As with synchronization licenses for motion pictures and television programs and electrical transcriptions for radio programs, commercial synchronization licenses do not permit the *performance* of music; accordingly, separate performance fees are payable by radio and television stations that broadcast performances of commercials containing copyrighted music.

### B. The Value of the Song

#### *1. Nature of the Product or Service*

Publishers and writers should consider the possibility that associating a hit song with a commercial product might harm the future earning potential of the song. A song that has become associated with a particular product in the mind of consumers may become less attractive to recording artists considering whether to include a song on a new album, to producers considering the use of the music in a motion picture, or to other advertisers considering the use of the music in connection with another product. For this reason, a publisher will charge a *premium* (i.e., higher than average fee) if he believes that an identification with a specific product might adversely affect the song's future mechanical, synchronization, or commercial advertising revenues. In addition, a publisher would be warranted in demanding a premium if the song has never before been made available for use in commercial advertising.

#### *2. Reluctance to License*

Because they understand and appreciate the maturing life of their copyright, older composers, and the surviving family of deceased composers, tend to make no objection to, and often encourage, the exploitation of their musical compositions in commercial advertising. It remains a mystery why many contemporary artists have an aversion to permitting the use of their music in commercial advertising. Where these artists have the right to approve such uses in their music publishing contracts, they tend to deny approval. If an artist's song should fall into disuse, the value of the copyright will decline over time, along with the number of people who may still remember it. Modern artists who find their popularly on the wane will soon regret their decision to withhold their approval of licensing their music for commercial purposes. A more prudent course would be to take the long-term view and recognize the importance of licensing music in advertising.

### *3. Overcoming Reluctance*

An advertiser who comes across a copyright owner who is reluctant to license music for commercial advertising should remind the copyright owner of the revenues arising from the public performances of the music. The performance royalties earned from a performing rights society (e.g., ASCAP, BMI) on public performances of the commercial on radio and television can be substantial and will act as a multiplier on the synchronization license fee. The use of music in commercials will also maintain that special relationship between a song and the listening public. This is particularly important with respect to older songs, such as those songs written in the 1930s and 1940s, as well as songs written more recently, including songs written in the 1950s and 1960s. As the public gets older, unless there is some medium through which the song is continually exposed to the public — such as the classic movie, *Casablanca*, which features the standard song, *As Time Goes By* — there will be, as time goes by, fewer and fewer people who will recognize and appreciate the song. Maintaining continual exposure through commercial advertising will likely lead to other uses of the song by new generations.

If the copyright owner otherwise willing to grant a license for a commercial advertising use informs you that he is unable to obtain the consent of the songwriter for the use you are requesting, (i) you should not blame your troubles on the music publisher (who is probably just as frustrated as you are) and (ii) you should attempt to approach the artist or the artist's representatives directly to determine just what the specific objection is and how you can overcome it. If the objections cannot be overcome, you should ask the publisher to recommend another song in his catalog that would serve as an adequate substitute for your needs.

## C. The Importance of the Song in Relation to Its Intended Use

### *1. Nature of the Product or Service*

The central question an advertiser will be asked concerns the nature of the product or service the song will be used to promote. By first asking the reason a particular song was chosen, the music copyright owner may discover the importance of the song in relation to its intended commercial use, and thereby find a reason to ask for a premium for the use.

Sometimes a variety of songs may fit the need of the advertiser. For example, a commercial bank producing a television commercial may desire to use *We're In the Money.* Should that song not be available, the bank may well use in its place, *Pennies From Heaven*, or *With Plenty of Money and You.* When a variety of substitutes are available, a premium fee will be difficult to obtain.

Every once in a while, however, one, and only one, particular song will best fit the message of the advertiser. That just may have been the case when an advertiser selected the song, *Anticipation* by Carly Simon for television advertisements of Heinz catsup to help dramatize the "anticipation" on the faces of people as they wait for the thick, tasty concoction of tomatoes and 57 varieties of spices to slowly come dripping out of the bottle. It would be difficult to imagine a more fitting song for the commercial.

The more closely a song is related to the message of the advertising campaign, the less likely it is that close substitutes for the song are available to the advertiser, and the higher the license fee the publisher can command. Even when only one song will do, however, an advertiser may consider using an old negotiating technique when haggling over the license fee: tell the copyright owner that the music is only one of several, alternative songs under consideration. It may be an old ploy,[2] but it often works.

---

[2] See, for example, Stendhal, *The Red and the Black*, Ch. 5, "Coming to Terms" (1830).

### *2. Nature of the Use*

Some of the same questions relevant in granting a synchronization license for the use of music in motion pictures and television programs will also apply here. For example, whether the music is to be used in a vocal rendition or merely instrumental; whether the music is used as background music or foreground music; whether the intended use relates to how the composition was originally presented to the public; and whether the music is used to help tell the story, or in the case with commercials, directly used to help promote the product or just used to set the mood. As with synchronization licenses, a foreground use will generally command a higher license fee than a background use.

Some licenses specify the length and number of the commercials in which the music is licensed. For example, a license might limit the use to "a maximum of three thirty-second television commercials" or "one fifteen second radio commercial." Most advertisers, however, desire a greater amount of flexibility in producing differing versions of a commercial, particularly those used in extensive national advertising campaigns. Publishers would generally have no objection to providing such flexibility, provided the boundaries of the use are specified in the license.

Commercial synchronization licenses generally have no limitation on the number of times a commercial may be broadcast during the term of the license. This lack of a limitation is for good reason: as far as the publisher is concerned, the more times a commercial is broadcast, the more performance royalties the publisher is likely to earn. This underscores the role commercial advertising plays in generating and sustaining the performance royalties and license terms should be crafted to recognize this.

### *3. Use of Original Recordings*

If the producer desires to use an original sound recording in the commercial, he would normally be required to obtain a separate license to do so from the owner of the recording, such as a record company. If the original hit version is being licensed, a music publisher, having recognized the advertiser's acute interest in a particular recording, may quote a higher fee.

### *4. Use of Sound-Alike Recordings*

To protect the music copyright owners against claims by recording artists and other entertainers from tortious claims concerning unauthorized use of their "name, voice, or likeness," publishers are advised to include a prohibition in their commercial synchronization licenses against the use of *sound-alike* recordings. These are recordings in which professional singers and studio musicians perform the composition in such a manner as to imitate or simulate an earlier recorded performance of the composition by an artist who may have made a distinctive popular recording of the song. Such recordings are perfectly legal, even where they are substantially similar to the original recording, as long as they are comprised of entirely new sounds (i.e., not sampled from the original recording).[3] Prohibiting the use of sound-alike recordings by this contractual means is particularly important where the music publisher has, and wants to maintain, a business relationship with the particular artist/songwriter sought to be simulated.

### *5. Lyric Changes*

Generally, music copyright owners are prepared to permit changes or additions to the original lyrics of a composition, as long as such changes or additions are subject to the publisher's final written approval. Lyric changes should be approved only after the publisher has taken care to make certain it has the right to authorize the change. A publisher may be under a contractual obligation to consult with or obtain the approval of the songwriter prior to authorizing any changes to lyrics of the song.

The conditions under which a songwriter would be willing to agree to a modification in lyrics are unpredictable. If changes to lyrics are to be approved, the exact nature of the new lyrics should be specified in the license or final approval should be withheld until the exact lyric is determined. One experience should illustrate the point: Ira Gershwin gave his permission for the use of the song *I Got Rhythm* in a commercial advertisement for a chain of supermarkets in New York. He also permitted the use of a parody lyric in place of the original, but when he learned that the new lyric used the words, "*I've* Got Rhythm,"

---

[3] 17 U.S.C. Sec. 114. See also Chapter 24, on *The Digital Sampling Controversy.*

he insisted that it be changed back to "*I* Got Rhythm." Ira said he deliberately chose the phrase "*I* Got Rhythm" instead of "*I've* Got Rhythm" for the title and lyrics of the composition written by his brother George, not because of its colloquial sound, but because it emphasized the powerful rhythmic structure his brother gave the music.

Even when a publisher is under no contractual obligation to obtain the permission of the songwriter, the publisher should at least consult with the writer on any proposed changes. Changes to any artistic work may evoke some emotional reaction from the artist. Informing the writer in advance of proposed changes, at the very least, may avoid some surprise and embarrassment. Going the extra mile to satisfy any objections of the writer is also a good way to help build a long-term relationship with the writer, which may be important down the road, when it comes time for negotiating with the writer for a further grant of renewal rights or terminated rights under the 19-year extension period or the 35-year termination rule.

Performing rights societies, such as BMI and ASCAP, will pay performance royalties even when a new or parody lyric is used; however, the credits received may be less than if the original lyric is used. Nevertheless, the lower performance credits per use should not deter a decision to grant permission to alter the lyrics.

#### *6. Use of the Song's Title*

If the song's title is used for a special purpose, such as the name of the product, the importance of the song in relation to its intended use becomes obvious. Some additional consideration for the use of the music could be considered, as well as a separate fee for the use of the song as the name of the product.

The ability of the publisher to command a fee for the use of the song's title as the name of the product, whether or not the music is used, will depend upon the distinctiveness of the title.[4] For example, if the name of the song is merely a common word, such as *Misty*, then it might be difficult to command a fee for the use of the word "Misty" as the name of a product. It would, however, be quite reasonable to ask for a premium for the use of the song *Misty* or its lyrics in advertisements of

[4] On the protection of song titles, see *Tomlin v. Walt Disney Productions*, 18 Cal.App.3d 226 (1971).

the product. On the other hand, if the title of the song is distinctive, because either it consists of a wholly fictitious word or phrase or it contains some distinctive or recognizable grammatical error or misspelling, a fee for the use of the title may be demanded. For example, the titles "Supercalifragilisticexpialidocious" and "Ain't Misbehavin" could probably not be used as the name of a product without the permission of the owner of the song's copyright.

## D. Scope of the Intended Use

### *1. Media and Distribution Channels*

Generally, commercial synchronization licenses should be narrowly drawn to permit the recording of the music in conjunction with radio or television commercials solely for radio or television broadcast. The license may also be expanded to permit "off-air" or non-broadcast trade uses, such as performance of the commercial at a trade show, for over-the-counter use in retail stores, and on websites or Internet advertising that promotes the product.

Advertisers who conduct a television and radio advertising campaign will usually try to place print ads that *tie in* with the broadcast messages. If such is the case, the advertiser will ask for a license to print any lyrics used in the television or radio commercials in printed advertising published during the term. Music copyright owners will generally grant permission to do so for an additional fee. Occasionally, the only permission that is sought is for the use of the lyrics in a print advertisement. A simplified license for such a use is set forth as Form 20.3 found on the CD-ROM.

### *2. Term*

The term of a commercial synchronization license will customarily commence upon the first broadcast of the commercial embodying the licensed musical composition, and will last for one week, one month, thirteen weeks, or other term negotiated between the parties, but will not normally endure for more than one year, unless options are negotiated. Because the success of advertising campaigns are difficult to predict, advertisers should always attempt to negotiate options to extend the term for one or two renewal periods upon payment of additional license fees. An advertiser may wish to test market the advertisement with the particular song, in which case it would request a short-term license with options to renew. An option to renew one-year term must usually be exercised at least 30 days before the expiration of the initial term.

### *3. Territory*

The territory for commercial advertising use varies depending upon the business of the advertiser. The territory of nationally advertised products is generally limited to the United States and Canada, although where a regional test of the advertising is contemplated, the territory may be restricted to a specific region with an option to expand the territory as appropriate, upon the payment of additional license fees.

When issuing a license whose territory is limited to the United States and Canada, keep in mind that certain television networks, such as CNN and Fox News, are broadcast worldwide via satellite. Accordingly, music copyright owners should be careful to exclude advertising on CNN if his right to license such use is contractually limited or he is otherwise unwilling to permit the use of the music in advertising outside the United States and Canada. By the same token, when the territory of the license is intended to be restricted to a certain region or city, such as the vicinity of Atlanta, Georgia, the music copyright owner should be careful to exclude advertising on "superstations" such as WTBS, which is a local station in Atlanta that is broadcast nationwide via satellite to local cable television operators. Other superstations include WOR in New York and WGN in Chicago. Where the advertising is specifically intended to be broadcast on superstations, the music publisher should become familiar with the number of markets into which the superstations' broadcasts are retransmitted and price the license accordingly. In other words, license fees for use of compositions on superstations should tend to be nearly the same as fees for use nationwide, because the superstations are usually transmitted to cable stations across the country.

Certain regions, such as New York City and Southern California, are larger, and comprise larger markets, than others, and can therefore command higher license fees. If you are a music copyright owner, keep in mind that if you receive a request for use of music in advertising to be broadcast in, for example, Newark, New Jersey, don't be fooled — such advertising could be received by viewers in the greater New York area, one of the largest television markets in the country.

Advertisers of products that have international appeal may request options for the use of music in additional countries. Consideration should be given to local subpublishing contracts or local publishing affiliate control over the music licensed for commercial advertising that takes place in their local markets.

### *4. Exclusivity*

An advertiser paying a substantial fee for a commercial synchronization license may well request the exclusive right to use the song for commercial purposes during the license term. Music copyright owners are normally willing to agree to some form of limited exclusivity. For example, the music publisher may agree not to license the song in connection with the commercial advertising of products that directly compete with the advertisers licensed product.

An advertiser would normally find that acceptable, but, in addition, may request that the publisher not license the song in connection with products that not only "compete with" the licensed product or service, but "relate to" the licensed product or service — that is, products that are complementary, not necessarily competing with the licensed products. Thus, for example, a sporting goods manufacturer licensing a song for use in advertising its line of *golf clubs* may well expect that the publisher would not license the song to another sporting goods manufacturer for use in connection with the advertising of its *golf balls.*

It should be evident that there is some degree of ambiguity inherent in phrases such as "compete with" or "relate to." To avoid ambiguity, a publisher may phrase the restriction in terms of precisely what kind of product(s) or service(s) in connection with which the publisher will not grant a license to use the song. For example, instead of providing that "The license is exclusive with respect to products that compete with stuffed animals," music copyright owners would be advised to state instead, "During the Term of the license, Publisher will not grant a license to use the Composition in the Territory in connection with the advertising of stuffed animals." While the former provision might be construed as preventing the license of the song in connection with dolls — on the basis that dolls are directly competitive with stuffed animals — the latter provision would be more narrowly construed to prevent the license of the song in connection with only those items that could reasonably be called a "stuffed animal." If the advertiser believes such a restriction is too narrow, the publisher should ask the advertiser to list the kinds of products it believes should be within the scope of the restriction, leaving it to the advertiser, who is in a better position to foresee potential conflicts, to take the risk of leaving a product off the list.

Care should also be taken in choosing the name of the product for which exclusivity is sought. For example, if the advertised product is aspirin, the copyright owner should try to limit the scope of the exclusivity to "aspirin." It might be reasonable for the advertiser to request that the exclusivity cover "pain relievers," which would include non-aspirin pain relievers, but a request for coverage of "pharmacology products," which might include cosmetics, would be too broad. Similarly, if the product advertised is beer, the scope of exclusivity should not be "all beverages," but "alcoholic beverages" or "domestic beer." In some rare cases, the advertiser may be willing to pay the extremely high premium required to obtain a broader scope of exclusivity.

Finally, if a songwriter or recording artist is being asked to perform the song in the commercial, the advertiser will typically require that, during the term of the license, the publisher will not grant to another a license to use any other song composed or recorded by the artist in the publisher's catalog for the purpose of advertising a competing product. This restriction, of course, will have little effect if many of the artist's popular songs are controlled by a different music publisher.

## III. PRINT ADVERTISING

The considerations described above regarding television and radio advertising apply also to print advertising, although the latter generally involves the more limited use of lyrics. Sometimes a television or radio advertising campaign will be supported by print advertising and a commercial synchronization license may include a provision allowing the use of lyrics in print advertising, product brochures, and point-of-sale displays.

## IV. CONCLUSION

As we have seen, advertisers spend about $300 billion a year promoting their products in the United States alone. Although some songwriters and recording artists are reluctant to permit the licensing of their music in connection with advertising, the revenue potential from commercial uses is often too large to ignore. Artists at the height of their career may have good reason to delay advertising uses, but at some point they would be foolish to decline these opportunities solely for artistic reasons. The choice, ultimately, is theirs (assuming they've reserved a right of consent under their contracts). But they should keep in mind the fact that if a song should fall into disuse, the value of the copyright will decline over time, along with the number of people who may still remember it. Songwriters should remember the importance of maintaining a relationship between the song and the listening public — something that will not only promote performance income, but future licensing opportunities as well. The most prudent course would be to take the long-term view and recognize the importance of licensing music in advertising.

# Appendix to Chapter 20
# Licensing Music in Television, Radio, Print, and Internet Advertising

Forms (On CD-Rom Only)

CHAPTER 21

# LICENSES FOR MUSIC BOXES, CONSUMER MUSICAL PRODUCTS, AND OTHER MERCHANDISE

SUMMARY

CHAPTER 21

# LICENSES FOR MUSIC BOXES, CONSUMER MUSICAL PRODUCTS, AND OTHER MERCHANDISE

From time to time, a music publisher will receive a request for permission to use a musical composition in a consumer product. The variety of merchandise in which music is being employed is ever increasing and hardly a month goes by without an innovative use of music being brought to the attention of a publisher for licensing consideration.

This chapter will explore the considerations in licensing music in music boxes and other consumer musical products.

## I. BACKGROUND

As noted in Chapter 13, on *Licensing Music in Sound Recordings*, a *music box* is a mechanical instrument whose sounds are produced by the spring activated rotation of a cylinder having specially placed protruding pins that pluck the teeth of a metal comb. The music box was the first mechanical device designed to perform music and is used today in jewelry boxes, figurines, novelty items, and children's toys.

Modern technology has spawned new, innovative applications of the music box idea. For example, a toy manufacturer has marketed a musical coin bank, called the *Musical Bogie Bank* that plays the melody of the song *As Time Goes By* whenever a coin is deposited in its slot. A greeting card containing a special sound-capable computer chip may perform, for example, a few bars of *My Funny Valentine* when the card is opened. An exercise machine may play the melody of *Chariots of Fire* while the user is cycling or running in place. A doll bearing the likeness of the movie character, *Mary Poppins* might sing the *A Spoonful of Sugar* when the child pulls a string or claps his or her hands.

Other consumer musical products may use music in a way that does not involve a performance of the melody. For example, a tea kettle might bear the imprint of the words and musical notation of the song, *Tea For Two* by Irving Caesar and Vincent Youmans. And a greeting card may contain the printed lyric of the song, *I Love You Truly*.

## II. CONSIDERATIONS IN GRANTING AND CLEARING MUSICAL PRODUCT LICENSES

In granting permission to use a song in connection with a consumer product, a music copyright owner will consider many of the same points applicable to determining the appropriate rate to charge for use of his music in television, radio, or print advertising (see Chapter 26), including the fee structure, value of the song, the importance of the song in relation to its intended use, and the scope of the use. These factors are discussed below.

One of the first considerations, however, for a music publisher is whether there is any restriction in the publisher's agreement with the songwriter pertaining to the licensing of the song in consumer products. A publisher would be advised to determine whether the songwriter's consent is required before issuing such a license.

### A. Fee Structure

Music copyright owners typically charge some percentage of the sales of the consumer music product in exchange for the license. The percentage may be a portion of the suggested retail price, wholesale price, or net revenues (gross revenues less product returns). Because the price charged for the musical product by its manufacturer is completely within the discretion of the manufacturer, the copyright owner may establish some minimum fixed penny or dollar amount per copy. The fixed amount per copy will often serve as a *floor*, or minimum fee, below which the royalty will not fall, regardless of what the manufacturer charges for the product. The copyright owner will also seek an advance against royalties payable upon the execution of the license. *See* Forms 21.1 and 21.2 on the CD-ROM for model licenses for music boxes and musical product licenses.

A person seeking to clear a license for a musical product might attempt to negotiate a one-time flat fee for the use during the term of the license. However, music copyright owners would be reluctant to grant such licenses on a flat fee basis, because of the absence of any means to share in the economic success of the work in which the music will be included. For example, the television broadcast of a young child playing with a *Mary Poppins* doll that sings *A Spoonful of Sugar* will earn the song's copyright owner performance fees that are in addition to any initial licensee fee charged for the synchronization of the song to the advertisement. By contrast, the child's playing with the doll day after day at home does not earn the music copyright owner any additional fees, no matter how popular the doll becomes with little girls. This is because all performances of the song in the home are *private* performances. These performances are not subject to the permission of the copyright owners, and, because there are no fees collectable for private performances, the music copyright owner will seek alternative means to share the economic success of the use. It has therefore been the practice of music publishers to charge a royalty for the use based on the number of units of the products sold or the revenues derived from sales of the product.

If, at the same time you are seeking to clear a musical product license, you are seeking to clear a synchronization license for the use of the music in television commercials to advertising the musical product, you may be able to negotiate a flat fee rate, or in any event, better terms for the musical product license, if you can persuade the copyright owner that your use of the song will significantly increase the copyright owner's income during the term of the license. The copyright owner may also accept a flat fee if it is high enough to overcome the copyright owner's fear of making a "bad deal."

### *1. Applicability of Compulsory License Provision*

Before a person seeking to clear a license for a musical product accepts any terms offered by a music copyright owner, he should first determine whether the compulsory license provision of the Copyright Act applies to the particular use intended.[1] If the compulsory license provision does apply, then the licensee would be entitled to compel the copyright owner to issue a license for a fee limited to the *statutory rate* existing at the time the sales of the product occur. Currently, the statutory rate is 9.1 cents per copy for the use of songs up to 5 minutes in length. The music copyright owner is free to negotiate better terms only if the compulsory license statute does not apply.

Technically, when a music box or a musical greeting card *plays* a song, the performance is not accompanied by motion pictures or some other form of audiovisual work. Accordingly, one might assert that the purely mechanical reproduction of the song in the music box or greeting card appears to be subject to the compulsory mechanical licensing provision.

A music copyright owner might argue that the compulsory license provision only applies to phonorecords, or record albums as they are customarily understood, and does not apply to devices that might technically contain a phonorecord, such as a sound chip, but are incorporated into a consumer product. In addition, some musical products only use an edited version of the song, using the most identifying portion of the melody, perhaps looping it. Music publishers may also argue that such editing would put the use outside the purview of the compulsory license provision.[2] In addition, since the incorporation of music into a consumer product commercially ties the music to the product, and can be considered in the nature of an endorsement of the product, something more is present than the mere incorporation of the music in a phonorecord for private use.

It is not clear how this question would be decided if ever tested in court. It is not likely to be decided as long as the royalty rates customarily charged for the use of music in consumer products remains reasonably consistent with the statutory rate.

Note, however, that the reprinting of lyrics is clearly not a mechanical reproduction and therefore is clearly not subject to the

[1] 17 U.S.C. Sec. 115. See Chapter 13, on *Licensing Music in Sound Recordings*.

[2] A similar argument was rejected by the U.S. Copyright Office when it ruled that ringtone downloads, even though they typically contain abbreviated versions of the songs they render, constitute digital phonorecord deliveries that are subject to the compulsory license provision.

compulsory license provisions. Nor is music embodied in a product that contains an audiovisual work a mechanical reproduction of the music subject to compulsory licensing. Accordingly, if the lyrics are used, with or without the music, or the music is used in connection with moving pictures, the compulsory license provision of the Copyright Act would not apply and the publisher would clearly be free to negotiate more favorable terms.

## B. Value of the Song

As in the consideration of licensing music for use in advertising commercial products, discussed in Chapter 20, music copyright owners in considering licensing music for use in the products themselves should consider the possibility that associating a hit song with a commercial product might harm the future earning potential of the song. A song that has become associated with a particular product may become less attractive to recording artists considering whether to make new recordings of the song, to producers considering whether to use the music in motion pictures, or to other advertisers considering whether to use the music in the marketing or advertising of other products. For these reasons, a publisher would consider charging a premium if he believes that an identification with a specific product might adversely affect the song's future revenues from other sources. In addition, a publisher would be warranted in demanding a premium if the song has never before been made available for use in a consumer product.

A person seeking to clear a license for musical products would do well to remind a reluctant copyright owner of the importance of maintaining continual exposure of the song to the listening public, despite the lack of public performances arising from the license. Licensing music for a toy music box or wind-up doll will expose the music to a new generation and will increase the likelihood that licenses for use and performance of the song will continue over the full life of the copyright.

## C. Importance of the Song in Relation to Its Intended Use

Again, the music copyright owner should ask himself, or the potential licensee, why *this* particular song? When one, and only one, particular song will best fit the use in the product, the copyright owner may have a good reason to ask for a premium fee. As previously noted, the fewer substitutes that are available for the use, the more the licensee may be willing to pay. For example, there may be only a limited number of songs or themes logically available for a musical doll based on a popular motion picture or television program character. Also, if the song's title will be used as the name of the product, a separate fee for that use should be considered, though the music copyright owner's ability to charge a fee for the use of the song's title will depend upon the distinctiveness of the title.

## D. Scope of Use

### *1. Media*

The product in which the music will be embodied should be described with particularity. To this end, the copyright owner should ask for a full description of the product at the time the license is being sought.

### *2. Term*

The term of musical product licenses are, generally, for a period of one to three years, with a provision to allow the manufacturer to sell off his inventory for a period of no more than six months after the expiration of the term. A person seeking to clear such a license should be able to negotiate options to renew the term upon the payment of additional advances against future royalties.

### *3. Territory*

The territory that the licensee is permitted to distribute the licensed product is limited to the local market in which the license is issued, such as the United States and Canada. Options permitting the export of the musical product to other countries may be available, but a music publisher may require that such licenses be sought from the local music publishers in each of the countries in which the licensee intends to market the product.

### *4. Exclusivity*

When requested, product exclusivity is often granted. The principals of the exclusivity discussion set forth in Chapter 20, with respect to commercial advertising, apply equally to consumer product licenses, though exclusivity may not be as important here as it is to the licensee in establishing a product identity in the course of a commercial advertising campaign. An exclusivity provision of a musical product license should, of course, be narrow in scope and worded with great care to assure the license reflects the intent of the parties.

## III. PRINTING OF MUSIC OR LYRICS

Makers of some consumer musical products merely require permission to print the lyrics on or in the product. For example, a tea kettle might bear the imprint of the words and musical notation of the song, *Tea For Two* or a greeting card may contain the printed lyric of the song, *I Love You Truly*. In each instance, the music copyright owner will generally grant permission under terms and conditions similar to those described in the previous section.

However, music copyright owners should first reflect upon whether they have the right to grant such a license to begin with. If the copyright owner previously granted to a print music publisher the exclusive rights to make copies of the music in printed form, then, unless the grant of rights in the print music publishing agreement excluded uses for consumer products or reprints of lyrics in books and other products, then the copyright owner may be required to refer the person who is seeking the musical product license to the owner of the exclusive print rights of the music.

# Appendix to Chapter 21
# Licenses for Music Boxes, Consumer Musical Products, and Other Merchandise

Forms (On CD-Rom Only)

CHAPTER 22

# LICENSING MUSIC IN VIDEOGAMES, OTHER NEW MEDIA, MULTIMEDIA DEVICES, AND ONLINE VERSIONS

## SUMMARY

# CHAPTER 22

# LICENSING MUSIC IN VIDEOGAMES, OTHER NEW MEDIA, MULTIMEDIA DEVICES, AND ONLINE VERSIONS

When you listen to a sound recording or watch a television program or a movie, you tend to watch from beginning to the end. By contrast, when you play a videogame or use entertainment software, you might start at the beginning, but the similarity with traditional forms of media ends there: you begin to interact with the game or software and the beginning, middle, and the end are given new meaning. The distinction between media through which entertainment programming has been traditionally distributed (e.g., radio, television, theatrical exhibition, CD, videocassettes, and DVD) and new forms of distribution (e.g., interactive CD-ROMS, karaoke, videogame cartridges, web-based digital download and streaming) is becoming blurred, but one characteristic that may provide a useful distinction is the interactivity afforded by these new forms of delivery (CD-ROMs and web-based transmission) and the interactive nature of the content itself (e.g., videogames).

The *non-linear* nature of these products and services presents special licensing challenges to the music copyright owner. For example, a use of music may no longer be always a fixed number of seconds, as it is in a motion picture, but may "loop" numerous times in a critical juncture of an interactive work. In addition, a song may be one of several in a motion picture, but one of hundreds in an interactive device, such as a CD-ROM or website. Finally, these devices allow new combinations of copyrighted works, such as the performance of a song with synchronized display of its lyrics, and new forms of music licenses have evolved to address the new uses.

This chapter will sketch some of the developments in multimedia technology before the advent of the Internet, such as computer software, multimedia CD-ROMs, karaoke, videogames, and other new media products, and will then discuss considerations in granting and clearing licenses for the use of music in those products in general, as well as licenses for the use of music in videogame devices and web-based forms of videogames.

## I. TECHNOLOGICAL DEVELOPMENTS

The advent of the microchip, a device that can pack hundreds of thousands of "transistors" onto a sliver of silicon the size of a thumbnail, has spawned several entirely new categories of commercial and consumer products. A greeting card that plays a song when you open it (see Chapter 21) is just one simple example of a musical application of the computer chip. These chips have become so powerful that computing power previously reserved for the large refrigerated rooms that housed large mainframe computers are now available in personal computers and videogame players that you can buy for a few hundred dollars. The computer chip is, indeed, the electronic "brain" upon which all of these technological developments rely.

### A. Multimedia Products

It has been said that we are now in an "age of information" and nothing could be better evidence of that than the advent of new technologies that are revolutionizing the way we accumulate, store, retrieve, analyze, and interact with the vast amounts of information being generated by modern society. One of the most exciting developments that have emerged in this new era has been the convergence of various audio, visual, and database technologies to form what has been called, appropriately, *multimedia.*

We use the term multimedia here to describe a certain class of products that combine the attributes of several different traditional media, such as motion pictures, still photographs, recorded sounds, printed text, computer generated sounds and graphics, and the like. Most multimedia programs are designed to be used in an *interactive* way, with the user controlling the sequence and organization of the information or entertainment that is to be produced or generated.

One of the earliest applications of music in multimedia products was the use of music in educational software products, discussed below. Examples include *Mozart's The Magic Flute*, a CD-ROM disc for the Apple Macintosh; *Beethoven's Ninth Symphony*, a CD-ROM disc for IBM-compatible computers; and *Louis Armstrong: An American Songbook*, a CD-I disc for the now obsolete Philips or Sony home CD-I players. Early non-music related multimedia products included *Dinosaur Adventure*, developed by Knowledge Adventures, which was founded by entrepreneurs Billy and Larry Gross.

Another exciting development in the field of interactive media was the advent of the electronic encyclopedia. One early example was a multimedia version of *Compton's Encyclopedia* for use on Apple Macintosh and IBM-compatible personal computers. Later, Microsoft entered the field with its *Encarta* CD-ROM product. Soon after, the Encyclopedia Britannica released multi-disk CD-ROM and later DVD versions of its popular encyclopedia. Encyclopedia Britannica is now available online.

Music copyright owners should expect to see in the future the creation of multimedia encyclopedias dedicated to music, such as an encyclopedia of jazz and popular music. The *electronic discography* that might be included in such a work could allow the user to listen to clips from the listed recordings, or read the music notation or lyrics of any particular song, at the mere press of a button.

All of these encyclopedia services may eventually be subsumed within or replaced by the fast growing Wikipedia.

## B. New Media Products

The term new media is used here to encompass a variety of products that are just coming on the market, as well as products that have not yet been invented. Several new technologies are only now converging and the result has been and will continue to be the establishment of new markets for licensing musical works and new means of distributing these works. The best example of these is karaoke.

### *1. Karaoke*

In the 1940s, the Ben Yost singers made popular *sing-along* performances in night clubs of that era. Later, Mitch Miller further popularized the idea with a highly successful television program called, "Sing-along with Mitch." The modern-day equivalent of these sing-along programs is *karaoke* (pronounced "Kara-OK"), which has become quite a phenomenon in Japanese night life. Meaning literally "empty orchestra," karaoke became the sing-along of the 1990s. In Japan, a businessman may take his guests to a small bar, where they may imbibe western spirits and take turns at karaoke singing.

A karaoke system is composed of special hardware, which combines a stereo amplifier with a compact disc player, hooked to a television monitor. Recordings of standard songs are digitally recorded without the lead vocal, often fully orchestrated with back-up singers. The disc also contains the lyrics for the lead vocal. In a typical Japanese karaoke bar, a patron, usually after having imbibed a few drinks to acquire the nerve necessary to volunteer,[1] chooses a song from a list of titles, walks up to a small stage, faces the audience (of other bar patrons), and views a small television monitor facing him on the stage. When the music starts, the lyrics begin to scroll onto the monitor, highlighted, line by line, in tempo with the music to cue the performer when to sing the appropriate line. The karaoke players come equipped with special features, such as echo, reverb, and pitch control, which can make even the worst voice seem listenable. The lyrics are usually displayed in the foreground of random motion pictures of popular American scenes, such as surfing, and other amusement scenes. A video camera may be focused on the performer and the performer's image may be displayed on video monitors located throughout the bar. The karaoke bars, where performances of music by karaoke take place, are licensed by performance rights societies.

This technology has been marketed in several novel ways. Consumers at a shopping mall may now go to what is called a *karaoke booth* where they can render a live karaoke performance and purchase a videotape of their performance to take home. Complete karaoke systems for home use made by companies such as Pioneer and the Daiicho Kosho Co. are now available for less than $1,000. Karaoke discs for playback on these machines are available for under $20. Being that there are several uses to which the term karaoke has been applied, a license to permit karaoke use of music should carefully define precisely

[1] Confirmed by personal experience one late night in Tokyo — Bob.

what forms of karaoke use is permitted. *See* Form 22.5 on the CD-ROM for an example of a Karaoke license agreement.

Though karaoke bars and home karaoke devices remain popular, karaoke has now moved to the Internet. The first online karaoke service was KSolo.com (now, MySpace Karaoke), started by Israeli-entrepreneur, Nimrod Lev. Licensing for online karaoke is discussed in more detail later in this chapter and in Chapter 12, on *Licensing Music in Print and Digital Print.*

## C. Computer Software

The term computer program, or *computer software*, refers to the set of instructions given to a machine to bring about a certain result. The copyright law provides the same protection to computer software that is afforded to literary works.[2] It is important not to confuse the computer with the software that instructs the computer what to do. The computer is the physical machine, or *hardware*, that performs certain limited kinds of tasks; the *software* is the copyrighted work that provides the instructions that tells the machine what tasks to perform. An apropos analogy that best illustrates the relationship between computer hardware and computer software is one that suggests that you conceive the software as the *record album* and the hardware as the *record player and stereo system* that plays the music embodied in the record album. Just as the record player cannot play music without the record, a computer cannot perform any meaningful tasks without the computer software that instructs it.

The following outlines the various kinds of computer software being marketed for use on computers in use today, including educational software, music software for professional and amateur musicians, musical instrument digital interface (MIDI) software, and business software, and videogame software (sometimes referred to as interactive entertainment software).

### *1. Educational Software*

We have barely seen the tip of the proverbial iceberg of potential educational applications to which computers can be put to use, and

[2] 17 U.S.C. Sec. 101, 117.

music is expected to play an important role in the development of these applications. We are beginning to see computer software that teaches the alphabet and reading by phonics, electronic books that contain lyrics or play music, software that teaches you how to play the piano, and software that explores the boundaries of music appreciation.

The recording of popular music in even non-music specific software, such as the early geography software, *Where in the World is Carmen San Diego*, and history program, *Where in Time is Carmen San Diego?* (published by Broderbund Software) is likely to greatly enhance the educational experience these programs aim to provide.

One of the first products to demonstrate the marvels of applying computer technology in education was a program called *The Magic Flute*, a set of three CD-ROM optical discs for use on an Apple Macintosh personal computer equipped with a CD-ROM drive or player. Published by Warner New Media, a division of AOL Time-Warner, Inc., the program contained a digital recording of Mozart's opera, enhanced by more than one hour of commentary, additional music, and more than 7,000 screens of information. While listening to the opera, or any portion of the opera, a user may simultaneously read the English or German libretto, or put the program on hold to read the story, look up a definition in the glossary, explore a character analysis, or view a complete map of the opera, and then, of course, take a final exam.

*Beethoven: The Ninth Symphony* was another early interactive optical disc program for Microsoft Windows. With this program, the user could see and hear everything from an overview of the symphonic form to an in-depth analysis of each movement of the Ninth symphony. The program included biographical material, examples of Beethoven's other works, and an interactive game for one to four players to test your musical knowledge.

*Luciano Pavorotti: O Sole Mio*, *Louis Armstrong: An American Songbook*, and *Mozart: A Musical Biography* were released by the MusicWorks team at Philips Interactive Media of America. These programs were playable on a regular CD player, but with a CD-I equipped player, a special interactive media player that works with a television set, users could explore all the interactive features that the CD-I format affords.

The CD-I format is now obsolete, but many interactive educational programs like these have moved to the Internet.

### 2. *Music Software*

Some personal computer software programs were specifically designed for professional or amateur composing and playback of musical compositions. These programs present on the computer screen the five-line musical staff, and give the user the ability to place on the staff musical notes, including whole, half, quarter, eighth, sixteenth, etc., and all of the customary musical notation terminology. The user may arrange his own notes on the musical scale or load into the computer pre-arranged notes. The user can then "play" the notes in sequence, rendering a performance of the song so arranged, and store or "save" the music in the computer's hard disk, together with any changes made to the music by the user, so that it can later be played back. Any notation of the songs that are presented on the computer screen can be printed out on the user's printer, and, depending on the resolution of the user's computer printer, the print-out may have a quality approaching that of printed sheet music. When played, the music may be heard through the speaker provided with the computer, or an external speaker.

More sophisticated music software programs provide the user with the capability to completely automate the music creation process. An early example was Midisoft's STUDIO, which operated on Microsoft Windows. While you are playing an electronic keyboard, or any properly equipped musical instrument, the program displays your exact musical performance instantly on the screen as standard musical notation. With powerful editing features, you can rearrange your music, combine parts, change instruments, replay your changes, print it out, or save your performance to a file on your computer disk for later playback.

Later, more sophisticated programs were developed, including *Sibelius*, now owned by DigiDesign, the makers of ProTools music editing software.

### 3. *Musical Instrument Digital Interface (MIDI) Software*

The magic behind the process in Midisoft's STUDIO and DigiDesign's Sibelius is something called the *musical instrument digital interface* (*MIDI*). MIDI is the standard computer format or protocol for transmitting music data electronically. Most electronic instruments today, such as electronic piano keyboards and synthesizers, are MIDI equipped. Even sounds from acoustic instruments (including the human voice) can be converted to MIDI with special hardware and software. Compared to digitized audio, MIDI data is significantly more compact and more easily manipulated without loss of sound quality.

The significant aspect of this new technology is that it allows you to store the equivalent of a live performance on a computer disk. Since all of these music computer *files* are stored in digital magnetic form, they can be easily copied from one computer diskette to another, and can even be transmitted over telephone lines.

This is not expensive technology. Midisoft's STUDIO 6.0 program has a suggested retail price of less than $100, and a MIDI interface card can also be installed into any PC for about $100, and reasonably powerful PCs are available for less than $2000.

Programs such as these, and the music files they can produce, raise several interesting music licensing questions with which the music industry is just beginning to grapple.

For example, is a MIDI computer file a mechanical reproduction the distribution of which requires a mechanical license subject to the compulsory license statute, or is it a copy of an audiovisual work, the distribution of which may be negotiated, such as the terms of a synchronization or videogram license? The Harry Fox Agency has considered the fixation of music in MIDI files and, to deal with the increasing number of requests for this new form of license, has developed a special form MIDI license, a copy of which is set forth as Form 22.4 on the CD-ROM.

Is a computer file that contains the ability to display music notation on the screen of a personal computer and to print out the notation on a computer printer the equivalent of printed sheet music? Is it a combination of sheet music and mechanical reproduction or audiovisual work? The question becomes significant, because many music copyright owners have granted to print publishers the rights to distribute their music in printed form, such as sheet music and folios, on an exclusive basis. If the music copyright owner grants permission for the reproduction of MIDI files, and those files have the capability of printing out musical notation on laser printers, a print publisher who holds exclusive print rights in the music might take the position that the granting of the license was a breach of its exclusive print rights contract.

The Harry Fox license set forth as Form 22.4 on the CD-ROM states that the license does not grant permission to the licensee "to program into the MIDI sequence [file] the capability of making any other use of the Composition not expressly authorized" by the license. One of the permissions not granted to the licensee is the license to print the licensed composition in sheet music form. Further, the license requires that a warning notice be placed conspicuously on each copy of the MIDI file stating that it is a violation of copyright law to print the file in the form of standard music notation without the permission of the copyright owner. While it is clear that the music copyright owner can limit the scope of the license to prevent the licensee from distributing laser-printed copies of musical notation displayed by a licensed MIDI file, it is not clear how one who distributes files that operate with, for example, Midisoft's STUDIO program, would practically be able to comply with a requirement of making a file that is capable of displaying musical notation on a computer screen incapable of having that notation printed out on a printer.

It would appear that the distribution of MIDI files containing copyrighted music notation capable of being printed out would not be within the scope of the license and the only way one seeking to clear a license for such use would be to also obtain clearance from the owners of the exclusive print rights. This, obviously, is a burdensome solution, and perhaps one that might not be worth the effort.

It seems that the purpose of the scope of the Harry Fox MIDI license is to protect music copyright owners from breach of contract claims of holders of exclusive print rights in their music. Should such a breach of contract dispute ever occur, the resolution of the case may well depend upon what was meant by the term "print" or "sheet music" at a time when the only means of distributing copies of music notation were on paper. An analysis of the question would parallel those considered in Chapter 17, on *Old Licenses, New Uses.* We suspect that, unless there is language in these contracts specifically covering electronic forms of printed music, the courts would narrowly construe "print" and "sheet" music as being limited to distribution on paper form. Perhaps distribution of sheet music via telecopier, or "fax," machines would still be considered a form of distribution on paper, but files that are only usable with the aid of a machine or device (i.e., a computer) take on an entirely different character. If this does, in fact, become the result of these cases, then obtaining clearance of publishers who hold exclusive print rights to music for distribution of MIDI files containing printable music notation would become unnecessary.

Finally, a MIDI file distributor would probably have no need to be concerned with potential violations of exclusive print rights by purchasers and users of MIDI files, because it is not likely that a music copyright owner could legally prevent a purchaser of a licensed MIDI file from printing out a copy of the musical notation for personal use, and not for distribution. The printing out of MIDI files by the end user would be akin to the home taping of sound recordings, a practice that was specifically condoned by Congress when considering the Copyright Act of 1976.

Other software publishers, such as Macromedia, have developed computer programs that allow you to create animated cartoons that can be performed on your computer screen. The animation produced can, of course, be synchronized with music. The publishers of such programs may well wish to include arrangements of copyrighted musical compositions on the disks distributed with the software. Independent software publishers, sometimes referred to as publishers of "addon" software, may wish to separately sell diskettes that contain copyrighted music that can be played back by the user of such programs. Users may wish to exchange songs stored on disk with other users. Since computer software files may easily be transferred over telephone lines, such song files may well find themselves on one or more electronic bulletin board services or Internet "Web sites," which allow callers to transfer, or *download*, these files to their own personal computers over the telephone. Music copyright owners are beginning to see more and more requests for these forms of uses, but few standards have yet emerged on how best music copyright owners can respond to these requests.

#### *4. Business Software*

The variety of applications to which powerful desktop and home computers can be applied is limited only by the imagination of the people who are writing the software for use on these machines. Today, the largest segment of the market for personal computer software is software designed for business uses, such as word processing, electronic spreadsheets, and database management systems.

Few personal computer software programs designed for business, however, require music. Nevertheless, some business programs may lend themselves to the application of music in unexpected ways. For example, business graphics programs, used by executives to make business presentations, have the capability to perform a variety of special effects. Microsoft's *Powerpoint* is a graphics presentation program that allows the user to place sound effects in business presentations. Customized sound effects, including public domain and copyrighted music, have become an after-market product sold by independent software publishers to users of these programs.

If a software publisher wished to distribute a set of "sound files" on diskette which, when combined with such a presentation graphics software program, performs copyrighted music, would the use of the music require a mechanical reproduction license or a synchronization license? If the "slide show" presentation is an audiovisual work, then the use would not be a mechanical reproduction and the compulsory license provision of the copyright act would not apply.

*Audiovisual works*, as that term is defined in the copyright law, comprise:

> works that consist of a series of related images which are intrinsically intended to be shown by the use of machines or devices such as projectors, viewers, or electronic equipment, together with accompanying sounds, if any, regardless of the nature of the material objects, such as films or tapes, in which the works are embodied.

Clearly, a computer generated slide show constitutes an audiovisual work. Thus, a synchronization license, likely to be in the form of one of the non-theatrical synchronization or videogram licenses, set forth on the CD-ROM as part of Chapter 15, would be required.

Under what circumstances would a *performance license* be required for a business presentation, which used such sound files? If the performance of the slide show constituted a *public* performance, then a performance license, usually acquired on a blanket basis, would be required.

### D. Videogame or Interactive Entertainment Software

Increasingly, producers of *videogames*, or *interactive entertainment software* as they prefer to call it, are recognizing the value of music as an integral part of the entertainment mix provided to users of videogames. For example, the enjoyment of a simple electronic table tennis game, such as *Pong*, may be enhanced if the game could be instructed to play a victory jingle, such as the theme from the movie *Rocky*, each time the player succeeds at performing a certain score or level of competence. Certainly, the absence of the music from the movie *Star Wars* would be conspicuous if it were not an element of a videogame based upon the movie.

Because of the popularity of videogames among youth, the promotion of new music in videogames can often be more valuable than radio airplay.

### *1. Videogame Arcades*

Initially, videogames were incorporated exclusively in large game machines, which contain their own television monitors and control systems (e.g., joy stick, buttons, pedals). These machines are normally distributed to pin-ball arcades, now called *video arcades.* Makers of these machines require synchronization licenses for the incorporation of music in the videogames programmed into these machines. Most video arcades obtain performance licenses from ASCAP or BMI and any music that may emanate from a videogame machine at an arcade would be covered by the arcade's performance license.

### *2. Videogame Software and Cartridges*

Later, videogames were sold in the form of floppy disks and CDs for use on personal computers and game cartridges for use on home videogame machines, such as Nintendo and Sony's PlayStation. While games sold on floppy disk and CD were subject to copying and sharing, cartridge-based games carried with them strong forms of copy protection, which discouraged a large amount of end-user piracy.

### *3. Dedicated Portable Videogame Devices*

A new generation of portable videogame devices, or *handheld videogame consoles*, such as the Nintendo *Gameboy* and DS, and Sony *Playstation Portable* (PSP), have become quite popular. The importance of the audio or musical aspects of these games is evidenced by the earphone attachments that these game machines now support. Some of these devices now play movies and music videos.

#### *4. Mobile Videogames*

A large variety of videogames, such as Tetris, are available for download over the air (i.e., by wireless from your telephone carrier) directly to mobile phones that support them. Games may be purchased *a la carte* or downloaded as part of a user's subscription. More recently, videogames have been developed specifically for download to Apple's iPhone and iTouch products and to the recently released Palm Pre devices.

#### *5. Online Videogames*

The fastest growing type of game is the online versions of popular software or cartridge games and newly developed games for multiplayer use over the Internet. These games are usually made available by subscription. New revenue models, however, have been developing. For example, Kartrider, a popular online multiplayer racing game developed in Korea by Nexon, earns revenues by selling virtual items in the in-game shop, including different types of vehicle and spraypaint. Over 15 million people have played Kartrider, and Nexon is pulling in over $200 million a year in revenue from its online games.

#### *6. Music Videogames*

In recent years, a new form of videogame — completely dedicated to music — has come to market, the best examples of which are *Guitar Hero* and *Rock Band.* Guitar Hero features a controller shaped like a guitar, which the player uses to emulate the playing of a popular guitar made by Gibson. While musical notes are scrolling on the player's TV monitor, the player presses buttons on the guitar controller, which produces the sounds of rock music from an array of rock genres. Inspired by Guitar Hero, Rock Band allows up to four players to emulate the performance of popular rock music using controllers that simulate a lead guitar, bass guitar, drums, and a microphone for vocal accompaniment. Songs may be purchased on game discs or downloaded directly to the device's console. Copyright owners publish their songs on the Rock Band Network. A version of Rock Band featuring the songs and likenesses of the Beatles has recently been released. The franchise is responsible for hundreds of millions of dollars in music sales.

## II. CONSIDERATIONS IN GRANTING AND CLEARING LICENSES FOR DEVICES CONTAINING MULTIMEDIA PROGRAMS — IN GENERAL

Licensing the use of music in such products requires consideration of some of the same basic factors discussed in preceding chapters, including the fee structure, the value of the song, the importance of the song in relation to its intended use, and the scope of the intended use.

### A. Fee Structure

#### *1. Flat Fee*

In certain limited circumstances, it may be appropriate for a music copyright owner to charge a one-time, flat fee, for the use of music in certain computer software, multimedia, or new media works. Such a fee structure would be appropriate where the software will not be offered for sale.

Interactive multimedia is being increasingly used for corporate training purposes, and the use of music in such works, where relatively few copies will be made and none sold, would warrant a flat fee, much like a synchronization fee for nontheatrical motion pictures. However, the music copyright owner should be sure to either (i) define the license narrowly to assure that a subsequent decision by the licensee to distribute copies of the work for commercial sale would require further permission of the copyright owner, or (ii) structure the fee so that if the licensee elects to commercially release the work, royalties will be paid on the basis of each unit distributed or revenues derived from such sales. The form of license for such arrangements would be similar to Forms 15.4 and 15.5 found on the CD-ROM as part of Chapter 15, on *Licensing Music in Audiovisual Works.*

#### *2. Royalty*

Like the use of music in consumer products, the performance of music in the course of using computer software, videogames, multimedia programs, and new media products will usually be *private*, not public. Because no fees are collectible for private performances of music, the music copyright owner will seek alternative means to share the economic success of the use. The most common means is collecting a royalty based on the sales of the work embodying the music.

The fee structure for most uses of music in computer software, multimedia, and new media products is, therefore, much the same as that found in videogram licenses and licenses for consumer musical products. *See* Forms 15.1 through 15.7 on the CD-ROM as part of Chapter 15, on *Licensing Music in Audiovisual Works*, and Forms 20.1 and 20.2 on the CD-ROM as part of Chapter 20, on *Licensing Music in Television, Radio, Print, and Internet Advertising.*

For karaoke recordings, publishers charge a fixing fee of between $100 and $250 per track plus a royalty of 10¢ and 20¢ per copy. Many of these karaoke recordings have recently been made available on the Internet for download and streaming. Should they be made available with lyrics or other audiovisual works displayed, publishers will charge 12% to 15% of revenues. When the recordings are made without their lyrics, such as a typical MP3 download, the owners of the karaoke recordings have been able to obtain compulsory mechanical licenses under the compulsory license section of the Copyright Act.[3]

### *3. Pro Rata*

Licenses to use music in certain computer software, multimedia, new media products poses a special problem that usually does not arise in the case of other consumer products, such as music boxes, exercise machines, and greeting cards. In each of the latter three examples, it is unlikely that more than one song will be required. With respect to computer software, multimedia programs, and new media products, it is likely that several songs, perhaps hundreds of songs will be used in the work. For example, a single CD-ROM laser disc, or a website, may contain hundreds or thousands of files, each containing music in a format capable of being performed with the aid of a computer (e.g., MIDI, MP3, MP4, Windows Media). Similarly, a multimedia encyclopedia reproduced on laser discs

---

[3] 17 U.S.C. Sec. 115. See Chapter 13, *Licensing Music in Sound Recordings.*

may also contain portions of thousands of songs in mechanical or an "electronic print" format.

In instances where there is more than one song involved in the work, music copyright owners will typically request a royalty, using a percentage of net revenues *prorated* among the number of copyrighted musical compositions in the work. For example, if there are 10 songs in the computer software or new media program, and the royalty percentage charged is 5%, the royalty for the use of one particular song would be 1/10 of 5% of the net revenues that the producer of the computer software program receives on sales of the work. Of course, this does not mean that the owners of the nine other musical compositions used in the software will receive the same fee. Each owner would negotiate his own pro rata percentage or other license fee for the use of the music.

A copyright owner granting a license containing a provision for the payment of royalties on the basis of a pro rata share in relation to all of the musical compositions in the work should be certain the license provides that only *copyrighted, royalty-bearing* musical compositions be used in calculating the share. In other words, songs in the public domain, such as *The Star Spangled Banner*, should not be counted in determining the number of songs in the work. This is to prevent the licensee from adding several, or hundreds, of public domain songs to the work at no cost for the purpose of reducing the amount of royalties payable to owners of licensed musical compositions in the work. Nor should sound recordings be included in the calculation of the number of songs used to prorate the royalties — only musical compositions.

A person seeking to clear a license to use a song in a work containing hundreds or thousands of songs should be prepared to come across one or more music copyright owners unfamiliar with multimedia technologies. A copyright owner inexperienced with licensing music for use in such works may insist upon receiving a royalty rate on par with rates normally obtained when licensing music for works containing one or just a few compositions. For example, if the music copyright owner asks for an un-prorated 5% of net revenues for the use of a song in a work that will contain several hundred songs, you may have to devote some further time educating the copyright owner about the nature of the use.

Pro rating the royalty based upon the number of songs, or copyrighted songs, appearing in the work, may not always be the optimal or fairest method of structuring a fee for a particular use of a composition. Either the music copyright owner or the producer, depending upon the circumstances, could take the position that it would not be fair to prorate the fee on a straight-line basis (i.e., dividing the fee strictly by the number of songs in the work), without accounting for the duration that each song appears in the work or the quality of the use.

But alternative methods of pro rating fees among works are often ineffective or inefficient. Some have suggested that the duration of each song used be a factor, but this would favor long symphonic works over shorter more popular compositions. Others have suggested an allocation on the basis of how much *real estate*, or memory space, each work uses on the disk containing the work, but this poses special problems. The amount of disk space used by a MIDI file that can generate a performance with the aid of a computer is significantly less than the disk space required by an analog or even digital recording of the very same performance. Thus, some recordings would be favored over others on a purely arbitrary basis.

Producers of multimedia works have suggested that music copyright owners should not forget that permission must be cleared to use a multitude of other types of media works in the multimedia program. They have proposed that the disk space used by all the music on the disk should be compared with the disk space used by all other materials, such as text, photographs, moving pictures, dialogue, and other sounds. Under this method, the producer might propose to budget 20% of revenues to royalties and suggest that an allocation be made among the various types of works used on the disk, as for example, 25% to music, 25% to visuals, 25% to text, and 25% to monologue or dialogue. Leaving aside the merits of this proposal, it still leaves open the question of how the percentage paid for music would be allocated among the owners of the music (and sound recording) copyrights used in the multimedia program.

Perhaps the soundest method of allocation, and perhaps the easiest to administer, is the straight-line proration based on the number of *copyrighted, royalty-bearing* songs used in the work and adjusting for the relative importance of the song in relation to its intended use by raising or lowering the percentage charged for the particular song. For example, a valuable song that is used each time the work is accessed might command 7% of the net revenues prorated among the number of copyrighted songs in the work; a less valuable song that plays a minor role in the work would receive 3% of the net revenues prorated among the number of total copyrighted songs in the work.

Perhaps another compromise that preserves the simplicity of the *pro rata* method, but one that still takes into consideration the particular value of the song and the importance in relation to its intended use, could be to provide that the use of an important song in a substantial way is assigned a value of two songs in calculating the pro ration and that less valuable songs used in less substantial ways or duration could be assigned a value of a fraction of one song. Of course, multimedia producers tend to avoid any formula that might complicate their business or produce accounting errors. At the same time, copyright owners might consider that it is just not worth negotiating what it takes to account for these finer distinctions, and that it is more important to just make sure the song is included in the work and that he will be paid some fair amount for its use.

### *4. Applicability of the Compulsory License Provision*

Almost all interactive multimedia programs will contain some audiovisual information, with either moving images or a series of still images. The same is true for videogames and is likely to be true for most educational software. Accordingly, licenses for recording music on such works will normally not be subject to the compulsory license provision of the Copyright Act.[4]

But what if an interactive program consists solely of text and music, with no pictures or other visual images? Would the mere text displayed on a computer screen be considered a visual image for the purpose of determining whether the compulsory license provision applies? For example, would the use of music in a software program that consists of music performances and the display of plain text on a computer screen (with no motion pictures or other visual images) merely require a mechanical license? More specifically, suppose a publisher produces an electronic discography of every popular recording made in the 1960s that allows the user to select any recording on the list and hear several bars of the recording for identification. Would the text appearing on the screen be considered a "motion picture" or other "audiovisual work" for purposes of determining whether the compulsory license statute is applicable?

[4] 17 U.S.C. Sec. 115.

The answer was unclear for many years, but a recent case involving karaoke has provided some guidance. In a case regarding whether a karaoke recording is subject to the compulsory license statute, a court held that the recorded performance of a song is considered an *audiovisual* work, not a sound recording when the song's lyrics are shown on a screen while the recording is played.[5] The fact that the visual images comprise only the lyrics does not preclude a finding that the recording is audiovisual.

But what if the text were not the lyrics, but something entirely different, such as the words of an eBook? Text presented on a computer screen would seem no different from text contained in the package that comes along with a standard compact disc. However, the user interface of computer software has been held to be an audiovisual work.[6] Thus, the user interface of the computer software that permits you to access the textual material may constitute a sufficient audiovisual work that accompanies the recording that would remove the recorded music from the scope of the compulsory license provision.

### B. Value of the Song

As in the consideration of licensing music for use in consumer products, music copyright owners should consider the potential impact of associating a hit song with computer software or new media software product on the future earning potential of the song. However, it should be noted that associating a song with a computer or new media product, unlike with a consumer product or commercial advertising, is more likely to enhance the earnings potential of the song than to harm it.

Just as one might get a negative impression by associating a song with a personally or politically undesirable consumer product (e.g., milk of magnesia, nuclear energy), one is likely to get a positive impression from the association of a song with a more popular or culturally laudable product (e.g., electronic children's book), a product that is conceived as being on the "cutting edge" of high technology (e.g., computer software, electronic encyclopedia), or a product that is clearly making a contribution to scholarship or historical research (e.g., an electronic discography).

---

[5] *Leadsinger, Inc. v. BMG Music Publishing*, 512 F.3d 522 (9th Cir. 2008).

[6] *Computer Associates v. Altai*, 982 F.2d 693 (2d Cir. 1992).

A music copyright owner who is offered to have his song placed in a work such as an electronic encyclopedia or discography should seize the opportunity, because the value of the copyright will benefit from merely the exposure provided by inclusion of the song in such a work. In an information explosion, the competition for the *share of mind* of the listening public is intense. Licensing the song, even for a momentary use in an encyclopedia or other interactive product, particularly those that are likely to be used as reference works in libraries, in business, and in the home, will help maintain the relationship between the song and the listening public, and increase the likelihood that future requests for licenses of the song will continue.

For these reasons, a music copyright owner should not allow the difficulties and complexities of setting a proper fee for new media works to get in the way of consummating a license and providing the song with a means of continual exposure to the listening public.

## C. Importance of the Song in Relation to Its Intended Use

Again, why is a license being sought for *this* particular song? The fewer substitutes for the song that are available, the more the licensee is willing to pay. In contrast with the limited number of songs or themes logically available for a musical doll based on a character of a popular motion picture or television program, there is more likely to be a large variety of songs available to provide in an electronic encyclopedia a demonstration of the kind of music that was popular in the 1930s. Of course, a limited universe of songs will be available for a videogame software program based upon, for example, *Star Wars*. Careful consideration should be given to the particular circumstances in evaluating the importance of the song in relation to its intended use in computers, multimedia programs and new media products.

### *1. Special Nature of Interactive Works*

A special problem may arise in using the usual means of establishing the appropriate license fees for use of music in interactive multimedia works, and this involves an important difference between interactive media devices and traditional works: traditional media are *linear*, while interactive media are *non-linear*.

Traditional media, such as record albums and videotapes, are linear in the sense that they are generally listened to or viewed from beginning to end. By contrast, interactive media, such as compact discs and CD-ROMs, are generally non-linear, in the sense that one can gain immediate access to any portion of the work by skipping from any one point in the work to any other point in the work.

In a traditional work, such as a motion picture, the music that the producer chooses to play over the main title and opening credits of the work will remain the same for every performance of the motion picture and the viewer will hear the music every time he watches the movie (unless he intentionally skips over, or *fast forwards* through, the main title). By contrast, in an interactive work, an excerpt of the song may be played back under a variety of different circumstances. For example, the new media work may be set up so that a few bars of the song, *Tea For Two* is rendered only when a picture of Irving Caesar and Vincent Youmans, the song's writer and composer, appear on the screen. If the user never goes to the part of the work that displays the picture of Irving Caesar and Vincent Youmans, the song will never be performed, even though the work as a whole might be used as much as on a daily basis. It may be impossible to gauge just how much one particular song would be performed, or where it will most likely appear, in relation to the balance of the work. On the other hand, the producer of the interactive work can arrange for the song to be played every time the work is started up by the user, no matter what use will be made of the interactive work in any particular session. Further, the producer can allow the user to customize the work, so that any number of songs can be played every time the user starts up the work. They may alternate randomly or the user can choose to hear only one particular song over and over again.

In other words, the importance of the song in relation to its intended use may depend entirely upon the use put to the work *by the user.* This makes it very difficult to determine just how valuable the music is likely to be in relation to the work in which it is to be incorporated.

### *2. Traditional Factors*

As discussed in Chapter 14, a licensor should consider a variety of factors in determining an appropriate fee for a standard synchronization license (for use of a composition in a motion picture or television program). Such factors may include whether the use is a vocal rendition or merely instrumental; whether the use is of the entire song or just a few bars; whether the music is used as background music or foreground music; whether the use is at a prominent point in the motion picture, such as over the main title or credits; whether the intended use relates to how the composition was originally presented to the public; and whether the music is used to help tell the story. These are all factors that help determine the importance of the song in relation to its intended use. If, for example, the song will be played at the beginning of the motion picture over the main title of the film, or in its entirety at any point in the film, the use would command a premium fee.

A synchronization license for a traditional work, such as a motion picture, will typically limit the number of seconds the licensed song may be used in the picture. This customary restriction generally causes no difficulties in the context of a motion picture or television program, where the performance of the audiovisual work is usually linear — played from one point in time to another, at one or several instances in the picture. In the context of interactive media, however, difficult questions arise from the fact that, depending upon the interaction between the user and the new media work, there may be no one readily identifiable period of time in which the composition is played during the performance of the work.

Under these circumstances, the rules for determining the appropriate fees for use in traditional works do not lend themselves very well to application in this new media. In a synchronization license for a motion picture, a music copyright owner may use as a rule of thumb the number of seconds the music will be performed in the movie, yet there may be no way of determining that number in an interactive work.

With a variety of possibilities such as these, it behooves the music copyright owner who wishes to maximize the value of his property to gain as much understanding as possible about the media and the particular program in which the music will be licensed. Asking for "most favored nation" status will not work in situations where, as here, it would be virtually impossible to determine whether the licensor of some other song appearing in the work received more favorable terms for its use.

The music copyright owner should learn as much about the particular multimedia work as possible and simply do the best he can to determine the value of the song and the importance of the song in relation to its intended use. It should also be remembered that licensing a few bars of a song for use in an electronic encyclopedia is not the equivalent of licensing the entire song in a work in which the song will always be played from beginning to end. A license fee that is significantly less than the statutory rate for a mechanical license could well be appropriate where only enough of the song is used to allow the listener to recognize the melody, as opposed to the rendering of the entire song.

## D. Scope of the Use

### *1. Media*

A copyright owner would want the license to fully describe the product in which the music will be embodied. The work should be referenced by title, or tentative title, and any other useful information to describe the work, thereby defining the scope of the license as narrowly as possible.

### *2. Term*

It is always in the interest of copyright owners to limit the duration of music licenses. Music copyright owners generally try to limit these licenses to five years, sometimes giving an option to extend for an additional three to five years upon the payment of an additional advance against royalties. The term of most karaoke licenses is currently about seven years.

Insisting upon a fixed limited term, however, might not always be practical. The producer of an interactive encyclopedia, for example, might convincingly argue that it cannot predict just how long the edition of the encyclopedia will remain "in print" and to require a new license between the publication of editions would not be practical. In that event, the music copyright owner might suggest that the term be limited to the one edition and its reprints (including foreign language versions) however long new printings are made, but that a new license would be required for subsequent editions. But even this would not be a practical solution in some cases. Because of the ease with which these works can be electronically *updated* (i.e., revised), a new "edition" can be published every month or even every week!

### *3. Exclusivity*

The principles of exclusivity discussed in connection with commercial advertising do not apply equally to computer software, educational software, videogames, multimedia, and other new media works. Using music to help establish a product identity is no more a factor in the use of music in an electronic encyclopedia or videogame than it is in the use of music in a motion picture or television program. As is true for synchronization licenses for motion pictures, television, and video, exclusivity is rarely granted for uses in interactive media and software.

Accordingly, a music copyright owner would be quite reluctant to provide any form of exclusivity in connection with the licensing of music in computer software or multimedia programs. If exclusivity were considered, the scope of the exclusivity should be very narrowly defined. For example, granting "exclusivity for educational software" when the intent is for works to be distributed in the K-12 educational market, might be construed to cover electronic encyclopedia and even adult training programs. The types of educational software could vary to such a degree that it may be impossible to narrowly circumscribe the terms of exclusivity. In any event, software and new media is usually differentiated sufficiently that a licensee would not normally require exclusivity to the music in order to help differentiate his product in the software market.

### *4. Territory*

Copyright owners have tried to restrict the territory of these licenses to the United States and Canada and require that separate licenses be obtained for use in other territories from their affiliated subpublishers around the world. The world, however, has changed dramatically from the days of locally produced sheet music and phonograph records, and music copyright owners are under increasing pressure to grant worldwide licenses.

It has become the practice of computer software and multimedia producers to establish facilities at one or two locations in the world, such as Singapore or Ireland, where virtually all copies of their products, in various language versions, are made and distributed to their subsidiaries and affiliates around the world. This is a much more efficient method of operation than the traditional means of distributing record albums with which music publishers are familiar. The technology itself is facilitating the trend toward a one world marketplace: the vast amounts of memory capacity of optical laser discs permit the storage of multiple language versions of a single program all on the same disc, vastly facilitating the distribution of such works overseas. Accordingly, music publishers are beginning to accept proposals for licensing on a worldwide basis to reflect these new technologies and business practices.

Music publishers should, of course, first consider whether they are under any contractual restriction with its songwriters or international co-publishers that would preclude them from issuing a worldwide license without special clearance. Where rights are split by territory (*see* Chapters 5 and 6), the co-administrators of the copyright should work out a deal by which royalties from worldwide licenses may be split in some equitable manner.

Music publishers and those with whom they share music rights overseas should work these deals out among themselves and not try to place unreasonable burdens on the prospective licensee, such as requesting the licensee to account for sales on a territory-by-territory basis. The rights owner in each territory has a great incentive to cooperate in working out such an arrangement. Rather than provide territory-by-territory accounting, a producer will accept licenses for the territories he can get and simply choose not to sell directly into territories for which he cannot obtain a license. In an environment with multiple distribution channels, producers cannot control the territories in which their products will end up. Consequently, the owner of rights for a territory that refuses to license will discover he receives no royalties for products that end up being sold in his territory.

The music publishers have created much of the bind they are in because of the way they structured their subpublishing deals in the past. Now that the world has changed, they should work out administrative solutions to facilitate the efficient licensing of their copyrights. Anything less would be a disservice to the songwriters they are supposed to represent.

## III. CONSIDERATIONS IN GRANTING AND CLEARING LICENSES FOR USE OF EXISTING MUSIC IN VIDEOGAMES

Because product managers overseeing the development of popular videogames are typically in the early 20s, there may be good opportunities to pitch to him existing music recorded by emerging rock bands, which he believes would be appropriate for players of the game. While the band may be paid little for the videogame license itself, the promotion value could break the act. For example, the use of recordings by the band Breaking Benjamin in the videogame Halo II resulted in millions of dollars in download and CD sales. These younger game developers may also be looking for standard songs from particular genres and might look to befriend synch license managers at the music publishers.

Licensing the use of existing musical work in videogames requires consideration of many of the same basic factors discussed in preceding sections and chapters, including the fee structure, the value of the song, the importance of the song in relation to its intended use, and the scope of the intended use.

## A. Fee Structure

### *1. Flat Fee*

Like the use of music in consumer products, the performance of music in the course of using a videogame device will usually be *private*, not public. Because no fees are collectible for private performances of music, the music copyright owner will seek alternative means to share the economic success of the use. The most common means is collecting a royalty based on the sales of the work embodying the music.

Traditionally, however, most videogame publishers have flat out refused to pay a royalty for the use of music in videogame devices. Since they were already accustomed to paying royalties to the developers of the games, their reluctance to pay for music on the same basis was probably more a reflection on their view of the importance of the music to the game experience than any real business concern about paying a royalty. Setting a precedent for paying a royalty for music may have also played a role in the delay, but these days game publishers are increasingly aware of the connection their users and subscribers have to popular music and are more likely to pay what they have to obtain the music that they believe will help them acquire new customers and subscribers and maintain them.

Where flat fees are still demanded, they range anywhere from $1,000 to $25,000, depending upon whether the fee includes online uses, related uses, and the other factors discussed below.

### 2. *Royalty*

Where a game publisher is willing to pay a royalty on each cartridge or copy, rates will vary between 9¢ to 18¢ per song, per copy distributed. For online videogames, some music publishers have attempted to obtain a percentage of the subscription fees, but game publishers have resisted, saying that the music publisher will be able to obtain a share of the economic success of the work through any public performance fees it may earn from the Internet transmissions of the game.

When a game is all about the music, such as *Guitar Hero* or *Rock Band*, music publishers will not accept a penny rate per song, as they would with a traditional video game where music is only incidental. Unfortunately, no rate standards have yet emerged for these uses.

For such large video arcade machines retailing from $1,000 to $3,000 per unit, a fee of 1/2% to 1% of the retail selling price might be considered. Alternatively, the music publisher might accept a maximum per unit royalty of $10 or $15 per unit. Performance rights are not included and it is the responsibility of the arcade to get appropriate performance rights from ASCAP and BMI.

## B. Value of the Song

As in the consideration of licensing music for use in consumer products and commercial advertising, a music copyright owner should consider the potential impact of associating a hit song with a particular videogame on the future earning potential of the song. By the same token, associating a song with a popular videogame, unlike with a consumer product or commercial advertising, is more likely to enhance the earnings potential of the song than to harm it. Some relatively unknown songs have become large commercial hits as a result of the exposure it received as part of a videogame.

## C. Importance of the Song in Relation to Its Intended Use

Videogames based upon feature films, such as *The Godfather* and *Star Wars*, have an obvious need for the use of music, particularly the music used in the original films. Typically, the film producer will control the rights in the film's score and will be able to provide a music license, together with the general license provided to create the videogame version of the film. However, where a separate license is required from a particular music publisher for the use of a song closely associated with the film (e.g., *When You Wish Upon A Star*), the publisher may have extra leverage, as there may be fewer substitutes available to create the optimal game experience.

## D. Exclusivity

The principles of exclusivity discussed in connection with commercial advertising do not apply equally to videogames. As is true for synchronization licenses for motion pictures, television, and video, exclusivity is rarely granted for these uses. Of course, videogame producers are always looking for ways of differentiating their products. Where the song is new, granting exclusivity for use in videogames for a period of years may be warranted if it provides the opportunity for exposure to the right audience in a popular game.

## E. Media

A copyright owner would want the license to fully describe the videogame in which the music will be embodied, how the music will be used in the games, and the types of media configurations used for the delivery of the game. The work should be referenced by title, or tentative title, and any other useful information to describe the work. In addition, the license should state whether the configurations are limited to embodying in physical devices, such as cartridges, CD-ROM, DVD, intended for distribution to the public or whether the game will be made available on the Internet for use with home computers and game devices connected to the Internet.

Game producers will require the ability to use the music in advertising and other materials that promote the videogame. These uses may include use in television commercials, websites, in-store promotions, trailers in DVDs.

## F. Duration of Use

The license should also state the length of time the song, or a portion of the song, will be used. The license may state "up to the entire length" of the song and because of the interactive nature of the game, the license will typically permit a rendering of a potentially infinite number of loops of the song while the game is being played.

### G. Term

Music copyright owners desire to limit the term to a period of years, typically five to ten years, and will often agree to options to renew for additional three-year periods upon payment of an additional license fee or advance against royalties.

Game developers typically insist on use for the "life of copyright" in either the song or the game or, failing that, for as long as the game is available in distribution or for the "commercial life of game." If the term is limited to a period of years, the game developer will get a six to twelve month post-termination period in which to sell-off existing inventory.

### H. Territory

Copyright owners have tried to restrict the territory of these licenses to the United States and Canada and require that separate licenses be obtained for use in other territories from their affiliated subpublishers around the world. The world, however, has changed dramatically from the days of locally produced sheet music and phonograph records, and music copyright owners are under increasing pressure to grant worldwide licenses, particularly where Internet versions of the game are contemplated.

### I. Changes

The license typically permits the game developer to edit the song so that it plays at the appropriate time during the course of the game. Indecent language may also be subject to editing. In addition, some uses require the stripping out of the vocal track, so the ultimate use may be purely instrumental. Where the videogame permits the end user to remix or otherwise alter the recording of the song, the game developer should be sure the license permits such use.

### J. Credit

Copyright owners should request credit for the composition somewhere in the videogame package and any website used to promote the videogame.

## IV. CONSIDERATIONS IN ENTERING INTO COMPOSER AGREEMENTS FOR THE USE OF MUSIC IN VIDEOGAMES

The development of a new online videogame often takes years of work across closely coordinated teams of writers, designers, product managers, and software programmers. A videogame may have as much as 80 hours of play time, so the scoring of music for these programs requires an enormous amount of effort and close work with those responsible for the development. In film production, the composer typically steps in at the post-production stage of a film's development, which may be for several months. In game production, the relationship with the composer may last as long as 18 months.

In addition, the use of music to elicit emotion in the player is becoming an increasingly important part of the game experience. Game developers, in some respects, have a greater challenge than film directors, because in games there is usually no dialogue to help set the mood. Music can really help here. Finally, the interactive nature of the videogame poses large challenges to the use of music. You're on a battlefield, the music stops at the end of the battle. You now can choose among four new paths, each requiring a different kind of music and each path has to sound like a composed film score. Then, of course, some players play faster than others. New composing styles must be invented to perfect the use of music in these games. A good composer will understand the meaning of the game and how music will work in it.

For this reason, game companies have looked to engage professional composers to help them plan for the use of music in new games. Composers engaged to work with development teams are typically hired on a work-for-hire basis, but some composers are able to maintain their writer's share and some game companies have established music publishing companies to do what's necessary to attract talented composers. For example, Microsoft has established a music publishing company that is administered by Warner Chappell.

### A. Fees

Composers working on a work-for-hire basis may get as much as \$100,000 or more per project, payable upon completing milestones. Additional fees may be payable upon the release of editions for various game devices or for significant new online versions. Royalties may also be payable on soundtrack albums, which may do very well on iTunes and other download services.

### B. Credit

Composers will typically get credit for their contributions in the screens of the game where credit is provided to others working on the project.

## V. ADDITIONAL CONSIDERATIONS IN CLEARING LICENSES FOR MULTIMEDIA AND NEW MEDIA PRODUCTS

### A. Understanding All the Rights Involved

As noted in Chapter 11, persons seeking to clear licenses for multimedia programs or new media products can avoid difficulties by first fully understanding all of the potential rights that may be involved in the use. For example, if you are seeking permission to use a particular recording in your multimedia program, don't overlook the fact that you will require two separate licenses, one under the copyright in the sound recording and another under the copyright in the underlying musical composition. A license to use the underlying composition may be obtained from the music publisher; the license to use the sound recording may be sought by conferring with the record company who owns the recording.

In some cases, more than two licenses to use a certain piece of material will need to be cleared. For example, the use of a simple film clip from a motion picture may require separate permission from each of several parties holding various rights underlying the clip. As noted in Chapter 11, any of the following rights may be hidden beneath the surface of an apparently simple clearance problem: a copyright in the underlying song featured in the clip, a copyright in the recording of the song performed in the clip, the copyright in the motion picture from which the clip was excerpted, a copyright in any choreography appearing in the clip, a copyright in a literary work upon which the clip is based (where the film from which the clip was taken is based upon a novel, non-fiction book, newspaper article, biography, autobiography, etc.), a copyright in a theatrical production (such as a musical play, opera, or ballet) performed in the clip, a copyright in an animated character, a copyright in a still photograph appearing in the clip, a copyright of a translation or arrangement of a work in the public domain, a right of privacy (i.e., the right one has "to be left alone") of one or more individuals appearing in the clip, or a right of publicity (i.e., the exclusive right an individual has to the use of one's name, voice, photograph, and likeness) of one or more individuals appearing in the clip.

Considerations in granting and clearing rights to use works other than musical compositions is beyond the scope of this book. However, an example of a license to use a film clip is set forth as Form 22.6 on the CD-ROM. Form 22.8 on the CD-ROM is an example of a license typically used by record companies and motion picture producers for the synchronization of sound recordings in audiovisual works. An example of a license to use a still photograph is set forth as Form 22.7 and a location release is set forth as Form 22.9 on the CD-ROM.

### B. Educate the Music Copyright Owner

Finally, where necessary, persons seeking to clear licenses for complex works, such as multimedia and new media works, should take the time to educate the music copyright owner on just how the music is intended to be used. A substantial number of people in society still remain frightened or distrustful of computers and high technology, but a simple live demonstration of a multimedia application could go a long way to promote the understanding and trust required to persuade a music copyright owner, fearful of making a bad deal, to grant the license you desire.

# APPENDIX TO CHAPTER 22
# LICENSING MUSIC IN VIDEOGAMES, OTHER NEW MEDIA, MULTIMEDIA DEVICES, AND ONLINE VERSIONS

FORMS (ON CD-ROM ONLY)

Chapter 23

# Licensing of Sound Recordings (Master Use Licenses, Digital Downloading and Digital Audio Transmissions)

## Summary

# CHAPTER 23

# LICENSING OF SOUND RECORDINGS (MASTER USE LICENSES, DIGITAL DOWNLOADING AND DIGITAL AUDIO TRANSMISSIONS)

The preceding chapters were primarily devoted to the licensing of *musical works* — the songs that underlie sheet music and guitar tabs, and which are performed in motion pictures and other recordings and at live venues, such as nightclubs and stadiums. In this chapter, however, we take a brief detour to explore the business and licensing aspects of the *sound recording*, a work of authorship that is entirely separate from the musical work and one that is a relative newcomer to copyright, as it owes its existence to the advent of recording technology developed a little more than a century ago by Thomas Edison.

The U.S. Copyright Act defines the term as follows:

> "Sound recordings" are works that result from the fixation of a series of musical, spoken, or other sounds, but not including the sounds accompanying a motion picture or other audiovisual work, regardless of the nature of the material objects, such as disks, tapes, or other phonorecords, in which they are embodied.[1]

We will begin by exploring the fundamental rights that need to be cleared for the creation of a sound recording and then we will look at the kinds of licenses that are typically granted by owners of sound recordings in order to earn a living from them.

[1] 17 U.S.C. Sec. 101.

## I. CREATING SOUND RECORDINGS

To create a sound recording of a singer or musician's performance of a copyrighted musical work, you must clear two fundamental rights: (1) the exclusive rights in the song to be recorded and (2) the exclusive right the singer or musician has to authorize the recording of his or her performance. The exclusive rights in the song that needs to be cleared is the copyright owner's exclusive rights, under the Copyright Act, to make derivative works and to reproduce copies and phonorecords of the song.[2] The exclusive right a performer has in his or her performance is derived from the common law.

Should the creator of a new sound recording wish to use a digital sample of an existing sound recording, a third right comes into play: the exclusive right of a record company or other owner of a copyright in the existing recording to make derivative works and reproduce copies and phonorecords of the sampled recording. Licensing of digital samples is discussed at length in Chapter 24.[3]

### A. Mechanical Reproduction of the Underlying Musical Work

One of a copyright owner's exclusive rights under copyright is the exclusive right to reproduce copies of the song into copies and phonorecords and another is the exclusive right to make derivative works of the song. A *derivative work* is "a work based upon one or more preexisting works, such as a translation, *musical arrangement*, dramatization, fictionalization, motion picture version, *sound recording*, art reproduction, abridgment, condensation, *or any other form in which a work may be recast, transformed, or adapted.*" Thus, a sound recording of a song is a derivative work of the song and the process of recording a song — i.e., saving the sounds of some or all of the notes of the song onto a tangible medium of expression (e.g., a magnetic tape or hard disk) — is a reproduction of the song in a phonorecord.

Thus, before you can even consider distributing copies of another's song, you must first get permission from the copyright owner to make a

[2] 17 U.S.C. Sec. 106.

[3] Note, as discussed in Chapter 24, when sampling from a sound recording owned by another, it does not matter how little you sample — taking even one bit or byte of data constitutes copyright infringement in the sound recording from which you are sampling.

derivative work of the song and the initial recording — i.e., recording the sounds of some or all of the notes of the song onto a tangible medium of expression (e.g., a magnetic tape or hard disk).[4]

In practice, however, getting permission to make a derivative work of a song, not written or controlled by the recording artist, prior to making the recording is not always done.[5] The exigencies of creating complex forms of entertainment, such as commercial recordings, sometimes do not allow for the time and effort required to negotiate a license before the production process has begun. As a practical matter, however, the recording artist often also controls the rights to the song, in which case the license is set forth in his recording agreement or permission is implied.

In the case of a song controlled by another, the artist or producer knows that it may compel the song's owner to grant a mechanical reproduction license. Under the compulsory license provision, the fee is set by statute and the license need only be obtained prior to distribution, not prior to recording.[6] Thus, the risks of making a recording prior to obtaining a license are minimal, given the fact that a compulsory mechanical license may be obtained within 30-days after the recording and the damages to the copyright owner for such technical infringement would be minimal.[7]

---

[4] Technically, you need not even make that copy to infringe a copyright owner's exclusive right to make derivative works. For example, a dance routine may be a derivative work of written instructions on how to perform the dance. Simply to perform the dance from its copyrighted choreographic notation would be a derivative work of the dance, and therefore an infringement of the choreographic work, even if no copy was made in the course of creating the derivative work (i.e., the performance). 1976 Copyright Act, House Report at 62.

[5] Record companies typically obtain the mechanical licenses they need from an artist/songwriter under the recording agreement with the artist. Where the artist records a cover song, however, the mechanical license is often obtained after the recording is made, but before copies are distributed. Certainly, anyone making an arrangement of a song and recording it at home for non-commercial purposes could rely on the defense of fair use of copyright (at least until he or she begins to share copies with friends or begins uploading a copy to YouTube or some such other site).

[6] Any person who wishes to obtain a compulsory license under this section shall, before *or within thirty days after making, and before distributing any phonorecords of the work*, serve notice of intention to do so on the copyright owner. 17 U.S.C. Sec. 115(b)(1).

[7] Note, however, that the compulsory license provision of the Copyright Act does not apply to the use of the song in audiovisual works, only sound recordings (which, by definition, are audio only). If the recording of a song to be used in a motion picture is

Business and legal considerations in granting mechanical licenses are discussed at length in Chapter 13, on *Licensing Music in Sound Recordings.*

## B. Performer's Exclusive Right to Record a Performance

A performer's exclusive right to control (i.e., legally prevent or permit) the recording of his or her performance arises from the common law. That is, it is not a right arising under the Copyright Act, but rather one arising from the courts' recognition of such a right by a series of legal decisions.

The U.S. Supreme Court specifically recognized the exclusive right of a performer to control the recording of his performance in a case brought by a performer whose 15-second "human cannonball" act, in which he was shot from a cannon into a net some 200 feet away, was, without his consent, videotaped in its entirety and televised on a news program later that day.[8] The court held that the broadcast of the performer's entire act posed a substantial threat to the economic value of his performance and the television station had no privilege to televise the performance.

Recognizing a performer's exclusive right to control his performance, the Supreme Court stated, "The State's interest in permitting a 'right of publicity' is in protecting the proprietary interest of the individual in his act in part to encourage such entertainment."[9] The broadcast of the entertainer's "entire performance . . . goes to the heart of [the performer's] ability to earn a living as an entertainer." The entertainer's control over his performance even extends to the news media. "No social purpose is served by having the [broadcaster] get free some aspect of the plaintiff that would have market value and for which he would normally pay."

---

likely to be expensive (e.g., performed by a large orchestra or with the aid of an otherwise elaborate studio recording) an appropriate license might be sought before the recording is made, as a producer may wish to be certain that an appropriate synch license can be obtained at a reasonable cost before incurring further the production expense.

[8] *Zacchini v. Scripps-Howard Broadcasting Co.*, 433 U.S. 562 (1977).

[9] *Citing Ettore v. Philco Television Broadcasting Corp.*, 229 F.2d 481 at 486 (1956), discussed in Chapter 17, on *Old Licenses, New Uses.*

Many states have specifically codified a performer's exclusive right to control recordings of his performances.[10] For example, in the state of Illinois,

> A person commits unlawful use of recorded sounds or images when he: . . . (4) Intentionally, knowingly or recklessly transfers or causes to be transferred without the consent of the owner, any live performance with the purpose of selling or causing to be sold, or using or causing to be used for profit the sound or audio visual recording to which the performance is transferred.

California has enacted a more general statute intended to cover any proprietary right of performers that would not be preempted by the Copyright Act:

> The author of any original work of authorship that is not fixed in any tangible medium of expression has an exclusive ownership in the representation or expression thereof as against all persons except one who originally and independently creates the same or similar work. A work shall be considered not fixed when it is not embodied in a tangible medium of expression or when its embodiment in a tangible medium of expression is not sufficiently permanent or stable

[10] Illinois: *http://law.justia.com/illinois/codes/chapter53/60665.html.* See also statutes enacted by Kansas: *http://law.justia.com/kansas/codes/chapter21/statute_11640.html* ("Piracy of recordings is knowingly, and without the consent of the owner, duplicating or causing to be duplicated any sounds recorded on a phonograph record, disc, wire, tape, film or other article on which sounds are recorded, or recording or causing to be recorded any live performance, with the intent to sell, rent or cause to be sold or rented, any such duplicated sounds or any such recorded performance, or to give away such duplicated sounds or recorded performance as part of a promotion for any product or service."); Texas: *http://law.justia.com/texas/codes/bc/004.00.000035.00.html* ("A person commits an offense if the person: . . . (2) with the intent to sell for commercial advantage or private financial gain records or fixes or causes to be recorded or fixed on a recording a live performance with the knowledge that the live performance has been recorded or fixed without the consent of the owner."); Alabama: *http://law.justia.com/alabama/codes/13297/13a-8-81.html* ("In the absence of a written agreement or operation of law to the contrary, the performer or performers of the live performance shall be presumed to own the rights to record or authorize the recording of the live performance."); and similar statutes in Kentucky, Florida, West Virginia, and Louisiana: *http://law.justia.com/kentucky/codes/434-00/445.html*, *http://law.justia.com/florida/codes/TitleXXXIII/ch0540.html*, *http://law.justia.com/westvirginia/codes/61/wvc61-3-50.html*, *http://law.justia.com/louisiana/codes/146/78370.html.*

> to permit it to be perceived, reproduced, or otherwise communicated for a period of more than transitory duration, either directly or with the aid of a machine or device. California Civil Code 980(a)(1).

A number of states have also enacted laws to protect by statute a performer's "right of publicity." For example, in California:

> Any person who knowingly uses another's name, voice, signature, photograph, or likeness, in any manner, on or in products, merchandise, or goods, or for purposes of advertising or selling, or soliciting purchases of, products, merchandise, goods or services, without such person's prior consent, or, in the case of a minor, the prior consent of his parent or legal guardian, shall be liable for any damages sustained by the person or persons injured as a result thereof.[11]

The courts have also ruled that the Copyright Act does not preempt state laws protecting the exclusive right to an entertainer's performances.[12] Under Section 301(a) of the Copyright Act "all legal or equitable rights that are equivalent to any of the exclusive rights within the general scope of copyright . . . that are fixed in a tangible medium of expression and come within the subject matter of copyright" are preempted by the Copyright Act. Accordingly, "No person is entitled to any such right or equivalent right in any such work under the common law or statutes of any State."

However, Section 301(b), which represents the reverse of Section 301(a), expressly allows the states to confer common law copyright protection upon works that do not come within the subject matter of copyright, including works of authorship not fixed in any tangible medium of expression. Unrecorded performances *per se* are not fixed in tangible form. Examples of works not fixed in tangible form include "choreography that has never been filmed or notated, an extemporaneous speech, 'original works of authorship' communicated solely through conversations or live broadcasts, and a dramatic sketch or

[11] Cal. Civil Code Sec. 3344.

[12] *Baltimore Orioles, Inc. v. Major League Baseball Players Association*, 805 F.2d 663 at fn 22 (7th Cir. 1986) (citing *Zacchini*, held that the use of a tape of a broadcast of a ballgame without the consent of the ballplayers would violate their rights of publicity if an authorized tape was not made simultaneous with the performance of the game).

musical composition improvised or developed from memory and without being recorded or written down."[13] Because such works are not fixed in tangible form, rights in such works are not subject to preemption under § 301(a).[14]

Nonetheless, once a performance is reduced to tangible form, there is no distinction between the performance and the recording of the performance for the purpose of preemption under Section 301(a).[15] Thus, if a baseball game was broadcast without being recorded, the ball players' performances similarly would not be fixed in tangible form and their rights of publicity would not be subject to preemption. By virtue of being videotaped, however, the performances are fixed in tangible form, and any rights of publicity in their performances that are equivalent to the rights contained in the copyright of the telecast are preempted.

The *Zacchini* case was decided before the Copyright Act of 1976 took effect, but in *Baltimore Orioles*, the court opined that Section 301(a) would have not preempted state law protection of the human cannonball's performance:

> Assuming that Zacchini did not videotape or otherwise record his performance, his human cannonball act would not be fixed in tangible form and could not be copyrighted. Nonetheless, because the work in which he asserts rights would *not be fixed* in a tangible *medium* of expression, his right of publicity in his performance would not be subject to preemption. Thus, if a television station were to broadcast his act, he still could sue successfully for violation of his right of publicity in his performance. Merely that the television station might videotape its telecast would not grant the station a copyright in the broadcast of Zacchini's performance or preempt Zacchini's right of publicity. To be "fixed" in tangible form, a work must be recorded "by or under the authority of the *author*," here Zacchini. *See* 17 U.S.C. § 101 (definition of "fixed"). Because Zacchini did not consent to the telecast, the broadcast could not be "fixed" for the

[13] House Report at 131.

[14] *Baltimore Orioles, Inc. v. Major League Baseball Players Association*, 805 F.2d at note 22.

[15] *Id.*

purpose of copyrightability and Zacchini's right of publicity would not be subject to preemption.[16] (emphasis in the original).

## C. Federal Protection Against Recording of Live Musical Performances

On December 8, 1994, Congress revised the Copyright Act by enacting a new right under copyright: the exclusive right to make — or, to put it another way, the right to exclude others from making — an audio or video recording of a live musical performance.[17] It is important to note that this is not a right in a musical composition nor is it a right in any existing and authorized sound recording, but a right to make recordings of the *live performance* itself. It is, in short, a right in a *live musical performance.*[18]

### *1. What the Anti-Bootlegging Statute Prohibits*

The new anti-bootlegging law, set forth in the appendix to this chapter, prohibits four types of conduct:

- the making of audio or video recordings of live musical performances, without the consent of the performers involved;
- the reproduction of unauthorized audio or video recordings of live musical performances;
- the distribution of unauthorized audio or video recordings of live musical performances; and
- the transmission of live musical performances to the public, without the consent of the performers involved.

---

[16] *Id.*

[17] 17 U.S.C. Sec. 1101, the entire text of which is set forth in the appendix of this chapter.

[18] Much of the remainder of this section on the anti-bootlegging statute was borrowed verbatim from the article by Lionel Sobel, "*Bootleggers Beware: Copyright Law Now Protects Live Musical Performances, but New Law Leaves Many Questions Unanswered,*" 17 Entertainment Law Reporter, No. 2, p. 6 (July, 1995). Copyright © 1995 Entertainment Law Reporter. Used with permission.

While these provisions seem clear enough, some points are worth emphasizing. The new law applies to live *musical* performances only, not to speeches, lectures, or poetry readings, nor even to purely dramatic performances. Congress didn't focus on musical performances because it considered them worthier of protection than non-musical performances. Instead, the law focuses on musical performances for the same reason it was enacted in the first place — a point that will be covered below.

The new law applies to live musical performances only, not to recordings of musical performances. This is because making and distributing unauthorized recordings and reproductions of recordings already was prohibited by the Copyright Act. That practice is known as "piracy" rather than "bootlegging," and piracy has been prohibited by federal copyright law since 1972.

By its own terms, the new law is violated by doing any of the prohibited acts "without the consent of the performer or performers involved." Thus, if consent is obtained, no violation occurs. But the law says nothing whatsoever about how consent should or may be obtained. Thus, it appears that consent does not have to be in writing. Oral and even implied consent should be sufficient (though oral and especially implied consent are often more difficult to prove than written consent).

Those who violate the new law are vulnerable to civil liability and even criminal penalties.

On the civil side, virtually all of the remedies that are available in other types of copyright infringement cases are now available in bootlegging cases as well. These remedies include injunctions, impounding and destruction of infringing recordings and videos, damages, profits, costs and attorneys' fees. These are the remedies that have long been specified in Sections 502 through 505 of the Copyright Act; and the new law makes these remedies available in bootlegging cases simply by providing that bootleggers "shall be subject to the remedies provided in Sections 502 through 505, to the same extent as an infringer of copyright."

On the criminal side, the new bootlegging law provides for penalties that include imprisonment, fines, and seizure, forfeiture and destruction of infringing recordings and videos. The substantive actions that constitute a criminal violation are the same as those that amount to a civil violation, with one important exception: the acts must be committed "knowingly and for purposes of commercial advantage or private financial gain" in order to be a criminal violation. (This is the same distinction that has long been made between civil and criminal copyright infringements of all kinds.)

### *2. Why the Anti-Bootlegging Statute Was Enacted*

The bootlegging law was required by the international agreement on Trade Related Aspects of Intellectual Property Rights — commonly known as "TRIPs" — which is an annex to the Uruguay Round revision of the General Agreement on Tariffs and Trade (commonly known as "GATT"). The reason the bootlegging law was enacted as part of a much larger statute is that the Uruguay Round agreement required changes in countless areas of U.S. law, and those changes literally dwarf — in bulk — the changes that were required in copyright law.

There are two primary reasons the United States sought an intellectual property code within GATT — two reasons, in other words, why the United States found the Berne Convention to be insufficient for the protection of U.S. copyrights. The first reason is that although the Berne Convention requires its members to provide a high level of substantive protection for copyrights, it requires very little in the way of remedies for infringements. Countries are eligible for Berne membership even if the only remedy found in their copyright laws is the remedy of seizure and destruction of infringing goods after they have been found to be infringing as a result of a civil lawsuit. Berne does not require countries to provide for the recovery of damages, profits, costs or attorneys' fees, nor does it require countries to provide for preliminary injunctive relief or criminal penalties. The second reason is that the Berne Convention does not provide dispute resolution mechanisms for cases where one country (such as the United States) claims that another country is failing to comply with its obligations under Berne.

Because Berne is inadequate when it comes to remedies, the United States has resorted to "self-help" measures in dealing with some countries. The United States has imposed trade sanctions — or has threatened to — against countries that have not been providing adequate and effective protection for U.S. copyrights (and other types of intellectual property). The United States has found this to be an effective method for improving protection for U.S. copyrights abroad, because the United States is the world's leading customer for goods made in other countries. The imposition of tariffs on goods made in countries that do not respect U.S. copyrights — or the threat to impose tariffs on such goods — has been helpful in getting those countries to improve their copyright policies. However, some other countries have responded by asserting that the United States violates its own obligations under GATT when it imposes tariffs in response to copyright protection complaints, because prior to the Uruguay Round, GATT was not concerned with intellectual property at all. Now, by making respect for copyright a GATT obligation of all WTO members, the failure to respect copyright is a violation of GATT; and in due course that violation authorizes the imposition of trade sanctions as a matter of GATT law itself.

The United States also sought an intellectual property code as part of GATT because GATT did (and the WTO now does) have formal procedures for the resolution of disputes (unlike the Berne Convention which doesn't and never did).

The new bootlegging law is a direct consequence of TRIPs, because protection against bootlegging is one of the intellectual property rights which TRIPs requires WTO members to provide. The requirement is found in Article 14(1) of TRIPs, which mandates that performers have the right to prevent three things: the unauthorized audio recordings of their live performances, the reproduction of such audio recordings, and the unauthorized broadcasting of their live performances.

The actual language of TRIPs is somewhat awkward, but is worth quoting because it explains in part why Congress limited bootlegging rights to live musical performances, and did not grant such rights to lecturers or actors. TRIPs Article 14(a) states: "In respect of a fixation of their performance on a phonogram performers shall have the possibility of preventing . . . the fixation of their unfixed performance and the reproduction of such fixation . . . [and] the broadcasting . . . and . . . communication to the public of their live performance." When Congress implemented this provision of TRIPs in the new bootlegging law, Congress did more than TRIPs required, and arguably less too. Congress did more than TRIPs requires, because the bootlegging law prohibits both audio and video recordings of live musical performances without the consent of the performers, while

TRIPs itself only requires countries to prohibit unauthorized audio recordings. TRIPs' focus on audio recordings is reflected by its use of the word "phonograms." The word "'phonograms' means any exclusively aural fixation of sounds of a performance or of other sounds." (This definition does not appear in TRIPs itself; it is quoted from Article 3 of the Rome Convention. The U.S. Copyright Act refers to phonograms as "sound recordings.")

Congress arguably did less than TRIPs requires, because TRIPs mandates that "performers" have the right to prevent the bootlegging of their "performance." TRIPs does not confine its benefits to musical performers nor limit its applicability to musical performances. Apparently, Congress concluded that the only types of performances that would be recorded on phonograms are musical performances; and no doubt, most performances recorded on phonograms are musical. But not all. Audio recordings of lectures may be made without the consent of the lecturer, as might audio recordings of dramatic performances and poetry readings. TRIPs requires that lecturers, actors, and poets be given the right to prevent unauthorized audio recordings of their performances. The new bootlegging law fails to do so. Neither the law nor its legislative history explains why.

It is easier to explain why the bootlegging law grants performance rights for live performances only, and does not give performers (or their record companies) the right to prevent (or be compensated for) the unauthorized public performance or broadcast of their pre-recorded musical performances. The reason simply is that TRIPs only requires protection for live musical performances; it does not require a public performance right for the public performance of recordings. (In this respect, TRIPs differs from the Rome Convention which does require compensation for the broadcast or other public performance of "phonograms." U.S. copyright law does not contain such a right at the present time, and never has; and that is why the United States has never adhered to the Rome Convention.)

### 3. *The Constitutionality of the Anti-Bootlegging Statute*

TRIPs explicitly requires that performers be given the right to prevent unauthorized recordings "of their *unfixed* performances," and the new bootlegging law fulfills this requirement by giving them the right to prevent unauthorized recordings of their "*live* musical performances." The words "unfixed" and "live" in the two clauses just quoted are italicized, because these words raise a fundamental Constitutional issue insofar as U.S. copyright law is concerned.

In the United States, copyright protection has been available only to works that have been "fixed in [a] tangible medium of expression," and not to unfixed works. The fixation requirement appears in Section 102(a) of the current Copyright Act, but it has been a feature of U.S. law for more than 200 years. The fixation requirement arises from the Constitutional source of Congress' power to enact copyright legislation in the first place — namely, Article I, Section 8 of the Constitution, which gives Congress the power to grant authors the exclusive right to their "Writings." While Congress and the Supreme Court have defined the word "Writings" broadly — so that it includes, for example, photographs and sound recordings — "Writings" has always been construed to mean something that is tangible — something, in other words, that is written or recorded or otherwise "fixed in [a] tangible medium." When Congress decided to grant copyright protection to live television broadcasts — in response to the fervent requests of sports teams and leagues whose games are televised live — Article I, Section 8 of the Constitution required Congress to grant such protection to a live broadcast only if "a fixation" of the broadcast "is being made simultaneously with its transmission."

The new bootlegging law abandons any pretext of requiring live musical performances to be fixed in order for performers to be protected. Congress did not, in other words, require performers to record their performances as they were being given. Because Congress only has the power to protect fixed works under Article I, Section 8 of the Constitution, the Constitutional basis for Congress' power to enact the bootlegging law must be some other provision of the Constitution. Neither the law, nor its meager legislative history, mentions this issue in any way.

This does not mean that the bootlegging law is unconstitutional. It simply means that another Constitutional basis for it must be found. The Commerce Clause is certainly an adequate Constitutional basis for the bootlegging law. Indeed, reliance on the Commerce Clause to amend the Copyright Act opens the door to all types of additional amendments that until now have been thought to be beyond the reach of copyright law. Now that Congress has shown it is willing to exercise its Commerce Clause power to create new rights of copyright protection for all manner of unfixed works — including lectures, dramatic performances, and improvisational comedy — are possible. Moreover, under the Commerce Clause, Congress would have the power to enact legislation granting copyright protection to works that reflect industrious effort but no "creativity" of the kind previously required — protection for works such as comprehensive data bases and alphabetically arranged telephone directories.

### *4. The Effect of the Anti-Bootlegging Statute on State Law*

Finally, it is important to note that, by its own terms, the anti-bootlegging statute does not preempt state laws that purport to provide the same protections.

> (d) STATE LAW NOT PREEMPTED. — Nothing in this section may be construed to annul or limit any rights or remedies under the common law or statutes of any State.

Thus, all of the statutes set forth in the previous section, and the common law of other states that offer the same protections to performers, remain in full force and effect. The effect of the new federal statute is merely to offer additional federal remedies to performers whose live performances are recorded without their permission.

## II. FINANCING AND DISTRIBUTING SOUND RECORDINGS

Having established a performer's exclusive right to control the recording of his or her performances, we now turn to the common ways in which performers finance the creation of such recordings and how those recordings are typically exploited commercially.

There are two basic ways sound recordings are financed and distributed: (1) a performer creates his or her own recording and sells physical or digital copies to consumers (a) by direct sale, (b) through intermediaries or (c) both, or (2) a performer enters into a recording agreement with a record company, who produces the recording and distributes copies through the record company's physical and digital distribution channels.

The ability of an act or group to finance the creation of its own recordings, or to otherwise lean on a record label for assistance, is a function of their personal financial position and the genre of music they desire to produce. At one extreme, a singer creating a recording accompanied solely by an acoustic guitar or a DJ producing a recording with sophisticated software each benefit from fairly low recording costs as compared with, at the other extreme, a symphony orchestra recording a piano concerto. Somewhere in between may be pop, jazz, hip-hop, rock, and alternative rock recordings, which require a good recording studio, as well as sophisticated software and production expertise, to produce commercially satisfactory recordings.

Layered on top of the technical aspects of creating recordings are legal aspects relating to the proper clearance of songs underlying those recordings and of any digital samples used from other recordings. The piano concerto, being in the public domain, may not require a mechanical license, but an album of cover recordings by a hip-hop artist may require a substantial amount of legal clearance. The transaction costs of negotiating with music publishers demanding a copyright interest in songs modified by the artist and with record companies requiring royalty payments for digital samples can get high. An artist would certainly benefit from the experience of a record label's legal affairs staff.

The performer's choice is not always between self-publishing and signing with a record label. Sometimes there's no choice at all, which is the case with a performer who has no offer from a record label, having little choice but to begin their careers on the self-publishing route. Years ago, with the costs of creating a professional recording far higher than they are today, and access to distribution nearly all locked up by traditional means controlled by the record labels, performers had little choice but to get signed to a label or be cast off into oblivion. Today, however, self-publication is a realistic, though not ideal, choice.

Moreover, the choice is not limited to self-publication or signing with a label: there are a variety of variations and combinations of these models. Some artists, for example, form a relationship with a recording studio, record producer, or music publisher to create a professionally produced recording, and then together or separately seek a means of marketing the act and distributing its recordings. Others may produce a recording through a label operated by their personal manager, or through a label that is co-owned (i.e., a joint venture) with their manager, record label, or distributor. Other acts form their own record label, finance their own production, and negotiate their own distribution deals. Some of these, where they've been successful, even sign other acts, leveraging the path they forged for themselves. The means chosen will vary, depending upon the stage of the artist's career (e.g., new artist, superstar, well-known artist making a comeback), the artist's negotiating leverage, and, of course, the size of the artist's bank account or source of financing.

Leaving aside variations and combinations of relationships that can lead to the production and distribution of professional recordings, the remainder of this section will provide an overview of the basic ways a recording artist may produce a recording and make them available on a commercial basis to their fans.

## A. Performer Creates Own Recording and Self-Publishes Direct to Consumer

Since the advent of inexpensive digital recording and record editing technology, such as personal computers equipped with Pro Tools software and other audio recording equipment, performers today typically make their own first recordings, either for demonstration purposes or for actual commercial distribution.

Once the recording is made, the recording artist has a variety of options for offering the copies of the recordings for sale. If the artist records 10 or 12 recordings, he can compile them into an album and create the cover art necessary for the manufacture of professional looking CDs. The artist can engage a CD manufacturer to press as few as 300 copies, which the artist may use for demonstration or promotional purposes, or actually sell, at live performances or on the artist's website.

An act may also sell its recordings directly to consumers by digital download by using a number of Internet software tools designed specifically for that purpose, such as software widgets that allow you to sell digital downloads (typically in the MP3 file format) on the artist's website, MySpace, and similar web destinations.

## B. Performer Creates Own Recording and Self-Publishes Through Online Retailers & Digital Distributors

An act may do well selling its CDs at live performances or on its website, but unless it gains publicity at the level of a winner of American Idol, the act is not likely to attract enough of an audience to its live performances or visitors to its own website, or Facebook page, to make a living selling its recordings. At some point, an act will want to have its recordings available where music buyers visit all the time: Amazon.com, the iTunes store, eMusic, Rhapsody, and similar music services.

*Physical Distribution.* In addition to selling its CDs on their website, a band may enter into a relationship with Amazon.com to make the CDs available to anyone doing a search for the band on the Amazon website. Amazon.com offers programs that allow for the act to engage in its own fulfillment of orders; alternatively, Amazon will stock a small inventory of CDs, orders for which Amazon will fulfill for you. Recordings artists should check the Amazon.com website for details on the relative merits of these services.

*Press-On-Demand.* Amazon also offers a service in which they, instead of carrying an inventory of ready-made CDs, will even press a CD and ship it on-demand — that is, the CD is pressed and packaged shortly after the customer enters the order. Recordings artists should check the Amazon.com website for details on this service.

*Digital Distribution.* Perhaps the best means an artist has of making his recordings widely available is to have them distributed by popular online music services, such as iTunes, eMusic, AmazonMP3, Rhapsody, Napster, and others. Though some artists with high bargaining power may be able to strike deals directly with these services, most online services are reluctant to enter direct deals with individual artists and even small record labels. To save costs, most large online music services prefer to deal with service organizations that specialize in digital distribution.

There are basically five types of organizations that provide digital distribution services: (1) the major record companies, (2) independent distributors offering digital distribution services along side of physical distribution services, (3) aggregators or pure digital distributors who provide solely digital distribution services, (4) service providers who provide solely content delivery services, and (5) service providers who specialize in distributing the recordings of unsigned artists.

### *1. Major Record Companies*

For a major record company (i.e., Universal, Sony, Warner, EMI) to perform digital distribution services for you, you must either be signed to one of the major's labels or to an independent label that uses the major distributor for digital distribution. The major record companies typically charge independent labels a distribution fee of 15% to 20% of gross revenues for this service, but you must be a fairly large independent record label to obtain such a distribution relationship with a major record company, which will typically insist on the right to distribute the label's repertoire both in physical form (e.g., CDs) and digitally (e.g., download and streaming).

### *2. Independent Distributors*

For an independent distributor (e.g., E1, formerly Koch Distribution, in the United States; PIAS in Europe) to perform digital distribution services for you, you must be signed to one of independent record companies distributed by the distributor. Independent distributors typically charge independent labels a distribution fee of 15% to 25% of gross revenues for this service.

### *3. Digital Distributors for Independent Labels*

Many independent labels are too small to be signed to any of the major or independent distributors and therefore need to find an alternative means of getting their repertoire posted to the online download and on-demand services. Some of these labels turn to what have become known as "aggregators" or "digital distributors." These include The Orchard, IODA, InGrooves, IRIS, and BFM Digital, all of which are based in the United States, but provide their services on a worldwide basis, either directly or via relationships with other digital distributors overseas (such as Wild Palm in France and Zebralution in Germany).

These organizations offer complete digital distribution services; in other words, they will "rip" your CDs and cover art to a digital format (e.g., lossless and bitmap), store the files, upload them to the various services (e.g., iTunes, eMusic, AmazonMP3, Rhapsody, including the overseas websites of each of them), and collect the income and receive digital revenue reports from each of these services. They pay you the income received on a monthly or quarterly basis, less their distribution fee, which can be as much as 30%, though more typically 15% to 20%. These deals are always exclusive and typically require a minimum of three years.

Many individual artists who have produced their own CDs and have created their own "labels," are often successful at persuading these digital distributors to treat them as a real label and accept distribution of the recordings.

#### *4. Content Delivery Service Companies*

Many independent labels have been able to retain the digital distribution rights to their recordings. Thus, they use a major or independent distributor solely for physical distribution of CDs, and choose an alternative means of delivering their content to the online services. Some of these labels use their own in-house staff to deliver their content to the online services. Others use organizations such as Consolidated Independent, a U.K.-based firm that provides content delivery services. CI will rip and store your content for a fee, and for an additional fee, deliver the content to the online service you desire. While these services are great for large independent labels who have their own direct deals with the online music services, such arrangements are now almost impossible for a small independent record label or individual artist to get. Large music services such as iTunes and Amazon prefer to work with digital aggregators rather than small labels and individual artists (unless you happen to be the Beatles).

In addition, the independent label has to have a solution to the problem of collecting and aggregating the digital revenue files, containing millions of transactions often worth only a fraction of a cent each, produced by the online services every month. For this, many labels turn to RoyaltyShare, a firm with offices in California, New York, and London, who will aggregate the data for the label and help ingest the data into the label's accounting systems. RoyaltyShare performs this service for two of the major record companies and over 200 independent record labels worldwide. RoyaltyShare also provides full royalty processing services through a web-based platform that produces for the label the artist/producer and mechanical royalty statements.

### *5. Digital Distributors for Individual Artists*

Individual artists who can't obtain digital distribution services by another means frequently turn to services designed with the individual artist in mind. Services such as CD Baby, Tunecore, and Songcast offer individual recording artists an inexpensive means to make available their sound recordings on iTunes, Rhapsody, eMusic, Napster, AmazonMP3, and a variety of other online retailers or subscription services operating around the world.

## C. Performer Enters into a Recording Agreement with a Record Company

The most common way that most successful commercial recordings are made is by virtue of a relationship with a major or independent record company. The record company finances the production of the recording, helps promote and market the act, and distributes the recordings, on an exclusive basis, through its channels of physical and digital distribution.

### *1. The Majors and Independents*

Record companies can be distinguished primarily by their size, the breadth of the channels they use to distribute their recordings, and the amount of financing and marketing resources they can devote to backing recording artists. They break down into (1) the major record companies and (2) the independent record labels.

#### *a. Major Record Companies*

Years of consolidation have boiled down the major record companies to the following four organizations: Universal Music Group (owned by Vivendi, a French conglomerate), Sony (owned by Sony Corporation, a public company based in Japan), Warner Music Group (a public company based in the United States), and EMI (a privately owned company based in the United Kingdom). For the year 2005, the U.S. market shares of these companies were 31.71%, 25.61%, 15%, and 9.55%, respectively (according to Neilsen Sound-Scan; their worldwide market shares were 25.5%, 21.5%, 11.3%, and 13.4% (according to the International Federation of the Phonographic Industry (IFPI)).

Each of the four majors owns and operates their own distribution company, which facilitates the distribution of CDs to wholesalers and retailers and the digital distribution of their respective recordings to online retailers around the world. Each major also operates several "labels," or organizations that engage in the A&R activities (i.e., *artist and repertoire* — the function of discovering and nurturing new recording artists and the managing of all recordings artists signed to the label) and marketing and promotion activities. For example, Universal Music Group operates several labels, including Interscope, A&M, Geffen, Island/Def Jam, and Motown; Sony operates Columbia, Epic, Jive, and RCA Records; Warner Music Group operates Warner Bros. and Atlantic; and EMI operates Capitol and Virgin Records. Each label may focus on a particular genre of music (e.g., pop, hip-hop, classical, etc.) and each may have counterparts around the world focusing on regional acts.

### *b. Independent Record Labels*

Independent record companies are those record companies that are not wholly owned by the majors. They represent between 18% and 28% of record industry revenues, though that percentage may be as much as 10 percentage points higher, depending upon how you categorize the revenue.[19] Independent labels may be further broken down into those whose recordings are (1) distributed by one of the distribution companies owned by the major record labels, (2) distributed by an independent distributor, and (3) distributed through a combination of major or independent distributor and self-distribution.

---

[19] The American Association of Independent Music ($A^2IM$), a U.S. trade association established in 2005 to represent the interests of independent record labels, estimates that the U.S. market share of independent labels for the year 2008 was approximately 32%. Their calculation includes recordings produced by independent labels and distributed through the distribution companies owned by the major record companies.

Each of the four major record companies, in addition to owning and operating their own distribution companies, also owns and operates a distribution company dedicated to the distribution of recordings owned by independent record companies. Universal Music Group operates Fontana Distribution; Sony operates RED; Warner Music Group operates ADA; and EMI operates Caroline Distribution.

Each of these major-owned, independent distributors will enter into distribution agreements with independent labels. Under these agreements, the independent label manufactures its own CDs and ships to the distributor an inventory of CDs on a consignment basis. When the distributor sells CDs to record retailers, the distributor collects the revenue and pays it over to the independent label, less a distribution fee of 15% to 30%, but more typically 18% to 22% for physical (and 15% for digital) distribution. The distributor also typically maintains, for six months to a year after the sale, a reserve of 20% to 30% of revenues for returns.

In some cases, the independent label may enter into a P&D (i.e., production and distribution) deal, under which the independent labels engage the distributor to manufacturing an inventory of CDs for distribution. The distributor maintains a price list for the manufacture of the various parts of the CD, including the jewel-case, booklet, and "tray card" that comprises the typical CD package.

As mentioned above, many independent labels have retained their digital distribution rights, using a major or independent distributor solely for physical distribution of CDs. For deliveries of content to the online services, they may use their own IT departments or use organizations that specialize in content delivery. Organizations like Consolidated Independent, based in the United Kingdom, will rip and store your content for an annual fee, and for an additional fee, will deliver the content to the online service you desire. The problem with these services is that you have to have your own deals with the online services, which, as we have mentioned, is quite difficult for a small independent record label or individual artist to obtain.

In addition, whether you are a large or a small label, you still have the problem of aggregating and processing the large digital revenue data files produced by the online services every month. For this, many labels turn to RoyaltyShare, which aggregates the revenue data for the label and helps the label ingest the data into its accounting system.

RoyaltyShare also provides full royalty processing services through a web-based platform that produces for the label the artist/producer and mechanical royalty statements it is obligated to provide periodically under its recording contracts and mechanical license agreements.

### 2. *Organization of a Record Company*

Though the organization of a record company will vary considerably depending upon its size, the typical record label will be organized along four basic functional areas: *labels, shared-services, special products*, and *new businesses* (e.g., merchandising, artist management services).

#### *a. Labels*

Each major record company maintains several distinct label operations. Traditionally, when a major record company acquired an independent record label, the label's identity was maintained, allowing the managers of the label and their relationship with the artists acquired in the transactions to continue uninterrupted. As time went on, the reason to maintain separate identities among labels faded while the need to reduce the costs associated with maintaining the separate entities has given way to a considerable amount of consolidation. Labels now tend to focus on particular genres of music and back catalogs of labels have been transferred to organizations within the record company focused on their exploitation in secondary markets.

The labels that have survived continue to focus on the creative and promotional aspects of the record companies operations, and get involved in operational aspects to the extent necessary to assure the proper coordination of new releases.

#### (1) Creative — The A&R Department

The creative activities of a record label are generally lead by the company's A&R Department. The domain of the *A&R manager* includes: discovering new acts, negotiating their recording contract, matching the recording artist with record producers and songwriters, nurturing the talent, and dealing with the day-to-day creative and business affairs between the record company and the act. The A&R manager also works with many other departments of the record label in connection with the production, marketing and promotion of the act's recordings. Larger labels separate out some of these coordination activities and assign them to a *product manager.*

### (2) Marketing, Promotion, & Digital Media

*Marketing Department.* Although the A&R manager and product manager will be deeply involved in both the promotion and marketing of the recordings, particularly new releases, the marketing department will frequently get involved in the creation of the "cover art" of an act's albums, which is closely aligned with advertising materials, in-store displays, promotional merchandise, and the like.

*Promotion Department.* It is estimated that over 80% of record sales are driven by radio airplay, so it should be no surprise that major record labels have promotion departments dedicated to getting their recordings played on AM and FM radio.

*Digital Media.* As terrestrial radio airplay has been substituted by web radio, satellite radio, and other means of music discovery, promotion departments are increasingly devoting their time to the promotion of acts and recordings via new means, such as social networking websites and Internet-based networks (e.g., MySpace Music, Facebook, Twitter). Since the shift from physical distribution to digital has become so pronounced recently, many of the major record companies have consolidated much of the decision-making on digital promotion and digital distribution into wide-ranging digital media departments. Some of the more promotional aspects of digital distribution have remained within the label and some of the more technical aspects have been moved to shared-services, usually as a stand-along digital media department, separate from physical distribution.

### (3) Business Affairs

Depending upon the record company, some labels retain their own *business affairs* department. At other record companies, the business affairs function has been moved under one roof within shared-services. Wherever it resides, the business and legal affairs department of a record company performs many of the same functions of a typical corporate in-house legal department. These include the drafting and negotiation of many of the label's recording agreements and agreements with other third parties. The business and legal affairs department will work closely with the A&R department on the business aspects of artist relations and will often oversee many outbound licensing functions, such as issuing licenses for the use of recordings in the label's *back catalog* of recordings — by other labels producing compilation albums, motion picture producers, television producers, and other potential licensees. Record companies with large back catalogs will establish a separate department, often called *Special Products*, specializing in the exploitation of the back catalog (discussed below).

The business and legal affairs department may also oversee any inbound licensing necessary to the operation of the label, such as clearing mechanical licenses for the use of songs in recordings and licenses for the use of digital samples from recordings owned by others. One of the most important things for an in-house lawyer to keep in mind in drafting or negotiating any agreement is to *preserve your ability to change your mind.* This may be as simple as including an *out* clause (e.g., termination for convenience) or preferring nonexclusive over exclusive arrangements. If in each transaction a lawyer would ask, "What happens if we change our mind?", a solution will come to mind that will allow the label to negotiate, in advance, a satisfactory way out should circumstances change later on.

In addition to drafting and negotiating agreements, a responsible business and legal affairs department will assume a law enforcement role, making sure the label's activities are conducted within the dictates of the law. The management of a music publisher should look to its legal department as its *corporate conscience* and should respect not only the legal, but the ethical aspects of the advice given. Smaller labels, as with smaller businesses, not large enough to support this function in house, will rely primarily on the services of a law firm specializing in entertainment and copyright, for its legal affairs function.

### *b. Shared Services*

The shared services part of the record company — named because each label shares in some manner the services offered by the various parts of the shared-service organization — comprises all the administrative activities necessary to carry out the objectives of the record company. These include finance, human resources, IT, royalty accounting, legal, corporate communications, sales, global marketing, distribution, digital distribution, and industry and government relations.

*Finance.* The finance department is responsible for all aspects of the organizations accounting, including accounts receivable, accounts payable, billing, payroll, maintenance of the general ledger, and other matters. It is also responsible for the organization's IT needs, as well as its royalty accounting function, which in many labels is a department of its own, and sometimes multiple departments in many of the major record companies.

*Royalty Accounting.* The royalty accounting department is responsible for periodically (e.g., usually every six months for artist royalties and three months for mechanical royalties) producing royalty statements showing the amount of royalties owed to recording artists, producers, other record labels, and music publishers for the recordings sold or otherwise exploited by the label during the period. The revenue data that comes in to the label may be managed by the accounts receivable department, the IT department or the royalty department itself.

*IT Department.* With an increasing proportion of a label's revenue being derived from digital revenue sources, comprising hundreds of millions of small transactions, each often far less than 1 cent each, the record company's IT department has begun to take a greater role in the pre-processing of much of the digital revenue. Once pre-processed, the revenue files are ingested into the label's royalty processing software, which is programmed with the appropriate royalty splits. Because of the increased volume of transactions that must be handled, many legacy software systems can no longer handle the load. To reduce costs, many labels have outsourced the pre-processing of their digital revenue data to RoyaltyShare, which helps the label aggregate revenue from all digital sources, match each transaction properly to the metadata of albums and tracks in the label's catalog, and identify and match any exceptions that could not be matched automatically.

*Distribution.* As mentioned above, each of the four major record companies has its own distribution facilities for the distribution of physical CDs. With the emergence of digital, each of the majors has also built facilities for the delivery of its content to the various online services and ringtone carriers with the aggregation of digital revenue data from the services. This mass duplication of effort is unfortunate, as the independent record companies have worked with a number of organizations who handle the problem on an outsourced basis.

*International.* Each of the major record companies owns subsidiaries in each of the major music markets around the world. Independent record companies have traditionally sublicensed their recordings on an exclusive basis to other record labels or independent distributors overseas on a country-by-country basis, but the advent of digital is beginning to change the nature of these relationships. A U.S. independent label now has direct access to virtually every online music service in the world, either through a direct relationship or through an aggregator or digital distributor. As digital sales receive an increasingly higher share of revenue relative to physical CD sales, the need for independent representation overseas for the distribution of recording will decline in importance.

According to the IFPI, over 85% of the total revenue from recordings worldwide is derived from 20 countries in the proportions shown in the chart below.[20]

| | *Country* | *Share of World Market* |
|---|---|---|
| 1 | United States | 30-35% |
| 2 | Japan | 16-19% |
| 3 | United Kingdom | 6.4-9.1% |
| 4 | Germany | 6.4-5.3% |
| 5 | France | 5.4-6.3% |
| 6 | Canada | 1.9-2.8% |
| 7 | Australia | 1.5-2.0% |
| 8 | Brazil | 1.1-3.1% |
| 9 | Italy | 1.5-2.0% |
| 10 | Spain | 1.4-1.8% |
| 11 | Netherlands | 1.3-1.8% |
| 12 | Mexico | 0.8-1.8% |

[20] "Digital Music Report 2009," IFPI.

| | *Country* | *Share of World Market* |
|---|---|---|
| 13 | Belgium | 0.8-1.2% |
| 14 | Switzerland | 0.8-1.1% |
| 15 | Austria | 0.8-1.0% |
| 17 | Russia | 0.5-1.4% |
| 18 | Taiwan | 0.5-1.1% |
| 19 | Argentina | 0.5-1.0% |
| 20 | Denmark | 0.5-0.8% |

*c. Special Products*

Each of the major record companies operates what was traditionally known as a "special products" division, a group that provides centralized management and licensing of its back catalog of recordings. These special products or catalog management divisions work closely with the labels to develop special products, such as box-sets, "best of" albums and other compilations, reissues, premiums, and other products. They also license individual recordings to third parties for use in motion picture sound track albums and other compilations.

These divisions are often responsible for negotiating and licensing of back catalog recordings for use in motion pictures, television programs, home video, videogames, commercial advertising, and other media. To best exploit the back catalog, people in special products develop relationships with motion picture studios, independent music supervisors, advertising agencies, and other licensees.

*d. New Businesses*

*Merchandising.* Each of the major labels, and many indies, have gone into the business of developing and marketing licensed merchandise, such as t-shirts, coffee mugs, posters, and other products that exploit the brands of the artists in their respective repertoires. These products are sold on live tours and distributed through selected retail outlets and web-based stores. The merchandising division also licenses rights to third-party licensees around the world.

*Artist Services.* Looking for new sources of revenue, record companies became envious of the 10% to 15% fees that personal managers earn when representing recording artists. Universal Music became the first major record company to get into the artist management business when it acquired Sanctuary Group in 2007. Universal now operates several artist management firms, including Twenty-First Artists (Elton John and James Blunt), Trinifold (Robert Plant and the Who), and Helter Skelter (Pet Shop Boys and Amy Winehouse).

#### *3. The Record Deal*

The business and legal considerations in negotiating artist recording agreements typically offered by the major record companies and most large independent record labels is currently beyond the scope of this book. Several good books cover the subject in great depth, including Don Passman's *All You Need to Know About the Music Business, 7th Edition* (Simon & Schuster, November 2009).

## III. SOURCES OF RECORD COMPANY REVENUES

The sources of a record company's revenues can be divided into three categories: (1) revenues derived from the distribution of physical phonorecords (e.g., CDs, vinyl albums), (2) revenues derived from digital distribution, including permanent download, on-demand music services and certain other kinds of digital audio transmissions, and (3) revenue from other forms of licensing. A fourth source of revenue, income from general public performances of sound recordings, is only available for recordings produced outside the United States.

### A. Revenue from the Distribution of Physical Product

By the end of 2009, it is estimated that between 30% and 40% of a record label's revenues will be derived from digital sources, such as download, subscription and ringtone services. By the end of 2010, less than 50% of a label's income will be from physical CD sales. Until recently, the transition from physical to digital has been far slower than many expected, but the effect on how labels conduct business, market their acts and recordings, and manage their operations has been profound.

## B. Revenue from Digital Distribution and Transmission

The fastest growing source of record company revenue is comprised of recordings offered to consumers by download and streaming by online music services. These include permanent downloads sold by services such as iTunes, eMusic, and AmazonMP3; on-demand streams and limited downloads offered by subscription services such as Rhapsody and Napster and by advertising-based services, such as iMeem and Qtrax; ringtones and ringbacks offered by the major telephone carriers and through aggregators such as Thumbplay; and webcasting by organizations such as Live365, Pandora, and Clear Channel.

From 2006 to 2007, digital sales have increased nearly 50% year over year while physical sales have declined nearly 25% over the same period. Unfortunately, the increase in digital revenue has not yet made up for the decline in physical CD sales, but the industry is hopeful that an inflection point will be reached where the high margins afforded by digital distribution, which does not suffer from bloated inventories or returns, will make way for a sound stable record industry, provided that piracy can be kept under some reasonable degree of control.

## C. Revenue from Other Licensed Sources

It is estimated that over one-half of a major label's revenues are derived from the exploitation of recordings in its back catalog. While developing new acts and making hits drive the future of a record company, the revenue derived from a label's back catalog — revenue used to finance new acts and their recordings — cannot be ignored. The following list of a record label's other sources of income is not intended to be exhaustive:

- Licensing Sound Recordings in Other Albums — Compilations & Special Products
- Licensing Sound Recordings in Motion Pictures, Television Programs, and Other Audiovisual works
- Licensing Sound Recordings in Commercial Advertisements
- Licensing Sound Recordings in Videogames, Multimedia and Other New Media Products

- Licensing Sound Recordings in Other Sound Recordings — Digital Sampling
- Licensing Sound Recordings for Public Performance

Some of the foregoing sources of income, and the respective licensing practices that concern them, will be discussed below.

## IV. LEGAL BACKGROUND

Before proceeding to an analysis of several specific activities that require licenses from owners of sound recordings, this section outlines two important legal concepts that underlie the discussion in the remainder of this chapter.

### A. Sound Recording Copyright vs. Musical Work Copyright

It is axiomatic that anyone seeking to obtain permission (i.e., a license) to use a sound recording must first appreciate that his or her use will normally involve not one, but two separate copyrights: (a) the copyright in the sound recording and (b) the copyright in the underlying song, or musical work. The copyright in a *sound recording*, a particular series of sounds, is completely separate from the copyright in the underlying *song* featured in the sound recording.

There exists, for example, a valid copyright in the song *I've Got You Under My Skin* by Cole Porter and the copyright is owned by Warner/Chappell Music, Inc., a music publishing company. At the same time, several recordings of *I've Got You Under My Skin* have been produced by a number of recording artists over the years, including Frank Sinatra, Ella Fitzgerald, and Bono in duet with Frank Sinatra. A completely separate copyright exists for each particular recording — the sequence of sounds that make up the performance of the song by a singer and orchestra. These recordings are owned by the respective record companies that commissioned their creation. For example, the 1956 version of Frank Sinatra's recording of *I've Got You Under My Skin* is owned by Capitol Records.

Thus, if you wished to obtain permission to use Sinatra's 1956 recording of *I've Got You Under My Skin*, you would require the permission of Capitol to use the recording *and* the permission of Warner/Chappell to use the underlying song. You could not use the recording without permission from both companies. If you wished to make a new recording of the song *I've Got You Under My Skin*, you would require permission from Warner/Chappell, but you would not require permission from Capitol Records or any other record company who happens to own a recording of the song.

Accordingly, whenever you transmit a sound recording, either by a streaming transmission (i.e., where no copy is made at the recipient's end) or by a digital delivery (i.e., where a copy is made at the recipient's end), the first thing to understand is that the transmission concerns two different works of authorship: (a) a *song* and (b) a *sound recording* of a song. Who is required to clear the license to use the underlying song when embodied in a sound recording will be discussed below.

## B. Reproduction Right vs. Performance Right

Another important concept underlying the following analysis involves the difference between what is known as the *reproduction right* and the *public performance right.*

### *1. The Reproduction Right*

As we have seen, one of the most important exclusive rights provided by the Copyright Act to the owner of a copyright is the exclusive right "to *reproduce* the copyrighted work in *copies* or *phonorecord.*"

The right is enjoyed by owners of both musical works and sound recordings. When a musical work is fixed in a tangible medium of expression, the material object in which the work is fixed is called a *copy.* When a sound recording is fixed in a tangible medium of expression, the material object in which the work is fixed is called a *phonorecord.*

Thus, for example, the reproduction of (i.e., the act of reproducing) a musical work in copies of *sheet music* requires the permission of the copyright owner of the musical work; the reproduction of a sound recording in phonorecords (e.g., CDs, digital audio files) requires permission of the owner of copyright of the sound recording. Further, while a work may be fixed in a copy or phonorecord, the ownership of copyright in the work, or any of the exclusive rights under the copyright, is distinct from ownership of any material object (that is, the copy or phonorecord) in which the work is embodied. Thus, a person may own an album or CD, but not own the copyright in any musical works or sound recordings it contains, and *vice versa.*

#### *2. The Public Performance Right*

One of the other important exclusive rights provided by the Copyright Act to owners of a copyright is the exclusive right to *publicly perform* the copyrighted work. To perform a work means to recite, render, play, dance, or act it, either directly or by means of any device or process.[21] To perform a work publicly means to (1) perform it at a place open to the public or at any place where a substantial number of persons outside of a normal circle of a family and its social acquaintances is gathered; or (2) transmit or otherwise communicate a performance or display of the work to a place specified by clause (1) or to the public, by means of any device or process.[22]

When you sing the song in your living room or in your shower, you are rendering a *performance.* When a performer sings the song, *I've Got You Under My Skin* in a nightclub, he is rendering a performance that is *public.* When you hear a recording of *I've Got You Under My Skin* on the radio, the radio station is rendering a performance of both the song and the recording, but the transmission by the station is not comprised of sounds directly audible by the human ear, but of electromagnetic waves sent through space, which are converted to audible sounds by a radio receiver. The copyright law makes it clear that these transmissions, or broadcasts, also constitute performances: To "transmit" a performance is to communicate it by any device or process whereby images or sounds are received beyond the place from which they are sent.[23]

Historically, in the United States, copyright owners of sound recordings did not enjoy a public performance right. Thus, when a radio station plays a song over the airwaves, it pays a public performance royalty to the owner of the musical work, but not to the owner of

[21] 17 U.S.C. Sec. 101.

[22] *Id.*

[23] *Id.*

the sound recording. This is not the case in most countries outside the United States; most other countries recognize what are called *neighboring rights* in sound recordings, and record companies, through local collection societies, such as PPL in the United Kingdom, disburse revenues collected from terrestrial radio stations and others who engage in the public performance of sound recordings.

For many years, the U.S. recording industry has lobbied Congress to amend the Copyright Act to provide to owners of sound recordings an exclusive right of public performance. In 1995, the recording industry won an important step toward that end when Congress passed the Digital Performance Rights in the Sound Recording Act of 1995.

## C. The Evolution of the Digital Audio Transmission Right and Its Limitations

The advent of digital transmissions have caused those who create and distribute recorded entertainment to question whether the laws designed to protect their copyrighted content, such as musical works and sound recordings, will effectively be enforceable in the digital world. Copyright owners became uneasy about the potential for receivers of digital transmissions being technically enabled to make perfect digital copies of the transmitted recordings. To the extent perfect digital copies of these transmissions could easily be made, then the transmissions posed a threat to the market for the purchase of phonorecords and permanent downloads.

To specifically address these concerns, Congress enacted the Digital Performance Rights in Sound Recordings Act of 1995 (the "1995 Act").

### *1. Digital Performance Rights in Sound Recordings Act of 1995*

This important legislation made two significant, but distinct, changes affecting the licensing of musical works and sound recordings under U.S. copyright law: (1) to address the questions raised by *downloadable music* files, it broadened the Copyright Act's existing compulsory mechanical license provision to include the reproduction and delivery of musical works in sound recordings by digital transmission and (2) to address the questions raised by *webcasting* and other forms of digital audio transmission of sound recordings, it created a new, but limited, digital public performance right for sound recordings, which gave owners of sound recordings, not a general public performance right, but an exclusive right to publicly perform the sound recordings by *digital audio transmission.*

The expansion of the compulsory license for the use of musical works in digital downloads is described in Chapter 13, on *Licensing Music in Sound Recordings.* The remainder of this section will focus on this new exclusive right given to owners of sound recordings to make digital audio transmissions and the limitations on that right. It should be noted, however, that the record industry has begun a renewed effort to expand its new-found limited right to make digital audio transmissions into a full public performance right, covering all forms of broadcast transmission, including any analog, terrestrial broadcasts.

### *2. A New Exclusive Right for Owners of Sound Recordings*

The 1995 Act created a limited public performance right in sound recordings by adding a new right to the list of exclusive rights afforded copyright owners under Section 106 of the Copyright Act:

> (6) in the case of sound recordings, to perform the copyrighted work publicly by means of a digital audio transmission.

This new public performance right didn't affect terrestrial radio or other kinds of analog broadcasts; it concerned transmissions of sound recordings, such as on-demand streams and webcasts transmitted by digital means. Thus, to constitute a digital audio transmission, the transmission must be (a) digital, (b) audio, and (c) a transmission.

*Digital.* First, the right applies only to *digital* public performances. In other words, it does not apply to *analog* transmissions, such as standard FM or AM broadcasts. Congress was apparently persuaded by the broadcasters that the transmission of recordings by non-digital means would not result in copies that are likely to displace sales of high quality digital recordings. Thus, analog radio stations continue to have no obligation to pay royalties for the public performances of sound recordings they render.

*Audio.* Second, the right applies only to the transmission of *audio-only* public performances — i.e., of *sound recordings.* Thus, it does not apply to performances of *audiovisual works*, such as television programs, motion pictures, and music videos. This does not mean that the audiovisual works, or audio portions of audiovisual works, have no public performance protection — owners of audiovisual works have always enjoyed an exclusive right of public performance, even if only the audio portion of the audiovisual work is broadcast.[24]

*Transmission.* Finally, the right applies only to *transmissions*, which is defined as communications that are received beyond the place from which they are sent. Thus, performing a sound recording from a CD on your stereo, whether in your home or out in public (e.g., at a public park), is not a transmission and is not covered by the new performance right. In addition, the limited exclusive performance right in sound recordings does not cover live performances or other performances of recordings that are not transmitted beyond the place from which they are sent. Though possible, it is not likely that a live performance of a copyrighted sound recording through loudspeakers will result in the unauthorized reproduction of a high quality recording of the sound recording (as compared to a digital transmission). But, note the above discussion, regarding a performer's right to record his or her performance and the prohibition against the taping of live musical performances.

### 3. *Limitations on the Digital Audio Transmission Right*

This new exclusive right, however, came with some severe limitations by virtue of several provisions that were simultaneously added to Section 114 of the Copyright Act, governing limitations on the rights of the owners of sound recordings.[25]

Recall that the underpinnings of the new digital audio transmission right involved the potential that digital transmissions of copyrighted recordings could easily become the basis for perfect digital copies of the sound recordings being transmitted. Because of the threat these transmissions posed to the market for phonorecords and permanent

[24] 17 U.S.C. Sec. 106(4).

[25] Section 114 in its current form is set forth in full in the appendix to this chapter.

downloads of recordings, the record companies wanted an unrestricted right to charge what it wanted for these new digital audio transmissions.

Broadcasters and webcasters, however, were concerned that since free terrestrial, analog radio broadcasts do not require a payment of license fees to record companies, neither should radio services broadcast digitally or over the Internet. The record companies countered that digital transmissions create a threat to their livelihood and that the business models for terrestrial radio were based on the collection of advertising revenue, while Internet-based technology allowed services to charge a subscription fee — which is an altogether different business.

A compromise was reached, which exempted all digital audio transmissions that constituted *nonsubscription* transmissions from the sound recording owner's exclusive right. Thus, any broadcast transmission, and anyone with a website who didn't charge a subscription fee was able to make an unlimited amount of digital audio transmissions of copyrighted sound recordings without permission or payment to record companies.

In what appeared to be a major blunder by the recording industry, authors of the 1995 Act appear to have assumed that webcasting, or the broadcasting of digital radio stations over the web, would be primarily supported by subscription fees. As the Internet evolved shortly after the 1995 Act was passed, it became increasing clear that webcasting on the Internet, like terrestrial radio, was going to be substantially supported by advertising revenue.

By the late 1990s, hundreds of web radio stations began operation under what they believed was an exemption from a sound recording copyright owner's exclusive right of digital audio transmission. Section 114, under the 1995 Act, exempted *nonsubscription transmissions*, and since these web radio stations appeared to fall within this exemption, they needed nothing more than the appropriate performance licenses from ASCAP/BMI/SESAC in order to engage in their services.

In June 1998, the Recording Industry Association of America (the "RIAA") sent a letter to about 40 web radio stations stating that they require licenses from record companies for the "webcasting" of their sound recordings over the Internet. "I write," stated Steve Marks, the RIAA's vice president and deputy general counsel of that time, "because our record company members are the copyright owners of the sound recordings that you are transmitting, and we want to ensure that you have secured the appropriate permission to Webcast those recordings."

In a brief article I (Bob Kohn) wrote and published on the website, MP3.com in June, 1998, we pointed out that the RIAA letter neglected to state that only certain types of webcasts of copyrighted sound recordings require licenses from record companies, and we attempted to explain why many of them do not. Specifically, we stated that the 1995 Act exempted *noninteractive, nonsubscription* digital audio transmissions of sound recordings, such as those produced by Internet radio stations, from any requirement of a license from their owners.

A lawyer for the RIAA responded to that article in a formal letter to the authors of this book dated July 1, 1998, which he then distributed for publication on the web and elsewhere. In this new letter, he attempted to explain why the RIAA believes the 1995 Act does not exempt noninteractive, nonsubscription digital audio transmissions of sound recordings from the copyright owner's exclusive rights. A few weeks later, we posted an article on the web that refuted the RIAA's analysis.

Meanwhile, on July 1, 1998, Hilary Rosen, President and CEO of the RIAA wrote a blistering letter to the CEOs of the top webcasting companies, including RealNetworks, makers of software that facilitates digital audio transmissions, and Mark Cuban's Broadcast.com, a leading Internet publisher of digital audio transmissions, such as retransmissions of radio broadcasts (later purchased by Yahoo). A month earlier RealNetworks and Broadcast.com had formed the Digital Media Association (or, "DiMA") to serve as a voice in Washington on behalf of Internet audio companies. In her letter, Rosen accused these companies of, among other things, "stabbing [the recording industry] in the back." DiMA responded to that Rosen's letter by letter dated July 8, 1998, suggesting that one of the reasons DiMA was formed in the first place was that RIAA had gone around the backs of webcasters by lobbying to eliminate the ephemeral recording exception these companies had been relying on to facilitate their webcasting activities. DiMA, however, was not comfortable being on the receiving end of the shrill of accusations being made by the RIAA, and offered to sit down with the RIAA to reach a compromise.

Toward the end of July, 1998, DiMA and the RIAA met to discuss ways of compromising their differences. Within days, they reached an agreement in principle that would (1) eliminate the exemption for webcasters set forth in Section 114(d)(1) of the Copyright Act, (2) add a compulsory license scheme for limited kinds of "eligible" transmissions (i.e., those made by webcasters having the profile of members of DiMA), and (3) add language to Section 112 that would make it clear the "eligible" webcasters could make ephemeral recordings of sound recordings for the purposes of facilitating their webcasts.

On Thursday, July 23, 1998, representatives of the RIAA and DiMA and other music industry groups met at the U.S. Copyright Office in Washington, D.C. and were told by the Register of Copyrights that they had until the following Friday, July 31, 1998, to draft the legislation they were seeking. Miraculously, on August 4, 1998, the House of Representatives passed an amendment to the DMCA that included the legislation drafted and agreed upon by the RIAA and DiMA just days, and perhaps hours, earlier. The DMCA, in the form negotiated by the RIAA and DiMA, was enacted into law later that year.

#### *4. The RIAA Pulls a Fast One*

Thus, as a result of last minute lobbying by the RIAA and DiMA, the Digital Millennium Copyright Act (DMCA) was passed with an amendment that eliminated the exemption for webcasters of nonsubscription transmissions.

Should the exemption for noninteractive, nonsubscription transmissions have been eliminated? From the record companies' perspective, the answer to that question is clearly, yes, but other interests may not have fared as well. First, under the 1995 Act, and before the DMCA, music publishers and songwriters had a direct interest in promoting as many noninteractive, nonsubscription web radio stations as possible. This would have allowed the performance societies to issue far more blanket licenses for the use of music on these sites with minimum fees that could have amounted to millions of dollars. Thus, it appears that the changes made to Section 114 by the DMCA may well have been against the interests of music publishers.

Presumably, in the 1995 Act, Congress took into consideration the interests of the performance rights societies and their members when determining the kinds of transmissions that should be considered exempt, which should be subject to a compulsory license, and which should be subject to a voluntary license. Given the particular circumstances of the DMCA's passage, it is not likely the Congress took anything into consideration, except the fact that two powerful lobbying organizations came to an agreement on the subject.

### *5. The NAB Gets Outmaneuvered*

While the DMCA eliminated what the 1995 Act previously established as an exemption (from a sound recording owner's exclusive rights) for a "nonsubscription transmission other than a retransmission," the DMCA preserved the exemption for "a nonsubscription *broadcast transmission.*" A "broadcast transmission" is defined as "a transmission made by a terrestrial broadcast station licensed as such by the Federal Communications Commission." Thus, any audio or *digital* transmission by a terrestrial broadcast station licensed by the FCC would be exempt from liability to owners of sound recordings.

Believing that they were now exempted from the record companies' new right of public performance by digital audio transmission, broadcast radio stations that desired to webcast their on-the-air broadcasts of sound recordings over the Internet have argued that, under the DMCA, they remain exempt from licensing requirements. It may well be asked, why should webcasters who don't own radio stations licensed by the FCC be put at a competitive disadvantage to those who do? It would at first appear that any large webcasting company could use their size and resources to purchase FCC licensed radio stations in order to webcast sound recordings over the web without payment to record companies. But, when negotiating changes to the DMCA, the RIAA put one over on not only the large webcasters, but the owners of FCC licensed radio stations! Their representative, the National Association of Broadcasters (NAB) were either asleep at the switch or weren't even at the table when the changes were proposed last minute by the RIAA and DiMA.

Here's how: when the RIAA and DiMA added (or should we say, recommended to Congress to add) a brief phrase to the definition of eligible subscription transmissions, the FCC licensed radio stations lost their ability to retransmit their terrestrial broadcasts digitally over the Internet without payment to the record companies:

> An "eligible nonsubscription transmission" is a noninteractive, nonsubscription transmission made as part of a service that provides

> audio programming consisting, in whole or in part, of performances of sound recordings, *including retransmissions of broadcast transmissions*, if the primary purpose of the service is to provide to the public such audio or other entertainment programming, and the primary purpose of the service is not to sell, advertise, or promote particular products or services other than sound recordings, live concerts, or other music-related events. (emphasis added).

The italicized language makes it clear that *retransmissions of broadcast transmissions* constitutes an *eligible nonsubscription transmission* eligible for, and apparently subject to, a compulsory license, rather than being exempt, as was thought by the radio station owners. In other words, while an analog or digital radio broadcast from a terrestrial radio station is exempt from the exclusive rights of the sound recording owner to digital audio transmissions, if the terrestrial radio station attempted to retransmit its broadcasts, whether they were originally transmitted by digital or analog means, over the Internet, such retransmissions would be subject to the sound recording owners' new exclusive right of digital audio transmissions. Surprise!

And, what accounts for the distinction between those making "eligible" nonsubscription transmissions and those who make noneligible ones? Looking down the list of members of DiMA, it's striking that all of them would appear to be engaging in eligible nonsubscription transmissions, yet that organization appeared instrumental in eliminating the exemption for all other kinds of webcasters, including FCC-licensed radio stations. Why would members of DiMA support the elimination of this exemption for nonsubscription transmissions? Large webcasters must make large number of server copies of the recordings to facilitate their transmissions. Concerned that making these server copies would not be exempt from the copyright owner's reproduction right, DiMA negotiated changes in the law, through the DMCA, that would enable them to make *ephemeral copies* (discussed below) to facilitate their digital audio transmissions. They may have also enjoyed the resulting reduced competition from small webcasters who would not otherwise be able to afford to pay and account for royalties from their webcasting activities.

Assuming that all nonsubscription transmissions (including broadcast transmissions) were subject to a compulsory license, a level playing field would only result if the compulsory license was as easy to obtain and administer as the performance licenses that are offered by ASCAP or BMI. If, on the other hand, anything akin to the requirements of the compulsory license for subscription transmissions is instituted for non-subscription transmissions — for "Interim Regulations on Notice and Recordkeeping for Digital Subscription Transmissions, Docket No. RM 96-3B, only large, well-financed webcasters will, as a practical matter, have access to sound recordings for nonsubscription transmissions.

Perhaps the ideal of a level playing field is not politically possible today, given the tenacity of the lobbying organizations involved, the complexities of the issues, and the amount of money that is at stake. Certainly, the new technologies provide more than enough challenges to the music and recording industries, and giving the content creators the benefit of the doubt, at least at the current time, may be just what is needed to maintain the incentives necessary to promote the creation of creative works of authorship. In the end, however, the ideal of a level playing field may best be accomplished by the granting of a general public performance right in sound recordings coupled with a fairly easy to administer compulsory license, such as those offered by ASCAP and BMI.

### *6. The Ephemeral Copy Problem Solved*

Transmitting organizations, such as radio and television broadcasters, have long found it necessary to make copies of the recordings they transmit, typically by making a tape of a recording that was first provided in another medium (such as a vinyl album or CD), to facilitate the transmission. Recall that under the Copyright Act, a copyright owner has the exclusive right to reproduce the work in copies and phonorecords. Thus, unless there was an exemption from the copyright owner's exclusive right, a transmitting organization who makes such copies even just to facilitate its legitimate transmissions would risk being sued for copyright infringement.

For that reason, the Copyright Act provides an exemption for what are called *ephemeral recordings*, and that exemption is set forth in Section 112 as follows:

> Notwithstanding the provisions of section 106, . . . it is not an infringement of copyright for a transmitting organization entitled to

> transmit to the public a performance or display of a work, under a license or transfer of the copyright or under the limitations on exclusive rights in sound recordings specified by section 114(a), to make no more than one copy or phonorecord of a particular transmission program embodying the performance or display, if —
>
> (1) the copy or phonorecord is retained and used solely by the transmitting organization that made it, and no further copies or phonorecords are reproduced from it; and
>
> (2) the copy or phonorecord is used solely for the transmitting organization's own transmissions within its local service area, or for purposes of archival preservation or security; and
>
> (3) unless preserved exclusively for archival purposes, the copy or phonorecord is destroyed within six months from the date the transmission program was first transmitted to the public.

For some time, the RIAA took the position that the foregoing exemption only applies to reproductions embodying performances made under license, transfer of copyright ownership or the Section 114(a) exception to the general performance right of Section 106(4). The exemption, they said, did not apply to reproductions embodying performances made by means of digital audio transmissions, which are subject to the performance right of Section 106(6). This argument is refuted easily by pointing out that Section 112 begins, "Notwithstanding the provisions of section 106 . . ." — meaning, all of Section 106, not just Section 106(4), but all of 106.

The RIAA had also asserted that the fact that Congress, when it enacted the 1995 Act, did not amend Section 112 at the same time, is "evidence that Congress intended not to extend the ephemeral recording exemption to digital audio transmissions." Of course, the same omission is also evidence that Congress thought the ephemeral recording exemption certainly did apply to webcasters and, therefore, felt no need to add anything to Section 112 to that effect. Moreover, why would Congress have created an exemption for nonsubscription transmissions, but leave no practical way for anyone to use the exemption?

Finally, the RIAA took the position that: even if Section 112 is applicable to digital audio transmissions, the copies by this section are to be used only for transmissions within the transmitting organization's "local service area."

The legislative history of the Copyright Act defines the term "local service area" in only three contexts: in the case of a television broadcast station, in the case of a low power television station, and in the case of a radio broadcast station. It does not refer to Internet websites, naturally, because they did not exist in 1976 when the Copyright Act was passed. But this does not mean that websites are not covered; it only means that the extent of the local service area is not defined. Where they are defined, the legislative history seems to contemplate that transmissions may be sent by wire beyond the place where the primary broadcast transmission takes place. In the case of television stations, for example, the local service area comprises the area in which such station is entitled to insist upon its signal being transmitted by a cable system pursuant to the rules and regulations of the Federal Communications Commission.

Thus, the term "local service area" does not confine the transmission to a service area which is "local," but, in the case of television and radio stations licensed by the FCC, such transmissions are con-fined to those areas permitted by the FCC. Since web stations are not so regulated, the local service area appears to be throughout the Internet, but perhaps not beyond, such as through analog radio broadcasts. The local services area of a shortwave broadcast is worldwide, no different from a webcast, but I would be surprised to learn if broadcasters have been operating under the assumption that the ephemeral recording exemption applies only to small regional or "local" broadcasters.

Granted, Section 112 only permits the making of "no more than one copy or phonorecord of a particular transmission program." This, according to the RIAA, makes is problematic for webcasters who wish to install copies on multiple servers. While this may be problematic for large, commercial webcasters, one copy would certainly be sufficient for the many thousands of small websites who wish to take advantage of the exemption provided in Section 114(d)(1) and offer noninteractive, nonsubscription transmissions.

As a result of negotiations between the RIAA and the National Association of Broadcasters (NAB), a *Senate* version of the Digital Millennium Copyright Act (Senate Bill 2037) would have amended Section 112 to provide a specific exemption only for broadcast radio or television stations licensed by the FCC who provide "a performance of a sound recording in a digital format on a nonsubscription basis."

According to information obtained by the Digital Media Association (DiMA), the NAB initially proposed that the ephemeral recording exemption be revised to make it clear it applied to all lawful digital transmissions, but the RIAA had explicitly demanded that the exemption not apply to cable, satellite, or Internet broadcasters. If the bill had passed as so amended, the RIAA could have taken the position that by only exempting broadcast radio and television stations, the legislation could have been construed as not exempting webcasters. Webcasters might then need to rely on the less specific exemption offered by the "fair use" provisions set forth in Section 107 of the Copyright Act.

As a result of negotiations between the RIAA and DiMA, discussed above, the final version of the DMCA amended Section 112 to include provisions for the compulsory license of ephemeral recordings that are made by transmitting organizations entitled to transmit public performances of sound recordings under Section 114 (discussed above). A statutory rate or license fee for such copies would be set under a procedure established by the Librarian of Congress (and now, the Copyright Royalty Board).

## D. The New Webcasting Regime

This section will describe the statutory limitations on this new limited digital audio transmission right, which the 1995 Act, as amended by the DMCA, afforded owners of sound recordings.

### *1. Theoretical Underpinnings*

Recall that the impetus for granting the limited public performance right to begin with was the concern that receivers of digital transmissions could make perfect digital copies of the transmitted recordings, which posed a threat to the market for the purchase of phonorecords and permanent downloads. Thus, it may be useful to think about what Congress did in extending this limited public performance right in terms of (1) the several kinds of performances that are possible and (2) the likelihood that each kind of performance will facilitate unauthorized reproduction of works by recipients of the performance — to wit, (a) performances involving a *high* risk of reproduction, (b) performances involving a *low* risk of reproduction, and (c) performances involving a *moderate* risk of reproduction.

*a. Performances Involving a High Risk of Reproduction*

Interactive transmissions, such as on-demand streams, which would allow a member of the public to download selected sound recordings in digital form as and when they want them, would greatly facilitate the capture of such streams, ending up in high quality phonorecords for reuse. This activity, if uncompensated, would obviate the need for the consumer to purchase a CD or digital download to obtain the same value and would adversely affect the ability of sound recording copyright owners, and recording artists, to reap the reward intended by the Copyright Act. Accordingly, the Copyright Act provides that all interactive, or on-demand, digital audio transmissions must be licensed through voluntary negotiations with the owner of the sound recording.

*b. Performances Involving a Low Risk of Reproduction*

Analog transmissions are not likely to result in the kind of perfect duplication that copyright owners are concerned about with respect to digital transmission. Accordingly, analog transmissions are excluded from the public performance right by definition (i.e., the public performances of sound recordings that are produced are only those audio transmissions that are *digital*).

Certain types of public performances of sound recordings, which may have fallen within the definition of "digital audio transmission," are nevertheless exempt from the new digital audio performance right in sound recordings. Performances that are exempt do not require permission from the owner of the sound recording. These include (1) nonsubscription broadcast transmissions, (2) certain other transmissions.

*Nonsubscription broadcast transmissions.* Transmissions to the public by terrestrial radio stations licensed by the Federal Communications Commission, for which there is no charge, such as digital or "HD" radio broadcasts are exempt from licensing requirements. Because these radio broadcasts do not usually provide listeners with advance warning about what recordings are going to be broadcast, and do not usually include broadcasts of all the recordings of a particular CD album, it is felt that traditional radio broadcasting, even by digital transmission, is not likely to facilitate the wide scale taping of recordings and therefore poses little threat to the sale of CDs and digital downloads.

*Other transmissions.* Other transmissions of sound recordings are exempt, such as a transmission to or within a business establishment for use in the ordinary course of its business (e.g. background music services), provided the business does not retransmit the transmission outside its premises or the immediately surrounding vicinity. Again, these transmissions are not likely to facilitate the wide-scale duplication of sound recordings by consumers.

#### c. *Performances Involving a Moderate Risk of Reproduction*

Because of the moderate risk that they will result in an unauthorized reproduction, other types of public performances, though not excluded or exempt from the new public performance right, were made subject to a compromise. These performances are not exempt from licensing fees, yet the record companies are not free to set royalty rates as they wish nor may they refuse to license their recordings for these transmissions — in other words, they are subject to a statutory license,[26] similar to the compulsory license applicable to the reproduction of musical works in phonorecords, allowing a transmitter to compel the owner of the sound recording to grant a license under terms set by statute or administrative oversight. The kinds of transmissions that fall into this middle category are discussed below.

### 2. *Statutory Categories of Digital Audio Transmissions*

Digital audio transmissions are either (a) subject to a voluntary license, which they must obtain from the copyright owner exempt from licensing, (b) subject to a compulsory license, provided they comply with the statutory requirements, or (c) exempt from any requirement of a license. Whether the transmission is subject to a voluntary license or a compulsory license, or is otherwise exempt depends upon the category under which transmissions fall.

Transmissions may first be divided up into either (a) those made by interactive services and (b) those make by noninteractive services. All interactive services, such as services that provide public performances by digital audio transmissions "on-demand" must license the recordings used directly from their copyright owners, the record companies.

---

[26] 17 U.S.C. Sec. 114(d)(2).

Certain noninteractive services — those that conform to the requirements of the compulsory license set forth in Section 114 of the Copyright Act — may qualify for a statutory license, which compels the record companies to provide licenses at rates established by the government.

### a. *Interactive Services*

Interactive services are those that provide transmissions more or less "on-demand" — such as an on-demand streaming or limited download service. The Copyright Act defines the term as follows:

> An "interactive service" is one that enables a member of the public to receive a transmission of a program specially created for the recipient, or on request, a transmission of a particular sound recording, whether or not as part of a program, which is selected by or on behalf of the recipient. The ability of individuals to request that particular sound recordings be performed for reception by the public at large, or in the case of a subscription service, by all subscribers of the service, does not make a service interactive, if the programming on each channel of the service does not substantially consist of sound recordings that are performed within 1 hour of the request or at a time designated by either the transmitting entity or the individual making such request. If an entity offers both interactive and noninteractive services (either concurrently or at different times), the noninteractive component shall not be treated as part of an interactive service.

Because the kinds of on-demand transmissions that these interactive services offer involve a relatively high risk of easy reproduction, anyone wishing to provide interactive transmission services, must obtain permission from the record companies, which the record companies can refuse to provide or provide on terms they see fit.

Distinguishing between interactive services and noninteractive services is not always easy. As will be discussed further below, services that allow the listener to provide feedback to the service, which the webcaster then uses to customize future transmissions to the listener, are not necessarily interactive.

Typical fees charged by record companies for these voluntary licenses for on-demand transmissions are set forth below.

*b. Exempt Services*

As noted above, performances that are exempt do not require permission from the owner of the sound recording. These include (1) nonsubscription broadcast transmissions, (2) certain other transmissions.

The act defines a *broadcast transmission* as a "transmission made by a terrestrial radio station licensed as such by the Federal Communications Commission." Digital transmissions, such as HD radio, made by terrestrial radio stations licensed by the FCC that are nonsubscription — i.e., for which there is no charge — are exempt from licensing requirements. Such transmission must be "non-subscription," defined by the Act as "any transmission that is not a subscription transmission."[27] A *subscription transmission* is defined as "a transmission that is controlled and limited to particular recipients, and for which consideration is paid or otherwise given by or on behalf of the recipient to receive the transmission or a package of transmissions including a transmission."[28]

Other transmissions of sound recordings are exempt, such as a transmission "within a business establishment, confined to its premises or the immediately surrounding vicinity," for use in the ordinary course of its business.

*c. Noninteractive Services Eligible for the Compulsory License*

The Copyright Act has afforded prospective licensees of the kinds of digital audio transmissions that only have a moderate risk of unlawful reproduction a means of compelling owners of sound recording copyrights to provide a license at a statutory rate. Licensees eligible for the compulsory license include (a) pre-existing satellite digital audio radio services, (b) pre-existing subscription service, (c) new subscription services, and (d) eligible nonsubscription transmission services.

**(1) Eligible Nonsubscription Transmission Services**

An *eligible nonsubscription transmission* is "a noninteractive, nonsubscription transmission made as part of a service that provides audio

[27] 17 U.S.C. Sec. 114 (j)(9).

[28] 17 U.S.C. Sec. 114 (j)(14).

programming consisting, in whole or in part, of performances of sound recordings, including retransmissions of broadcast transmissions, if the primary purpose of the service is to provide to the public such audio or other entertainment programming, and the primary purpose of the service is not to sell, advertise, or promote particular products or services other than sound recordings, live concerts, or other music-related events."

### (2) New Subscription Services

A *new subscription service* is a service that performs sound recordings by means of noninteractive subscription digital audio transmissions and that is not a pre-existing subscription service or a pre-existing satellite digital audio service.

### (3) Pre-Existing Subscription Services

A *pre-existing subscription service* is "a service that performs sound recordings by means of noninteractive audio-only subscription digital audio transmissions, which was in existence and was making such transmissions to the public for a fee on or before July 31, 1998, and may include a limited number of sample channels representative of the subscription service that are made available on a nonsubscription basis in order to promote the subscription service." For example, certain *cable radio* services and Internet radio services that offer on a subscription basis that were in existence prior to July 31, 1998, would fall into this category. The only service we know of that fits into this category is Music Choice.

### (4) Pre-Existing Satellite Digital Audio Radio Services

A *pre-existing satellite digital audio radio service* is defined in the Act as "a subscription satellite audio radio service provided pursuant to a satellite digital audio radio service license issued by the FCC on or before July 31, 1998, and any renewal of such license to the extent the scope of the original license, and may include a limited number of sample channels representative of the subscription service that are made available on a nonsubscription basis in order to promote the subscription service." This is, in essence, referring to Sirius/XM satellite radio.

### 3. *Compulsory License Requirements for Eligible Nonsubscription Transmissions and New Subscription Services*

The four kinds of services eligible for the compulsory license under Section 114 — pre-existing satellite digital audio radio services, pre-existing subscription services, new subscription services, and eligible nonsubscription transmission services — must comply with all of the statutes requirements to qualify for the compulsory license.

#### *a. Registering Notice with the U.S. Copyright Office*

To qualify for a compulsory license under Section 114, all services must register with the U.S. Copyright Office by filing a Notice of Use of Sound Recordings Under Statutory License. This must be done before the digital transmission of recordings commences. If the service is making multiple streams available from the same website, a single filing can be made.

On the form, the service must indicate whether a Section 114 (for digital audio transmissions) or Section 112 (for ephemeral recordings that facilitate the transmission) license is being sought. The service will almost always require both. (A small webcaster which makes transmissions from single copies purchased by download could presumably do without the Section 112 license.)

The service must also indicate whether the service will be on a subscription (i.e., a fee will be charged to transmission recipients) or nonsubscription basis (e.g., the service will be financially supported by advertisements). Finally, the service must indicate whether it is a "pre-existing subscription service," one that existed before July 1, 1998. The form, together with instructions for completing it, is available on the Copyright Office's website at copyright.gov.

#### *b. Performance Restrictions*

In addition to filing the proper notice with the U.S. Copyright Office, to qualify for the compulsory license, a service must comply with a number of restrictions concerning how the sound recordings are transmitted. Consistent with the theoretical basis for the compulsory license, these restrictions are intended to make it more difficult for a listener of a webcast transmission to anticipate what recordings will be played next, thereby making it more difficult for the listener to make unauthorized permanent copies of selected recordings. The restrictions on the transmissions include the following:

### (1) The transmission service must not be interactive

The definition of an *interactive service* is set forth in the previous section. In general, the transmission service must not allow the listener to select specific recordings on demand and must not develop a program "specially created for" the listener. The service may receive play requests from listeners, as long as the service decides which requests to play and when they will be played.

That being said, for some time, it was not altogether clear the extent to which a webcasting service could offer some amount of interactivity — e.g., providing users with individual radio stations, the content of which can be affected by users' rating of songs, artists and albums — yet remain fully compliant with the conditions of the compulsory license. For example, Launch Media operated a service called, Launch.com (later acquired by Yahoo, which changed the name to LaunchCast), which provided radio-like webcasts of sound recordings that allowed the listener to provide feedback to the LaunchCast, which the webcaster used to facilitate the customization of future transmissions to that user. Pandora, another popular partially interactive webcast service, uses a similar mechanism for customizing the playlists for its users. If these transmissions were to be deemed *interactive*, then a compulsory license would not be available to these webcasters for these transmissions.

The question of where to draw the line between interactive and noninteractive webcast services was brought before the federal courts in May, 2001 when the major record companies filed suit against Launch Media. After over eight years of litigation, the Federal Court of Appeals for the Second Circuit ruled that LaunchCast was not an interactive service within the meaning of Section 114 of the Copyright Act.[29]

[29] *Arista Records LLC v. Launch Media, Inc.*, Docket No. 07-2576-cv (2d Cir. August 21, 2009).

An interactive service is defined as a service "that enables a member of the public to receive a transmission of a program specially created for the recipient, or on request, a transmission of a particular sound recording . . . , which is selected by or on behalf of the recipient."[30] Thus, a webcasting service is interactive under the statute if a user can either (1) request and have played a particular sound recording or (2) receive a transmission of a program "specially created" for the user. Since a user of LaunchCast cannot request and expect to hear a particular recording on demand, LaunchCast does not meet the first definition of interactive. The major record companies argued, however, that LaunchCast constitutes an interactive service, because it meets the second definition — that is, LaunchCast is designed and operated to enable members of the public to receive transmissions of programs *specially created* for them.

After describing how LaunchCast operates in generating playlists influenced by the user's input, the court found that LaunchCast does not provide a specially created program within the meaning of Section 114, "because the webcasting service does not provide sufficient control to users such that playlists are so predictable that users will choose to listen to the webcast in lieu of purchasing music, thereby — in the aggregate — diminishing record sales."

Thus, as a noninteractive service, LaunchCast need not obtain individual, voluntary license from the record companies, but need only pay the compulsory or statutory licensing fee set by the Copyright Royalty Board.

### (2) The transmission programming must not exceed the "sound recording performance complement"

The webcast must comply with a specific set of rules regarding how often recordings from the same artist or from the same album may be played within specified time frames. These restrictions are called the "sound recording performance complement," which is comprised of two basic components:

*Artist Restriction*: The transmission programming may not include more than four different selections by the same recording artist, or from

[30] 17 U.S.C. Sec. 114(j)(7).

any set or compilation, on a particular channel within any three-hour period, and no more than three such selections may be played consecutively.

Album Restriction: The transmission programming may not include more than three selections from any one album on a particular channel within any three-hour period, and no more than two such selections may be played consecutively.

The full statutory definition of the term is as follows:

> The "sound recording performance complement" is the transmission during any 3-hour period, on a particular channel used by a transmitting entity, of no more than —
>
> (A) 3 different selections of sound recordings from any one phonorecord lawfully distributed for public performance or sale in the United States, if no more than 2 such selections are transmitted consecutively; or
>
> (B) 4 different selections of sound recordings —
>
> (i) by the same featured recording artist; or
>
> (ii) from any set or compilation of phonorecords lawfully distributed together as a unit for public performance or sale in the United States, if no more than three such selections are transmitted consecutively:
>
> Provided, That the transmission of selections in excess of the numerical limits provided for in clauses (A) and (B) from multiple phonorecords shall nonetheless qualify as a sound recording performance complement if the programming of the multiple phonorecords was not willfully intended to avoid the numerical limitations prescribed in such clauses.

These restrictions have been relaxed for certain over-the-air broadcasters as a result of a settlement reached on February 15, 2009 between SoundExchange and the NAB. Broadcasters who opted into the settlement by April 2, 2009, may retransmit their over-the-air broadcasts over the Internet (i.e., *simulcast*) without complying with many of the restrictions set forth in the sound recording performance complement. Provided that the "substantial majority" of the audience is over-the-air listeners and a broadcast does not materially depart from "typical over-the-air programming practices," broadcasters simulcasting their over-the-air broadcasts will not be subject to restrictions on consecutive performance of recordings by the same artist or album so long as not more than one-half of a single album is played consecutively. In connection with such broadcasts, the broadcaster may announce the song title and artist before a song is played, provided that a written or visual schedule does not specify the time of a particular performance and the broadcaster does not post its playlists on any website. The settlement agreement also eliminated the requirement that such broadcasters retain for six months records of their ephemeral recordings.

#### (3) The transmission service must not publish a program schedule or playlist in advance

The service may not publish a program schedule or playlist, or otherwise identify in advance when a specific recording, album, or artist will be played. The service may announce that particular recording or artist is in the cue, but the exact time or order of recordings may not be provided. A limited exception to this restriction is available to certain noncommercial classical music radio stations that had published program guides prior to 1998.

#### (4) The transmission service must transmit copyright information while the recordings are playing

While the recordings are being transmitted, the service must identify in text on its website certain information, including the title of the recording, the album from which it came, and the artist featured in the performance. This information may not be displayed before the recording is transmitted. Also, to the extent technically feasible, the transmissions must be accompanied by information that is encoded in the recordings by the copyright owner, including information identifying the title of the recordings, the artists featured in them, and related information about the recordings.

#### (5) The transmission service must not automatically cause any device receiving the transmission to switch channels

The service may not automatically and intentionally cause the device receiving the transmission to switch from one program channel to another. An exception has been made to this restriction for transmissions to a business establishment, such as transmissions by background music services.

Note also, the compulsory license does not inure to the benefit of any webcaster, only those whose "primary purpose" is "not to sell, advertise, or promote particular products or services other than sound recordings, live concerts, or other music-related events." Anyone else must obtain a license from the owners of the sound recordings, which may be offered at any negotiated fee or not at all, by the record companies.

Services complying with these restrictions and all of the conditions of the compulsory license may compel the record companies to provide them with the license set forth in Section 114(f), under procedures established and fees determined by the Copyright Royalty Board. Such services also qualify for a statutory license under Section 112(e) to make multiple "ephemeral" recordings (i.e., temporary copies of sound recordings for the purpose of facilitating the transmissions permitted under the Section 114 license). Services that do not comply, and are not exempt under Section 114(d)(1), must obtain voluntary licenses from the record companies for the right to make digital audio transmissions and ephemeral reproductions of their recordings, meaning the record companies may charge what they want, demand advances against royalties, or refuse to license altogether.

### 4. *Development of the Statutory Fee Regime for Eligible Nonsubscription Transmissions and New Subscription Services Under the Compulsory License*

The 1995 Act and the DMCA created a procedure to set royalty rates for the compulsory licenses established under the amendments to Sections 112 and 114 of the Copyright Act. The Librarian of Congress was authorized to convene a Copyright Royalty Arbitration Panel (CARP) to take testimony from interested parties and recommend statutory royalty rates under the compulsory licenses. At the conclusion of the proceedings, the CARP issues a report the Librarian, who, upon recommendation of the Copyright Office, will adopt the fees proposed by the CARP unless it determines the fees recommended are arbitrary or contrary to copyright law. If the Librarian rejects the fees recommended by the CARP, he may, after an examination and an additional 30 days, issue an order setting them. The Librarian's decision may be appealed by an aggrieved party to the U.S. Court of Appeals for the D.C. Circuit.[31]

### a. *Webcasting I — The CARP Decision*

On February 20, 2002, the CARP issued a lengthy report, based on thousands of pages of testimony and evidence, with its recommendations for statutory royalties for eligible nonsubscription transmissions.[32] The CARP proposed a public performance fee of 0.14¢ per performance (under the Section 114 license) and an ephemeral license fee of 9% of performance fees (under the Section 112 license). For simultaneous Internet transmission of over-the-air AM or FM radio broadcasts, the CARP proposed a performance fee of .07¢ per performance and an ephemeral license fee of 9% of performance fees due. Fees for noncommercial broadcasters (i.e., those not affiliated with the Corporation for Public Broadcasting) who simulcast over the Internet their over-the-air AM or FM broadcasts recommended as .02¢ per performance and an ephemeral license fee of 9% of performance fees due.

While webcasters and broadcasters were arguing for fees to be set strictly on a percentage basis, the CARP ruled that "a 'per performance' royalty metric is preferable to a percentage of revenue option because, in part, many webcasters were generating very little revenue at that time. "Basing royalties on percentage of revenue," said the CARP, "could result in an undesirable situation where copyright owners are forced to allow extensive use of their property with little or no compensation."

### b. *Webcasting I — The Librarian of Congress Overrules*

The CARP's decision became immediately controversial, with many service providers claiming that the proposed rate would "kill" the development of webcasting. On May 15, 2002, the Senate Judiciary

[31] 17 U.S.C. Sec. 114(d)(1), which was subsequently amended. This is no longer the procedure.

[32] *In re rate setting for Digital Performance Right in Sound Recordings and Ephemeral Recordings* (February 20, 2002), a copy of which is available at copyright.gov.

Committee held a hearing over the proposed rates. On May, 21, 2002, upon recommendation of the Register of Copyrights, the Librarian of Congress rejected the CARP's proposed rates. On June 20, 2002, the Librarian issued Final Regulations that established new rates as follows: the performance fees were reduced from $0.14¢ to $0.07¢ per performance, per listener (i.e., the same rate as set for simulcasts of over-the-air broadcasts) and ephemeral fees were reduced from 9% to 8.8% of performance fees due.

*c. Small Webcasters Settlement Act of 2002*

The action taken by the Librarian of Congress did not end the controversy (one that continued, as we shall see, until July 7, 2009). Members of Congress reacted to the Final Regulation by introducing bills entitled, "Internet Radio Fairness Act" and "Small Webcasters Amendments Act of 2002." On December 4, 2002, President Bush signed into law the "Small Webcasters Settlement Act of 2002" (SWSA), which extended the due date for royalty payments and contemplated more rate options than those established by the Librarian's order, including the possibility of royalties payable by small webcasters on a percentage of revenue basis. Subsequent to the passage of the SWSA, a compromise was reached by the recording and webcasting industries on alternative rates that were effective through the end of 2005. The compromise provided small webcasters with an option to pay on the basis of a percentage of their revenues, subject to certain minimums.

*d. Replacement of CARP with Copyright Royalty Board*

Meanwhile, Congress enacted the Copyright Royalty and Distribution Reform Act of 2004, which replaced the CARP system with a Copyright Royalty Board (CRB) to be composed of three Copyright Royalty Judges.[33] Under the Copyright Act as amended, interested parties are encouraged to negotiate a settlement agreement during a three-month period, after which, failing such a settlement, the CRB is authorized to conduct hearings, gathering evidence and testimony, and issue a ruling on the statutory rates.

[33] 17 U.S.C. Sec. 804.

*e. Webcasting II — CRB Decision on Rates*

On March 9, 2007, after holding extensive hearings, the CRB issued its decision, published as a Final Rule and Order on May 1, 2007,[34] a copy of which is set forth in the appendix to this chapter. The order established the following rates for the period spanning January 1, 2006 through December 31, 2010:

| | |
|---|---|
| For commercial webcasters: | 2006: $.0008 per performance<br>2007: $.0011 per performance<br>2008: $.0014 per performance<br>2009: $.0018 per performance<br>2010: $.0019 per performance |
| For noncommercial webcasters: | For Internet transmission totaling less than 159,140 Aggregate Tuning Hours (ATH) per month, an annual per channel or per station performance royalty of $500 in each of the years 2006, 2007, 2008, 2009, and 2010.<br><br>For Internet transmission totaling more than 159,140 Aggregate Tuning Hours (ATH) per month, a performance royalty of<br><br>2006: $.0008 per performance<br>2007: $.0011 per performance<br>2008: $.0014 per performance<br>2009: $.0018 per performance<br>2010: $.0019 per performance |
| Minimum Fee: | Commercial and noncommercial webcasters will be subject to an annual, nonrefundable minimum fee of $500 for each calendar year or part thereof. |

[34] Library of Congress, Copyright Royalty Board, *Digital Performance Right in Sound Recordings and Ephemeral Recordings*, 72 F.R. 24084 (May 1, 2007). See 37 C.F.R. Part 380.

These fees included the fees for making ephemeral recordings under Section 112. The rate structure, however, did not make any special provision for "small webcasters." Yet, perhaps the most controversial part of the decision was that the performance royalties above were made subject to an annual, nonrefundable minimum fee of $500 *per channel or station* for each calendar year or part thereof:

> "This annual minimum fee is payable for each individual channel and each individual station maintained by Commercial Webcasters and Noncommercial Webcasters and is also payable for each individual Side Channel maintained by Broadcasters who are Licensees."

A definition of "channel" or "station" was not provided in the CRB's order, but webcasters often maintain multiple channels covering a large variety of music genres. Large commercial webcasters such as Yahoo, RealNetworks, and Pandora transmit thousands of channels of programming.

*f. Webcaster Settlement Act of 2008*

The reaction to the decision from the webcasting community — including small and large webcasters and commercial and noncommercial broadcasters — was quite negative and vociferous. On May 30, 2007, the Digital Media Association, National Public Radio, and others filed suit in the U.S. Court of Appeals for the D.C. Circuit, appealing the decision. Two bills were introduced in the 110th Congress — both entitled, the "Internet Radio Equality Act" — that would have overturned the CRB's decision and instituted a new rate regime. Neither passed, but Congress enacted the Webcaster Settlement Act of 2008, which was signed into law by President Bush on October 16, 2008. The purpose of the law was to provide statutory authority for SoundExchange to negotiate and enter into an alternative royalty structure satisfactory to the webcasters. Such agreements, if any, would become "binding on all copyright owners of sound recordings and other persons entitled to payment" in lieu of the CRB's rate decision.

*g. Industry-Negotiated Rates for Simulcasts by Public Broadcasting Entities*

Under the Webcaster Settlement Act of 2008, SoundExchange's authority to negotiate such settlements expired on February 15, 2009.

On that date, SoundExchange and the Corporation for Public Broadcasting (CPB) announced a comprehensive settlement on royalty rates to be paid for Internet streaming of sound recordings by approximately 450 public radio webcasters, including CPB-supported station websites, National Public Radio (NPR), members of NPR, member of the National Federation of Community Broadcasters, American Public Media, Public Radio Exchange, and Public Radio International. This agreement replaces the rates determined by the CRB and covers the period spanning January 1, 2005 through December 31, 2010 for these webcasters.

Under the settlement, CPB agreed to (a) pay SoundExchange a single, up-front flat-fee of $1.85 million, (b) provide to SoundExchange with consolidated usage and playlist reports, which SoundExchange would use to properly allocate payments to performers and sound recording copyright owners, and (c) drop its appeal of the CRB's rate decision.

On August 12, 2009, an agreement was reached extending the agreement through December 31, 2015 under modified terms, which are summarized in the next section.

#### *h. Industry-Negotiated Rates for Commercial Broadcasting Simulcasts*

Over-the-air digital audio transmissions (and all analog transmission, for that matter) made by terrestrial radio stations licensed by the Federal Communications Commission are exempt from any payment requirement to owners of sound recordings. Thus, HD (i.e., high definition over-the-air digital audio broadcasts) radio transmissions are exempt from payment. (Of course, radio stations must continue to pay for the public performances of musical works contained in such sound recordings, but until a general right of public performance is given to record labels, AM & FM radio stations need not pay for their use of sound recordings.)

As discussed above, however, terrestrial radio and National Association of Broadcasters were blind-sided by a change in the copyright law they overlooked at the time the DMCA was passed. Under the 1995 Act, terrestrial radio broadcast transmissions of sound recordings that were retransmitted over the Internet (i.e., Internet *simulcasts* of over-the-air broadcasts) were exempt from the requirement of obtaining a performance, or digital audio transmission, license. All that a radio station required to make such transmissions was a performance license for the underlying musical works, which was easily obtainable from the performance rights societies such as ASCAP and BMI.

Soon after they discovered this change, the broadcasters petitioned the Copyright Office for an interpretation of the DMCA. In December 2000, the Copyright Office ruled that the public performance of sound recordings by means of digital audio transmissions, such as over the Internet, were not exempt from copyright liability. Thus, radio stations would require sound recording licenses to transmit their broadcasts over the Internet, and in order to obtain a compulsory license, those transmissions would need to comply with the detailed playlist requirements set forth in Section 114 of the Copyright Act.

Shortly after that decision, some terrestrial broadcasters ceased their simulcast transmissions over the Internet, and tried to lobby Congress for a change in the law that would re-institute the exemption they briefly enjoyed under the 1995 Act. AM & FM radio had long since resigned to defeat, but when the CRB Final Rule of May 1, 2007 was announced, the high rates caused a special sting to radio stations desiring to simulcast their over-the-air broadcasts. The best they could hope for was a negotiated settlement with SoundExchange.

Thus, on February 15, 2009, SoundExchange and the NAB announced a settlement for terrestrial AM or FM radio broadcasters licensed by the FCC who simulcast their over-the-air broadcasts over the Internet.[35] Covering an extended period spanning January 1, 2006 through December 31, 2015, the agreement provides that each broadcaster will pay an annual minimum fee of $500 for each of its channels, with a cap of $50,000 per broadcaster against performance fee per listen that ranges from $.0008 in 2006 to $.0025 per performance in 2015.

The broadcasters are also required to submit each month a report to SoundExchange detailing on a "census" basis, which recordings were transmitted over the Internet, identified by the title of the recording, the artist featured, the album, number of times the recording was transmitted, and the number of listeners for each transmission. Small broadcasters, those who stream less than 27,777 aggregate tuning hours per

[35] 74 F.R. 9293, 9300 (Mar. 3, 2009).

year, may pay $100 to obtain a waiver from the reporting requirement. The details of these agreements are summarized in the next section.

*i. Industry-Negotiated Rates for Small Webcasters*

Also, on February 15, 2009, SoundExchange announced a settlement with a number of "small" webcasters.[36] The rate for these webcasters, which covers the period spanning January 1, 2006 through December 31, 2015, is as follows:

| Transmissions Not Exceeding 5 Million Aggregate Tuning Hours (ATH) per month | Transmissions Exceeding 5 Million Aggregate Tuning Hours (ATH) per month |
|---|---|
| The greater of:<br>• 10% of the small webcaster's first $250,000 in gross revenues, or 12% of any gross revenues in excess of $250,000, or<br>• 7% of the small webcaster's annual expenses | Either:<br>• the rates provided by the CRB for the royalty period spanning January 1, 2006 through December 31, 2010 or<br>• the then applicable commercial webcasting rates for the royalty period spanning 2011–2015 |

The above rates are subject to a minimum annual fee varying between $500 and $5,000, depending upon gross revenues. Small webcasters who have less than $50,000 in annual gross revenues are subject to a minimum fee of $2,000 per year; those with more than $50,000 in annual gross revenues are subject to a $5,000 per year minimum. Microcasters, who have annual gross revenues below $5,000 and whose transmissions do not exceed 18,067 ATH, need only pay a fee of $500 per year, plus a $100 per year fee to be exempt from the census reporting requirements — they are not subject to the royalty rates set forth in the above table.

[36] 74 F.R. 9293, 9303 (Mar. 3, 2009).

*j. Webcaster Settlement Act of 2009*

On June 30, 2009, President Obama signed into law the Webcaster Settlement Act of 2009, which extended the industry's authority to enter into privately negotiated rate settlements until July 30, 2009.

*k. Industry-Negotiated Rates for Large and Small "Pureplay" Commercial Webcasters*

Webcasters whose sole business is to offer an eligible nonsubscription or new subscription service not mixed with other services, such as web-portal services, are considered "pureplay" webcasters. SoundExchange was willing to provide these pureplay webcasters with special rates, because these webcasters, not having separate sources of revenue from non-streaming activities, would be unable to "game the system" (i.e., balance revenue from streaming with revenue from other sources to minimize royalty obligations for streaming activity).

On July 7, 2009, SoundExchange and a number of large and small commercial pureplay webcasters reached an agreement[37] that make these services eligible for rates that are substantially below the rates under the CRB Final Rule of May 1, 2007. Under the agreement, which are retroactive back to January 1, 2006 and expire on December 31, 2015, large commercial webcasters — defined as those with annual revenues exceeding $1.25 million — pay the greater of 25% of their gross U.S. revenues or the newly agreed upon per performance rates set forth below:

2006: $.0008 per performance, per listener
2007: $.00084 per performance, per listener
2008: $.00088 per performance, per listener
2009: $.00093 per performance, per listener
2010: $.00097 per performance, per listener

Rates beyond 2010 will be those set by the CRB. Webcasters with less than $1.25 million in annual revenues may be 12% of their first $250,000 in gross U.S. revenues, and 14% of revenues above that.

[37] Notification of Agreement Under the Webcaster Settlement Act of 2009, 74 F.R. 34796, 34797 (July 17, 2009) (will not be codified in C.F.R.).

Subsequent to the announcement of the settlement, Pandora, which provides a popular user-influenced eligible nonsubscription service, announced that its heaviest listeners of its free service would be subject to a 40-hour per month limit. Any user who reaches that limit may opt for unlimited listening for the remainder of that month for a $.99 fee. Alternatively, users may switch to Pandora One, a monthly subscription-based version of the service.

*l. Webcasting III*

On January 5, 2009, the Copyright Royalty Board announced that it would begin a third proceeding to determine royalty rates for digital audio transmissions subject to the statutory licenses, which would be applicable for the period spanning January 1, 2010 through December 31, 2015. The settlement agreements reached between SoundExchange and various segments of the webcasting industry will be, according to the CRB, non-precedential, meaning they "shall not be admissible as evidence or otherwise taken into account in any administrative, judicial, or other proceeding" involving the setting or adjustment of royalties rates under the statutory licenses.[38]

### 5. Compulsory License Requirements for New Subscription Services

As mentioned above, a *new subscription service* is "a service that performs sound recordings by means of noninteractive subscription digital audio transmissions and that is not a pre-existing subscription service or a pre-existing satellite digital audio radio service." A new subscription service must conform to the same performance requirements as eligible nonsubscription transmission services, described above.

Rates for new subscription services were set by the CRB in its Final Rule published on May 1, 2007.

Earlier, however, at the behest of a petition filed by XM Satellite Radio, which intended to launch a special form of *new subscription service* that bundled audio services with satellite television services,

---

[38] Copyright Royalty Board, Library of Congress, *Digital Performance in Sound Recordings and Ephemeral Recordings*, 74 F.R. 318 (January 5, 2009).

the Copyright Royalty Board commenced proceedings on December 5, 2005, to determine rates for this new subscription service. Sirius Satellite Radio, MTV Networks, and Sound Exchange later joined the hearing as interested parties. On September 10, 2007, XM, Sirius, and MTV reached a settlement with SoundExchange and, on December 19, 2007, the CRB published a Final Rule on rates for this special form of new subscription service.

Rates for the period ending December 31, 2010 were set based on whether the audio service was to be bundled with other (e.g., video) content licensed by the licensee to a video programming distributor (e.g., Dish Network, EchoStar) or unbundled (e.g., "Stand-Alone Contracts").

For Bundled Contracts, the rate was set at 15% of revenue, subject to a monthly minimum payment per subscriber as follows:

| | |
|---|---|
| From inception through 2006: | $0.0075 |
| 2007: | $0.0075 |
| 2008: | $0.0075 |
| 2009: | $0.0125 |
| 2010: | $0.0150 |

For Stand-Alone contracts, the rate was set at 15% of revenue or the following monthly minimum payment per subscriber:

| | |
|---|---|
| From inception through 2006: | $0.0220 |
| 2007: | $0.0220 |
| 2008: | $0.0220 |
| 2009: | $0.0220 |
| 2010: | $0.0250 |

No later than January 20 of each year, the service shall pay an advance of $100,000, recoupable from royalties payable during such year only.

### 6. *Compulsory License Requirements for Pre-Existing Subscription Services*

As mentioned above, a *pre-existing subscription service* is "a service that performs sound recordings by means of noninteractive audio-only subscription digital audio transmissions, which was in existence and was making such transmissions to the public for a fee on or before July 31, 1998, and may include a limited number of sample channels representative of the subscription service that are made available on a nonsubscription basis in order to promote the subscription service." For example, certain *cable radio* services, such as Music Choice, and Internet radio services offer on a subscription basis that were in existence prior to July 31, 1998, would fall into this category.

The performance requirements for pre-existing subscription services are slightly less demanding than those required of other transmission services eligible for the compulsory license. Pre-existing subscription services must comply with only the following two requirements:

(i) the transmission does not exceed the sound recording performance complement, and
(ii) the transmitting entity does not cause to be published by means of an advance program schedule or prior announcement the titles of the specific sound recordings or phonorecords embodying such sound recordings to be transmitted.

On January 9, 2006, the Copyright Royalty Board commenced proceedings to determine rates for pre-existing subscription services and pre-existing satellite radio services. The only pre-existing subscription service that was a party to those proceedings was Music Choice, which subsequently reached a settlement with SoundExchange on June 12, 2007. The CRB published a Final Rule relating to pre-existing subscription services on December 19, 2007.

For the period commencing January 1, 2008 through December 31, 2011, pre-existing subscription services shall pay a royalty fee of 7.5% of monthly gross revenues resulting from residential services in the United States. For the period spanning January 1, 2012 through December 31, 2012, such fee shall be increased to 7.5%. No later than January 20 of each year, the service shall pay an advance of $100,000, recoupable from royalties payable during such year only.

### *7. Compulsory License Requirements for Pre-Existing Satellite Radio Subscription Services*

As mentioned above, a *pre-existing satellite digital audio radio service* is defined in the Act as "a subscription satellite audio radio service provided pursuant to a satellite digital audio radio service license issued by the FCC on or before July 31, 1998, and any renewal of such license to the extent the scope of the original license, and may include a limited number of sample channels representative of the subscription service that are made available on a nonsubscription basis in order to promote the subscription service." This is, in essence, referring to Sirius/XM satellite radio.

A pre-existing satellite digital audio radio service must conform to the same performance requirements as eligible nonsubscription transmission services, described above.

On January 9, 2006, the Copyright Royalty Board commenced proceedings to determine rates for pre-existing subscription services and pre-existing satellite radio services. The only pre-existing satellite audio radio services that were parties to those proceedings were Sirius Satellite Radio and XM Satellite Radio, which have since merged.

The CRB published a Final Rule relating to pre-existing satellite audio radio services on January 24, 2008, announcing the following rates for the period spanning January 1, 2007 through December 31, 2012:[39]

| Year | Percent of gross revenue |
|---|---|
| 2007 | 6.0% |
| 2008 | 6.0% |
| 2009 | 6.5% |
| 2010 | 7.0% |
| 2011 | 7.5% |
| 2012 | 8.0% |

Gross revenues include all revenues paid to the service, excluding both subscription and advertising revenue associated with channels or programming that use only "incidental" performances of sound recordings as part of their programming.

The fees cover both the compulsory license to make the transmissions (under Section 114) and the making of server copies to facilitate those transmissions (under Section 112). Fees and reports are due on a monthly basis, on or before the 45th day after the end of the month for

[39] 73 CFR Part 382.

which the fees are due, and are subject to a late fee of 1½% per month. All payments are to be rounded to the nearest cent.

Detailed rules of recordkeeping for the use of sound recordings under the statutory license have been proposed by the CRB in a notice of proposed rulemaking announced in the Federal Register on December 30, 2008. 73 CFR 250, page 79727.

### *8. Administration of the Compulsory Licenses — SoundExchange*

When the Copyright Act was amended in 1995 to provide owners of sound recordings with an exclusive right to publicly perform their works by digital audio transmission and to provide webcasters with a compulsory license to make certain eligible transmissions of sound recordings, it allowed owners of sound recordings and recording artists to designate agents to represent them in negotiations and in the collection and distribution of royalties arising from these transmissions.

Initially, the Librarian of Congress designated the RIAA as the agent for receiving payments and reporting under the statutory license. In 2000, the RIAA created SoundExchange, an unincorporated division of the trade organization, to assume those responsibilities. In September 2003, SoundExchange was spun off as an independent non-profit corporation under Section 501(c)(6) of the Internal Revenue Code. SoundExchange is controlled by an 18 member Board of Directors composed of equal numbers of representatives of recording artists and sound recording copyright owners, which oversees its operations and approves its distribution methodologies and administrative expenses.

Since its founding, SoundExchange has sought to become the sole collective representing sound recordings owners and recording artists under the statutory license regimes of Sections 112 and 114. Despite arguments presented by prospective alternatives to SoundExchange that all interested parties would benefit from competition among designated agents (such as there is competition among ASCAP, BMI, and SESAC among performance rights societies representing musical works), the Copyright Royalty Board has appointed SoundExchange as the sole designated collecting agent for these licenses and fees under the various compulsory license regimes. The CRB felt that a single collective would be a more efficient means of representing the copyright owners and recording artists. It has been argued that authority of the CRB to make such an appointment appears to be in direct conflict with the statute. The CRB's authority to appoint SoundExchange as the sole collective, as well as the constitutionality of the CRB itself, has been challenged in the federal courts.[40]

### *9. Licenses Required to Use Musical Works in Digital Audio Transmissions of Sound Recordings*

Fees for the use of musical works in digital audio transmissions of sound recordings are subject to the compulsory license provision of Section 115 of the Copyright Act. The statutory rates established for these transmissions are discussed at length in Chapter 13, *Licensing Music in Sound Recordings.*

*On-Demand Transmissions.* The statutory rate payable for making mechanical reproductions of musical works in connection with services that conduct limited downloads and on-demand streams is, for the most part, 10.5% of service revenue less the amount of licensee fees paid for the public performances of such musical works in connection with such services, subject to certain minimum royalties depending upon the licensed activity, subject to subscriber minimums varying between 14.53% to 22% (depending upon several factors) of the royalties payable to owners of sound recordings for the streaming activity.

*Transmissions Subject to Section 114 Compulsory Licensing.* The use of musical works in transmissions of sound recordings that are subject to compulsory licensing under Section 114 of the Copyright Act, such as subscription transmissions and eligible nonsubscription transmissions, only require public performance licenses, which are obtained from the performance rights societies (e.g., ASCAP, BMI, SESAC).

---

[40] See *Live365, Inc. v. Copyright Royalty Board*, Case No. 1:09-vc-01662 (RBW) (U.S. District Court, District of Columbia, September 28, 2009); *http://www.scribd.com/doc/20378900/Motion-for-Preliminary-Injunction-in-Live365-v-CRB*; *http://www.scribd.-com/doc/20377680/Order-denying-preliminary-injunction-in-Live365-v-CRB.*

## V. CONSIDERATIONS IN GRANTING LICENSES FOR THE USE OF SOUND RECORDINGS

This section will analyze several specific activities that will require licenses from the owner of sound recordings. These include:

A. Permanent Downloads (i.e., digital phonorecord deliveries in general)

B. Music On Demand (i.e., on-demand streaming, limited/tethered downloads and other interactive services)

C. Webcasting (eligible nonsubscription transmission and new subscription services)

D. Pre-Existing Subscription Services (Music Choice)

E. Pre-Existing Digital Audio Radio Subscription Services (Sirius/XM)

F. Background Music Services

G. Licensing Sound Recordings in Other Albums — Compilations & Special Products

H. Licensing Sound Recordings in Films, Television Programs and Other Audiovisual works

I. Licensing Sound Recordings in Commercial Advertising

J. Licensing Sound Recordings in Videogames, Multimedia and Other New Media Devices and Online Versions

K. Digital Sampling

L. ISP Licensing

M. Public Performances

### A. Permanent Downloads (i.e., Digital Phonorecord Deliveries in General)

#### *1. Definition*

A permanent download is the reproduction of a sound recording that is sold or given away to a consumer for his or her permanent, private use by means of transmitting to the consumer over the Internet or wirelessly a digital data file embodying the recording. Anyone desiring to offer permanent downloads must obtain a license from the owners of the recordings, typically a record company (which license would be in addition to any applicable mechanical licenses that may be necessary from music publishers for simultaneously reproducing underlying musical work). Examples include permanent downloads offered by online services such as iTunes, AmazonMP3, and eMusic

### *2. Legal Background*

This activity of authorizing the download of a sound recording for permanent use by a consumer is formally known as transmitting a sound recording by *digital phonorecord delivery,* a term defined in the Copyright Act as:

> each individual delivery of a phonorecord by digital transmission of a sound recording which results in a specifically identifiable reproduction by or for any transmission recipient of a phonorecord of that sound recording, regardless of whether the digital transmission is also a public performance of the sound recording or any nondramatic musical work embodied therein.

Again, keep in mind that each digital phonorecord delivery concerns potentially two separate kinds of copyrights — the copyright in the sound recording and the copyright in the musical work embodied in the sound recording. This is important, because, in the United States, the *owner of the sound recording* is under an obligation to obtain a mechanical license to the songs embodied in the sound recordings prior to authorizing permanent digital phonorecord deliveries of the recording; outside the United States, the *online music service* is responsible for obtaining the mechanical reproduction licenses required to offer permanent downloads. The mechanical licensing of musical works in sound recordings for digital delivery is discussed at length in Chapter 13.

As discussed in Chapter 13, on mechanical licensing, there is some controversy in the United States as to whether a permanent download service requires, in addition to a mechanical reproduction license, a public performance license. One court has ruled that only a reproduction license is required.[41] This is not the case in countries overseas, which generally recognize a copyright owner's exclusive right to communicate the work to the public, a right that must be cleared together with the mechanical reproduction license.

When an online music service desires to license a *sound recording* for the purpose of making permanent downloads, it must look to the owner of the sound recording, typically a record company or an aggregator representing the record company, for such license.

### *3. Technical Protection/Digital Rights Management*

Technology used to control the unauthorized copying of digital files containing content, such as sound recordings and audiovisual works is known generally as *digital rights management* or "DRM." Some permanent download services employ it and some don't. While there was a time when major record companies where reluctant to license their music for download without DRM, today all the major record companies permit it.

### *4. Fee Structure and License Terms*

Unlike licenses for the right to effect digital deliveries of the underlying song, a compulsory license is not available for those wishing to offer permanent downloads of sound recordings. In other words, you must obtain permission from the record company and the record company can charge whatever it likes or even refuse to grant you permission to make the transmission. This also means that the record label can not only set the fee, but also require an advance against royalties, which they often demand to ensure against an online service going out of business before ever generating royalties for sales made.

The basic license fee per digital download varies by service, but the following examples, while not exhaustive, are representative of the kinds of fees paid by several of the most popular online services offering permanent downloads. Note, in recent months, the fee structures have been changing rapidly, so the examples below may become dated by the publication date of this book and inquiry should be made directly with the service or an applicable digital distributor.

[41] *United States v. ASCAP,* 485 F. Supp. 2d 438 (S.D.N.Y. 2007).

The following services, as of the time of this writing, each offer solely permanent downloads. Services that offer both permanent downloads and on-demand streams will be discussed in the next section. In addition, this section will cover the license fees typically required for the interactive digital audio transmission in the United States.

*a. iTunes*

iTunes, operated by Apple Computer, is the most popular online music store and enjoys an approximate 80% share of the download market. The store is accessed through a web-browser, but only via the iTunes media player, which can also be used to organize and play music and video files, and to manage content on iPods and iPhones. Though initially offering downloads only in its proprietary DRM format known as "Fairplay," iTune offers both DRM and non-DRM versions of recorded music files, though the non-DRM version still employs the AAC, not MP3, compression format. iTunes offers music in virtually all genres and operates stores in the following territories: Australia, Canada, Europe, Japan, New Zealand, United Kingdom, and the United States. (Retail pricing and royalty rates below are for the United States.)

*Retail Pricing.* For DRM-encased tracks, iTunes charges U.S. consumers $.99 per track and between $9.99 and $11.99 for full length albums. For non-DRM, iTunes charges $1.29 per track and $14.99 per album. Special editions, which may include video, may cost as much as $29.99 per album.

*Royalty Rates.* The Apple iTunes store pays to record labels the greater of 70% of retail and $.70 per track. There was a time when iTunes paid independent record labels only $.65 per download, but that practice ended in 2005 when $A^2$Im, a trade association representing independent labels, was mobilized to seek pricing parity for the independents. Originally, iTunes paid a royalty of $7 per album. Now, royalty rates for albums vary: Front-line Plus, $8.40; Mid-line/Front-line, $7.00; Back catalog, $5.60; and Budget line, $4.20. The royalty on EPs is $2.80; Mini-EPs is $1.40.

*b. Amazon*

Amazon currently ranks No. 2 in digital music download sales after Apple iTunes. The store is integrated with Amazon's CD store with links to digital albums appearing on CD product pages and search results. MySpace Music directs users to Amazon for downloads. Amazon is also available on T-Mobile's G1 (Google) phone. The store offers music in all genres and operates separate stores in a growing number of countries, including United States, France, and Germany. Unlike iTunes, it offers files in the MP3 format and encodes them at a high bit rate of 256kbs, which increases their size slightly, but offers an excellent sound quality.

*Retail Pricing.* Amazon charges between $.89 and $.99 per track, and offers promotions to get the price down significantly lower. Albums sell for between $5.99 and $9.99.

*Royalty Rates.* Amazon pays $.63 or $.70 per track, depending upon the price tier chosen by the label for the particular album. Album royalties are $4.00 to 7.00, depending upon the price tier.

### c. *eMusic*

EMusic.com, Inc.,[42] the first commercial supplier of popular music by permanent download, has entered into license agreements with over 1,000 independent record labels for the exclusive rights to make digital deliveries of their sound recordings. These deals were originally on an exclusive basis for a period of three to five years, and included all of the sound recordings in the label's catalog at the time the license was signed, plus all recordings that the label acquired the right to distribute during the term of the agreement. Most of eMusic's deals with labels today are on a non-exclusive basis. In 2009, eMusic licensed certain recordings from the back catalog of Sony Music. eMusic operates stores in Canada, Europe, the United Kingdom, and the United States.

*Subscription Pricing.* Originally, eMusic sold recordings for 99¢ per track, but later switched to subscription based pricing. Price tiers under eMusic's subscription regime have changed several times over

[42] Co-author Bob Kohn was founder of EMusic.com, Inc. (formerly NASDAQ: EMUS), and served as its Chairman until the company was sold to Vivendi/Universal in May 2001.

the years, but as of the time of this writing, subscribers could select from one of three subscription plans:

| | |
|---|---|
| $29.95 | for the right to download up to 20 tracks per month up to a total of 60 tracks over each three-month period; |
| $59.95 | for the right to download up to 20 tracks per month up to a total of 120 tracks over each six-month period; or |
| $119.95 | for the right to download up to 20 tracks per month up to a total of 240 tracks over each one-year month period. |

Under each of these plans, it appears that each track can cost the consumer as little as 49.9¢ per track, assuming the consumer downloads every track that he or she is entitled to download each month. It is not clear what the eMusic website means when it states, "Songs as low as 25 cents after free trial," which includes the right to download 25 tracks for free.

*Royalty Rates.* eMusic pays independent record labels between 50% and 60% of revenues after first deducting certain costs, which include the costs of effecting the transaction, such as VISA and MasterCard clearance fees, the cost of any mechanical royalties eMusic must pay, patent royalties, and commissions paid to affiliates who drive subscribers to the service. A license having similar terms is set forth as Form 23.3 on the CD-ROM.

It is not clear if eMusic is offering the same terms to independent labels as it has offered Sony. In addition, eMusic's promotional download policy has changed over the years and it is no longer clear what limitations there are in the amount of tracks the service may give away without compensation to the label. In addition, if consumers can pay as little as 25¢ per track, and eMusic does not pay any mechanical royalty that may be due as a result, the label may find itself with very little left for itself and its recording artist after payment of the mechanical royalty obligation.

#### *d. Beatport*

Beatport is a permanent download service devoted to selling recordings in the electronic or dance genres, and it is the recognized leader for electronic dance music downloads by DJs and fans. The Beatport store offers recordings in the MP3, M4A, and WAV formats, the latter of which are popular for DJ remixing.

*Retail Pricing.* Beatport charges between $1.89 and $2.49 per track, depending upon the file format, with the WAV format being the most expensive. Album prices vary considerably.

*Royalty Rates.* Beatport, following the eMusic model, pays 60% of revenues after deducting certain costs, including transaction fees, any mechanical royalties payable, and affiliate fees.

##### *e. Amie Street*

Amie Street sells tracks in the MP3 format, but under a unique pricing model called *demand-based pricing* under which the price per track increases with the track's popularity.

*Retail Pricing.* Tracks are initially sold for free but the price increases based on the number of purchases to a maximum of $0.98.

*Royalty Rates.* Amie Street pays labels 70% of net revenue.

### B. Music On Demand (i.e., On-demand Streaming, Limited/ Tethered Downloads and Other Interactive Services)

#### *1. In General*

Music "on demand" denotes the delivery of recorded music in a way that allows the consumer to select which individual recording he wants to hear when he wants to hear it, but the consumer is not permitted to maintain a copy of the recording on a permanent basis.

The on-demand experience may be effected by (a) a *streaming* of the recording, where no more than a buffer of a portion of the recording may reside on the consumer's device while the recording is being listened to or (b) a *limited download* of the recording, in which a copy of the full recording is downloaded to the consumer's device for a limited period (e.g., as short as the time it takes to listen to the recording, for some specified time, such as 30 days, or for as long as the consumer continues to pay a subscription fee) or for a limited number of plays. The limitation on the time period over which the consumer may play the recording, or how many times the consumer may play it, is effected through a form of digital rights management (DRM) that is connected, or tethered, to the servers maintained by the online music service. For this reason, limited downloads are also referred to as *tethered downloads.*

Examples include authorizing the streaming or limited download of recordings on online music services such as Rhapsody, Napster, iMeem, LaLa, Qtrax, Slacker, and other subscription or advertising-based on-demand music services.

### *2. Legal Background*

As with permanent downloads, it is important to note the difference between the licensing of the sound recording and the underlying musical work. The sound recording and underlying musical work used in on-demand services must each be licensed separately, from separate entities, under separate license regimes.

#### *a. Sound Recordings*

When evaluating what kind of license a streaming service requires, you must first come to some conclusion about the nature of the streaming transmission itself: Is it purely interactive (e.g., where the user gets to listen to a particular recording "on demand" — immediately after selecting it), or is the transmission in the nature of a radio program (e.g., where the user is constrained by the playlist established by the website operator). Transmissions of the first kind are considered part of an *interactive service*, defined in the Copyright Act as "one that enables a member of the public to receive, on request, a transmission of a particular sound recording chosen by or on behalf of the recipient."

Transmissions that are like radio programs, primarily noninteractive transmissions that conform to the requirements of a subscription transmission or an eligible nonsubscription transmission under the compulsory license provisions of Section 114 (discussed above), are eligible for statutory licensing, which compels the owners of sound recordings to provide a license at a rate established by the government.

One who desires to operate an *interactive*, or *on-demand* music service — whether offering the recordings by on-demand stream or limited download, or both — or any radio-like service that does not conform to the requirements of a subscription transmission or an eligible nonsubscription transmission under the compulsory license provisions of Section 114, must obtain a license directly from the owner of the recordings, typically a record company. Such permission is obtained under a *voluntary license*, meaning the record company may charge what it wishes for these transmissions or may refuse to provide a license at all.

#### *b. Musical Works*

As discussed in the mechanical licensing chapter, in the United States and overseas, on demand music services must obtain both a mechanical reproduction license, as well as a public performance license, to make on-demand streams or limited downloads of songs embodied in sound recordings. Overseas, the reproduction and performance license are obtained together. In the United States, the former is obtained directly from the music publishers and the latter from performance rights societies.

Licensing of musical work for interactive, on-demand transmissions is discussed at length in Chapter 13, on *Licensing Music in Sound Recordings.* Briefly, the statutory rate payable to music publishers for making mechanical reproductions of musical works in connection with services that conduct limited downloads and on-demand streams is, for the most part, 10.5% of service revenue less the amount of licensee fees paid for the public performances of such musical works in connection with such services, subject to certain minimum royalties depending upon the licensed activity, subject to subscriber minimums varying between 14.53% and 22% (depending upon several factors) of the royalties payable to owners of sound recordings for the streaming activity.

The following discussion will be restricted to the licensing of sound recordings (as opposed to musical works) in these interactive or "on-demand" music services.

### *3. Fee Structure and License Terms*

Online music services offering recordings on a streaming or limited download basis have traditionally charged users a monthly subscription fee for access to the services. More recently, however, several online services have begun experimenting with a purely advertising-based business model. The fee structures varies by service, but the following examples, while not exhaustive, are representative of the kinds of fees paid by several of the most popular online services offering recordings on a streaming or limited download basis in the United States. Some streaming services also offer permanent downloads.

*Royalties Payable to Labels.* The major record companies tend to charge all streaming/limited download services at the same rate, but new services typically have to pay the major labels large advances for initial access to their catalogs. In general, the labels receive (a) 50% of the gross revenues from the streaming/limited download service or (b) 1¢ per stream/limited download, whichever is greater. In addition, for the copies required to be made and placed on servers to facilitate the streaming/limited downloading, the labels typically get 2¢ per copy, up to a maximum of 10¢ per sound recording. An example of an interactive streaming license is set forth as Form 23.4 on the CD-ROM.

#### *a. Rhapsody*

Rhapsody, operated by RealNetworks, offers a subscription streaming service through Rhapsody.com, a download and streaming service through the Rhapsody Music Software (PCs only), a portable subscription service supporting select players, a free streaming service, and a streaming service through stand-alone players like Sonos and Squeezebox. Rhapsody also powers Comcast, RollingStone.com, and most recently, Verizon's mobile music subscription service.

*Retail Pricing.* For its streaming service, Rhapsody currently charges a subscription fee of $12.95 to $14.99 per month, depending upon the plan. For downloads, it charges $.99 per track and prices for albums vary.

*Royalty Rates.* For its streaming services, Rhapsody pays the greater of 50% of gross revenue or 1¢ per stream or limited download. For downloads purchased by subscribers, Rhapsody pays the label $.60 per track; for tracks downloaded by nonsubscribers, $.65 per track. For albums downloaded by subscribers, it pays $6.00 for frontline albums, and $4.20 for catalog albums. For albums downloaded by nonsubscribers, it pays $13.00 for frontline albums, $6.50 for catalog albums, and $5.85 for budget albums.

#### *b. Napster*

Napster, owned by BestBuy, offers a subscription streaming and download service, a portable subscription service (NapsterToGo), and a free streaming service (FreeNapster) online, as well as a mobile service (Napster Mobile) providing over-the-air downloads on AT&T, Cellular One, and US Cellular.

*Retail Pricing.* For its streaming service, Napster currently charges a subscription fee of $12.95 to $14.95 per month, depending upon the plan. For downloads, it charges $.99 per track and prices for albums begin at $6.95.

*Royalty Rates.* For its streaming services, Napster pays the label the greater of 50% of gross revenue or 1¢ per stream or limited download. For downloads, Napster pays the label $.70 per track, except that for downloads delivered over the air (OTA), they pay the greater of $1 or 50% of retail. For albums, they pay $7.00 for frontline albums and $5.00 for catalog albums. In addition, they pay 50% of advertising revenues derived from any of their services.

#### *c. MediaNet*

MediaNet, formerly MusicNet, powers a number of streaming and download services in the United States, Canada, the United Kingdom and Europe, including f.y.e., HMV Digital, iMesh, La Curacao, Music Gremlin, Samsung, and, until 2009, Microsoft Zune. Through its API and Web Components service, MediaNet can now be used by any website who wishes to operate a music streaming or download service with over 7 million tracks to choose from. Each of MediaNet's affiliated stores choose what price to charge for access to the recordings. MediaNet charges a fee to its affiliate for its service, beginning at $.10 per track downloaded, plus the royalty fees payable to the record companies.

*Royalty Rates.* For its streaming services, MediaNet pays the label the greater of 40% of gross revenue or 1/5 of 1¢ per stream. (The rate payable to major record companies may be higher.) For downloads, MediaNet pays the label $.65 per track and $6.50 per album.

#### d. *Nokia Music*

Nokia Music provides online download and mobile music services powering a number of European stores including Coketunes, MSN, MTV, Musica, NTL, Nokia Music Store, Packard Bell, Planet, and Wanadoo.

*Retail Pricing.* For downloads, it charges €.60 per track, €1.20 for a 2 or 3 track bundle, and €2.20 for a 4 to 5 track bundle. For full length albums, it charges €6.00 per album.

*Royalty Rates.* For track and album downloads, Nokia pays the label 80% of retail. For ringtones, they pay 30% of net revenue. For streams, they pay €.01 per stream.

## C. Webcasting (Eligible Nonsubscription Transmission and New Subscription Services)

Noninteractive digital audio transmissions are those that a consumer may listen to much like listening to a traditional, terrestrial (e.g., AM & FM) radio station — while the listener may select the general genre or station, the webcaster forms the specific playlist of recordings. The consumer may not select the individual tracks and may not significantly influence the playlist other than by making a general request, much like calling in to a radio station and requesting that a particular recording be added to the day's playlist (or "voting" on whether you like a particular recording, which will then influence the kinds of recordings the service will transmit to the consumer in the future). Like on-demand music services, the consumer does not get to keep a permanent copy of any of the recordings in the webcast. Examples of webcasting services include Live365, AOL Music, and Yahoo Music.

Recall, from the discussion above, that digital audio transmissions of sound recordings, such as subscription transmissions and eligible nonsubscription transmissions that conform to the statutory licensing requirements of Section 114 need not be licensed directly from the record labels, but are instead eligible for Section 114's compulsory license at the statutory rates established by the Copyright Royalty Board. Webcasters eligible for the statutory license pay royalty fees to SoundExchange, a collective appointed by the CRB to distribute royalties collected from webcasters to record companies and performing artists.

The rate structures for the various forms of webcasting have become increasingly complex. Agreeing that the CRB may have set webcasting rates too high, SoundExchange and various forms of webcasters have entered into a series of settlement agreements modifying the fees and fee structures for the respective forms of webcasts.

This section will summarize the statutory fees required for *eligible nonsubscription transmission* services and *new subscription services* under the compulsory licenses of Sections 112 and 114 of the Copyright Act. As mentioned earlier in this chapter, by order published on May 1, 2007,[43] the Copyright Royalty Board established fees for such compulsory licenses for the period spanning January 1, 2006 through December 31, 2010. Subsequent to that, several groups of webcasters entered into their own agreements, effectively superseding the rates set by the CRB. This section will summarize the rates as determined by the CRB, followed by the settlements that various groups of webcasters subsequently negotiated with SoundExhange.

### *1. Rate Set by the Copyright Royalty Board*

As discussed in the previous section, on May 1, 2007, the CRB established rates for eligible subscription transmissions and new subscription services for the period spanning January 1, 2006 through December 31, 2010. These terms and conditions serve as the default for all such transmissions and services, unless separate terms and conditions have been negotiated under the Webcaster Settlement Acts. The following is a summary of the terms of the CRB's Final Rule:

| **Term** | 2006-2010 |
|---|---|
| **Date of Publication** | May 1, 2007 |
| **Signatories** | n/a |

[43] Library of Congress, Copyright Royalty Board, *Digital Performance Right in Sound Recordings and Ephemeral Recordings*, 72 F.R. 24084 (May 1, 2007). See 37 C.F.R. Part 380.

| Eligible Services | Commercial webcaster — a Licensee, other than a Noncommercial Webcaster, that makes eligible nonsubscription transmissions or is a new subscription service.<br>Noncommercial webcaster — a Licensee that makes eligible digital audio transmissions and: (i) is exempt from taxation under Section 501 of the Internal Revenue Code, (ii) has applied in good faith for tax exempt status, or (iii) is operated by a State or possession or any governmental entity or subordinate thereof, or by the United States or District of Columbia, for exclusively public purposes. |
|---|---|
| **Election Process** | N/A |
| **Rate** | Commercial Webcasters<br>2006-$.0008 per performance<br>2007-$.0011<br>2008-$.0014<br>2009-$.0018<br>2010-$.0019<br><br>Noncommercial Webcasters<br>Same as commercial rates, but only pay for transmissions in excess of 159,140 aggregate tuning hours in a month |
| **Minimum Fee** | $500 per station or channel per year |
| **Payment Due Date** | 45th day after the end of each month |
| **Late Fees** | 1.5% per month late (late fees applicable to payments and statements of account) |
| **Reporting Waiver** | None |
| **Data** | Reporting provided in a format in accordance with current CRB regulations |

| | |
|---|---|
| **Format** | (1) name of service<br>(2) transmission category<br>(3) featured artist<br>(4) song title<br>(5) ISRC or album title and marketing label<br>(6) actual total performances (on a per station basis) or ATH, channel or program name, and play frequency |
| **Census or Sample** | Sample |
| **Frequency** | Quarterly |
| **Due Date** | 45th day after the end of each quarter |

### *2. Large Broadcasters Settlement with SoundExhange*

As mentioned above, the NAB negotiated a reduced rate applicable to Internet simulcasts of their over-the-air transmissions for the period spanning January 1, 2006 through December 31, 2015. The following is a summary of the terms of the settlement:

| **Term** | 2006-2015 |
|---|---|
| **Date of Publication** | March 3, 2009 |
| **Signatories** | National Association of Broadcasters |
| **Eligible Services** | Commercial "Broadcasters" (i.e., webcasters that also own and operate one or more FCC licensed terrestrial stations) |
| **Election Process** | Notice of Election is binding for the entire term; must be submitted by April 2, 2009 (for new services: 30 days after the Broadcaster begins making transmissions) |

| **Rate** | 2006 $0.0008 per performance<br>2007 $0.0011<br>2008 $0.0014<br>2009 $0.0015<br>2010 $0.0016<br>2011 $0.0017<br>2012 $0.0020<br>2013 $0.0022<br>2014 $0.0023<br>2015 $0.0025 |
|---|---|
| **Minimum Fee** | $500 per station or channel per year ($50,000 cap) |
| **Payment Due Date** | Minimum Fees: January 31<br>Monthly Royalties: 45th day after the end of each month<br>For 2006-Feb. 28, 2009: April 30, 2009 (payment shall include late fees from orig. due date) |
| **Late Fees** | 1.5% per month, compounded (late fees applicable to payments, statements of account, and reports of use) |
| **Reporting Waiver** | None. |
| **Data** | - Reporting in a format in accordance with current CRB regs, with headers<br>- Playlist and ATH permitted for a portion of their programming hours at the following percentages:<br><br>2009 20%<br>2010 18%<br>2011 16%<br>2012 14%<br>2013 12%<br>2014 10%<br>2015 8% |

| | |
|---|---|
| **Format** | (1) name of service<br>(2) transmission category<br>(3) featured artist<br>(4) song title<br>(5) ISRC or album title and marketing label<br>(6) actual total performances (on a per station basis)<br>(NOTE: Playlist and ATH permitted for the percentages noted above) |
| **Census or Sample** | Census |
| **Frequency** | Monthly |
| **Due Date** | 45th day after end of each month |

### *3. Small Broadcasters Settlement with SoundExchange*

The NAB negotiated a further reduction in rates for its smaller radio stations, summarizes as follows:

| | |
|---|---|
| **Term** | 2006-2015 |
| **Date of Publication** | March 3, 2009 |
| **Signatories** | National Association of Broadcasters |
| **Eligible Services** | Stations or channels with less than 27,777 total ATH in the prior year and expect to have less than 27,777 ATH in the applicable year. (Individual channels that retransmit broadcast transmissions may qualify as small broadcasters; all of a broadcaster's Internet-only channels must be considered in aggregate.) (The "Small Broadcaster" station may be a part of a larger station group.) |

| | |
|---|---|
| **Election Process** | Annual notice is required for each year during the term; elections must certify prior year's ATH and include each station's format or genre<br>For 2006-2009: Due by April 2, 2009<br>For 2010-2015: Due by January 31 of each year |
| **Rate** | 2006 $0.0008 per performance<br>2007 $0.0011<br>2008 $0.0014<br>2009 $0.0015<br>2010 $0.0016<br>2011 $0.0017<br>2012 $0.0020<br>2013 $0.0022<br>2014 $0.0023<br>2015 $0.0025 |
| **Minimum Fee** | $500 per station or channel per year ($50,000 cap) |
| **Payment Due Date** | Minimum Fees: January 31<br>Monthly Royalties: 45th day after the end of each month<br>For 2006-Feb. 28, 2009: April 30, 2009 (payment shall include late fees from orig. due date) |
| **Late Fees** | 1.5% per month, compounded (late fees applicable to payments and statements of account) |
| **Reporting Waiver** | Small Broadcasters may pay a $100 proxy fee at the beginning of each year in lieu of providing reporting; otherwise the broadcaster reporting is required |
| **Data** | |
| **Format** | |
| **Census or Sample** | |
| **Frequency** | |
| **Due Date** | |

### *4. Commercial Webcasters Settlement with SoundExchange*

As mentioned above, SiriusXM satellite radio negotiated a special rate for the simulcasts of its transmissions, and others like it, over the Internet. These terms are summarized as follows:

| **Term** | 2009-2015 |
|---|---|
| **Date of Publication** | August 12, 2009 |
| **Signatories** | SiriusXM |
| **Eligible Services** | Commercial webcasters as defined in 17 U.S.C. Sec. 114(f)(5)(E)(iii) that is not a "Broadcaster." |
| **Election Process** | Election is binding for the entire term.<br>Due Date for current services: 15 days after publication of rates and terms in Federal Register<br>Due Date for new services: 30 days after launching service |
| **Rate** | 2009 $0.0016 per performance<br>2010 $0.0017<br>2011 $0.0018<br>2012 $0.0020<br>2013 $0.0021<br>2014 $0.0022<br>2015 $0.0024 |
| **Minimum Fee** | $500 per station or channel per year ($50,000 cap) |
| **Payment Due Date** | Minimum Fees: January 31<br>Monthly Royalties: 45th day after the end of each month |
| **Late Fees** | 1.5% per month (late fees applicable to payments and statements of account) |
| **Reporting Waiver** | None. |

| | |
|---|---|
| **Data** | Reporting data provided in a format in accordance with current CRB regs (SiriusXM shall continue to provide census reporting per a side letter between SX and SiriusXM) |
| **Format** | (1) name of service<br>(2) transmission category<br>(3) featured artist<br>(4) song title<br>(5) ISRC or album title and marketing label<br>(6) actual total performances (on a per station basis) or ATH, channel or program name, and play frequency |
| **Census or Sample** | Sample |
| **Frequency** | Quarterly |
| **Due Date** | 45th day after the end of each quarter |

### *5. Large Pureplay Webcasters Settlement with SoundExchange*

As discussed in the previous section, webcasters whose sole business is to offer an eligible nonsubscription or new subscription service not mixed with other services, such as web-portal services, are considered "pureplay" webcasters. SoundExchange was willing to provide these pureplay webcasters with special rates, because these webcasters, not having separate sources of revenue from non-streaming activities, would be unable to "game the system" (i.e., balance revenue from streaming with revenue from other sources to minimize royalty obligations for streaming activity).

On July 7, 2009, SoundExchange and a number of large and small commercial pureplay webcasters reached an agreement[44] that make these services eligible for rates that are substantially below the rates under the CRB Final Rule of May 1, 2007. The effect of this settlement was to reduce the royalty costs of these pureplay services by about

[44] Notification of Agreement Under the Webcaster Settlement Act of 2009, 74 F.R. 34796, 34797 (July 17, 2009) (will not be codified in C.F.R.).

one-third of what they would have been under the CRM Final Rule. The terms of this settlement is summarized as follows:

<table>
<tr><td>Term</td><td colspan="2">2006-2015</td></tr>
<tr><td>Date of Publication</td><td colspan="2">July 17, 2009</td></tr>
<tr><td>Signatories</td><td colspan="2">Accuradio.com; Digitally Imported; IO World Media</td></tr>
<tr><td>Eligible Services</td><td colspan="2">Commercial webcasters as defined in 17 U.S.C. Sec. 114(f)(5)(E)(iii).</td></tr>
<tr><td>Election Process</td><td colspan="2">Annual notice is required each year during the term<br>For 2006-2009: Due by the 30th day after publication of rates and terms in Federal Register<br>For 2010-2015: Due by January 31 of each year</td></tr>
<tr><td>Rate</td><td><u>Nonsubscription Services</u><br>Greater of —<br>25% of Gross Revenues from activities in the United States<br>OR, the following per performance rates:<br>2006 $0.00080 per performance<br>2007 $0.00084<br>2008 $0.00088<br>2009 $0.00093<br>2010 $0.00097<br>2011 $0.00102<br>2012 $0.00110<br>2013 $0.00120<br>2014 $0.00130<br>2015 $0.00140</td><td><u>Subscription/ Bundled Services</u><br>2006 $0.0008 per performance<br>2007 $0.0011<br>2008 $0.0014<br>2009 $0.0015<br>2010 $0.0016<br>2011 $0.0017<br>2012 $0.0020<br>2013 $0.0022<br>2014 $0.0023<br>2015 $0.0025</td></tr>
</table>

| Minimum Fee | $25,000 per year |
|---|---|
| Payment Due Date | Minimum Fees: January 31<br>"Past Periods": 60 days after publication in Fed. Reg. (payment shall include late fees from original due date)<br>Prospectively: 45th day after the end of month |
| Late Fees | 1.5% per month, compounded (late fees applicable to payments, statements of account, and reports of use) |
| Reporting Waiver | None. |
| Data | Reporting data provided in a format in accordance with current CRB regs |
| Format | (1) name of service<br>(2) transmission category<br>(3) featured artist<br>(4) song title<br>(5) ISRC or album title and marketing label<br>(6) actual total performances (on a per station basis) |
| Census or Sample | Census |
| Frequency | Monthly |
| Due Date | 45th day after the end of each month |

### *6. Small Pureplay Webcasters Settlement with SoundExchange*

Small pureplay webcasters are defined as those whose annual gross revenues are less than $1.25 million and whose aggregate tuning hours of transmission are below certain thresholds. These small pureplay webcasters-negotiated even further reduced rates, which are summarized below:

| Term | 2006-2014 |
|---|---|
| Date of Publication | July 17, 2009 |
| Signatories | Accuradio.com; Digitally Imported; IO World Media |

| **Eligible Services** | Commercial webcasters as defined in 17 U.S.C. Sec. 114(f)(5)(E)(iii) that have annual gross revenues of less than $1.25 million and usage less than the following:<br>2006–2008-7 million ATH<br>2009-8 million ATH<br>2010-8.5 million ATH<br>2011-9 million ATH<br>2012-2014-10 million ATH |
|---|---|
| **Election Process** | Annual notice is required each year during the term<br>For 2006-2009: Due by the 30th day after publication of rates and terms in Federal Register<br>For 2010-2015: Due by January 31 of each year |
| **Rate** | 2006–2008<br>Greater of — 10% of first $250,000 in gross revenues, and 12% of gross revenues in excess of $250,000 OR 7% of expenses<br>2009-2014<br>Greater of — 12% of the first $250,000 in gross revenues, and 14% of gross revenues in excess of $250,000 OR 7% of expenses |
| **Minimum Fee** | $25,000 per year |
| **Payment Due Date** | Minimum Fees: January 31<br>"Past Periods": 60 days after publication in Fed. Reg. (payment shall include late fees from original due date)<br>Prospectively: 45th day after the end of month |
| **Late Fees** | 1.5% per month, compounded (late fees applicable to payments, statements of account, and reports of use) |
| **Reporting Waiver** | None. |
| **Data** | Reporting data provided in a format in accordance with current CRB regulations |

| Format | (1) name of service<br>(2) transmission category<br>(3) featured artist<br>(4) song title<br>(5) ISRC or album title and marketing label<br>(6) actual total performances (on a per station basis) |
|---|---|
| **Census or Sample** | Census |
| **Frequency** | Monthly |
| **Due Date** | 45th day after the end of each month |

### 7. *Small Commercial Webcasters Settlement with SoundExchange*

Commercial webcasters who in any calendar year have annual gross revenues from the operation of new subscription services of not more than $1,250,000 are eligible for reduced rates under their settlement with SoundExchange spanning the period commencing January 1, 2006 through December 31, 2015. Terms and conditions for these small commercial webcasters are set forth below:

| **Term** | 2006-2015 |
|---|---|
| **Date of Publication** | March 3, 2009 |
| **Signatories** | 18 small commercial webcasters: Attention Span Radio; BlogMusik; Christmas Music 247; Club 80s; Forever Cool; Indiwaves; Ludlow Media; My Jazz Network; Soulsvilleonline.com; taintradio; Voice of Country; WFMT-FM; Born Again Radio; Dark Horse Productions; Edgewater; Musical Justice; PartiRadio; Playacofi Jukebox |

| | |
|---|---|
| **Eligible Services** | Commercial Webcasters who in any calendar year have, together with its affiliates, annual gross revenues plus third party participation revenues and revenues from the operation of new subscription services of not more than $1,250,000. |
| **Election Process** | Annual notice is required each year during the term<br>For 2006-2009: Due by April 30, 2009<br>For 2010-2015: Due by the 45th day after the end of the month in which the service first makes transmissions in a given year |
| **Rate** | Greater of — 10% of SCW's first $250,000 in gross revenue and 12% of any gross revenues in excess of $250,000 OR 7% of webcaster's expenses during applicable year. (Subject to a usage cap of 5M ATH; CRB per performance rates paid for usage above 5M ATH.) |
| **Minimum Fee** | $2000 — services with no more than $50,000 in gross revenues in prior year or applicable year.<br>$5000 — services with more than $50,000 in gross revenues in prior year or applicable year. |
| **Payment Due Date** | Minimum Fees: January 31<br>Monthly Royalties: 45th day after the end of each month<br>For 2006-Feb. 28, 2009: April 30, 2009 (payment shall include late fees from orig. due date) |
| **Late Fees** | 1.5% per month (late fees applicable to payments, statements of account, and reports of use) |

| Reporting Waiver | None. |
|---|---|
| Data | Reporting data provided in a format in accordance with current CRB regs |
| Format | (1) featured artist<br>(2) song title<br>(3) album title (or in the case of compilations, the name of the album upon which the track was originally released)<br>(4) marketing label<br>(5) ISRC<br>(6) copyright owner information provided in copyright notice on product (or in the case of compilations, the copyright notice for the individual track)<br>(7) ATH on a monthly basis for each channel as computed by a recognized industry ratings service or as computed from the small webcaster's server logs;<br>(8) channel name<br>(9) start date and time of each transmission of each sound recording |
| Census or Sample | Census |
| Frequency | Monthly |
| Due Date | 45th day after the end of each month |

### *8. Microcasters Settlement with SoundExchange*

Very small commercial webcasters, aptly named *microcasters*, having annual gross revenues of not more than $5,000, annual expenses of not more than $10,000, and aggregate tuning hours of not more than 18,067 are eligible for even lower rates, and may exempt themselves from normal reporting requirements with the payment of an annual fee of $100. The details of this settlement, applicable for the period spanning January 1, 2006 through December 31, 2015, is set forth below:

| **Term** | 2006-2015 |
|---|---|
| **Date of Publication** | March 3, 2009 |
| **Signatories** | 18 small commercial webcasters: Attention Span Radio; BlogMusik; Christmas Music 247; Club 80s; Forever Cool; Indiwaves; Ludlow Media; My Jazz Network; Soulsvilleonline.com; taintradio; Voice of Country; WFMT-FM; Born Again Radio; Dark Horse Productions; Edgewater; Musical Justice; PartiRadio; Playacofi Jukebox |
| **Eligible Services** | Eligible Small Webcasters that together with its affiliates, had in the previous year (i) annual gross revenues plus third party participation revenues of not more than $5,000; (ii) expenses of not more than $10,000; and (iv) ATH not exceeding 18,067 ATH. |
| **Election Process** | Annual notice is required each year during the term; elections must certify prior year's gross revenues, third party participation revenues, and ATH<br>For 2006-2009: Due by April 30, 2009<br>For 2010-2015: Due by the 45th day after the end of the month in which the service first makes transmissions in a given year |
| **Rate** | To be eligible for the Microcaster rates and terms, services must have ATH less than or equal to 18,067 (i.e., an amount equal to the $500 minimum fee). As long as services stay within this threshold, they would not need to pay any royalties above the minimum fee. |
| **Minimum Fee** | $500 per year |

| | |
|---|---|
| **Payment Due Date** | Minimum Fees: January 31<br>For 2006-Feb. 28, 2009: April 30, 2009 (payment shall include late fees from orig. due date) |
| **Late Fees** | 1.5% per month |
| **Reporting Waiver** | NOTE: Microcasters can pay an additional $100 proxy fee at the beginning of each year in lieu of providing reporting; otherwise the small webcaster reporting is required |
| **Data** | |
| **Format** | |
| **Census or Sample** | |
| **Frequency** | |
| **Due Date** | |

### *9. Noncommercial Webcasters Settlement with SoundExchange*

Noncommercial webcasters negotiated a separate settlement with SoundExchange, the terms of which are summarized below:

| | |
|---|---|
| **Term** | 2006-2015 |
| **Date of Publication** | August 12, 2009 |
| **Signatories** | Northwestern College (NRBNMLC) |
| **Eligible Services** | Noncommercial webcasters as defined in 17 U.S.C. Sec. 114(f)(5)(E)(i). |
| **Election Process** | Annual election, except that an election for any calendar year shall apply to subsequent years unless service revokes the election<br>For 2006-2009: Due by September 15, 2009<br>For 2010-2015: Due by January 31 of each year or 30 days after the service launches |

| | |
|---|---|
| **Rate** | Noncommercial webcasters shall only pay for transmissions in excess of 159,140 aggregate tuning hours per month at the following:<br>For 2006-2010: $0.0002176 per performance or $0.00251 per ATH ($0.0002 per ATH for news/talk programming)<br>For 2011–2015:<br>2011-$0.00057 per performance (1/3 "NAB rates")<br>2012-$0.00067<br>2013-$0.00073<br>2014-$0.00077<br>2015-$0.00083 |
| **Minimum Fee** | $500 per station or channel |
| **Payment Due Date** | Minimum Fees: January 31<br>"Past Periods": September 15, 2009<br>Prospective Usage Fees: 45th day after the applicable month |
| **Late Fees** | 1.5% per month, compounded (late fees applicable to payments, statements of account, and reports of use) |
| **Reporting Waiver** | None. |
| **Data** | Reporting data provided in a format in accordance with then applicable regulations |
| **Format** | (1) name of service<br>(2) transmission category<br>(3) featured artist<br>(4) song title<br>(5) ISRC or album title and marketing label<br>(6) ATH, channel or program name, and play frequency |
| **Census or Sample** | Sample (for services within 159,140 ATH per month)<br>Census (for services whose monthly average ATH exceeds 159,149 ATH (beginning in 2011)) |

| **Frequency** | Quarterly |
|---|---|
| **Due Date** | 45th day after the end of each quarter |

### *10. Noncommercial Microcasters Settlement with SoundExchange*

Very small noncommercial webcasters also negotiated a separate settlement with SoundExchange, including terms allowing them to waive reporting requirements for annual fee of $100. The terms of the settlement are summarized below:

| **Term** | 2006-2015 |
|---|---|
| **Date of Publication** | August 12, 2009 |
| **Signatories** | Northwestern College (NRBNMLC) |
| **Eligible Services** | Noncommercial webcaster as defined in 17 U.S.C. Sec. 114(f)(5)(E)(i) that (i) during the prior year did not exceed usage of 44,000 ATH and (ii) during the applicable year does not expect to exceed usage of 44,000 ATH |
| **Election Process** | Annual notice is required each year during the term<br>For 2006-2009: Due by September 15, 2009<br>For 2010-2015: Due by January 31 of each year or 30 days after the service launches |
| **Rate** | To be eligible for the noncommercial microcaster rates and terms, services must have annual usage of less than 44,000 ATH. As a result, services would not need to pay anything above the minimum fee and proxy fee for reporting waiver. |
| **Minimum Fee** | $500 per station or channel |
| **Payment Due Date** | Minimum Fees: January 31<br>"Past Periods": September 15, 2009 |

| | |
|---|---|
| **Late Fees** | 1.5% per month, compounded (late fees applicable to payments, statements of account) |
| **Reporting Waiver** | NOTE: Noncommercial microcasters must pay a $100 proxy fee in lieu of providing reports of use |
| **Data** | |
| **Format** | |
| **Census or Sample** | |
| **Frequency** | |
| **Due Date** | |

### *11. Noncommercial Educational Webcaster Settlement with SoundExchange*

Noncommercial webcasters, such as college radio stations, negotiated a separate settlement for the period spanning January 1, 2011 through December 31, 2015. These terms are summarized below:

| | |
|---|---|
| **Term** | 2011-2015 (reporting terms retroactive to 2009) |
| **Date of Publication** | August 12, 2009 |
| **Signatories** | Collegiate Broadcasters Inc. |
| **Eligible Services** | Noncommercial webcasters that are directly operated by, or are affiliated with and officially sanctioned by, and the digital audio transmission operations of which are staffed substantially by students enrolled at, a domestically acrredited degree-granting educational institution, and is not a CPB-qualified station. |
| **Election Process** | Annual notice is required each year during the term. |

| Rate | Noncommercial webcasters shall only pay for transmissions in excess of 159,140 aggregate tuning hours per month at the following:<br><br>2011 $0.0017 per performance (same as NAB rates)<br>2012 $0.0020<br>2013 $0.0022<br>2014 $0.0023<br>2015 $0.0025 |
|---|---|
| **Minimum Fee** | $500 per station or channel |
| **Payment Due Date** | Minimum fees: January 31<br>Usage fees: 45th day after the end of the applicable month |
| **Late Fees** | 1.5% per month, compounded (late fees applicable to payments, statements of account, and reports of use) |
| **Reporting Waiver** | NOTE: Noncommercial Educational Webcasters with less than 55,000 total ATH per channel per month in the previous year and expect to have less than 55,000 ATH per channel per month in the applicable year can elect a reporting waiver and pay a $100 proxy fee in lieu of providing reports of use |
| **Data** | Reporting data provided in a format in accordance with then applicable regulations |
| **Format** | (1) name of service<br>(2) transmission category<br>(3) featured artist<br>(4) song title<br>(5) ISRC or album title and marketing label<br>(6) channel or program name, and play frequency (ATH not required) |

| | |
|---|---|
| **Census or Sample** | Reporting Waiver (for services with fewer than 55,000 total ATH per channel per month)<br>Sample (for services within 159,140 ATH per month)<br>Census (for services whose monthly average ATH exceeds 159,149 ATH) |
| **Frequency** | Quarterly |
| **Due Date** | 45th day after the end of each quarter |

### *12. Corporation for Public Broadcasting Settlements with SoundExchange*

The Corporation for Public Broadcasting negotiated a separate settlement for it and its affiliated public broadcasting entities that reduced its costs of simulcasting their over-the-air transmissions over the Internet. Two separate settlements, one for the period spanning 2005 though 2010, and the other spanning 2011 through 2015, are set forth below:

(a) For the period spanning January 1, 2005 through December 31, 2010:

| **Term** | 2005-2010 |
|---|---|
| **Date of Publication** | March 3, 2009 |
| **Signatories** | Corporation for Public Broadcasting |
| **Eligible Services** | Up to 450 originating public radio stations (and side channels) between 2005 and 2007; 10% growth in number of stations between 2008 and 2010, not to exceed 480 |
| **Election Process** | Stations identified by CPB |
| **Rate** | — flat payment of $1.85 million for entire term<br>— true-up payment due if aggregate ATH in the last three years exceeds 764,600,000 @ $.00251/ATH for ATH above threshold |

| **Minimum Fee** | N/A |
|---|---|
| **Payment Due Date** | — flat payment: 10 days after publication of agreement<br>— overage true-up: March 1, 2011 |
| **Late Fees** | 1.5% per month |
| **Reporting Waiver** | NOTE: All reporting to be consolidated and provided by CPB |
| **Data** | For 2004: Mediaguide playlist data along with Music ATH provided in 2004 NPR Census<br>For 2005-2008: Mediaguide playlist data along with Music ATH provided in 2007 NPR Census<br>For 2009: Station playlist data along with Music ATH representing at least 60% of total Music ATH (music ATH to be broken out by station and format)<br>For 2010: Station playlist data along with Music ATH representing at least 80% of total Music ATH (music ATH to be broken out by station and format) |
| **Format** | (1) name of station<br>(2) song title<br>(3) featured artist<br>(4) album title<br>(5) marketing label<br>(6) play frequency<br>NOTE: ATH to be provided separately broken out by station and format |
| **Census or Sample** | For 2004: N/A<br>For 2005-2008: N/A<br>For 2009: Sample (census from stations representing highest 20% of music ATH)<br>For 2010: Sample (census from stations representing highest 30% of music ATH) |

| **Frequency** | For 2009 and 2010: Quarterly |
|---|---|
| **Due Date** | For 2004-2008: N/A<br>For 2009 and 2010: First 2009 reports due 7/12/2009; thereafter reports are due within 30 days after the end of the quarter to which they pertain |

(b) For the period spanning January 1, 2010 through December 31, 2015:

| **Term** | 2011-2015 |
|---|---|
| **Date of Publication** | August 12, 2009 |
| **Signatories** | Corporation for Public Broadcasting |
| **Eligible Services** | Up to 490 originating public radio stations (and side channels); 10% annual growth in number of stations, not to exceed 530 |
| **Election Process** | Stations identified by CPB |
| **Rate** | — flat payment of $2,400,000 payable in five equal installments of $480,000 per year<br>— true-up payments due as set forth below, if aggregate annual ATH exceeds the following:<br><br>Year / ATH Cap / Per performance rate above cap<br>2011 / 279,500,000 / $0.00057 per performance<br>2012 / 280,897,500 / $0.00067<br>2013 / 282,301,988 / $0.00073<br>2014 / 283,713,497 / $0.00077<br>2015 / 285,132,065 / $0.00083<br><br>— true-up payments shall not exceed $480,000 in the aggregate for the term |

| Minimum Fee | N/A |
|---|---|
| Payment Due Date | — annual payment: December 31 of each year beginning in 2010<br>— overage true-up: March 1 of the year after the year in which they go over the cap |
| Late Fees | 1.5% per month |
| Reporting Waiver | NOTE: All reporting to be consolidated and provided by CPB |
| Data | Station playlist data along with Music ATH from all covered entities |
| Format | (1) station<br>(2) sound recording title<br>(3) featured artist<br>(4) album<br>(5) marketing label<br>(6) play frequency<br>(7) music ATH |
| Census or Sample | Sample (census from stations representing the highest 30% of reported music ATH) |
| Frequency | Quarterly |
| Due Date | 30 days after the end of each quarter |

### D. Pre-Existing Subscription Services (Music Choice)

As mentioned above, a *pre-existing subscription service* is "a service that performs sound recordings by means of noninteractive audio-only subscription digital audio transmissions, which was in existence and was making such transmissions to the public for a fee on or before July 31, 1998, and may include a limited number of sample channels representative of the subscription service that are made available on a nonsubscription basis in order to promote the subscription service." For example, certain *cable radio* services, such as Music Choice, and any other Internet radio services offered on a subscription basis that were in existence prior to July 31, 1998, would fall into this category.

On January 9, 2006, the Copyright Royalty Board commenced proceedings to determine rates for pre-existing subscription services and pre-existing satellite radio services. The only pre-existing subscription service that was a party to those proceedings was Music Choice, which subsequently reached a settlement with SoundExchange on June 12, 2007. The CRB published a Final Rule relating to pre-existing subscription services on December 19, 2007.

For the period commencing January 1, 2008 through December 31, 2011, pre-existing subscription services shall pay a royalty fee of 7.5% of monthly gross revenues resulting from residential services in the United States. For the period spanning January 1, 2012 through December 31, 2012, such fee shall be increased to 7.5%. No later than January 20 of each year, the service shall pay an advance of $100,000, recoupable from royalties payable during such year only.

## E. Pre-Existing Digital Audio Radio Subscription Services (Sirius/XM)

### *1. In General*

Users of satellite digital audio services listen to a broadcast using a receiver designed to capture audio transmissions coming, not from terrestrial based transmitters, but from transmitters residing on one or more satellites orbiting the earth. As they do with terrestrial radio stations, the listener may select the general genre or station, but the satellite broadcaster selects the specific playlist of recordings. The consumer may not select the individual tracks and may not influence the playlist other than by making a general request, much like calling in to a radio station and requesting that a particular recording be added to the day's playlist. Nor may the consumer get to keep a permanent copy of any of the recordings in the webcast.

Examples of satellite digital audio radio services include XM Satellite Radio and Sirius Satellite Radio, the firms that merged in 2008.

### *2. Legal Background*

Because broadcasts by satellite digital audio radio services are akin to traditional radio services — by virtue of their being noninteractive — consumers are less likely to record these broadcasts. Accordingly,

Congress has provided these services with a compulsory license under which they may compel owners of sound recordings to grant a license in exchange for a rate established by statute, and more specifically, the Copyright Royalty Board.

The compulsory license provision for these services is the same as those for "preexisting subscription services" and is set forth in Section 114(d)2 of the Copyright Act. In addition, these services have, under Section 112 — the ephemeral recording exemption — the right to make "server copies" of sound recordings licensed under Section 114 to facilitate their transmissions.

### 3. *Fee Structure and License Terms*

On January 24, 2008, the CRB issued a ruling setting the following rates for the period spanning 2007 though 2012:

| Year | Percent of gross revenue |
|---|---|
| 2007 | 6.0% |
| 2008 | 6.0% |
| 2009 | 6.5% |
| 2010 | 7.0% |
| 2011 | 7.5% |
| 2012 | 8.0% |

Gross revenues include all revenues paid to the service, excluding both subscription and advertising revenue associated with channels or programming that use only "incidental" performances of sound recordings as part of their programming. 73 Federal Register 382.11.

The fees cover both the compulsory license to make the transmissions (under Section 114) and the making of server copies to facilitate those transmissions (under Section 112). Fees and reports are due on a monthly basis, on or before the 45th day after the end of the month for which the fees are due, and are subject to a late fee of 1½% per month. All payments are to be rounded to the nearest cent.

The CRB has appointed SoundExchange as the sole designated collecting agent for these licenses and fees through 2012. The authority of the CRB to make such an appointment appears to be in direct conflict with the statute and their authority to do so has been challenged in the federal courts.

Detailed rules of recordkeeping for the use of sound recordings under the statutory license have been proposed by the CRB in a notice of proposed rulemaking announced in the Federal Register on December 30, 2008. 73 CFR 250, page 79727.

Notwithstanding the statutory rates set by the CRB, the parties are free to negotiate their own rates and terms should they wish to do so.

### F. Background Music Services

As discussed in Chapter 14, background music services provide public performances of music that are intended as "unobtrusive accompaniment to work, shopping, conversation, dining and relaxation" — more humorously referred to as "elevator" music. Muzak and DMX are the two largest background music services in the United States, each serving the music needs of hundreds of thousands of business establishments, including most of the major retail chains, restaurants, hotels, and other public establishments and businesses.

Transmissions by these services are usually analog transmissions, and therefore are not subject to any restrictions, because sound recording copyright owners, such as record companies, do not have an exclusive right of public performance in analog transmissions. Even where such transmissions are digital, they are exempt under Section 114(d)(1)(C)(ii) and (iv) to the extent they are delivered to business establishments. However, even though background music services may not be subject to any public performance right, they remain subject to the *reproduction rights* of the record companies. Thus, if the service needs to make copies to facilitate their transmissions — i.e., electrical transcriptions — then they must obtain a license from the record companies.

As described in Chapter 14, background music services deliver their programming to businesses by one of two means: delivery of physical copies for use on-premises or transmission by broadcast. For the reproduction of copies (i.e., phonorecords) of *sound recordings* offered by background music services, record companies typically receive the following:

On-premise: 5% to 10% (or more) of net revenues derived from subscription fees received prorated among the recordings used

Broadcast: Where the broadcast is made from CDs playing by computer control on industrial jukeboxes, no payment is made for making copies of the recordings, because none are being made to facilitate the broadcast transmissions; where tape or server copies are made, 5% to 10% (or more) of net revenues derived from subscription fees received prorated among the recordings used.

Some background music services broadcast their programming through subscription satellite services, such as EchoStar or the Dish Network. Since these broadcasts are digital audio transmissions, public performance payments may be due. To the extent such programming is transmitted to consumer for private use, the background music service, or its satellite service partner, must pay the statutory fees due to SoundExchange under the CRB Final Rule or applicable settlement under the Webcasting Settlement Act. To the extent such transmissions are received by business establishments, and meet the sound recording performance complement, they are exempt under Section 114(d) and no public performance fees would be payable to SoundExchange.

## G. Licensing Sound Recordings in Other Albums — Compilations & Special Products

As mentioned above, one of the most important and potential lucrative source of high margin revenue comes from the licensing of the record company's back catalog of recordings. Often performed by special *products divisions* of major record companies, or the business affairs staff of independent labels, labels will license individual recordings to third parties for use in motion picture sound track albums and other compilations. Fees vary, but a label may ask for an advance of between $1,000 and $5,000 against a royalty of $0.10 to $0.15 per track per copy.

## H. Licensing Sound Recordings in Films, Television Programs, and Other Audiovisual Works

A record company's special products division or a label's business affairs department is often responsible for the negotiating and licensing of back catalog recordings for use in motion pictures, television programs, home video, videogames, commercial advertising, and other media.

Licensing sound recordings in films, televisions, and other media is very similar to licensing musical compositions in such works. Many of the same considerations used by music publishers in determining the fees, structure, and scope of their *synchronization* licenses are applicable to record companies who issue master use licenses for the use of their recordings in films and television programs.

Like music publishers, record companies will demand a significant flat fee for the reproduction and distribution of the recording in the film or television program. Unlike music publishers, who have a general right of public performance in their musical works, record companies will not participate in the success of the motion picture, because they will not collect performance income in the United States when the film or television program is performed publicly. However, record companies can typically expect to receive about the same flat fee for the recording as the music publisher receives for the underlying musical work. In addition, many motion picture producers will developer a soundtrack album of the recordings and music featured in the film and record companies can expect to particulate in the success of the film to the extent it generates royalties from sales of the soundtrack album.

Licensing recordings in films also serves to reconnect an audience, or create a whole new audience, for a band or a particular recording. One example is the revival of the song *Louie Louie,* written by Richard Berry in 1955. Its best known recording was by The Kingsmen released in 1963. By the 1970s, the song and recording had long become a golden oldie, but they found an entirely new audience when both were licensed for a foreground use in a party scene in the comedy film *Animal House.* No doubt sales of the recording since that time have been far higher than they would have been had the record company declined to license the recording to the film's producers. An example of a song used in a popular television program was Frank Sinatra's recording of the song, *Love and Marriage*, used as the title theme for a television sitcom of the same name.

## I. Licensing Sound Recordings in Commercial Advertising

Licensing sound recordings in commercial advertising is also very much like licensing musical works in advertising, covered in detail in Chapter 20. Typically, the advertiser, either directly or through their agency, first identifies the musical work it would like to use in its commercial, which may or may not involve a particular recording of the song. Then, they might seek a license to the song from the appropriate music publisher. Once it is determined that a license fee is within their budget, they would then consider whether they would like to record their own version of the song or seek out a license to existing, popular recording — in which case, they would contact the applicable record company.

The license fee for the use of the recording is typically about the same as the fee paid for the use of the underlying song, unless the underlying song is relatively obscure and the recording artist is relatively famous. If the particular song is far more important to the advertiser than the original popular recording, then the advertiser's option to do a cover recording provides it with leverage to keep the costs of a master use license for the original recording down.

Sometimes, however, the song and the recording are equally indispensable and those situations — to quote Chico Marx (from the movie, *Animal Crackers)* — "that will run into money." In 1995, Microsoft was about to launch Windows '95, the new version of its popular operating system. One of the first recognizable features of the software, after its graphical user interface, was a control menu on the lower left corner of the screen, which bore simply the word, "Start."

Apparently, someone had the idea to base the advertising campaign on the popular Rolling Stones song and recording, "Start Me Up." Microsoft was keen to spend upwards of $200 million dollars on the launch of Windows '95 and, when it came to music, money, apparently, was no object. Now, the Rolling Stones had never before licensed their songs for commercial use, and the legend has it that when Microsoft came calling for a license to the song, the Stones, through their publisher and record company, quoted $4 million, thinking that at such a rate, Microsoft would just go away. But Microsoft was undeterred; to quote Chico again (from the contract negotiation scene from "Night at the Opera"), they said, "I'll take it."

When the Wall Street Journal called us to see if this was the highest amount ever paid for a song and recording, we confirmed that it was, indeed, higher than any license fee we ever heard of. The next day, the Journal reported:

> Companies don't usually rush to buy ads in another company's infomercial, and the Rolling Stones don't usually sell rights to their songs for television ads. But, then, none of the old rules seem to apply to the selling of Windows 95. Microsoft Corp. has already caused a marketing frenzy in the computer world. . . . Now is it orchestrating a buzz that is reaching far beyond the tech world, including a wide range of business partners — including the Stones, whose "Start Me Up" will be a sort of Windows 95 theme song. . . . It is the first time Stones songwriters Mick Jagger and Keith Richards have allowed commercial use of songs to which they own copyright . . .
>
> British press reports said Mr. Jagger set a price of $12 million for the use of the song, but one person familiar with the matter put the true figure closer to $4 million, an amount that would still be a record in the field. Microsoft declined comment on the price. "You can't always get what you want, but if you're Microsoft, you get what you need," said Al Kohn, a music licensing expert and retired vice president of Time Warner's Warner/Chappell Music unit.[45]

Record companies will typically require permission from the recording artist before authorizing the use in a commercial advertisement; this may be because of a contractual restriction in the artist's recording agreement or a desire to maintain good relations with the artist. Even if there's no contractual provision in the artist's contract, the artist might take the position that the use of his recording in a commercial advertisement may suggest that the artist himself has endorsed the product or service that is the subject of the advertisement.

## J. Licensing Sound Recordings in Videogames, Multimedia and Other New Media Devices, and Online Versions

As discussed in Chapter 22, on *Licensing Music in Videogames*, videogame producers are becoming increasingly aware of the

---

[45] Don Clark, "Windows 95 Buzz Will Get Even Louder," *Wall Street Journal* (August 18, 1995).

importance of music in either creating a mood or in entertaining the audience they are trying to reach. Traditionally, videogame producers have sought to engage composers on a work-for-hire basis, but they are now turning to existing recordings and recordings of up-and-coming rock bands who might appeal to the young game players.

Considerations for the licensing of existing sound recordings in video games are much like those of licensing existing musical works. Game producers who pay flat fees for the use of musical works — in the range of $1,000 to $25,000 for a buy-out or a royalty of 9¢ to 18¢ per copy — are likely to pay a similar amount for the use of a sound recording. New rock bands might accept a buy-out in the lower end of the range in exchange for the promotional value of being in the game, which might equal or exceed traditional radio airplay.

Rock bands featured on music-dedicated games such as *Guitar Hero* and *Rock Band* get paid very significant amounts of money (in the millions for the Beatles, for example) for the use of their likenesses in these games and for attending a one-time motion-capture of a typical performance. The major record companies, however, who control the original recordings by these bands have had a harder time monetizing their catalogs on these games. While the game company would greatly prefer to use the original recording, a close substitute that may be acceptable would be a recently made cover recording by the band itself. If the band were no longer under a re-recording restriction in its record contract, it could supply such a cover recording for far less than the license fees being sought by the record company for the original version. While some record companies have come to agreement with the producers of these games, others, such as Warner Music Group, are holding out for license fees, which they believe reflect the value of what they are providing.

## K. Digital Sampling

As discussed at length in Chapter 24, on *Digital Sampling*, when a recording artist uses a digital sample — even a *de minimus* amount of sound — from a copyrighted recording owned by another, he must seek permission from the copyright owner. The issuance of master use licenses for digital samples has now become commonplace — either on a one-time flat fee basis or on a royalty basis. Flat fees typically start at $2,500 and can go as high as $20,000. Royalty rates range from ½ ¢ to 5¢ per unit, with advances starting at $5,000.

### L. ISP Licensing

The mass use of peer-to-peer file-sharing software to facilitate the unauthorized downloading of popular recordings has cost the recording industry billions of dollars in lost CD and download sales. Because nearly all of the unauthorized files travel through the networks of the world's Internet Service Providers (ISPs) operated by the telephone or telecommunications carriers, record companies and music publishers have suggested that the immunity from liability for such illegal traffic that these ISPs have enjoyed should be revisited. If the ISPs were required to charge a premium, or additional flat monthly fee added to its monthly access fee, such money could be passed to music copyright owners to compensate them for the illegal use of their works.

The international recording industry has begun to put pressure on governments to require the ISPs to bear some responsibility for the piracy problem. In 2006, the government of France proposed to require users of ISP services to pay an additional monthly fee that would be distributed to the music industry as compensation for losses due to piracy. It was rejected by the French Parliament, which did support a proposal to require ISPs to disconnect broadband access to persistent pirates.

In 2007, the Belgium music rights society SABAM filed suit against Scarlet, a division of the Italy-based ISP, Tiscali.[46] A lower court in Belgium ruled that the ISP must make efforts to stop illegal file-sharing on its network by using file filtering systems. In doing so, the court had to reconcile two conflicting EU directives: the E-Commerce Directive, which declared that ISPs were not liable for the content on the websites it hosts and the later Copyright Directive, which suggested that ISPs could be responsible for copyright infringement if websites using their services were being used for unauthorized copying.

[46] SABAM v. S.A. Tiscali (Scarlet), District Court of Brussels, No. 04/8975/A (June 29, 2007), an English translation of which may be found at *http://www.cardozoaelj.net/issues/08/case001.pdf.*

With pressure increasing at the ISPs, some initial steps are being taken at the ISP level to address the problem. For example, in one of the first experiments of its kind, TDC, the Denmark-based Nordic telecommunications company, has cooperated with the major record companies in offering a "PLAY" package under which subscribers to the ISP in Nordic countries can make an unlimited number of DRM-protected downloads from a catalog of over 1 million tracks.

In January 2009, the Isle of Man, an outpost of the British Commonwealth located in the Irish Sea, proposed that its 80,000 residents would be able to download unlimited amounts of music — using even the illegal peer-to-peer networks — in exchange for a nominal fee of £1 (about $1.40) per month to be paid to their ISPs. The proposal has not yet been enacted.

In the United States, Warner Music Group has begun an initiative dubbed "Choruss," being managed by music industry veteran, Jim Griffin. Choruss, now backed by three of the major record labels, hopes to issue blanket licenses (or "covenants not to sue") to universities and, eventually, residential ISPs, to immunize the universities and ISPs for the illegal music file-sharing occurring on their networks. Choruss hopes to motivate universities to cooperate by appealing to their moral obligation "to do the right thing" and also by providing them with information upon which to base research in the fields of student behavior, network analysis, music marketing, and more. Choruss intends to work with several technology companies to track the music and recordings shared over the networks and to ensure that fees it receives from its licensing are properly distributed to copyright holders.

Other proposals, such as one that would allow ISPs to bundle "free" music services with their other offerings, have surfaced. While it is too soon to tell whether these efforts will be successful, the problem is likely to be more politically acute for the ISPs, as eBooks and full-length motion pictures come to suffer the same fate as music and recordings.

## M. Public Performances

As discussed above, historically, copyright owners of sound recordings in the United States did not enjoy an exclusive right to publicly perform their sound recordings. When a radio station plays a song over the airwaves, it pays a public performance royalty to music publishers (i.e., owners of the musical works), but not to record companies (i.e., the owners of the sound recordings). This has not been the case in most countries outside of the United States; most other countries recognize what are called *neighboring rights* in sound recordings, and record companies, through local collection societies, such as PPL in the United Kingdom (ppluk.com), disburse revenues collected from terrestrial radio stations and others who engage in the public performance of sound recordings.

For many years, the U.S. recording industry has lobbied Congress to amend the Copyright Act to provide to owners of sound recordings an exclusive right of public performance. In 1995, the recording industry won an important step toward that end when Congress passed the Digital Performance Rights in Sound Recording Act of 1995, the public performance right added to the Copyright Act was limited to those public performances made *by means of a digital audio transmission.*

Record companies are closer than ever before to persuading Congress, over the objections of the broadcasting industry, a full public performance right in sound recordings. Should such legislation be enacted, it is likely that Sound Exchange would become the collective administrator for licensing and collection of performance royalties in much the same way it does today with respect to digital audio transmissions under the compulsory license under the Copyright Act.

## VI. CONCLUSION

This chapter was intended to provide an overview of the licensing of sound recordings, with emphasis on the legal basis of their creation and their exploitation in the digital and, to some lesser extent, physical or traditional realms. As the shift from physical distribution to digital transmission continues, the record industry is going to become increasingly like the music publishing industry, with more emphasis on licensing and accounting and less on distribution. The use of technology to help market and exploit recordings, and track their income, will become increasingly important as this transition continues.

# APPENDIX TO CHAPTER 23 — LICENSING OF SOUND RECORDINGS (MASTER USE LICENSES, DIGITAL DOWNLOADING AND DIGITAL AUDIO TRANSMISSIONS)

# LAW 23.1

## 17 U.S.C. SECTION 1101 — UNAUTHORIZED FIXATION AND TRAFFICKING IN SOUND RECORDINGS AND MUSIC VIDEOS

**(a) Unauthorized Acts.** — Anyone who, without the consent of the performer or performers involved —

**(1)** fixes the sounds or sounds and images of a live musical performance in a copy or phonorecord, or reproduces copies or phonorecords of such a performance from an unauthorized fixation,

**(2)** transmits or otherwise communicates to the public the sounds or sounds and images of a live musical performance, or

**(3)** distributes or offers to distribute, sells or offers to sell, rents or offers to rent, or traffics in any copy or phonorecord fixed as described in paragraph (1), regardless of whether the fixations occurred in the United States, shall be subject to the remedies provided in sections 502 through 505, to the same extent as an infringer of copyright.

**(b) Definition.** — In this section, the term "traffic" has the same meaning as in section 2320 (e) of title 18.

**(c) Applicability.** — This section shall apply to any act or acts that occur on or after the date of the enactment of the Uruguay Round Agreements Act.

**(d) State Law Not Preempted.** — Nothing in this section may be construed to annul or limit any rights or remedies under the common law or statutes of any State.

# LAW 23.2

## 17 U.S.C. SECTION 106 — EXCLUSIVE RIGHTS IN COPYRIGHTED WORKS

### § 106. Exclusive rights in copyrighted works

Subject to sections 107 through 122, the owner of copyright under this title has the exclusive rights to do and to authorize any of the following:

**(1)** to reproduce the copyrighted work in copies or phonorecords;

**(2)** to prepare derivative works based upon the copyrighted work;

**(3)** to distribute copies or phonorecords of the copyrighted work to the public by sale or other transfer of ownership, or by rental, lease, or lending;

**(4)** in the case of literary, musical, dramatic, and choreographic works, pantomimes, and motion pictures and other audiovisual works, to perform the copyrighted work publicly;

**(5)** in the case of literary, musical, dramatic, and choreographic works, pantomimes, and pictorial, graphic, or sculptural works, including the individual images of a motion picture or other audiovisual work, to display the copyrighted work publicly; and

**(6)** in the case of sound recordings, to perform the copyrighted work publicly by means of a digital audio transmission.

# LAW 23.3

## 17 U.S.C. SECTION 114 — SCOPE OF EXCLUSIVE RIGHTS IN SOUND RECORDINGS

### § 114. Scope of exclusive rights in sound recordings

**(a)** The exclusive rights of the owner of copyright in a sound recording are limited to the rights specified by clauses (1), (2), (3) and (6) of section 106, and do not include any right of performance under section 106 (4).

**(b)** The exclusive right of the owner of copyright in a sound recording under clause (1) of section 106 is limited to the right to duplicate the sound recording in the form of phonorecords or copies that directly or indirectly recapture the actual sounds fixed in the recording. The exclusive right of the owner of copyright in a sound recording under clause (2) of section 106 is limited to the right to prepare a derivative work in which the actual sounds fixed in the sound recording are rearranged, remixed, or otherwise altered in sequence or quality. The exclusive rights of the owner of copyright in a sound recording under clauses (1) and (2) of section 106 do not extend to the making or duplication of another sound recording that consists entirely of an independent fixation of other sounds, even though such sounds imitate or simulate those in the copyrighted sound recording. The exclusive rights of the owner of copyright in a sound recording under clauses (1), (2), and (3) of section 106 do not apply to sound recordings included in educational television and radio programs (as defined in section 397 of title 47) distributed or transmitted by or through public broadcasting entities (as defined by section 118 (g)):[1] Provided, That copies or phonorecords of said programs are not commercially distributed by or through public broadcasting entities to the general public.

**(c)** This section does not limit or impair the exclusive right to perform publicly, by means of a phonorecord, any of the works specified by section 106 (4).

**(d) Limitations on Exclusive Right.** — Notwithstanding the provisions of section 106 (6) —

**(1) Exempt transmissions and retransmissions.** — The performance of a sound recording publicly by means of a digital audio transmission, other than as a part of an interactive service, is not an infringement of section 106 (6) if the performance is part of —

**(A)** a nonsubscription broadcast transmission;

**(B)** a retransmission of a nonsubscription broadcast transmission: Provided, That, in the case of a retransmission of a radio station's broadcast transmission —

**(i)** the radio station's broadcast transmission is not willfully or repeatedly retransmitted more than a radius of 150 miles from the site of the radio broadcast transmitter, however —

**(I)** the 150 mile limitation under this clause shall not apply when a nonsubscription broadcast transmission by a radio station licensed by the Federal Communications Commission is retransmitted on a nonsubscription basis by a terrestrial broadcast station, terrestrial translator, or terrestrial repeater licensed by the Federal Communications Commission; and

**(II)** in the case of a subscription retransmission of a nonsubscription broadcast retransmission covered by subclause (I), the 150 mile radius shall be measured from the transmitter site of such broadcast retransmitter;

**(ii)** the retransmission is of radio station broadcast transmissions that are —

**(I)** obtained by the retransmitter over the air;

**(II)** not electronically processed by the retransmitter to deliver separate and discrete signals; and

**(III)** retransmitted only within the local communities served by the retransmitter;

**(iii)** the radio station's broadcast transmission was being retransmitted to cable systems (as defined in section 111 (f)) by a satellite carrier on January 1, 1995, and that retransmission was being retransmitted by cable systems as a separate and discrete signal, and the satellite carrier obtains the radio station's broadcast transmission in an analog format: Provided, That the broadcast transmission being retransmitted may embody the programming of no more than one radio station; or

**(iv)** the radio station's broadcast transmission is made by a noncommercial educational broadcast station funded on or after January 1, 1995, under section 396(k) of the Communications Act of 1934 (47 U.S.C. 396 (k)), consists solely of noncommercial educational and cultural radio programs, and the retransmission, whether or not simultaneous, is a nonsubscription terrestrial broadcast retransmission; or

**(C)** a transmission that comes within any of the following categories —

**(i)** a prior or simultaneous transmission incidental to an exempt transmission, such as a feed received by and then retransmitted by an exempt transmitter: Provided, That such incidental transmissions do not include any subscription transmission directly for reception by members of the public;

**(ii)** a transmission within a business establishment, confined to its premises or the immediately surrounding vicinity;

**(iii)** a retransmission by any retransmitter, including a multichannel video programming distributor as defined in section 602(12)[1] of the Communications Act of 1934 (47 U.S.C. 522 (12)), of a transmission by a transmitter licensed to publicly perform the sound recording as a part of that transmission, if the retransmission is simultaneous with the licensed transmission and authorized by the transmitter; or

**(iv)** a transmission to a business establishment for use in the ordinary course of its business: Provided, That the business recipient does not retransmit the transmission outside of its premises or the immediately surrounding vicinity, and that the transmission does not exceed the sound recording performance complement. Nothing in this clause shall limit the scope of the exemption in clause (ii).

**(2) Statutory licensing of certain transmissions.** — The performance of a sound recording publicly by means of a subscription digital audio transmission not exempt under paragraph (1), an eligible nonsubscription transmission, or a transmission not exempt under paragraph (1) that is made by a preexisting satellite digital audio radio service shall be subject to statutory licensing, in accordance with subsection (f) if —

**(A)**

**(i)** the transmission is not part of an interactive service;

**(ii)** except in the case of a transmission to a business establishment, the transmitting entity does not automatically and intentionally cause any device receiving the transmission to switch from one program channel to another; and

**(iii)** except as provided in section 1002 (e), the transmission of the sound recording is accompanied, if technically feasible, by the information encoded in that sound recording, if any, by or under the authority of the copyright owner of that sound recording, that identifies the title of the sound recording, the featured recording artist who performs on the sound recording, and related information, including information concerning the underlying musical work and its writer;

**(B)** in the case of a subscription transmission not exempt under paragraph (1) that is made by a preexisting subscription service in the same transmission medium used by such service on July 31, 1998, or in the case of a transmission not exempt under paragraph (1) that is made by a preexisting satellite digital audio radio service —

**(i)** the transmission does not exceed the sound recording performance complement; and

**(ii)** the transmitting entity does not cause to be published by means of an advance program schedule or prior announcement the titles of the specific sound recordings or phonorecords embodying such sound recordings to be transmitted; and

**(C)** in the case of an eligible nonsubscription transmission or a subscription transmission not exempt under paragraph (1) that is made by a new subscription service or by a preexisting subscription service other than in the same transmission medium used by such service on July 31, 1998 —

**(i)** the transmission does not exceed the sound recording performance complement, except that this requirement shall not apply in the case of a retransmission of a broadcast transmission if the retransmission is made by a transmitting entity that does not have the right or ability to control the programming of the broadcast station making the broadcast transmission, unless —

**(I)** the broadcast station makes broadcast transmissions —

**(aa)** in digital format that regularly exceed the sound recording performance complement; or

**(bb)** in analog format, a substantial portion of which, on a weekly basis, exceed the sound recording performance complement; and

**(II)** the sound recording copyright owner or its representative has notified the transmitting entity in writing that broadcast transmissions of the copyright owner's sound recordings exceed the sound recording performance complement as provided in this clause;

**(ii)** the transmitting entity does not cause to be published, or induce or facilitate the publication, by means of an advance program schedule or prior announcement, the titles of the specific sound recordings to be transmitted, the phonorecords embodying such sound recordings, or, other than for illustrative purposes, the names of the featured recording artists, except that this clause does not disqualify a transmitting entity that makes a prior announcement that a particular artist will be featured within an unspecified future time period, and in the case of a retransmission of a broadcast transmission by a transmitting entity that does not have the right or ability to control the programming of the broadcast transmission, the requirement of this clause shall not apply to a prior oral announcement by the broadcast station, or to an advance program schedule published, induced, or facilitated by the broadcast station, if the transmitting entity does not have actual knowledge and has not received written notice from the copyright owner or its representative that the broadcast station publishes or induces or facilitates the publication of such advance program schedule, or if such advance program schedule is a schedule of classical music programming published by the broadcast station in the same manner as published by that broadcast station on or before September 30, 1998;

**(iii)** the transmission —

**(I)** is not part of an archived program of less than 5 hours duration;

**(II)** is not part of an archived program of 5 hours or greater in duration that is made available for a period exceeding 2 weeks;

**(III)** is not part of a continuous program which is of less than 3 hours duration; or

**(IV)** is not part of an identifiable program in which performances of sound recordings are rendered in a predetermined order, other than an archived or continuous program, that is transmitted at —

**(aa)** more than 3 times in any 2-week period that have been publicly announced in advance, in the case of a program of less than 1 hour in duration, or

**(bb)** more than 4 times in any 2-week period that have been publicly announced in advance, in the case of a program of 1 hour or more in duration, except that the requirement of this subclause shall not apply in the case of a retransmission of a broadcast transmission by a transmitting entity that does not have the right or ability to control the programming of the broadcast transmission, unless the transmitting entity is given notice in writing by the copyright owner of the sound recording that the broadcast station makes broadcast transmissions that regularly violate such requirement;

**(iv)** the transmitting entity does not knowingly perform the sound recording, as part of a service that offers transmissions of visual images contemporaneously with transmissions of sound recordings, in a manner that is likely to cause confusion, to cause mistake, or to deceive, as to the affiliation, connection, or association of the copyright owner or featured recording artist with the transmitting entity or a particular product or service advertised by the transmitting entity, or as to the origin, sponsorship, or approval by the copyright owner or featured recording artist of the activities of the transmitting entity other than the performance of the sound recording itself;

**(v)** the transmitting entity cooperates to prevent, to the extent feasible without imposing substantial costs or burdens, a transmission recipient or any other person or entity from automatically scanning the transmitting entity's transmissions alone or together with transmissions by other transmitting entities in order to select a particular sound recording to be transmitted to the transmission recipient, except that the requirement of this clause shall not apply to a satellite digital audio service that is in operation, or that is licensed by the Federal Communications Commission, on or before July 31, 1998;

**(vi)** the transmitting entity takes no affirmative steps to cause or induce the making of a phonorecord by the transmission recipient, and if the technology used by the transmitting entity enables the transmitting entity to limit the making by the transmission recipient of phonorecords of the transmission directly in a digital format, the transmitting entity sets such technology to limit such making of phonorecords to the extent permitted by such technology;

**(vii)** phonorecords of the sound recording have been distributed to the public under the authority of the copyright owner or the copyright owner authorizes the transmitting entity to transmit the sound recording, and the transmitting entity makes the transmission from a phonorecord lawfully made under the authority of the copyright owner, except that the requirement of this clause shall not apply to a retransmission of a broadcast transmission by a transmitting entity that does not have the right or ability to control the programming of the broadcast transmission, unless the transmitting entity is given notice in writing by the copyright owner of the sound recording that the broadcast station makes broadcast transmissions that regularly violate such requirement;

**(viii)** the transmitting entity accommodates and does not interfere with the transmission of technical measures that are widely used by sound recording copyright owners to identify or protect copyrighted works, and that are technically feasible of being transmitted by the transmitting entity without imposing substantial costs on the transmitting entity or resulting in perceptible aural or visual degradation of the digital signal, except that the requirement of this clause shall not apply to a satellite digital audio service that is in operation, or that is licensed under the authority of the Federal Communications Commission, on or before July 31, 1998, to the extent that such service has designed, developed, or made commitments to procure equipment or technology that is not compatible with such technical measures before such technical measures are widely adopted by sound recording copyright owners; and

**(ix)** the transmitting entity identifies in textual data the sound recording during, but not before, the time it is performed, including the title of the sound recording, the title of the phonorecord embodying such sound recording, if any, and the featured recording artist, in a manner to permit it to be displayed to the transmission recipient by the device or technology intended for receiving the service provided by the transmitting entity, except that the obligation in this clause shall not take effect until 1 year after the date of the enactment of the Digital Millennium Copyright Act and shall not apply in the case of a retransmission of a broadcast transmission by a transmitting entity that does not have the right or ability to control the programming of the broadcast transmission, or in the case in which devices or technology intended for receiving the service provided by the transmitting entity that have the capability to display such textual data are not common in the marketplace.

**(3) Licenses for transmissions by interactive services. —**

**(A)** No interactive service shall be granted an exclusive license under section 106 (6) for the performance of a sound recording publicly by means of digital audio transmission for a period in excess of 12 months, except that with respect to an exclusive license granted to an interactive service by a licensor that holds the copyright to 1,000 or fewer sound recordings, the period of such license shall not exceed 24 months: Provided, however, That the grantee of such exclusive license shall be ineligible to receive another exclusive license for the performance of that sound recording for a period of 13 months from the expiration of the prior exclusive license.

**(B)** The limitation set forth in subparagraph (A) of this paragraph shall not apply if —

**(i)** the licensor has granted and there remain in effect licenses under section 106 (6) for the public performance of sound recordings by means of digital audio transmission by at least 5 different interactive services: Provided, however, That each such license must be for a minimum of 10 percent of the copyrighted sound recordings owned by the licensor that have been licensed to interactive services, but in no event less than 50 sound recordings; or

**(ii)** the exclusive license is granted to perform publicly up to 45 seconds of a sound recording and the sole purpose of the performance is to promote the distribution or performance of that sound recording.

**(C)** Notwithstanding the grant of an exclusive or nonexclusive license of the right of public performance under section 106 (6), an interactive service may not publicly perform a sound recording unless a license has been granted for the public performance of any copyrighted musical work contained in the sound recording: Provided, That such license to publicly perform the copyrighted musical work may be granted either by a performing rights society representing the copyright owner or by the copyright owner.

**(D)** The performance of a sound recording by means of a retransmission of a digital audio transmission is not an infringement of section 106 (6) if —

**(i)** the retransmission is of a transmission by an interactive service licensed to publicly perform the sound recording to a particular member of the public as part of that transmission; and

**(ii)** the retransmission is simultaneous with the licensed transmission, authorized by the transmitter, and limited to that particular member of the public intended by the interactive service to be the recipient of the transmission.

**(E)** For the purposes of this paragraph —

**(i)** a "licensor" shall include the licensing entity and any other entity under any material degree of common ownership, management, or control that owns copyrights in sound recordings; and

**(ii)** a "performing rights society" is an association or corporation that licenses the public performance of nondramatic musical works on behalf of the copyright owner, such as the American Society of Composers, Authors and Publishers, Broadcast Music, Inc., and SESAC, Inc.

**(4) Rights not otherwise limited. —**

**(A)** Except as expressly provided in this section, this section does not limit or impair the exclusive right to perform a sound recording publicly by means of a digital audio transmission under section 106 (6).

**(B)** Nothing in this section annuls or limits in any way —

**(i)** the exclusive right to publicly perform a musical work, including by means of a digital audio transmission, under section 106 (4);

**(ii)** the exclusive rights in a sound recording or the musical work embodied therein under sections 106 (1), 106 (2) and 106 (3); or

**(iii)** any other rights under any other clause of section 106, or remedies available under this title, as such rights or remedies exist either before or after the date of enactment of the Digital Performance Right in Sound Recordings Act of 1995.

**(C)** Any limitations in this section on the exclusive right under section 106 (6) apply only to the exclusive right under section 106 (6) and not to any other exclusive rights under section 106. Nothing in this section shall be construed to annul, limit, impair or otherwise affect in any way the ability of the owner of a copyright in a sound recording to exercise the rights under sections 106 (1), 106 (2) and 106 (3), or to obtain the remedies available under this title pursuant to such rights, as such rights and remedies exist either before or after the date of enactment of the Digital Performance Right in Sound Recordings Act of 1995.

**(e) Authority for Negotiations. —**

**(1)** Notwithstanding any provision of the antitrust laws, in negotiating statutory licenses in accordance with subsection (f), any copyright owners of sound recordings and any entities performing sound recordings affected by this section may negotiate and agree upon the royalty rates and license terms and conditions for the performance of such sound recordings and the proportionate division of fees paid among copyright owners, and may designate common agents on a nonexclusive basis to negotiate, agree to, pay, or receive payments.

**(2)** For licenses granted under section 106 (6), other than statutory licenses, such as for performances by interactive services or performances that exceed the sound recording performance complement —

**(A)** copyright owners of sound recordings affected by this section may designate common agents to act on their behalf to grant licenses and receive and remit royalty payments: Provided, That each copyright owner shall establish the royalty rates and material license terms and conditions unilaterally, that is, not in agreement, combination, or concert with other copyright owners of sound recordings; and

**(B)** entities performing sound recordings affected by this section may designate common agents to act on their behalf to obtain licenses and collect and pay royalty fees: Provided, That each entity performing sound recordings shall determine the royalty rates and material license terms and conditions unilaterally, that is, not in agreement, combination, or concert with other entities performing sound recordings.

**(f) Licenses for Certain Nonexempt Transmissions. —**

**(1)**

**(A)** Proceedings under chapter 8 shall determine reasonable rates and terms of royalty payments for subscription transmissions by preexisting subscription services and transmissions by preexisting satellite digital audio radio services specified by subsection (d)(2) during the 5-year period beginning on January 1 of the second year following the year in which the proceedings are to be commenced, except in the case of a different transitional period provided under section 6(b)(3) of the Copyright Royalty and Distribution Reform Act of 2004, or such other period as the parties may agree. Such terms and rates shall distinguish among the different types of digital audio transmission services then in operation. Any copyright owners of sound recordings, preexisting subscription services, or preexisting satellite digital audio radio services may submit to the Copyright Royalty Judges licenses covering such subscription transmissions with respect to such sound recordings. The parties to each proceeding shall bear their own costs.

**(B)** The schedule of reasonable rates and terms determined by the Copyright Royalty Judges shall, subject to paragraph (3), be binding on all copyright owners of sound recordings and entities performing sound recordings affected by this paragraph during the 5-year period specified in subparagraph (A), a transitional period provided under section 6(b)(3) of the Copyright Royalty and Distribution Reform Act of 2004, or such other period as the parties may agree. In establishing rates and terms for preexisting subscription services and preexisting satellite digital audio radio services, in addition to the objectives set forth in section 801 (b)(1), the Copyright Royalty Judges may consider the rates and terms for comparable types of subscription digital audio transmission services and comparable circumstances under voluntary license agreements described in subparagraph (A).

**(C)** The procedures under subparagraphs (A) and (B) also shall be initiated pursuant to a petition filed by any copyright owners of sound recordings, any preexisting subscription services, or any preexisting satellite digital audio radio services indicating that a new type of subscription digital audio transmission service on which sound recordings are performed is or is about to become operational, for the purpose of determining reasonable terms and rates of royalty payments with respect to such new type of transmission service for the period beginning with the inception of such new type of service and ending on the date on which the royalty rates and terms for subscription digital audio transmission services most recently determined under subparagraph (A) or (B) and chapter 8 expire, or such other period as the parties may agree.

**(2)**

**(A)** Proceedings under chapter 8 shall determine reasonable rates and terms of royalty payments for public performances of sound recordings by means of eligible nonsubscription transmission services and new subscription services specified by subsection (d)(2) during the 5-year period beginning on January 1 of the second year following the year in which the proceedings are to be commenced, except in the case of a different transitional period provided under section 6(b)(3) of the Copyright Royalty and Distribution Reform Act of 2004, or such other period as the parties may agree. Such rates and terms shall distinguish among the different types of eligible nonsubscription transmission services and new subscription services then in operation and shall include a minimum fee for each such type of service. Any copyright owners of sound recordings or any entities performing sound recordings affected by this paragraph may submit to the Copyright Royalty Judges licenses covering such eligible nonsubscription transmissions and new subscription services with respect to such sound recordings. The parties to each proceeding shall bear their own costs.

**(B)** The schedule of reasonable rates and terms determined by the Copyright Royalty Judges shall, subject to paragraph (3), be binding on all copyright owners of sound recordings and entities performing sound recordings affected by this paragraph during the 5-year period specified in subparagraph (A), a transitional period provided under section 6(b)(3) of the Copyright Royalty and Distribution[2] Act of 2004, or such other period as the parties may agree. Such rates and terms shall distinguish among the different types of eligible nonsubscription transmission services then in operation and shall include a minimum fee for each such type of service, such differences to be based on criteria including, but not limited to, the quantity and nature of the use of sound recordings and the degree to which use of the service may substitute for or may promote the purchase of phonorecords by consumers. In establishing rates and terms for transmissions by eligible nonsubscription services and new subscription services, the Copyright Royalty Judges shall establish rates and terms that most clearly represent the rates and terms that would have been negotiated in the marketplace between a willing buyer and a willing seller. In determining such rates and terms, the Copyright Royalty Judges shall base its[3] decision on economic, competitive and programming information presented by the parties, including —

**(i)** whether use of the service may substitute for or may promote the sales of phonorecords or otherwise may interfere with or may enhance the sound recording copyright owner's other streams of revenue from its sound recordings; and

**(ii)** the relative roles of the copyright owner and the transmitting entity in the copyrighted work and the service made available to the public with respect to relative creative contribution, technological contribution, capital investment, cost, and risk.

In establishing such rates and terms, the Copyright Royalty Judges may consider the rates and terms for comparable types of digital audio transmission services and comparable circumstances under voluntary license agreements described in subparagraph (A).

**(C)** The procedures under subparagraphs (A) and (B) shall also be initiated pursuant to a petition filed by any copyright owners of sound recordings or any eligible nonsubscription service or new subscription service indicating that a new type of eligible nonsubscription service or new subscription service on which sound recordings are performed is or is about to become operational, for the purpose of determining reasonable terms and rates of royalty payments with respect to such new type of service for the period beginning with the inception of such new type of service and ending on the date on which the royalty rates and terms for preexisting subscription digital audio transmission services or preexisting satellite digital radio audio services, as the case may be, most recently determined under subparagraph (A) or (B) and chapter 8 expire, or such other period as the parties may agree.

**(3)** License agreements voluntarily negotiated at any time between 1 or more copyright owners of sound recordings and 1 or more entities performing sound recordings shall be given effect in lieu of any decision by the Librarian of Congress or determination by the Copyright Royalty Judges.

**(4)**

**(A)** The Copyright Royalty Judges shall also establish requirements by which copyright owners may receive reasonable notice of the use of their sound recordings under this section, and under which records of such use shall be kept and made available by entities performing sound recordings. The notice and recordkeeping rules in effect on the day before the effective date of the Copyright Royalty and Distribution Reform Act of 2004 shall remain in effect unless and until new regulations are promulgated by the Copyright Royalty Judges. If new regulations are promulgated under this subparagraph, the Copyright Royalty Judges shall take into account the substance and effect of the rules in effect on the day before the effective date of the Copyright Royalty and Distribution Reform Act of 2004 and shall, to the extent practicable, avoid significant disruption of the functions of any designated agent authorized to collect and distribute royalty fees.

**(B)** Any person who wishes to perform a sound recording publicly by means of a transmission eligible for statutory licensing under this subsection may do so without infringing the exclusive right of the copyright owner of the sound recording —

**(i)** by complying with such notice requirements as the Copyright Royalty Judges shall prescribe by regulation and by paying royalty fees in accordance with this subsection; or

**(ii)** if such royalty fees have not been set, by agreeing to pay such royalty fees as shall be determined in accordance with this subsection.

**(C)** Any royalty payments in arrears shall be made on or before the twentieth day of the month next succeeding the month in which the royalty fees are set.

**(5)**

**(A)** Notwithstanding section 112 (e) and the other provisions of this subsection, the receiving agent may enter into agreements for the reproduction and performance of sound recordings under section 112 (e) and this section by any 1 or more small commercial webcasters or noncommercial webcasters during the period beginning on October 28, 1998, and ending on December 31, 2004, that, once published in the Federal Register pursuant to subparagraph (B), shall be binding on all copyright owners of sound recordings and other persons entitled to payment under this section, in lieu of any determination by a copyright arbitration royalty panel or decision by the Librarian of Congress. Any such agreement for small commercial webcasters shall include provisions for payment of royalties on the basis of a percentage of revenue or expenses, or both, and include a minimum fee. Any such agreement may include other terms and conditions, including requirements by which copyright owners may receive notice of the use of their sound recordings and under which records of such use shall be kept and made available by small commercial webcasters or noncommercial webcasters. The receiving agent shall be under no obligation to negotiate any such agreement. The receiving agent shall have no obligation to any copyright owner of sound recordings or any other person entitled to payment under this section in negotiating any such agreement, and no liability to any copyright owner of sound recordings or any other person entitled to payment under this section for having entered into such agreement.

**(B)** The Copyright Office shall cause to be published in the Federal Register any agreement entered into pursuant to subparagraph (A). Such publication shall include a statement containing the substance of subparagraph (C). Such agreements shall not be included in the Code of Federal Regulations. Thereafter, the terms of such agreement shall be available, as an option, to any small commercial webcaster or noncommercial webcaster meeting the eligibility conditions of such agreement.

**(C)** Neither subparagraph (A) nor any provisions of any agreement entered into pursuant to subparagraph (A), including any rate structure, fees, terms, conditions, or notice and recordkeeping requirements set forth therein, shall be admissible as evidence or otherwise taken into account in any administrative, judicial, or other government proceeding involving the setting or adjustment of the royalties payable for the public performance or reproduction in ephemeral phonorecords or copies of sound recordings, the determination of terms or conditions related thereto, or the establishment of notice or recordkeeping requirements by the Librarian of Congress under paragraph (4) or section 112 (e)(4). It is the intent of Congress that any royalty rates, rate structure, definitions, terms, conditions, or notice and recordkeeping requirements, included in such agreements shall be considered as a compromise motivated by the unique business, economic and political circumstances of small webcasters, copyright owners, and performers rather than as matters that would have been negotiated in the marketplace between a willing buyer and a willing seller, or otherwise meet the objectives set forth in section 801 (b).

**(D)** Nothing in the Small Webcaster Settlement Act of 2002 or any agreement entered into pursuant to subparagraph (A) shall be taken into account by the United States Court of Appeals for the District of Columbia Circuit in its review of the determination by the Librarian of Congress of July 8, 2002, of rates and terms for the digital performance of sound recordings and ephemeral recordings, pursuant to sections 112 and 114.

**(E)** As used in this paragraph —

**(i)** the term "noncommercial webcaster" means a webcaster that —

**(I)** is exempt from taxation under section 501 of the Internal Revenue Code of 1986 (26 U.S.C. 501);

**(II)** has applied in good faith to the Internal Revenue Service for exemption from taxation under section 501 of the Internal Revenue Code and has a commercially reasonable expectation that such exemption shall be granted; or

**(III)** is operated by a State or possession or any governmental entity or subordinate thereof, or by the United States or District of Columbia, for exclusively public purposes;

**(ii)** the term "receiving agent" shall have the meaning given that term in section 261.2 of title 37, Code of Federal Regulations, as published in the Federal Register on July 8, 2002; and

**(iii)** the term "webcaster" means a person or entity that has obtained a compulsory license under section 112 or 114 and the implementing regulations therefor to make eligible nonsubscription transmissions and ephemeral recordings.

**(F)** The authority to make settlements pursuant to subparagraph (A) shall expire December 15, 2002, except with respect to noncommercial webcasters for whom the authority shall expire May 31, 2003.

**(g) Proceeds From Licensing of Transmissions. —**

**(1)** Except in the case of a transmission licensed under a statutory license in accordance with subsection (f) of this section —

**(A)** a featured recording artist who performs on a sound recording that has been licensed for a transmission shall be entitled to receive payments from the copyright owner of the sound recording in accordance with the terms of the artist's contract; and

**(B)** a nonfeatured recording artist who performs on a sound recording that has been licensed for a transmission shall be entitled to receive payments from the copyright owner of the sound recording in accordance with the terms of the nonfeatured recording artist's applicable contract or other applicable agreement.

**(2)** An agent designated to distribute receipts from the licensing of transmissions in accordance with subsection (f) shall distribute such receipts as follows:

**(A)** 50 percent of the receipts shall be paid to the copyright owner of the exclusive right under section 106 (6) of this title to publicly perform a sound recording by means of a digital audio transmission.

**(B)** 21/2 percent of the receipts shall be deposited in an escrow account managed by an independent administrator jointly appointed by copyright owners of sound recordings and the American Federation of Musicians (or any successor entity) to be distributed to nonfeatured musicians (whether or not members of the American Federation of Musicians) who have performed on sound recordings.

**(C)** 21/2 percent of the receipts shall be deposited in an escrow account managed by an independent administrator jointly appointed by copyright owners of sound recordings and the American Federation of Television and Radio Artists (or any successor entity) to be distributed to nonfeatured vocalists (whether or not members of the American Federation of Television and Radio Artists) who have performed on sound recordings.

**(D)** 45 percent of the receipts shall be paid, on a per sound recording basis, to the recording artist or artists featured on such sound recording (or the persons conveying rights in the artists' performance in the sound recordings).

**(3)** A nonprofit agent designated to distribute receipts from the licensing of transmissions in accordance with subsection (f) may deduct from any of its receipts, prior to the distribution of such receipts to any person or entity entitled thereto other than copyright owners and performers who have elected to receive royalties from another designated agent and have notified such nonprofit agent in writing of such election, the reasonable costs of such agent incurred after November 1, 1995, in —

**(A)** the administration of the collection, distribution, and calculation of the royalties;

**(B)** the settlement of disputes relating to the collection and calculation of the royalties; and

**(C)** the licensing and enforcement of rights with respect to the making of ephemeral recordings and performances subject to licensing under section 112 and this section, including those incurred in participating in negotiations or arbitration proceedings under section 112 and this section, except that all costs incurred relating to the section 112 ephemeral recordings right may only be deducted from the royalties received pursuant to section 112.

**(4)** Notwithstanding paragraph (3), any designated agent designated to distribute receipts from the licensing of transmissions in accordance with subsection (f) may deduct from any of its receipts, prior to the distribution of such receipts, the reasonable costs identified in paragraph (3) of such agent incurred after November 1, 1995, with respect to such copyright owners and performers who have entered with such agent a contractual relationship that specifies that such costs may be deducted from such royalty receipts.

**(h) Licensing to Affiliates. —**

**(1)** If the copyright owner of a sound recording licenses an affiliated entity the right to publicly perform a sound recording by means of a digital audio transmission under section 106 (6), the copyright owner shall make the licensed sound recording available under section 106 (6) on no less favorable terms and conditions to all bona fide entities that offer similar services, except that, if there are material differences in the scope of the requested license with respect to the type of service, the particular sound recordings licensed, the frequency of use, the number of subscribers served, or the duration, then the copyright owner may establish different terms and conditions for such other services.

**(2)** The limitation set forth in paragraph (1) of this subsection shall not apply in the case where the copyright owner of a sound recording licenses —

**(A)** an interactive service; or

**(B)** an entity to perform publicly up to 45 seconds of the sound recording and the sole purpose of the performance is to promote the distribution or performance of that sound recording.

**(i) No Effect on Royalties for Underlying Works. —** License fees payable for the public performance of sound recordings under section 106 (6) shall not be taken into account in any administrative, judicial, or other governmental proceeding to set or adjust the royalties payable to copyright owners of musical works for the public performance of their works. It is the intent of Congress that royalties payable to copyright owners of musical works for the public performance of their works shall not be diminished in any respect as a result of the rights granted by section 106 (6).

**(j) Definitions. —** As used in this section, the following terms have the following meanings:

**(1)** An "affiliated entity" is an entity engaging in digital audio transmissions covered by section 106 (6), other than an interactive service, in which the licensor has any direct or indirect partnership or any ownership interest amounting to 5 percent or more of the outstanding voting or non-voting stock.

**(2)** An "archived program" is a predetermined program that is available repeatedly on the demand of the transmission recipient and that is performed in the same order from the beginning, except that an archived program shall not include a recorded event or broadcast transmission that makes no more than an incidental use of sound recordings, as long as such recorded event or broadcast transmission does not contain an entire sound recording or feature a particular sound recording.

**(3)** A "broadcast" transmission is a transmission made by a terrestrial broadcast station licensed as such by the Federal Communications Commission.

**(4)** A "continuous program" is a predetermined program that is continuously performed in the same order and that is accessed at a point in the program that is beyond the control of the transmission recipient.

**(5)** A "digital audio transmission" is a digital transmission as defined in section 101, that embodies the transmission of a sound recording. This term does not include the transmission of any audiovisual work.

**(6)** An "eligible nonsubscription transmission" is a noninteractive nonsubscription digital audio transmission not exempt under subsection (d)(1) that is made as part of a service that provides audio programming consisting, in whole or in part, of performances of sound recordings, including retransmissions of broadcast transmissions, if the primary purpose of the service is to provide to the public such audio or other entertainment programming, and the primary purpose of the service is not to sell, advertise, or promote particular products or services other than sound recordings, live concerts, or other music-related events.

**(7)** An "interactive service" is one that enables a member of the public to receive a transmission of a program specially created for the recipient, or on request, a transmission of a particular sound recording, whether or not as part of a program, which is selected by or on behalf of the recipient. The ability of individuals to request that particular sound recordings be performed for reception by the public at large, or in the case of a subscription service, by all subscribers of the service, does not make a service interactive, if the programming on each channel of the service does not substantially consist of sound recordings that are performed within 1 hour of the request or at a time designated by either the transmitting entity or the individual making such request. If an entity offers both interactive and noninteractive services (either concurrently or at different times), the noninteractive component shall not be treated as part of an interactive service.

**(8)** A "new subscription service" is a service that performs sound recordings by means of noninteractive subscription digital audio transmissions and that is not a preexisting subscription service or a preexisting satellite digital audio radio service.

**(9)** A "nonsubscription" transmission is any transmission that is not a subscription transmission.

**(10)** A "preexisting satellite digital audio radio service" is a subscription satellite digital audio radio service provided pursuant to a satellite digital audio radio service license issued by the Federal Communications Commission on or before July 31, 1998, and any renewal of such license to the extent of the scope of the original license, and may include a limited number of sample channels representative of the subscription service that are made available on a nonsubscription basis in order to promote the subscription service.

**(11)** A "preexisting subscription service" is a service that performs sound recordings by means of noninteractive audio-only subscription digital audio transmissions, which was in existence and was making such transmissions to the public for a fee on or before July 31, 1998, and may include a limited number of sample channels representative of the subscription service that are made available on a nonsubscription basis in order to promote the subscription service.

**(12)** A "retransmission" is a further transmission of an initial transmission, and includes any further retransmission of the same transmission. Except as provided in this section, a transmission qualifies as a "retransmission" only if it is simultaneous with the initial transmission. Nothing in this definition shall be construed to exempt a transmission that fails to satisfy a separate element required to qualify for an exemption under section 114 (d)(1).

**(13)** The "sound recording performance complement" is the transmission during any 3-hour period, on a particular channel used by a transmitting entity, of no more than —

**(A)** 3 different selections of sound recordings from any one phonorecord lawfully distributed for public performance or sale in the United States, if no more than 2 such selections are transmitted consecutively; or

**(B)** 4 different selections of sound recordings —

**(i)** by the same featured recording artist; or

**(ii)** from any set or compilation of phonorecords lawfully distributed together as a unit for public performance or sale in the United States,

if no more than three such selections are transmitted consecutively:

Provided, That the transmission of selections in excess of the numerical limits provided for in clauses (A) and (B) from multiple phonorecords shall nonetheless qualify as a sound recording performance complement if the programming of the multiple phonorecords was not willfully intended to avoid the numerical limitations prescribed in such clauses.

**(14)** A "subscription" transmission is a transmission that is controlled and limited to particular recipients, and for which consideration is required to be paid or otherwise given by or on behalf of the recipient to receive the transmission or a package of transmissions including the transmission.

**(15)** A "transmission" is either an initial transmission or a retransmission.

---

[1] See References in Text note below.

[2] So in original. Probably should be followed by "Reform".

[3] So in original. Probably should be "their".

# LAW 23.4

## 17 U.S.C. SECTION 112 — LIMITATION ON EXCLUSIVE RIGHTS — EPHEMERAL RECORDINGS

### § 112. Limitations on exclusive rights: Ephemeral recordings

**(a)**

**(1)** Notwithstanding the provisions of section 106, and except in the case of a motion picture or other audiovisual work, it is not an infringement of copyright for a transmitting organization entitled to transmit to the public a performance or display of a work, under a license, including a statutory license under section 114 (f), or transfer of the copyright or under the limitations on exclusive rights in sound recordings specified by section 114 (a), or for a transmitting organization that is a broadcast radio or television station licensed as such by the Federal Communications Commission and that makes a broadcast transmission of a performance of a sound recording in a digital format on a nonsubscription basis, to make no more than one copy or phonorecord of a particular transmission program embodying the performance or display, if —

**(A)** the copy or phonorecord is retained and used solely by the transmitting organization that made it, and no further copies or phonorecords are reproduced from it; and

**(B)** the copy or phonorecord is used solely for the transmitting organization's own transmissions within its local service area, or for purposes of archival preservation or security; and

**(C)** unless preserved exclusively for archival purposes, the copy or phonorecord is destroyed within six months from the date the transmission program was first transmitted to the public.

**(2)** In a case in which a transmitting organization entitled to make a copy or phonorecord under paragraph (1) in connection with the transmission to the public of a performance or display of a work is prevented from making such copy or phonorecord by reason of the application by the copyright owner of technical measures that prevent the reproduction of the work, the copyright owner shall make available to the transmitting organization the necessary means for permitting the making of such copy or phonorecord as permitted under that paragraph, if it is technologically feasible and economically reasonable for the copyright owner to do so. If the copyright owner fails to do so in a timely manner in light of the transmitting organization's reasonable business requirements, the transmitting organization shall not be liable for a violation of section 1201 (a)(1) of this title for engaging in such activities as are necessary to make such copies or phonorecords as permitted under paragraph (1) of this subsection.

**(b)** Notwithstanding the provisions of section 106, it is not an infringement of copyright for a governmental body or other nonprofit organization entitled to transmit a performance or display of a work, under section 110 (2) or under the limitations on exclusive rights in sound recordings specified by section 114 (a), to make no more than thirty copies or phonorecords of a particular transmission program embodying the performance or display, if —

**(1)** no further copies or phonorecords are reproduced from the copies or phonorecords made under this clause; and

**(2)** except for one copy or phonorecord that may be preserved exclusively for archival purposes, the copies or phonorecords are destroyed within seven years from the date the transmission program was first transmitted to the public.

**(c)** Notwithstanding the provisions of section 106, it is not an infringement of copyright for a governmental body or other nonprofit organization to make for distribution no more than one copy or phonorecord, for each transmitting organization specified in clause (2) of this subsection, of a particular transmission program embodying a performance of a nondramatic musical work of a religious nature, or of a sound recording of such a musical work, if —

**(1)** there is no direct or indirect charge for making or distributing any such copies or phonorecords; and

**(2)** none of such copies or phonorecords is used for any performance other than a single transmission to the public by a transmitting organization entitled to transmit to the public a performance of the work under a license or transfer of the copyright; and

**(3)** except for one copy or phonorecord that may be preserved exclusively for archival purposes, the copies or phonorecords are all destroyed within one year from the date the transmission program was first transmitted to the public.

**(d)** Notwithstanding the provisions of section 106, it is not an infringement of copyright for a governmental body or other nonprofit organization entitled to transmit a performance of a work under section 110 (8) to make no more than ten copies or phonorecords embodying the performance, or to permit the use of any such copy or phonorecord by any governmental body or nonprofit organization entitled to transmit a performance of a work under section 110 (8), if —

**(1)** any such copy or phonorecord is retained and used solely by the organization that made it, or by a governmental body or nonprofit organization entitled to transmit a performance of a work under section 110 (8), and no further copies or phonorecords are reproduced from it; and

**(2)** any such copy or phonorecord is used solely for transmissions authorized under section 110 (8), or for purposes of archival preservation or security; and

**(3)** the governmental body or nonprofit organization permitting any use of any such copy or phonorecord by any governmental body or nonprofit organization under this subsection does not make any charge for such use.

**(e) Statutory License. —**

**(1)** A transmitting organization entitled to transmit to the public a performance of a sound recording under the limitation on exclusive rights specified by section 114 (d)(1)(C)(iv) or under a statutory license in accordance with section 114 (f) is entitled to a statutory license, under the conditions specified by this subsection, to make no more than 1 phonorecord of the sound recording (unless the terms and conditions of the statutory license allow for more), if the following conditions are satisfied:

**(A)** The phonorecord is retained and used solely by the transmitting organization that made it, and no further phonorecords are reproduced from it.

**(B)** The phonorecord is used solely for the transmitting organization's own transmissions originating in the United States under a statutory license in accordance with section 114 (f) or the limitation on exclusive rights specified by section 114 (d)(1)(C)(iv).

**(C)** Unless preserved exclusively for purposes of archival preservation, the phonorecord is destroyed within 6 months from the date the sound recording was first transmitted to the public using the phonorecord.

**(D)** Phonorecords of the sound recording have been distributed to the public under the authority of the copyright owner or the copyright owner authorizes the transmitting entity to transmit the sound recording, and the transmitting entity makes the phonorecord under this subsection from a phonorecord lawfully made and acquired under the authority of the copyright owner.

**(2)** Notwithstanding any provision of the antitrust laws, any copyright owners of sound recordings and any transmitting organizations entitled to a statutory license under this subsection may negotiate and agree upon royalty rates and license terms and conditions for making phonorecords of such sound recordings under this section and the proportionate division of fees paid among copyright owners, and may designate common agents to negotiate, agree to, pay, or receive such royalty payments.

**(3)** Proceedings under chapter 8 shall determine reasonable rates and terms of royalty payments for the activities specified by paragraph (1) during the 5-year period beginning on January 1 of the second year following the year in which the proceedings are to be commenced, or such other period as the parties may agree. Such rates shall include a minimum fee for each type of service offered by transmitting organizations. Any copyright owners of sound recordings or any transmitting organizations entitled to a statutory license under this subsection may submit to the Copyright Royalty Judges licenses covering such activities with respect to such sound recordings. The parties to each proceeding shall bear their own costs.

**(4)** The schedule of reasonable rates and terms determined by the Copyright Royalty Judges shall, subject to paragraph (5), be binding on all copyright owners of sound recordings and transmitting organizations entitled to a statutory license under this subsection during the 5-year period specified in paragraph (3), or such other period as the parties may agree. Such rates shall include a minimum fee for each type of service offered by transmitting organizations. The Copyright Royalty Judges shall establish rates that most clearly represent the fees that would have been negotiated in the marketplace between a willing buyer and a willing seller. In determining such rates and terms, the Copyright Royalty Judges shall base their decision on economic, competitive, and programming information presented by the parties, including —

**(A)** whether use of the service may substitute for or may promote the sales of phonorecords or otherwise interferes with or enhances the copyright owner's traditional streams of revenue; and

**(B)** the relative roles of the copyright owner and the transmitting organization in the copyrighted work and the service made available to the public with respect to relative creative contribution, technological contribution, capital investment, cost, and risk.

In establishing such rates and terms, the Copyright Royalty Judges may consider the rates and terms under voluntary license agreements described in paragraphs (2) and (3). The Copyright Royalty Judges shall also establish requirements by which copyright owners may receive reasonable notice of the use of their sound recordings under this section, and under which records of such use shall be kept and made available by transmitting organizations entitled to obtain a statutory license under this subsection.

**(5)** License agreements voluntarily negotiated at any time between 1 or more copyright owners of sound recordings and 1 or more transmitting organizations entitled to obtain a statutory license under this subsection shall be given effect in lieu of any decision by the Librarian of Congress or determination by the Copyright Royalty Judges.

**(6)**

**(A)** Any person who wishes to make a phonorecord of a sound recording under a statutory license in accordance with this subsection may do so without infringing the exclusive right of the copyright owner of the sound recording under section 106 (1) —

**(i)** by complying with such notice requirements as the Copyright Royalty Judges shall prescribe by regulation and by paying royalty fees in accordance with this subsection; or

**(ii)** if such royalty fees have not been set, by agreeing to pay such royalty fees as shall be determined in accordance with this subsection.

**(B)** Any royalty payments in arrears shall be made on or before the 20th day of the month next succeeding the month in which the royalty fees are set.

**(7)** If a transmitting organization entitled to make a phonorecord under this subsection is prevented from making such phonorecord by reason of the application by the copyright owner of technical measures that prevent the reproduction of the sound recording, the copyright owner shall make available to the transmitting organization the necessary means for permitting the making of such phonorecord as permitted under this subsection, if it is technologically feasible and economically reasonable for the copyright owner to do so. If the copyright owner fails to do so in a timely manner in light of the transmitting organization's reasonable business requirements, the transmitting organization shall not be liable for a violation of section 1201 (a)(1) of this title for engaging in such activities as are necessary to make such phonorecords as permitted under this subsection.

**(8)** Nothing in this subsection annuls, limits, impairs, or otherwise affects in any way the existence or value of any of the exclusive rights of the copyright owners in a sound recording, except as otherwise provided in this subsection, or in a musical work, including the exclusive rights to reproduce and distribute a sound recording or musical work, including by means of a digital phonorecord delivery, under sections 106 (1), 106 (3), and 115, and the right to perform publicly a sound recording or musical work, including by means of a digital audio transmission, under sections 106 (4) and 106 (6).

**(f)**

**(1)** Notwithstanding the provisions of section 106, and without limiting the application of subsection (b), it is not an infringement of copyright for a governmental body or other nonprofit educational institution entitled under section 110 (2) to transmit a performance or display to make copies or phonorecords of a work that is in digital form and, solely to the extent permitted in paragraph (2), of a work that is in analog form, embodying the performance or display to be used for making transmissions authorized under section 110 (2), if —

**(A)** such copies or phonorecords are retained and used solely by the body or institution that made them, and no further copies or phonorecords are reproduced from them, except as authorized under section 110 (2); and

**(B)** such copies or phonorecords are used solely for transmissions authorized under section 110 (2).

**(2)** This subsection does not authorize the conversion of print or other analog versions of works into digital formats, except that such conversion is permitted hereunder, only with respect to the amount of such works authorized to be performed or displayed under section 110 (2), if —

**(A)** no digital version of the work is available to the institution; or

**(B)** the digital version of the work that is available to the institution is subject to technological protection measures that prevent its use for section 110 (2).

**(g)** The transmission program embodied in a copy or phonorecord made under this section is not subject to protection as a derivative work under this title except with the express consent of the owners of copyright in the preexisting works employed in the program.

Chapter 24

# The Digital Sampling Controversy

## Summary

# CHAPTER 24

# THE DIGITAL SAMPLING CONTROVERSY

A cold chill raced across the face of the recording industry when a federal district court in New York invoked the Seventh Commandment[1] in a lawsuit filed by British recording artist and songwriter Gilbert O'Sullivan against the rap music recording artist Biz Markie and his record company Cold Chillin' Records, after Markie included in his rap album entitled *I Need a Haircut* a *digital sample* of three words and their accompanying music taken from the popular recording of O'Sullivan's hit song *Alone Again (Naturally)*.[2] Markie's album might as well have been entitled *I Need a Lawyer*, as the court proceeded to enjoin all sales of the album and specifically referred the matter to the United States Attorney for consideration of prosecution under the provisions of federal law that make such infringements criminal acts subject to fines and imprisonment.[3]

This chapter will sketch the technical and legal background of digital sampling and will outline some of the practices currently emerging in connection with the licensing of and settlement of disputes about sampling activities.

## I. Technical Background

The term *digital sampling*, or *sampling,* refers to the recording of a sound, or a portion of a previously existing sound recording, with the aid of a device that can store the recording in binary form in the memory of

[1] "Thou shalt not steal," Exodus, Chapter 20: Verse 15.

[2] *Grand Upright Music Limited v. Warner Bros. Records, Inc.*, 780 F. Supp. 182 (S.D.N.Y. 1991). Interestingly, Markie's next album was entitled "All Samples Cleared."

[3] 17 U.S.C. Sec. 506(a) and 18 U.S.C. Sec. 2319.

a computer. Sampling was made possible by the emergence of digital sound and computer technology developed in the 1960 and 1970 and has been made practical in the 1980 and 1990 by the widespread availability of inexpensive sampling-capable digital synthesizers and personal computers.

In scientific terms, music is a series of sound waves that emanate from a musical instrument (e.g., violin, vocal chords). These waves cause *analogous* vibrations on the human eardrum, which are then transmitted to the human brain and, by act of Providence, perceived by the human mind. Sound waves may be recorded in tangible media, such as a phonograph record or a tape recorder, by various technological means. These recordings may be made in *analog* form — analogously reflecting the vibrations of the analog sound waves, such as the grooves of a vinyl phonograph record — or in *digital* form, recorded on tape or on compact disc.

An analog performance, or a recording of an analog performance, may be converted to digital form with the aid of a device that converts the analog sound waves into a *digital code*. This is accomplished by breaking down the sound waves into small bits of information that are represented in the form of the binary numbering system (i.e., numbers comprised of solely 0s and 1s). This is the numbering system, or *machine language*, which forms the basis of modern computing. Digital sampling can be viewed as the "high tech" equivalent of several non-digital or physical sampling techniques, such as scratching and needle-dropping. The term *scratching* refers to the process of making or recording the sounds produced by turning back and forth a vinyl record while the needle is still in the grooves. The term *needledropping*, also referred to as *looping*, refers to the process of taking a portion of a magnetic tape recording, joining together the beginning and the ending of the selected portion of the tape to form a continuous loop, and playing the loop so that the selected portion of the recording is played over and over. What distinguishes scratching and needledropping, on the one hand, from digital sampling, on the other, is what amounts to the proverbial Pandora's box of sampling: the digital, binary, or machine language of computers.

The significance of the digital format is this: any information that can be stored in a computer in digital form may be readily displayed, modified, copied, or transmitted to an extremely exacting degree of flexibility. Recording artists today have access to a sophisticated array of equipment capable of manipulating digitized sound recordings. For example, using a triggering instrument, such as an electronic keyboard or specially modified set of drums, guitar, or reed instrument, an artist may replay sampled sounds at their original pitch (i.e., vibrations per second) or any other pitch desired. The artist can increase or decrease the speed at which the sampled sound is rendered, add new sounds, eliminate sounds, add echo effects, and, by reversing the sequence of the digital information, can even play the notes backwards. The waveform of a sampled sound may even be displayed on a computer screen and modifications may be made in the waveform to more precisely change the characteristics of the sound it produces.

Sounds may be sampled from live performances or from recorded sources such as magnetic tapes and compact discs. An artist can sample his own voice, the sounds made by an individual instrument, or the crescendo of an entire orchestra. Because digital samples can be stored for future use, they may easily be stored on servers and distributed on the Internet, allowing artists to create and distribute libraries of sampled sounds for reuse by others. The question to which we now turn is whether we can find Hope at the bottom of this Pandora's box.

## II. RECENT RECORDING PRACTICES

If sampling were performed solely by amateur musicians or computer hobbyists intending only to perform their sampled recordings privately in their own homes, there would be no controversy. Digital sampling has become, however, an attractive practice among young professional recording artists and their producers.

Sampling the sound recording of another artist for use with original material affords the professional recording artist or producer a way to more economically complete the task of producing pop records within tight recording budgets. For many artists, it is easier to select the "right" sound than to produce it from scratch, and using samples of existing recordings obviates the need to employ the talents of live musicians who could otherwise, albeit at greater expense, produce the desired performance or sound mix. Theoretically, a song can be composed entirely by the mere combination of sampled elements of existing recordings.

Though artists will use samples of existing recordings to save money and time, a more common and compelling reason why sampling is often employed stems from a desire to use the distinctive sound of a successful song or recording artist for the express purpose of giving sampling artist's original work a familiar element that listeners will quickly recognize.

## III. LEGAL BACKGROUND

It has been the practice of many artists to engage in sampling under the assumption that sampling is not a copyright infringement, believing that the act of sampling is somehow a *fair use* of copyright. As discussed below, this assumption is invalid, as now confirmed by the courts.[4]

### A. Multiple Copyright Infringement

Unauthorized sampling may be an infringement of both (i) the sound recording from which the sample is taken and (ii) the song underlying the sampled recording. As noted in Chapter 1, the copyright in a sound recording is completely separate from the copyright in the underlying song featured in the sound recording, and the underlying song should not be overlooked when considering the use of a sound recording.

It has been suggested that the standards for infringement of copyright for sound recordings and musical works may be different.[5] The standards for determining infringement by sampling for each will be discussed in the following sections.

---

[4] *Grand Upright Music, supra*, with respect to infringement of musical works by digital sampling. See *Bridgeport Music, Inc. v. Dimension Films*, 440 F.3d 792 (6th Cir. 2005) (citing the Third Edition of Kohn On Music Licensing in support of the 6th Circuit's establishing a "bright line" test for determining copyright infringement of sound recordings by digital sampling).

[5] See Broussard, *Current and Suggested Business Practices for the Licensing of Digital Samples*, 11 Loyola Entertainment Law Journal 479, 484 (1991).

### *1. Infringement of the Music*

In general, to prove copyright infringement, a person must show that he owns a copyright in the work and that the alleged infringer has copied it.[6] The question whether a valid copyright subsists in a song or a sound recording will rarely be at issue in a sampling case; this leaves the issue of whether work was copied. To prove that his work was *copied* a person must show that the alleged infringer had *access* to the work and that the work and the allegedly infringing work are *substantially similar*. Whether the alleged infringer had *access* to the work will also rarely be at issue in a sampling case, as access will either be admitted or easily proven. The extent of similarity, which constitutes a *substantial* and hence infringing similarity, has presented difficulties that have long challenged courts engaged in deciding these cases and lawyers engaged in advising their clients on the extent to which a particular use is legally permissible under the law.

Courts have approached the issue of substantial similarity in a variety of ways. Some courts have broken the question down into two parts: (1) whether the work was physically copied and (2) whether the copying was illicit or improper. In the case of sampling, whether the work was physically copied will either be admitted or an easy matter of proof. But proof of physical copying will not end the inquiry. A determination must still be made as to whether the copying was illicit or improper, or, in other words, whether extent of similarity is sufficiently *substantial* to constitute infringement.

In making this determination, courts will inquire whether the portion copied was a *qualitatively substantial* portion of the work from which it was taken.[7] Courts will find infringement where the quality of the portion taken was "the whole meritorious part of the song,"[8] "so much of what is pleasing to the ears of lay listeners,"[9] "that portion of the [copied work] upon which its popular appeal, and hence, its commercial success,

---

[6] See generally 3 Nimmer On Copyright, Sec. 13 (1995).

[7] *M. Witmark & Sons v. Pastime Amusement Co.*, 298 F. 470 (E.D.S.C. 1924), *aff'd*, 2 F.2d 1020 (4th Cir. 1924).

[8] *Northern Music Corp. v. King Record Distrib. Co.*, 105 F. Supp. 393, 397 (S.D.N.Y. 1952).

[9] *Arnstein v. Porter*, 154 F.2d 464, 473, *aff'd on reh'g*, 158 F.2d 795 (2d Cir. 1946).

depends,"[10] or "the very part that makes [the copied work] popular and valuable."[11]

In determining what kinds of short portions of musical compositions are qualitatively substantial and hence protectable by copyright law, it will be useful to divide the universe of potential samples into those tending to be clearly infringing and those tending to be noninfringing, recognizing, however, that there will always be those cases in that "gray area" in which the parties may find themselves subject to the most precisely applicable standard ever developed by the courts, "I know it when I see it."[12]

#### a. *Clearly Infringing Samples*

The chorus is often the heart of a song. Because of its brevity, repetitiveness, and frequent placement at the end of the song, the chorus tends to be the most memorable part of the song. In many cases, it would not be difficult for a court to find that the chorus is the very part that makes the song "popular and valuable." Accordingly, should a digital sample be made of a recognizable portion of a chorus, its unauthorized use is likely to be held infringing.

Other phrases of a musical composition that are distinctive and memorable are likely to be deemed qualitatively substantial parts of the song. This may include any phrase that is repeated often in a composition or placed at the beginning or end of the song.

Even a very short phrase from a musical composition could be infringed by the use of a sample of that phrase if the sampled phrase is repeated through substantial portions of the sampler's new work. For example, if the digital sample contains six notes from a song that repeats those six notes fifteen times, and the digital sample of the six notes is repeated ten times in the sampler's new work, then the sampler has taken sixty notes, not six. In such a case, the sampler's work is more likely to be held substantially similar to the copied work and the

[10] *Robertson v. Batten, Barton, Durstine & Osborne, Inc.*, 146 F. Supp. 795, 798 (S.D. Cal. 1956).

[11] *Johns & Johns Printing Co. v. Paull-Pioneer Music Corp.*, 102 F.2d 282, 283 (8th Cir. 1939).

[12] *Jacobellis v. Ohio*, 378 U.S. 184 (1964).

unauthorized distribution of the sampler's new work would constitute copyright infringement.

Finally, the unauthorized use of any sample which is clearly identifiable as having been taken from another copyrighted composition or which an average person would immediately associate with another copyrighted composition is likely to be held an infringement.

### *b. Clearly Non-Infringing Samples*

Because there are only a limited number of ways in which a short number of musical notes may be expressed, copyright protection does not subsist in exceedingly short phrases of music. Clearly, a single musical note is not protectable by copyright. For the same reason, a two-note phrase is not protectable, and the same is probably true for a three-note phrase. The more notes that are appropriated, the more likely the appropriation will constitute an infringement, but where will the courts draw the line on the use of extremely short phrases?

The smallest appropriation from a musical composition ever held to be infringing was a phrase consisting of six notes.[13] In that case, the two songs before the court were "considerably different, both in theme and execution, except as to [the] phrase, 'I hear you calling me.' " This phrase, and the music accompanying the words, in both compositions, were "practically identical" and the court held that the use of the phrase was a copyright infringement, because the phrase, despite its brevity, had what "causes audiences to listen, applaud, and buy copies in the corridor on the way out of the theatre." Nevertheless, samplers should take note[14] of a more recent case in which a court determined that the use of a four-note phrase, together with three of the words accompanying those notes, would have been sufficient to constitute infringement. In *Elsmere Music, Inc. v. NBC*,[15] the song *I Love New York* became the basis of the parody composition, *I Love Sodom*, performed by the "not-ready-for-prime-time-players" on NBC's *Saturday Night Live* television program. In both compositions, the four-note phrase was continually repeated and was referred to by the court as "the heart of the

[13] *Boosey v. Empire Music Co., Inc.*, 224 F. 646 (S.D.N.Y. 1915).

[14] Pun intended.

[15] *Elsmere Music, Inc. v. NBC*, 482 F. Supp. 741 (S.D.N.Y. 1980), *aff'd*, 623 F.2d (2d Cir. 1980).

composition." The court concluded that the use did not constitute infringement, because it was part of a satire, permissible under the doctrine of *fair use* (discussed below). However, the court stated that the taking was of a "substantial nature," "easily recognizable," and "capable of rising to the level of a copyright infringement."

Accordingly, while the sampling of a single note or a phrase of two notes would appear not to be an infringement of a musical composition, the sampling of three notes may be the *sine qua non* of permissible song sampling, at least where the sample includes the words accompanying the music. Thus, a single shout rendered by a singer, two chords, or three notes from a nonessential bass line would probably not be qualitatively substantial parts of musical compositions, and therefore not protectable. Commercially insignificant phrases and commonly used phrases would also fall outside the scope of protection.

As noted below, however, sound recordings may be afforded significantly stronger protection than the underlying music, meaning that an infringement of a sound recording may still be found in a sample that appropriates elements that would not constitute an infringement of the underlying musical composition.

### 2. *Infringement of the Sound Recording*

Shortly after the publication of the third edition of *Kohn On Music Licensing* in 2002, the Federal Court of Appeals for the Sixth Circuit addressed a question of first impression: What is the legal standard for infringement by digital sampling of a copyrighted sound recording?[16]

In *Bridgeport*, the court determined that a two-second sample from a guitar solo in the recording of the composition, "Get Off Your Ass and Jam" used without permission in the recording, "100 Miles and Runnin'" constituted copyright infringement. Establishing for the first time a legal standard for infringement of sound recordings by digital sampling, the court held that a sound recording is infringed when the actual recording — or portions of it (no matter how *de minimis*) — is used without permission, regardless of whether the recordings at issue are substantially similar. In support of its opinion, the court quoted

---

[16] *Bridgeport Music, Inc. v. Dimension Films*, 440 F.3d 792 (6th Cir. 2005)

a number of texts, including the following paragraphs from the Third Edition of Kohn on Music Licensing:[17]

> Certain provisions of the copyright law, however, do suggest that broader protection against unauthorized sampling may be available for owners of sound recordings than for the owners of musical compositions that may be embodied in those sound recordings.
>
> For example, the copyright act states that, "The exclusive rights of the owner of copyright in a sound recording . . . do not extend to the making or duplication of another sound recording that consists *entirely* of an independent fixation of other sounds, even though such sounds imitate or simulate those in the copyrighted sound recording" (emphasis added).[18] By using the words "*entirely* of an independent fixation" in referring to sound recordings which may imitate or simulate the sounds of another, Congress may have intended that a recording containing *any* sounds of another recording would constitute infringement. Thus, it would appear that any unauthorized use of a digital sample taken from another's copyrighted recording would be an infringement of the copyrighted recording.
>
> In fact, the copyright law specifically provides that the owner of copyright in a sound recording has the exclusive right to prepare a derivative work "in which the actual sounds fixed in the sound recording are rearranged, remixed, or otherwise altered in sequence or quality." A recording that embodies samples taken from the sound recording of another is by definition a "rearranged, remixed, or otherwise altered in sequence or quality."
>
> It has been suggested that the strong protection implied by the foregoing provisions could be mitigated by a judicially applied standard which permits some degree of *de minimis* copying or copying where the sampled portion of the resulting work is not substantially similar to the copied work.[19] For example, a court could determine that the taking of a millisecond of sound from another's copyrighted recording, or the taking of a more extensive portion that has been modified to the point of being completely unrecognizable or impossible to associate with the copied recording, does not constitute infringement. It is believed, however, that the courts should take what appears to be a

[17] *Bridgeport*, 440 F.3d at 803, fn 18.

[18] 17 U.S.C. Sec. 114(b).

[19] Broussard, Current and Suggested Business Practices for the Licensing of Digital Samples, at 492.

> rare opportunity to follow a "bright line" rule specifically mandated by Congress. This would result in a substantial reduction of litigation costs and uncertainty attending disputes over sampling infringement of sound recordings and would promote a faster resolution of these disputes.
>
> While the question whether an unauthorized use of a digital sample infringes a musical composition may require a full substantial similarity analysis, the question whether the use of a sample constitutes infringement of a sound recording could end upon a determination that the sampler physically copied the copyrighted sound recording of another. If the sampler physically copied any portion of another's copyrighted sound recording, then infringement should be found. If the sampler did not physically copy, then there could be no infringement (even if the resulting recording substantially simulates or imitates the original recording).

Our treatise went on to say, "Even if the courts choose to apply a de minimis standard, or a substantial similarity analysis, the courts are likely to find infringing those samples of recordings that appropriate the style of an artist's performance. This would include any part of the performance that is unique or sufficiently distinctive or identifiable with the artist. Examples may include the distinctive 'whoa' of Michael Jackson, shriek of James Brown, snare of Phil Collins, etc. — anything that might be considered a *signature sound* of an artist. None of these would be considered copyrightable as musical compositions, but would clearly be protectable under the copyright of a sound recording."

The court concluded that "The music industry, as well as the courts, are best served if something approximating a bright-line test can be established. Not necessarily a 'one size fits all' test, but one that, at least adds clarity to what constitutes actionable infringement with regard to the digital sampling of copyrighted sound recordings."

### B. No Fair Use

The doctrine of *fair use* of copyright will not justify sampling for most purposes. In particular, the unauthorized use of the typical digital sample made for the purpose of giving the sampling artist's work a familiar element from another artist's distinctive sound would clearly not be considered a fair use of the copyrighted composition and sound recording from which the sample was taken.

The doctrine of fair use is generally limited to several specific kinds of circumstances defined in the copyright law,[20] such as criticism, news reporting, teaching, or research. Fair use has also been recognized for works created for the purposes of parody and satire, on the basis that society benefits the social and literary commentary contributed by these kinds of works. The copyright law lists the following four factors to be used by the courts in determining whether the use made of a work in any particular case is a fair use:

(1) the purpose and character of the use, including whether such use is of a commercial nature or is for nonprofit educational purposes;

(2) the nature of the copyrighted work;

(3) the amount and substantiality of the portion used in relation to the copyrighted work as a whole; and

(4) the effect of the use upon the potential market for or value of the copyrighted work.

The application of the first factor would militate against a finding of fair use in a digital sample case, because the purpose and character of the sampler's recording is generally commercial, rather than nonprofit. In applying the second factor, the courts give greater flexibility to those desiring to use portions of informational works, such as compilations of facts or data. Being that musical compositions and sound recordings of musical compositions are purely creative or imaginative works, the second factor is also likely to weigh heavily against a finding of fair use for samplings of those works. The third factor would imply that if the material that was sampled was slight and was not qualitatively substantial, the application of the factor could support a finding of fair use. Of course, all samples that are deemed to have taken a qualitatively substantial part of an existing musical work under a substantial similarity analysis would fail to meet these criteria. Thus, this factor might only apply to de minimis use of sound recordings. The fourth factor has been interpreted as including a consideration of whether the use would have a detrimental effect if the practice were widespread. Further, the U.S. Supreme Court has held that "if the defendant's work adversely

[20] 17 U.S.C. Sec. 107; See Chapter 25, on *The Fair Use Controversy*.

affects the value of *any of the rights* in the copyrighted work . . . the use is not fair" (emphasis added).[21] One of the rights an owner has in a copyrighted work is the exclusive right to make derivative works. Since one of the sampling would adversely affect the potential market for similar derivative uses of the song or recording, the fourth factor would not support a finding of fair use.

As recently confirmed by the U.S. Supreme Court in the *Pretty Woman* case, discussed in Chapter 25, the use of music may be a fair use if the use is for the purpose of parody or satire. The courts have determined that parody and satire are works that should be encouraged and their creation would often not be possible without the doctrine of fair use. It should be clear, however, that unless the sample is being used for some form of criticism, news reporting, teaching, research, parody, satire, or some nonprofit use, the doctrine of fair use is not likely to provide a valid defense to copyright infringement.

### C. Permission Required

Record companies have tended to be quite tolerant of other record companies whose artists engage in the sampling of their recordings. This tolerance has afforded each record company the informal privilege of tolerating the sampling practices of their own recording artists and producers under contract. As more and more artists become outraged by the sampling of their works, record companies should begin to become less sanguine about these practices.

Music publishers and songwriters, however, have taken a much dimmer view of sampling practices. At least one prominent music publisher has begun reviewing new recordings to listen for samples that may infringe their copyrights. It also should be noted that Gilbert O'Sullivan's record company was not a plaintiff in the songwriter's action against Biz Markie and Markie's record company. Mr. O'Sullivan filed the lawsuit through his own music publishing company, taking on the expense of the litigation himself. As his lawyer explained in a recent music trade magazine, "This case was not brought by some megacompany . . . . This case was brought by a solitary artistic person who did not like the idea that somebody was using the song that *he* wrote and the recording that *he* made without his permission. . . . He could have made a deal early on.

[21] *Harper & Row v. Nation Enters.*, 471 U.S. 539, 568 (1985).

But that wasn't what he wanted. What he wanted was the recording that he did not like off the market, and that is what he got. If you are a creator, shouldn't that be your right?"

With music publishers searching for authorized samples and filing lawsuits, a recording artist can no longer assume that no one will notice his use of a sample. Nor should the artist assume that he will be absolved of liability as long as an average lay person would not recognize his use of an authorized sample. While it is true the courts have found infringement where the quality of the portion taken was "so much of what is pleasing to the ears of lay listeners" and will often rely on the ears of lay juries to determine whether an average person would clearly identify a sample as having been taken from another song, it is still quite possible that a court could hold a sampler's work an infringement even where an association of the sample with the copied composition is only noticeable by experts or others with trained or sophisticated perceptions. Samplers would therefore be advised to seek permission of the copyright owners even if it is believed that an association could be made only by an expert or that the association is only mildly noticeable. If the sampler knows he physically copied another song or recording, he should seek permission.

Artists intending to use samples from another's copyrighted recording would be strongly advised to maintain a record of the samples used in their recordings and obtain permission from the copyright owners before any distribution takes place. Once the sample is used in a recording that has been distributed to the public, the bargaining leverage of the copyright owner of the composition or recording from which the sample was taken increases significantly.

Finally, samplers seeking the proper clearance should not overlook the fact that two copyrights may be involved in each particular sample. Copyrights in sound recordings are generally owned by the record companies that financed or distributed them, and songs are owned by music publishers. These are rarely the same entities.

## IV. CONSIDERATIONS IN GRANTING AND CLEARING LICENSES FOR DIGITAL SAMPLES

This section sketches the considerations in granting and clearing licenses for the use of portions of copyrighted musical compositions and recordings by digital sampling.

## A. Music Licensing

When a sampling artist wishes to make copies of a recording containing the sampled musical composition of another, permission will be required from the copyright owner of the musical composition. The permission, if granted without further conditions, will normally be in the form of a mechanical license.

### *1. Applicability of Compulsory License Provision*

The use of a sample containing the copyrighted song of another will not, however, be subject to the compulsory license provision of the copyright law.[22] As noted in Chapter 13, Congress specifically recognized the legitimate interests of songwriters who might wish to prevent their musical works from being "perverted, distorted, or travestied."[23] Accordingly, the compulsory license provision provides, "A compulsory license includes the privilege of making a musical arrangement of the work to the extent necessary to conform it to the style or manner of interpretation of the performance involved, but the arrangement shall not change the basic melody or fundamental character of the work . . . except with the express consent of the copyright owner."[24]

Because mechanical licenses for song samples are not subject to the compulsory license provision, the fees and other terms of licenses to make and distribute samples containing copyrighted compositions may be freely negotiated. Even if the compulsory license statute should apply with respect to a given sample — i.e., the sample recording does not change the basic melody or fundamental character of the song — the consequences of a sampling artist not complying with the express terms of the compulsory license provision will have the same effect. It has been the common practice of many sample artists to release their recordings before seeking to obtain the proper mechanical license. The compulsory license provision provides that any person who wishes to obtain a compulsory license shall, before

[22] 17 U.S.C. Sec. 115.

[23] House Report of the Copyright Act of 1976, No. 94-1476, at page 109 (September 3, 1976).

[24] 17 U.S.C. Sec. 115 (a) (2).

or within 30 days after making, and before distributing any copies of the work, serve notice of intention to do so on the copyright owner. Once a recording containing the musical work of another is distributed without compliance with the compulsory license provision and without the consent of the copyright owner, a compulsory license is no longer available, and the copyright owner is free to negotiate the terms of the mechanical license without regard to the restrictions set forth in the compulsory license provision.

### 2. *Alternatives of the Music Copyright Owner*

When a copyright owner is faced with the circumstances of an artist having included a portion of his musical composition in an otherwise original song, the alternatives available to the copyright owner are to (a) do nothing, (b) refuse to license, (c) grant a mechanical license for a one-time flat fee, (d) grant a mechanical license for a royalty, (e) grant a mechanical license for a royalty and take a share in a percentage of the performance royalties of the new composition containing the sample, (f) seek a co-ownership interest in the new composition, or (g) seek an assignment of the copyright in the new composition.

Which of these alternatives the copyright owner chooses will depend upon the circumstances, including the circumstances under which the sampling came to his attention, the value of the song, the importance of the song in relation to its intended use, the leverage he perceives he has over the sampling artist, and the fortitude that may be required to justify his position.

The ability of the music copyright owner to demand a license for the use of a sample containing a portion of his musical composition will depend upon whether the sampling artist's unauthorized use of the sample would constitute an infringement of the copyrighted music. As noted above, in determining whether an unauthorized use of the sample would constitute an infringement of a music copyright, courts will inquire whether the portion copied was a *qualitatively substantial* portion of the work from which it was taken. If it is determined that the portion copied was *qualitatively substantial,* then the inquiry turns to *how* substantial. At this point, the music copyright owner would turn to basic considerations of music licensing, including the value of the song sampled, the importance of the sample in relation to its intended use, and the scope of the use. The outcome of an analysis of these factors will result in a perception about the leverage the copyright owner has over the sampling artist in bargaining for a license. Other factors affecting the copyright owner's leverage include the circumstances under which the sampling came to his attention. For example, if the sampling artist attempts to obtain permission for the use before releasing the recording, then the availability of other samples containing substitute music will preserve for the sampling artist the ability to walk away from the negotiations. If, however, the recording containing the sample is already on the market when the music copyright owner is engaging in his analysis, the result of the *Grand Upright* case should impress upon both parties the significantly higher bargaining leverage of the copyright owner.

A copyright owner's leverage in bargaining with the sampling artist will influence his fortitude or willingness to take the actions required, up to and including the filing of a lawsuit, to justify his choice among the following alternatives, including the structure of any deal, or the amount of any license fee, which he may settle upon.

*a. Do Nothing*

When a music copyright owner discovers that an artist has made and distributed recordings containing a sampled portion of his copyrighted composition, he may choose to do nothing. This would only be likely in one or more of the following circumstances: the material sampled was not a qualitatively substantial part of the copyright owner's song, or the similarity between the owner's musical work and the sampling artist's work was so slight as to render the similarity unrecognizable by the listening public or even a trained ear, if the sampling was so slight that it may be difficult to prove the similarity of the compositions was the result of sampling at all. In any of these circumstances, the copyright owner just may decide it is not worth the trouble to take any further action, if, in fact, he had any action he could take.

If, however, the sampling artist's new composition has become a hit and is receiving a significant amount of airplay and record sales, or if it is merely included in a record album that has become a top seller, it may be worth the trouble for the copyright owner to take steps to enforce his rights under the appropriate circumstances.

*b. Refuse to License*

Should the music copyright owner be approached by a sampling artist seeking permission to make and distribute recordings containing a sampled portion of the owner's composition, the copyright owner may refuse to grant a license. This may be a sampling artist's worst nightmare. To repeat the statement made by Gilbert O'Sullivan's attorney, O'Sullivan "could have made a deal early on. But that wasn't what he wanted. What he wanted was the recording that he did not like off the market, and that is what he got."

It has been suggested that Congress consider a compulsory license scheme for the licensing of digital samples similar to the regime currently in place for recordings under Section 115 of the copyright law.[25] This suggestion, however, unreasonably ignores the rights of the creative artist's right not to have his work "perverted, distorted, or travestied," a right that Congress has enacted into law by the express terms of Section 115(a)(2). This section compels music copyright owners to grant licenses for other recordings, but only after the copyright owner already has once permitted the public distribution of recordings of the composition (in audio form only — licensing the work for inclusion in audiovisual works and motion picture soundtracks and other audiovisual works would not be considered a distribution for the purpose of this provision). Until that first distribution is made, if ever, the law respects the right of the copyright owner to refuse to permit the distribution of recordings of his copyrighted composition. And, even after such recordings are first distributed, the law compels the copyright owner to license only those recordings that have arrangements that do not change the basic melody or the fundamental character of the owner's musical composition.

Nevertheless, unless the copyright owner has a compelling reason not to license, he should consider licensing his music in sampled recordings. A reasonable reason to refuse to license may be that the recording in which the sample is intended to be used contains indecent, racist, or other opprobrious language. Another reason to refuse to license may be that the sampler's work uses the owner's composition in a way that

[25] Note, *A New Spin on Music Sampling: A Case of Fair Play*, 105 Harvard Law Review 726, 742 (1992).

mutilates the composition or otherwise offends the creative sensitivities of the songwriter. Note, however, that a songwriter's refusal to license, for whatever reason, may be overcome if the sampler can establish that his sampling constitutes a *fair use* of the composition, such as a use in a parody or satire.[26]

Even if the songwriter does not have a contractual right of consent over such uses, a music publisher should avoid licensing music in a sampled recording if that action would harm his business or personal relationship with the songwriter. Leaving aside such circumstances, a music copyright owner should not view sampling as a form of stealing, but as a new market in which to derive revenue for the songs in his catalog.

### c. *Grant a Mechanical License for a One-Time Flat Fee*

If the copyright owner who discovers the unauthorized use of his musical composition in a sampled recording decides to do something about it, such as write a letter demanding that the sampling artist's record company cease and desist distribution of the offending recording, the response he receives will depend upon whether the sampling artist or record company perceives that the recording constitutes an infringement of copyright in the owner's musical composition. An indignant reply from the artist's attorney telling the copyright owner, in a more or less dignified manner, to go away, should require no explanation as to the artist's perception of the use or evaluation of the copyright owner's position.

If the copyright owner's position is, under the circumstances, a weak one, the parties may wish to settle upon the issuance of a mechanical license in exchange for a one time flat fee. Even if the copyright owner's perception of his case is stronger than the record company's perception of it, the copyright owner may still be unwilling to bear the expense of taking the matter to court, and may accept such an arrangement. The artist or record company may be willing to pay some amount on a flat fee basis, even where it is felt the music copyright

[26] See the discussion of *Campbell v. Acuff-Rose* (the "Pretty Woman case") in Chapter 25, on *The Fair Use Controversy*.

owner's position is weak, to avoid the costs and risks associated with any litigation that would be necessary to defend their position. A form effecting this kind of flat fee arrangement is set forth as Form 24.1 found on the CD-ROM.[27]

On occasion, a copyright owner may be asked to grant such a license on a *gratis* basis — that is, without charge. Music copyright owners, once persuaded to issue a license, will generally charge at least some nominal fee sufficient to cover the administrative costs of issuing the license. This may range from $50 to $100.

### *d. Grant a Mechanical License for a Royalty*

If, in light of all the circumstances regarding the qualitative substantiality of the music sampled and the importance of its contribution to the recording in which it is used, the sampling artist is persuaded that the copyright owner has a strong position and the fortitude to support that position with legal action, the parties may negotiate a more substantial arrangement.

A straightforward arrangement under which sampled music may be licensed is the issuance of a mechanical license in exchange for a royalty based upon the number of copies of the recording distributed. The royalty in these arrangements is usually a function of the *statutory rate* set forth in the compulsory license provision in the copyright law, as modified from time to time by the Copyright Royalty Board. The sampling artist, however, would take the position that it is unfair for his publisher to pay the full statutory rate, because the amount of material sampled from the copyright owner's work represents only a small part of the original musical work in which it is embodied. A copyright owner might therefore be persuaded to accept half of the statutory rate or less, and, in fact, this has become the standard practice. The percentage is typically set between 10% and 50%, with the prevailing rate in average sampling cases being about 30% of statutory.

[27] Many of the forms relating to sampling at the end of this chapter are courtesy of Martin Cohen, Esq., of Los Angeles, California, and Ira B. Selsky, Esq., of New York, New York.

#### e. *Grant a Mechanical License for a Royalty and Take a Share in a Percentage of the Performance Royalties of the New Composition*

Nevertheless, the foregoing arrangement may still not be satisfactory to the copyright owner, who would understandably assert that he should not only receive a portion of the mechanical royalty for copies made and distributed of the recording, but should also share a portion of the performance royalties resulting from the broadcast of the music on radio and television and other public performances.

The most common arrangement under which sampled music is licensed are deals in which the copyright owner grants a mechanical license at some percentage below the statutory rate and the sampling artist agrees that the copyright owner is entitled to receive some percentage of the performance royalties payable by performance rights societies. Even where a significantly substantial amount of the copyright owner's music is sampled, the copyright owner may be willing to accept a mechanical royalty at lower than the statutory rate in exchange for a significant share of the performance royalties, because the latter often represents a greater source of income than mechanical royalties.

A form effecting this kind of sample licensing arrangement is set forth as Form 24.2 on the CD-ROM.

A special problem arises where the sampling artist does not own the composition containing the sampled song. For example, a sampling artist may include a sample of song in a recording of a song owned by another copyright owner, adding no original material of his own. Under these circumstances, the solution described in this section will not work, because the sampling artist would be entitled to no performance royalties with which to share with the copyright owner. This problem is revisited below.

The solution may also be unsatisfactory to the copyright owner for another reason: mechanical and performance royalties are not the only sources of music publishing revenue. The copyright owner would want an arrangement that assures that he receives a fair share of all sources of subsidiary revenue derived from the composition containing his copyrighted music, including revenue from commercial advertising, motion picture and television synchronization and other licenses. Form 24.2 attempts to address this problem by making all licenses other than mechanical and performance licenses subject to the further permission of the copyright owner. However, the copyright owner might not be convinced that this sufficiently secures his interest in the additional revenue and the sampling artist may feel no assurance that the copyright owner will seek only a fair portion of the additional revenue.

#### *f. Seek a Co-Ownership Interest in the New Composition*

Where the sampling artist can be persuaded that the copyright owner has a very strong position and the fortitude to support that position with legal action, the parties may negotiate an arrangement that satisfies the copyright owner's desire to share in all sources of subsidiary revenue derived from the new composition.

The most elegant way to assure that the copyright owner and the sampling artist each receive the proper share of all music publishing income derived from the exploitation of the new composition is for the parties to enter into a co-publishing agreement. Under this arrangement, the copyright owner is granted a co-ownership interest in the new composition containing the sampled material. This has become a fairly common solution to the sampling problem.

Under this arrangement, the percentage of the undivided copyright in the new composition granted to the copyright owner of the sampled material would reflect the qualitative substantiality of the music sampled and the importance of its contribution to the new work as a whole.

When these deals are struck, copyright owners commonly acquire a 25% to 50% co-ownership interest in the new composition. Exclusive administration rights are generally left to the sampling artist's music publisher, who is often more experienced in exploiting music in the same genre of new composition. However, this point is open to negotiation.

Three forms each effecting this kind of licensing arrangement are set forth as Forms 24.3, 24.4, and 24.5 on the CD-ROM. Form 24.4 is a short-form agreement that allows each owner to grant mechanical license to others, subject to accounting to the other co-owner of its share of the revenues, but neither may license other uses unless the other has failed to object after receiving notice. Form 24.3, a short-form letter agreement, requires each party to obtain the consent of the other prior to issuing licenses for each of their respective shares. Form 24.5, the long-form, entitles each co-owner to administer its own respective share. None of these solutions seem desirable. The problems arising from ownership of copyrights split in this manner are discussed at length in Chapter 6.

*g. Seek an Assignment of the Copyright in the New Composition*

If the copyright owner feels he has the leverage and all the fortitude and money necessary to engage in litigation, then he may insist in nothing less than a complete ownership interest in the new composition. An extreme position such as this may be justified in cases where the sampled recording adds little original material to the owner's copyrighted song. This may be the case where the new composition is merely a modern arrangement of the song, the instrumental portion of the composition with modified or new lyrics, or the song's lyrics sung to a newly composed music.

In such cases, the music copyright owner could seek to enjoin the sampling artist from collecting any music publishing income in connection with the recording and collect damages for copyright infringement. The result of such a lawsuit could be severe and the sampling artist or its recording company could choose to quickly settle the claim by just assigning all rights in the work over to the copyright owner.

## B. Sound Recording Licensing

When a sampling artist wishes to make copies of a recording containing the sampled sound recording of another, permission will be required from the copyright owner of the sound recording. The permission, if granted without further conditions, will normally be in the form of a *master use license*.

The alternatives available to the owner of a sound recording faced with an artist having included a portion of his sound recording in an otherwise original sound recording are quite similar to those of the owner of the copyright in the underlying music. Those alternatives need not be repeated here, but a few important differences between practices in sound recording and music licenses for sampling will be pointed out in the context of licenses for sampled recordings.

### *1. Flat Fee Licenses*

As noted, the owner of the sound recording may often have a much stronger case for infringement than the owner of the music underlying the recording, but record companies, who generally own the recordings, are more tolerant of sampling, because they know that artists in their own repertoire frequently engage in similar practices. Thus, it might not always be in the best interests of recording companies to do anything that would unreasonably restrain customary practices or help establish legal case law that supports strong protection against the use of sound recordings or musical compositions in digital samples.

Record companies therefore typically accept one-time flat fee payments for the use of samples from their recordings. Where the sampling is insubstantial or virtually unrecognizable, a record company may grant a license on a gratis or nominal fee basis. Examples of licenses to use a recording sample on a flat fee basis are set forth as Forms 24.6 and 24.7 on the CD-ROM.

### *2. Royalties*

Where the sampling is substantial or recognizable, or if the success of the sampler's recording can clearly be attributed to the distinctive features of the sampled recording, a record company may demand a royalty. In fact, a record company may actually be under an obligation, albeit an implied one, under its recording contract with the recording artists who created the original recording, to use good faith efforts to generate income from sampled uses of the recording. Royalty rates for samples of sound recordings typically range from 1/2 cent to 5 cents per unit, with advances typically starting at about $5,000. An example of a license to use a recording sample on a royalty basis is set forth as Form 24.8 on the CD-ROM. The record company should review its contract with the artist to determine whether any consent is required prior to issuing such a license.

## C. Where Sampling Artist's Additional Musical Material Is Owned by Another

As previously noted, a special problem may arise where the sampling artist does not own the composition containing the sampled song.

For example, a sampling artist may include a sample of song in a recording of a song owned by another copyright owner, adding no original material of his own.

If the sampling artist does not own, or claim to own, the new musical composition embodied in his original recording, a co-ownership agreement may be the only solution to a serious sampling problem the artist has created for the several copyright owners affected. In such circumstances, the owners of the two musical compositions used in the unauthorized creation of the new work will need to work out a co-publishing agreement among themselves. This may be a difficult negotiation, because it would seem that none of the parties involved would have any particular leverage over any of the others. Yet, if the resulting composition became a hit or was included in a hit album, the parties involved would have a great incentive to reach a co-ownership arrangement clarifying where lucrative mechanical royalties, performance royalties, and royalties from subsidiary uses should be paid.

Worse yet, where the work of one party was copied in virtually its entirety and that party is already receiving a mechanical royalty at full statutory rate and all the performance credits, negotiations for a fair share of royalties attempted by a party whose work was subjected to only a small sampling would seem most difficult. The party who is already receiving full royalties — one who has done no wrongdoing — would appear to have little incentive to negotiate, except to avoid the expense of a lawsuit or to maintain good relations with another member of a small industry.

The National Music Publishers' Association (NMPA) will offer its services to help mediate or arbitrate disputes between members and can provide a forum with knowledgeable industry veterans to help resolve the dispute in a quick, fair, amicable, and inexpensive way. Music publishers faced with a situation such as that described above should seriously consider inquiring with the NMPA or a similar organization about how they may help the parties resolve such a matter.

## V. CONCLUSION

It has been the practice of sampling artists to sample under the assumption that sampling is not an infringement or with the knowledge that their activity was illegal, but thought their sampling would not be discovered. With music publishers listening carefully for samples containing their copyrighted works, artists can no longer assume their activity will not be noticed. An artist who has incorporated in his recording a digital sample from a song or sound recording of another is likely to be held to have infringed two copyrights — that in a sound recording and that in the song embodied in the recording.

The first federal judge to have issued a ruling on the issue of such infringement enjoined all sales of the recording and took the unusual step of referring the matter to the U.S. Attorney's office for criminal prosecution. Thus, it is now clear that sampling is illegal and will be dealt with seriously by the law.

A sampler is therefore strongly advised to seek permission whenever he knows he physically copied the sounds of another song. Careful records should be maintained of all samples used during the creation of a recording so that the appropriate permissions can be cleared. Permission should always be cleared *before* any distribution of the recording takes place. By following these procedures, a sampling artist may avoid the substantial risks and consequences of violating the legitimate rights of other songwriters and artists.

# Appendix to Chapter 24
# The Digital Sampling Controversy

Forms (On CD-Rom Only)

| | |
|---|---|
| **Form 24.1** | **Letter in Lieu of Mechanical License for Use of Digital Sample from a Musical Composition for a Flat Fee** |
| **Form 24.2** | **Side Letter for Use of Digital Sample from a Musical Composition – To Be Used in Conjunction with a Mechanical License (See Forms 13.1, 13.2 and 13.3)** |
| **Form 24.3** | **Letter Agreement for Co-Ownership of a Musical Composition Containing a Digital Sample from Another Musical Composition** |
| **Form 24.4** | **Short Form Licensing and Co-Publishing Agreement for a Musical Composition Containing Sampled Material Taken from Another Musical Composition** |
| **Form 24.5** | **Long Form Licensing and Co-Publishing Agreement for a Musical Composition Containing Sampled Material Taken from Another Musical Composition** |
| **Form 24.6** | **Short Form Master License for Use of Sound Recording Sample on a Flat Fee Basis** |
| **Form 24.7** | **Long Form Master License for Use of Sound Recording Sample on a Flat Fee Basis** |
| **Form 24.8** | **Long Form Master License for Use of Sound Recording Sample on a Royalty Basis** |

## CHAPTER 25

# THE FAIR USE CONTROVERSY

## SUMMARY

# CHAPTER 25

# THE FAIR USE CONTROVERSY

As pointed out in our chapter on clearing licenses, one does not always require a license to use a particular musical work. Besides obtaining the express permission to use the music owned by another, originating the music yourself, or buying the copyright in the composition outright, you can have the necessary legal privilege to use a musical work by either using a song that is entirely in the *public domain* (i.e., taking steps to assure the music is not subject to any legal rights of another),[1] or by making a *fair use* of another's copyrighted composition.

This chapter will explore the standards used in determining whether a use of a copyrighted song is considered a *fair use*, a use that would otherwise constitute an infringement of copyright, but by virtue of the purpose of the use does not require permission of the copyright owner. Our discussion will be limited, however, to those fair use issues that typically arise in the context of commercial music licensing (i.e., excluding other areas, such as home video and audio taping, which, though important, are outside the scope of this book). We will begin with a brief overview of the fair use provision of the U.S. Copyright Act.

## I. Legal Background

The purpose of copyright protection, in the words of the Constitution, is to "promote the Progress of Science and useful Arts." That Progress, and thereby the public interest, is promoted by granting to authors the exclusive rights to reproduce their works, which, being the

[1] Considerations used in determining whether a work is in the public domain are discussed in Chapter 7, on *The Language of Music Licensing*. See also Chapter 9, on the *Duration of Copyright, Assignments of Copyright, and Licenses.*

means by which they may reap personal gains from their creations, provides authors with the incentive to create. The right to exclude, or the legal monopoly, created by copyright thus provides a mechanism for rewarding the individual author in order to benefit the public.

## A. Fair Use as a Balance Between Copyright and Freedom of Speech

There are circumstances, however, in which strict enforcement of this monopoly would inhibit the very Progress that copyright is intended to promote. For example, the work of a scholar who may depend upon the use of quotes from the works of predecessors may suffer if permission to use the quotes could not be obtained at an acceptable price. Consequently, the courts have recognized a balance between enforcing the monopoly to provide authors with the incentive to create, and not enforcing the monopoly, to provide other authors the means by which their creative efforts may advance the very Progress sought to be encouraged. The tension, under the U.S. Constitution, is also one between the copyright owner's monopoly, intended to promote creative efforts, and the First Amendment's guarantee of freedom of speech. Copyright, after all, is a limitation on speech enforceable by the courts by virtue of an act of Congress.

But where does one draw the line between the incentive afforded by the enforcement of a monopoly on certain forms of speech and the exercise of free speech that promotes creative efforts, which would not otherwise be possible if the monopoly were strictly enforced? Drawing that line is the purpose of the *doctrine of fair use*.

## B. Fair Use in the Copyright Act

The doctrine of fair use had long been a child of *case law* (i.e., court decisions ruling upon individual lawsuits), until it was first given express statutory recognition in Section 107 of the Copyright Act of 1976.[2] Because all the forms of potential fair use of copyright cannot be anticipated by a statute, the U.S. Congress could only provide some guidelines, including a list of several categories of fair use and four factors to be used by the courts in determining whether the use made of a

---

[2] 17 U.S.C. Sec. 107.

work in any particular case is a fair use. Section 107, which sets forth those factors, reads as follows:

> **Section 107. Limitations on exclusive rights: Fair use.** Notwithstanding the provisions of sections 106 and 106A [regarding the exclusive rights in copyrighted works and rights of certain authors to attribution and integrity], the fair use of a copyrighted work, including such use by reproduction in copies or phonorecords or by any other means specified by that section, for purposes such as criticism, comment, news reporting, teaching (including multiple copies for classroom use), scholarship, or research, is not an infringement of copyright. In determining whether the use made of a work in a particular case is a fair use the factors to be considered shall include —
>
> (1) the purpose and character of the use, including whether such use is of a commercial nature or is for nonprofit educational purposes;
>
> (2) the nature of the copyrighted work;
>
> (3) the amount and substantiality of the portion used in relation to the copyrighted work as a whole; and
>
> (4) the effect of the use upon the potential market for or value of the copyrighted work.
>
> The fact that a work is unpublished shall not itself bar a finding of fair use if such finding is made upon consideration of all of the above factors.

These factors, as they may be applied in any particular case, have been called "the most troublesome in the whole law of copyright."[3] When Congress enacted Section 107, it stated the general intention behind the provision as follows:

> The statement of the fair use doctrine in section 107 offers some guidance to users in determining when the principles of the doctrine apply. However, the endless variety of situations and combinations of circumstances that can rise in particular cases precludes the formulation of exact rules in the statute. The bill endorses the purpose and general scope of the judicial doctrine of fair use, but there is no disposition to freeze the doctrine in the statute, especially during a period of

[3] See *Sony Corp. of America v. Universal City Studios, Inc.* 464 U.S. 417 (1984).

> rapid technological change. Beyond a very broad statutory explanation of what fair use is and some of the criteria applicable to it, the courts must be free to adapt the doctrine to particular situations on a case-by-case basis. Section 107 is intended to restate the present judicial doctrine of fair use, not to change, narrow, or enlarge it in any way.[4]

The application of the doctrine of fair use in any particular case will, therefore, be largely judgmental, and the best a lawyer can do is to review the case books for any cases on point and making an assessment of the risk his client takes by using a work without the permission of the copyright owner. Often those risks are less influenced by what is "right" than by the potential attorneys' fees that could be incurred in connection with the defense of any action taken, rightly or wrongly, by the copyright owner.

## II. FAIR USE IN MUSIC LICENSING

As mentioned above, a *fair use* does not require permission of the copyright owner, which is to say that one making a fair use of a copyrighted work does not require a license to do so. The issue of whether a particular use of a song constitutes a *fair use* generally arises in the following licensing contexts:

(a) photocopying of sheet music,

(b) the use of music in connection with criticism, comment, and news reporting,

(c) the use of music for satire, parody, or burlesque,

(d) use of a few lines of a song's lyrics in a book,

(e) the use of a few bars of music in a recording or audiovisual work, and

(f) the use of a digital sample of a sound recording containing copyrighted music.

We will review each of these in the foregoing order.

---

[4] 1976 House Report 94-1476, pp. 65, 66

## A. Photocopying

Most would agree that when a person at home, or at school, writes out by hand the lyrics to a song or a musical arrangement of a popular recording for use in playing the song on their piano, the copy made in each case is a *fair use* of the song's copyright. But what if, for the same purpose, a music teacher makes a single photocopy of the sheet music of the song and gives it to a student? What if the teacher makes 30 copies for use by an entire class?

Reproduction of copyrighted works for purposes of teaching (including multiple copies for classroom use), scholarship, or research are among the examples of fair use that are specifically set forth in the fair use provision of the copyright law. Nevertheless, the statute does not specify the extent to which particular types or volumes of copying would be considered beyond the bounds of what would be considered an acceptable fair use.

In a joint letter dated April 30, 1976, representatives of the music publishing industry and several associations of music schools and teachers submitted to the House Judiciary Subcommittee responsible for enacting the 1976 Copyright Act, a set of guidelines addressing both the interests of the music copyright owners and the needs of users of music in the academic community. Those guidelines were included in the House Report[5] and are set forth in full as follows:

*Guidelines for Educational Uses of Music*

> The purpose of the following guidelines is to state the minimum and not the maximum standards of educational fair use under Section 107 of HR 2223. The parties agree that the conditions determining the extent of permissible copying for educational purposes may change in the future; that certain types of copying permitted under these guidelines may not be permissible in the future, and conversely that in the future other types of copying not permitted, under these guidelines may be permissible under revised guidelines.
>
> Moreover, the following statement of guidelines is not intended to limit the types of copying permitted under the standards of fair use

[5] *Id.* at pp. 70, 71, 78.

under judicial decision and which are stated in Section 107 of the Copyright Revision Bill. There may be instances in which copying which does not fall within the guidelines stated below may nonetheless be permitted under the criteria of fair use.

*A. Permissible Uses*

1. Emergency copying to replace purchased copies which for any reason are not available for an imminent performance provided purchased replacement copies shall be substituted in due course.

2. (a) For academic purposes other than performance, multiple copies of excerpts of works may be made, provided that the excerpts do not comprise a part of the whole which would constitute a performable unit such as a section, movement or aria, but in no case more than 10% of the whole work. The number of copies shall not exceed one copy per pupil.

(b) For academic purposes other than performance, a single copy of an entire performable unit (section, movement, aria, etc.) that is, (1) confirmed by the copyright proprietor to be out of print or (2) unavailable except in a larger work, may be made by or for a teacher solely for the purpose of his or her scholarly research or in preparation to teach a class.

3. Printed copies which have been purchased may be edited or simplified provided that the fundamental character of the work is not distorted or the lyrics, if any, altered or lyrics added if none exist.

4. A single copy of recordings of performances by students may be made for evaluation or rehearsal purposes and may be retained by the educational institution or individual teacher.

5. A single copy of a sound recording (such as a tape, disc or cassette) of copyrighted music may be made from sound recordings owned by an educational institution or an individual teacher for the purpose of constructing aural exercises or examinations and may be retained by the educational institution or individual teacher. (This pertains only to the copyright of the music itself and not to any copyright which may exist in the sound recording.)

*B. Prohibitions*

1. Copying to create or replace or substitute for anthologies, compilations or collective works.

2. Copying of or from works intended to be "consumable" in the course of study or of teaching such as workbooks, exercises, standardized tests and answer sheets and like material.

3. Copying for the purpose of performance, except as in A(1) above.

4. Copying for the purpose of substituting for the purchase of music, except as in A (1) and A (2) above.

5. Copying without inclusion of the copyright notice which appears on the printed copy.

Though these guidelines have been criticized in some corners of academia as too restrictive, they are instructive insofar as they state the music publishing industry's views as to the general boundaries of permissible fair use of copyrighted music for educational purposes. Uses that exceed these boundaries are likely to pose legal risks to the user who chooses not to seek a license.

## B. Criticism, Comment, and News Reporting

Criticism, comment, and news reporting are also among the examples of fair use that are specifically set forth in the fair use provision of the copyright law, but, again, the confines of the doctrine must be determined on a case-by-case basis. A music critic's use of a few lyrics in a newspaper or magazine column, written for the purpose of reviewing the song from which the lyrics were taken, would clearly constitute a fair use.

The fair use defense relying on criticism and commentary is not limited to use in newspapers and magazines, but could also be used in books and websites. Suppose, for example, we included in this book and on our website, *Kohn on Music Licensing*,[6] the lyrics of songs, *Oh,*

[6] http://www.kohnmusic.com

*Pretty Woman* and its rap parody, *Pretty Woman*, as part of an illustration of the U.S. Supreme Court's application of the doctrine of fair use in *Campbell v. Acuff-Rose Music.*[7] Such a use would certainly be criticism and commentary, constituting fair use. If we were to take 30-second clips from the sound recordings of each of these songs and include them on our website, we would think that such use would also constitute a fair use.

### *1. The Yoko Ono Case*

Imagine using a Beatles song in a motion picture without permission and getting away way with it! That's just what happened when the producers of a documentary motion picture used 15 seconds of the song, *Imagine*, without permission[8] over the objections of the widow and children of John Lennon.

The documentary, entitled *Expelled*, was a 1-hour 39-minute nationally released theatrical movie that addressed the debate between proponents of intelligent design and the scientific theory of evolution. The producers of the film obtained licenses for all the music used in the film, except for the song *Imagine*. Approximately 1 hour and 5 minutes into the film, the 15-second excerpt of the song is heard and the 10 words from the lyrics that are heard appear on the screen:

*Nothing to kill or die for/*
*And no religion too.*

Immediately preceding the excerpt, several people interviewed are shown expressing negative views about religion and the narrator comments that the last of the interviewees was "merely lifting a page out of John Lennon's songbook." Then the 15-second excerpt plays and the above lyrics appear on the screen. The movie then cuts to another interviewee commenting on withdrawal of faith.

The court stepped through the analysis of the four factors for determining fair use set forth in Section 107. (A closer examination of the four factors is set forth in the following section.) In short, applying the first factor, the court determined that the use of the song was

---

[7] 510 U.S. 569 (1994).

[8] *Yoko Ono Lennon v. Premise Media Corp.*, 556 F. Supp. 2d 310 (2008).

"transformative" in that the film incorporates the excerpt for purposes of criticism and commentary. Specifically, the purpose was to "criticize the song's message."[9]

"To be transformative, it is not necessary that defendants alter the music or lyrics of the song."[10] Even though the use was not strictly necessary, the use of *Imagine* was "transformative because it does not 'merely supersede the objects of the original creation" but rather "adds something new, with a further purpose or different character, altering the first with new expression, meaning, or message."[11] The fact that defendants obtained permission to use other music in the movie did not alter that conclusion.[12] In sum, the use "would better serve the copyright law's goal of promoting the Progress of Science and useful Arts . . . than would prevent it."[13]

### *2. News Reporting Without Criticism*

How far, however, would the fair use doctrine extend if the use were entirely unrelated to any criticism of the song?

In 1940, a court held that the use of 12 lines of the lyrics from the 1914 song, *Poor Pauline*, by the *New Yorker* magazine in a brief comment in its "Talk of the Town" section about the death of film actress, Pauline White, was a fair use of the lyric.[14] Similarly, the following year, a court held that the quotation of the eight line chorus of the "official song" of the Green Bay Packer football team in a four-page article appearing in the *Saturday Evening Post* was a fair use.

Is a televised news report of a parade showing a marching band performing copyrighted music a fair use? Provided the broadcast is truly televised for purposes of reporting the news, and not for mere entertainment purposes, it probably is. However, if the newscast were to be taped for future commercial use, a synchronization license would be required.

---

[9] *Id.* at 327.

[10] *Id.* at 324.

[11] Quoting *Campbell*, 510 U.S. at 579.

[12] *Lennon* at 325.

[13] *Id.* at 327.

[14] *Broadway Music Corp. v. F-R Publishing Corp.*, 31 F. Supp. 817 (S.D.N.Y. 1940).

## C. Satire, Parody, and Burlesque

Perhaps the most litigated and controversial issues involving the doctrine of fair use have stemmed from the use of music for the purpose of parody, satire, or burlesque. Fair use has generally been recognized for works created for the purposes of parody, satire, or burlesque on the basis that society benefits from the social and literary commentary contributed by these kinds of works.[15] Nevertheless, determining whether a particular use qualifies for the defense must still be made on a case-by-case basis.

A case-by-case analysis will be aided by an understanding of the rationale underlying some of the key court decisions in this area.

### *1. The Case of MAD Magazine*

One of the first cases to deal with the extent to which song parodies constitute a fair use of copyright was *Berlin v. E. C. Publications, Inc.*[16] The prose of Judge Kaufman, writing for the U.S. Court of Appeals for the Second Circuit, was too entertaining to resist quoting him here at length:

> **Irving R. Kaufman, Circuit Judge.** Through depression and boom, war and peace, Tin Pan Alley has light-heartedly insisted that "the whole world laughs" with a laughter, and that "the best things in life are free." In an apparent departure from these delightful sentiments, the owners of the copyrights upon some twenty-five popular songs instituted this action against the publishers, employees, and distributors of "Mad Magazine," alleging that Mad's publication of satiric parody lyrics to plaintiffs' songs infringed the copyrighted originals, despite Mad's failure to reproduce the music of plaintiffs' compositions in any form whatsoever. . . .
>
> . . . The parodies were published as a "special bonus" to the Fourth Annual Edition of Mad, whose cover characterized its contents as "More Trash From Mad — A Sickening Collection of Humor and Satire From Past Issues," and almost prophetically carried this admonition for its readers: "For Solo or Group Participation (Followed by Arrest)."

[15] See, 3 Nimmer On Copyright, Sec. 13.05[C] (2000).

[16] 329 F.2d 57 (2d Cir. 1964).

> Defendants' efforts were billed as "a collection of parody lyrics to 57 old standards which reflect the idiotic world we live in today." Divided into nine categories, ranging from "Songs of Space & The Atom," to "Songs of Sports," they were accompanied by the notation that they were to be "Sung to" or "Sung to the tune of" a well-known popular song — in twenty-five cases, the plaintiffs' copyrighted compositions. So that this musical direction might feasibly be obeyed, the parodies were written in the same meter as the original lyrics.
>
> The District Court observed that the theme and content of the parodies differed markedly from those of the originals. Thus, *The Last Time I Saw Paris*, originally written as a nostalgic ballad which tenderly recalled pre-war France, became in defendant's hands, "The Last Time I Saw Maris," a caustic commentary upon the tendency of a baseball hero to become a television pitchman, more prone to tempt injury with the razor blade which he advertises than with the hazards of the game which he plays. Similarly, defendants transformed the plaintiffs' *A Pretty Girl is Like a Melody*, into "Louella Schwartz Describes Her Malady"; what was originally a tribute to feminine beauty became a burlesque of a feminine hypochondriac troubled with sleeplessness and a propensity to tell the world of her plight. As might be inferred from the range of categories presented and the foregoing examples of defendants' works, the parodies were as diverse in their targets for satire as they were broad in their humor.

After providing an analysis of the relative "substantiality — in terms of both quality and quantity — of the material taken from the original," (which analysis included a notable lampoon of one of the plaintiffs — "We doubt that even so eminent a composer as plaintiff Irving Berlin should be permitted to claim a property interest in iambic pentameter"), the court concluded,

> We believe that parody and satire *are* deserving of substantial freedom — both as entertainment and as a form of social and literary criticism. As readers of Cervantes's "Don Quixote" and Swift's "Gulliver's Travels," or the parodies of a modern master such as Max Beerbohm well know, many a true word is spoken in jest. At the very least, where, as here, it is clear that the parody has neither the intent nor the effect of fulfilling the original, and where the parodist does not appropriate a greater amount of the original work than is

necessary to "recall or conjure up" the object of his satire, a finding of infringement would be improper.

### *2. The Case of Saturday Night Live*

A late night television performance of the *Not Ready for Prime Time Players* kicked off a court battle that culminated in a 1980 decision by the U.S. Court of Appeals for the Second Circuit upholding a finding of fair use.[17] The entire opinion of the court is set forth as follows:

> This copyright infringement suit concerns a skit, shown on the television program, "Saturday Night Live," poking fun at New York City's public relations campaign and its theme song. In the four minute skit the town fathers of Sodom discuss a plan to improve their city's image. The satire ends with the singing of "I Love Sodom" to the tune of the theme song, *I Love New York*. The District Court for the Southern District of New York (Gerard L. Goettel, Judge) rejected appellant's claim of copyright infringement, concluding that the parody was protected fair use. Believing that, in today's world of often unrelieved solemnity, copyright law should be hospitable to the humor parody, and that the District Court correctly applied the doctrine of fair use, we affirm on Judge Goettel's thorough opinion.[18]

The decision contained the following lone, but instructive, footnote:

> The District Court concluded, among other things, that the parody did not make more extensive use of appellant's song than was necessary to "conjure up" the original. 482 F. Supp. at 747. While we agree with this conclusion, we note that the concept of "conjuring up" an original came into the copyright law not as a limitation on how much of an original may be used, but as a recognition that a parody frequently needs to be more than a fleeting evocation of an original in order to make its humorous point. *Columbia Pictures Corp. v. National Broadcasting Co.*, 137 F. Supp. 348, 354 (S.D. Cal. 1955). A parody is entitled at least to "conjure up" the original. Even more extensive use would still be fair use, provided the parody

---

[17] *Elsmere Music, Inc. v. National Broadcasting Co.*, 623 F.2d 252 (2d Cir. 1980).

[18] Referring to *Elsmere Music, Inc. v. National Broadcasting Co.*, 482 F. Supp 741 (1979).

> builds upon the original, using the original as a known element of modern culture and contributing something new for humorous effect or commentary.

Thus, a parody may constitute a fair use even where it uses more material than is necessary to merely conjure up the original, provided that the parody builds upon the original.

But what if the commentary expressed by the parody is not directed at the original work, but rather at another work or person, or at society in general? Within that question lies the subtle difference between a *parody* and a *satire*. One court defined *parody* as a work in which the language or style of another work is closely imitated or mimicked for comic effect or ridicule and in which some critical comment or statement about the original work is made, and *satire* as a work which holds up or exposes the vices or shortcomings of an individual or institution to ridicule or derision, usually with an intent to stimulate change.[19] Thus, parody both mimics and comments upon the original; satire mimics the original, but the object of its comment or ridicule may be the original work or another work, person, or institution.

In the *Elsmire* case, the court recognized that the target of the parody was both New York City's public relations campaign and the *I Love New York* theme song. Would a fair use defense protect the use of the theme song for the purpose of making a satire upon something entirely unrelated to the song or its subject?

### *3. The Case of the Boogie Woogie Bugle Boy*

That question was briefly addressed in the case of *MCA v. Wilson*, the X-rated facts of which were summarized by the court as follows:

> From January 1974 until July 1976, a show called "Let My People Come" was performed at the Village Gate, a cabaret in the Greenwich Village section of New York City. Thereafter, it had short runs in several other cabarets and legitimate theaters. The producers, perhaps wisely, refrained from seeking reviews from established theater critics. However, columnists who viewed the production described it, among

---

[19] *Metro-Goldwyn-Mayer, Inc. v. Showcase Atlanta Co-op Productions, Inc.*, 479 F. Supp. 351 (1979). *Compare, Acuff Rose v. Campbell*, cited below.

> other things, as an "erotic nude show" with "sex content raunchy enough to satisfy the most jaded porno palate," a show whose "main concern is not fornication but fellatio and cunnilingus."
>
> The music in the show was said by one columnist to sound "like something we've heard before but definitely not with these words." One of the songs, described by reporters as a "take-off on the Andrews Sisters' and Bette Midler's renditions of "Boogie Woogie Bugle Boy" is the subject of this litigation.
>
> . . . Boogie Woogie Bugle Boy is the alliterative description of a soldier in "Company B" who hailed from Chicago. During early rehearsals for Let My People Come, defendant Wilson played for the cast a rough version of the song he had composed which alliteratively described the "Cunnilingus Champion of Company C" who came from Memphis or maybe St. Joe.

One might conjure a valid defense that the language and style of the song *Boogie Woogie Bugle Boy* was closely imitated for comic effect or ridicule, including some critical comment or statement about the original, but the court found that this was simply not proven at trial and rejected the application of the fair use defense given the facts before it.

At the trial, the defendant testified that, sometime during the rehearsals that followed the song's unveiling, he formed the intent that the song would be a burlesque of the music of the 1940. The plaintiff contended that, since *Cunnilingus Champion* did not parody the song, *Boogie Woogie Bugle Boy*, it could not be a parody entitled to fair use. The court, however, agreed with the defendant, and stated,

> [A] permissible parody need not be directed solely to the copyrighted song but may also reflect life in general.

Nevertheless, the evidence showed that, *at the time he originally wrote* the song, *Cunnilingus Champion*, the defendant did not intend it to be either a burlesque or a satire. Moreover,

> When this action was commenced in July 1974, defendants did not contend that they were making a fair use of plaintiff's song. Instead,

> they simply denied plaintiff's allegation that Cunnilingus Champion was substantially copied from plaintiff's copyrighted work.

As a result, the court held that the defendants' song was neither a parody nor a burlesque *of Boogie Woogie Bugle Boy*, and concluded:

> We are not prepared to hold that a commercial composer can plagiarize a competitor's copyrighted song, substitute dirty lyrics of his own, perform it for commercial gain, and then escape liability by calling the end result a parody or satire on the mores of society.

#### *4. The Case of Rick Dees*

A case involving radio disc jockey Rick Dees and the '50's song, *When Sunny Gets Blue*, is also instructive.[20] In 1984, a lawyer representing Dees contacted one of the song's composers and requested permission to use all or a part of the music to create an inoffensive, comedic version. The composer refused to grant permission, and, a few months later, Dees released a comedy album called *Put It Where the Moon Don't Shine*. The album included, *When Sonny Sniffs Glue*, a parody which copied the first 6 of the original song's 38 bars of music — its recognizable main theme. In addition, it changed the original's opening lyrics — "When Sonny gets blue, her eyes get gray and cloudy, then the rain begins to fall" to "When Sonny sniffs glue, her eyes get red and bulgy, then her hair begins to fall." The parody ran for 29 seconds of the approximately 40 minutes of material on Dee's album.

The composers asserted that the parody, although it borrowed from the original work, was not "directed" at the original. Though the court assumed that a humorous or satiric work deserved protection under the fair use doctrine only if the copied work is "at least partly the target of the work in question" — a conclusion that was later refined by the Supreme Court (see below) — the court found that Dees's parody was intended to poke fun at the composer's song *and* at Johnny Mathis's rather singular vocal range.

In analyzing the "purpose and character" of the use, the court cited the principle earlier established by the U.S. Supreme Court that "every

[20] *Fisher v. Dees*, 794 F.2d 432 (9th Cir. 1986).

commercial use of copyrighted material is presumptively an unfair exploitation of the monopoly privilege that belongs to the owner of the copyright,"[21] but pointed out that the defendant can rebut the presumption by convincing the court that the parody does not unfairly diminish the economic value of the original. In assessing the economic effect of the parody upon the potential market or value of the copyrighted work, the court stated that the parody's critical impact must be excluded. Through its critical function, a "parody may quite legitimately aim at garroting the original, destroying it commercially as well as artistically."[22]

> Accordingly, the economic effect of a parody with which we are concerned is not its potential to destroy or diminish the market for the original — any bad review can have that effect — but rather whether it fulfills the demand for the original. Biting criticism suppresses demand; copyright infringement usurps it. Thus, infringement occurs when a parody supplants the original in markets the original is aimed at, or in which the original is, or has reasonable potential to become, commercially viable.[23]

With that guidance in mind, the court proceeded to hold that the two songs did not fulfill the same demand.

> "When Sunny Gets Blue" is "a lyrical song concerning or relating to a woman's feelings about lost love and her change for . . . happiness again." [citation omitted] By contrast, the parody is a 29-second recording concerning a woman who sniffs glue, which "ends with noise and laughter mixed into the song." [citation omitted] We do not believe the consumers desirous of hearing a romantic and nostalgic ballad such as the composer's song would be satisfied to purchase the parody instead. Nor are those fond of parody likely to consider "When Sunny Gets Blue" a source of satisfaction.

In analyzing the "amount and substantiality of the taking," the court explored the boundaries of a test it articulated in an earlier opinion: "whether the parodist has appropriated a greater amount of the

---

[21] *Sony Corp. of America v. Universal City Studios, Inc.*, 464 U.S. 417 (1984); *Harper & Row, Publishers, Inc. v. Nation Enters.*, 471 U.S. 539 (1985).

[22] B. Kaplan, *An Unhurried View of Copyright* 69 (1967).

[23] 794 F.2d at 438.

original work than is necessary to 'recall or conjure up' the object of his satire."[24] The composers interpreted this test to limit the amount of permissible copying to that necessary to evoke only *initial* recognition by the listener. In rejecting this rigid view, the court found itself in accord with the lone footnote of *Elsmere Music, Inc. v. National Broadcasting Company* set forth above — i.e., a parody is entitled *at least* to conjure up the original.

The court listed three considerations it thought important in determining whether a taking was excessive under the circumstances: the degree of public recognition of the original, the ease of conjuring up the original work in the chosen medium, and the focus of the parody. The court found that, in creating parodies of music, there is a special need for accuracy, because, like a speech, a song is difficult to parody effectively without exact or near-exact copying. Though the license to copy is not limitless, a parody that accomplishes its purpose by taking no more than is necessary to reasonably accomplish its parodic purpose is a fair use.

### *5. The Case of the Pretty Woman*

On March 7, 1994, the U.S. Supreme Court strolled down the proverbial street of fair use parody by publishing a decision in a case over whether the song, *Oh Pretty Woman*, by Roy Orbison and William Dees was infringed by a song entitled, *Pretty Woman*, recorded by rap recording group, 2 Live Crew.[25]

At the outset of its discussion of the four factors of fair use set forth in the copyright law, the court quoted an early distillation of "fair use" rendered by Justice Story in *Folsom v. Marsh*:

> look to the nature and objects of the selections made, the quantity and value of the materials used, and the degree in which the use may prejudice the sale, or diminish the profits, or supersede the objects, of the original work.[26]

The court then proceeded to explore each of the four factors set forth in Section 107 and applied them to the facts of the case.

[24] *Walt Disney Productions v. Air Pirates*, 581 F.2d 751, 757 (9th Cir. 1978).

[25] *Campbell v. Acuff-Rose*, 510 U.S. 569 (1994).

[26] *Folsom v. Marsh*, 9 F Cas 342, 348 (No. 4,901 (CCD Mass 1841).

*a. First Factor — "The purpose and character of the use, including whether such use is of a commercial nature or is for nonprofit educational purposes."*

The central purpose of this investigation, said the court, is to see whether the new work merely supersedes the objects of the original creation or instead adds something new, with a further purpose or different character, altering the first with new expression, meaning or message; it asks, in other words, whether and to what extent the new work is *transformative*. Although a transformative use is not necessary for a finding of fair use, the more transformative the new work, the less will be the significance of other factors, such as commercialism, that may weigh against a finding of fair use.

The court then confirmed that parody has an obvious claim to transformative value, as it can provide social benefit by shedding light on an earlier work, and, in the process, create a new one. Recognizing the difference between *parody* and *satire*, quoting two standard dictionary definitions of each word, the court shed some light on the question of the extent to which a parody qualifying for the fair use defense must be directed at the original work:

> For the purposes of copyright law, the nub of the definitions, and the heart of any parodist's claim to quote from existing material, is the use of some elements of a prior author's composition to create a new one that, at least in part, comments on that author's works. See, e.g., *Fisher v. Dees*, supra, at 437; *MCA, Inc. v. Wilson*, 677 F.2d 180, 185 (CA2 1981). If, on the contrary, the commentary has no critical bearing on the substance or style of the original composition, which the alleged infringer merely uses to get attention or to avoid the drudgery in working up something fresh, the claim to fairness in borrowing from another's work diminishes accordingly (if it does not vanish), and other factors, like the extent of its commerciality, loom larger. Parody needs to mimic an original to make its point, and so has some claim to use the creation of its victim's (or collective victims') imagination, whereas satire can stand on its own two feet and so requires justification for the very act of borrowing. See Ibid.; Bisceglia, *Parody and Copyright Protection: Turning the Balancing Act Into a Juggling Act*, in ASCAP, Copyright Law Symposium, No. 34, p. 25 (1987).

Thus, whether the parody is directed at the original is not definitive. The extent to which the parody is directed at the original must be placed on a sliding scale and considered with the other fair use factors, such as the extent to which the parody has an economic effect upon the potential market or value of the original. If the parody borrows from the original and the original is the object of the criticism, the parodist requires less justification and may have more leeway to adversely affect the potential market or value of the original. A satire, the criticism of which is directed entirely at an object other than the original work, or the creators of the original work, has a steeper hill to climb in laying claim to copying the original work.[27]

Further, the court made it clear that whether parody is in "good taste or bad" does not and should not matter to fair use. The threshold question when fair use is raised in defense of parody is "whether a parodic character may reasonably be perceived."

In applying the first factor to the facts of the case, the court found that,

> While we might not assign a high rank to the parodic element here, we think it fair to say 2 Live Crew's song reasonably could be perceived as commenting on the original or criticizing it, to some degree. 2 Live Crew juxtaposes the romantic musings of a man whose fantasy comes true, with degrading taunts, a bawdy demand for sex, and a sigh of relief from paternal responsibility. The later words can be taken as a comment on the naivete′ of the original of an earlier day, as a rejection of its sentiment that ignores the ugliness of street life and the

[27] Political or social satire, such as that conveyed in the hilarious song parodies written and performed by the Capitol Steps, tend to be directed less at the lyrics or composers of the copyrighted song parodied and more at the vices or shortcomings of individuals and institutions unrelated to the subject of the original song. In a friend-of-the-court brief filed in the Pretty Woman case by Capitol Steps Production, Inc., the amici pointed out that the particular music selected to convey the satirical message will often evoke a mood, setting, or juxtaposition of sentiments that either adds a musical joke to the satirical lyrics or otherwise enhances their effectiveness. Such a contribution by the copyrighted material to an otherwise unrelated satire would appear to supply that which is necessary to justify the claim to fairness. The Capitol Steps were joined in their efforts before the Supreme Court by, among others, nationally syndicated radio host Dr. Demento, whose popular broadcasts regularly include song parodies submitted by talented professional and amateur comedic artists, as well as comedian Mark Russell, whose many appearances on public television demonstrate that political satire need not necessarily be funny to constitute a fair use of copyright.

debasement that it signifies. It is this joinder of reference and ridicule that marks off the author's choice of parody from the other types of comment and criticism that traditionally have had a claim to fair use protection as transformative works.

Before turning to the other factors, the court made some other instructive observations. For example, the court noted that 2 Live Crew need not have labeled its song, or the album on which it appeared, a parody, in order to claim fair use protection. "Parody," said the court, "serves its goals whether labeled or not, and there is no reason to require parody to state the obvious (or even the reasonably perceived)." Further, it did not matter that 2 Live Crew had never recorded a parody before. However, the court pointed out that the use of a copyrighted work to advertise a product, even in a parody, will be entitled to less indulgence under the first factor of the fair use enquiry, than the sale of a parody for its own sake, let alone one performed a single time by students in a school.

*b. Second Factor — "the nature of the copyrighted work."*

This factor, said the court, calls for recognition that some works are closer to the core of intended copyright protection than others,[28] with the consequence that fair use is more difficult to establish when the former works are copied. Clearly, Roy Orbison's *Oh Pretty Woman* falls well within this core. However, the court said this was "not much help in this case, or ever likely to help much in separating the fair use sheep from the infringing goats in a parody case, since parodies almost invariably copy publicly known, expressive works."

*c. Third Factor — "The amount and substantiality of the portion used in relation to the copyrighted work as a whole."*

The attention here, said the court, turns to the persuasiveness of a parodist's justification for the particular copying done. Further, this enquiry will harken back to first of the statutory factors, because the extent

[28] Examples of works that are further away from the "core of intended copyright protection" include works comprised primarily of historical facts, information databases, and other compilations, as well as works of a utilitarian nature, such as computer programs.

of permissible copying varies with the purpose and character of the use, and will tend to have a bearing on the fourth factor, by revealing the degree to which the parody may serve as a market substitute for the original or potentially licensed derivatives. We now quote the court at length:

> Parody presents a difficult case. Parody's humor, or in any event its comment, necessarily springs from recognizable allusion to its object through distorted imitation. Its art lies in the tension between a known original and its parodic twin. When parody takes aim at a particular original work, the parody must be able to "conjure up" at least enough of that original to make the object of its critical wit recognizable. See, *e. g., Elsmere Music*, 623 F. 2d, at 253, n. 1; *Fisher v. Dees*, 794 F. 2d, at 438-439. What makes for this recognition is quotation of the original's most distinctive or memorable features, which the parodist can be sure the audience will know. Once enough has been taken to assure identification, how much more is reasonable will depend, say, on the extent to which the song's overriding purpose and character is to parody the original or, in contrast, the likelihood that the parody may serve as a market substitute for the original. But using some characteristic features cannot be avoided.
>
> We think the Court of Appeals was insufficiently appreciative of parody's need for the recognizable sight or sound when it ruled 2 Live Crew's use unreasonable as a matter of law. It is true, of course, that 2 Live Crew copied the characteristic opening bass riff (or musical phrase) of the original, and true that the words of the first line copy the Orbison lyrics. But if quotation of the opening riff and the first line may be said to go to the "heart" of the original, the heart is also what most readily conjures up the song for parody, and it is the heart at which parody takes aim. Copying does not become excessive in relation to parodic purpose merely because the portion taken was the original's heart. If 2 Live Crew had copied a significantly less memorable part of the original, it is difficult to see how its parodic character would have come through. See *Fisher v. Dees*, 794 F. 2d, at 439.
>
> This is not, of course, to say that anyone who calls himself a parodist can skim the cream and get away scot free. In parody, as in news reporting, see *Harper & Row*, supra, context is everything, and the question of fairness asks what else the parodist did besides go to the heart of the original. It is significant that 2 Live Crew not only

> copied the first line of the original, but thereafter departed markedly from the Orbison lyrics for its own ends. 2 Live Crew not only copied the bass riff and repeated it, but also produced otherwise distinctive sounds, interposing "scraper" noise, overlaying the music with solos in different keys, and altering the drum beat. See 754 F. Supp., at 1155. This is not a case, then, where "a substantial portion" of the parody itself is composed of a "verbatim" copying of the original. It is not, that is, a case where the parody is so insubstantial, as compared to the copying, that the third factor must be resolved as a matter of law against the parodists.
>
> Suffice it to say here that, as to the lyrics, we think the Court of Appeals correctly suggested that "no more was taken than necessary," 972 F. 2d, at 1438, but just for that reason, we fail to see how the copying can be excessive in relation to its parodic purpose, even if the portion taken is the original's "heart." As to the music, we express no opinion whether repetition of the bass riff is excessive copying, and we remand to permit evaluation of the amount taken, in light of the song's parodic purpose and character, its transformative elements, and considerations of the potential for market substitution sketched more fully below.

*d. Fourth Factor — "The effect of the use upon the potential market for or value of the copyrighted work."*

The final factor, said the court, requires courts to consider not only the extent of market harm caused by the particular actions of the alleged infringer, but also whether unrestricted and widespread conduct of the sort engaged in by the defendant would result in a substantial adverse impact on the potential market for the original. The enquiry must take account not only of the harm to the original but also of harm to the market for derivative works of the original.

Correcting the primary error made by the lower court, the court held that there is no presumption that uses intended for commercial gain are likely to have a substantial adverse impact on the potential market for the original. On the contrary, the more transformative the use, such as a pure parody or satire, the more likely it is that the new work will *not* affect the market for the original. This is so because the parody and the original usually serve different market functions.

Nevertheless, the analysis cannot stop there, as even a transformative work may have characteristics beyond those of parodic or satiric criticism. For example, the 2 Live Crew song, besides being a parody, is also rap music. Thus, a relevant inquiry is whether the rap nature of the 2 Live Crew song will have a substantial adverse impact upon rap derivatives of the original Orbison version.[29]

Since there was no evidence in the record upon which the Supreme Court could base a decision on this question, it remanded the case to the lower courts where the "evidentiary hole will doubtless be plugged." Thus, in contrast to news reports holding that the Supreme Court held the 2 Live Crew song to be a fair use and not infringing the Orbison hit, the court actually remanded the case back to the lower courts for a redetermination of fair use in light of the court's discussion of the law.

### *6. The Case of Ghostface Killah*

The song *What a Wonderful World*, the best known rendition of which was recorded by Louis Armstrong and which subscribes to the message of a pastoral world of "skies of blue and clouds of white," was taken to task by rap artist known professionally as Ghostface Killah. The original song opens with the lines:

> I see trees of green, red roses, too
> I see them bloom for me and you
> And I think to myself, what a wonderful world.

In 2001, Ghostface Killah wrote and recorded a song called, *The Forest*, for inclusion in an album entitled, Bulletproof Wallets. *The Forest* portrays a dark view of the world by imagining popular cartoon characters (including, Daffy Duck, the Simpsons, and Snow White) in a "wonderland," engaged in acts of violence, sex, and theft. *The Forest* opens, however, with an off-key rendition of the first verse of *What*

---

[29] Having the characteristics of a rap musical recording, the 2 Live Crew parody actually receives radio airplay and enjoys CD sales as a musical recording intended to be enjoyed as such. Arguably, this substantial, non-parody characteristic may tip the scales against a finding of fair use. By contrast, if the parody were instead primarily intended as a comedy recording, to be enjoyed as such, then, notwithstanding the radio airplay and CD sales it may receive, it is less likely the parody recording would affect the market for the original, tipping the scales in favor of a finding of fair use.

*a Wonderful World*, the lyrics of which were changed to include references to marijuana:

> I see buds that are green, red roses, too
> I see them blunts for me and you
> And I think to myself, what a wonderful world.

After a pause, the rap begins,

> It's the illest little story for all the girls and boys/Wonderland you should see it . . .

The owners of the song *What a Wonderful World* filed suit for copyright infringement[30] and the court granted defendant's motion for summary judgment, holding that the use was a fair use of copyright. Closely following the Supreme Court's analysis in *Campbell*, the court found that *The Forest* indisputably intended to parody the message of the *What a Wonderful World* and would be so perceived by any listener familiar with the song. It therefore had an obvious claim to transformative value.

> Given the small portion of *What a Wonderful World* quoted in *The Forest*, and the transformative nature of the song's use, Ghostface Killah's parody presents little danger of impairing plaintiff's right to exploit their copyright. Disallowing this use of *What a Wonderful World* would contravene copyright's purpose of allowing new works to acknowledge influence and react to what has gone before, and would allow copyright owners to quash parodies and other forms of transformation and comment of which they do not approve."

### *7. The Case of Barbie Doll*

Does the doctrine of fair use extend to protect a song when the object of its parody or satire is not another song, or even another copyrighted work, but a product or trademark of a product?

---

[30] *Abilene Music, Inc. v. Sony Music Entertainment, Inc.*, 320 F.Supp.2d 84 (2003).

That question was tested by the 1997 release of the song, *Barbie Girl* by the Danish band, Aqua, and subsequent suit[31] by Mattel, the makers of the Barbie doll, a long-legged, blond doll — a cultural icon that has become a symbol of American girlhood. In the song, a female band member impersonates Barbie and a male member impersonates Barbie's friend, Ken, who entices Barbie to "go party."

The lyrics of the song *Barbie Girl* were set forth in the court's opinion as follows[32]:

-Hiya Barbie!
-Hi Ken!
-You wanna go for a ride?
-Sure, Ken!
-Jump in!
-Ha ha ha ha!

I'm a Barbie girl, in my Barbie world
Life in plastic, it's fantastic
You can brush my hair, undress me everywhere
Imagination, life is your creation
Come on Barbie, let's go party!

I'm a blonde bimbo girl, in a fantasy world
Dress me up, make it tight, I'm your dolly
You're my doll, rock and roll, feel the glamour in pink
Kiss me here, touch me there, hanky-panky
You can touch, you can play
If you say "I'm always yours," ooh ooh

Come on, Barbie, let's go party, ah ah ah yeah
Come on, Barbie, let's go party, ooh ooh, ooh ooh
Come on, Barbie, let's go party, ah ah ah yeah
Come on, Barbie, let's go party, ooh ooh, ooh ooh
Make me walk, make me talk, do whatever you please
I can act like a star, I can beg on my knees
Come jump in, be my friend, let us do it again
Hit the town, fool around, let's go party

[31] *Mattel, Inc. v. MCA Records, Inc.*, 296 F.3d 894 (9th Cir. 2002).

[32] Copyright © 1997 Universal Music. Used without permission.

You can touch, you can play
You can say "I'm always yours"
You can touch, you can play
You can say "I'm always yours"

-Oh, I'm having so much fun!
-Well, Barbie, we're just getting started!
-Oh, I love you Ken!

The song became a Top 40 hit, but Mattel was not amused and filed suit alleging the song and its title (a) infringe Mattel's federal trademark in the name, "Barbie," (b) constitute a "false designation of origin" under the Lanham Act, and (c) dilute the trademark under the Federal Trademark Dilution Act. In an opinion for the Ninth Circuit Federal Court of Appeals written by Judge Kozinski, the court held that *Barbie Girl* did not violate Mattel's rights in its famous trademark.

*a. Trademark Infringement*

As with copyright law, there exists a tension between trademark law and the First Amendment's guarantee of freedom of speech.

> A trademark is a word, phrase or symbol that is used to identify a manufacturer or sponsor of a good or the provider of a service. *See New Kids on the Block* v. *News Am. Publ'g, Inc.*, 971 F.2d 302, 305 (9th Cir. 1992). It's the owner's way of preventing others from duping consumers into buying a product they mistakenly believe is sponsored by the trademark owner. A trademark "informs people that trademarked products come from the same source." *Id.* at 305 n.2. Limited to this core purpose — avoiding confusion in the marketplace — a trademark owner's property rights play well with the First Amendment. "Whatever first amendment rights you may have in calling the brew you make in your bathtub 'Pepsi' are easily outweighed by the buyer's interest in not being fooled into buying it." *Trademarks Unplugged*, 68 N.Y.U.L. Rev. 960, 973 (1993).
>
> . . . The First Amendment may offer little protection for a competitor who labels its commercial good with a confusingly similar mark, but "trademark rights do not entitle the owner to quash an unauthorized use of the mark by another who is communicating

ideas or expressing points of view." *L.L. Bean, Inc.* v. *Drake Publishers, Inc.*, 811 F.2d 26, 29 (1st Cir. 1987). Were we to ignore the expressive value that some marks assume, trademark rights would grow to encroach upon the zone protected by the First Amendment. *See Yankee Publ'g, Inc.* v. *News Am. Publ'g, Inc.*, 809 F. Supp. 267, 276 (S.D.N.Y. 1992) ("When unauthorized use of another's mark is part of a communicative message and not a source identifier, the First Amendment is implicated in opposition to the trademark right."). Simply put, the trademark owner does not have the right to control public discourse whenever the public imbues his mark with a meaning beyond its source-identifying function. *See Anti-Monopoly, Inc.* v. *Gen. Mills Fun Group*, 611 F.2d 296, 301 (9th Cir. 1979) ("It is the source-denoting function which trademark laws protect, and nothing more.").

The court then ruled that the use of the trademark Barbie in the title of the song, Barbie Girl, did not infringe Mattel's trademark, because the song's title "conveys a message to consumers about what they can expect to discover in the song itself." Further, the song "pokes fun at Barbie and the values that Aqua contends she represents." "Where an artistic work targets the original and does not merely borrow another's property to get attention, First Amendment interests weigh more heavily in the balance."[33]

*b. False Designation of Origin*

The court also held that the song's title does not constitute a false designation of origin in violation of the Lanham Act. In doing so, the court adopted a standard earlier established by the Second Circuit Federal Court of Appeals that "literary titles do not violate the Lanham Act "unless the title has no artistic relevance to the underlying work whatsoever, or, if it has some artistic relevance, unless the title explicitly misleads as to the source or content of the work."[34] The court found that song title clearly is relevant to the underlying work and the song is

[33] Citing *Dr. Seuss Enters. v. Penguin Books USA, Inc.*, 109 F.3d 1394 (9th Cir. 1997). (The court distinguished the result in Dr. Seuss where the court held that the book *The Cat NOT In The Hat* borrowed Dr. Seuss's trademarks and lyrics to get attention rather than to mock *The Cat In The Hat*. In *Mattel*, the song did not use the Barbie mark to poke fun at another subject but targeted Barbie herself.)

[34] Citing *Rogers v. Grimaldi*, 875 F.2d 994 (2d Cir. 1989).

about Barbie and the values Aqua claims she represents. The song title "did not explicitly mislead as to the source of the work; it does not, explicitly or otherwise, suggest that it was produced by Mattel."

#### c. *Dilution of Trademark*

Trademark *dilution* refers to the weakening of a trademark when it is used to identify different products. For example, few would be misled into thinking that "Tylenol snowboards" are manufactured by a major pharmaceutical company, but the use of the Tylenol mark in that context would weaken the commercial value of the pharmaceutical company's Tylenol mark. By contrast to trademark infringement, the injury from dilution usually occurs when consumers are *not* confused about the source of a product. Even if no one suspects that the maker of analgesics has entered into the snowboard business, the Tylenol mark will now bring to mind two products, not one.

The court held that the use of the mark Barbie in the title of the song Barbie Girl did not constitute trademark dilution, because under the Federal Trademark Dilution Act there is an exemption for *noncommercial* uses. At first blush, it would seem that a commercially released song would constitute a commercial use, but the legislative history of the Act makes it clear that noncommercial use refers to a use that consists entirely of noncommercial, or fully constitutionally protective speech. *See* 2 Jerome Gilson et al., *Trademark Protection and Practice* § 5.12[1][c][vi] at 5-240 (this exemption "is intended to prevent the courts from enjoining speech that has been recognized to be [fully] constitutionally protected," "such as parodies").

The court found that, although the song used Barbie's name to sell copies of the song, the song also "lampoons the Barbie image and comments humorously on the cultural values that Aqua claims she represents. Use of the Barbie mark in the song Barbie Girl therefore falls within the noncommercial use exemption to the FTDA. For precisely the same reasons, use of the mark in the song's title is also exempted."

### *8. The Case of The Family Guy*

The owner of the song, *When You Wish Upon A Star*, written for the animated Disney classic, *Pinocchio*, filed suit against the creators and producers of "The Family Guy," an animated, comedic television series, broadcast on the Fox Network, among others, which frequently pokes fun at popular culture, movies, songs, and celebrities.

The focus of the complaint was an episode entitled, *When You Wish Upon A Weinstein*, an episode about how the show's father, Peter, has difficulty managing his family's finances. After hearing friends about how men with Jewish-sounding names have helped them to achieve financial success, Peter decides that he "needs a Jew" to help him with his finances. The point of the episode was that Peter's beliefs based upon racial stereotypes, even potentially positive ones, are ridiculous. At the end of the Episode, Peter says to his wife, Lois, "I see what you're saying. The Jewish are just like us. No better, no worse." According to the show's creators, "one of the comedic values present is that although this is an obvious concept, it was not obvious to Peter."

The scene at issue in the case was when Peter is depicted looking out of a window up at the night sky in a manner similar to that of the toymaker Gepetto in Pinocchio when Gepetto is wishing for a "real boy." Peter begins to sing a song entitled, *I Need A Jew*, the first four notes of which are identical to the first four notes in *When You Wish Upon A Star* and the lyrics of which are as follows:

> Nothing else has worked so far, So I'll wish upon a star,
> Wondrous dancing speck of light, I need a Jew.
> Lois makes me take the rap, 'Cause our check-book looks like crap,
> Since I can't give her a slap, I need a Jew.
>
> Where to find a Baum or Steen or Stein,
> To teach me how to whine and do my taxes?
> Though by many they're abhorred, Hebrew people I've adored.
> Even though they killed my Lord I need a Jew.

The cartoon accompanying the song depicts "Jews as magical creatures that come to Peter in the form of a magical spaceship that turns into a flying dreidel." Oy.

Before proceeding with its analysis of the four factors to be considered in any fair use analysis, the court explored whether the use here constituted a parody or a satire, a distinction that turns on the object of the commentary made by the infringing work. In holding that *I Need*

*A Jew* constituted a parody — one which comments, at least in part, on the original work — the court found:

> . . . that by juxtaposing the "saccharin sweet" song "When You Wish Upon a Star" with "I Need a Jew" the Defendants do more than just comment on racism and bigotry generally, as Plaintiff contends. Rather, Defendants' use of "When You Wish Upon a Star" calls to mind a warm and fuzzy view of the world that is ultimately nonsense; wishing upon a star does not, in fact, make one's dreams come true. By pairing Peter's "positive," though racist, stereotypes of Jewish people with that fairy tale world-view, "I Need a Jew" comments both on the original work's fantasy of stardust and magic, as well as Peter's fantasy of the "superiority" of Jews. The song can be "reasonably perceived" to be commenting that any categorical view of a race of people is childish and simplistic, just like wishing upon a star.
>
> This interpretation of "I Need a Jew" is supported by the visual elements on screen at the time the song is being sung by Peter in the Episode. The visual elements, depicting Peter staring out a window at a starry night, echo the equivalent scene in *Pinocchio* in which Gepetto is wishing for a real boy. It is undisputed that *Pinocchio* is the original context of the song "When You Wish Upon a Star". . . . The visual reference to *Pinocchio* makes plain that this is not a case in which the creators simply substituted new lyrics for a known song "to get attention or to avoid the drudgery in working up something fresh". *Campbell*, 510 U.S. at 580; *cf. MCA, Inc. v. Wilson*, 425 F.Supp. 443, 453 (D.C.N.Y. 1976), *Dr. Seuss Enters., L.P. v. Penguin Books USA, Inc.*, 109 F.3d 1394 (9th Cir. 1997). The creators of the Episode were clearly attempting to comment in some way on the wishful, hopeful scene in Pinocchio with which the song is associated. Consequently, "I Need a Jew" is properly understood as a parody of "When You Wish Upon a Star."
>
> The Court's finding is further supported by Defendants' proffered evidence that the song in the Episode makes an additional comment, or "inside joke," about the "widespread belief" that Walt Disney was anti-Semitic. . . . Defendants argue that, "[t]he creators of the Family Guy Song thought it would be the perfect, cutting commentary to use the iconic song most closely-associated with Walt Disney, Wish Upon a Star, in a parodic reverie where the main character 'wishes upon a star' for, of all things, a Jew."

Applying the four factor analysis to the parody, the court had no trouble finding the work to be transformative. In addition, given evidence of an internal, creative dispute as to how much of the original to use, the court found that the amount of the borrowing was necessary to allow the parodic character of the defendants' work to come through. Finally, the court held "there can be no question that *I Need A Jew* does not usurp the market for *When You Wish Upon A Star*, as they serve different market functions. Affording little weight to the second factor, and finding factors one, three and four to be weighing heavily in defendants' favor, the court held the use to constitute a fair use."

> [T]he owner of the rights to a well-known work "must expect, or at least tolerate, a parodist's deflating ridicule."[35] . . . Plaintiff reaps the benefit of their song's association with *Pinocchio* and Disney, and enjoys its reputation for wholesomeness; it is precisely that beneficial association that opens the song up to ridicule by parodists seeking to take the wind out of such lofty, magical, or pure associations. The Supreme Court found that such deflating uses serve the important social function of shedding light on the earlier work. . . . Transformative uses of a copyrighted work, such as the Family Guy parody here, "lie at the heart of the fair use doctrine's guarantee of breathing space within the confines of copyright."

## D. Lyric Quotes

Though the quoting of a copyrighted song lyric in a student's term paper would clearly constitute a fair use, the quoting of even a few short lines of the lyric in a book intended for commercial sale would generally not be permitted under the fair use doctrine, unless the use was specifically for the purpose of comment or criticism. When Dr. Sigmund Spaeth, in his book on American Popular music, *Read 'Em and Weep*, quoted the words and music of the copyright song, *Ta-Ra-Ra-Boom-Der-E*, a court in 1932 rejected his fair use defense on the basis that the use was "obviously more than quotation and comment."[36]

---

[35] Citing *Leibovitz v. Paramount Pictures Corporation*, 137 F.3d 109, 114-115 (2d Cir. 1998).

[36] *Sayers v. Spaeth*, 20 Copyr. Dec. 625 (S.D.N.Y. 1932).

### E. A Few Bars

For most uses of music, unless the music is being used directly for some form of criticism, news reporting, teaching, research, parody, satire, or some other nonprofit use, the doctrine of fair use is not likely to provide a valid defense to copyright infringement, even if the use consists of only a few short bars of the copyrighted music. Thus, the whistling of even a few bars of a song in a motion picture will require permission from the copyright owner.

### F. Digital Sampling

Fair use has been unsuccessfully advanced as a defense to digital sampling. For a further discussion, the reader is referred to Chapter 24, on *The Digital Sampling Controversy*.

### G. 30-Second Samples

Fair use has also been unsuccessfully advanced as a defense to online retailers who use 30-second streamed performances of recordings to promote the sales of permanent music downloads, ring tones, and ring backs.[37] Accordingly, 30-second samples streamed over the Internet to promote the online sales of recordings require a performance license from the performance rights societies.

## III. Should You Ask for Permission?

As suggested at the outset of this chapter, the application of the doctrine of fair use in any particular case will largely be judgmental. All a good lawyer can do is review the casebooks for any legal decisions on point and make an independent assessment of the risk his client takes by using a work without the permission of the copyright owner. Of course, the risk of using a work owned by another can be eliminated by asking and obtaining permission for the use. Suppose, however, you attempt to

---

[37] *United States of America v. ASCAP* (In the Matter of AT&T Wireless), 599 F. Supp. 2d 415 (2009).

clear the use, but permission is denied. Should you make use of the work anyway? Was it a mistake to have asked for permission in the first place? Indeed, in the case of a parody or satire, what is the likelihood that permission will actually be granted?[38]

Many lawyers advise against seeking permission where circumstances suggest a reasonable basis supporting the fair use defense. Asking for permission, they say, may be construed as an admission that the defense is not applicable, and, by using a work after permission has been denied is likely to increase the chances of litigation — a jilted copyright owner seeking retribution for the audacity of your client.

In the case of Rick Dees, however, the court did not fault Dees for using the song after the composers expressly refused permission:

> Parodists will seldom get permission from those whose works are parodied. . . . Moreover, to consider Dees blameworthy because he asked permission would penalize him for this modest show of consideration. Even though such gestures are predictably futile, we refuse to discourage them.[39]

Contrast this with the court's reaction in *Grand Upright Music Limited v. Warner Bros.*, discussed in Chapter 24, on *The Digital Sampling Controversy*.

> [T]he most persuasive evidence that the copyrights are valid and owned by the plaintiff comes from the actions and admissions of the defendants. Prior to the time that Biz Markie's album was released, the various defendants apparently discussed among themselves the need to obtain a license. They decided to contact O'Sullivan and wrote to his brother/agent, enclosing a copy of the tape. . . . In writing this letter, counsel for Biz Markie admittedly was seeking "terms" for the use of the material. One would not agree to pay to use the material of another unless there was a valid copyright! What more persuasive evidence can there be![40]

---

[38] "People ask . . . for criticism, but they only want praise." S. Maugham, Of Human Bondage 241 (Penguin ed. 1992).

[39] 794 F.2d at 437 (9th Cir. 1986).

[40] 780 F. Supp. 182, 184 (S.D.N.Y 1991).

Does this mean that if you're in New York, don't ask; if you're in California, ask — it couldn't hurt? No, because subsequent to these decisions, the Supreme Court sided with "ask":

> [W]e reject Acuff-Rose's argument that 2 Live Crew's request for permission to use the original should be weighed against a finding of fair use. Even if good faith were central to fair use, 2 Live Crew's actions do not necessarily suggest that they believed their version was not fair use; the offer may simply have been made in a good faith effort to avoid litigation. If the use is otherwise fair, then no permission need be sought or granted. Thus, being denied permission to use a work does not weigh against finding of fair use. *See Fisher v. Dees*, 794 F2d 432, 437 (CA9 1986).[41]

So, should you ask for permission in doubtful cases? Yes, but we suggest that, in your letter to the copyright owner, you set forth your position on fair use, and state that you are writing in good faith in an effort to avoid litigation. By the same token, failing or neglecting to ask for permission should not hurt a good fair use defense.

---

[41] The Southern District of New York appears now to be in accord. See *Abilene Music, Inc. v. Sony Music Entertainment, Inc.*, 320 F. Supp. 2d 84 (S.D.N.Y. 2003) (defendants initially sought a license from the music publisher to use *When You Wish Upon A Star*, but was refused).

CHAPTER 26

# TYPICAL LICENSE FEES

## SUMMARY

## III. Mechanical License Fees

A. Statutory Rate

1. Physical Phonorecords and Permanent Downloads
2. Ringtones
3. Incidental Digital Phonorecord Deliveries

B. Special Rates

## IV. Electrical Transcription Fees

A. Syndicated Radio Shows

B. Radio Transcriptions (for programming introductions, themes, background music and breaks, etc.)

C. Background Music Services

1. Reproduction License
2. Performance License

## V. Synchronization Fees

A. Television Synchronization License Fees

B. Theatrical Motion Picture Synchronization License Fees — Major Studio

C. Theatrical Motion Picture Synchronization License Fees — Independent, Low Budget, Non-Profit or Student Films

D. Non-Theatrical Film Synchronization License Fees

E. Television Synchronization License for Music Videos

F. Synchronization License for Feature Film Trailers

G. Videogram Synchronization License Fees

H. Video Download Synchronization License Fees

## VI. Commercial Advertising License Fees

A. Television Commercial Synchronization License

B. Radio Commercial Electrical Transcription License

C. Print Advertising

## VII. Music Boxes and Commercial Product License

A. Royalty

B. Advance

## VIII. VIDEOGAMES, COMPUTER SOFTWARE, MULTIMEDIA

A. Videogames
   1. Video Arcade Games
   2. Video Game Cartridges and Online Versions
   3. Video Games Dedicated to Music

B. Multimedia Programs

C. MIDI Software

D. Karaoke
   1. Karaoke Discs
   2. Online Karaoke

## IX. NEEDLEDROP OR PRODUCTION MUSIC LIBRARY

A. Television and Non-Theatrical License
   1. Local
   2. National (including Worldwide)

B. Theatrical Motion Pictures; Pay or Subscriber T.V.; Videocassette (U.S. use only)

C. Other (including CD-ROMs)

## X. LIVING STAGE PERFORMANCE FEES

## XI. THEME PARK LICENSE FEES

A. Permanent Attractions

B. Single Additional Attractions

C. Live Stage Show in Theme Park

## XII. DIGITAL SAMPLING LICENSE FEES

A. Music

B. Sound Recordings

# CHAPTER 26

# TYPICAL LICENSE FEES

Having explored the various types of licenses by which permission to use music is granted and the considerations involved in negotiating the terms of those licenses, we need only consider the license fees that are typically charged for the various uses of music. This chapter provides some of the ranges within which license fees have tended to fall at the time this edition went to print in the fall of 2009.

## I. Overview

It should be noted that, in many cases, the fee ranges set forth in this chapter are based upon some broad generalizations and assumptions. Consequently, many of the fees stated do not take into consideration some of the key considerations discussed in this book, including the countervailing factors of (i) the importance of the song in relation to its intended use and (ii) the availability of close substitutes for the song.

For example, if a song is needed to merely establish the setting of a scene in the 1940s, the song *As Time Goes By* from the motion picture *Casablanca* might fulfill that need quite well. However, songs such as *Boogie Woogie Bugle Boy* and *I'll Be with You in Apple Blossom Time* (made popular by the Andrews Sisters) may serve that purpose just as well. If the licensor of *As Time Goes By* were to quote too high a license fee, the producer may choose one of the other ready alternatives. If, on the other hand, the song is required for a movie such as Woody Allen's *Play It Again, Sam*, virtually no close substitutes for the song, *As Time Goes By* will suffice, and it is more likely the producer would expect to pay a license fee in the high end of the range, if not above the range, for this particular use of that song.

Nevertheless, despite the generalizations made and the likelihood that these ranges will, *As Time Goes By*, become obsolescent, the fees stated in this chapter may still be useful for the information they provide about relative values — that is, the fees as they relate in proportion to each other — which is not likely to change significantly over time.

## II. PRINT AND DIGITAL PRINT LICENSE FEES

Presently, publishers are using the following formula for sheet music, folios, and other printed items such as orchestrations for dance orchestras, brass bands, and vocal arrangements:

### A. Standard Publishing Agreement Between Songwriter and Music Publisher

Music publishers typically agree to pay the songwriter the following amounts:

#### *1. Sheet Music*

6¢ to 12¢ per copy, with the median average being 7¢ or 8¢ per copy.

The cents per copy structure for sheet music has long been considered a "sacred cow" and exceptions are rarely made. Where, however, the writer has an unusual amount of leverage, he or she may be able to persuade the publisher to provide 10% to 15% of the publisher's wholesale price, or 20% of the retail list price, on revenues from sheet music. Many old publishing contracts provide for rates as low as 2¢ or 3¢ per copy, but the days of 50¢ sheet music went out with high button shoes, and perhaps in this era of inflation, the percentage royalty structure is more appropriate.

#### *2. Arrangements*

10% to 15% of the retail selling price of the item, with 12.5% being quite common.

#### *3. Folios*

10% to 15% of the retail selling price of the item, with 12.5% being quite common, pro rated over the number of copyrighted, royalty-bearing songs in the folio.

#### *4. Educational and Concert Editions*

12.5% of the established retail selling price of the item.

### B. Agreement Between Music Publisher and Independent Print Publisher

A print publisher typically agrees to pay the music publisher the following amounts:

#### *1. Sheet Music*

20% of the suggested retail selling price, which is typically $3.95, but can be $2.95 or $4.95. Thus, a music publisher should expect to receive between $0.50 to $1.00 per copy.

#### *2. Folios*

10% to 15%, but most often 12.5%, of the suggested retail price pro rated over the number of copyrighted, royalty-bearing songs used in the folio.

#### *3. Personality Folio*

10% to 15% but most often 12.5%, of the suggested retail price pro rated over the number of copyrighted, royalty-bearing songs used in the folio, plus additional 2.5% to 5% for the right to publish the photograph, likeness, and biographical material about the artist. Advance against royalty: $500–1,000.

#### *4. Educational and Concert Editions*

12.5% of the suggested retail price.

#### *5. Lyric Reprints on Internet Websites*

$1,000 per year.

### C. Printing of Lyrics

#### *1. Books*

$50 to $1,000, plus two copies of the book upon publication, to quote a lyric from a copyrighted song in a novel, textbook, or other works of fiction or non-fiction. The fee may vary based upon the size of anticipated print run, with large publishing houses charged more than those producing self-published books. Similar fees for other editions, such as paperback, book club, and abridgments.

*2. Magazine Advertising*

$2,500 to $5,000 per year.

*3. Greeting Cards*

5% of the retail selling price of the item.

*4. Record Albums*

2¢ to 5¢ per lyric per album copy.

*5. Promotional Albums*

Free

*6. Lyric Magazines*

$150 per song for 1 year; additional $100 if the song reaches Hot 100 song listing in Billboard Magazine.

*7. Lyric Reprints on Internet Websites*

$1,000 per year for use of lyrics on website to promote motion picture in which the lyrics appear.

**D. Digital Print**

*1. Lyric Reprints on Websites*

For permission to reprint lyrics on Internet websites, $1,000 per year.

*2. Digital Sheet Music*

25% of retail or 50% of gross receipts, whichever is higher.

### 3. *Digital Guitar Tabs*

50% of gross receipts (including any subscription fees, advertising revenues, etc.). The sites provide reports to the publisher showing the amount of "hits" or "views" of the guitar tabs and pro rate the license fees among the songs and their respective owners accordingly. Some deals require the online retailer to pay a penny rate for each hit or view of the guitar tab.

### 4. *Digital Lyric Database Websites*

50% of gross receipts (including any subscription fees, advertising revenues, etc.). The sites provide reports to the publisher showing the amount of "hits" or "views" of the lyrics and pro rate the license fees among the songs and their owners accordingly.

### 5. *Online Karaoke*

12% to 15% of gross revenues, for the use of lyrics and music.

# III. MECHANICAL LICENSE FEES

## A. Statutory Rate

### 1. *Physical Phonorecords and Permanent Downloads*

As of January 1, 2009, the statutory rate was 9.1¢ for recordings up to five minutes in length and, if over five minutes, 1.75¢ per minute of playing time. The same rate applies to both physical phonorecords (e.g., CDs, LPs, cassettes, etc.) and permanent digital downloads (e.g., digital phonorecord deliveries in general).

### 2. *Ringtones*

The statutory rate to be paid for each digital phonorecord delivery constituting a ringtone made during the period beginning March 1, 2009 and ending when modified by the CRB in a future rate proceeding, is 24¢.

#### *3. Incidental Digital Phonorecord Deliveries*

Rates for incidental digital phonorecord deliveries (e.g., on-demand streams and limited downloads) are set forth in Chapter 13.

Note: The Harry Fox Agency, which administers mechanical licensing in the United States for many music publishers, has announced an intention to apply this new rate to all phonorecords made and distributed on or after January 1, 1996, *regardless of the date upon which the mechanical license under which such records are manufactured was issued, or the date upon which the recording was first released*, unless the licensee can prove that the licensee is contractually entitled to a lower rate.

### B. Special Rates

50% to 75% of statutory for budget line records. (Rates are often provided for physical CDs, especially compilation albums, but rarely for permanent digital downloads.)

## IV. ELECTRICAL TRANSCRIPTION FEES

### A. Syndicated Radio Shows

$100 per copy; does not include performance license.

### B. Radio Transcriptions (for programming introductions, themes, background music and breaks, etc.)

Free. These are distributed free of charge to encourage radio stations to use them and thereby generate lucrative performance fees.

### C. Background Music Services

#### *1. Reproduction License*

The royalty is 1% of net income, pro rated amongst all copyrighted songs used during a period of three (3) months. Music publishers normally authorize the Harry Fox Agency to issue this type of license. Where the broadcast is made from CDs playing by computer control on industrial jukeboxes, no payment is made for electrical transcriptions, because none are being made to facilitate the broadcast transmissions.

### 2. *Performance License*

In addition to the above reproduction fees, the background music service must also pay fees for the public performance of the musical works arising from the transmissions emanating from the service or on the premises at the business establishment subscribers. Such fees are typically $6.50 to $6.75 per month per location, regardless of whether the performances are from on-premise or broadcast transmissions.

## V. SYNCHRONIZATION FEES

### A. Television Synchronization License Fees

The typical fees for background use of a song in a network television program, including certain options that may be negotiated as part of a step deal, are as follows:

| | *Term* | *Territory* | *Media* | *Fee* |
|---|---|---|---|---|
| Base license | 5 year | U.S. only | Free television | $2,000-2,500 |
| Option | 5-year renewal | | | +100% of base fee |
| Option | | Rest of World | | +50% of base fee |
| Base license | Life of copyright | U.S. only | Free television | $4,000-5,000 |
| Option | | | Pay TV | +30% of base fee |
| Base license | Life of copyright | Worldwide | All television | $8,000-12,000 |
| Option | Life of copyright | Worldwide | Home video devices | +10,000-$12,500 |
| Option | Life of copyright | Worldwide | Internet video streaming & download | +10,000-$15,000 |
| Option | Life of copyright | Worldwide | Airlines, etc. | +2,500-5,000 |
| Option | Life of copyright | Worldwide | Foreign theatrical | +2,500-5,000 |
| Base license | Life of copyright | Worldwide | All media, excluding U.S. theatrical | $20,000-50,000 |
| Base license | Life of copyright | Worldwide | Broad rights | $50,000-100,000 |

Note, the use assumed has been *background* — that is where no one on the screen is seen performing the song, either instrumentally or vocally. If use is foreground (i.e., song performed on screen instrumentally or vocally), add 20% to the above amounts. If the song is featured, such as used over the title of a particular episode or over the closing credits, add 25% to 50%.

Use of the title of the song as the title of the television series or an episode would warrant an additional 50% to 100%; however, music publishers typically reduce the above fees by 25% if the song is used in every episode of the series (thereby increasing the performance fees significantly). On the other hand, if the producer wishes to use an established hit song as the theme song for the series, the publisher must consider the detrimental effect the use may have on potential commercial uses of the song in the future. Unless the publisher doesn't think the song would otherwise have a lucrative commercial future, the publisher may ask for a significant premium for such a use. If the story of an episode is a dramatization of the song's lyrics, add anywhere from 100% to 200% and consider other uses, such as sequels, spin-offs, and the like.

Multiple uses of the song in the same episode, even if the total time performed on screen is less than an entire performance of the song, will warrant a premium of 10% to 25% of the base fee. Certain variety and award shows use an unusually high number of songs in the program; in such cases, a reduced fee may be warranted. Reduced fees are also warranted when the producer is reviving an old television series for television syndication, home video, or Internet downloading or streaming.

Where a producer desires to use the song in an advertising campaign, including spots on radio, television, and Internet advertising, a music publisher may typically charge between $1,000 and $5,000 per week, depending upon whether the use is *in context* or *out of context.* Adding theatrical use in the United States, or licensing so-called *broad rights* (i.e., all media, worldwide, for life of copyright) should be considered and negotiated, as though it were a theatrical synchronization license.

### B. Theatrical Motion Picture Synchronization License Fees — Major Studio

The typical fees for use of a song in a theatrical motion picture, including certain options that may be negotiated as part of a step deal, are as follows:

| *Term* | *Territory* | *Media* | *Background* | *Foreground — Visual/Vocal* | *Featured* |
|---|---|---|---|---|---|
| Life of copyright | Worldwide | Theatrical exhibition | $5,000-25,000 | $7,500-$50,000 | $15,000-$100,000 |
| Life of copyright | Worldwide | Television broadcast | + 5,000-25,000 | + 7,500-$50,000 | + 50,000-$100,000 |
| Life of copyright | Worldwide | Internet Streaming | + 5,000-25,000 | + 7,500-$50,000 | + 50,000-$100,000 |
| Life of copyright | Worldwide | Home video & Internet download royalty | + $.10-$.20 per copy against advance of $5,000-$10,000 | | |
| Life of copyright | Worldwide | Home video & Internet download Buy-out | + 10,000-25,000 | + 15,000-$50,000 | + 25,000-$250,000 |
| Life of copyright | Worldwide | Broad Rights Buy-out (includes all of above) | $15,000-100,000 | $25,000-$200,000 | $50,000-$500,000 |

*Duration and Territory.* The duration of theatrical synch licenses issued to films produced or distributed by the major studios are almost always life of copyright and the territory is almost always worldwide (or the "universe"). Where a shorter term is negotiated, such as a 5-year term, the term will commence upon the first commercial theatrical exhibition of the film.

*Featured Use.* A *featured use* is where the song performed over the opening title sequence or becomes an important part of the presentation of a character or turning point in the film's plot. A featured use could warrant double the usual synch fee. Use of the song over the closing credits will also command a premium, though not as high as for the opening title sequence.

*Lyric Changes.* Lyric changes will also command a premium, but the publisher should (i) carefully consider the long term effect on the song if the film becomes a hit or classic and (ii) obtain any permission that may be required from the songwriter(s).

*Use of Song Title.* Use of the title of the song as the title of the motion picture should bring an additional 50-100% over the fees above, or more if the song is a standard and its title fairly unique or closely identified with an important act.

*Multiple Uses.* Multiple uses of the song, even if the total time performed on screen is less than an entire performance of the song, will warrant a premium of 10-25% of the base fee.

*Broad rights.* Broad rights include use all media, including U.S. and overseas theatrical release, all television and home video devices, such as videocassettes and DVDs, and Internet download and streaming for *in context* use. Thus, because the synch fee includes a buy-out of the home video rights, no additional royalties would be payable for distribution of videocassettes, DVDs, or BluRay discs. Because Internet downloads could eventually replace home video devices, and perhaps threaten the classic television or theatrical performance itself, a music publisher would be wise to try to exclude Internet use (i.e., video streaming and download). A publisher might give up on getting a carve out for video streaming, provided that the performances inherent in such streams are subject to license by the appropriate performance rights society. Video downloads are another matter and publishers should be wary of issuing long term licenses until the market for downloads matures. A five or even ten year term for video download use, from the publisher's perspective, would be far better than life of copyright.

*Performance Fees.* To remain consistent with the antitrust consent decrees with performance rights societies in the U.S., the synch license will include a license component to permit performances in movie theaters in the United States. Unless the license specifies the synchronization component and performance component separately, the music publisher usually considers that 1/2 of the stated fee is allocated to U.S. performance rights. Nevertheless, public performances in theaters in other countries will be subject to theaters having appropriate performance licenses from their local performance rights societies.

The television exhibition component of the license will also be subject to broadcast on stations licensed by the appropriate U.S. performance rights society (e.g., ASCAP, BMI, SESAC), but some producers try to insist on obtaining the necessary performance licenses directly from the publisher as part of the synch license. A publisher might agree to this only to the extent a television station for some reason does have an ASCAP, BMI or SESAC license or those societies are legally prohibited from issuing television performance license.

*Trailers.* The above fees will also include use in trailers, even if used in an advertising campaign (including spots on radio, television, and Internet advertising), provided they are *in context*, as discussed above.

*Out of Context Use.* If the use is *out of context*, a music publisher may typically charge between $1,000-5,000 per week. If the song is not used in the motion picture, but the producer wishes to use the song in a trailer for publicizing the film, a music publisher may charge $1,000-5,000 per week (less, if only performed on radio) or anywhere from $10,000 to $100,000 for the life of copyright.

### C. Theatrical Motion Picture Synchronization License Fees — Independent, Low Budget, Non-Profit or Student Films

A low budget film is one with a production budget of between $500,000 and $5 million. Student films, of course, may have production budgets that are significantly lower. Because of the limited ability of the producer to fully pay the going rate for a song up front, music publishers will often agree to a step deal — one that closely approximates the one set forth in Section A above, except that the steps may be triggered by the number of screens to which the film is distributed (e.g., over 1,000) or certain levels of box office receipts (e.g., $5 million, $10 million, $25 million, etc ).

A true student film may warrant the granting of a license for a nominal fee, with step deal terms in the event the film eventually becomes successful. Alternatively, a license could be granted for free or for a nominal fee, but could be limited to exhibition at film festivals or a very limited theatrical engagement within a specified period of time. Music publishers should be encouraged to permit the use of their music in student films as a means of supporting budding film-makers while taking the opportunity to educate them on the terms typically required for the use of music in motion pictures.

### D. Non-Theatrical Film Synchronization License Fees

The fee for the use of a musical composition in a corporate video to be used for in-house training or trade show convention use ranges from $3,000 to $5,000. The term is generally for one year. A quote should be dependent on the audience size, number of meetings, and size of the convention or show city. User is normally authorized to retain one copy of the video for archival purposes.

### E. Television Synchronization License for Music Videos

When a popular song video is to be televised purely for promotional purposes, a publisher will generally charge a handling fee of $100. However, one can expect these fees to increase as the broadcast of these videos are becoming less promotional and more for pure entertainment. This initial license should not include the distribution of the video in videocassettes, DVDs, or Blu-ray discs for the home market.

### F. Synchronization License for Feature Film Trailers

For a well-known musical composition not originally used in the motion picture to be advertised (i.e., *out-of-context* use), a typical fee would be $25,000. Unless the producer obtained broad rights, which would include this use, for a musical composition used (perhaps as background) and not "featured" in the motion picture being advertised, a typical fee would be $15,000. For the use of a song on the radio to promote a motion picture, a typical fee may be $1,000 per week.

## G. Videogram Synchronization License Fees

*Motion Pictures.* Recently, it has been the practice of motion picture producers to ask for terms that would allow them to buy out the videogram license for a one time flat fee payment. While music publishers have resisted this, a producer might typically pay, in addition to the standard synchronization license fee, a flat fee videogram license buy-out of $25,000 to $35,000. Since no public performance fees are collected on performances in the home, publishers will normally make every effort to avoid offering a buy-out provision and may suggest instead an advance that would cover 20,000 or more units, which should be more than sufficient to cover a normal home video release of the motion picture.

Where the publisher can negotiate a royalty per unit, the average per unit royalty for each song used in a videocassette, DVD, or other home video device is currently between 10¢ and 15¢. The actual per unit royalty would vary according to the considerations set forth above, such as whether the use is background, foreground, or special. A publisher will generally require an advance against royalties of about $5,000 to $10,000. Sometimes, a publisher may also negotiate a roll-over advance, in which case the producer must pay an additional advance (e.g., $12,500) when a certain number of copies are sold (e.g., 100,000).

*Music Videos.* Standards for licensing of music videos for home video distribution have still not yet fully emerged. Synchronization licenses will continue to provide a short-term, perhaps two years, license for a flat fee with additional negotiations at the end of the term, with a buy-out of between $10,000 and $25,000.

*Video Yearbooks.* There is a $50 buyout fee for high school, $100 for college, per song.

*Corporate Videos.* There is a fixing fee of $1,000; royalty of $.10 per unit; buy-out of royalty about $5,000. Term can be up to five years.

## H. Video Download Synchronization License Fees

As we discussed above, it is very important for music publishers to consider that, when it issues a license to use a song in audiovisual works distributed by home video devices (e.g., DVD, Blu-ray) on a flat fee basis, it is foregoing an opportunity to participate in the economic success of the audiovisual work in which it was embodied — no royalties are paid to the publisher on copies sold and no public performance income accrues to the publisher for the private performances of the work in the home. This is especially so when the duration of such a license is for the life of the copyright.

Providing a videogram license on a flat fee basis may be acceptable, home video devices are likely to become obsolete, replaced by streaming video and video downloads. But if streaming and downloading becomes the technological end of the road, then to provide licenses for permanent downloads on anything other than some form of royalty basis — or, alternatively, on a flat fee basis combined with public performance or public communication rights income — would be to forever forego an economic stake in the success of the audiovisual work in which the song appeared. The music publisher's only hope would be the exercise of the public communication right overseas and the passage of a new exclusive right of public communication in the United States.

Where a publisher has the leverage to demand and obtain a royalty, the royalty may well be very similar to that which is typically received upon the distribution and sale of home video devices: currently between 10¢ and 15¢. Again, the actual per unit royalty would vary according to the considerations set forth above, such as whether the use is background, foreground, or special. A publisher will generally require an advance against royalties of about $5,000 to $10,000. Sometimes, a publisher may also negotiate a roll-over advance, in which case the producer must pay an additional advance (e.g., $12,500) when a certain number of copies are downloaded (e.g., 100,000). Films that use a relatively high number of songs may command a lesser rate per song, and in such instances a publisher may provide a reduced rate with some form of most favored nations provision.

Where a producer is still insistent upon a full video download license on a flat fee basis, one solution would be to limit the term of the license to five or ten years, to preserve the right to charge some form of royalty or fee based upon the number of transmissions at some later date.

## VI. Commercial Advertising License Fees

### A. Television Commercial Synchronization License

It is difficult to describe what a "typical" fee would be for the use of a song in a television commercial, because terms and conditions for such licenses vary widely.

In Chapter 20, we posed the question why so many contemporary composers have had an aversion to permitting the use of their music in television advertising. For example, Mick Jagger and Keith Richards of the Rolling Stones had long declined requests for the use of their music in television commercials. However, when software maker Microsoft called for permission to use *Start Me Up* in TV spots to advertise the launch of the Windows95 operating system software, the Stones' writers agreed. On the question of the fee involved, I was quoted in an article written by Don Clark, which appeared in the *Wall Street Journal* on August 18, 1995, as follows:

British press reports said Mr. Jagger set a price of $12 million for use of the song, but one person familiar with the matter put the true figure at closer to $4 million, an amount that would still be considered a record in the field. Microsoft declined comment on the price. "You can't always get what you want, but if you're Microsoft you get what you need," said Al Kohn, a music licensing expert and retired vice president of Time Warner's Warner/Chappell Music unit.

Leaving that unusual situation aside, we have formed a more typical baseline to assist our readers in determining the appropriate license fee for a variety of commercial advertising uses. While the fee will vary from song to song, the baseline should be useful for determining the relative fees for other works and uses under other circumstances.

Let us assume you are licensing the standard song, *As Time Goes By*, the song made famous by the classic motion picture, *Casablanca*. The fee for a non-exclusive license for the use of the song for one year in a television commercial for network broadcast in the United States and Canada might be $150,000 to $200,000. If the use were limited to a particular average-sized state, the fee might be $50,000. If the use were limited to a major metropolitan area, such as New York City or Southern California, the fee might be $25,000, and for other medium-sized to large cities, the fee might be $10,000 to $15,000. Use in smaller cities and towns is generally requested for a shorter period of time; in these cases, the fee might be $5,000 per week, but you must be careful that the town is not within the broadcast range of a major city, in which case a higher fee may be warranted. When licenses of a duration shorter than one year are requested, the above fees can be pro rated. For example, during a recent economic recession, advertising agencies began requesting for their clients licenses of six months in length. The quote for such a license may be 75% of what you would normally charge for the same license of one year duration. However, it is not unusual to obtain fees for thirteen (13) week television spots (USA and Canada) between $50,000 and $100,000.

It is important to limit the duration of these licenses to one year or less. A song that becomes too closely associated with a nationally advertised product could lose its value as a commercial vehicle for other products. If an advertiser wants to continue to use the song for a long term, you can better evaluate what you need to charge by giving yourself an opportunity to reevaluate the fee each year. You lose this flexibility by giving longer term licenses, such as for five or more years. If an advertiser insists on a longer term license, consider providing an option to renew, upon which an additional license fee is to be paid. For the reason just mentioned, you should require a premium for the option itself, and you should try to limit the renewal to one option year.

When advertisers request exclusivity, the better policy is to avoid providing it altogether. Nevertheless, if the circumstances require it, and you can be careful to narrowly define the scope of the exclusivity as suggested in Chapter 20, you can demand a premium of as much as 100% of the normal fee for the license. Remember, that if you provide exclusivity to a local advertiser, you may have restricted your ability to enter into a more lucrative nationwide license with an advertiser of a competing product. All exclusive licenses, of whatever duration, should be entered into with extreme care.

### B. Radio Commercial Electrical Transcription License

Normal nationwide radio license for a one-year term national should cost between $50,000 and $75,000.

Short-term regional radio broadcasts, not within the broadcast range of major cities, would be $1,000 to $3,000 per week.

### C. Print Advertising

On occasion, an advertising agency, on behalf of its client, would request a quote for the use of a lyric to promote its client's product in magazine and newspaper advertisements. The typical fee for such use in an advertisement would be $5,000 to $10,000, for a term of one year.

## VII. MUSIC BOXES AND COMMERCIAL PRODUCT LICENSE

### A. Royalty

5% of the retail selling price per unit

### B. Advance

$1,000 to $5,000

Note: A licensee may take the position that the fee should be governed by the compulsory license provision of the copyright law (17 U.S.C. Sec. 115, set forth in the appendix Law 13.1 on the CD-ROM), because the recordings are not accompanied by an audiovisual work. The statutory rate is likely to be significantly less than a percentage of the retail price. However, most publishers will insist upon some percentage of the suggested retail selling price of the item, and, as a practical matter, the manufacturer can either accept the publisher's terms or attempt to obtain a compulsory license under the copyright statute; however, the administrative burdens of complying with the compulsory license provision may outweigh its advantages, and manufacturers often accept the publisher's terms.

## VIII. VIDEOGAMES, COMPUTER SOFTWARE, MULTIMEDIA

### A. Videogames

#### *1. Video Arcade Games*

For such large video arcade games retailing from $1,000 to $3,000 per unit, a fee of 1/2% to 1% of the retail selling price might be considered. Publishers might accept a maximum per unit royalty of $10 or $15 per unit. Performance rights are not included and it is the responsibility of the arcade to get appropriate performance rights from ASCAP and BMI.

### *2. Video Game Cartridges and Online Versions*

For normal videogames, where the music is incidental to the action, rates will vary between 9¢ to 18¢ per song, per copy distributed, with a buy-out ranging from $1,000 to $25,000, depending upon whether the fee includes online uses, related uses, and other factors.

### *3. Video Games Dedicated to Music*

For games dedicated to music, such as *Guitar Hero* and *Rock Band*, rates are considerably higher, but no standards have yet emerged.

## B. Multimedia Programs

**Royalty:** 5% of the retail selling price per unit.

**Pro Ration:** When more than one song is used in a particular product, the fee should be pro rated among all the copyrighted, royalty-bearing songs used.

**Advance:** $1,000 to $5,000

Should the music publisher and multimedia producer be unable to come to terms on an agreeable royalty, a compromise may be reached in a manner similar to that reached by many music publishers and motion picture producers shortly after the advent of videocassettes for distribution to the home video market. A music publisher with a substantial catalog could package together a number of popular compositions, and the multimedia producer, recognizing that his program may have a limited life anyway, could agree to a license having a 3- to 5-year term, in exchange for a flat fee of $5,000 to $10,000, depending upon the number of songs licensed in the package.

## C. MIDI Software

**Royalty:** 5% of retail selling price per unit, or 50¢ per unit per song.

**Pro Ration:** When more than one song is used in a particular product, and the royalty is based upon a percentage of the retail selling price, the fee should be pro rated among all the copyrighted, royalty bearing songs used.

**Advance:** $500 to $1,000

### D. Karaoke

#### *1. Karaoke Discs*

For karaoke recordings, publishers charge a fixing fee of between $100 and $250 per track plus a royalty of 10¢ and 20¢ per copy.

#### *2. Online Karaoke*

For online karaoke, publishers typically charge 12% to 15% of revenues for the use of lyrics and music.

## IX. NEEDLEDROP OR PRODUCTION MUSIC LIBRARY

As mentioned in Chapter 1, a large variety of *canned* music is available from several production music libraries. The following is a schedule of fees typically charged by these libraries, though all are negotiable.

### A. Television and Non-Theatrical License

#### *1. Local*

Use of Single Cues $400 to $500
Not in excess of 30 minutes $500 to $1,000
T.V. Spot Commercials $250 to $500
Radio and Slide Films $100 to $200
Radio Commercials $250 to $500

#### *2. National (including Worldwide)*

Use of Single Cues $750 to $1,200
Not in excess of 30 minutes $1,000 to $3,000
T.V. Spot Commercials (U.S./Canada only)
$500 to $1,000 Radio and Slide Films $50 to $100
Radio Commercials (U.S./Canada only)
$500 to $1,000 Theatrical Trailer $600 to $1,000

### B. Theatrical Motion Pictures; Pay or Subscriber T.V.; Videocassette (U.S. use only)

Use of Single Cues (each of above): $750 to $1,500
Per film 30 minutes to full length $2,500 to $7,500

### C. Other (including CD-ROMs)

Because CD-ROMs can run from 10 cues to as many as 150 cues or more, using production music can be very economical. Fees start at $50 per cue, but a "Max Cap" may be negotiated in advance. For example, the fee can be $50 per cue with a $3,000 to $5,000 maximum for as many cues as needed for a single CD-ROM program.

The same structure is available for industrial or corporate slide shows and in-house videos. Corporations may often negotiate a blanket license renewable on a yearly basis. Yearly fees for blanket licenses vary considerably, depending on the amount of music contained by the library.

## X. LIVING STAGE PERFORMANCE FEES

Fees for a performance of a song in a "revue" or regular Broadway-type show would depend upon the strength of the use and size of the theater.

The royalty rate for a visual vocal performance in an Off-Off Broadway theater (99 seats or less) could be $5 to $10 per performance.

Off Broadway theaters (up to 500 seats) fees could range from $75 to $200 per week. A major performance of a work over 4 or 5 minutes in duration, a special additional fee up to $250 might be in order.

On-Broadway, a good fee would be $250 to $500 per 8 performance week per song or 5% of the gross receipts pro rated among all copyrighted songs in the play.

Publishers licensing works for the living stage must remember they are not granting a grand performance license, which may only be obtained from the owners of the show.

## XI. Theme Park License Fees

### A. Permanent Attractions

Flat fee of $25,000 to $50,000 per year, covering use of the song in any and all attractions in the original and branch theme parks, cruise ships, resorts, and other entertainment centers worldwide.

### B. Single Additional Attractions

Synchronizing a song with, for example, audioanimatronic figures (such as Disneyland's *It's a Small World*), a flat fee of $5,000 to $10,000 per year, covering the use of the song in a single attraction.

### C. Live Stage Show in Theme Park

Flat fee of $1,000 per week for run of the show.

## XII. Digital Sampling License Fees

### A. Music

Buy-outs: $2,500 to $10,000
Mechanical: 20% to 50% of the statutory rate
Co-ownership: 25% to 50% interest

### B. Sound Recordings

Buy outs: $2,500 to $20,000
Royalties: 20% to 50% of the statutory rate for the music

# Index

## C

## M

## O

## R

## S

**W**